RAILWAY

PSYCHOLOGICAL/APTITUDE TEST

मनोवैज्ञानिक / अभिरुचि परीक्षण

STATION MASTER

(METRO/MOTOR MAN/DFCCIL)

BILINGUAL

BASED ON LATEST PATTERN OF RRB NTPC

MANOJ KUMAR MODI

A Distinguished Teacher of Psychological Test

&

N. BHARTI

S. CHAND PUBLISHING

S Chand And Company Limited

(ISO 9001 Certified Company)

S Chand And Company Limited

(ISO 9001 Certified Company)

Head Office: D-92, Sector – 02, Noida 201301, U.P. (India), Ph. 91-120-4682700

Registered Office: A-27, 2nd Floor, Mohan Co-operative Industrial Estate, New Delhi – 110 044

Phone: 011-49731800

www.**schandpublishing.com;** e-mail: **info@schandpublishing.com**

Marketing Offices:

Chennai	:	Ph: 044-2363 2120, chennai@schandpublishing.com
Guwahati	:	Ph: 0361-4066 369, guwahati@schandpublishing.com
Hyderabad	:	Ph: 040-4018 6018, hyderabad@schandpublishing.com
Jalandhar	:	Ph: 0181-4645 630, jalandhar@schandpublishing.com
Kolkata	:	Ph: 033-2335 7458 kolkata@schandpublishing.com
Lucknow	:	Ph: 0522-400 3633, lucknow@schandpublishing.com
Mumbai	:	Ph: 022-2500 0297, mumbai@schandpublishing.com
Patna	:	Ph: 0612-4011400, patna@schandpublishing.com

First Edition 2026

ISBN : 978-93-7359-353-1

Product Code: H2RPA

PRINTED IN INDIA

By Shri Shyamlal Printing Press Private Limited, Plot 20/4, Site-IV, Industrial Area Sahibabad, Ghaziabad – 201 010 and Published by S Chand And Company Limited, A-27, 2nd Floor, Mohan Co-operative Industrial Estate, New Delhi – 110 044

लेखक की कलम से...

इस पुस्तक के माध्यम से मैंने रेलवे भर्ती बोर्ड की परीक्षाओं में मनोवैज्ञानिक परीक्षण से सम्बन्धित पूछे गये प्रश्नों को सरलतापूर्वक हल करने के लिए अपने विचारों और अनुभवों को साझा करने की कोशिश की है साथ ही साथ इसमें सफलता के लिए अनेक तरह के फूलों को संग्रहित कर माला पिरोया है, जिससे पाठकों का सपना साकार होने में कहीं बाधा उत्पन्न न हो। इस पुस्तक का मुख्य उद्देश्य पाठकों के लिए अच्छे मार्गदर्शन, दिशा-निर्देशन, एकाग्रता एवं सफलता प्रदान करना है।

यह पुस्तक मेरे जीवन के २३ वर्षों के अनुभव और शोध के अध्ययन के परिणामों का संग्रह है जिसमें रेलवे भर्ती बोर्ड के मनोवैज्ञानिक परीक्षण परीक्षा के विगत वर्षों में पूछे गये प्रश्नों को सरलता एवं सुगमतापूर्वक हल करने के विभिन्न तरीकों की समावेश किया गया है जिससे की परीक्षा में परीक्षार्थी समय पर सारे प्रश्नों को हल कर सके। साथ ही साथ इस पुस्तक के माध्यम से मैंने मनोवैज्ञानिक/अभिरुचि परीक्षण की तैयारी करने वाले उम्मीदवारों की विभिन्न विषयों जैसे- बुद्धि मापन परीक्षण, चयनात्मक अवधान मापन परीक्षण, स्थानिक क्षमता मापन परीक्षण और व्यक्तित्व मापन परीक्षण इत्यादि को समझाने की भरपूर कोशिश की है।

यह पुस्तक रेलवे भर्ती बोर्ड की तैयारी कर रहे समस्त उम्मीदवारों को समर्पित है जिसमें बोर्ड की आवश्यकताओं के अनुसार विभिन्न प्रकार के प्रश्नों एवं उनके उत्तरों को सहज एवं सरल भाषा में शामिल किया गया है ताकि उन्हें तैयारी करने में मदद मिल सके।

मुझे आशा ही नहीं बल्कि पूर्ण विश्वास है कि इस पुस्तक के माध्यम से रेलवे भर्ती बोर्ड द्वारा आयोजित स्टेशन मास्टर पद की परीक्षा में सफल होने के लिए मार्गदर्शन प्रदान करेगी। मैंने यह महसूस किया कि यह पुस्तक हिन्दी, अंग्रेजी भाषा में उपलब्ध कराया जाय ताकि अधिक से अधिक परीक्षार्थी इसका लाभ उठा सके। जिस कारण मैं इस पुस्तक को दोनों भाषाओं में प्रकाशित करा रहा हूँ।

मैं अपने परिवार, मित्रों एवं सहयोगियों का आभार व्यक्त करता हूँ जिसने मुझे पुस्तक को लिखने को प्रेरित किया साथ ही साथ एस. चन्द प्रकाशन को साधुवाद देता हूँ। जिनके सहयोग से पुस्तक प्रकाशित हो सका।

मानव से त्रुटियाँ रहना स्वाभाविक है एवं संशोधन से विकास प्रक्रिया निरंतर चलती रहती है। नवीन संस्करण हेतु आपका सुझाव सादर आमंत्रित हैं।

धन्यवाद

आपका लेखक
मनोज कुमार मोदी
एन. भारती

From the Author's Pen...

Through this book, I have attempted to share my thoughts and experiences to help candidates easily solve the questions related to psychological test asked in Railway Recruitment Board examinations. I have also compiled various tips and strategies for success, ensuring that readers' dreams are not hindered in any way. The main objective of this book is to provide readers with good guidance, direction, focus, and ultimately, success.

This book is a compilation of my 23 years of experience and research, incorporating various methods to easily and efficiently solve the questions asked in previous years' Railway Recruitment Board psychological aptitude test, enabling candidates to complete all questions within the allotted time. Furthermore, through this book, I have made every effort to explain various topics to candidates preparing for psychological/ aptitude test, such as intelligence measurement tests, selective attention measurement test, spatial scanning measurement test, and personality measurement test, etc.

This book is dedicated to all candidates preparing for the Railway Recruitment Board examinations. It includes various types of questions and their answers in simple and easy-to-understand language, in accordance with the board's requirements, to assist them in their preparation.

I not only hope but am fully confident that this book will provide guidance for success in the Station Master examination conducted by the Railway Recruitment Board. I felt that this book should be available in both Hindi and English so that more candidates can benefit from it. Therefore, I am publishing this book in both languages.

I express my gratitude to my family, friends, and colleagues who inspired me to write this book, and I also thank S. Chand Publishing for their cooperation in publishing this book.

It is natural for humans to make mistakes, and the process of improvement continues through revisions. Your suggestions for the new edition are cordially invited.

Thank you

Your Author
Manoj Kumar Modi
N. Bharti

Preface of Book

From the Author's Pen...

I take immense pleasure in presenting before you the bilingual version of the Psychological Aptitude Test. This book is a complete book of Psychological test for Station Master. Almost all latest patterns are given in this book.

Based on my extensive experience and research of 23 years, I have designed this book in such a manner that students will certainly have clear understanding of concepts and feel confident by practicing. All chapters have been explained comprehensively for better understanding.

Based on Memory, many questions that have been asked in examinations in the previous years have been arranged chapter-wise in this book, So that students are ready for Psycho Test for any division of India.

I am thankful to all my friends, colleagues, N. Bharti, Ayushman Modi, Manya Shree, Binay Singh, Abhay Kumar, Niraj Kumar, Shireen Nathaniel and well wishers who have contributed in the framing of this book.

Your suggestions to make this book more useful and easy are most welcome, I am confident that this remarkable book will play an

Key Features of Books :

1. सरल और स्पष्ट भाषा।
2. विस्तृत उदाहरण और स्पष्टीकरण।
3. विशेषज्ञों के 23 वर्षों का अनुभव।
4. अभ्यास एवं विगत प्रश्नों के साथ उत्तर का संग्रह।
5. स्पष्ट चित्रों और आरेखों का उपयोग।
6. अद्यतन और नवीनतम जानकारी।

1. Simple and clear language.
2. Detailed Examples and Explanations.
3. 23 years of experience of experts.
4. Collection of exercise & previous questions with answers.
5. Use of clear picture and Diagrams.
6. Updated and latest information.

मनोवैज्ञानिक/अभिरूचि परीक्षण की तैयारी कैसे करें

How to Prepare for Psychological / Aptitude Test

रेलवे भर्ती बोर्ड के द्वारा आयोजित स्टेशन मास्टर (SM) पद के लिए ऑनलाईन पैटर्न के अनुसार तीन चरणों में परीक्षाएँ सम्पन्न होती है। ये परीक्षाएँ एक-दूसरे से पूर्णत: भिन्न होती है। प्रथम (CBT-1) एवं द्वितीय (CBT-2) की परीक्षाएँ पूर्णत: कम्प्यूटर आधारित होती है तथा तृतीय चरण में मनोवैज्ञानिक/अभिरूचि परीक्षण कम्प्यूटर बेस्ड एप्टीच्यूट टेस्ट (CBAT) आधारित होती है। दोनों कम्प्यूटर आधारित परीक्षाओं (CBT-1 और CBT-2) में सफल होने के बाद मनोवैज्ञानिक/ अभिरुचि परीक्षण (CBAT) में सफल होना अनिवार्य है।

स्टेशन मास्टर के मनोवैज्ञानिक परीक्षण के लिए दिशा-निर्देश और परीक्षण के मुख्य घटक–

यह परीक्षण आमतौर पर पाँच या छ: बैटरी टेस्ट में विभाजित होता है। इस परीक्षण से अभ्यर्थियों की मानसिक क्षमताओं और व्यवहारिक पहलूओं का मूल्यांकन करना होता है। यह सुनिश्चित करने के लिए होता है कि उम्मीदवार रेलवे के परिचालन से संबंधित काम के लिए मानसिक रूप से तैयार है–

❊ **इंटेलिजेंस टेस्ट :** यह आपकी सामान्य बुद्धि, तर्क करने की क्षमता और समस्याओं को हल करने की क्षमता का मापन करता है।

❊ **सेलेक्टिव अटेंशन टेस्ट :** यह परीक्षण आपकी एकाग्रता और चयनात्मक ध्यान (Selective Attention) की जाँच करता है।

❊ **स्पासीएल स्कैनिंग टेस्ट :** यह परीक्षण उम्मीदवारों की स्थानिक संबंधों को समझने और जटिल रास्तों को खोजने की क्षमता का मूल्यांकन करना होता है। इस परीक्षण को एकाग्रता, शीघ्रता और अपने विवेक से प्रश्नों को हल करना होता है।

❊ **निर्देश समझ सकने की क्षमता टेस्ट :** इस परीक्षण के द्वारा उम्मीदवारों की तार्किक क्षमता, सोचने की क्रमबद्धता, निर्देशों के अनुसार कार्य करने की योग्यता का मापन किया जाता है।

❊ **पर्सनालिटी टेस्ट :** यह परीक्षण आपके व्यवहार संबंधी पहलूओं, जैसे नेतृत्व क्षमता, निर्णय लेने की क्षमता और तनाव प्रबंधन का मूल्यांकन करता है। इस परीक्षण में सफल होने वाले अभ्यर्थियों को व्यक्तित्व के दोनों आयामों में उत्तीर्ण होना अनिवार्य होगा। यदि कोई अभ्यर्थी एक आयाम में असफल होता है तो उसे असफल माना जाएगा।

Psychological/Aptitude Test The examinations for the Station Master (SM) post, conducted by the Railway Recruitment Board, are held in three stages according to the online pattern. These examinations are completely different from each other. The first (CBT-1) and second (CBT-2) examinations are entirely computer-based, while the third stage, the psychological/aptitude test, is a Computer-Based Aptitude Test (CBAT). Passing both computer-based examinations (CBT-1 and CBT-2) is mandatory before appearing for and passing the psychological/ aptitude test (CBAT).

Guidelines and Main Components of the Station Master's Psychological Test:

This test is usually divided into five or six battery tests. This test evaluates the candidates' mental abilities and behavioral aspects. This is to ensure that the candidate is mentally prepared for work related to railway operations:

❊ **Intelligence Test :** This measures your general intelligence, reasoning ability, and problem-solving skills.

❊ **Selective Attention Test :** This test checks your concentration and selective attention.

❊ **Spatial Scanning Test :** This test evaluates the candidates' ability to understand spatial relationships and navigate complex routes. This test requires concentration, speed, and the ability to solve questions judiciously.

❊ **Ability to Understand Instructions Test :** This test measures the candidates' logical ability, systematic thinking, and ability to follow instructions.

❊ **Personality Test:** This test evaluates your behavioral aspects, such as leadership qualities, decision-making ability, and stress management. Candidates who pass this test must qualify in both dimensions of personality. If a candidate fails in one dimension, they will be considered unsuccessful.

Computer Based Aptitude Test (CBAT) की विधि :

Method of Computer Best Aptitude Test (CBAT)

1. यह परीक्षण **Computer Based Aptitude (CBAT) Test** पर आधारित है।
2. इस परीक्षण में कुल पाँच या छः परीक्षण होंगे। सारे परीक्षण हिन्दी और अंग्रेजी माध्यम में होते हैं।
3. परीक्षण प्रारम्भ होने से पूर्व **Computer Screen** पर निर्देश आएगा। जिसे हल करने का तरीका तथा निर्धारित समय -सीमा के साथ कुछ उदाहरणों को सहायता से प्रश्नों का हल दिया रहता है। जिन्हें समझकर आप प्रत्येक परीक्षण को यथासम्भव एवं यथाशीघ्र हल करें।
4. निर्देश समाप्त होने के बाद **Computer Screen** पर प्रथम परीक्षण शुरू हो जाएगा। प्रश्नों को एकाग्रता तथा शीघ्रता से पढ़ें और समझने की कोशिश करें।
5. प्रत्येक परीक्षण के लिए अलग-अलग समय सीमा निर्धारित होती है। जो आपको परीक्षण सत्र के दौरान दिखाई देती रहेगी।
6. प्रत्येक परीक्षण में आप प्रश्नों **Computer Mouse** की मदद से ऊपर-नीचे, बाएँ-दाएँ करके अपनी सुविधानुसार हल कर सकते हैं।
7. परीक्षण-स्क्रीन पर ऊपर दाएँ कोने की तरफ समय-सीमा दिखेगी जो परीक्षण की जानकारी मिनटों और सेकंडों में दिखती रहेगी।
8. परीक्षण स्क्रीन पर समय सीमा शून्य हो जाने पर परीक्षण स्वतः समाप्त हो जाता है और दूसरे परीक्षण का निर्देश परीक्षण स्क्रीन पर दिखने लगता है। इसी तरह से पाँच परीक्षण की प्रक्रिया होती रहती है।
9. उत्तर देने के लिए एक से अधिक उत्तर विकल्प **(Answer Option)** होते हैं। सबसे सही विकल्प का चयन कर माउस की सहायता से **Click** करें।
10. प्रत्येक **Click** के बाद आपका उत्तर स्वतः सुरक्षित **(Save)** हो जाएगा। कुछ परीक्षण में **Save & Next** करने की आवश्यकता पड़ती है।
11. गलत उत्तर होने पर एक से अधिक विकल्पों में सही विकल्प का चयन कर माउस की सहायता से पुनः **Click** कर उत्तर बदल सकते हैं।

सुझाव : ऑनलाइन मनोवैज्ञानिक/अभिरूचि परीक्षण में शामिल होनेवाले अभ्यर्थियों के लिए आवश्यक सुझाव :-

✽ परीक्षण से पहले अच्छी तैयारी करें।
✽ परीक्षण से पहले निर्देश को ध्यानपूर्वक पढ़ें और समझें।
✽ परीक्षा में समय सीमा बहुत सीमित है, इसलिए ऑनलाइन मौक टेस्ट के अभ्यास के दौरान सही समय का प्रबंधन करें।
✽ उत्तर देने से पहले विकल्पों का मूल्यांकन अच्छी ढंग से करें।

1. This test is based on Computer Based Aptitude (CBAT) Test.
2. There will be a total of five or six test in this test. All the tests are conducted in Hindi and English medium.
3. Before the test starts, instructions will appear on the computer screen. The solution to the questions is given with the help of some examples along with the method to solve it and the prescribed time limit Understanding these, you should solve each test as quickly and as possible.
4. After the instructions are over, the first test will start on the computer screen. Read the questions with concentration and quickly and try to understand.
5. There is a separate time allotted for each test, which will be visible to you during the testing session.
6. In each test, you can solve the questions as per your convenience by moving up, down, left and right with the help of computer mouse.
7. A time limit will be visible on the right upper corner of the test screen which will display the test information in minutes and seconds.
8. When the time limit on the indirect screen reaches zero, the test authmatically ends and instructions for next test appear on the test screen, Similarity, the process of five tests continues.
9. There is more than one answer option to answer. Select the most correct option and click with the help of the mouse.
10. After every click, your answer will be automatically saved. Some test require Save & Next.
11. If there is a wrong answer, you can change the answer by selecting the correct option from more than one option and clicking again with the help of

Suggestion : Computer Based Aptitude Test Important suggestions for candidates participating in the online psychological/ aptitude test:

✽ Prepare well before the test.
✽ Read and understand the instructions carefully before the test.
✽ The time limit for the exam is very limited, so manage your time effectively while practicing with online mock tests.
✽ Carefully evaluate the options before answering.

STATION MASTER

modirailwaypsychotestclasses.in | E-mail : manojmodinwd@gmail.com

ANSWER SHEET

स्मृति पर आधारित BASED ON MEMORY

Test परीक्षण 1

TEST ID परीक्षण अभिज्ञान Ⓐ Ⓑ Ⓒ Ⓓ Ⓔ Ⓕ

TEST CODE परीक्षण कूट I ① II ② III ③ IV ④ V ⑤ VI ⑥ VII ⑦ VIII ⑧

1 ① ② ③ ④ ⑤ ⑥ ⑦ ⑧
2 ① ② ③ ④ ⑤ ⑥ ⑦ ⑧
3 ① ② ③ ④ ⑤ ⑥ ⑦ ⑧
4 ① ② ③ ④ ⑤ ⑥ ⑦ ⑧
5 ① ② ③ ④ ⑤ ⑥ ⑦ ⑧
6 ① ② ③ ④ ⑤ ⑥ ⑦ ⑧
7 ① ② ③ ④ ⑤ ⑥ ⑦ ⑧
8 ① ② ③ ④ ⑤ ⑥ ⑦ ⑧
9 ① ② ③ ④ ⑤ ⑥ ⑦ ⑧
10 ① ② ③ ④ ⑤ ⑥ ⑦ ⑧
11 ① ② ③ ④ ⑤ ⑥ ⑦ ⑧
12 ① ② ③ ④ ⑤ ⑥ ⑦ ⑧
13 ① ② ③ ④ ⑤ ⑥ ⑦ ⑧
14 ① ② ③ ④ ⑤ ⑥ ⑦ ⑧
15 ① ② ③ ④ ⑤ ⑥ ⑦ ⑧
16 ① ② ③ ④ ⑤ ⑥ ⑦ ⑧
17 ① ② ③ ④ ⑤ ⑥ ⑦ ⑧
18 ① ② ③ ④ ⑤ ⑥ ⑦ ⑧
19 ① ② ③ ④ ⑤ ⑥ ⑦ ⑧
20 ① ② ③ ④ ⑤ ⑥ ⑦ ⑧
21 ① ② ③ ④ ⑤ ⑥ ⑦ ⑧
22 ① ② ③ ④ ⑤ ⑥ ⑦ ⑧
23 ① ② ③ ④ ⑤ ⑥ ⑦ ⑧
24 ① ② ③ ④ ⑤ ⑥ ⑦ ⑧
25 ① ② ③ ④ ⑤ ⑥ ⑦ ⑧
26 ① ② ③ ④ ⑤ ⑥ ⑦ ⑧
27 ① ② ③ ④ ⑤ ⑥ ⑦ ⑧
28 ① ② ③ ④ ⑤ ⑥ ⑦ ⑧
29 ① ② ③ ④ ⑤ ⑥ ⑦ ⑧
30 ① ② ③ ④ ⑤ ⑥ ⑦ ⑧
31 ① ② ③ ④ ⑤ ⑥ ⑦ ⑧
32 ① ② ③ ④ ⑤ ⑥ ⑦ ⑧
33 ① ② ③ ④ ⑤ ⑥ ⑦ ⑧
34 ① ② ③ ④ ⑤ ⑥ ⑦ ⑧
35 ① ② ③ ④ ⑤ ⑥ ⑦ ⑧
36 ① ② ③ ④ ⑤ ⑥ ⑦ ⑧
37 ① ② ③ ④ ⑤ ⑥ ⑦ ⑧
38 ① ② ③ ④ ⑤ ⑥ ⑦ ⑧
39 ① ② ③ ④ ⑤ ⑥ ⑦ ⑧
40 ① ② ③ ④ ⑤ ⑥ ⑦ ⑧
41 ① ② ③ ④ ⑤ ⑥ ⑦ ⑧
42 ① ② ③ ④ ⑤ ⑥ ⑦ ⑧
43 ① ② ③ ④ ⑤ ⑥ ⑦ ⑧
44 ① ② ③ ④ ⑤ ⑥ ⑦ ⑧
45 ① ② ③ ④ ⑤ ⑥ ⑦ ⑧
46 ① ② ③ ④ ⑤ ⑥ ⑦ ⑧
47 ① ② ③ ④ ⑤ ⑥ ⑦ ⑧
48 ① ② ③ ④ ⑤ ⑥ ⑦ ⑧
49 ① ② ③ ④ ⑤ ⑥ ⑦ ⑧
50 ① ② ③ ④ ⑤ ⑥ ⑦ ⑧

Test परीक्षण 2

TEST ID परीक्षण अभिज्ञान Ⓐ Ⓑ Ⓒ Ⓓ Ⓔ Ⓕ

TEST CODE परीक्षण कूट I ① II ② III ③ IV ④ V ⑤ VI ⑥ VII ⑦ VIII ⑧

1 ① ② ③ ④ ⑤ ⑥ ⑦ ⑧
2 ① ② ③ ④ ⑤ ⑥ ⑦ ⑧
3 ① ② ③ ④ ⑤ ⑥ ⑦ ⑧
4 ① ② ③ ④ ⑤ ⑥ ⑦ ⑧
5 ① ② ③ ④ ⑤ ⑥ ⑦ ⑧
6 ① ② ③ ④ ⑤ ⑥ ⑦ ⑧
7 ① ② ③ ④ ⑤ ⑥ ⑦ ⑧
8 ① ② ③ ④ ⑤ ⑥ ⑦ ⑧
9 ① ② ③ ④ ⑤ ⑥ ⑦ ⑧
10 ① ② ③ ④ ⑤ ⑥ ⑦ ⑧
11 ① ② ③ ④ ⑤ ⑥ ⑦ ⑧
12 ① ② ③ ④ ⑤ ⑥ ⑦ ⑧
13 ① ② ③ ④ ⑤ ⑥ ⑦ ⑧
14 ① ② ③ ④ ⑤ ⑥ ⑦ ⑧
15 ① ② ③ ④ ⑤ ⑥ ⑦ ⑧
16 ① ② ③ ④ ⑤ ⑥ ⑦ ⑧
17 ① ② ③ ④ ⑤ ⑥ ⑦ ⑧
18 ① ② ③ ④ ⑤ ⑥ ⑦ ⑧
19 ① ② ③ ④ ⑤ ⑥ ⑦ ⑧
20 ① ② ③ ④ ⑤ ⑥ ⑦ ⑧
21 ① ② ③ ④ ⑤ ⑥ ⑦ ⑧
22 ① ② ③ ④ ⑤ ⑥ ⑦ ⑧
23 ① ② ③ ④ ⑤ ⑥ ⑦ ⑧
24 ① ② ③ ④ ⑤ ⑥ ⑦ ⑧
25 ① ② ③ ④ ⑤ ⑥ ⑦ ⑧
26 ① ② ③ ④ ⑤ ⑥ ⑦ ⑧
27 ① ② ③ ④ ⑤ ⑥ ⑦ ⑧
28 ① ② ③ ④ ⑤ ⑥ ⑦ ⑧
29 ① ② ③ ④ ⑤ ⑥ ⑦ ⑧
30 ① ② ③ ④ ⑤ ⑥ ⑦ ⑧
31 ① ② ③ ④ ⑤ ⑥ ⑦ ⑧
32 ① ② ③ ④ ⑤ ⑥ ⑦ ⑧
33 ① ② ③ ④ ⑤ ⑥ ⑦ ⑧
34 ① ② ③ ④ ⑤ ⑥ ⑦ ⑧
35 ① ② ③ ④ ⑤ ⑥ ⑦ ⑧
36 ① ② ③ ④ ⑤ ⑥ ⑦ ⑧
37 ① ② ③ ④ ⑤ ⑥ ⑦ ⑧
38 ① ② ③ ④ ⑤ ⑥ ⑦ ⑧
39 ① ② ③ ④ ⑤ ⑥ ⑦ ⑧
40 ① ② ③ ④ ⑤ ⑥ ⑦ ⑧
41 ① ② ③ ④ ⑤ ⑥ ⑦ ⑧
42 ① ② ③ ④ ⑤ ⑥ ⑦ ⑧
43 ① ② ③ ④ ⑤ ⑥ ⑦ ⑧
44 ① ② ③ ④ ⑤ ⑥ ⑦ ⑧
45 ① ② ③ ④ ⑤ ⑥ ⑦ ⑧
46 ① ② ③ ④ ⑤ ⑥ ⑦ ⑧
47 ① ② ③ ④ ⑤ ⑥ ⑦ ⑧
48 ① ② ③ ④ ⑤ ⑥ ⑦ ⑧
49 ① ② ③ ④ ⑤ ⑥ ⑦ ⑧
50 ① ② ③ ④ ⑤ ⑥ ⑦ ⑧

Example Test-1

1 ① ② ③ ④ ⑤ ⑥ ⑦ ⑧
2 ① ② ③ ④ ⑤ ⑥ ⑦ ⑧
3 ① ② ③ ④ ⑤ ⑥ ⑦ ⑧
4 ① ② ③ ④ ⑤ ⑥ ⑦ ⑧
5 ① ② ③ ④ ⑤ ⑥ ⑦ ⑧

Example Test-2

1 ① ② ③ ④ ⑤ ⑥ ⑦ ⑧
2 ① ② ③ ④ ⑤ ⑥ ⑦ ⑧
3 ① ② ③ ④ ⑤ ⑥ ⑦ ⑧
4 ① ② ③ ④ ⑤ ⑥ ⑦ ⑧
5 ① ② ③ ④ ⑤ ⑥ ⑦ ⑧

Test परीक्षण 3

TEST ID परीक्षण अभिज्ञान Ⓐ Ⓑ Ⓒ Ⓓ Ⓔ Ⓕ

TEST CODE परीक्षण कूट I ① II ② III ③ IV ④ V ⑤ VI ⑥ VII ⑦ VIII ⑧

1 ①②③④⑤⑥⑦⑧⑨⑩
2 ①②③④⑤⑥⑦⑧⑨⑩
3 ①②③④⑤⑥⑦⑧⑨⑩
4 ①②③④⑤⑥⑦⑧⑨⑩
5 ①②③④⑤⑥⑦⑧⑨⑩
6 ①②③④⑤⑥⑦⑧⑨⑩
7 ①②③④⑤⑥⑦⑧⑨⑩
8 ①②③④⑤⑥⑦⑧⑨⑩
9 ①②③④⑤⑥⑦⑧⑨⑩
10 ①②③④⑤⑥⑦⑧⑨⑩
11 ①②③④⑤⑥⑦⑧⑨⑩
12 ①②③④⑤⑥⑦⑧⑨⑩
13 ①②③④⑤⑥⑦⑧⑨⑩
14 ①②③④⑤⑥⑦⑧⑨⑩
15 ①②③④⑤⑥⑦⑧⑨⑩
16 ①②③④⑤⑥⑦⑧⑨⑩
17 ①②③④⑤⑥⑦⑧⑨⑩
18 ①②③④⑤⑥⑦⑧⑨⑩
19 ①②③④⑤⑥⑦⑧⑨⑩
20 ①②③④⑤⑥⑦⑧⑨⑩
21 ①②③④⑤⑥⑦⑧⑨⑩
22 ①②③④⑤⑥⑦⑧⑨⑩
23 ①②③④⑤⑥⑦⑧⑨⑩
24 ①②③④⑤⑥⑦⑧⑨⑩
25 ①②③④⑤⑥⑦⑧⑨⑩
26 ①②③④⑤⑥⑦⑧⑨⑩
27 ①②③④⑤⑥⑦⑧⑨⑩
28 ①②③④⑤⑥⑦⑧⑨⑩
29 ①②③④⑤⑥⑦⑧⑨⑩
30 ①②③④⑤⑥⑦⑧⑨⑩
31 ①②③④⑤⑥⑦⑧⑨⑩
32 ①②③④⑤⑥⑦⑧⑨⑩
33 ①②③④⑤⑥⑦⑧⑨⑩
34 ①②③④⑤⑥⑦⑧⑨⑩
35 ①②③④⑤⑥⑦⑧⑨⑩
36 ①②③④⑤⑥⑦⑧⑨⑩
37 ①②③④⑤⑥⑦⑧⑨⑩
38 ①②③④⑤⑥⑦⑧⑨⑩
39 ①②③④⑤⑥⑦⑧⑨⑩
40 ①②③④⑤⑥⑦⑧⑨⑩

Example Test-3

1 ① ② ③ ④ ⑤ ⑥ ⑦ ⑧
2 ① ② ③ ④ ⑤ ⑥ ⑦ ⑧
3 ① ② ③ ④ ⑤ ⑥ ⑦ ⑧
4 ① ② ③ ④ ⑤ ⑥ ⑦ ⑧
5 ① ② ③ ④ ⑤ ⑥ ⑦ ⑧

STATION MASTER

ANSWER SHEET स्मृति पर आधारित BASED ON MEMORY

Test परीक्षण 4

TEST ID परीक्षण अभिज्ञान Ⓐ Ⓑ Ⓒ Ⓓ Ⓔ Ⓕ

TEST CODE परीक्षण कूट: I ① II ② III ③ IV ④ V ⑤ VI ⑥ VII ⑦ VIII ⑧

1	① ② ③ ④ ⑤ ⑥ ⑦ ⑧	26	① ② ③ ④ ⑤ ⑥ ⑦ ⑧
2	① ② ③ ④ ⑤ ⑥ ⑦ ⑧	27	① ② ③ ④ ⑤ ⑥ ⑦ ⑧
3	① ② ③ ④ ⑤ ⑥ ⑦ ⑧	28	① ② ③ ④ ⑤ ⑥ ⑦ ⑧
4	① ② ③ ④ ⑤ ⑥ ⑦ ⑧	29	① ② ③ ④ ⑤ ⑥ ⑦ ⑧
5	① ② ③ ④ ⑤ ⑥ ⑦ ⑧	30	① ② ③ ④ ⑤ ⑥ ⑦ ⑧
6	① ② ③ ④ ⑤ ⑥ ⑦ ⑧	31	① ② ③ ④ ⑤ ⑥ ⑦ ⑧
7	① ② ③ ④ ⑤ ⑥ ⑦ ⑧	32	① ② ③ ④ ⑤ ⑥ ⑦ ⑧
8	① ② ③ ④ ⑤ ⑥ ⑦ ⑧	33	① ② ③ ④ ⑤ ⑥ ⑦ ⑧
9	① ② ③ ④ ⑤ ⑥ ⑦ ⑧	34	① ② ③ ④ ⑤ ⑥ ⑦ ⑧
10	① ② ③ ④ ⑤ ⑥ ⑦ ⑧	35	① ② ③ ④ ⑤ ⑥ ⑦ ⑧
11	① ② ③ ④ ⑤ ⑥ ⑦ ⑧	36	① ② ③ ④ ⑤ ⑥ ⑦ ⑧
12	① ② ③ ④ ⑤ ⑥ ⑦ ⑧	37	① ② ③ ④ ⑤ ⑥ ⑦ ⑧
13	① ② ③ ④ ⑤ ⑥ ⑦ ⑧	38	① ② ③ ④ ⑤ ⑥ ⑦ ⑧
14	① ② ③ ④ ⑤ ⑥ ⑦ ⑧	39	① ② ③ ④ ⑤ ⑥ ⑦ ⑧
15	① ② ③ ④ ⑤ ⑥ ⑦ ⑧	40	① ② ③ ④ ⑤ ⑥ ⑦ ⑧
16	① ② ③ ④ ⑤ ⑥ ⑦ ⑧	41	① ② ③ ④ ⑤ ⑥ ⑦ ⑧
17	① ② ③ ④ ⑤ ⑥ ⑦ ⑧	42	① ② ③ ④ ⑤ ⑥ ⑦ ⑧
18	① ② ③ ④ ⑤ ⑥ ⑦ ⑧	43	① ② ③ ④ ⑤ ⑥ ⑦ ⑧
19	① ② ③ ④ ⑤ ⑥ ⑦ ⑧	44	① ② ③ ④ ⑤ ⑥ ⑦ ⑧
20	① ② ③ ④ ⑤ ⑥ ⑦ ⑧	45	① ② ③ ④ ⑤ ⑥ ⑦ ⑧
21	① ② ③ ④ ⑤ ⑥ ⑦ ⑧	46	① ② ③ ④ ⑤ ⑥ ⑦ ⑧
22	① ② ③ ④ ⑤ ⑥ ⑦ ⑧	47	① ② ③ ④ ⑤ ⑥ ⑦ ⑧
23	① ② ③ ④ ⑤ ⑥ ⑦ ⑧	48	① ② ③ ④ ⑤ ⑥ ⑦ ⑧
24	① ② ③ ④ ⑤ ⑥ ⑦ ⑧	49	① ② ③ ④ ⑤ ⑥ ⑦ ⑧
25	① ② ③ ④ ⑤ ⑥ ⑦ ⑧	50	① ② ③ ④ ⑤ ⑥ ⑦ ⑧

Test परीक्षण 5

TEST ID परीक्षण अभिज्ञान Ⓐ Ⓑ Ⓒ Ⓓ Ⓔ Ⓕ

TEST CODE परीक्षण कूट: I ① II ② III ③ IV ④ V ⑤ VI ⑥ VII ⑦ VIII ⑧

1	① ② ③ ④ ⑤ ⑥ ⑦ ⑧	26	① ② ③ ④ ⑤ ⑥ ⑦ ⑧
2	① ② ③ ④ ⑤ ⑥ ⑦ ⑧	27	① ② ③ ④ ⑤ ⑥ ⑦ ⑧
3	① ② ③ ④ ⑤ ⑥ ⑦ ⑧	28	① ② ③ ④ ⑤ ⑥ ⑦ ⑧
4	① ② ③ ④ ⑤ ⑥ ⑦ ⑧	29	① ② ③ ④ ⑤ ⑥ ⑦ ⑧
5	① ② ③ ④ ⑤ ⑥ ⑦ ⑧	30	① ② ③ ④ ⑤ ⑥ ⑦ ⑧
6	① ② ③ ④ ⑤ ⑥ ⑦ ⑧	31	① ② ③ ④ ⑤ ⑥ ⑦ ⑧
7	① ② ③ ④ ⑤ ⑥ ⑦ ⑧	32	① ② ③ ④ ⑤ ⑥ ⑦ ⑧
8	① ② ③ ④ ⑤ ⑥ ⑦ ⑧	33	① ② ③ ④ ⑤ ⑥ ⑦ ⑧
9	① ② ③ ④ ⑤ ⑥ ⑦ ⑧	34	① ② ③ ④ ⑤ ⑥ ⑦ ⑧
10	① ② ③ ④ ⑤ ⑥ ⑦ ⑧	35	① ② ③ ④ ⑤ ⑥ ⑦ ⑧
11	① ② ③ ④ ⑤ ⑥ ⑦ ⑧	36	① ② ③ ④ ⑤ ⑥ ⑦ ⑧
12	① ② ③ ④ ⑤ ⑥ ⑦ ⑧	37	① ② ③ ④ ⑤ ⑥ ⑦ ⑧
13	① ② ③ ④ ⑤ ⑥ ⑦ ⑧	38	① ② ③ ④ ⑤ ⑥ ⑦ ⑧
14	① ② ③ ④ ⑤ ⑥ ⑦ ⑧	39	① ② ③ ④ ⑤ ⑥ ⑦ ⑧
15	① ② ③ ④ ⑤ ⑥ ⑦ ⑧	40	① ② ③ ④ ⑤ ⑥ ⑦ ⑧
16	① ② ③ ④ ⑤ ⑥ ⑦ ⑧	41	① ② ③ ④ ⑤ ⑥ ⑦ ⑧
17	① ② ③ ④ ⑤ ⑥ ⑦ ⑧	42	① ② ③ ④ ⑤ ⑥ ⑦ ⑧
18	① ② ③ ④ ⑤ ⑥ ⑦ ⑧	43	① ② ③ ④ ⑤ ⑥ ⑦ ⑧
19	① ② ③ ④ ⑤ ⑥ ⑦ ⑧	44	① ② ③ ④ ⑤ ⑥ ⑦ ⑧
20	① ② ③ ④ ⑤ ⑥ ⑦ ⑧	45	① ② ③ ④ ⑤ ⑥ ⑦ ⑧
21	① ② ③ ④ ⑤ ⑥ ⑦ ⑧	46	① ② ③ ④ ⑤ ⑥ ⑦ ⑧
22	① ② ③ ④ ⑤ ⑥ ⑦ ⑧	47	① ② ③ ④ ⑤ ⑥ ⑦ ⑧
23	① ② ③ ④ ⑤ ⑥ ⑦ ⑧	48	① ② ③ ④ ⑤ ⑥ ⑦ ⑧
24	① ② ③ ④ ⑤ ⑥ ⑦ ⑧	49	① ② ③ ④ ⑤ ⑥ ⑦ ⑧
25	① ② ③ ④ ⑤ ⑥ ⑦ ⑧	50	① ② ③ ④ ⑤ ⑥ ⑦ ⑧

Example Test-4		Example Test-5	
1	① ② ③ ④ ⑤ ⑥ ⑦ ⑧	1	① ② ③ ④ ⑤ ⑥ ⑦ ⑧
2	① ② ③ ④ ⑤ ⑥ ⑦ ⑧	2	① ② ③ ④ ⑤ ⑥ ⑦ ⑧
3	① ② ③ ④ ⑤ ⑥ ⑦ ⑧	3	① ② ③ ④ ⑤ ⑥ ⑦ ⑧
4	① ② ③ ④ ⑤ ⑥ ⑦ ⑧	4	① ② ③ ④ ⑤ ⑥ ⑦ ⑧
5	① ② ③ ④ ⑤ ⑥ ⑦ ⑧	5	① ② ③ ④ ⑤ ⑥ ⑦ ⑧

उत्तर देने का सही तरीका :- ✗ ✗ ✗ ✓ ✗

Based on Latest Pattern Book

निर्देश : INSTRUCTIONS :

★ नीले बाल प्वाइंट पैन से भरें।
★ Marks By Blue Ball Point Pen.
★ दिए गए उत्तर बदलने की अनुमति नहीं है लेकिन Online Exam में उत्तर बदलने की अनुमति है।
★ No change in answer permited But changing is allowed in online Exam.
★ उत्तर पत्र पर अन्य किसी जगह कोई निशान न लगायें।
★ Do not make any stray marks on this form.

MODI CLASSES NAWADA
Mob.: 09334610185
09973120503

रौल नं॰ अंकों (In Figures)

रौल नं॰ शब्दो में (In Words)..

निम्न क्रम में परीक्षा होती है:-
1. Classification Test
2. Add/Counting of Odd No. Test
3. Shortest Route Test
4. Information Ordering Test
5. Personality Test

SYLLABUS FOR PSYCHOLOGICAL APTITUDE TEST (SM/DFCCIL)
(Based on Memory)

Battery Test	Chapters (CBAT) Name	No. of Questions	Time About (Online)	Time About (Offline)
1	Test For Measuring Your Intelligence (बुद्धि मापन हेतु परीक्षण) Classification Test (वर्गीकरण परीक्षण)	35	10 Min.	10 Min.
2	Test For Measuring Selective Attention (चयनात्मक अवधान मापन हेतु परीक्षण) (A) Add of Odd No. Test (विषम संख्याओं का योग परीक्षण) (B) Counting of Odd No. Test (विषम संख्याओं का गणन परीक्षण)	30	07-08 Min.	10 Min.
3	Test For Measuring Spatial Scanning (स्थानिक क्षमता मापन हेतु परीक्षण) Shortest Route Test (संक्षिप्त रास्ता परीक्षण)	40	05-08 Min.	05 Min.
4	Test For Measuring Information Ordering Test (निर्देश समझ सकने की योग्यता का परीक्षण)	25	06-08 Min.	10 Min.
5	Test For Measuring Personality Test (व्यक्तित्व समझ सकने की योग्यता का परीक्षण) Personality Test (व्यक्तित्व परीक्षण)	35	12-15 Min.	15 Min.
	Total	165	40-49 Min.	50 Min.

PSYCHO EXAM PATTERN (SM/DFCCIL)
(Based on Memory)

Battery Test	CBAT Exam Process	Time (about) (Minutes)	No. of Questions (about)
1	**Intelligence Test Instructions**	05	
	Inteligence Test	10	35
	Break	01	
2	**Selective Attention Test Instruction**	05	
	Selective Attention Test	07-08	30
	Break	01	
3	**Spatial Scanning Test Instruction**	05	
	Spatial Scanning Test	05 - 08	40
	Break	01	
4	**Information Ordering Test Instruction**	05	
	Information Test Ordering	06 - 08	25
	Break	01	
5	**Personality Test Instruction**	05	35
	Personality Test	12-15	
	Total	69 - 78	165
	Feed Back	06	14

CONTENTS
विषय-सूची

MODI CLASSES NAWADA

Station Master / Metro Railway / Asst. Loco Pilot
के पद पर चयनित अभ्यर्थी

1 TEST FOR MEASURING YOUR INTELLIGENCE

Classification Test (वर्गीकरण परीक्षण)

रेलवे मनोवैज्ञानिक परीक्षण के अन्तर्गत बुद्धि मापन परीक्षण स्टेशन मास्टर पद के लिए महत्वपूर्ण परीक्षण है जो व्यक्ति की बौद्धिक क्षमता, तर्कशक्ति क्षमता, समस्या समाधान का आकलन करता है।

दिए गए बुद्धि मापन परीक्षण में कुल 35 प्रश्न होंगे जिसे हल करने के लिए 10 मिनट का समय दिया जाऐंगे। इस परीक्षण के प्रत्येक प्रश्न में पाँच आकृतियाँ हैं जिसमें से चार में कुछ समानता है, आपको एक आकृति को खोजना है जो चारों से भिन्न है, वही भिन्न आकृति आपका उत्तर होगा जिसे दिए गए उत्तर-पत्रक में गोले को काला/माउस की सहायता से क्लिक करना होता है।

The Intelligence Test, part of the Railway Psychological Test, is an important test for the post of Station Master, which assesses a person's intellectual ability, reasoning ability, and problem-solving.

The Intelligence Test consists of a total of 35 questions, with a 10 minute time limit. Each question contains five figures, four of which have some similarity. You must find the one that is different from the other four. The different figure will be your answer by clicking on the black circle on the answer sheet or using the mouse.

नीचे दिए गए उदाहरणों के द्वारा इसे समझें :-

Example for understanding :-

A B C D E

1.
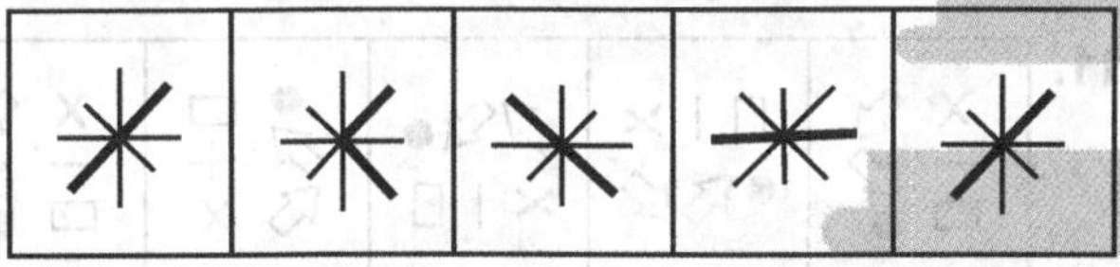

2.
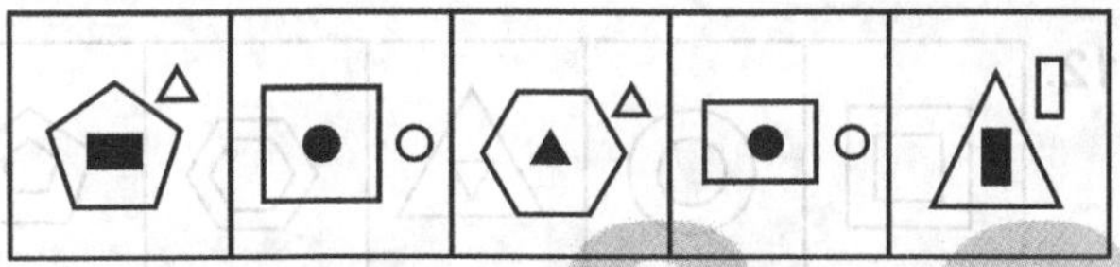

3.
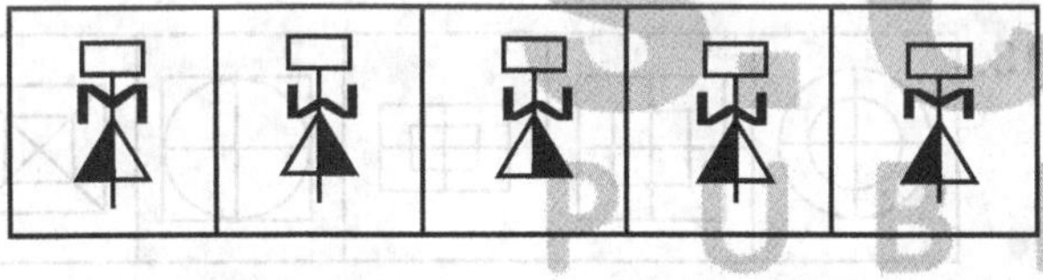

4.
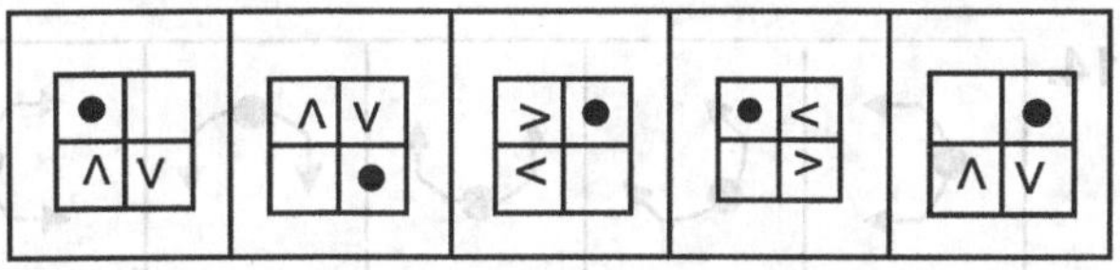

5.
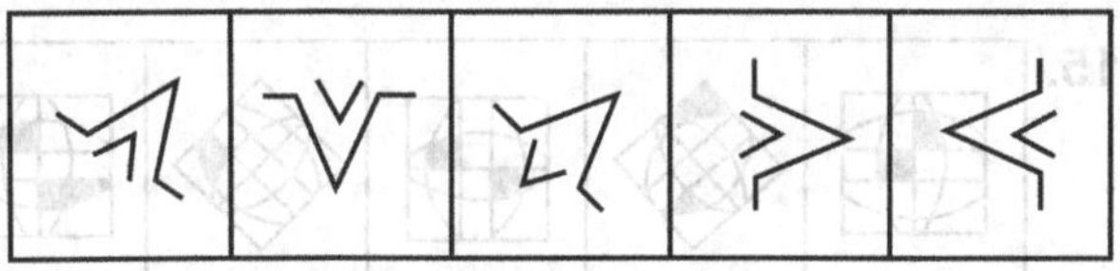

6.
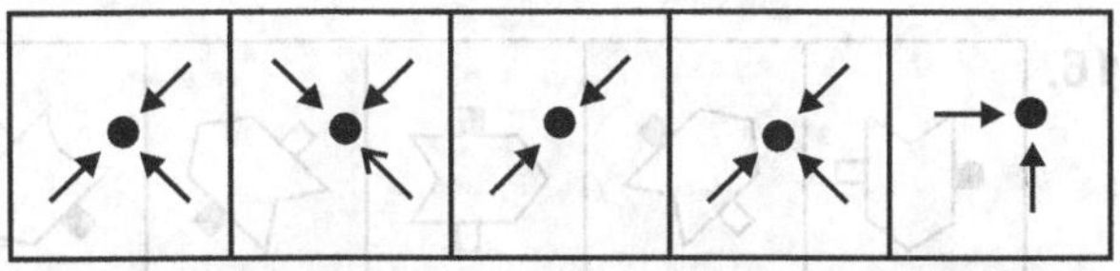

A B C D E

7.
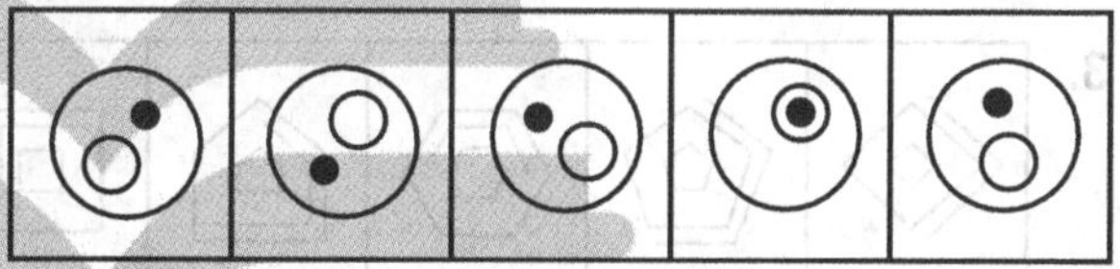

8.
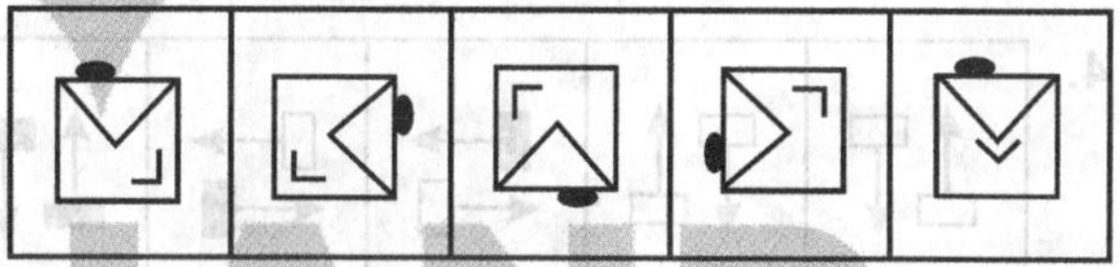

9.
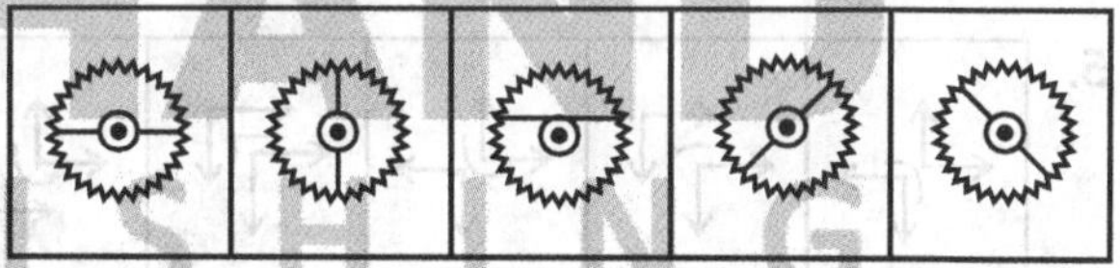

10.
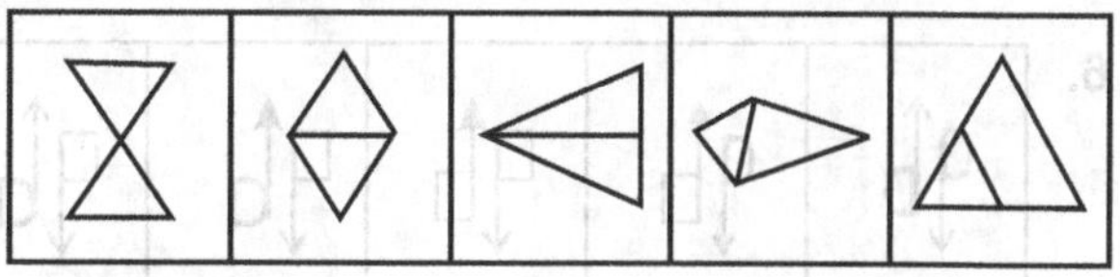

11.
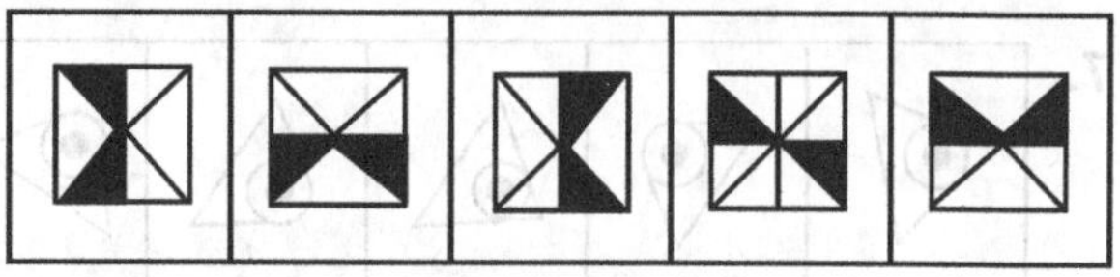

12.
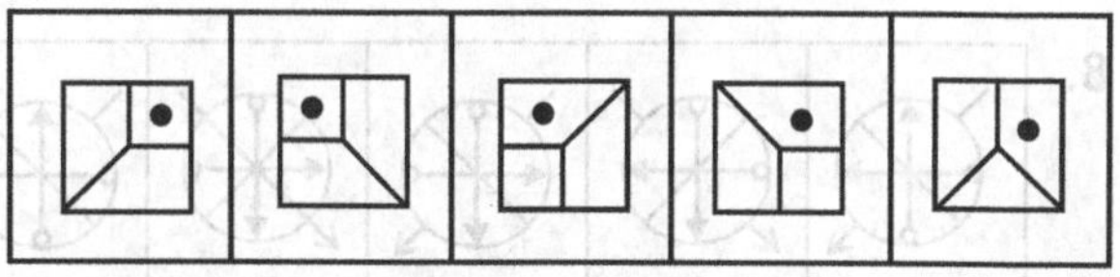

Ans.: 1. (B), 2. (A), 3. (C), 4. (E), 5. (C), 6. (B), 7. (D), 8. (E), 9. (C), 10. (E), 11. (D), 12. (E)

PRACTICE SET-1

Total Ques.- 35
Time - 10 Min.

निर्देश : (प्रश्न 1–35) बुद्धिमापन परीक्षण के प्रत्येक प्रश्न में पाँच आकृतियाँ दिए जाते हैं जिसमें से चार आकृतियाँ में कुछ समानता और कोई एक आकृति अन्य चारों से भिन्न है वही भिन्न आकृति आपका उत्तर होगा जिसे दिए गए उत्तर-पत्रक में गोले को काला/माउस की सहायता से क्लिक करना होता है और इसके लिए 10 मिनट का समय दिया जाता है।

Instructions : (Questions 1–35) : Each question in the Intelligence Test consists of five figures, four of which have some similarity, and one that is different from the other four is your answer. You must click on the black circle on the answer sheet or using the mouse. You are given 10 minutes to complete the test.

A B C D E

1. 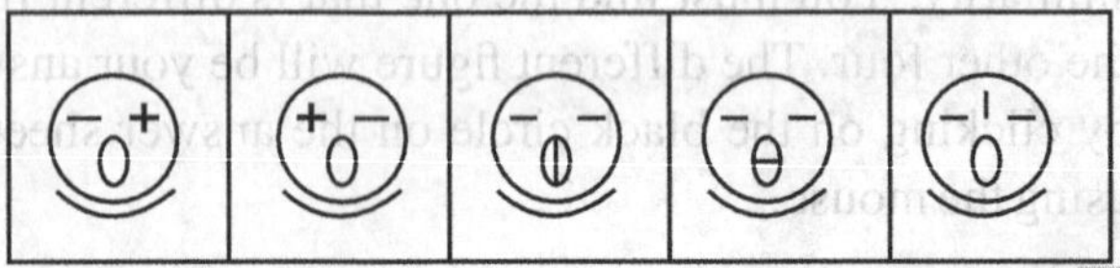

2. 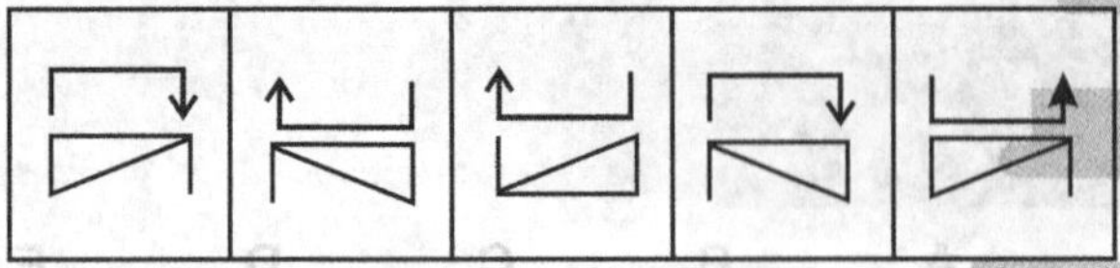

3. 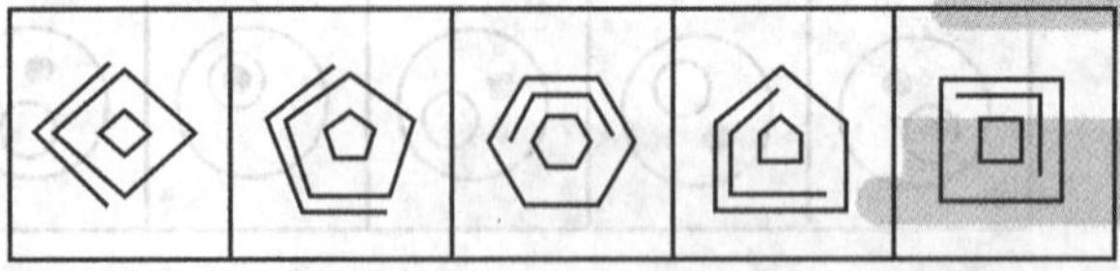

4. 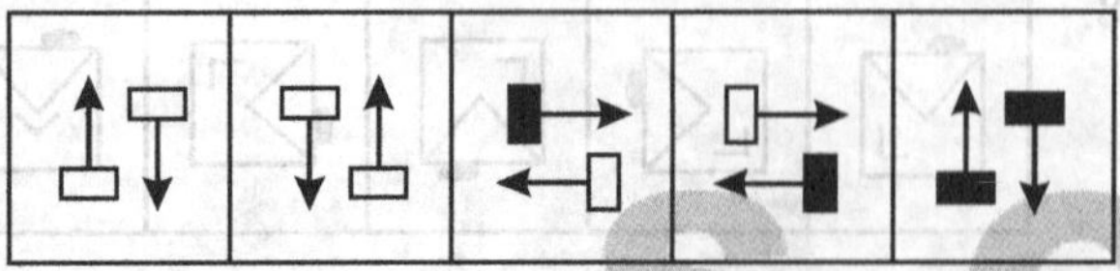

5. 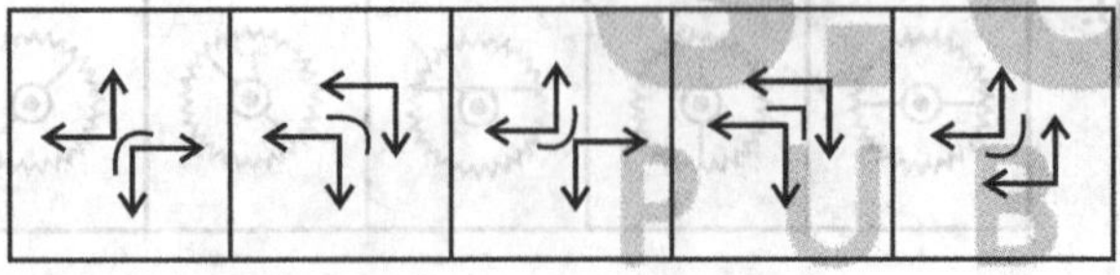

6. 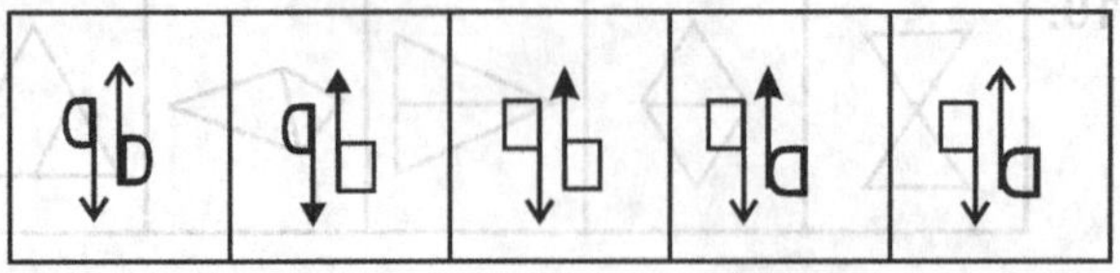

7. 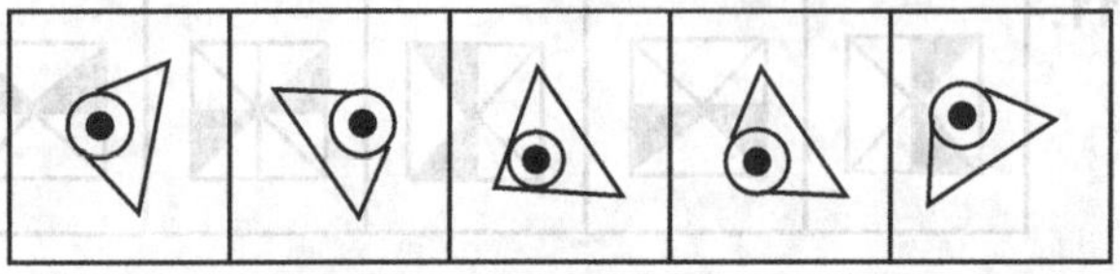

8. 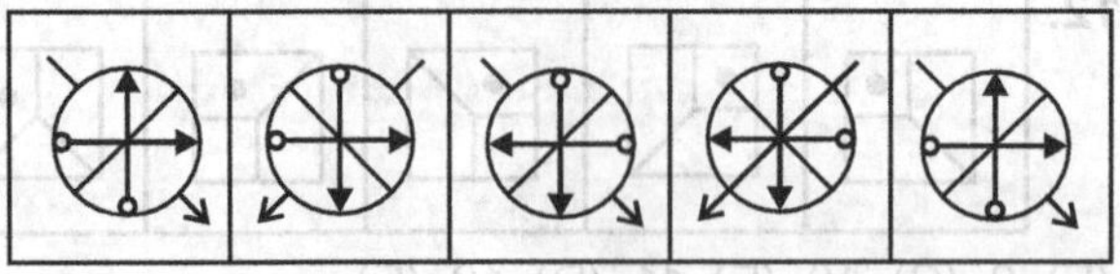

A B C D E

9. 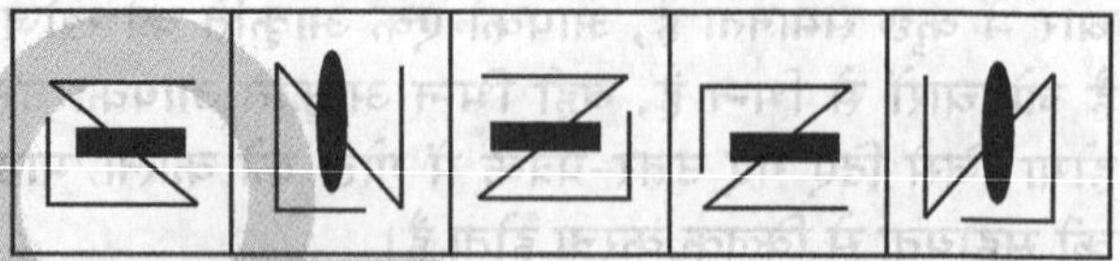

10. 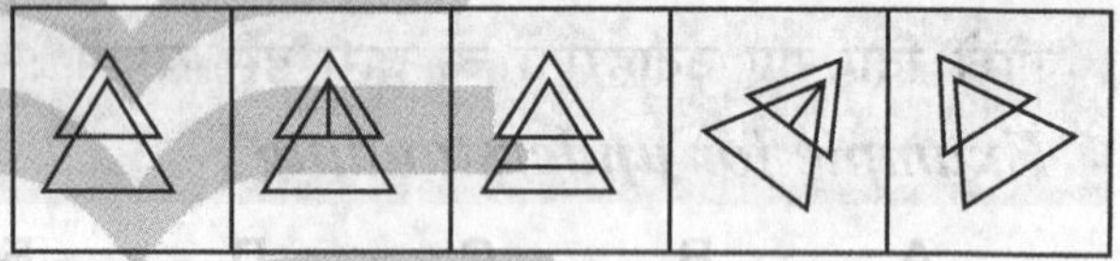

11. 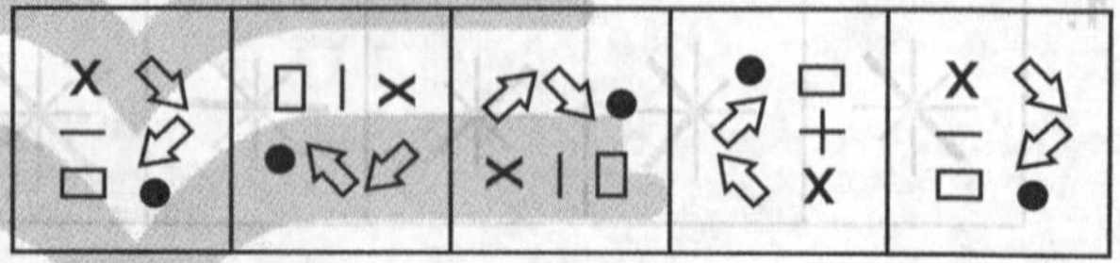

12. 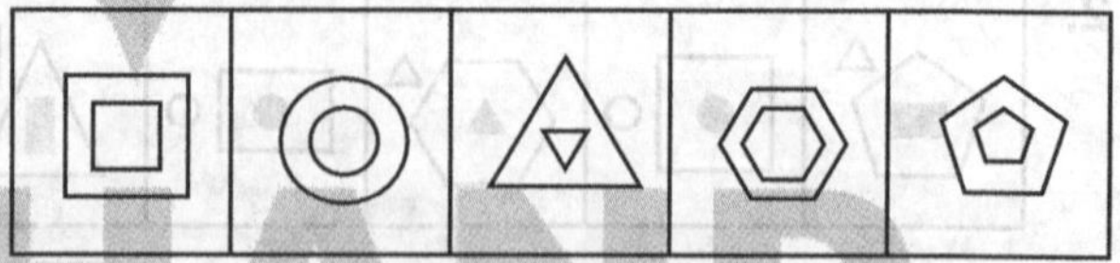

13. 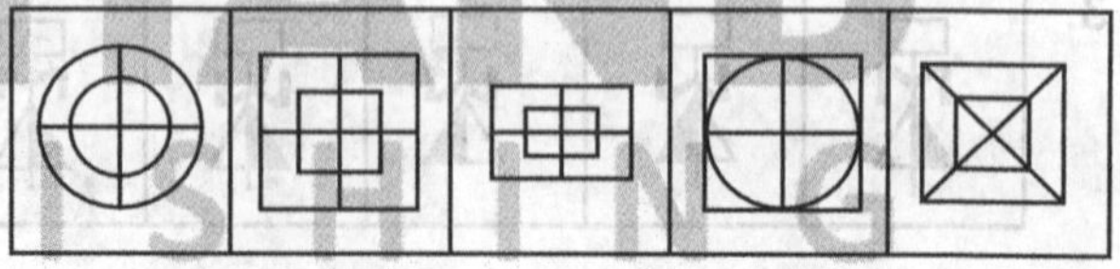

14. 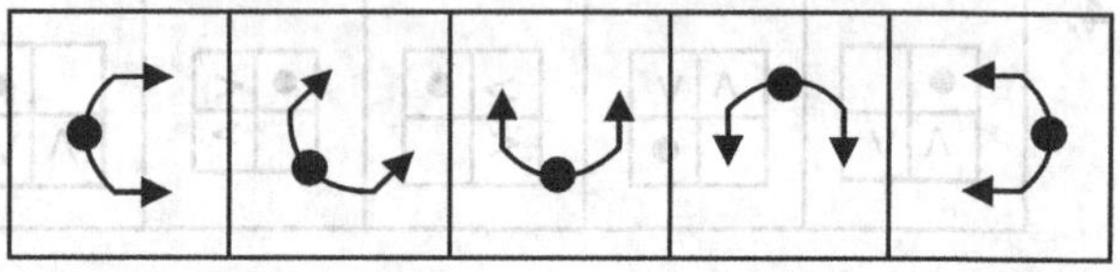

15. 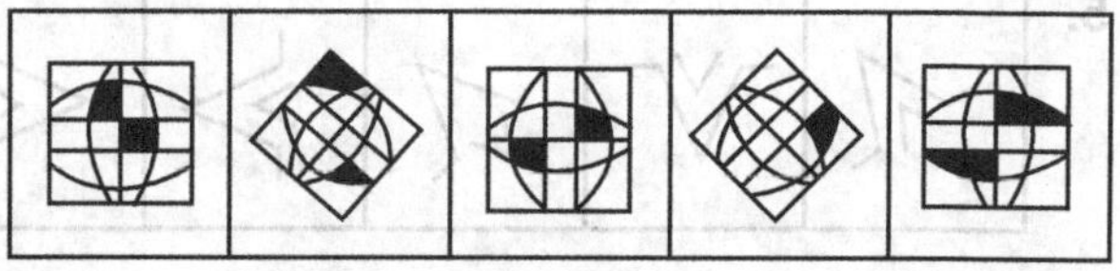

16. 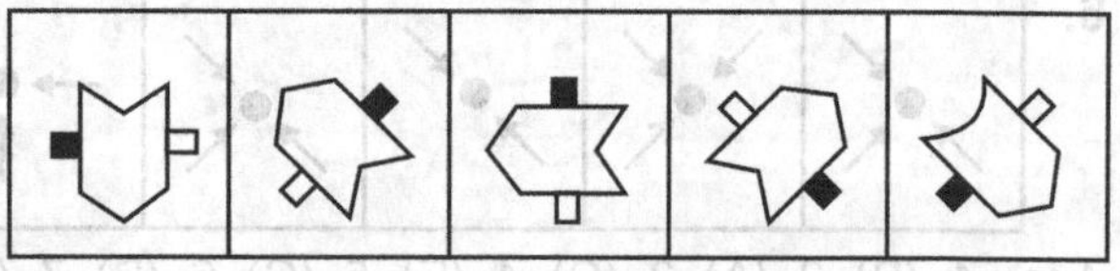

A B C D E

17.
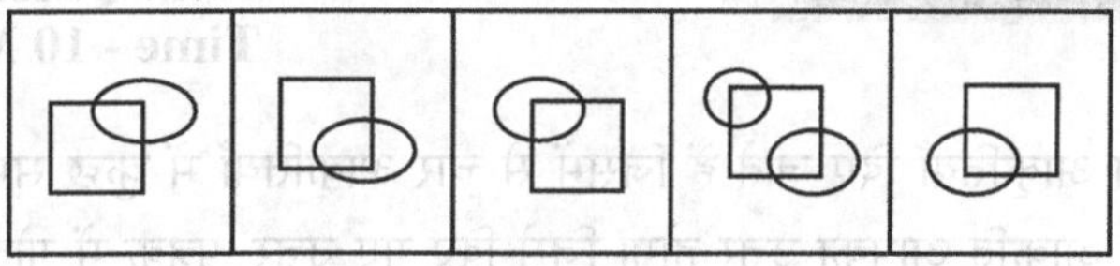

18.
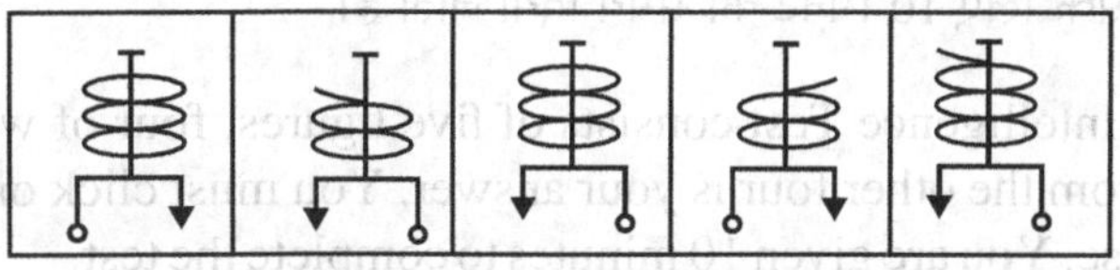

19.
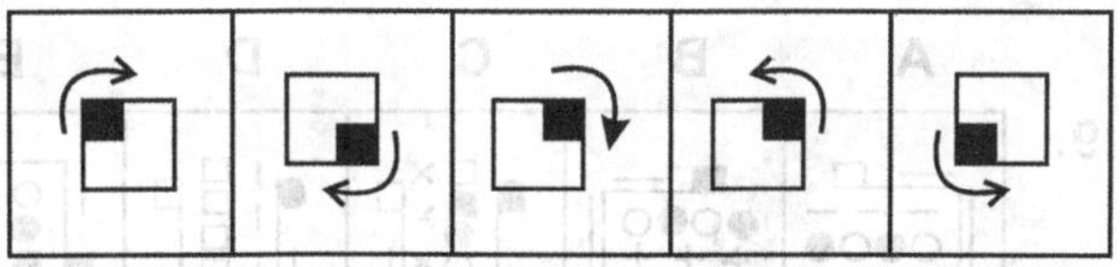

20.
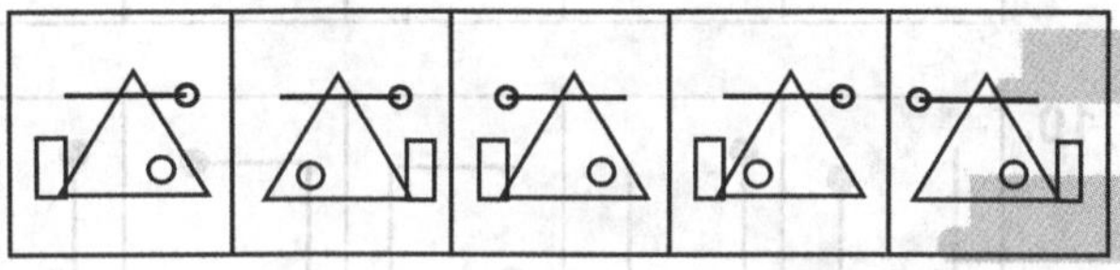

21.
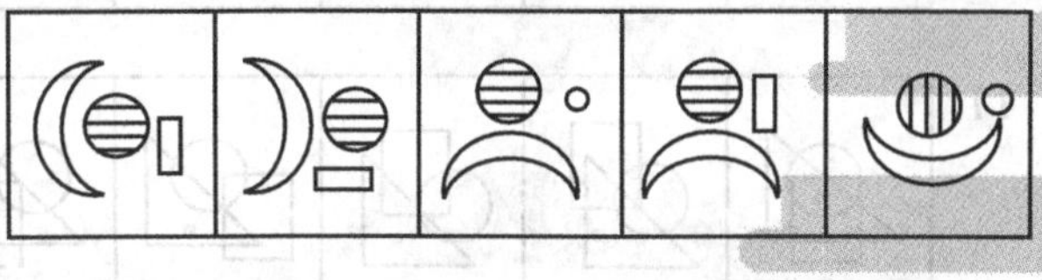

22.
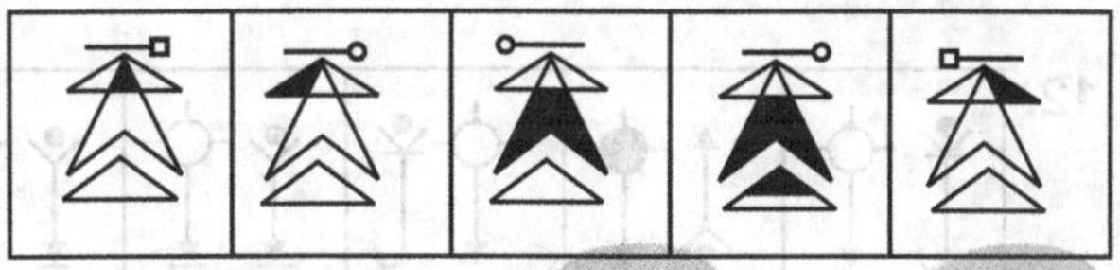

23.
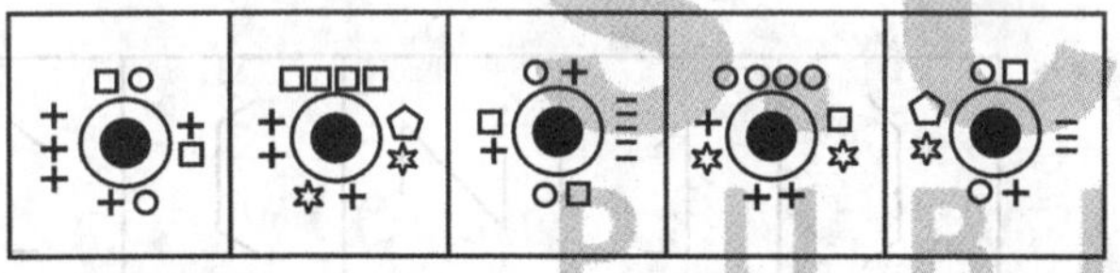

24.
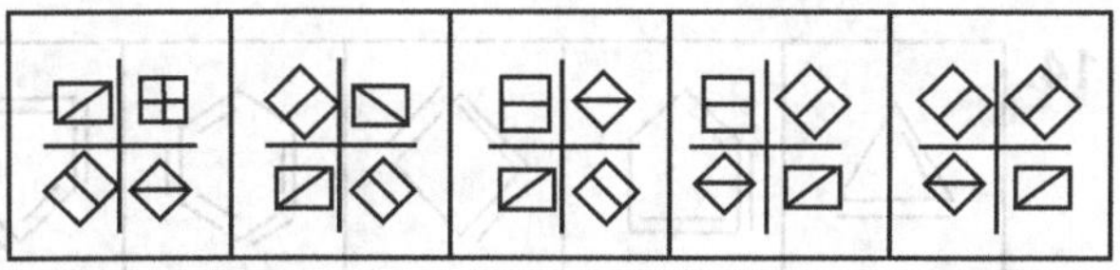

25.
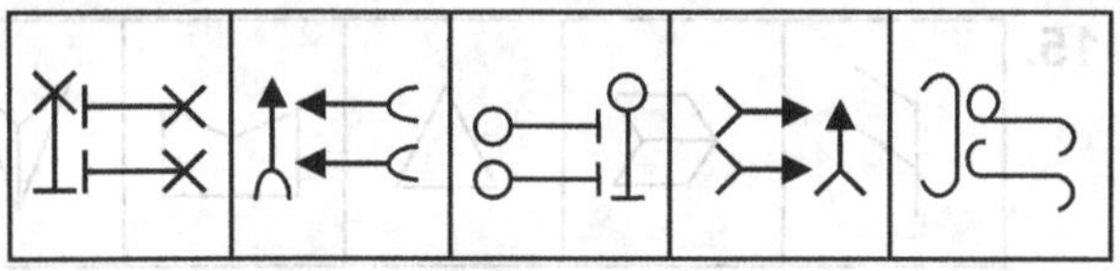

26.
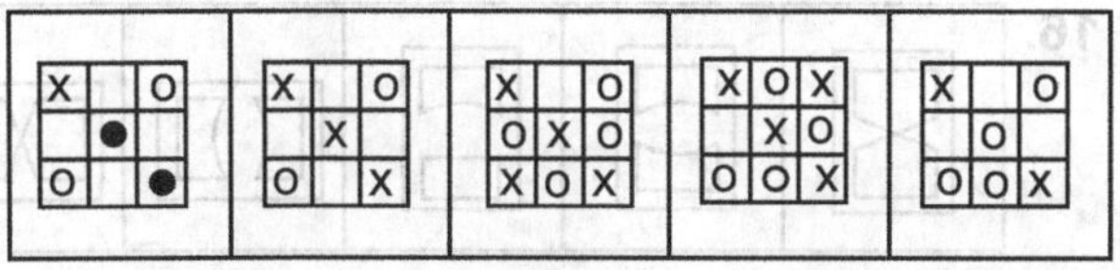

A B C D E

27.
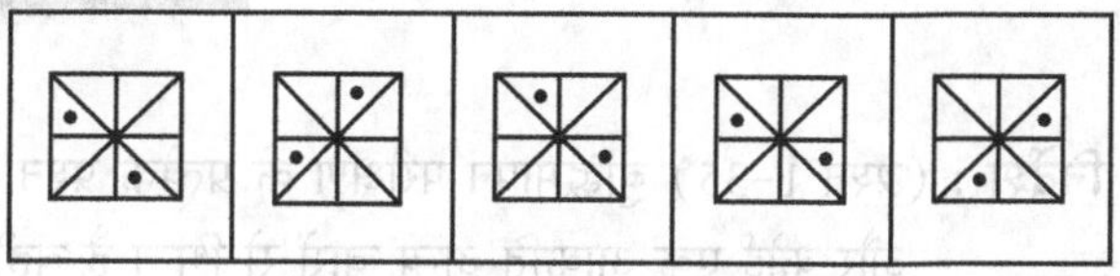

28.
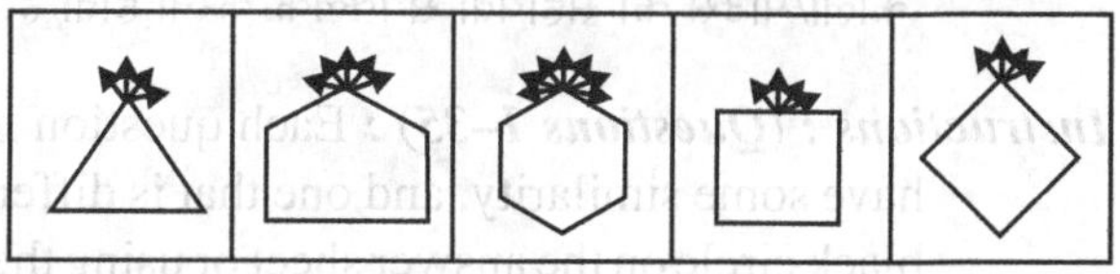

29.
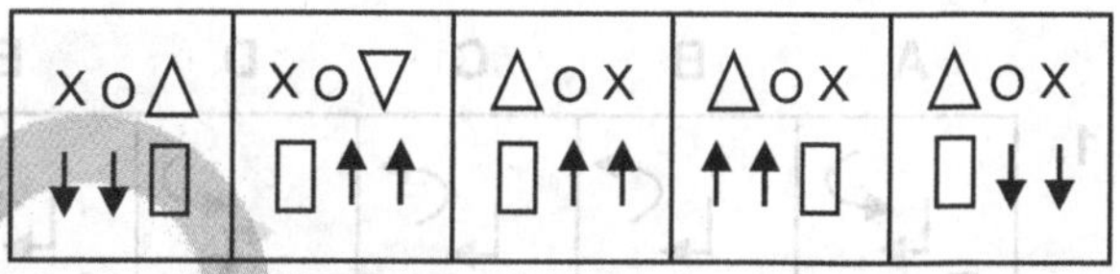

30.
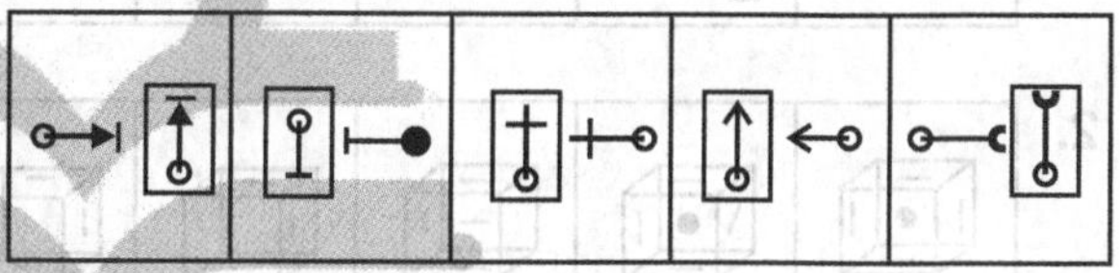

31.
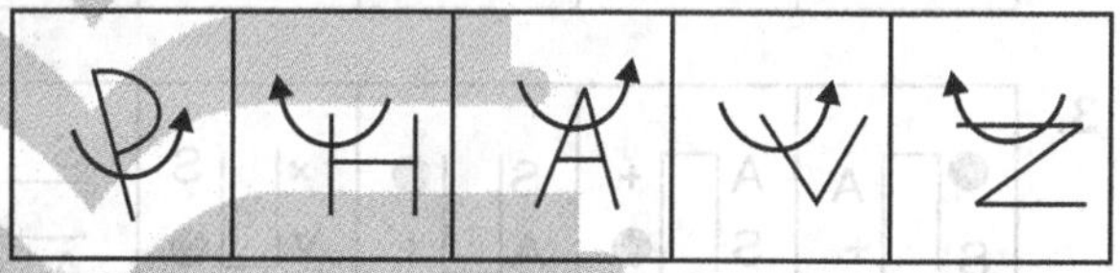

32.
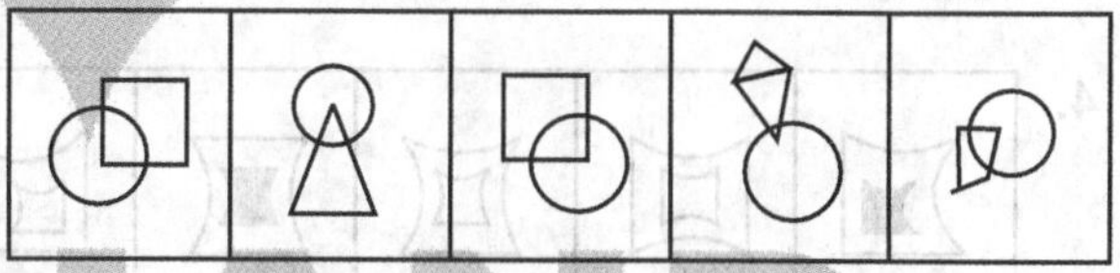

33.
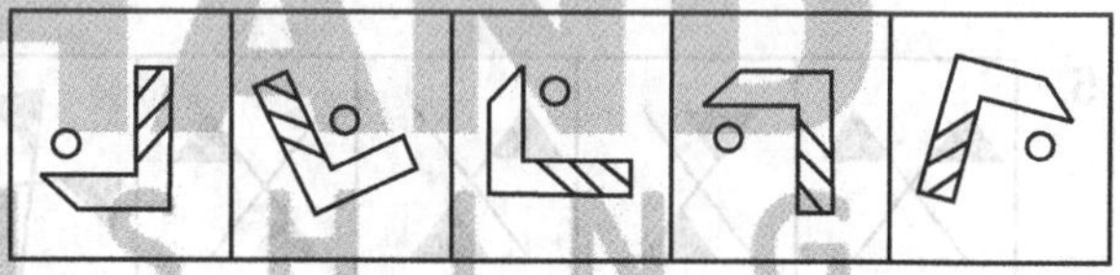

34.
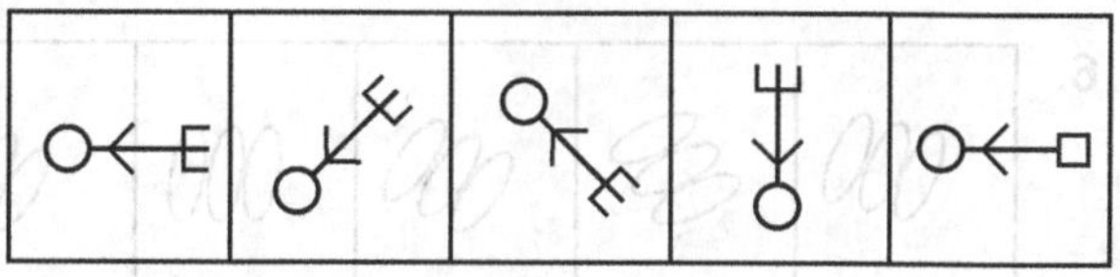

35.
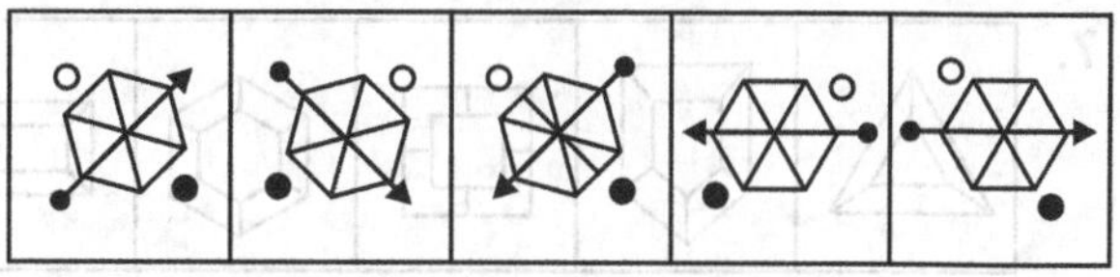

PRACTICE SET-2

Total Ques.- 35
Time - 10 Min.

निर्देश : (प्रश्न 1–35) बुद्धिमापन परीक्षण के प्रत्येक प्रश्न में पाँच आकृतियाँ दिए जाते हैं जिसमें से चार आकृतियाँ में कुछ समानता और कोई एक आकृति अन्य चारों से भिन्न है वही भिन्न आकृति आपका उत्तर होगा जिसे दिए गए उत्तर–पत्रक में गोले को काला/माउस की सहायता से क्लिक करना होता है और इसके लिए 10 मिनट का समय दिया जाता है।

Instructions : (Questions 1–35) : Each question in the Intelligence Test consists of five figures, four of which have some similarity, and one that is different from the other four is your answer. You must click on the black circle on the answer sheet or using the mouse. You are given 10 minutes to complete the test.

A B C D E

1. 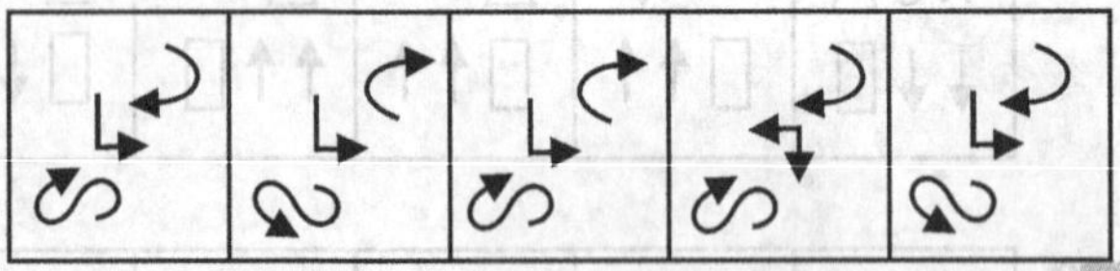

2. 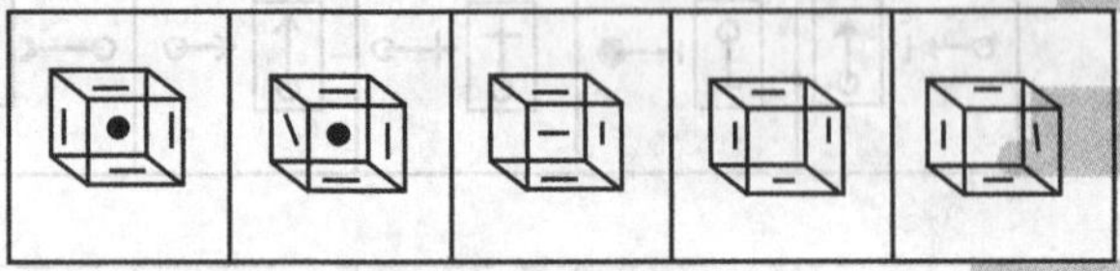

3. 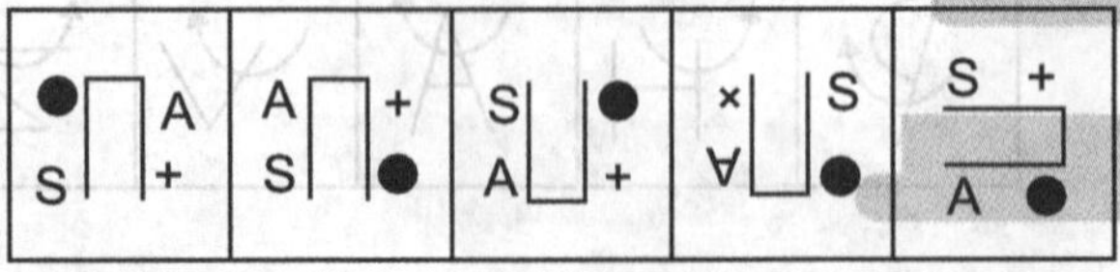

4. 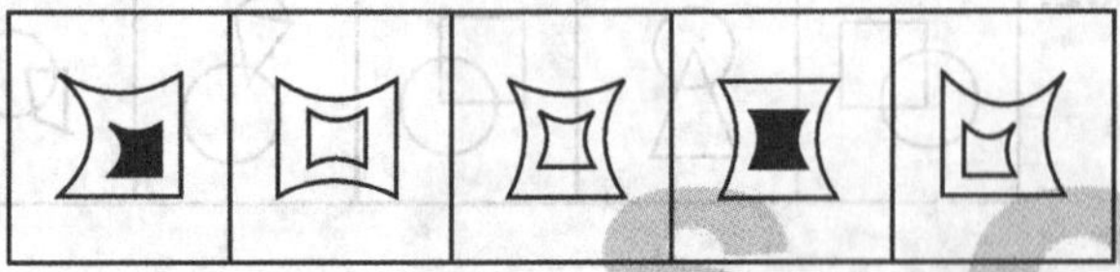

5. 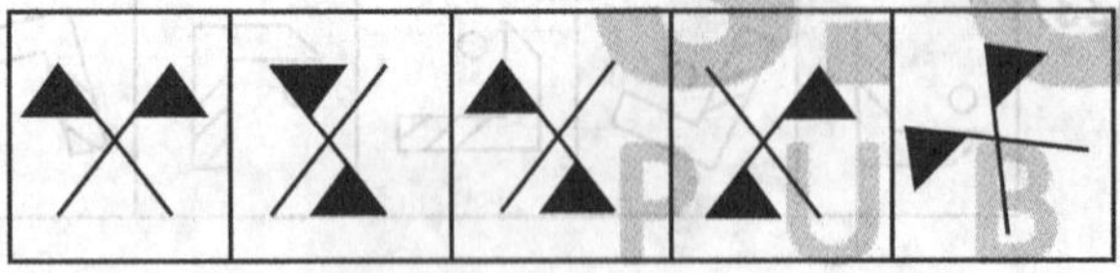

6. 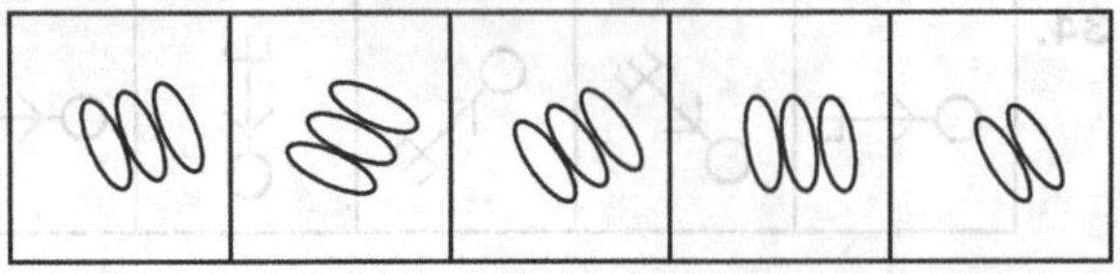

7. 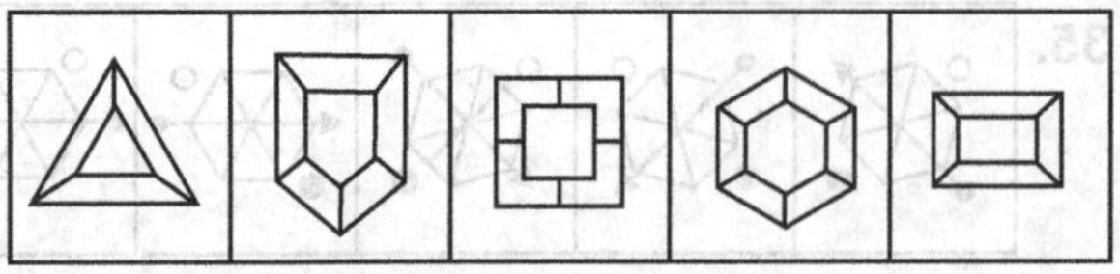

8. 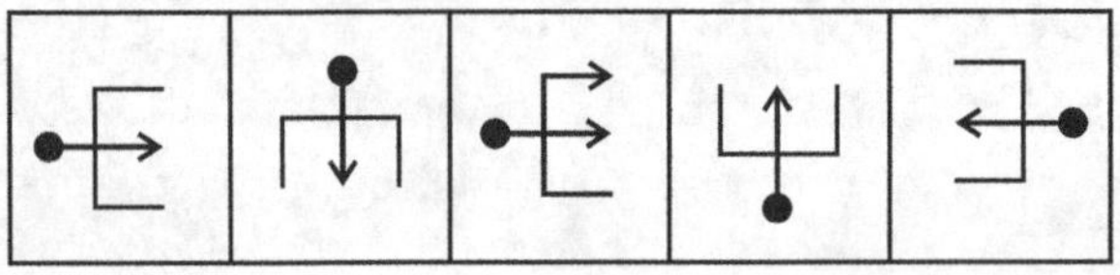

A B C D E

9. 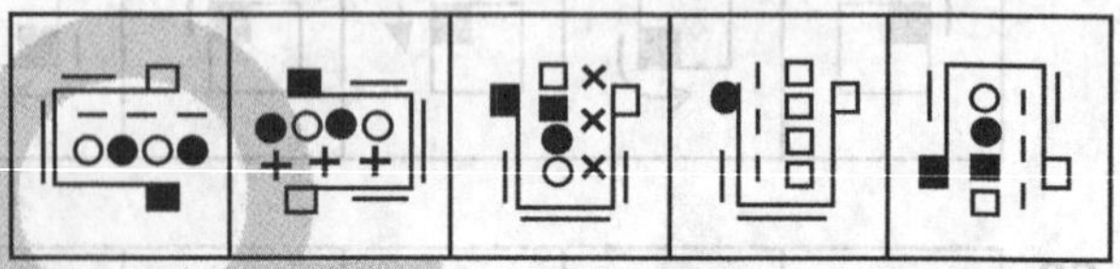

10. 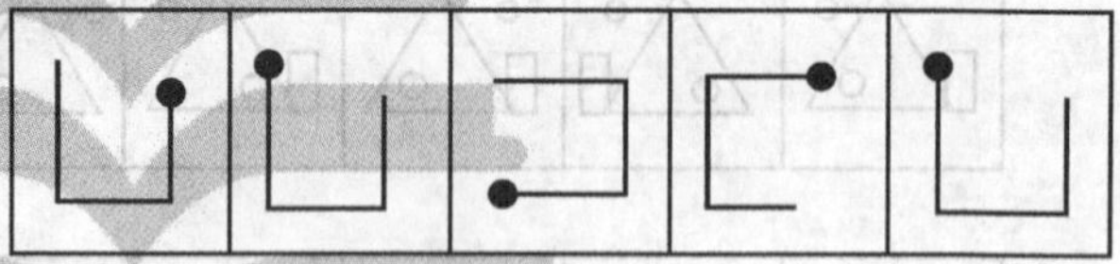

11. 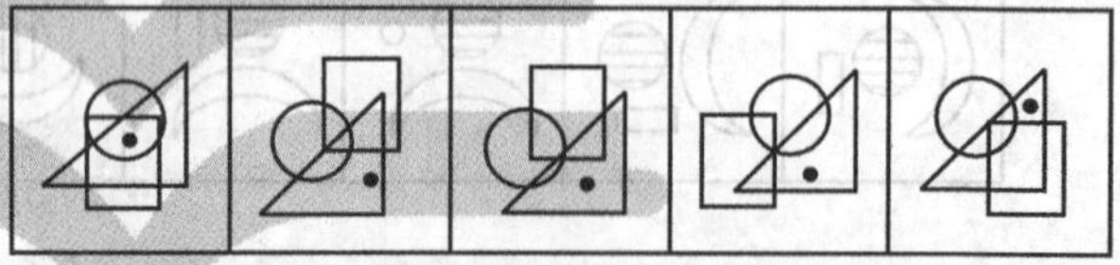

12. 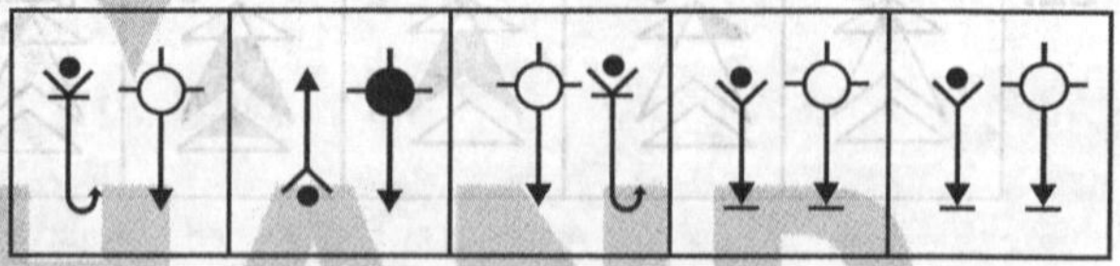

13. 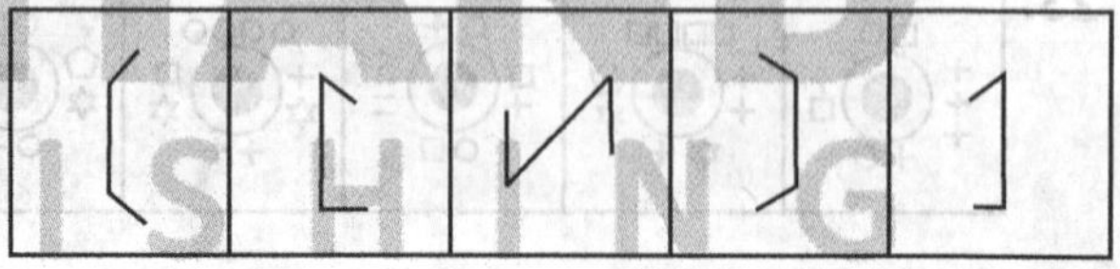

14. 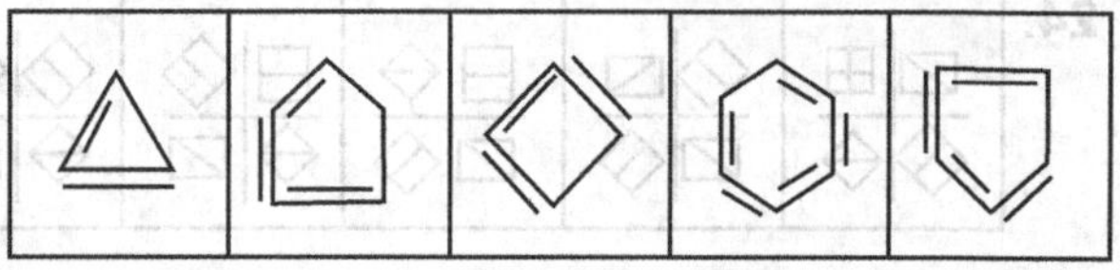

15. 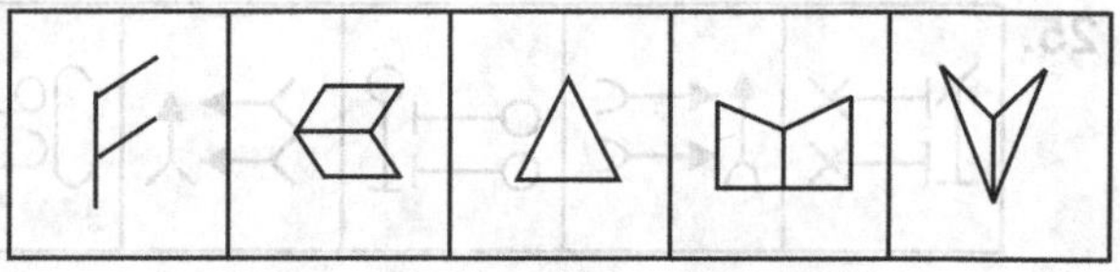

16. 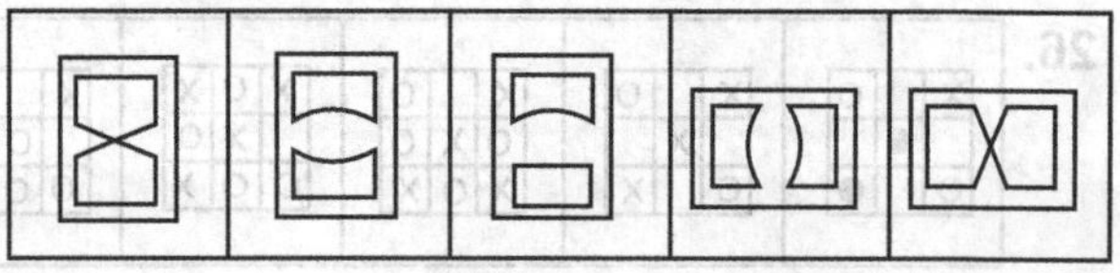

A B C D E

17. 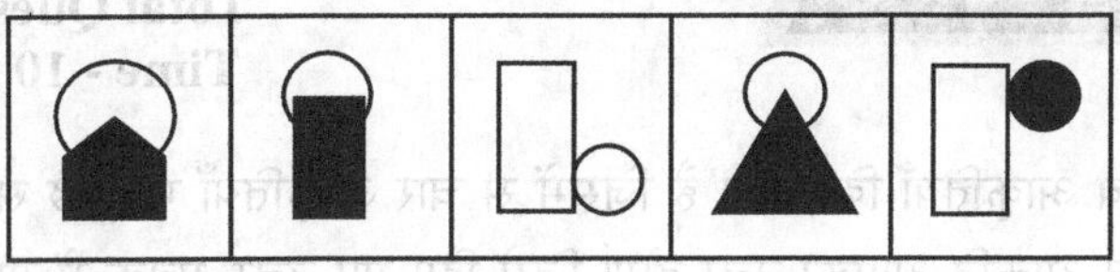

18. 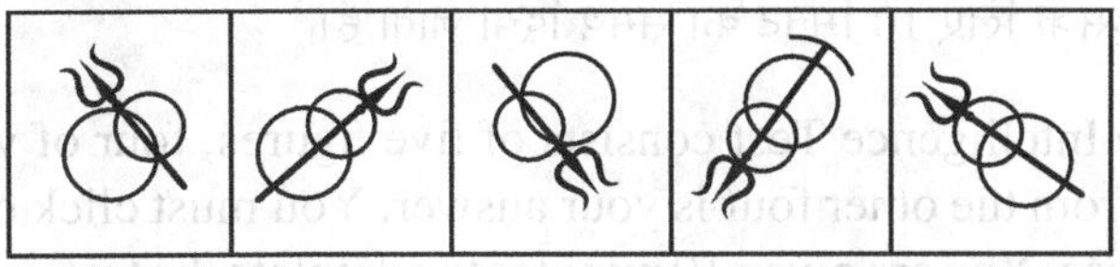

19.

A	B	C	D	E
UR	PE	KI	BM	OD

20. 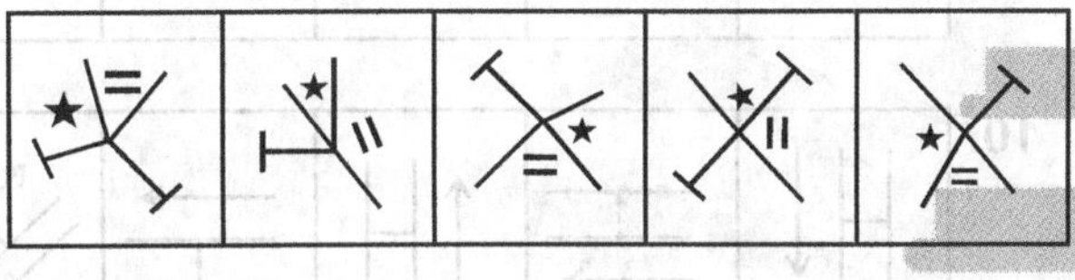

21. 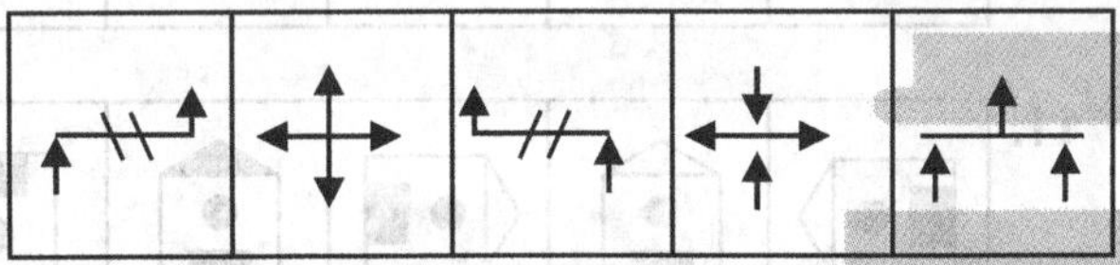

22. 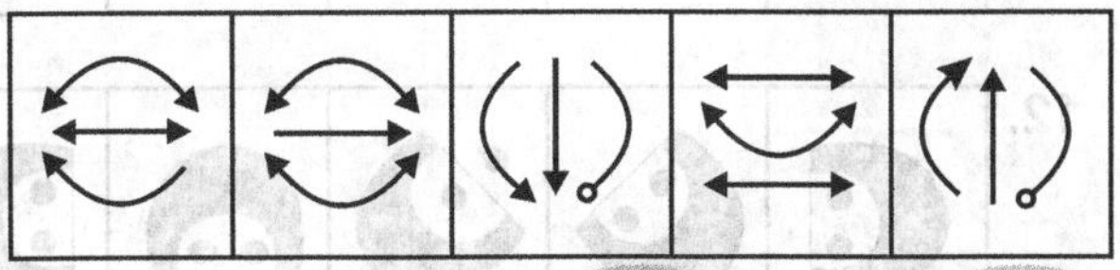

23. 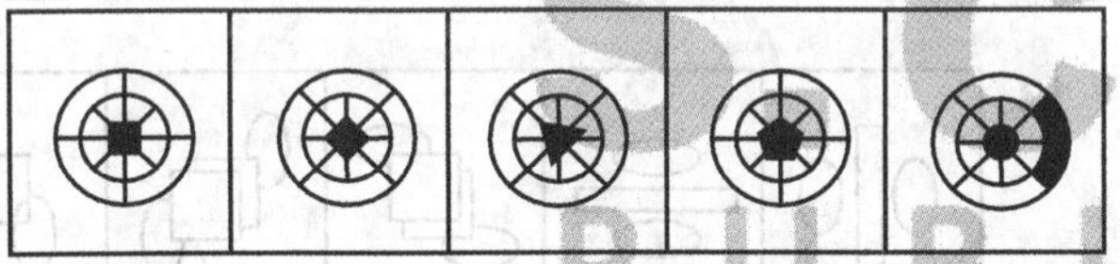

24. 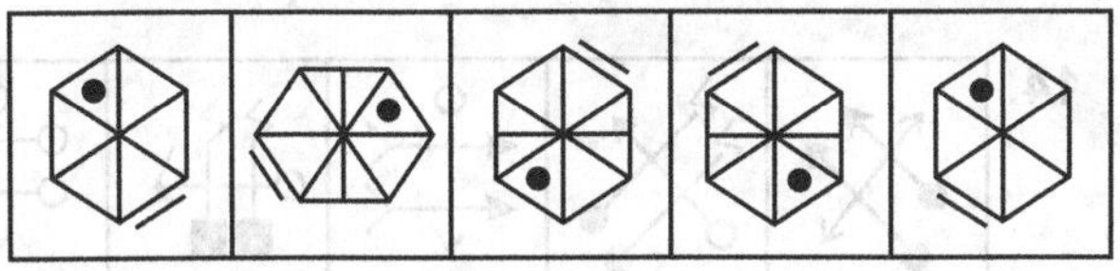

25. 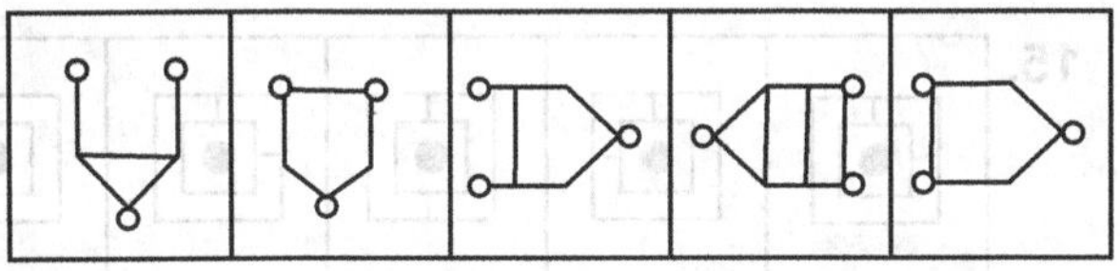

26. 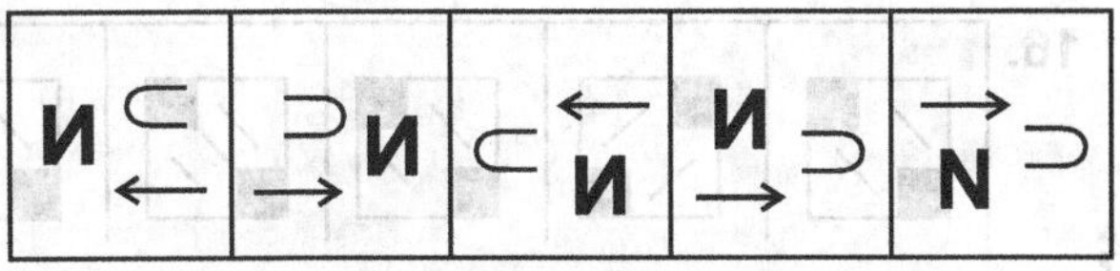

A B C D E

27. 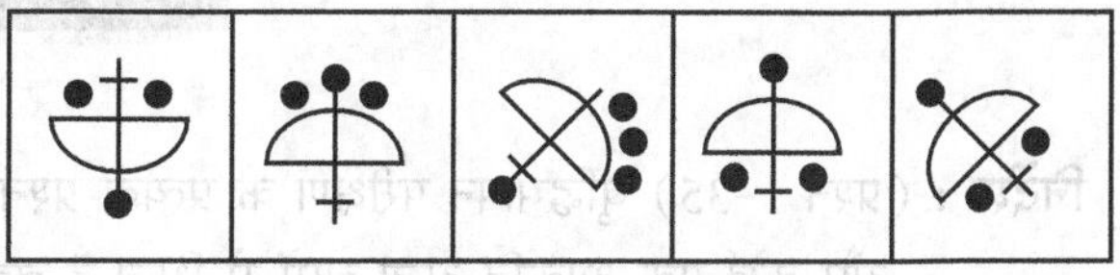

28. 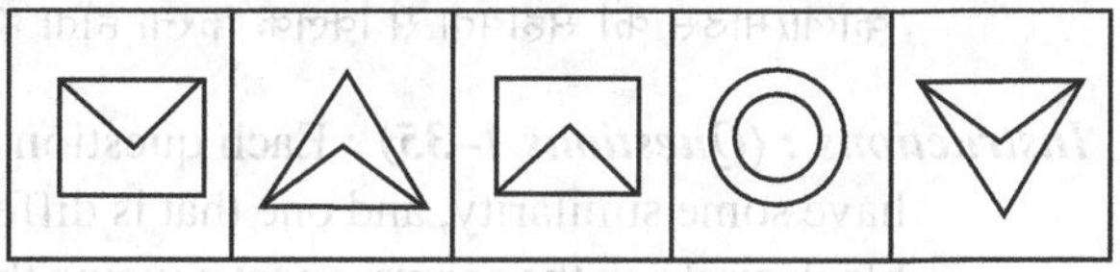

29. 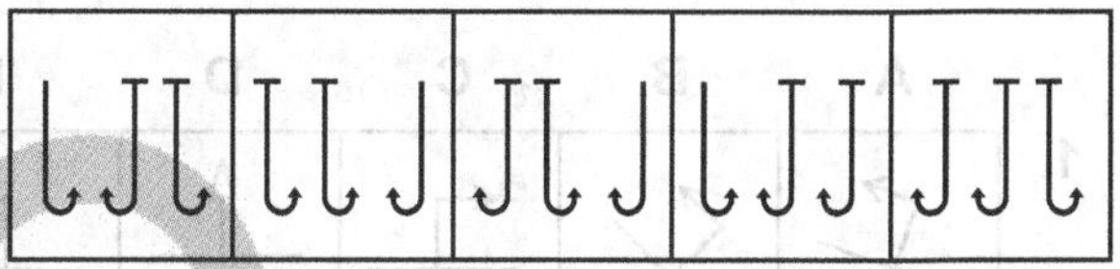

30. 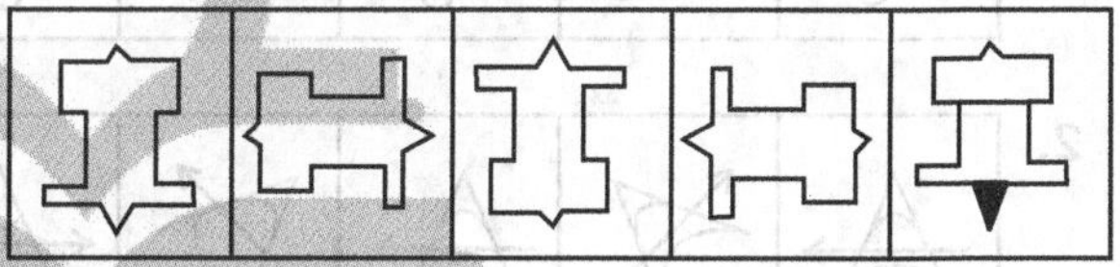

31. 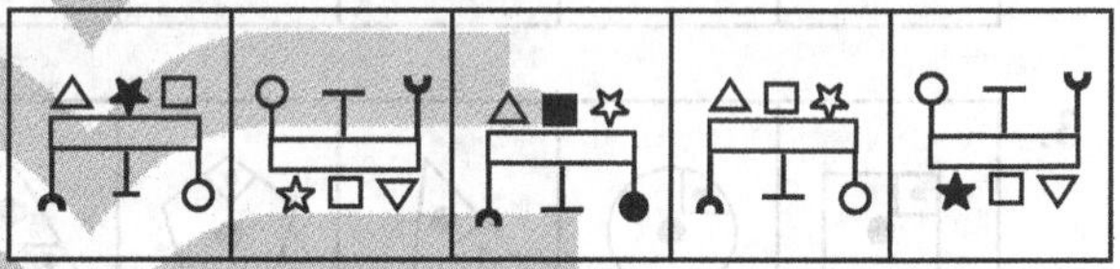

32. 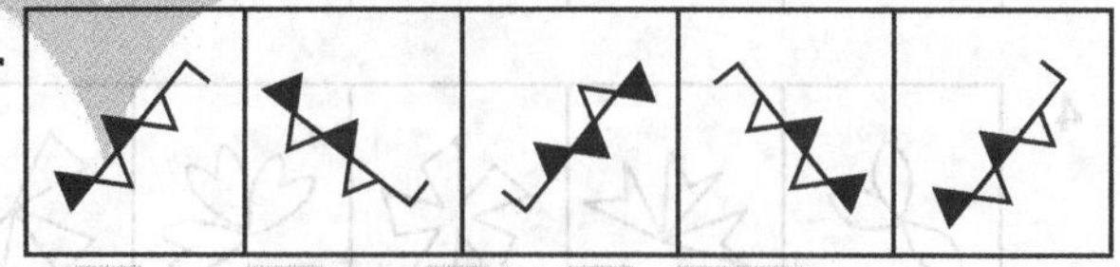

33. 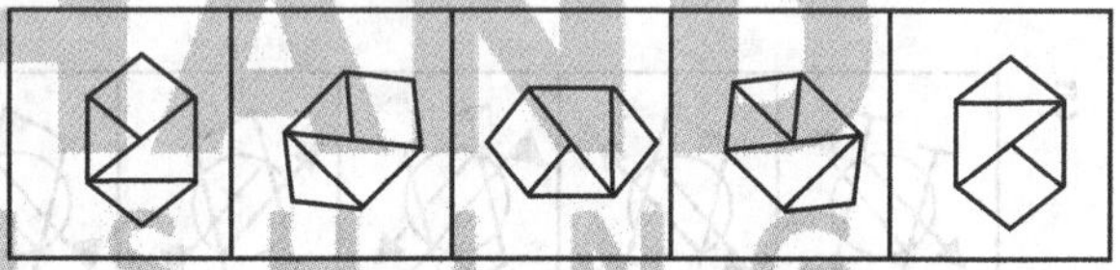

34. 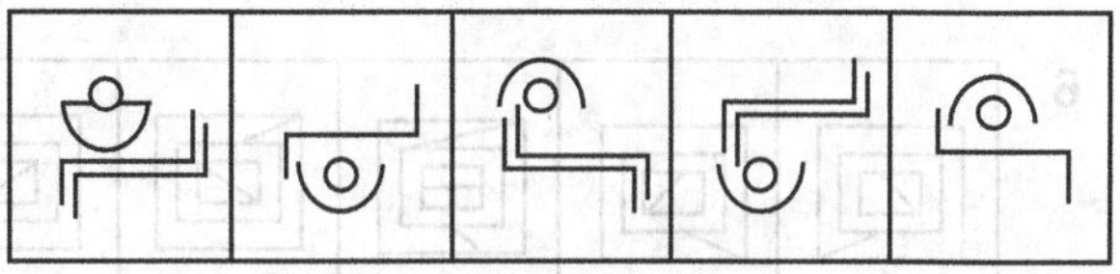

35. 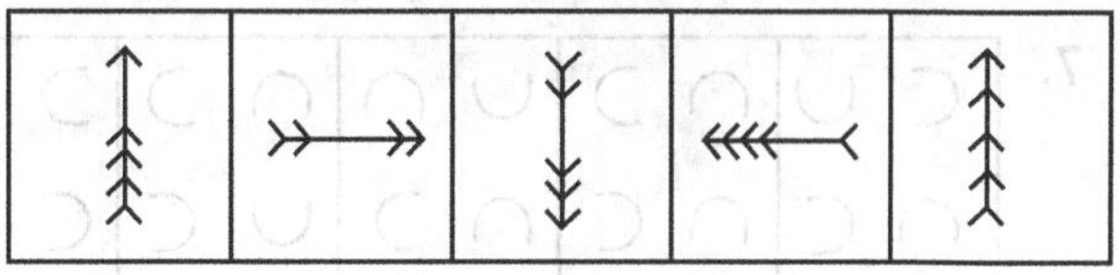

PRACTICE SET-3

Total Ques.- 35
Time - 10 Min.

निर्देश : (प्रश्न 1-35) बुद्धिमापन परीक्षण के प्रत्येक प्रश्न में पाँच आकृतियाँ दिए जाते हैं जिसमें से चार आकृतियाँ में कुछ समानता और कोई एक आकृति अन्य चारों से भिन्न है वही भिन्न आकृति आपका उत्तर होगा जिसे दिए गए उत्तर-पत्रक में गोले को काला/माउस की सहायता से क्लिक करना होता है और इसके लिए 10 मिनट का समय दिया जाता है।

Instructions : (Questions 1–35) : Each question in the Intelligence Test consists of five figures, four of which have some similarity, and one that is different from the other four is your answer. You must click on the black circle on the answer sheet or using the mouse. You are given 10 minutes to complete the test.

A B C D E

1. 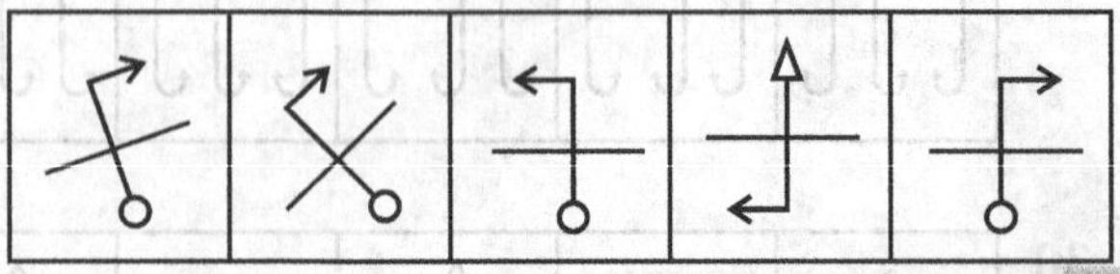

2. 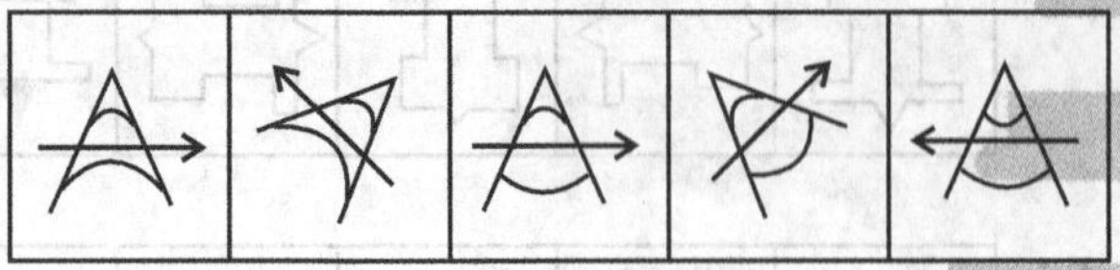

3. 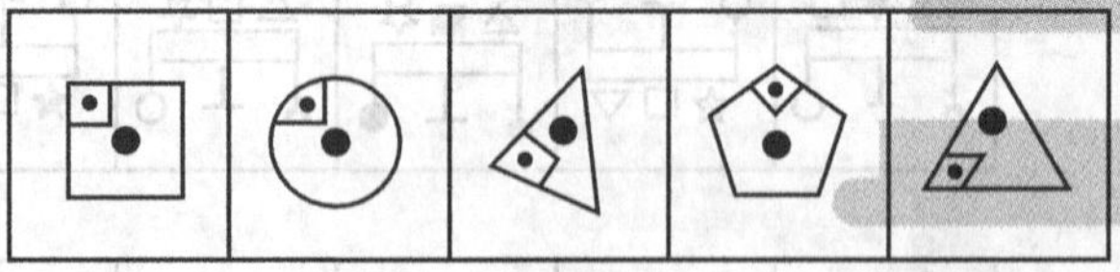

4. 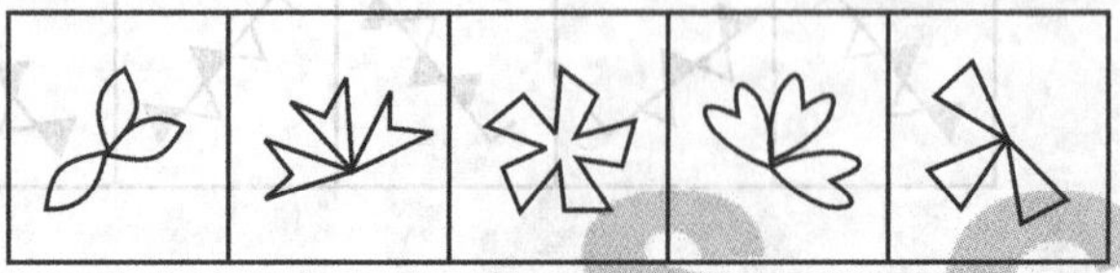

5. 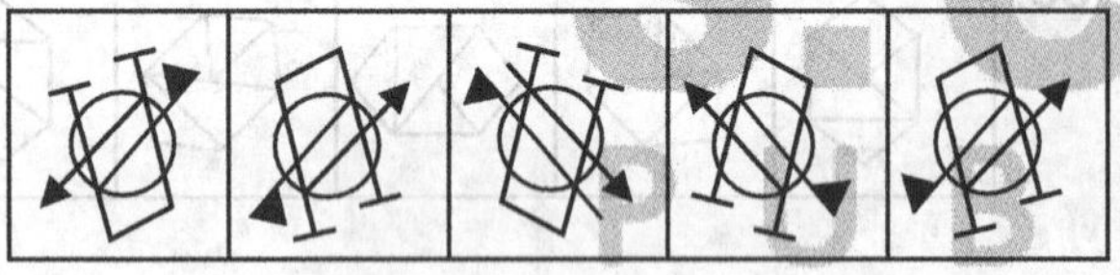

6. 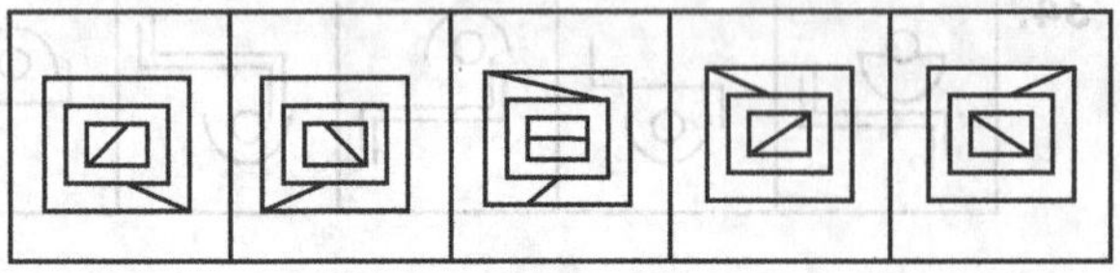

7. 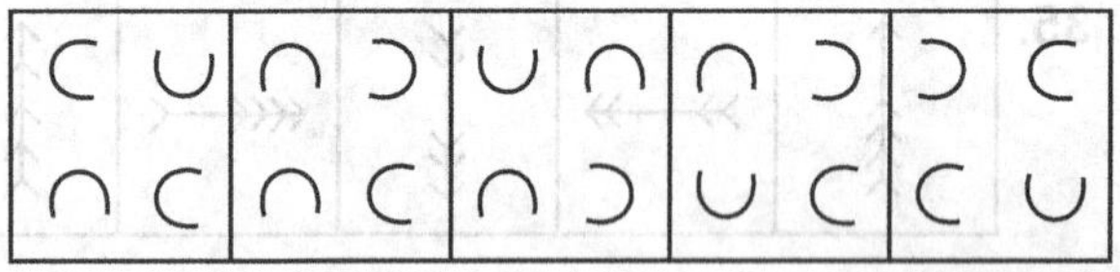

8. 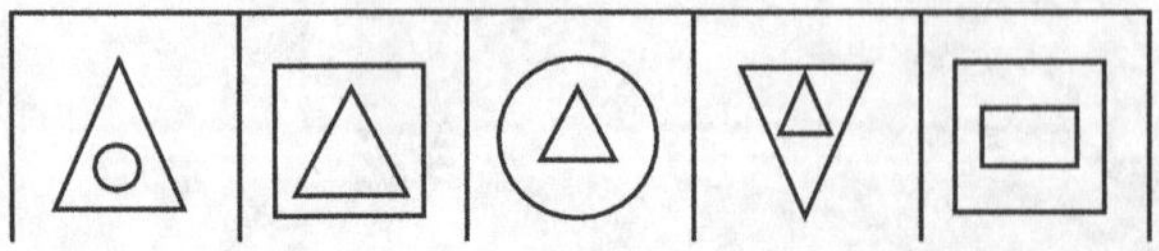

A B C D E

9. 

10. 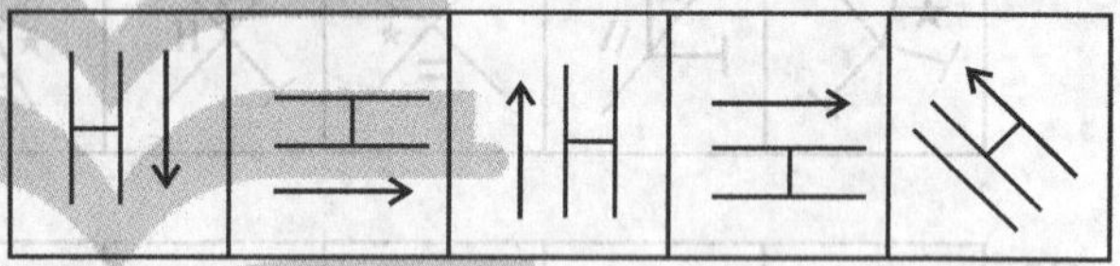

11. 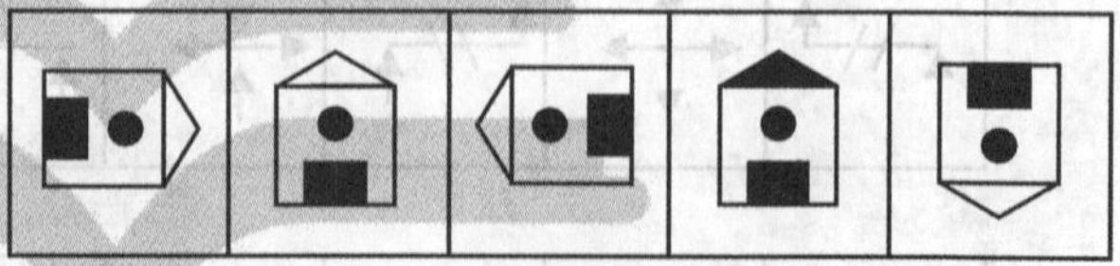

12. 

13. 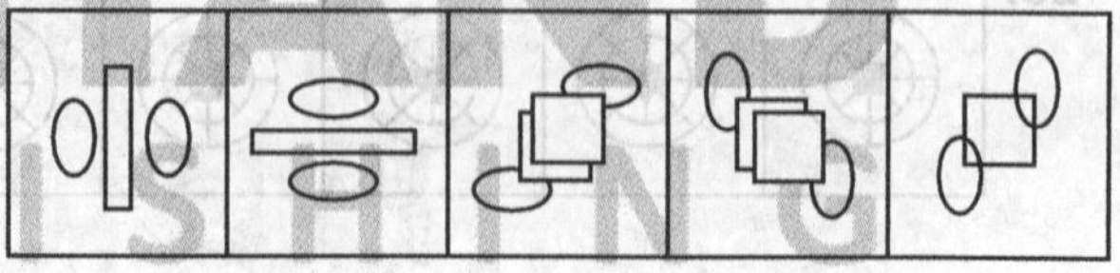

14. 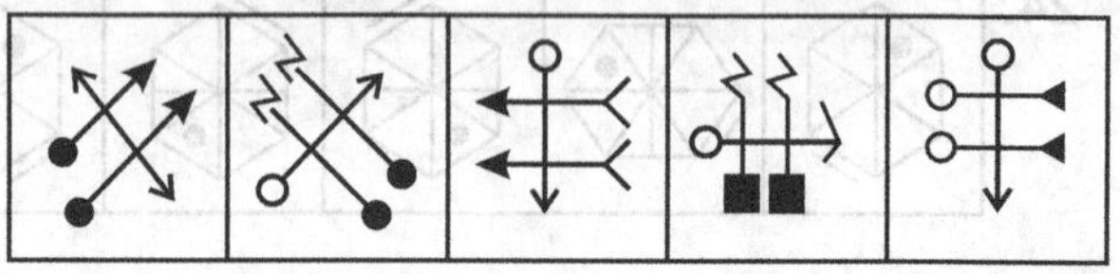

15. 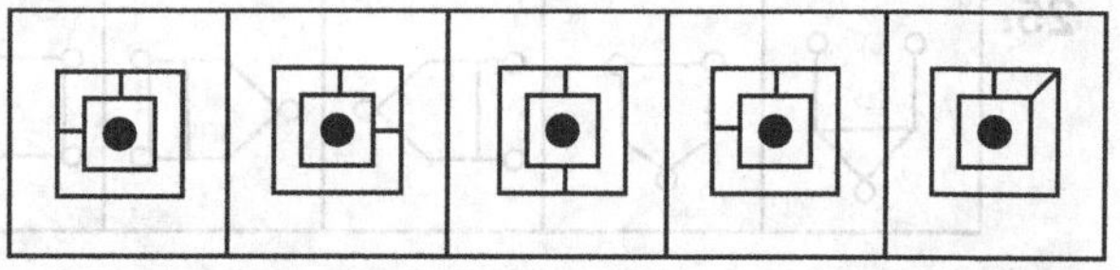

16. 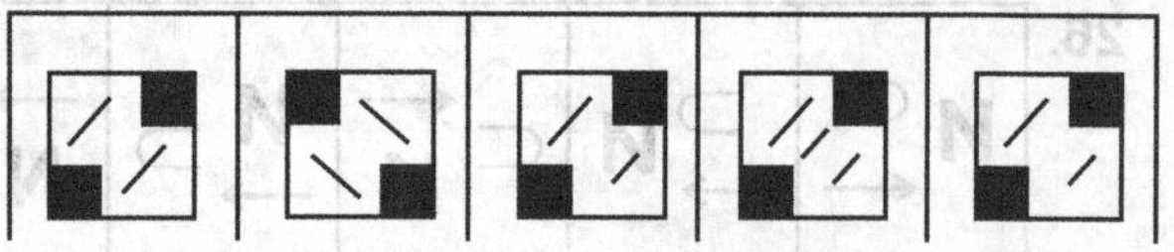

A B C D E

17.
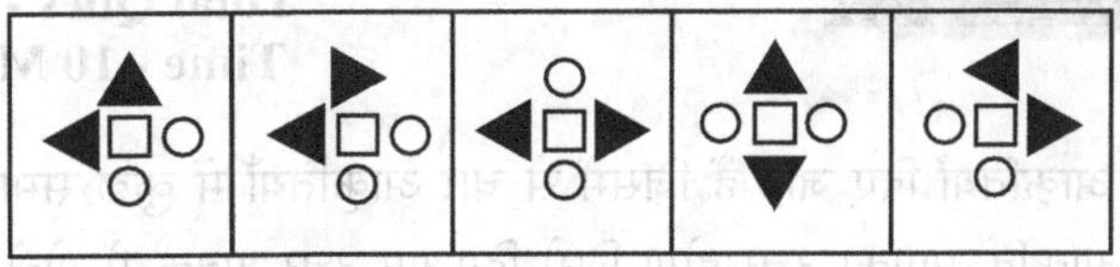

18.
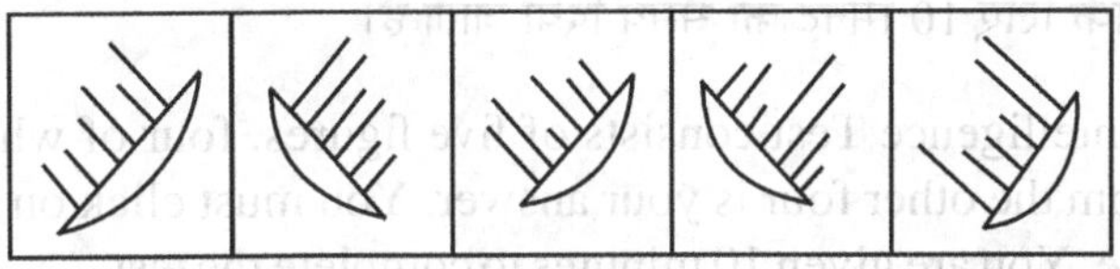

19.
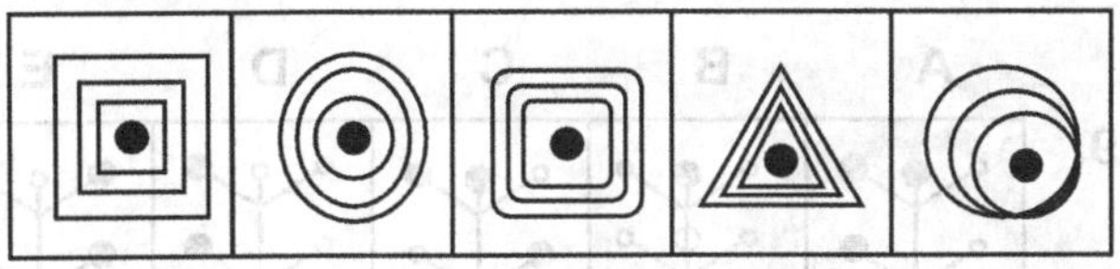

20.
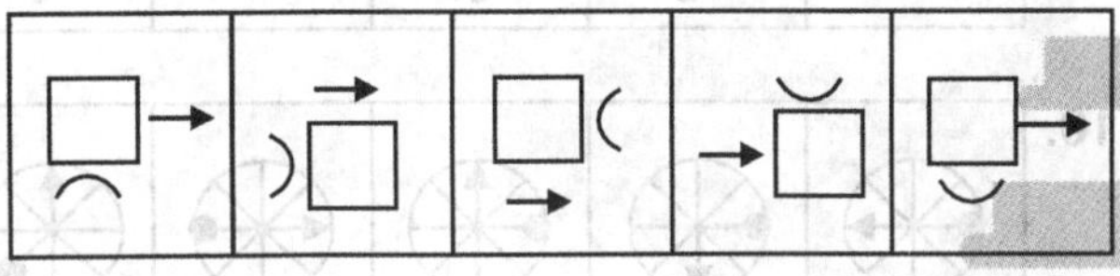

21.
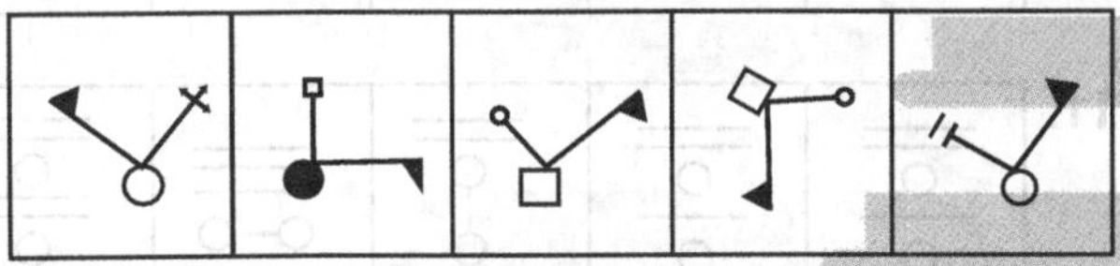

22.
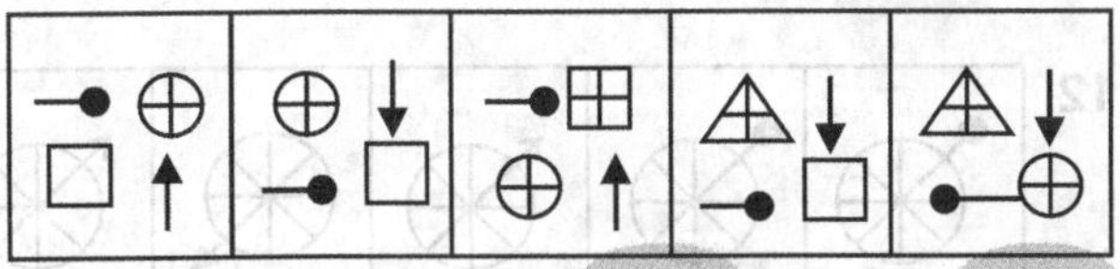

23.
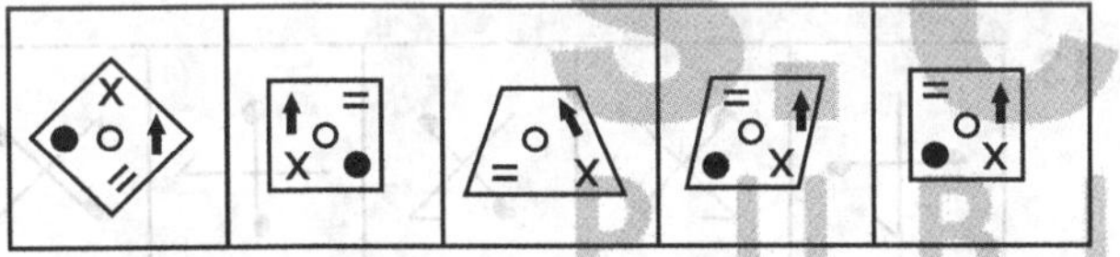

24.
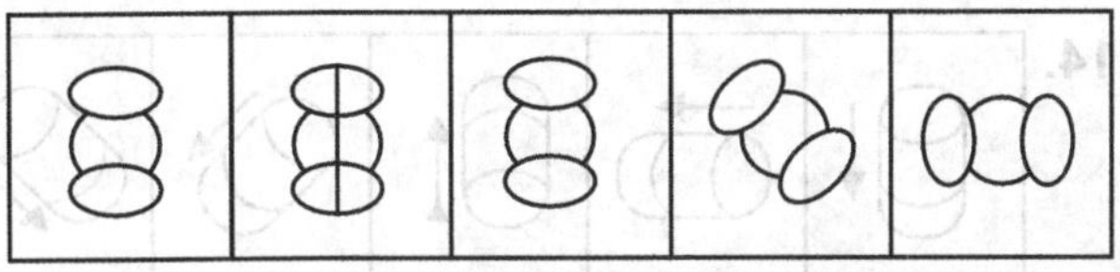

25.
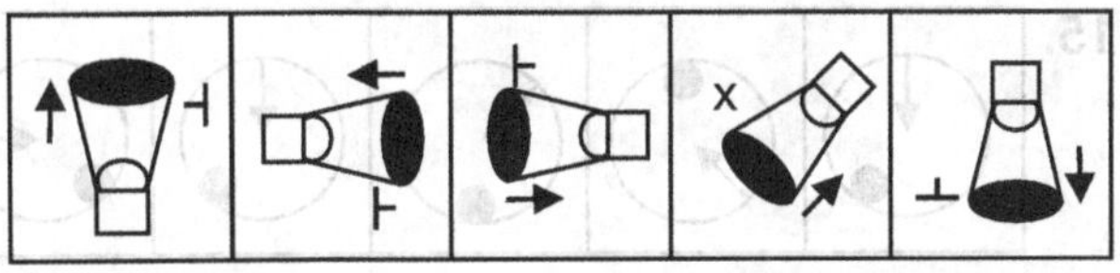

26.
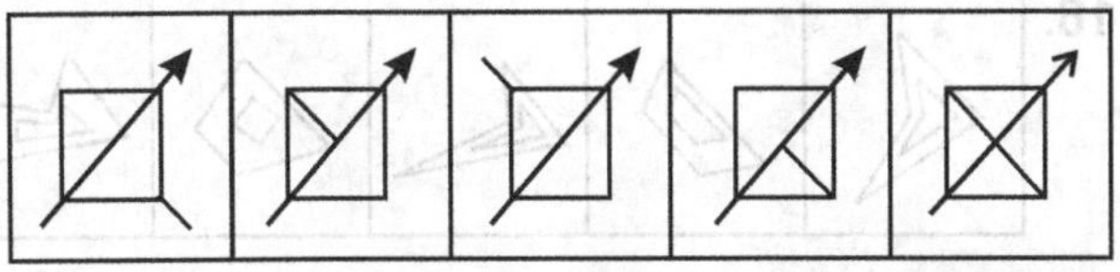

A B C D E

27.
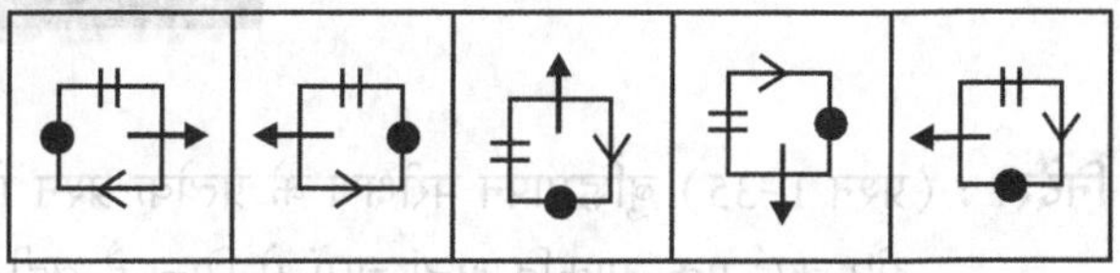

28.
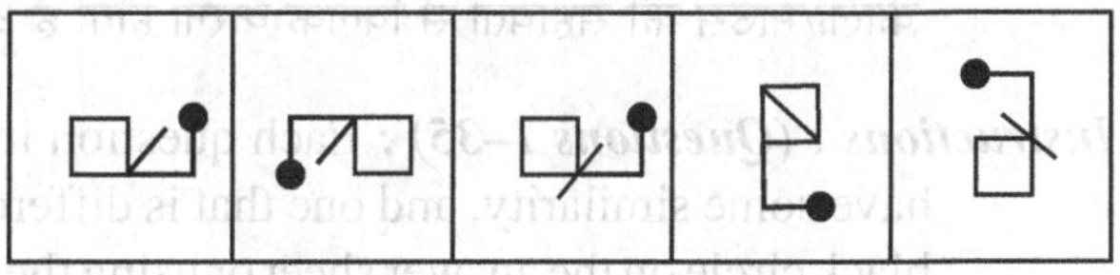

29.
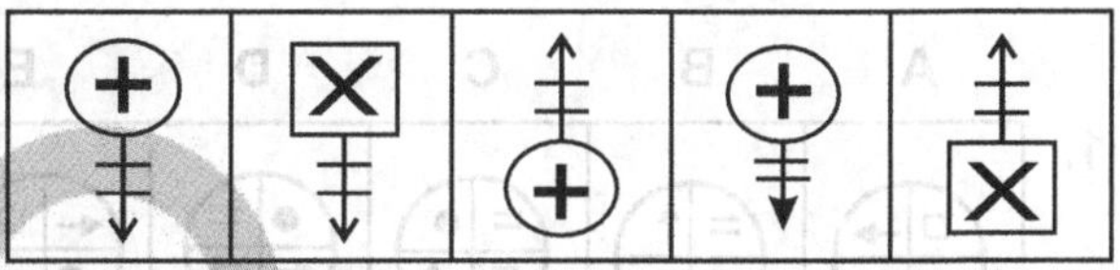

30.
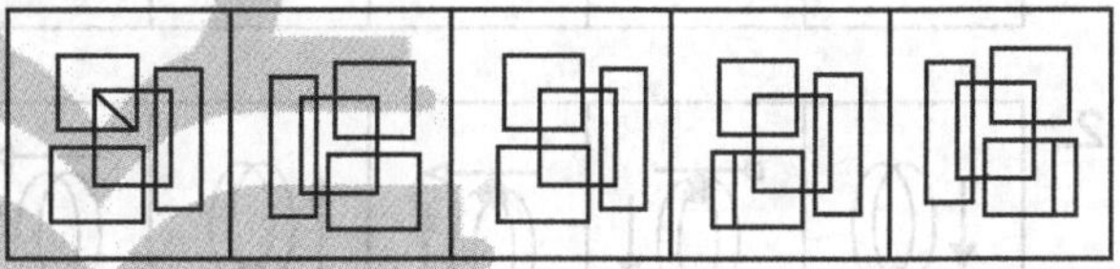

31.
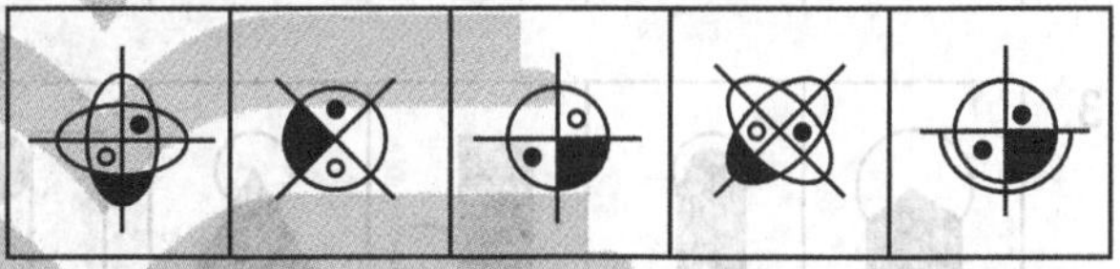

32.

33.
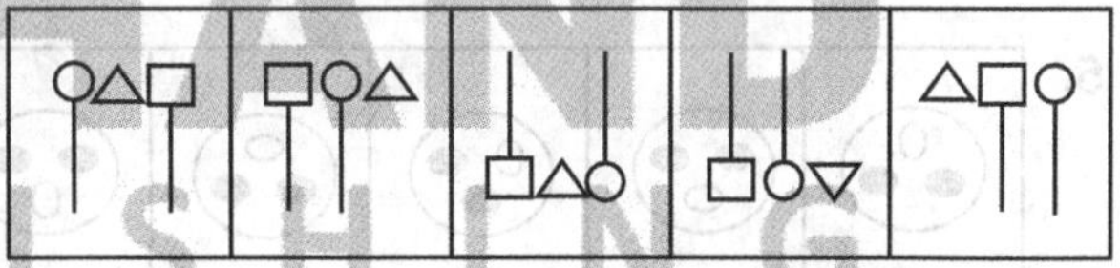

34.
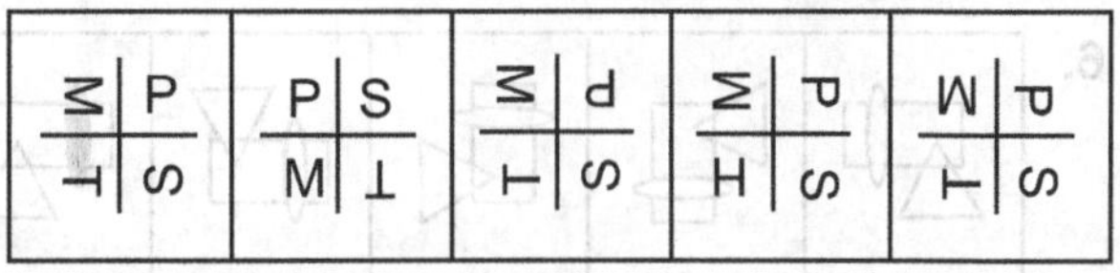

35.
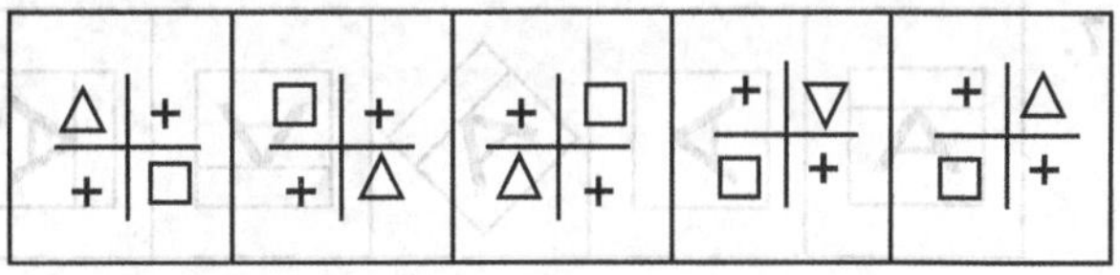

PRACTICE SET-4

Total Ques.- 35
Time - 10 Min.

निर्देश : (प्रश्न 1–35) बुद्धिमापन परीक्षण के प्रत्येक प्रश्न में पाँच आकृतियाँ दिए जाते हैं जिसमें से चार आकृतियाँ में कुछ समानता और कोई एक आकृति अन्य चारों से भिन्न है वही भिन्न आकृति आपका उत्तर होगा जिसे दिए गए उत्तर-पत्रक में गोले को काला/माउस की सहायता से क्लिक करना होता है और इसके लिए 10 मिनट का समय दिया जाता है।

Instructions : (Questions 1–35) : Each question in the Intelligence Test consists of five figures, four of which have some similarity, and one that is different from the other four is your answer. You must click on the black circle on the answer sheet or using the mouse. You are given 10 minutes to complete the test.

A B C D E

1.
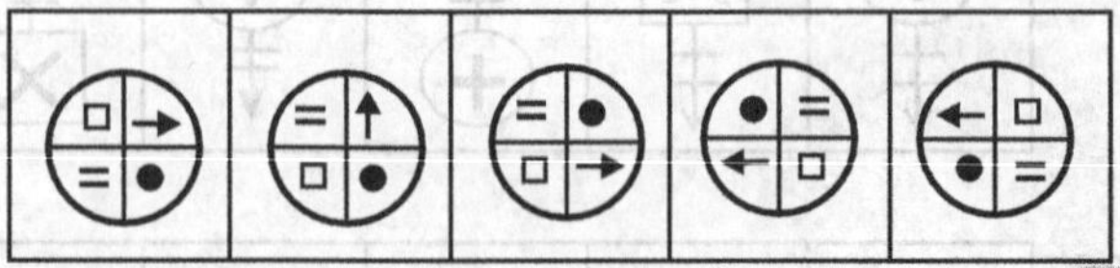

2.
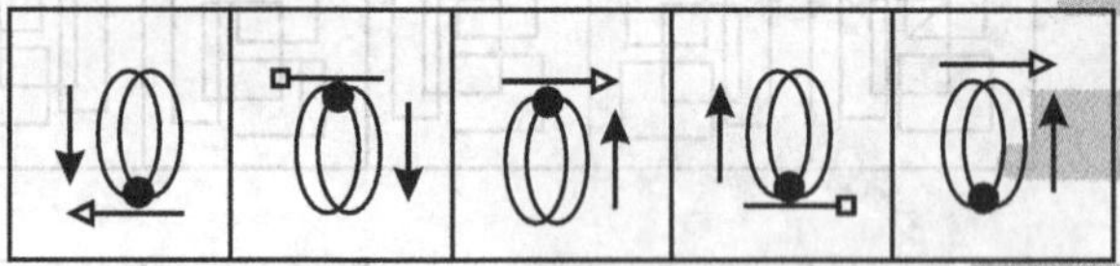

3.
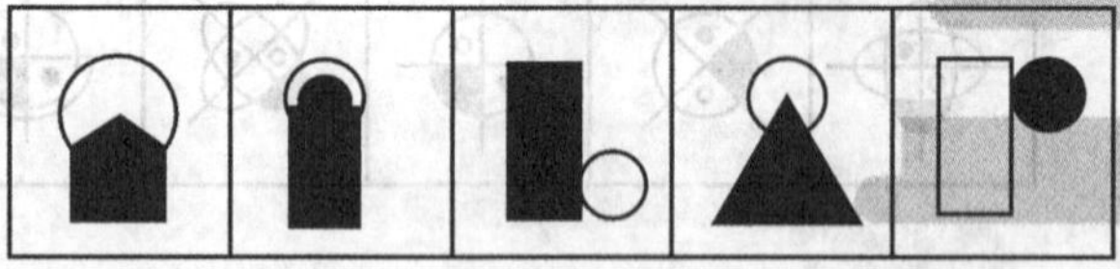

4.
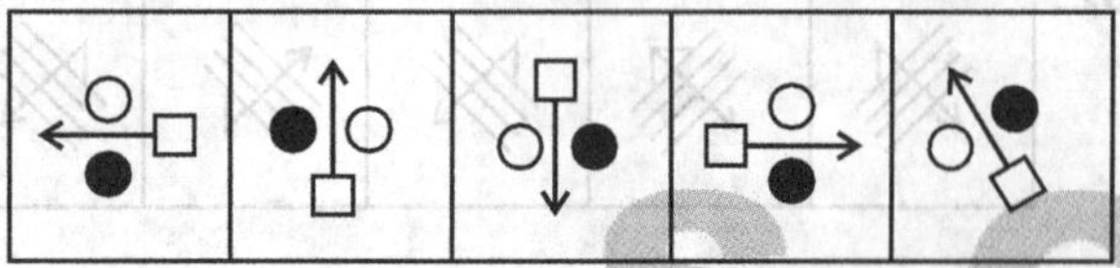

5.
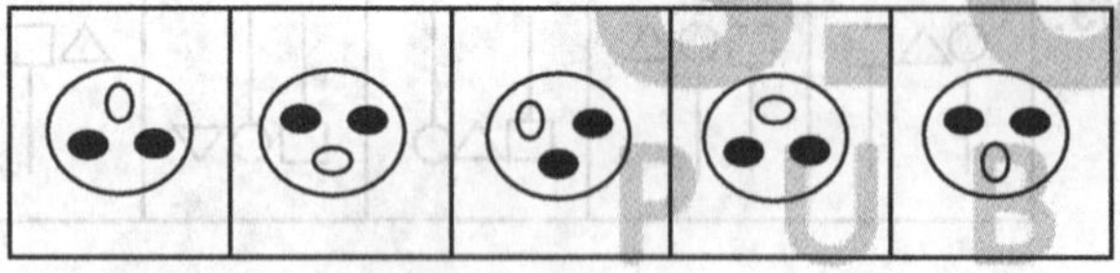

6.
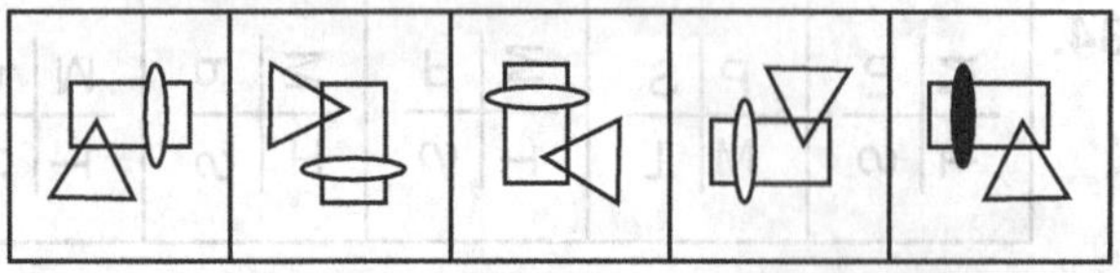

7.

8.
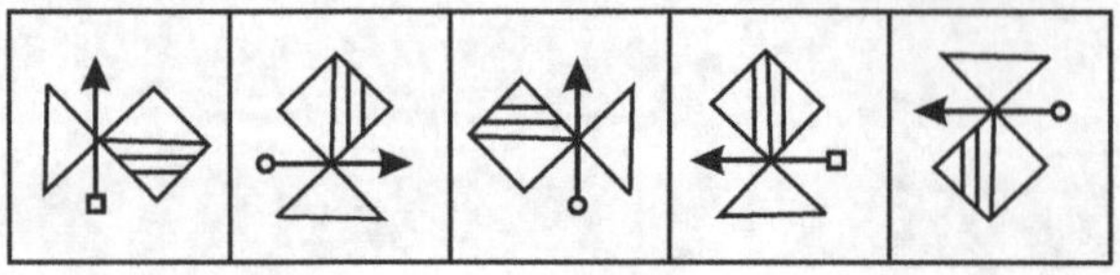

A B C D E

9.
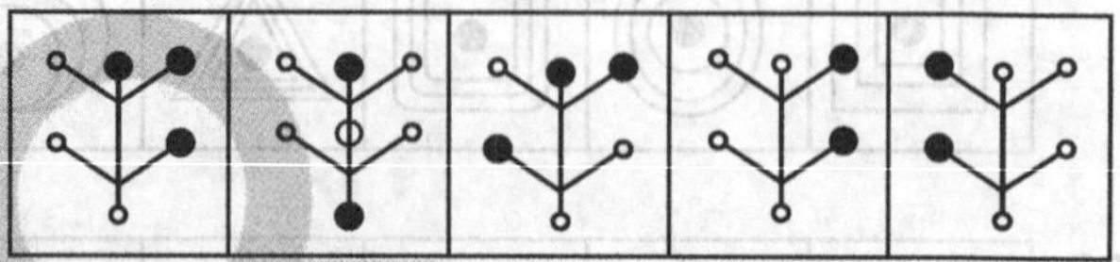

10.
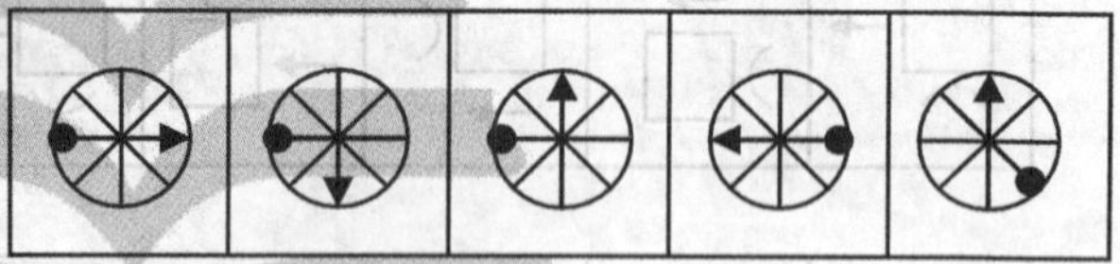

11.
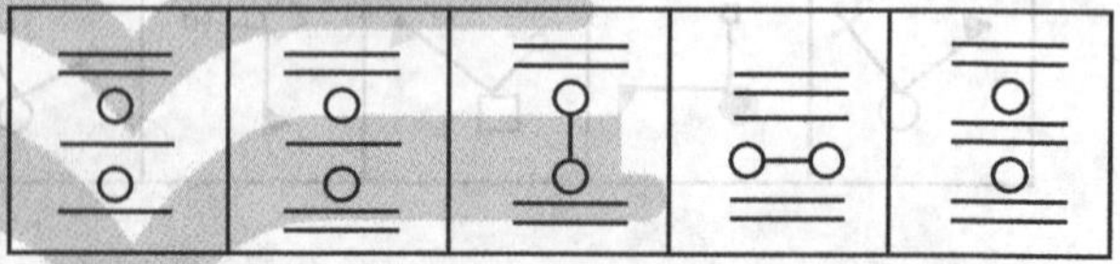

12.

13.
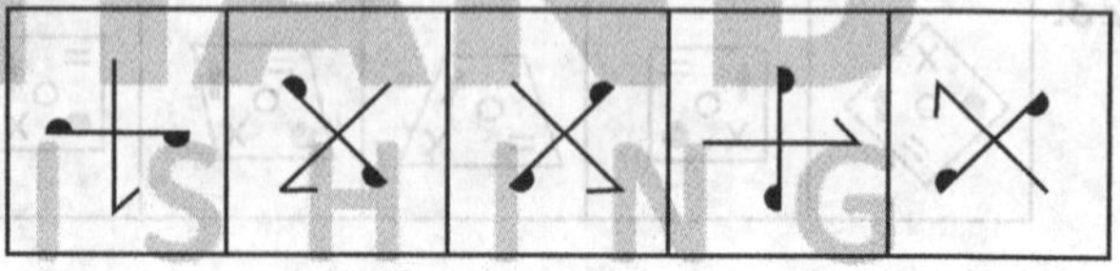

14.
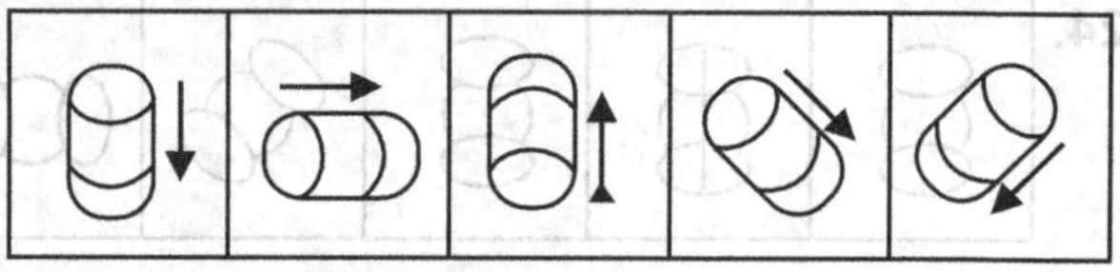

15.
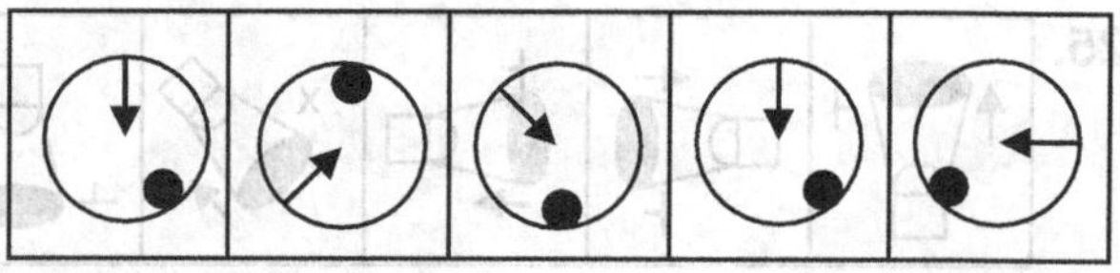

16.
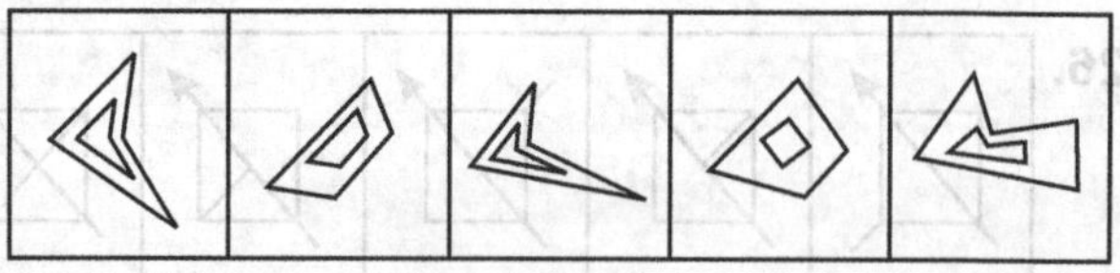

A B C D E

17. 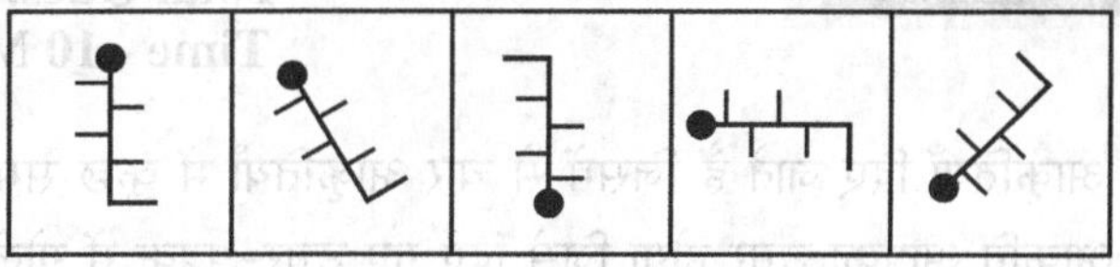

18. 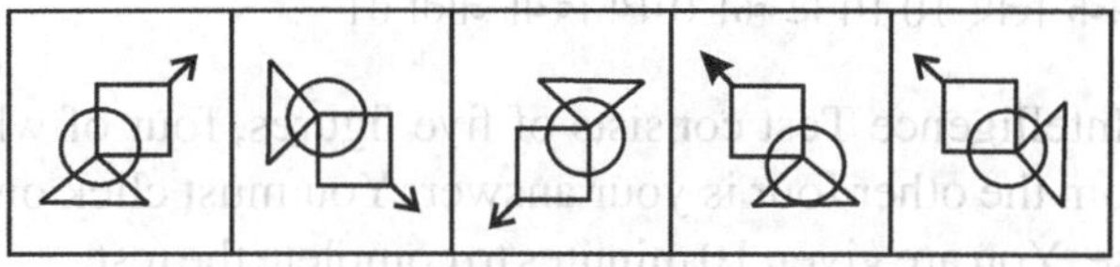

19. 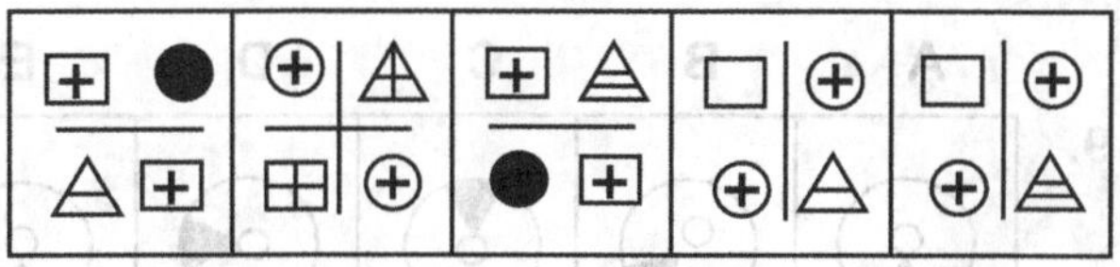

20. 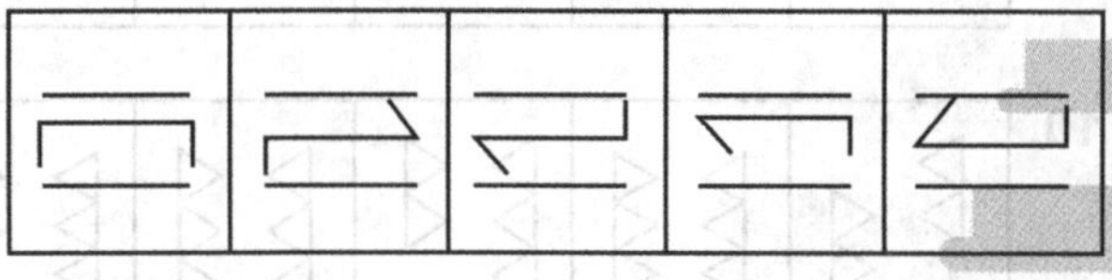

21. 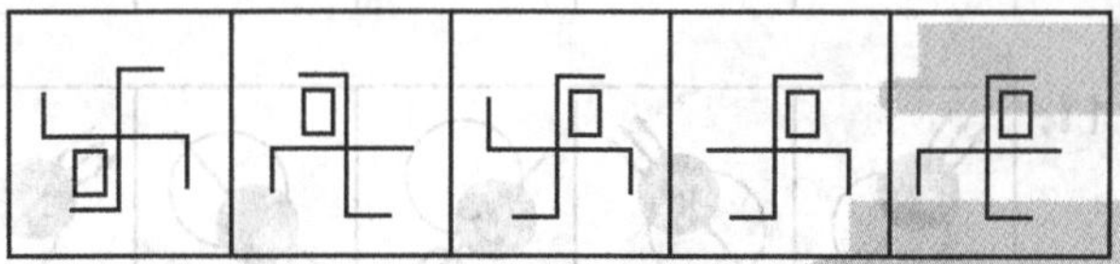

22. 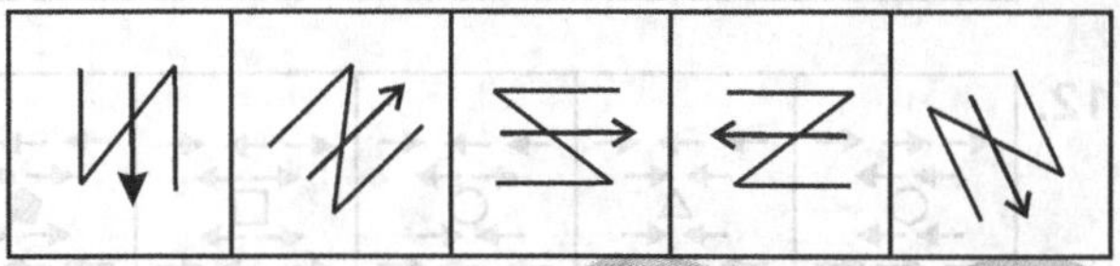

23. 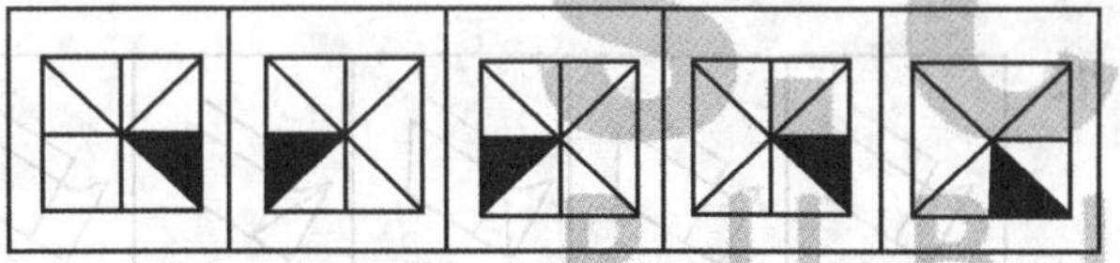

24. 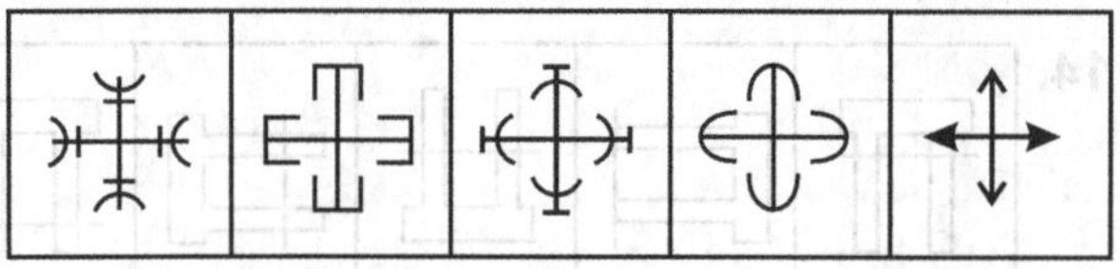

25. 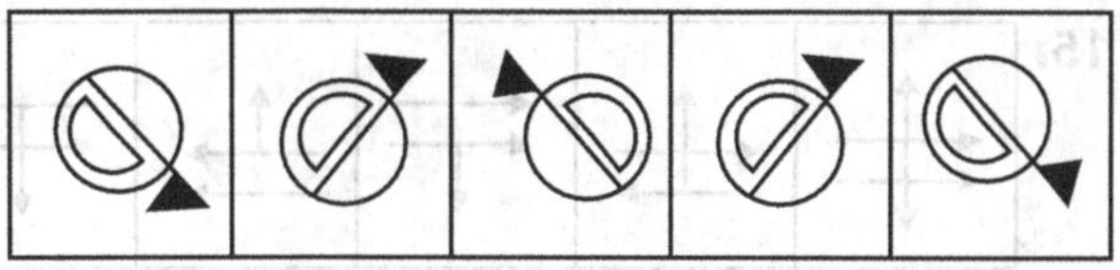

26. 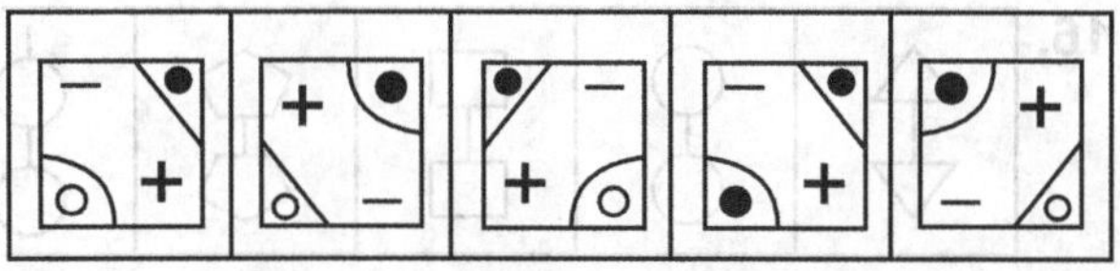

A B C D E

27. 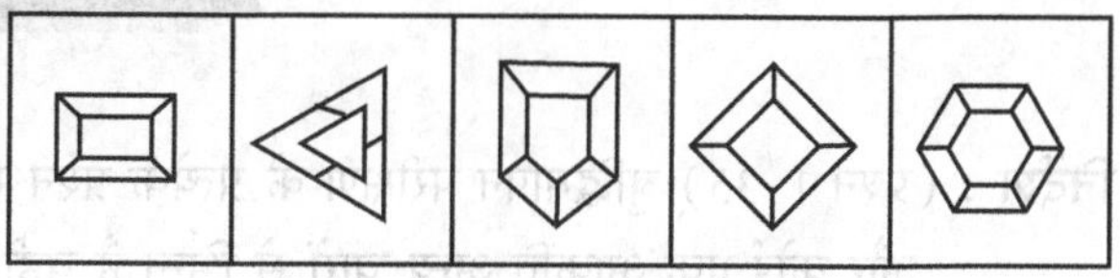

28. 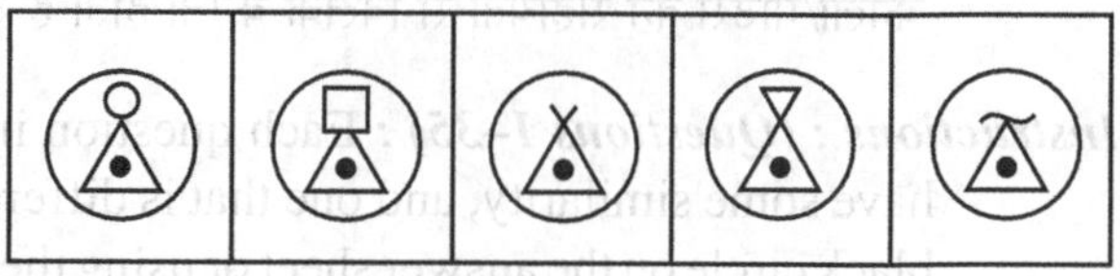

29. 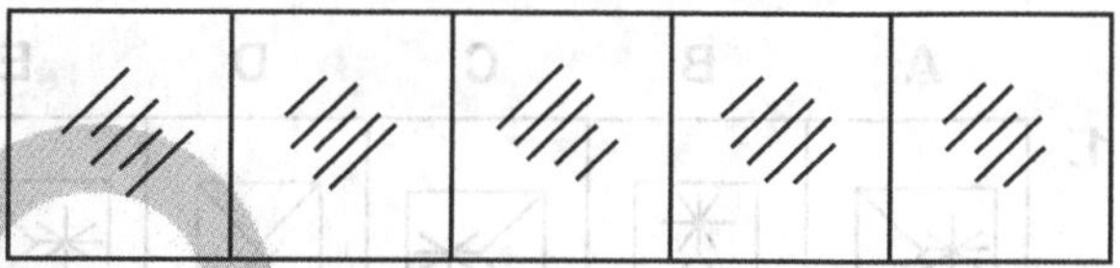

30. 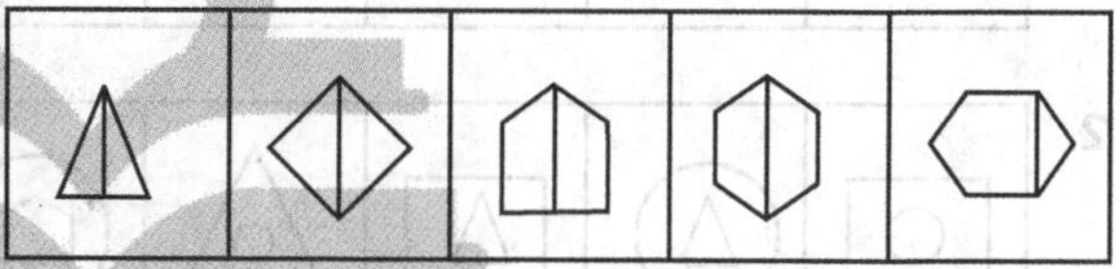

31. 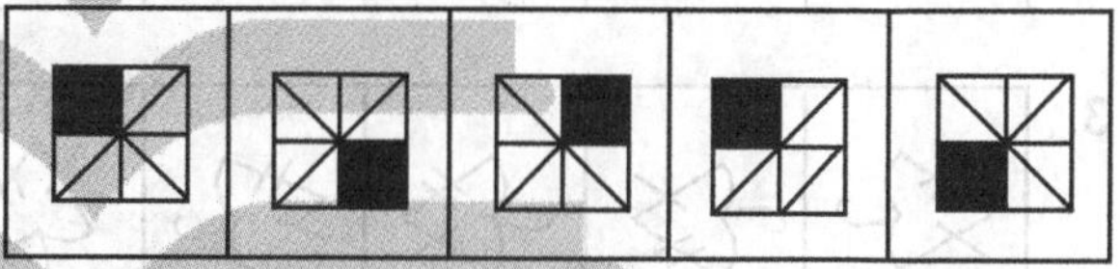

32. 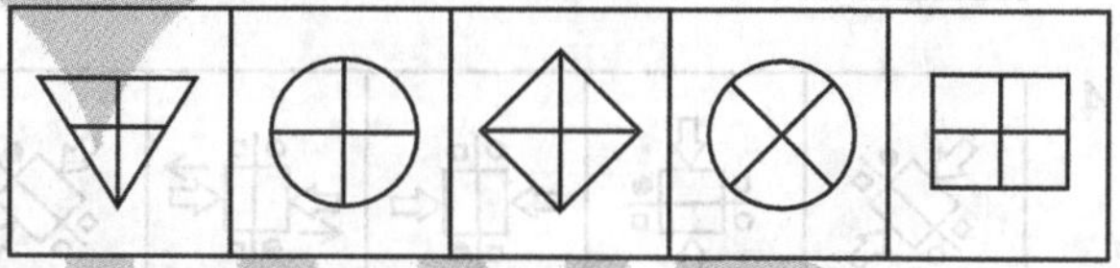

33. 

34. 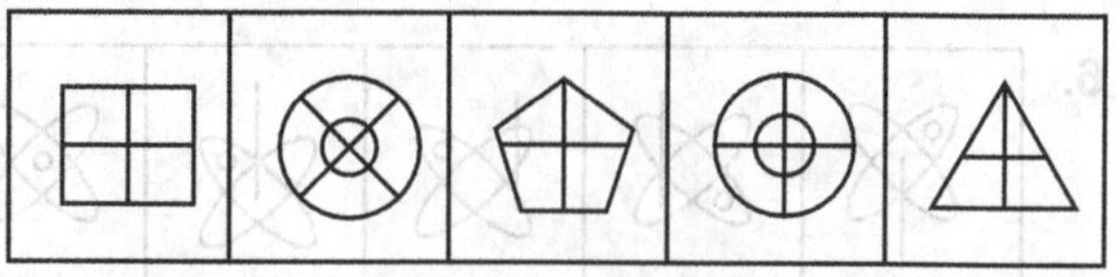

35. 

PRACTICE SET-5

Total Ques.- 35
Time - 10 Min.

निर्देश : (प्रश्न 1–35) बुद्धिमापन परीक्षण के प्रत्येक प्रश्न में पाँच आकृतियाँ दिए जाते हैं जिसमें से चार आकृतियाँ में कुछ समानता और कोई एक आकृति अन्य चारों से भिन्न है वही भिन्न आकृति आपका उत्तर होगा जिसे दिए गए उत्तर-पत्रक में गोले को काला/माउस की सहायता से क्लिक करना होता है और इसके लिए 10 मिनट का समय दिया जाता है।

Instructions : (Questions 1–35) : Each question in the Intelligence Test consists of five figures, four of which have some similarity, and one that is different from the other four is your answer. You must click on the black circle on the answer sheet or using the mouse. You are given 10 minutes to complete the test.

A B C D E

1. 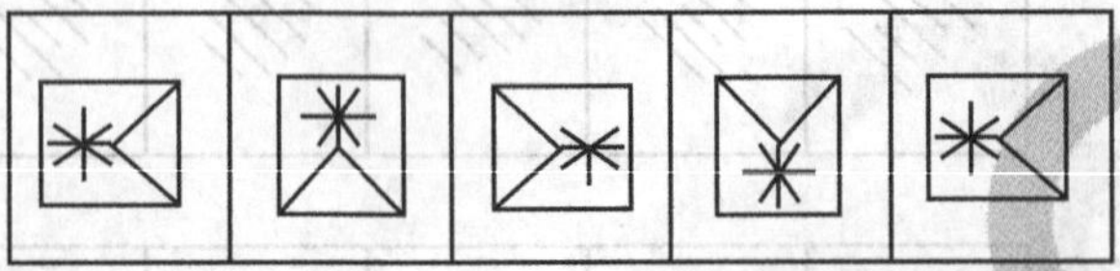

2. 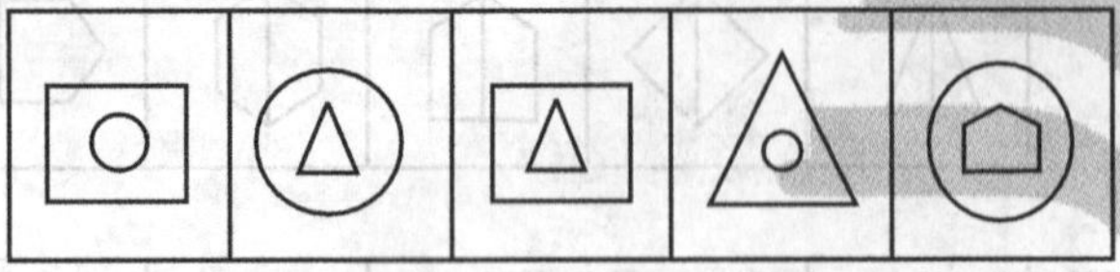

3. 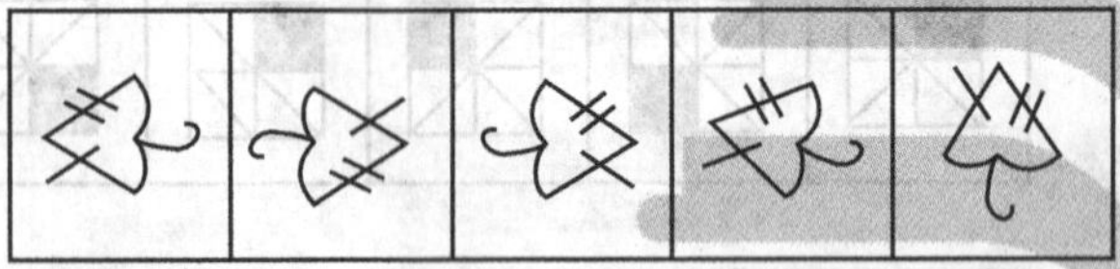

4. 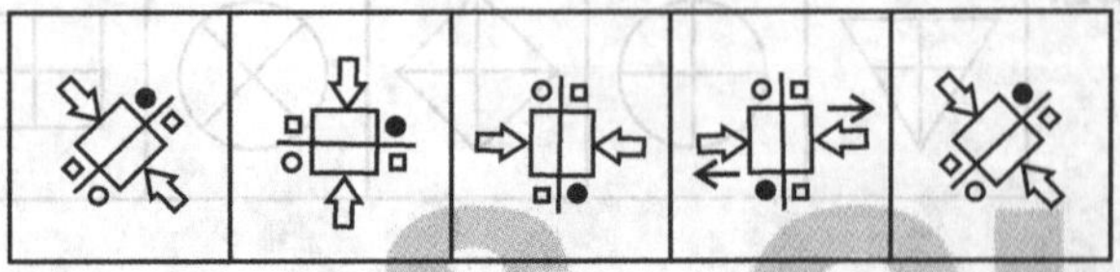

5. 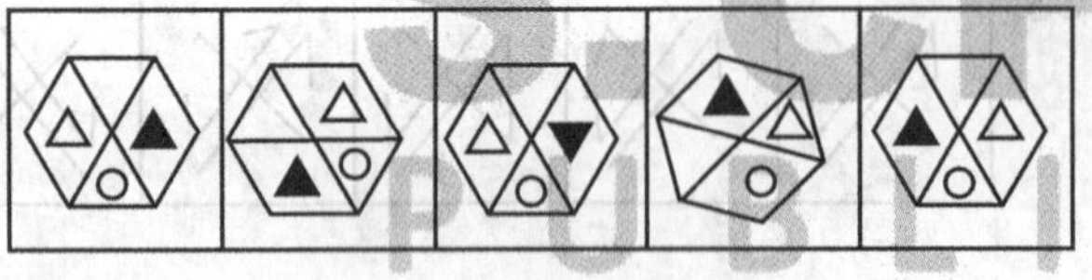

6. 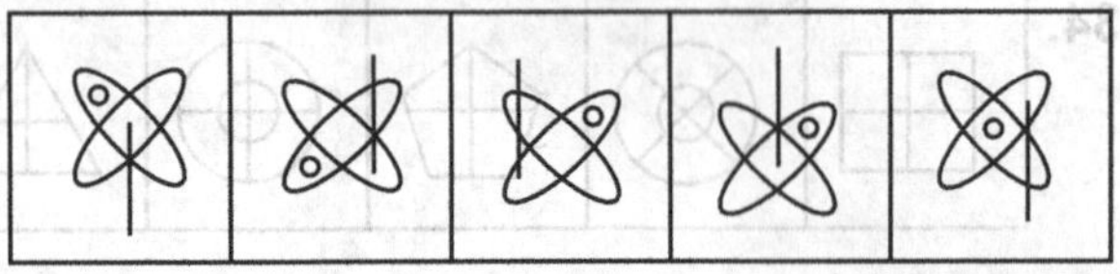

7. 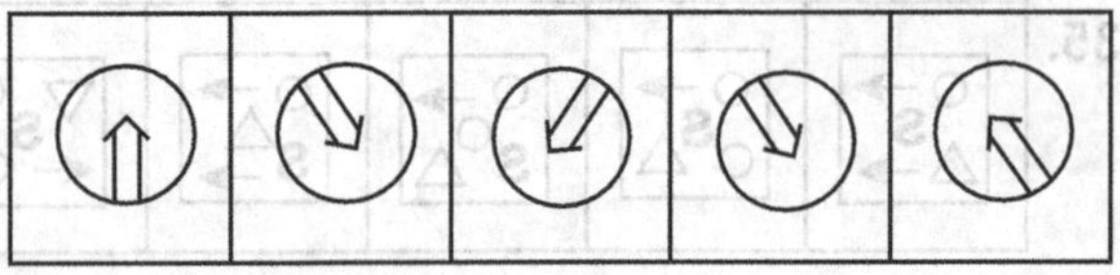

8. 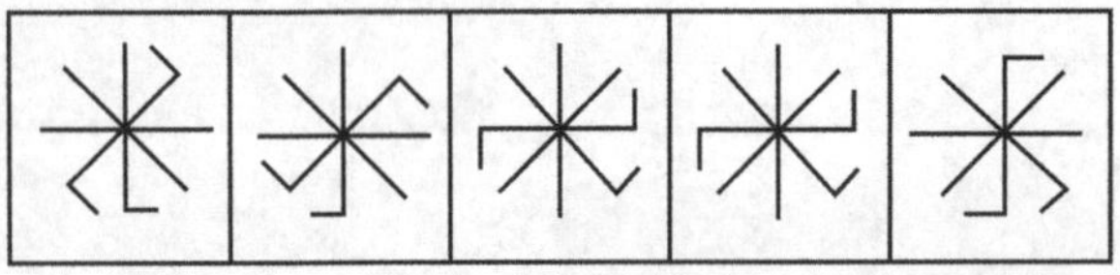

A B C D E

9. 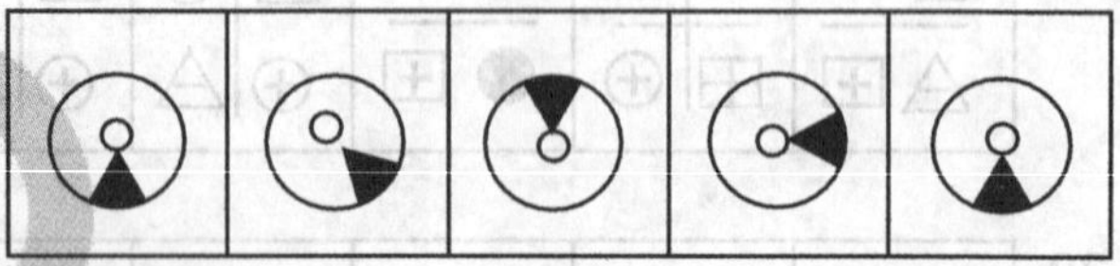

10. 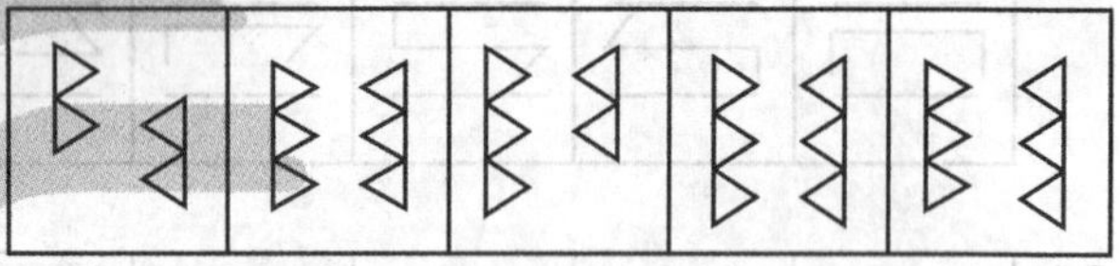

11. 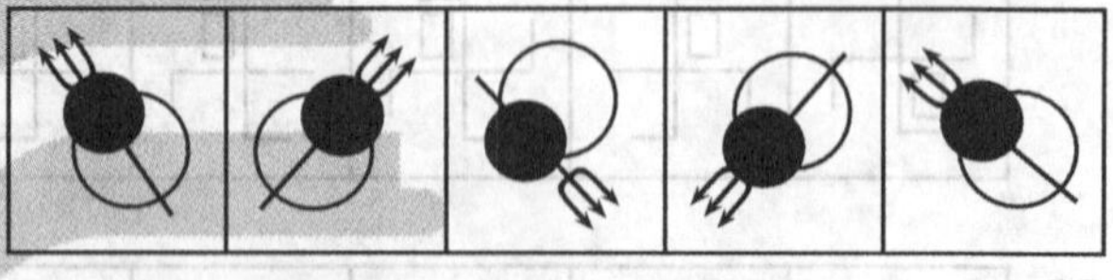

12. 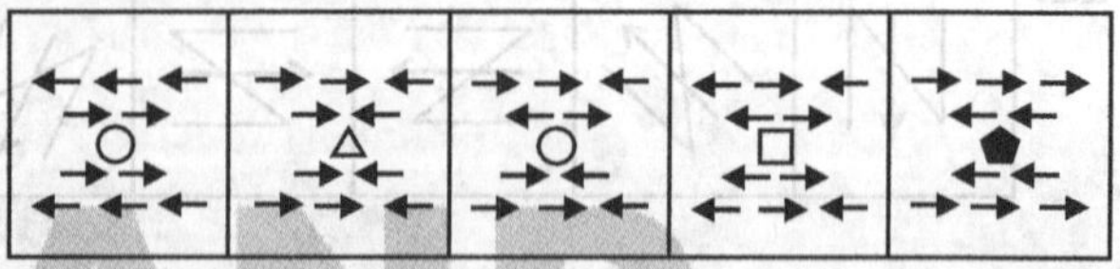

13. 

14. 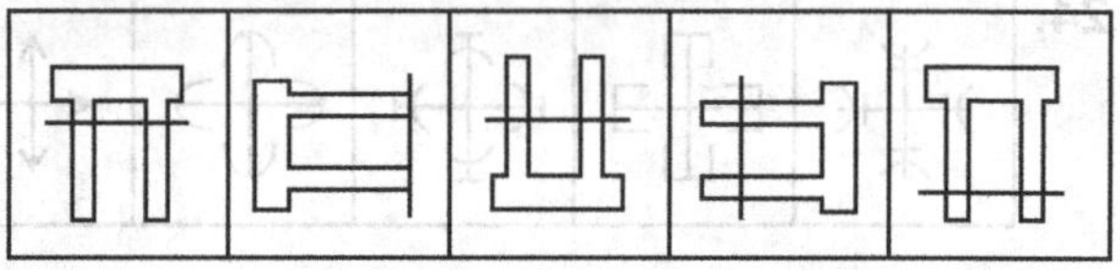

15. 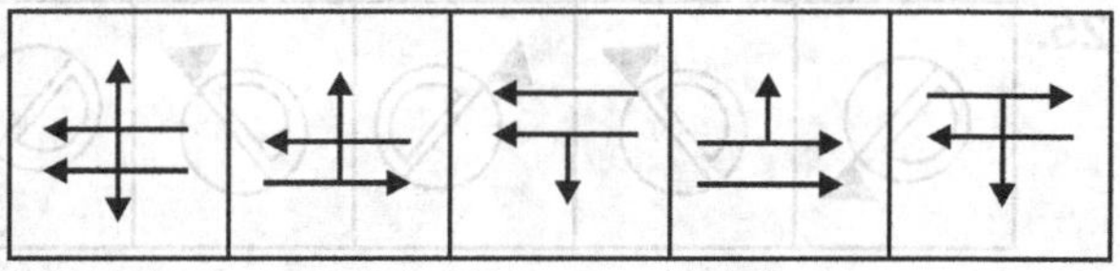

16. 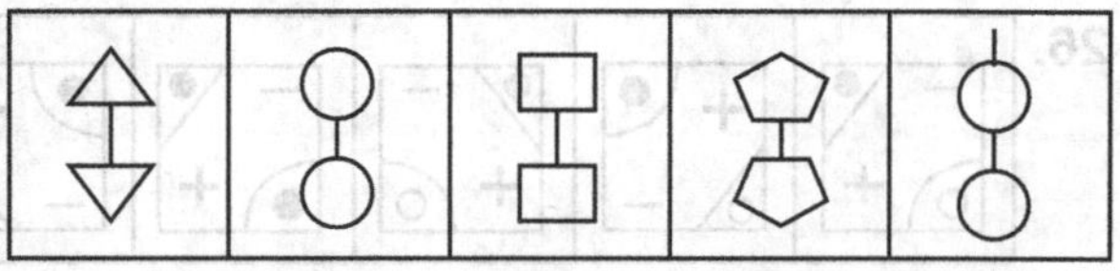

A B C D E

17.
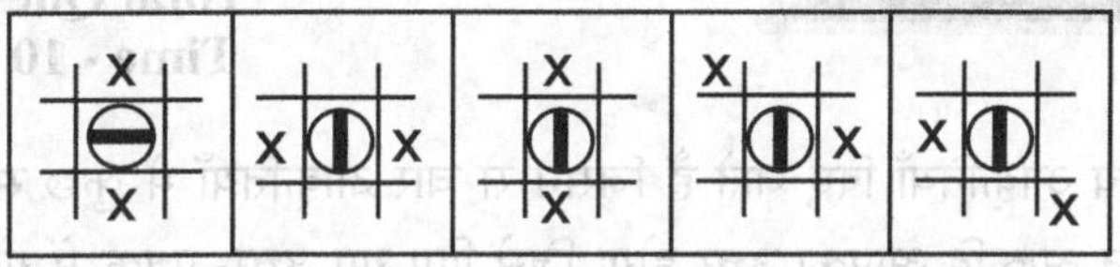

18.
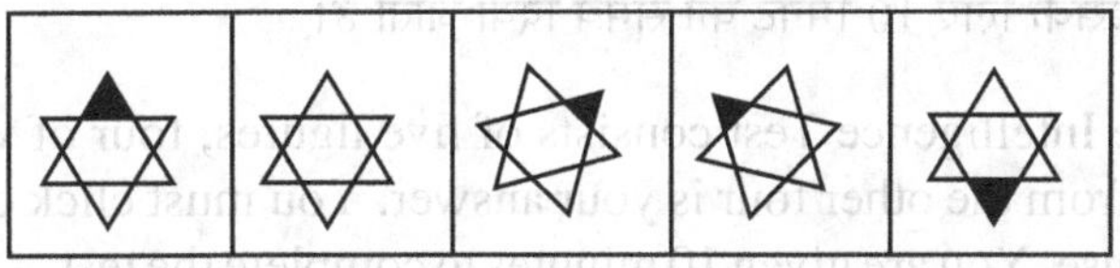

19.
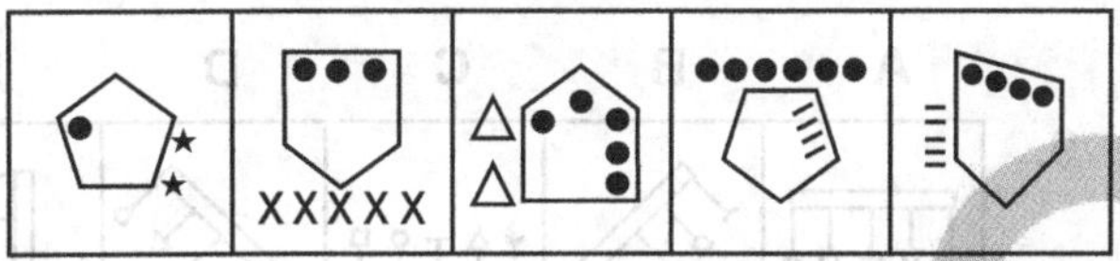

20.
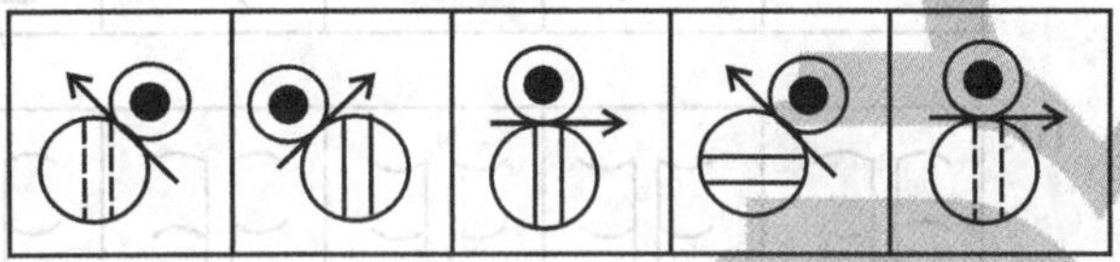

21.

22.
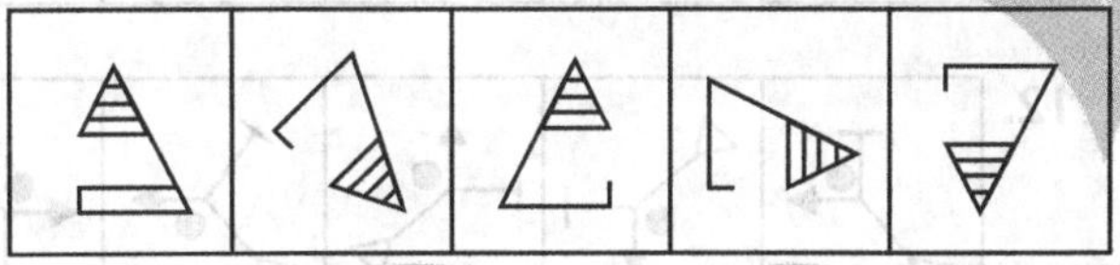

23.
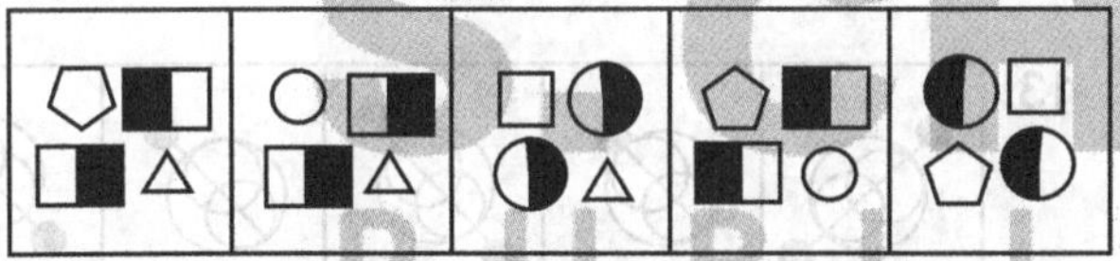

24.
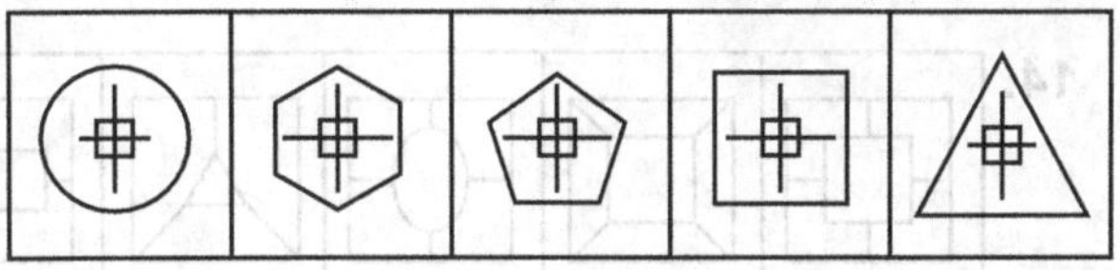

25.
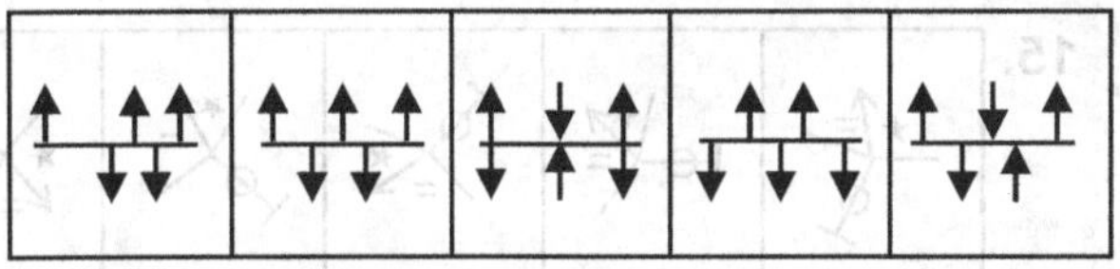

26.
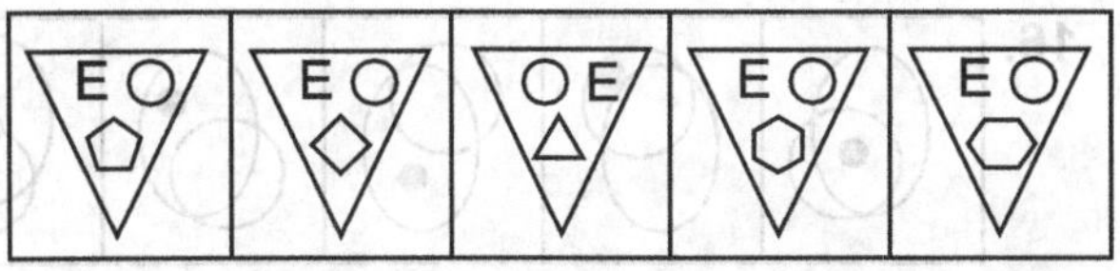

A B C D E

27.
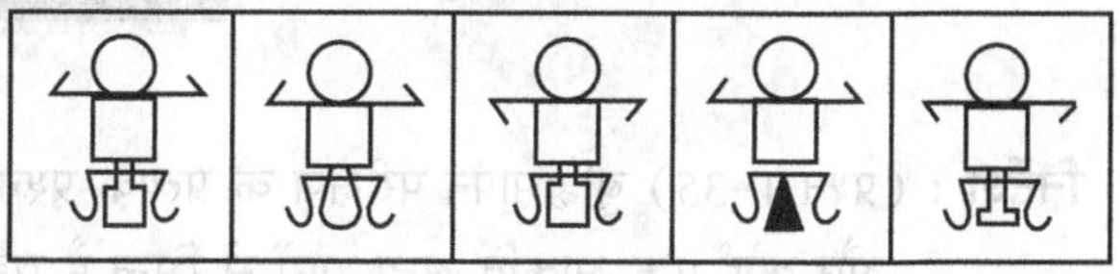

28.
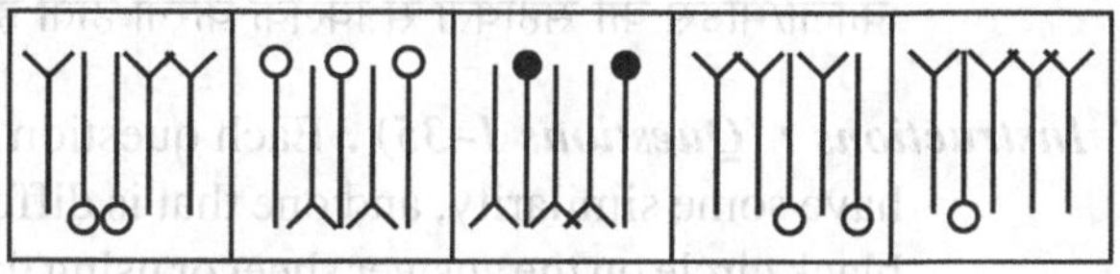

29.
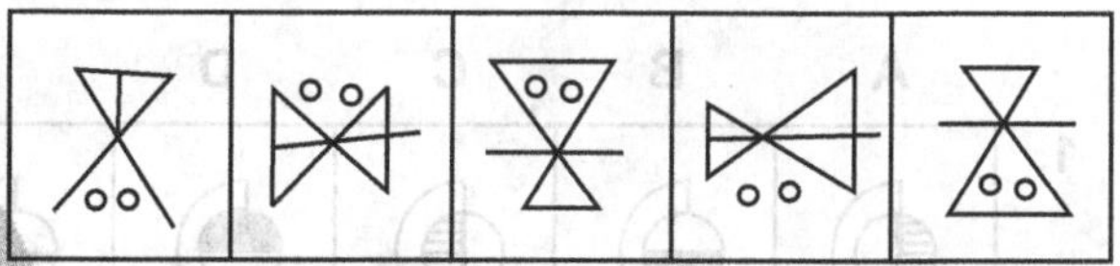

30.
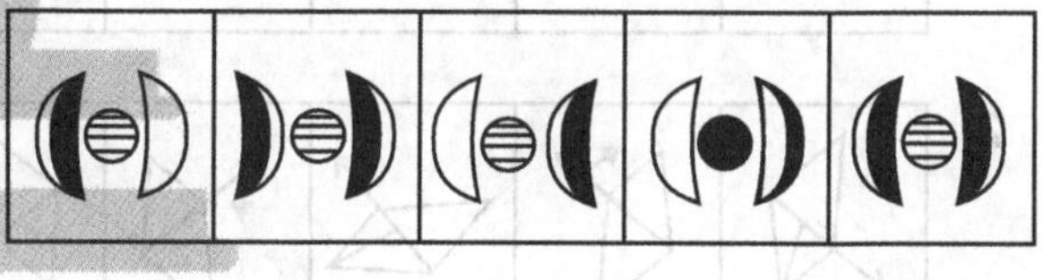

31.
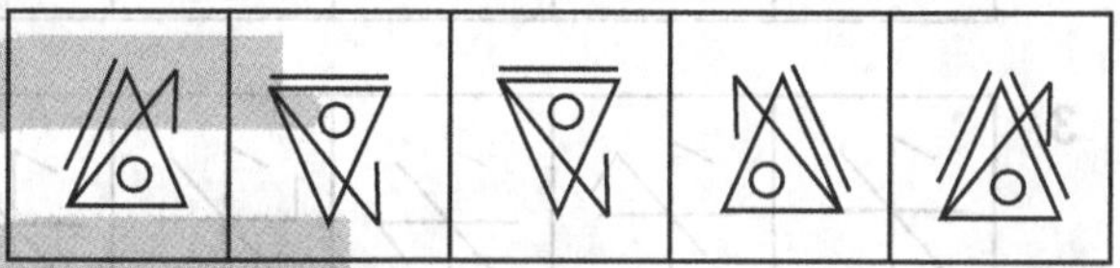

32.
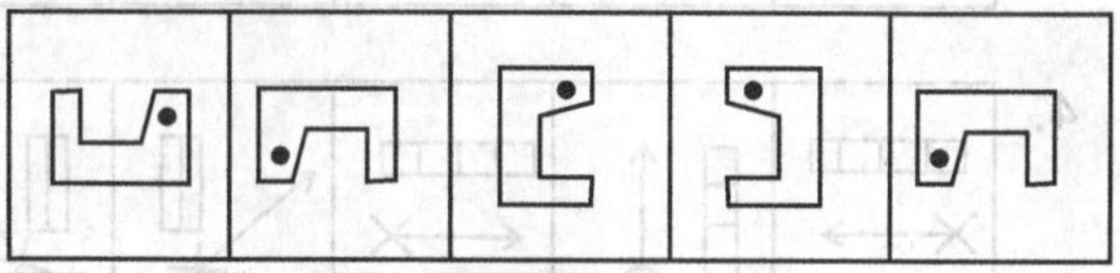

33.
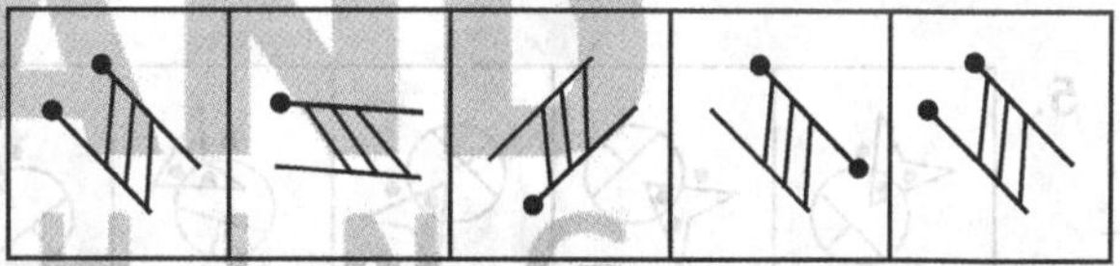

34.
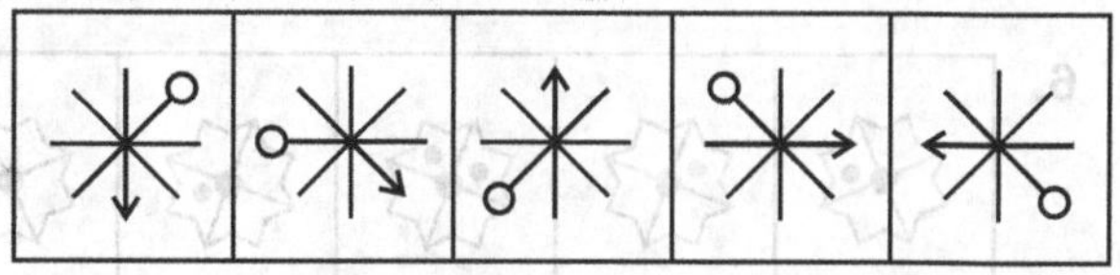

35.
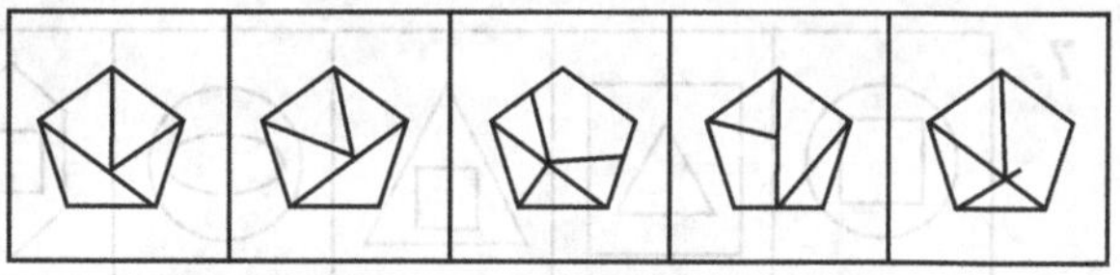

PRACTICE SET-6

Total Ques.- 35
Time - 10 Min.

निर्देश : (प्रश्न 1-35) बुद्धिमापन परीक्षण के प्रत्येक प्रश्न में पाँच आकृतियाँ दिए जाते हैं जिसमें से चार आकृतियाँ में कुछ समानता और कोई एक आकृति अन्य चारों से भिन्न है वही भिन्न आकृति आपका उत्तर होगा जिसे दिए गए उत्तर-पत्रक में गोले को काला/माउस की सहायता से क्लिक करना होता है और इसके लिए 10 मिनट का समय दिया जाता है।

Instructions : (Questions 1–35) : Each question in the Intelligence Test consists of five figures, four of which have some similarity, and one that is different from the other four is your answer. You must click on the black circle on the answer sheet or using the mouse. You are given 10 minutes to complete the test.

A B C D E

1. 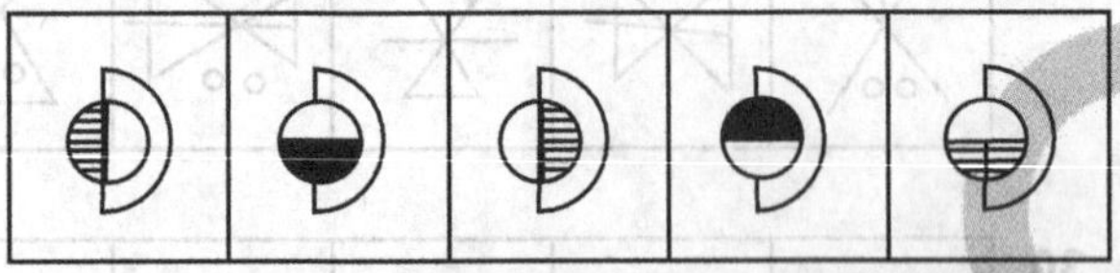

2. 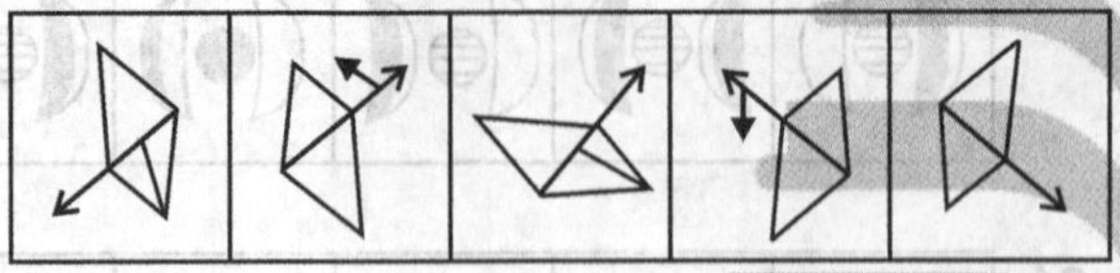

3. 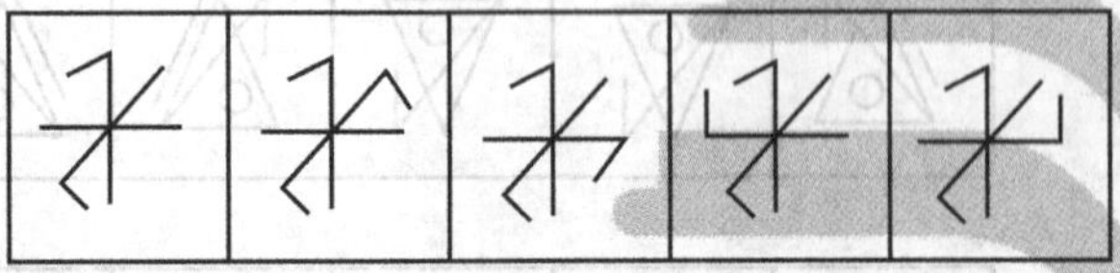

4. 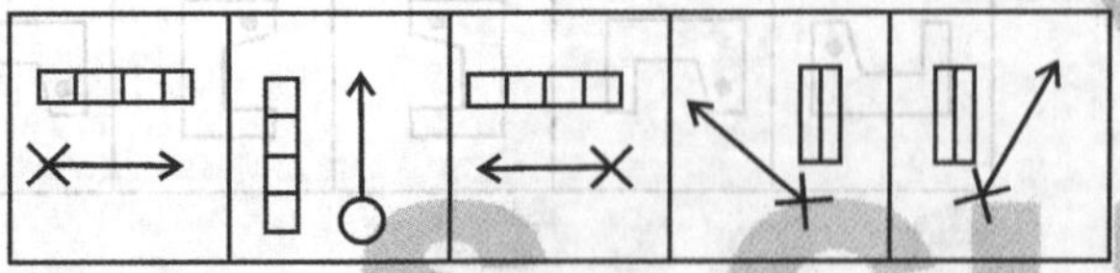

5. 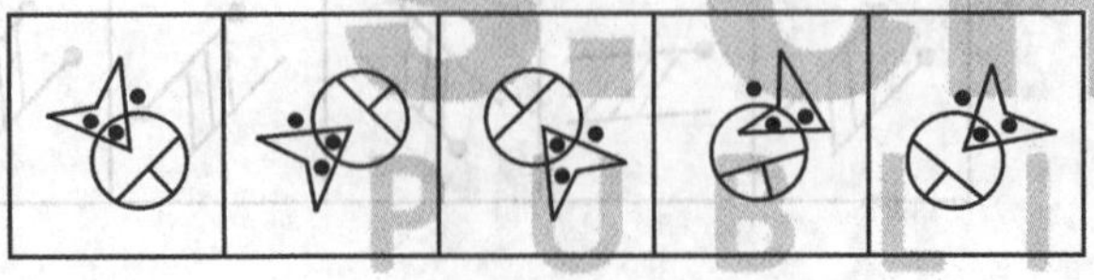

6. 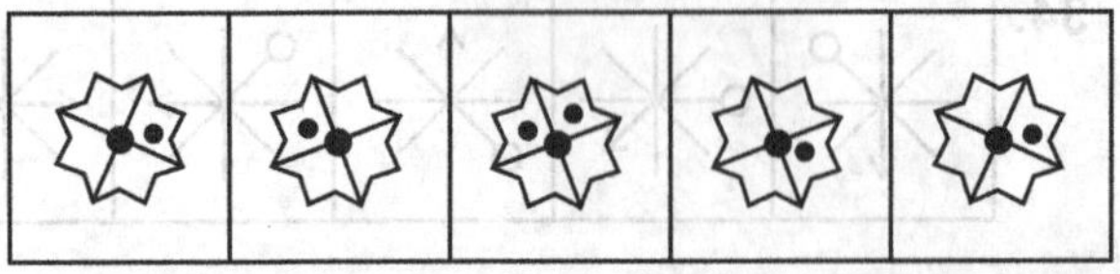

7. 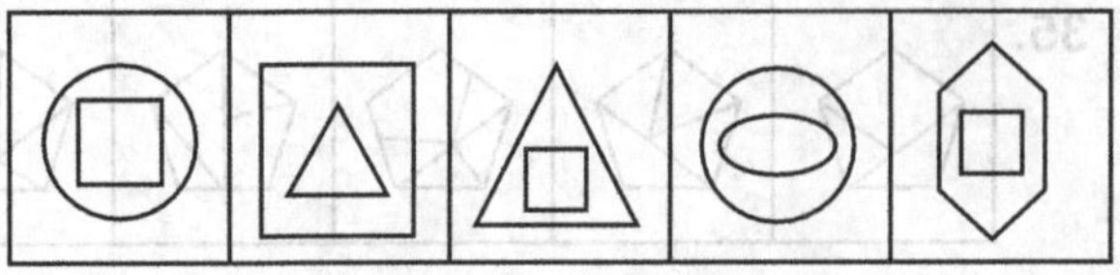

8. 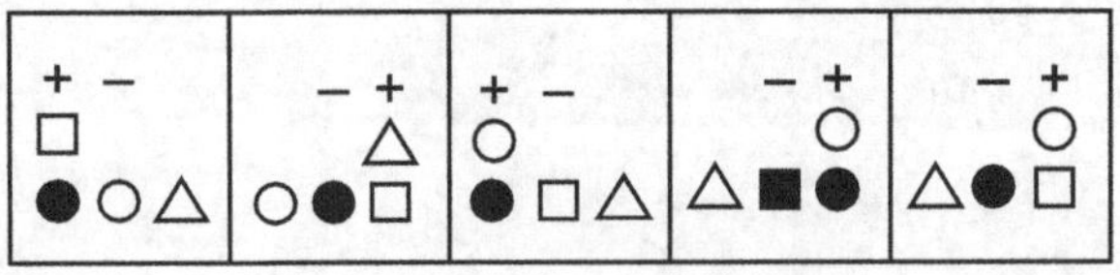

A B C D E

9. 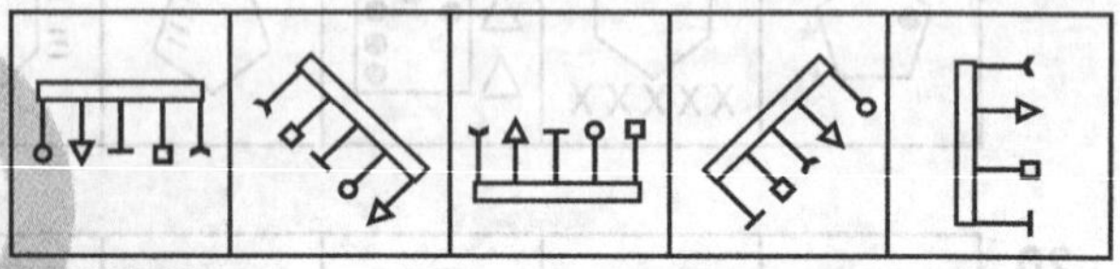

10. 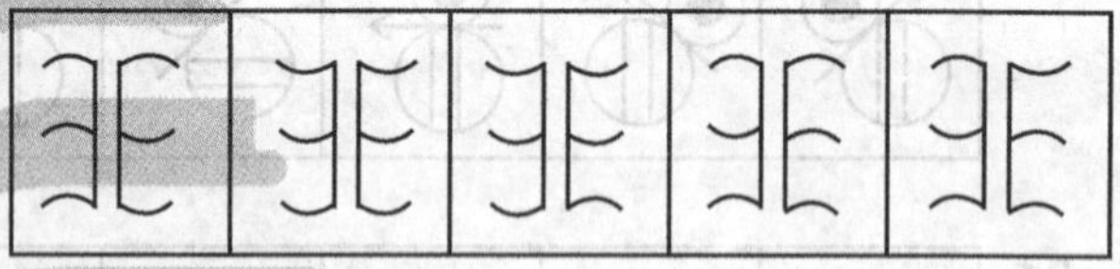

11. 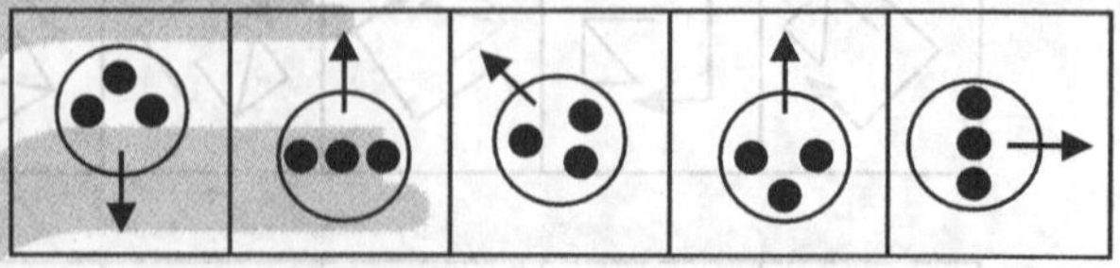

12. 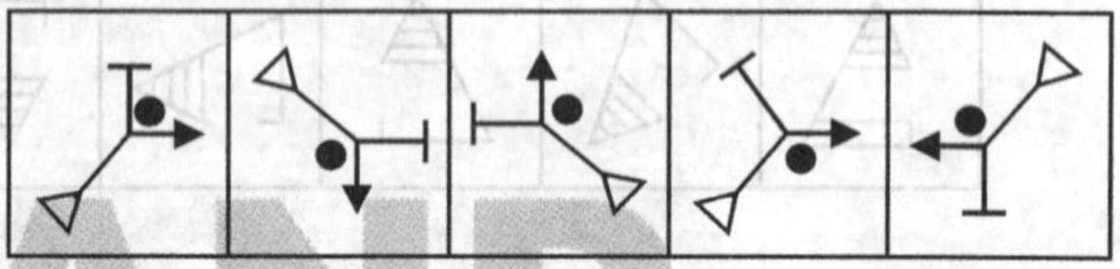

13. 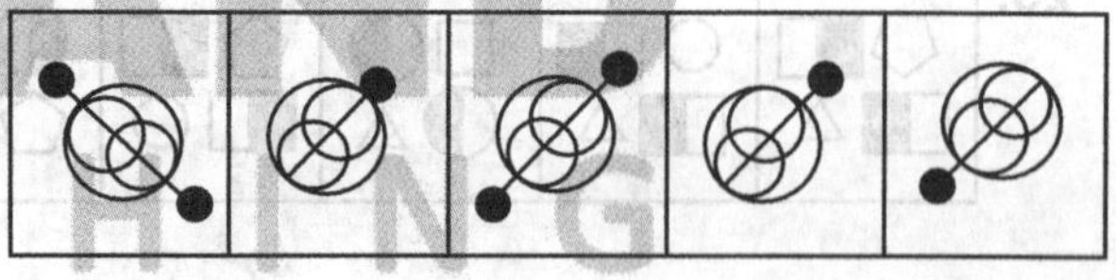

14. 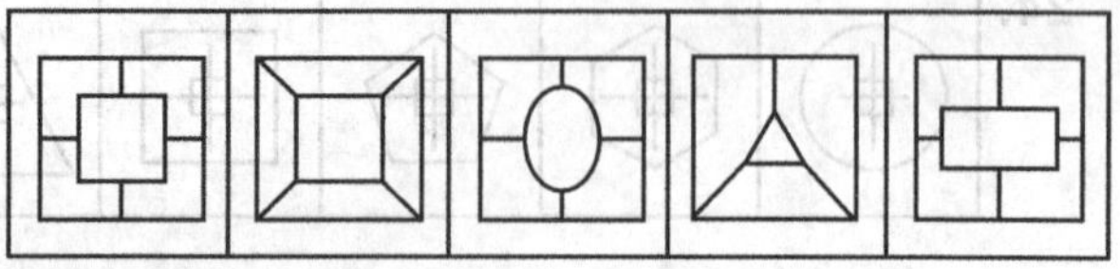

15. 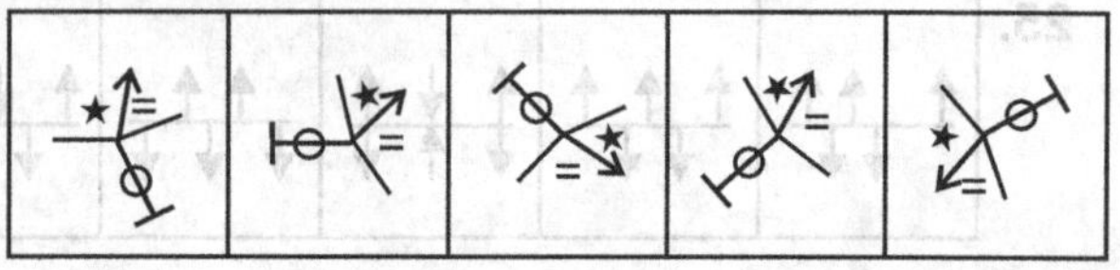

16. 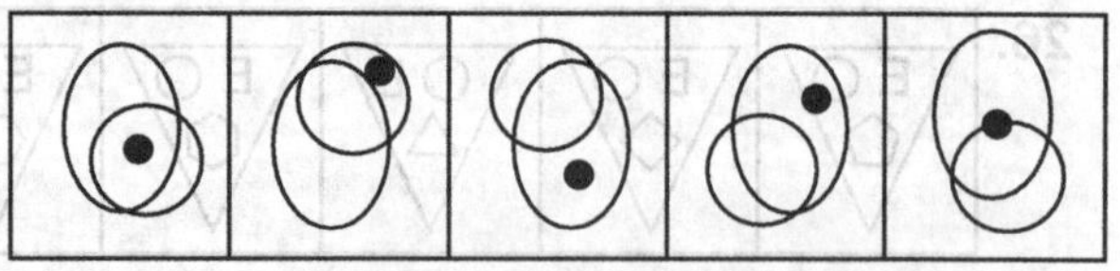

A B C D E

17.

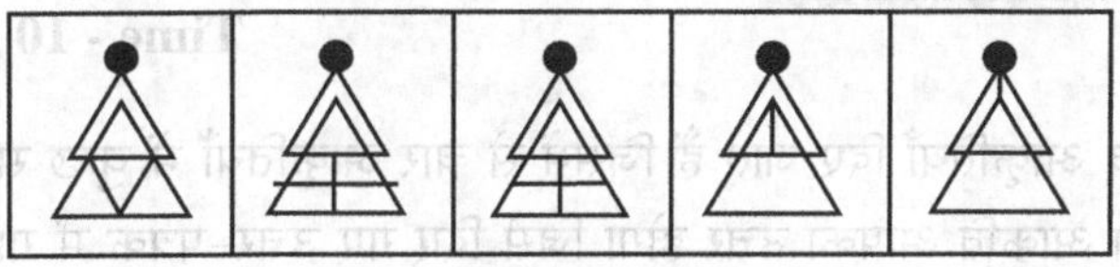

18.

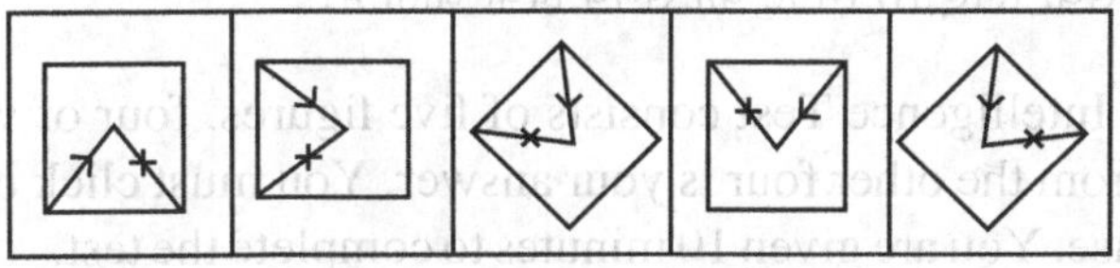

19.

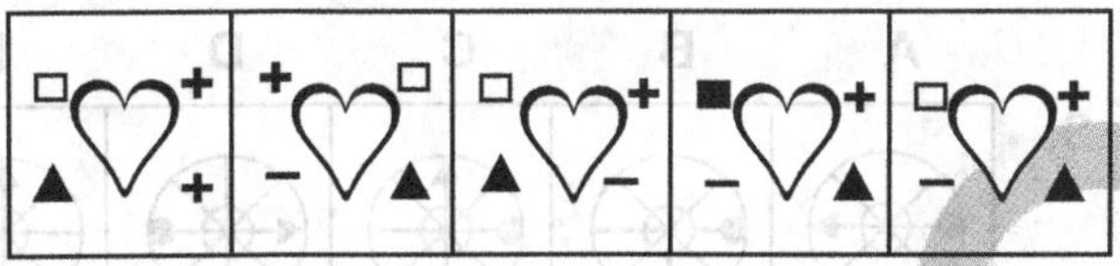

20.

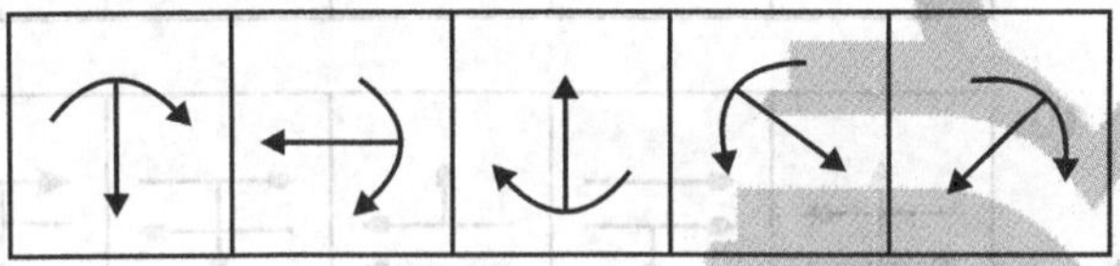

21.

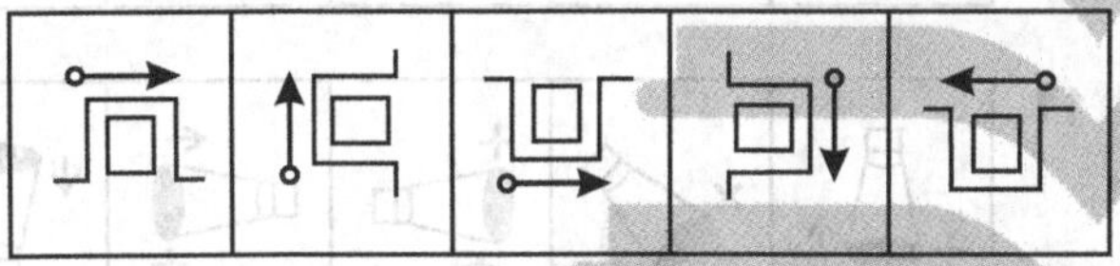

22.

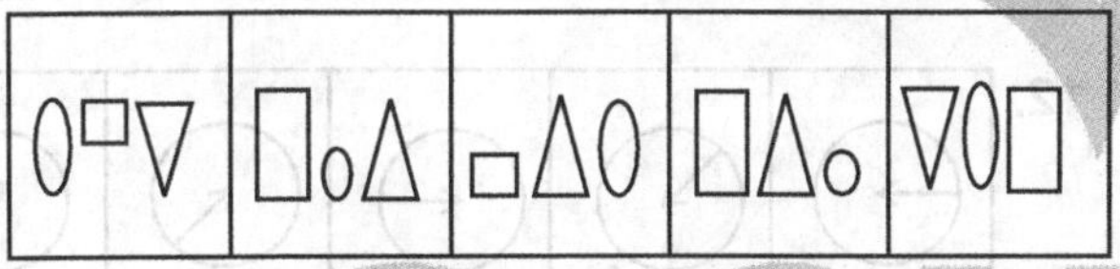

23.

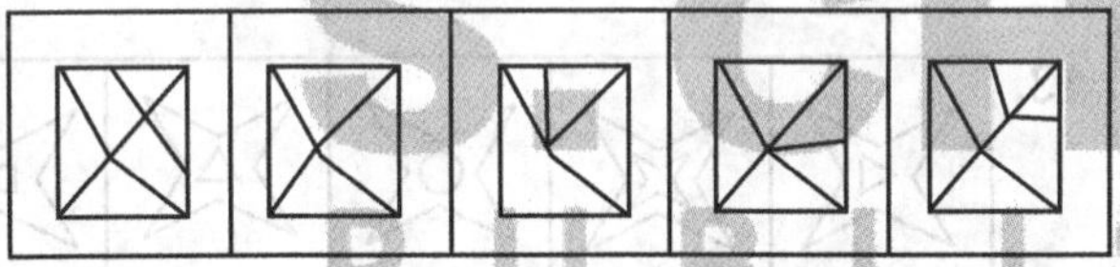

24.

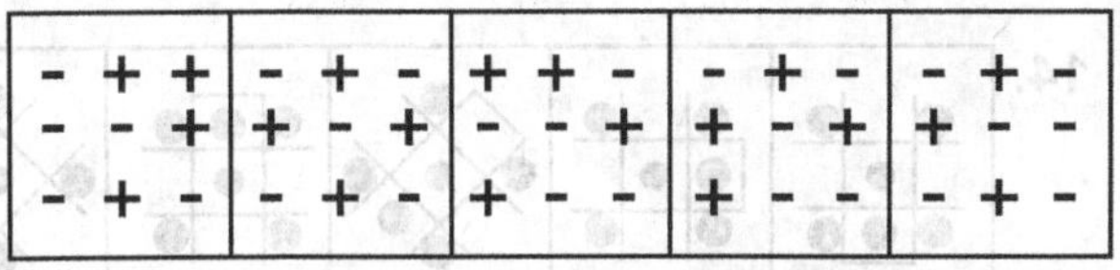

25.

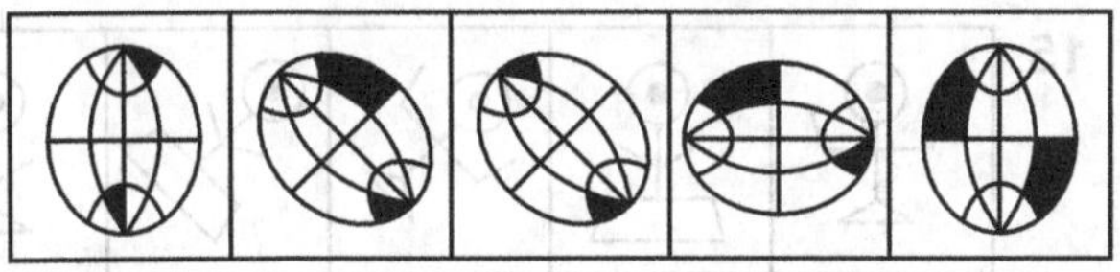

26.

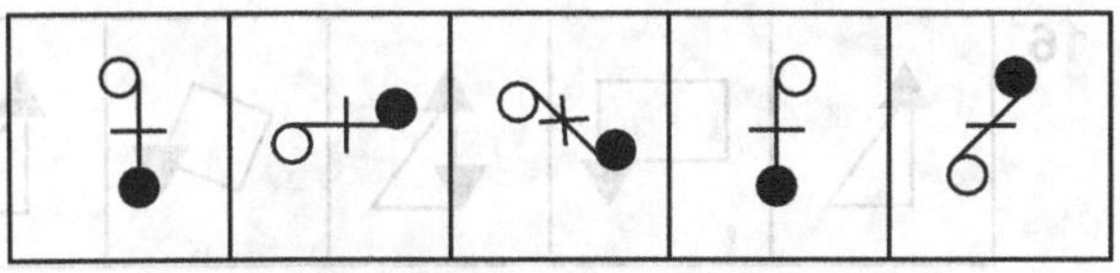

A B C D E

27.

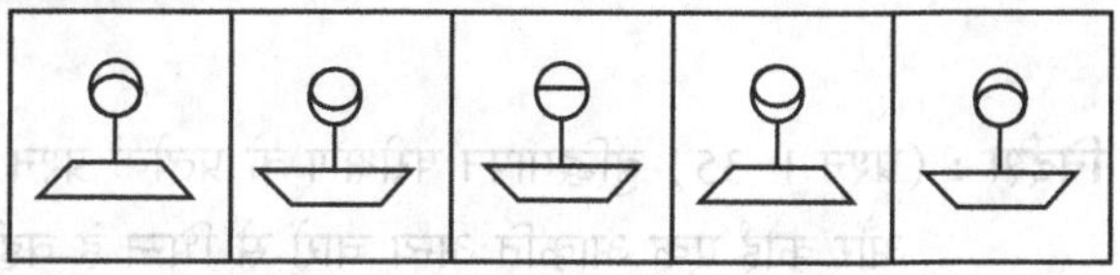

28.

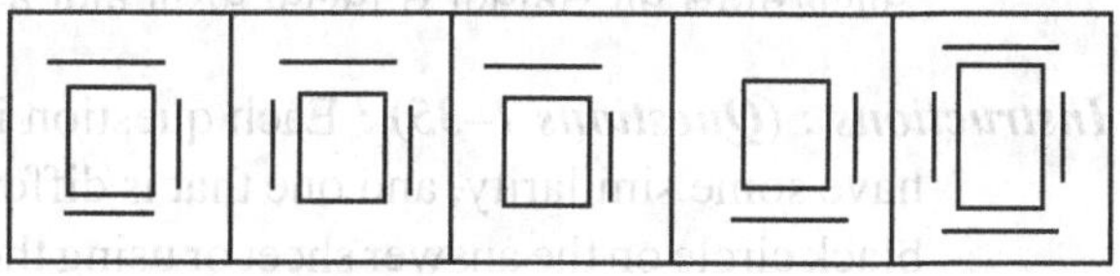

29.

30.

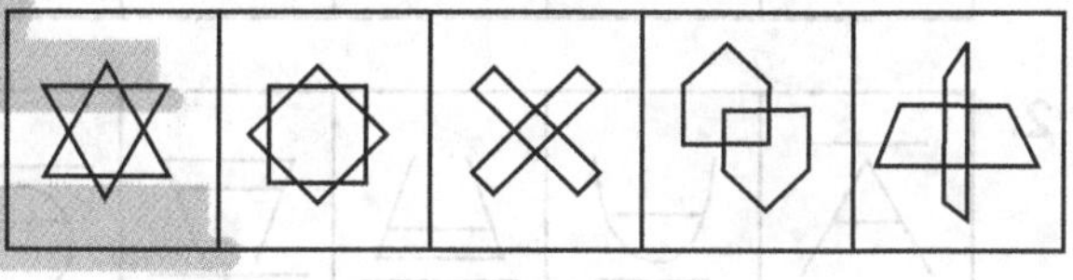

31.

32.

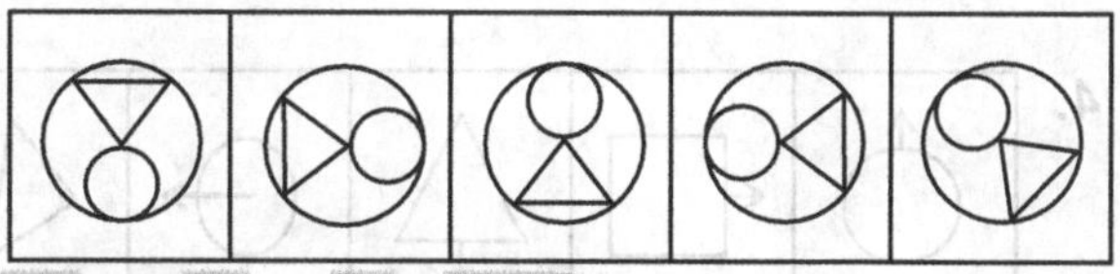

33.

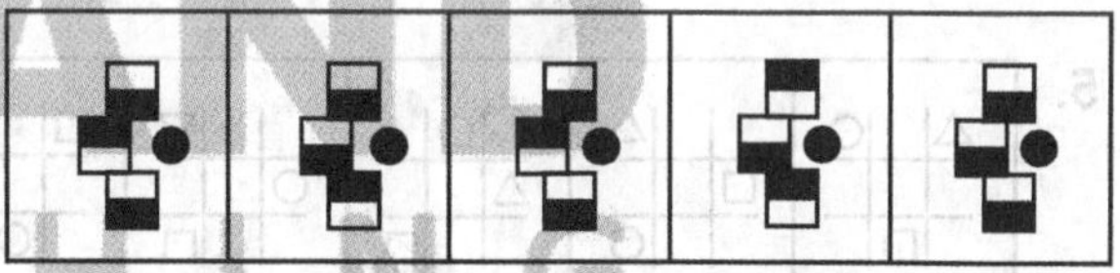

34.

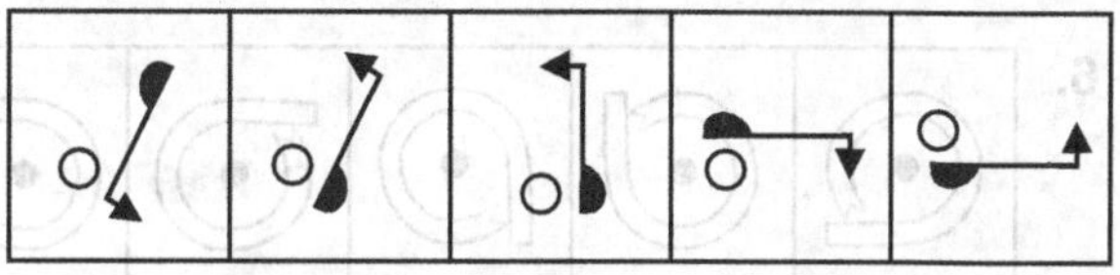

35.

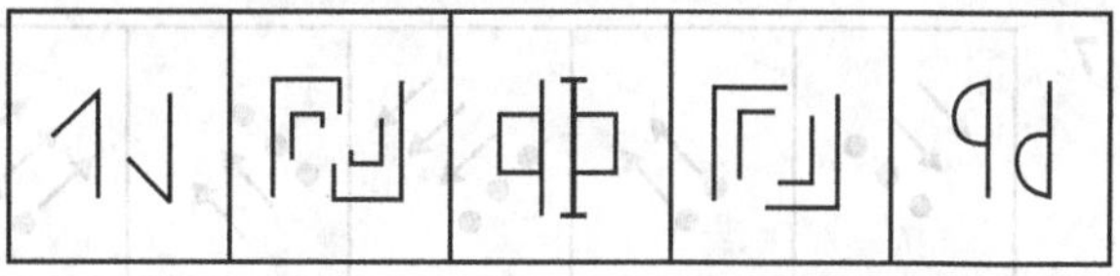

PRACTICE SET-7

Total Ques.- 35
Time - 10 Min.

निर्देश : (प्रश्न 1–35) बुद्धिमापन परीक्षण के प्रत्येक प्रश्न में पाँच आकृतियाँ दिए जाते हैं जिसमें से चार आकृतियाँ में कुछ समानता और कोई एक आकृति अन्य चारों से भिन्न है वही भिन्न आकृति आपका उत्तर होगा जिसे दिए गए उत्तर-पत्रक में गोले को काला/माउस की सहायता से क्लिक करना होता है और इसके लिए 10 मिनट का समय दिया जाता है।

Instructions : (Questions 1–35) : Each question in the Intelligence Test consists of five figures, four of which have some similarity, and one that is different from the other four is your answer. You must click on the black circle on the answer sheet or using the mouse. You are given 10 minutes to complete the test.

A B C D E

1. 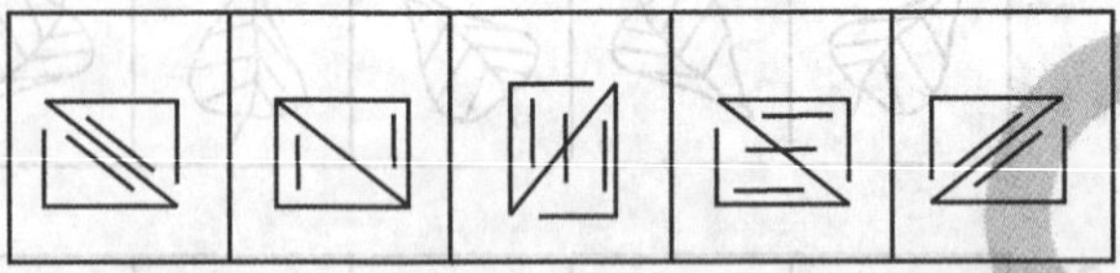

2. 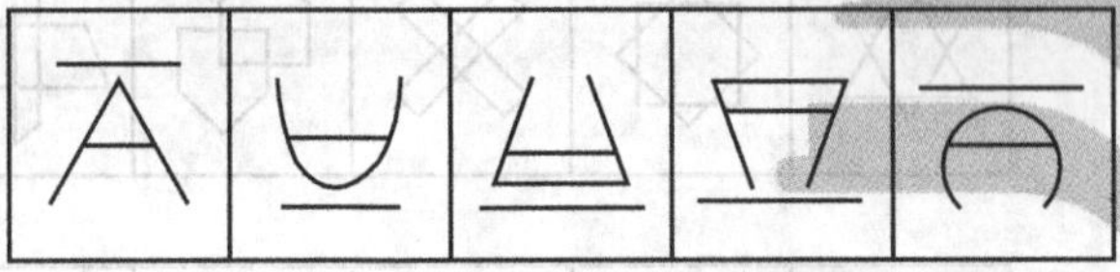

3. 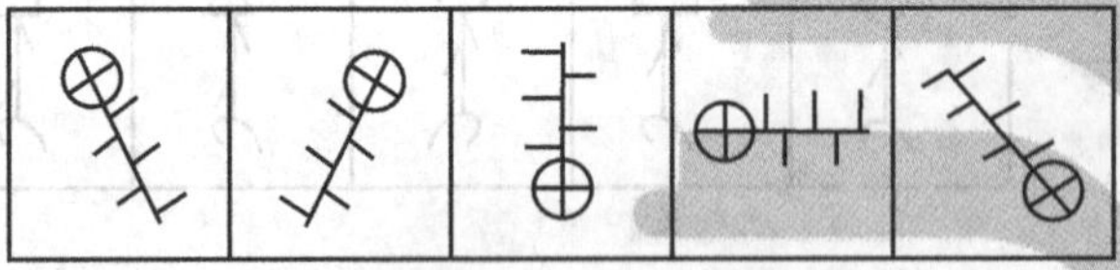

4. 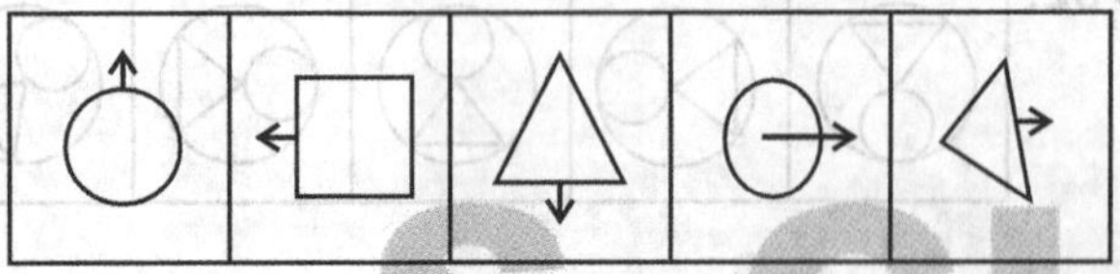

5. 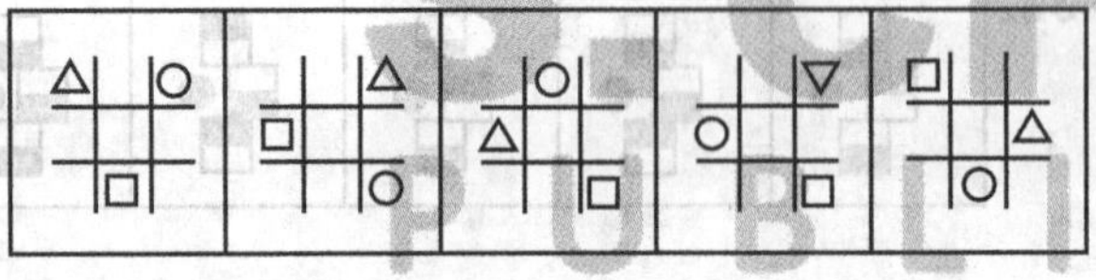

6. 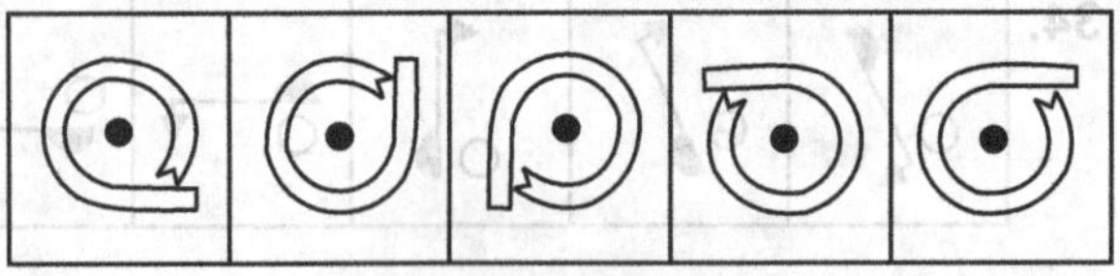

7. 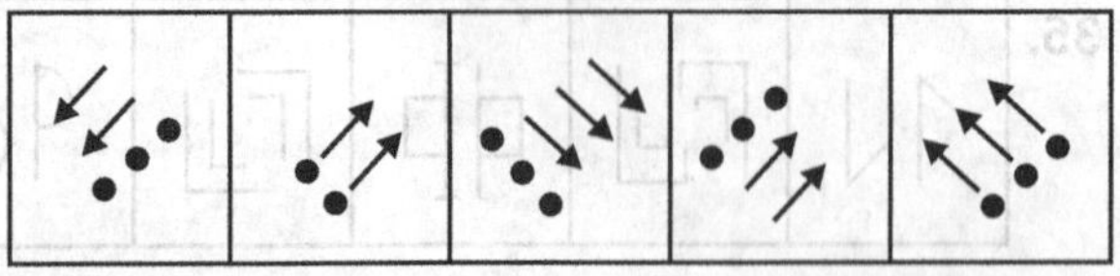

8. 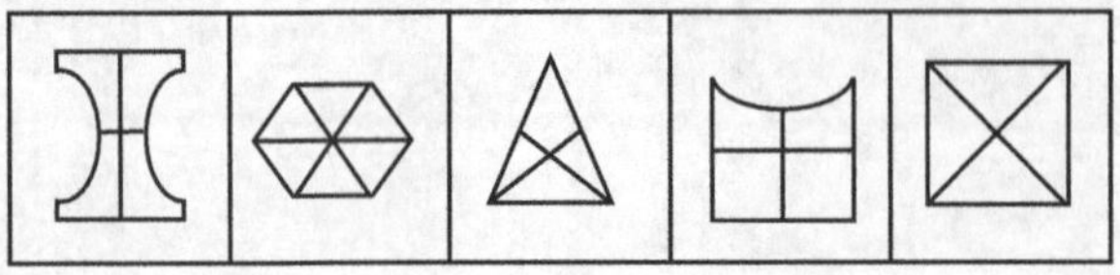

A B C D E

9. 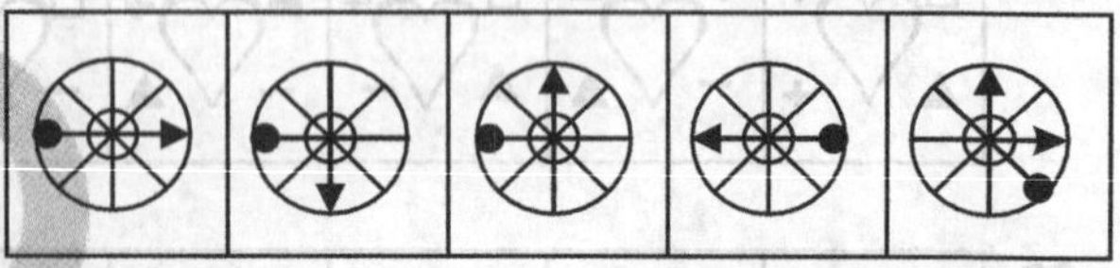

10. 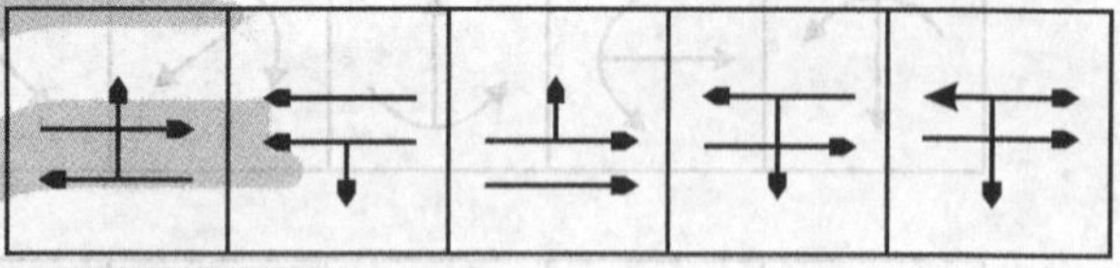

11. 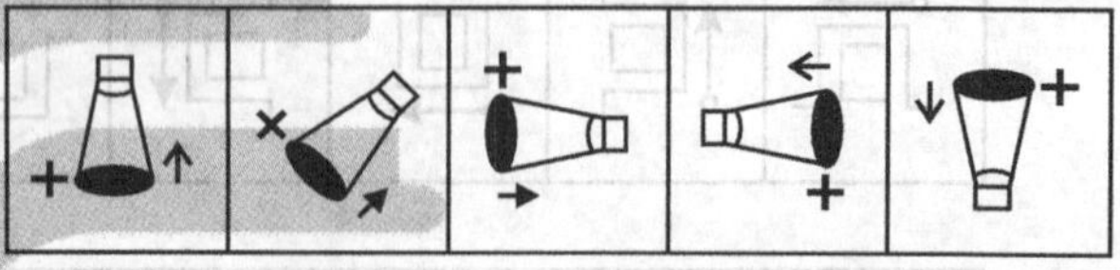

12. 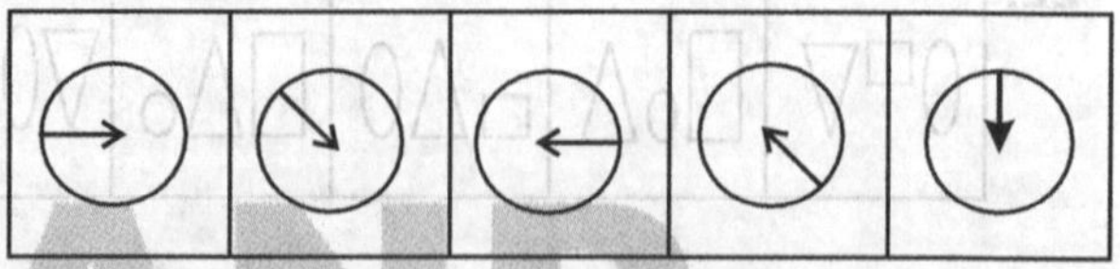

13. 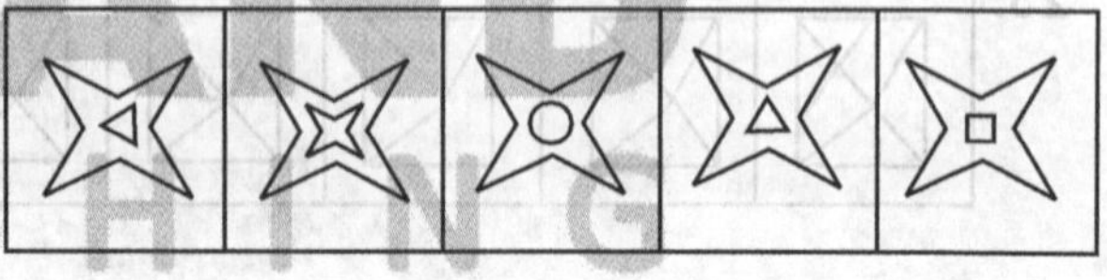

14. 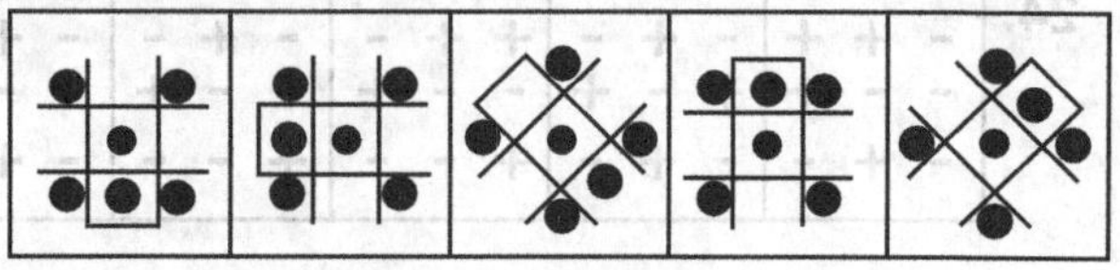

15. 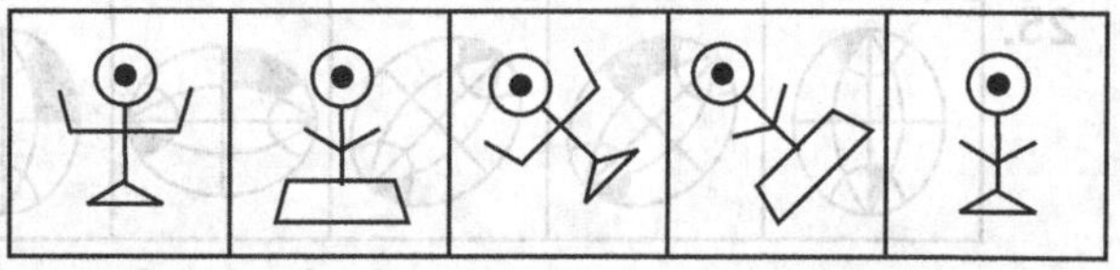

16. 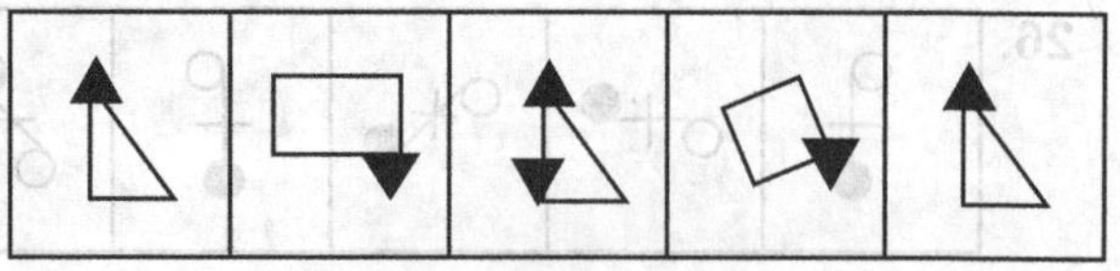

A B C D E

17.
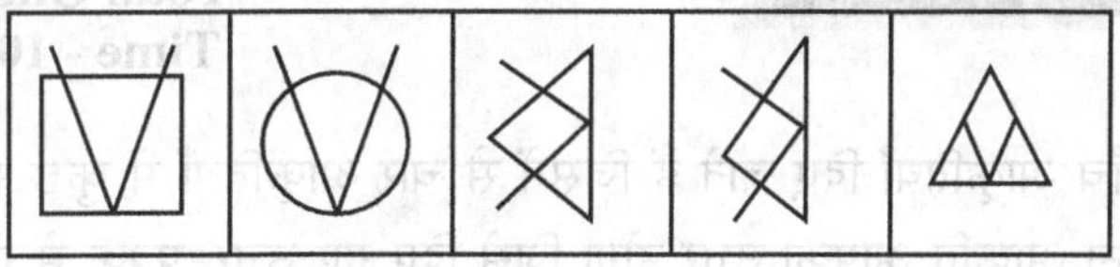

18.
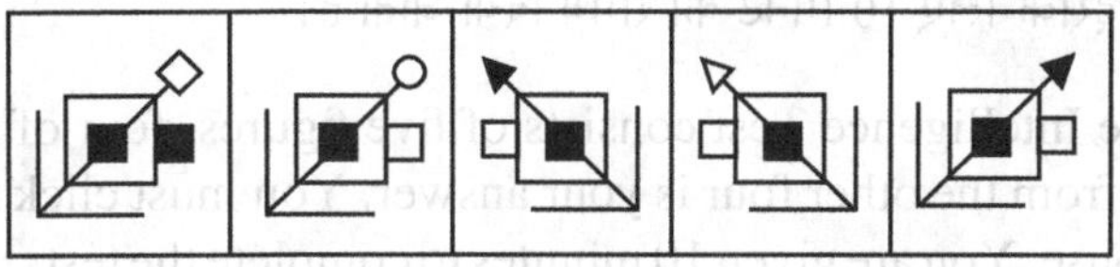

19.
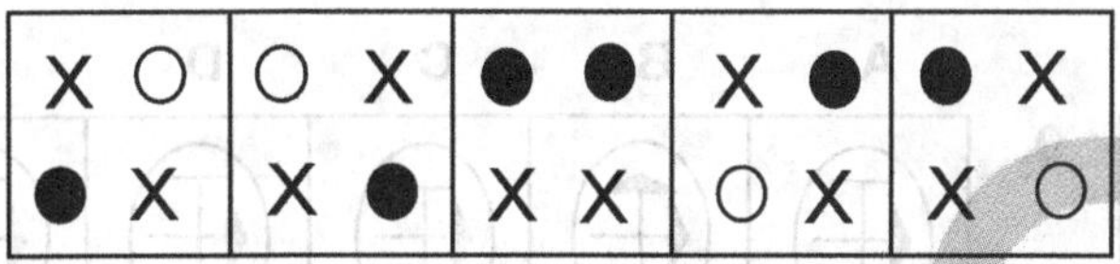

20.
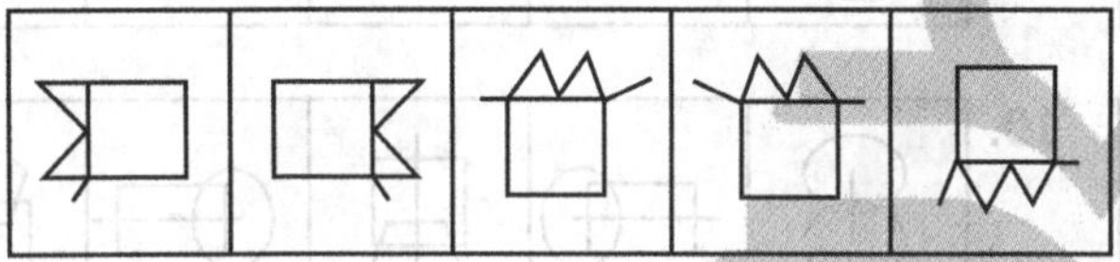

21.
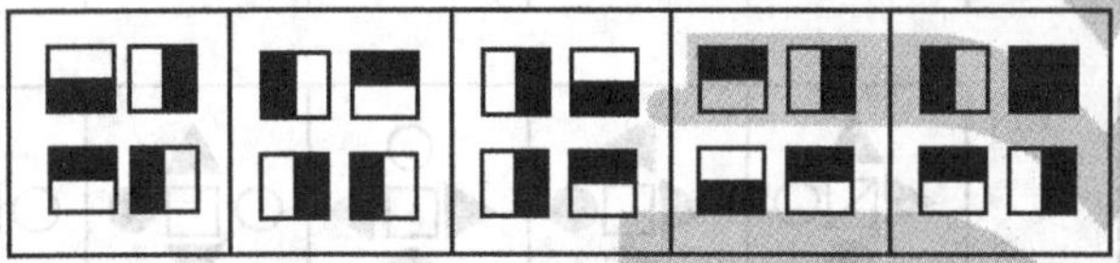

22.
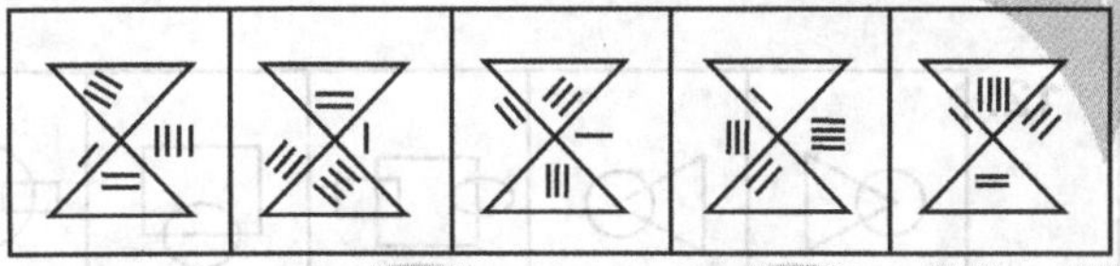

23.
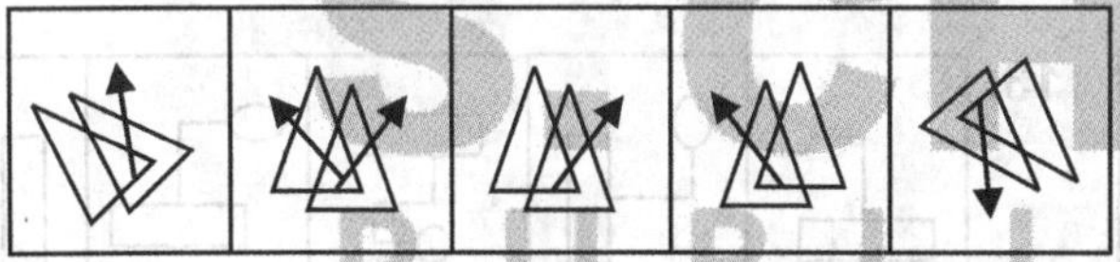

24.
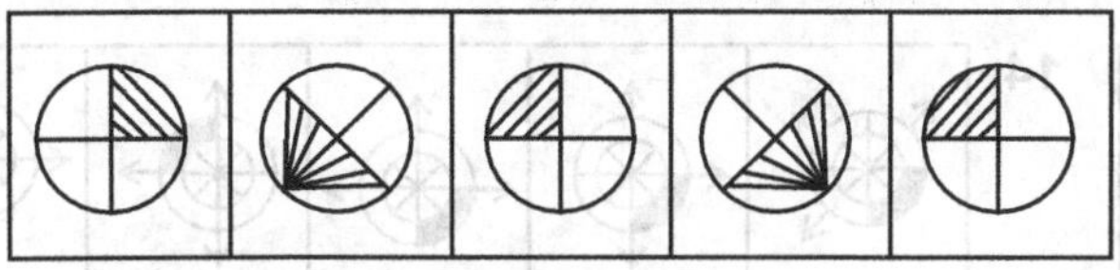

25.
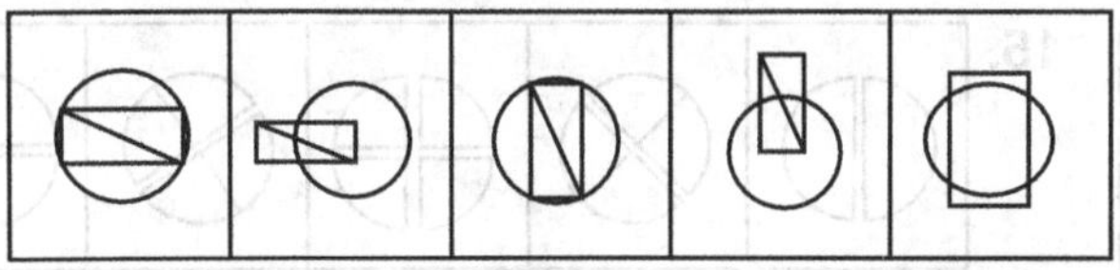

26.
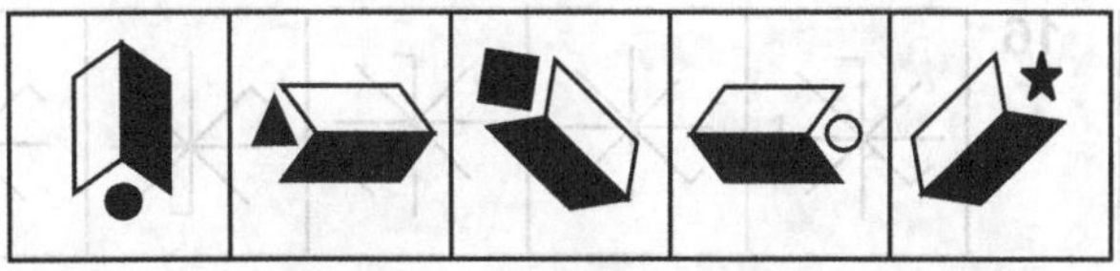

A B C D E

27.
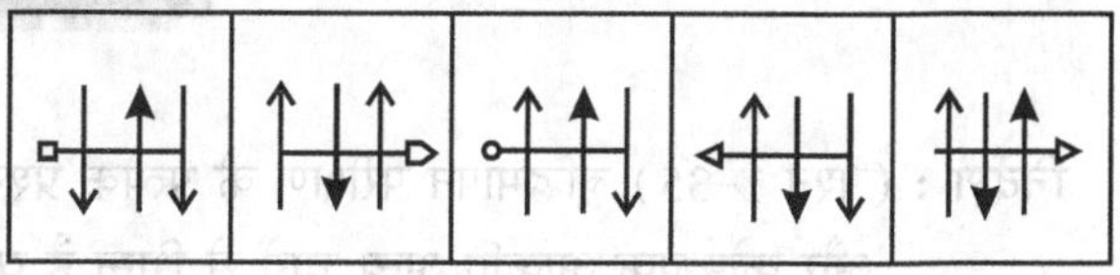

28.
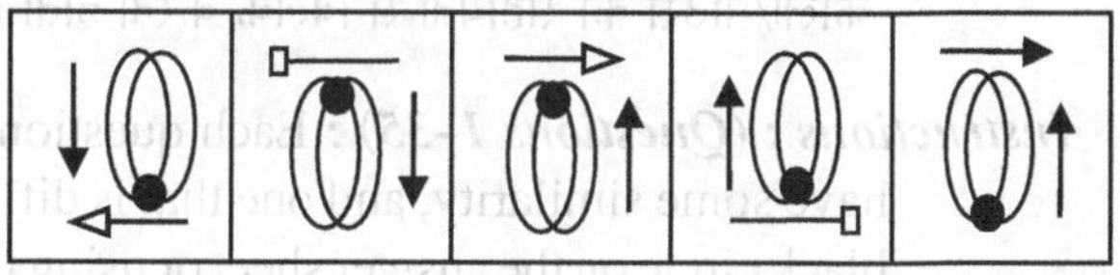

29.
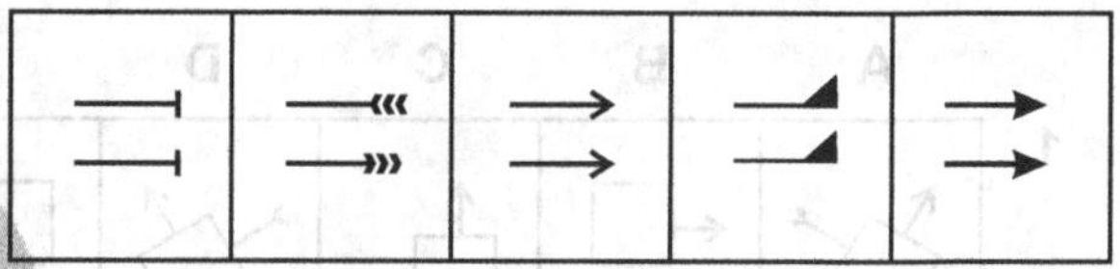

30.
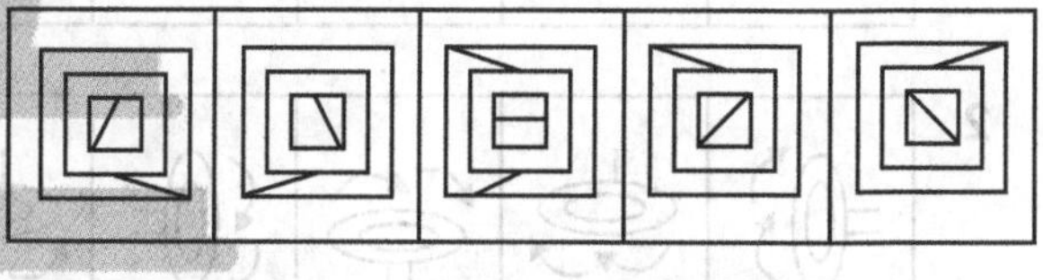

31.
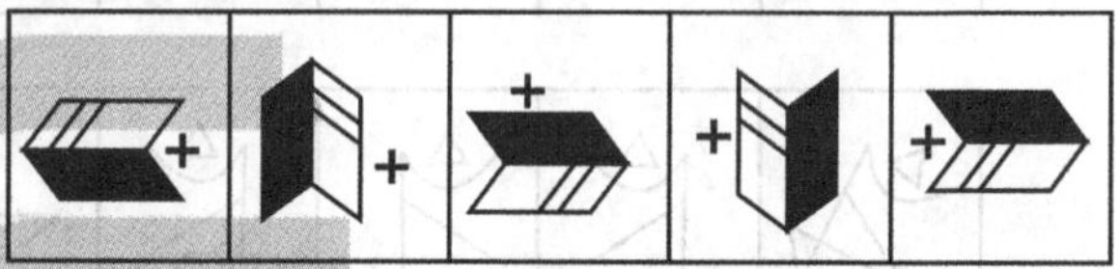

32.
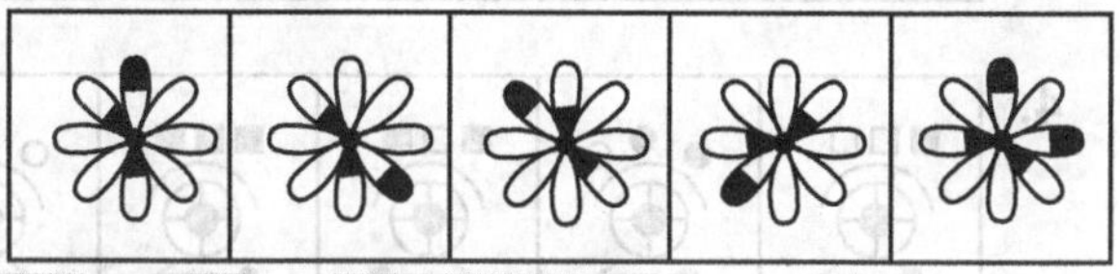

33.
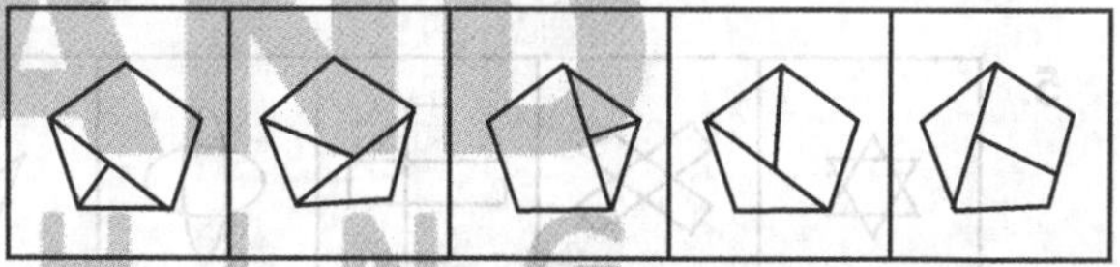

34.
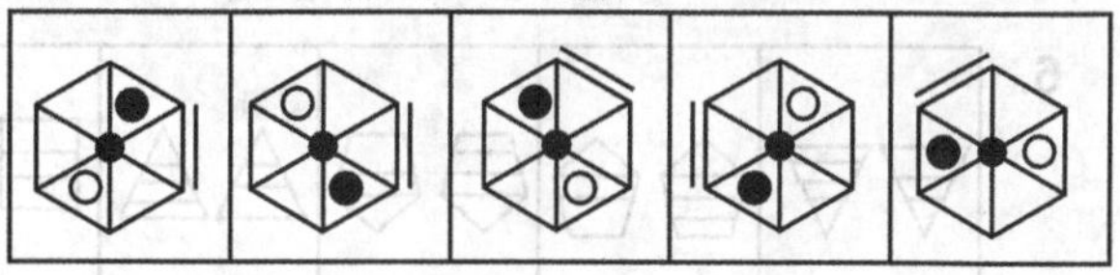

35.
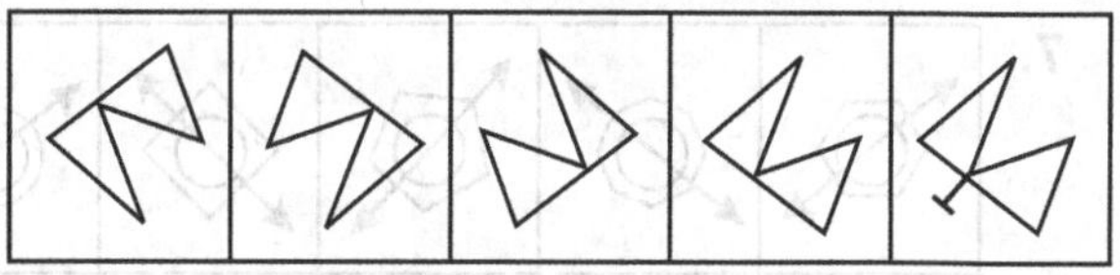

PRACTICE SET-8

Total Ques.- 35
Time - 10 Min.

निर्देश : (प्रश्न 1–35) बुद्धिमापन परीक्षण के प्रत्येक प्रश्न में पाँच आकृतियाँ दिए जाते हैं जिसमें से चार आकृतियाँ में कुछ समानता और कोई एक आकृति अन्य चारों से भिन्न है वही भिन्न आकृति आपका उत्तर होगा जिसे दिए गए उत्तर-पत्रक में गोले को काला/माउस की सहायता से क्लिक करना होता है और इसके लिए 10 मिनट का समय दिया जाता है।

Instructions : (Questions 1–35) : Each question in the Intelligence Test consists of five figures, four of which have some similarity, and one that is different from the other four is your answer. You must click on the black circle on the answer sheet or using the mouse. You are given 10 minutes to complete the test.

A B C D E

1.
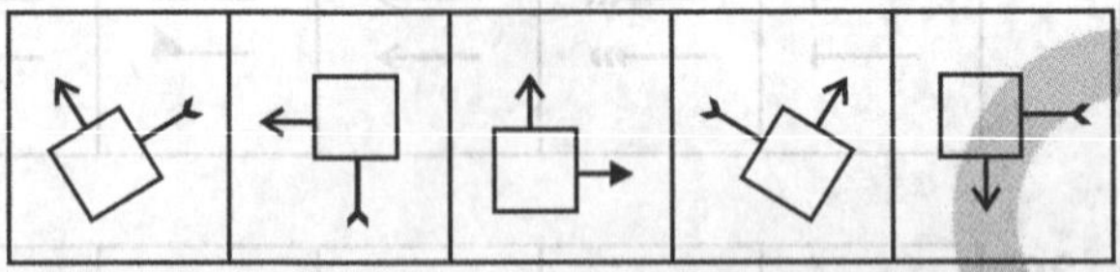

2.

3.
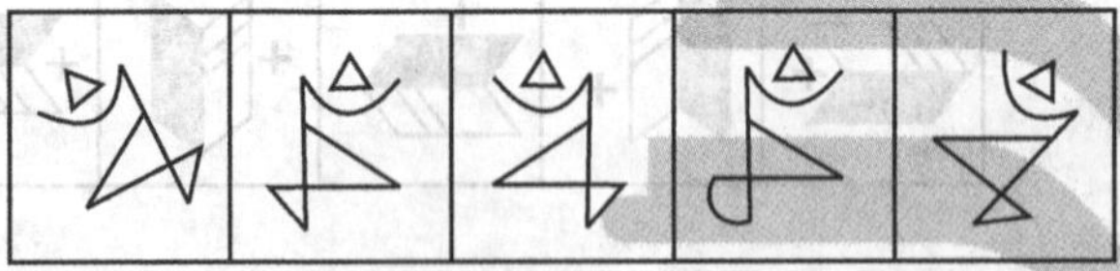

4.
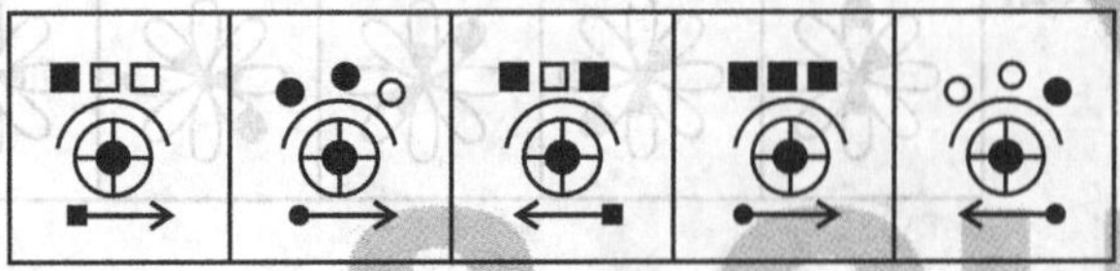

5.
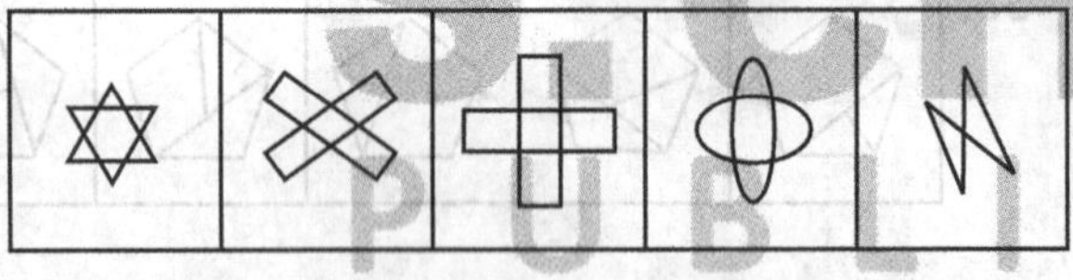

6.
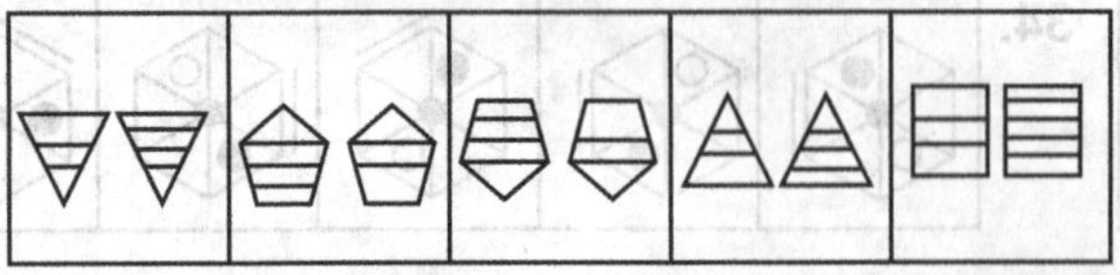

7.
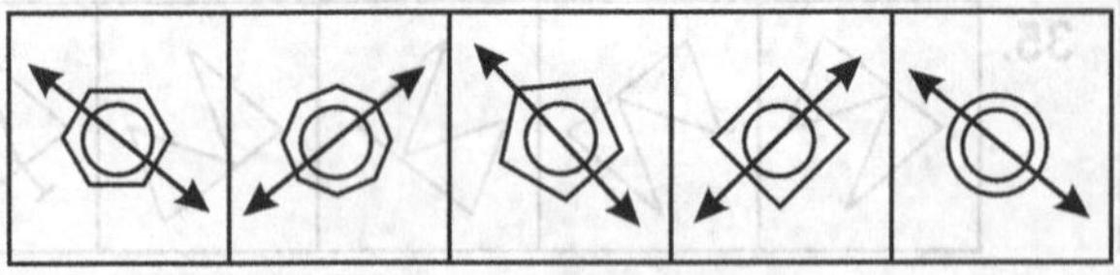

8.
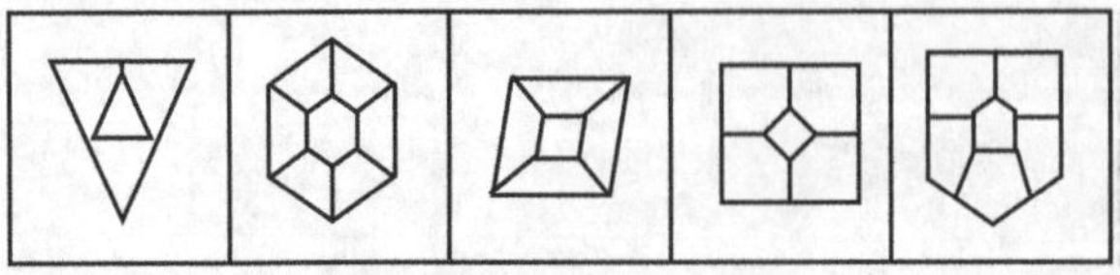

A B C D E

9.
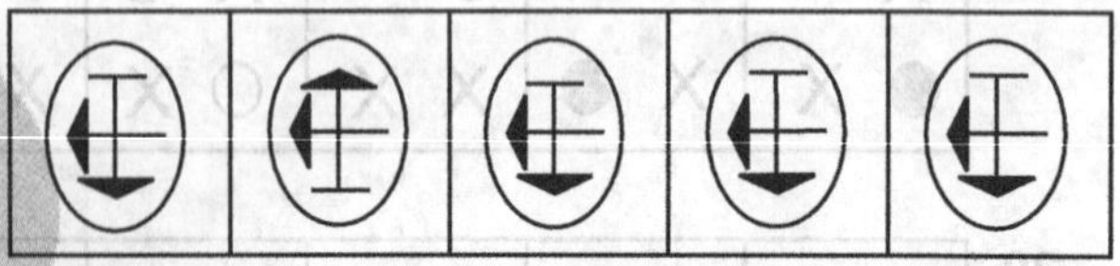

10.
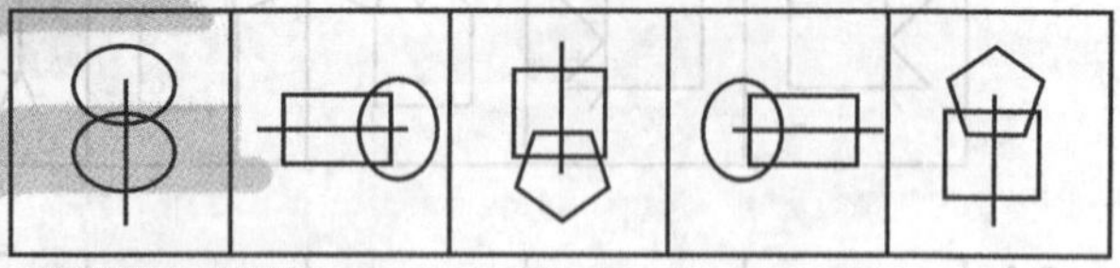

11.
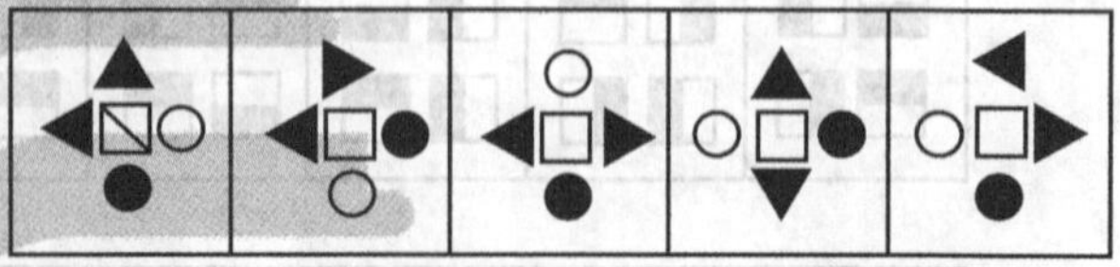

12.
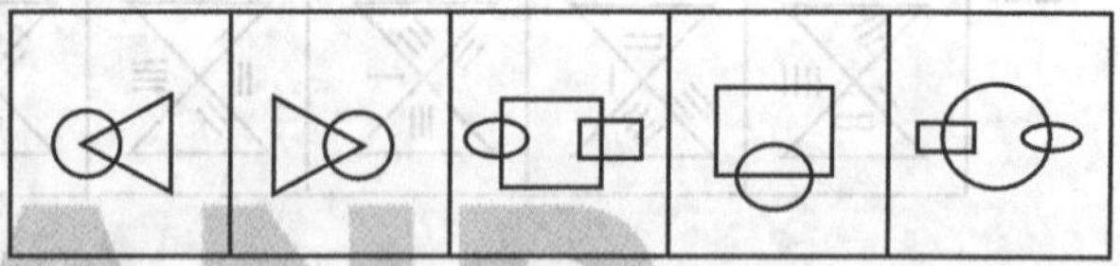

13.
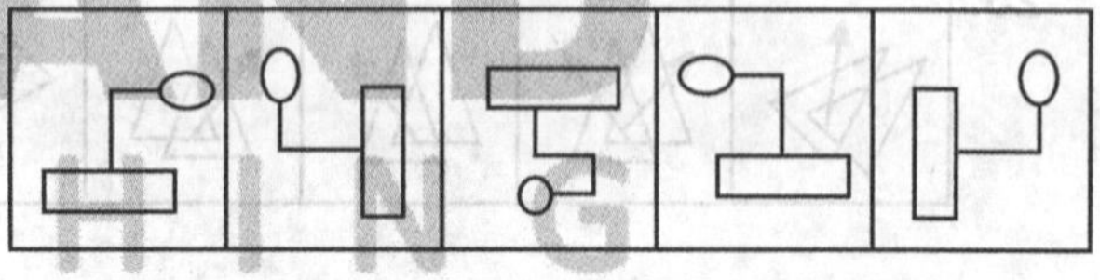

14.
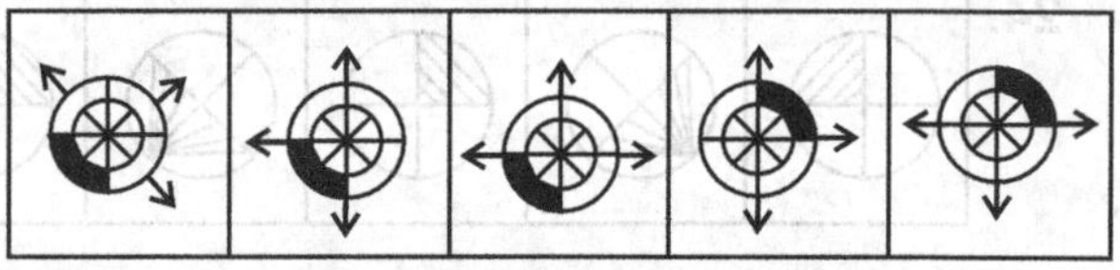

15.
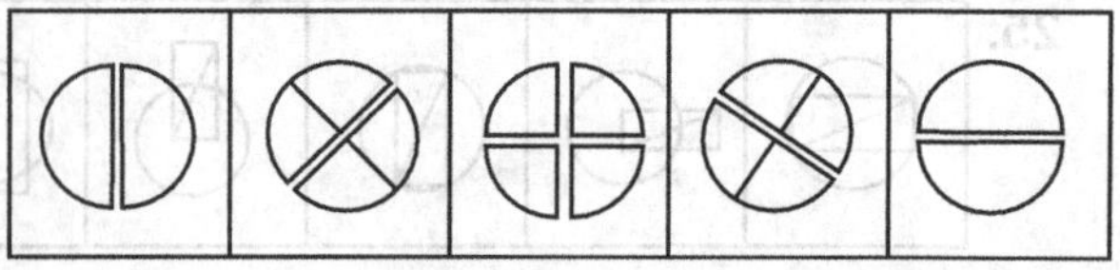

16.
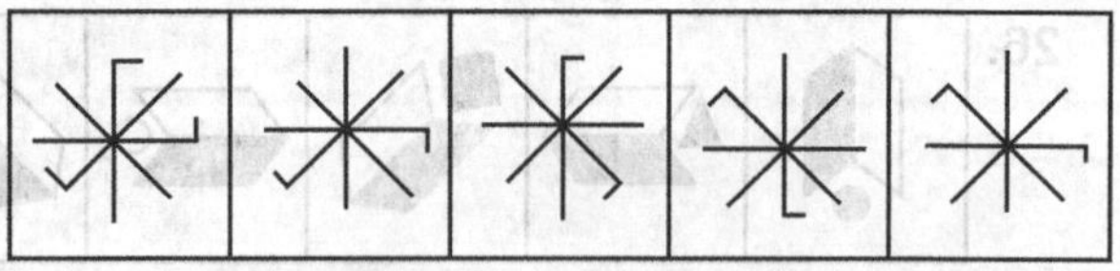

A B C D E

17. 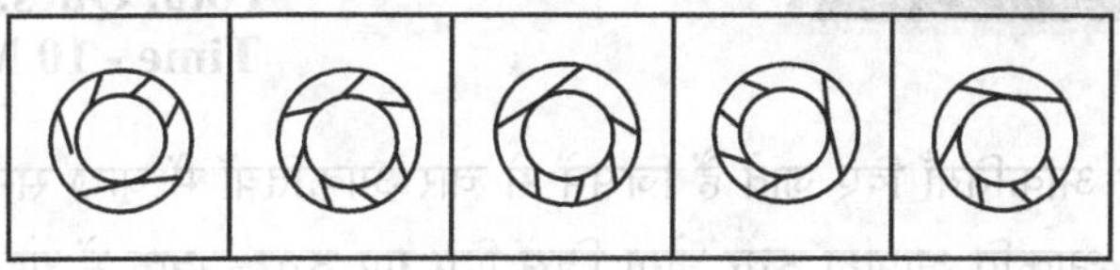

18. 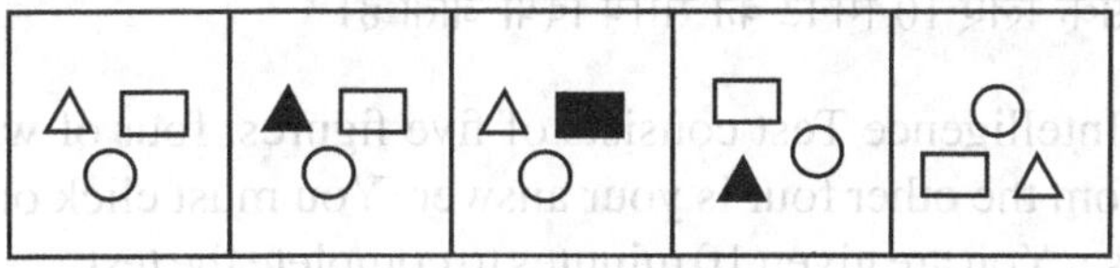

19. 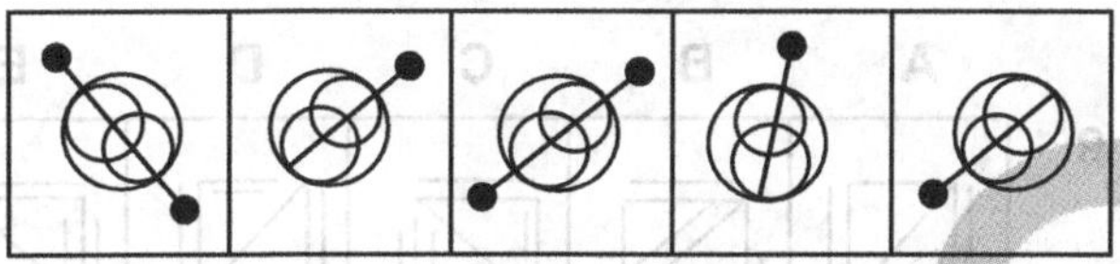

20. 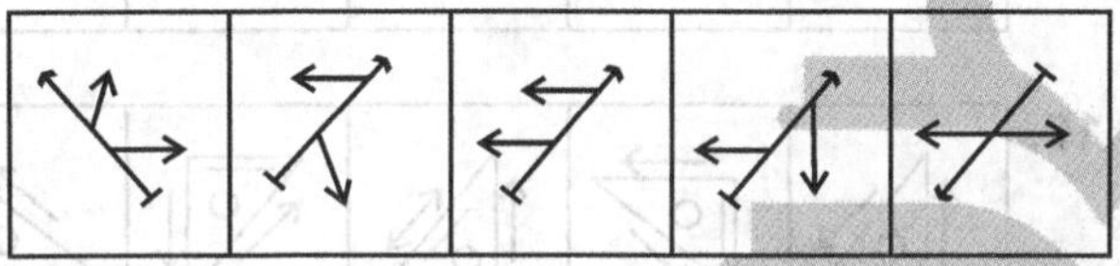

21. 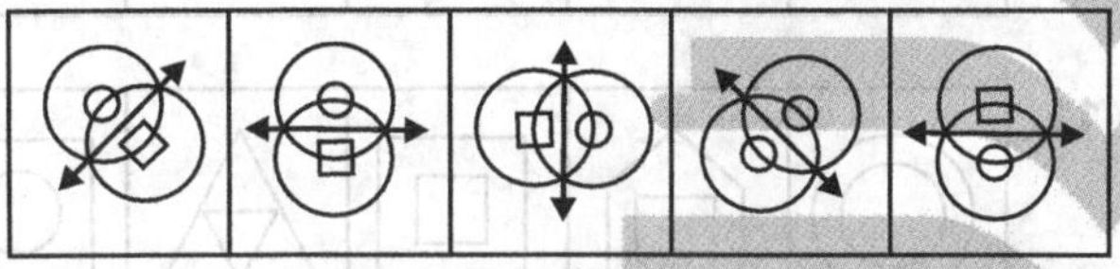

22. 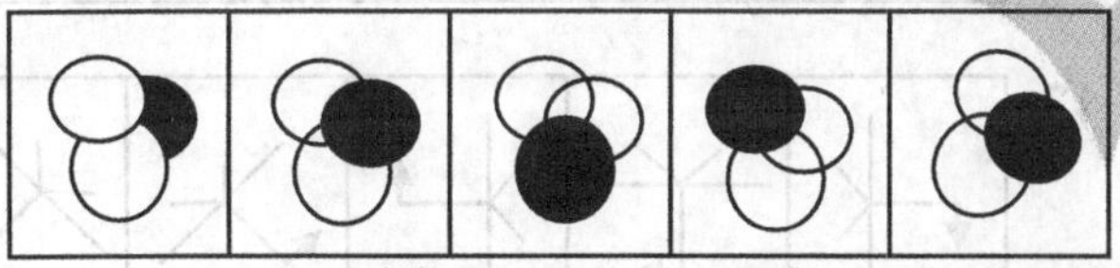

23. 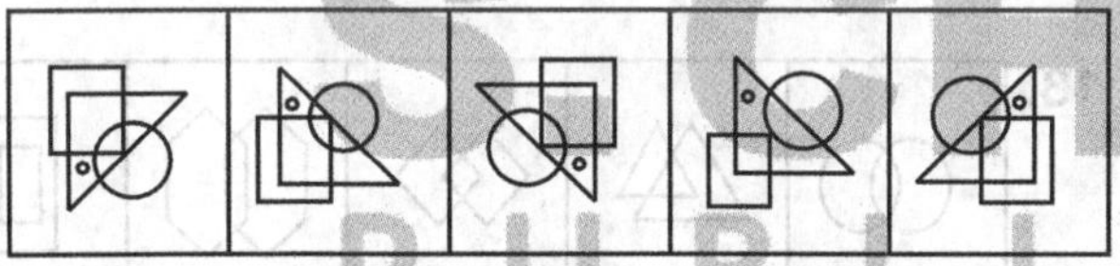

24. 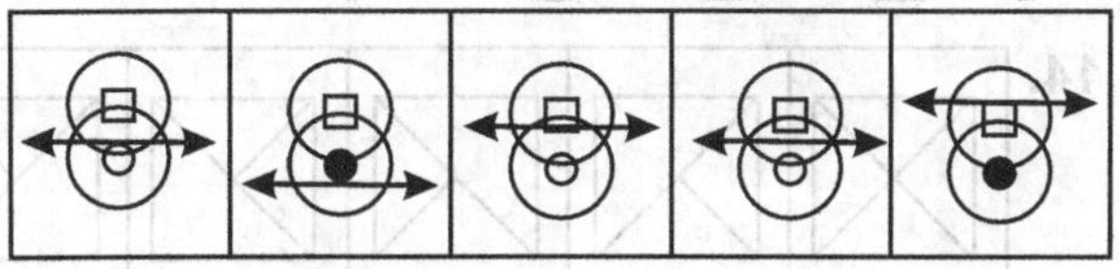

25. 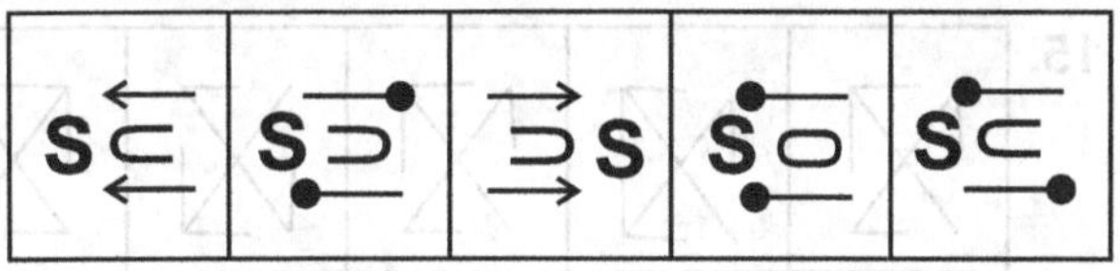

26. 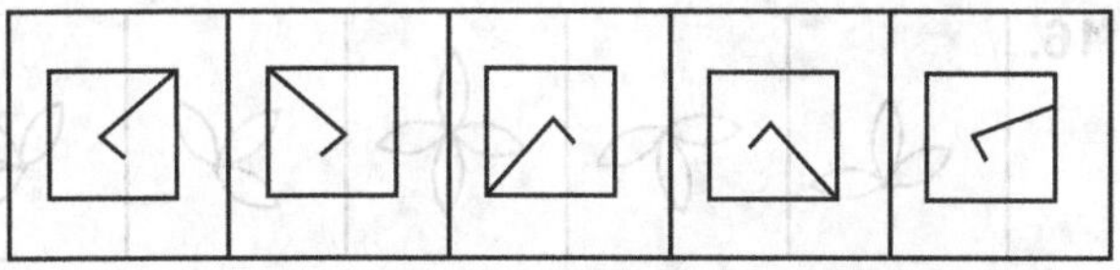

A B C D E

27. 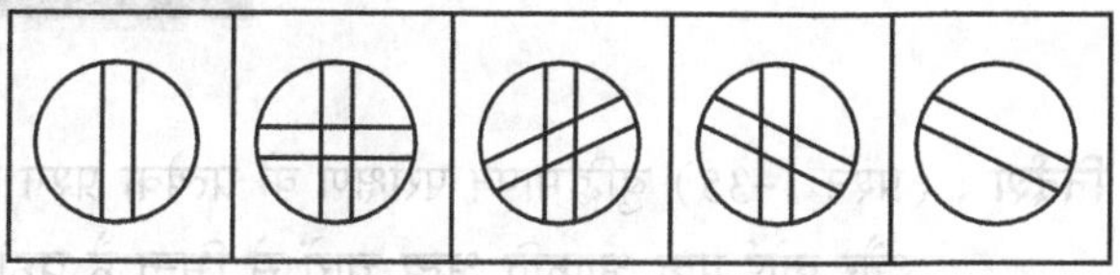

28. 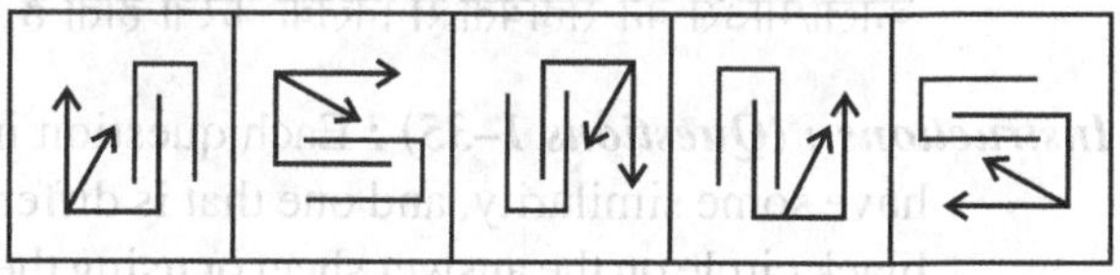

29. 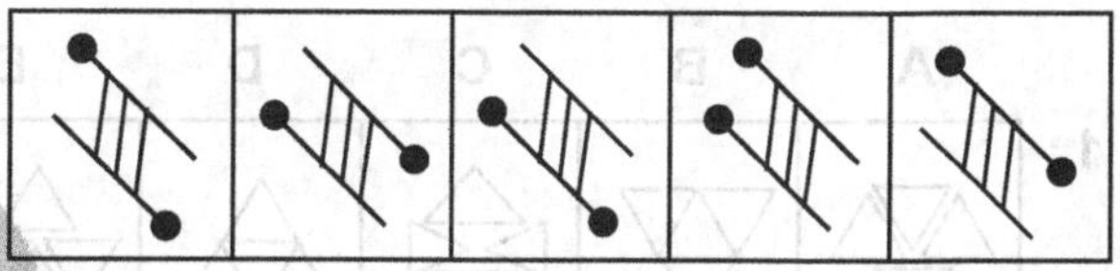

30. 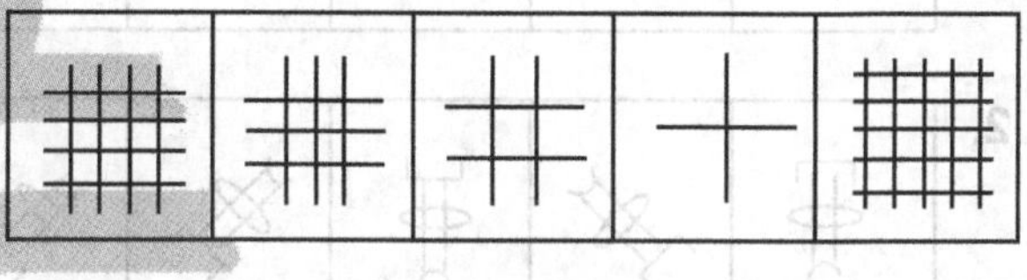

31. 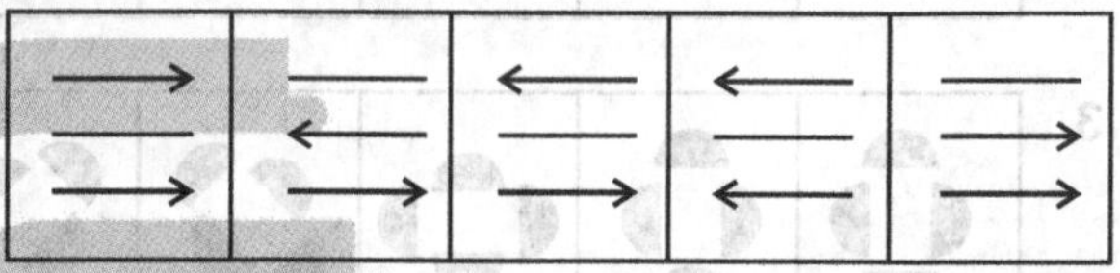

32. 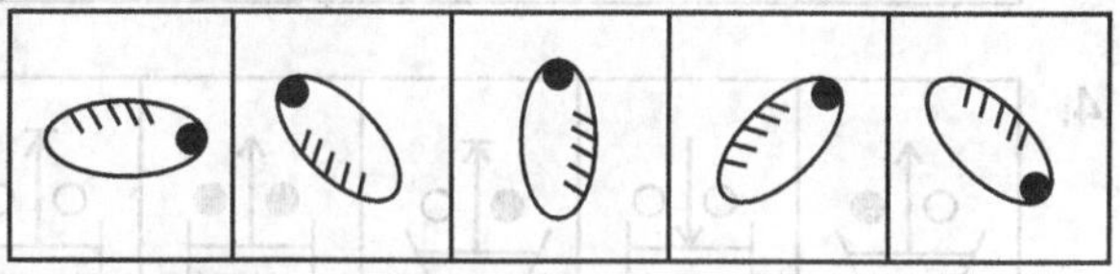

33. 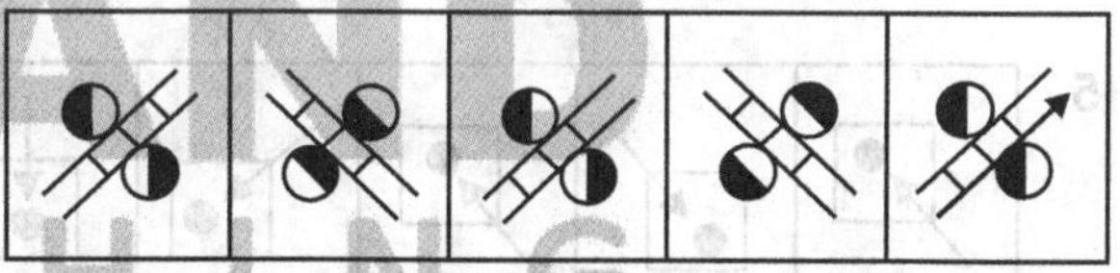

34. 

35. 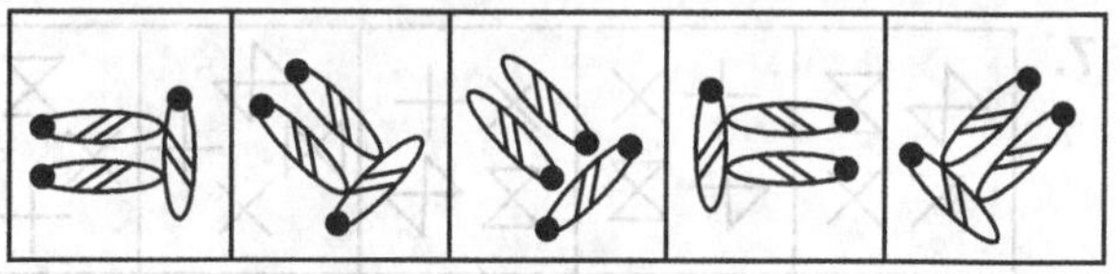

PRACTICE SET-9

Total Ques.- 35
Time - 10 Min.

निर्देश : (प्रश्न 1–35) बुद्धिमापन परीक्षण के प्रत्येक प्रश्न में पाँच आकृतियाँ दिए जाते हैं जिसमें से चार आकृतियाँ में कुछ समानता और कोई एक आकृति अन्य चारों से भिन्न है वही भिन्न आकृति आपका उत्तर होगा जिसे दिए गए उत्तर-पत्रक में गोले को काला/माउस की सहायता से क्लिक करना होता है और इसके लिए 10 मिनट का समय दिया जाता है।

Instructions : (Questions 1–35) : Each question in the Intelligence Test consists of five figures, four of which have some similarity, and one that is different from the other four is your answer. You must click on the black circle on the answer sheet or using the mouse. You are given 10 minutes to complete the test.

A B C D E

1. 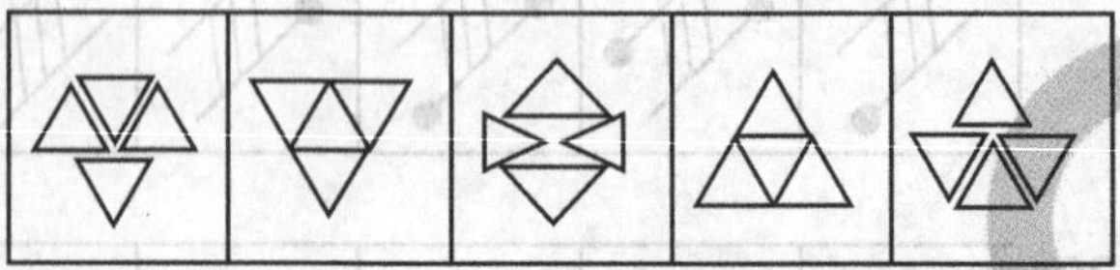

2. 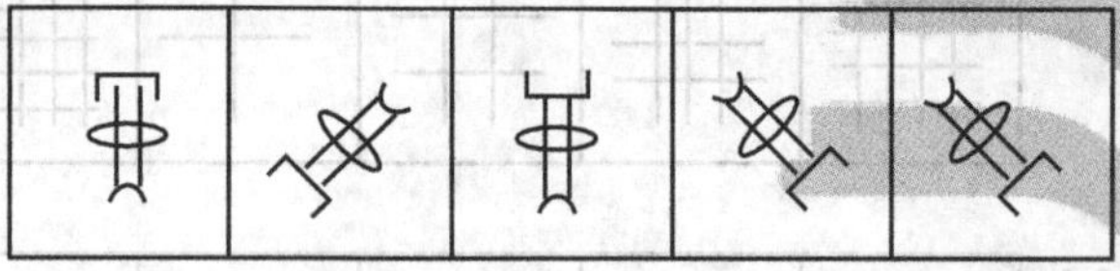

3. 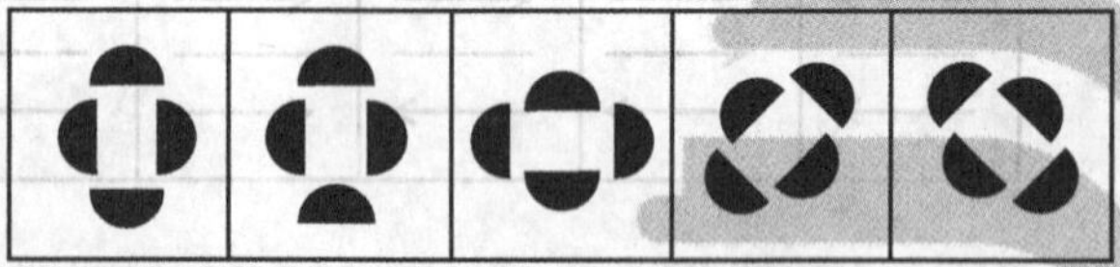

4. 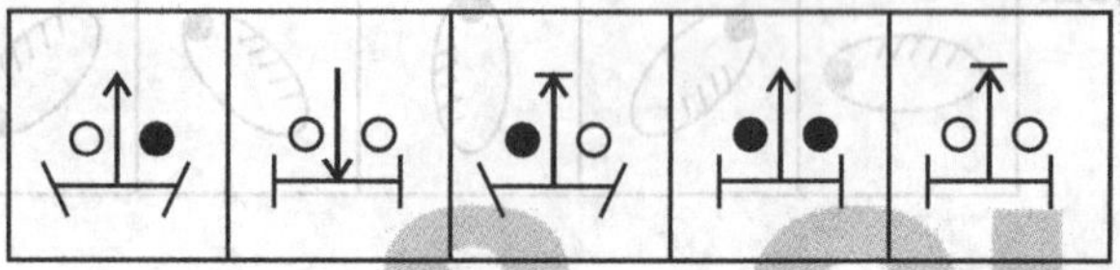

5. 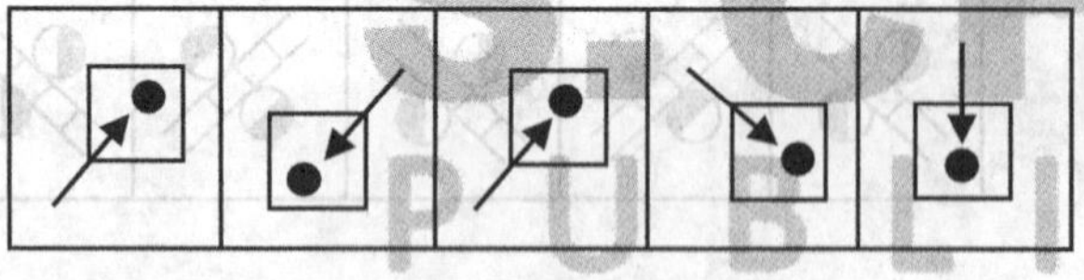

6. 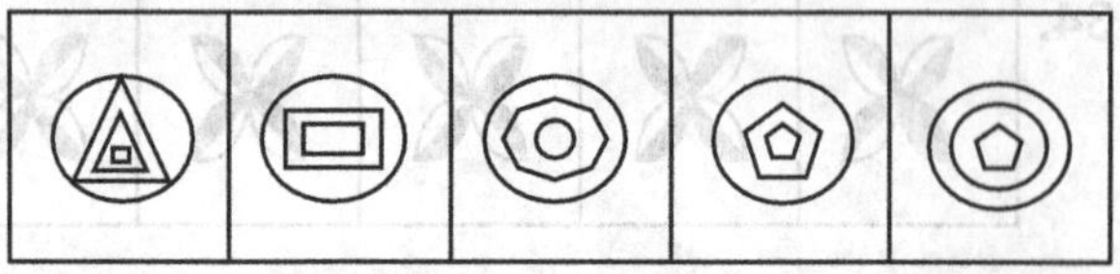

7. 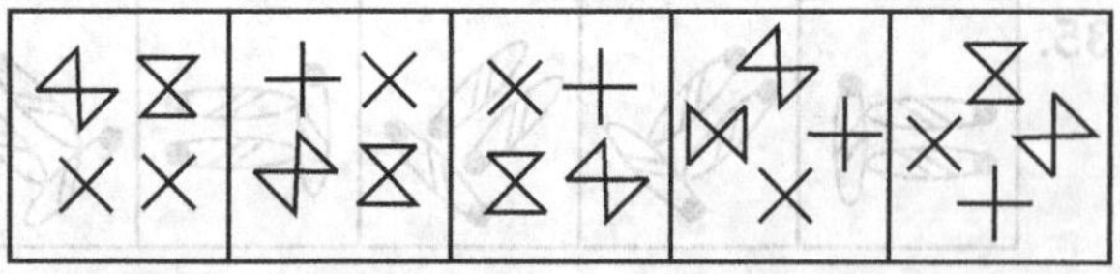

8. 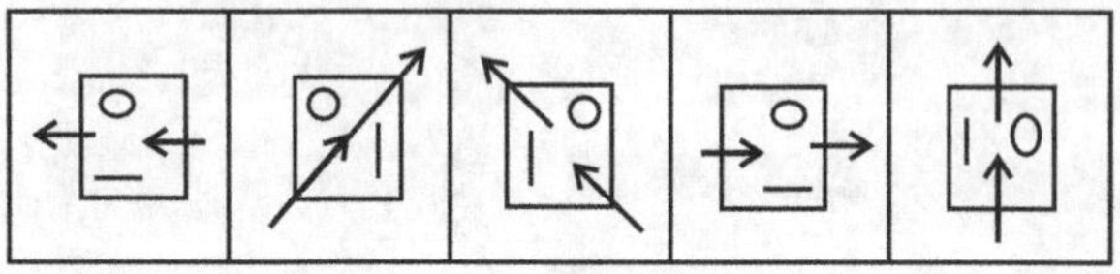

A B C D E

9. 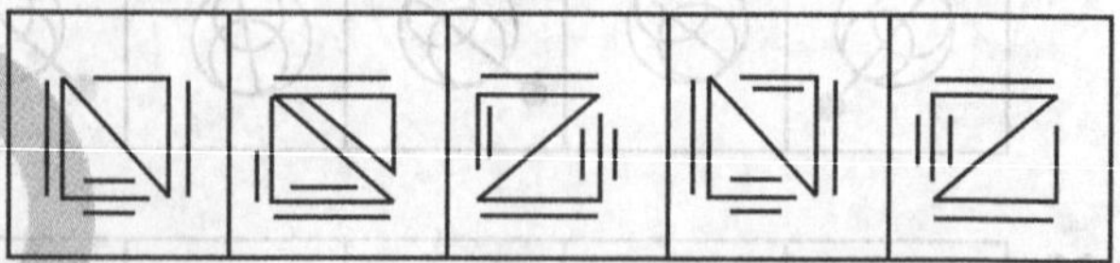

10. 

11. 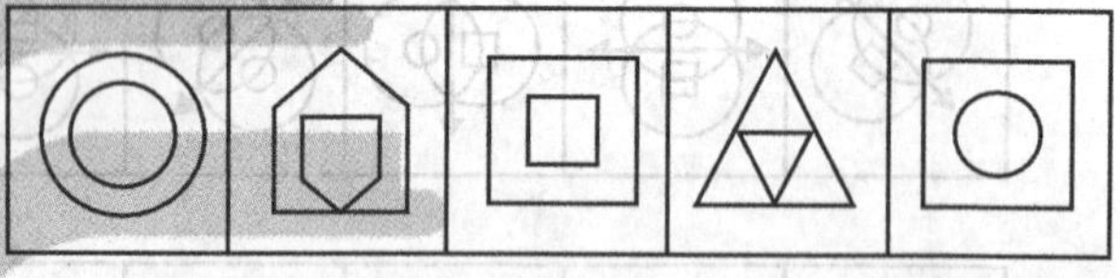

12. 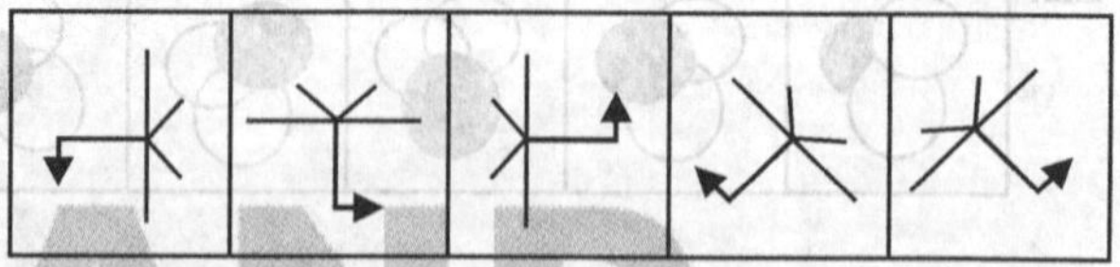

13. 

14. 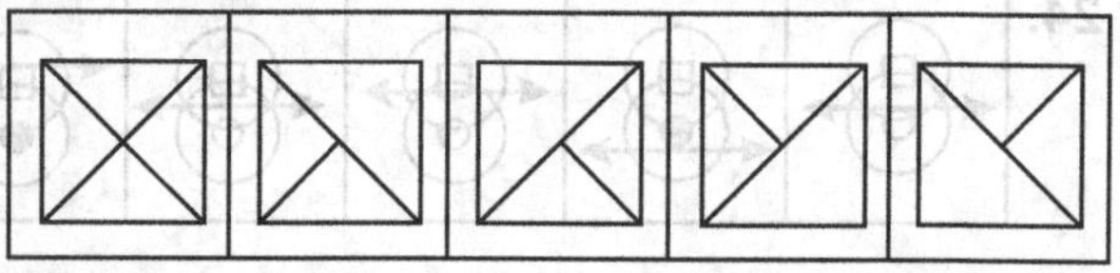

15. 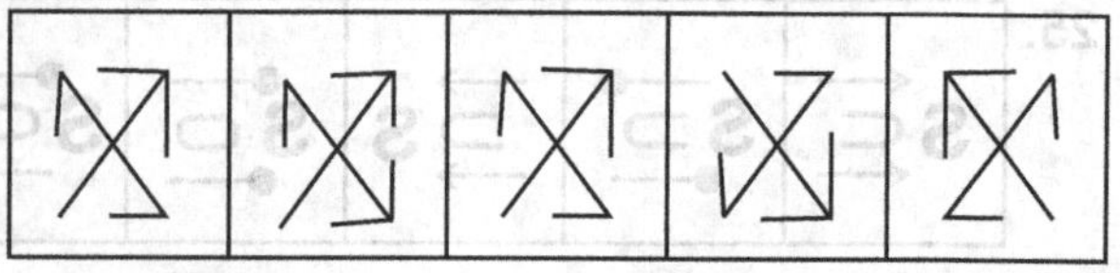

16. 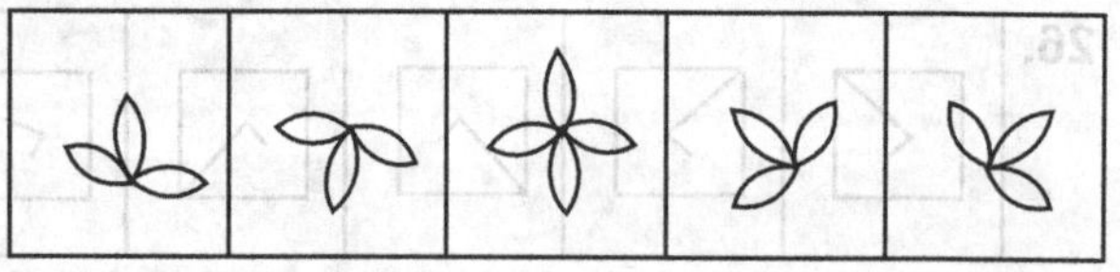

A B C D E

17. 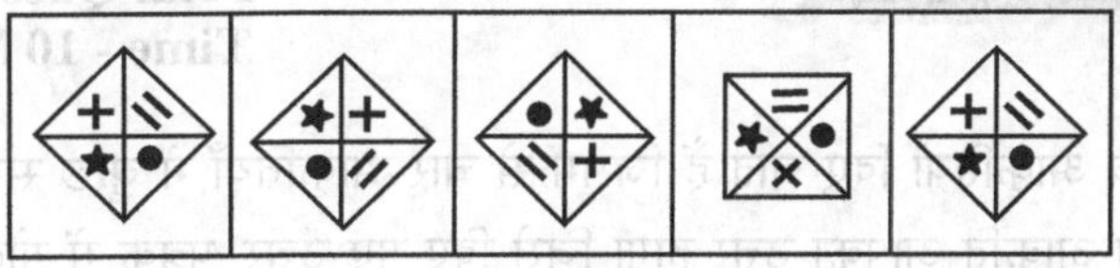

18. 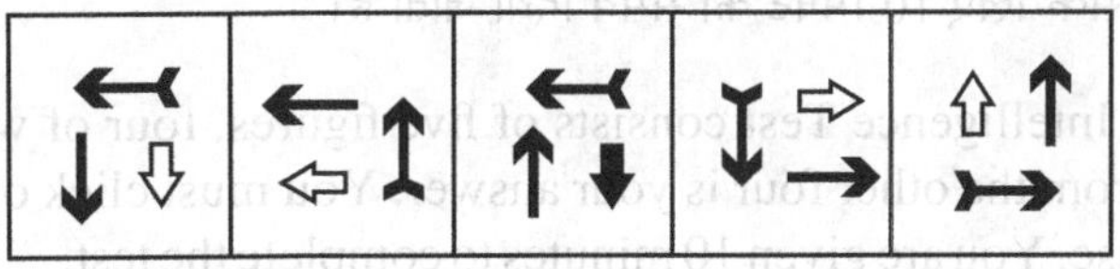

19. 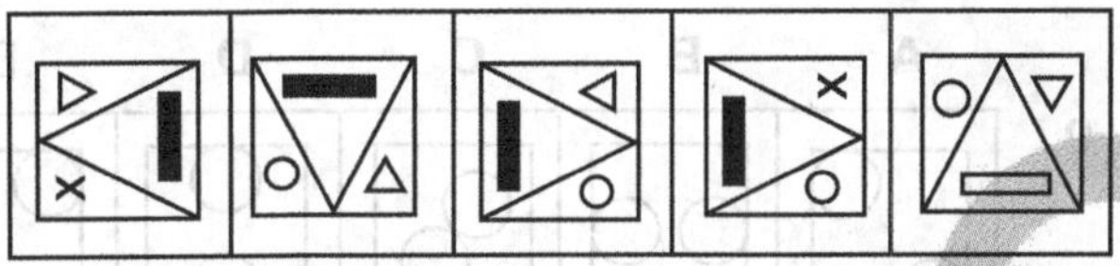

20. 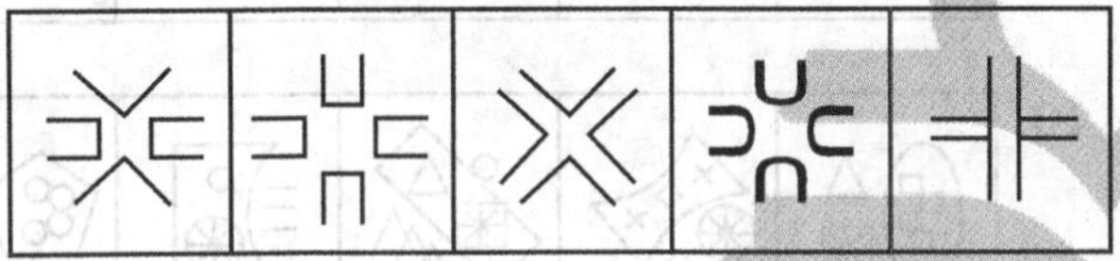

21. 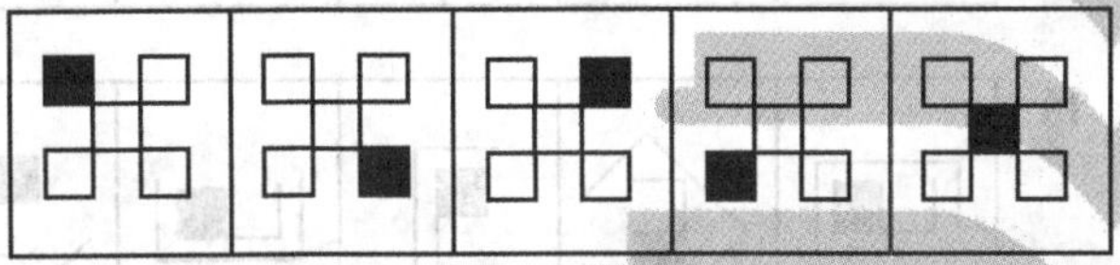

22. 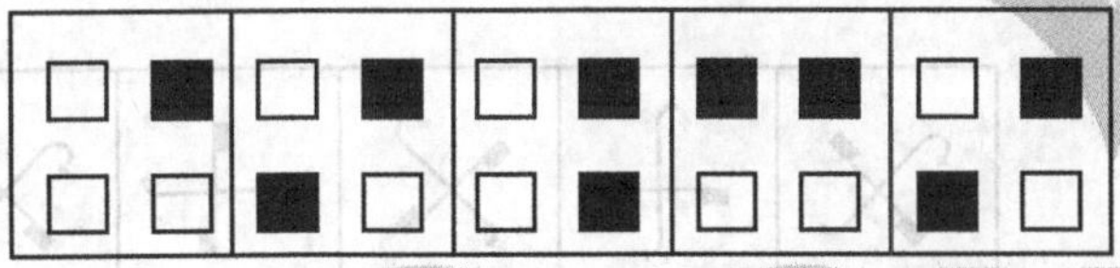

23. 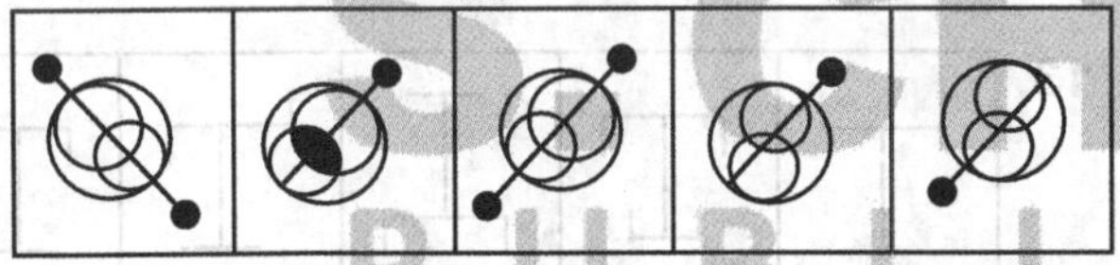

24. 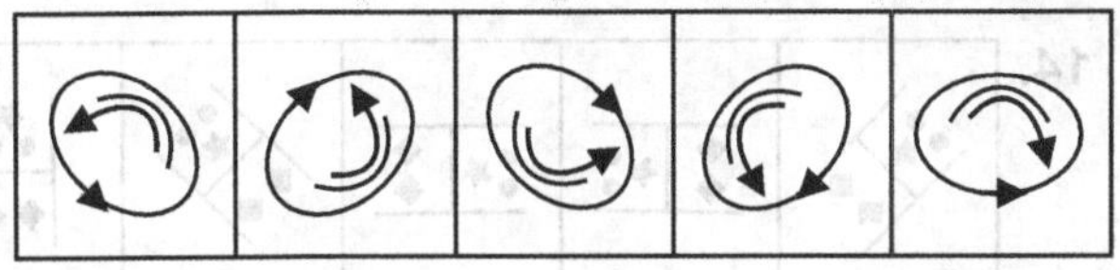

25. 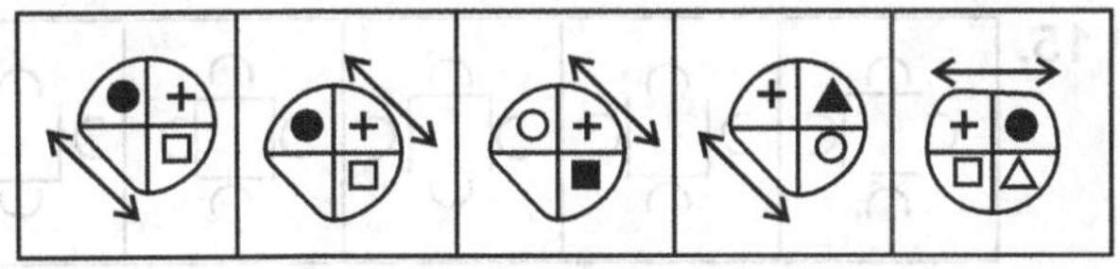

26. 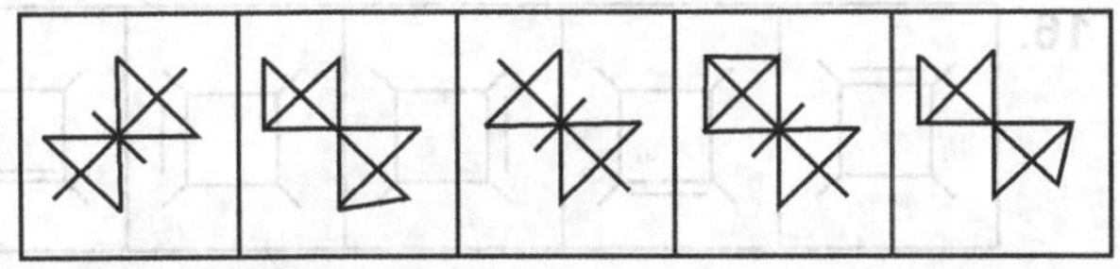

A B C D E

27. 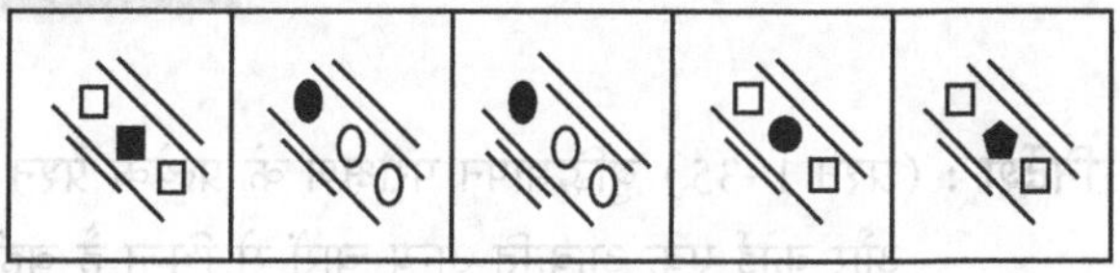

28. 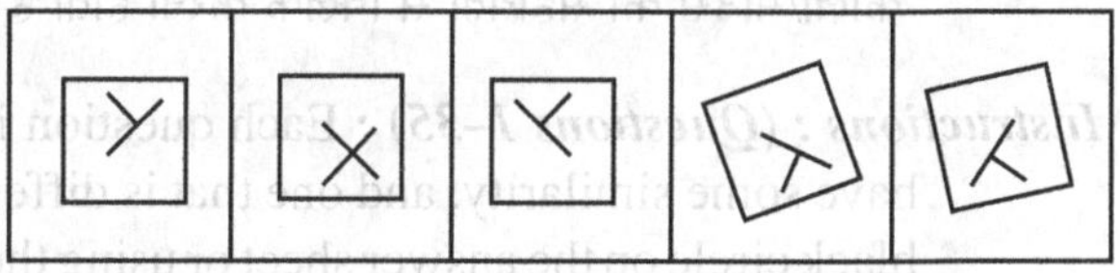

29. 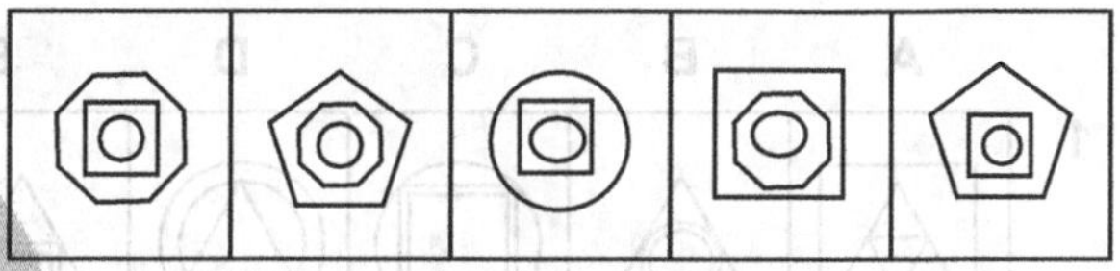

30. 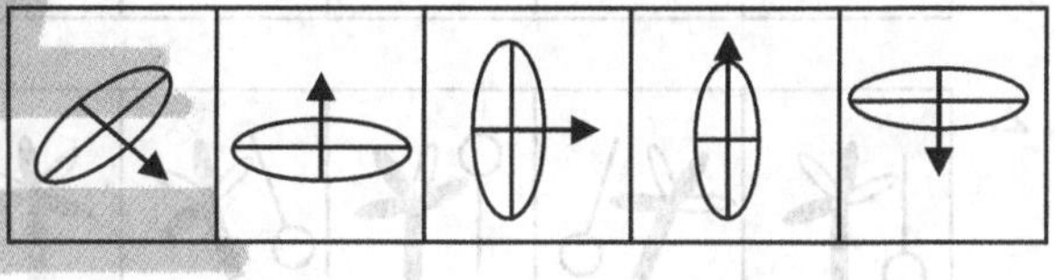

31. 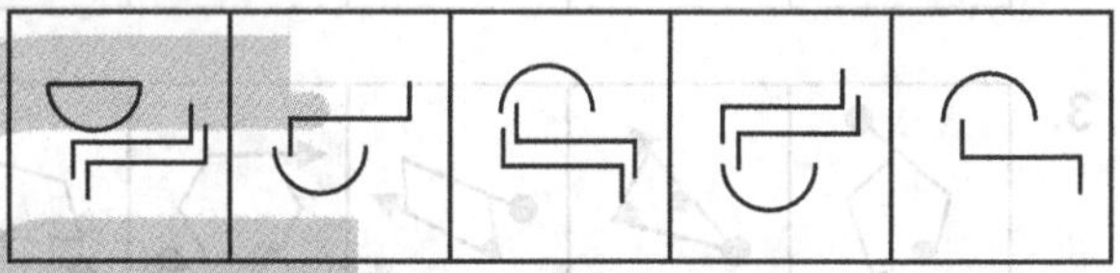

32. 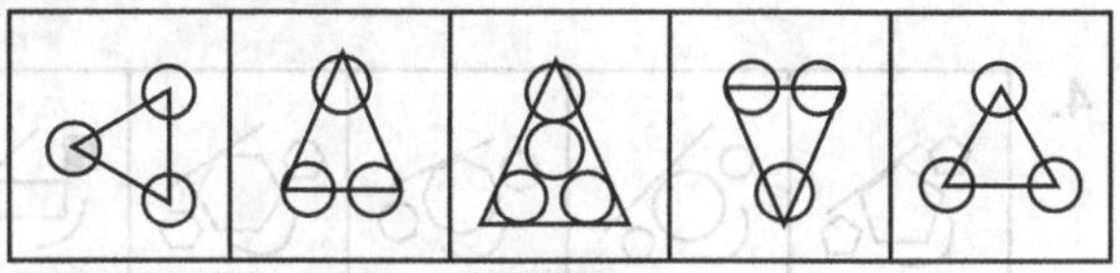

33. 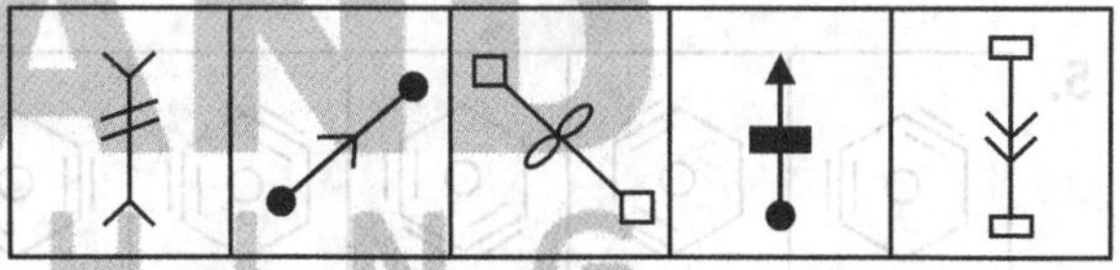

34. 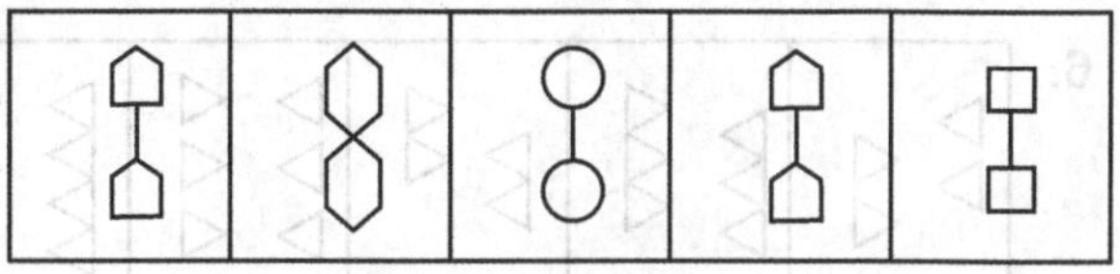

35. 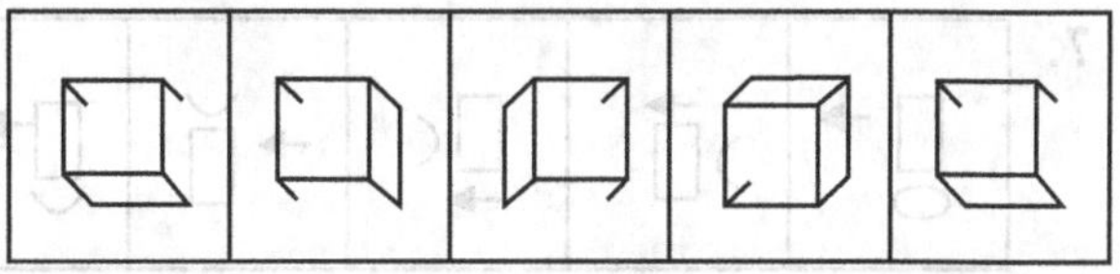

PRACTICE SET-10

Total Ques.- 35
Time - 10 Min.

निर्देश : (प्रश्न 1-35) बुद्धिमापन परीक्षण के प्रत्येक प्रश्न में पाँच आकृतियाँ दिए जाते हैं जिसमें से चार आकृतियाँ में कुछ समानता और कोई एक आकृति अन्य चारों से भिन्न है वही भिन्न आकृति आपका उत्तर होगा जिसे दिए गए उत्तर-पत्रक में गोले को काला/माउस की सहायता से क्लिक करना होता है और इसके लिए 10 मिनट का समय दिया जाता है।

Instructions : (Questions 1–35) : Each question in the Intelligence Test consists of five figures, four of which have some similarity, and one that is different from the other four is your answer. You must click on the black circle on the answer sheet or using the mouse. You are given 10 minutes to complete the test.

A B C D E

1. 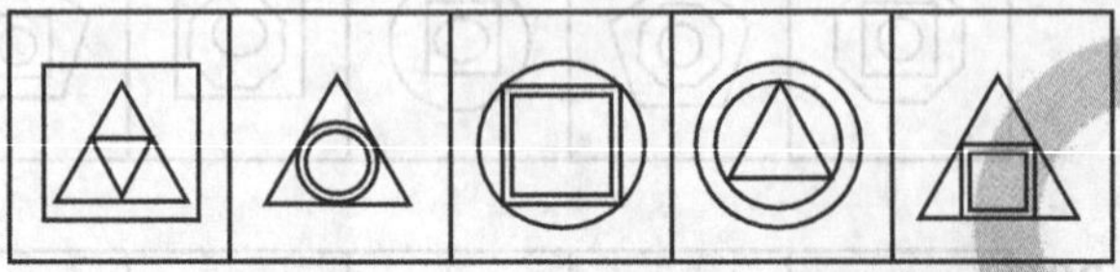

2. 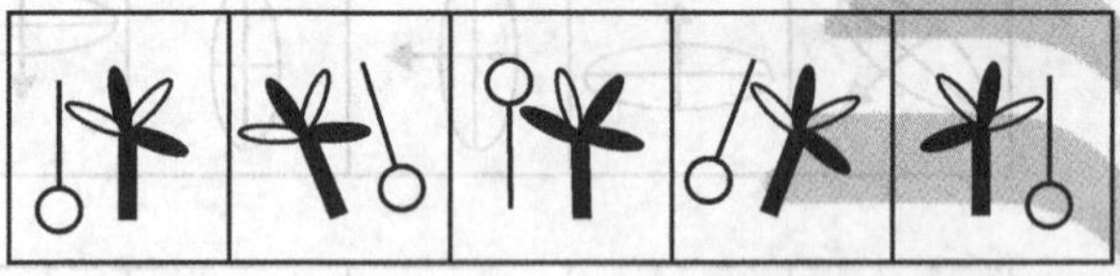

3. 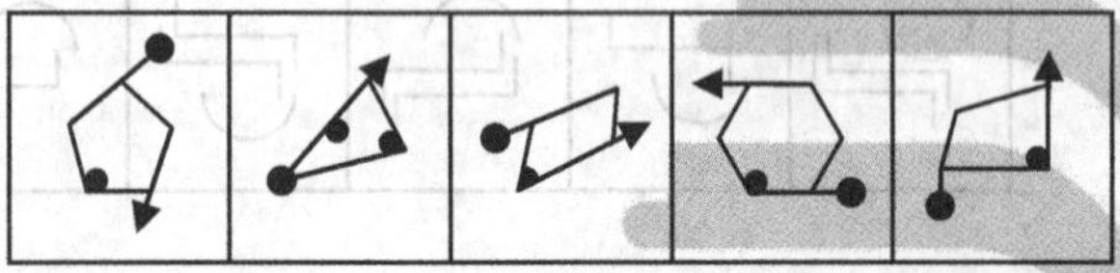

4. 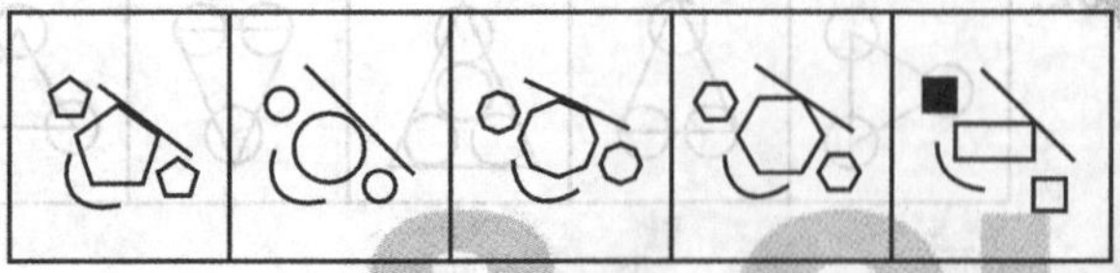

5. 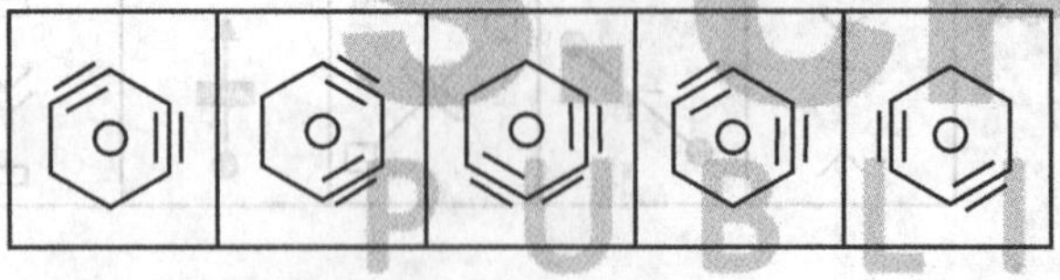

6. 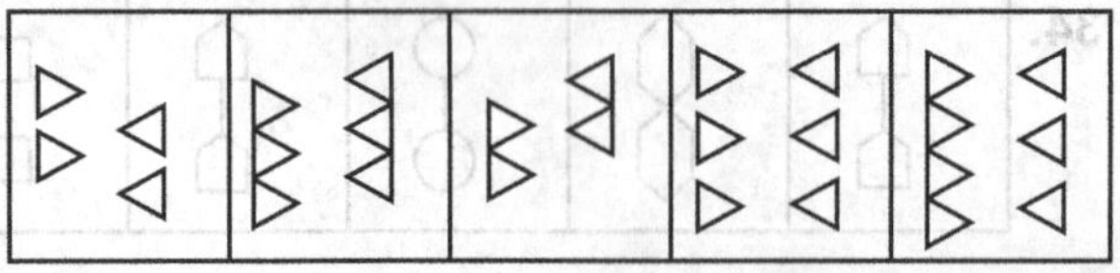

7. 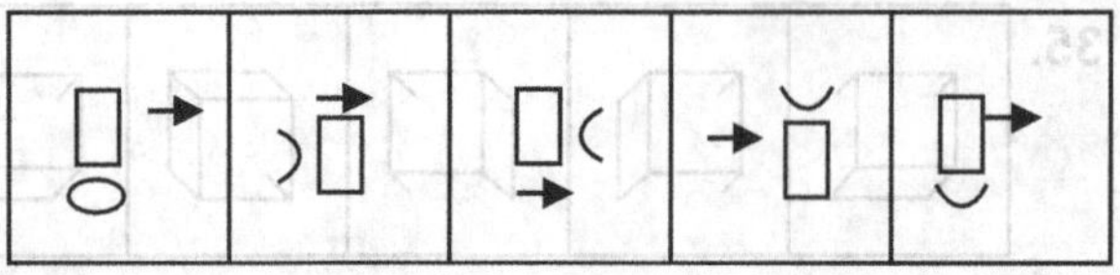

8. 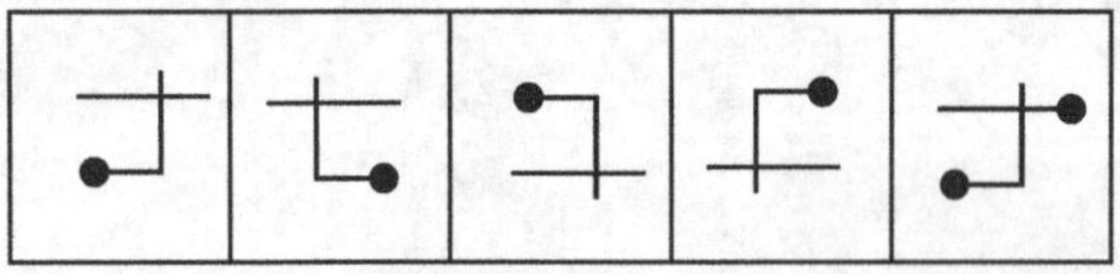

A B C D E

9. 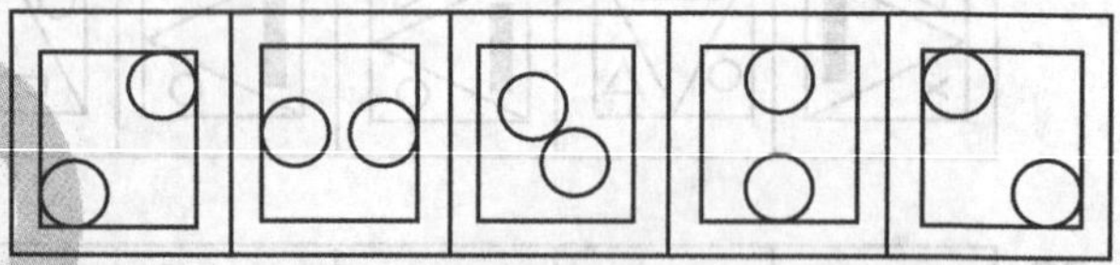

10. 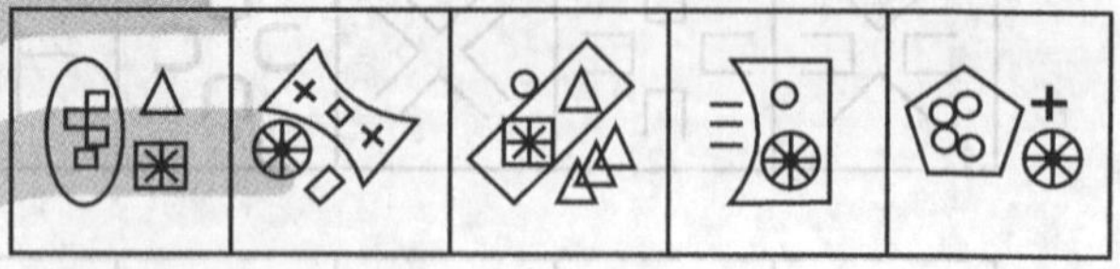

11. 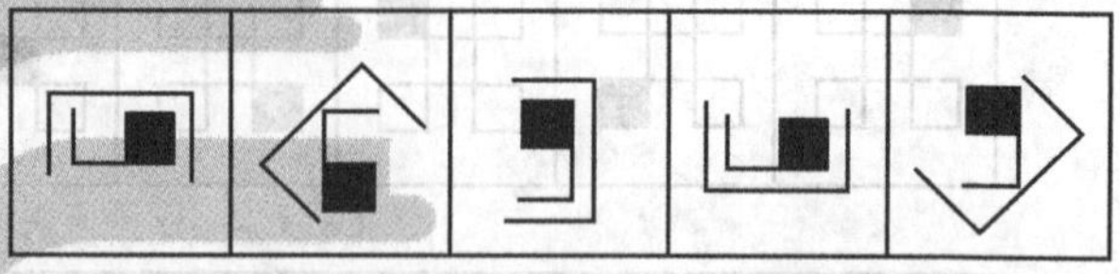

12. 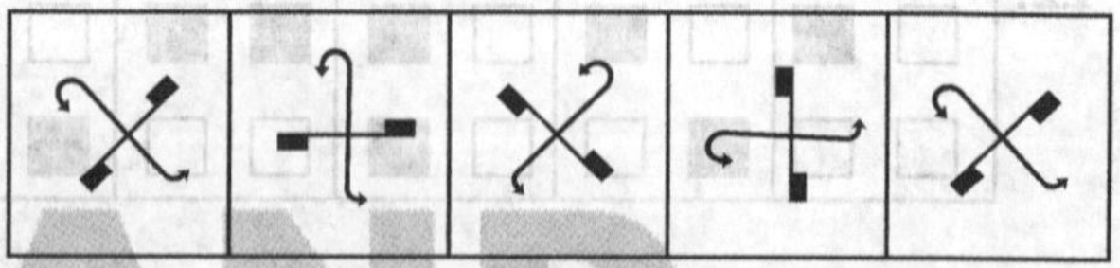

13. 

14. 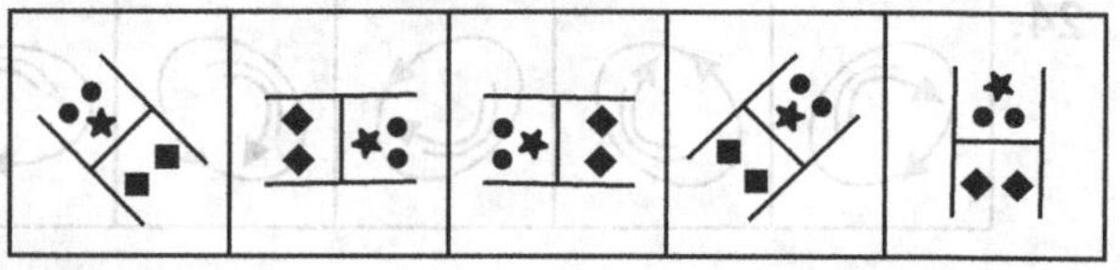

15. 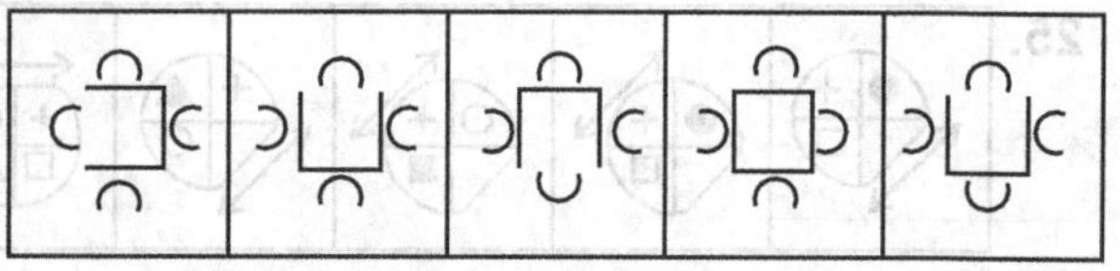

16. 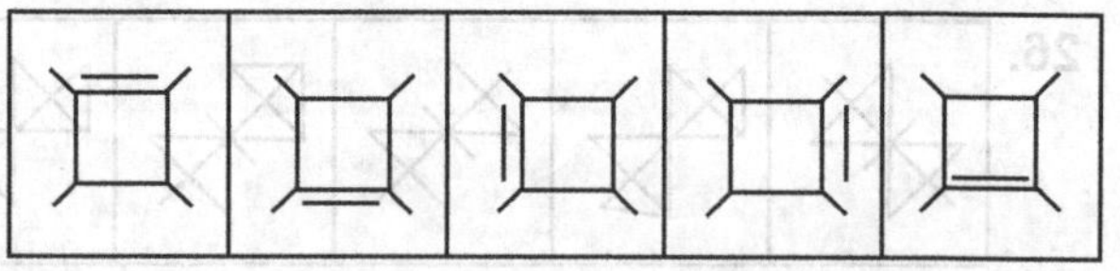

A B C D E

17. 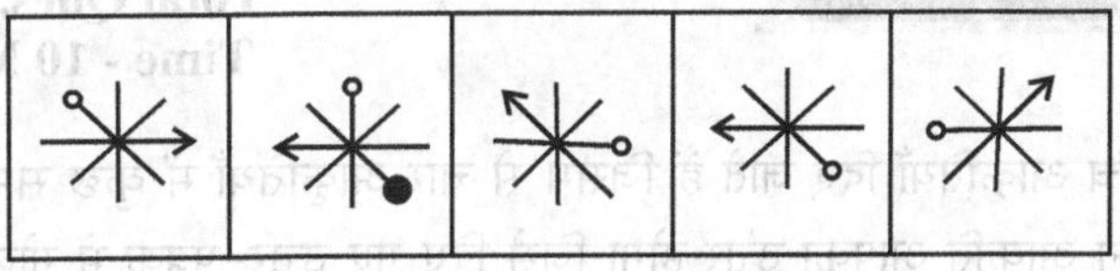

18. 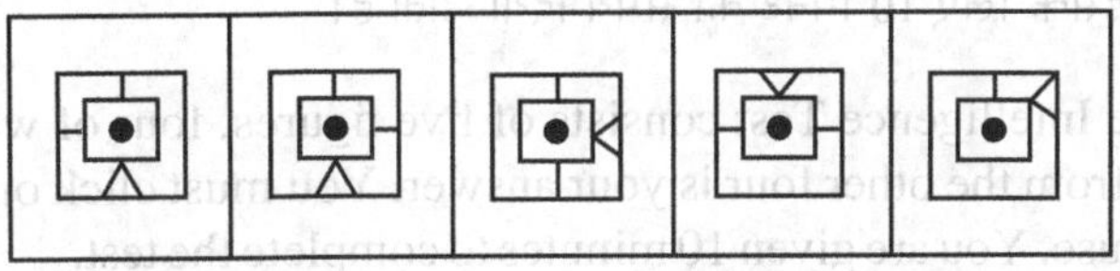

19. 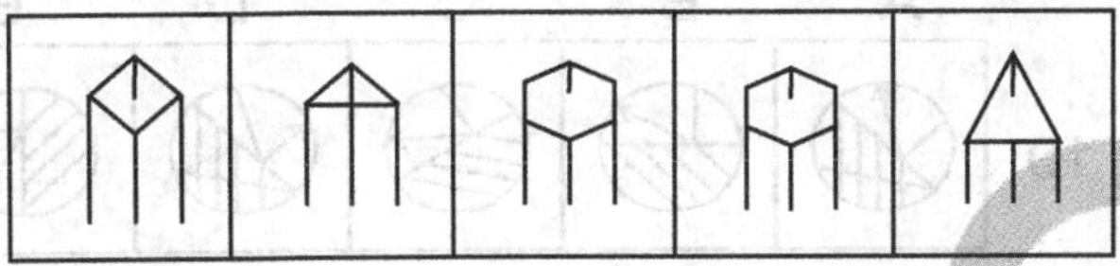

20. 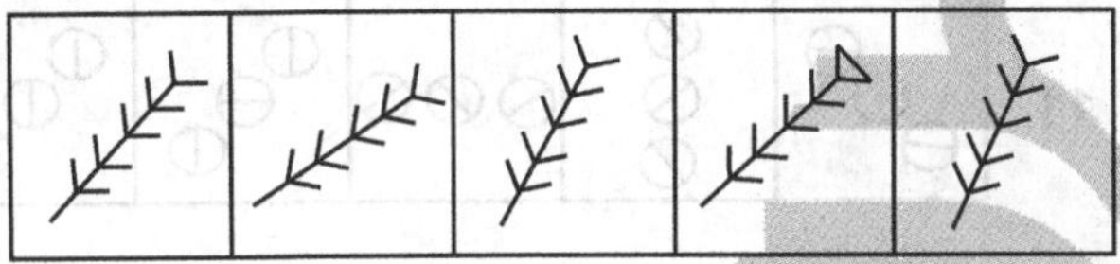

21. 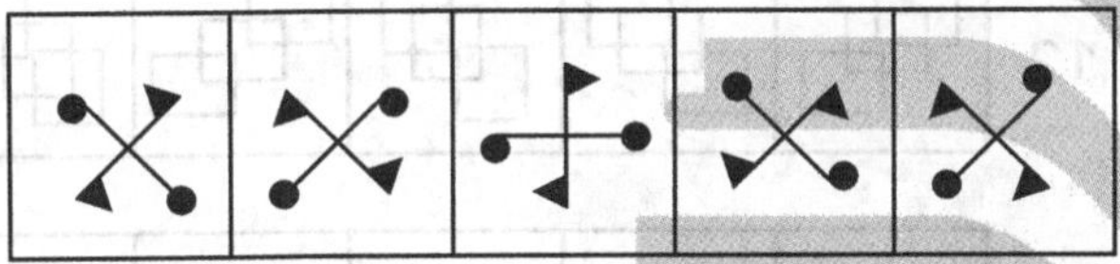

22. 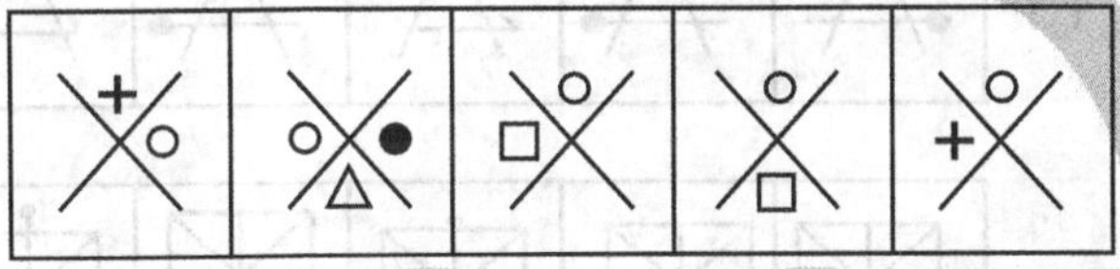

23. 

24. 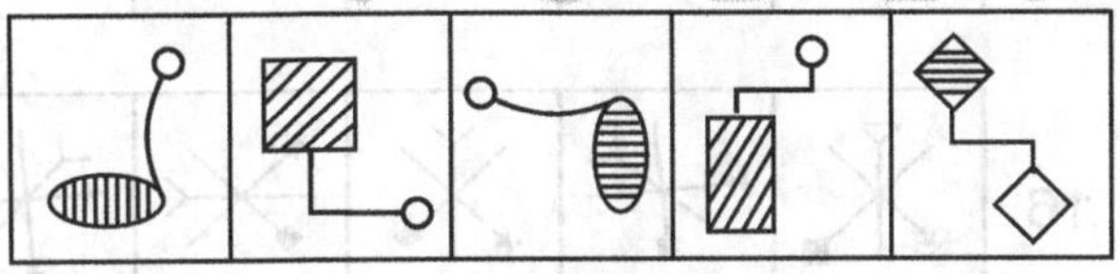

25. 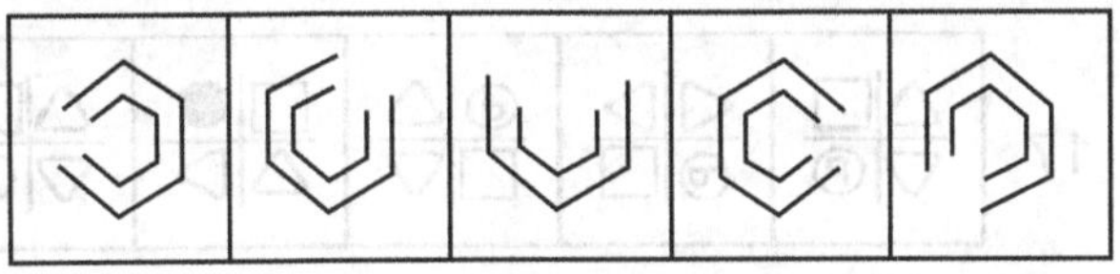

26. 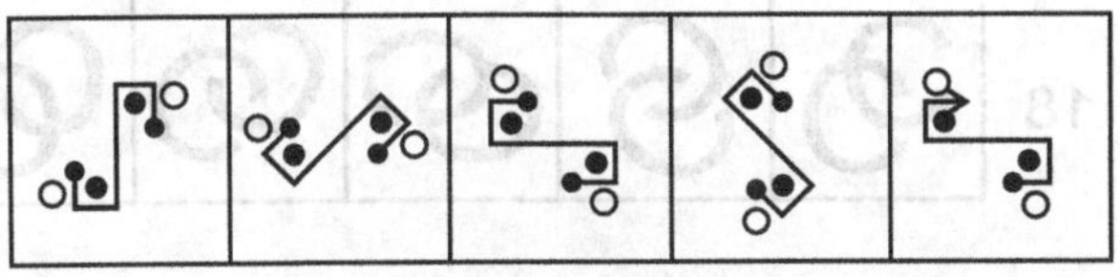

A B C D E

27. 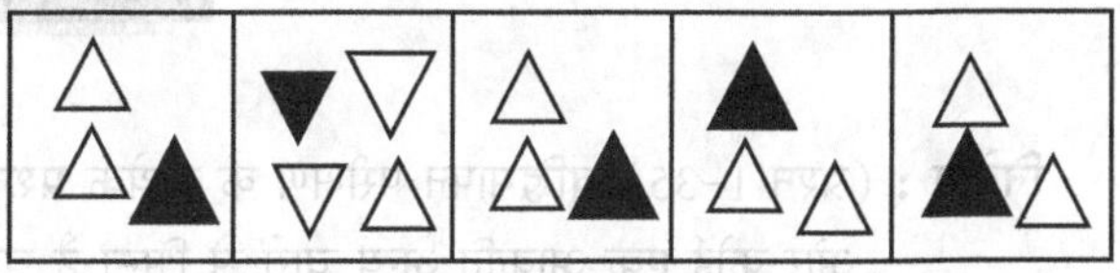

28. 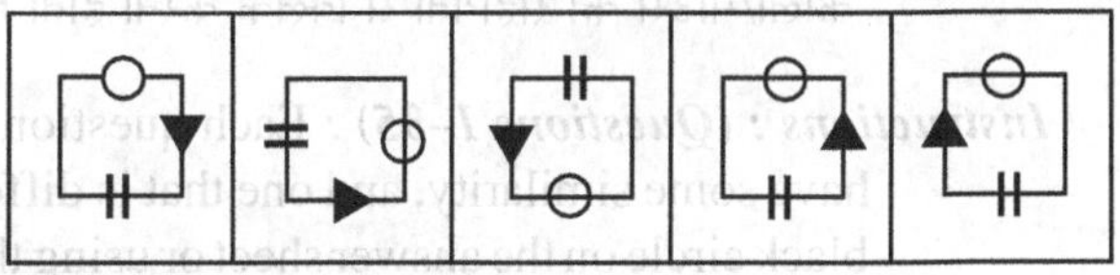

29. 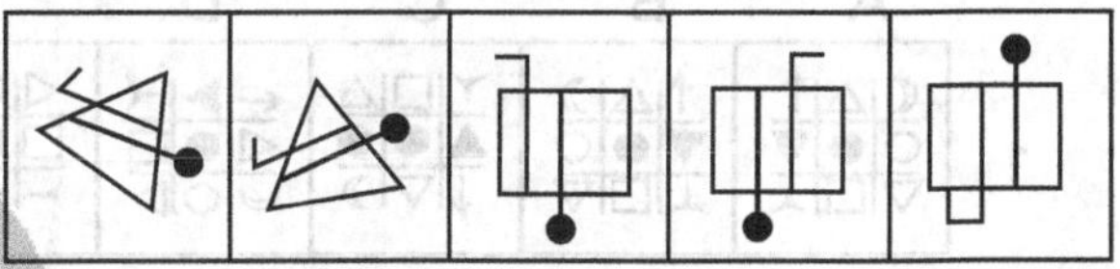

30. 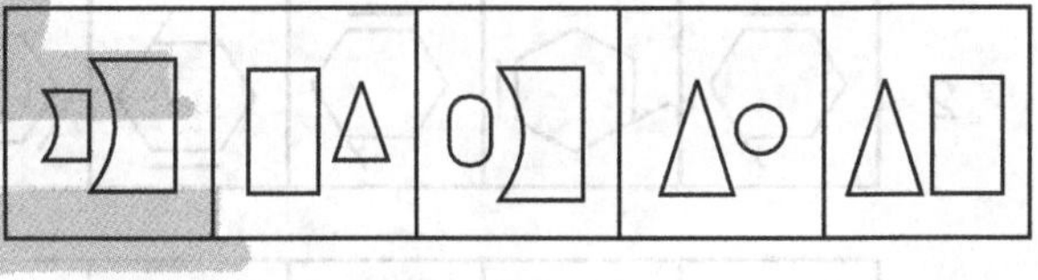

31. 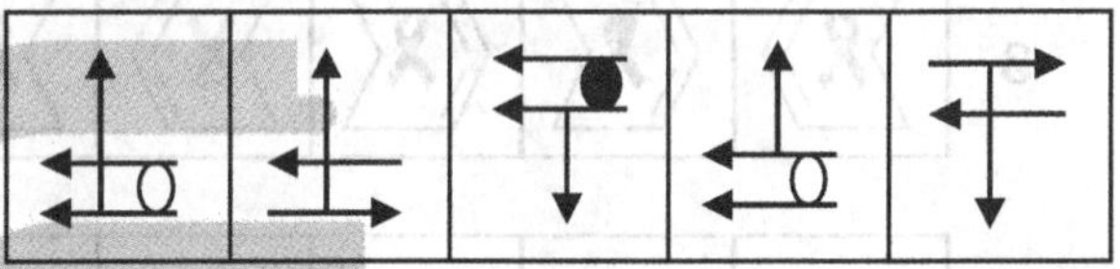

32. 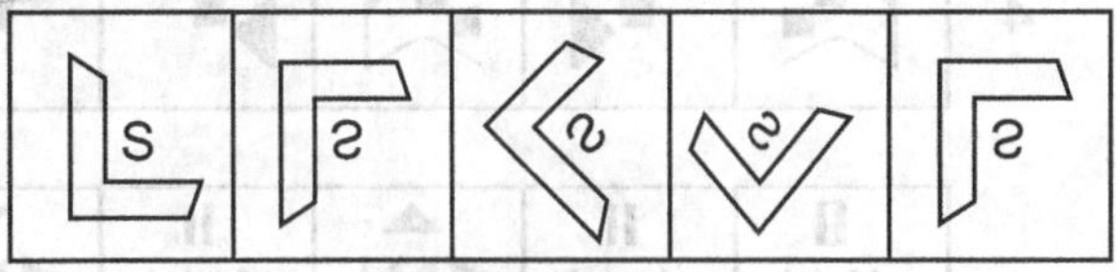

33. 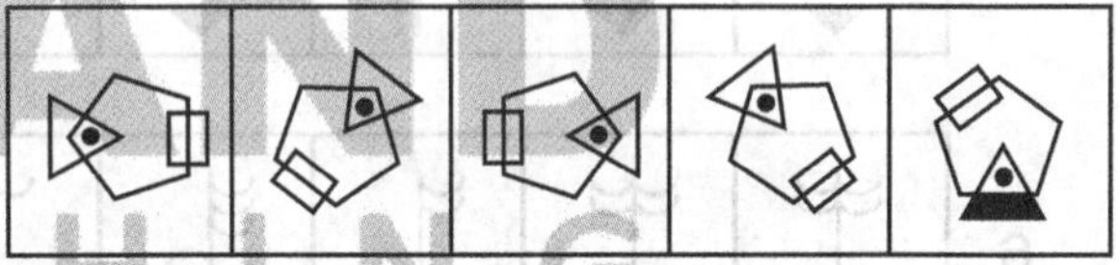

34. 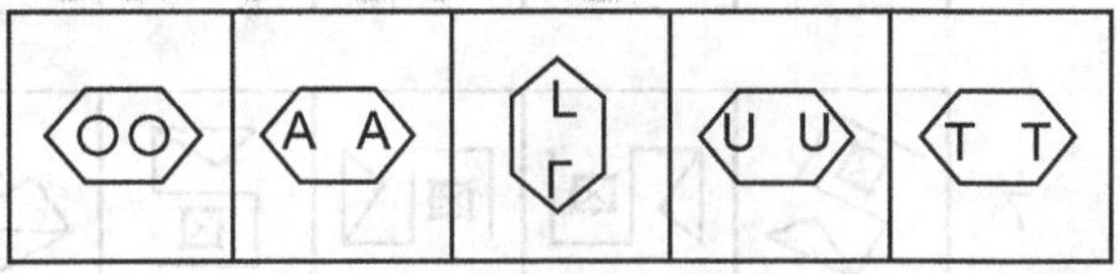

35. 

PRACTICE SET-11

Total Ques.- 35
Time - 10 Min.

निर्देश : (प्रश्न 1–35) बुद्धिमापन परीक्षण के प्रत्येक प्रश्न में पाँच आकृतियाँ दिए जाते हैं जिसमें से चार आकृतियाँ में कुछ समानता और कोई एक आकृति अन्य चारों से भिन्न है वही भिन्न आकृति आपका उत्तर होगा जिसे दिए गए उत्तर-पत्रक में गोले को काला/माउस की सहायता से क्लिक करना होता है और इसके लिए 10 मिनट का समय दिया जाता है।

Instructions : (Questions 1–35) : Each question in the Intelligence Test consists of five figures, four of which have some similarity, and one that is different from the other four is your answer. You must click on the black circle on the answer sheet or using the mouse. You are given 10 minutes to complete the test.

A B C D E

1
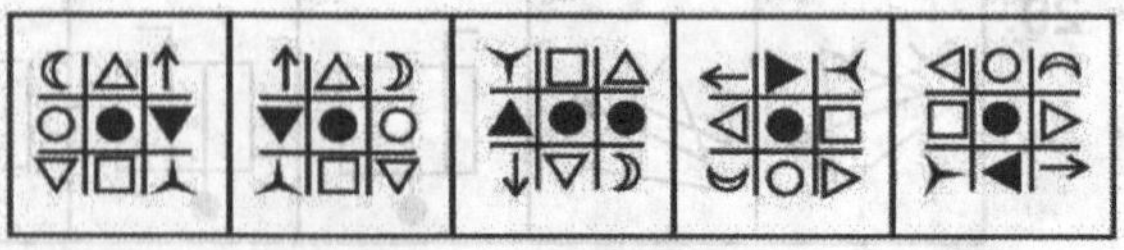

2
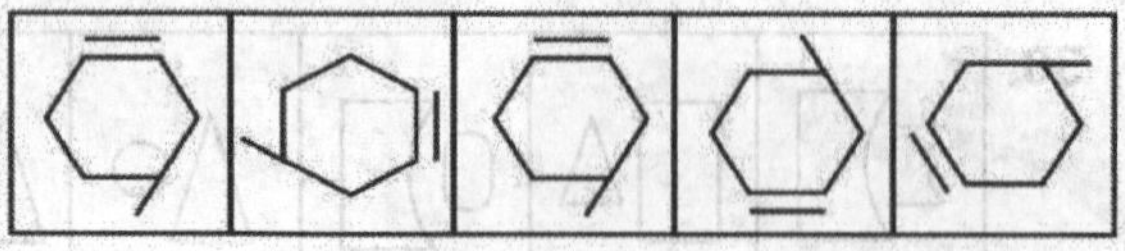

3

4

5

6
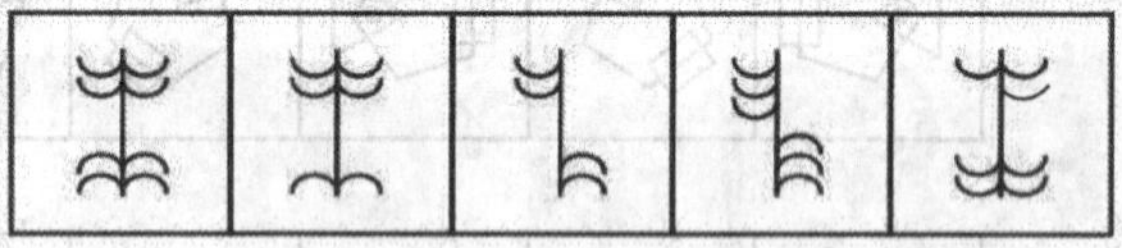

7
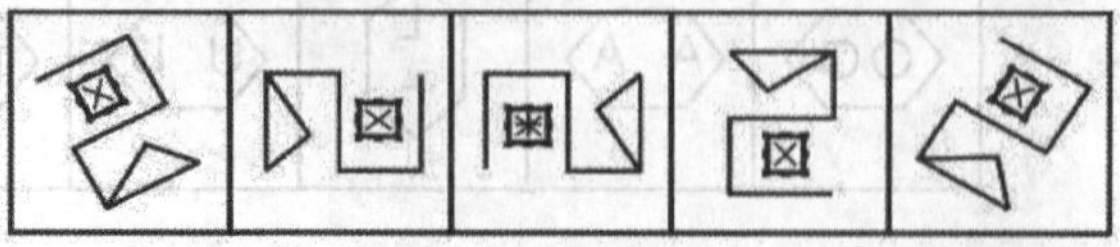

8

9
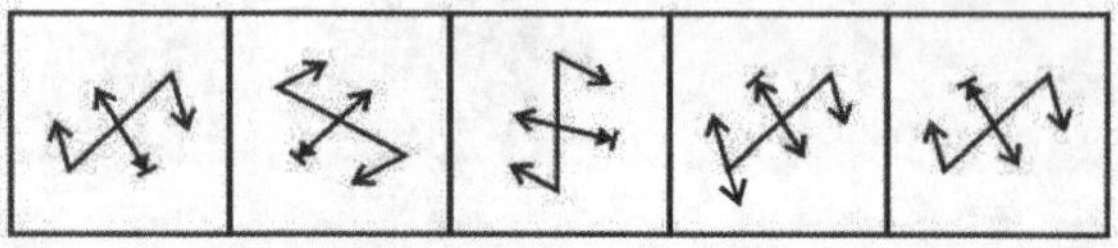

A B C D E

10
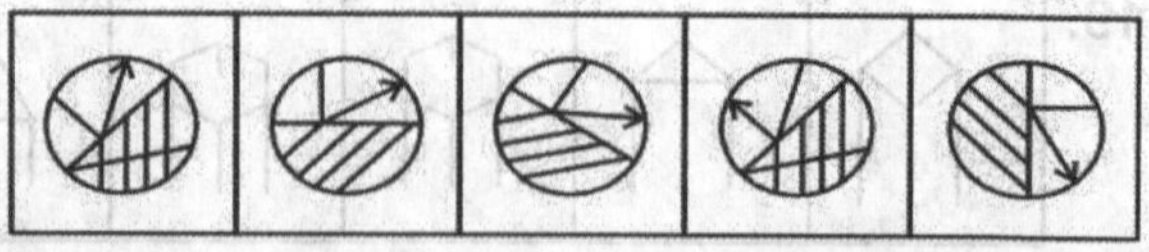

11
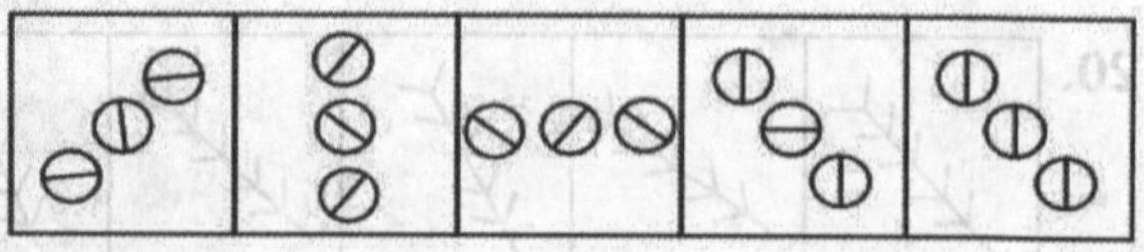

12
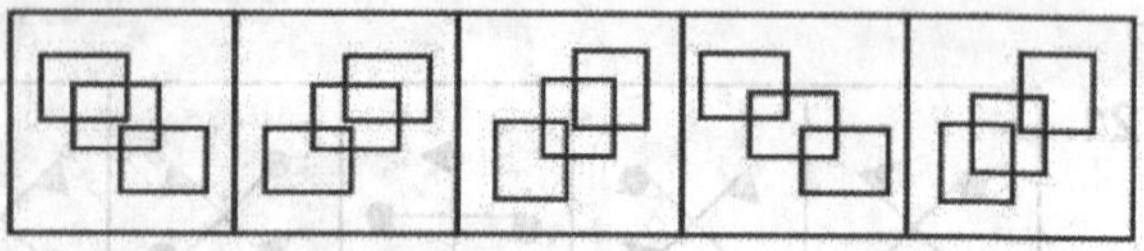

13
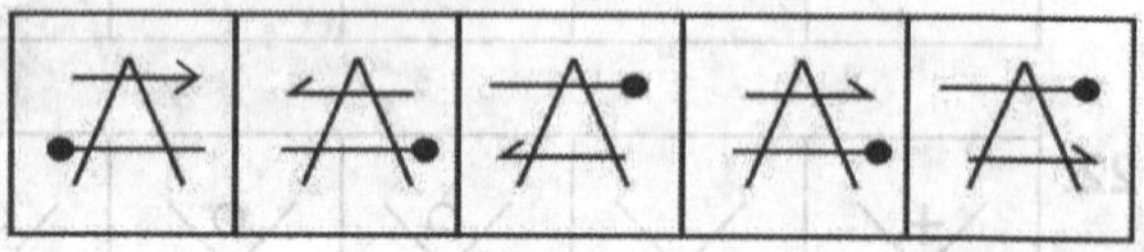

14
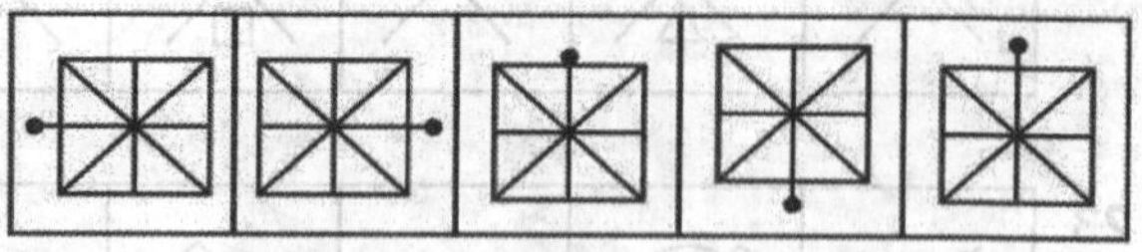

15
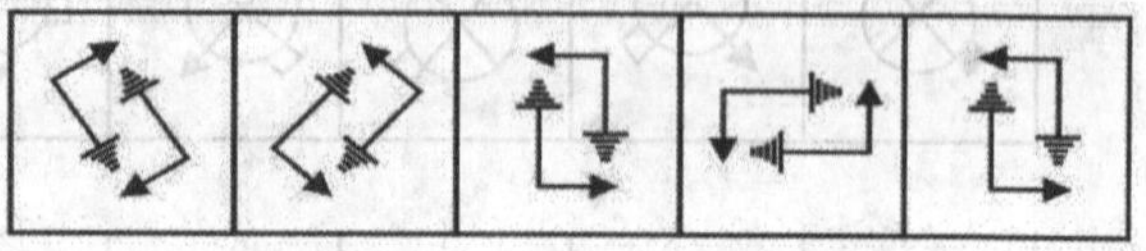

16
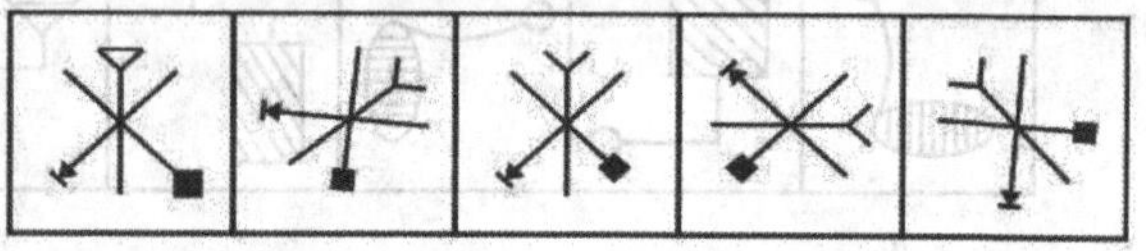

17

18

A B C D E

19 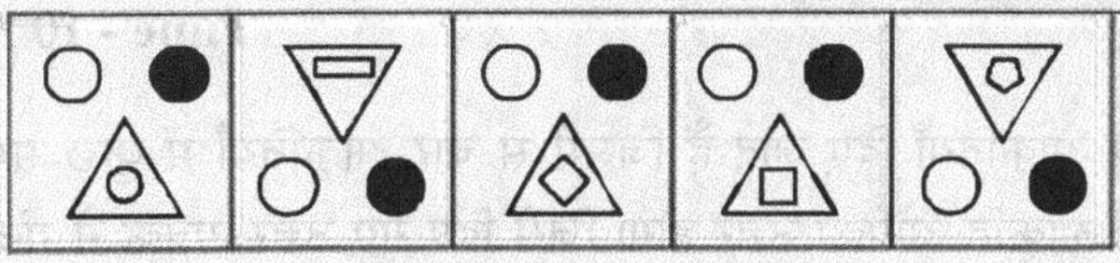

20 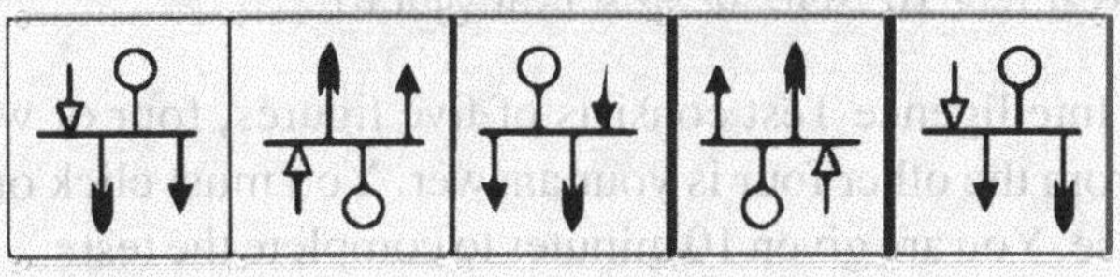

21 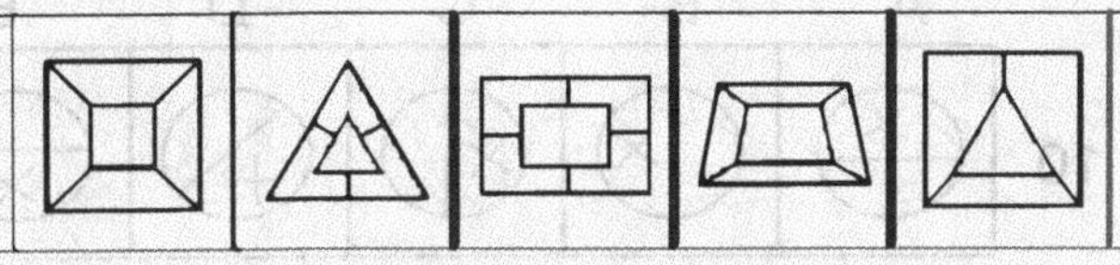

22 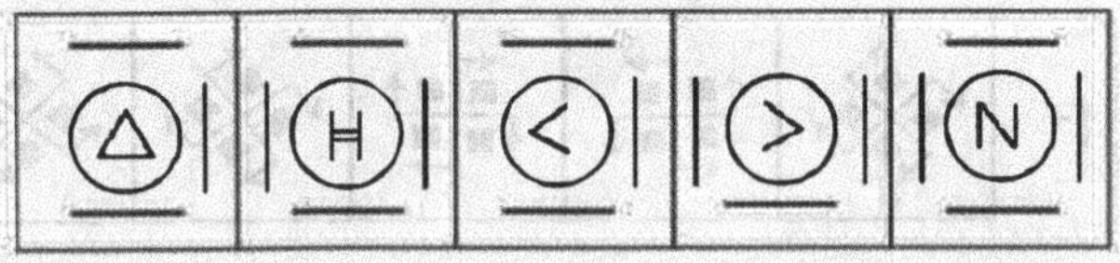

23 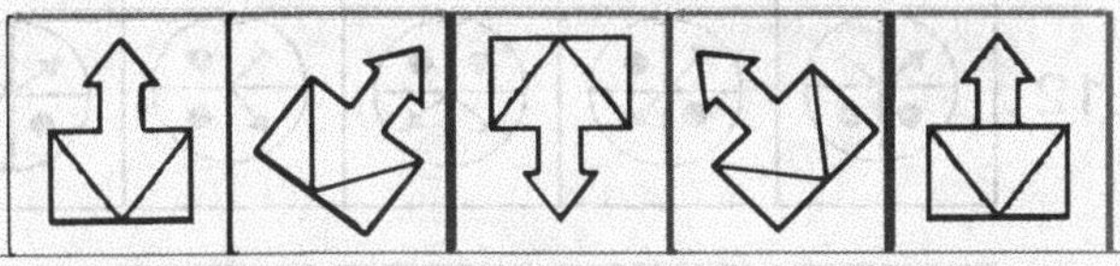

24 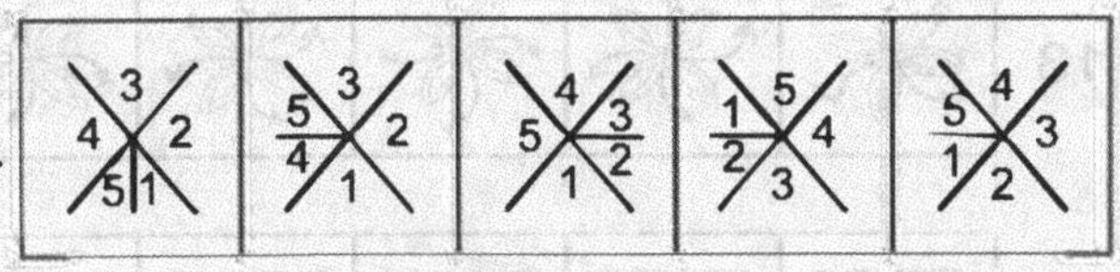

25 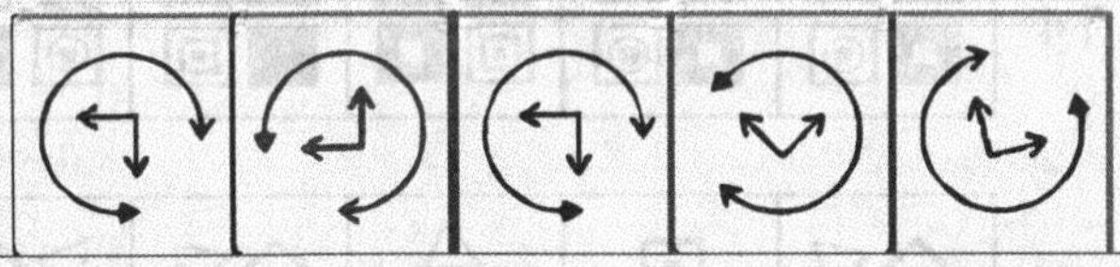

26 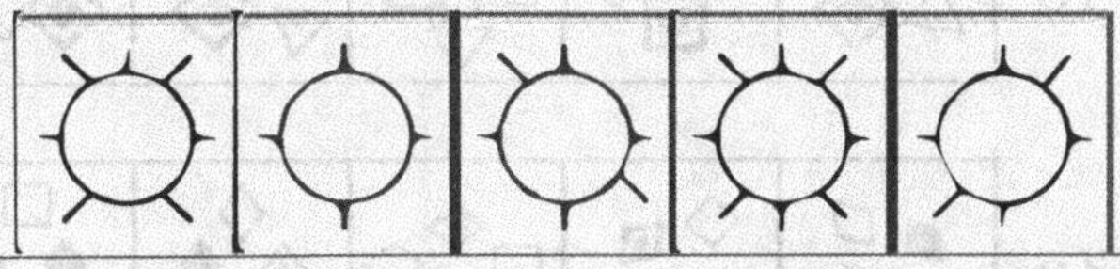

27 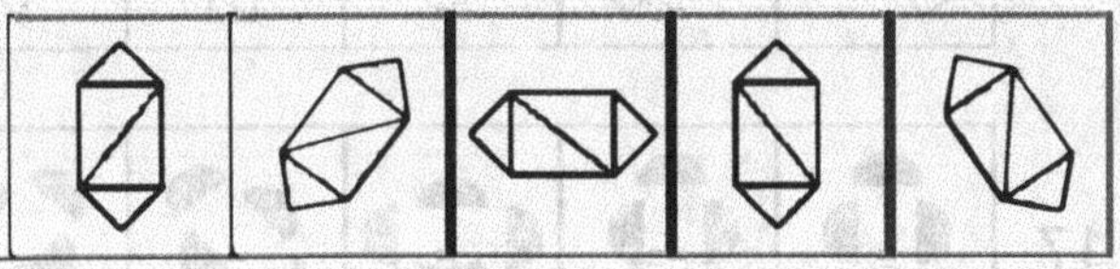

A B C D E

28 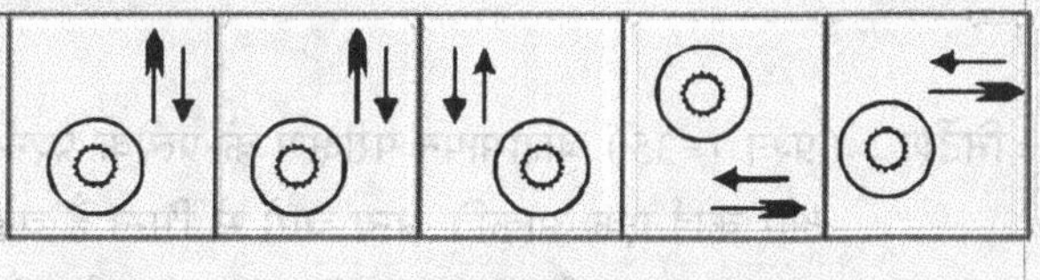

29 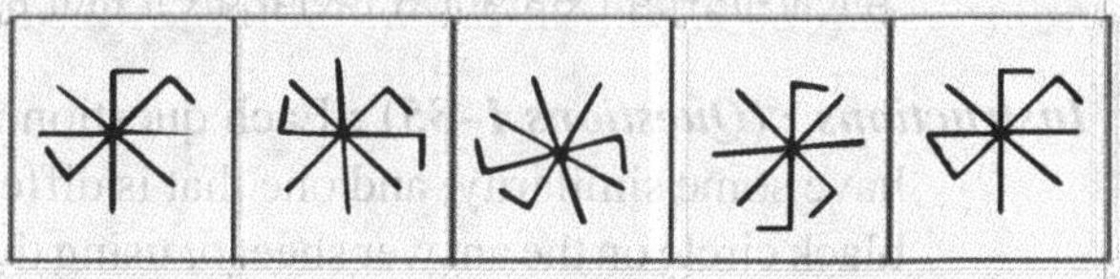

30 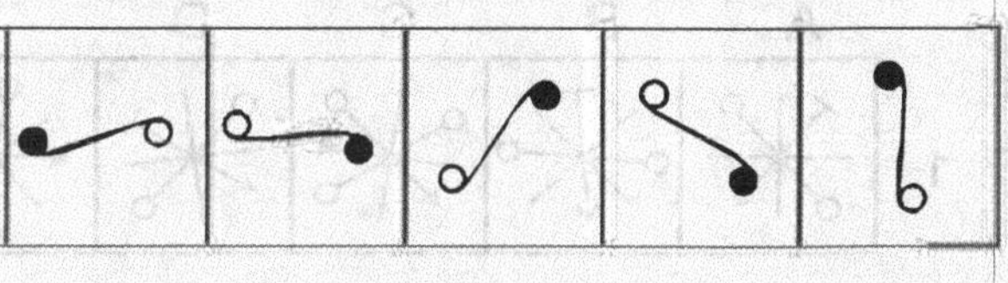

31 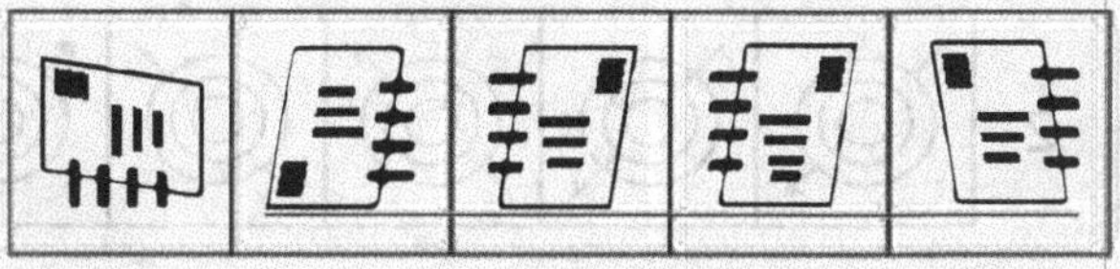

32 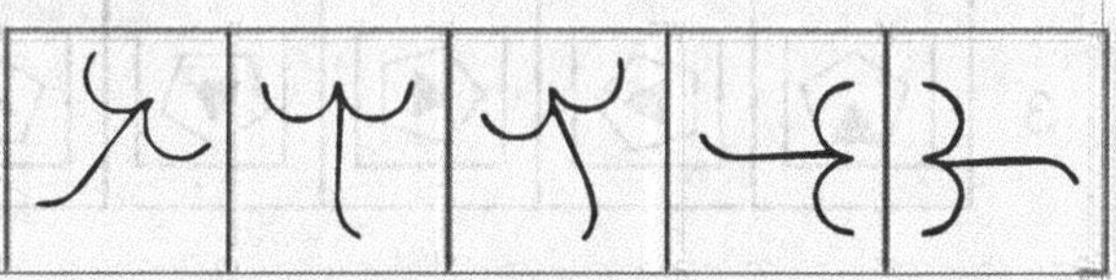

33 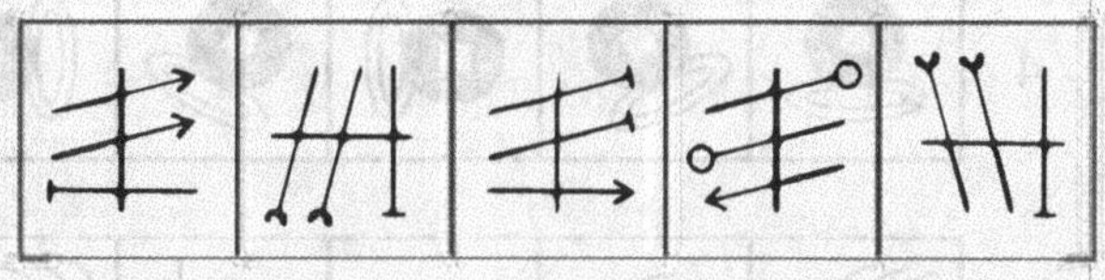

34 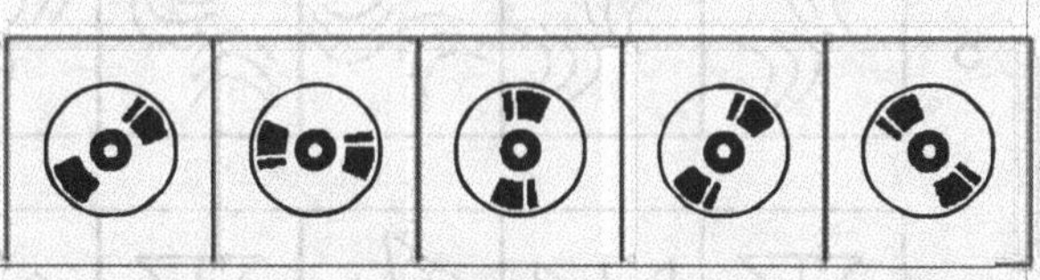

35 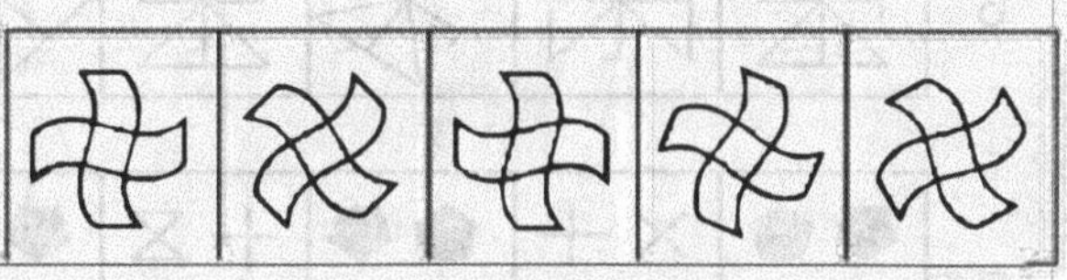

PRACTICE SET-12

Total Ques.- 35
Time - 10 Min.

निर्देश : (प्रश्न 1-35) बुद्धिमापन परीक्षण के प्रत्येक प्रश्न में पाँच आकृतियाँ दिए जाते हैं जिसमें से चार आकृतियाँ में कुछ समानता और कोई एक आकृति अन्य चारों से भिन्न है वही भिन्न आकृति आपका उत्तर होगा जिसे दिए गए उत्तर-पत्रक में गोले को काला/माउस की सहायता से क्लिक करना होता है और इसके लिए 10 मिनट का समय दिया जाता है।

Instructions : (Questions 1–35) : Each question in the Intelligence Test consists of five figures, four of which have some similarity, and one that is different from the other four is your answer. You must click on the black circle on the answer sheet or using the mouse. You are given 10 minutes to complete the test.

A B C D E

1 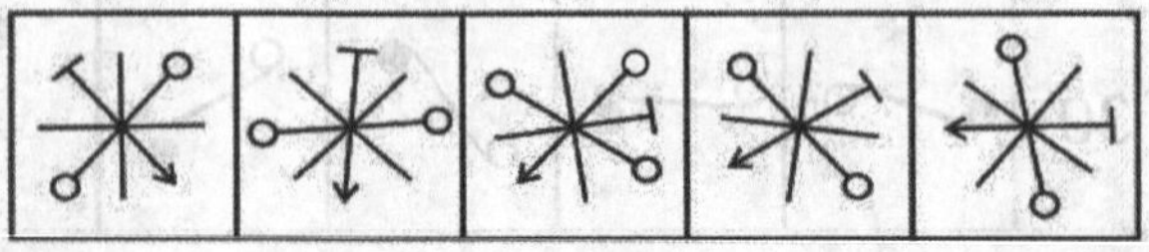

2 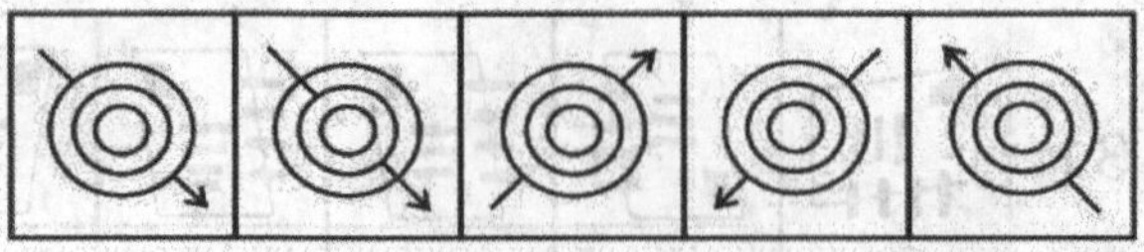

3 

4 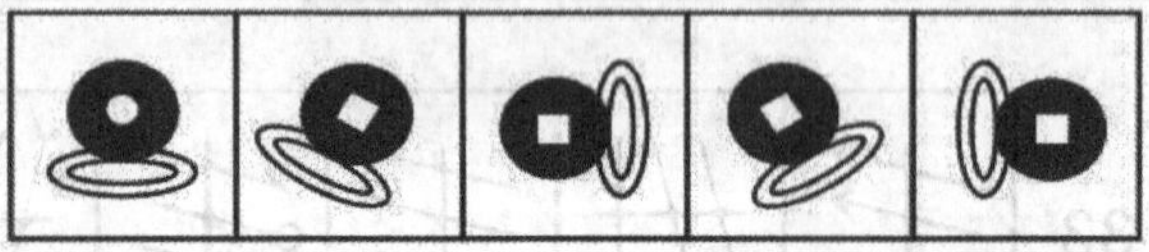

5 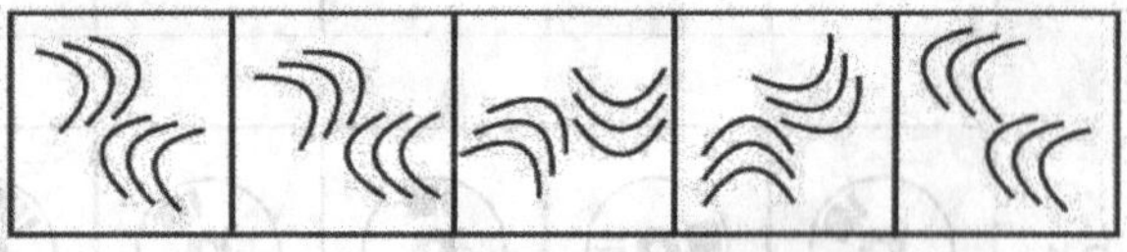

6 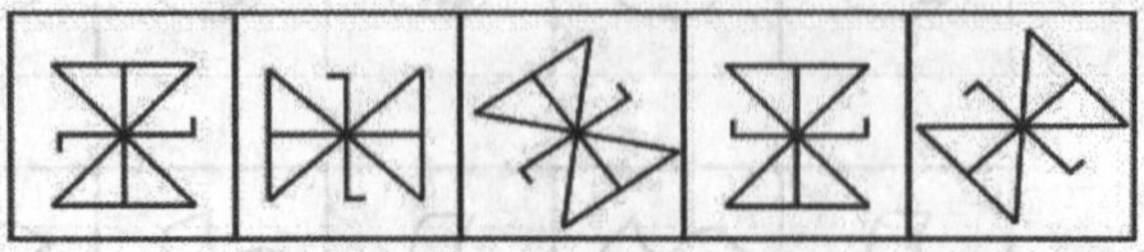

7 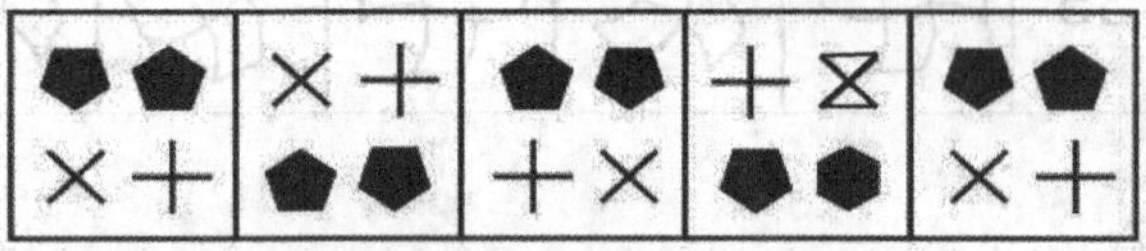

8 

9 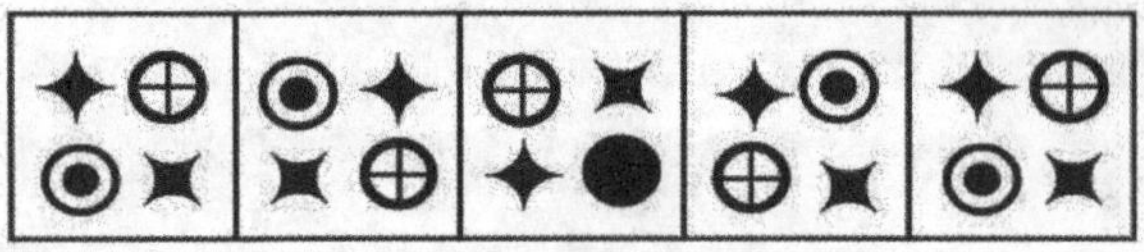

A B C D E

10 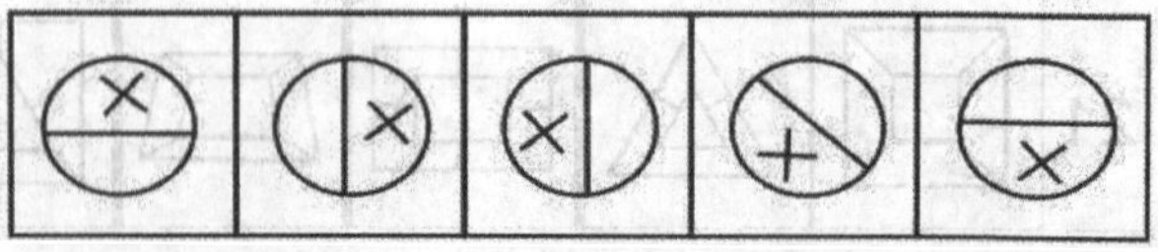

11 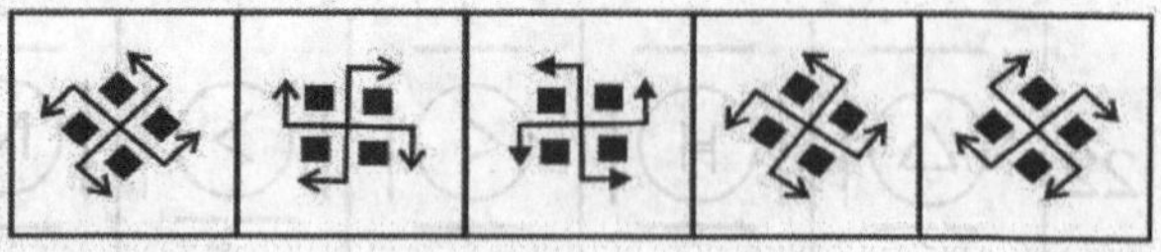

12 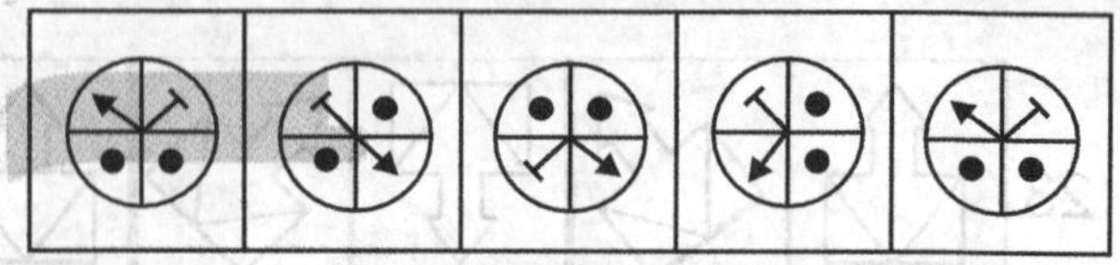

13 

14 

15 

16 

17 

18 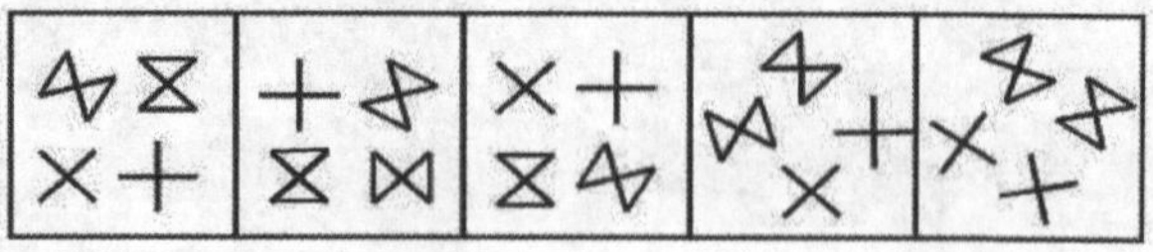

A B C D E

19
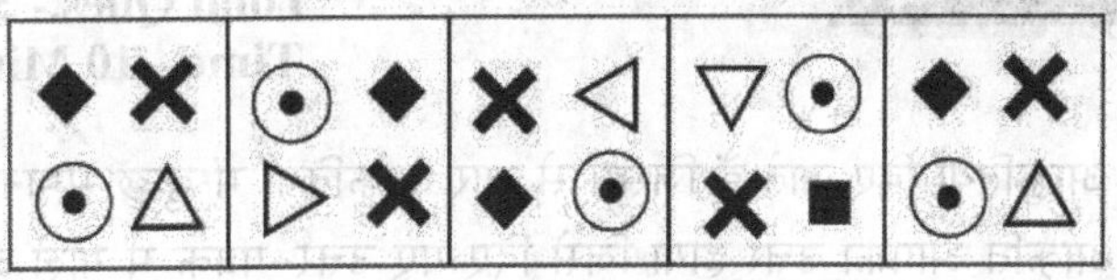

20
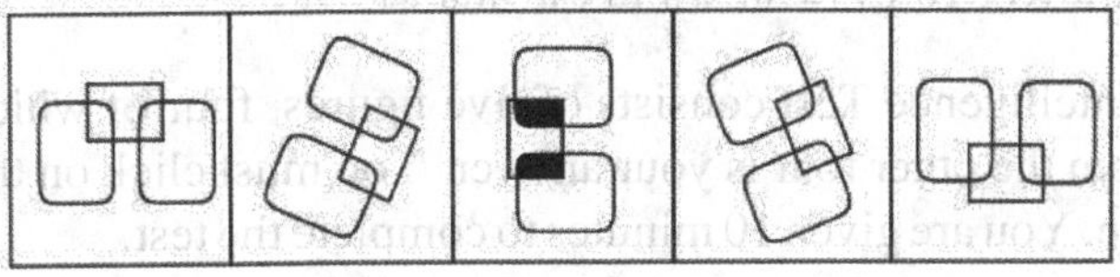

21
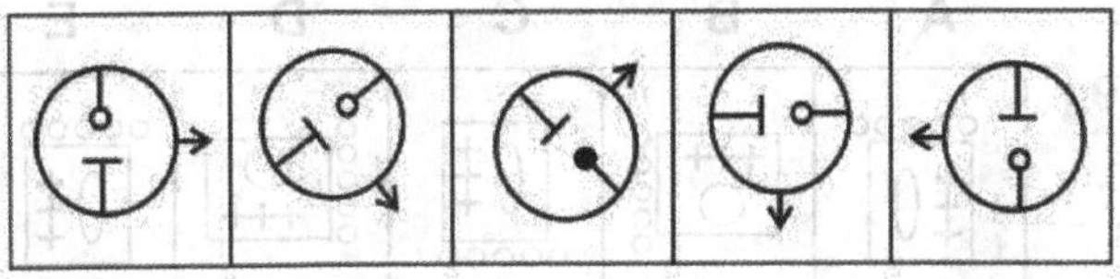

22
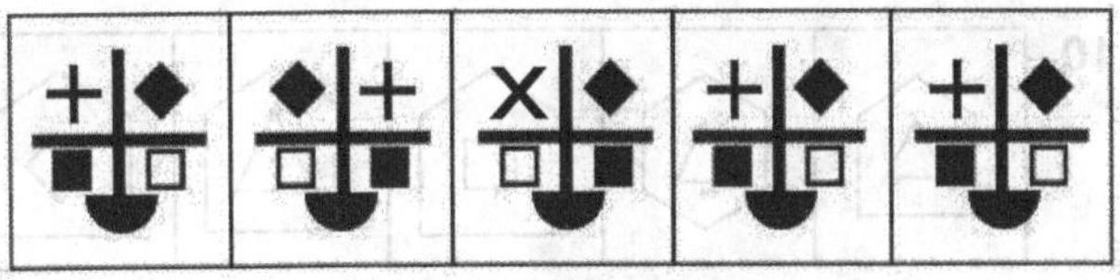

23
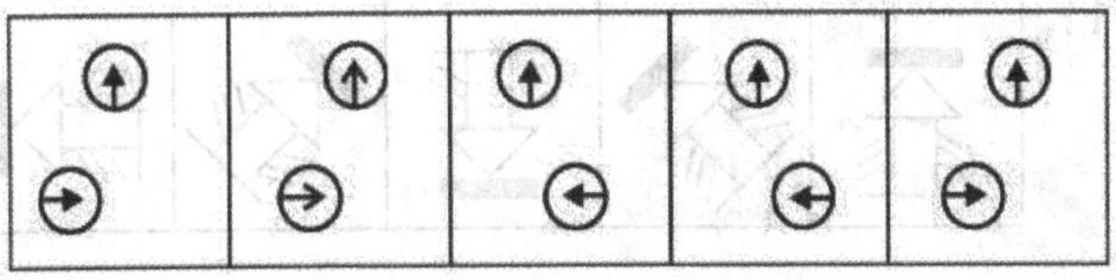

24
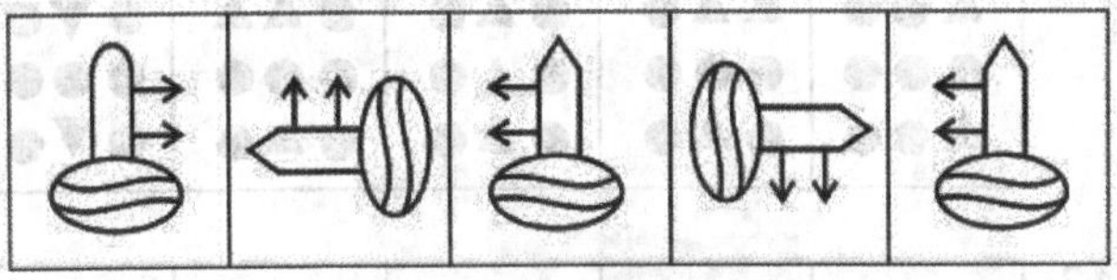

25
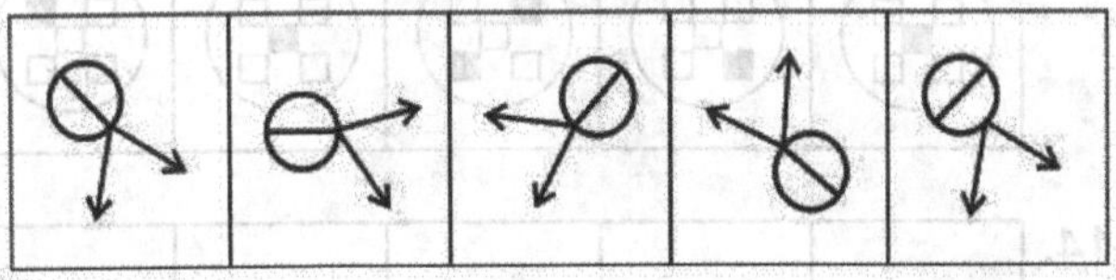

26
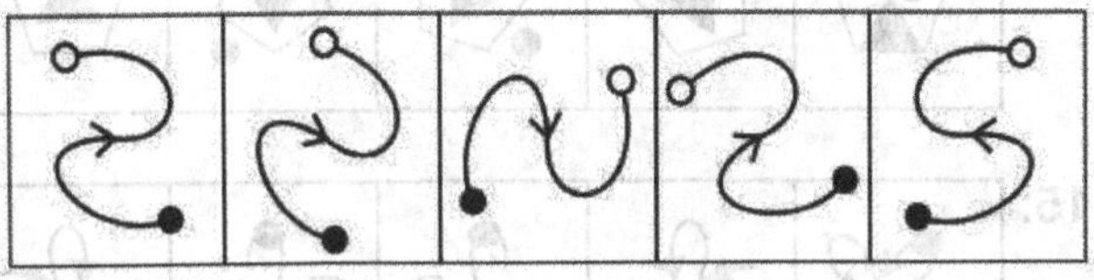

27
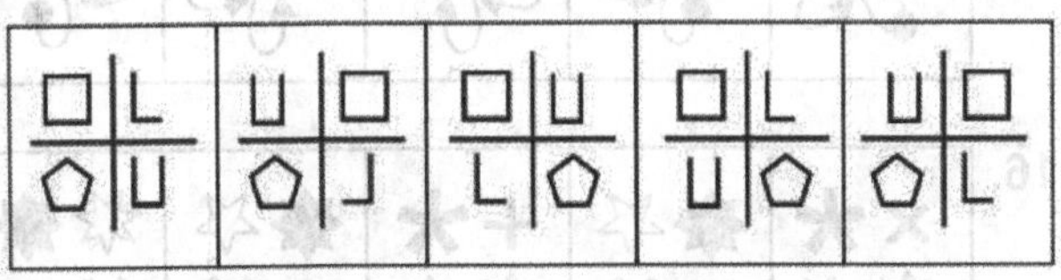

A B C D E

28
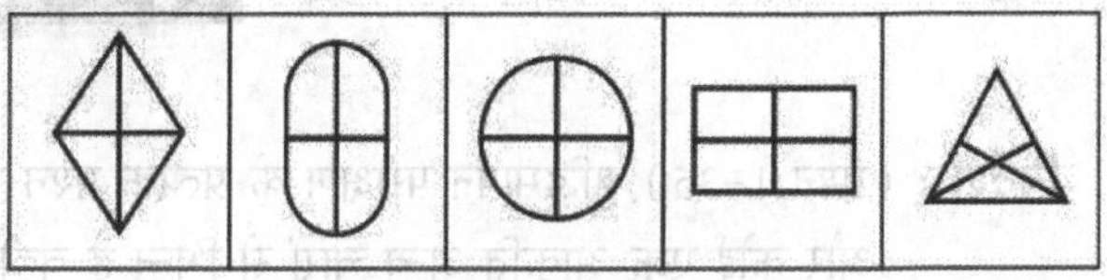

29
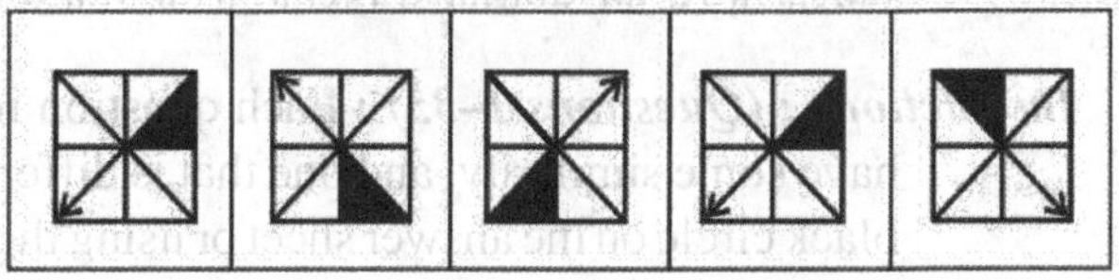

30
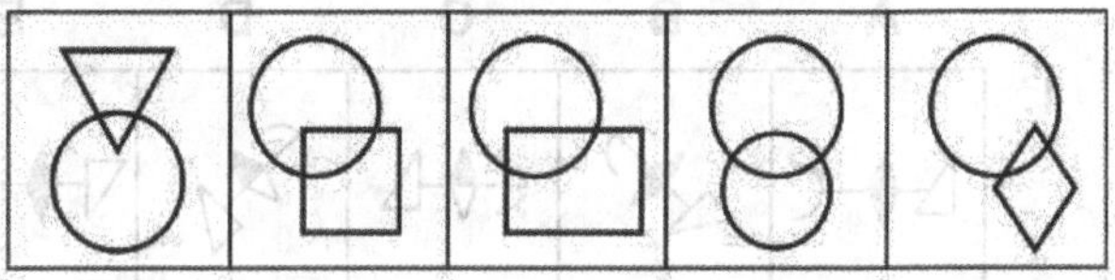

31
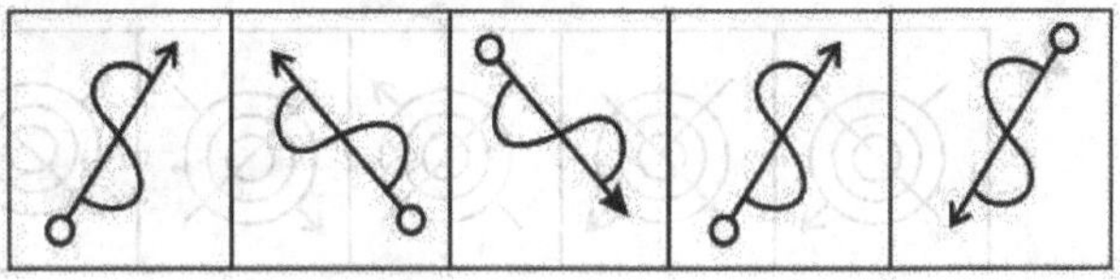

32
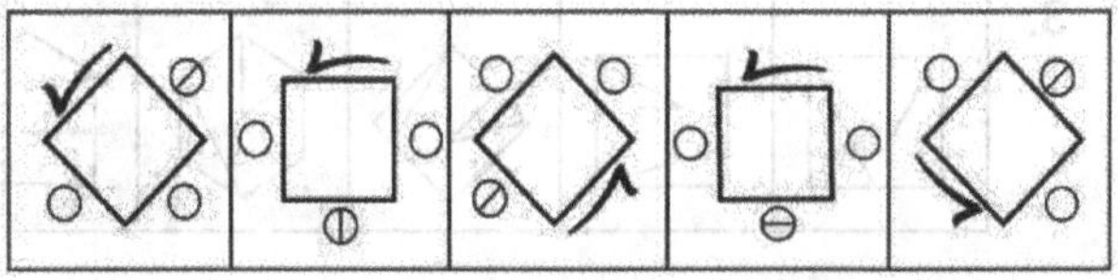

33
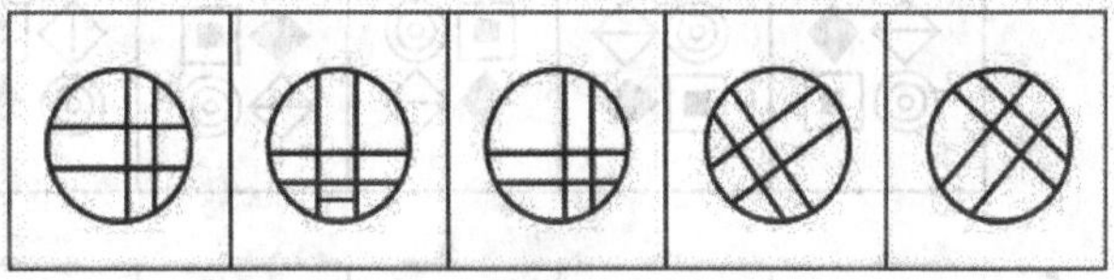

34
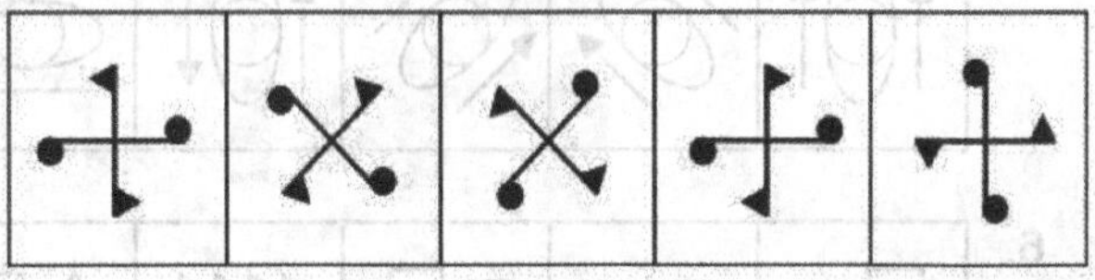

35
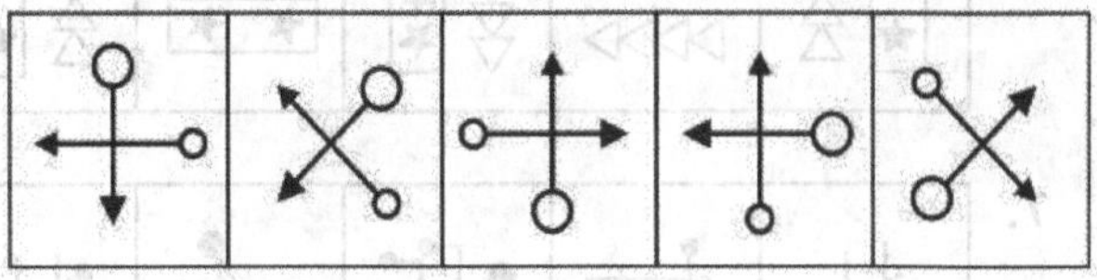

PRACTICE SET-13

Total Ques.- 35
Time - 10 Min.

निर्देश : (प्रश्न 1–35) बुद्धिमापन परीक्षण के प्रत्येक प्रश्न में पाँच आकृतियाँ दिए जाते हैं जिसमें से चार आकृतियाँ में कुछ समानता और कोई एक आकृति अन्य चारों से भिन्न है वही भिन्न आकृति आपका उत्तर होगा जिसे दिए गए उत्तर-पत्रक में गोले को काला/माउस की सहायता से क्लिक करना होता है और इसके लिए 10 मिनट का समय दिया जाता है।

Instructions : (Questions 1–35) : Each question in the Intelligence Test consists of five figures, four of which have some similarity, and one that is different from the other four is your answer. You must click on the black circle on the answer sheet or using the mouse. You are given 10 minutes to complete the test.

A B C D E

1. 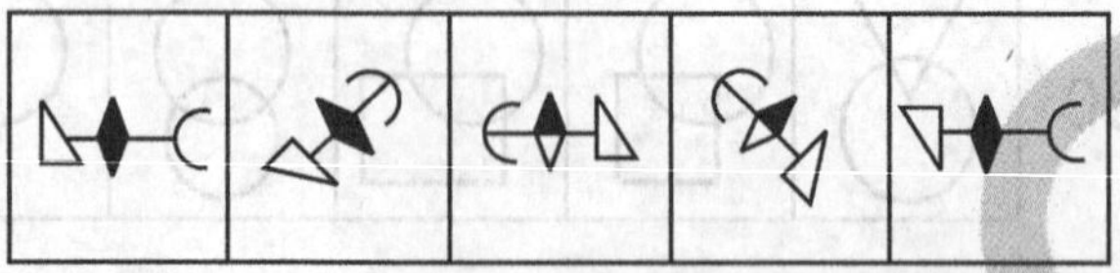

2. 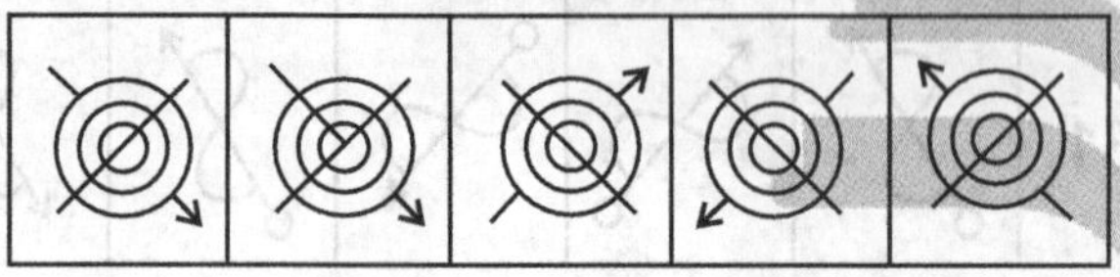

3. 

4. 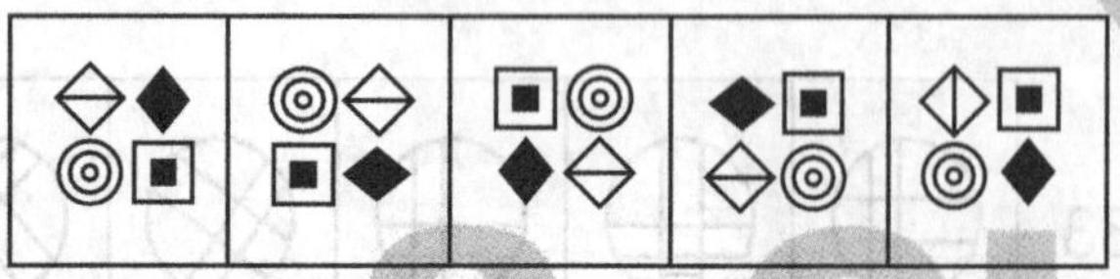

5. 

6. 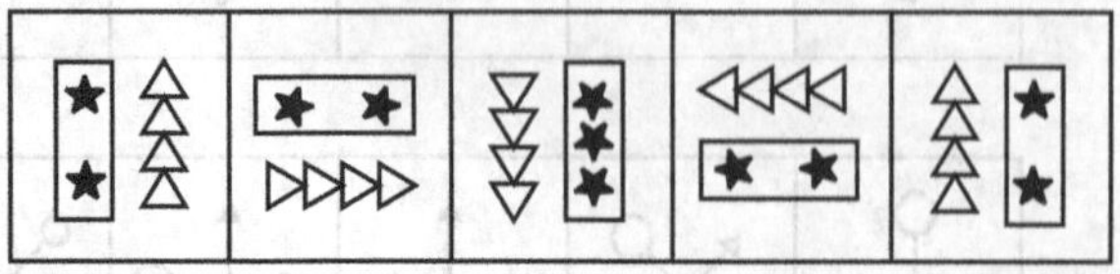

7. 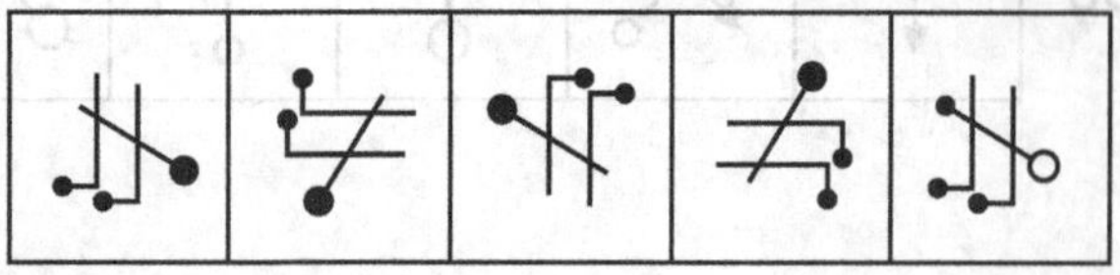

8. 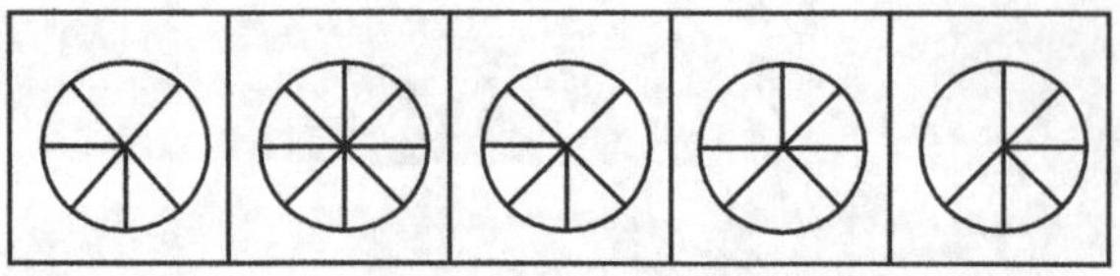

A B C D E

9. 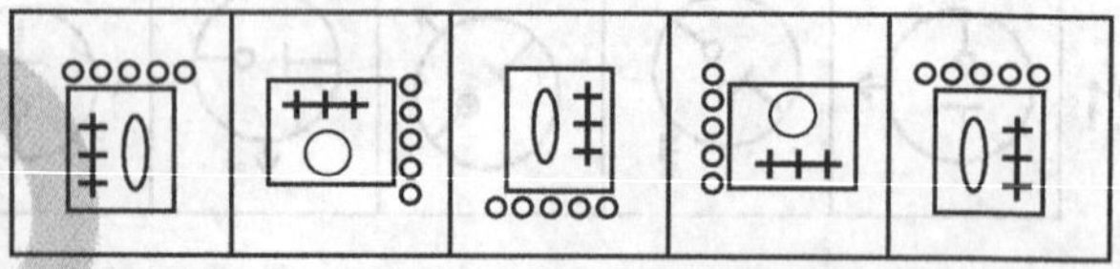

10. 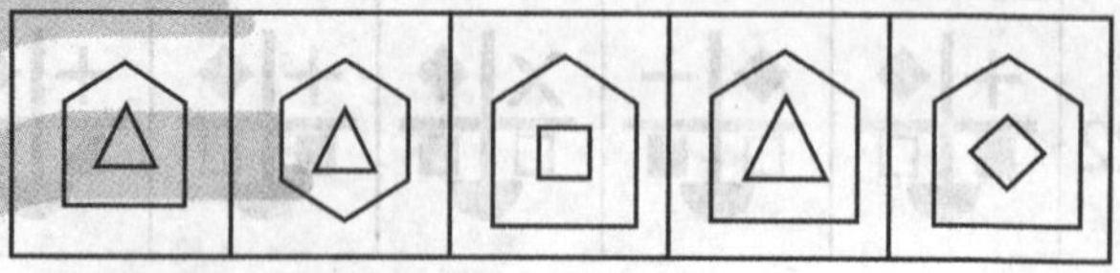

11. 

12. 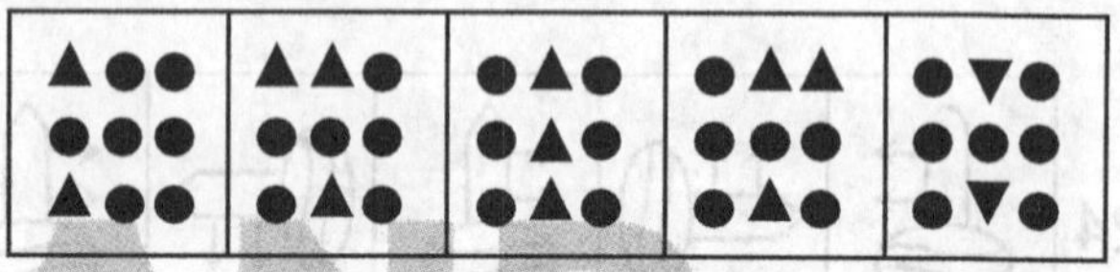

13. 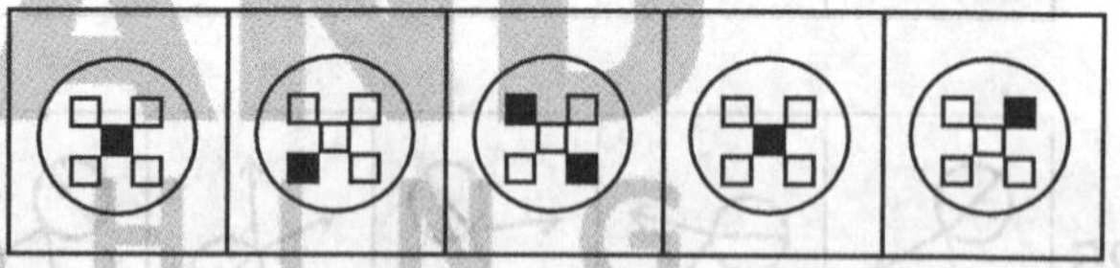

14. 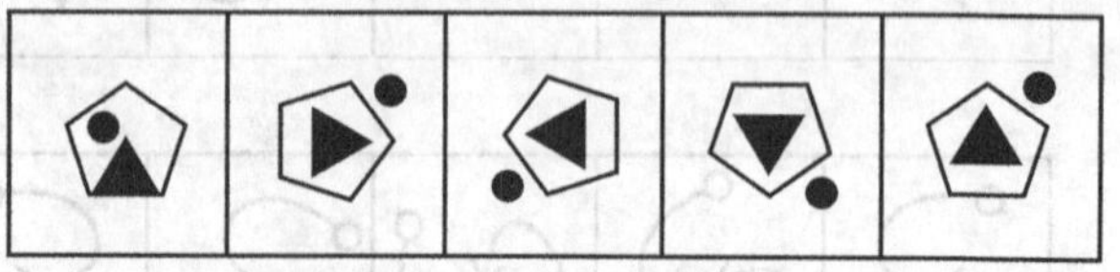

15. 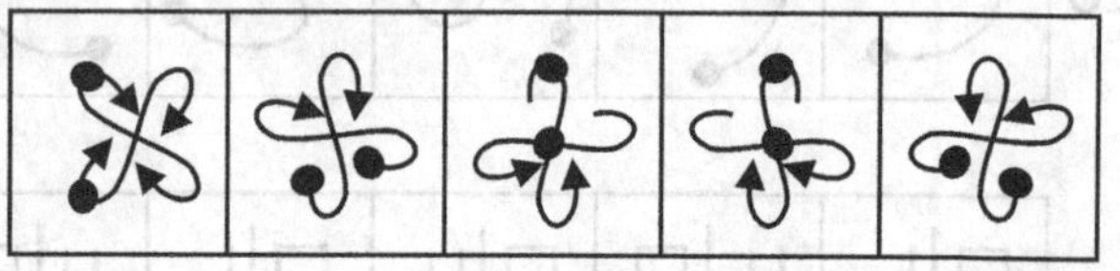

16. 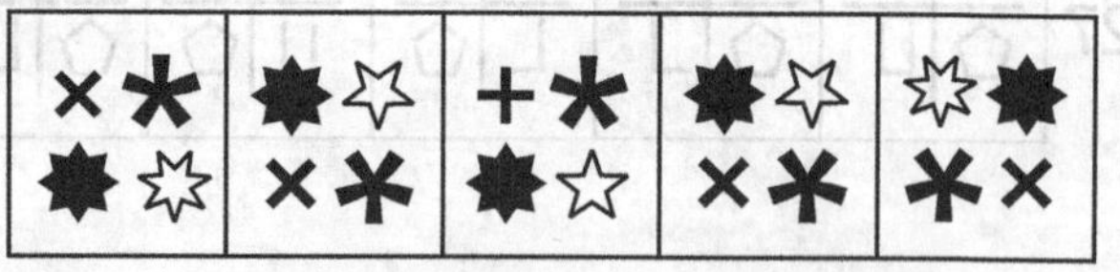

A B C D E

17. 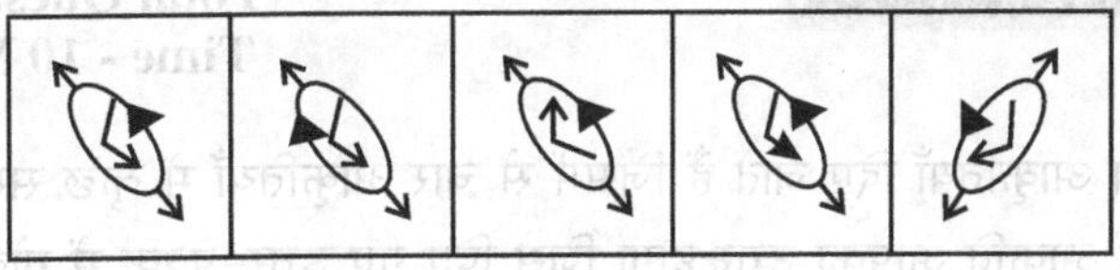

18. 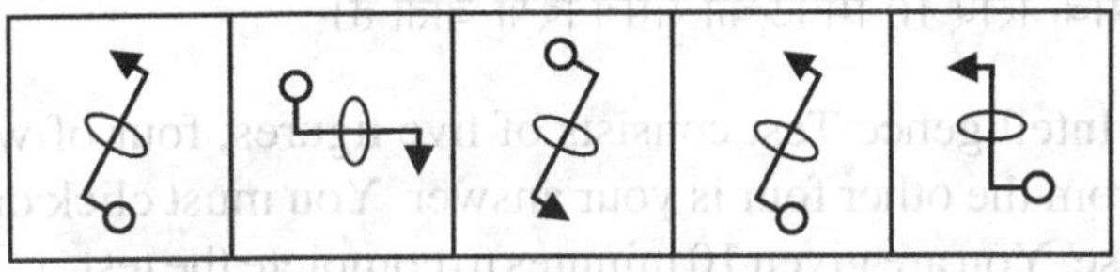

19. 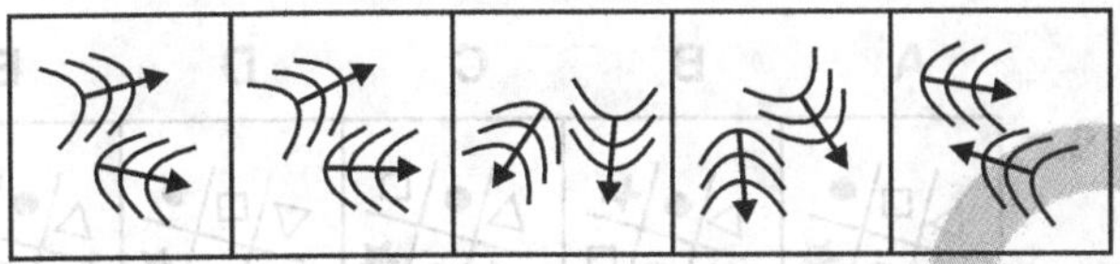

20. 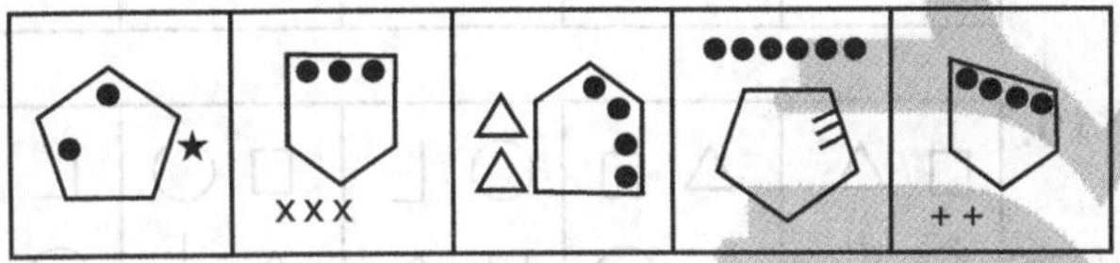

21. 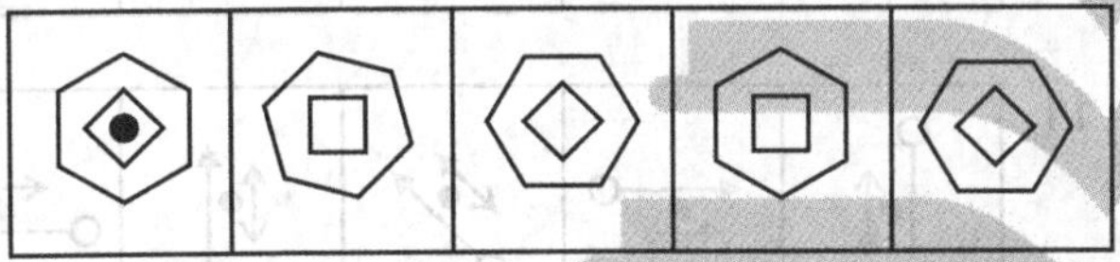

22. 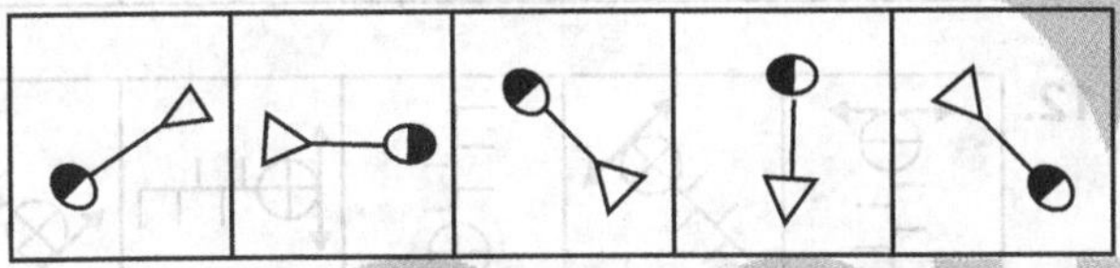

23. 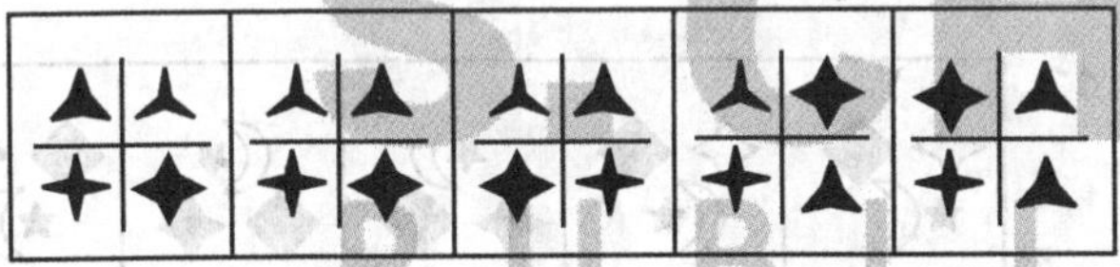

24. 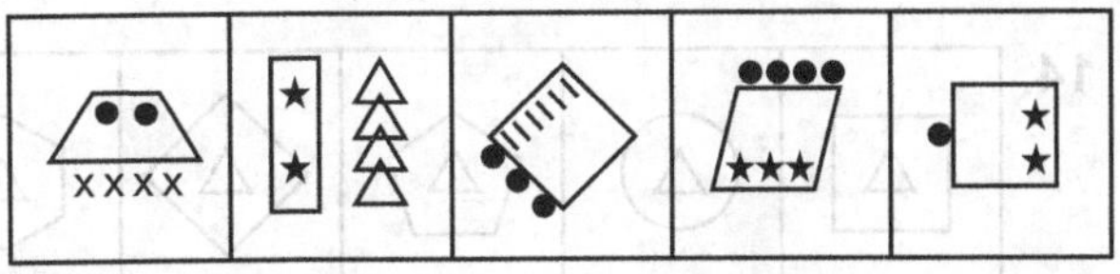

25. 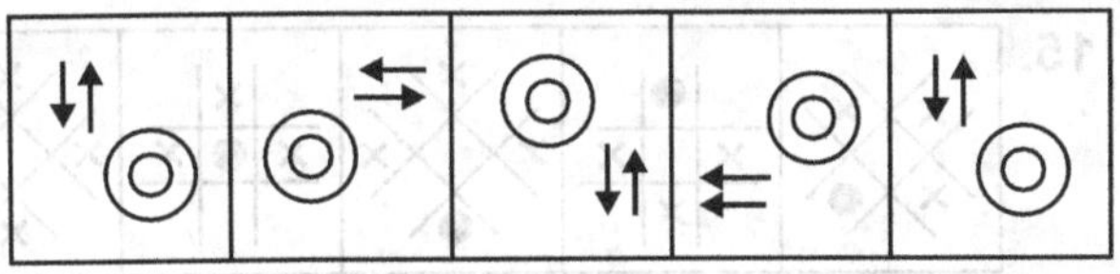

26. 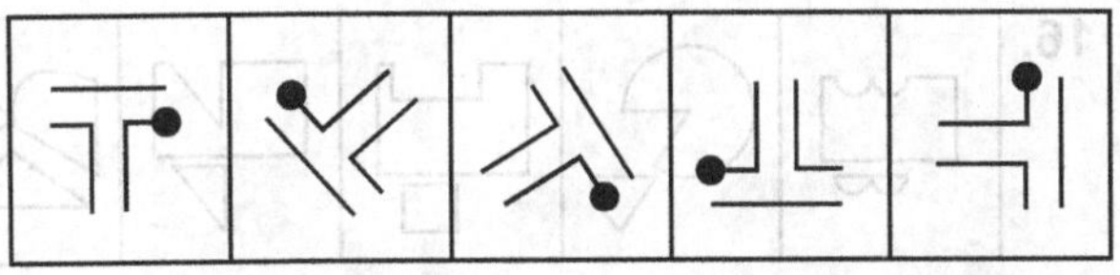

A B C D E

27. 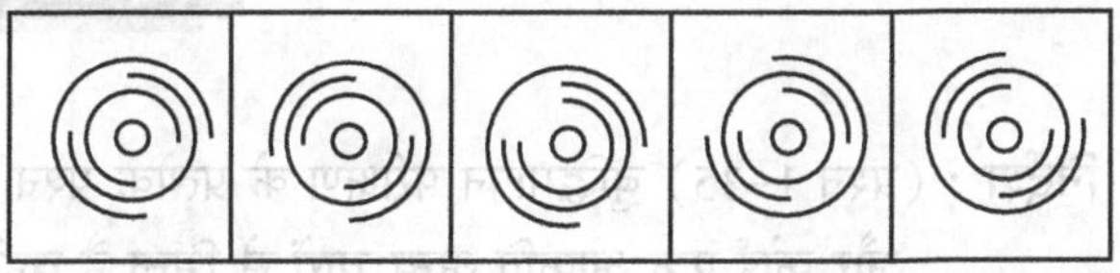

28. 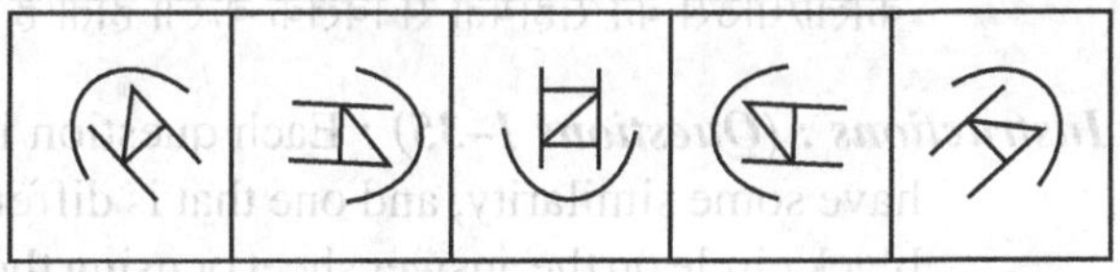

29. 

30. 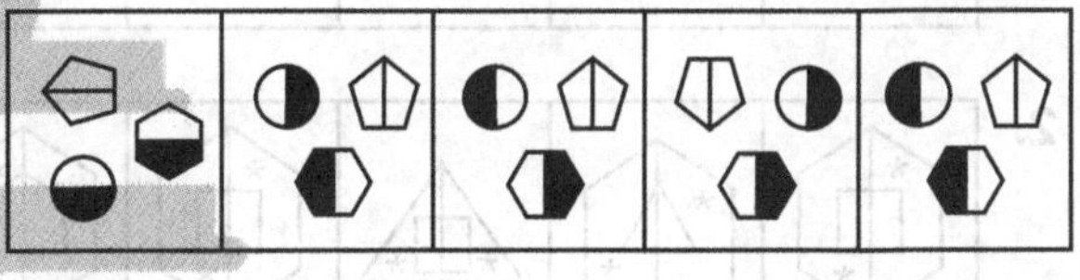

31. 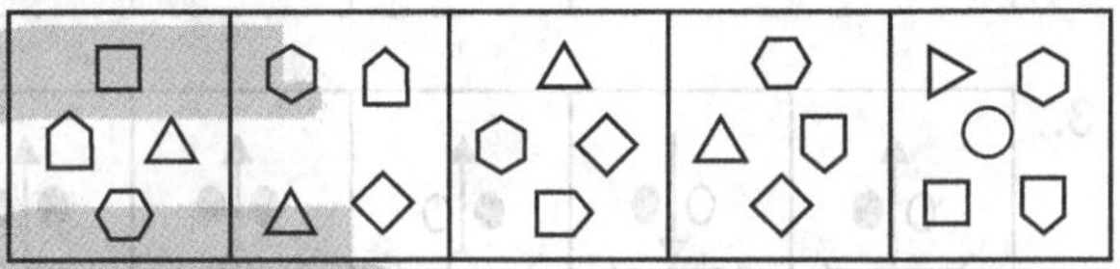

32. 

33. 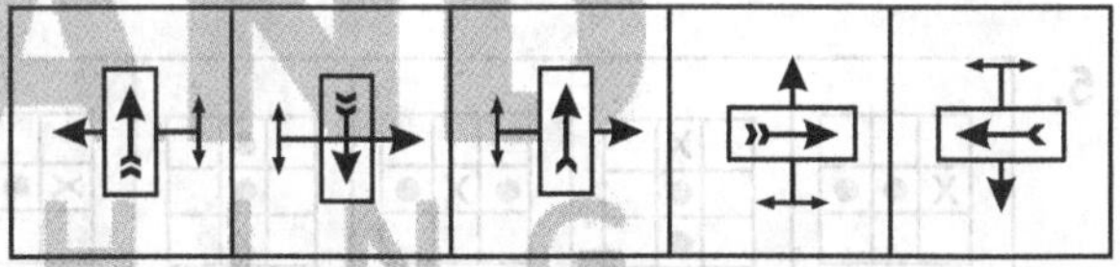

34. 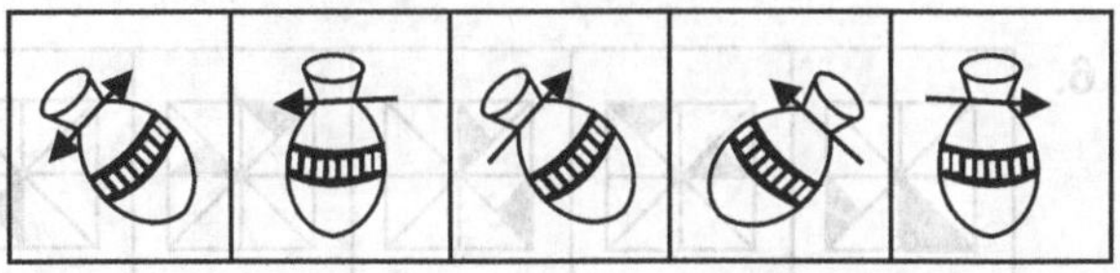

35. 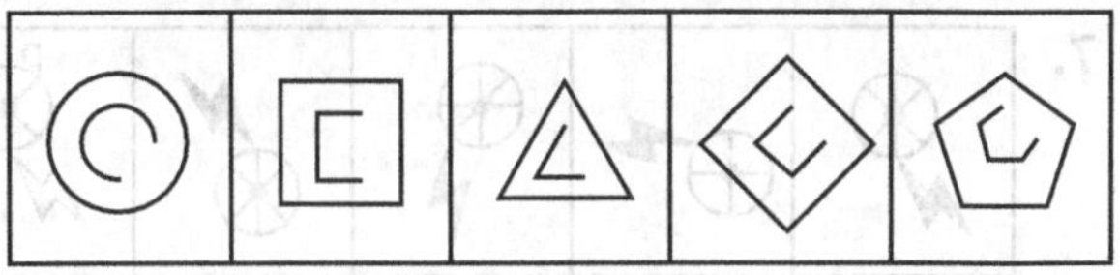

PRACTICE SET-14

Total Ques.- 35
Time - 10 Min.

निर्देश : (प्रश्न 1–35) बुद्धिमापन परीक्षण के प्रत्येक प्रश्न में पाँच आकृतियाँ दिए जाते हैं जिसमें से चार आकृतियाँ में कुछ समानता और कोई एक आकृति अन्य चारों से भिन्न है वही भिन्न आकृति आपका उत्तर होगा जिसे दिए गए उत्तर–पत्रक में गोले को काला/माउस की सहायता से क्लिक करना होता है और इसके लिए 10 मिनट का समय दिया जाता है।

Instructions : (Questions 1–35) : Each question in the Intelligence Test consists of five figures, four of which have some similarity, and one that is different from the other four is your answer. You must click on the black circle on the answer sheet or using the mouse. You are given 10 minutes to complete the test.

A B C D E

1. 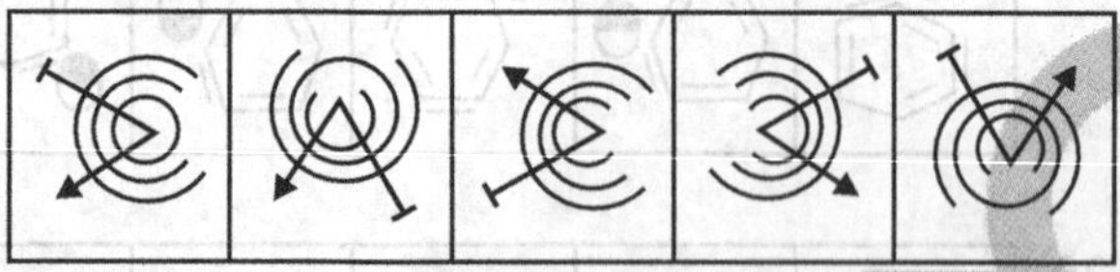

2. 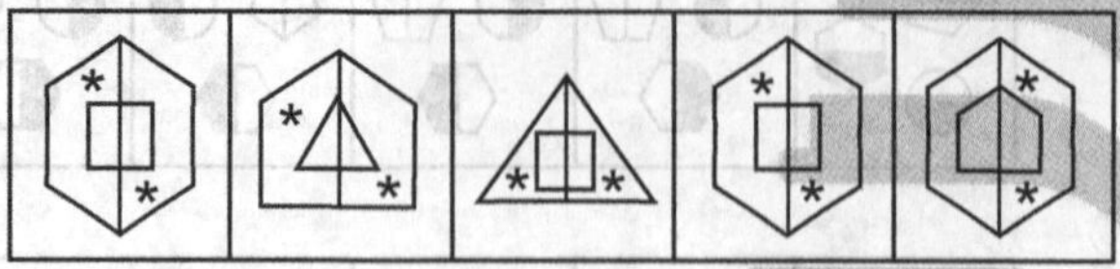

3. 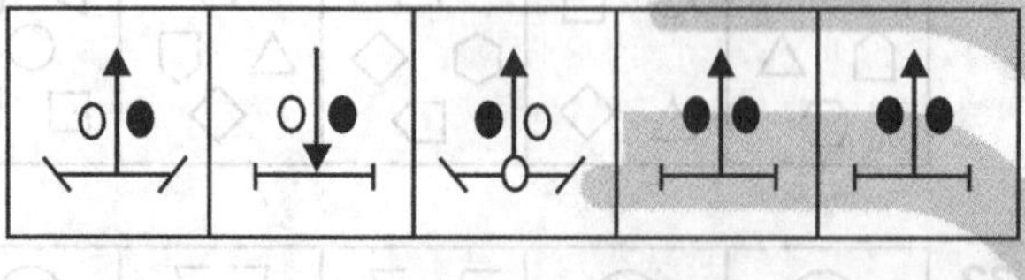

4. 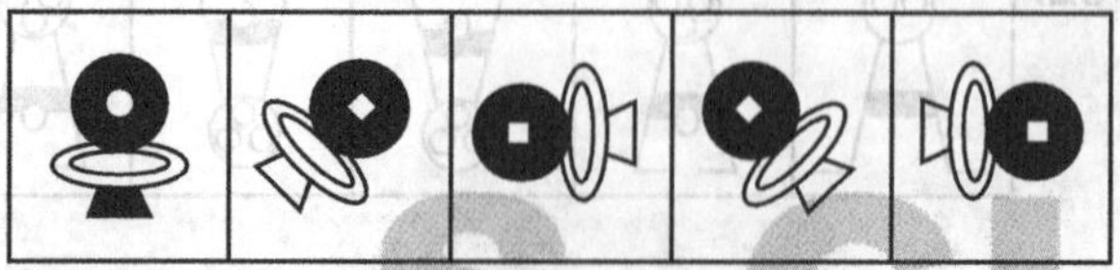

5. 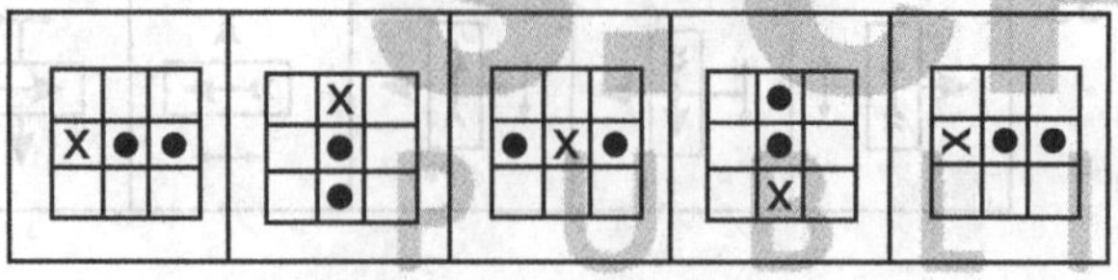

6. 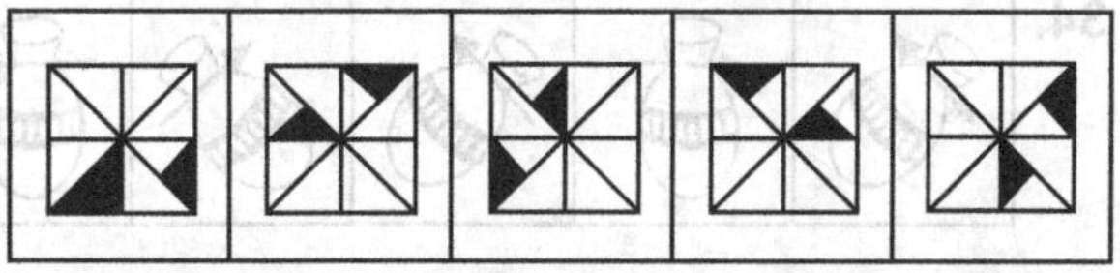

7. 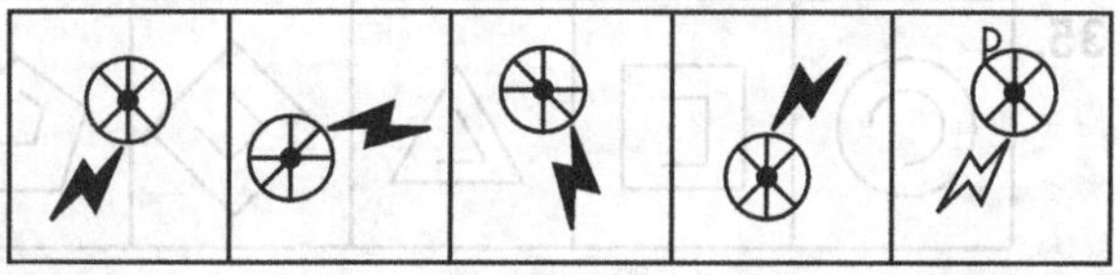

8. 

A B C D E

9. 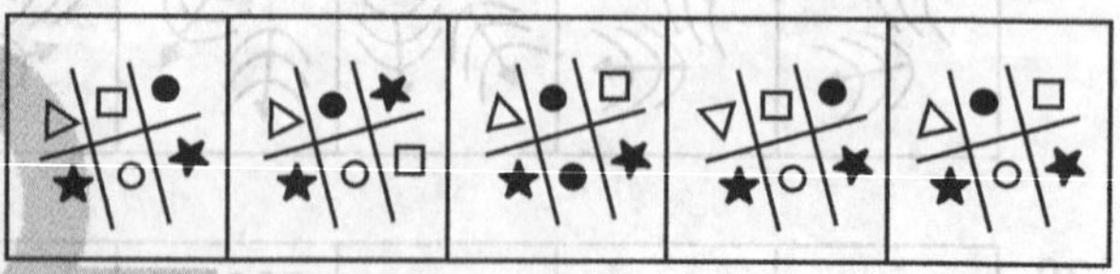

10. 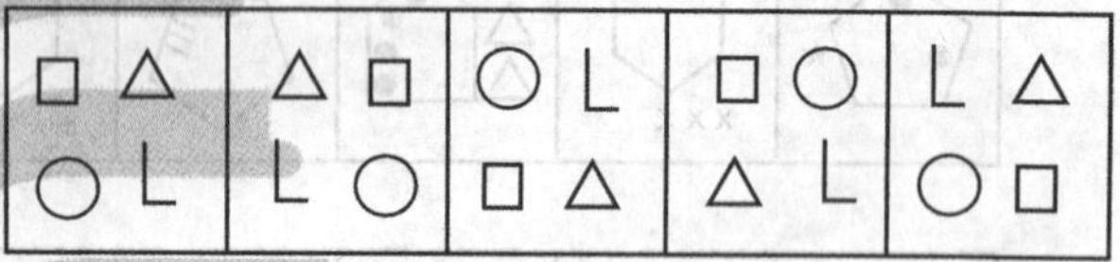

11. 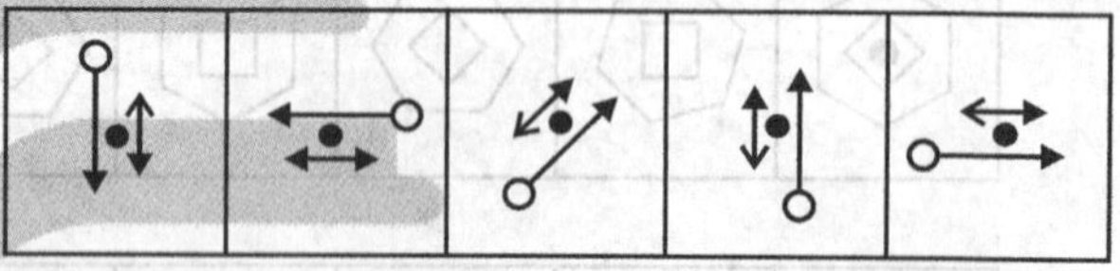

12. 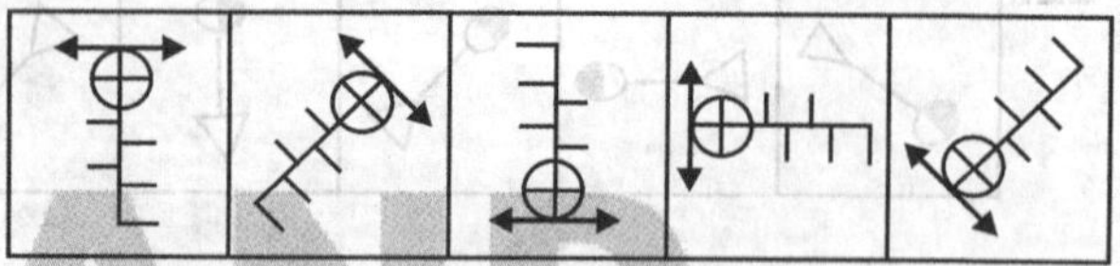

13. 

14. 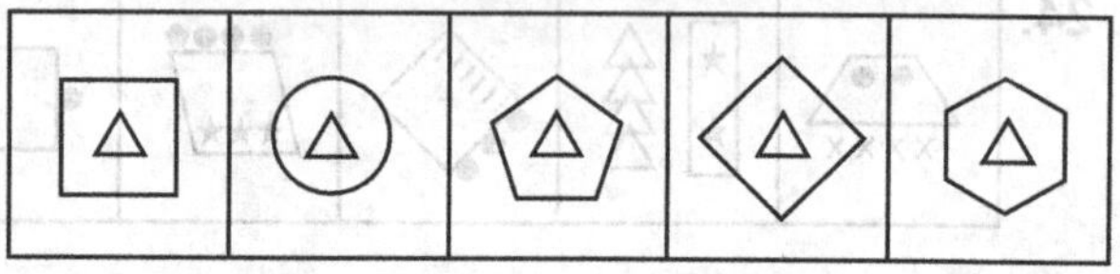

15. 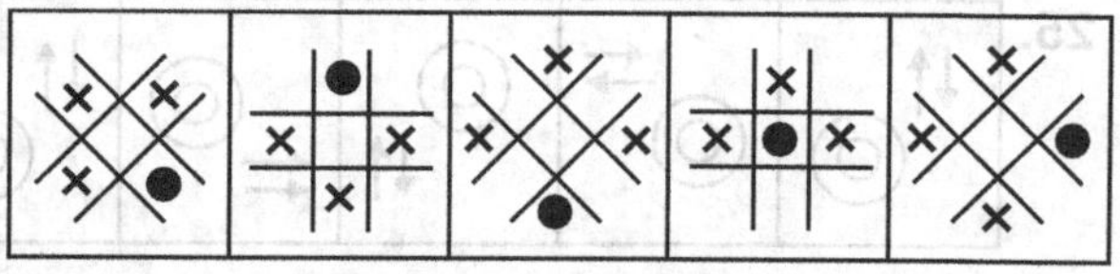

16. 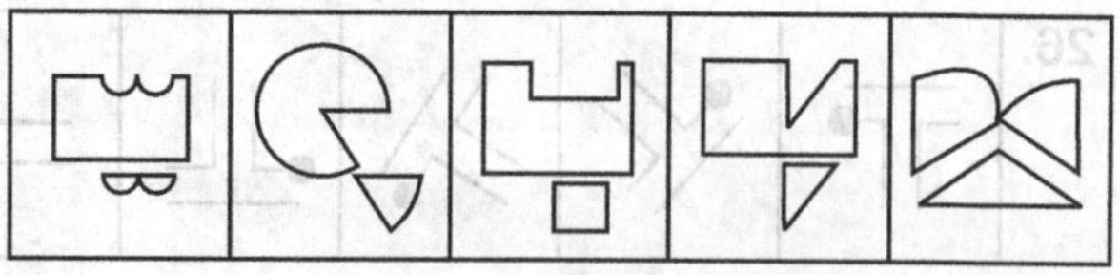

A B C D E

17.
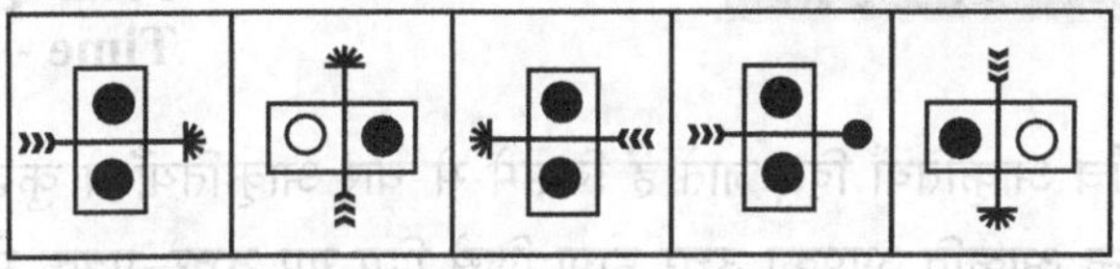

18.
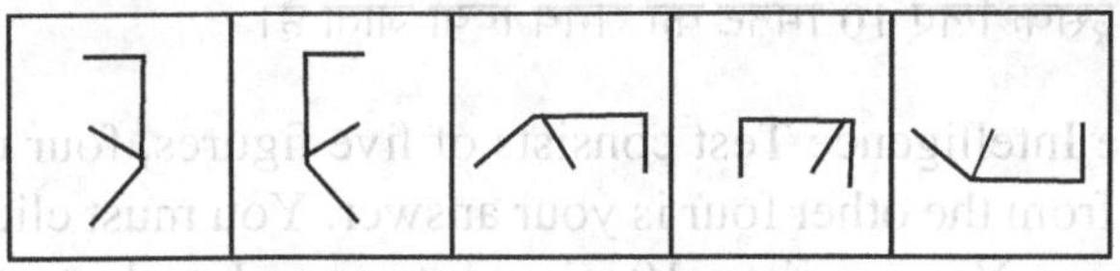

19.
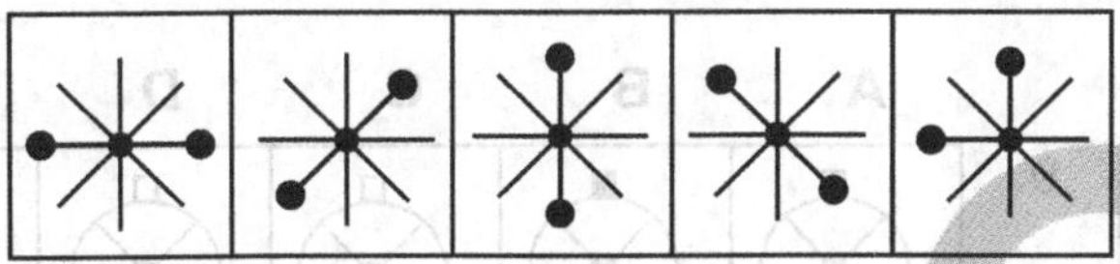

20.
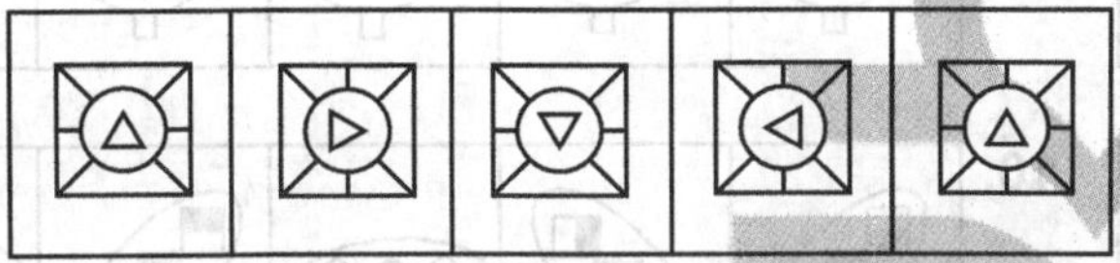

21.
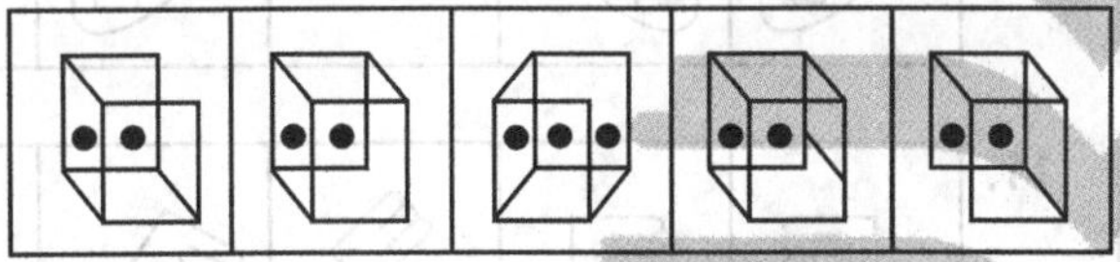

22.
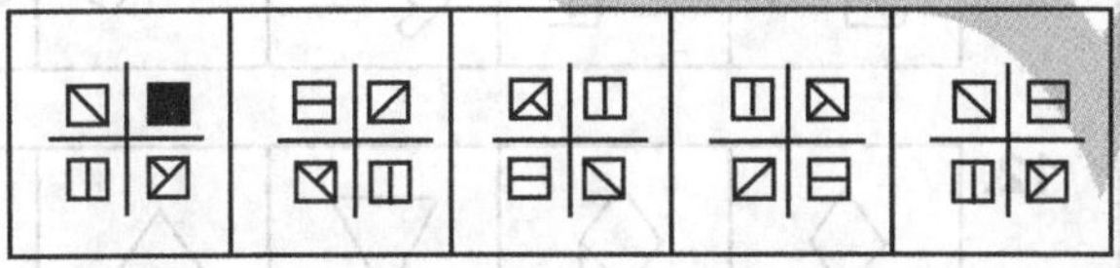

23.
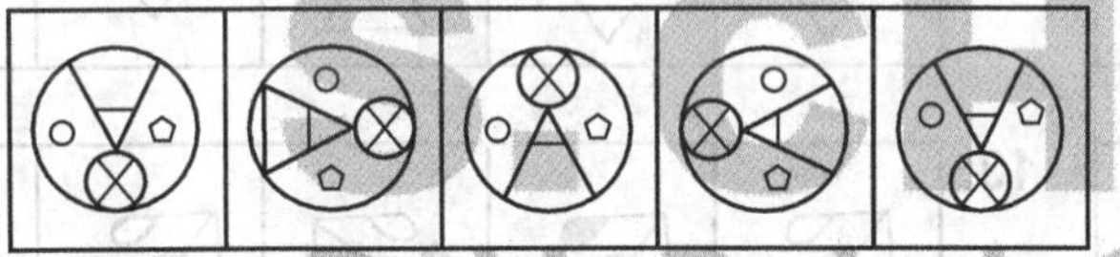

24.
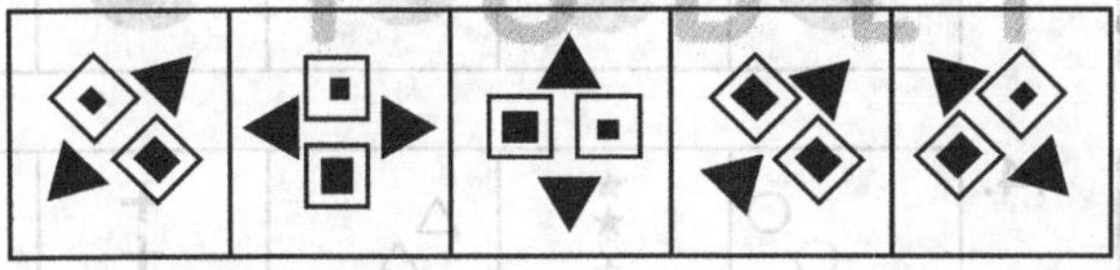

25.
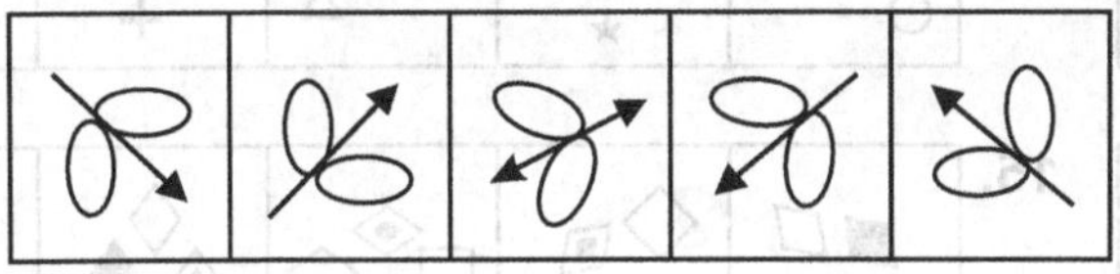

26.
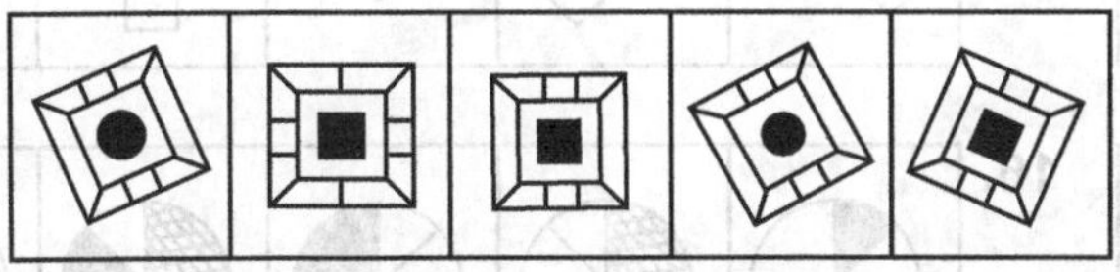

A B C D E

27.
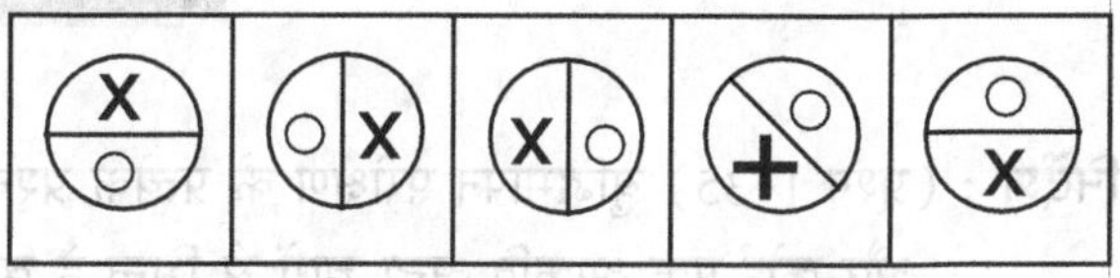

28.
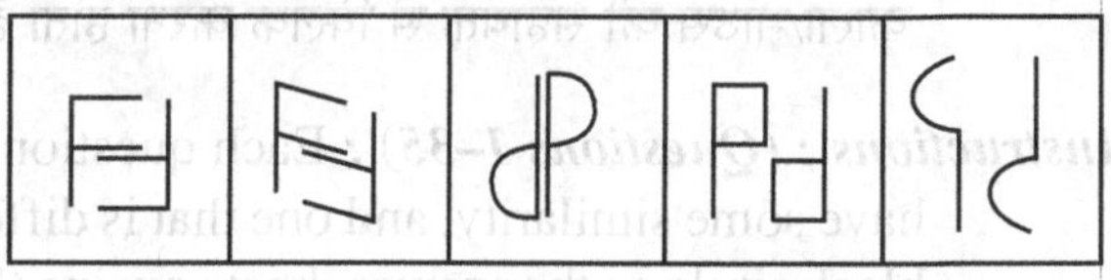

29.
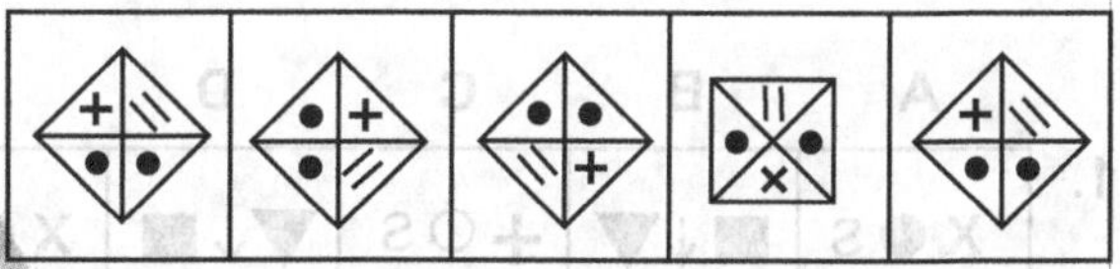

30.
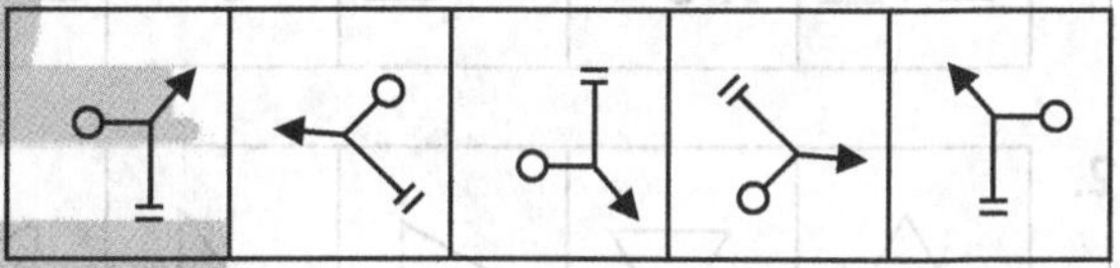

31.
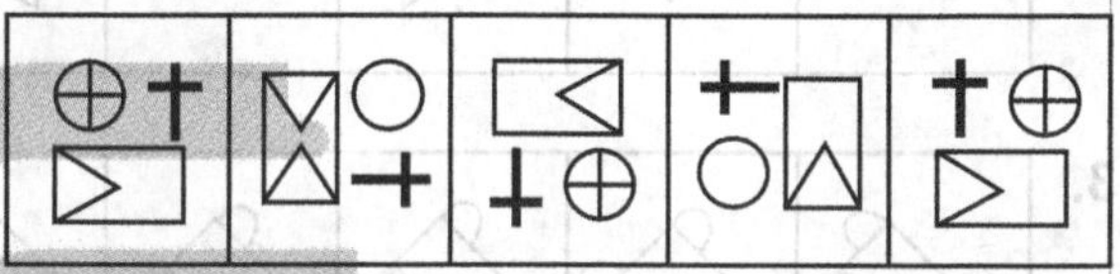

32.
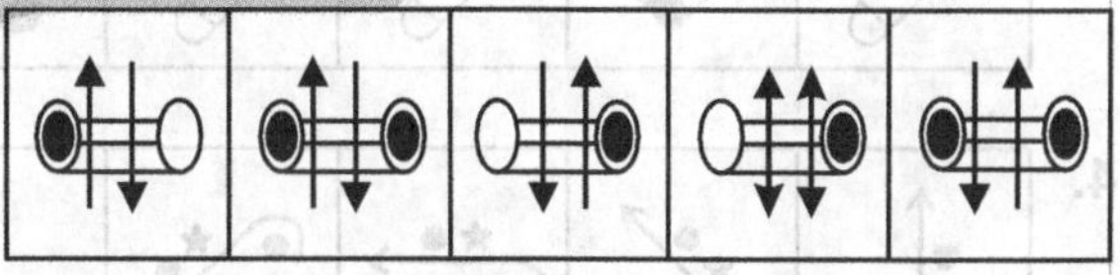

33.
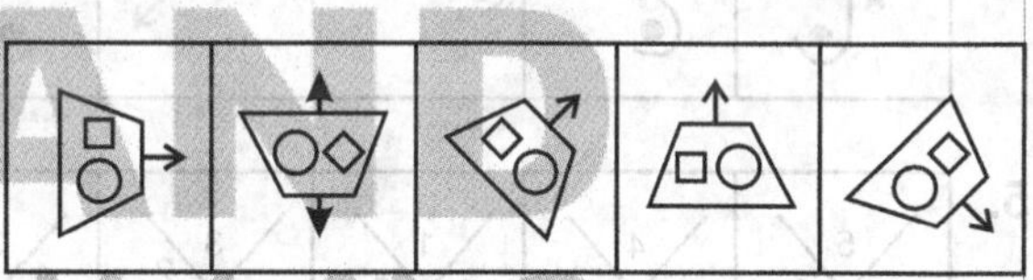

34.
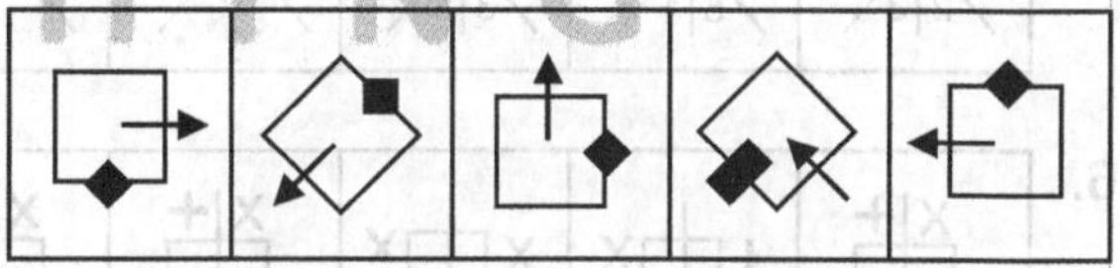

35.
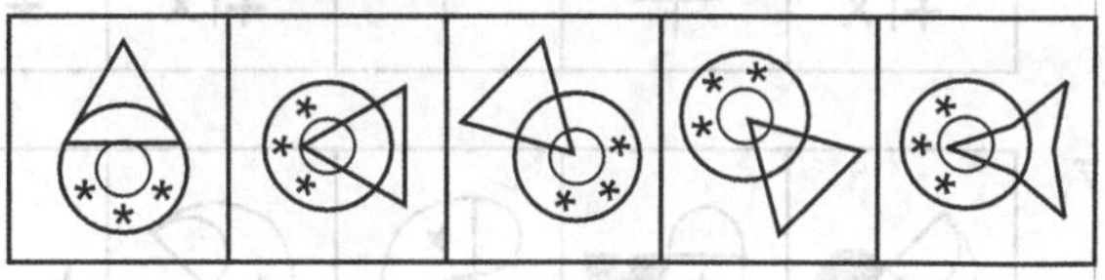

PRACTICE SET-15

Total Ques.- 35
Time - 10 Min.

निर्देश : (प्रश्न 1-35) बुद्धिमापन परीक्षण के प्रत्येक प्रश्न में पाँच आकृतियाँ दिए जाते हैं जिसमें से चार आकृतियाँ में कुछ समानता और कोई एक आकृति अन्य चारों से भिन्न है वही भिन्न आकृति आपका उत्तर होगा जिसे दिए गए उत्तर-पत्रक में गोले को काला/माउस की सहायता से क्लिक करना होता है और इसके लिए 10 मिनट का समय दिया जाता है।

Instructions : (Questions 1–35) : Each question in the Intelligence Test consists of five figures, four of which have some similarity, and one that is different from the other four is your answer. You must click on the black circle on the answer sheet or using the mouse. You are given 10 minutes to complete the test.

A B C D E

1. 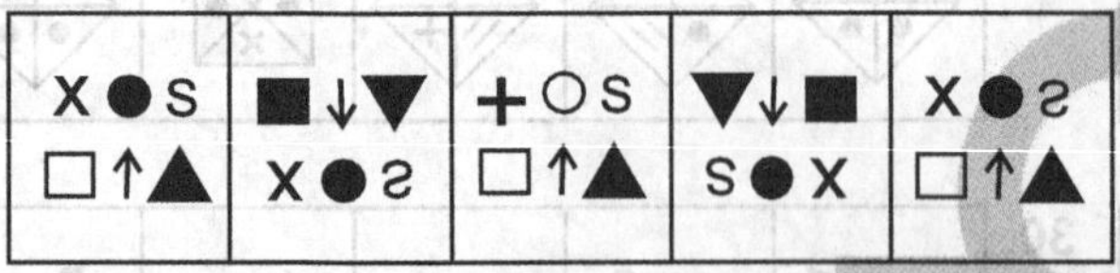

2. 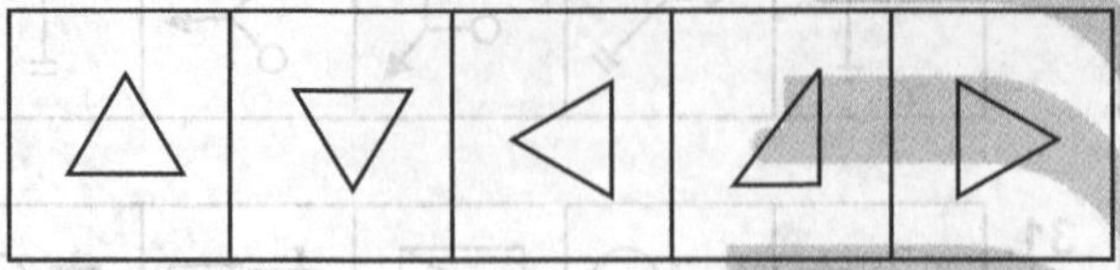

3. 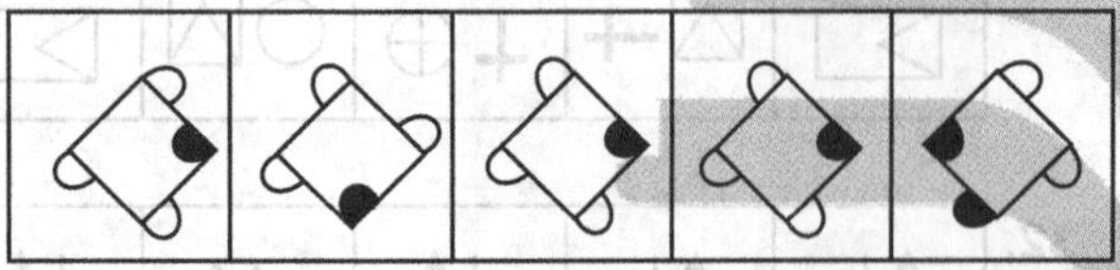

4. 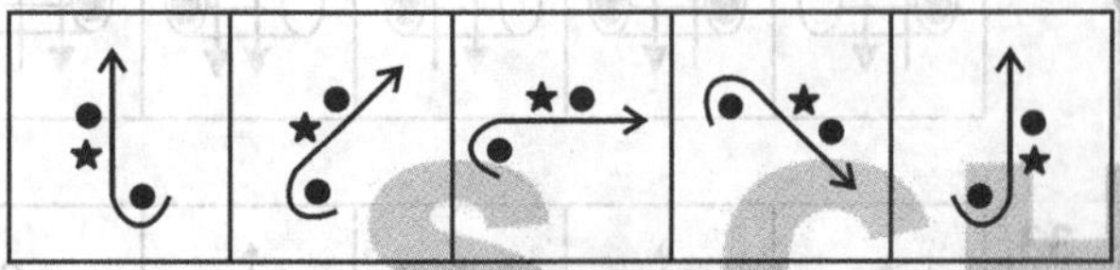

5. 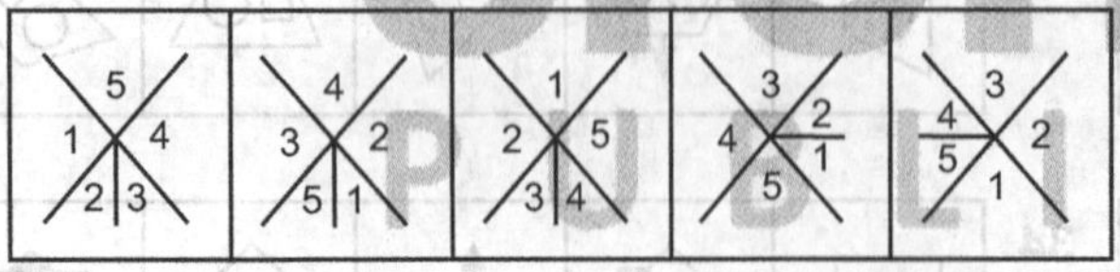

6. 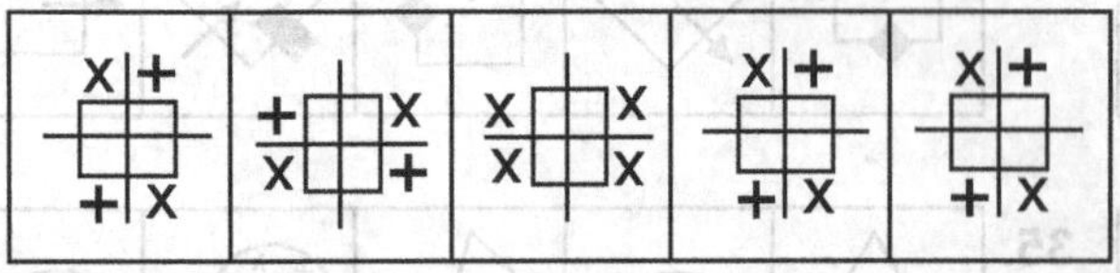

7. 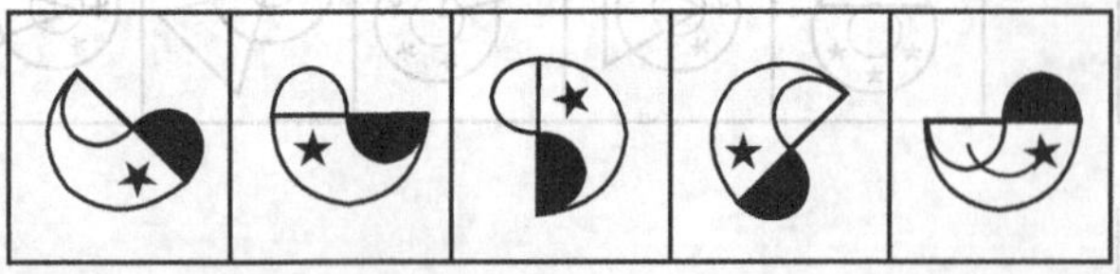

8. 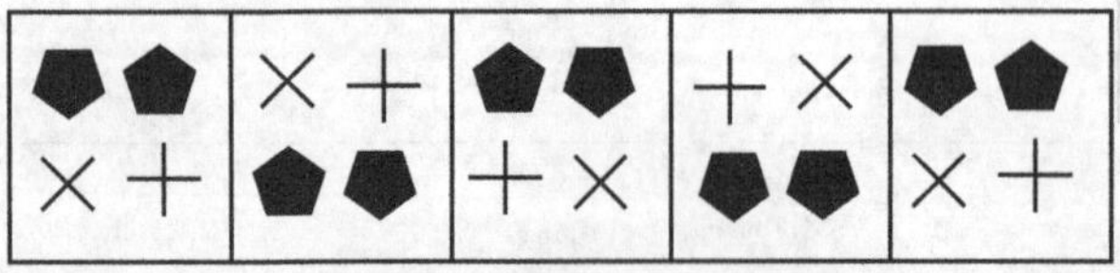

A B C D E

9. 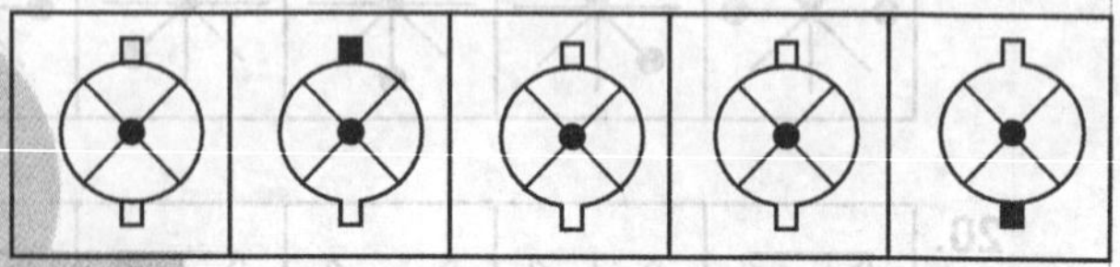

10. 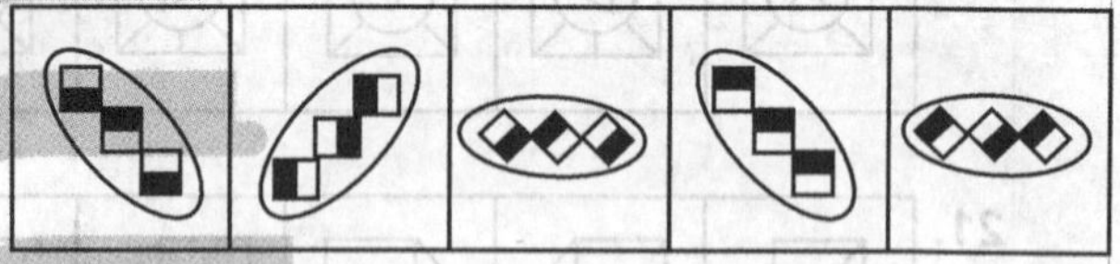

11. 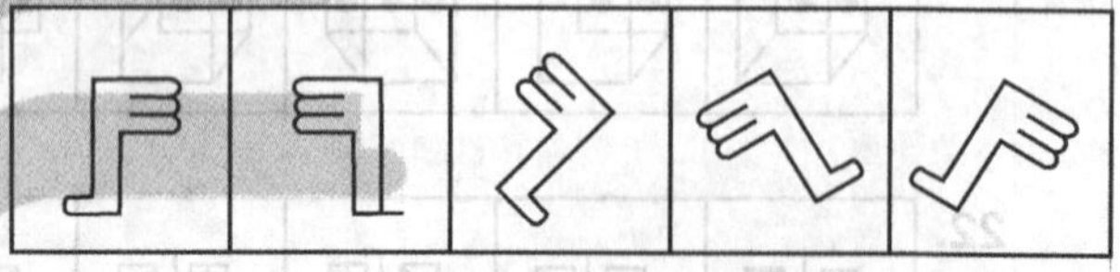

12. 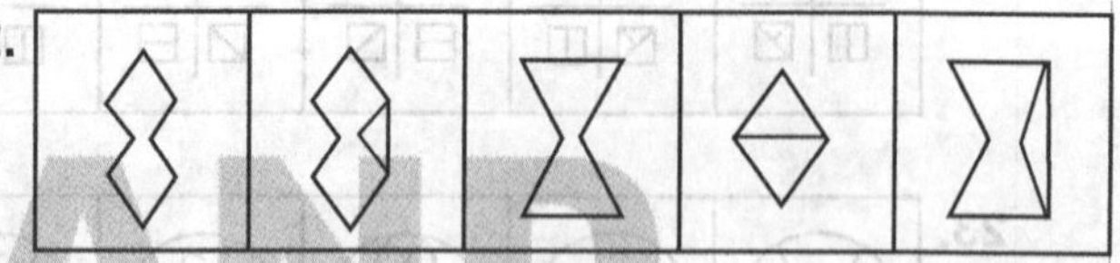

13. 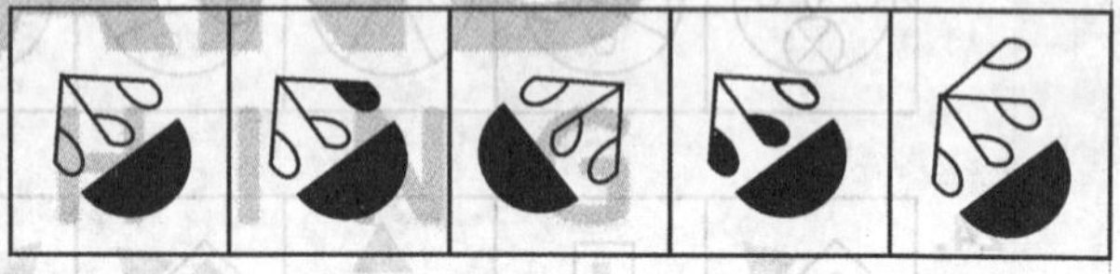

14. 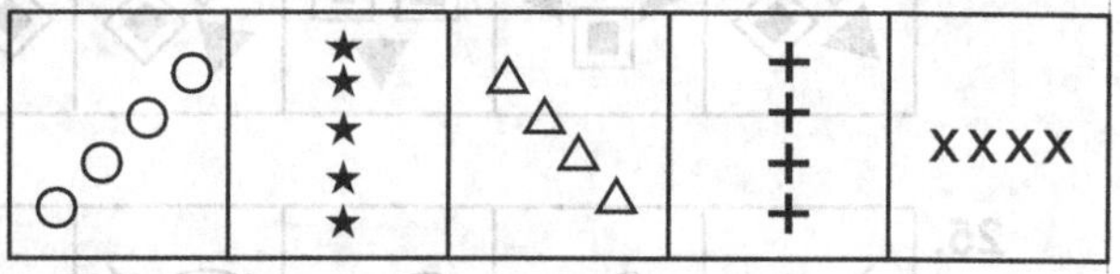

15. 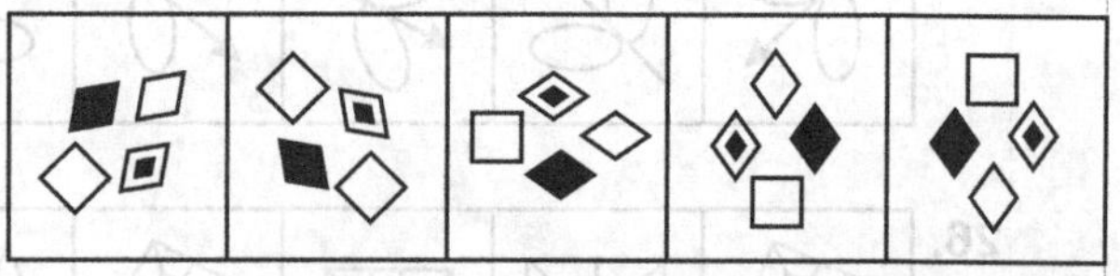

16. 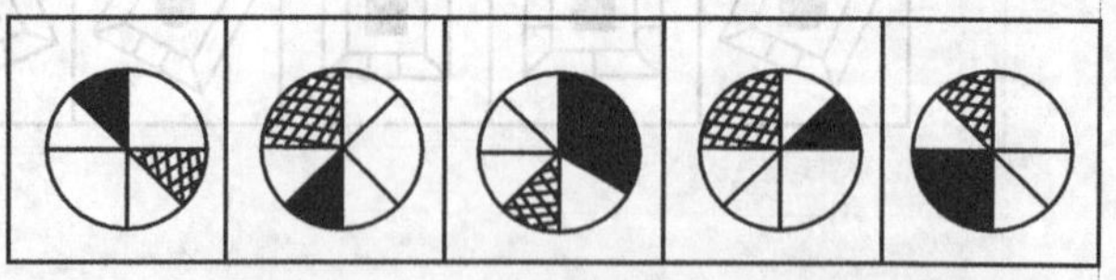

A B C D E

17. 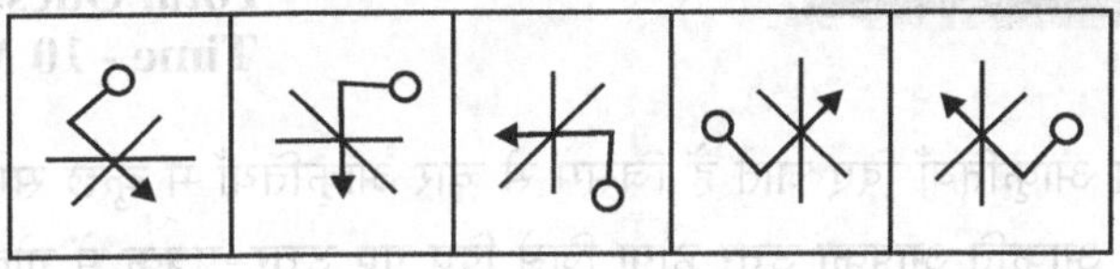

18. 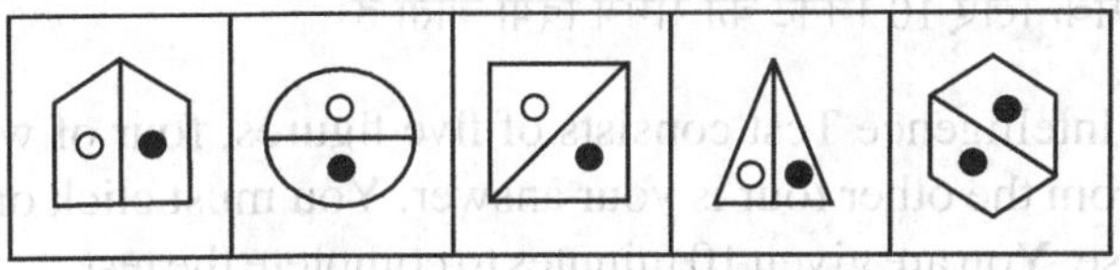

19. 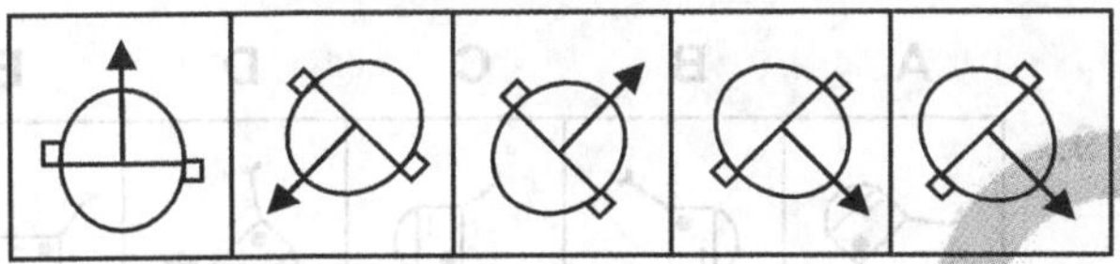

20. 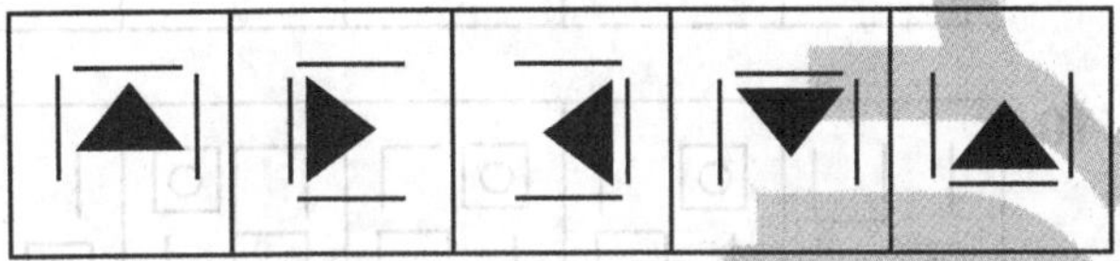

21. 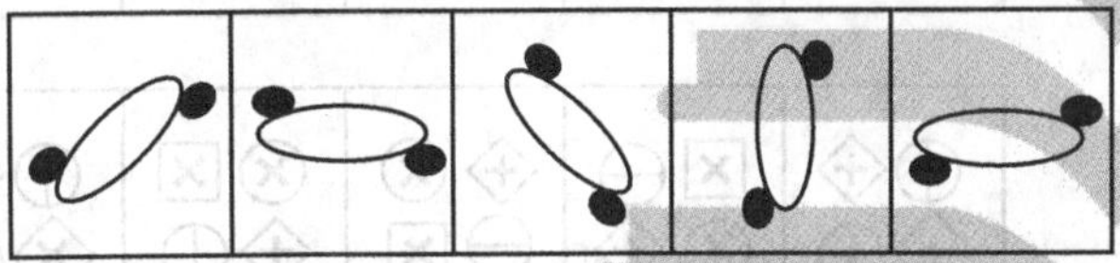

22. 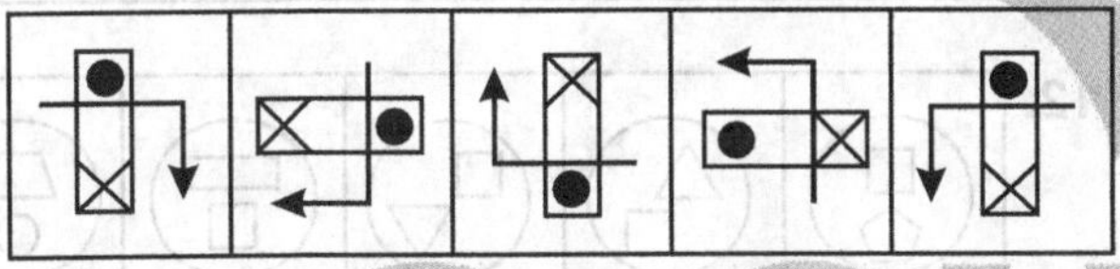

23. 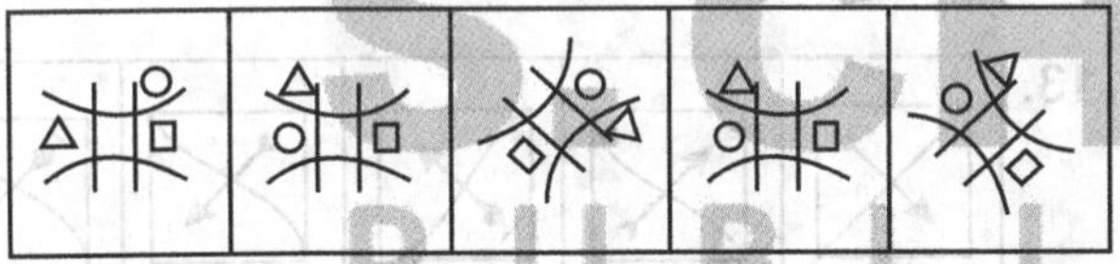

24. 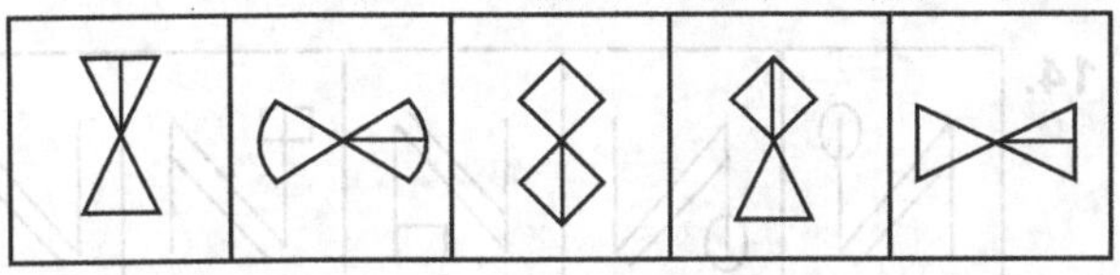

25. 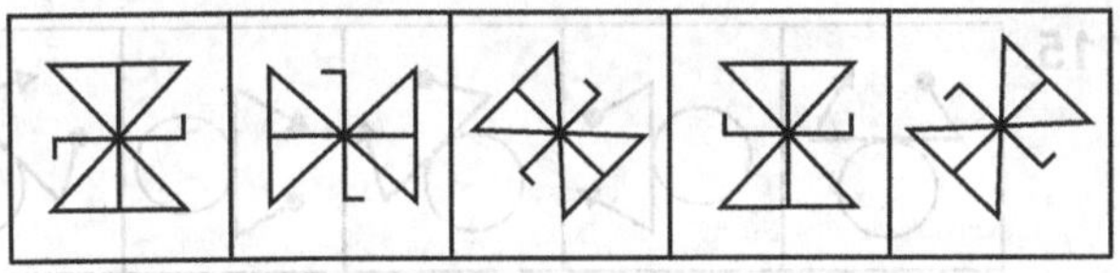

26. 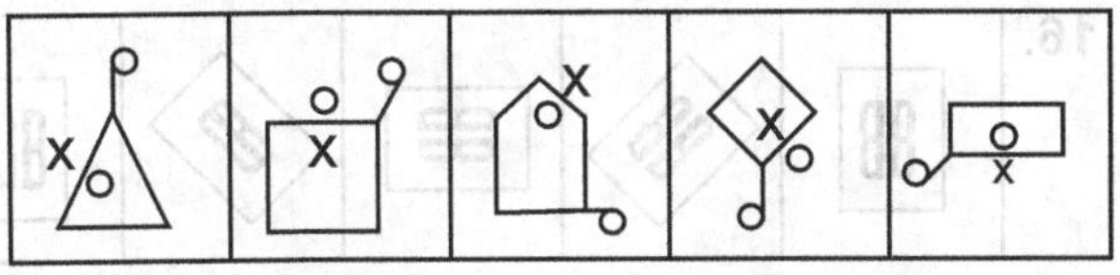

A B C D E

27. 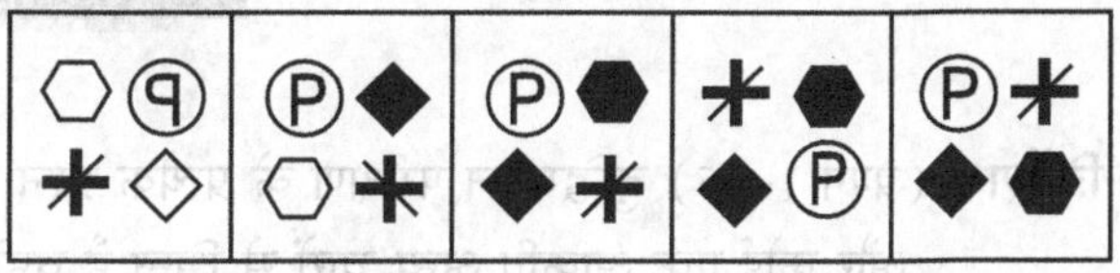

28. 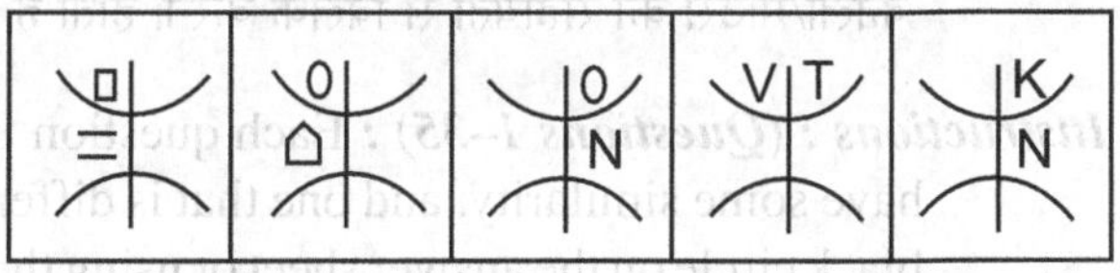

29. 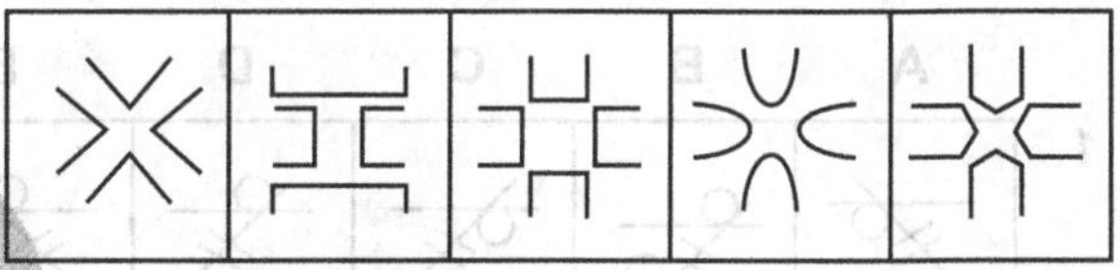

30. 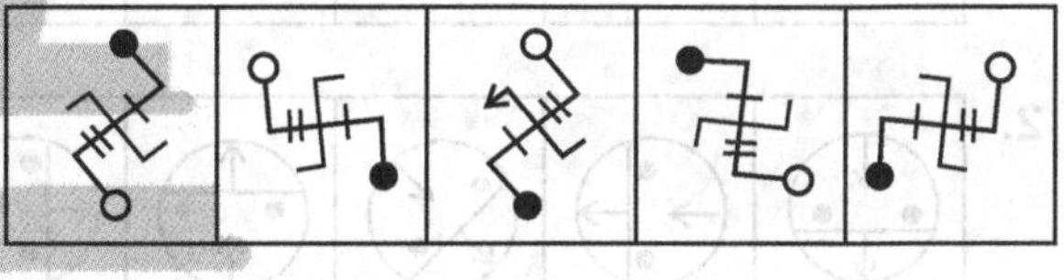

31. 

32. 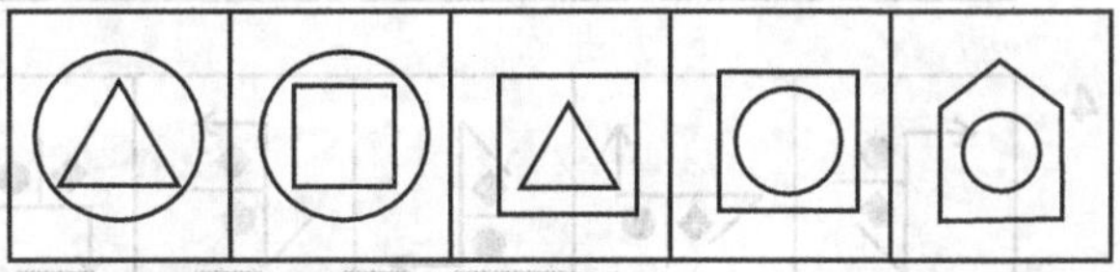

33. 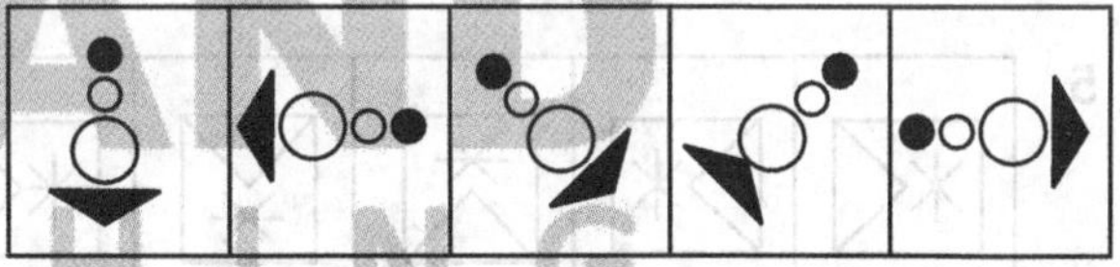

34. 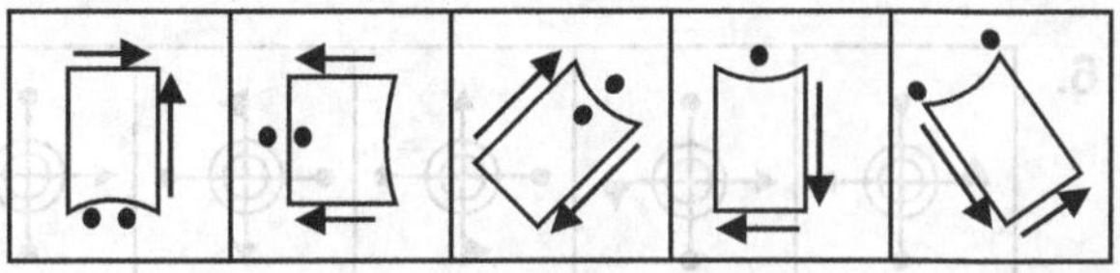

35. 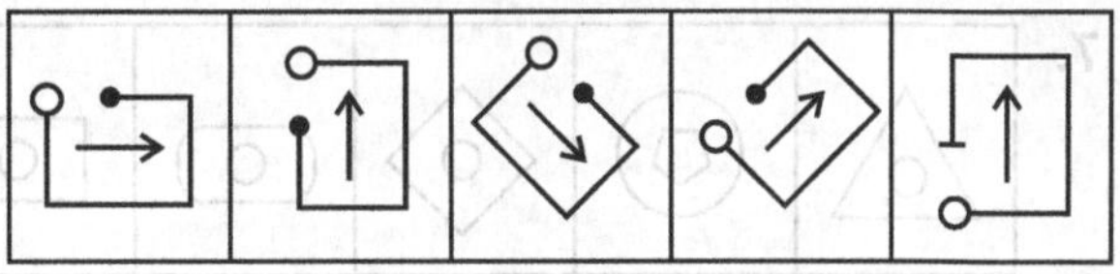

PRACTICE SET-16

Total Ques.- 35
Time - 10 Min.

निर्देश : (प्रश्न 1-35) बुद्धिमापन परीक्षण के प्रत्येक प्रश्न में पाँच आकृतियाँ दिए जाते हैं जिसमें से चार आकृतियाँ में कुछ समानता और कोई एक आकृति अन्य चारों से भिन्न है वही भिन्न आकृति आपका उत्तर होगा जिसे दिए गए उत्तर-पत्रक में गोले को काला/माउस की सहायता से क्लिक करना होता है और इसके लिए 10 मिनट का समय दिया जाता है।

Instructions : (Questions 1–35) : Each question in the Intelligence Test consists of five figures, four of which have some similarity, and one that is different from the other four is your answer. You must click on the black circle on the answer sheet or using the mouse. You are given 10 minutes to complete the test.

A B C D E

1. 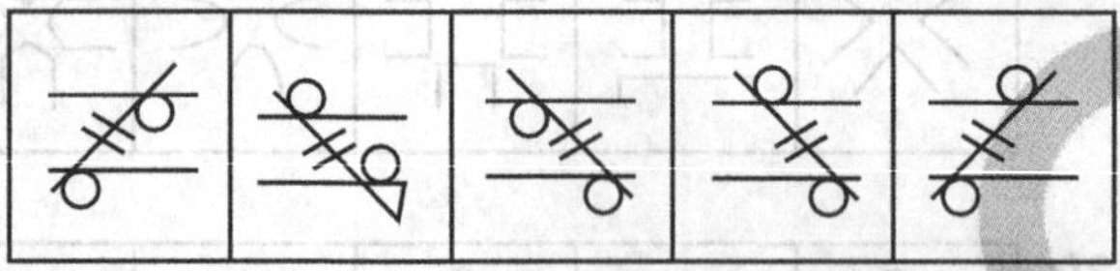

2. 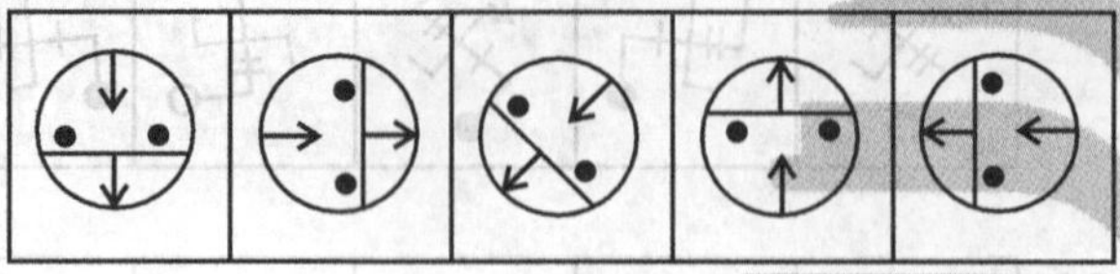

3. 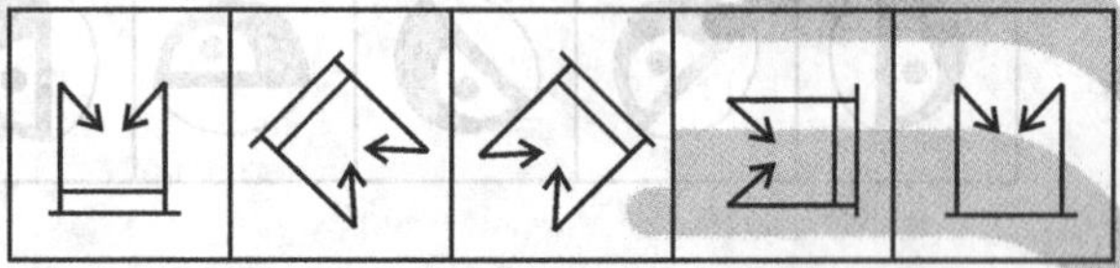

4. 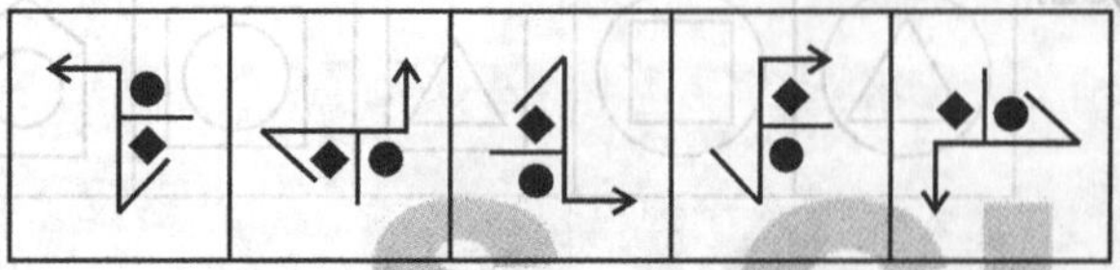

5. 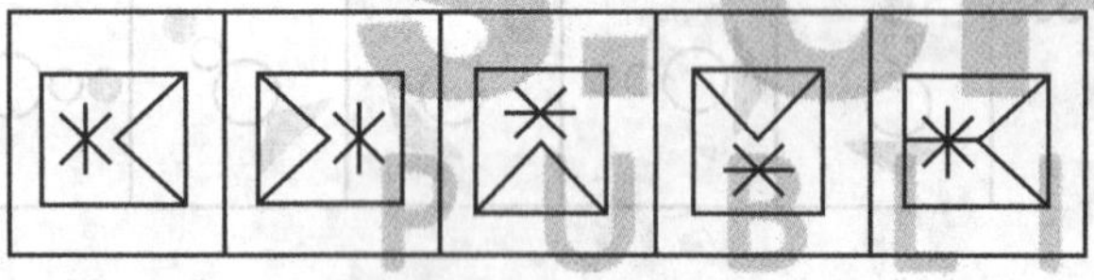

6. 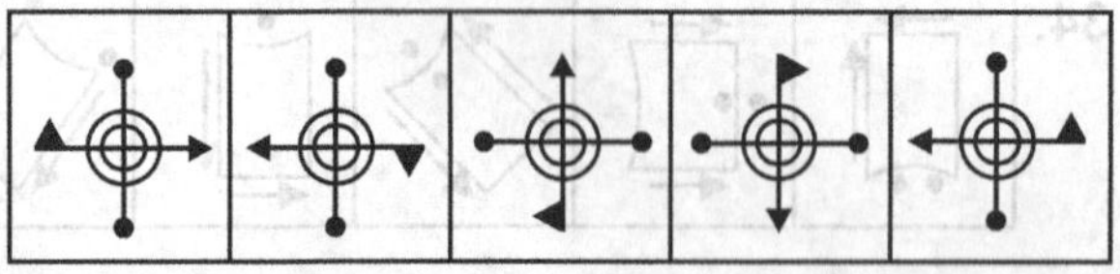

7. 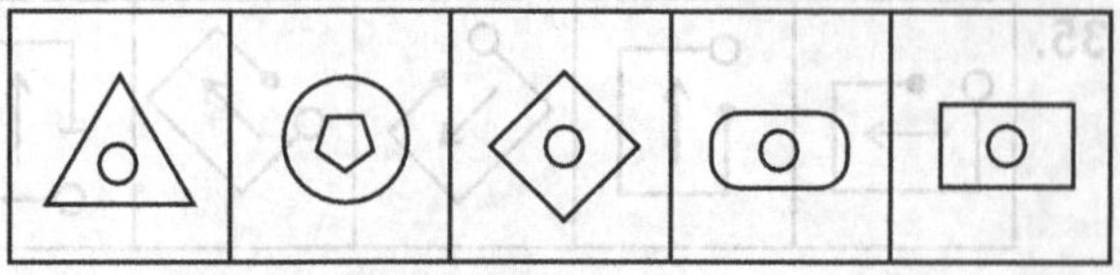

8. 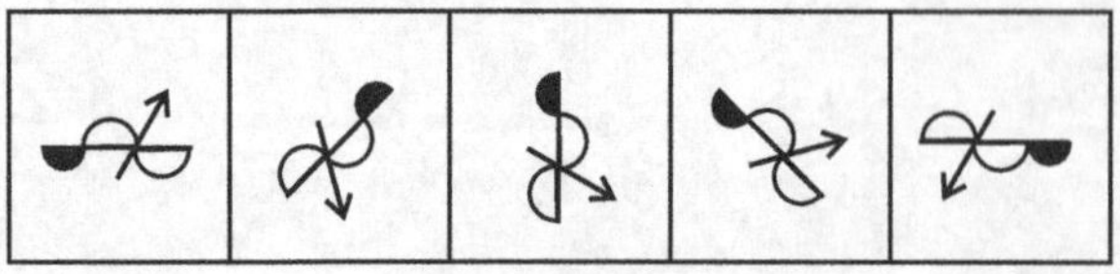

A B C D E

9. 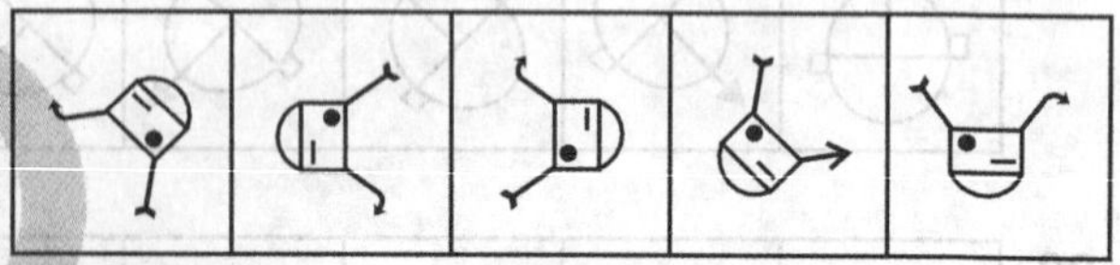

10. 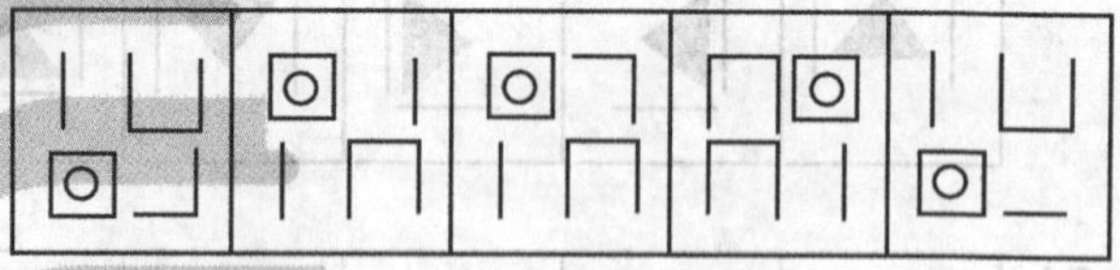

11. 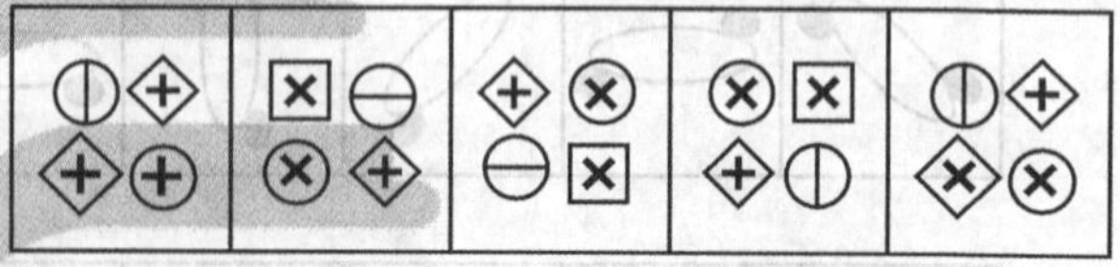

12. 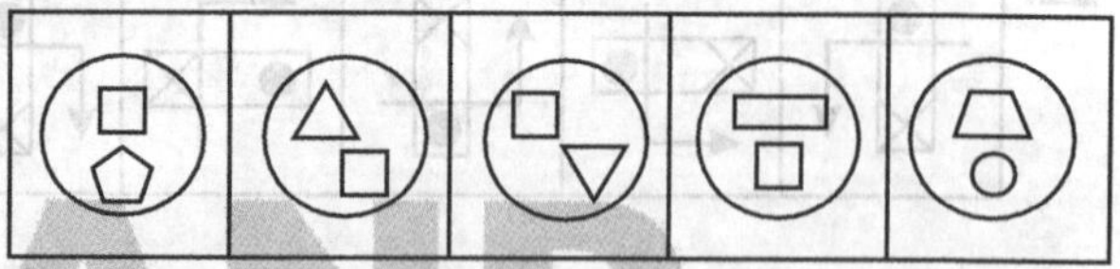

13. 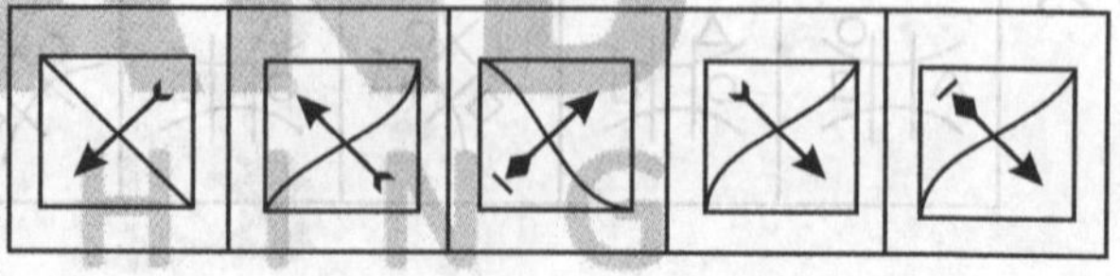

14. 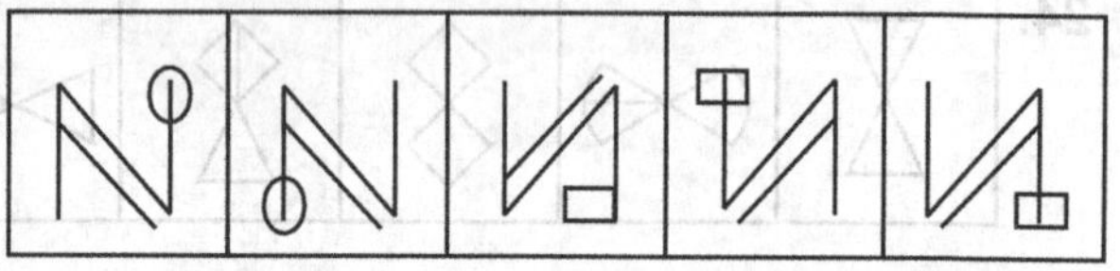

15. 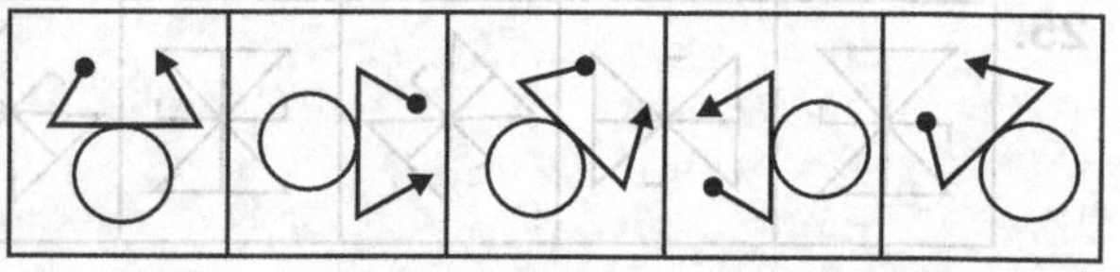

16. 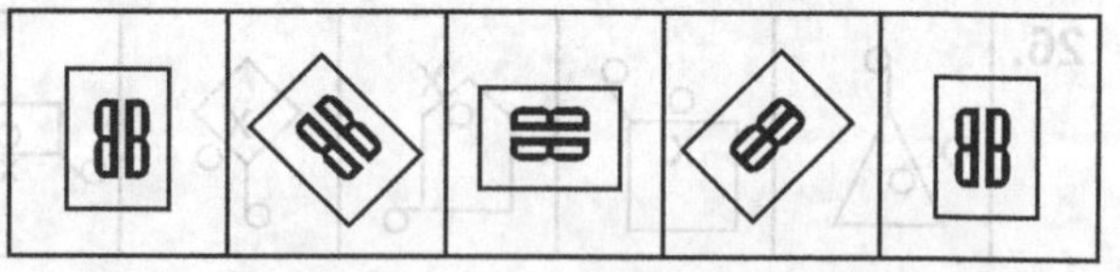

A B C D E

17.
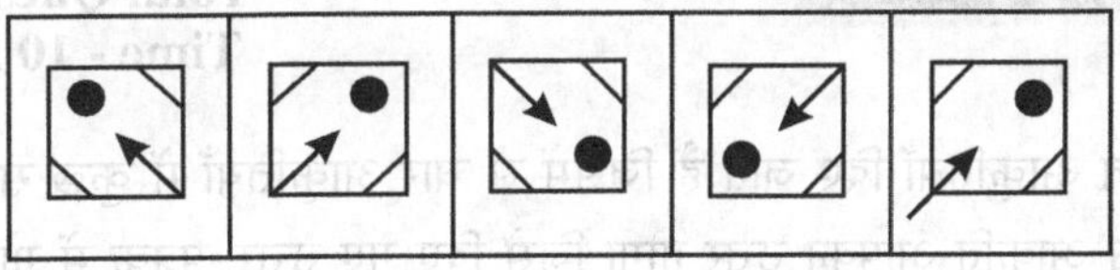

18.
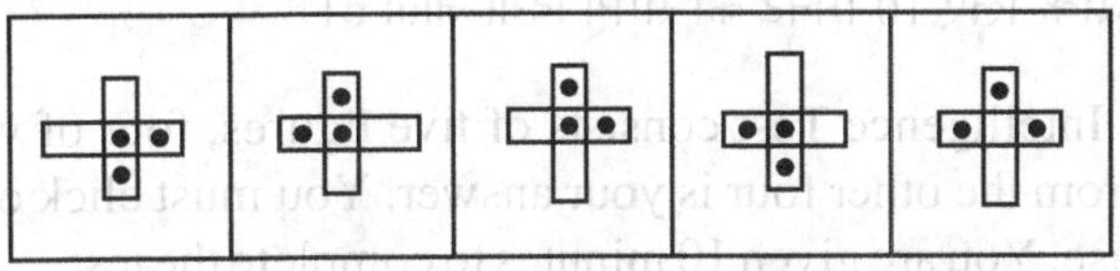

19.
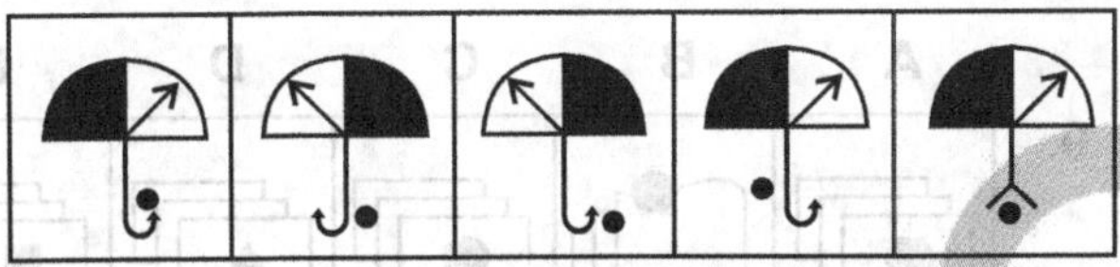

20.
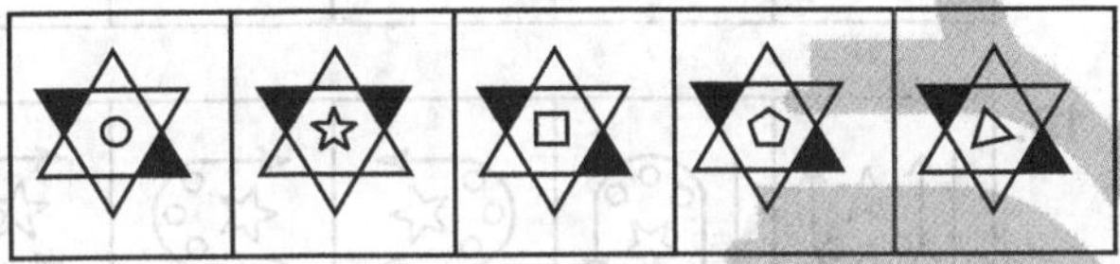

21.
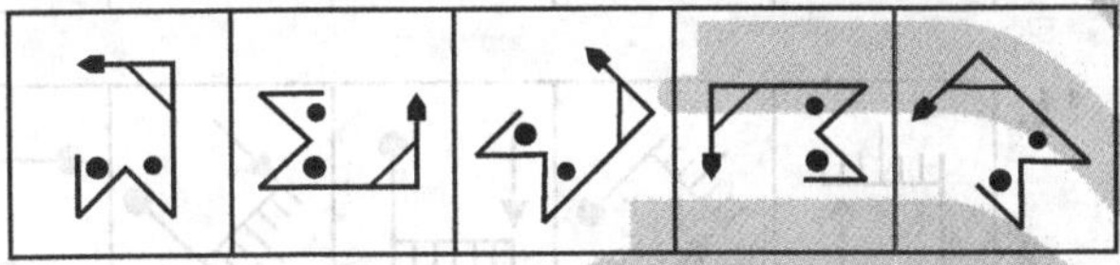

22.
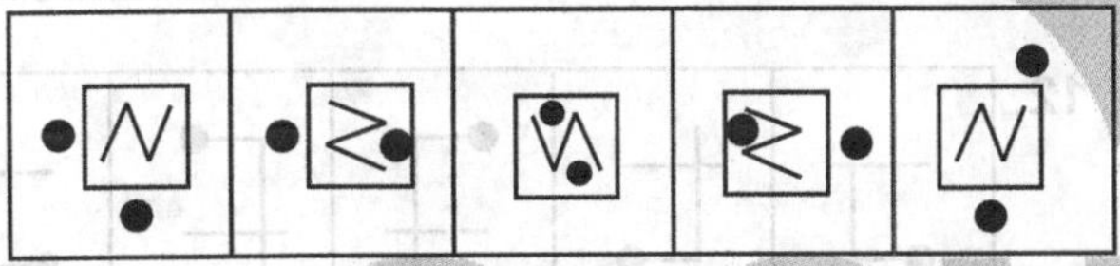

23.
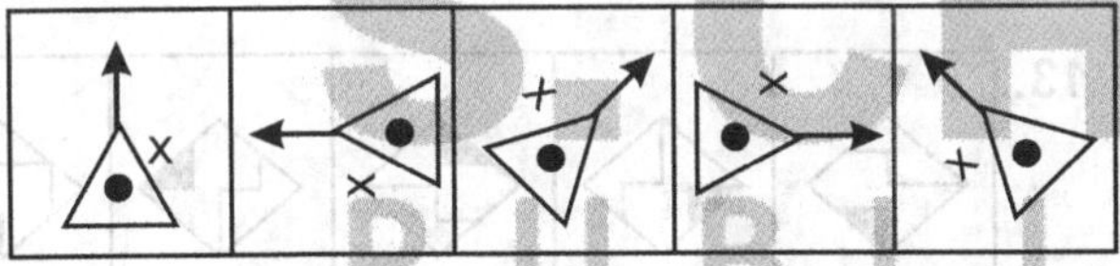

24.
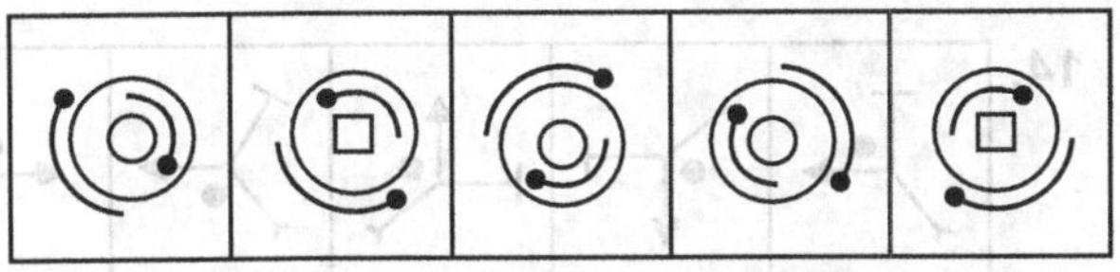

25.
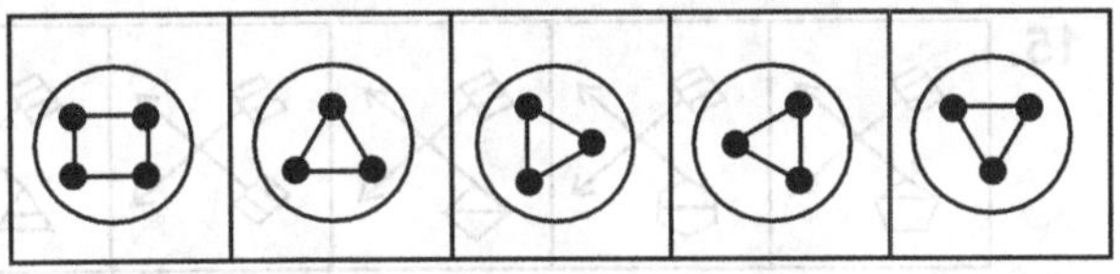

26.
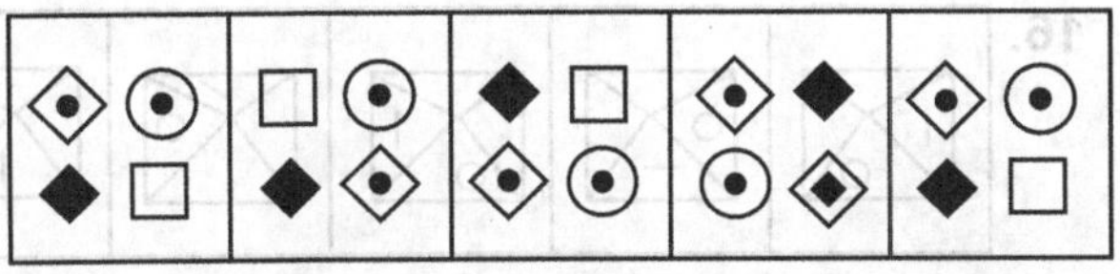

A B C D E

27.
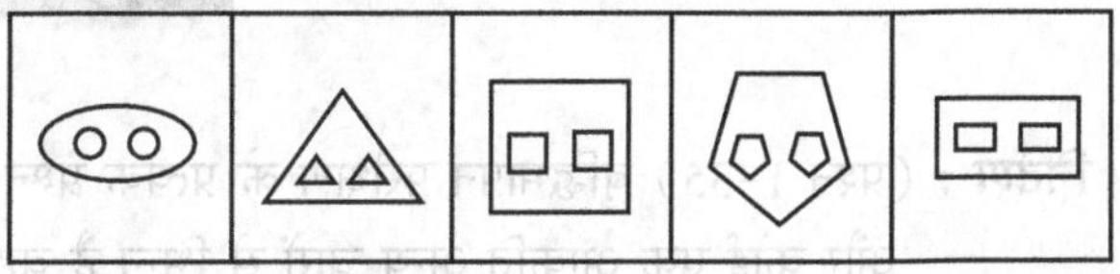

28.
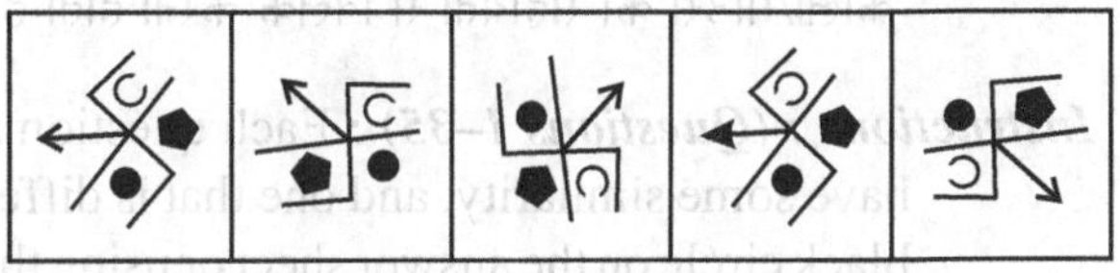

29.
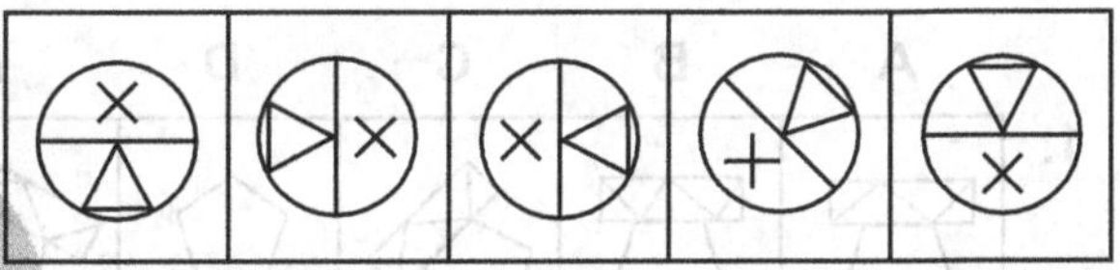

30.
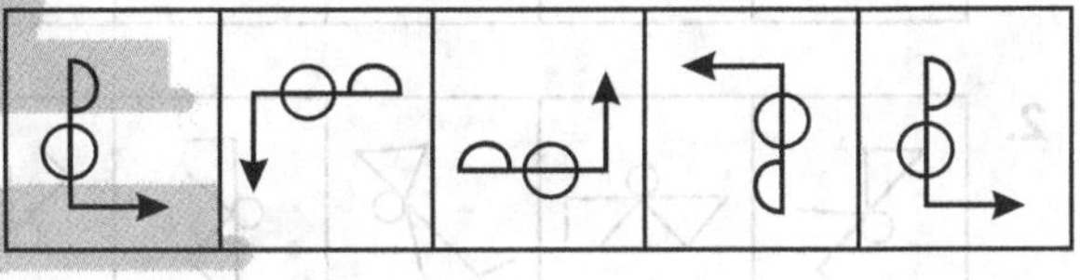

31.
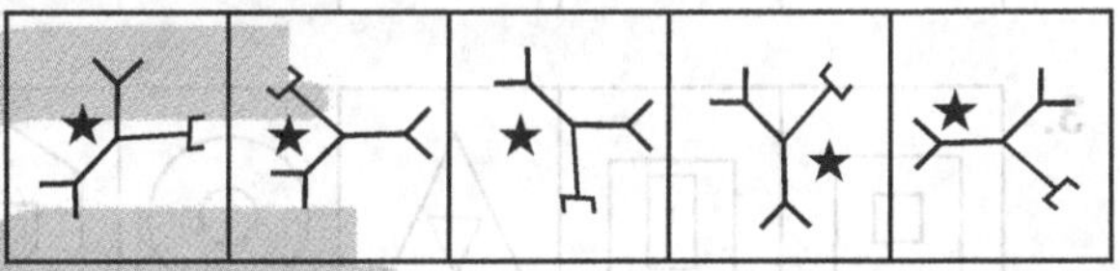

32.
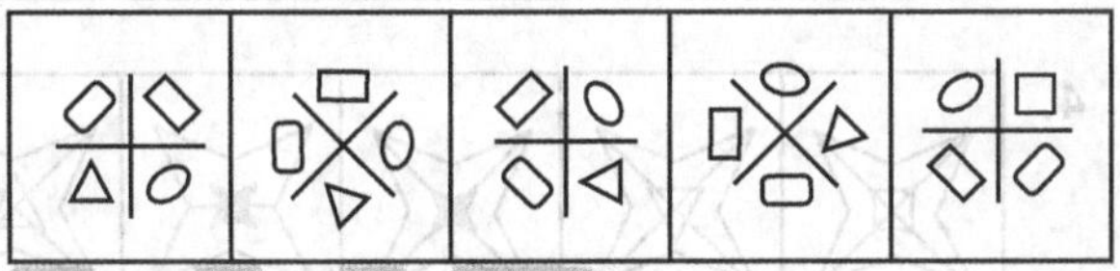

33.
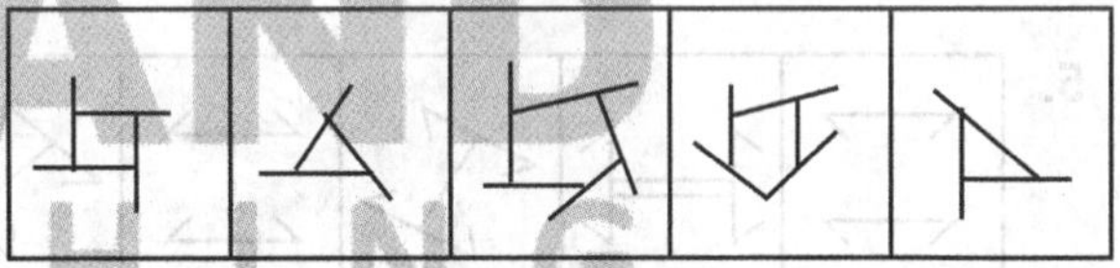

34.
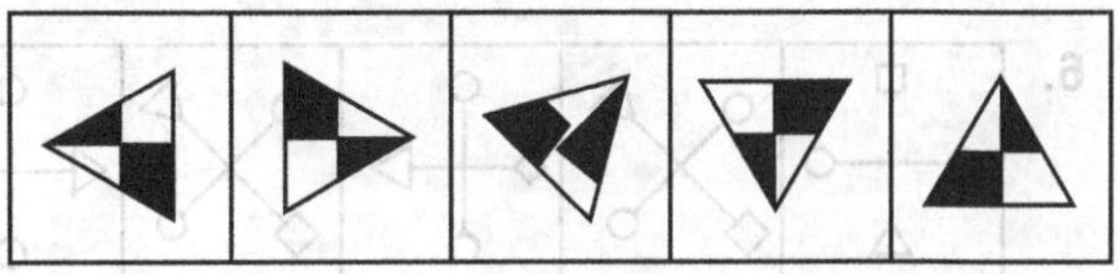

35.
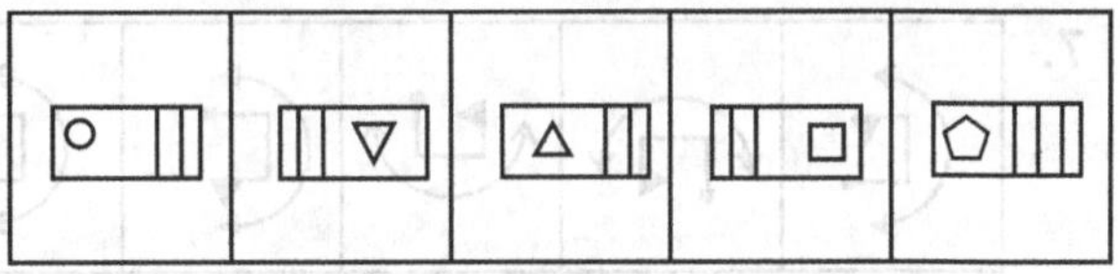

PRACTICE SET-17

Total Ques.- 35
Time - 10 Min.

निर्देश : (प्रश्न 1-35) बुद्धिमापन परीक्षण के प्रत्येक प्रश्न में पाँच आकृतियाँ दिए जाते हैं जिसमें से चार आकृतियाँ में कुछ समानता और कोई एक आकृति अन्य चारों से भिन्न है वही भिन्न आकृति आपका उत्तर होगा जिसे दिए गए उत्तर-पत्रक में गोले को काला/माउस की सहायता से क्लिक करना होता है और इसके लिए 10 मिनट का समय दिया जाता है।

Instructions : (Questions 1–35) : Each question in the Intelligence Test consists of five figures, four of which have some similarity, and one that is different from the other four is your answer. You must click on the black circle on the answer sheet or using the mouse. You are given 10 minutes to complete the test.

A B C D E

1. 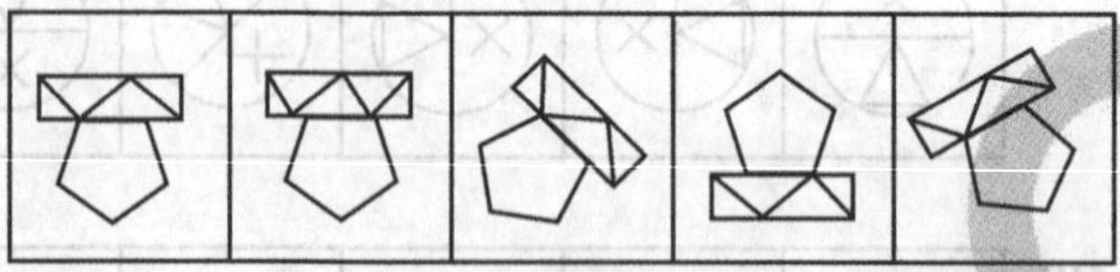

2. 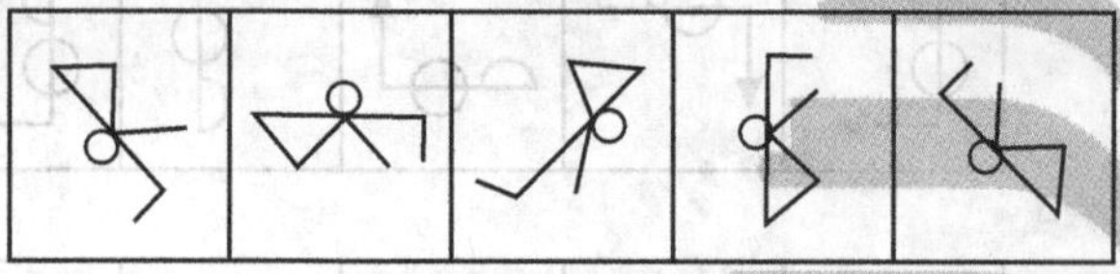

3. 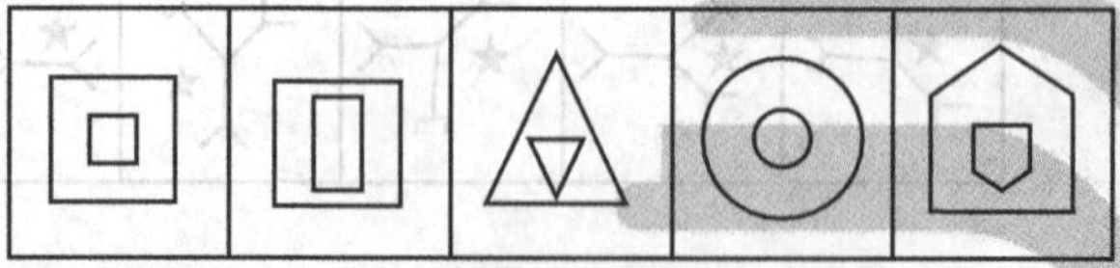

4. 

5. 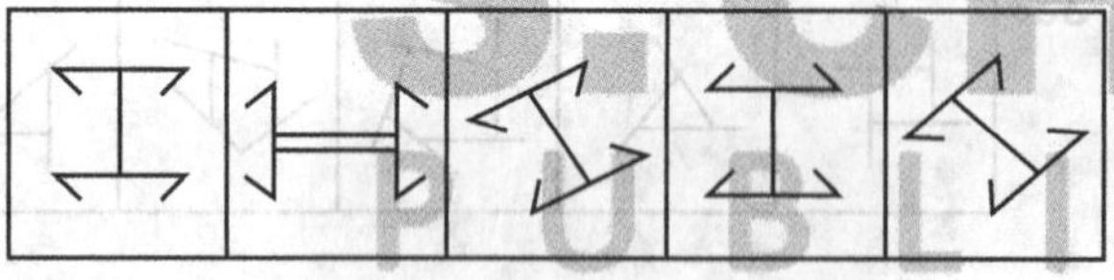

6. 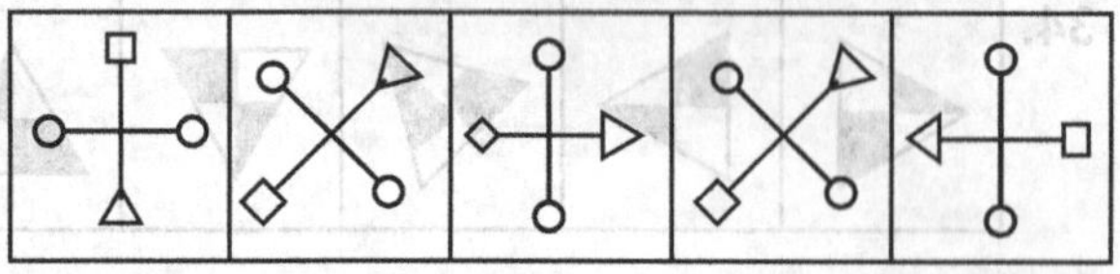

7. 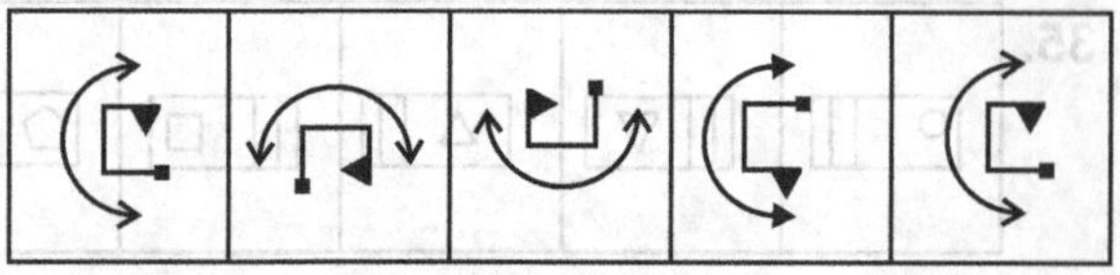

8. 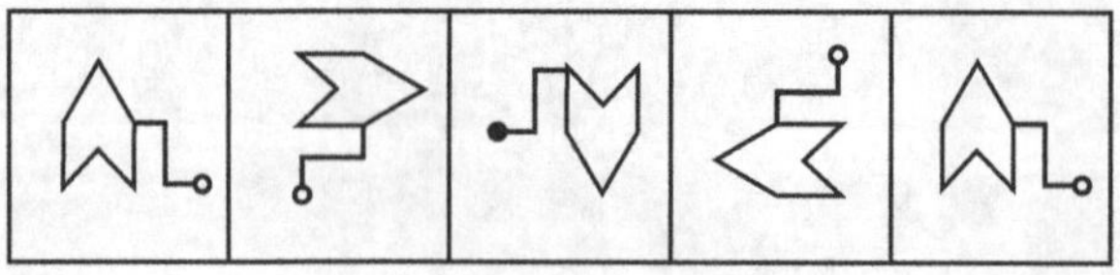

A B C D E

9. 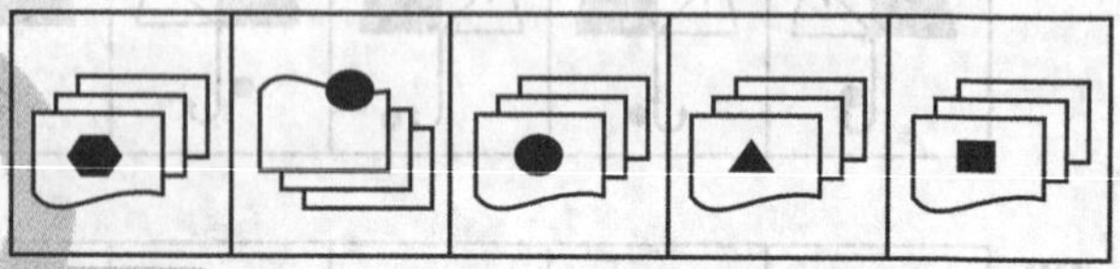

10. 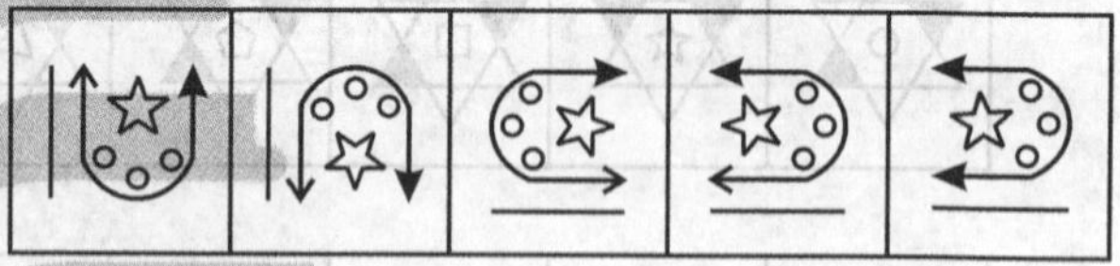

11. 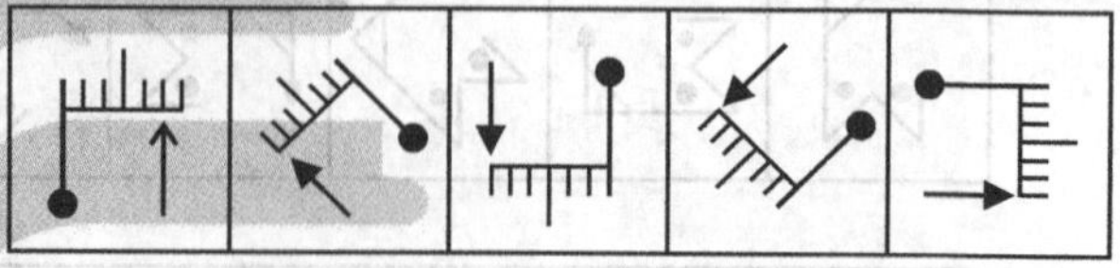

12. 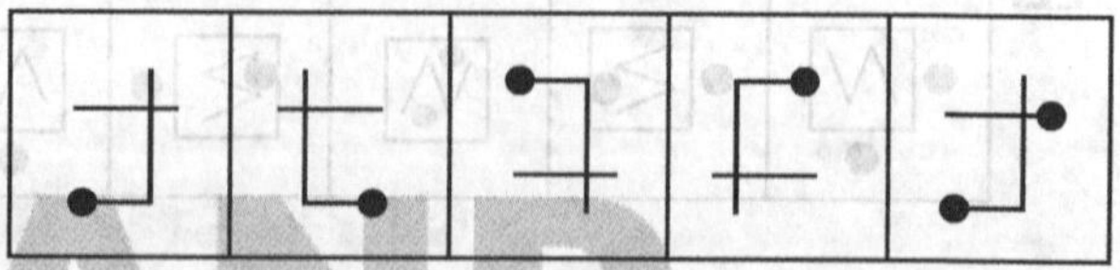

13. 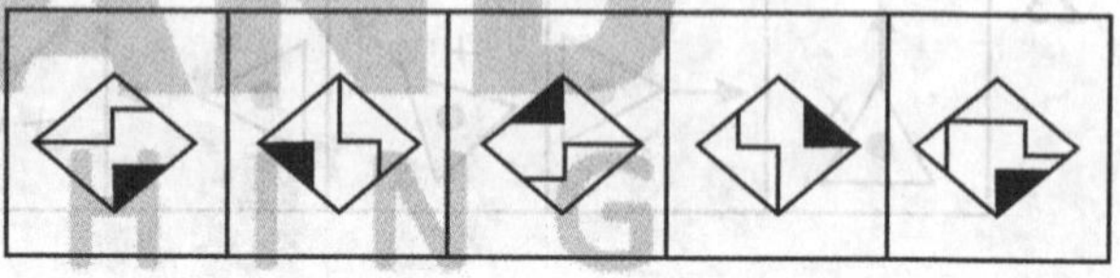

14. 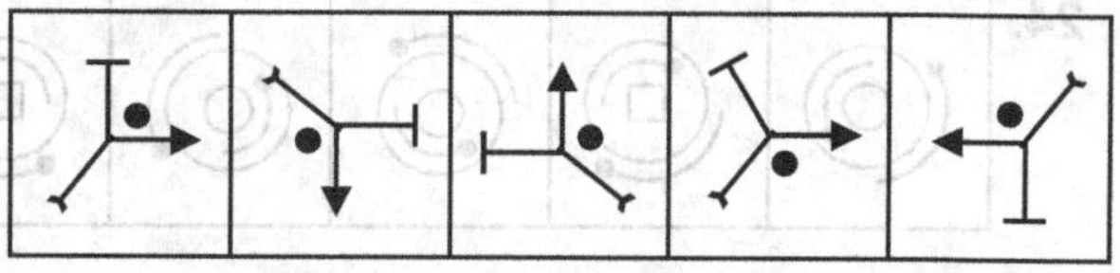

15. 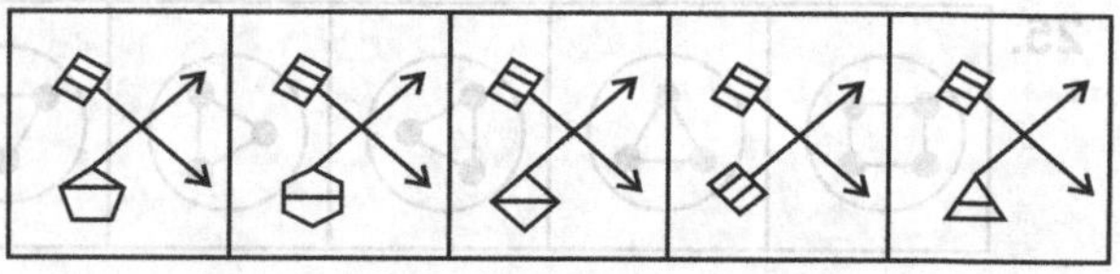

16. 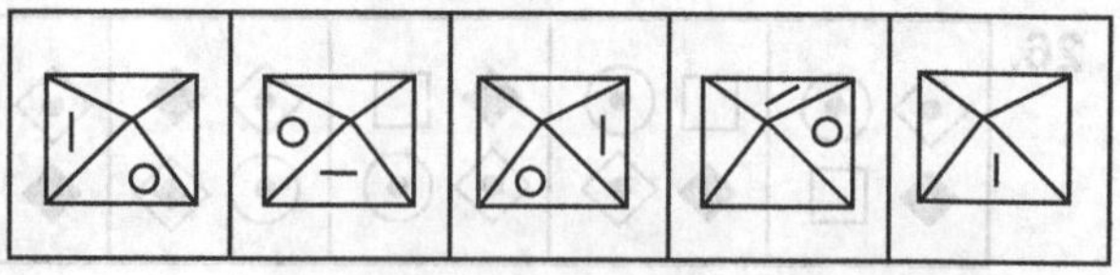

A B C D E

17.
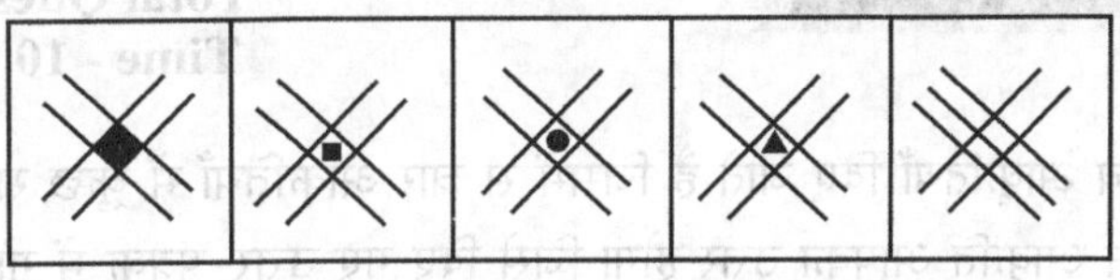

18.
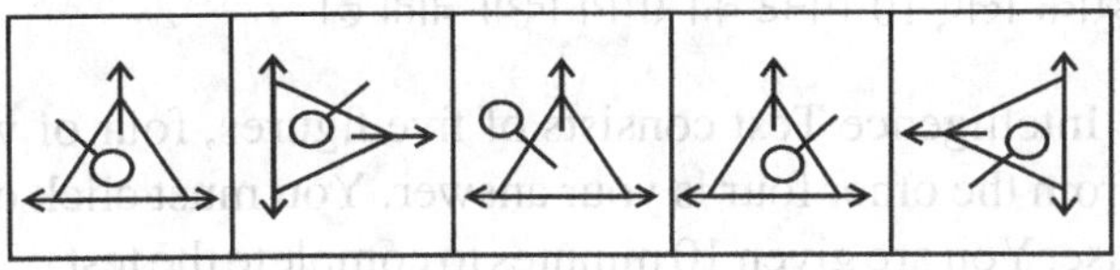

19.
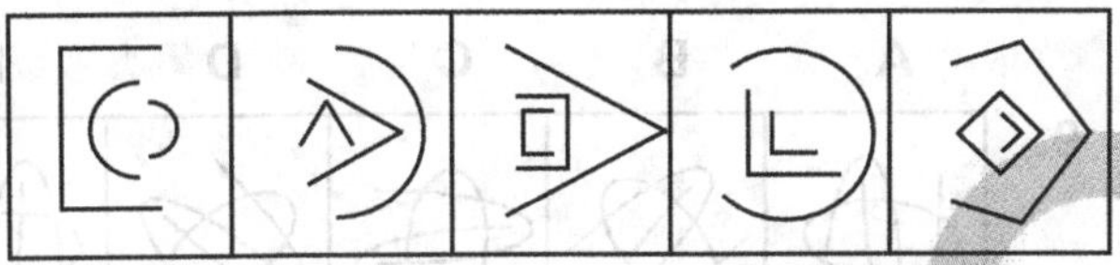

20.
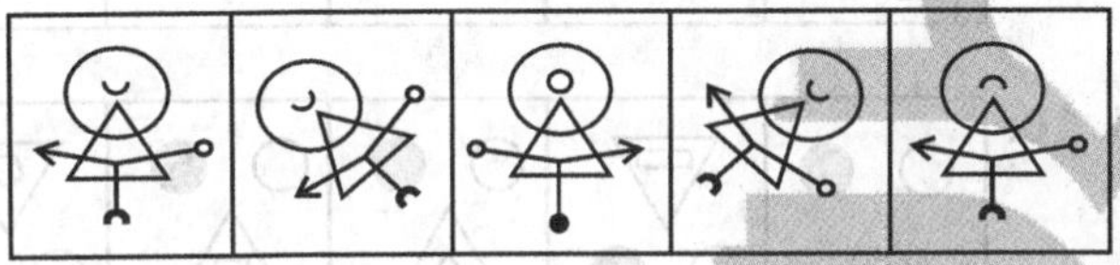

21.
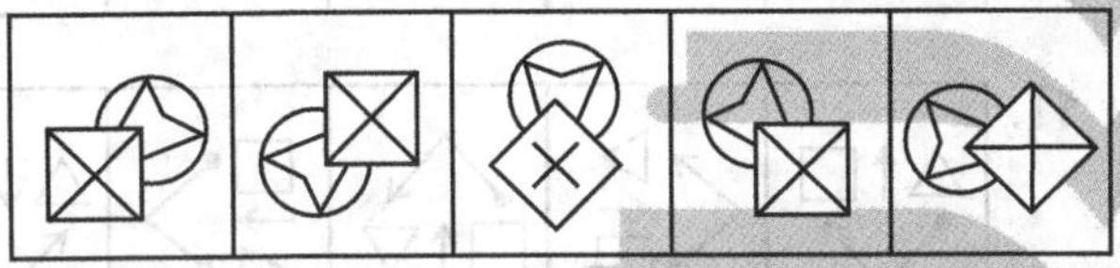

22.
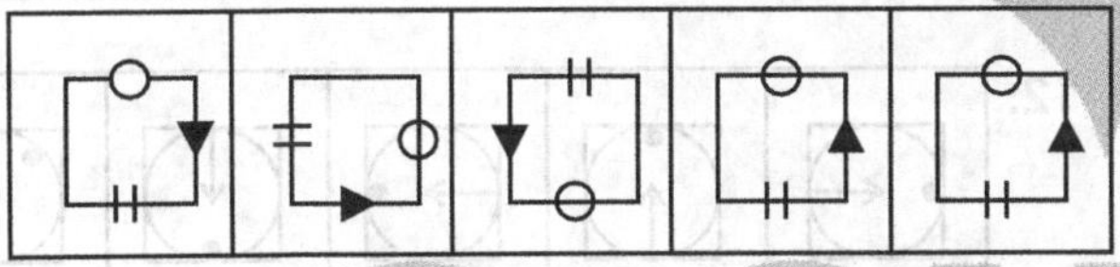

23.
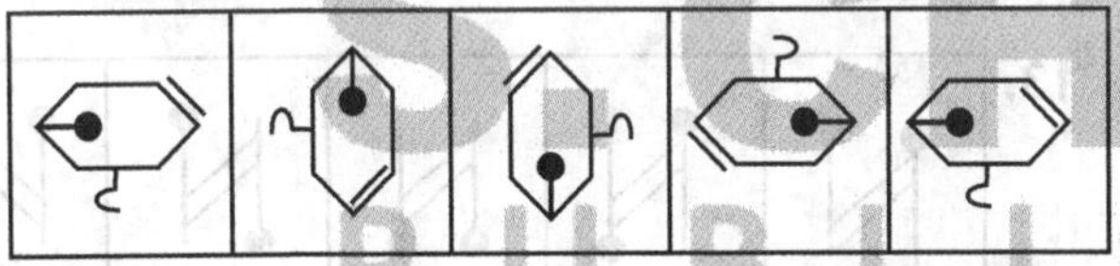

24.
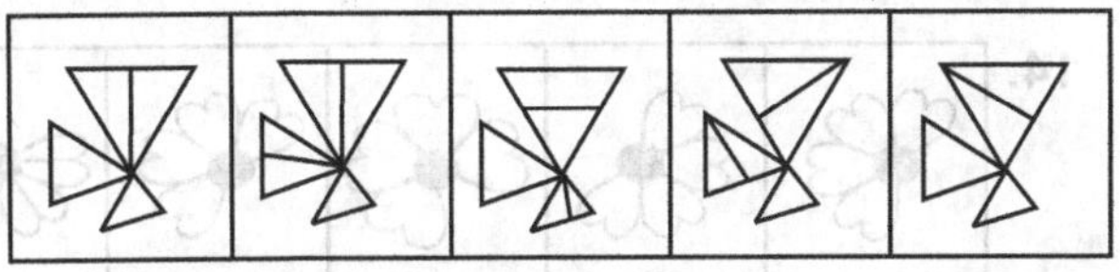

25.
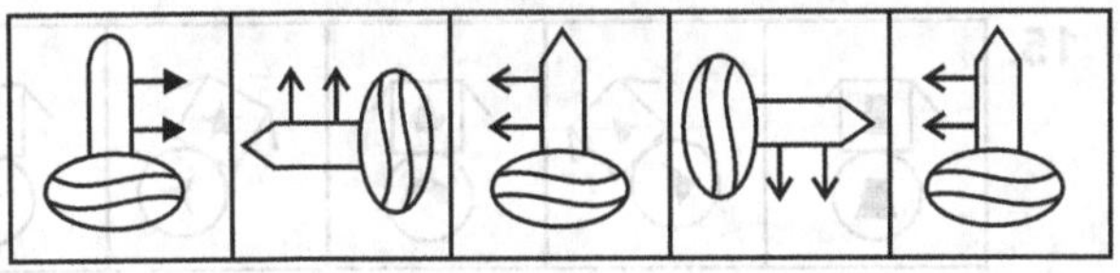

26.
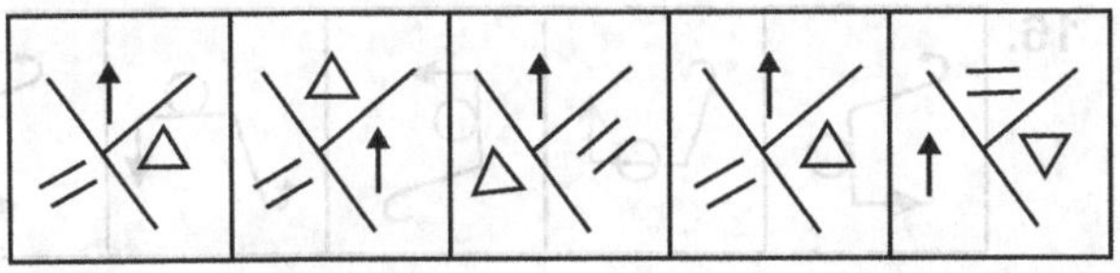

A B C D E

27.
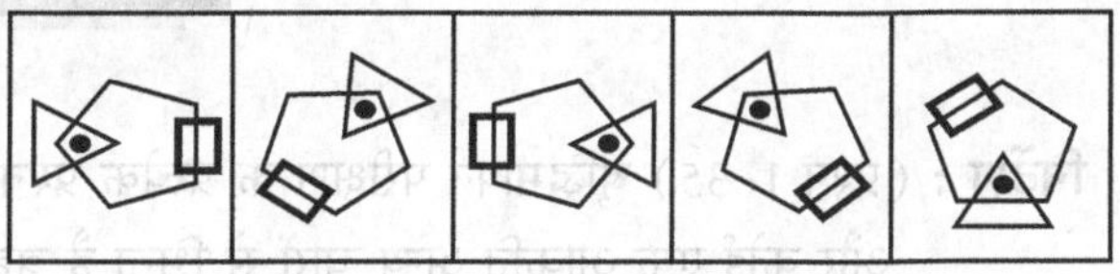

28.
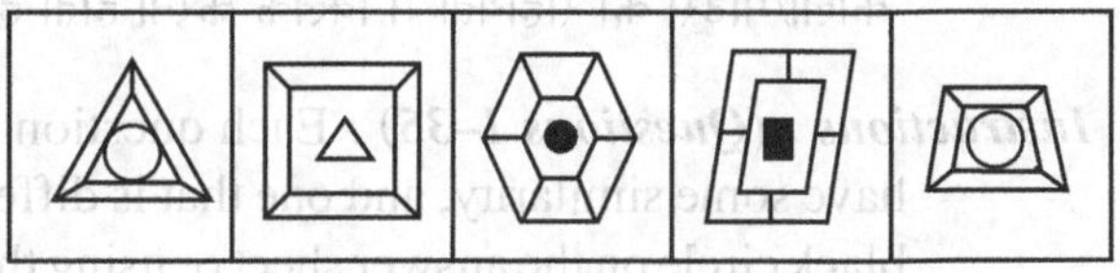

29.
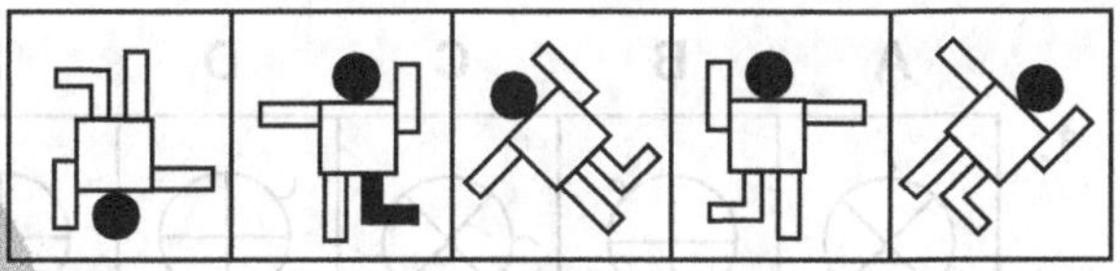

30.
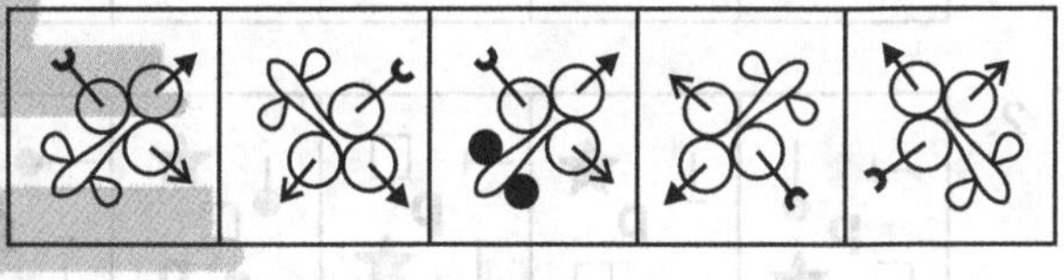

31.
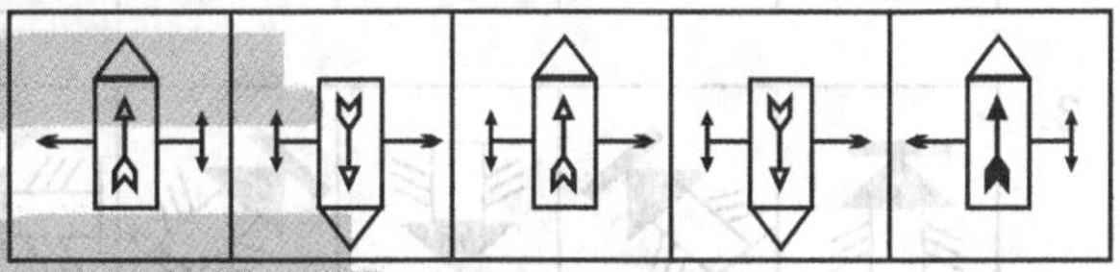

32.
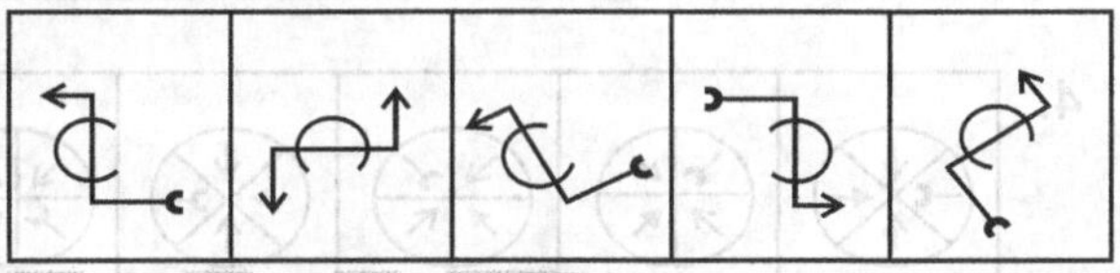

33.
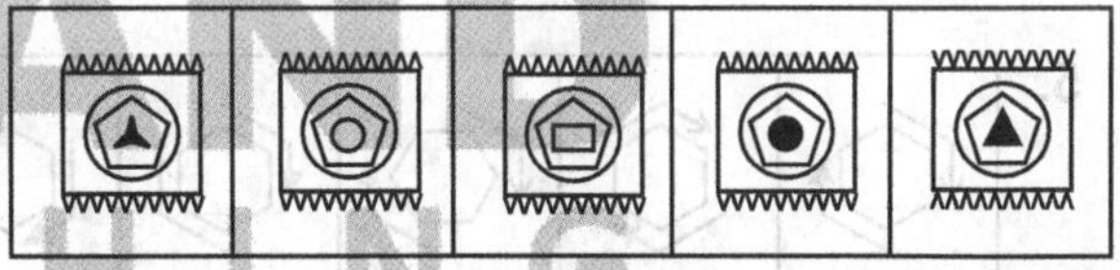

34.
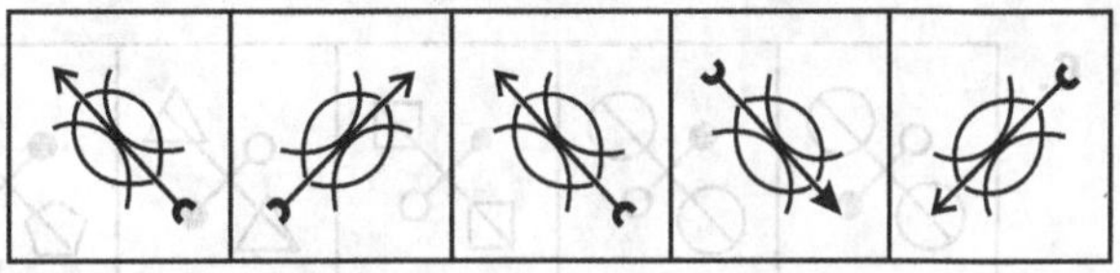

35.
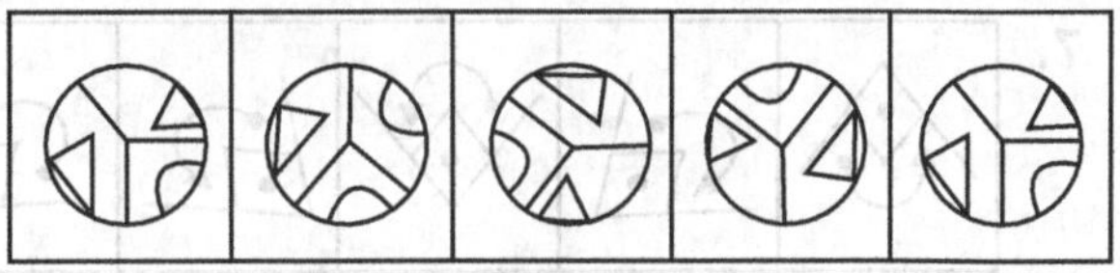

PRACTICE SET-18

Total Ques.- 35
Time - 10 Min.

निर्देश : (प्रश्न 1-35) बुद्धिमापन परीक्षण के प्रत्येक प्रश्न में पाँच आकृतियाँ दिए जाते हैं जिसमें से चार आकृतियाँ में कुछ समानता और कोई एक आकृति अन्य चारों से भिन्न है वही भिन्न आकृति आपका उत्तर होगा जिसे दिए गए उत्तर-पत्रक में गोले को काला/माउस की सहायता से क्लिक करना होता है और इसके लिए 10 मिनट का समय दिया जाता है।

Instructions : (Questions 1–35) : Each question in the Intelligence Test consists of five figures, four of which have some similarity, and one that is different from the other four is your answer. You must click on the black circle on the answer sheet or using the mouse. You are given 10 minutes to complete the test.

A B C D E

1. 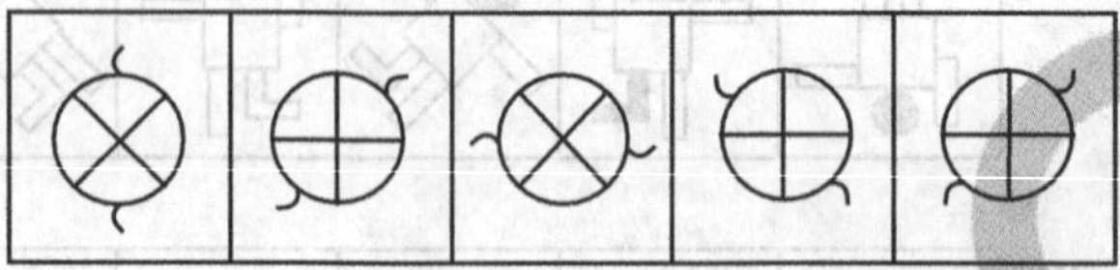

2. 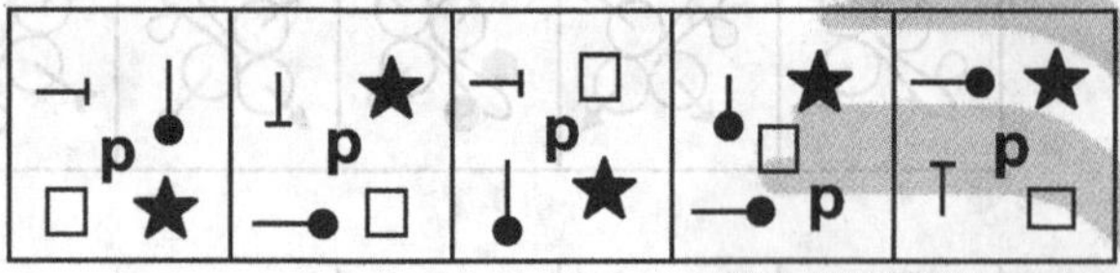

3. 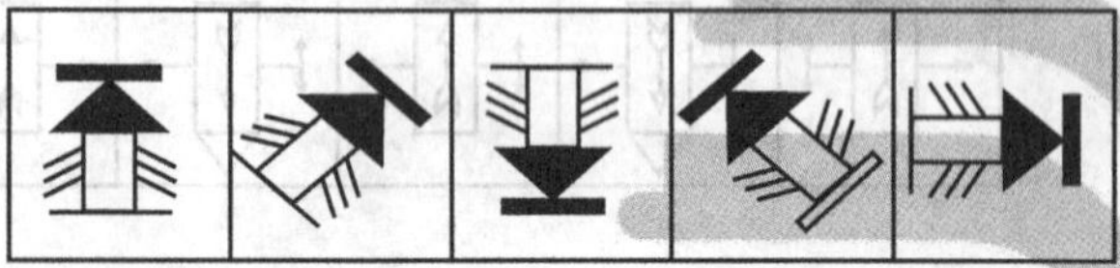

4. 

5. 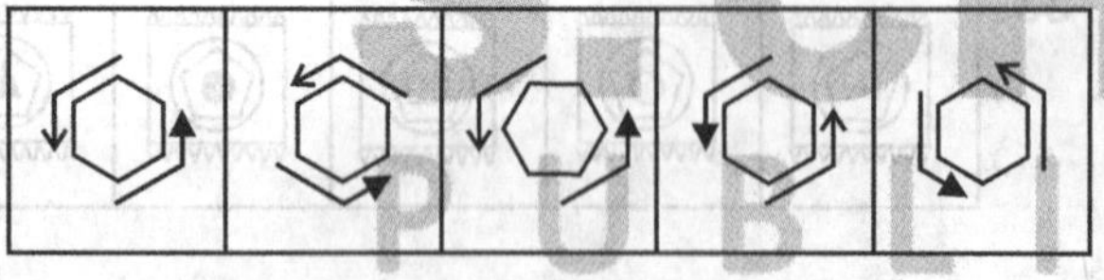

6. 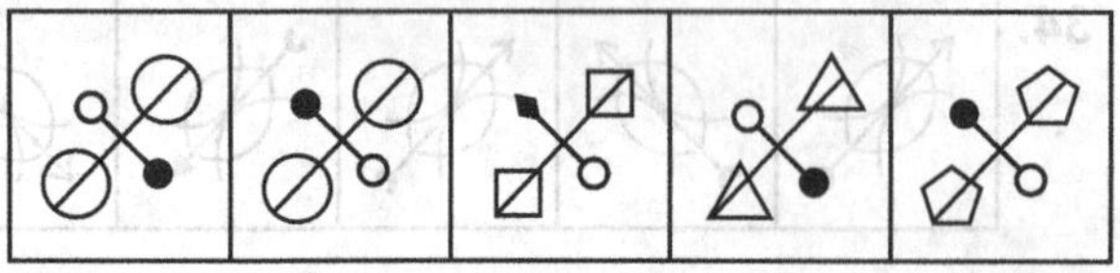

7. 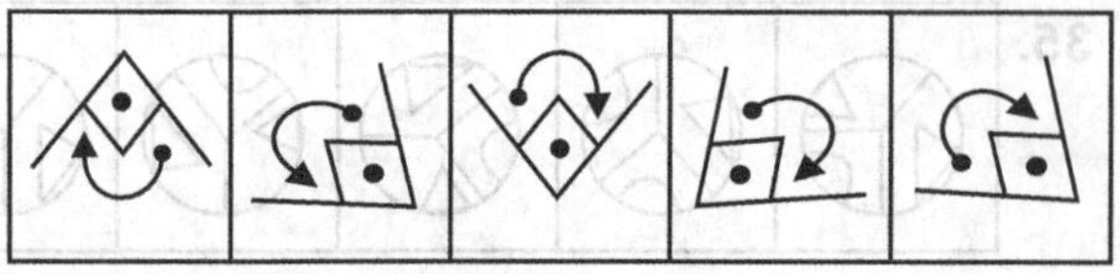

8. 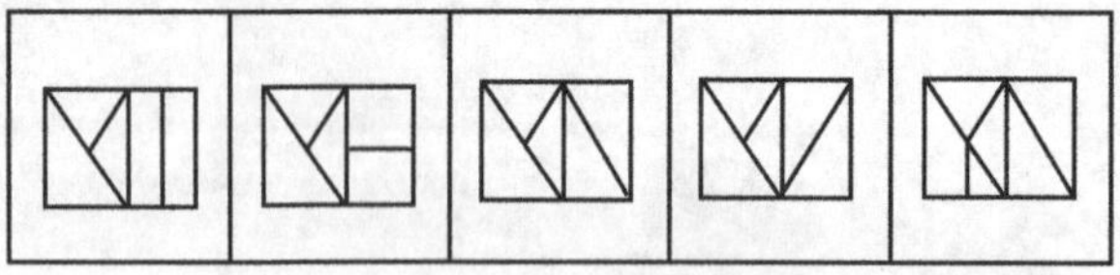

A B C D E

9. 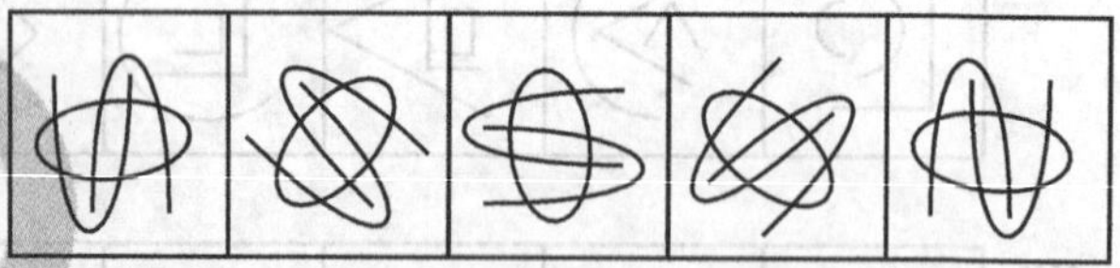

10. 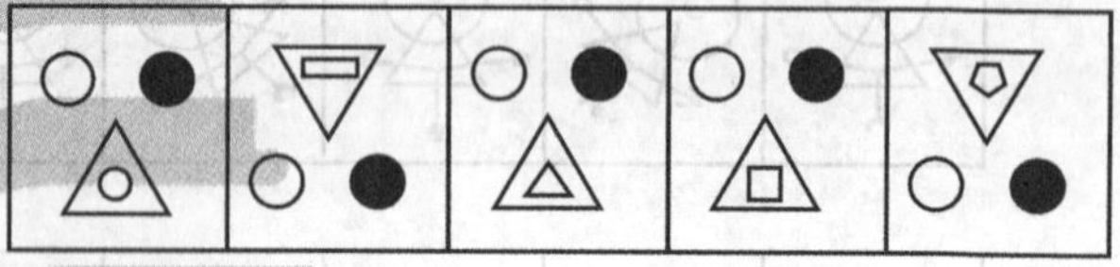

11. 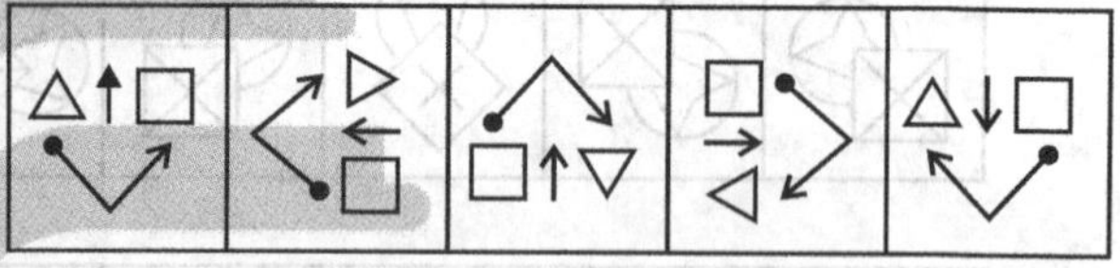

12. 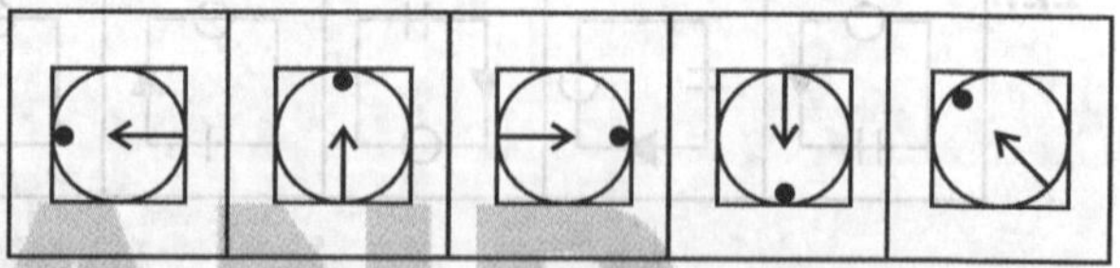

13. 

14. 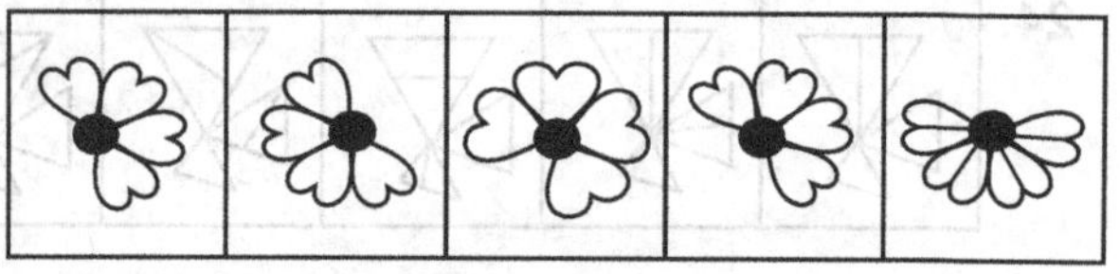

15. 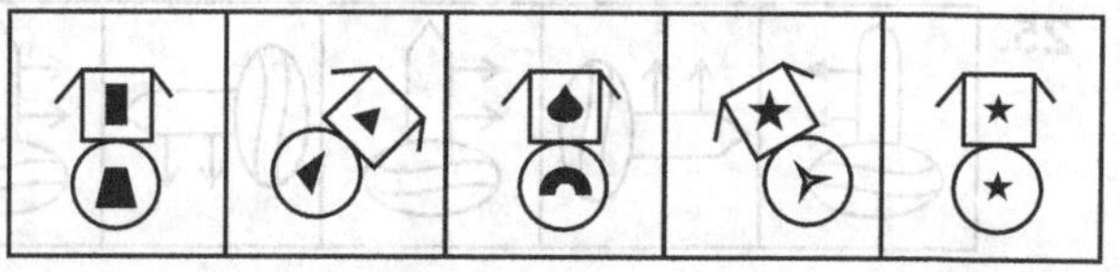

16. 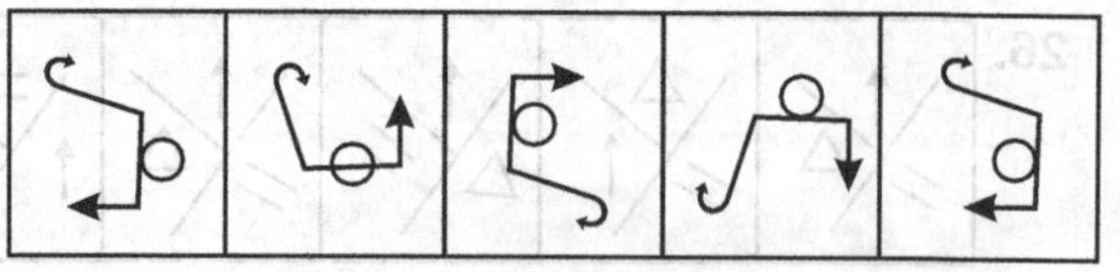

	A	B	C	D	E
17.	A	T	C	U	O

18.
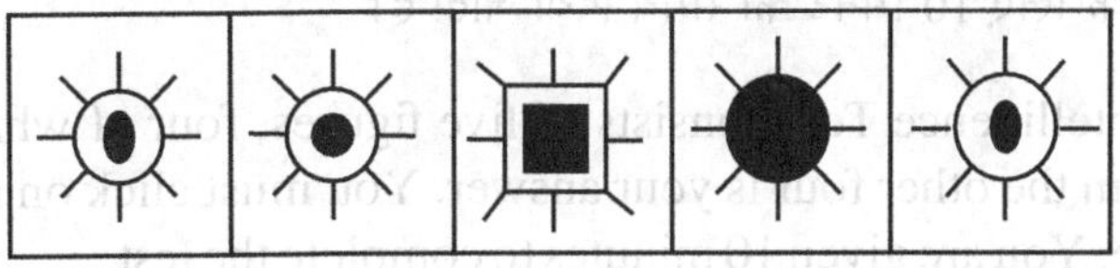

19.
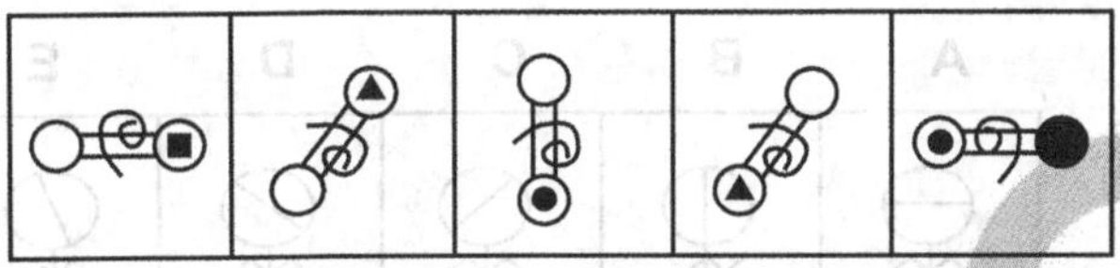

20.
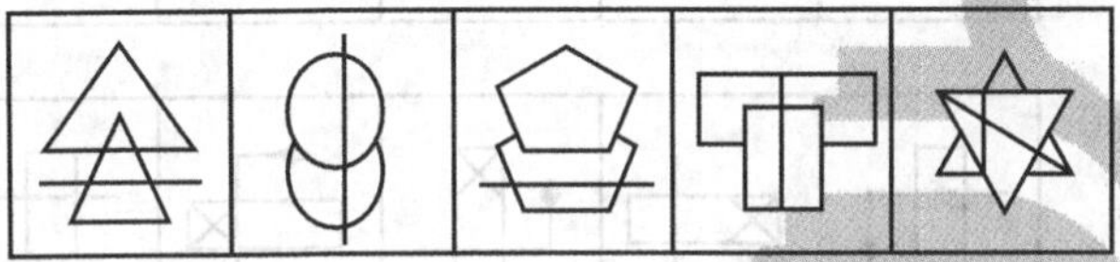

21.
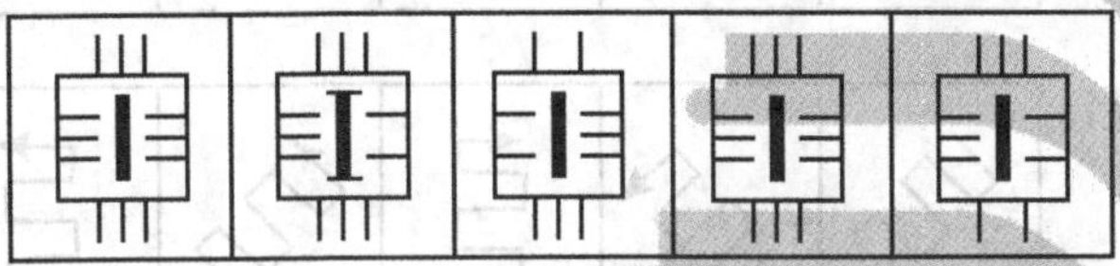

22.
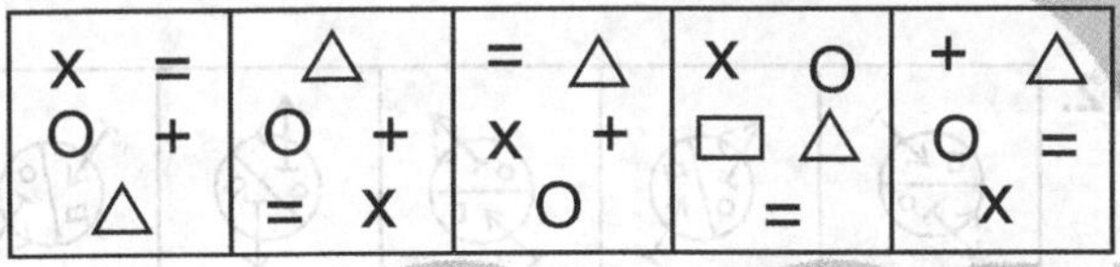

23.
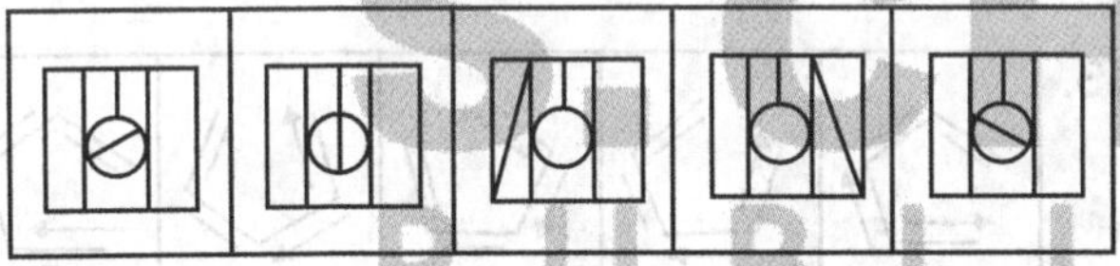

24.
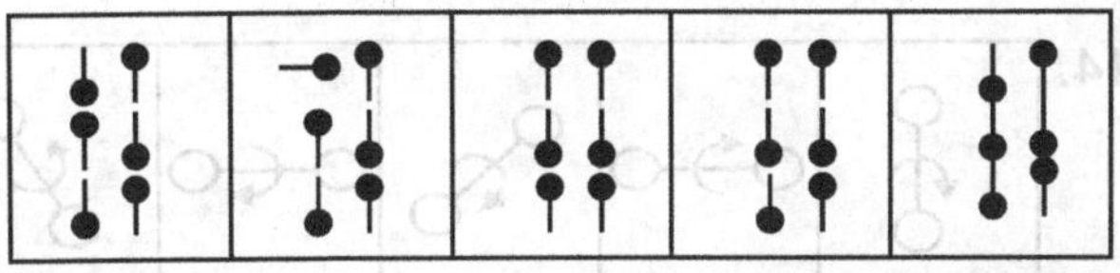

25.
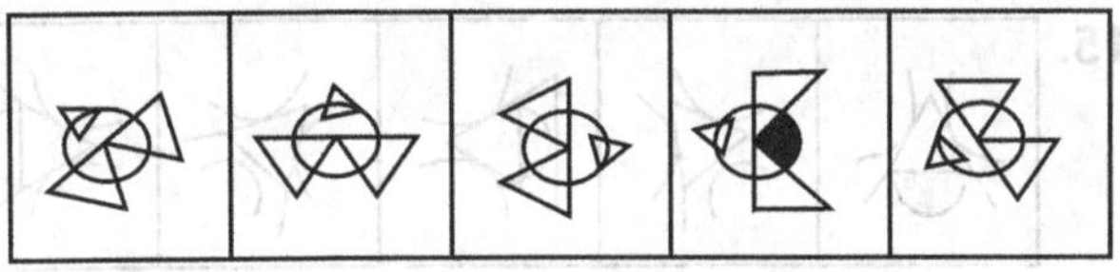

26.
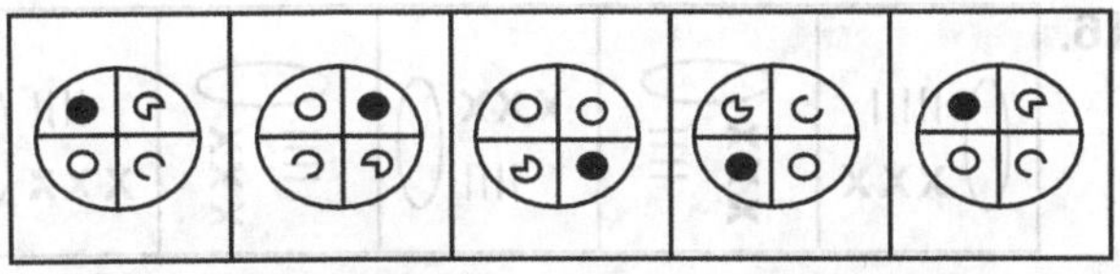

27.
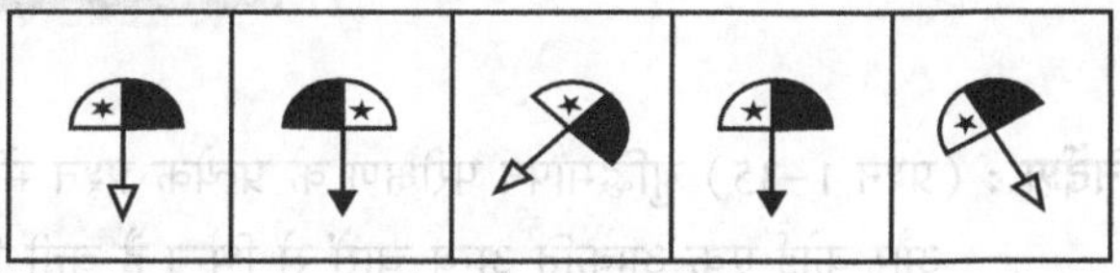

28.
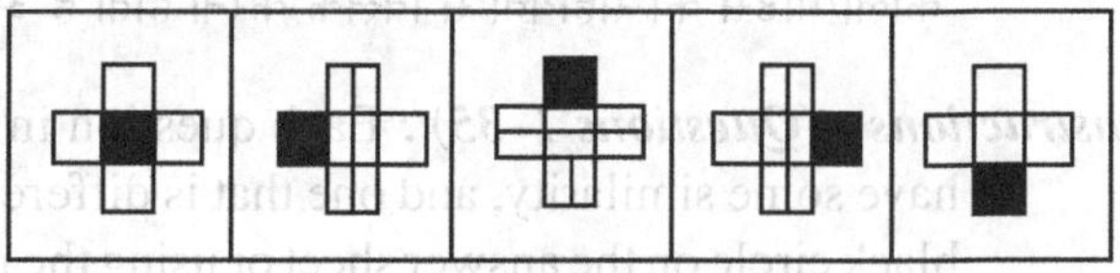

29.
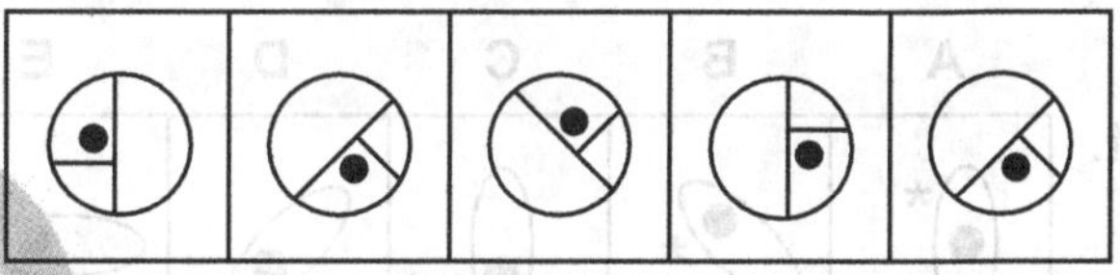

30.
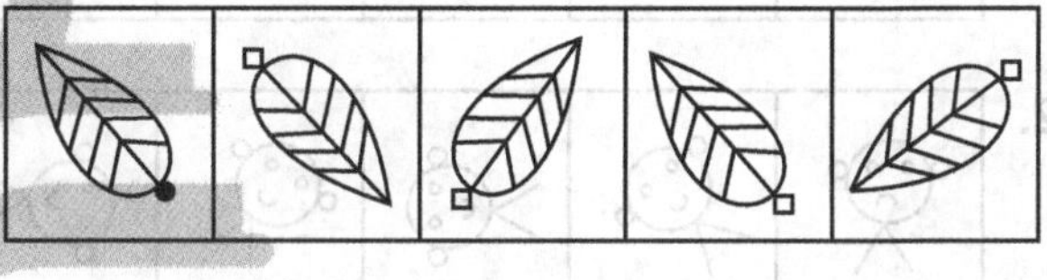

31.
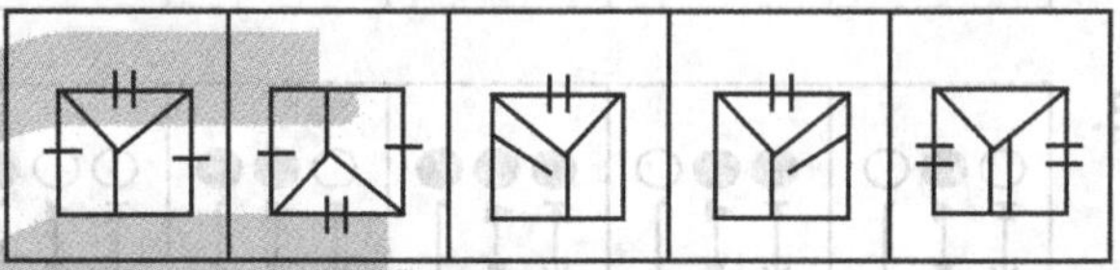

32.
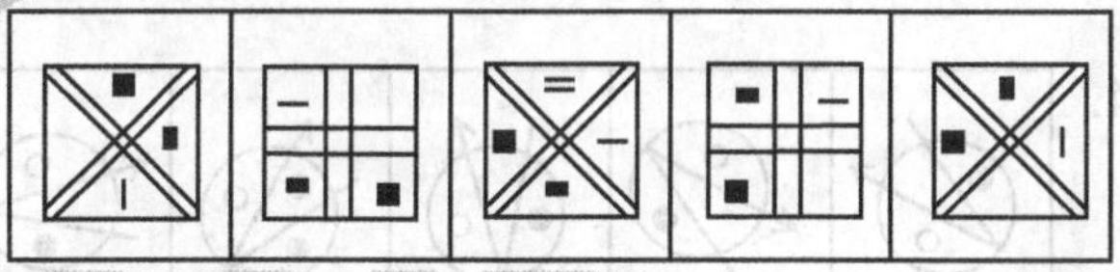

33.
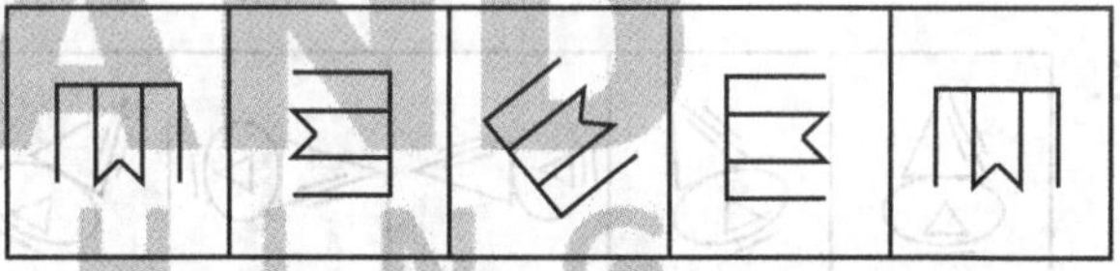

34.
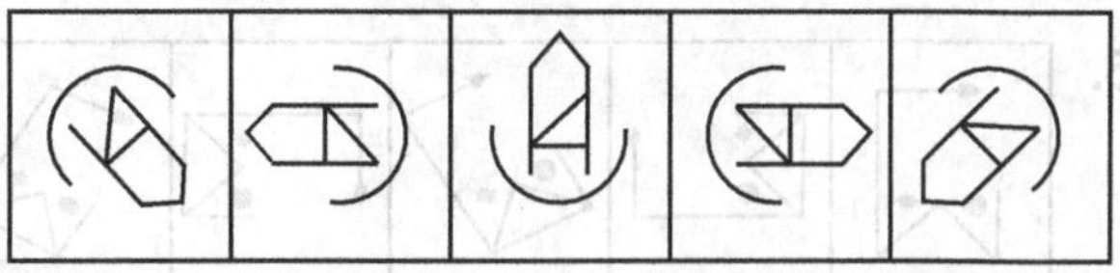

35.
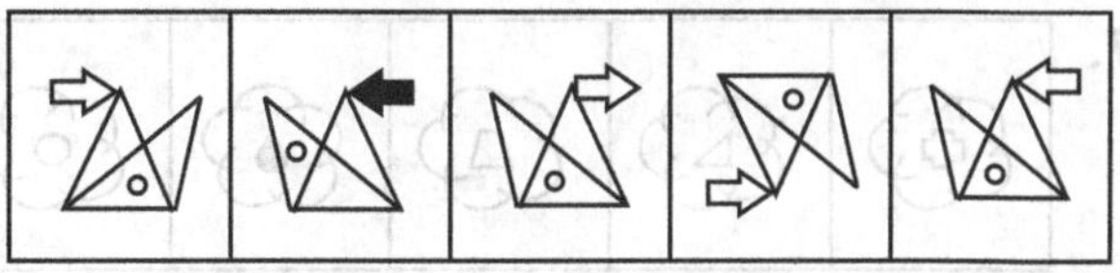

PRACTICE SET-19

Total Ques.- 35
Time - 10 Min.

निर्देश : (प्रश्न 1–35) बुद्धिमापन परीक्षण के प्रत्येक प्रश्न में पाँच आकृतियाँ दिए जाते हैं जिसमें से चार आकृतियाँ में कुछ समानता और कोई एक आकृति अन्य चारों से भिन्न है वही भिन्न आकृति आपका उत्तर होगा जिसे दिए गए उत्तर-पत्रक में गोले को काला/माउस की सहायता से क्लिक करना होता है और इसके लिए 10 मिनट का समय दिया जाता है।

Instructions : (Questions 1–35) : Each question in the Intelligence Test consists of five figures, four of which have some similarity, and one that is different from the other four is your answer. You must click on the black circle on the answer sheet or using the mouse. You are given 10 minutes to complete the test.

A B C D E

1. 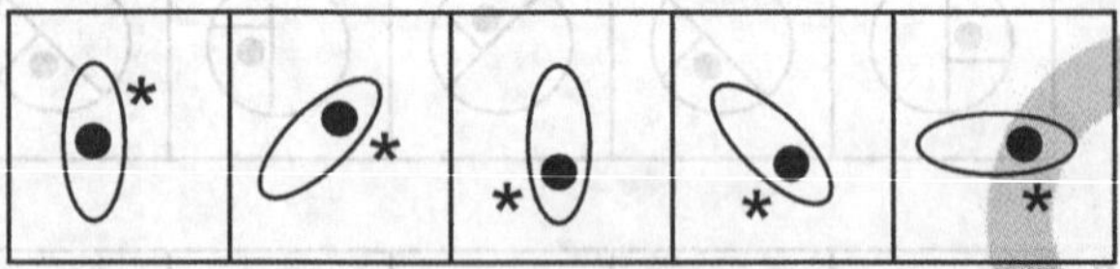

2. 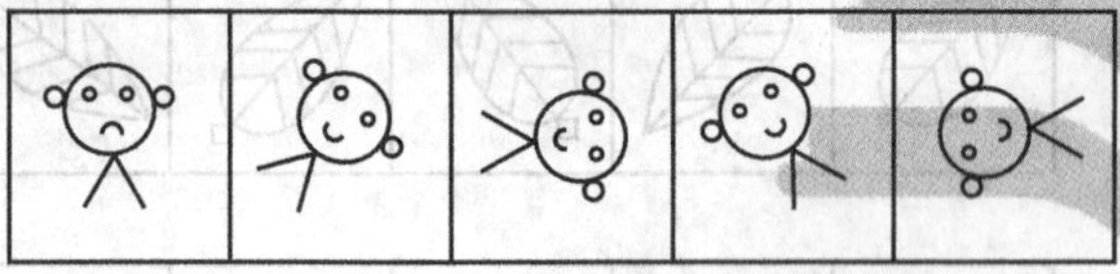

3. 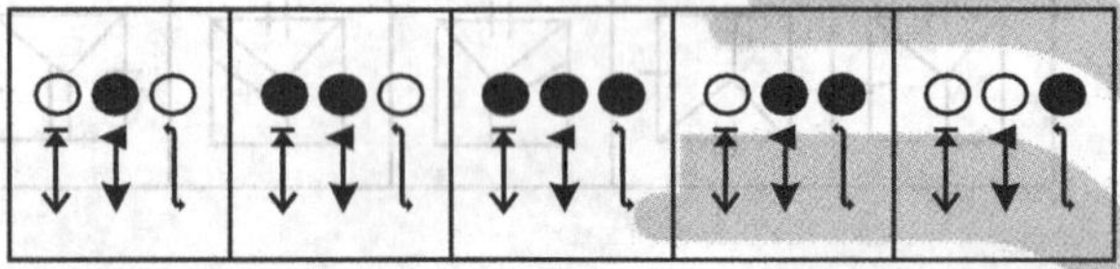

4. 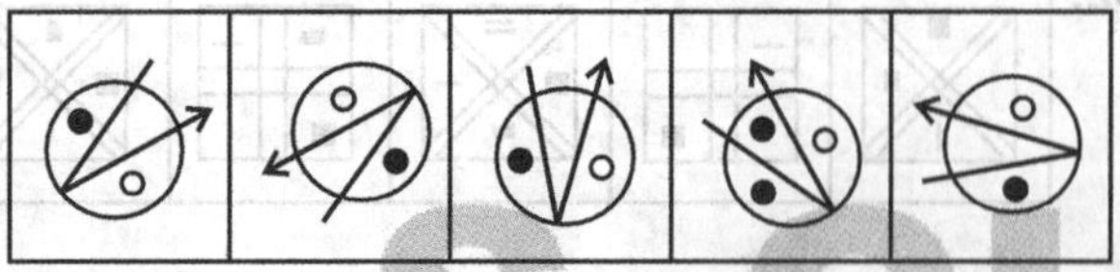

5. 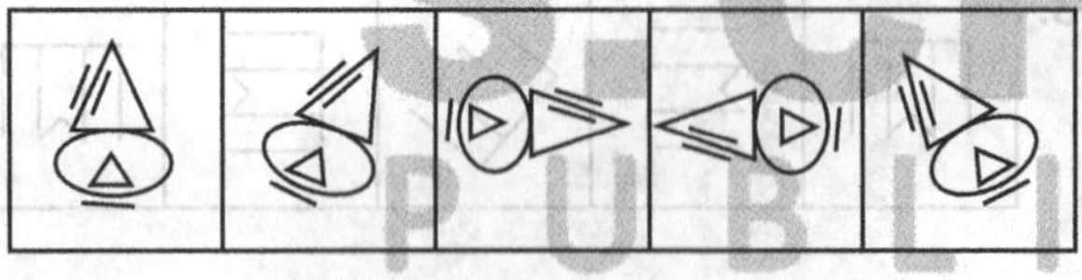

6. 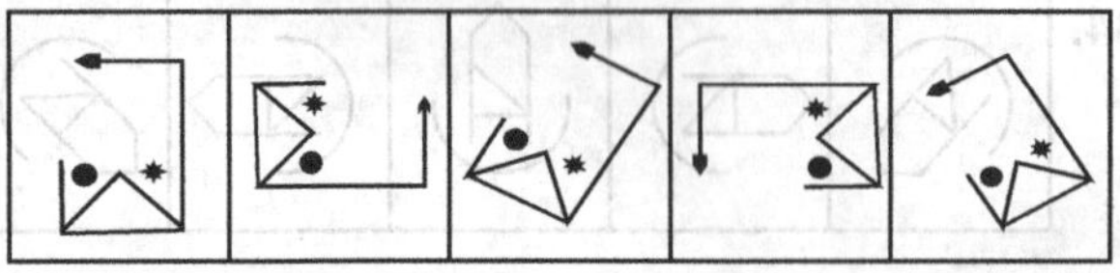

7. 

8. 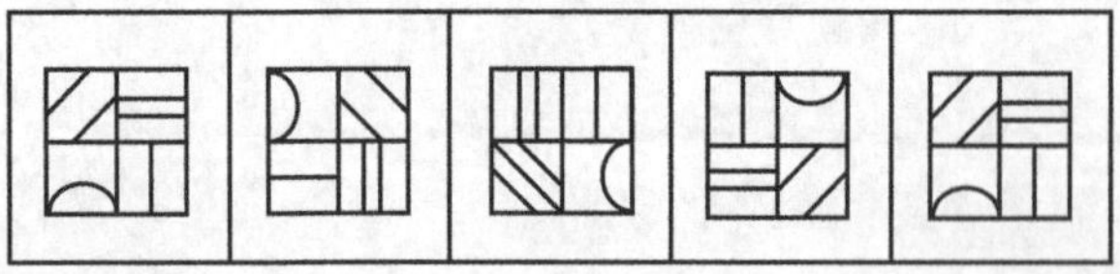

A B C D E

9. 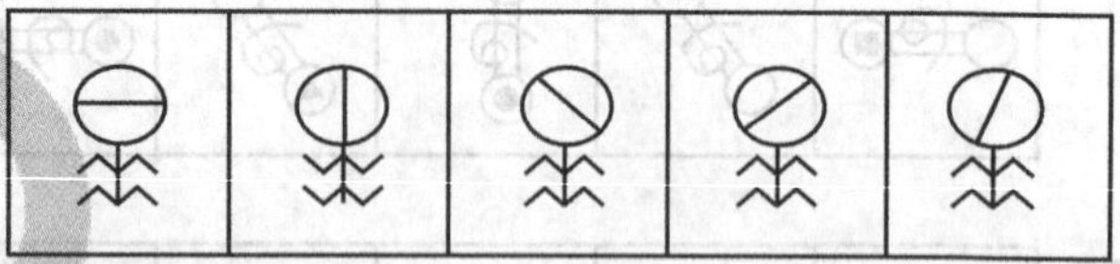

10. 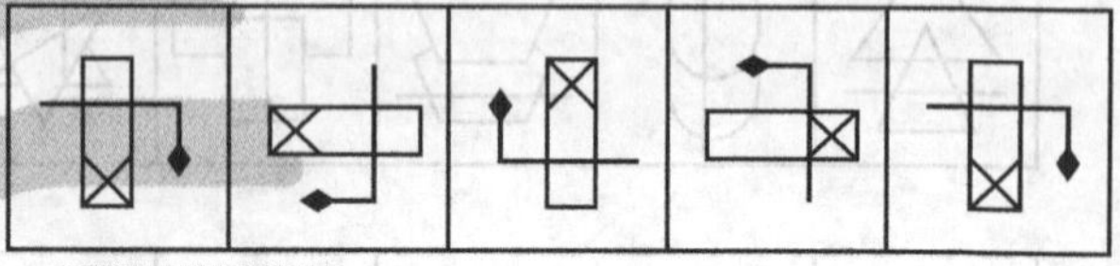

11. 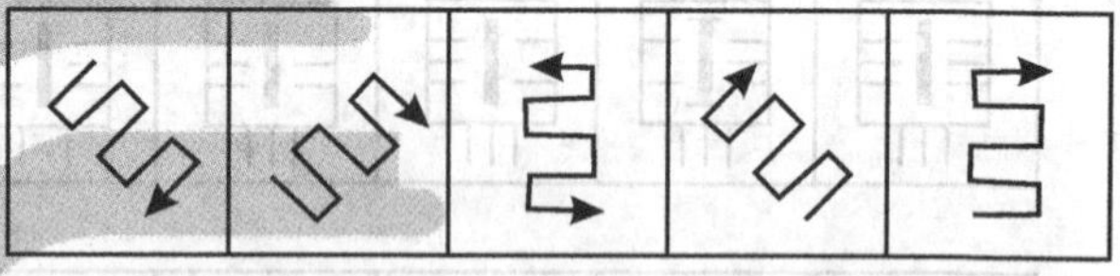

12. 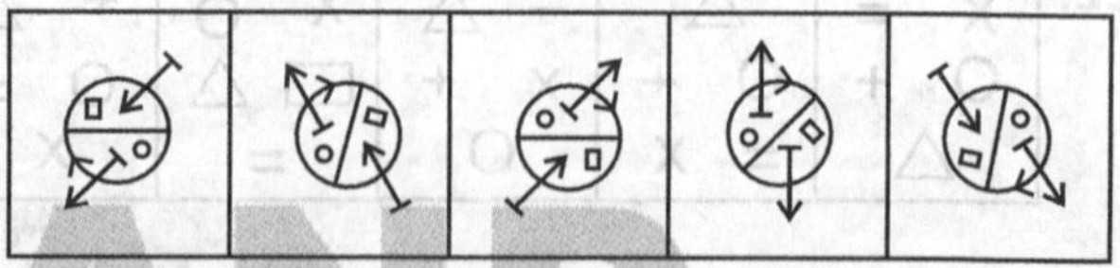

13. 

14. 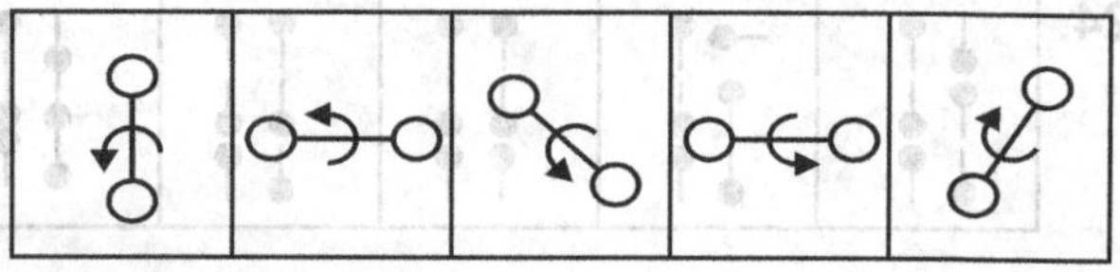

15. 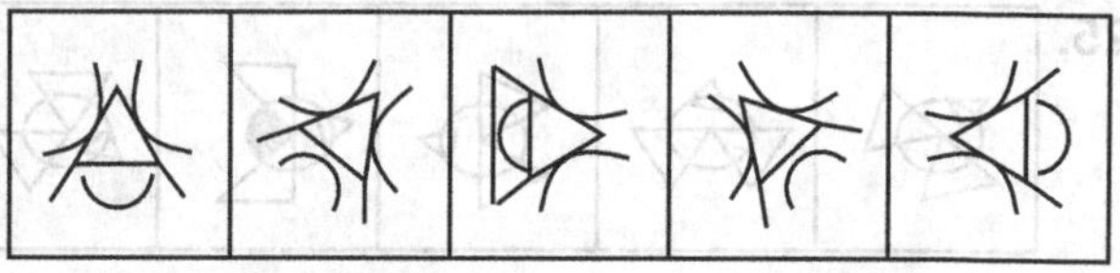

16. 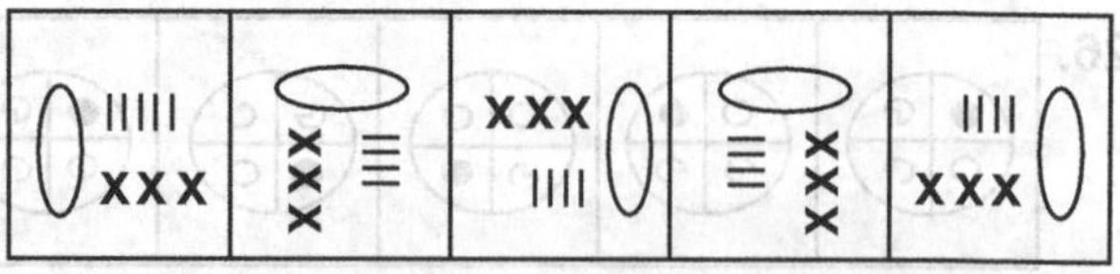

A B C D E

17. 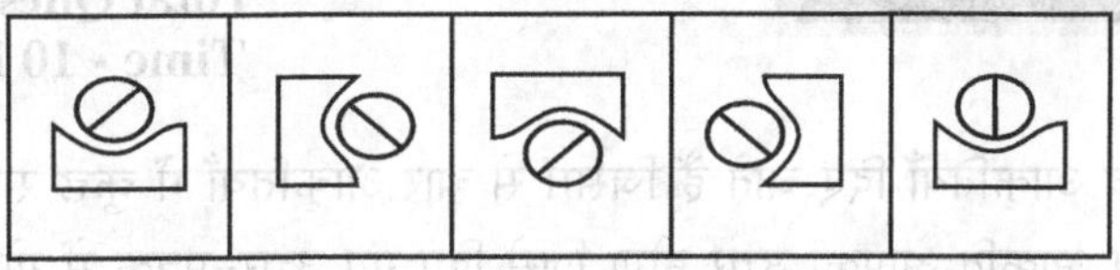

18. 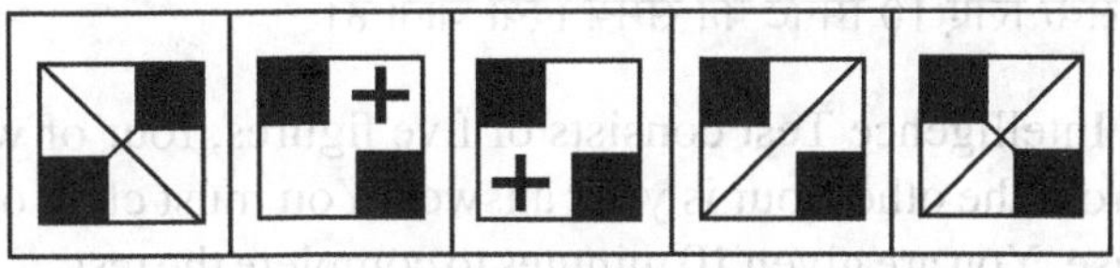

19. 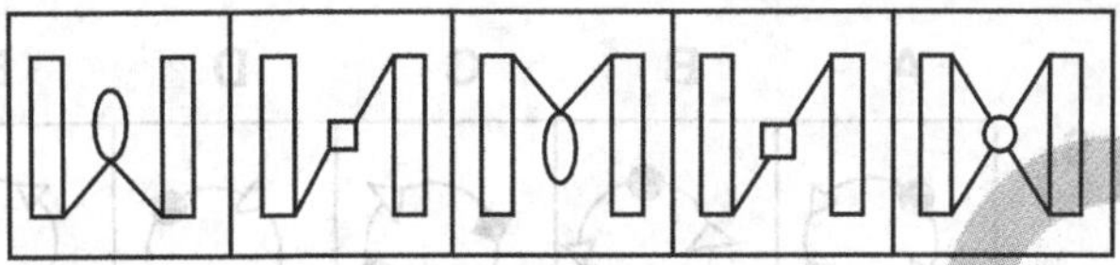

20. 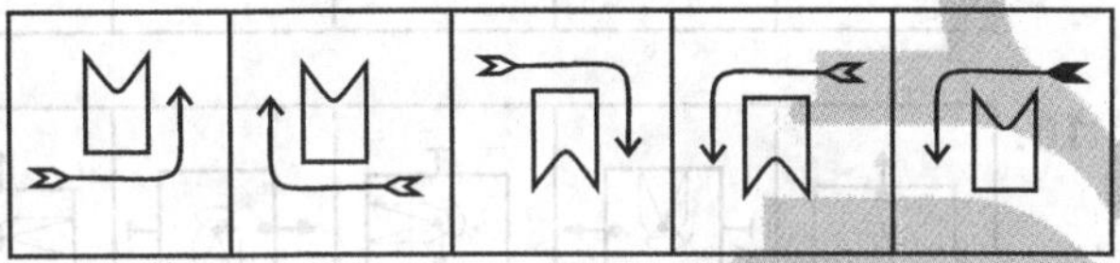

21. 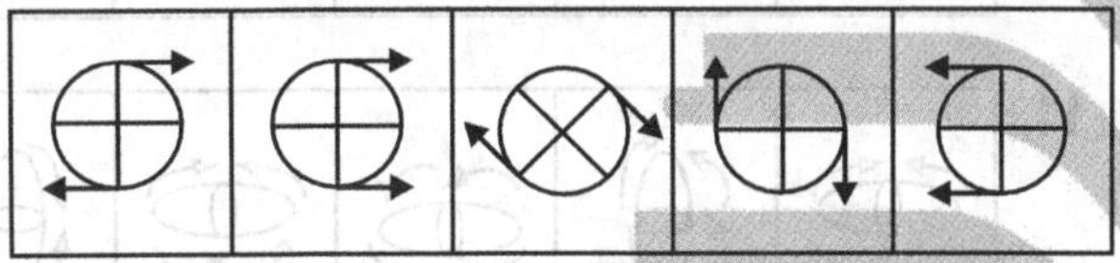

22. 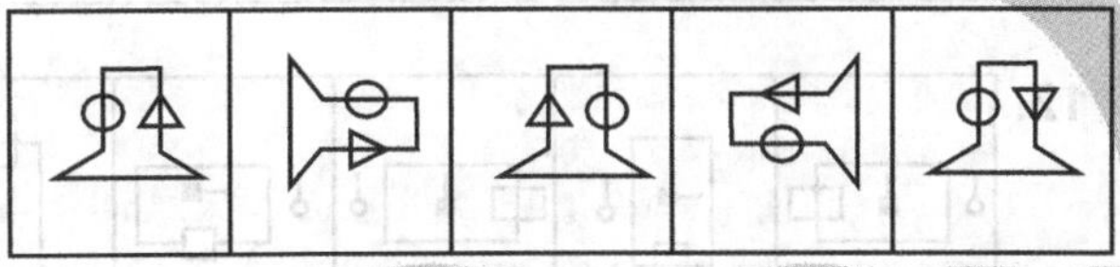

23. 

24. 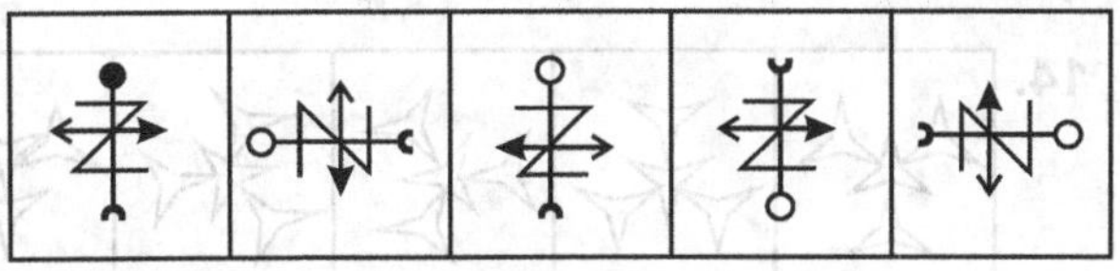

25. 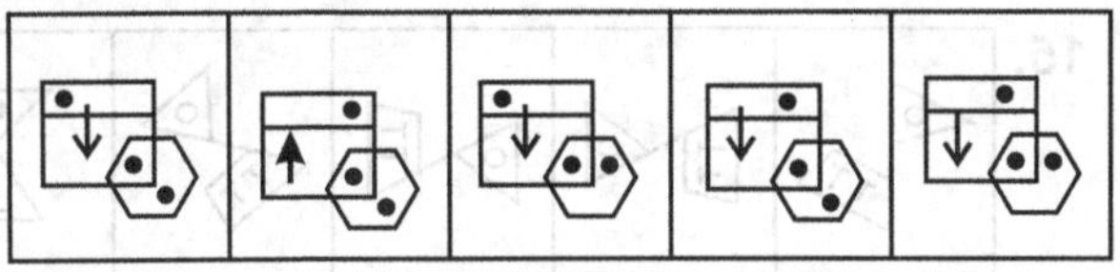

26. 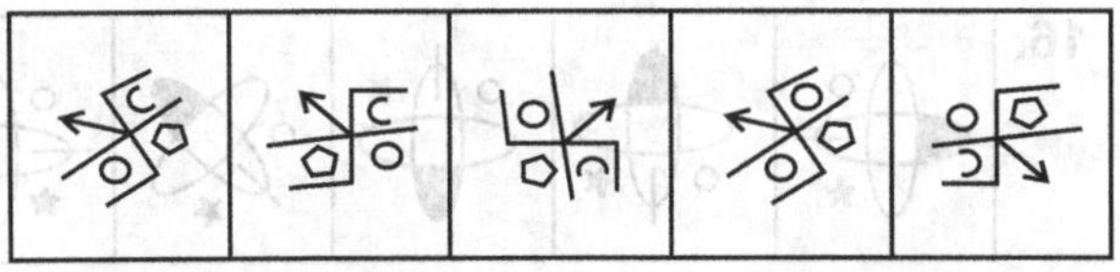

A B C D E

27. 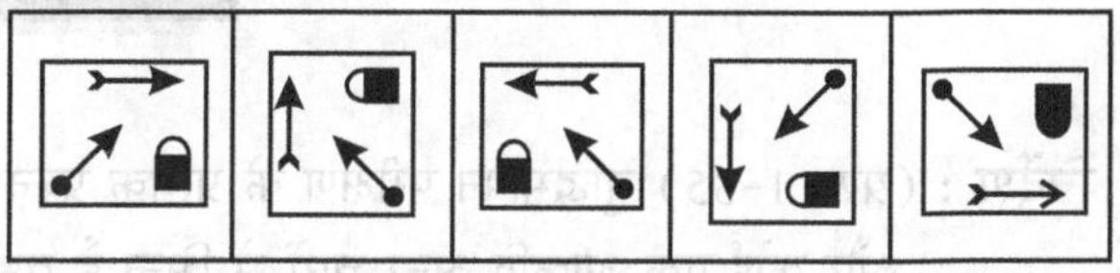

28. 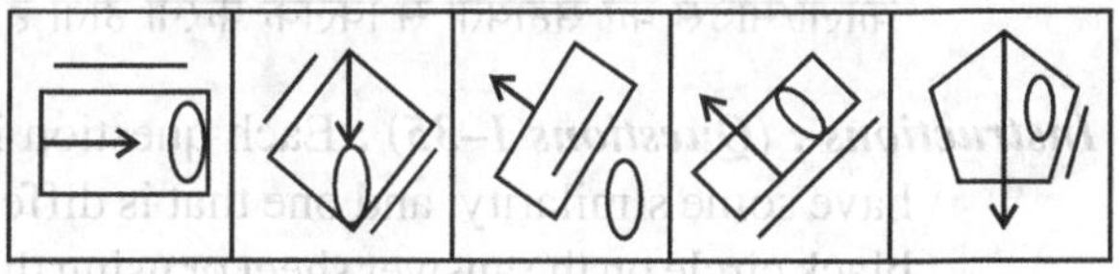

29. 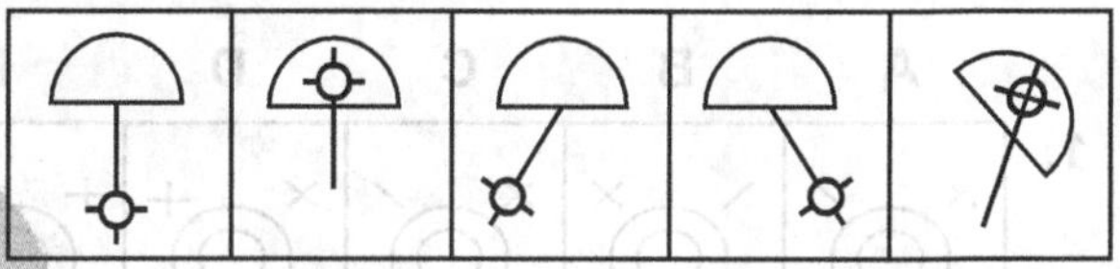

30. 

31. 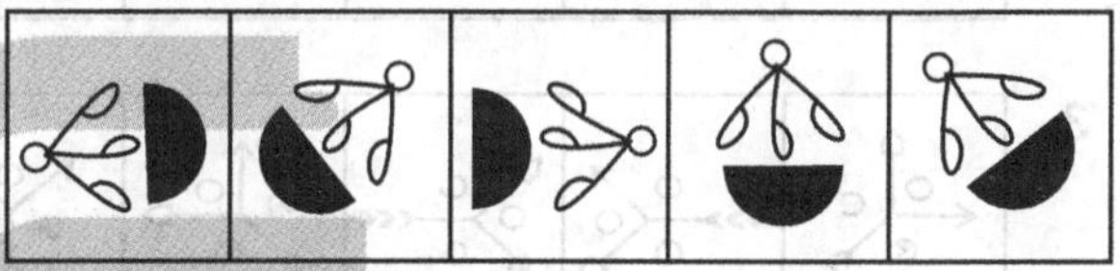

32. 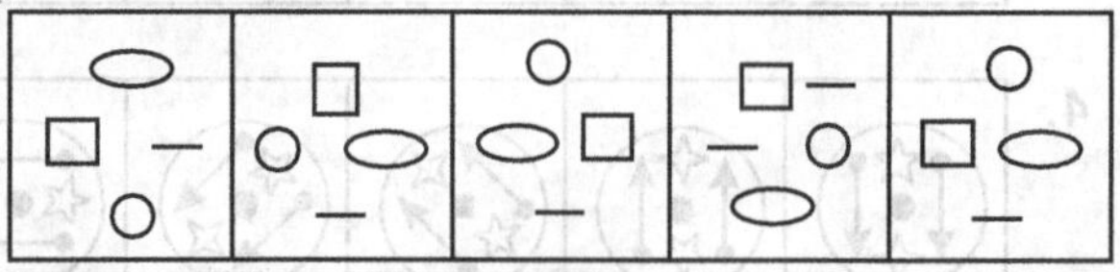

33. 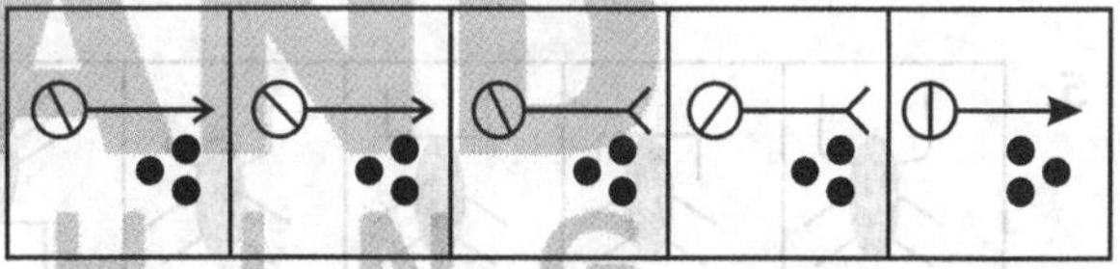

34. 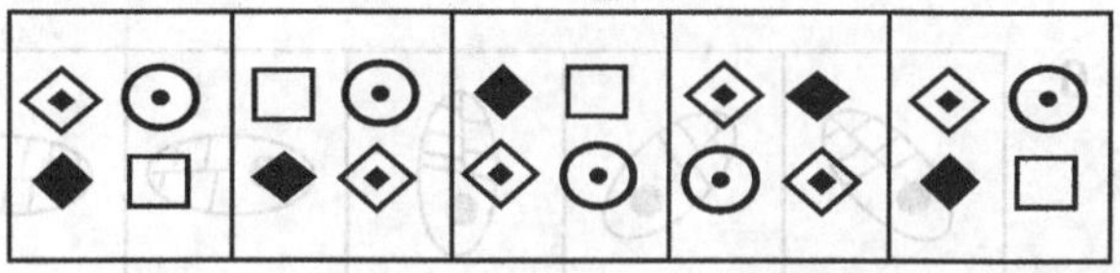

35. 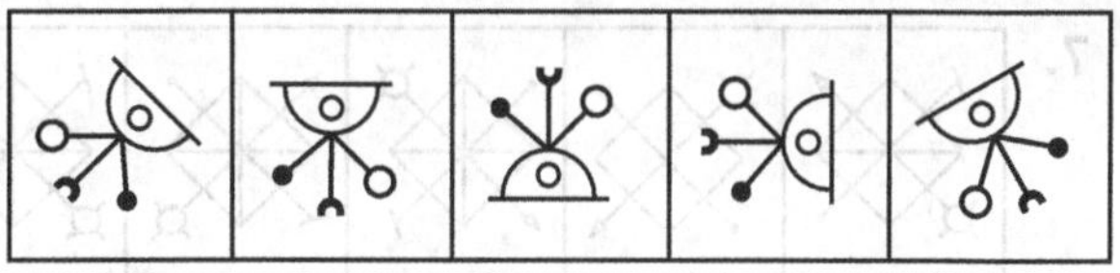

PRACTICE SET-20

Total Ques.- 35
Time - 10 Min.

निर्देश : (प्रश्न 1-35) बुद्धिमापन परीक्षण के प्रत्येक प्रश्न में पाँच आकृतियाँ दिए जाते हैं जिसमें से चार आकृतियाँ में कुछ समानता और कोई एक आकृति अन्य चारों से भिन्न है वही भिन्न आकृति आपका उत्तर होगा जिसे दिए गए उत्तर-पत्रक में गोले को काला/माउस की सहायता से क्लिक करना होता है और इसके लिए 10 मिनट का समय दिया जाता है।

Instructions : (Questions 1–35) : Each question in the Intelligence Test consists of five figures, four of which have some similarity, and one that is different from the other four is your answer. You must click on the black circle on the answer sheet or using the mouse. You are given 10 minutes to complete the test.

A B C D E

1. 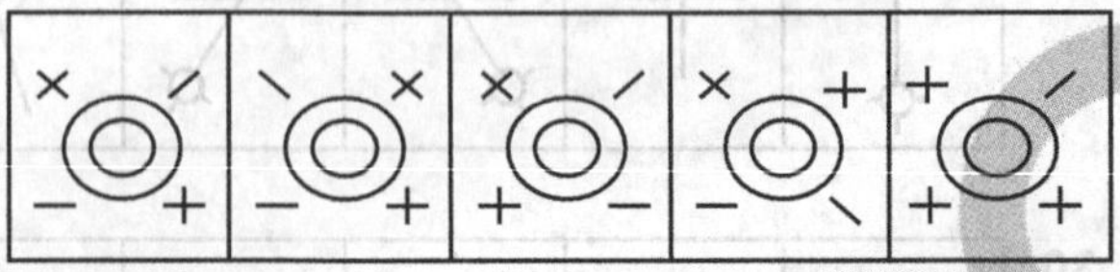

2. 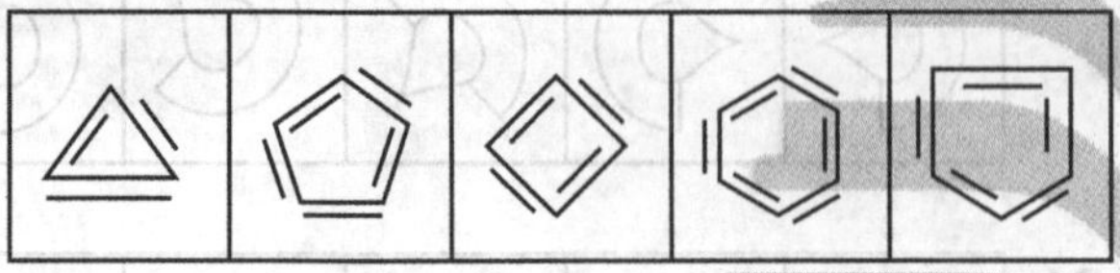

3. 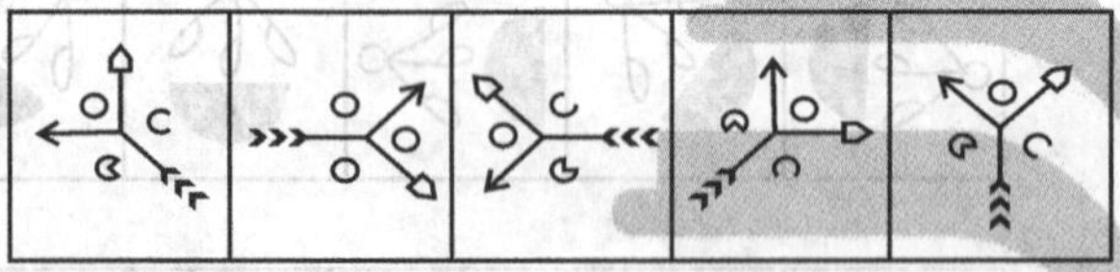

4. 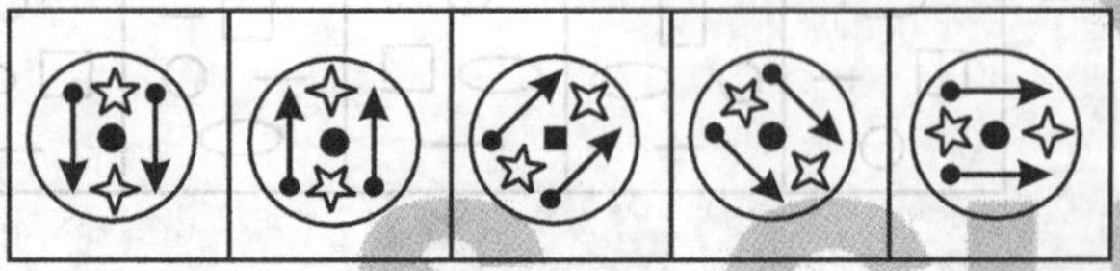

5. 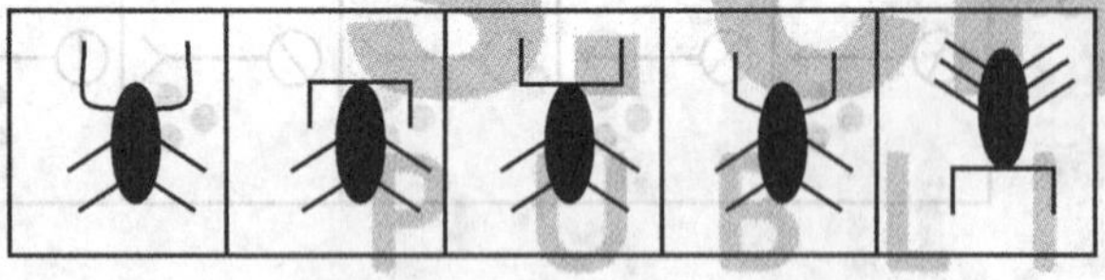

6. 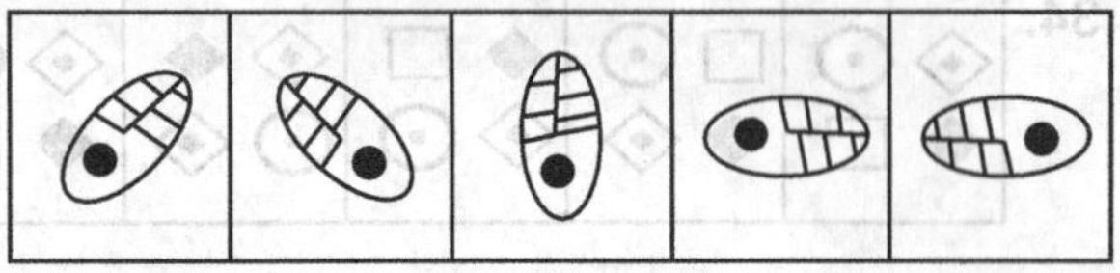

7. 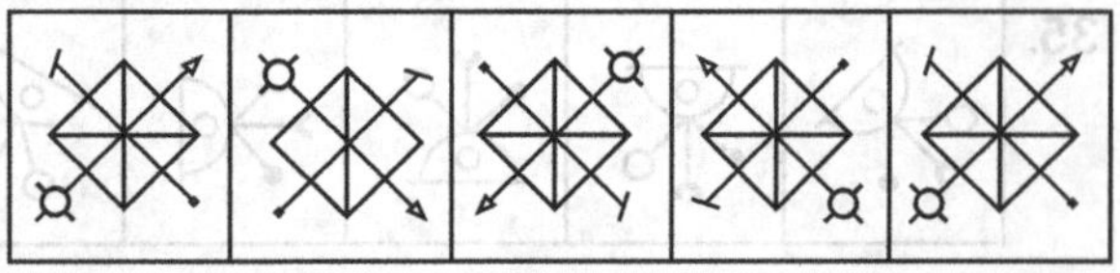

8. 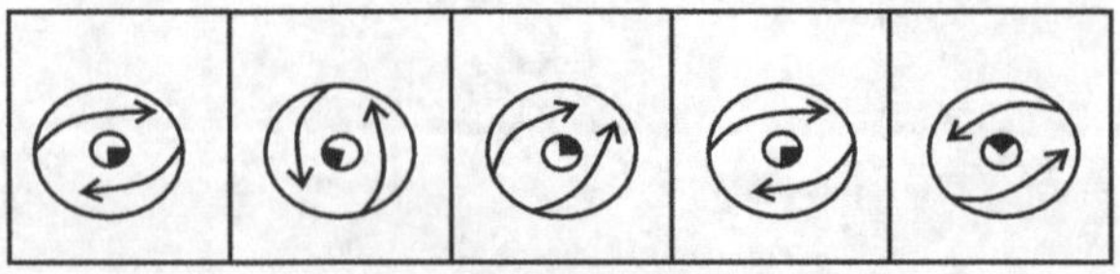

A B C D E

9. 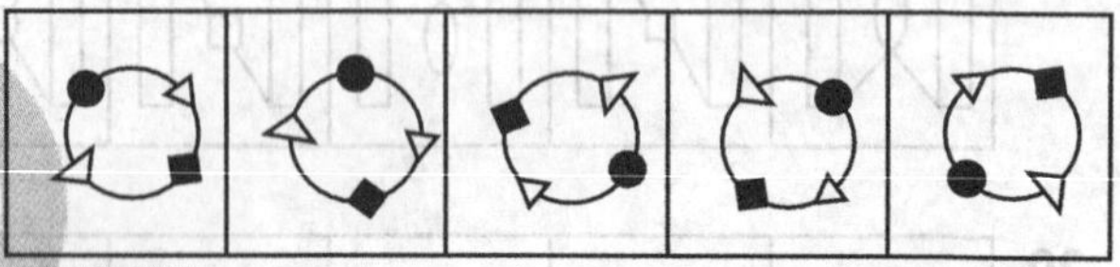

10. 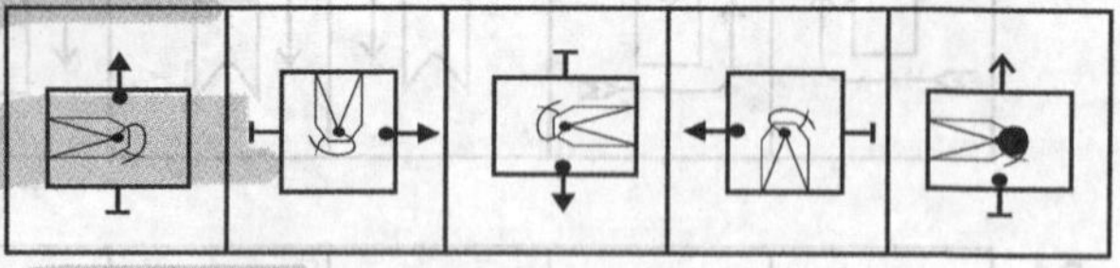

11. 

12. 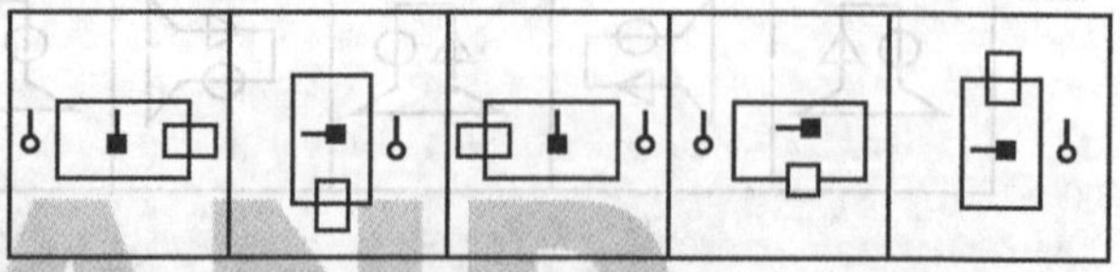

13. 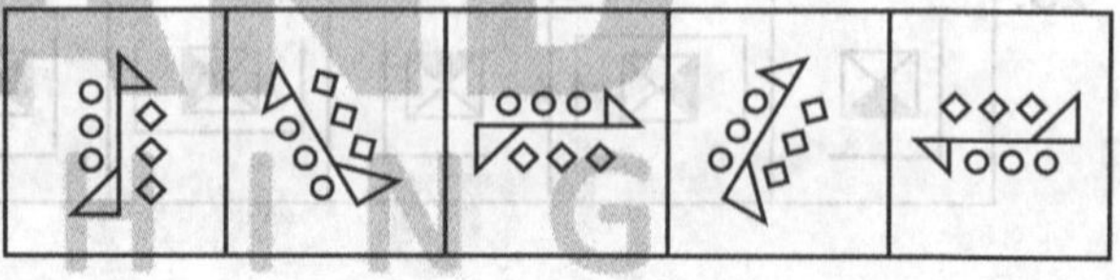

14. 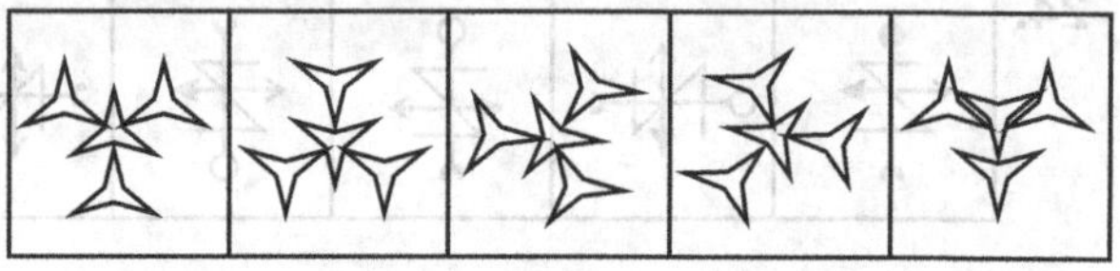

15. 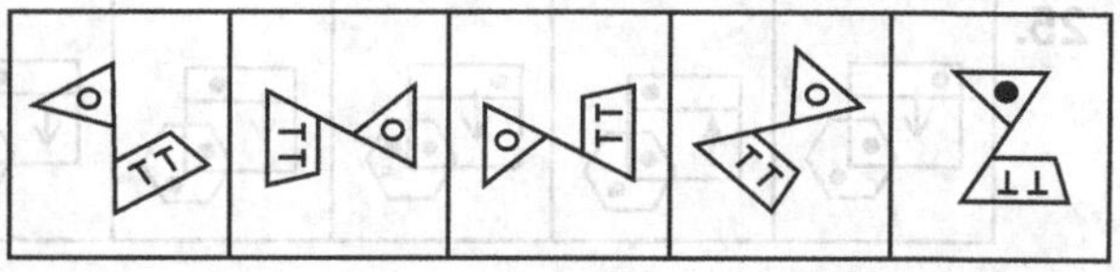

16. 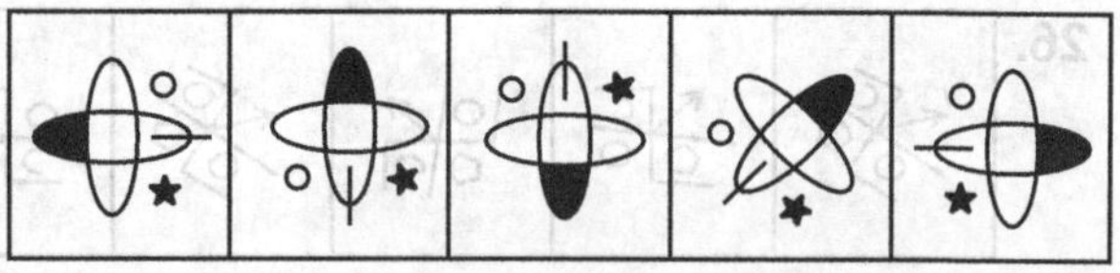

A B C D E

17.
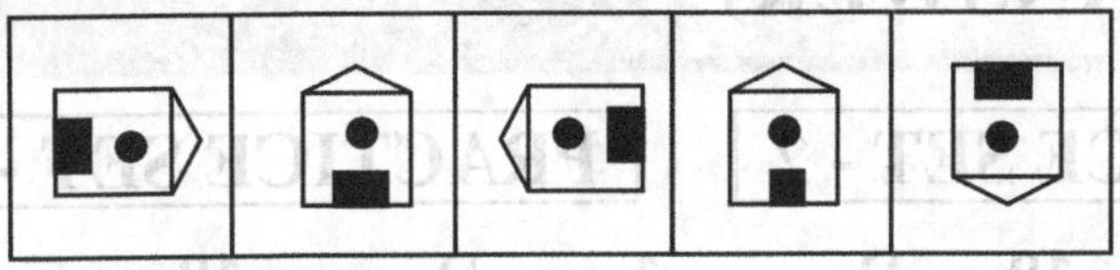

18.
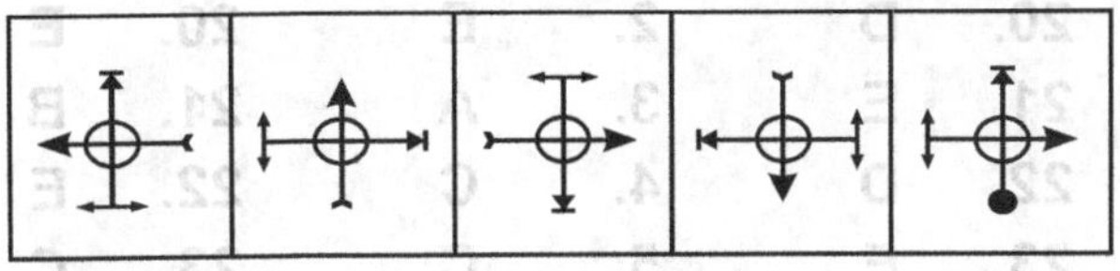

19.
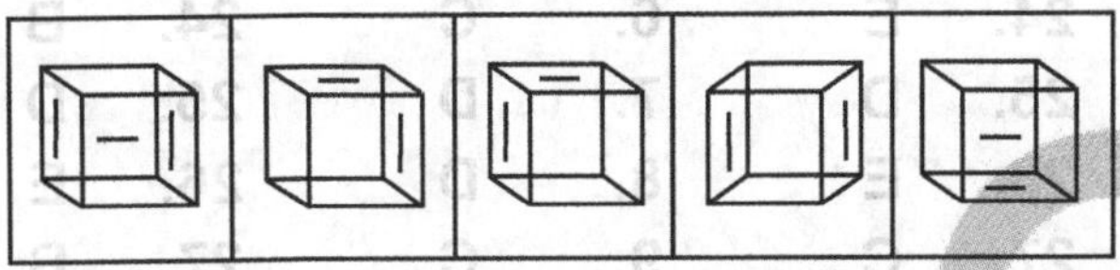

20.
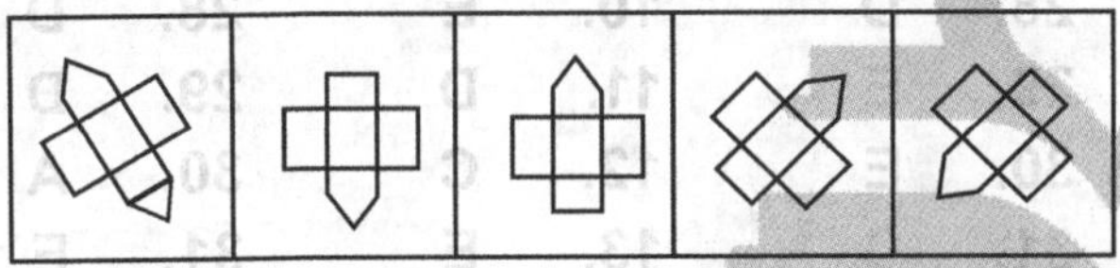

21.
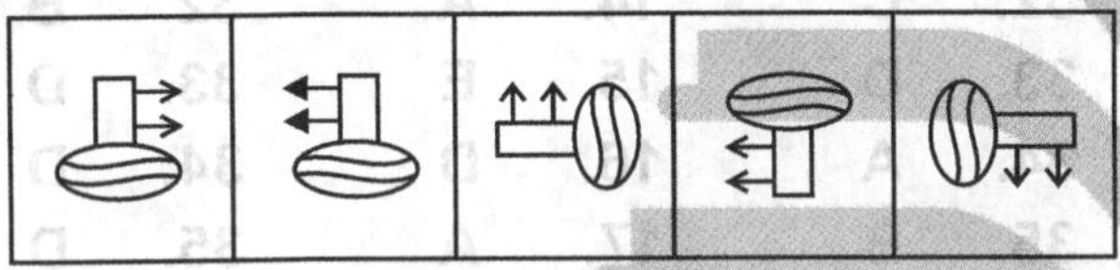

22.
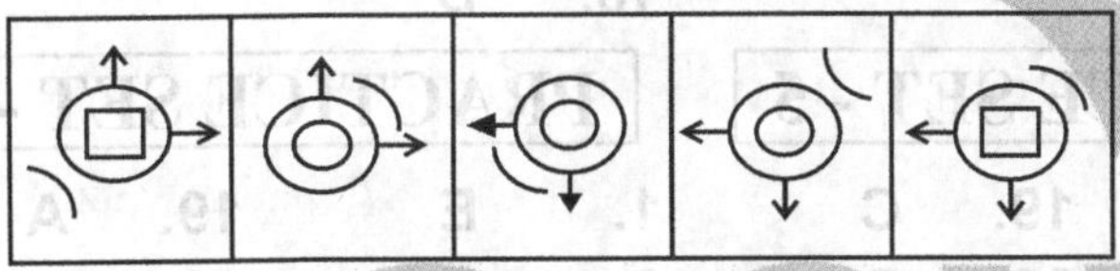

23.
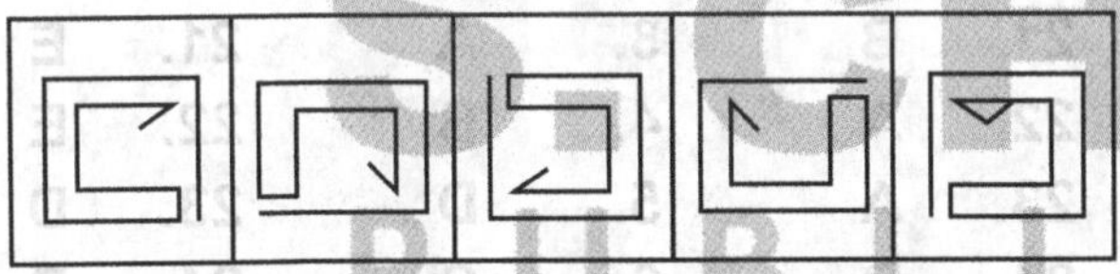

24.
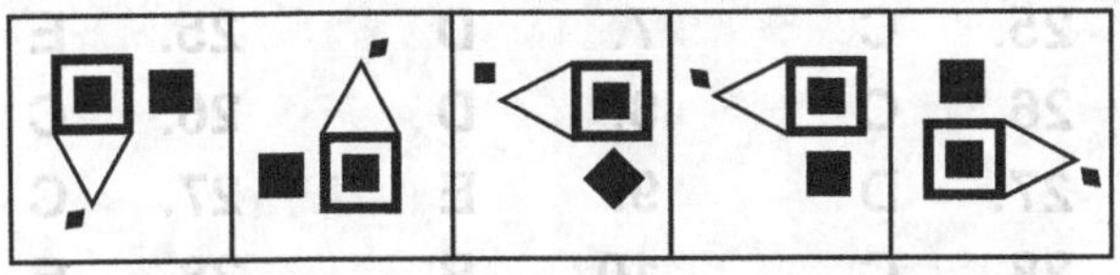

25.
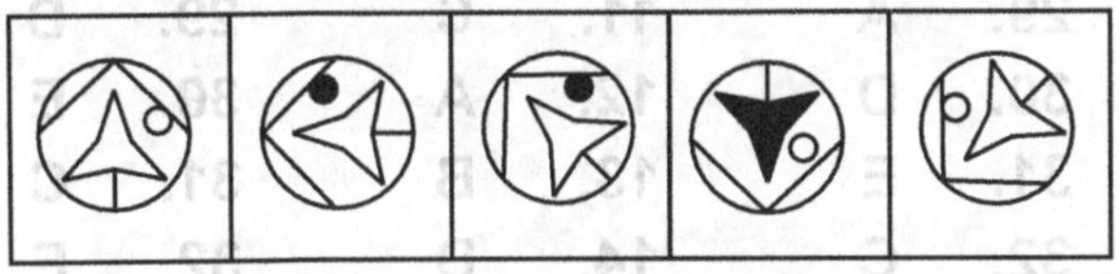

26.
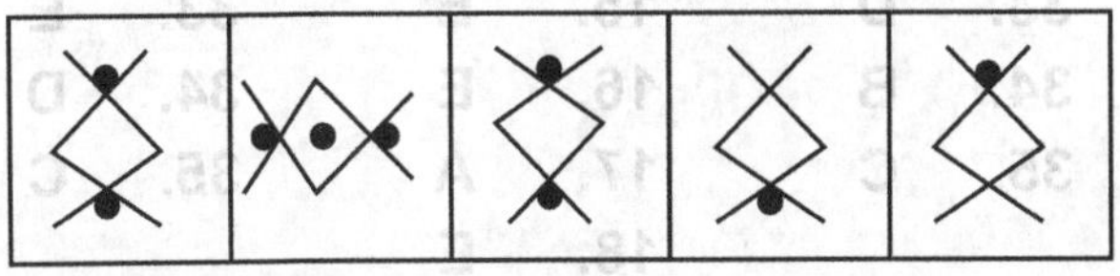

A B C D E

27.
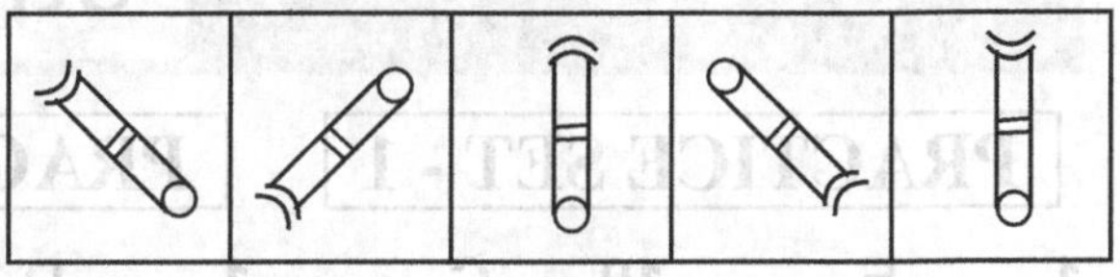

28.
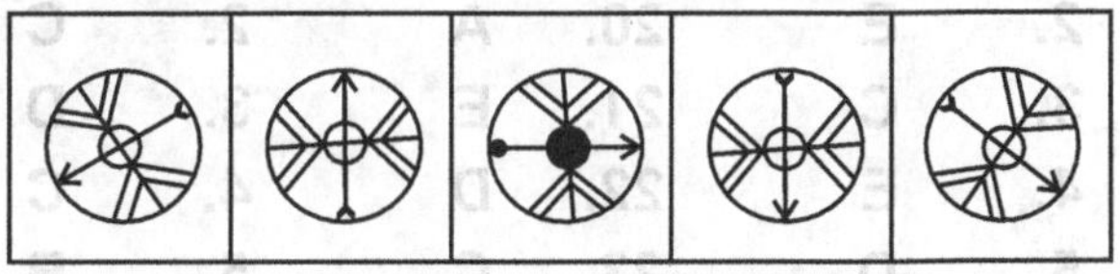

29.

30.
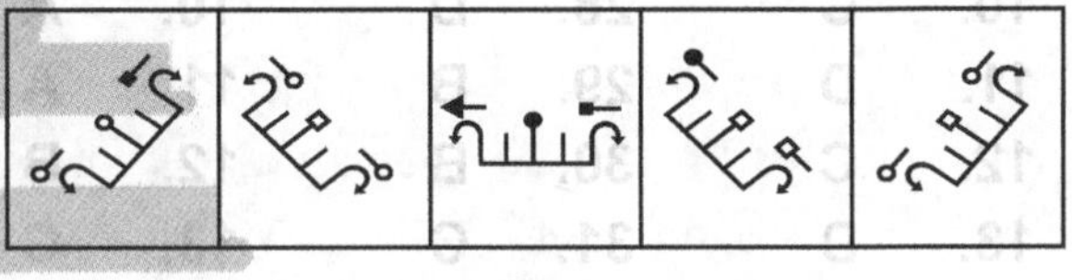

31.
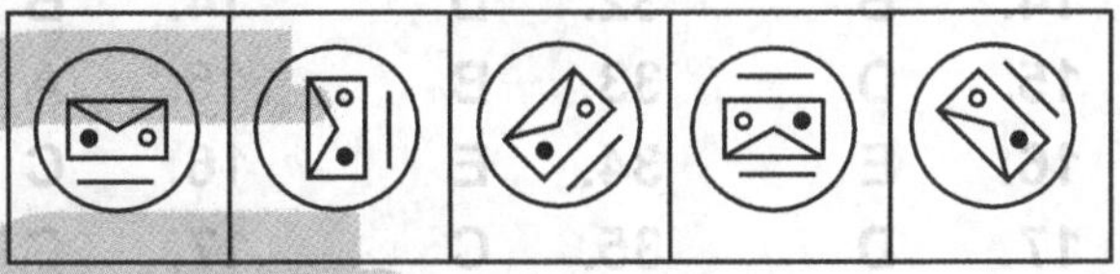

32.
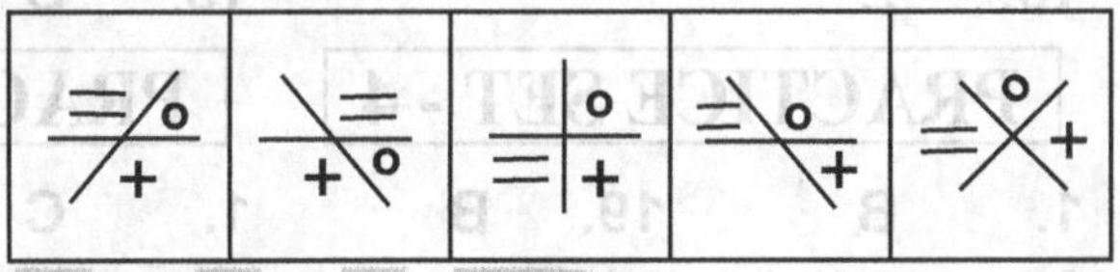

33.

34.
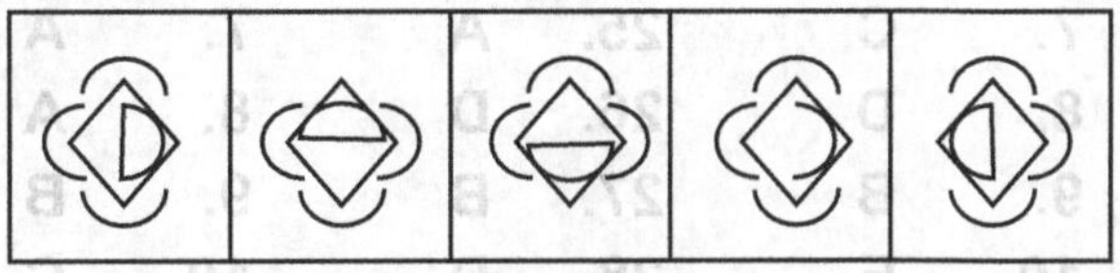

35.
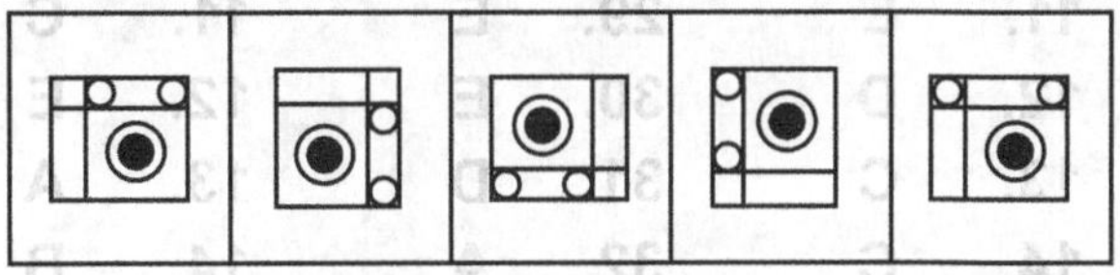

उत्तर (ANSWER)

PRACTICE SET - 1

1.	E	19.	C
2.	E	20.	A
3.	C	21.	E
4.	E	22.	D
5.	D	23.	C
6.	B	24.	A
7.	C	25.	E
8.	D	26.	A
9.	D	27.	D
10.	C	28.	D
11.	D	29.	B
12.	C	30.	B
13.	D	31.	C
14.	B	32.	D
15.	D	33.	B
16.	E	34.	E
17.	D	35.	C
18.	E		

PRACTICE SET - 2

1.	D	19.	D
2.	C	20.	D
3.	D	21.	E
4.	C	22.	D
5.	B	23.	E
6.	E	24.	E
7.	C	25.	D
8.	C	26.	E
9.	D	27.	C
10.	A	28.	D
11.	A	29.	E
12.	B	30.	E
13.	C	31.	C
14.	B	32.	C
15.	A	33.	D
16.	C	34.	A
17.	C	35.	B
18.	D		

PRACTICE SET - 3

1.	D	19.	E
2.	E	20.	E
3.	A	21.	B
4.	C	22.	E
5.	C	23.	C
6.	C	24.	B
7.	D	25.	D
8.	D	26.	E
9.	C	27.	B
10.	E	28.	D
11.	D	29.	D
12.	C	30.	A
13.	E	31.	E
14.	A	32.	B
15.	E	33.	D
16.	D	34.	D
17.	A	35.	D
18.	D		

PRACTICE SET - 4

1.	B	19.	B
2.	E	20.	A
3.	B	21.	E
4.	E	22.	A
5.	C	23.	E
6.	E	24.	E
7.	C	25.	A
8.	D	26.	D
9.	B	27.	B
10.	E	28.	D
11.	E	29.	E
12.	D	30.	E
13.	C	31.	D
14.	C	32.	A
15.	C	33.	D
16.	D	34.	A
17.	D	35.	E
18.	D		

PRACTICE SET - 5

1.	C	19.	C
2.	C	20.	D
3.	C	21.	B
4.	D	22.	A
5.	C	23.	A
6.	E	24.	D
7.	A	25.	C
8.	A	26.	C
9.	B	27.	D
10.	C	28.	C
11.	C	29.	A
12.	E	30.	D
13.	A	31.	E
14.	B	32.	C
15.	A	33.	D
16.	E	34.	B
17.	A	35.	C
18.	B		

PRACTICE SET - 6

1.	E	19.	A
2.	E	20.	D
3.	A	21.	E
4.	B	22.	E
5.	D	23.	D
6.	C	24.	E
7.	D	25.	E
8.	D	26.	C
9.	E	27.	C
10.	B	28.	E
11.	C	29.	D
12.	A	30.	E
13.	B	31.	C
14.	D	32.	E
15.	E	33.	E
16.	E	34.	D
17.	A	35.	C
18.	E		

उत्तर (ANSWER)

PRACTICE SET - 7

1.	B	19.	C
2.	D	20.	E
3.	E	21.	E
4.	D	22.	C
5.	D	23.	B
6.	E	24.	E
7.	B	25.	E
8.	B	26.	D
9.	E	27.	E
10.	E	28.	E
11.	B	29.	B
12.	E	30.	C
13.	B	31.	C
14.	C	32.	E
15.	E	33.	E
16.	C	34.	B
17.	E	35.	E
18.	A		

PRACTICE SET - 8

1.	C	19.	D
2.	E	20.	E
3.	D	21.	D
4.	D	22.	A
5.	E	23.	D
6.	E	24.	D
7.	E	25.	D
8.	A	26.	E
9.	B	27.	B
10.	A	28.	D
11.	A	29.	D
12.	D	30.	D
13.	C	31.	E
14.	A	32.	C
15.	C	33.	E
16.	A	34.	A
17.	B	35.	C
18.	C		

PRACTICE SET - 9

1.	C	19.	E
2.	A	20.	E
3.	B	21.	E
4.	B	22.	A
5.	E	23.	B
6.	A	24.	A
7.	A	25.	E
8.	B	26.	D
9.	B	27.	C
10.	C	28.	B
11.	E	29.	C
12.	D	30.	D
13.	E	31.	A
14.	A	32.	C
15.	B	33.	D
16.	C	34.	B
17.	D	35.	D
18.	C		

PRACTICE SET - 10

1.	A	19.	B
2.	C	20.	D
3.	B	21.	E
4.	E	22.	B
5.	C	23.	A
6.	E	24.	E
7.	A	25.	C
8.	E	26.	E
9.	C	27.	B
10.	C	28.	A
11.	A	29.	E
12.	E	30.	A
13.	B	31.	C
14.	E	32.	A
15.	D	33.	E
16.	E	34.	C
17.	B	35.	E
18.	E		

PRACTICE SET - 11

1.	C	19.	A
2.	D	20.	C
3.	A	21.	E
4.	E	22.	B
5.	C	23.	E
6.	E	24.	B
7.	C	25.	E
8.	D	26.	A
9.	D	27.	D
10.	D	28.	C
11.	E	29.	E
12.	D	30.	E
13.	A	31.	D
14.	C	32.	B
15.	A	33.	D
16.	A	34.	A
17.	D	35.	C
18.	C		

PRACTICE SET - 12

1.	C	19.	D
2.	B	20.	C
3.	A	21.	C
4.	A	22.	C
5.	E	23.	B
6.	D	24.	A
7.	D	25.	E
8.	E	26.	E
9.	C	27.	B
10.	D	28.	E
11.	C	29.	C
12.	B	30.	D
13.	B	31.	C
14.	B	32.	D
15.	D	33.	B
16.	B	34.	D
17.	B	35.	C
18.	B		

उत्तर (ANSWER)

PRACTICE SET - 13

1.	A	19.	E
2.	B	20.	B
3.	D	21.	A
4.	E	22.	D
5.	D	23.	E
6.	C	24.	D
7.	E	25.	D
8.	B	26.	E
9.	E	27.	C
10.	B	28.	C
11.	D	29.	E
12.	E	30.	A
13.	C	31.	E
14.	A	32.	A
15.	A	33.	B
16.	C	34.	A
17.	D	35.	A
18.	B		

PRACTICE SET - 14

1.	A	19.	E
2.	E	20.	E
3.	C	21.	C
4.	A	22.	A
5.	C	23.	B
6.	A	24.	D
7.	E	25.	C
8.	C	26.	B
9.	C	27.	D
10.	A	28.	E
11.	B	29.	D
12.	D	30.	A
13.	A	31.	B
14.	B	32.	D
15.	D	33.	B
16.	C	34.	D
17.	D	35.	A
18.	D		

PRACTICE SET - 15

1.	C	19.	A
2.	D	20.	A
3.	E	21.	E
4.	E	22.	D
5.	B	23.	A
6.	C	24.	D
7.	E	25.	D
8.	D	26.	B
9.	A	27.	A
10.	D	28.	D
11.	B	29.	B
12.	D	30.	C
13.	E	31.	A
14.	B	32.	C
15.	B	33.	D
16.	C	34.	D
17.	E	35.	E
18.	E		

PRACTICE SET - 16

1.	B	19.	E
2.	C	20.	B
3.	E	21.	B
4.	D	22.	C
5.	E	23.	A
6.	E	24.	B
7.	B	25.	A
8.	E	26.	D
9.	D	27.	A
10.	D	28.	D
11.	A	29.	D
12.	E	30.	B
13.	A	31.	B
14.	C	32.	E
15.	A	33.	A
16.	D	34.	C
17.	E	35.	E
18.	E		

PRACTICE SET - 17

1.	B	19.	E
2.	C	20.	C
3.	B	21.	C
4.	D	22.	A
5.	B	23.	C
6.	C	24.	C
7.	D	25.	A
8.	C	26.	E
9.	B	27.	E
10.	E	28.	D
11.	A	29.	B
12.	E	30.	C
13.	E	31.	E
14.	A	32.	B
15.	D	33.	B
16.	E	34.	D
17.	E	35.	B
18.	C		

PRACTICE SET - 18

1.	A	19.	E
2.	D	20.	E
3.	D	21.	B
4.	B	22.	D
5.	C	23.	B
6.	C	24.	B
7.	B	25.	D
8.	E	26.	C
9.	E	27.	B
10.	C	28.	C
11.	A	29.	C
12.	E	30.	A
13.	E	31.	E
14.	E	32.	C
15.	E	33.	C
16.	B	34.	C
17.	C	35.	B
18.	D		

उत्तर (ANSWER)

PRACTICE SET - 19

1.	A	19.	E
2.	A	20.	E
3.	C	21.	C
4.	D	22.	E
5.	D	23.	E
6.	B	24.	A
7.	D	25.	B
8.	C	26.	D
9.	B	27.	E
10.	D	28.	B
11.	C	29.	E
12.	D	30.	E
13.	E	31.	C
14.	E	32.	D
15.	C	33.	E
16.	A	34.	D
17.	E	35.	B
18.	D		

PRACTICE SET - 20

1.	E	19.	A
2.	A	20.	A
3.	B	21.	B
4.	C	22.	C
5.	E	23.	E
6.	C	24.	C
7.	B	25.	D
8.	C	26.	B
9.	B	27.	C
10.	E	28.	C
11.	B	29.	E
12.	D	30.	C
13.	A	31.	D
14.	E	32.	C
15.	E	33.	D
16.	D	34.	D
17.	D	35.	E
18.	E		

2 (A) TEST FOR MEASURING SELECTIVE ATTENTION

Add of Odd Number Test (विषम संख्याओं का योग परीक्षण)

रेलवे मनोवैज्ञानिक परीक्षण के अन्तर्गत चयनात्मक अवधान मापन हेतु परीक्षण जिसे विषम संख्याओं का योग परीक्षण भी कहा जाता है। यह स्टेशन मास्टर पद के लिए बहुत महत्वपूर्ण अध्याय है। यह परीक्षण आपकी एकाग्रता और चयनात्मक ध्यान की जाँच करता है। इस परीक्षण के लिए कुल 30 प्रश्न दिए होते हैं, जिसे हल करने के लिए 8 या 10 मिनट का समय दिया जाता है। इस परीक्षण के प्रश्न में सम और विषम संख्याओं को मिलाकर एक श्रृंखला दिया रहता है जिसमें विषम संख्या 1, 3, 5 आदि को जोड़ना होता है। इस श्रृंखला में सम संख्या को जोड़ना नहीं होता है। विषम संख्याओं को जोड़ने के बाद नीचे दिए गए पाँच विकल्पों (A, B, C, D और E) में से एक सही विकल्प को ढूंढना होता है जिससे दिए गए उत्तर पत्रक में गोले को काला/माउस की सहायता से क्लिक करना होता है।

As part of the Railway psychological Test for the post of Station Master, the Odd Number Add Test is an important section to measure selective attention. This test checks your concentration and selective attention. The test consists of 30 questions, which must be completed in 8 or 10 minutes. Each question presents a series of even and odd numbers. You are required to add only the odd numbers (1, 3, 5, etc.) in the series. Even numbers should not be added. After adding the odd numbers, select the correct option from the five given choices (A, B, C, D & E). The correct option will be your answer.

Mark your answer by filling the circle on the answer sheet or by clicking on it using the mouse.

नीचे दिए गए उदाहरणों के द्वारा इसे समझें :-
Example for understanding :-

1. 6 2 2 8 5 2 3 2 1 1 2 3 6 6 8 4 1 2 5 2 1 2 3 2 1 5 4 1 2 3 5 1 2
   (A) 40 (B) 37 (C) 39 (D) 38 (E) 41
2. 6 5 2 1 5 2 3 4 2 3 2 1 3 2 5 4 1 8 2 3 6 2 8 2 4 1 8 6 5 2 1
   (A) 36 (B) 38 (C) 35 (D) 39 (E) 37
3. 5 4 2 8 6 5 3 2 6 1 6 2 4 1 2 8 6 3 3 4 2 1 4 2 2 1 2 6 5 2 1
   (A) 42 (B) 44 (C) 29 (D) 45 (E) 40
4. 2 3 5 4 2 1 8 4 6 2 5 1 2 3 1 1 2 4 1 1 2 3 5 2 1 5 2 1 4 1 2 3 5 1
   (A) 46 (B) 42 (C) 44 (D) 47 (E) 45
5. 2 1 4 2 5 2 2 4 6 8 3 4 1 2 3 6 5 8 5 2 1 4 1 2 5 6 2 2 3 2 8 4 1 2
   (A) 33 (B) 32 (C) 36 (D) 35 (E) 34
6. 1 2 2 4 6 3 5 4 8 6 3 2 5 4 1 7 1 1 8 6 2 5 4 1 2 1 2 1 4 5 2 1
   (A) 43 (B) 41 (C) 39 (D) 44 (E) 42
7. 2 3 6 5 2 3 2 1 4 2 1 3 8 2 6 8 4 1 2 3 2 2 1 2 1 6 2 4 1 8 4
   (A) 22 (B) 19 (C) 20 (D) 21 (E) 23
8. 3 5 2 3 6 8 4 1 2 2 2 6 4 2 3 3 6 8 2 3 1 5 6 2 3 8 4 1 2
   (A) 36 (B) 32 (C) 29 (D) 31 (E) 33

Ans.: 1. (C) 2. (E) 3. (C) 4. (D) 5. (E) 6. (B) 7. (E) 8. (D)

PRACTICE SET-1

Total Ques.- 30
Time - 8 or 10 Min.

निर्देश : (प्रश्न 1–30) विषम संख्याओं को योग परीक्षण के प्रत्येक प्रश्न में सम और विषम संख्याओं को मिलाकर एक श्रृंखला दिया रहता है। इस श्रृंखला में प्रदत्त केवल विषम संख्या 1, 3, 5 आदि को जोड़ने के बाद नीचे दिए गए पाँच विकल्पों (A, B, C, D और E) में कोई एक सही विकल्प को ढूंढना होता है जिसे दिए गए उत्तर-पत्रक में गोले को काला/माउस की सहायता से क्लिक करना होता है।

Directions: (Questions 1–30) : Each question in the Odd Number Adding Test presents a series of even and odd numbers. You need to add the total number of odd numbers 1, 3, 5 etc. in the given series. After adding, select the correct option from the five choices (A, B, C, D & E) provided. Mark your answer by filling the circle on the answer sheet or by clicking on it using the mouse.

1. 5 4 2 8 6 5 3 2 6 1 6 2 4 1 2 8 6 3 3 4 2 1 4 2 2 1 2 6 5 2 1
(A) 42 (B) 44 (C) 29 (D) 45 (E) 40

2. 1 2 2 4 6 3 5 4 8 6 3 2 5 4 1 7 1 1 8 6 2 5 4 1 2 1 2 1 4 5 2 1
(A) 43 (B) 41 (C) 39 (D) 44 (E) 42

3. 3 5 2 3 6 8 4 1 2 2 2 6 4 2 3 3 6 8 2 3 1 5 6 2 3 8 4 1 2
(A) 36 (B) 32 (C) 29 (D) 31 (E) 33

4. 5 2 2 3 6 2 5 8 4 1 2 2 2 3 5 8 1 2 6 8 2 6 8 4 2 5 1 2 3 1 2 1
(A) 33 (B) 31 (C) 29 (D) 36 (E) 34

5. 3 5 2 1 6 5 2 1 8 4 1 2 3 8 5 2 1 4 2 1 3 5 1 2 6 2 1 1 1 2 3 4 4 2
(A) 40 (B) 39 (C) 42 (D) 46 (E) 41

6. 2 3 5 4 2 1 8 4 6 2 5 1 2 3 1 1 2 4 1 1 2 3 5 2 1 5 2 1 4 1 2 3 5 1
(A) 46 (B) 42 (C) 44 (D) 47 (E) 45

7. 6 2 2 8 5 2 3 2 1 1 2 3 6 6 8 4 1 2 5 2 1 2 3 2 1 5 4 1 2 3 5 1 2
(A) 40 (B) 37 (C) 39 (D) 38 (E) 41

8. 8 5 2 1 6 5 2 3 2 1 4 5 2 1 4 5 3 2 1 2 1 3 2 5 1 2 5 8 4 1 2 2 1 2
(A) 48 (B) 47 (C) 46 (D) 45 (E) 49

9. 2 3 6 5 2 3 2 1 4 2 1 3 8 2 6 8 4 1 2 3 2 2 1 2 1 6 2 4 1 8 4
(A) 22 (B) 19 (C) 20 (D) 21 (E) 23

10. 6 5 2 1 5 2 3 4 2 3 2 1 3 2 5 4 1 8 2 3 6 2 8 2 4 1 8 6 5 2 1
(A) 36 (B) 38 (C) 35 (D) 39 (E) 37

11. 8 5 4 1 2 6 1 2 3 6 8 4 1 2 3 2 1 3 2 1 4 2 3 5 1 2 5 8 5 2 3 6 2 2
(A) 41 (B) 39 (C) 42 (D) 40 (E) 43

12. 2 1 4 2 5 2 2 4 6 8 3 4 1 2 3 6 5 8 5 2 1 4 1 2 5 6 2 2 3 2 8 4 1 2
(A) 33 (B) 32 (C) 36 (D) 35 (E) 34

13. 2 5 6 3 2 1 5 8 4 6 8 5 2 3 2 2 4 1 2 3 6 8 5 1 2 1 2 8 2 6
(A) 32 (B) 33 (C) 31 (D) 34 (E) 30

14. 6 5 2 3 5 8 4 1 2 5 1 2 3 6 3 2 1 4 8 5 4 1 2 3 6 8 2 4 1 8
(A) 38 (B) 39 (C) 35 (D) 37 (E) 36

15. 5 8 4 5 2 3 2 4 1 2 5 6 2 8 4 1 2 5 2 1 3 6 3 8 4 1 2 3 5 1 2
(A) 40 (B) 41 (C) 42 (D) 39 (E) 38

16. 5 8 4 2 1 2 4 8 2 3 6 5 2 6 8 4 2 3 2 1 1 1 2 2 3 3 3 6 8 2
(A) 29 (B) 28 (C) 27 (D) 30 (E) 31

17. 8 5 4 1 2 3 6 6 2 1 4 8 4 1 2 5 3 6 6 2 1 5 2 1 4 8 5 2 8 6 5 2
(A) 37 (B) 38 (C) 36 (D) 35 (E) 34

18. 3 3 2 6 3 4 1 8 5 6 2 3 2 1 4 8 4 1 2 3 2 2 1 6 8 2 4 1 2 1 8
(A) 28 (B) 25 (C) 24 (D) 27 (E) 26

19. 6 5 8 6 2 3 2 4 1 3 6 5 2 1 8 4 2 6 2 1 5 8 4 1 2 1 3 2 4 1
(A) 32 (B) 30 (C) 31 (D) 29 (E) 28

20. 1 4 5 8 1 2 1 6 5 8 5 2 1 4 2 1 1 4 8 6 5 2 3 1 3 4 1 2 3 5 4 6 8
(A) 44 (B) 40 (C) 43 (D) 42 (E) 41

21. 4 6 2 8 2 4 1 2 6 8 5 2 1 3 6 2 1 4 8 5 2 5 6 8 2 1 3 3 2 1 8 1 1
(A) 31 (B) 32 (C) 30 (D) 33 (E) 29

22. 8 5 4 1 2 6 8 2 1 2 1 4 4 6 3 6 8 5 2 1 3 2 1 2 5 1 1 2 2 1 4 6
(A) 31 (B) 30 (C) 29 (D) 28 (E) 27

23. 6 5 8 4 4 1 2 3 6 8 5 2 1 5 4 2 1 8 5 2 1 6 3 2 5 8 4 1 2 8
(A) 37 (B) 38 (C) 35 (D) 34 (E) 36

24. 8 5 4 1 2 3 6 2 2 6 6 2 1 5 4 1 2 8 4 1 2 3 2 1 4 1 6 2 8 5 2 1
(A) 29 (B) 28 (C) 27 (D) 30 (E) 31

25. 2 5 1 4 2 1 3 6 1 8 4 6 8 4 6 2 6 1 3 2 1 4 2 3 5 1 8 5 2 1
(A) 30 (B) 29 (C) 28 (D) 31 (E) 32

26. 3 3 2 5 2 1 6 6 6 6 8 5 4 1 2 5 1 2 0 2 1 3 5 1 4 8 1 2 5 4
(A) 40 (B) 42 (C) 39 (D) 41 (E) 37

27. 3 2 5 8 5 2 2 3 2 3 3 3 2 6 5 2 1 8 8 8 4 1 2 1 5 4 1 2 5
(A) 40 (B) 39 (C) 44 (D) 37 (E) 42

28. 3 5 2 6 8 5 4 1 2 5 4 1 2 6 4 8 5 2 1 4 2 5 4 1 2 5 2 1 4 8 2 6
(A) 37 (B) 35 (C) 40 (D) 41 (E) 38

29. 2 3 2 1 4 8 6 2 1 3 5 2 1 4 3 6 8 2 1 3 5 8 4 1 2 6 3 8 2 1 1
(A) 30 (B) 32 (C) 33 (D) 31 (E) 29

30. 3 2 6 5 8 4 1 2 3 2 6 8 4 1 2 5 6 3 2 1 4 8 5 2 1 3 5 8 4 1
(A) 35 (B) 38 (C) 36 (D) 37 (E) 34

PRACTICE SET-2

Total Ques.- 30
Time - 8 or 10 Min.

निर्देश : (प्रश्न 1–30) विषम संख्याओं को योग परीक्षण के प्रत्येक प्रश्न में सम और विषम संख्याओं को मिलाकर एक श्रृंखला दिया रहता है। इस श्रृंखला में प्रदत्त केवल विषम संख्या 1, 3, 5 आदि को जोड़ने के बाद नीचे दिए गए पाँच विकल्पों (A, B, C, D और E) में कोई एक सही विकल्प को ढूंढना होता है जिसे दिए गए उत्तर-पत्रक में गोले को काला/माउस की सहायता से क्लिक करना होता है।

Directions: (Questions 1–30) : Each question in the Odd Number Adding Test presents a series of even and odd numbers. You need to add the total number of odd numbers 1, 3, 5 etc. in the given series. After adding, select the correct option from the five choices (A, B, C, D & E) provided. Mark your answer by filling the circle on the answer sheet or by clicking on it using the mouse.

1. 2 4 2 8 2 6 1 6 2 4 1 2 8 2 1 4 2 2 1 2 6 5 2 1 6 5 3 2 6 3 3 4
(A) 24 (B) 22 (C) 26 (D) 25 (E) 23

2. 1 2 2 2 3 1 5 6 2 3 8 4 1 2 4 6 3 5 4 81 2 1 4 5 2 1
(A) 37 (B) 30 (C) 39 (D) 42 (E) 33

3. 3 5 2 3 6 8 4 5 2 2 3 6 2 5 8 4 1 2 2 2 3 5 8 1 2 2 2 6 4 2 3 3 6 8
(A) 40 (B) 42 (C) 45 (D) 39 (E) 41

4. 6 3 2 5 4 1 7 1 1 8 6 2 5 4 1 2 1 2 6 8 2 6 8 4 2 5 1 2 3 1 2 1
(A) 27 (B) 28 (C) 36 (D) 30 (E) 32

5. 3 5 2 1 6 5 2 1 8 3 1 1 2 4 1 2 3 2 1 5 2 1 4 1 2 4 2 3 8 2 1 4 2 2
(A) 35 (B) 34 (C) 33 (D) 36 (E) 21

6. 2 3 5 4 2 2 1 2 3 2 1 5 4 1 2 3 1 2 1 3 5 1 2 6 2 1 1 1 2 3 5 1
(A) 48 (B) 47 (C) 44 (D) 42 (E) 45

7. 6 2 2 8 5 2 3 2 1 1 2 3 4 4 8 4 6 2 5 1 2 3 6 6 8 4 1 2 5 5 1 2
(A) 33 (B) 36 (C) 35 (D) 34 (E) 38

8. 8 5 2 1 2 1 3 2 5 1 2 5 8 4 1 2 2 1 6 5 2 3 2 1 4 5 2 1 4 5 3 2 1 2
(A) 46 (B) 49 (C) 47 (D) 48 (E) 45

9. 2 3 6 5 2 2 3 2 2 1 2 1 6 2 3 2 1 4 2 1 3 8 2 6 8 4 14 1 8 4
(A) 22 (B) 23 (C) 25 (D) 28 (E) 20

10. 6 5 2 1 5 2 3 2 3 2 1 1 4 2 3 5 1 2 8 2 3 6 2 4 2 3 2 1 3 2 5 4 1
(A) 44 (B) 46 (C) 43 (D) 40 (E) 41

11. 8 2 3 6 2 8 2 4 1 8 6 5 2 1 8 5 2 2 4 1 2 6 1 2 3 6 8 4 2
(A) 19 (B) 20 (C) 17 (D) 21 (E) 23

12. 2 1 4 2 5 2 2 4 2 4 1 2 3 6 8 1 2 1 2 8 6 8 4 1 2 3 6 5 8 8 4 1 2
(A) 23 (B) 21 (C) 22 (D) 19 (E) 20

13. 2 5 6 3 5 2 1 4 1 2 5 6 2 2 3 2 2 1 5 8 4 6 8 5 2 3 2 6
(A) 33 (B) 31 (C) 35 (D) 34 (E) 37

14. 6 5 2 3 5 2 1 3 6 3 8 4 1 2 3 5 1 5 8 4 1 2 5 1 2 3 6 3 8

(A) 47 (B) 43 (C) 46 (D) 49 (E) 48

15. 5 8 4 5 2 1 4 8 5 4 1 2 3 6 8 2 4 1 2 3 2 4 1 2 5 6 2 8 4 1 2 2

(A) 30 (B) 33 (C) 31 (D) 32 (E) 29

16. 5 8 4 1 1 4 8 6 5 2 3 1 3 4 1 6 8 2 1 4 2 3 5 4 6 2 1 2 4 8 2

(A) 30 (B) 32 (C) 31 (D) 29 (E) 24

17. 8 5 4 1 2 2 3 6 5 2 6 8 4 2 3 2 1 1 1 2 2 3 3 3 6 8 3 6 6 2 6 5 2

(A) 36 (B) 37 (C) 35 (D) 38 (E) 39

18. 3 3 2 6 3 4 1 4 8 4 1 2 5 3 6 1 5 2 1 4 8 5 2 8 1 8 5 6 2 3 2

(A) 36 (B) 34 (C) 40 (D) 33 (E) 32

19. 6 5 2 1 5 8 4 1 2 1 3 8 6 2 3 2 4 1 3 6 5 2 1 8 4 2 6 2 4 1

(A) 29 (B) 28 (C) 27 (D) 30 (E) 31

20. 1 4 5 8 1 2 1 1 4 8 4 1 2 3 2 2 1 6 8 2 4 1 2 8 5 2 1 4 2 8

(A) 18 (B) 19 (C) 25 (D) 23 (E) 21

21. 4 6 2 6 8 5 2 1 3 2 1 2 5 1 1 2 8 2 4 1 2 6 8 5 3 3 2 1 8 1 1

(A) 41 (B) 33 (C) 35 (D) 32 (E) 37

22. 8 5 2 1 3 6 2 1 4 8 5 2 5 6 8 2 1 8 2 1 2 1 4 4 6 3 1 4 6

(A) 28 (B) 33 (C) 27 (D) 29 (E) 32

23. 6 5 8 2 4 1 3 2 1 3 5 1 4 8 1 2 3 2 1 8 4 4 1 3 6 8 5 2 1 5 8

(A) 38 (B) 39 (C) 37 (D) 36 (E) 40

24. 8 5 4 1 2 3 6 2 2 6 8 4 6 2 6 1 3 2 5 1 8 5 6 6 1 5 4 8 2 8 2 1

(A) 31 (B) 32 (C) 35 (D) 38 (E) 29

25. 2 5 1 4 2 1 3 4 2 1 8 1 4 2 3 5 2 1 6 3 2 5 8 4 1 2 6 1 8 4 6 1

(A) 30 (B) 32 (C) 33 (D) 35 (E) 37

26. 3 3 2 2 1 4 2 5 4 1 2 5 2 1 4 5 2 1 6 1 6 6 8 5 4 1 2 5 1 2 4

(A) 37 (B) 36 (C) 38 (D) 34 (E) 35

27. 3 2 5 8 5 2 2 2 4 1 6 2 3 2 3 3 3 2 6 5 2 2 1 8 4 1 2 5

(A) 39 (B) 33 (C) 35 (D) 38 (E) 40

28. 3 5 2 8 8 4 1 2 1 6 8 5 4 1 2 5 1 8 6 4 1 2 6 4 8 5 8 2 6

(A) 27 (B) 26 (C) 25 (D) 24 (E) 28

29. 2 3 2 1 4 1 4 8 5 2 1 3 4 1 2 6 8 6 2 1 3 2 1 4 3 6 3 8 2 1 1

(A) 25 (B) 27 (C) 29 (D) 28 (E) 30

30. 3 2 6 8 2 1 3 2 8 4 1 2 6 5 8 4 1 4 3 2 6 8 4 1 2 5 6 3 2 8 4 1

(A) 29 (B) 25 (C) 27 (D) 26 (E) 28

PRACTICE SET-3

Total Ques.- 30
Time - 8 or 10 Min.

निर्देश : (प्रश्न 1-30) विषम संख्याओं को योग परीक्षण के प्रत्येक प्रश्न में सम और विषम संख्याओं को मिलाकर एक श्रृंखला दिया रहता है। इस श्रृंखला में प्रदत्त केवल विषम संख्या 1, 3, 5 आदि को जोड़ने के बाद नीचे दिए गए पाँच विकल्पों (A, B, C, D और E) में कोई एक सही विकल्प को ढूंढना होता है जिसे दिए गए उत्तर-पत्रक में गोले को काला/माउस की सहायता से क्लिक करना होता है।

Directions: (Questions 1–30) : Each question in the Odd Number Adding Test presents a series of even and odd numbers. You need to add the total number of odd numbers 1, 3, 5 etc. in the given series. After adding, select the correct option from the five choices (A, B, C, D & E) provided. Mark your answer by filling the circle on the answer sheet or by clicking on it using the mouse.

1. 2 4 2 8 2 4 8 6 2 3 1 4 2 1 3 2 8 2 6 5 4 1 2 1 2 1
   (A) 16 (B) 13 (C) 15 (D) 19 (E) 17
2. 1 2 2 2 3 1 5 6 2 3 86 2 8 4 1 2 3 5 2 1 4 8 1 3 2
   (A) 25 (B) 27 (C) 26 (D) 29 (E) 28
3. 3 5 2 3 6 8 4 5 2 8 4 1 2 6 8 4 5 1 2 1 2 2 2 6 4 2 3 3 6 8
   (A) 33 (B) 31 (C) 30 (D) 32 (E) 35
4. 6 3 2 5 4 1 7 1 3 2 4 1 2 8 6 2 1 4 8 2 5 1 2 3 1 2 1
   (A) 29 (B) 25 (C) 23 (D) 33 (E) 27
5. 3 6 2 8 4 2 5 1 2 1 4 1 2 3 2 1 5 2 1 4 1 2 4 2 3 8 2 1 4 2 2
   (A) 25 (B) 24 (C) 27 (D) 30 (E) 26
6. 2 3 5 4 2 2 3 6 8 2 4 1 2 6 8 2 3 1 2 1 4 2 1 2 1 1 1 2 3 5 1
   (A) 30 (B) 32 (C) 35 (D) 29 (E) 31
7. 6 2 2 8 56 2 8 4 2 1 5 4 1 2 1 2 1 2 3 6 6 8 1 2 5 5 1 2
   (A) 27 (B) 29 (C) 28 (D) 30 (E) 31
8. 8 8 4 6 8 4 1 2 3 6 8 5 4 1 2 1 4 2 1 3 2 1 4 5 2 1 4 5 3 2 1 2
   (A) 34 (B) 33 (C) 35 (D) 36 (E) 31
9. 2 3 6 6 2 5 8 4 1 2 3 2 1 2 3 2 1 4 8 5 4 8 6 6 4 1 4 1 8 4
   (A) 23 (B) 27 (C) 25 (D) 24 (E) 26
10. 6 5 2 5 4 1 2 2 1 5 2 3 2 3 2 1 1 4 2 3 5 1 2 6 2 8 4 1 2 4 1
    (A) 35 (B) 33 (C) 38 (D) 39 (E) 36
11. 3 6 2 8 4 1 2 6 8 4 1 2 5 1 8 5 2 2 4 1 2 6 1 2 3 6 8 4 2
    (A) 20 (B) 17 (C) 19 (D) 21 (E) 23
12. 2 1 4 2 6 3 8 4 2 1 6 8 4 1 2 1 3 6 8 4 1 2 3 6 5 8 8 4 1 2
    (A) 18 (B) 19 (C) 20 (D) 21 (E) 22
13. 2 5 2 1 4 8 4 2 1 6 3 5 2 1 4 1 2 5 6 6 8 2 4 1 3 1 5 2 3 2 6
    (A) 36 (B) 35 (C) 33 (D) 34 (E) 37

14. 6 2 8 4 1 2 5 8 4 2 1 5 4 2 1 3 5 6 3 5 1 5 8 4 1 2 5 1 2 3 6 3 8
(A) 48 (B) 49 (C) 50 (D) 47 (E) 46

15. 6 2 8 4 1 2 3 5 8 4 1 2 1 5 1 2 1 2 3 2 4 1 2 5 6 2 8 4 1 2 2
(A) 29 (B) 28 (C) 27 (D) 26 (E) 25

16. 5 3 4 1 6 8 2 1 4 2 3 5 4 6 8 4 1 1 8 6 5 2 3 1 2 1 2 4 8 2
(A) 33 (B) 30 (C) 29 (D) 28 (E) 32

17. 8 5 4 1 2 2 3 3 3 6 8 3 6 6 2 6 2 3 6 5 2 6 8 4 2 3 2 1 1 1 2 5 2
(A) 38 (B) 39 (C) 36 (D) 37 (E) 40

18. 3 3 2 1 5 2 1 4 8 5 2 8 1 8 5 6 3 4 1 4 8 4 1 2 5 3 6 6 2 3 2
(A) 33 (B) 40 (C) 35 (D) 36 (E) 32

19. 6 5 3 6 5 2 1 8 4 2 6 2 4 1 2 1 5 8 4 1 2 1 3 8 6 2 3 2 4 1
(A) 32 (B) 29 (C) 31 (D) 33 (E) 30

20. 1 6 8 2 4 1 2 8 5 2 1 4 5 8 1 2 1 1 4 8 4 1 2 3 2 21 4 2 8
(A) 21 (B) 23 (C) 19 (D) 17 (E) 25

21. 4 6 2 4 1 2 6 8 5 3 3 2 1 8 1 2 6 8 5 2 1 3 2 1 2 5 1 1 2 8 1
(A) 33 (B) 36 (C) 32 (D) 28 (E) 29

22. 8 2 1 8 2 1 2 1 4 4 8 5 2 1 3 6 2 1 4 8 5 2 5 6 6 3 1 4 6
(A) 26 (B) 28 (C) 29 (D) 27 (E) 25

23. 6 5 2 1 8 4 4 1 3 6 8 5 2 1 5 8 2 4 1 3 2 1 3 5 1 4 8 1 2 3 8
(A) 39 (B) 38 (C) 35 (D) 41 (E) 43

24. 8 5 4 5 6 6 1 5 4 8 2 1 2 3 6 2 2 6 8 4 6 2 6 1 3 2 5 1 8 8 2 1
(A) 30 (B) 32 (C) 33 (D) 29 (E) 31

25. 2 5 6 3 2 5 8 4 1 2 6 1 8 4 1 4 2 1 3 4 2 1 8 1 4 2 3 5 2 1 6 1
(A) 28 (B) 31 (C) 32 (D) 29 (E) 30

26. 2 1 6 1 6 6 8 5 4 1 2 3 3 2 2 1 4 2 5 4 1 2 5 2 1 4 5 5 1 2 4
(A) 38 (B) 35 (C) 34 (D) 32 (E) 31

27. 3 2 3 3 3 2 6 5 2 2 1 8 4 1 5 8 5 2 2 2 4 1 6 2 3 2 2 5
(A) 39 (B) 34 (C) 37 (D) 38 (E) 36

28. 3 5 8 6 4 1 2 6 4 8 5 2 8 8 4 1 2 1 6 8 5 4 1 2 5 1 8 2 6
(A) 29 (B) 28 (C) 27 (D) 30 (E) 31

29. 2 3 2 1 3 2 1 4 3 6 3 8 2 2 1 4 1 4 8 5 2 1 3 4 1 2 6 8 61 1
(A) 27 (B) 30 (C) 31 (D) 32 (E) 28

30. 3 2 6 4 1 4 3 2 6 8 4 1 2 5 8 2 1 3 2 8 4 1 2 6 5 8 6 3 2 8 4 1
(A) 25 (B) 28 (C) 27 (D) 26 (E) 30

PRACTICE SET-4

Total Ques.- 30
Time - 8 or 10 Min.

निर्देश : (प्रश्न 1–30) विषम संख्याओं को योग परीक्षण के प्रत्येक प्रश्न में सम और विषम संख्याओं को मिलाकर एक श्रृंखला दिया रहता है। इस श्रृंखला में प्रदत्त केवल विषम संख्या 1, 3, 5 आदि को जोड़ने के बाद नीचे दिए गए पाँच विकल्पों (A, B, C, D और E) में कोई एक सही विकल्प को ढूंढना होता है जिसे दिए गए उत्तर-पत्रक में गोले को काला/माउस की सहायता से क्लिक करना होता है।

Directions: (Questions 1–30) : Each question in the Odd Number Adding Test presents a series of even and odd numbers. You need to add the total number of odd numbers 1, 3, 5 etc. in the given series. After adding, select the correct option from the five choices (A, B, C, D & E) provided. Mark your answer by filling the circle on the answer sheet or by clicking on it using the mouse.

1. 2 4 2 2 1 3 2 8 2 6 5 4 8 2 4 8 6 2 3 1 4 1 2 1 2 1
   (A) 16 (B) 15 (C) 13 (D) 14 (E) 17
2. 2 8 4 1 2 3 5 2 1 4 1 2 2 2 3 1 5 6 2 3 8 6 8 1 3 2
   (A) 29 (B) 28 (C) 27 (D) 26 (E) 24
3. 3 5 8 4 5 1 2 1 2 4 2 6 4 2 3 3 2 3 6 8 4 5 2 8 4 2 6 6 8
   (A) 23 (B) 22 (C) 21 (D) 29 (E) 25
4. 2 8 6 2 1 4 8 2 5 1 6 3 2 5 4 1 3 6 1 4 3 2 4 1 2 3 1 2 1
   (A) 33 (B) 28 (C) 30 (D) 32 (E) 29
5. 3 6 4 1 2 6 8 2 1 2 1 4 2 1 2 1 1 2 8 4 2 5 1 2 1 4 1 2 3 2 1 5
   (A) 22 (B) 26 (C) 24 (D) 21 (E) 20
6. 2 3 5 4 2 2 1 4 1 2 4 2 3 8 2 1 4 2 2 2 3 6 8 2 5 1
   (A) 23 (B) 25 (C) 27 (D) 22 (E) 20
7. 6 5 4 1 2 1 2 1 2 3 6 6 8 1 2 5 2 2 8 5 6 2 8 4 2 1 5 1 2
   (A) 28 (B) 27 (C) 29 (D) 26 (E) 30
8. 4 2 1 3 2 1 4 5 2 1 8 8 4 6 8 4 1 2 3 6 8 5 4 1 2 1 4 5 3 2 1 2
   (A) 30 (B) 31 (C) 32 (D) 29 (E) 28
9. 2 3 6 8 5 4 8 6 6 4 1 4 1 8 6 2 5 8 4 1 2 3 2 1 2 3 2 1 4 4
   (A) 25 (B) 24 (C) 23 (D) 22 (E) 26
10. 6 5 2 5 4 1 3 5 1 2 6 2 8 4 1 2 1 5 2 3 2 3 2 1 1 4 2 1 2 4 1
    (A) 35 (B) 36 (C) 38 (D) 37 (E) 39
11. 3 2 2 4 1 2 6 1 2 3 6 8 6 2 8 4 1 2 6 8 4 1 2 5 1 8 5 4 2
    (A) 25 (B) 19 (C) 21 (D) 22 (E) 23
12. 2 1 3 6 8 4 1 2 3 6 2 1 4 26 3 3 4 2 1 6 8 4 1 5 8 8 4 1 2
    (A) 21 (B) 23 (C) 19 (D) 18 (E) 24
13. 2 2 5 6 6 8 2 4 1 3 1 5 2 3 5 2 1 4 8 4 2 1 6 3 5 2 1 4 1 2 6
    (A) 33 (B) 36 (C) 37 (D) 35 (E) 34

14. 6 2 6 3 5 1 5 8 4 1 2 5 1 8 4 1 2 5 8 4 2 1 5 4 2 1 3 5 2 3 6 3 8
(A) 46 (B) 49 (C) 50 (D) 47 (E) 48

15. 6 2 3 2 4 1 2 5 6 2 8 4 1 2 8 4 1 2 3 5 8 4 1 2 1 5 1 2 1 2 2
(A) 30 (B) 31 (C) 34 (D) 26 (E) 28

16. 5 3 2 6 8 4 2 1 6 3 4 1 4 8 4 1 2 5 3 6 6 2 3 2 4 1 6 8 2 1 4 2
(A) 27 (B) 26 (C) 25 (D) 29 (E) 30

17. 6 8 4 1 1 8 6 5 2 3 1 2 1 2 4 8 2 6 2 6 8 4 2 3 2 1 1 1 2 5 2
(A) 21 (B) 23 (C) 24 (D) 25 (E) 20

18. 8 5 4 1 2 2 3 3 3 6 8 3 3 5 4 3 3 2 1 5 2 1 4 8 5 2 8 1 8 5
(A) 50 (B) 49 (C) 50 (D) 51 (E) 52

19. 6 5 3 8 4 1 2 1 3 8 6 2 3 2 4 3 6 5 2 1 8 4 2 6 2 4 1 2 1 1
(A) 26 (B) 27 (C) 29 (D) 28 (E) 30

20. 1 3 2 6 8 5 3 3 2 1 8 1 2 8 5 1 6 8 2 4 1 2 8 4 1 2 3 2 4 2 8
(A) 26 (B) 29 (C) 30 (D) 25 (E) 28

21. 4 6 2 4 8 5 2 1 4 5 8 1 2 2 1 3 2 1 2 5 1 1 2 8 1
(A) 23 (B) 24 (C) 25 (D) 26 (E) 27

22. 2 1 4 8 5 2 5 6 5 2 1 8 4 1 3 6 8 2 1 5 8 2 4 8 2 6 6 3 1 4 6
(A) 29 (B) 31 (C) 33 (D) 30 (E) 32

23. 1 8 2 1 2 1 4 4 8 5 2 1 3 6 1 3 2 1 3 5 1 4 8 1 2 3 8
(A) 31 (B) 33 (C) 32 (D) 30 (E) 29

24. 8 6 4 1 2 6 1 8 4 1 4 2 1 3 3 5 2 5 4 5 6 6 1 5 4 8 2 1 2 3 6 2 2
(A) 35 (B) 37 (C) 36 (D) 34 (E) 33

25. 2 5 6 2 1 4 2 5 4 1 2 2 5 2 1 4 6 8 4 6 2 6 1 3 2 5 1 1 6 1
(A) 29 (B) 31 (C) 33 (D) 32 (E) 30

26. 2 1 8 8 2 1 3 2 5 6 1 6 6 8 5 4 1 2 3 3 2 5 5 1 2 4
(A) 37 (B) 36 (C) 34 (D) 35 (E) 33

27. 1 5 8 5 2 2 2 4 1 6 3 2 3 3 3 2 6 5 2 2 1 8 4 2 3 2 2 5
(A) 37 (B) 38 (C) 39 (D) 40 (E) 41

28. 3 5 6 8 5 4 1 2 5 1 8 2 6 8 6 4 1 2 6 5 8 5 2 8 8 4 1 2 1
(A) 34 (B) 32 (C) 31 (D) 33 (E) 30

29. 2 1 4 1 4 8 5 2 1 3 4 2 3 2 1 3 2 1 4 3 6 3 8 2 1 2 6 8 6 1 1
(A) 27 (B) 29 (C) 30 (D) 28 (E) 25

30. 3 2 3 2 8 4 1 2 6 5 8 8 3 2 8 6 4 1 4 3 2 6 8 4 1 2 3 8 2 1 4 1
(A) 25 (B) 20 (C) 21 (D) 26 (E) 27

PRACTICE SET-5

Total Ques.- 30
Time - 8 or 10 Min.

निर्देश : (प्रश्न 1–30) विषम संख्याओं को योग परीक्षण के प्रत्येक प्रश्न में सम और विषम संख्याओं को मिलाकर एक श्रृंखला दिया रहता है। इस श्रृंखला में प्रदत्त केवल विषम संख्या 1, 3, 5 आदि को जोड़ने के बाद नीचे दिए गए पाँच विकल्पों (A, B, C, D और E) में कोई एक सही विकल्प को ढूंढना होता है जिसे दिए गए उत्तर-पत्रक में गोले को काला/माउस की सहायता से क्लिक करना होता है।

Directions: (Questions 1–30) : Each question in the Odd Number Adding Test presents a series of even and odd numbers. You need to add the total number of odd numbers 1, 3, 5 etc. in the given series. After adding, select the correct option from the five choices (A, B, C, D & E) provided. Mark your answer by filling the circle on the answer sheet or by clicking on it using the mouse.

1. 8 4 2 6 5 2 3 1 5 4 2 3 6 2 1 1 1 2 3 2 8 4 5 2 6 2 3 6
(A) 30 (B) 31 (C) 32 (D) 34 (E) 3

2. 2 8 4 6 3 2 8 4 5 1 4 1 2 1 3 2 5 4 2 4 8 2 1 1 8 6 8 1 3 2
(A) 25 (B) 26 (C) 23 (D) 24 (E) 27

3. 3 5 8 4 5 6 1 4 3 2 4 1 2 2 8 4 1 3 1 2 1 4 1 2 1 2 4 2 6 6 8
(A) 27 (B) 28 (C) 26 (D) 29 (E) 31

4. 2 2 6 4 2 3 3 2 3 6 8 4 5 2 8 4 8 6 2 1 4 8 2 5 1 6 3 2 5 4 1 3
(A) 29 (B) 32 (C) 31 (D) 33 (E) 28

5. 3 6 2 8 4 2 5 1 2 1 2 3 5 4 2 2 3 6 8 4 1 2 4 2 3 8 2 4 1 2 3 2 1 5
(A) 31 (B) 33 (C) 29 (D) 34 (E) 35

6. 4 1 2 6 8 2 1 2 1 4 2 1 2 1 1 1 4 2 2 2 8 5 1 2 3 6 8 2 5 1
(A) 21 (B) 23 (C) 22 (D) 25 (E) 20

7. 6 5 4 1 2 1 2 1 2 3 6 6 8 2 1 3 2 1 4 5 2 1 8 8 4 4 1 2 1 2 5 2
(A) 22 (B) 29 (C) 27 (D) 25 (E) 23

8. 4 3 6 2 8 5 6 2 8 4 2 1 2 8 6 1 5 1 2 6 8 5 4 1 2 1 4 5 3 2 1 2
(A) 32 (B) 30 (C) 33 (D) 31 (E) 29

9. 2 5 8 4 1 2 3 3 2 3 5 2 3 2 3 2 1 1 4 2 1 2 4 1 2 1 2 3 2 1 4 4
(A) 35 (B) 30 (C) 32 (D) 36 (E) 34

10. 6 5 2 5 4 1 3 5 1 3 6 2 8 4 2 3 6 8 5 4 8 6 6 4 1 4 1 8 6
(A) 31 (B) 33 (C) 35 (D) 37 (E) 30

11. 3 2 1 4 2 6 3 3 4 2 1 6 8 4 2 4 1 2 6 1 2 3 6 8 6 2 8 8 5 4 2
(A) 20 (B) 23 (C) 21 (D) 22 (E) 25

12. 2 1 3 4 1 2 6 8 4 1 2 5 1 6 8 4 1 2 3 6 2 1 5 8 8 4 1 2
(A) 22 (B) 21 (C) 23 (D) 25 (E) 20

13. 2 2 5 6 4 1 2 5 8 4 2 1 5 4 2 1 3 5 6 8 2 4 1 3 1 5 2 3
(A) 37 (B) 42 (C) 40 (D) 41 (E) 39

14. 6 2 6 3 5 1 5 8 4 1 5 2 1 4 8 4 2 1 6 3 5 2 1 6 2 5 1 3 6 3 8
(A) 40 (B) 41 (C) 42 (D) 44 (E) 43

15. 6 2 8 4 1 2 1 5 1 2 1 2 3 2 4 1 2 5 6 2 8 4 1 2 8 4 1 2 3 5 2
(A) 26 (B) 29 (C) 28 (D) 27 (E) 30

16. 5 3 2 2 4 8 2 6 2 6 8 4 2 3 2 1 1 1 2 5 2 6 8 4 2 1 4 2
(A) 19 (B) 18 (C) 20 (D) 21 (E) 17

17. 6 6 3 4 1 4 8 4 1 2 5 3 6 6 2 3 2 4 6 8 2 1 8 4 1 6 5 2 1 2 1
(A) 25 (B) 26 (C) 24 (D) 21 (E) 23

18. 8 5 4 1 8 2 1 5 8 2 4 8 2 6 2 6 3 1 4 6 2 2 3 3 3 6 1 8 5
(A) 30 (B) 32 (C) 33 (D) 31 (E) 29

19. 6 5 3 8 4 1 2 1 3 8 6 2 3 2 4 3 5 2 1 8 4 2 6 2 4 1 2 1 1
(A) 26 (B) 27 (C) 25 (D) 29 (E) 28

20. 4 3 2 1 3 3 5 2 5 4 5 6 6 1 4 8 2 1 2 3 2 1 8 1 2 8 5 1 2 8
(A) 39 (B) 38 (C) 37 (D) 36 (E) 40

21. 4 6 2 4 8 5 2 1 4 5 8 2 4 1 2 2 1 3 2 1 2 5 1 1 2 8 1
(A) 21 (B) 22 (C) 25 (D) 26 (E) 27

22. 2 1 8 3 3 5 4 3 3 2 1 5 2 4 8 5 2 6 4 8 5 2 5 6 5 2 1 8 4 1 3 6
(A) 47 (B) 49 (C) 57 (D) 50 (E) 53

23. 1 8 2 1 2 1 4 4 8 5 2 1 4 3 6 1 3 2 1 3 5 1 4 8 1 2 3 8
(A) 29 (B) 31 (C) 28 (D) 32 (E) 30

24. 8 6 4 1 2 6 8 2 4 1 4 6 2 8 4 1 2 3 2 4 6 6 1 8 4 1 4 4 2 2
(A) 6 (B) 7 (C) 9 (D) 8 (E) 10

25. 2 5 6 2 1 4 6 5 2 2 4 1 8 4 2 3 2 4 2 5 8 4 1 2 2 5 2
(A) 26 (B) 25 (C) 24 (D) 22 (E) 28

26. 2 1 8 8 2 1 3 2 5 2 6 1 6 2 6 8 5 4 1 2 3 3 2 2 5 5 1 2 4
(A) 31 (B) 34 (C) 33 (D) 35 (E) 32

27. 1 5 1 4 6 8 4 6 2 6 1 3 2 5 1 1 6 1 8 5 2 2 2 4 1 6 3 2 3 3 3 2
(A) 38 (B) 36 (C) 35 (D) 37 (E) 33

28. 3 5 6 4 3 6 3 8 2 1 2 6 8 6 8 5 4 1 2 5 1 8 2 6 8 62 8 8 4 1 2 1
(A) 28 (B) 27 (C) 29 (D) 30 (E) 31

29. 2 1 4 1 4 4 1 2 6 5 8 5 4 1 4 3 2 6 8 8 5 2 1 3 3 6 6 8 5 3 2 1 1 1
(A) 40 (B) 41 (C) 42 (D) 43 (E) 44

30. 3 2 3 2 8 4 1 2 6 5 8 8 3 2 8 4 2 3 2 1 3 6 4 1 2 3 8 2 1 4 1
(A) 27 (B) 26 (C) 25 (D) 28 (E) 24

PRACTICE SET-6

Total Ques.- 30
Time - 8 or 10 Min.

निर्देश : (प्रश्न 1-30) विषम संख्याओं को योग परीक्षण के प्रत्येक प्रश्न में सम और विषम संख्याओं को मिलाकर एक श्रृंखला दिया रहता है। इस श्रृंखला में प्रदत्त केवल विषम संख्या 1, 3, 5 आदि को जोड़ने के बाद नीचे दिए गए पाँच विकल्पों (A, B, C, D और E) में कोई एक सही विकल्प को ढूंढना होता है जिसे दिए गए उत्तर-पत्रक में गोले को काला/माउस की सहायता से क्लिक करना होता है।

Directions: (Questions 1–30) : Each question in the Odd Number Adding Test presents a series of even and odd numbers. You need to add the total number of odd numbers 1, 3, 5 etc. in the given series. After adding, select the correct option from the five choices (A, B, C, D & E) provided. Mark your answer by filling the circle on the answer sheet or by clicking on it using the mouse.

1. 4 4 1 2 1 4 2 1 2 1 1 1 4 2 2 2 8 5 1 2 3 6 8 2 5 1 6
(A) 21 (B) 25 (C) 20 (D) 18 (E) 23

2. 2 8 2 2 8 4 1 3 1 2 1 4 1 2 1 2 3 2 8 4 5 1 4 1 2 1 3 1 3 2
(A) 28 (B) 26 (C) 24 (D) 20 (E) 27

3. 3 5 8 2 5 4 2 4 8 2 1 1 8 6 8 4 5 6 1 4 3 2 4 1 2 6 6 8
(A) 20 (B) 27 (C) 25 (D) 22 (E) 28

4. 2 2 6 4 2 3 6 8 4 1 2 4 2 3 8 2 4 1 2 3 2 5 6 8 8 4 5 2 3
(A) 28 (B) 22 (C) 19 (D) 24 (E) 26

5. 3 6 8 4 8 6 2 1 4 1 6 3 2 5 4 1 2 8 4 2 1 2 3 5 4 2 2 3 1 5
(A) 30 (B) 35 (C) 28 (D) 33 (E) 32

6. 4 8 4 2 6 2 3 1 4 2 3 6 2 1 1 1 2 3 2 8 4 5 2 6 2 3 1 2 6 8 2
(A) 18 (B) 20 (C) 25 (D) 22 (E) 23

7. 6 5 4 1 2 1 2 1 2 3 6 6 8 2 1 3 2 1 4 5 2 1 8 8 4 4 1 2 1 2 5 2
(A) 25 (B) 28 (C) 29 (D) 32 (E) 30

8. 4 3 2 6 8 4 6 1 4 2 1 2 4 1 2 1 2 3 2 1 2 8 5 6 2 8 4 2 1 2
(A) 15 (B) 17 (C) 20 (D) 22 (E) 18

9. 2 5 8 2 4 6 2 8 6 1 5 1 2 6 8 5 4 1 2 1 4 5 3 2 1 4 3 2 1 4 4
(A) 32 (B) 30 (C) 29 (D) 35 (E) 33

10. 6 5 1 4 2 6 3 3 4 2 1 6 8 4 2 4 1 2 6 1 2 3 6 8 6 2 8 4 1 8 6
(A) 17 (B) 19 (C) 21 (D) 23 (E) 20

11. 3 2 2 4 4 2 3 6 2 1 2 2 4 5 8 8 3 6 8 5 4 8 6 6 4 1 4 5 4 2
(A) 20 (B) 24 (C) 26 (D) 28 (E) 31

12. 2 1 1 6 3 5 2 1 6 2 5 1 1 2 3 3 2 3 5 2 3 2 2 5 1 6 8 4 14 1 2
(A) 40 (B) 45 (C) 42 (D) 43 (E) 47

13. 2 2 5 6 4 1 2 5 8 4 2 1 5 4 6 8 4 1 1 3 5 6 8 2 4 1 3 1 5 2 3
(A) 38 (B) 36 (C) 43 (D) 46 (E) 40

14. 6 2 6 1 2 5 6 2 8 4 1 2 8 4 1 2 8 4 1 5 2 1 4 8 4 2 3 6 3 8
(A) 18 (B) 20 (C) 23 (D) 21 (E) 25

15. 6 2 8 4 1 2 1 5 8 2 5 4 1 3 5 1 3 6 2 8 1 2 1 2 3 2 4 3 5 2
(A) 37 (B) 36 (C) 38 (D) 34 (E) 35

16. 5 3 2 3 2 4 6 8 2 1 8 4 2 8 4 1 6 5 2 1 2 1 8 4 2 1 4 2
(A) 19 (B) 20 (C) 21 (D) 22 (E) 23

17. 6 2 4 8 2 6 2 6 8 4 2 3 2 1 1 2 6 6 3 4 1 4 8 4 1 2 5 3 6 6 2
(A) 16 (B) 18 (C) 19 (D) 20 (E) 21

18. 8 5 4 2 4 3 5 2 1 8 4 2 6 2 4 1 2 1 1 1 8 2 1 5 8 2 4 8 2 8 5
(A) 25 (B) 30 (C) 27 (D) 29 (E) 28

19. 6 5 26 2 6 3 1 4 6 2 2 3 3 3 6 1 2 4 3 8 4 1 2 1 3 8 6 2
(A) 29 (B) 27 (C) 31 (D) 32 (E) 26

20. 4 3 2 1 3 3 8 2 4 1 2 2 1 3 2 1 2 5 1 2 8 5 2 5 4 5 8 5 1 2 8
(A) 41 (B) 42 (C) 43 (D) 44 (E) 45

21. 4 6 6 6 1 4 8 2 1 2 3 2 1 4 4 2 8 1 2 2 4 8 5 2 1 4 4 1
(A) 15 (B) 19 (C) 12 (D) 14 (E) 13

22. 8 1 4 3 6 1 3 2 1 3 5 1 4 8 1 2 3 8 2 1 8 3 3 3 2 1 5 2 4 8 3 6
(A) 40 (B) 39 (C) 38 (D) 42 (E) 41

23. 1 8 2 5 2 6 4 8 5 2 5 6 5 2 1 8 4 1 1 2 1 4 4 8 2 2 4 5 2
(A) 30 (B) 31 (C) 29 (D) 28 (E) 32

24. 2 3 2 6 6 1 2 1 4 6 5 2 2 4 1 8 4 1 2 6 8 2 4 1 4 6 2 8 4 1
(A) 13 (B) 19 (C) 16 (D) 15 (E) 14

25. 2 5 6 2 8 4 1 2 6 8 6 2 8 8 1 3 3 6 6 8 4 4 2 5 8 4 1 2 2 5 2
(A) 24 (B) 23 (C) 21 (D) 25 (E) 27

26. 2 1 8 8 2 1 3 2 5 1 8 5 2 2 2 4 1 2 2 6 1 6 2 6 8 5 5 5 1 2 4
(A) 32 (B) 33 (C) 34 (D) 35 (E) 36

27. 1 5 1 4 6 8 4 1 2 3 3 2 2 4 6 2 6 1 3 2 5 1 1 6 3 3 3 2
(A) 36 (B) 34 (C) 33 (D) 31 (E) 39

28. 3 5 6 4 3 63 5 4 3 8 2 2 1 2 6 8 6 8 5 4 1 2 5 1 8 4 1 2 1
(A) 36 (B) 35 (C) 34 (D) 37 (E) 33

29. 2 1 4 2 6 5 1 3 6 4 1 2 31 4 4 1 2 6 5 8 5 4 1 4 3 2 1 1 1
(A) 32 (B) 33 (C) 31 (D) 30 (E) 35

30. 3 2 3 2 3 2 6 8 8 5 2 5 8 4 1 2 6 5 8 8 3 2 8 4 2 3 2 8 2 1 4 1
(A) 28 (B) 29 (C) 33 (D) 31 (E) 32

PRACTICE SET-7

Total Ques.- 30
Time - 8 or 10 Min.

निर्देश : (प्रश्न 1–30) विषम संख्याओं को योग परीक्षण के प्रत्येक प्रश्न में सम और विषम संख्याओं को मिलाकर एक श्रृंखला दिया रहता है। इस श्रृंखला में प्रदत्त केवल विषम संख्या 1, 3, 5 आदि को जोड़ने के बाद नीचे दिए गए पाँच विकल्पों (A, B, C, D और E) में कोई एक सही विकल्प को ढूंढना होता है जिसे दिए गए उत्तर-पत्रक में गोले को काला/माउस की सहायता से क्लिक करना होता है।

Directions: (Questions 1–30) : Each question in the Odd Number Adding Test presents a series of even and odd numbers. You need to add the total number of odd numbers 1, 3, 5 etc. in the given series. After adding, select the correct option from the five choices (A, B, C, D & E) provided. Mark your answer by filling the circle on the answer sheet or by clicking on it using the mouse.

1. 4 5 2 4 6 1 4 3 2 4 1 2 6 6 8 4 4 1 2 1 4 2 1 2 2 5 1 6
(A) 19 (B) 17 (C) 15 (D) 16 (E) 20

2. 2 8 4 2 3 8 2 4 1 2 3 2 5 6 8 2 2 8 4 1 3 1 2 1 4 1 2 1 2 3 2 3 2
(A) 24 (B) 26 (C) 22 (D) 21 (E) 20

3. 3 5 1 1 1 4 2 2 2 8 5 1 2 3 6 8 8 2 5 4 2 4 8 2 1 1 8 6 8
(A) 27 (B) 26 (C) 24 (D) 25 (E) 28

4. 2 2 6 4 2 8 4 5 1 4 1 2 2 2 1 3 13 6 8 4 1 8 4 5 2 3
(A) 22 (B) 21 (C) 24 (D) 23 (E) 20

5. 3 6 1 1 1 2 3 2 8 4 5 2 6 2 3 8 4 8 6 2 1 4 1 6 3 2 5 2 2 3 1 5
(A) 32 (B) 30 (C) 36 (D) 33 (E) 35

6. 4 8 4 2 4 1 2 8 2 4 4 2 1 2 3 5 4 6 2 3 1 4 2 3 6 2 8 2
(A) 14 (B) 16 (C) 13 (D) 17 (E) 15

7. 6 1 2 1 2 3 2 1 2 8 5 6 2 8 4 2 5 1 2 1 2 3 6 6 8 1 2 1 2 5 2
(A) 24 (B) 26 (C) 28 (D) 29 (E) 27

8. 4 3 2 2 1 3 2 1 4 5 2 1 8 8 4 4 6 8 4 6 1 4 2 1 2 4 1 2
(A) 16 (B) 15 (C) 14 (D) 17 (E) 13

9. 2 5 8 2 2 1 6 5 1 4 2 6 3 3 4 2 1 6 8 4 2 4 1 2 6 4 6 3 2 1 4 4
(A) 20 (B) 25 (C) 23 (D) 21 (E) 24

10. 6 1 5 1 2 6 8 5 4 2 8 4 5 3 2 1 4 1 1 2 3 6 8 6 2 8 4 1 8 6
(A) 26 (B) 28 (C) 25 (D) 27 (E) 29

11. 3 2 2 8 6 6 4 1 4 5 4 4 4 2 3 6 2 1 2 2 4 5 8 8 3 6 8 5 4 2
(A) 23 (B) 27 (C) 21 (D) 24 (E) 26

12. 2 5 1 1 2 3 3 2 3 5 2 3 1 1 6 3 5 2 1 6 2 2 2 5 1 6 8 4 1 4 1 2
(A) 45 (B) 40 (C) 42 (D) 43 (E) 44

13. 2 2 2 8 4 1 2 8 4 1 5 2 1 4 8 5 6 4 1 2 5 8 4 2 1 5 3 1 5 2 3
(A) 34 (B) 35 (C) 37 (D) 39 (E) 36

14. 6 2 6 1 4 6 8 4 1 1 3 5 6 8 2 4 1 2 5 6 2 8 4 1 4 2 3 6 3 8
(A) 21 (B) 24 (C) 26 (D) 23 (E) 25

15. 6 2 2 8 1 2 1 2 3 2 4 8 4 1 2 1 5 8 2 5 4 1 3 5 1 3 6 3 5 2
(A) 41 (B) 40 (C) 38 (D) 39 (E) 42

16. 5 2 3 2 1 1 2 6 6 3 4 1 4 8 4 1 2 5 3 3 2 3 2 4 6 8 2 1 8 4 2 8
(A) 33 (B) 30 (C) 31 (D) 32 (E) 34

17. 6 2 4 4 1 6 5 2 1 2 2 5 8 1 8 4 2 1 4 2 8 2 6 2 6 8 4 6 6 2
(A) 13 (B) 15 (C) 14 (D) 11 (E) 16

18. 8 5 4 2 4 3 5 2 1 8 4 2 6 2 4 1 2 1 1 1 8 2 1 5 8 2 4 8 2 8 5
(A) 29 (B) 31 (C) 30 (D) 28 (E) 32

19. 6 8 1 2 3 8 2 1 8 3 3 3 2 1 5 2 5 2 6 2 6 3 1 4 6 2 1 3 8 6 2
(A) 35 (B) 30 (C) 33 (D) 34 (E) 32

20. 4 3 2 1 3 3 8 2 4 1 2 2 1 3 2 1 2 5 1 2 8 5 2 5 4 5 8 5 1 2 8
(A) 44 (B) 46 (C) 45 (D) 41 (E) 43

21. 4 6 6 6 1 4 8 2 1 2 3 2 1 4 4 2 8 1 2 2 4 8 5 2 1 4 4 1
(A) 15 (B) 14 (C) 18 (D) 16 (E) 19

22. 8 1 4 3 2 2 3 2 4 6 1 2 4 3 8 4 1 6 1 3 2 1 3 5 1 4 4 8 3 6
(A) 33 (B) 30 (C) 32 (D) 29 (E) 31

23. 6 8 2 5 2 6 4 8 5 2 5 6 5 2 1 8 4 1 1 2 1 4 4 8 2 2 4 5 2
(A) 27 (B) 29 (C) 28 (D) 31 (E) 33

24. 2 3 4 6 1 6 2 6 8 5 5 5 1 2 4 1 2 6 8 2 4 1 4 6 2 8 4 1
(A) 23 (B) 26 (C) 25 (D) 22 (E) 21

25. 2 5 6 2 8 4 1 2 6 8 6 2 8 8 1 3 3 6 6 8 4 4 2 5 8 4 1 2 2 5 2
(A) 23 (B) 22 (C) 21 (D) 24 (E) 25

26. 2 1 8 8 2 1 3 2 2 6 6 1 2 1 4 6 4 6 2 4 1 8 5 1 8 5 2 2 2 4 1 2 2
(A) 18 (B) 19 (C) 21 (D) 23 (E) 20

27. 1 5 3 6 8 5 4 1 2 5 1 1 4 6 8 4 1 2 3 3 2 2 5 1 1 6 3 3 3 2
(A) 40 (B) 43 (C) 45 (D) 47 (E) 46

28. 3 5 6 4 5 8 3 2 8 4 2 3 2 8 2 1 3 3 5 4 3 8 2 1 2 6 8 8 4 1 2 1
(A) 37 (B) 39 (C) 38 (D) 35 (E) 36

29. 2 1 5 8 5 4 1 4 3 2 4 4 2 6 5 1 3 6 2 4 1 2 31 4 4 1 2 61 1 1
(A) 31 (B) 32 (C) 30 (D) 33 (E) 34

30. 3 2 3 2 3 2 6 8 8 5 2 5 8 4 1 4 2 6 4 4 6 2 6 1 3 2 6 4 1
(A) 21 (B) 24 (C) 25 (D) 27 (E) 26

PRACTICE SET-8

Total Ques.- 30
Time - 8 or 10 Min.

निर्देश : (प्रश्न 1–30) विषम संख्याओं को योग परीक्षण के प्रत्येक प्रश्न में सम और विषम संख्याओं को मिलाकर एक श्रृंखला दिया रहता है। इस श्रृंखला में प्रदत्त केवल विषम संख्या 1, 3, 5 आदि को जोड़ने के बाद नीचे दिए गए पाँच विकल्पों (A, B, C, D और E) में कोई एक सही विकल्प को ढूंढना होता है जिसे दिए गए उत्तर-पत्रक में गोले को काला/माउस की सहायता से क्लिक करना होता है।

Directions: (Questions 1–30) : Each question in the Odd Number Adding Test presents a series of even and odd numbers. You need to add the total number of odd numbers 1, 3, 5 etc. in the given series. After adding, select the correct option from the five choices (A, B, C, D & E) provided. Mark your answer by filling the circle on the answer sheet or by clicking on it using the mouse.

1. 2 2 8 4 2 5 1 2 1 2 3 6 6 8 1 2 1 2 5 2 4 5 2 4 6 4 6
   (A) 21 (B) 23 (C) 22 (D) 24 (E) 26
2. 2 8 4 1 3 1 2 1 4 1 2 1 2 8 4 2 3 8 2 4 1 2 3 6 8 2 3 2 3 2
   (A) 20 (B) 21 (C) 24 (D) 25 (E) 23
3. 3 8 8 2 5 4 2 4 8 2 1 1 5 1 1 1 4 2 2 2 8 5 1 2 3 8 6 8
   (A) 25 (B) 26 (C) 29 (D) 30 (E) 27
4. 2 2 6 4 4 5 2 6 2 3 8 4 8 6 4 1 6 3 2 5 2 2 4 6 8 4 5 1 2 3
   (A) 27 (B) 29 (C) 25 (D) 26 (E) 31
5. 4 1 2 2 2 1 3 13 6 8 4 1 8 4 5 3 6 1 1 1 2 3 2 8 3 1 5
   (A) 30 (B) 33 (C) 31 (D) 35 (E) 34
6. 4 8 4 2 4 1 2 8 2 4 4 2 1 2 3 5 4 6 2 3 1 4 2 3 6 2 8 2
   (A) 15 (B) 13 (C) 17 (D) 16 (E) 19
7. 6 1 4 3 2 4 1 2 6 6 8 4 4 1 2 1 4 2 1 2 2 5 1 1 2 1 2 3 2 1 5 6
   (A) 24 (B) 23 (C) 21 (D) 19 (E) 25
8. 4 3 2 2 6 8 4 2 4 1 2 6 4 6 3 2 1 3 2 1 4 5 2 2 4 1 8 6 2
   (A) 20 (B) 19 (C) 16 (D) 18 (E) 17
9. 2 5 8 2 6 3 3 4 2 1 8 2 2 1 6 4 6 8 4 6 1 4 2 1 2 4 5 1 4 4 4
   (A) 21 (B) 19 (C) 20 (D) 23 (E) 22
10. 6 2 1 4 1 1 2 3 6 6 2 2 5 1 2 6 8 5 4 2 8 4 5 3 4 1 8 6
    (A) 32 (B) 20 (C) 26 (D) 25 (E) 29
11. 3 2 2 2 4 5 8 8 3 6 8 5 2 8 6 6 4 1 4 5 4 4 4 2 3 6 2 1 4 2
    (A) 25 (B) 21 (C) 23 (D) 27 (E) 26
12. 2 5 3 5 2 1 6 2 2 2 5 1 6 1 1 2 3 3 2 3 3 1 1 3 8 4 1 4 1 2
    (A) 41 (B) 43 (C) 45 (D) 39 (E) 37
13. 2 6 4 1 2 5 8 4 2 1 5 3 1 8 4 1 2 8 4 1 5 2 1 4 8 5 5 2 3
    (A) 36 (B) 34 (C) 38 (D) 39 (E) 37

14. 6 2 4 1 2 5 6 2 8 1 2 1 2 3 2 4 8 6 1 4 6 8 4 1 4 2 3 6 3 8
(A) 19 (B) 20 (C) 21 (D) 22 (E) 23

15. 6 2 2 8 4 14 1 2 1 5 6 8 1 3 5 6 8 2 5 4 1 3 5 1 3 6 3 5 2
(A) 41 (B) 42 (C) 43 (D) 44 (E) 45

16. 3 2 5 4 1 8 6 4 2 1 5 8 5 2 3 1 4 5 2 3 6 2 4 1 5 4 1 2 3 6 2 1
(A) 43 (B) 42 (C) 39 (D) 40 (E) 41

17. 8 4 2 1 6 5 2 1 5 4 2 3 1 2 5 4 1 2 1 4 2 8 2 6 2 6 8 4 6 6 2
(A) 22 (B) 23 (C) 25 (D) 21 (E) 20

18. 6 2 3 5 2 1 4 2 1 3 1 5 4 1 6 5 2 3 1 1 8 2 1 5 8 2 4 2 8 5
(A) 40 (B) 39 (C) 41 (D) 42 (E) 43

19. 5 6 5 2 3 1 2 3 5 8 4 1 2 6 8 2 2 5 2 6 2 6 3 1 1 3 8 6 2
(A) 38 (B) 37 (C) 34 (D) 36 (E) 35

20. 4 3 2 1 3 3 8 2 4 1 3 6 2 1 4 8 2 1 4 2 1 6 8 2 8 5 1 2 8
(A) 25 (B) 23 (C) 24 (D) 22 (E) 21

21. 4 6 8 1 2 2 4 8 5 2 1 2 6 6 1 4 8 2 1 2 3 2 1 4 4 2 4 4 1
(A) 13 (B) 11 (C) 14 (D) 17 (E) 16

22. 8 1 3 2 1 3 5 1 4 1 4 3 2 2 3 2 4 3 6 1 2 4 3 8 4 1 6 4 8 3 6
(A) 31 (B) 33 (C) 30 (D) 32 (E) 29

23. 6 8 1 1 2 1 4 4 8 2 2 4 5 2 5 2 6 4 8 5 2 5 6 5 2 1 8 4 2
(A) 27 (B) 28 (C) 31 (D) 30 (E) 29

24. 2 3 4 1 2 6 8 2 4 1 4 6 4 6 1 6 2 6 8 5 5 5 1 2 2 8 4 1
(A) 21 (B) 25 (C) 23 (D) 24 (E) 22

25. 2 5 6 6 8 4 4 2 5 8 4 1 2 2 5 6 2 8 4 1 2 6 8 6 2 8 8 1 3 3 2
(A) 23 (B) 21 (C) 19 (D) 24 (E) 25

26. 2 1 2 4 1 8 5 1 8 5 2 2 8 8 2 1 3 2 2 6 6 1 2 1 4 6 4 6 2 4 1 2 2
(A) 17 (B) 19 (C) 21 (D) 22 (E) 20

27. 1 5 3 2 3 3 2 2 5 1 1 6 3 6 8 5 4 1 2 5 1 1 4 6 8 4 1 3 3 2
(A) 46 (B) 47 (C) 43 (D) 45 (E) 44

28. 3 5 6 3 8 2 1 2 6 8 8 4 5 8 3 2 8 4 2 3 2 8 2 1 3 3 5 4 1 2 1
(A) 32 (B) 30 (C) 29 (D) 28 (E) 37

29. 2 1 6 2 4 1 2 3 1 4 4 1 2 6 5 8 5 4 1 4 3 2 4 4 2 6 5 1 3 1 1 1
(A) 30 (B) 31 (C) 35 (D) 34 (E) 33

30. 3 2 6 4 4 6 2 6 1 3 2 3 2 3 2 6 8 8 5 2 5 8 4 1 4 2 6 4 1
(A) 25 (B) 26 (C) 27 (D) 23 (E) 21

PRACTICE SET-9

Total Ques.- 30
Time - 8 or 10 Min.

निर्देश : (प्रश्न 1–30) विषम संख्याओं को योग परीक्षण के प्रत्येक प्रश्न में सम और विषम संख्याओं को मिलाकर एक श्रृंखला दिया रहता है। इस श्रृंखला में प्रदत्त केवल विषम संख्या 1, 3, 5 आदि को जोड़ने के बाद नीचे दिए गए पाँच विकल्पों (A, B, C, D और E) में कोई एक सही विकल्प को ढूंढना होता है जिसे दिए गए उत्तर-पत्रक में गोले को काला/माउस की सहायता से क्लिक करना होता है।

Directions: (Questions 1–30) : Each question in the Odd Number Adding Test presents a series of even and odd numbers. You need to add the total number of odd numbers 1, 3, 5 etc. in the given series. After adding, select the correct option from the five choices (A, B, C, D & E) provided. Mark your answer by filling the circle on the answer sheet or by clicking on it using the mouse.

1. 4 2 2 2 8 5 1 2 3 8 6 8 2 5 4 8 1 3 2 2 4 5 2 4 6 4 6
   (A) 21 (B) 22 (C) 24 (D) 25 (E) 23
2. 2 3 6 8 4 1 8 4 5 3 6 1 1 1 2 8 4 1 3 1 2 1 4 1 2 1 2 3 2 3 2
   (A) 29 (B) 27 (C) 28 (D) 30 (E) 31
3. 3 8 1 8 2 5 4 2 4 8 2 1 1 2 2 8 4 1 2 1 2 3 6 6 8 1 2 5 1 1 1
   (A) 25 (B) 26 (C) 27 (D) 23 (E) 21
4. 2 2 6 4 5 2 6 2 3 8 4 8 4 1 6 3 2 5 2 2 4 6 8 4 5 1 2 3
   (A) 25 (B) 26 (C) 27 (D) 28 (E) 29
5. 4 1 2 2 2 1 3 1 8 4 2 3 8 2 4 1 2 3 6 8 2 3 2 8 3 1 5
   (A) 27 (B) 23 (C) 25 (D) 26 (E) 20
6. 4 8 4 2 4 1 2 8 2 4 4 2 1 2 3 5 4 6 2 3 1 4 2 3 6 2 8 2
   (A) 16 (B) 14 (C) 15 (D) 18 (E) 17
7. 6 1 4 3 1 2 2 5 1 1 2 1 2 3 2 4 1 2 6 6 8 4 4 1 2 4 2 2 1 5 6
   (A) 22 (B) 23 (C) 25 (D) 24 (E) 26
8. 4 3 3 2 1 4 5 2 2 4 1 8 6 2 2 6 8 2 4 2 4 1 2 6 4 6 3 2 1 2
   (A) 16 (B) 18 (C) 19 (D) 17 (E) 20
9. 2 6 8 4 6 1 4 2 1 2 4 5 8 2 6 3 3 4 2 1 8 2 2 1 6 4 1 4 4 4
   (A) 16 (B) 17 (C) 19 (D) 20 (E) 15
10. 6 2 8 5 4 2 8 4 5 3 4 1 8 1 4 1 1 2 2 6 3 6 6 2 2 5 1 2 6 6
    (A) 21 (B) 25 (C) 26 (D) 28 (E) 29
11. 3 1 4 5 4 4 4 2 3 6 2 2 2 4 5 8 8 3 6 8 5 2 8 6 6 4 2 1 4 2
    (A) 25 (B) 23 (C) 21 (D) 27 (E) 26
12. 2 5 3 2 3 3 1 1 3 8 4 1 4 1 3 5 2 1 6 2 2 2 5 1 6 1 1 2 3 2
    (A) 40 (B) 39 (C) 42 (D) 41 (E) 43
13. 2 8 4 1 5 2 1 4 8 5 2 6 4 1 2 5 8 4 2 1 5 3 1 8 4 1 5 2 3
    (A) 35 (B) 37 (C) 36 (D) 33 (E) 34

14. 6 2 4 6 1 4 6 8 4 1 4 2 3 6 1 2 5 6 2 8 1 2 1 2 3 2 4 8 3 8

(A) 18 (B) 17 (C) 16 (D) 19 (E) 20

15. 6 2 2 8 4 1 3 5 1 3 6 4 1 4 1 2 1 5 6 8 1 3 5 6 8 2 5 3 5 2

(A) 41 (B) 42 (C) 43 (D) 44 (E) 45

16. 6 5 2 1 4 8 5 2 1 3 6 5 2 1 4 2 1 3 6 2 4 1 5 4 1 2 3 6 2 1

(A) 38 (B) 33 (C) 34 (D) 36 (E) 35

17. 8 4 2 6 8 2 4 1 2 5 8 4 1 2 3 2 5 3 5 8 2 6 2 6 8 4 6 6 2

(A) 22 (B) 21 (C) 23 (D) 25 (E) 24

18. 4 1 2 5 6 5 2 1 4 2 3 8 4 2 1 5 2 3 1 1 8 2 1 5 8 2 4 2 8 5

(A) 35 (B) 37 (C) 38 (D) 36 (E) 33

19. 5 6 5 2 3 1 2 3 5 8 4 1 6 2 5 8 4 1 2 3 2 5 5 4 1 2 8 2

(A) 43 (B) 40 (C) 41 (D) 42 (E) 44

20. 4 3 2 1 3 2 5 8 4 1 2 5 1 2 3 5 8 4 1 2 1 6 8 2 8 5 1 2 8

(A) 35 (B) 36 (C) 33 (D) 32 (E) 34

21. 2 5 6 5 8 4 1 2 3 5 1 2 1 4 2 1 5 4 2 1 2 3 2 1 4 4 2 4 4 1

(A) 31 (B) 32 (C) 35 (D) 33 (E) 34

22. 3 5 8 5 4 1 2 6 5 8 4 1 2 6 5 2 1 4 1 2 4 3 8 4 1 6 4 8 3 6

(A) 33 (B) 37 (C) 34 (D) 35 (E) 36

23. 5 2 6 4 8 5 2 5 6 6 8 1 1 2 1 4 4 8 2 2 4 5 2 5 2 1 8 4 2

(A) 27 (B) 29 (C) 30 (D) 31 (E) 28

24. 2 6 2 6 8 5 5 5 1 2 2 8 3 4 1 2 6 8 2 4 1 4 6 4 6 1 4 1

(A) 23 (B) 19 (C) 17 (D) 16 (E) 15

25. 6 2 8 4 1 2 6 8 6 2 2 5 6 6 8 4 2 5 8 4 1 2 2 5 8 8 1 3 3 2

(A) 22 (B) 23 (C) 24 (D) 25 (E) 26

26. 2 1 8 2 1 3 2 2 6 6 1 2 1 4 6 4 6 2 4 2 4 1 8 5 1 8 5 2 2 8 1 2 2

(A) 19 (B) 18 (C) 17 (D) 20 (E) 15

27. 1 5 3 2 4 6 8 4 1 3 3 3 2 2 5 1 1 6 3 6 8 5 4 1 2 5 1 1 3 2

(A) 46 (B) 47 (C) 44 (D) 43 (E) 45

28. 3 3 2 8 4 2 3 2 8 2 1 3 3 5 4 1 2 5 6 3 8 2 1 2 6 8 8 4 5 8 1

(A) 36 (B) 38 (C) 37 (D) 39 (E) 40

29. 4 1 4 3 2 4 4 2 6 5 2 1 6 2 4 1 2 3 1 4 4 1 2 6 5 8 5 1 3 1 1 1

(A) 32 (B) 33 (C) 31 (D) 34 (E) 35

30. 3 2 3 2 6 8 8 5 2 5 8 4 1 4 2 6 4 6 4 4 6 2 6 1 3 2 3 2 1

(A) 25 (B) 27 (C) 24 (D) 23 (E) 28

PRACTICE SET-10

Total Ques.- 30
Time - 8 or 10 Min.

निर्देश : (प्रश्न 1-30) विषम संख्याओं को योग परीक्षण के प्रत्येक प्रश्न में सम और विषम संख्याओं को मिलाकर एक श्रृंखला दिया रहता है। इस श्रृंखला में प्रदत्त केवल विषम संख्या 1, 3, 5 आदि को जोड़ने के बाद नीचे दिए गए पाँच विकल्पों (A, B, C, D और E) में कोई एक सही विकल्प को ढूंढना होता है जिसे दिए गए उत्तर-पत्रक में गोले को काला/माउस की सहायता से क्लिक करना होता है।

Directions: (Questions 1–30) : Each question in the Odd Number Adding Test presents a series of even and odd numbers. You need to add the total number of odd numbers 1, 3, 5 etc. in the given series. After adding, select the correct option from the five choices (A, B, C, D & E) provided. Mark your answer by filling the circle on the answer sheet or by clicking on it using the mouse.

1. 4 4 1 2 3 6 8 2 3 2 8 3 1 5 4 5 3 1 1 8 5 2 2 2 8 5 6 4 6
   (A) 35 (B) 37 (C) 34 (D) 33 (E) 36
2. 5 6 2 4 1 8 4 2 1 6 8 2 1 2 3 2 1 3 1 2 1 4 1 2 1 2 3 2 3 2
   (A) 25 (B) 26 (C) 27 (D) 28 (E) 29
3. 3 8 1 8 2 5 4 2 3 6 8 2 1 4 6 5 2 8 1 4 2 6 8 1 2 5 1 1 1
   (A) 27 (B) 29 (C) 26 (D) 25 (E) 28
4. 2 2 6 2 6 5 2 8 4 1 2 3 5 2 1 4 6 5 3 2 5 2 2 4 6 8 4 5 1 2 3
   (A) 37 (B) 38 (C) 39 (D) 40 (E) 41
5. 4 1 2 2 2 3 8 4 6 5 2 1 3 2 5 8 4 1 2 5 4 1 2 6 4 2 3 8 2
   (A) 27 (B) 29 (C) 30 (D) 32 (E) 28
6. 4 8 3 5 2 6 8 4 1 2 3 5 8 4 1 2 3 6 4 6 2 3 1 3 2 3 6 2 8 2
   (A) 35 (B) 33 (C) 31 (D) 34 (E) 36
7. 6 1 4 3 1 2 2 6 8 2 1 4 8 4 1 2 5 6 5 8 4 1 2 2 2 4 2 2 1 5 6
   (A) 23 (B) 22 (C) 25 (D) 24 (E) 26
8. 4 3 3 2 1 1 6 5 2 1 4 8 4 1 2 3 6 8 4 1 2 1 3 6 4 6 3 2 1 2
   (A) 25 (B) 27 (C) 29 (D) 28 (E) 26
9. 2 6 8 2 6 3 3 4 2 1 8 2 3 1 6 4 1 8 4 6 1 4 2 1 2 4 3 4 4 4
   (A) 18 (B) 19 (C) 17 (D) 20 (E) 21
10. 4 1 1 2 2 6 3 6 6 2 2 5 2 8 5 4 2 8 4 5 3 4 1 8 1 4 5 3 2 6 6
    (A) 31 (B) 32 (C) 34 (D) 33 (E) 35
11. 3 1 4 5 3 6 8 5 2 8 6 6 4 5 4 1 4 2 3 6 2 2 2 4 5 8 8 2 1 4 2
    (A) 33 (B) 32 (C) 31 (D) 34 (E) 35
12. 2 5 2 1 6 2 2 2 5 1 6 1 1 2 3 2 3 3 1 3 3 8 4 1 4 1 3 5 3 2
    (A) 42 (B) 47 (C) 43 (D) 46 (E) 45
13. 2 8 4 2 1 5 3 1 8 2 2 1 4 1 5 2 1 4 8 5 2 6 4 1 2 5 83
    (A) 31 (B) 36 (C) 34 (D) 32 (E) 33

14. 6 2 4 6 8 4 1 3 5 1 3 6 4 1 4 1 1 4 6 1 4 2 3 6 1 2 5 6 3 8
(A) 27 (B) 28 (C) 26 (D) 30 (E) 29

15. 6 2 8 2 5 3 5 2 2 1 5 6 2 2 2 4 5 8 1 3 5 6 8 2 5 3 5 2
(A) 45 (B) 47 (C) 46 (D) 48 (E) 49

16. 6 5 2 1 3 2 2 1 4 2 1 5 4 2 1 2 3 2 1 4 4 2 4 4 1 2 3 6 2 1
(A) 25 (B) 27 (C) 26 (D) 30 (E) 31

17. 8 4 2 6 4 8 5 2 5 1 3 6 5 2 1 4 2 1 3 6 2 4 1 5 4 1 26 2
(A) 34 (B) 31 (C) 32 (D) 35 (E) 29

18. 4 1 2 5 6 5 6 5 2 3 1 4 2 3 8 4 2 1 3 1 8 2 1 5 8 2 4 2 8 5
(A) 39 (B) 40 (C) 41 (D) 42 (E) 43

19. 5 2 3 1 8 2 3 4 1 2 5 8 4 1 2 3 2 5 3 4 1 2 3 2 5 4 1 2 8 2
(A) 42 (B) 43 (C) 41 (D) 40 (E) 39

20. 4 3 2 1 3 2 5 8 4 3 1 2 5 8 1 2 5 1 2 3 5 1 6 8 2 8 5 1 2 8
(A) 42 (B) 44 (C) 45 (D) 41 (E) 43

21. 2 5 6 5 2 1 4 1 2 4 3 8 5 2 6 4 8 5 2 5 2 5 2 4 5 8 4 1 2 3 5 1
(A) 51 (B) 52 (C) 50 (D) 49 (E) 48

22. 3 5 8 5 4 1 2 6 5 8 2 6 4 1 2 6 5 2 1 4 1 2 4 3 8 4 1 6 4 8 3 6
(A) 35 (B) 34 (C) 33 (D) 32 (E) 31

23. 6 6 8 1 1 2 1 2 3 5 8 4 1 6 4 4 8 2 2 4 5 2 5 2 8 4 1 2 1 8 4 2
(A) 25 (B) 28 (C) 27 (D) 24 (E) 26

24. 2 6 2 6 85 8 2 6 5 8 8 1 3 3 6 8 4 6 2 6 5 2 1 4 6 4 6 1 4 1
(A) 24 (B) 23 (C) 22 (D) 21 (E) 25

25. 6 2 8 4 1 2 6 4 2 4 2 1 3 2 2 6 6 1 2 1 1 8 5 1 8 5 2 4 2 5 8 4 1 2 2
(A) 25 (B) 28 (C) 26 (D) 24 (E) 23

26. 2 1 8 8 6 2 2 5 5 5 1 2 2 8 3 4 1 2 6 8 2 4 5 64 6 2 2 8 1 2 2
(A) 23 (B) 27 (C) 25 (D) 26 (E) 30

27. 1 5 3 2 4 6 8 4 1 3 3 3 2 2 2 3 2 8 2 1 3 3 5 1 1 5 1 1 3 2
(A) 50 (B) 52 (C) 47 (D) 46 (E) 40

28. 3 3 2 8 4 4 1 2 6 5 8 6 3 6 8 5 4 1 2 8 2 1 2 6 8 8 4 5 8 1
(A) 26 (B) 28 (C) 27 (D) 25 (E) 23

29. 4 1 4 3 2 4 4 2 4 4 2 6 1 6 5 2 1 6 2 6 8 4 6 3 1 4 5 1 3 1 1 1
(A) 27 (B) 25 (C) 26 (D) 28 (E) 22

30. 3 2 3 2 6 8 8 5 2 4 1 2 5 6 5 8 4 1 4 2 6 4 6 3 2 3 2 1
(A) 29 (B) 31 (C) 32 (D) 33 (E) 30

PRACTICE SET-11

Total Ques.- 30
Time - 8 or 10 Min.

निर्देश : (प्रश्न 1-30) विषम संख्याओं को योग परीक्षण के प्रत्येक प्रश्न में सम और विषम संख्याओं को मिलाकर एक श्रृंखला दिया रहता है। इस श्रृंखला में प्रदत्त केवल विषम संख्या 1, 3, 5 आदि को जोड़ने के बाद नीचे दिए गए पाँच विकल्पों (A, B, C, D और E) में कोई एक सही विकल्प को ढूंढना होता है जिसे दिए गए उत्तर-पत्रक में गोले को काला/माउस की सहायता से क्लिक करना होता है।

Directions: (Questions 1–30) : Each question in the Odd Number Adding Test presents a series of even and odd numbers. You need to add the total number of odd numbers 1, 3, 5 etc. in the given series. After adding, select the correct option from the five choices (A, B, C, D & E) provided. Mark your answer by filling the circle on the answer sheet or by clicking on it using the mouse.

1. 4 4 1 2 1 2 1 4 1 2 1 2 3 2 3 2 3 6 8 2 3 2 2 8 5 6 4 6
   (A) 22 (B) 23 (C) 24 (D) 25 (E) 26
2. 5 6 2 4 1 2 8 3 1 5 4 3 1 1 8 5 2 8 4 2 1 6 8 2 1 2 3 2 1 3
   (A) 32 (B) 34 (C) 33 (D) 31 (E) 29
3. 3 8 1 8 2 5 1 4 6 5 3 2 5 2 2 4 6 4 2 3 6 8 2 1 4 6 5 2 1 1 1
   (A) 33 (B) 34 (C) 36 (D) 35 (E) 32
4. 2 2 6 2 8 1 4 2 6 8 1 2 5 6 5 2 8 4 1 2 3 5 2 8 4 5 1 2 3
   (A) 32 (B) 28 (C) 29 (D) 30 (E) 31
5. 4 1 2 2 2 2 3 1 3 2 3 6 2 3 8 4 6 5 2 1 1 2 6 4 2 3 8 2
   (A) 25 (B) 26 (C) 27 (D) 28 (E) 24
6. 4 8 3 2 5 8 4 1 2 5 4 3 5 2 6 8 4 1 2 3 5 8 4 1 2 3 6 4 6 8 2
   (A) 37 (B) 38 (C) 40 (D) 35 (E) 39
7. 6 1 4 1 2 1 3 6 4 6 3 3 1 2 2 6 8 2 1 4 8 4 1 2 5 2 2 1 5 6
   (A) 25 (B) 24 (C) 26 (D) 23 (E) 27
8. 4 3 3 2 1 1 6 5 8 4 1 2 2 2 4 6 5 2 1 4 8 4 1 2 3 6 8 4 2 1 2
   (A) 26 (B) 25 (C) 24 (D) 23 (E) 29
9. 2 6 2 3 1 6 4 1 8 4 6 1 6 6 2 2 5 2 8 5 4 4 2 1 2 4 3 4 4 4
   (A) 20 (B) 21 (C) 22 (D) 23 (E) 24
10. 4 1 1 2 2 6 3 2 8 4 8 2 6 3 3 4 2 1 8 2 5 3 4 1 8 1 4 5 3 2 6 6
    (A) 31 (B) 32 (C) 30 (D) 33 (E) 34
11. 3 1 4 2 3 5 3 1 3 3 8 4 1 4 1 3 5 5 3 6 8 5 2 8 6 6 4 5 4 1 4 2 3
    (A) 55 (B) 54 (C) 53 (D) 56 (E) 52
12. 6 2 2 2 4 5 8 8 2 1 4 2 2 5 2 1 6 2 2 2 5 1 6 1 1 2 3 3 2
    (A) 25 (B) 24 (C) 27 (D) 26 (E) 23
13. 2 8 1 1 4 6 1 4 2 3 6 1 2 5 6 4 2 1 5 3 1 8 2 2 1 4 1 5 5 8 3
    (A) 38 (B) 39 (C) 36 (D) 35 (E) 37

14. 6 2 4 2 1 4 8 5 2 6 4 1 2 6 8 4 1 3 5 1 3 6 4 1 4 3 8
(A) 21 (B) 22 (C) 24 (D) 31 (E) 30

15. 6 2 3 5 6 8 2 5 3 8 2 5 3 5 2 2 1 5 6 2 2 2 4 5 8 1 5 2
(A) 46 (B) 42 (C) 47 (D) 43 (E) 48

16. 6 5 3 8 5 2 6 4 8 5 2 5 2 5 2 4 5 8 4 1 2 1 2 1 2 3 6 2 1
(A) 39 (B) 41 (C) 40 (D) 42 (E) 37

17. 8 4 2 3 2 5 3 4 1 2 3 2 5 4 1 5 2 6 4 8 5 6 4 1 3 2 6 2
(A) 34 (B) 35 (C) 36 (D) 33 (E) 32

18. 4 1 2 5 6 5 6 5 2 3 1 4 2 3 8 4 2 1 3 1 8 2 1 5 8 2 4 2 8 5
(A) 35 (B) 34 (C) 36 (D) 37 (E) 39

19. 5 2 3 1 3 1 2 5 2 3 5 8 6 4 4 8 2 2 4 5 2 5 2 8 4 1 2 1 8 2 8 2
(A) 37 (B) 40 (C) 39 (D) 38 (E) 36

20. 4 3 2 1 3 2 5 8 4 3 1 2 5 8 1 2 5 1 2 3 5 1 6 8 2 8 5 1 2 8
(A) 44 (B) 43 (C) 42 (D) 41 (E) 40

21. 2 2 3 2 5 2 1 4 2 1 5 4 2 1 2 3 2 1 4 4 2 4 4 5 6 5 2 1 4 1
(A) 32 (B) 35 (C) 36 (D) 37 (E) 38

22. 3 5 8 5 8 4 6 2 6 1 4 6 4 6 1 4 1 2 6 5 8 2 6 4 1 2 6 5 8 3 6
(A) 23 (B) 26 (C) 22 (D) 27 (E) 30

23. 6 6 8 3 4 1 2 5 8 4 1 2 2 5 1 3 6 5 2 1 4 2 1 3 6 2 4 1 4 2
(A) 26 (B) 27 (C) 28 (D) 29 (E) 30

24. 2 6 2 6 8 5 1 1 8 5 1 8 5 2 4 2 5 8 8 2 6 5 8 8 1 3 3 6 4 1
(A) 28 (B) 27 (C) 36 (D) 31 (E) 32

25. 6 2 8 4 1 2 2 1 4 1 2 4 3 8 4 1 6 4 2 4 2 1 3 2 2 6 6 1 2 4 1 2 2
(A) 15 (B) 19 (C) 17 (D) 13 (E) 11

26. 2 1 8 8 6 2 2 5 5 5 1 2 2 8 3 4 1 8 2 4 5 6 4 6 2 2 8 1 2 2
(A) 26 (B) 27 (C) 29 (D) 31 (E) 30

27. 1 5 3 2 4 6 2 1 2 6 8 8 4 5 8 4 6 8 4 1 3 3 3 2 2 3 3 2
(A) 32 (B) 33 (C) 34 (D) 30 (E) 31

28. 3 3 2 8 4 2 6 8 4 6 3 1 4 5 1 4 1 2 6 5 8 6 3 6 8 5 4 1 2 8 1
(A) 33 (B) 32 (C) 31 (D) 34 (E) 35

29. 4 1 4 3 2 4 4 2 4 4 2 6 1 5 8 4 1 4 2 6 4 6 3 2 3 6 5 2 1 6 3 1 1 1
(A) 23 (B) 26 (C) 27 (D) 29 (E) 24

30. 3 2 3 2 2 3 2 8 2 1 3 3 5 1 1 5 1 1 6 8 8 5 2 4 1 2 5 6 2 1
(A) 31 (B) 30 (C) 29 (D) 42 (E) 33

PRACTICE SET-12

Total Ques.- 30
Time - 8 or 10 Min.

निर्देश : (प्रश्न 1–30) विषम संख्याओं को योग परीक्षण के प्रत्येक प्रश्न में सम और विषम संख्याओं को मिलाकर एक श्रृंखला दिया रहता है। इस श्रृंखला में प्रदत्त केवल विषम संख्या 1, 3, 5 आदि को जोड़ने के बाद नीचे दिए गए पाँच विकल्पों (A, B, C, D और E) में कोई एक सही विकल्प को ढूंढना होता है जिसे दिए गए उत्तर-पत्रक में गोले को काला/माउस की सहायता से क्लिक करना होता है।

Directions: (Questions 1–30) : Each question in the Odd Number Adding Test presents a series of even and odd numbers. You need to add the total number of odd numbers 1, 3, 5 etc. in the given series. After adding, select the correct option from the five choices (A, B, C, D & E) provided. Mark your answer by filling the circle on the answer sheet or by clicking on it using the mouse.

1. 4 8 4 2 1 6 8 2 1 5 3 2 1 3 4 1 2 1 2 1 4 1 2 6 5 6 4 6
(A) 21 (B) 20 (C) 23 (D) 24 (E) 25

2. 5 6 2 4 1 2 1 2 3 2 3 2 3 6 8 2 3 2 2 8 3 1 5 4 3 5 1 8 5 2
(A) 42 (B) 35 (C) 36 (D) 38 (E) 39

3. 3 8 1 8 3 6 8 2 1 4 6 2 8 1 4 2 6 8 1 2 5 6 5 6 5 2 1 1 1
(A) 25 (B) 27 (C) 28 (D) 29 (E) 31

4. 2 2 2 8 4 2 5 1 4 6 5 3 2 5 2 2 4 6 4 2 1 5 2 8 4 5 1 2 3
(A) 30 (B) 32 (C) 33 (D) 34 (E) 35

5. 4 1 3 8 4 6 5 2 1 1 2 4 1 2 5 4 3 5 2 6 8 6 4 2 3 8 2
(A) 25 (B) 28 (C) 27 (D) 29 (E) 30

6. 4 8 3 2 5 8 4 1 2 2 5 3 1 3 2 3 6 2 5 8 4 1 2 3 6 4 6 8 2
(A) 30 (B) 33 (C) 32 (D) 29 (E) 31

7. 6 1 4 2 2 6 8 2 1 4 8 4 5 8 4 1 2 2 2 4 6 5 2 1 5 2 2 1 5 6
(A) 24 (B) 23 (C) 25 (D) 27 (E) 26

8. 4 3 3 2 5 4 4 2 1 2 4 1 1 6 8 1 2 1 6 3 3 1 4 1 2 3 6 8 4 2 1 2
(A) 25 (B) 27 (C) 29 (D) 28 (E) 30

9. 2 6 2 3 1 6 4 1 2 6 3 2 8 4 8 2 8 4 6 1 6 6 2 2 5 2 8 4 4
(A) 10 (B) 13 (C) 12 (D) 15 (E) 14

10. 4 1 1 2 6 3 3 4 8 5 2 8 6 6 4 1 8 2 5 3 4 1 8 1 4 5 3 2 6 6
(A) 30 (B) 32 (C) 34 (D) 35 (E) 36

11. 3 1 2 5 1 6 1 1 2 3 3 3 1 3 3 8 4 1 4 1 3 5 5 3 6 5 4 1 4 2 3
(A) 55 (B) 50 (C) 53 (D) 54 (E) 49

12. 6 2 2 2 4 5 8 8 2 1 4 2 1 2 5 6 4 2 1 5 3 1 8 2 2 5 2 1 6 2 22
(A) 25 (B) 23 (C) 28 (D) 27 (E) 29

13. 2 8 1 1 4 2 1 4 8 5 2 6 4 1 2 4 6 1 4 2 3 6 2 1 4 1 5 5 8 3
(A) 30 (B) 32 (C) 27 (D) 28 (E) 29

14. 6 2 6 8 4 1 3 5 4 2 1 4 8 5 2 6 4 1 2 1 3 6 4 1 4 3 8
(A) 20 (B) 23 (C) 24 (D) 26 (E) 28

15. 6 2 3 5 6 8 2 5 3 8 2 5 3 5 2 2 1 5 6 2 2 2 4 5 8 1 5 2
(A) 40 (B) 45 (C) 44 (D) 48 (E) 46

16. 5 8 4 3 1 2 2 1 2 3 2 1 4 4 2 4 4 5 6 5 2 1 4 1 2 3 6 2 1
(A) 30 (B) 29 (C) 28 (D) 31 (E) 32

17. 8 4 2 3 2 5 6 5 3 8 5 2 6 4 8 5 2 5 2 5 1 2 1 2 1 4 1 3 2 6 2
(A) 41 (B) 43 (C) 42 (D) 44 (E) 40

18. 4 1 2 3 4 1 2 3 2 5 2 6 8 5 3 1 4 5 4 1 5 2 6 4 8 5 62 8 5
(A) 46 (B) 45 (C) 43 (D) 44 (E) 42

19. 5 6 5 6 5 2 3 1 4 2 3 8 4 2 1 8 2 1 5 8 2 4 8 4 1 2 1 8 2 8 2
(A) 29 (B) 31 (C) 30 (D) 32 (E) 28

20. 4 3 2 1 3 2 5 8 4 3 1 2 5 8 1 2 5 1 2 3 5 1 6 8 2 8 5 1 2 8
(A) 44 (B) 42 (C) 40 (D) 41 (E) 43

21. 5 2 3 1 3 1 2 5 2 3 5 8 6 4 8 2 2 4 5 2 5 3 2 5 2 1 4 2 1 5 4 2
(A) 49 (B) 50 (C) 48 (D) 51 (E) 52

22. 1 3 6 5 2 1 4 2 1 3 6 3 5 8 5 8 4 6 2 6 1 4 6 4 6 1 4 1 2 68 3 6
(A) 30 (B) 31 (C) 33 (D) 34 (E) 35

23. 5 8 2 6 4 1 2 6 5 6 6 8 3 4 1 2 5 8 4 1 2 2 52 4 1 4 2
(A) 27 (B) 28 (C) 26 (D) 29 (E) 30

24. 4 2 4 2 1 3 2 2 6 6 1 2 4 6 2 2 8 5 1 8 5 1 8 5 2 4 2 5 4 1
(A) 26 (B) 28 (C) 27 (D) 29 (E) 30

25. 8 2 6 5 8 8 1 3 3 6 2 8 4 3 2 2 1 4 1 2 4 3 8 4 1 6 4 2 2
(A) 17 (B) 20 (C) 21 (D) 22 (E) 23

26. 4 1 8 2 4 5 6 4 6 24 6 2 1 2 6 8 8 4 4 6 8 2 1 2 8 1 2 2
(A) 10 (B) 7 (C) 8 (D) 9 (E) 11

27. 1 5 3 2 8 8 6 2 2 5 5 5 1 2 2 8 3 4 1 3 3 3 2 2 3 3 2
(A) 45 (B) 42 (C) 41 (D) 43 (E) 44

28. 3 6 5 8 6 3 6 4 4 2 6 1 5 8 4 1 4 2 6 3 2 8 4 2 8 5 4 1 2 8 1
(A) 29 (B) 27 (C) 28 (D) 30 (E) 26

29. 4 1 4 3 6 8 8 5 2 4 1 2 5 6 2 2 6 8 4 6 3 1 4 5 1 4 1 2 3 1
(A) 32 (B) 30 (C) 31 (D) 29 (E) 28

30. 3 2 4 6 3 2 3 6 5 2 1 6 3 1 3 2 2 3 2 8 2 1 3 3 5 1 1 5 1 5 1
(A) 51 (B) 50 (C) 48 (D) 49 (E) 52

PRACTICE SET-13

Total Ques.- 30
Time - 8 or 10 Min.

निर्देश : (प्रश्न 1-30) विषम संख्याओं को योग परीक्षण के प्रत्येक प्रश्न में सम और विषम संख्याओं को मिलाकर एक श्रृंखला दिया रहता है। इस श्रृंखला में प्रदत्त केवल विषम संख्या 1, 3, 5 आदि को जोड़ने के बाद नीचे दिए गए पाँच विकल्पों (A, B, C, D और E) में कोई एक सही विकल्प को ढूंढना होता है जिसे दिए गए उत्तर-पत्रक में गोले को काला/माउस की सहायता से क्लिक करना होता है।

Directions: (Questions 1–30) : Each question in the Odd Number Adding Test presents a series of even and odd numbers. You need to add the total number of odd numbers 1, 3, 5 etc. in the given series. After adding, select the correct option from the five choices (A, B, C, D & E) provided. Mark your answer by filling the circle on the answer sheet or by clicking on it using the mouse.

1. 6 8 2 3 2 2 8 3 1 5 4 3 5 13 4 6 8 5 2 4 8 4 2 1 6 6
   (A) 30 (B) 29 (C) 27 (D) 31 (E) 28
2. 5 6 2 8 2 1 3 2 1 3 4 1 2 1 2 1 4 1 2 6 5 6 4 4 1 2 1 2 3 2 3 2 3
   (A) 32 (B) 33 (C) 29 (D) 30 (E) 31
3. 6 5 3 2 5 2 2 4 6 4 2 1 5 2 8 4 5 1 2 3 3 8 1 5 6 5 6 5 2 1 1 1
   (A) 49 (B) 51 (C) 50 (D) 52 (E) 47
4. 2 2 8 3 6 8 2 1 4 6 2 8 1 5 8 4 2 6 8 1 2 2 8 4 2 5 1 4
   (A) 20 (B) 19 (C) 18 (D) 17 (E) 16
5. 4 5 4 3 2 4 5 2 4 8 3 2 5 8 4 1 2 2 5 3 1 6 8 6 4 2 3 8 2
   (A) 37 (B) 35 (C) 31 (D) 33 (E) 34
6. 3 2 3 1 3 8 4 5 6 5 2 1 1 2 4 1 2 3 6 2 5 8 4 1 2 3 6 4 6 8 2
   (A) 36 (B) 37 (C) 38 (D) 35 (E) 34
7. 6 1 6 8 1 2 1 6 3 3 1 4 1 2 3 6 8 4 2 1 2 2 6 8 2 1 2 2 1 5 6
   (A) 24 (B) 23 (C) 22 (D) 21 (E) 20
8. 4 3 3 4 8 4 5 8 4 1 2 2 2 4 6 5 2 1 5 2 5 4 4 2 1 2 4 1 2
   (A) 29 (B) 30 (C) 31 (D) 32 (E) 33
9. 8 2 8 4 6 1 6 2 2 4 5 8 8 2 1 4 2 1 2 5 6 2 6 2 3 2 5 2 8 4 4
   (A) 21 (B) 22 (C) 25 (D) 24 (E) 23
10. 4 1 8 2 5 1 6 1 1 2 3 3 3 1 3 3 8 4 1 3 4 1 8 1 4 5 3 2 6 6
    (A) 38 (B) 39 (C) 36 (D) 35 (E) 40
11. 3 1 2 5 1 2 6 3 3 4 8 5 2 8 6 6 4 1 4 1 3 5 5 3 6 5 4 1 4 2 3
    (A) 48 (B) 46 (C) 45 (D) 49 (E) 51
12. 6 2 6 4 1 2 6 3 2 8 4 4 2 1 5 3 1 8 2 2 5 2 1 6 2 2 2
    (A) 21 (B) 19 (C) 20 (D) 18 (E) 22
13. 2 8 6 4 1 2 1 3 6 4 1 4 3 1 1 4 2 1 4 8 5 2 4 5 5 8 3
    (A) 31 (B) 32 (C) 29 (D) 28 (E) 30

14. 6 2 6 1 4 5 6 2 2 2 4 6 4 1 2 5 8 1 5 2 3 6 2 1 4 1 5 2 8
(A) 29 (B) 28 (C) 27 (D) 26 (E) 30

15. 6 2 3 6 8 4 1 3 5 4 2 1 4 8 5 6 8 2 5 3 8 2 5 3 5 2 2 1 2
(A) 41 (B) 39 (C) 42 (D) 40 (E) 43

16. 5 8 4 3 2 6 8 5 3 1 4 5 4 1 5 2 6 4 8 5 2 1 2 3 2 1 4
(A) 31 (B) 33 (C) 38 (D) 34 (E) 32

17. 8 4 2 4 4 5 6 5 2 1 4 1 2 3 6 2 14 2 3 2 5 6 2 1 4 1 3 2 6 2
(A) 30 (B) 28 (C) 27 (D) 29 (E) 31

18. 4 5 3 8 5 2 6 4 8 5 2 5 2 5 1 2 1 1 2 3 4 1 2 3 2 5 8 5
(A) 46 (B) 49 (C) 48 (D) 47 (E) 50

19. 5 6 5 6 5 2 3 1 4 2 3 8 4 2 1 8 2 1 5 8 2 4 8 4 1 2 1 8 2 8 2
(A) 34 (B) 31 (C) 33 (D) 32 (E) 30

20. 4 3 5 8 6 4 8 2 2 4 5 2 5 3 2 5 2 1 4 2 2 1 3 3 1 2 5 8 1 1 2 8
(A) 41 (B) 40 (C) 43 (D) 42 (E) 44

21. 5 2 3 2 2 5 1 2 3 5 1 6 8 2 8 5 3 1 3 1 2 5 2 3 1 5 4 2
(A) 49 (B) 53 (C) 50 (D) 51 (E) 48

22. 1 3 6 3 4 1 2 5 8 4 1 2 2 4 5 2 1 4 2 1 3 6 3 5 4 1 2 68 3 6
(A) 36 (B) 39 (C) 38 (D) 37 (E) 35

23. 5 8 8 5 8 4 6 5 3 2 6 1 4 6 4 6 1 2 6 4 1 1 2 6 5 6 1 4 2
(A) 29 (B) 30 (C) 27 (D) 26 (E) 28

24. 4 2 5 8 8 1 3 3 6 2 8 4 3 2 2 1 4 8 5 1 8 5 1 2 4 2 5 4 1
(A) 33 (B) 36 (C) 37 (D) 35 (E) 34

25. 8 2 6 4 1 3 1 5 4 8 3 2 2 6 3 6 1 2 4 2 4 3 8 4 1 6 4 2 2
(A) 21 (B) 20 (C) 18 (D) 19 (E) 22

26. 4 1 2 8 8 6 2 2 5 5 5 1 2 2 6 8 8 4 4 6 8 2 1 2 8 1 2 2
(A) 16 (B) 19 (C) 15 (D) 17 (E) 18

27. 1 5 3 2 4 5 6 4 5 6 8 4 2 6 2 4 6 2 13 4 1 3 3 3 2 2 3 3 2
(A) 58 (B) 37 (C) 39 (D) 35 (E) 34

28. 3 6 5 2 6 3 2 84 1 4 3 6 8 8 5 2 4 1 2 5 6 4 2 8 5 4 1 2 8 1
(A) 32 (B) 33 (C) 35 (D) 31 (E) 34

29. 2 2 6 8 8 6 3 6 4 4 2 6 1 5 8 4 6 3 1 4 5 1 4 1 2 3 1
(A) 23 (B) 22 (C) 20 (D) 24 (E) 25

30. 3 2 4 6 3 2 3 3 5 1 1 5 3 6 5 2 1 6 3 1 4 6 3 1 2 8 2 1 1 5 1
(A) 48 (B) 49 (C) 47 (D) 45 (E) 50

PRACTICE SET-14

Total Ques.- 30
Time - 8 or 10 Min.

निर्देश : (प्रश्न 1–30) विषम संख्याओं को योग परीक्षण के प्रत्येक प्रश्न में सम और विषम संख्याओं को मिलाकर एक श्रृंखला दिया रहता है। इस श्रृंखला में प्रदत्त केवल विषम संख्या 1, 3, 5 आदि को जोड़ने के बाद नीचे दिए गए पाँच विकल्पों (A, B, C, D और E) में कोई एक सही विकल्प को ढूंढना होता है जिसे दिए गए उत्तर-पत्रक में गोले को काला/माउस की सहायता से क्लिक करना होता है।

Directions: (Questions 1–30) : Each question in the Odd Number Adding Test presents a series of even and odd numbers. You need to add the total number of odd numbers 1, 3, 5 etc. in the given series. After adding, select the correct option from the five choices (A, B, C, D & E) provided. Mark your answer by filling the circle on the answer sheet or by clicking on it using the mouse.

1. 1 2 3 3 8 1 5 6 5 6 5 2 1 1 1 6 8 2 3 2 2 4 8 4 2 1 6 6
(A) 29 (B) 31 (C) 30 (D) 32 (E) 33

2. 6 8 4 2 1 2 2 6 8 2 2 8 2 1 3 2 1 3 4 1 2 1 2 1 4 1 2 3 2 3 2 3
(A) 25 (B) 22 (C) 21 (D) 23 (E) 24

3. 6 1 1 2 4 1 2 3 6 2 5 8 4 1 2 5 3 2 5 2 2 4 6 4 2 1 5 2 8 4 5
(A) 35 (B) 36 (C) 37 (D) 38 (E) 39

4. 2 2 8 3 6 8 2 1 4 6 2 8 1 5 8 4 2 6 8 1 2 2 8 4 2 5 1 4
(A) 17 (B) 18 (C) 19 (D) 20 (E) 21

5. 8 3 2 5 8 4 1 2 2 5 3 1 6 8 4 5 4 3 2 4 5 2 4 6 4 2 3 8 2
(A) 33 (B) 34 (C) 36 (D) 37 (E) 32

6. 3 2 8 3 1 5 4 3 5 1 3 4 6 8 5 2 3 1 3 8 4 5 6 5 6 4 6 8 2
(A) 39 (B) 41 (C) 42 (D) 46 (E) 43

7. 6 1 6 6 5 6 4 4 1 2 1 2 8 1 2 1 6 3 3 1 4 1 2 3 2 2 1 5 6
(A) 26 (B) 29 (C) 27 (D) 30 (E) 31

8. 8 4 1 3 4 1 8 15 2 5 6 1 3 1 2 4 4 5 3 5 4 4 2 1 2 4 1 2
(A) 36 (B) 38 (C) 39 (D) 37 (E) 35

9. 8 4 8 5 2 8 6 6 4 1 4 1 3 5 4 6 1 6 2 2 4 5 8 8 2 2 8 4 4
(A) 21 (B) 25 (C) 23 (D) 29 (E) 19

10. 4 1 8 2 5 1 4 3 3 4 8 4 5 8 4 2 4 6 5 2 1 2 3 3 3 1 3 3 2 6 6
(A) 41 (B) 42 (C) 43 (D) 44 (E) 40

11. 3 1 1 4 2 1 2 5 6 2 6 2 3 2 52 5 1 2 6 3 3 5 3 6 5 4 1 4 2 3
(A) 48 (B) 47 (C) 49 (D) 46 (E) 50

12. 6 2 6 4 1 2 6 3 1 4 8 5 2 4 5 5 2 8 4 5 4 2 3 1 5 2 2
(A) 33 (B) 35 (C) 32 (D) 30 (E) 34

13. 2 8 3 1 8 2 2 5 2 1 6 2 6 4 1 2 1 3 6 4 1 4 3 1 1 4 2 8 3
(A) 21 (B) 23 (C) 24 (D) 25 (E) 27

14. 6 2 4 1 2 5 8 3 6 8 4 1 3 5 4 2 1 4 1 5 2 3 6 2 1 4 1 5 2 8
(A) 39 (B) 37 (C) 33 (D) 35 (E) 31

15. 6 2 8 5 6 1 4 5 6 2 2 2 4 6 6 8 2 5 3 8 2 5 3 5 2 2 1 2
(A) 35 (B) 33 (C) 36 (D) 32 (E) 31

16. 1 4 2 3 2 5 6 2 1 4 1 3 2 6 2 4 4 5 6 5 2 1 2 4 3 3 2 1 4
(A) 31 (B) 33 (C) 32 (D) 35 (E) 30

17. 8 4 2 5 8 4 3 2 6 8 5 3 1 4 5 4 1 5 2 6 4 8 2 1 2 4 1 2 3 6 2
(A) 33 (B) 30 (C) 31 (D) 32 (E) 35

18. 4 5 2 3 4 1 2 3 2 5 8 3 8 5 2 6 4 8 5 2 5 2 5 1 2 1 1 5
(A) 47 (B) 46 (C) 49 (D) 50 (E) 48

19. 5 6 2 1 5 8 2 4 8 6 4 8 2 2 4 5 2 5 3 2 2 4 1 2 1 8 2 8 2
(A) 28 (B) 26 (C) 27 (D) 25 (E) 24

20. 4 3 1 4 2 5 6 5 2 3 1 4 2 3 8 4 2 1 8 2 1 3 3 1 2 5 8 1 2 8
(A) 34 (B) 35 (C) 37 (D) 38 (E) 36

21. 5 2 6 3 4 1 2 5 8 4 1 2 5 2 1 4 2 1 3 6 3 2 3 5 1 6 8 2 8 5 4 2
(A) 42 (B) 41 (C) 40 (D) 34 (E) 43

22. 1 3 3 1 3 1 4 4 3 2 2 5 1 2 5 2 3 1 5 4 5 4 2 2 1 2 68 3 6
(A) 46 (B) 44 (C) 45 (D) 47 (E) 43

23. 5 8 3 2 2 1 4 8 5 1 8 5 8 4 6 5 3 2 6 1 4 6 4 6 1 2 6 4 1 1
(A) 30 (B) 26 (C) 28 (D) 32 (E) 27

24. 4 2 6 5 6 1 4 2 2 5 8 8 1 3 3 6 2 8 4 8 5 1 2 4 2 5 4 1
(A) 30 (B) 33 (C) 32 (D) 31 (E) 29

25. 8 2 6 4 1 3 1 5 5 2 6 8 4 1 2 1 4 8 3 2 2 6 3 6 1 2 4 2
(A) 25 (B) 23 (C) 24 (D) 26 (E) 27

26. 4 1 1 3 4 1 3 3 3 2 2 8 8 6 2 2 5 5 5 1 2 2 4 2 8 1 2 2
(A) 34 (B) 29 (C) 31 (D) 33 (E) 32

27. 1 5 3 6 8 8 4 4 6 8 1 4 6 3 1 2 8 2 1 2 4 5 6 4 5 6 3 2
(A) 26 (B) 28 (C) 27 (D) 29 (E) 30

28. 3 2 5 6 4 1 5 8 4 6 3 1 4 2 8 5 2 2 8 8 5 2 4 1 4 1 2 8 1
(A) 31 (B) 30 (C) 29 (D) 32 (E) 33

29. 2 2 6 8 8 6 3 6 4 4 2 6 6 5 2 6 3 2 8 4 1 4 3 6 5 1 4 1 2 3 1
(A) 27 (B) 25 (C) 24 (D) 26 (E) 28

30. 8 4 2 6 2 4 6 2 3 3 2 4 6 3 2 3 3 5 1 1 5 3 6 5 2 1 6 3 2 1 1 5 1
(A) 49 (B) 46 (C) 45 (D) 48 (E) 47

PRACTICE SET-15

Total Ques.- 30
Time - 8 or 10 Min.

निर्देश : (प्रश्न 1–30) विषम संख्याओं को योग परीक्षण के प्रत्येक प्रश्न में सम और विषम संख्याओं को मिलाकर एक श्रृंखला दिया रहता है। इस श्रृंखला में प्रदत्त केवल विषम संख्या 1, 3, 5 आदि को जोड़ने के बाद नीचे दिए गए पाँच विकल्पों (A, B, C, D और E) में कोई एक सही विकल्प को ढूंढना होता है जिसे दिए गए उत्तर-पत्रक में गोले को काला/माउस की सहायता से क्लिक करना होता है।

Directions: (Questions 1–30) : Each question in the Odd Number Adding Test presents a series of even and odd numbers. You need to add the total number of odd numbers 1, 3, 5 etc. in the given series. After adding, select the correct option from the five choices (A, B, C, D & E) provided. Mark your answer by filling the circle on the answer sheet or by clicking on it using the mouse.

1. 1 2 3 1 2 5 3 1 2 1 4 1 2 3 2 3 2 5 4 3 3 8 1 5 6 5 2 1 6 6
(A) 41 (B) 40 (C) 43 (D) 45 (E) 47

2. 6 8 4 2 6 5 2 1 1 6 8 2 3 2 2 4 8 4 1 6 8 2 2 8 2 1 3 2 1 3 4 3
(A) 23 (B) 22 (C) 21 (D) 25 (E) 27

3. 6 1 2 4 6 4 2 1 5 2 8 4 1 2 4 1 2 3 6 2 5 8 4 1 2 5 3 2 5 2 5
(A) 31 (B) 33 (C) 35 (D) 37 (E) 36

4. 2 4 2 6 8 4 1 2 2 5 3 1 6 8 4 51 2 2 8 4 5 6 4 2 5 1 4
(A) 27 (B) 29 (C) 30 (D) 25 (E) 26

5. 8 3 2 5 8 4 2 8 3 6 8 2 1 4 6 2 8 1 5 8 3 2 4 5 2 4 6 4 2 3 8 2
(A) 29 (B) 28 (C) 27 (D) 26 (E) 25

6. 3 2 8 3 3 1 4 1 2 3 2 3 1 5 4 3 5 1 3 4 6 8 5 2 3 1 3 8 2
(A) 40 (B) 41 (C) 42 (D) 47 (E) 43

7. 6 1 6 8 4 5 6 5 6 4 6 6 5 6 4 4 1 2 1 2 8 1 2 1 6 2 1 5 6
(A) 27 (B) 26 (C) 30 (D) 31 (E) 32

8. 8 4 4 6 1 6 2 2 4 5 8 8 2 1 3 4 1 8 1 5 2 1 3 1 2 4 4 1 2
(A) 25 (B) 27 (C) 23 (D) 29 (E) 25

9. 8 4 8 5 3 5 4 4 2 1 2 4 5 2 8 6 6 4 1 4 1 3 5 2 8 4 4
(A) 30 (B) 31 (C) 35 (D) 27 (E) 29

10. 4 1 8 1 2 5 6 2 6 2 3 2 5 1 4 3 2 1 2 3 3 3 1 3 3 2 6 6
(A) 36 (B) 33 (C) 34 (D) 35 (E) 37

11. 3 1 1 4 2 1 2 6 3 3 4 8 4 5 8 4 2 4 6 5 3 5 3 6 5 4 1 4 2 3
(A) 41 (B) 40 (C) 39 (D) 42 (E) 43

12. 6 2 5 2 4 5 5 2 8 4 5 2 5 2 1 6 2 6 4 14 2 3 1 5 2 2
(A) 41 (B) 36 (C) 39 (D) 37 (E) 38

13. 2 8 3 1 8 2 2 1 3 66 4 1 2 6 3 1 4 8 4 1 4 3 1 1 4 2 8 3
(A) 26 (B) 25 (C) 24 (D) 23 (E) 22

14. 6 2 4 5 4 2 1 4 1 5 2 8 5 6 1 4 5 6 2 2 2 3 6 2 1 4 1 5 2 8
(A) 33 (B) 30 (C) 31 (D) 32 (E) 34

15. 6 2 4 6 6 8 2 51 2 5 8 3 6 8 4 1 3 3 8 2 5 3 5 2 2 1 2
(A) 37 (B) 36 (C) 34 (D) 33 (E) 35

16. 1 4 5 6 5 2 1 2 4 3 3 2 4 2 3 2 5 6 2 1 4 1 3 2 6 2 4
(A) 30 (B) 32 (C) 31 (D) 33 (E) 34

17. 8 4 1 5 2 6 4 8 2 1 2 4 5 8 4 3 2 6 8 5 3 1 4 5 1 2 3 6 2
(A) 33 (B) 34 (C) 30 (D) 32 (E) 31

18. 4 5 2 2 4 5 2 5 3 2 2 4 1 2 1 8 2 8 2 1 2 3 2 5 8 3 8 5 2 1 5
(A) 43 (B) 45 (C) 46 (D) 42 (E) 41

19. 5 6 4 8 5 2 5 2 5 1 4 5 6 8 2 2 1 6 2 1 5 8 2 4 8 6 4 8 2
(A) 31 (B) 32 (C) 33 (D) 35 (E) 34

20. 4 3 4 2 1 8 2 4 5 8 2 1 6 1 4 4 3 2 2 5 3 3 2 1 2 5 8 1 2 8
(A) 30 (B) 33 (C) 32 (D) 31 (E) 35

21. 5 3 2 6 1 4 6 4 6 1 2 6 4 5 2 6 3 4 1 2 1 2 5 4 2 1 3 8 5 4 2
(A) 37 (B) 34 (C) 36 (D) 35 (E) 38

22. 1 3 3 1 3 1 1 2 5 1 4 2 5 6 5 2 3 1 4 2 3 8 6 8 3 6
(A) 38 (B) 42 (C) 41 (D) 39 (E) 40

23. 5 8 6 3 2 3 5 1 6 8 2 3 2 2 1 4 8 5 1 8 5 8 4 6 1 1
(A) 35 (B) 36 (C) 37 (D) 39 (E) 34

24. 8 1 3 3 6 2 8 2 6 4 1 3 1 5 5 2 6 8 4 1 2 1 8 5 1 2 4 2 5 4 1
(A) 36 (B) 37 (C) 38 (D) 39 (E) 40

25. 3 4 8 3 2 4 2 6 5 2 8 6 1 4 2 2 5 8 2 6 2 3 6 1 2 4 2
(A) 17 (B) 19 (C) 23 (D) 25 (E) 21

26. 4 1 1 3 6 8 8 4 2 2 4 6 8 1 4 6 5 5 1 2 2 4 2 8 1 2 2
(A) 18 (B) 19 (C) 21 (D) 23 (E) 25

27. 3 1 2 8 2 1 4 1 3 3 3 2 2 8 8 6 2 2 1 5 3 4 5 6 4 5 6 3 2
(A) 35 (B) 37 (C) 36 (D) 38 (E) 39

28. 3 2 5 5 2 2 8 8 5 1 1 5 3 6 5 2 1 6 3 2 1 1 5 2 4 1 4 1 2 8 1
(A) 46 (B) 45 (C) 47 (D) 48 (E) 49

29. 2 2 3 2 8 6 4 1 5 8 4 6 3 1 4 2 8 4 1 4 3 6 5 1 4 1 2 3 1
(A) 27 (B) 25 (C) 23 (D) 28 (E) 29

30. 8 4 6 8 8 6 3 6 4 6 6 5 2 6 2 6 2 4 6 2 3 3 2 4 6 3 2 3 3 1
(A) 21 (B) 22 (C) 23 (D) 25 (E) 24

PRACTICE SET-16

Total Ques.- 30
Time - 8 or 10 Min.

निर्देश : (प्रश्न 1–30) विषम संख्याओं को योग परीक्षण के प्रत्येक प्रश्न में सम और विषम संख्याओं को मिलाकर एक श्रृंखला दिया रहता है। इस श्रृंखला में प्रदत्त केवल विषम संख्या 1, 3, 5 आदि को जोड़ने के बाद नीचे दिए गए पाँच विकल्पों (A, B, C, D और E) में कोई एक सही विकल्प को ढूंढना होता है जिसे दिए गए उत्तर-पत्रक में गोले को काला/माउस की सहायता से क्लिक करना होता है।

Directions: (Questions 1–30) : Each question in the Odd Number Adding Test presents a series of even and odd numbers. You need to add the total number of odd numbers 1, 3, 5 etc. in the given series. After adding, select the correct option from the five choices (A, B, C, D & E) provided. Mark your answer by filling the circle on the answer sheet or by clicking on it using the mouse.

1. 1 2 3 2 3 6 2 5 8 4 1 2 5 3 2 5 2 1 2 3 1 2 1 4 1 2 3 1 6
(A) 36 (B) 38 (C) 40 (D) 37 (E) 33

2. 6 8 4 2 6 5 2 1 1 6 8 2 3 2 2 8 4 5 6 4 2 5 1 2 2 4 8 4 1 6 3
(A) 21 (B) 24 (C) 26 (D) 27 (E) 25

3. 6 1 2 4 4 1 2 1 2 8 1 2 1 6 2 1 6 4 2 1 5 2 8 4 1 2 4 1
(A) 10 (B) 14 (C) 11 (D) 12 (E) 15

4. 8 2 2 8 2 1 3 2 1 3 4 2 4 2 6 8 4 1 2 2 5 3 1 6 8 4 5 1 4
(A) 24 (B) 23 (C) 21 (D) 22 (E) 26

5. 8 3 2 5 8 4 2 8 3 6 8 2 1 4 8 1 5 8 3 2 4 5 2 4 6 4 2 3 8 2
(A) 28 (B) 29 (C) 27 (D) 30 (E) 31

6. 3 2 6 8 4 5 6 5 6 4 6 6 4 3 1 4 1 2 3 2 3 1 5 4 3 1 3 8 2
(A) 35 (B) 36 (C) 37 (D) 38 (E) 39

7. 6 1 2 2 3 5 1 3 4 6 8 5 2 3 2 5 4 3 3 8 1 5 6 5 2 5 6
(A) 46 (B) 47 (C) 49 (D) 50 (E) 48

8. 8 4 4 6 1 8 6 6 4 1 4 1 3 5 2 6 2 2 4 5 8 8 2 1 3 4 1 4 1 2
(A) 23 (B) 20 (C) 21 (D) 22 (E) 19

9. 8 4 8 5 8 1 5 2 1 3 1 2 3 4 2 4 3 5 4 4 2 1 2 4 5 2 8 4 4
(A) 32 (B) 34 (C) 33 (D) 36 (E) 35

10. 4 1 5 3 5 3 6 5 4 1 4 8 1 2 5 6 2 6 2 3 2 5 1 4 3 2 1 6
(A) 42 (B) 41 (C) 40 (D) 39 (E) 43

11. 3 1 2 3 3 3 1 3 3 2 6 1 4 2 1 2 6 3 3 4 8 4 5 8 4 2 4 6 2 3
(A) 31 (B) 32 (C) 33 (D) 34 (E) 36

12. 6 2 5 2 4 2 6 4 8 3 1 8 2 2 4 1 2 6 3 1 4 8 1 4 2 3 1 5 2 2
(A) 20 (B) 21 (C) 22 (D) 24 (E) 25

13. 2 8 3 1 8 2 2 1 3 6 6 4 5 5 2 8 4 5 2 5 2 1 6 1 4 3 1 1 4 2 8 3
(A) 39 (B) 38 (C) 37 (D) 40 (E) 41

14. 6 2 4 5 4 8 3 6 8 4 1 3 3 5 2 1 4 1 5 2 8 5 6 1 4 5 6 2 2 8
(A) 36 (B) 39 (C) 38 (D) 37 (E) 35

15. 6 2 4 6 2 2 3 6 2 2 5 6 1 4 1 5 6 8 2 5 1 2 5 2 2 1 2
(A) 26 (B) 28 (C) 29 (D) 30 (E) 27

16. 1 4 1 4 5 6 8 2 2 1 6 2 1 5 8 2 4 8 6 5 6 3 2 4 2 3 2 4
(A) 23 (B) 24 (C) 25 (D) 22 (E) 21

17. 8 4 5 6 2 1 4 1 3 2 6 2 1 5 2 6 4 2 4 8 2 1 2 4 2 3 6 2
(A) 18 (B) 19 (C) 21 (D) 20 (E) 22

18. 4 5 2 2 4 5 2 5 3 2 2 4 1 2 1 5 2 1 2 8 4 6 3 2 4 1 5
(A) 34 (B) 33 (C) 36 (D) 37 (E) 35

19. 5 6 5 8 1 2 5 1 4 2 5 6 5 2 3 1 4 2 3 5 1 4 8 5 2 5 2 5 4 8 2
(A) 54 (B) 56 (C) 55 (D) 57 (E) 58

20. 4 3 4 2 1 8 2 4 5 8 2 1 6 1 4 4 3 2 2 5 3 3 2 1 2 5 8 1 2 8
(A) 31 (B) 32 (C) 33 (D) 34 (E) 35

21. 5 3 2 6 1 4 6 4 1 2 3 2 2 1 4 3 5 1 8 5 8 4 6 1 2 6 4 5 2 6 8 5 4 2
(A) 39 (B) 38 (C) 37 (D) 36 (E) 35

22. 1 8 2 8 2 1 2 3 8 4 3 2 6 8 5 3 1 4 2 5 8 3 8 3 3 1 3 1 6 8 3 6
(A) 37 (B) 36 (C) 39 (D) 38 (E) 40

23. 5 8 5 2 1 2 4 3 3 4 1 2 1 2 5 4 2 1 3 6 3 2 3 5 1 6 8 6 1 1
(A) 40 (B) 41 (C) 44 (D) 42 (E) 43

24. 8 1 1 2 5 4 6 6 4 3 6 5 1 4 1 2 8 4 1 2 1 8 5 1 2 4 2 5 4 1
(A) 30 (B) 33 (C) 27 (D) 28 (E) 31

25. 1 4 6 5 5 1 2 2 4 2 8 3 4 8 3 4 6 8 8 2 4 2 6 5 2 8 6 1 2 4 2
(A) 21 (B) 22 (C) 24 (D) 23 (E) 25

26. 4 1 4 2 2 5 8 2 6 2 3 6 1 5 1 1 3 6 8 8 4 2 2 4 6 8 1 2 2
(A) 21 (B) 20 (C) 19 (D) 18 (E) 17

27. 4 6 2 1 4 1 3 3 3 2 3 3 2 2 6 4 4 6 3 2 3 3 1 2 8 2 3 2
(A) 29 (B) 32 (C) 30 (D) 31 (E) 33

28. 3 2 5 5 2 2 8 8 5 1 1 5 3 6 5 2 1 6 3 2 1 1 5 2 4 1 4 1 2 8 1
(A) 46 (B) 48 (C) 39 (D) 42 (E) 47

29. 2 2 3 2 8 6 4 3 3 6 2 8 2 6 4 1 3 1 5 5 8 4 6 3 1 4 2 8 3 1
(A) 29 (B) 30 (C) 32 (D) 31 (E) 33

30. 2 8 8 6 2 2 1 5 3 4 5 6 4 5 6 8 6 3 6 4 6 6 5 2 6 2 6 2 3 1
(A) 31 (B) 30 (C) 32 (D) 33 (E) 29

PRACTICE SET-17

Total Ques.- 30
Time - 8 or 10 Min.

निर्देश : (प्रश्न 1–30) विषम संख्याओं को योग परीक्षण के प्रत्येक प्रश्न में सम और विषम संख्याओं को मिलाकर एक श्रृंखला दिया रहता है। इस श्रृंखला में प्रदत्त केवल विषम संख्या 1, 3, 5 आदि को जोड़ने के बाद नीचे दिए गए पाँच विकल्पों (A, B, C, D और E) में कोई एक सही विकल्प को ढूंढना होता है जिसे दिए गए उत्तर-पत्रक में गोले को काला/माउस की सहायता से क्लिक करना होता है।

Directions: (Questions 1–30) : Each question in the Odd Number Adding Test presents a series of even and odd numbers. You need to add the total number of odd numbers 1, 3, 5 etc. in the given series. After adding, select the correct option from the five choices (A, B, C, D & E) provided. Mark your answer by filling the circle on the answer sheet or by clicking on it using the mouse.

1. 6 5 6 4 6 6 4 3 1 4 1 2 3 2 3 1 8 2 1 2 3 2 3 6 4 1 2 3 1 6
   (A) 26 (B) 27 (C) 29 (D) 30 (E) 31
2. 6 8 2 1 6 4 2 1 5 2 8 4 1 2 4 2 6 5 2 1 6 8 2 3 2 2 8 4 1 6 3
   (A) 22 (B) 29 (C) 25 (D) 21 (E) 27
3. 6 1 2 4 6 4 2 5 1 2 2 4 1 2 6 3 8 4 1 2 1 2 8 1 2 1 6 4 1
   (A) 15 (B) 16 (C) 14 (D) 13 (E) 11
4. 8 2 2 8 2 1 3 2 3 1 3 3 2 6 1 4 8 4 5 3 4 2 6 8 4 5 1 4
   (A) 29 (B) 28 (C) 27 (D) 30 (E) 31
5. 8 3 2 8 1 2 5 6 2 6 2 3 2 5 1 4 3 2 8 4 2 8 3 6 8 2 1 4 8 1
   (A) 25 (B) 24 (C) 23 (D) 22 (E) 26
6. 3 2 5 8 4 1 2 5 3 2 5 3 1 4 8 1 4 2 1 2 3 1 2 1 2 6 8 4 5
   (A) 37 (B) 36 (C) 38 (D) 35 (E) 34
7. 6 1 5 4 3 3 8 1 5 6 5 2 2 3 5 2 3 4 1 3 4 6 8 5 2 2 5 6
   (A) 47 (B) 48 (C) 46 (D) 45 (E) 44
8. 8 4 4 8 1 5 2 1 3 1 2 3 4 2 4 3 5 6 1 4 5 8 8 2 1 3 4 1 4 1 2
   (A) 34 (B) 36 (C) 37 (D) 33 (E) 35
9. 8 4 8 5 4 4 8 6 6 4 1 4 1 3 5 2 6 2 2 2 1 2 4 5 2 8 4 4
   (A) 19 (B) 17 (C) 16 (D) 21 (E) 22
10. 4 1 5 8 3 2 4 5 2 4 6 4 2 3 8 2 5 3 5 3 6 5 4 1 4 1 6
    (A) 40 (B) 36 (C) 35 (D) 34 (E) 33
11. 3 1 8 4 1 3 3 2 2 6 8 4 1 8 2 5 1 2 5 2 5 3 8 4 2 4 6 2 3
    (A) 35 (B) 36 (C) 37 (D) 30 (E) 34
12. 6 2 5 2 5 4 2 4 6 6 4 8 3 1 8 2 2 4 1 2 6 1 5 2 2
    (A) 19 (B) 17 (C) 21 (D) 16 (E) 20
13. 2 8 3 1 8 2 2 1 3 6 6 4 5 5 2 8 4 5 2 5 2 1 4 3 1 1 4 2 8 3
    (A) 37 (B) 38 (C) 39 (D) 36 (E) 35

14. 6 2 4 2 5 4 1 3 5 4 8 3 6 5 2 5 2 8 5 6 1 4 5 6 2 2 8
(A) 31 (B) 32 (C) 37 (D) 38 (E) 35

15. 6 2 4 3 2 5 6 4 8 1 2 8 6 2 2 3 6 2 2 5 6 1 4 1 5 6 2 1 2
(A) 21 (B) 25 (C) 27 (D) 23 (E) 20

16. 5 2 1 4 8 5 2 6 2 1 4 2 3 6 4 2 1 4 6 3 2 6 5 6 3 2 4 2 3 2 4
(A) 29 (B) 31 (C) 33 (D) 35 (E) 30

17. 8 4 2 5 6 3 2 1 2 1 6 4 5 2 1 2 4 2 4 8 2 1 2 4 2 3 6 2
(A) 18 (B) 20 (C) 19 (D) 17 (E) 21

18. 4 5 2 2 6 3 2 1 4 8 5 2 1 4 3 6 4 1 2 1 2 8 4 6 3 2 4 1 5
(A) 29 (B) 28 (C) 27 (D) 26 (E) 23

19. 6 3 2 1 4 5 8 2 1 4 2 1 3 6 4 4 2 3 5 1 4 8 5 2 5 2 5 4 8 2
(A) 33 (B) 36 (C) 34 (D) 36 (E) 38

20. 3 6 2 1 4 2 1 8 4 5 4 1 4 4 3 2 2 5 3 3 2 1 2 5 8 1 2 8
(A) 33 (B) 31 (C) 32 (D) 30 (E) 35

21. 6 3 2 1 4 8 5 2 1 4 1 2 3 5 4 1 2 3 1 2 4 6 4 5 2 6 8 5 4 2
(A) 31 (B) 34 (C) 35 (D) 33 (E) 32

22. 2 1 4 8 2 3 6 5 2 1 4 5 4 2 6 8 5 3 1 4 2 8 3 3 1 3 1 6 8 3 6
(A) 39 (B) 40 (C) 38 (D) 41 (E) 43

23. 5 2 1 2 5 4 6 1 8 2 1 3 6 3 2 3 5 1 6 8 5 2 1 2 4 3 3 4 1 1
(A) 40 (B) 42 (C) 41 (D) 39 (E) 45

24. 4 1 2 8 4 1 2 3 4 8 3 4 6 8 8 2 4 2 2 8 6 1 8 5 1 2 4 2 5 4 1
(A) 21 (B) 20 (C) 19 (D) 18 (E) 17

25. 1 4 6 5 5 1 2 2 4 2 8 8 1 1 2 5 4 6 6 4 3 6 5 1 1 2 4 2
(A) 28 (B) 27 (C) 26 (D) 29 (E) 30

26. 4 1 3 6 8 1 3 3 3 2 3 3 2 2 6 4 4 1 8 4 2 2 4 6 8 1 2 2
(A) 18 (B) 17 (C) 22 (D) 20 (E) 21

27. 4 6 2 1 4 4 2 2 5 8 2 6 2 3 6 1 5 1 6 3 2 3 3 1 2 8 2 3 2
(A) 28 (B) 30 (C) 31 (D) 27 (E) 29

28. 3 2 5 5 8 6 4 3 6 2 8 2 6 4 1 3 1 2 6 3 2 1 5 2 4 1 4 1 2 8 1
(A) 33 (B) 30 (C) 31 (D) 35 (E) 34

29. 2 2 3 2 5 5 8 2 8 8 5 1 1 5 3 6 6 5 2 1 4 6 3 1 4 2 8 3 1
(A) 41 (B) 40 (C) 39 (D) 42 (E) 43

30. 2 8 8 6 6 3 6 4 6 6 5 2 6 2 2 1 5 3 4 5 6 4 5 6 8 2 6 2 3 1
(A) 34 (B) 33 (C) 31 (D) 32 (E) 30

PRACTICE SET-18

Total Ques.- 30
Time - 8 or 10 Min.

निर्देश : (प्रश्न 1-30) विषम संख्याओं को योग परीक्षण के प्रत्येक प्रश्न में सम और विषम संख्याओं को मिलाकर एक श्रृंखला दिया रहता है। इस श्रृंखला में प्रदत्त केवल विषम संख्या 1, 3, 5 आदि को जोड़ने के बाद नीचे दिए गए पाँच विकल्पों (A, B, C, D और E) में कोई एक सही विकल्प को ढूंढना होता है जिसे दिए गए उत्तर-पत्रक में गोले को काला/माउस की सहायता से क्लिक करना होता है।

Directions: (Questions 1–30) : Each question in the Odd Number Adding Test presents a series of even and odd numbers. You need to add the total number of odd numbers 1, 3, 5 etc. in the given series. After adding, select the correct option from the five choices (A, B, C, D & E) provided. Mark your answer by filling the circle on the answer sheet or by clicking on it using the mouse.

1. 2 5 4 2 1 8 5 3 6 5 2 1 3 2 1 4 2 1 4 3 6 4 1 2 3 1 6
(A) 34 (B) 33 (C) 31 (D) 30 (E) 32

2. 3 6 8 2 1 4 5 2 1 4 6 5 2 1 3 6 5 2 1 6 8 2 3 2 2 8 4 1 6 3
(A) 31 (B) 33 (C) 35 (D) 34 (E) 32

3. 6 1 2 4 6 4 2 5 3 2 5 2 1 4 8 4 6 3 2 1 5 4 1 2 1 6 4 1
(A) 27 (B) 26 (C) 25 (D) 24 (E) 23

4. 8 2 2 8 4 2 8 3 6 8 2 1 4 2 8 2 1 3 2 3 1 3 6 8 4 5 1 4
(A) 19 (B) 23 (C) 25 (D) 27 (E) 21

5. 8 3 2 3 2 6 1 4 8 4 5 3 4 2 8 1 2 5 6 2 6 2 2 5 1 4 3 8 1
(A) 31 (B) 29 (C) 30 (D) 32 (E) 28

6. 3 6 5 2 3 5 2 3 4 1 3 4 6 8 2 5 8 4 1 2 5 3 5 3 1 4 6 8 4 5
(A) 47 (B) 46 (C) 49 (D) 51 (E) 48

7. 6 1 5 8 1 4 2 1 2 3 1 2 1 2 4 3 3 8 2 3 5 4 1 5 5 2 2 5 6
(A) 41 (B) 45 (C) 43 (D) 44 (E) 40

8. 5 2 6 2 2 2 1 2 8 4 4 8 1 5 2 1 3 1 2 3 4 2 1 3 4 1 4 1 2
(A) 25 (B) 26 (C) 24 (D) 23 (E) 27

9. 8 4 8 4 3 5 6 1 4 5 8 8 2 5 4 4 8 6 6 4 1 4 1 3 4 4
(A) 25 (B) 26 (C) 27 (D) 24 (E) 23

10. 4 2 3 3 1 8 4 1 3 3 2 6 8 8 2 5 8 2 5 3 5 3 6 5 4 1 4 1 6
(A) 33 (B) 42 (C) 35 (D) 31 (E) 37

11. 1 2 4 2 1 5 8 3 2 4 5 2 4 6 5 2 5 3 8 4 2 4 6 2 3
(A) 31 (B) 30 (C) 29 (D) 32 (E) 33

12. 4 8 3 1 5 8 2 2 1 3 6 6 4 5 5 2 8 2 4 1 2 6 1 5 2 2
(A) 29 (B) 30 (C) 31 (D) 32 (E) 33

13. 8 3 6 5 2 5 2 8 5 6 1 4 2 8 3 1 4 5 5 2 5 4 2 4 4 2 8 3
(A) 43 (B) 42 (C) 41 (D) 39 (E) 37

14. 6 6 2 5 2 1 4 3 1 1 6 2 4 2 5 4 1 3 5 4 5 6 2 2 8
(A) 32 (B) 33 (C) 29 (D) 30 (E) 31

15. 6 2 4 2 5 6 1 4 1 5 6 3 2 5 6 4 8 1 2 8 6 2 2 3 6 2 2 1 2
(A) 26 (B) 24 (C) 25 (D) 23 (E) 27

16. 5 3 6 3 2 3 5 1 6 8 5 2 1 2 4 3 3 2 1 4 8 5 2 6 2 1 4 2
(A) 37 (B) 36 (C) 39 (D) 40 (E) 41

17. 8 4 6 3 2 1 2 5 4 6 1 8 2 1 4 1 2 4 2 4 8 2 1 2 4 2 3 6 2
(A) 16 (B) 13 (C) 15 (D) 17 (E) 19

18. 4 5 3 6 4 2 1 4 6 3 2 6 5 6 3 2 4 2 3 2 2 6 3 2 1 4 8 4 1 5
(A) 31 (B) 34 (C) 35 (D) 33 (E) 37

19. 6 3 2 1 4 5 8 2 1 4 2 1 3 6 4 4 2 3 5 1 4 8 5 2 5 2 5 4 8 2
(A) 37 (B) 36 (C) 38 (D) 39 (E) 41

20. 3 6 2 2 3 1 2 4 6 4 5 2 6 8 4 6 8 1 4 2 1 8 4 5 4 1 4 4 3 8
(A) 23 (B) 29 (C) 28 (D) 26 (E) 31

21. 6 3 2 1 2 2 5 3 3 2 1 2 5 8 1 2 4 8 5 2 1 4 1 2 3 5 4 1 5 4 2
(A) 41 (B) 40 (C) 39 (D) 44 (E) 43

22. 2 1 4 3 2 1 8 2 3 6 5 4 6 2 5 2 1 4 2 1 4 5 4 2 6 8 5 3 8 3 6
(A) 36 (B) 37 (C) 39 (D) 40 (E) 41

23. 5 2 1 4 2 8 3 2 5 6 2 1 6 4 5 2 1 4 3 1 3 1 6 3 6 4 1 2 1 2 8 1
(A) 33 (B) 37 (C) 35 (D) 39 (E) 34

24. 4 1 2 8 4 1 2 3 4 8 3 4 6 8 8 2 4 2 2 8 6 1 8 5 1 2 4 2 5 4 1
(A) 20 (B) 21 (C) 22 (D) 23 (E) 24

25. 1 4 6 5 6 3 2 4 6 2 2 5 8 2 6 2 5 5 4 6 6 4 3 6 5 1 1 2 4 2
(A) 33 (B) 29 (C) 35 (D) 34 (E) 28

26. 4 1 3 6 6 2 8 2 6 4 1 3 8 1 3 3 3 2 3 3 2 2 4 8 1 2 2
(A) 24 (B) 23 (C) 21 (D) 26 (E) 25

27. 4 6 2 1 4 4 3 6 1 5 1 6 2 4 2 8 8 1 1 2 3 2 3 3 1 2 8 2 3 2
(A) 30 (B) 29 (C) 23 (D) 26 (E) 25

28. 3 2 4 4 1 8 4 2 5 5 8 6 4 3 1 2 6 3 2 1 5 2 4 1 4 1 2 8 1
(A) 33 (B) 30 (C) 31 (D) 29 (E) 27

29. 2 2 3 4 5 6 4 5 6 8 2 2 8 8 5 1 1 5 3 6 5 2 1 4 6 3 1 4 2 8 3 1
(A) 41 (B) 43 (C) 44 (D) 42 (E) 46

30. 2 8 6 5 4 8 2 3 2 5 5 8 8 6 6 3 6 4 6 6 5 2 6 2 2 1 5 3 2 3 1
(A) 35 (B) 39 (C) 36 (D) 37 (E) 38

PRACTICE SET-19

Total Ques.- 30
Time - 8 or 10 Min.

निर्देश : (प्रश्न 1-30) विषम संख्याओं को योग परीक्षण के प्रत्येक प्रश्न में सम और विषम संख्याओं को मिलाकर एक श्रृंखला दिया रहता है। इस श्रृंखला में प्रदत्त केवल विषम संख्या 1, 3, 5 आदि को जोड़ने के बाद नीचे दिए गए पाँच विकल्पों (A, B, C, D और E) में कोई एक सही विकल्प को ढूंढना होता है जिसे दिए गए उत्तर-पत्रक में गोले को काला/माउस की सहायता से क्लिक करना होता है।

Directions: (Questions 1–30) : Each question in the Odd Number Adding Test presents a series of even and odd numbers. You need to add the total number of odd numbers 1, 3, 5 etc. in the given series. After adding, select the correct option from the five choices (A, B, C, D & E) provided. Mark your answer by filling the circle on the answer sheet or by clicking on it using the mouse.

1. 6 3 2 1 5 4 1 2 1 6 4 1 2 5 4 2 1 8 5 3 6 5 4 1 2 3 1 6
   (A) 33 (B) 35 (C) 34 (D) 36 (E) 30
2. 1 3 2 3 1 3 6 8 4 3 6 8 2 1 4 5 2 1 4 6 5 2 1 3 6 5 2 6 3
   (A) 37 (B) 36 (C) 38 (D) 39 (E) 40
3. 2 1 3 2 1 4 2 1 4 3 6 6 1 2 4 6 4 2 5 3 2 5 2 1 2 1 4 8 4
   (A) 26 (B) 27 (C) 30 (D) 25 (E) 29
4. 1 6 8 2 3 2 2 8 4 1 8 2 2 8 4 2 8 3 6 8 2 1 4 2 8 2 5 1 4
   (A) 16 (B) 17 (C) 13 (D) 14 (E) 15
5. 4 1 3 4 6 8 2 5 8 4 1 8 3 2 3 4 2 8 1 2 5 6 2 6 2 2 5 1 4 3 8 1
   (A) 31 (B) 29 (C) 32 (D) 33 (E) 35
6. 3 6 5 2 3 5 2 3 6 1 4 8 4 5 2 5 3 2 6 1 6 5 3 1 4 6 8 4 5
   (A) 47 (B) 48 (C) 49 (D) 50 (E) 51
7. 2 1 2 3 1 2 8 4 4 8 1 5 2 1 6 1 5 4 3 6 8 2 3 5 4 1 5 5 2 2 5 6
   (A) 45 (B) 46 (C) 47 (D) 48 (E) 50
8. 5 2 6 2 2 8 1 4 2 1 4 6 2 3 1 3 1 2 3 4 2 1 3 4 1 4 1 2
   (A) 23 (B) 25 (C) 24 (D) 26 (E) 29
9. 8 1 4 5 8 8 2 5 4 8 4 1 3 3 2 6 8 8 4 8 6 6 4 1 4 1 3 4 4
   (A) 23 (B) 31 (C) 33 (D) 30 (E) 35
10. 4 2 3 2 1 4 8 4 3 5 6 8 2 5 3 5 3 6 5 4 1 4 1 6
    (A) 36 (B) 34 (C) 33 (D) 35 (E) 37
11. 1 2 4 5 2 4 6 5 8 2 2 1 3 6 2 5 2 4 5 3 8 4 2 4 6 2 3
    (A) 30 (B) 32 (C) 31 (D) 33 (E) 29
12. 4 8 3 1 6 4 5 5 2 4 2 1 5 8 3 2 8 2 4 1 2 6 1 5 2 2
    (A) 30 (B) 29 (C) 31 (D) 28 (E) 32
13. 4 2 8 3 1 4 2 1 4 3 1 1 6 2 4 5 5 2 5 4 2 4 4 2 8 3
    (A) 26 (B) 25 (C) 29 (D) 28 (E) 30

14. 6 6 2 5 2 8 3 6 5 2 5 2 8 5 6 1 5 4 1 3 5 4 5 6 2 2 8
(A) 41 (B) 40 (C) 43 (D) 42 (E) 44

15. 8 5 2 1 4 3 6 4 8 1 2 8 6 2 2 3 6 1 4 1 5 6 3 2 5 6 6 2 2 1 2
(A) 30 (B) 31 (C) 32 (D) 33 (E) 29

16. 5 3 6 2 1 4 1 8 6 6 3 6 4 6 6 5 2 6 2 2 1 5 3 2 1 4 2
(A) 25 (B) 26 (C) 28 (D) 30 (E) 31

17. 8 1 4 2 1 3 6 4 4 2 3 5 1 4 8 5 6 1 8 2 4 2 4 8 2 1 2 4 2 3 6 2
(A) 20 (B) 24 (C) 22 (D) 25 (E) 26

18. 4 5 3 6 4 2 1 4 6 3 2 6 5 6 3 2 4 2 3 2 2 6 3 2 1 4 8 4 1 5
(A) 33 (B) 30 (C) 32 (D) 28 (E) 29

19. 6 3 2 1 3 2 3 5 1 6 8 5 2 1 2 4 3 3 2 1 4 8 5 2 6 5 4 8 2
(A) 38 (B) 39 (C) 36 (D) 40 (E) 42

20. 3 6 2 2 3 1 2 4 6 4 5 2 6 8 4 6 8 1 4 2 1 8 4 5 4 1 4 4 3 8
(A) 20 (B) 22 (C) 23 (D) 25 (E) 26

21. 6 3 2 1 2 2 5 3 3 2 1 2 5 8 1 2 4 8 5 2 1 4 1 2 3 5 4 1 5 4 2
(A) 40 (B) 42 (C) 44 (D) 43 (E) 45

22. 3 1 6 3 6 4 1 2 1 2 2 1 4 3 2 1 8 2 3 6 5 4 6 2 5 2 1 4 2 1 8 3 6
(A) 30 (B) 29 (C) 33 (D) 35 (E) 32

23. 5 2 1 4 5 4 2 6 8 5 3 2 5 2 4 2 8 3 2 5 6 2 1 6 4 5 4 3 1 8 1
(A) 43 (B) 40 (C) 39 (D) 41 (E) 42

24. 4 1 2 8 4 6 3 8 5 1 2 2 3 4 1 5 2 1 2 5 4 4 5 8 2 4 2 5 4 1
(A) 33 (B) 34 (C) 35 (D) 37 (E) 36

25. 1 4 6 5 6 3 2 4 6 2 2 5 8 2 6 2 5 5 4 6 6 4 3 6 5 1 1 2 4 2
(A) 34 (B) 35 (C) 36 (D) 33 (E) 31

26. 4 1 3 6 6 2 8 2 6 4 1 3 8 1 3 3 3 2 3 3 2 2 4 8 1 2 2
(A) 23 (B) 26 (C) 25 (D) 27 (E) 29

27. 4 6 2 1 4 4 3 6 1 5 1 6 3 1 2 6 3 2 1 5 2 4 1 2 4 2 8 8 1 3 2
(A) 28 (B) 27 (C) 26 (D) 29 (E) 30

28. 3 2 4 4 3 6 5 2 1 4 6 3 3 2 6 1 8 4 2 5 5 8 6 4 4 1 2 8 1
(A) 32 (B) 31 (C) 33 (D) 30 (E) 35

29. 2 2 3 4 5 6 4 5 6 1 2 3 2 1 2 8 2 1 2 2 8 8 5 1 1 5 1 4 2 8 3 1
(A) 35 (B) 39 (C) 40 (D) 33 (E) 36

30. 2 8 6 4 1 2 3 4 8 3 4 6 8 8 2 4 2 2 8 6 1 4 8 2 3 2 5 5 8 2 3 1
(A) 25 (B) 26 (C) 27 (D) 23 (E) 21

PRACTICE SET-20

Total Ques.- 30
Time - 8 or 10 Min.

निर्देश : (प्रश्न 1-30) विषम संख्याओं को योग परीक्षण के प्रत्येक प्रश्न में सम और विषम संख्याओं को मिलाकर एक श्रृंखला दिया रहता है। इस श्रृंखला में प्रदत्त केवल विषम संख्या 1, 3, 5 आदि को जोड़ने के बाद नीचे दिए गए पाँच विकल्पों (A, B, C, D और E) में कोई एक सही विकल्प को ढूंढना होता है जिसे दिए गए उत्तर-पत्रक में गोले को काला/माउस की सहायता से क्लिक करना होता है।

Directions: (Questions 1–30) : Each question in the Odd Number Adding Test presents a series of even and odd numbers. You need to add the total number of odd numbers 1, 3, 5 etc. in the given series. After adding, select the correct option from the five choices (A, B, C, D & E) provided. Mark your answer by filling the circle on the answer sheet or by clicking on it using the mouse.

1. 5 3 6 2 6 1 6 5 3 2 6 8 1 4 6 8 4 5 3 6 5 4 1 2 3 1 6
   (A) 36 (B) 35 (C) 33 (D) 30 (E) 31
2. 1 3 2 32 4 6 4 2 5 3 2 5 2 1 2 1 1 3 6 8 2 3 5 4 3 6 8 6 3
   (A) 39 (B) 40 (C) 41 (D) 37 (E) 42
3. 2 1 2 1 4 5 2 1 4 6 5 2 1 3 6 5 2 3 2 1 4 2 1 4 3 6 6 1 4 8 4
   (A) 31 (B) 30 (C) 29 (D) 32 (E) 33
4. 1 6 2 8 3 6 8 1 8 3 2 3 4 2 8 1 2 5 6 8 2 1 4 2 8 2 5 1 4
   (A) 23 (B) 24 (C) 25 (D) 26 (E) 21
5. 4 1 3 4 6 2 6 2 2 5 18 2 3 2 2 8 4 1 8 2 2 8 4 4 3 8 1
   (A) 18 (B) 17 (C) 16 (D) 15 (E) 20
6. 3 6 5 3 2 1 5 4 1 6 4 1 2 5 4 2 1 8 5 2 3 5 2 3 6 1 4 8 4 5 2
   (A) 46 (B) 45 (C) 47 (D) 48 (E) 49
7. 2 1 2 1 4 6 2 3 4 2 1 3 2 3 1 2 8 4 4 8 1 5 2 1 6 1 5 5 6
   (A) 30 (B) 31 (C) 33 (D) 35 (E) 34
8. 5 2 4 3 6 8 2 3 2 4 3 5 4 1 5 5 2 2 6 2 2 8 1 4 4 1 4 1 2
   (A) 30 (B) 32 (C) 33 (D) 34 (E) 35
9. 8 1 6 8 2 5 3 5 3 6 5 4 1 4 4 5 8 8 2 5 4 8 4 1 3 4 4
   (A) 31 (B) 37 (C) 33 (D) 35 (E) 36
10. 4 2 1 3 3 2 6 8 8 4 8 6 6 4 1 4 3 2 1 4 8 4 3 5 1 6
    (A) 19 (B) 18 (C) 21 (D) 20 (E) 22
11. 2 5 2 4 5 3 1 6 4 5 5 2 4 2 1 5 8 3 2 1 2 4 5 2 8 4 2 4 6 2 3
    (A) 41 (B) 40 (C) 43 (D) 42 (E) 44
12. 4 8 3 4 6 5 8 2 2 1 3 6 8 5 4 6 8 1 2 2 6 2 4 1 2 6 1 5 2 2
    (A) 21 (B) 22 (C) 25 (D) 23 (E) 24
13. 4 5 5 2 6 2 2 3 6 1 4 1 5 6 3 2 5 6 6 2 2 1 5 4 2 4 4 2 8 3
    (A) 35 (B) 36 (C) 38 (D) 39 (E) 37

14. 6 6 2 1 4 2 1 4 3 1 1 6 2 6 1 5 4 1 3 5 4 5 6 2 2 8
(A) 27 (B) 22 (C) 23 (D) 24 (E) 29

15. 8 5 5 2 8 3 6 5 2 5 2 8 5 4 2 8 3 2 1 4 3 6 4 8 1 2 8 2
(A) 38 (B) 37 (C) 34 (D) 35 (E) 36

16. 5 2 6 2 5 5 4 6 6 4 3 6 5 1 1 2 3 6 2 1 4 1 2 2 1 5 3 2 1 4 2
(A) 40 (B) 39 (C) 38 (D) 37 (E) 36

17. 8 2 4 8 5 2 1 4 1 2 3 5 4 1 5 4 2 1 4 2 1 3 6 4 4 2 2 4 2 3 6 2
(A) 28 (B) 27 (C) 29 (D) 25 (E) 30

18. 4 5 3 8 6 6 6 4 2 1 4 6 3 2 6 3 6 4 6 6 5 6 3 2 8 4 1 5
(A) 28 (B) 31 (C) 30 (D) 29 (E) 27

19. 6 3 2 1 3 2 3 5 1 6 8 5 2 1 2 4 3 3 2 1 4 8 5 2 6 5 4 8 2
(A) 41 (B) 37 (C) 40 (D) 38 (E) 39

20. 3 6 2 2 3 1 2 4 6 4 5 2 6 8 4 6 8 1 5 2 1 8 4 5 4 1 4 4 3 8
(A) 27 (B) 26 (C) 29 (D) 28 (E) 30

21. 6 3 2 1 4 2 3 2 2 6 3 2 3 4 2 1 6 4 2 4 2 2 5 3 3 2 1 2 5 8 1
(A) 31 (B) 33 (C) 32 (D) 34 (E) 35

22. 3 1 6 3 6 4 2 4 8 2 12 2 5 8 1 2 1 2 2 1 4 3 2 1 8 8 3 6
(A) 21 (B) 20 (C) 22 (D) 25 (E) 23

23. 5 2 1 4 5 4 2 6 8 5 3 2 5 2 4 2 8 3 2 5 6 2 1 6 4 5 4 3 1 8 1
(A) 40 (B) 44 (C) 45 (D) 43 (E) 41

24. 4 1 2 8 4 6 3 8 4 1 2 3 4 8 3 4 6 8 8 2 4 2 2 5 1 2 1 5 2 5 4 1
(A) 28 (B) 27 (C) 29 (D) 30 (E) 31

25. 1 4 6 5 6 3 2 4 6 3 2 3 6 5 4 6 2 1 4 2 1 5 1 4 8 5 6 1 8 2 4 4 2
(A) 33 (B) 34 (C) 35 (D) 36 (E) 31

26. 4 1 1 8 4 2 5 5 8 6 4 4 1 3 6 6 2 8 2 6 4 1 3 8 8 1 2 2
(A) 22 (B) 16 (C) 17 (D) 19 (E) 21

27. 4 6 2 1 4 4 3 6 1 5 1 6 3 1 2 6 3 2 1 5 2 4 1 2 4 2 8 8 1 3 2
(A) 27 (B) 26 (C) 25 (D) 29 (E) 30

28. 3 2 4 1 2 5 6 1 2 3 2 1 2 8 2 2 8 2 8 8 5 1 1 5 1 4 4 3 6 2 8 1
(A) 29 (B) 30 (C) 31 (D) 32 (E) 33

29. 2 2 3 4 5 5 2 1 4 6 3 3 2 6 1 3 3 3 2 3 3 2 2 2 4 6 4 3 1
(A) 39 (B) 40 (C) 41 (D) 42 (E) 38

30. 2 8 6 8 1 2 5 4 4 5 8 2 4 2 6 1 4 8 2 3 2 5 5 8 2 3 1
(A) 29 (B) 27 (C) 26 (D) 30 (E) 31

उत्तर (ANSWER)

PRACTICE SET - 1

1.	C	16.	A
2.	B	17.	C
3.	D	18.	E
4.	E	19.	B
5.	E	20.	D
6.	D	21.	A
7.	C	22.	C
8.	B	23.	E
9.	E	24.	B
10.	E	25.	D
11.	A	26.	A
12.	E	27.	C
13.	B	28.	E
14.	D	29.	B
15.	C	30.	D

PRACTICE SET - 2

1.	A	16.	A
2.	B	17.	B
3.	A	18.	C
4.	C	19.	D
5.	D	20.	E
6.	E	21.	D
7.	D	22.	C
8.	C	23.	B
9.	B	24.	A
10.	A	25.	B
11.	B	26.	C
12.	C	27.	D
13.	E	28.	E
14.	E	29.	D
15.	C	30.	C

PRACTICE SET - 3

1.	A	16.	B
2.	B	17.	D
3.	C	18.	B
4.	D	19.	E
5.	E	20.	A
6.	A	21.	C
7.	B	22.	D
8.	E	23.	A
9.	D	24.	E
10.	E	25.	C
11.	D	26.	A
12.	C	27.	D
13.	B	28.	B
14.	A	29.	E
15.	B	30.	C

PRACTICE SET - 4

1.	A	16.	A
2.	C	17.	B
3.	D	18.	C
4.	E	19.	D
5.	B	20.	E
6.	A	21.	C
7.	C	22.	B
8.	B	23.	D
9.	B	24.	A
10.	D	25.	E
11.	C	26.	C
12.	B	27.	B
13.	D	28.	D
14.	E	29.	D
15.	E	30.	A

PRACTICE SET - 5

1.	B	16.	C
2.	A	17.	A
3.	C	18.	D
4.	D	19.	E
5.	E	20.	B
6.	C	21.	C
7.	B	22.	B
8.	A	23.	E
9.	A	24.	D
10.	B	25.	A
11.	C	26.	B
12.	C	27.	D
13.	E	28.	C
14.	E	29.	A
15.	C	30.	D

PRACTICE SET - 6

1.	A	16.	C
2.	B	17.	B
3.	C	18.	D
4.	D	19.	B
5.	E	20.	C
6.	D	21.	D
7.	C	22.	E
8.	B	23.	A
9.	A	24.	E
10.	B	25.	A
11.	C	26.	C
12.	D	27.	B
13.	E	28.	D
14.	D	29.	B
15.	C	30.	C

उत्तर (ANSWER)

PRACTICE SET - 7

1.	A	16.	B
2.	B	17.	C
3.	A	18.	A
4.	C	19.	C
5.	C	20.	E
6.	D	21.	B
7.	C	22.	D
8.	D	23.	B
9.	E	24.	A
10.	D	25.	D
11.	E	26.	E
12.	D	27.	C
13.	C	28.	A
14.	B	29.	D
15.	C	30.	C

PRACTICE SET - 8

1.	C	16.	A
2.	B	17.	B
3.	E	18.	C
4.	D	19.	D
5.	B	20.	B
6.	C	21.	C
7.	E	22.	D
8.	D	23.	E
9.	A	24.	C
10.	C	25.	D
11.	E	26.	E
12.	A	27.	D
13.	E	28.	E
14.	A	29.	E
15.	C	30.	A

PRACTICE SET - 9

1.	E	16.	D
2.	A	17.	C
3.	A	18.	B
4.	B	19.	A
5.	C	20.	A
6.	E	21.	D
7.	D	22.	C
8.	B	23.	B
9.	A	24.	A
10.	C	25.	C
11.	E	26.	D
12.	D	27.	E
13.	B	28.	C
14.	D	29.	B
15.	C	30.	A

PRACTICE SET - 10

1.	E	16.	C
2.	A	17.	B
3.	E	18.	A
4.	A	19.	D
5.	E	20.	E
6.	C	21.	C
7.	D	22.	B
8.	B	23.	D
9.	C	24.	E
10.	D	25.	A
11.	B	26.	B
12.	C	27.	D
13.	D	28.	B
14.	E	29.	A
15.	C	30.	E

PRACTICE SET - 11

1.	A	16.	C
2.	B	17.	B
3.	D	18.	E
4.	D	19.	D
5.	E	20.	B
6.	D	21.	A
7.	C	22.	E
8.	B	23.	E
9.	A	24.	C
10.	C	25.	D
11.	B	26.	B
12.	D	27.	E
13.	E	28.	B
14.	C	29.	D
15.	A	30.	D

PRACTICE SET - 12

1.	C	16.	A
2.	A	17.	B
3.	C	18.	C
4.	D	19.	B
5.	B	20.	E
6.	B	21.	D
7.	C	22.	C
8.	D	23.	A
9.	E	24.	B
10.	B	25.	C
11.	A	26.	D
12.	C	27.	E
13.	D	28.	C
14.	C	29.	B
15.	E	30.	A

उत्तर (ANSWER)

PRACTICE SET - 13

1.	A	16.	C
2.	B	17.	D
3.	C	18.	C
4.	D	19.	B
5.	E	20.	D
6.	D	21.	C
7.	C	22.	A
8.	B	23.	E
9.	A	24.	E
10.	B	25.	A
11.	A	26.	B
12.	C	27.	C
13.	E	28.	B
14.	B	29.	D
15.	D	30.	B

PRACTICE SET - 14

1.	C	16.	C
2.	B	17.	A
3.	B	18.	E
4.	A	19.	B
5.	B	20.	E
6.	D	21.	A
7.	C	22.	B
8.	A	23.	D
9.	A	24.	A
10.	E	25.	C
11.	A	26.	E
12.	E	27.	B
13.	C	28.	A
14.	D	29.	D
15.	B	30.	E

PRACTICE SET - 15

1.	D	16.	C
2.	B	17.	A
3.	E	18.	A
4.	A	19.	C
5.	A	20.	C
6.	D	21.	B
7.	B	22.	D
8.	C	23.	E
9.	E	24.	A
10.	A	25.	E
11.	D	26.	A
12.	B	27.	B
13.	E	28.	C
14.	A	29.	D
15.	E	30.	E

PRACTICE SET - 16

1.	D	16.	C
2.	E	17.	D
3.	B	18.	E
4.	A	19.	C
5.	B	20.	B
6.	C	21.	A
7.	E	22.	C
8.	D	23.	D
9.	C	24.	E
10.	A	25.	C
11.	E	26.	A
12.	D	27.	C
13.	B	28.	E
14.	C	29.	C
15.	E	30.	A

PRACTICE SET - 17

1.	C	16.	E
2.	D	17.	B
3.	B	18.	A
4.	A	19.	E
5.	E	20.	C
6.	C	21.	B
7.	B	22.	C
8.	A	23.	B
9.	D	24.	A
10.	A	25.	D
11.	E	26.	C
12.	C	27.	E
13.	A	28.	A
14.	D	29.	D
15.	B	30.	C

PRACTICE SET - 18

1.	B	16.	C
2.	E	17.	A
3.	A	18.	D
4.	E	19.	C
5.	A	20.	A
6.	D	21.	E
7.	C	22.	A
8.	B	23.	C
9.	D	24.	B
10.	B	25.	D
11.	A	26.	E
12.	B	27.	D
13.	C	28.	B
14.	D	29.	D
15.	C	30.	B

उत्तर (ANSWER)

PRACTICE SET - 19

1.	D	16.	C
2.	C	17.	B
3.	D	18.	A
4.	E	19.	B
5.	C	20.	C
6.	B	21.	D
7.	A	22.	E
8.	C	23.	A
9.	A	24.	E
10.	D	25.	A
11.	C	26.	C
12.	A	27.	D
13.	D	28.	B
14.	C	29.	E
15.	E	30.	A

PRACTICE SET - 20

1.	A	16.	A
2.	B	17.	C
3.	A	18.	D
4.	B	19.	E
5.	A	20.	D
6.	C	21.	C
7.	B	22.	E
8.	C	23.	D
9.	B	24.	C
10.	C	25.	B
11.	D	26.	E
12.	C	27.	D
13.	E	28.	C
14.	A	29.	B
15.	E	30.	A

2 (B) TEST FOR MEASURING SELECTIVE ATTENTION

Counting of Odd Number Test (विषम संख्याओं का गणन परीक्षण)

स्टेशन मास्टर पद के लिए रेलवे मनोवैज्ञानिक परीक्षण के अन्तर्गत चयनात्मक अवधान मापन हेतु परीक्षण में 'विषम संख्याओं का गणन परीक्षण' एक महत्वपूर्ण अध्याय है। यह परीक्षण आपकी एकाग्रता और चयनात्मक ध्यान की जाँच करता है। इस परीक्षण के लिए 30 प्रश्न दिए होते हैं जिसे 8 या 10 मिनट में हल करना होता है। इस परीक्षण के प्रश्न में सम और विषम संख्याओं को मिलाकर एक श्रृंखला दिया रहता है। जिसमें विषम संख्या 1, 3, 5 आदि को गणन करना होता है। इस श्रृंखला में सम संख्याओं को गणना नहीं करना होता है। विषम संख्याओं को गणना करने के बाद नीचे दिए गए पाँच विकल्पों (A B C D और E) में से कौन-सा एक सही विकल्प है। ढूँढे गए सही विकल्प ही आपका उत्तर होगा जिसे उत्तर-पत्रक में दिए गए

As part of the Railway Psychological Test for the post of Station Master, the Odd Number Counting Test is an important section to measure selective attention. This test checks your concentration and selective attention. The test consists of 30 questions, to be completed in 8 or 10 minutes. Each question presents a series of even and odd numbers. You are required to count only the odd numbers (1, 3, 5, etc.) in the series. Even numbers are not to be counted. After counting the odd numbers, identify the correct option from the five given choices (A B C D & E). Mark your answer by filling the circle on the answer sheet or by clicking on it using the mouse.

नीचे दिए गए उदाहरणों के द्वारा इसे समझें :-
Example for understanding :-

1. 1 2 2 2 1 2 5 4 1 4 1 5 4 2 3 5 2 6 5 4 2 1 2 3 5 6 3 2 5 2
   (A) 22 (B) 24 (C) 14 (D) 12 (E) 15
2. 2 3 2 5 2 1 2 5 4 1 2 1 2 3 6 4 4 1 2 5 3 2 1 5 2 1 2 5 4 2 6
   (A) 10 (B) 13 (C) 11 (D) 14 (E) 17
3. 2 2 5 4 1 2 3 1 4 5 2 1 3 2 5 1 2 3 5 6 4 1 2 5 1 4 5 2
   (A) 17 (B) 19 (C) 21 (D) 15 (E) 25
4. 5 2 1 6 2 3 2 5 2 1 4 1 2 5 4 4 1 2 3 2 1 2 1 4 5 4 1 2 3
   (A) 23 (B) 14 (C) 19 (D) 17 (E) 25
5. 5 2 1 2 2 3 5 2 1 2 5 3 2 5 4 1 2 3 2 5 6 2 5 2 1 1 2
   (A) 17 (B) 16 (C) 20 (D) 14 (E) 15
6. 3 2 4 1 2 5 3 2 1 5 2 1 3 2 5 4 1 2 3 2 5 1 2 4 1 4 5 2 1
   (A) 13 (B) 20 (C) 14 (D) 18 (E) 16
7. 6 2 3 2 1 4 5 6 5 2 3 1 2 5 4 5 2 3 5 2 1 2 5 6 2 1
   (A) 10 (B) 11 (C) 16 (D) 18 (E) 13
8. 6 5 2 3 2 2 3 2 5 2 1 2 3 2 15 4 1 2 5 4 2 3 1 2 5 1 2
   (A) 14 (B) 11 (C) 16 (D) 12 (E) 20

Ans.: 1. (C) 2. (D) 3. (D) 4. (B) 5. (D) 6. (E) 7. (E) 8. (A)

PRACTICE SET-1

Total Ques.- 30
Time - 8 or 10 Min.

निर्देश : (प्रश्न 1-30) विषम संख्याओं का गणना परीक्षण के प्रत्येक प्रश्न में सम और विषम संख्याओं को मिलाकर एक श्रृंखला दिया जाता है। दिए गए संख्याओं में जितने विषम संख्या है उन्हें गणना करना होता है। गणना करने के बाद नीचे दिए गए पाँच विकल्पों (A, B, C, D और E) में एक सही विकल्प को ढूंढना होता है। जिसे उत्तर पत्रक में दिए गए गोले को काला या माउस की सहायता से क्लिक करना होता है।

Directions: (Questions 1–30) : Each question in the Odd Number Counting Test presents a series of even and odd numbers. You need to count the total number of odd numbers in the given series. After counting, select the correct option from the five choices (A, B, C, D & E) provided. Mark your answer by filling the circle on the answer sheet or by clicking on it using the mouse.

1. 1 5 4 2 3 5 2 6 1 2 4 1 2 6 5 3 3 3 2 1 4 5 2 1 5 2 6 5 2 1
   (A) 16 (B) 20 (C) 21 (D) 18 (E) 19
2. 2 3 5 6 4 1 2 4 1 2 3 2 1 5 2 1 4 1 2 5 3 2 5 1 4 2 3 2 1
   (A) 15 (B) 18 (C) 23 (D) 29 (E) 16
3. 5 2 1 4 2 3 2 1 5 2 6 3 2 1 5 4 1 2 1 2 5 2 6 3 4 2 1 5 2 4
   (A) 10 (B) 11 (C) 13 (D) 14 (E) 16
4. 4 5 2 1 3 2 5 6 2 1 2 5 4 3 6 2 1 5 2 3 2 1 4 1 2 5 3 2 5 2
   (A) 20 (B) 26 (C) 15 (D) 18 (E) 23
5. 6 2 3 5 2 1 2 2 2 3 4 4 1 2 5 2 3 2 1 1 1 5 2 3 2 5 6 2 5 1
   (A) 12 (B) 13 (C) 15 (D) 17 (E) 18
6. 4 1 2 5 2 3 2 5 4 1 2 5 2 1 2 3 2 5 2 1 6 2 3 2 1 4 5 2 1 3
   (A) 16 (B) 23 (C) 17 (D) 15 (E) 19
7. 3 2 1 2 5 2 1 2 5 4 6 2 3 6 2 5 4 1 2 3 2 5 1 2 4 2 3 2 5 6
   (A) 10 (B) 11 (C) 23 (D) 18 (E) 13
8. 1 2 2 5 4 2 3 5 2 6 5 4 2 1 2 3 5 6 2 1 2 5 4 1 4 1 3 2 5 2
   (A) 22 (B) 14 (C) 28 (D) 12 (E) 15
9. 2 3 2 5 2 1 4 1 2 5 3 2 1 2 5 4 1 2 1 2 3 6 5 2 1 2 5 4 2 6
   (A) 09 (B) 10 (C) 13 (D) 14 (E) 17
10. 2 1 4 5 2 1 3 2 5 1 2 3 5 6 4 1 2 5 1 2 5 4 1 2 3 4 5 2
    (A) 15 (B) 17 (C) 21 (D) 19 (E) 23
11. 5 2 1 4 1 2 3 2 1 2 1 4 5 6 2 3 2 5 2 1 4 1 2 5 4 1 2 3
    (A) 22 (B) 17 (C) 19 (D) 14 (E) 25
12. 5 2 1 2 3 2 5 4 1 2 3 2 5 6 2 5 2 1 1 2 2 3 5 2 1 2 5
    (A) 14 (B) 16 (C) 15 (D) 17 (E) 21
13. 3 2 5 4 1 2 3 2 5 1 2 4 1 2 5 3 2 1 5 2 1 3 2 1 4 5 2 1
    (A) 13 (B) 18 (C) 14 (D) 16 (E) 20

14. 6 5 2 3 1 2 5 4 5 6 2 3 2 1 4 5 2 3 5 2 1 2 5 6 2 1
(A) 11 (B) 10 (C) 13 (D) 18 (E) 16

15. 6 5 2 3 2 5 4 1 2 5 4 2 3 1 2 3 2 5 1 2 3 2 1 2 5 1 2
(A) 16 (B) 11 (C) 20 (D) 12 (E) 14

16. 3 3 2 1 4 5 2 1 5 2 6 5 2 1 2 1 5 4 2 3 5 2 6 1 2 4 1 2 6 5 3
(A) 18 (B) 20 (C) 19 (D) 16 (E) 21

17. 2 5 3 2 5 1 4 2 3 5 6 3 2 1 5 2 1 4 1 2 2 3 2 1 6 4 1 2 4 1 2
(A) 16 (B) 18 (C) 23 (D) 27 (E) 15

18. 4 2 3 2 1 5 2 6 3 2 1 5 2 1 6 6 5 4 1 2 2 1 5 2 4 1 2 5 2 6 3 4
(A) 14 (B) 11 (C) 13 (D) 16 (E) 10

19. 4 4 6 2 1 5 2 3 2 1 4 1 2 5 3 2 5 2 4 5 2 1 3 2 5 6 2 1 2 5 4 3
(A) 20 (B) 15 (C) 18 (D) 22 (E) 23

20. 1 1 1 5 2 3 2 5 6 2 6 2 3 5 2 1 2 2 2 3 4 4 1 2 5 2 3 2 2 5 1
(A) 17 (B) 13 (C) 15 (D) 18 (E) 18

21. 4 1 2 3 2 5 2 1 6 2 3 2 5 2 3 2 5 4 1 2 5 2 1 2 6 1 4 5 2 1 3
(A) 16 (B) 19 (C) 15 (D) 21 (E) 17

22. 3 2 1 2 4 5 4 1 2 3 2 5 1 2 4 25 2 1 2 5 4 6 2 3 6 2 3 2 5 6
(A) 13 (B) 11 (C) 18 (D) 21 (E) 10

23. 1 2 2 5 4 2 3 5 2 6 5 4 2 1 2 3 5 6 2 1 2 5 4 1 4 1 3 2 5 2
(A) 12 (B) 14 (C) 26 (D) 15 (E) 21

24. 2 2 5 3 2 1 2 5 4 1 2 1 2 3 3 2 5 2 1 4 1 2 6 5 2 1 2 5 4 2 6
(A) 09 (B) 10 (C) 17 (D) 13 (E) 14

25. 5 1 2 5 4 1 2 3 4 2 1 4 5 2 1 3 2 5 1 2 3 5 6 4 1 2 6 5 2
(A) 19 (B) 15 (C) 24 (D) 17 (E) 23

26. 2 1 4 5 6 2 3 2 5 2 1 4 5 2 1 4 1 2 2 5 4 1 2 3 3 2 1 4 1 2
(A) 14 (B) 17 (C) 19 (D) 21 (E) 25

27. 1 1 2 2 3 5 2 1 2 5 5 2 1 2 2 3 2 5 4 2 3 2 5 4 1 6 2 5 2
(A) 14 (B) 16 (C) 15 (D) 17 (E) 21

28. 3 2 4 1 2 5 3 2 1 5 2 1 5 4 1 2 5 2 1 3 2 5 1 2 6 3 2 1 4
(A) 16 (B) 18 (C) 13 (D) 14 (E) 28

29. 64 5 2 3 5 2 1 2 5 2 3 12 3 2 2 2 5 4 5 6 1 4 5 6 2 1
(A) 11 (B) 10 (C) 16 (D) 18 (E) 13

30. 2 1 2 5 1 2 2 6 5 2 3 4 2 3 1 4 2 5 4 1 2 52 3 2 5 1 2 3
(A) 16 (B) 11 (C) 24 (D) 12 (E) 14

PRACTICE SET-2

Total Ques.- 30
Time - 8 or 10 Min.

निर्देश : (प्रश्न 1-30) विषम संख्याओं का गणना परीक्षण के प्रत्येक प्रश्न में सम और विषम संख्याओं को मिलाकर एक श्रृंखला दिया जाता है। दिए गए संख्याओं में जितने विषम संख्या है उन्हें गणना करना होता है। गणना करने के बाद नीचे दिए गए पाँच विकल्पों (A, B, C, D और E) में एक सही विकल्प को ढूंढना होता है। जिसे उत्तर पत्रक में दिए गए गोले को काला या माउस की सहायता से क्लिक करना होता है।

Directions: (Questions 1–30) : Each question in the Odd Number Counting Test presents a series of even and odd numbers. You need to count the total number of odd numbers in the given series. After counting, select the correct option from the five choices (A, B, C, D & E) provided. Mark your answer by filling the circle on the answer sheet or by clicking on it using the mouse.

1. 1 5 4 2 1 4 5 2 1 5 2 4 2 3 5 2 6 1 2 4 1 2 6 5 3 3 3 2 6 5 2 1
   (A) 16 (B) 22 (C) 20 (D) 18 (E) 19
2. 2 3 2 2 4 1 2 3 2 1 5 2 1 4 5 6 4 1 2 1 2 5 3 2 2 5 1 4 2 3 2 1
   (A) 30 (B) 18 (C) 23 (D) 15 (E) 16
3. 5 25 2 6 3 4 2 1 5 2 4 2 1 4 2 3 2 1 5 2 6 3 2 1 5 4 1 2 1 2
   (A) 10 (B) 11 (C) 16 (D) 14 (E) 13
4. 4 3 6 2 1 5 2 3 2 1 5 2 1 3 2 5 6 2 1 2 5 4 2 4 1 2 5 3 2 5 2
   (A) 20 (B) 29 (C) 15 (D) 18 (E) 23
5. 6 2 4 1 2 5 2 3 2 1 1 1 5 2 3 2 5 6 2 5 1 3 5 2 1 2 2 2 3 4 4
   (A) 12 (B) 13 (C) 15 (D) 17 (E) 21
6. 3 2 5 2 1 6 2 3 2 1 4 1 2 5 2 3 2 5 4 1 2 5 2 1 2 4 5 2 1 3
   (A) 15 (B) 16 (C) 17 (D) 23 (E) 19
7. 2 5 4 6 2 3 6 2 5 4 3 2 1 2 5 2 1 1 2 3 2 5 1 2 4 2 3 2 5 6
   (A) 18 (B) 11 (C) 10 (D) 22 (E) 13
8. 1 2 2 2 1 2 5 4 1 4 1 5 4 2 3 5 2 6 5 4 2 1 2 3 5 6 3 2 5 2
   (A) 22 (B) 24 (C) 14 (D) 12 (E) 15
9. 2 3 2 5 2 1 2 5 4 1 2 1 2 3 6 4 4 1 2 5 3 2 1 5 2 1 2 5 4 2 6
   (A) 10 (B) 13 (C) 11 (D) 14 (E) 17
10. 2 2 5 4 1 2 3 1 4 5 2 1 3 2 5 1 2 3 5 6 4 1 2 5 1 4 5 2
    (A) 17 (B) 19 (C) 21 (D) 15 (E) 25
11. 5 2 1 6 2 3 2 5 2 1 4 1 2 5 4 4 1 2 3 2 1 2 1 4 5 4 1 2 3
    (A) 23 (B) 14 (C) 19 (D) 17 (E) 25
12. 5 2 1 2 2 3 5 2 1 2 5 3 2 5 4 1 2 3 2 5 6 2 5 2 1 1 2
    (A) 17 (B) 16 (C) 20 (D) 14 (E) 15
13. 3 2 4 1 2 5 3 2 1 5 2 1 3 2 5 4 1 2 3 2 5 1 2 4 1 4 5 2 1
    (A) 13 (B) 20 (C) 14 (D) 18 (E) 16

14. 6 2 3 2 1 4 5 6 5 2 3 1 2 5 4 5 2 3 5 2 1 2 5 6 2 1
(A) 10 (B) 11 (C) 16 (D) 18 (E) 13

15. 6 5 2 3 2 2 3 2 5 2 1 2 3 2 15 4 1 2 5 4 2 3 1 2 5 1 2
(A) 14 (B) 11 (C) 16 (D) 12 (E) 20

16. 1 5 3 2 6 5 2 2 3 2 3 5 2 6 1 1 2 3 2 1 4 5 2 1 2 6 5 2 1 2 6 5 3
(A) 29 (B) 26 (C) 17 (D) 21 (E) 16

17. 2 3 2 1 6 4 1 2 4 1 2 2 4 1 2 3 2 5 1 4 2 3 5 6 4 1 2 4 1 2
(A) 25 (B) 23 (C) 19 (D) 12 (E) 13

18. 3 4 2 1 5 2 6 4 2 3 2 2 1 5 2 4 1 2 5 2 6 3 2 1 5 2 1 6 6 5 4 1
(A) 14 (B) 20 (C) 15 (D) 23 (E) 19

19. 5 2 3 2 1 4 1 2 5 3 2 4 4 6 2 1 5 2 4 5 2 1 3 2 5 6 2 1 2 5 4 3
(A) 21 (B) 25 (C) 22 (D) 15 (E) 17

20. 1 2 2 3 4 4 1 3 5 2 1 2 3 2 2 2 5 2 1 1 5 2 3 2 5 6 2 6 2 5 1
(A) 10 (B) 15 (C) 12 (D) 17 (E) 26

21. 5 4 1 2 3 2 5 4 1 2 5 2 2 1 6 2 3 2 5 2 3 2 1 2 6 1 4 5 2 1 3
(A) 31 (B) 27 (C) 23 (D) 15 (E) 19

22. 3 4 5 4 1 2 6 2 3 2 1 3 2 5 1 2 4 2 5 2 1 2 5 4 2 6 2 3 2 5 6
(A) 11 (B) 12 (C) 17 (D) 10 (E) 13

23. 1 2 2 2 3 5 2 6 5 4 2 1 4 1 5 6 2 1 2 5 4 1 5 4 2 3 3 2 5 2
(A) 22 (B) 13 (C) 14 (D) 18 (E) 21

24. 2 5 4 2 6 3 2 1 2 2 5 4 1 2 6 5 2 1 2 5 4 1 2 1 2 3 3 2 5 2 1
(A) 22 (B) 17 (C) 21 (D) 14 (E) 16

25. 2 3 5 6 4 4 1 2 3 4 2 1 5 1 2 5 5 2 1 3 2 5 1 4 1 2 6 5 2
(A) 23 (B) 21 (C) 15 (D) (E) 25

26. 2 1 4 1 4 1 5 6 2 3 2 5 2 1 4 5 2 5 4 1 2 3 3 2 2 1 4 1 2 2
(A) 16 (B) 14 (C) 18 (D) 19 (E) 22

27. 2 1 2 2 2 5 2 1 1 2 2 3 2 5 4 2 3 2 5 4 1 5 3 5 2 1 2 5 5
(A) 15 (B) 17 (C) 16 (D) 20 (E) 22

28. 3 2 4 2 5 1 2 1 3 2 5 2 1 1 5 5 3 2 1 5 4 1 2 5 2 1 3 1 5
(A) 21 (B) 19 (C) 23 (D) 20 (E) 26

29. 6 4 5 2 2 3 5 2 1 2 5 2 3 2 2 2 5 4 5 6 1 3 1 4 5 6 2 1
(A) 10 (B) 12 (C) 15 (D) 13 (E) 16

30. 2 1 3 4 2 3 1 2 5 1 2 3 2 5 1 4 2 5 4 1 2 5 2 3 2 2 6 5 2
(A) 24 (B) 22 (C) 18 (D) 14 (E) 16

PRACTICE SET-3

Total Ques.- 30
Time - 8 or 10 Min.

निर्देश : (प्रश्न 1-30) विषम संख्याओं का गणना परीक्षण के प्रत्येक प्रश्न में सम और विषम संख्याओं को मिलाकर एक श्रृंखला दिया जाता है। दिए गए संख्याओं में जितने विषम संख्या है उन्हें गणना करना होता है। गणना करने के बाद नीचे दिए गए पाँच विकल्पों (A, B, C, D और E) में एक सही विकल्प को ढूंढना होता है। जिसे उत्तर पत्रक में दिए गए गोले को काला या माउस की सहायता से क्लिक करना होता है।

Directions: (Questions 1–30) : Each question in the Odd Number Counting Test presents a series of even and odd numbers. You need to count the total number of odd numbers in the given series. After counting, select the correct option from the five choices (A, B, C, D & E) provided. Mark your answer by filling the circle on the answer sheet or by clicking on it using the mouse.

1. 2 3 5 2 6 1 2 4 1 2 6 5 3 3 3 2 6 5 2 1 1 5 4 2 1 4 5 2 1 5 2 4
(A) 22 (B) 20 (C) 15 (D) 14 (E) 16

2. 4 5 6 4 1 2 1 2 5 3 2 2 5 2 3 2 2 4 1 2 3 2 1 5 2 1 1 4 2 3 2 1
(A) 14 (B) 29 (C) 25 (D) 15 (E) 20

3. 5 2 2 1 4 2 3 2 1 5 2 6 3 2 1 5 4 1 5 2 6 3 4 2 1 5 2 4 2 1 2
(A) 19 (B) 18 (C) 13 (D) 14 (E) 16

4. 4 3 5 4 2 4 1 2 5 3 2 6 2 1 5 2 3 2 1 5 2 1 3 2 5 6 2 1 2 5 2
(A) 21 (B) 16 (C) 15 (D) 29 (E) 26

5. 6 2 4 2 5 1 3 5 2 1 2 2 2 3 4 1 2 5 2 3 2 1 1 1 5 2 3 2 5 6 4
(A) 18 (B) 12 (C) 31 (D) 15 (E) 22

6. 3 2 5 2 1 2 5 3 1 2 4 5 1 3 2 3 5 1 4 1 2 5 2 3 2 5 4 2 1 3
(A) 22 (B) 18 (C) 24 (D) 25 (E) 29

7. 2 5 4 6 2 3 2 5 1 2 4 2 3 2 5 6 2 3 6 2 5 4 3 2 1 2 5 2 1 1
(A) 26 (B) 22 (C) 18 (D) 13 (E) 16

8. 1 2 2 2 5 4 2 1 2 3 5 6 3 2 1 2 5 4 1 4 1 5 4 2 3 5 2 6 5 2
(A) 29 (B) 25 (C) 22 (D) 16 (E) 14

9. 2 3 2 6 4 4 1 2 5 3 2 1 5 2 1 2 5 4 2 6 5 2 1 2 5 4 1 2 1 2 3
(A) 18 (B) 24 (C) 22 (D) 14 (E) 15

10. 2 2 5 4 5 6 4 1 2 5 1 4 1 2 3 1 4 5 2 1 3 2 5 1 2 3 5 2
(A) 20 (B) 22 (C) 14 (D) 15 (E) 22

11. 5 2 4 1 2 3 2 1 2 1 4 5 4 1 2 3 1 6 2 3 2 5 2 1 4 1 2 5 4
(A) 16 (B) 20 (C) 18 (D) 14 (E) 15

12. 5 2 3 2 5 6 2 5 2 1 1 2 2 3 5 2 1 2 5 3 2 5 4 1 2 1 3 5 1
(A) 21 (B) 17 (C) 22 (D) 26 (E) 30

13. 3 2 1 2 3 2 5 1 2 4 1 4 5 2 4 1 2 5 3 2 1 5 2 1 3 2 5 4 1
(A) 28 (B) 22 (C) 23 (D) 16 (E) 32

14. 6 2 3 5 2 1 2 5 6 3 2 1 4 5 6 5 2 3 1 2 5 4 5 2 2 1
(A) 22 (B) 16 (C) 13 (D) 26 (E) 29

15. 6 5 2 1 5 4 1 2 5 4 2 3 1 2 5 1 3 2 2 3 2 2 3 2 5 2 1 2 3
(A) 15 (B) 18 (C) 22 (D) 26 (E) 28

16. 1 5 3 6 1 1 2 3 2 1 4 5 2 1 2 6 5 2 6 5 2 2 3 2 3 5 2 2 1 2 6 5 3
(A) 20 (B) 19 (C) 22 (D) 17 (E) 15

17. 2 3 2 1 6 4 1 2 2 3 5 6 4 1 2 4 1 2 2 4 1 2 3 2 5 1 4 4 1 2
(A) 18 (B) 11 (C) 12 (D) 19 (E) 20

18. 3 4 6 3 2 1 5 2 1 6 6 5 4 2 1 5 2 6 4 2 3 2 2 1 5 2 4 1 2 5 2 1
(A) 12 (B) 16 (C) 18 (D) 14 (E) 20

19. 6 2 1 5 2 4 5 2 1 3 2 5 5 2 3 2 1 4 1 2 5 3 2 4 4 6 2 1 2 5 4 3
(A) 20 (B) 12 (C) 18 (D) 16 (E) 15

20. 1 2 2 3 4 1 1 5 2 3 2 5 6 2 6 4 1 3 5 2 1 2 3 2 2 2 5 2 2 5 1
(A) 16 (B) 20 (C) 15 (D) 18 (E) 14

21. 5 4 5 2 2 1 6 2 3 2 5 2 3 2 1 2 1 2 3 2 5 4 1 2 6 1 4 5 2 1 3
(A) 13 (B) 16 (C) 18 (D) 15 (E) 20

22. 3 4 2 5 2 1 2 5 4 2 6 2 3 5 4 1 2 6 2 3 2 1 3 2 5 1 2 4 2 5 6
(A) 15 (B) 13 (C) 18 (D) 20 (E) 22

23. 1 2 2 1 2 5 4 1 5 4 2 3 3 2 5 2 3 5 2 6 5 4 2 1 4 1 5 6 2 2
(A) 10 (B) 12 (C) 18 (D) 14 (E) 20

24. 2 5 4 2 1 2 5 4 1 2 1 2 3 2 6 3 2 1 2 2 5 4 1 2 6 5 3 2 5 2 1
(A) 12 (B) 13 (C) 14 (D) 15 (E) 16

25. 2 3 5 5 2 1 3 2 5 1 4 1 2 6 5 6 4 4 1 2 3 4 2 1 5 1 2 5 2
(A) 19 (B) 17 (C) 16 (D) 14 (E) 15

26. 2 1 1 2 3 3 2 2 1 4 4 1 4 1 5 6 2 3 2 5 2 1 4 5 2 5 4 1 2 2
(A) 19 (B) 20 (C) 18 (D) 14 (E) 16

27. 2 1 3 2 5 4 1 6 3 5 2 1 2 5 2 2 2 5 2 1 1 2 2 3 2 5 4 2 5
(A) 20 (B) 18 (C) 15 (D) 12 (E) 14

28. 5 3 2 1 5 4 1 2 5 2 13 2 4 2 5 1 2 6 3 2 5 2 1 1 2 3 1 4
(A) 15 (B) 19 (C) 14 (D) 16 (E) 18

29. 6 5 4 5 6 13 1 4 5 6 2 1 4 5 2 2 3 5 2 1 2 5 2 3 2 2 2
(A) 14 (B) 15 (C) 16 (D) 13 (E) 20

30. 2 5 4 1 2 5 2 3 2 2 1 3 4 2 3 1 2 5 1 2 3 2 5 1 4 2 6 5 2
(A) 12 (B) 15 (C) 20 (D) 16 (E) 14

PRACTICE SET-4

Total Ques.- 30
Time - 8 or 10 Min.

निर्देश : (प्रश्न 1-30) विषम संख्याओं का गणना परीक्षण के प्रत्येक प्रश्न में सम और विषम संख्याओं को मिलाकर एक श्रृंखला दिया जाता है। दिए गए संख्याओं में जितने विषम संख्या है उन्हें गणना करना होता है। गणना करने के बाद नीचे दिए गए पाँच विकल्पों (A, B, C, D और E) में एक सही विकल्प को ढूंढना होता है। जिसे उत्तर पत्रक में दिए गए गोले को काला या माउस की सहायता से क्लिक करना होता है।

Directions: (Questions 1–30) : Each question in the Odd Number Counting Test presents a series of even and odd numbers. You need to count the total number of odd numbers in the given series. After counting, select the correct option from the five choices (A, B, C, D & E) provided. Mark your answer by filling the circle on the answer sheet or by clicking on it using the mouse.

1. 1 5 4 2 1 2 6 5 3 3 3 2 1 4 5 2 1 5 2 4 2 3 5 2 6 1 2 4 6 5 2 1
(A) 20 (B) 11 (C) 13 (D) 16 (E) 17

2. 2 3 2 2 5 3 2 2 5 1 4 2 3 2 1 2 4 1 2 3 2 1 5 2 1 4 5 6 4 1 2 1
(A) 12 (B) 14 (C) 15 (D) 16 (E) 21

3. 5 2 5 2 6 3 2 1 5 4 5 2 6 3 4 2 1 5 2 4 2 1 4 2 3 2 1 1 2 1 2
(A) 11 (B) 12 (C) 15 (D) 14 (E) 16

4. 4 3 6 2 2 5 4 2 4 1 2 5 3 2 5 2 1 5 2 3 2 1 5 2 1 3 2 5 6 2 1
(A) 12 (B) 14 (C) 18 (D) 15 (E) 20

5. 3 2 5 6 2 5 1 3 5 2 1 2 6 2 4 1 2 5 2 3 2 1 1 1 5 2 2 2 3 4 4
(A) 17 (B) 19 (C) 15 (D) 18 (E) 20

6. 3 1 2 5 2 3 2 5 4 1 2 5 2 1 2 5 2 1 6 2 3 2 1 4 2 4 5 2 1 3
(A) 17 (B) 14 (C) 16 (D) 18 (E) 15

7. 2 5 1 1 2 3 2 5 1 2 4 2 3 2 4 6 2 3 6 2 5 4 3 2 1 2 5 2 5 6
(A) 15 (B) 13 (C) 20 (D) 22 (E) 19

8. 1 5 2 6 5 4 2 1 2 3 5 2 2 2 1 2 5 4 1 4 1 5 4 2 3 6 3 2 5 2
(A) 20 (B) 18 (C) 15 (D) 14 (E) 16

9. 2 3 1 2 5 3 2 1 5 2 1 2 5 4 2 2 5 2 1 2 5 4 1 2 1 2 3 6 4 4 6
(A) 16 (B) 18 (C) 11 (D) 14 (E) 12

10. 2 2 2 3 5 6 4 1 2 5 5 4 1 2 3 1 4 5 2 1 3 2 5 1 1 4 5 2
(A) 20 (B) 19 (C) 17 (D) 15 (E) 16

11. 5 2 1 2 3 2 1 2 1 4 5 4 1 1 6 2 3 2 5 2 1 4 1 2 5 4 4 2 3
(A) 11 (B) 12 (C) 14 (D) 15 (E) 16

12. 5 2 1 2 3 2 5 6 2 5 1 2 2 3 5 2 1 2 5 3 2 5 4 2 1 1 2
(A) 12 (B) 14 (C) 20 (D) 18 (E) 16

13. 3 2 1 2 3 2 5 1 2 4 1 4 5 4 1 2 5 3 2 1 5 2 1 3 2 5 4 2 1
(A) 20 (B) 17 (C) 14 (D) 15 (E) 16

14. 6 2 3 5 2 3 5 2 1 2 2 1 4 5 6 5 2 3 1 2 5 4 5 6 2 1
(A) 18 (B) 19 (C) 20 (D) 16 (E) 13

15. 6 5 2 1 5 4 1 2 5 4 2 3 1 2 5 2 3 2 2 3 2 5 2 1 2 3 1 2
(A) 11 (B) 14 (C) 13 (D) 15 (E) 19

16. 1 5 3 2 6 5 2 1 2 6 5 3 6 5 2 2 3 2 3 5 2 6 1 2 2 4 5 2 1 2
(A) 18 (B) 13 (C) 15 (D) 14 (E) 16

17. 2 3 2 1 6 4 2 5 1 4 2 3 5 6 4 1 2 4 1 2 2 4 1 2 3 1 2 4 1 2
(A) 17 (B) 16 (C) 12 (D) 11 (E) 15

18. 3 4 4 1 2 5 2 6 3 2 1 5 2 1 6 6 2 1 5 2 6 4 2 3 2 2 1 5 2 5 4 1
(A) 13 (B) 15 (C) 18 (D) 16 (E) 14

19. 5 2 5 2 4 5 2 1 3 2 5 6 3 2 1 4 1 2 5 3 2 4 4 6 2 1 2 1 2 5 4 3
(A) 18 (B) 25 (C) 15 (D) 17 (E) 22

20. 1 2 2 3 2 1 1 5 2 3 2 5 6 2 6 4 4 1 3 5 2 1 2 3 2 2 2 5 2 5 1
(A) 23 (B) 21 (C) 19 (D) 17 (E) 15

21. 1 6 2 3 2 5 2 3 2 1 2 6 5 4 1 2 3 2 5 4 1 2 5 2 2 1 4 5 2 1 3
(A) 11 (B) 18 (C) 15 (D) 16 (E) 14

22. 3 4 5 1 2 4 2 5 2 1 2 5 4 2 6 2 6 3 1 1 2 6 2 3 2 1 3 2 5 3 2 5 6
(A) 12 (B) 15 (C) 13 (D) 16 (E) 11

23. 1 2 2 2 3 5 2 1 2 5 4 1 5 4 2 3 2 6 5 4 2 1 4 1 5 6 3 2 5 2
(A) 21 (B) 15 (C) 14 (D) 16 (E) 17

24. 2 5 4 2 1 2 5 4 1 2 1 2 3 2 6 3 2 1 2 2 5 4 1 2 6 5 3 2 5 2 1
(A) 19 (B) 20 (C) 18 (D) 14 (E) 15

25. 2 3 5 6 5 5 2 1 3 2 5 1 4 4 4 1 2 3 4 2 1 5 1 2 1 2 6 5 2
(A) 13 (B) 15 (C) 17 (D) 20 (E) 21

26. 2 1 2 5 4 1 2 3 3 2 2 1 4 4 1 4 1 5 6 2 3 2 5 2 1 4 5 1 2 2
(A) 12 (B) 14 (C) 13 (D) 17 (E) 20

27. 2 1 2 3 2 5 4 1 6 3 5 2 2 2 2 2 5 2 1 1 2 2 3 2 5 4 1 2 5 5
(A) 12 (B) 13 (C) 14 (D) 16 (E) 18

28. 3 2 4 2 1 5 4 1 2 5 2 1 3 2 5 1 2 6 3 2 5 2 1 1 2 5 3 1 4
(A) 21 (B) 15 (C) 16 (D) 18 (E) 17

29. 6 2 5 4 5 6 1 3 1 4 5 4 5 2 2 3 5 2 1 2 5 2 3 2 2 6 2 1
(A) 10 (B) 13 (C) 19 (D) 22 (E) 16

30. 2 1 3 5 4 1 2 5 2 3 2 2 4 2 3 1 2 5 1 2 3 2 5 1 4 2 6 5 2
(A) 15 (B) 14 (C) 20 (D) 23 (E) 19

PRACTICE SET-5

Total Ques.- 30
Time - 8 or 10 Min.

निर्देश : (प्रश्न 1-30) विषम संख्याओं का गणना परीक्षण के प्रत्येक प्रश्न में सम और विषम संख्याओं को मिलाकर एक श्रृंखला दिया जाता है। दिए गए संख्याओं में जितने विषम संख्या है उन्हें गणना करना होता है। गणना करने के बाद नीचे दिए गए पाँच विकल्पों (A, B, C, D और E) में एक सही विकल्प को ढूंढना होता है। जिसे उत्तर पत्रक में दिए गए गोले को काला या माउस की सहायता से क्लिक करना होता है।

Directions: (Questions 1–30) : Each question in the Odd Number Counting Test presents a series of even and odd numbers. You need to count the total number of odd numbers in the given series. After counting, select the correct option from the five choices (A, B, C, D & E) provided. Mark your answer by filling the circle on the answer sheet or by clicking on it using the mouse.

1. 1 5 4 2 6 5 3 3 3 2 6 5 2 1 2 1 4 5 2 1 5 2 4 2 3 5 2 6 1 2 4 1
   (A) 19 (B) 17 (C) 16 (D) 21 (E) 23
2. 1 4 5 6 4 1 2 1 2 5 3 2 2 5 1 4 2 3 2 2 4 1 2 3 2 1 5 2 2 3 2 1
   (A) 12 (B) 16 (C) 18 (D) 15 (E) 19
3. 5 2 5 2 5 2 6 3 2 1 5 4 1 6 3 4 2 1 5 2 4 2 1 4 2 3 2 1 2 1 2
   (A) 21 (B) 13 (C) 14 (D) 16 (E) 18
4. 4 3 6 2 6 2 1 2 5 4 2 4 1 2 1 5 2 3 2 1 5 2 1 3 2 5 5 3 2 5 2
   (A) 22 (B) 20 (C) 16 (D) 15 (E) 19
5. 6 2 4 1 2 5 2 3 2 5 4 1 2 5 2 5 2 3 2 1 1 1 5 2 3 2 5 2 2 3 4 4
   (A) 11 (B) 19 (C) 15 (D) 16 (E) 12
6. 3 2 5 2 1 6 2 6 3 4 2 1 2 4 1 2 4 1 2 4 4 6 5 2 1 3
   (A) 16 (B) 18 (C) 10 (D) 12 (E) 14
7. 2 3 2 1 2 5 2 1 1 2 5 4 6 2 3 6 2 5 4 3 2 5 1 2 4 2 3 2 5 6
   (A) 22 (B) 21 (C) 19 (D) 13 (E) 16
8. 1 2 2 2 1 2 5 4 1 2 3 5 6 3 2 5 2 4 1 5 4 2 3 5 2 6 5 4 2 1
   (A) 19 (B) 20 (C) 14 (D) 15 (E) 16
9. 2 3 2 5 22 5 3 2 1 5 2 1 2 5 1 2 5 4 1 2 1 2 3 6 4 4 1 4 2 6
   (A) 16 (B) 17 (C) 19 (D) 14 (E) 15
10. 2 2 5 1 2 3 5 6 4 1 2 5 4 1 2 3 1 4 5 2 1 3 2 5 1 4 5 2
    (A) 23 (B) 21 (C) 17 (D) 16 (E) 15
11. 4 1 2 5 4 4 1 2 3 2 1 2 5 2 1 6 2 3 2 5 2 1 1 4 5 4 1 2 3
    (A) 15 (B) 14 (C) 19 (D) 25 (E) 21
12. 3 2 5 4 1 2 3 2 5 5 2 1 2 2 3 5 2 1 2 5 6 2 5 2 1 1 2
    (A) 14 (B) 20 (C) 15 (D) 21 (E) 17
13. 3 2 4 1 3 2 5 1 2 4 1 4 5 2 2 5 3 2 1 5 2 1 3 2 5 4 1 2 1
    (A) 12 (B) 11 (C) 15 (D) 21 (E) 16

14. 6 2 3 5 4 5 2 3 5 2 1 2 1 4 5 6 5 2 3 1 2 2 5 6 2 1

(A) 11 (B) 17 (C) 21 (D) 13 (E) 15

15. 6 5 2 1 5 4 1 2 5 4 2 3 1 2 3 2 2 3 2 5 2 1 2 3 2 5 1 2

(A) 16 (B) 13 (C) 14 (D) 15 (E) 18

16. 1 5 3 2 6 2 3 2 1 4 5 2 3 3 4 1 3 2 3 5 2 6 1 1 1 2 6 5 2 1 2 6 5 3

(A) 22 (B) 20 (C) 19 (D) 17 (E) 23

17. 2 2 2 4 1 2 3 2 5 1 4 2 3 5 3 2 1 6 4 1 2 4 1 6 4 1 2 4 1 2

(A) 21 (B) 17 (C) 16 (D) 12 (E) 13

18. 3 4 2 1 2 1 5 2 1 6 6 5 2 6 4 2 3 2 2 1 5 2 4 1 2 5 2 6 3 5 4 1

(A) 23 (B) 22 (C) 14 (D) 15 (E) 19

19. 5 2 3 2 1 3 2 5 6 2 1 2 5 1 4 1 2 5 3 2 4 4 6 2 1 5 2 4 5 2 4 3

(A) 17 (B) 11 (C) 15 (D) 20 (E) 21

20. 1 2 2 3 4 5 2 3 2 5 6 2 6 2 5 1 4 1 3 5 2 1 2 3 2 2 2 5 2 1 1

(A) 13 (B) 15 (C) 14 (D) 19 (E) 22

21. 5 2 3 2 1 2 6 1 4 5 5 4 1 2 3 2 5 4 1 2 5 2 2 1 6 2 3 2 2 1 3

(A) 23 (B) 21 (C) 15 (D) 13 (E) 17

22. 3 4 4 2 5 2 1 2 5 4 2 6 2 3 2 5 6 5 4 1 2 6 2 3 2 1 3 2 5 1 2

(A) 22 (B) 13 (C) 19 (D) 12 (E) 14

23. 6 2 1 2 5 4 1 5 4 2 1 2 2 2 3 5 2 6 5 4 2 1 4 1 5 3 3 2 5 2

(A) 11 (B) 23 (C) 14 (D) 15 (E) 17

24. 2 5 4 2 12 5 4 1 2 1 2 3 3 2 2 6 3 2 1 2 2 5 4 1 2 6 5 5 2 1

(A) 17 (B) 22 (C) 19 (D) 14 (E) 15

25. 1 2 5 5 2 1 3 2 5 1 4 2 3 5 6 4 4 1 2 3 4 2 1 5 1 2 6 5 2

(A) 11 (B) 18 (C) 15 (D) 16 (E) 21

26. 2 1 5 2 5 4 1 2 3 3 2 2 1 4 1 4 1 4 1 5 6 2 3 2 5 2 1 4 2 2

(A) 21 (B) 18 (C) 14 (D) 16 (E) 17

27. 2 1 2 3 2 5 4 2 3 2 5 4 1 2 2 2 5 2 1 1 2 6 3 5 2 1 2 5 5

(A) 15 (B) 14 (C) 18 (D) 17 (E) 21

28. 2 5 3 2 1 5 4 1 2 5 2 3 2 4 2 5 1 2 6 3 2 5 2 1 1 1 3 1 4

(A) 15 (B) 19 (C) 16 (D) 21 (E) 12

29. 6 4 4 5 6 1 3 1 4 5 6 2 5 2 2 3 5 2 1 2 5 2 3 2 2 2 5 1

(A) 21 (B) 24 (C) 13 (D) 11 (E) 16

30. 2 1 3 4 2 3 5 4 1 2 5 2 3 2 1 1 3 2 2 5 1 2 3 2 5 1 4 2 2 6 5 2

(A) 19 (B) 15 (C) 16 (D) 17 (E) 23

PRACTICE SET-6

Total Ques.- 30
Time - 8 or 10 Min.

निर्देश : (प्रश्न 1–30) विषम संख्याओं का गणना परीक्षण के प्रत्येक प्रश्न में सम और विषम संख्याओं को मिलाकर एक श्रृंखला दिया जाता है। दिए गए संख्याओं में जितने विषम संख्या है उन्हें गणना करना होता है। गणना करने के बाद नीचे दिए गए पाँच विकल्पों (A, B, C, D और E) में एक सही विकल्प को ढूंढना होता है। जिसे उत्तर पत्रक में दिए गए गोले को काला या माउस की सहायता से क्लिक करना होता है।

Directions: (Questions 1–30) : Each question in the Odd Number Counting Test presents a series of even and odd numbers. You need to count the total number of odd numbers in the given series. After counting, select the correct option from the five choices (A, B, C, D & E) provided. Mark your answer by filling the circle on the answer sheet or by clicking on it using the mouse.

1. 1 5 4 2 6 5 3 3 3 2 6 5 2 1 4 5 2 1 5 2 4 2 3 5 2 6 1 2 4 1 2 1
   (A) 23 (B) 22 (C) 16 (D) 20 (E) 21
2. 2 3 2 1 2 1 2 5 3 2 2 5 1 2 4 1 2 3 2 1 5 2 1 4 5 6 4 4 2 3 2 1
   (A) 13 (B) 19 (C) 21 (D) 15 (E) 17
3. 5 2 5 2 6 3 2 1 5 4 1 2 3 4 2 1 5 2 4 2 1 4 2 3 2 1 5 2 6 1 2
   (A) 15 (B) 14 (C) 17 (D) 20 (E) 21
4. 4 3 5 6 2 1 2 5 4 2 4 1 2 5 6 2 1 5 2 3 2 1 5 2 1 3 2 3 2 5 2
   (A) 17 (B) 15 (C) 16 (D) 22 (E) 25
5. 6 2 2 3 2 5 6 2 5 1 3 5 2 4 1 2 5 2 3 2 1 1 1 5 1 2 2 2 3 4 4
   (A) 19 (B) 18 (C) 17 (D) 15 (E) 13
6. 3 3 2 5 4 1 2 5 2 1 2 2 5 2 1 6 2 3 2 1 4 1 2 5 2 4 5 2 1 3
   (A) 17 (B) 15 (C) 18 (D) 21 (E) 23
7. 2 5 4 6 2 3 2 5 1 2 4 2 3 2 3 6 2 5 4 3 2 1 2 5 2 1 1 2 5 6
   (A) 14 (B) 16 (C) 15 (D) 13 (E) 17
8. 1 2 2 2 1 6 5 4 2 1 2 3 5 2 5 4 1 4 1 5 4 2 3 5 2 6 3 2 5 2
   (A) 20 (B) 18 (C) 17 (D) 14 (E) 15
9. 2 3 2 5 2 1 2 5 3 2 1 5 2 1 2 1 2 5 4 1 2 1 2 3 6 4 4 5 4 2 6
   (A) 13 (B) 11 (C) 14 (D) 15 (E) 22
10. 5 2 1 3 2 5 1 2 3 2 2 5 4 1 2 3 1 4 6 4 1 2 5 1 4 5 2
    (A) 12 (B) 15 (C) 16 (D) 14 (E) 21
11. 5 2 1 6 2 3 2 5 2 3 2 1 2 1 4 5 4 1 1 4 1 2 5 4 4 1 2 2 3
    (A) 12 (B) 11 (C) 25 (D) 21 (E) 14
12. 5 5 4 1 2 3 2 5 6 2 5 2 1 2 2 3 5 2 1 2 5 3 2 2 1 1 2
    (A) 17 (B) 16 (C) 20 (D) 14 (E) 18
13. 3 2 4 2 4 1 4 5 2 1 1 2 5 3 2 1 5 2 1 3 2 5 4 1 2 3 2 5 1
    (A) 25 (B) 21 (C) 20 (D) 18 (E) 16

14. 6 2 3 2 1 2 5 4 5 2 3 5 2 1 2 1 4 5 6 5 2 3 5 6 2 1
(A) 12 (B) 15 (C) 23 (D) 13 (E) 17

15. 6 5 2 3 2 4 1 2 5 4 2 3 1 2 2 3 2 5 2 1 2 3 2 1 5 5 1 2
(A) 21 (B) 22 (C) 13 (D) 17 (E) 14

16. 3 5 2 6 1 1 2 3 2 1 4 1 5 3 2 6 5 2 2 3 2 5 2 1 2 6 5 2 1 2 6 5 3
(A) 15 (B) 27 (C) 25 (D) 17 (E) 11

17. 2 3 2 1 6 4 1 2 3 2 5 1 4 2 3 5 6 2 4 1 2 2 4 1 4 1 2 4 1 2
(A) 20 (B) 21 (C) 12 (D) 15 (E) 17

18. 3 4 2 1 5 2 4 1 2 5 2 2 1 5 2 6 4 2 3 2 6 3 2 1 5 2 1 6 6 5 4 1
(A) 13 (B) 15 (C) 14 (D) 17 (E) 20

19. 2 1 5 2 4 5 2 1 3 2 5 6 2 1 5 2 3 2 1 4 1 2 5 3 2 4 4 6 2 5 4 3
(A) 11 (B) 22 (C) 20 (D) 18 (E) 15

20. 1 2 2 3 5 2 3 2 5 6 2 6 2 5 1 4 4 1 3 5 2 1 2 3 2 2 2 5 2 1 1
(A) 10 (B) 11 (C) 23 (D) 16 (E) 15

21. 6 2 3 2 5 2 3 2 1 2 6 1 4 5 5 4 1 2 3 2 5 4 1 2 5 2 2 1 2 1 3
(A) 17 (B) 19 (C) 23 (D) 15 (E) 21

22. 3 4 5 1 2 5 4 2 6 2 3 2 5 6 4 1 2 6 2 3 2 1 3 2 5 1 2 4 2 5 2
(A) 15 (B) 16 (C) 13 (D) 22 (E) 21

23. 5 4 2 1 4 1 5 6 2 1 2 5 4 1 2 2 2 3 5 2 6 1 5 4 2 3 3 2 5 2
(A) 13 (B) 19 (C) 21 (D) 14 (E) 16

24. 2 5 4 2 1 2 5 4 1 2 1 2 3 3 2 6 3 2 1 2 2 5 4 1 2 6 5 2 5 2 1
(A) 11 (B) 14 (C) 13 (D) 16 (E) 17

25. 2 3 5 6 4 4 1 2 3 1 4 1 2 6 4 2 1 5 1 2 5 5 2 1 3 2 5 5 2
(A) 13 (B) 14 (C) 15 (D) 16 (E) 20

26. 2 1 4 1 2 3 3 2 2 1 4 1 2 2 4 1 4 1 5 6 2 3 2 5 2 1 4 5 2 5
(A) 18 (B) 22 (C) 15 (D) 14 (E) 16

27. 2 4 2 3 2 5 4 1 6 3 5 1 2 2 2 5 2 1 1 2 2 3 2 5 2 1 2 5 5
(A) 12 (B) 19 (C) 14 (D) 22 (E) 20

28. 3 2 4 2 1 5 4 1 2 5 2 1 3 2 5 1 2 6 3 2 5 2 1 1 2 5 3 1 4
(A) 15 (B) 14 (C) 16 (D) 18 (E) 19

29. 6 4 5 5 4 5 6 1 3 1 4 5 2 2 3 5 2 1 2 5 2 3 2 2 2 6 2 1
(A) 11 (B) 21 (C) 17 (D) 13 (E) 19

30. 2 1 2 5 4 1 2 5 2 3 2 2 3 4 2 3 1 2 5 1 2 3 2 5 1 4 6 5 2
(A) 18 (B) 14 (C) 20 (D) 22 (E) 23

PRACTICE SET-7

Total Ques.- 30
Time - 8 or 10 Min.

निर्देश : (प्रश्न 1-30) विषम संख्याओं का गणना परीक्षण के प्रत्येक प्रश्न में सम और विषम संख्याओं को मिलाकर एक श्रृंखला दिया जाता है। दिए गए संख्याओं में जितने विषम संख्या है उन्हें गणना करना होता है। गणना करने के बाद नीचे दिए गए पाँच विकल्पों (A, B, C, D और E) में एक सही विकल्प को ढूंढना होता है। जिसे उत्तर पत्रक में दिए गए गोले को काला या माउस की सहायता से क्लिक करना होता है।

Directions: (Questions 1–30) : Each question in the Odd Number Counting Test presents a series of even and odd numbers. You need to count the total number of odd numbers in the given series. After counting, select the correct option from the five choices (A, B, C, D & E) provided. Mark your answer by filling the circle on the answer sheet or by clicking on it using the mouse.

1. 1 5 4 2 6 1 2 4 1 2 6 5 3 3 3 2 3 1 2 1 4 5 2 1 5 2 3 5 6 5 2 1
   (A) 16 (B) 19 (C) 18 (D) 23 (E) 14
2. 2 3 1 2 5 3 2 2 5 1 4 2 3 2 1 5 3 2 2 4 1 2 3 2 1 5 2 1 4 5 6 4 1 2 1
   (A) 18 (B) 22 (C) 20 (D) 17 (E) 15
3. 5 2 5 2 2 6 3 2 1 5 4 1 2 6 3 4 2 1 5 2 4 2 1 4 2 3 2 1 5 1 2
   (A) 16 (B) 14 (C) 17 (D) 21 (E) 23
4. 4 3 6 2 2 4 1 2 5 3 2 5 2 1 5 2 3 2 1 5 2 1 3 2 5 6 2 1 2 5 4
   (A) 18 (B) 16 (C) 15 (D) 17 (E) 23
5. 6 2 4 1 2 5 2 2 2 3 4 2 3 2 1 1 1 5 2 3 2 5 6 2 5 1 3 5 2 1 4
   (A) 18 (B) 26 (C) 25 (D) 15 (E) 16
6. 1 2 5 2 3 2 5 4 1 2 5 2 1 3 2 5 2 1 6 2 3 2 1 4 2 4 5 2 1 3
   (A) 14 (B) 12 (C) 22 (D) 18 (E) 15
7. 2 5 4 3 2 5 1 2 4 2 3 2 6 2 3 6 2 5 4 3 2 1 2 5 2 1 1 2 5 6
   (A) 21 (B) 25 (C) 22 (D) 13 (E) 16
8. 1 2 5 2 6 5 4 2 1 2 3 5 2 2 1 2 5 4 1 4 1 5 4 2 3 6 3 2 5 2
   (A) 15 (B) 11 (C) 14 (D) 16 (E) 17
9. 2 3 2 3 2 1 5 2 1 2 5 4 2 5 2 1 2 5 4 1 2 1 2 3 6 4 4 1 2 5 6
   (A) 22 (B) 19 (C) 15 (D) 14 (E) 16
10. 2 2 5 4 1 2 3 5 6 4 1 2 5 1 2 3 1 4 5 2 1 3 2 5 1 4 5 2
    (A) 22 (B) 25 (C) 15 (D) 16 (E) 23
11. 5 2 1 2 3 2 1 2 1 4 5 4 1 6 2 3 2 5 2 1 4 1 2 5 4 4 1 2 3
    (A) 21 (B) 18 (C) 19 (D) 14 (E) 15
12. 5 2 4 1 2 3 2 5 6 2 5 1 2 2 3 5 2 1 2 5 3 2 5 2 1 1 2
    (A) 22 (B) 15 (C) 16 (D) 17 (E) 14
13. 3 2 3 2 5 1 2 4 1 4 5 4 1 2 5 3 2 1 5 2 1 3 2 5 4 1 2 2 1
    (A) 21 (B) 13 (C) 14 (D) 16 (E) 11

14. 6 2 3 5 4 5 2 3 5 2 1 2 1 4 5 6 5 2 3 1 2 2 5 6 2 1

(A) 25 (B) 19 (C) 13 (D) 17 (E) 22

15. 6 5 2 2 5 4 2 3 1 2 5 1 3 2 2 3 2 5 2 1 2 3 2 1 5 4 1 2

(A) 23 (B) 14 (C) 16 (D) 18 (E) 21

16. 2 1 4 5 2 1 2 6 5 2 1 1 5 3 2 6 5 2 2 3 2 3 5 2 6 1 1 2 3 2 6 5 3

(A) 16 (B) 13 (C) 17 (D) 21 (E) 23

17. 2 3 2 1 2 5 1 4 2 3 5 6 4 1 6 4 1 2 4 1 2 2 4 1 2 3 2 4 1 2

(A) 16 (B) 20 (C) 12 (D) 11 (E) 15

18. 3 1 5 2 1 6 6 5 4 4 2 1 5 2 6 4 2 3 2 2 1 5 2 4 1 2 5 2 6 3 2 1

(A) 13 (B) 14 (C) 15 (D) 17 (E) 19

19. 5 6 2 1 5 2 4 5 2 1 3 2 5 6 2 1 2 5 4 2 3 2 1 4 1 2 5 3 2 4 4 3

(A) 13 (B) 15 (C) 17 (D) 18 (E) 20

20. 2 5 2 1 1 5 2 3 2 5 1 2 2 3 4 4 1 3 5 2 1 2 3 2 2 6 2 6 2 5 1

(A) 15 (B) 17 (C) 19 (D) 20 (E) 20

21. 5 2 1 6 2 3 2 5 2 3 2 1 2 6 1 4 5 2 1 4 1 2 3 2 5 4 1 2 5 2 3

(A) 16 (B) 18 (C) 15 (D) 14 (E) 17

22. 3 2 1 2 5 4 2 6 2 3 4 5 4 1 2 6 2 3 2 1 3 2 5 1 2 4 2 5 2 5 6

(A) 15 (B) 17 (C) 24 (D) 22 (E) 13

23. 1 2 2 1 2 5 4 1 5 4 2 3 3 2 5 2 2 3 5 2 6 5 4 2 1 4 1 5 6 2

(A) 21 (B) 20 (C) 16 (D) 14 (E) 17

24. 2 5 4 1 2 1 2 3 3 2 5 4 2 6 3 2 1 2 2 5 4 1 2 6 5 2 1 2 5 2 1

(A) 22 (B) 24 (C) 12 (D) 16 (E) 14

25. 2 3 5 5 2 1 3 2 5 1 4 1 2 6 5 6 4 4 1 2 3 4 2 1 5 1 2 5 2

(A) 19 (B) 17 (C) 15 (D) 18 (E) 20

26. 2 1 1 4 5 2 5 4 1 2 3 3 2 2 1 4 1 2 4 1 4 1 5 6 2 3 2 5 2 2

(A) 18 (B) 21 (C) 13 (D) 14 (E) 16

27. 2 1 2 2 5 4 1 6 3 5 2 1 2 2 5 2 1 1 2 2 3 2 5 4 2 3 2 5 5

(A) 13 (B) 15 (C) 17 (D) 14 (E) 16

28. 3 2 3 2 1 5 4 1 2 5 2 1 3 1 4 4 2 5 1 2 6 3 2 5 2 1 1 2 5

(A) 18 (B) 16 (C) 20 (D) 23 (E) 19

29. 6 4 5 5 4 5 6 1 3 1 4 5 2 2 3 5 2 1 2 5 2 3 2 2 2 6 2 1

(A) 11 (B) 15 (C) 13 (D) 19 (E) 22

30. 2 1 2 5 4 1 2 5 2 3 2 2 6 5 2 3 4 2 3 1 2 5 1 2 3 2 5 1 4

(A) 16 (B) 14 (C) 17 (D) 20 (E) 19

PRACTICE SET-8

Total Ques.- 30
Time - 8 or 10 Min.

निर्देश : (प्रश्न 1-30) विषम संख्याओं का गणना परीक्षण के प्रत्येक प्रश्न में सम और विषम संख्याओं को मिलाकर एक श्रृंखला दिया जाता है। दिए गए संख्याओं में जितने विषम संख्या है उन्हें गणना करना होता है। गणना करने के बाद नीचे दिए गए पाँच विकल्पों (A, B, C, D और E) में एक सही विकल्प को ढूंढना होता है। जिसे उत्तर पत्रक में दिए गए गोले को काला या माउस की सहायता से क्लिक करना होता है।

Directions: (Questions 1–30) : Each question in the Odd Number Counting Test presents a series of even and odd numbers. You need to count the total number of odd numbers in the given series. After counting, select the correct option from the five choices (A, B, C, D & E) provided. Mark your answer by filling the circle on the answer sheet or by clicking on it using the mouse.

1. 2 4 1 2 6 5 3 3 3 2 1 5 4 2 1 4 5 2 1 5 2 4 2 3 5 2 6 1 2 1
(A) 18 (B) 22 (C) 15 (D) 17 (E) 19

2. 5 6 4 1 2 1 2 5 3 2 2 5 1 2 3 2 2 4 1 2 3 2 1 5 2 1 4 4 2 3 2 1
(A) 22 (B) 21 (C) 16 (D) 15 (E) 17

3. 5 2 5 2 6 2 6 3 2 1 5 4 3 4 2 1 5 2 4 2 1 4 2 3 2 1 5 1 2 1 2
(A) 17 (B) 19 (C) 15 (D) 14 (E) 16

4. 4 3 6 5 6 2 1 2 5 4 2 4 1 2 5 2 1 5 2 3 2 1 5 2 1 3 2 3 2 5 2
(A) 19 (B) 22 (C) 25 (D) 15 (E) 21

5. 1 5 2 3 2 5 6 2 5 1 3 6 2 4 1 2 5 2 3 2 1 1 5 2 1 2 2 2 3 4 4
(A) 17 (B) 16 (C) 15 (D) 22 (E) 18

6. 5 2 1 2 4 5 2 1 3 3 2 5 2 1 6 2 3 2 1 4 1 2 5 2 3 2 5 4 1 2
(A) 13 (B) 15 (C) 16 (D) 21 (E) 25

7. 2 1 2 5 2 1 1 2 3 2 5 1 2 5 4 6 2 3 6 2 5 4 3 2 4 2 3 2 5 6
(A) 15 (B) 17 (C) 19 (D) 13 (E) 16

8. 4 2 3 5 2 6 5 4 2 1 2 3 5 6 1 2 2 2 1 2 5 4 1 4 1 5 3 2 5 2
(A) 19 (B) 17 (C) 21 (D) 22 (E) 14

9. 2 1 2 3 6 4 4 1 2 5 3 2 1 5 2 1 2 3 2 5 2 1 2 5 4 12 5 4 2 6
(A) 11 (B) 14 (C) 22 (D) 25 (E) 13

10. 3 1 4 5 2 1 3 2 5 1 2 2 2 5 4 1 2 3 5 6 4 1 2 5 1 4 5 2
(A) 14 (B) 19 (C) 21 (D) 15 (E) 13

11. 5 4 4 1 2 3 2 1 2 5 2 1 6 2 3 2 5 2 1 4 1 2 1 4 5 4 1 2 3
(A) 13 (B) 22 (C) 19 (D) 14 (E) 17

12. 3 2 5 4 1 2 3 2 5 6 2 5 2 1 2 2 3 5 2 1 2 5 5 2 1 1 2
(A) 15 (B) 17 (C) 22 (D) 23 (E) 14

13. 4 1 2 3 2 5 1 2 4 1 3 2 4 1 2 5 3 2 1 5 2 1 3 2 5 4 5 2 1
(A) 19 (B) 25 (C) 18 (D) 11 (E) 16

14. 3 1 2 5 4 5 2 3 5 6 2 3 2 1 4 5 6 5 2 2 1 2 5 6 2 1
(A) 19 (B) 23 (C) 11 (D) 13 (E) 15

15. 6 5 2 3 2 5 4 2 3 1 2 5 1 2 2 2 3 2 5 2 1 2 3 2 1 5 4 1
(A) 23 (B) 21 (C) 14 (D) 16 (E) 19

16. 1 5 1 2 3 2 1 4 5 2 1 2 6 5 2 1 2 3 2 6 5 2 2 3 2 3 5 2 6 1 6 5 3
(A) 22 (B) 15 (C) 17 (D) 21 (E) 23

17. 2 4 1 2 3 2 5 1 4 2 3 5 2 3 2 1 6 4 1 2 4 1 2 6 4 1 2 4 1 2
(A) 17 (B) 21 (C) 23 (D) 12 (E) 16

18. 2 3 2 2 1 5 2 4 1 2 5 2 6 3 3 4 2 1 5 2 6 4 2 1 5 2 1 6 6 5 4 1
(A) 20 (B) 19 (C) 25 (D) 14 (E) 23

19. 4 4 6 2 1 5 2 4 5 2 1 3 2 5 2 3 2 1 4 1 2 5 3 2 5 6 2 1 2 5 4 3
(A) 23 (B) 12 (C) 15 (D) 17 (E) 21

20. 2 2 2 5 2 1 1 5 2 3 2 5 6 2 1 2 2 3 4 4 1 3 5 2 1 2 3 6 2 5 1
(A) 23 (B) 15 (C) 19 (D) 20 (E) 13

21. 1 6 2 3 2 5 2 3 2 1 2 6 1 4 5 5 4 1 2 3 2 5 4 1 2 5 2 2 2 1 3
(A) 17 (B) 22 (C) 15 (D) 14 (E) 13

22. 3 4 5 5 1 2 4 2 5 2 1 2 5 4 2 4 1 2 6 2 3 2 1 3 2 6 2 3 2 5 6
(A) 15 (B) 13 (C) 21 (D) 18 (E) 22

23. 1 2 2 4 2 3 3 2 5 2 3 5 2 6 5 4 2 1 4 1 5 6 2 1 2 5 4 1 5 2
(A) 17 (B) 14 (C) 15 (D) 22 (E) 24

24. 2 5 4 2 6 5 2 1 2 5 4 1 2 1 2 6 3 2 1 2 2 5 4 1 2 3 3 2 5 2 1
(A) 22 (B) 15 (C) 14 (D) 16 (E) 23

25. 2 3 1 5 1 2 5 5 2 1 3 2 5 1 4 1 5 6 4 4 1 2 3 4 2 2 6 5 2
(A) 16 (B) 15 (C) 22 (D) 25 (E) 21

26. 2 1 4 1 4 1 2 3 3 2 2 1 4 1 4 1 5 6 2 3 2 5 2 1 4 5 2 5 2 2
(A) 12 (B) 11 (C) 14 (D) 16 (E) 18

27. 2 2 2 3 2 5 4 2 3 2 5 4 1 6 1 2 2 2 5 2 1 1 3 5 2 1 2 5 5
(A) 20 (B) 14 (C) 15 (D) 16 (E) 11

28. 3 2 2 1 5 4 1 2 5 2 1 3 4 2 5 1 2 6 3 2 5 2 1 1 2 5 3 1 4
(A) 17 (B) 11 (C) 16 (D) 19 (E) 21

29. 6 4 4 5 6 1 3 1 4 5 6 2 5 2 2 3 5 2 1 2 5 2 3 2 2 2 5 1
(A) 11 (B) 14 (C) 23 (D) 13 (E) 15

30. 2 1 3 1 2 5 2 3 2 2 6 4 2 3 1 2 5 1 2 3 2 5 1 4 2 5 4 5 2
(A) 21 (B) 22 (C) 25 (D) 14 (E) 17

PRACTICE SET-9

Total Ques.- 30
Time - 8 or 10 Min.

निर्देश : (प्रश्न 1-30) विषम संख्याओं का गणना परीक्षण के प्रत्येक प्रश्न में सम और विषम संख्याओं को मिलाकर एक श्रृंखला दिया जाता है। दिए गए संख्याओं में जितने विषम संख्या है उन्हें गणना करना होता है। गणना करने के बाद नीचे दिए गए पाँच विकल्पों (A, B, C, D और E) में एक सही विकल्प को ढूंढना होता है। जिसे उत्तर पत्रक में दिए गए गोले को काला या माउस की सहायता से क्लिक करना होता है।

Directions: (Questions 1–30) : Each question in the Odd Number Counting Test presents a series of even and odd numbers. You need to count the total number of odd numbers in the given series. After counting, select the correct option from the five choices (A, B, C, D & E) provided. Mark your answer by filling the circle on the answer sheet or by clicking on it using the mouse.

1. 1 5 4 4 1 2 6 5 3 3 3 2 6 5 2 1 2 1 4 5 2 1 5 2 4 2 3 5 2 6 1 2
(A) 21 (B) 25 (C) 27 (D) 16 (E) 14

2. 2 3 2 2 1 2 1 2 5 3 2 2 5 1 4 1 2 3 2 1 5 2 1 4 5 6 4 4 2 3 2 1
(A) 21 (B) 24 (C) 15 (D) 14 (E) 18

3. 5 2 1 5 2 6 3 2 1 5 4 1 2 1 2 5 2 6 3 4 2 1 5 2 4 2 1 4 2 3 2
(A) 20 (B) 15 (C) 11 (D) 14 (E) 16

4. 6 2 1 2 5 4 2 4 1 2 4 3 6 2 1 5 2 3 2 1 5 2 1 3 2 5 5 3 2 5 2
(A) 25 (B) 22 (C) 20 (D) 17 (E) 15

5. 6 2 6 2 5 1 3 5 2 1 2 2 2 3 4 4 1 2 5 2 3 2 1 1 1 5 2 3 2 5 4
(A) 14 (B) 18 (C) 20 (D) 15 (E) 17

6. 3 2 5 4 1 2 5 2 1 2 4 5 2 5 2 1 6 2 3 2 1 4 1 2 5 2 3 2 1 3
(A) 11 (B) 23 (C) 15 (D) 17 (E) 21

7. 2 5 4 6 2 5 1 2 4 2 3 2 3 6 2 5 4 3 2 1 2 5 2 1 1 2 3 2 5 6
(A) 16 (B) 11 (C) 13 (D) 15 (E) 21

8. 1 2 2 5 4 2 1 2 3 5 6 3 2 5 2 2 1 2 5 4 1 4 1 5 4 2 3 5 2 6
(A) 17 (B) 14 (C) 16 (D) 22 (E) 19

9. 2 5 3 2 1 5 2 1 2 2 3 2 5 2 1 2 5 4 1 2 1 2 3 6 4 4 1 5 4 2 6
(A) 19 (B) 21 (C) 14 (D) 15 (E) 20

10. 1 2 3 5 6 4 1 2 5 2 2 5 4 1 2 3 1 4 5 2 1 3 2 5 1 4 5 2
(A) 11 (B) 15 (C) 17 (D) 21 (E) 23

11. 5 2 5 4 4 1 2 3 2 1 2 1 4 5 4 2 1 6 2 3 2 5 2 1 4 1 1 2 3
(A) 16 (B) 14 (C) 18 (D) 11 (E) 23

12. 5 4 1 2 3 2 5 6 2 5 5 2 1 2 2 3 5 2 1 2 5 3 2 2 1 1 2
(A) 13 (B) 14 (C) 19 (D) 25 (E) 18

13. 3 2 3 2 5 4 1 2 3 2 5 1 2 4 4 1 2 5 3 2 1 5 2 1 1 4 5 2 1
(A) 21 (B) 13 (C) 16 (D) 18 (E) 22

14. 5 4 5 2 3 5 2 1 2 6 2 3 2 1 4 5 6 5 2 3 1 2 5 6 2 1

(A) 16 (B) 15 (C) 19 (D) 13 (E) 12

15. 6 5 1 2 5 4 2 3 1 2 5 1 2 3 2 2 3 2 5 2 1 2 3 2 1 5 4 2

(A) 22 (B) 19 (C) 14 (D) 16 (E) 17

16. 1 5 3 2 2 1 4 5 2 1 2 6 5 2 1 2 6 6 5 2 2 3 2 3 5 2 6 1 1 2 3 5 3

(A) 25 (B) 18 (C) 17 (D) 19 (E) 23

17. 2 3 2 1 6 4 1 1 4 2 3 5 6 4 1 2 4 1 2 2 4 1 2 3 2 5 4 1 2

(A) 16 (B) 15 (C) 12 (D) 17 (E) 21

18. 3 4 2 2 5 2 6 3 2 1 5 2 1 6 6 1 5 2 6 4 2 3 2 2 1 5 2 4 1 5 4 1

(A) 17 (B) 14 (C) 19 (D) 22 (E) 25

19. 4 4 6 2 1 5 2 4 5 2 1 5 2 3 2 1 4 1 2 5 3 2 3 2 5 6 2 1 2 5 4 3

(A) 21 (B) 15 (C) 17 (D) 13 (E) 14

20. 1 3 5 2 1 2 3 2 2 2 5 2 1 1 2 2 3 4 4 1 5 2 3 2 5 6 2 6 2 5 1

(A) 18 (B) 14 (C) 15 (D) 22 (E) 23

21. 5 4 1 2 2 1 2 6 1 4 5 2 3 2 5 4 1 2 5 2 2 1 6 2 3 2 5 2 3 1 3

(A) 14 (B) 17 (C) 15 (D) 22 (E) 25

22. 3 4 5 4 1 4 2 6 2 3 2 5 6 2 6 2 3 2 1 3 2 5 1 2 4 2 5 2 1 2 5

(A) 11 (B) 14 (C) 13 (D) 16 (E) 17

23. 1 2 2 1 2 5 4 1 5 4 2 3 3 2 2 3 5 2 6 5 4 2 1 4 1 5 6 2 5 2

(A) 17 (B) 14 (C) 16 (D) 21 (E) 19

24. 2 5 4 2 4 1 2 1 2 3 3 2 5 2 1 6 3 2 1 2 2 5 4 1 2 6 5 2 1 2 5

(A) 22 (B) 11 (C) 14 (D) 17 (E) 20

25. 2 3 5 6 4 4 1 2 3 1 4 1 2 6 4 2 1 5 1 2 5 5 2 1 3 2 5 5 2

(A) 16 (B) 23 (C) 19 (D) 15 (E) 14

26. 2 1 4 4 1 2 3 3 2 2 1 4 1 1 4 1 5 6 2 3 2 5 2 1 4 5 2 5 2 2

(A) 17 (B) 14 (C) 27 (D) 21 (E) 23

27. 2 1 2 2 5 4 1 6 3 5 2 1 2 5 2 1 1 2 2 3 2 5 4 2 3 2 2 5 5

(A) 21 (B) 18 (C) 14 (D) 16 (E) 15

28. 3 2 4 1 5 4 1 2 5 2 1 3 1 4 2 5 1 2 6 3 2 5 2 1 1 2 5 3 2

(A) 21 (B) 16 (C) 18 (D) 22 (E) 25

29. 6 2 2 5 4 5 6 1 3 1 4 4 5 2 2 3 5 2 1 2 5 2 3 2 5 6 2 1

(A) 16 (B) 15 (C) 17 (D) 13 (E) 21

30. 2 1 2 5 4 1 2 5 2 3 2 2 6 5 3 4 2 3 1 2 5 1 2 3 2 5 1 4 2

(A) 18 (B) 14 (C) 17 (D) 22 (E) 25

PRACTICE SET-10

Total Ques.- 30
Time - 8 or 10 Min.

निर्देश : (प्रश्न 1-30) विषम संख्याओं का गणना परीक्षण के प्रत्येक प्रश्न में सम और विषम संख्याओं को मिलाकर एक श्रृंखला दिया जाता है। दिए गए संख्याओं में जितने विषम संख्या है उन्हें गणना करना होता है। गणना करने के बाद नीचे दिए गए पाँच विकल्पों (A, B, C, D और E) में एक सही विकल्प को ढूंढना होता है। जिसे उत्तर पत्रक में दिए गए गोले को काला या माउस की सहायता से क्लिक करना होता है।

Directions: (Questions 1–30) : Each question in the Odd Number Counting Test presents a series of even and odd numbers. You need to count the total number of odd numbers in the given series. After counting, select the correct option from the five choices (A, B, C, D & E) provided. Mark your answer by filling the circle on the answer sheet or by clicking on it using the mouse.

1. 1 5 4 2 1 4 5 6 5 3 3 3 2 6 2 1 5 2 4 2 3 5 2 6 1 2 4 1 2 5 2 1
   (A) 14 (B) 11 (C) 16 (D) 20 (E) 22
2. 2 3 2 2 2 1 2 5 3 2 2 5 1 4 2 3 2 4 1 2 3 2 1 5 2 1 4 5 6 4 1 1
   (A) 21 (B) 15 (C) 16 (D) 18 (E) 20
3. 5 2 5 2 6 2 1 5 2 6 3 2 1 5 4 3 4 2 1 5 2 4 2 1 4 2 3 1 2 1 2
   (A) 19 (B) 25 (C) 22 (D) 14 (E) 17
4. 4 3 6 5 4 2 4 1 2 5 3 2 5 2 1 5 2 3 2 1 5 2 1 3 2 5 6 2 1 2 2
   (A) 22 (B) 14 (C) 15 (D) 16 (E) 20
5. 6 2 4 1 2 5 5 1 3 5 2 1 2 2 2 3 2 1 1 1 5 2 3 2 5 6 2 2 3 4 4
   (A) 21 (B) 15 (C) 17 (D) 20 (E) 19
6. 3 2 5 1 2 5 2 1 2 4 5 2 2 1 6 2 3 2 1 4 1 2 5 2 3 2 5 4 1 3
   (A) 13 (B) 14 (C) 15 (D) 20 (E) 18
7. 2 5 4 6 2 3 6 2 2 3 2 5 1 2 4 2 5 4 3 2 1 2 5 2 1 1 3 2 5 6
   (A) 17 (B) 16 (C) 19 (D) 13 (E) 23
8. 1 2 2 2 6 5 4 2 1 2 3 5 1 2 5 4 1 4 1 5 4 2 3 5 2 6 3 2 5 2
   (A) 17 (B) 14 (C) 20 (D) 21 (E) 23
9. 2 3 2 5 2 1 3 2 1 5 2 1 2 5 4 2 5 4 1 2 1 2 3 6 4 4 1 2 5 2 6
   (A) 17 (B) 18 (C) 14 (D) 16 (E) 20
10. 2 2 5 4 5 1 2 3 5 6 4 1 2 1 2 3 1 4 5 2 1 3 2 5 1 4 5 2
    (A) 18 (B) 15 (C) 17 (D) 21 (E) 12
11. 5 2 1 3 2 1 2 1 4 5 4 1 6 2 3 2 5 2 1 4 1 2 5 4 4 1 2 2 3
    (A) 13 (B) 12 (C) 14 (D) 17 (E) 18
12. 5 2 1 2 2 2 3 2 5 6 2 4 5 2 3 5 2 1 2 5 3 2 5 4 1 1 1 2
    (A) 25 (B) 19 (C) 23 (D) 14 (E) 16
13. 3 2 4 1 2 5 1 2 4 1 4 5 2 5 3 2 1 5 2 1 3 2 5 4 1 2 3 2 1
    (A) 14 (B) 16 (C) 18 (D) 20 (E) 19

14. 6 2 3 2 1 2 5 4 5 2 3 5 2 1 4 5 6 5 2 3 1 2 5 6 2 1
(A) 17 (B) 15 (C) 13 (D) 21 (E) 25

15. 6 5 2 3 2 5 4 2 3 1 2 5 1 2 2 2 3 2 5 2 1 2 3 2 1 5 4 1
(A) 23 (B) 21 (C) 15 (D) 14 (E) 16

16. 1 5 3 3 2 1 4 5 2 1 2 6 5 2 1 2 6 5 2 2 3 2 3 5 2 6 1 1 2 2 6 5 3
(A) 19 (B) 16 (C) 17 (D) 23 (E) 25

17. 2 1 2 2 4 1 2 3 2 5 1 4 2 3 5 6 4 3 2 1 6 4 1 2 4 1 2 4 1 2
(A) 16 (B) 12 (C) 19 (D) 21 (E) 18

18. 3 4 2 4 1 2 5 2 6 3 2 1 5 2 1 5 2 6 4 2 3 2 2 1 5 2 1 6 6 5 4 1
(A) 16 (B) 15 (C) 21 (D) 14 (E) 18

19. 4 6 2 1 5 2 4 5 2 1 3 2 5 2 3 2 1 4 1 2 5 3 2 4 5 6 2 1 2 5 4 3
(A) 21 (B) 18 (C) 24 (D) 22 (E) 15

20. 1 2 2 2 1 1 5 2 3 2 5 6 2 6 3 4 4 1 3 5 2 1 2 3 2 2 2 5 2 5 1
(A) 16 (B) 21 (C) 15 (D) 22 (E) 23

21. 5 2 3 2 5 2 3 2 1 2 6 4 1 2 3 2 5 4 1 2 5 2 2 1 6 1 4 5 2 1 3
(A) 14 (B) 25 (C) 15 (D) 21 (E) 11

22. 3 4 5 4 1 2 6 2 1 2 5 4 2 6 2 3 2 2 3 2 1 3 2 5 1 2 4 2 5 5 6
(A) 16 (B) 13 (C) 17 (D) 22 (E) 25

23. 1 2 2 2 3 5 2 5 4 1 5 4 2 2 6 5 4 2 1 4 1 5 6 2 1 3 3 2 5 2
(A) 14 (B) 22 (C) 12 (D) 18 (E) 23

24. 2 5 4 2 4 1 2 1 2 3 3 2 5 6 3 2 1 2 2 5 4 1 2 6 5 2 1 2 5 2 1
(A) 19 (B) 21 (C) 14 (D) 16 (E) 15

25. 2 3 1 2 5 5 2 1 3 2 5 1 4 1 5 6 4 4 1 2 3 4 2 1 5 2 6 5 2
(A) 19 (B) 25 (C) 15 (D) 18 (E) 22

26. 2 1 4 5 4 1 2 3 3 2 2 1 4 1 5 6 2 3 2 5 2 1 4 5 2 1 4 1 2 2
(A) 23 (B) 21 (C) 22 (D) 14 (E) 16

27. 2 1 2 2 2 5 4 1 6 3 5 2 1 2 5 2 1 1 2 2 3 2 5 4 2 3 2 5 5
(A) 16 (B) 14 (C) 20 (D) 19 (E) 23

28. 3 2 4 2 5 1 5 4 1 2 5 2 1 2 6 3 2 5 2 1 1 2 5 3 2 1 3 1 4
(A) 27 (B) 18 (C) 19 (D) 16 (E) 23

29. 6 4 5 4 5 6 1 3 1 4 5 6 2 2 3 5 2 1 2 5 2 3 2 2 2 5 2 1
(A) 18 (B) 12 (C) 15 (D) 13 (E) 20

30. 2 2 5 1 4 2 5 4 1 2 5 2 3 2 2 1 3 4 2 3 1 2 5 1 2 3 6 5 2
(A) 22 (B) 14 (C) 16 (D) 23 (E) 19

PRACTICE SET-11

Total Ques.- 30
Time - 8 or 10 Min.

निर्देश : (प्रश्न 1-30) विषम संख्याओं का गणना परीक्षण के प्रत्येक प्रश्न में सम और विषम संख्याओं को मिलाकर एक श्रृंखला दिया जाता है। दिए गए संख्याओं में जितने विषम संख्या है उन्हें गणना करना होता है। गणना करने के बाद नीचे दिए गए पाँच विकल्पों (A, B, C, D और E) में एक सही विकल्प को ढूंढना होता है। जिसे उत्तर पत्रक में दिए गए गोले को काला या माउस की सहायता से क्लिक करना होता है।

Directions: (Questions 1–30) : Each question in the Odd Number Counting Test presents a series of even and odd numbers. You need to count the total number of odd numbers in the given series. After counting, select the correct option from the five choices (A, B, C, D & E) provided. Mark your answer by filling the circle on the answer sheet or by clicking on it using the mouse.

1. 1 5 4 2 1 4 1 2 6 5 3 3 3 2 4 5 2 1 5 2 4 2 3 5 2 6 1 2 6 5 2 1
(A) 22 (B) 21 (C) 16 (D) 23 (E) 15

2. 2 3 1 2 1 2 5 3 2 2 5 1 4 2 2 2 4 1 2 3 2 1 5 2 1 4 5 6 4 3 2 1
(A) 23 (B) 25 (C) 22 (D) 15 (E) 21

3. 5 2 5 1 5 2 6 3 2 1 5 4 1 2 1 2 2 6 3 4 2 1 5 2 4 2 1 4 2 3 2
(A) 18 (B) 14 (C) 23 (D) 15 (E) 16

4. 4 3 6 5 4 2 4 1 2 5 3 2 2 1 5 2 3 2 1 5 2 1 3 2 5 6 2 1 2 5 2
(A) 17 (B) 13 (C) 21 (D) 22 (E) 15

5. 6 2 4 1 2 5 5 6 2 5 1 3 5 2 1 2 2 3 2 1 1 1 5 2 3 2 2 2 3 4 4
(A) 22 (B) 21 (C) 25 (D) 15 (E) 14

6. 3 2 3 2 5 4 1 2 5 2 1 2 4 5 3 5 2 1 6 2 3 2 1 4 1 2 5 2 2 1 3
(A) 25 (B) 23 (C) 16 (D) 22 (E) 21

7. 2 5 2 1 1 2 3 2 5 1 2 4 6 2 3 6 2 5 4 3 2 1 2 5 4 2 3 2 5 6
(A) 20 (B) 14 (C) 15 (D) 13 (E) 19

8. 1 2 2 3 5 2 6 5 4 2 1 2 3 2 2 1 2 5 4 1 4 1 5 4 5 6 3 2 5 2
(A) 18 (B) 20 (C) 23 (D) 14 (E) 15

9. 2 3 2 2 5 3 2 1 5 2 1 2 5 2 1 2 5 4 1 2 1 2 3 6 4 4 1 5 4 2 6
(A) 21 (B) 25 (C) 27 (D) 16 (E) 14

10. 2 2 5 2 3 5 6 4 1 2 5 1 4 5 1 1 4 1 2 3 1 4 5 2 1 3 2 5 1 2
(A) 20 (B) 17 (C) 25 (D) 18 (E) 14

11. 5 2 1 4 6 3 2 1 2 1 4 5 2 3 4 2 6 5 2 1 4 1 4 2 5 4 4 1 2
(A) 23 (B) 27 (C) 14 (D) 12 (E) 15

12. 5 2 5 3 2 5 4 1 2 3 2 5 1 2 4 2 3 5 2 6 1 2 6 2 5 2 1 1 2
(A) 18 (B) 16 (C) 14 (D) 21 (E) 23

13. 3 2 4 1 2 5 1 2 4 1 4 5 2 2 5 3 2 1 5 2 1 3 2 5 4 1 2 3 1
(A) 14 (B) 16 (C) 15 (D) 22 (E) 19

14. 6 2 3 4 5 2 3 5 2 1 2 5 2 1 4 5 6 5 2 3 1 2 5 6 2 1

(A) 17 (B) 22 (C) 18 (D) 13 (E) 23

15. 6 5 2 3 2 5 4 2 3 1 2 5 2 2 3 2 5 2 1 2 3 2 1 5 4 1 1 2

(A) 18 (B) 14 (C) 22 (D) 21 (E) 19

16. 1 5 3 1 2 3 2 1 4 5 2 1 2 6 5 2 1 2 5 3 2 6 5 2 2 3 2 3 5 2 6 1 6 5 3

(A) 22 (B) 19 (C) 16 (D) 23 (E) 14

17. 2 3 2 4 1 2 3 2 5 1 1 2 1 6 4 1 2 4 1 2 4 2 3 5 6 4 1 2 4 1 2

(A) 18 (B) 13 (C) 21 (D) 25 (E) 19

18. 3 4 5 2 4 1 2 5 2 6 3 2 1 5 3 2 1 5 2 6 4 2 3 2 2 1 2 1 6 6 5 4 1

(A) 14 (B) 21 (C) 15 (D) 22 (E) 16

19. 5 2 3 2 1 4 1 2 5 3 2 3 2 5 6 2 1 4 4 6 2 1 5 2 4 5 2 1 5 1 2 5 4 3

(A) 25 (B) 14 (C) 17 (D) 22 (E) 24

20. 3 1 2 2 3 1 5 2 3 2 5 6 2 6 2 4 4 1 3 5 2 1 2 3 2 2 2 5 2 1 5 1

(A) 15 (B) 16 (C) 22 (D) 17 (E) 21

21. 5 4 1 1 6 2 3 2 5 2 3 2 1 2 6 2 3 2 5 4 1 2 5 2 2 1 4 5 2 1 3

(A) 22 (B) 15 (C) 18 (D) 21 (E) 19

22. 3 1 2 4 2 5 2 1 2 4 5 4 1 2 6 2 3 2 1 3 2 5 5 4 2 6 2 3 2 5 6

(A) 22 (B) 18 (C) 25 (D) 13 (E) 16

23. 1 2 2 2 1 5 6 2 1 2 5 4 1 5 4 3 5 2 6 5 4 2 1 4 2 3 3 2 5 2

(A) 19 (B) 14 (C) 17 (D) 11 (E) 15

24. 2 5 1 2 5 4 1 2 1 2 3 3 2 5 4 2 6 3 2 1 2 2 5 4 1 2 6 5 2 2 1

(A) 17 (B) 18 (C) 14 (D) 22 (E) 21

25. 2 3 5 1 3 2 5 1 4 1 2 6 5 6 4 4 1 2 3 4 2 1 5 1 2 5 5 2 2

(A) 18 (B) 22 (C) 15 (D) 21 (E) 23

26. 2 1 4 1 4 5 4 1 2 3 3 2 2 1 1 5 6 2 3 2 5 2 1 4 5 2 4 1 2 2

(A) 22 (B) 18 (C) 14 (D) 19 (E) 21

27. 2 5 4 1 6 3 5 2 1 2 1 2 2 2 5 2 1 1 2 2 3 2 5 4 2 3 2 5 5

(A) 20 (B) 18 (C) 15 (D) 21 (E) 14

28. 3 2 4 2 2 5 2 1 3 1 5 1 2 6 3 2 5 2 1 1 2 5 3 2 1 5 4 1 4

(A) 18 (B) 16 (C) 22 (D) 26 (E) 19

29. 6 4 2 5 4 5 6 1 3 1 4 5 6 5 2 2 3 5 2 1 2 5 2 3 2 2 2 1

(A) 15 (B) 13 (C) 11 (D) 23 (E) 19

30. 2 1 3 2 5 1 4 2 5 4 1 2 5 2 3 2 2 6 5 2 3 4 2 3 1 2 5 1 2

(A) 22 (B) 12 (C) 20 (D) 14 (E) 17

PRACTICE SET-12

Total Ques.- 30
Time - 8 or 10 Min.

निर्देश : (प्रश्न 1-30) विषम संख्याओं का गणना परीक्षण के प्रत्येक प्रश्न में सम और विषम संख्याओं को मिलाकर एक श्रृंखला दिया जाता है। दिए गए संख्याओं में जितने विषम संख्या है उन्हें गणना करना होता है। गणना करने के बाद नीचे दिए गए पाँच विकल्पों (A, B, C, D और E) में एक सही विकल्प को ढूंढना होता है। जिसे उत्तर पत्रक में दिए गए गोले को काला या माउस की सहायता से क्लिक करना होता है।

Directions: (Questions 1–30) : Each question in the Odd Number Counting Test presents a series of even and odd numbers. You need to count the total number of odd numbers in the given series. After counting, select the correct option from the five choices (A, B, C, D & E) provided. Mark your answer by filling the circle on the answer sheet or by clicking on it using the mouse.

1. 1 3 5 2 6 1 2 4 1 2 6 5 4 2 1 4 5 2 1 5 2 4 2 3 3 3 2 6 5 2 1
(A) 21 (B) 17 (C) 15 (D) 14 (E) 22

2. 2 3 2 2 2 5 3 2 2 5 1 4 2 4 1 2 3 2 1 5 2 1 4 5 6 4 1 2 1 3 2 1
(A) 14 (B) 15 (C) 11 (D) 21 (E) 17

3. 5 2 5 2 5 2 6 3 2 1 5 4 1 2 1 6 3 4 2 1 5 2 4 2 1 4 2 3 2 1 2
(A) 21 (B) 22 (C) 14 (D) 18 (E) 16

4. 4 3 6 2 2 5 4 2 4 1 2 5 3 1 5 2 3 2 1 5 2 1 3 2 5 6 2 1 2 5 2
(A) 18 (B) 22 (C) 21 (D) 15 (E) 23

5. 6 2 4 5 1 3 5 2 1 2 2 2 3 1 2 5 2 3 2 1 1 1 5 2 3 2 5 6 2 4 4
(A) 17 (B) 15 (C) 22 (D) 25 (E) 28

6. 3 3 2 5 4 1 2 5 2 1 2 2 5 2 1 6 2 3 2 1 4 1 2 5 2 4 5 2 1 3
(A) 22 (B) 19 (C) 15 (D) 17 (E) 18

7. 2 3 2 1 2 5 2 1 1 2 3 2 5 1 2 4 2 3 5 4 6 2 3 6 2 5 4 2 5 6
(A) 14 (B) 15 (C) 13 (D) 21 (E) 22

8. 1 2 2 5 4 2 1 2 3 5 6 3 2 2 1 2 5 4 1 4 1 5 4 2 3 5 2 6 5 2
(A) 18 (B) 14 (C) 22 (D) 16 (E) 23

9. 2 3 2 2 1 5 2 1 2 5 4 5 2 1 2 5 4 1 2 1 2 3 6 4 4 1 2 5 3 2 6
(A) 12 (B) 14 (C) 13 (D) 18 (E) 19

10. 2 2 2 3 5 6 4 1 2 5 1 4 5 5 4 1 2 3 1 4 5 2 1 3 2 5 1 2
(A) 23 (B) 15 (C) 22 (D) 25 (E) 28

11. 5 3 2 1 2 1 4 5 4 2 1 6 2 3 2 5 2 1 4 1 2 5 4 4 1 2 1 2 3
(A) 17 (B) 16 (C) 14 (D) 23 (E) 22

12. 5 2 1 2 3 2 5 6 2 5 2 1 6 4 1 2 2 3 5 2 1 2 5 3 2 5 4 1 2
(A) 29 (B) 23 (C) 18 (D) 14 (E) 20

13. 4 1 2 3 2 5 1 2 4 1 3 2 4 1 2 5 3 2 1 5 2 1 3 2 5 4 5 2 1
(A) 18 (B) 21 (C) 22 (D) 17 (E) 16

14. 6 5 2 3 1 2 5 4 5 2 3 6 5 2 1 4 2 3 2 1 4 5 6 2 5 6 2 1
(A) 16 (B) 19 (C) 22 (D) 11 (E) 13

15. 6 5 2 1 5 4 1 2 5 4 2 3 1 2 2 3 2 2 3 2 5 2 1 2 3 5 1 2
(A) 19 (B) 18 (C) 14 (D) 21 (E) 25

16. 1 5 3 2 6 2 1 4 5 2 1 2 6 5 2 1 2 6 5 2 2 3 2 3 5 2 6 1 1 2 3 5 3
(A) 22 (B) 14 (C) 19 (D) 15 (E) 17

17. 2 1 2 2 4 1 2 3 2 5 1 4 2 3 5 6 3 2 1 6 4 1 2 4 4 1 2 4 1 2
(A) 14 (B) 20 (C) 12 (D) 18 (E) 16

18. 1 5 2 6 4 2 3 2 2 1 5 2 4 1 2 5 2 6 3 2 1 5 2 1 6 3 4 2 6 5 4 1
(A) 18 (B) 14 (C) 17 (D) 23 (E) 19

19. 5 3 2 4 4 6 2 1 5 2 4 5 2 1 3 2 5 6 2 2 3 2 1 4 1 2 5 1 2 5 4 3
(A) 19 (B) 20 (C) 15 (D) 18 (E) 22

20. 2 1 1 5 2 3 2 5 6 2 6 1 2 2 3 4 4 1 3 5 2 1 2 3 2 2 2 5 2 5 1
(A) 20 (B) 14 (C) 13 (D) 15 (E) 21

21. 5 5 2 2 1 6 2 3 2 5 2 3 2 1 2 6 1 4 5 2 1 3 4 1 2 3 2 5 4 1 2
(A) 23 (B) 21 (C) 15 (D) 11 (E) 22

22. 2 4 2 5 2 1 2 5 4 2 6 2 3 4 5 4 1 2 6 2 3 2 1 3 2 5 1 3 2 5 6
(A) 20 (B) 13 (C) 16 (D) 11 (E) 15

23. 1 2 6 2 1 2 5 4 1 5 4 2 3 3 2 2 2 3 5 2 6 5 4 2 1 4 1 5 5 2
(A) 20 (B) 18 (C) 14 (D) 13 (E) 17

24. 2 2 1 2 2 5 4 1 2 6 5 2 1 2 5 4 1 2 1 2 5 4 2 6 3 3 3 2 5 2 1
(A) 21 (B) 14 (C) 23 (D) 18 (E) 15

25. 2 3 5 2 1 3 2 5 1 4 1 2 6 5 6 4 4 1 2 3 4 2 1 5 1 2 5 5 2
(A) 14 (B) 18 (C) 16 (D) 15 (E) 19

26. 2 1 4 3 2 2 1 4 1 1 4 1 5 6 2 3 2 5 2 1 4 5 2 5 4 1 2 3 2 2
(A) 13 (B) 14 (C) 23 (D) 18 (E) 12

27. 2 5 4 1 6 3 5 2 1 2 1 2 2 2 5 2 1 1 2 2 3 2 5 4 2 3 2 5 5
(A) 20 (B) 18 (C) 14 (D) 15 (E) 19

28. 3 2 2 1 5 4 1 2 5 2 1 3 1 4 4 2 5 1 2 6 3 2 5 2 1 1 2 5 3
(A) 14 (B) 13 (C) 11 (D) 16 (E) 15

29. 6 4 5 2 2 5 6 1 3 1 4 5 6 3 5 2 1 2 5 2 3 2 2 2 5 4 2 1
(A) 22 (B) 18 (C) 13 (D) 17 (E) 15

30. 2 1 5 4 1 2 5 2 3 2 2 6 5 2 3 4 2 3 1 2 5 1 2 3 2 5 1 4 2
(A) 17 (B) 14 (C) 15 (D) 18 (E) 22

PRACTICE SET-13

Total Ques.- 30
Time - 8 or 10 Min.

निर्देश : (प्रश्न 1-30) विषम संख्याओं का गणना परीक्षण के प्रत्येक प्रश्न में सम और विषम संख्याओं को मिलाकर एक श्रृंखला दिया जाता है। दिए गए संख्याओं में जितने विषम संख्या है उन्हें गणना करना होता है। गणना करने के बाद नीचे दिए गए पाँच विकल्पों (A, B, C, D और E) में एक सही विकल्प को ढूंढना होता है। जिसे उत्तर पत्रक में दिए गए गोले को काला या माउस की सहायता से क्लिक करना होता है।

Directions: (Questions 1–30) : Each question in the Odd Number Counting Test presents a series of even and odd numbers. You need to count the total number of odd numbers in the given series. After counting, select the correct option from the five choices (A, B, C, D & E) provided. Mark your answer by filling the circle on the answer sheet or by clicking on it using the mouse.

1. 1 5 4 1 2 6 5 3 3 3 2 6 2 1 4 5 2 1 5 2 4 2 3 5 2 6 1 2 4 5 2 1
   (A) 18 (B) 17 (C) 16 (D) 22 (E) 23
2. 2 3 6 4 1 2 1 2 5 3 2 2 5 1 4 2 3 2 2 4 1 2 3 2 1 5 2 1 4 5 2 1
   (A) 18 (B) 14 (C) 23 (D) 15 (E) 21
3. 5 2 5 5 2 6 3 2 1 5 4 1 2 1 2 6 3 4 2 1 5 2 4 2 1 4 2 3 2 1 2
   (A) 11 (B) 14 (C) 17 (D) 21 (E) 19
4. 4 3 6 2 2 1 2 5 4 2 4 1 2 5 1 5 2 3 2 1 5 2 1 3 2 5 6 3 2 5 2
   (A) 16 (B) 19 (C) 15 (D) 23 (E) 25
5. 6 2 2 5 1 3 5 2 1 2 2 2 3 4 4 1 2 5 2 3 2 1 1 1 5 2 3 2 5 6 4
   (A) 22 (B) 23 (C) 19 (D) 15 (E) 20
6. 3 2 5 4 1 2 5 2 1 2 4 2 1 6 2 3 2 1 4 1 2 5 2 3 2 5 5 2 1 3
   (A) 21 (B) 19 (C) 15 (D) 17 (E) 22
7. 2 5 1 1 2 3 2 5 1 2 4 2 3 2 5 4 6 2 3 6 2 5 4 3 2 1 2 5 2 6
   (A) 21 (B) 18 (C) 22 (D) 14 (E) 13
8. 1 2 2 4 2 1 2 3 5 6 3 2 1 2 5 4 1 4 1 5 4 2 3 5 2 6 5 2 5 2
   (A) 11 (B) 14 (C) 16 (D) 20 (E) 22
9. 2 3 1 2 5 3 2 1 5 2 1 2 5 4 6 2 5 2 1 2 5 4 1 2 1 2 3 6 4 4 2 6
   (A) 16 (B) 14 (C) 18 (D) 21 (E) 19
10. 2 2 1 2 3 5 6 4 1 2 5 5 4 1 2 6 3 1 4 5 2 1 3 2 5 4 1 4 5 2
    (A) 22 (B) 17 (C) 15 (D) 21 (E) 14
11. 5 3 2 1 2 1 4 5 4 6 1 2 2 1 6 2 3 2 5 2 1 4 1 2 5 4 4 1 2 3
    (A) 11 (B) 16 (C) 18 (D) 14 (E) 23
12. 5 2 1 2 2 3 2 5 6 2 5 2 2 3 5 2 1 2 5 3 2 5 4 1 1 1 2
    (A) 13 (B) 14 (C) 22 (D) 25 (E) 16
13. 3 2 4 3 2 5 1 2 4 1 4 5 2 1 2 5 3 6 2 1 5 2 1 3 2 5 4 1 2 1
    (A) 25 (B) 24 (C) 16 (D) 17 (E) 22

14. 6 2 3 5 2 3 5 2 1 2 2 1 4 5 6 5 4 2 3 1 2 5 4 5 6 2 1
(A) 18 (B) 17 (C) 13 (D) 16 (E) 20

15. 6 5 3 2 1 5 4 1 2 5 4 2 3 1 2 3 2 2 3 2 5 2 1 2 2 5 1 2
(A) 17 (B) 14 (C) 16 (D) 15 (E) 22

16. 1 5 3 2 2 1 4 5 2 1 2 6 5 2 1 2 6 5 2 2 3 2 3 5 2 6 1 1 2 3 6 5 3
(A) 18 (B) 16 (C) 21 (D) 17 (E) 20

17. 2 3 2 4 1 6 4 1 2 2 4 1 5 6 4 1 2 6 2 2 4 1 2 3 2 5 1 4 2 34 1 2
(A) 14 (B) 16 (C) 12 (D) 22 (E) 15

18. 3 4 2 1 5 2 6 4 2 2 1 4 2 3 2 5 6 2 1 2 5 4 1 6 5 2 1 6 6 5 4 1
(A) 20 (B) 22 (C) 18 (D) 13 (E) 15

19. 5 2 3 2 4 2 3 2 2 1 5 2 4 1 2 5 2 6 3 2 1 4 1 2 5 3 2 4 4 6 2 1 5 2 4 5 3
(A) 18 (B) 14 (C) 15 (D) 16 (E) 22

20. 1 2 2 3 4 4 1 2 1 1 5 2 3 2 5 6 3 5 2 1 2 3 2 2 2 5 2 6 2 5 1
(A) 16 (B) 14 (C) 15 (D) 18 (E) 20

21. 5 4 2 3 2 1 2 6 1 4 5 2 1 1 2 3 2 5 4 1 2 5 2 2 1 6 2 3 2 5 3
(A) 20 (B) 18 (C) 15 (D) 23 (E) 21

22. 3 4 5 2 5 2 1 2 5 4 2 6 2 3 4 1 2 6 2 3 2 1 3 2 5 1 2 4 2 5 6
(A) 16 (B) 18 (C) 20 (D) 13 (E) 19

23. 1 2 2 5 4 1 5 4 2 3 3 2 5 2 2 3 5 2 6 5 4 2 1 4 1 5 6 2 1 2
(A) 16 (B) 21 (C) 14 (D) 15 (E) 19

24. 6 5 2 1 2 5 4 1 2 1 2 2 5 4 2 6 3 2 1 2 2 5 4 1 2 3 3 2 5 2 1
(A) 21 (B) 22 (C) 14 (D) 15 (E) 19

25. 2 3 2 5 1 4 1 2 6 5 5 6 4 4 1 2 3 4 2 1 5 1 2 5 5 2 1 3 2
(A) 19 (B) 22 (C) 23 (D) 14 (E) 15

26. 2 1 4 1 5 2 5 4 1 2 3 3 2 2 4 1 5 6 2 3 2 5 2 1 4 1 4 1 2 2
(A) 18 (B) 17 (C) 21 (D) 14 (E) 23

27. 2 1 5 4 1 6 3 5 2 1 2 5 6 2 2 2 5 2 1 1 2 2 3 2 5 4 2 3 2 5
(A) 21 (B) 20 (C) 16 (D) 14 (E) 15

28. 3 3 2 1 5 4 1 2 5 2 1 2 4 2 5 1 2 6 3 2 5 2 1 1 2 5 3 1 4
(A) 22 (B) 16 (C) 18 (D) 21 (E) 19

29. 6 4 5 4 5 6 1 3 1 4 5 6 5 2 2 3 5 2 1 2 5 2 3 2 2 2 2 1
(A) 18 (B) 14 (C) 15 (D) 13 (E) 21

30. 2 1 4 2 5 4 1 2 5 2 3 2 3 4 2 3 1 2 5 1 2 3 2 5 1 2 6 5 2
(A) 17 (B) 16 (C) 14 (D) 19 (E) 20

PRACTICE SET-14

Total Ques.- 30
Time - 8 or 10 Min.

निर्देश : (प्रश्न 1-30) विषम संख्याओं का गणना परीक्षण के प्रत्येक प्रश्न में सम और विषम संख्याओं को मिलाकर एक श्रृंखला दिया जाता है। दिए गए संख्याओं में जितने विषम संख्या है उन्हें गणना करना होता है। गणना करने के बाद नीचे दिए गए पाँच विकल्पों (A, B, C, D और E) में एक सही विकल्प को ढूंढना होता है। जिसे उत्तर पत्रक में दिए गए गोले को काला या माउस की सहायता से क्लिक करना होता है।

Directions: (Questions 1–30) : Each question in the Odd Number Counting Test presents a series of even and odd numbers. You need to count the total number of odd numbers in the given series. After counting, select the correct option from the five choices (A, B, C, D & E) provided. Mark your answer by filling the circle on the answer sheet or by clicking on it using the mouse.

1. 1 5 4 6 1 2 4 1 2 6 5 3 3 3 2 2 1 4 5 2 1 5 2 4 2 3 5 2 6 5 2 1
   (A) 18 (B) 17 (C) 16 (D) 14 (E) 15
2. 2 3 2 2 1 2 5 3 2 2 5 1 4 1 2 3 2 1 5 2 1 4 5 6 4 1 2 4 2 3 2 1
   (A) 19 (B) 20 (C) 22 (D) 15 (E) 17
3. 5 2 5 2 1 5 2 6 3 2 1 5 4 1 2 2 6 3 4 2 1 5 2 4 2 1 4 2 3 1 2
   (A) 25 (B) 22 (C) 17 (D) 14 (E) 19
4. 4 3 6 2 5 4 2 4 1 2 5 3 2 1 5 2 3 2 1 5 2 1 3 2 5 6 2 1 2 5 2
   (A) 21 (B) 20 (C) 15 (D) 18 (E) 16
5. 6 2 2 5 6 2 5 1 3 5 2 1 2 2 2 3 4 1 2 5 2 3 2 1 1 1 5 2 3 4 4
   (A) 19 (B) 17 (C) 15 (D) 11 (E) 13
6. 3 2 5 4 1 2 5 2 1 2 4 2 1 6 2 3 2 1 4 1 2 5 2 3 2 5 5 2 1 3
   (A) 18 (B) 15 (C) 16 (D) 22 (E) 21
7. 2 2 1 1 2 3 2 5 1 2 4 2 3 2 5 4 6 2 3 6 2 5 4 3 2 1 2 5 5 6
   (A) 22 (B) 25 (C) 13 (D) 14 (E) 17
8. 1 2 2 5 4 2 1 2 3 5 6 3 2 2 1 2 5 4 1 4 1 5 4 2 3 5 2 6 5 2
   (A) 17 (B) 14 (C) 15 (D) 23 (E) 19
9. 2 3 2 1 2 5 3 2 1 5 2 1 2 5 2 1 2 5 4 1 2 1 2 3 6 4 4 5 4 2 6
   (A) 27 (B) 14 (C) 15 (D) 22 (E) 25
10. 2 2 3 5 6 4 1 2 5 1 4 5 2 5 4 1 2 3 1 4 5 2 1 3 2 5 1 2
    (A) 23 (B) 22 (C) 15 (D) 17 (E) 20
11. 2 5 4 4 1 2 3 2 1 5 2 1 6 2 3 2 5 2 1 4 1 2 1 4 5 4 1 2 3
    (A) 16 (B) 18 (C) 15 (D) 14 (E) 21
12. 3 2 5 4 1 2 3 2 4 5 6 5 2 2 1 2 2 4 3 5 2 1 2 5 2 5 2 1 1 2
    (A) 17 (B) 14 (C) 18 (D) 22 (E) 19
13. 3 2 4 2 5 1 2 4 1 4 5 21 2 5 3 2 1 5 2 1 3 2 5 4 1 2 3 1
    (A) 18 (B) 17 (C) 16 (D) 21 (E) 22

14. 2 3 1 2 5 4 5 2 3 5 2 6 2 3 2 1 4 5 6 5 6 1 2 5 6 2 1
(A) 19 (B) 20 (C) 14 (D) 13 (E) 15

15. 6 5 2 3 5 4 2 3 1 2 5 6 2 2 3 2 5 2 1 2 3 2 1 5 4 1 2 1 2
(A) 19 (B) 14 (C) 15 (D) 20 (E) 22

16. 2 4 1 2 5 2 6 3 2 1 5 2 1 1 1 2 3 2 1 4 5 2 1 2 6 5 2 1 2 6 5 3
(A) 19 (B) 16 (C) 15 (D) 14 (E) 21

17. 2 3 2 3 2 5 1 4 2 3 5 1 6 4 1 2 4 1 2 2 4 1 2 6 4 1 2 4 1 2
(A) 14 (B) 18 (C) 12 (D) 22 (E) 23

18. 3 4 2 1 5 2 6 4 5 2 1 2 6 3 1 5 5 2 1 2 3 2 2 1 5 6 6 5 4 1
(A) 25 (B) 21 (C) 22 (D) 15 (E) 17

19. 5 2 3 2 1 4 5 2 1 3 2 5 6 2 1 4 1 2 5 3 2 4 4 6 2 1 5 2 2 5 4 3
(A) 20 (B) 18 (C) 15 (D) 16 (E) 14

20. 1 2 2 2 1 1 5 2 3 2 5 6 2 3 4 4 1 3 5 2 1 2 3 2 2 2 5 6 2 5 1
(A) 18 (B) 14 (C) 13 (D) 15 (E) 19

21. 5 4 1 2 3 2 5 2 3 2 1 1 5 3 2 6 2 3 2 5 4 1 2 5 1 2 2 1 6 3
(A) 22 (B) 17 (C) 16 (D) 14 (E) 21

22. 3 4 5 5 1 2 4 2 5 2 2 5 6 4 1 2 1 2 5 4 2 6 2 3 6 2 3 2 1 3 2
(A) 17 (B) 16 (C) 14 (D) 13 (E) 19

23. 1 2 2 2 3 5 2 6 5 4 1 5 4 2 3 3 2 2 1 4 1 5 6 2 1 2 5 4 5 2
(A) 21 (B) 22 (C) 13 (D) 14 (E) 19

24. 2 5 4 1 2 1 2 3 3 2 5 2 1 4 2 6 3 2 1 2 2 5 4 1 2 6 5 2 1 2 5
(A) 19 (B) 12 (C) 14 (D) 17 (E) 20

25. 5 1 2 5 5 2 1 3 2 5 1 2 3 5 6 4 4 1 2 3 4 2 1 4 1 2 6 5 2
(A) 12 (B) 15 (C) 14 (D) 20 (E) 18

26. 2 5 4 1 2 3 3 2 2 1 4 1 2 2 1 4 1 4 1 5 6 2 3 2 5 2 1 4 5 2
(A) 15 (B) 19 (C) 14 (D) 16 (E) 22

27. 4 2 3 2 5 4 1 6 3 5 2 2 1 2 2 2 5 2 1 1 2 2 3 2 5 1 2 5 5
(A) 13 (B) 14 (C) 18 (D) 22 (E) 17

28. 3 2 3 2 1 5 4 1 2 5 2 1 3 1 4 2 5 1 2 6 3 2 5 2 1 1 2 5 4
(A) 23 (B) 18 (C) 16 (D) 14 (E) 19

29. 6 4 5 6 1 3 1 4 5 6 4 5 2 2 3 5 2 1 2 5 2 3 2 2 2 5 2 1
(A) 16 (B) 13 (C) 19 (D) 22 (E) 21

30. 2 1 3 2 5 4 1 2 5 2 3 2 2 6 5 4 2 3 1 2 5 1 2 3 2 5 1 4 2
(A) 11 (B) 14 (C) 17 (D) 22 (E) 25

PRACTICE SET-15

Total Ques.- 30
Time - 8 or 10 Min.

निर्देश : (प्रश्न 1-30) विषम संख्याओं का गणना परीक्षण के प्रत्येक प्रश्न में सम और विषम संख्याओं को मिलाकर एक श्रृंखला दिया जाता है। दिए गए संख्याओं में जितने विषम संख्या है उन्हें गणना करना होता है। गणना करने के बाद नीचे दिए गए पाँच विकल्पों (A, B, C, D और E) में एक सही विकल्प को ढूंढना होता है। जिसे उत्तर पत्रक में दिए गए गोले को काला या माउस की सहायता से क्लिक करना होता है।

Directions: (Questions 1–30) : Each question in the Odd Number Counting Test presents a series of even and odd numbers. You need to count the total number of odd numbers in the given series. After counting, select the correct option from the five choices (A, B, C, D & E) provided. Mark your answer by filling the circle on the answer sheet or by clicking on it using the mouse.

1. 1 5 4 4 1 2 6 5 3 3 3 2 6 5 2 2 1 4 5 2 1 5 2 4 2 3 5 2 6 1 2 1
   (A) 14 (B) 11 (C) 16 (D) 19 (E) 23
2. 2 3 2 2 5 3 2 2 5 1 4 2 4 1 2 3 2 1 5 2 1 4 5 6 4 1 2 1 2 3 2 1
   (A) 16 (B) 15 (C) 19 (D) 23 (E) 18
3. 5 2 5 2 6 3 2 1 5 4 1 2 1 2 5 2 6 3 4 2 1 5 2 4 2 1 4 2 3 2 1
   (A) 13 (B) 12 (C) 14 (D) 17 (E) 20
4. 2 1 2 5 4 2 4 1 2 5 4 3 6 2 1 5 2 3 2 1 5 2 1 3 2 5 6 3 2 5 2
   (A) 19 (B) 15 (C) 18 (D) 20 (E) 22
5. 6 2 4 5 1 3 5 2 1 2 2 2 3 4 1 2 5 2 3 2 1 1 1 5 2 3 2 5 6 2 4
   (A) 21 (B) 17 (C) 15 (D) 22 (E) 23
6. 3 2 5 2 5 4 1 2 5 2 1 2 4 1 6 2 3 2 1 4 1 2 5 2 3 2 5 2 1 3
   (A) 19 (B) 21 (C) 11 (D) 15 (E) 16
7. 2 5 4 6 2 3 2 5 1 2 4 2 3 2 2 3 6 2 5 4 3 2 1 2 5 2 1 1 5 6
   (A) 18 (B) 19 (C) 13 (D) 15 (E) 16
8. 1 2 2 6 5 4 2 1 2 3 5 6 2 1 2 5 4 1 4 1 5 4 2 3 5 2 3 2 5 2
   (A) 10 (B) 12 (C) 13 (D) 16 (E) 14
9. 2 3 2 4 4 1 2 5 3 2 1 5 2 1 2 5 2 1 2 5 4 1 2 1 2 3 6 5 4 2 6
   (A) 19 (B) 21 (C) 13 (D) 14 (E) 15
10. 5 1 2 3 5 6 4 1 2 2 2 5 4 1 2 3 1 4 5 2 1 3 2 5 1 4 5 2
    (A) 13 (B) 18 (C) 15 (D) 17 (E) 19
11. 5 2 1 2 3 2 1 2 1 4 5 4 1 2 3 6 2 3 2 5 2 1 4 1 2 5 4 4 1
    (A) 21 (B) 17 (C) 15 (D) 14 (E) 18
12. 1 2 3 2 5 6 2 5 2 5 2 1 2 2 3 5 2 1 2 5 3 2 5 4 1 1 2
    (A) 15 (B) 14 (C) 17 (D) 21 (E) 22
13. 3 2 3 2 5 1 2 4 1 4 5 2 4 1 2 5 3 2 1 5 2 1 3 2 5 4 1 2 1
    (A) 17 (B) 13 (C) 15 (D) 16 (E) 21

14. 6 2 3 3 5 2 1 2 5 6 2 1 4 5 6 5 2 3 1 2 5 4 5 2 2 1
(A) 16 (B) 13 (C) 15 (D) 21 (E) 18

15. 6 5 5 4 1 2 5 4 2 3 1 2 5 2 3 2 2 3 2 5 2 1 2 3 2 1 1 2
(A) 17 (B) 14 (C) 16 (D) 18 (E) 19

16. 1 5 5 2 3 2 5 6 2 6 2 5 1 6 1 1 2 3 2 1 4 5 2 1 2 6 5 2 1 2 6 5 3
(A) 20 (B) 18 (C) 19 (D) 17 (E) 21

17. 2 3 2 5 1 4 2 3 5 6 4 2 3 2 1 6 4 1 2 4 1 2 2 4 1 1 2 4 1 2
(A) 15 (B) 20 (C) 12 (D) 14 (E) 16

18. 3 5 2 4 1 2 5 2 6 3 4 2 1 5 2 6 4 2 3 2 2 1 2 1 5 2 1 6 6 5 4 1
(A) 17 (B) 13 (C) 20 (D) 14 (E) 15

19. 5 2 3 2 2 4 5 2 1 3 2 5 6 2 1 4 1 2 5 3 2 4 4 6 2 1 5 1 2 5 4 3
(A) 14 (B) 13 (C) 15 (D) 17 (E) 18

20. 1 2 2 3 4 4 1 3 5 2 1 3 2 6 5 2 2 3 2 3 5 2 2 3 2 2 2 5 2 1 1
(A) 19 (B) 16 (C) 15 (D) 14 (E) 20

21. 5 2 3 2 1 2 6 1 4 5 2 1 3 4 1 2 3 2 5 4 1 2 5 2 2 1 6 2 3 2 5
(A) 16 (B) 17 (C) 21 (D) 15 (E) 14

22. 5 1 2 4 2 5 2 1 2 5 4 3 4 5 4 1 2 6 2 3 2 1 3 2 2 6 2 3 2 5 6
(A) 19 (B) 14 (C) 13 (D) 21 (E) 23

23. 2 1 4 1 5 6 2 1 2 5 4 1 1 2 2 2 3 5 2 6 5 4 5 4 2 3 3 2 5 2
(A) 11 (B) 22 (C) 14 (D) 17 (E) 20

24. 2 5 1 2 5 4 1 2 1 2 3 3 2 5 2 4 2 6 3 2 1 2 2 5 4 1 2 6 5 2 1
(A) 16 (B) 14 (C) 18 (D) 19 (E) 11

25. 2 3 5 6 4 4 1 1 4 1 2 6 2 3 4 2 1 5 1 2 5 5 2 1 3 2 5 5 2
(A) 17 (B) 22 (C) 19 (D) 15 (E) 13

26. 2 1 4 1 2 3 3 2 2 1 4 1 2 4 1 5 6 2 3 2 5 2 1 4 5 2 5 4 1 2
(A) 12 (B) 14 (C) 18 (D) 19 (E) 15

27. 2 1 2 5 4 1 6 3 5 2 1 2 5 2 2 2 5 2 1 1 2 2 3 2 5 4 2 3 5
(A) 16 (B) 14 (C) 15 (D) 17 (E) 18

28. 3 2 4 2 5 1 2 1 5 4 1 2 5 2 2 6 3 2 5 2 1 1 2 5 3 1 3 1 4
(A) 14 (B) 22 (C) 16 (D) 18 (E) 20

29. 6 4 5 6 1 3 1 4 5 6 2 5 2 2 3 5 2 1 2 5 2 3 2 2 2 5 4 1
(A) 18 (B) 16 (C) 15 (D) 13 (E) 11

30. 2 1 3 4 2 2 5 2 3 2 2 3 1 2 5 1 2 3 2 5 1 4 2 5 4 1 6 5 2
(A) 22 (B) 15 (C) 14 (D) 17 (E) 20

PRACTICE SET-16

Total Ques.- 30
Time - 8 or 10 Min.

निर्देश : (प्रश्न 1-30) विषम संख्याओं का गणना परीक्षण के प्रत्येक प्रश्न में सम और विषम संख्याओं को मिलाकर एक श्रृंखला दिया जाता है। दिए गए संख्याओं में जितने विषम संख्या है उन्हें गणना करना होता है। गणना करने के बाद नीचे दिए गए पाँच विकल्पों (A, B, C, D और E) में एक सही विकल्प को ढूंढना होता है। जिसे उत्तर पत्रक में दिए गए गोले को काला या माउस की सहायता से क्लिक करना होता है।

Directions: (Questions 1–30) : Each question in the Odd Number Counting Test presents a series of even and odd numbers. You need to count the total number of odd numbers in the given series. After counting, select the correct option from the five choices (A, B, C, D & E) provided. Mark your answer by filling the circle on the answer sheet or by clicking on it using the mouse.

1. 2 3 5 2 6 1 2 4 1 2 6 1 5 4 2 1 4 5 2 1 5 2 4 5 3 3 3 2 6 5 2 1
   (A) 21 (B) 22 (C) 16 (D) 15 (E) 13
2. 2 3 2 2 4 1 2 1 2 5 3 2 2 5 1 4 2 3 4 1 2 3 2 1 5 2 1 4 5 6 2 1
   (A) 23 (B) 21 (C) 22 (D) 15 (E) 17
3. 5 2 5 2 1 5 2 6 3 2 1 5 4 1 2 1 6 3 4 2 1 5 2 4 2 1 4 2 3 2 2
   (A) 19 (B) 21 (C) 17 (D) 14 (E) 20
4. 4 3 6 6 2 1 2 5 4 2 4 1 2 2 1 5 2 3 2 1 5 2 1 3 2 5 5 3 2 5 2
   (A) 13 (B) 19 (C) 15 (D) 17 (E) 22
5. 6 2 6 2 5 1 3 5 2 1 2 2 2 3 4 4 1 2 5 2 3 2 1 1 1 5 2 3 2 5 4
   (A) 11 (B) 23 (C) 20 (D) 15 (E) 19
6. 3 2 5 5 4 1 2 5 2 1 2 4 2 1 6 2 3 2 1 4 1 2 5 2 3 2 5 2 1 3
   (A) 17 (B) 15 (C) 22 (D) 12 (E) 18
7. 2 5 5 2 1 1 2 3 2 5 1 2 4 2 3 2 5 4 6 2 3 6 2 5 4 3 2 1 2 6
   (A) 14 (B) 17 (C) 13 (D) 22 (E) 25
8. 1 2 2 5 4 2 1 2 3 5 6 2 1 2 5 4 1 4 1 5 4 2 3 5 2 6 3 2 5 2
   (A) 17 (B) 14 (C) 22 (D) 20 (E) 16
9. 2 3 1 2 5 3 2 1 5 2 1 2 5 4 2 6 2 5 2 1 2 5 4 1 2 1 2 3 6 4 4
   (A) 13 (B) 14 (C) 18 (D) 19 (E) 21
10. 2 2 2 3 5 6 4 1 2 5 1 5 4 1 2 3 1 4 5 2 1 3 2 5 1 4 5 2
    (A) 21 (B) 15 (C) 17 (D) 22 (E) 23
11. 5 2 2 3 2 1 2 1 4 5 4 1 2 1 6 2 3 2 5 2 1 4 1 2 5 4 4 1 3
    (A) 19 (B) 15 (C) 17 (D) 14 (E) 16
12. 5 2 1 3 2 5 6 2 5 2 1 2 2 3 5 2 1 2 5 3 2 5 4 1 2 1 2
    (A) 19 (B) 22 (C) 14 (D) 16 (E) 20
13. 3 1 2 3 2 5 1 2 4 1 4 5 2 2 4 1 2 5 3 2 1 5 2 1 3 2 5 4 1
    (A) 18 (B) 14 (C) 16 (D) 18 (E) 20

14. 5 4 5 2 3 5 2 1 2 6 2 3 2 1 4 5 4 6 5 2 3 1 2 6 2 5 6 2 1
(A) 15 (B) 13 (C) 19 (D) 22 (E) 21

15. 6 5 4 1 2 5 4 2 3 1 2 5 5 2 3 2 2 3 2 5 2 1 2 3 2 1 1 2
(A) 21 (B) 22 (C) 14 (D) 16 (E) 17

16. 1 5 3 2 6 1 2 3 2 1 4 5 2 2 6 5 3 1 5 2 2 3 2 3 5 2 6 1 2 6 5 2 1
(A) 25 (B) 24 (C) 17 (D) 22 (E) 21

17. 2 3 2 1 6 5 1 4 2 3 5 6 4 4 1 2 4 1 2 2 4 1 2 3 2 1 2 4 1 2
(A) 22 (B) 15 (C) 14 (D) 12 (E) 21

18. 3 5 2 4 1 2 5 2 4 2 1 5 2 6 4 2 3 2 2 1 6 3 2 1 5 2 1 6 6 5 4 1
(A) 19 (B) 15 (C) 14 (D) 17 (E) 16

19. 5 2 4 4 6 2 1 5 2 4 5 2 1 3 2 5 6 2 1 3 2 1 4 1 2 5 3 2 2 5 4 3
(A) 16 (B) 18 (C) 20 (D) 15 (E) 22

20. 1 2 3 2 2 2 5 2 1 1 5 2 3 1 2 2 3 4 4 1 3 5 2 2 5 6 2 6 2 5 1
(A) 17 (B) 20 (C) 15 (D) 22 (E) 23

21. 5 4 1 2 3 2 3 2 1 2 6 1 4 5 2 2 5 4 1 2 5 2 2 1 6 2 3 2 5 1 3
(A) 19 (B) 21 (C) 22 (D) 15 (E) 17

22. 3 4 5 4 1 2 6 2 1 2 5 4 2 6 2 3 3 2 1 3 2 5 1 2 4 2 5 2 2 5 6
(A) 14 (B) 13 (C) 17 (D) 22 (E) 19

23. 1 2 1 5 4 2 3 3 2 5 2 2 2 3 5 2 6 5 4 2 1 4 1 5 6 2 1 2 5 4
(A) 14 (B) 17 (C) 21 (D) 22 (E) 19

24. 2 5 4 2 1 2 5 4 1 2 1 2 3 2 6 3 2 1 2 2 5 4 1 2 6 5 3 2 5 2 1
(A) 18 (B) 16 (C) 14 (D) 22 (E) 15

25. 2 3 5 1 3 2 5 1 4 1 2 6 5 6 4 4 1 2 3 4 2 1 5 1 2 5 5 2 2
(A) 13 (B) 16 (C) 18 (D) 15 (E) 20

26. 1 4 5 2 5 4 1 2 3 3 2 2 1 4 1 4 1 5 6 2 3 2 5 2 2 1 4 1 2 2
(A) 14 (B) 16 (C) 17 (D) 22 (E) 19

27. 2 1 2 2 3 2 5 4 1 6 3 5 2 1 2 5 2 5 2 1 1 2 2 3 2 5 4 2 5
(A) 21 (B) 22 (C) 14 (D) 23 (E) 19

28. 3 2 5 2 1 2 2 1 2 5 3 4 3 2 6 4 2 4 5 2 1 4 2 6 2 1 3 2 1 4
(A) 14 (B) 12 (C) 16 (D) 18 (E) 19

29. 6 4 5 4 5 6 1 3 1 4 5 6 5 2 2 3 5 2 1 2 5 2 3 2 2 2 1
(A) 13 (B) 23 (C) 19 (D) 20 (E) 18

30. 2 2 5 4 1 2 5 2 3 2 2 1 3 4 2 3 1 2 5 1 2 3 2 5 1 4 6 5 2
(A) 11 (B) 12 (C) 14 (D) 16 (E) 15

PRACTICE SET-17

Total Ques.- 30
Time - 8 or 10 Min.

निर्देश : (प्रश्न 1–30) विषम संख्याओं का गणना परीक्षण के प्रत्येक प्रश्न में सम और विषम संख्याओं को मिलाकर एक श्रृंखला दिया जाता है। दिए गए संख्याओं में जितने विषम संख्या है उन्हें गणना करना होता है। गणना करने के बाद नीचे दिए गए पाँच विकल्पों (A, B, C, D और E) में एक सही विकल्प को ढूंढना होता है। जिसे उत्तर पत्रक में दिए गए गोले को काला या माउस की सहायता से क्लिक करना होता है।

Directions: (Questions 1–30) : Each question in the Odd Number Counting Test presents a series of even and odd numbers. You need to count the total number of odd numbers in the given series. After counting, select the correct option from the five choices (A, B, C, D & E) provided. Mark your answer by filling the circle on the answer sheet or by clicking on it using the mouse.

1. 2 1 5 4 2 1 3 5 2 6 1 2 4 1 2 6 5 3 4 5 2 1 5 2 4 2 3 3 2 6 5 2 1
   (A) 21 (B) 19 (C) 16 (D) 14 (E) 18
2. 2 3 2 2 3 2 2 4 1 2 3 2 5 5 1 4 2 3 1 5 2 1 4 5 6 4 1 2 1 2 2 1
   (A) 15 (B) 17 (C) 16 (D) 13 (E) 19
3. 5 2 5 2 6 3 2 1 5 2 6 3 2 1 5 4 4 2 1 5 2 4 2 1 4 2 3 1 2 1 2
   (A) 15 (B) 14 (C) 17 (D) 22 (E) 23
4. 4 3 6 6 2 1 2 5 4 2 4 1 2 2 1 5 2 3 2 1 5 2 1 3 2 5 5 3 2 5 2
   (A) 13 (B) 14 (C) 15 (D) 19 (E) 22
5. 6 2 4 1 3 2 5 6 2 5 1 3 5 3 2 5 2 3 2 1 1 1 5 2 2 1 2 2 2 3 4 4
   (A) 13 (B) 15 (C) 16 (D) 14 (E) 17
6. 3 2 3 2 5 4 1 2 5 2 1 2 4 5 1 1 2 5 2 1 6 2 3 2 1 4 1 2 5 2 1 3
   (A) 13 (B) 17 (C) 22 (D) 19 (E) 21
7. 2 5 4 6 2 3 2 5 1 2 4 2 3 3 6 2 5 4 3 2 1 2 5 2 1 1 2 2 5 6
   (A) 15 (B) 13 (C) 18 (D) 19 (E) 22
8. 1 2 4 2 3 5 2 6 5 4 2 1 2 2 1 2 5 4 1 4 1 5 1 3 5 2 1 2 5 2
   (A) 15 (B) 17 (C) 22 (D) 19 (E) 21
9. 2 3 2 5 2 1 2 5 4 1 5 2 1 2 5 4 2 1 2 3 6 4 4 1 2 5 3 2 1 2 6
   (A) 14 (B) 21 (C) 18 (D) 22 (E) 25
10. 2 2 5 2 3 5 6 4 1 2 5 4 1 2 3 1 4 5 2 1 3 2 5 1 1 4 5 2
    (A) 14 (B) 15 (C) 13 (D) 19 (E) 23
11. 5 2 1 2 1 2 1 4 5 4 1 2 6 2 3 2 5 2 1 4 1 2 5 4 4 1 2 3 3
    (A) 17 (B) 14 (C) 16 (D) 21 (E) 22
12. 5 2 1 2 2 3 5 2 5 6 2 5 2 2 1 2 5 3 2 5 4 1 2 3 1 1 2
    (A) 17 (B) 19 (C) 14 (D) 22 (E) 25
13. 3 2 4 2 3 2 5 1 2 4 1 4 1 2 5 3 2 1 5 2 1 3 2 5 4 1 5 2 1
    (A) 11 (B) 12 (C) 14 (D) 16 (E) 17

14. 6 2 3 2 5 4 5 2 3 5 2 1 1 4 5 6 5 2 3 1 2 2 5 6 2 1

(A) 16 (B) 13 (C) 17 (D) 19 (E) 20

15. 6 2 1 5 4 1 2 5 4 2 3 1 2 5 2 3 2 2 3 2 5 2 1 2 3 5 1 2

(A) 22 (B) 15 (C) 14 (D) 17 (E) 20

16. 2 2 3 2 3 1 5 3 2 6 5 1 2 6 5 3 5 2 6 1 1 2 3 2 1 4 5 2 1 2 6 5 2

(A) 19 (B) 22 (C) 17 (D) 13 (E) 12

17. 2 2 1 2 4 6 1 2 2 4 1 2 3 2 5 13 2 1 6 4 1 2 4 4 2 3 5 6 4 1 2

(A) 17 (B) 23 (C) 12 (D) 15 (E) 19

18. 3 4 2 2 2 1 5 2 4 1 2 5 2 6 3 2 1 5 2 6 4 2 3 1 5 2 1 6 6 5 4 1

(A) 14 (B) 16 (C) 17 (D) 19 (E) 21

19. 5 2 3 2 1 3 2 5 6 2 1 2 5 4 3 1 4 1 2 5 3 2 4 4 6 2 1 5 2 4 5 2

(A) 22 (B) 20 (C) 15 (D) 14 (E) 19

20. 2 1 2 3 2 2 2 5 2 1 1 2 2 3 4 4 1 3 5 1 5 2 3 2 5 6 2 6 2 5 1

(A) 15 (B) 16 (C) 19 (D) 22 (E) 13

21. 5 4 1 2 2 1 2 6 1 4 5 2 1 3 2 5 4 1 2 5 2 2 1 6 2 3 2 5 2 3 3

(A) 15 (B) 18 (C) 12 (D) 11 (E) 17

22. 3 4 5 2 1 2 5 4 2 6 2 3 2 4 1 2 6 2 3 2 1 3 2 5 1 2 4 2 5 5 6

(A) 17 (B) 13 (C) 15 (D) 22 (E) 25

23. 1 2 2 2 3 5 2 6 5 4 1 5 4 2 3 3 2 5 2 2 1 4 1 5 6 2 1 2 5 4

(A) 14 (B) 11 (C) 19 (D) 15 (E) 16

24. 2 5 4 2 6 2 3 3 2 5 2 3 2 1 2 2 5 4 1 2 6 5 2 1 2 5 4 1 2 1 1

(A) 14 (B) 17 (C) 23 (D) 16 (E) 12

25. 2 4 2 1 5 1 2 5 5 2 1 3 2 5 1 4 3 5 6 4 4 1 2 3 1 2 6 5 2

(A) 16 (B) 15 (C) 22 (D) 18 (E) 20

26. 2 1 4 1 2 3 3 2 2 1 4 1 2 2 1 4 1 5 6 2 3 2 5 2 1 4 5 2 5 4

(A) 13 (B) 12 (C) 14 (D) 18 (E) 20

27. 2 4 2 3 2 5 4 1 6 3 5 2 1 2 2 2 5 2 1 1 2 2 3 2 5 1 2 5 5

(A) 25 (B) 19 (C) 13 (D) 14 (E) 16

28. 3 2 4 2 5 1 4 1 2 5 2 1 3 1 2 6 3 2 5 2 1 1 2 5 3 2 1 5 4

(A) 16 (B) 18 (C) 20 (D) 21 (E) 23

29. 6 4 5 2 2 3 5 2 1 2 5 4 5 6 1 3 2 3 5 2 1 2 5 2 3 2 2 1 4 5 6 2 1

(A) 17 (B) 13 (C) 23 (D) 16 (E) 14

30. 2 1 3 4 1 2 5 2 3 2 2 6 2 3 1 2 5 1 2 3 2 5 1 4 2 5 5 2

(A) 14 (B) 11 (C) 18 (D) 20 (E) 15

PRACTICE SET-18

Total Ques.- 30
Time - 8 or 10 Min.

निर्देश : (प्रश्न 1-30) विषम संख्याओं का गणना परीक्षण के प्रत्येक प्रश्न में सम और विषम संख्याओं को मिलाकर एक श्रृंखला दिया जाता है। दिए गए संख्याओं में जितने विषम संख्या है उन्हें गणना करना होता है। गणना करने के बाद नीचे दिए गए पाँच विकल्पों (A, B, C, D और E) में एक सही विकल्प को ढूंढना होता है। जिसे उत्तर पत्रक में दिए गए गोले को काला या माउस की सहायता से क्लिक करना होता है।

Directions: (Questions 1–30) : Each question in the Odd Number Counting Test presents a series of even and odd numbers. You need to count the total number of odd numbers in the given series. After counting, select the correct option from the five choices (A, B, C, D & E) provided. Mark your answer by filling the circle on the answer sheet or by clicking on it using the mouse.

1. 1 5 4 4 1 2 6 5 3 3 3 2 6 5 2 2 1 4 5 1 5 2 4 2 3 5 2 6 1 2 1
   (A) 16 (B) 14 (C) 17 (D) 19 (E) 22
2. 2 3 2 2 4 1 2 3 5 3 2 2 5 1 4 2 2 1 5 2 1 4 5 6 4 1 2 1 2 3 2 1
   (A) 19 (B) 15 (C) 18 (D) 22 (E) 20
3. 5 2 5 2 6 6 3 2 1 5 4 1 2 1 3 4 2 1 5 2 4 2 1 4 2 3 2 1 5 2 2
   (A) 17 (B) 18 (C) 14 (D) 13 (E) 11
4. 4 3 6 2 1 5 2 1 2 5 4 2 4 1 2 2 3 2 1 5 2 1 3 2 5 6 5 3 2 5 2
   (A) 23 (B) 14 (C) 15 (D) 17 (E) 22
5. 6 2 4 1 5 2 1 2 2 2 3 4 4 2 5 2 3 2 1 1 1 5 2 3 2 5 6 2 5 1 3
   (A) 15 (B) 16 (C) 19 (D) 22 (E) 14
6. 3 2 5 2 1 6 2 5 4 1 2 5 2 1 2 3 2 1 4 1 2 5 2 3 2 4 5 2 1 3
   (A) 15 (B) 21 (C) 18 (D) 22 (E) 11
7. 2 5 4 6 2 2 5 1 2 4 2 3 2 5 3 6 2 5 4 3 2 1 2 5 2 1 1 2 3 6
   (A) 13 (B) 17 (C) 22 (D) 24 (E) 18
8. 1 2 2 2 1 2 2 6 5 4 2 1 2 3 5 5 4 1 4 1 5 4 2 3 5 6 3 2 5 2
   (A) 17 (B) 14 (C) 23 (D) 25 (E) 19
9. 2 3 2 1 2 5 3 2 1 5 2 1 2 5 4 5 2 1 2 5 4 1 2 1 2 3 6 4 4 2 6
   (A) 14 (B) 20 (C) 22 (D) 23 (E) 21
10. 2 2 2 1 3 2 5 1 2 3 5 5 4 1 2 3 1 4 5 6 4 1 2 5 1 4 5 2
    (A) 12 (B) 15 (C) 17 (D) 23 (E) 18
11. 5 2 5 2 2 1 6 2 3 1 2 1 4 5 4 1 2 1 4 1 2 5 4 4 1 2 3 2 3
    (A) 14 (B) 12 (C) 16 (D) 17 (E) 19
12. 5 2 3 2 5 6 2 5 2 2 1 2 2 3 5 2 1 2 5 3 2 5 4 1 1 1 2
    (A) 14 (B) 16 (C) 20 (D) 19 (E) 25
13. 3 2 4 3 2 5 1 2 4 1 4 5 2 1 2 5 3 2 1 5 2 1 3 2 5 4 1 2 1
    (A) 19 (B) 13 (C) 16 (D) 14 (E) 22

14. 6 2 3 2 1 4 5 2 3 5 2 1 2 5 6 5 2 3 1 2 5 4 5 6 2 1

(A) 11 (B) 13 (C) 23 (D) 21 (E) 15

15. 6 5 2 5 4 1 2 5 4 2 3 1 2 5 1 3 2 2 3 2 5 2 1 2 3 2 1 2

(A) 14 (B) 22 (C) 23 (D) 17 (E) 15

16. 1 5 3 2 6 5 2 2 3 2 3 5 6 4 1 2 4 4 5 2 1 2 6 5 2 1 2 6 5 3

(A) 14 (B) 16 (C) 21 (D) 11 (E) 13

17. 2 3 3 5 2 6 1 3 5 2 1 2 3 2 6 4 1 2 4 1 2 2 4 1 2 3 2 5 1 4 2 1 2

(A) 15 (B) 22 (C) 21 (D) 16 (E) 13

18. 3 4 2 1 5 2 6 4 2 3 2 2 1 5 2 4 1 2 5 2 6 3 2 1 5 2 1 6 6 5 4 1

(A) 19 (B) 14 (C) 16 (D) 15 (E) 18

19. 5 2 3 2 1 4 1 2 5 3 2 4 2 3 2 3 5 2 6 1 1 2 3 4 6 2 1 5 2 4 5 4 3

(A) 16 (B) 21 (C) 14 (D) 19 (E) 13

20. 1 2 2 3 4 1 1 2 3 2 1 2 1 4 2 2 5 2 1 1 5 2 3 2 5 6 2 6 2 5 1

(A) 13 (B) 15 (C) 14 (D) 17 (E) 22

21. 5 4 1 2 2 5 2 3 2 1 2 6 3 2 5 4 1 2 5 2 2 1 6 2 3 1 4 5 2 1 3

(A) 17 (B) 18 (C) 15 (D) 22 (E) 23

22. 3 4 5 4 1 2 6 2 5 2 1 2 5 4 2 6 2 2 3 2 1 3 2 5 1 2 4 3 2 5 6

(A) 21 (B) 24 (C) 11 (D) 13 (E) 14

23. 1 2 2 2 5 4 1 5 4 2 3 3 2 3 5 2 6 5 4 2 1 4 1 5 6 2 1 2 5 2

(A) 14 (B) 22 (C) 23 (D) 16 (E) 21

24. 2 6 5 2 1 2 5 4 1 2 1 2 5 4 2 6 3 2 1 2 2 5 4 1 2 3 3 2 5 2 1

(A) 14 (B) 15 (C) 22 (D) 18 (E) 19

25. 2 3 5 6 2 1 3 2 5 1 4 1 2 4 4 1 2 3 4 2 1 5 1 2 5 5 6 5 2

(A) 16 (B) 15 (C) 21 (D) 11 (E) 13

26. 2 1 4 1 4 5 2 5 4 1 2 3 3 2 1 4 1 5 6 2 3 2 5 2 2 1 4 1 2 2

(A) 22 (B) 21 (C) 14 (D) 16 (E) 17

27. 2 1 2 2 5 4 1 6 3 5 2 1 2 2 5 2 1 1 2 2 3 2 5 4 2 3 2 5 5

(A) 14 (B) 15 (C) 19 (D) 22 (E) 23

28. 3 2 4 2 5 3 2 1 5 4 1 2 2 5 1 2 6 3 2 5 2 1 1 5 2 1 3 1 4

(A) 14 (B) 16 (C) 18 (D) 22 (E) 23

29. 6 4 5 2 5 4 5 6 1 3 1 4 5 6 2 2 3 5 2 1 2 5 2 3 2 2 2 1

(A) 21 (B) 19 (C) 13 (D) 17 (E) 22

30. 2 1 3 4 2 5 4 1 2 5 2 3 4 2 3 1 2 5 1 2 3 2 5 1 2 2 6 5 2

(A) 11 (B) 13 (C) 14 (D) 17 (E) 21

PRACTICE SET-19

Total Ques.- 30
Time - 8 or 10 Min.

निर्देश : (प्रश्न 1-30) विषम संख्याओं का गणना परीक्षण के प्रत्येक प्रश्न में सम और विषम संख्याओं को मिलाकर एक श्रृंखला दिया जाता है। दिए गए संख्याओं में जितने विषम संख्या है उन्हें गणना करना होता है। गणना करने के बाद नीचे दिए गए पाँच विकल्पों (A, B, C, D और E) में एक सही विकल्प को ढूंढना होता है। जिसे उत्तर पत्रक में दिए गए गोले को काला या माउस की सहायता से क्लिक करना होता है।

Directions: (Questions 1–30) : Each question in the Odd Number Counting Test presents a series of even and odd numbers. You need to count the total number of odd numbers in the given series. After counting, select the correct option from the five choices (A, B, C, D & E) provided. Mark your answer by filling the circle on the answer sheet or by clicking on it using the mouse.

1. 1 5 4 2 1 4 5 2 1 2 6 5 3 3 3 2 1 5 2 4 2 3 5 2 6 1 2 4 6 5 2 1
   (A) 14 (B) 16 (C) 19 (D) 20 (E) 21
2. 2 3 2 2 4 1 2 5 3 2 2 5 1 4 2 3 1 2 3 2 1 5 2 1 4 5 6 4 1 2 2 1
   (A) 15 (B) 17 (C) 20 (D) 14 (E) 13
3. 5 2 5 2 6 1 5 2 6 3 2 1 5 4 1 3 4 2 1 5 2 4 2 1 4 2 3 2 2 1 2
   (A) 16 (B) 14 (C) 11 (D) 12 (E) 19
4. 4 3 6 2 1 2 5 4 2 4 1 2 5 3 1 5 2 3 2 1 5 2 1 3 2 5 6 2 2 5 2
   (A) 16 (B) 17 (C) 21 (D) 11 (E) 15
5. 6 2 4 1 2 5 1 3 5 2 1 2 2 2 5 2 3 2 1 1 1 5 2 3 2 5 6 2 3 4 4
   (A) 19 (B) 25 (C) 22 (D) 16 (E) 15
6. 3 2 5 2 3 2 5 4 1 2 5 2 2 5 2 1 6 2 3 2 1 4 1 1 2 4 5 2 1 3
   (A) 20 (B) 13 (C) 15 (D) 14 (E) 11
7. 2 5 4 2 5 1 2 4 2 3 2 6 2 3 6 2 5 4 3 2 1 2 5 2 1 1 2 3 5 6
   (A) 13 (B) 14 (C) 17 (D) 22 (E) 25
8. 1 5 2 6 5 4 2 1 2 3 5 2 2 2 1 2 5 4 1 4 1 5 4 2 3 6 3 2 5 2
   (A) 14 (B) 20 (C) 22 (D) 21 (E) 15
9. 2 3 4 1 2 5 3 2 1 5 2 1 2 5 2 5 2 1 2 5 4 1 2 1 2 3 6 4 4 2 6
   (A) 14 (B) 13 (C) 11 (D) 12 (E) 16
10. 1 3 2 5 1 2 3 5 6 4 1 2 2 5 4 1 2 3 1 4 5 2 2 5 1 4 5 2
    (A) 17 (B) 16 (C) 15 (D) 14 (E) 19
11. 5 2 1 6 1 2 1 4 5 4 1 2 3 2 3 2 5 2 1 4 1 2 5 4 4 1 2 3 2
    (A) 14 (B) 16 (C) 15 (D) 11 (E) 18
12. 5 2 1 2 2 2 3 2 5 6 2 5 3 5 2 1 2 5 3 2 5 4 1 2 1 1 2
    (A) 22 (B) 13 (C) 14 (D) 16 (E) 17
13. 3 2 4 1 2 3 2 5 1 2 4 1 4 5 2 5 3 2 1 5 2 1 3 2 5 4 1 2 1
    (A) 16 (B) 14 (C) 18 (D) 11 (E) 22

14. 6 2 3 2 5 4 5 2 3 5 4 2 1 2 6 2 1 4 5 6 5 2 3 1 6 5 6 2 1
(A) 16 (B) 13 (C) 11 (D) 10 (E) 15

15. 6 5 2 3 2 4 1 2 5 4 2 3 1 2 5 2 3 2 5 2 1 2 3 2 1 5 1 2
(A) 18 (B) 14 (C) 20 (D) 22 (E) 21

16. 1 5 3 2 6 5 2 2 3 2 2 1 2 6 5 2 1 2 6 3 5 2 6 1 1 2 3 2 1 4 5 5 3
(A) 19 (B) 20 (C) 17 (D) 14 (E) 13

17. 2 3 2 1 6 4 1 2 1 4 2 3 5 6 4 1 2 4 1 2 2 4 1 2 3 2 5 4 1 2
(A) 18 (B) 19 (C) 11 (D) 12 (E) 14

18. 3 4 2 1 5 2 1 6 6 5 4 2 1 5 2 6 4 2 3 2 2 1 5 2 4 1 2 5 2 6 3 1
(A) 14 (B) 17 (C) 22 (D) 25 (E) 16

19. 5 2 3 2 1 5 2 4 5 2 1 3 2 5 4 1 2 5 3 2 4 4 6 2 1 6 2 1 2 5 4 3
(A) 19 (B) 18 (C) 15 (D) 16 (E) 21

20. 1 2 2 2 3 2 5 6 2 6 2 3 4 4 1 3 5 2 1 2 3 2 2 2 5 2 1 1 5 5 1
(A) 14 (B) 17 (C) 15 (D) 20 (E) 19

21. 5 4 1 2 3 2 5 4 2 3 2 1 2 6 1 4 1 2 5 2 2 1 6 2 3 2 5 5 2 1 3
(A) 21 (B) 19 (C) 16 (D) 15 (E) 11

22. 3 4 5 2 1 2 5 4 2 6 2 3 2 5 4 1 2 6 2 3 2 1 3 2 5 1 2 4 2 5 6
(A) 13 (B) 15 (C) 17 (D) 22 (E) 18

23. 1 2 4 1 5 4 2 3 3 2 2 3 5 2 6 5 4 2 1 4 1 5 6 2 1 2 5 2 5 2
(A) 10 (B) 11 (C) 15 (D) 14 (E) 16

24. 2 5 4 2 6 5 4 1 2 1 2 3 3 3 2 1 2 2 5 4 1 2 6 5 2 1 2 2 5 2 1
(A) 20 (B) 15 (C) 17 (D) 16 (E) 14

25. 2 3 5 2 1 3 2 5 1 4 1 2 6 5 6 4 4 1 2 3 4 2 1 5 1 2 5 5 2
(A) 21 (B) 22 (C) 18 (D) 15 (E) 14

26. 1 2 3 1 2 3 3 2 2 1 4 1 2 1 2 3 3 2 2 1 4 1 2 3 2 2 1 4 1 2
(A) 17 (B) 15 (C) 23 (D) 14 (E) 13

27. 2 1 2 2 4 1 6 3 5 2 1 2 2 5 2 1 1 2 2 3 2 5 4 2 3 2 5 5 5
(A) 18 (B) 13 (C) 21 (D) 16 (E) 14

28. 3 2 4 2 5 1 2 6 2 1 5 4 1 2 5 2 3 2 5 2 1 1 2 5 3 1 3 1 4
(A) 12 (B) 15 (C) 16 (D) 17 (E) 19

29. 6 4 2 5 4 5 6 1 3 1 4 5 6 5 2 2 3 5 2 1 2 5 2 3 2 2 2 1
(A) 13 (B) 15 (C) 14 (D) 21 (E) 19

30. 2 1 3 4 2 4 2 5 4 1 2 5 2 3 1 2 5 1 2 3 2 5 1 3 2 2 6 5 2
(A) 14 (B) 12 (C) 16 (D) 19 (E) 20

PRACTICE SET-20

Total Ques.- 30
Time - 8 or 10 Min.

निर्देश : (प्रश्न 1-30) विषम संख्याओं का गणना परीक्षण के प्रत्येक प्रश्न में सम और विषम संख्याओं को मिलाकर एक श्रृंखला दिया जाता है। दिए गए संख्याओं में जितने विषम संख्या है उन्हें गणना करना होता है। गणना करने के बाद नीचे दिए गए पाँच विकल्पों (A, B, C, D और E) में एक सही विकल्प को ढूंढना होता है। जिसे उत्तर पत्रक में दिए गए गोले को काला या माउस की सहायता से क्लिक करना होता है।

Directions: (Questions 1–30) : Each question in the Odd Number Counting Test presents a series of even and odd numbers. You need to count the total number of odd numbers in the given series. After counting, select the correct option from the five choices (A, B, C, D & E) provided. Mark your answer by filling the circle on the answer sheet or by clicking on it using the mouse.

1. 1 5 4 2 1 4 1 2 6 5 3 3 3 2 4 5 2 1 5 2 4 2 3 5 2 6 1 2 6 5 2 1
   (A) 16 (B) 22 (C) 20 (D) 18 (E) 19
2. 2 3 2 1 2 1 2 5 3 2 2 5 1 4 2 3 2 4 1 2 3 2 1 5 2 1 4 5 6 4 2 1
   (A) 30 (B) 18 (C) 23 (D) 15 (E) 16
3. 5 2 1 5 2 6 3 2 1 5 4 1 2 1 2 5 2 6 3 4 2 1 5 2 4 2 1 4 2 3 2
   (A) 10 (B) 11 (C) 16 (D) 14 (E) 13
4. 5 6 2 1 2 5 4 2 4 1 2 4 3 6 2 1 5 2 3 2 1 5 2 1 3 2 5 3 2 5 2
   (A) 20 (B) 29 (C) 15 (D) 18 (E) 23
5. 6 3 2 5 6 2 5 1 3 5 2 1 2 2 2 2 4 1 2 5 2 3 2 1 1 1 5 2 3 4 4
   (A) 12 (B) 13 (C) 15 (D) 17 (E) 21
6. 3 2 4 1 2 5 2 1 2 4 5 2 5 2 1 6 2 3 2 1 4 1 2 5 2 3 2 5 1 3
   (A) 15 (B) 16 (C) 17 (D) 23 (E) 19
7. 2 5 4 1 2 3 2 5 1 2 4 2 6 2 3 6 2 5 4 3 2 1 2 5 2 1 3 2 5 6
   (A) 18 (B) 11 (C) 10 (D) 22 (E) 13
8. 1 2 6 5 4 2 1 2 3 5 6 3 2 2 2 1 2 5 4 1 4 1 5 4 2 3 5 2 5 2
   (A) 22 (B) 24 (C) 14 (D) 12 (E) 15
9. 2 3 2 5 4 4 1 2 5 3 2 1 5 2 2 1 2 5 4 1 2 1 2 3 6 1 2 5 4 2 6
   (A) 10 (B) 13 (C) 11 (D) 14 (E) 17
10. 2 2 2 3 5 6 4 1 2 5 1 4 5 5 4 1 2 3 1 4 5 2 1 3 2 5 1 2
    (A) 17 (B) 19 (C) 21 (D) 15 (E) 25
11. 5 2 1 6 1 2 3 2 1 2 1 4 2 3 2 5 2 1 4 1 2 5 4 4 5 4 1 2 3
    (A) 23 (B) 14 (C) 19 (D) 17 (E) 25
12. 5 2 1 2 2 5 6 2 5 2 1 3 5 2 1 2 5 3 2 5 4 1 2 3 2 1 2
    (A) 17 (B) 16 (C) 20 (D) 14 (E) 15
13. 3 2 1 2 3 2 5 1 2 4 4 1 2 5 3 2 1 5 2 1 3 2 5 4 1 4 5 2 1
    (A) 13 (B) 20 (C) 14 (D) 18 (E) 16

14. 6 5 2 3 1 2 5 4 5 2 3 5 2 3 2 1 4 5 6 2 1 2 5 6 2 1
(A) 10 (B) 11 (C) 16 (D) 18 (E) 13

15. 6 5 2 3 1 2 5 4 2 3 1 2 2 2 3 2 5 2 1 2 3 2 1 5 4 5 1 2
(A) 14 (B) 11 (C) 16 (D) 12 (E) 20

16. 1 5 2 6 1 1 2 3 2 1 4 5 2 1 2 6 5 3 2 6 5 2 2 3 2 3 5 2 1 2 6 5 3
(A) 15 (B) 17 (C) 20 (D) 21 (E) 22

17. 2 3 2 3 2 5 1 4 2 3 5 6 2 1 6 4 1 2 4 1 2 2 4 1 4 1 2 4 1 2
(A) 17 (B) 16 (C) 12 (D) 13 (E) 15

18. 3 4 4 1 2 5 2 6 3 2 1 5 2 1 2 1 5 2 6 4 2 3 2 2 1 5 2 6 6 5 4 1
(A) 16 (B) 20 (C) 19 (D) 14 (E) 15

19. 2 1 5 2 4 5 2 1 3 2 5 6 2 5 2 3 2 1 4 1 2 5 3 2 4 4 6 1 2 5 4 3
(A) 15 (B) 21 (C) 18 (D) 22 (E) 23

20. 1 2 2 3 1 1 5 2 3 2 5 6 2 6 4 4 1 3 5 2 1 2 3 2 2 2 5 2 2 5 1
(A) 21 (B) 19 (C) 15 (D) 13 (E) 11

21. 2 3 2 5 2 3 2 1 2 6 1 5 4 1 2 3 2 5 4 1 2 5 2 2 1 6 4 5 2 1 3
(A) 17 (B) 22 (C) 25 (D) 15 (E) 16

22. 3 4 5 2 1 2 5 4 2 6 2 3 4 1 2 6 2 3 2 1 3 2 5 1 2 4 2 5 2 5 6
(A) 15 (B) 13 (C) 12 (D) 14 (E) 20

23. 1 2 2 2 1 2 5 4 1 5 4 2 2 3 5 2 6 5 4 2 1 4 1 5 6 3 3 2 5 2
(A) 11 (B) 14 (C) 15 (D) 19 (E) 22

24. 2 5 4 5 4 1 2 1 2 3 3 2 5 2 6 3 2 1 2 2 5 4 1 2 6 5 2 1 2 2 1
(A) 13 (B) 14 (C) 16 (D) 20 (E) 21

25. 2 3 2 5 5 2 1 3 2 5 1 4 5 6 4 4 1 2 3 4 2 1 5 1 1 2 6 5 2
(A) 17 (B) 15 (C) 13 (D) 11 (E) 22

26. 2 1 4 5 4 1 2 3 3 2 2 1 4 1 1 4 1 5 6 2 3 2 5 2 1 4 5 2 2 2
(A) 13 (B) 12 (C) 11 (D) 14 (E) 16

27. 4 2 3 2 5 4 1 6 3 5 2 2 1 2 2 2 5 2 1 1 2 2 3 2 5 1 2 5 5
(A) 11 (B) 14 (C) 15 (D) 19 (E) 22

28. 3 2 4 2 1 5 4 1 2 5 2 1 3 1 4 2 5 1 2 6 3 2 5 2 1 1 2 5 3
(A) 19 (B) 11 (C) 13 (D) 16 (E) 14

29. 6 4 5 2 2 3 5 6 1 3 1 4 5 5 2 1 2 5 2 3 2 2 2 5 4 6 2 1
(A) 15 (B) 13 (C) 16 (D) 19 (E) 20

30. 2 1 5 4 1 2 5 2 3 2 2 6 3 4 2 3 1 2 5 1 2 3 2 5 1 4 2 5 2
(A) 17 (B) 21 (C) 14 (D) 15 (E) 11

उत्तर (ANSWER)

PRACTICE SET - 1

1.	A	16.	D
2.	A	17.	E
3.	D	18.	A
4.	C	19.	B
5.	C	20.	C
6.	D	21.	C
7.	E	22.	A
8.	B	23.	B
9.	D	24.	E
10.	A	25.	B
11.	D	26.	A
12.	A	27.	A
13.	D	28.	A
14.	C	29.	E
15.	E	30.	E

PRACTICE SET - 2

1.	A	16.	C
2.	D	17.	D
3.	D	18.	A
4.	C	19.	D
5.	C	20.	B
6.	A	21.	D
7.	E	22.	E
8.	C	23.	C
9.	D	24.	D
10.	D	25.	C
11.	B	26.	B
12.	D	27.	A
13.	E	28.	B
14.	E	29.	D
15.	A	30.	D

PRACTICE SET - 3

1.	E	16.	D
2.	D	17.	C
3.	D	18.	D
4.	C	19.	E
5.	D	20.	C
6.	B	21.	D
7.	D	22.	B
8.	E	23.	D
9.	D	24.	C
10.	D	25.	E
11.	D	26.	D
12.	B	27.	E
13.	D	28.	D
14.	C	29.	D
15.	A	30.	E

PRACTICE SET - 4

1.	D	16.	D
2.	C	17.	C
3.	D	18.	E
4.	D	19.	C
5.	C	20.	E
6.	E	21.	C
7.	B	22.	B
8.	D	23.	C
9.	D	24.	D
10.	D	25.	B
11.	C	26.	B
12.	B	27.	C
13.	E	28.	C
14.	E	29.	B
15.	B	30.	B

PRACTICE SET - 5

1.	C	16.	C
2.	D	17.	D
3.	C	18.	C
4.	D	19.	C
5.	C	20.	B
6.	C	21.	C
7.	D	22.	B
8.	C	23.	C
9.	D	24.	D
10.	E	25.	C
11.	B	26.	C
12.	A	27.	B
13.	E	28.	C
14.	D	29.	C
15.	C	30.	C

PRACTICE SET - 6

1.	C	16.	D
2.	D	17.	C
3.	B	18.	C
4.	B	19.	E
5.	D	20.	E
6.	B	21.	D
7.	D	22.	C
8.	D	23.	D
9.	C	24.	B
10.	D	25.	C
11.	E	26.	D
12.	D	27.	C
13.	E	28.	C
14.	D	29.	D
15.	E	30.	B

उत्तर (ANSWER)

PRACTICE SET - 7

1.	C	16.	C
2.	A	17.	C
3.	B	18.	B
4.	C	19.	B
5.	D	20.	A
6.	E	21.	C
7.	D	22.	E
8.	C	23.	D
9.	D	24.	E
10.	C	25.	C
11.	D	26.	D
12.	E	27.	D
13.	D	28.	B
14.	C	29.	C
15.	B	30.	B

PRACTICE SET - 8

1.	C	16.	C
2.	D	17.	D
3.	D	18.	D
4.	D	19.	C
5.	C	20.	B
6.	B	21.	C
7.	D	22.	B
8.	E	23.	B
9.	B	24.	C
10.	D	25.	B
11.	D	26.	C
12.	E	27.	B
13.	E	28.	C
14.	D	29.	D
15.	C	30.	D

PRACTICE SET - 9

1.	D	16.	C
2.	C	17.	C
3.	D	18.	B
4.	E	19.	B
5.	D	20.	C
6.	C	21.	C
7.	C	22.	C
8.	B	23.	B
9.	C	24.	C
10.	B	25.	D
11.	B	26.	B
12.	B	27.	C
13.	C	28.	B
14.	D	29.	D
15.	C	30.	B

PRACTICE SET - 10

1.	C	16.	C
2.	B	17.	B
3.	D	18.	D
4.	C	19.	E
5.	B	20.	C
6.	C	21.	C
7.	D	22.	B
8.	B	23.	A
9.	C	24.	C
10.	B	25.	C
11.	C	26.	D
12.	D	27.	B
13.	B	28.	D
14.	C	29.	D
15.	D	30.	B

PRACTICE SET - 11

1.	C	16.	B
2.	D	17.	B
3.	B	18.	C
4.	E	19.	C
5.	D	20.	B
6.	C	21.	B
7.	D	22.	D
8.	D	23.	B
9.	E	24.	C
10.	B	25.	C
11.	D	26.	C
12.	C	27.	E
13.	B	28.	B
14.	D	29.	B
15.	B	30.	D

PRACTICE SET - 12

1.	C	16.	E
2.	B	17.	C
3.	C	18.	B
4.	D	19.	C
5.	B	20.	D
6.	C	21.	C
7.	C	22.	B
8.	B	23.	C
9.	B	24.	B
10.	B	25.	D
11.	C	26.	B
12.	D	27.	C
13.	E	28.	D
14.	E	29.	C
15.	C	30.	B

उत्तर (ANSWER)

PRACTICE SET - 13

1.	C	16.	D
2.	D	17.	C
3.	B	18.	D
4.	C	19.	D
5.	D	20.	C
6.	C	21.	C
7.	E	22.	D
8.	B	23.	C
9.	B	24.	C
10.	C	25.	E
11.	D	26.	D
12.	B	27.	D
13.	C	28.	B
14.	C	29.	D
15.	B	30.	C

PRACTICE SET - 14

1.	C	16.	B
2.	D	17.	C
3.	D	18.	D
4.	C	19.	C
5.	C	20.	D
6.	B	21.	C
7.	C	22.	D
8.	B	23.	D
9.	B	24.	C
10.	C	25.	B
11.	D	26.	C
12.	B	27.	B
13.	C	28.	C
14.	D	29.	B
15.	B	30.	B

PRACTICE SET - 15

1.	C	16.	D
2.	B	17.	C
3.	C	18.	D
4.	B	19.	C
5.	C	20.	C
6.	D	21.	D
7.	C	22.	C
8.	E	23.	C
9.	D	24.	B
10.	C	25.	D
11.	D	26.	B
12.	B	27.	B
13.	D	28.	C
14.	B	29.	D
15.	B	30.	C

PRACTICE SET - 16

1.	C	16.	C
2.	D	17.	D
3.	D	18.	C
4.	C	19.	D
5.	D	20.	C
6.	B	21.	D
7.	C	22.	B
8.	B	23.	A
9.	B	24.	C
10.	B	25.	D
11.	D	26.	A
12.	C	27.	C
13.	C	28.	B
14.	B	29.	A
15.	C	30.	C

PRACTICE SET - 17

1.	C	16.	C
2.	A	17.	C
3.	B	18.	A
4.	C	19.	C
5.	C	20.	A
6.	B	21.	A
7.	B	22.	B
8.	A	23.	A
9.	A	24.	A
10.	B	25.	B
11.	B	26.	C
12.	C	27.	D
13.	D	28.	A
14.	B	29.	D
15.	C	30.	A

PRACTICE SET - 18

1.	A	16.	A
2.	B	17.	A
3.	C	18.	B
4.	C	19.	A
5.	A	20.	B
6.	A	21.	C
7.	A	22.	D
8.	B	23.	A
9.	A	24.	A
10.	B	25.	B
11.	A	26.	C
12.	A	27.	A
13.	C	28.	B
14.	B	29.	C
15.	A	30.	C

उत्तर (ANSWER)

PRACTICE SET - 19

1.	B	16.	C
2.	A	17.	D
3.	B	18.	A
4.	E	19.	C
5.	E	20.	C
6.	C	21.	D
7.	A	22.	A
8.	A	23.	D
9.	A	24.	E
10.	C	25.	D
11.	A	26.	B
12.	C	27.	E
13.	A	28.	C
14.	B	29.	A
15.	B	30.	A

PRACTICE SET - 20

1.	A	16.	B
2.	D	17.	C
3.	D	18.	D
4.	C	19.	A
5.	C	20.	C
6.	A	21.	D
7.	E	22.	B
8.	C	23.	B
9.	D	24.	B
10.	D	25.	B
11.	B	26.	D
12.	D	27.	B
13.	E	28.	D
14.	E	29.	B
15.	A	30.	C

3 TEST FOR MEASURING SPATIAL SCANNING

(स्थानिक क्षमता मापन हेतु परीक्षण)

Shortest Route Test (संक्षिप्त रास्ता परीक्षण)

रेलवे मनोवैज्ञानिक परीक्षण के अन्तर्गत स्थानिक क्षमता परीक्षण/संक्षिप्त रास्ता परीक्षण स्टेशन मास्टर पद के लिए बहुत महत्वपूर्ण अध्याय है। इस परीक्षण का तात्पर्य एक स्थान से दूसरे स्थान तक कम से कम दूरी का रास्ता तय कर शीघ्रता से खोजना होता है। इस परीक्षण में कुल 40 प्रश्न दिए होते हैं जिसे हल करने के लिए 5 या 8 मिनट का समय दिया जाता है।

इस परीक्षण को एकाग्रता, शीघ्रता और अपने विवेकपूर्वक से प्रश्नों को हल करना होता है।

कुछ महत्वपूर्ण जानकारियाँ :-

1. दिए गए चित्रों को ध्यानपूर्वक देखे जो A से Z तक निर्देशित किया गया है। इस तरह चार चित्र दिए गए हैं। प्रत्येक चित्र में एक स्थान से दूसरे स्थान तक पहुँचने के लिए कम से कम दूरी का रास्ता का चयन करना होता है जिसके बीच रास्ते में कई रूकावटें होते हें जिसे (—O—) से दर्शाया गया है। यह अवरोधक पूरे चित्र में कहीं भी हो सकते हैं।
2. दिए गए चित्रों में 1 से 10 तक नम्बरों वाले बॉक्स/घर (—|—) दिए होते हैं जो चार दिवारों से बने होते हैं बॉक्स के अंदर जो अंक दिए होते हैं उसे एक दिवार या दो दिवारों से गुजरना होता है।
3. **एक स्थान से दूसरे स्थान तक जाने हेतु आपको हमेशा एक ही घर मिलेगा चाहे वह एक दीवार हो या दो दिवार से स्पर्श करता हो, उस घर का नंबर ही आपका उत्तर होगा।**
4. **रास्ते में जाते समय किसी घर का कोने बिन्दु को दिवारों के गिनती के अन्तर्गत नहीं रख सकते ।**

Spatial Scanning Test / Shortest Route Test for the Post of Railway Station Master As part of the Railway Psychological Test, the Spatial Scanning Test (also called the Shortest Route Test) is a very important section for the post of Station Master.The purpose of this test is to quickly determine the shortest route from one location to another.The test consists of 40 questions, and candidates are given 5 or 8 minutes to complete it.

This test requires focus, speed and careful decision-making while solving the questions.

Important Information:

1. Observe the given diagrams carefully, which are labelled from A to Z. There are four diagrams in total. For each diagram, you need to select the shortest route from one point to another. The paths may have obstacles, represented by(—O—), which can appear anywhere in the diagram.
2. In the diagrams, there are boxes/houses numbered 1 to 10, each formed by four walls. The number inside the box indicates that you may need to pass through one or twowalls to reach it.
3. **To move from one location to another, you will always pass through only one house. Whether it touches one wall or two walls, the number of that house will be your answer.**
4. **While going on the road, the corner point of a house cannot be included in the count of walls.**

इसे उदाहरण के द्वारा समझें : *Example for understanding*

Corner Touch **(कोने स्पर्श) :-**

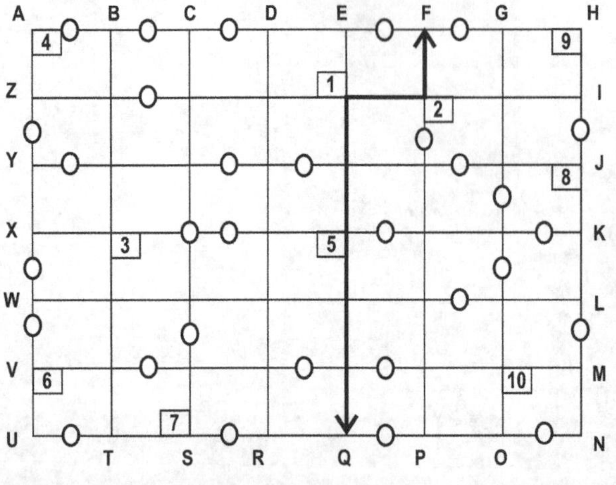

प्रश्न : F से Q तक जाने के लिए छोटा रास्ता कौन-सा होगा?

उत्तर : 5

व्याख्या : F से Q तक जाने के लिए रास्ते में पहला बॉक्स 2 दूसरा बॉक्स 1 और तीसरा बॉक्स 5 मिलता है। इस रास्ते में नंबर-2 और नंबर-1 वाले बॉक्स कॉर्नर स्पर्श से होते हुए नंबर-5 वाले बॉक्स के दिवार को स्पर्श करते हुए अपने निर्धारित स्थान पर पहुँच रहा है। अत: आपका सही उत्तर 5 होगा।

नोट : ध्यान रहे कि रास्ते में नंबर-2 और नंबर-1 दोनों कॉर्नर बिन्दु से होकर जा रहा है। इसलिए इसे सही उत्तर नहीं मान सकते हैं।

Que.: What would be the shortest route from F to Q?

Ans.: 5

Explanation: On the way from F to Q, the first box 2 the second box 1 and the third box 5 meet. In this route, boxes numbered 2 and 1 touch the corner, and boxes numbered 5 touch the wall of box, reaching their destination. Therefore, your correct answer is 5.

Note: Keep in mind that both boxes numbered 2 and 1 pass through corner points on the route. Therefore, this cannot be considered the correct answer.

उदाहरण/Example

1.

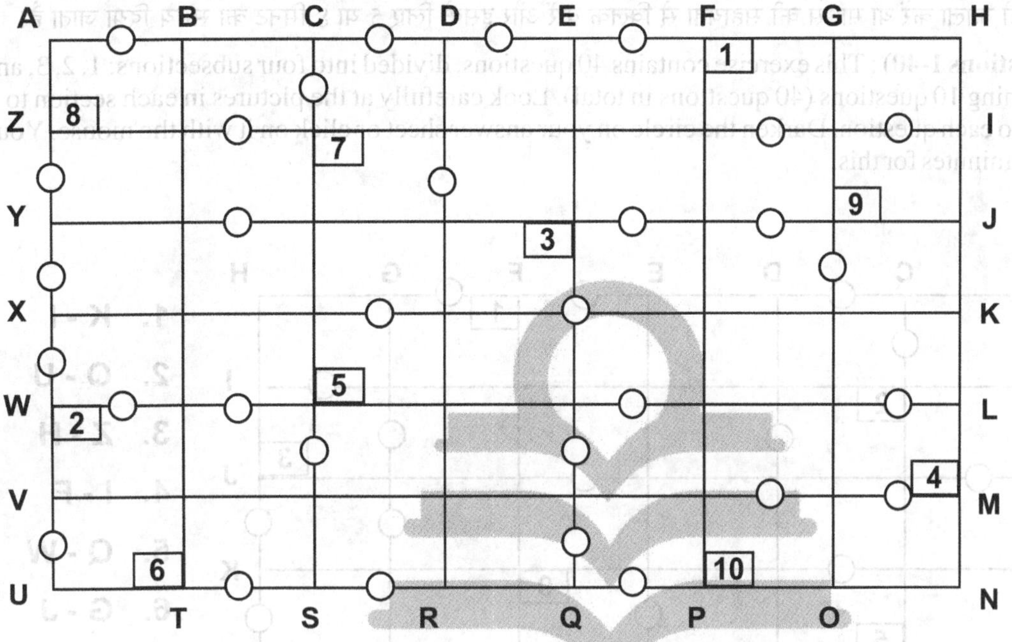

प्रश्न संख्या Q. No.	सबसे नजदीक का रास्ता The Shortest Route from
1.	I - J
2.	K - L
3.	R - X
4.	S - A
5.	D - X
6.	E - R
7.	R - U
8.	R - M
9.	H - E
10.	X - W

2.

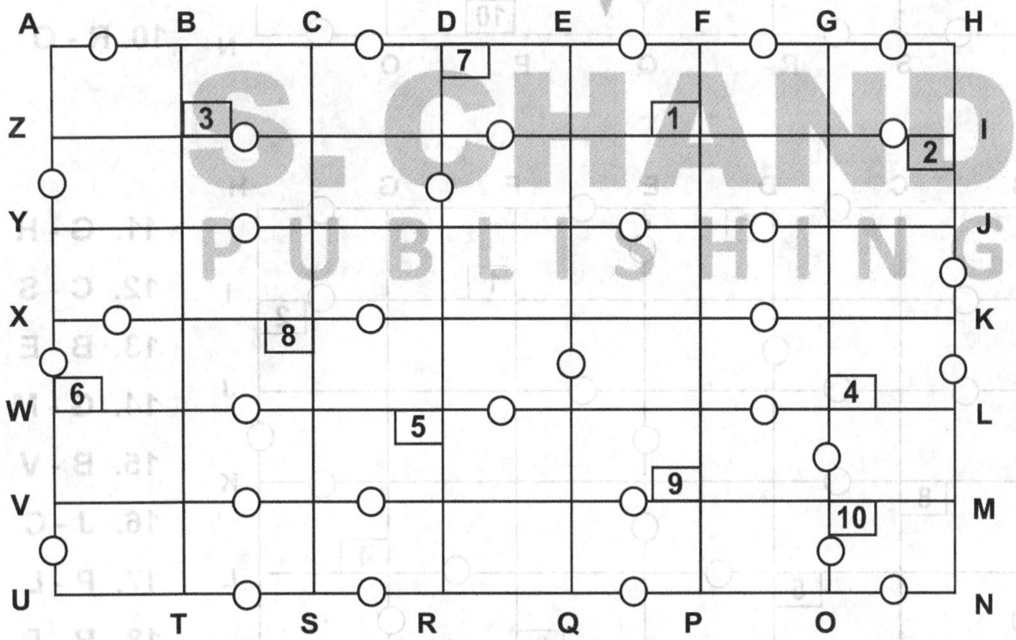

11.	H - G
12.	A - C
13.	S - R
14.	E - J
15.	C - E
16.	G - P
17.	M - J
18.	N - O
19.	A - W
20.	S - Y

Ans. 1. (9) 2. (4) 3. (5) 4. (8) 5. (7) 6. (3) 7. (6) 8. (10) 9. (1) 10. (2)
11. (2) 12. (3) 13. (5) 14. (1) 15. (7) 16. (9) 17. (4) 18. (10) 19. (6) 20. (8)

PRACTICE SET-1

Total Ques.- 40
Time - 5 or 8 Min.

निर्देश : (प्रश्न 1-40) इस अभ्यास में 40 प्रश्न दिए गए हैं जो चार उपखंडों 1, 2, 3 एवं 4 में 10-10 प्रश्नों (कुल 40 प्रश्न) के रूप में विभाजित है। प्रत्येक खण्ड के चित्रों को ध्यानपूर्वक देखकर दिए गए प्रत्येक प्रश्नों का उत्तर खोजकर अपने उत्तर-पत्रक में अंकित गोले को काला करें या माउस की सहायता से क्लिक करें और इसके लिए 5 या 8 मिनट का समय दिया जाता है।

Instructions: (Questions 1-40) : This exercise contains 40 questions, divided into four subsections: 1, 2, 3, and 4, each containing 10 questions (40 questions in total). Look carefully at the pictures in each section to find the answer to each question. Darken the circle on your answer sheet or click on it with the mouse. You are given 5 or 8 minutes for this.

उपखंड/Section-1

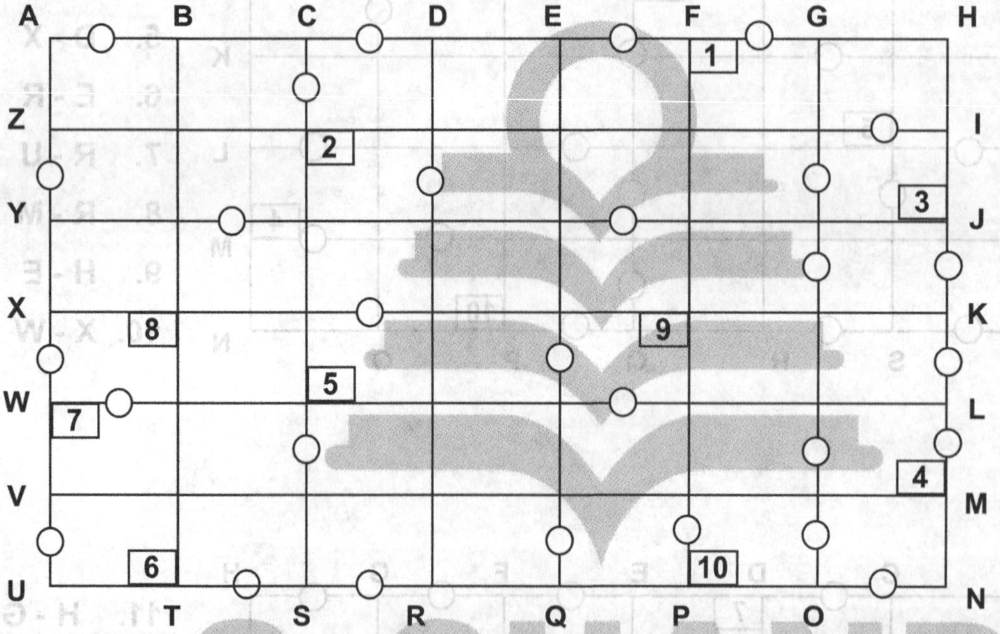

1. K - I
2. Q - U
3. Z - H
4. I - F
5. Q - W
6. G - J
7. B - V
8. K - L
9. S - M
10. R - O

उपखंड/Section-2

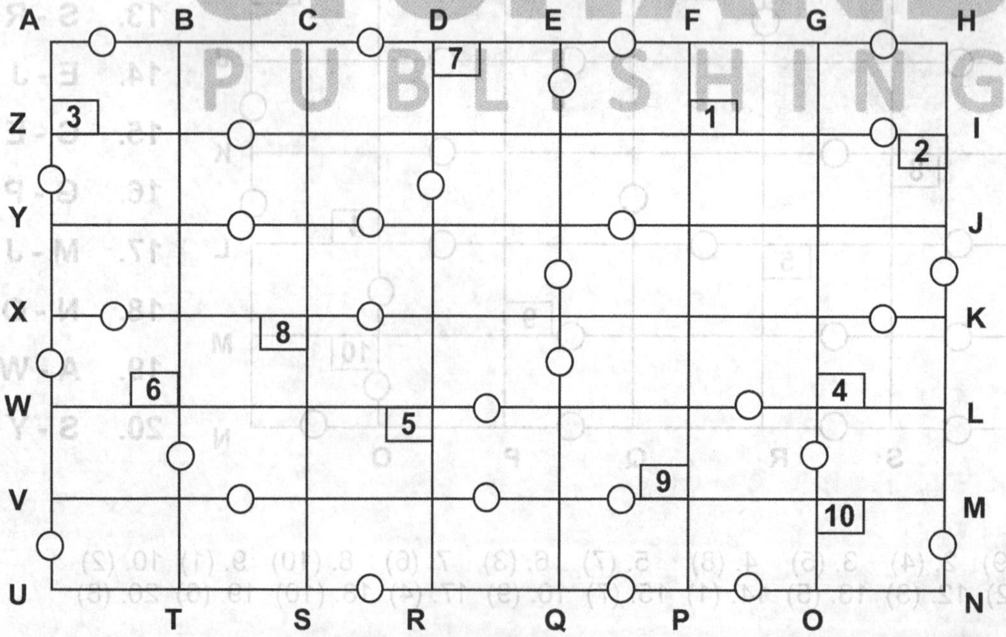

11. G - H
12. C - S
13. B - E
14. G - M
15. B - V
16. J - C
17. P - L
18. R - P
19. C - A
20. X - A

उपखंड/Section-3

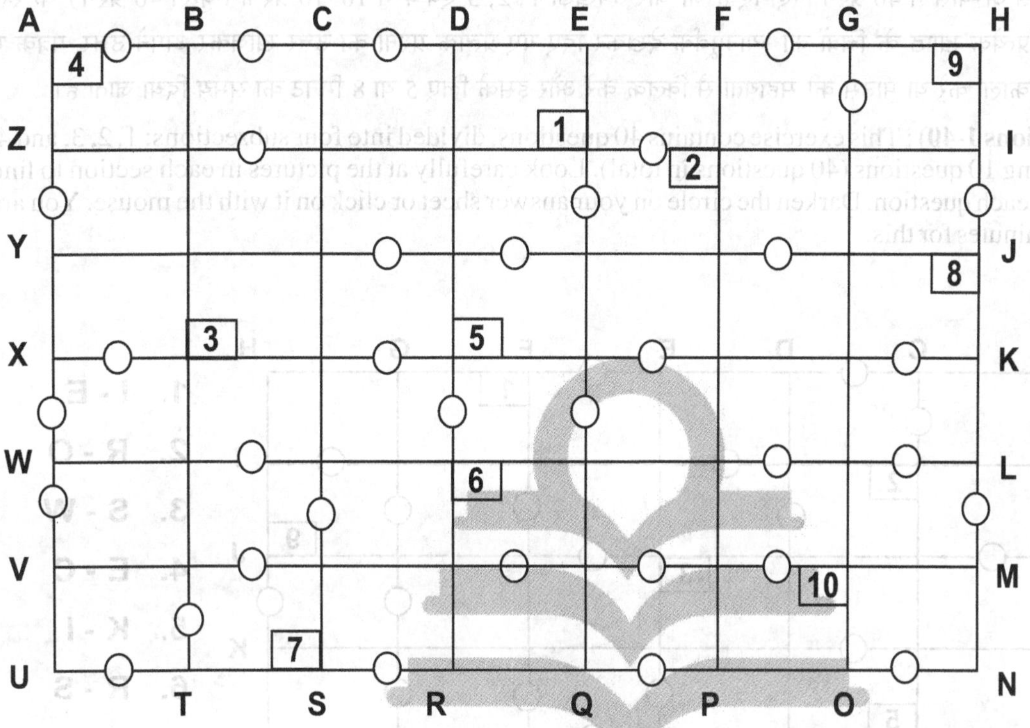

21. T - Q
22. N - Q
23. R - C
24. L - M
25. P - F
26. B - F
27. X - U
28. O - Q
29. D - A
30. F - H

उपखंड/Section-4

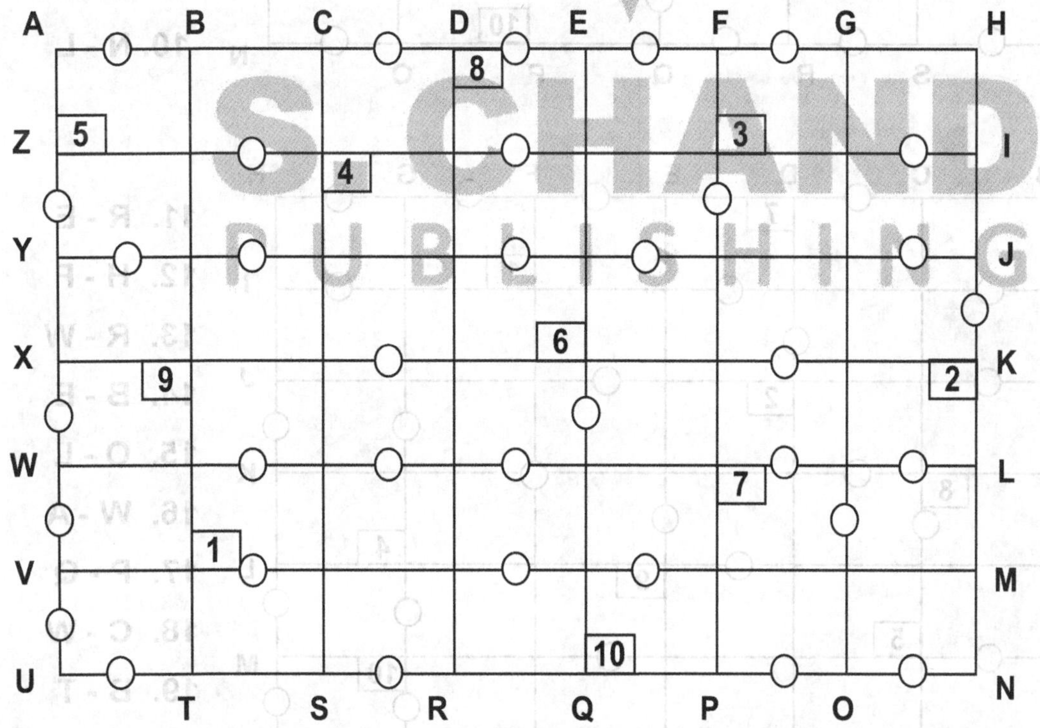

31. J - L
32. B - Y
33. E - R
34. R - C
35. P - G
36. P - G
37. R - D
38. I - E
39. S - C
40. N - R

PRACTICE SET-2

Total Ques.- 40
Time - 5 or 8 Min.

निर्देश : (प्रश्न 1-40) इस अभ्यास में 40 प्रश्न दिए गए हैं जो चार उपखंडों 1, 2, 3 एवं 4 में 10-10 प्रश्नों (कुल 40 प्रश्न) के रूप में विभाजित है। प्रत्येक खण्ड के चित्रों को ध्यानपूर्वक देखकर दिए गए प्रत्येक प्रश्नों का उत्तर खोजकर अपने उत्तर-पत्रक में अंकित गोले को काला करें या माउस की सहायता से क्लिक करें और इसके लिए 5 या 8 मिनट का समय दिया जाता है।

Instructions: (Questions 1-40) : This exercise contains 40 questions, divided into four subsections: 1, 2, 3, and 4, each containing 10 questions (40 questions in total). Look carefully at the pictures in each section to find the answer to each question. Darken the circle on your answer sheet or click on it with the mouse. You are given 5 or 8 minutes for this.

उपखंड/Section-1

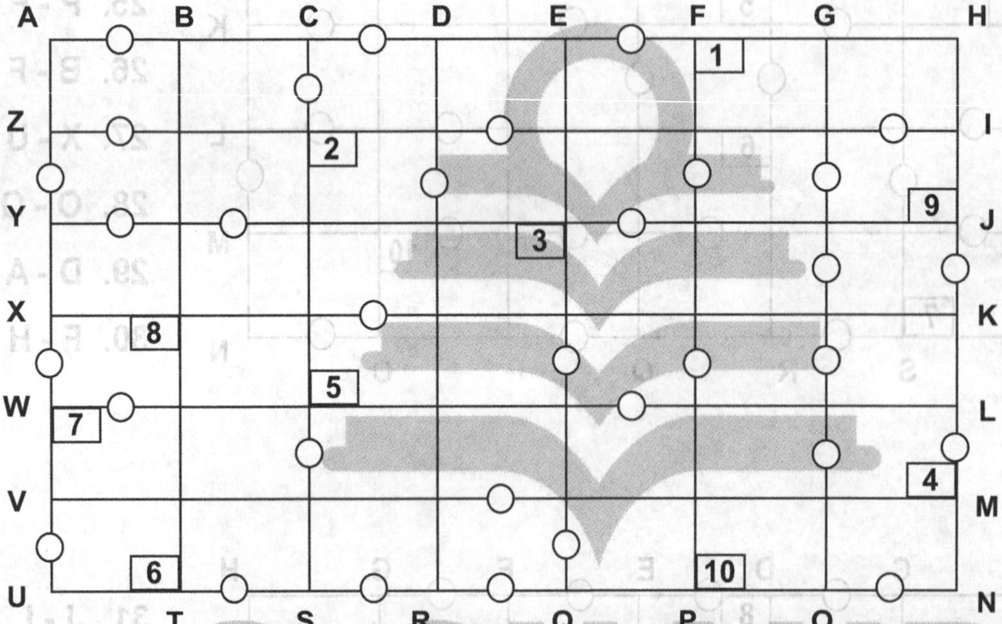

1. I - E
2. R - O
3. S - W
4. E - C
5. K - I
6. R - S
7. R - U
8. E - R
9. B - X
10. N - L

उपखंड/Section-2

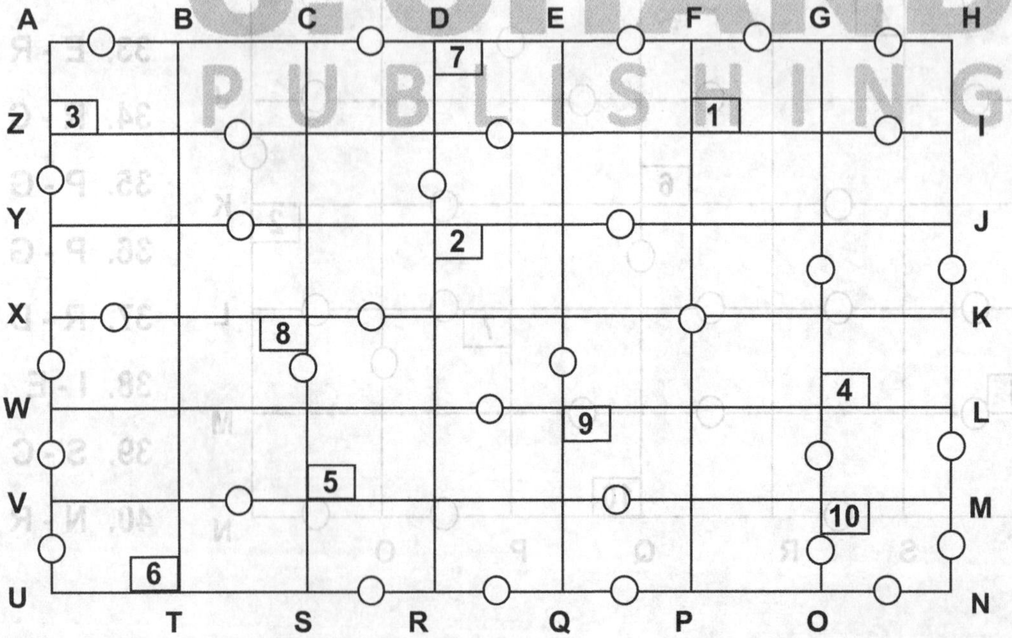

11. R - E
12. H - F
13. R - W
14. B - E
15. O - L
16. W - A
17. P - Q
18. C - W
19. B - T
20. O - M

उपखंड/Section-3

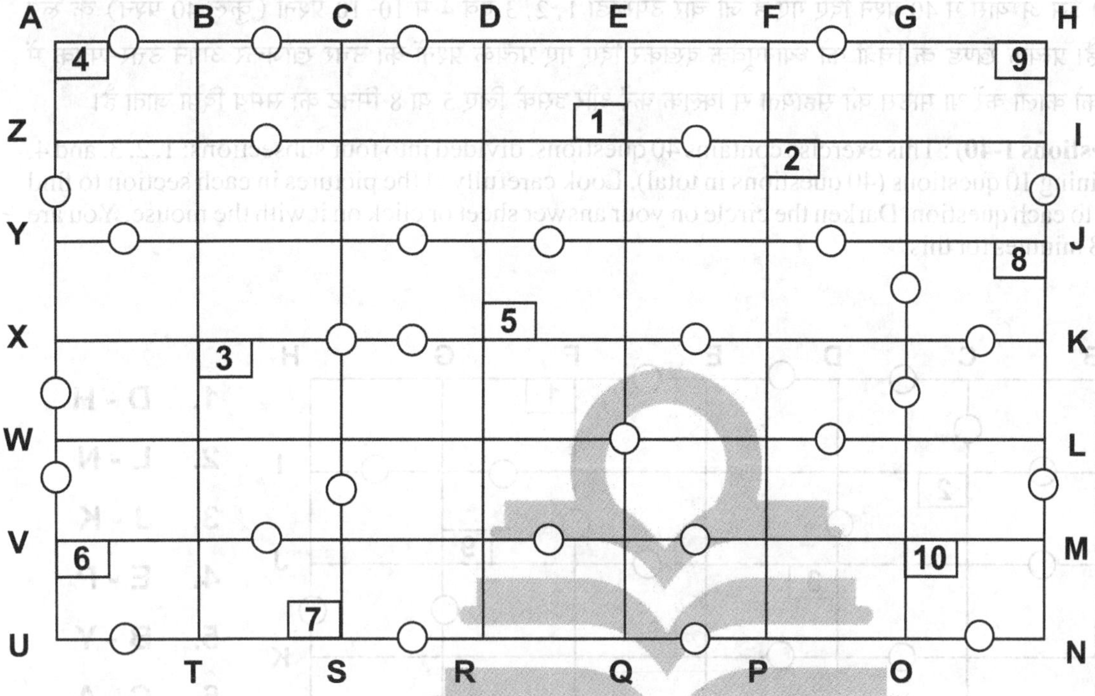

21. C - F
22. W - U
23. L - I
24. D - A
25. Q - T
26. D - Q
27. X - A
28. P - F
29. B - T
30. N - K

उपखंड/Section-4

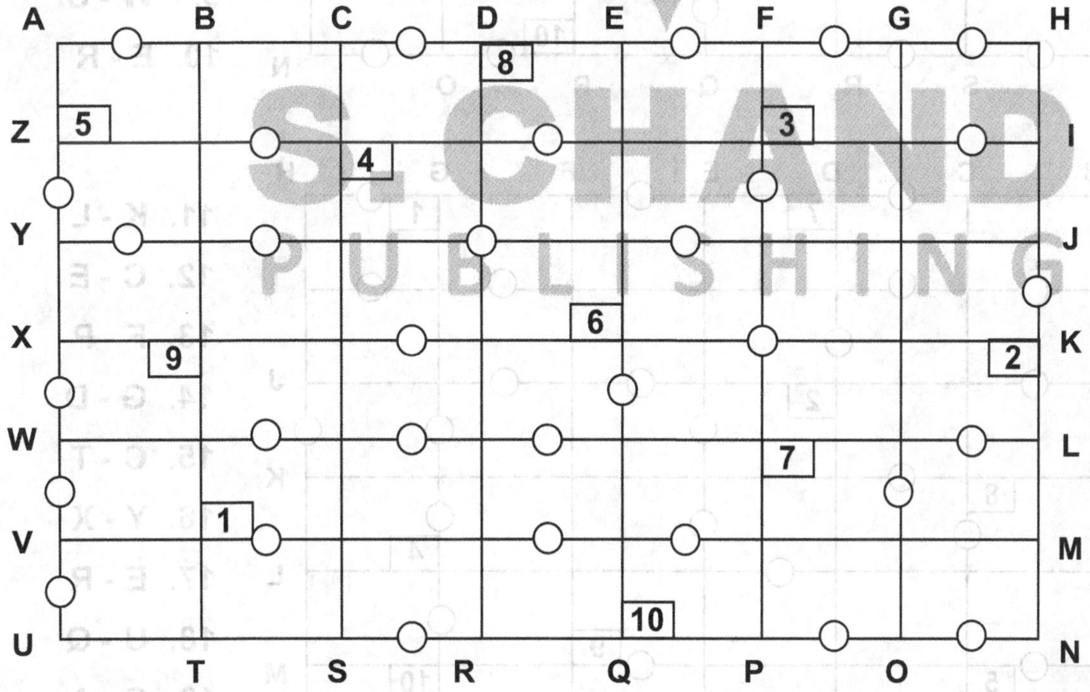

31. E - R
32. B - Y
33. E - J
34. O - R
35. P - G
36. C - S
37. M - R
38. W - U
39. C - A
40. N - J

PRACTICE SET-3

Total Ques.- 40
Time - 5 or 8 Min.

निर्देश : (प्रश्न 1-40) इस अभ्यास में 40 प्रश्न दिए गए हैं जो चार उपखंडों 1, 2, 3 एवं 4 में 10-10 प्रश्नों (कुल 40 प्रश्न) के रूप में विभाजित है। प्रत्येक खण्ड के चित्रों को ध्यानपूर्वक देखकर दिए गए प्रत्येक प्रश्नों का उत्तर खोजकर अपने उत्तर-पत्रक में अंकित गोले को काला करें या माउस की सहायता से क्लिक करें और इसके लिए 5 या 8 मिनट का समय दिया जाता है।

Instructions: (Questions 1-40) : This exercise contains 40 questions, divided into four subsections: 1, 2, 3, and 4, each containing 10 questions (40 questions in total). Look carefully at the pictures in each section to find the answer to each question. Darken the circle on your answer sheet or click on it with the mouse. You are given 5 or 8 minutes for this.

उपखंड/Section-1

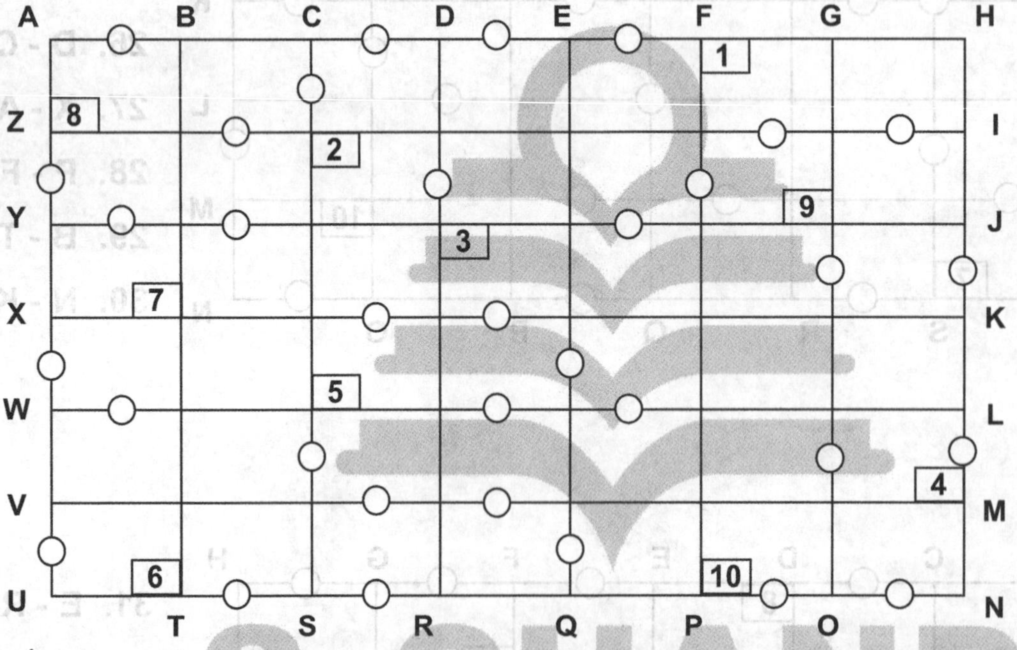

1. D - H
2. L - N
3. J - K
4. E - P
5. B - Y
6. C - A
7. I - E
8. R - S
9. W - U
10. E - R

उपखंड/Section-2

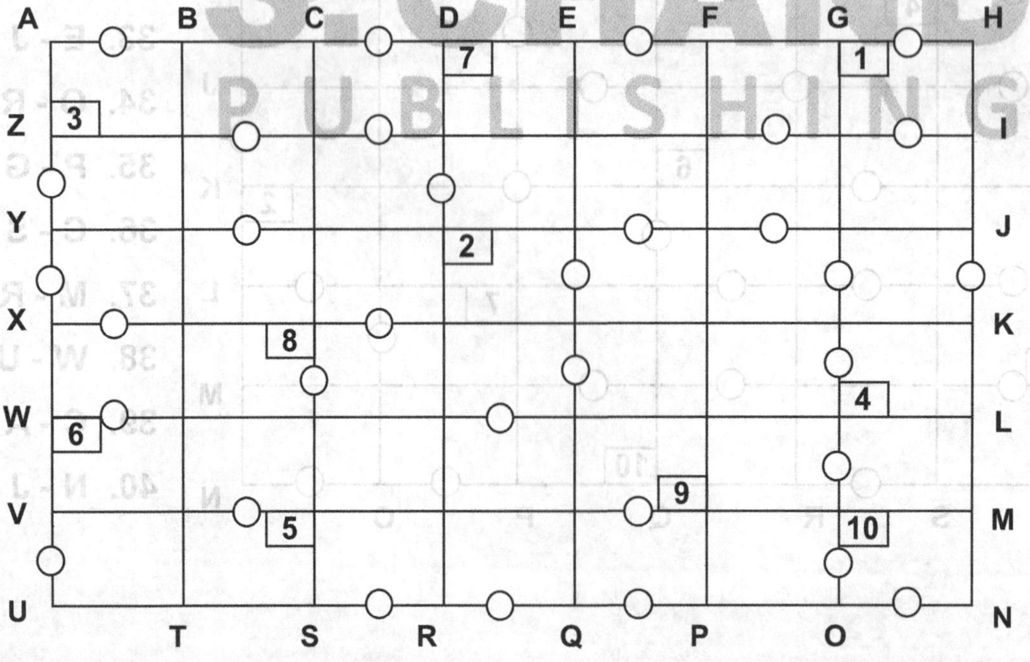

11. K - L
12. C - E
13. F - P
14. G - D
15. C - T
16. Y - X
17. E - R
18. U - Q
19. C - A
20. P - N

उपखंड/Section-3

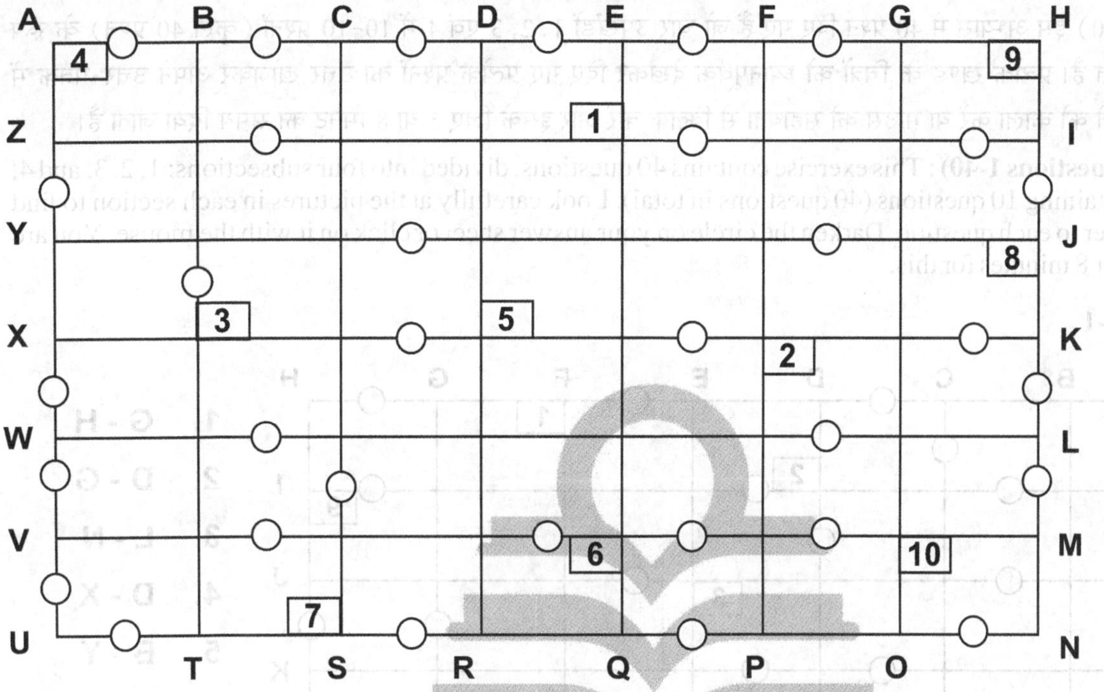

21. L - I
22. F - P
23. P - Q
24. X - S
25. K - L
26. X - A
27. C - E
28. D - R
29. P - N
30. C - X

उपखंड/Section-4

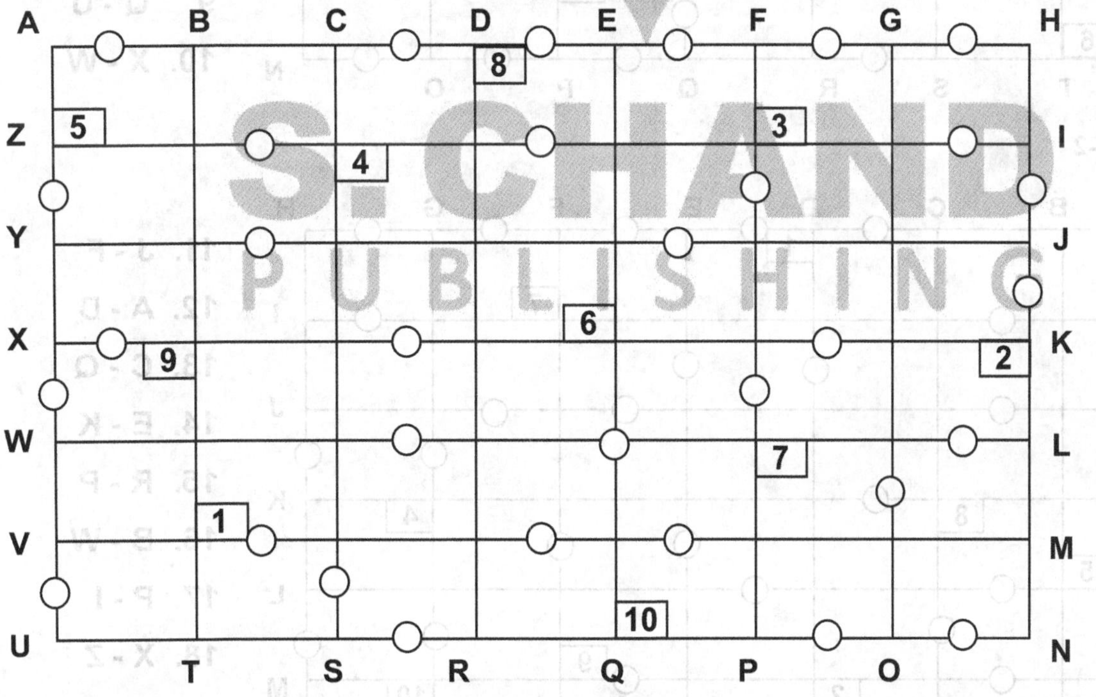

31. E - D
32. C - B
33. X - A
34. P - J
35. R - D
36. E - R
37. J - N
38. J - F
39. R - M
40. R - S

PRACTICE SET-4

Total Ques.- 40
Time - 5 or 8 Min.

निर्देश : (प्रश्न 1-40) इस अभ्यास में 40 प्रश्न दिए गए हैं जो चार उपखंडों 1, 2, 3 एवं 4 में 10-10 प्रश्नों (कुल 40 प्रश्न) के रूप में विभाजित है। प्रत्येक खण्ड के चित्रों को ध्यानपूर्वक देखकर दिए गए प्रत्येक प्रश्नों का उत्तर खोजकर अपने उत्तर-पत्रक में अंकित गोले को काला करें या माउस की सहायता से क्लिक करें और इसके लिए 5 या 8 मिनट का समय दिया जाता है।

Instructions: (Questions 1-40) : This exercise contains 40 questions, divided into four subsections: 1, 2, 3, and 4, each containing 10 questions (40 questions in total). Look carefully at the pictures in each section to find the answer to each question. Darken the circle on your answer sheet or click on it with the mouse. You are given 5 or 8 minutes for this.

उपखंड/Section-1

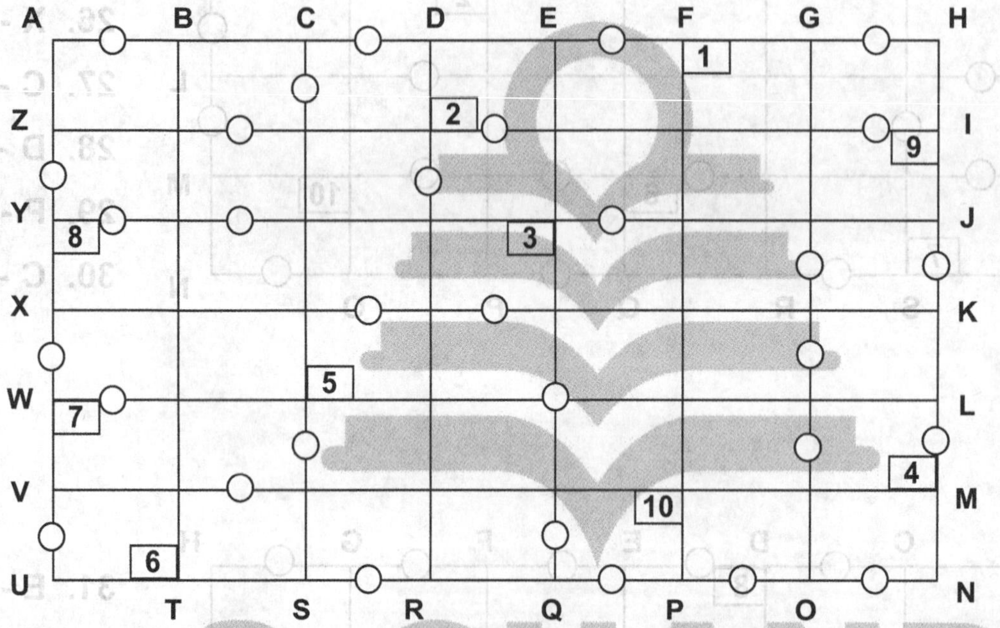

1. G - H
2. D - G
3. L - N
4. D - X
5. B - Y
6. E - R
7. R - O
8. B - T
9. Q - U
10. X - W

उपखंड/Section-2

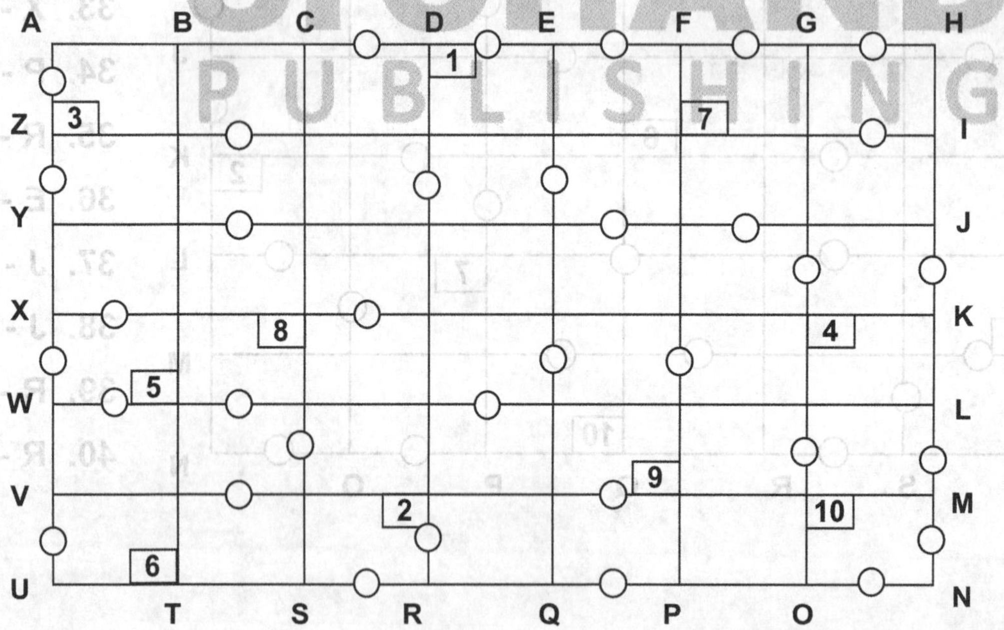

11. J - F
12. A - D
13. C - Q
14. E - K
15. R - P
16. B - W
17. P - L
18. X - Z
19. P - M
20. Q -T

उपखंड/Section-3

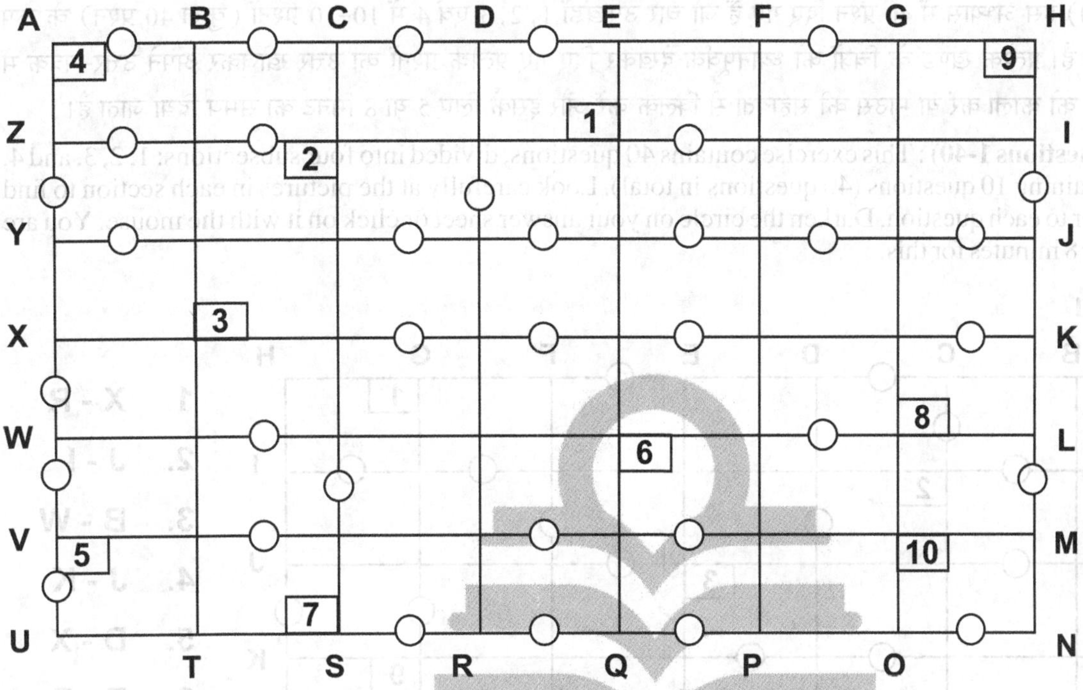

21. J - I
22. E - R
23. B - T
24. Y - V
25. B - D
26. E - I
27. R - U
28. F - Q
29. R - E
30. P - N

उपखंड/Section-4

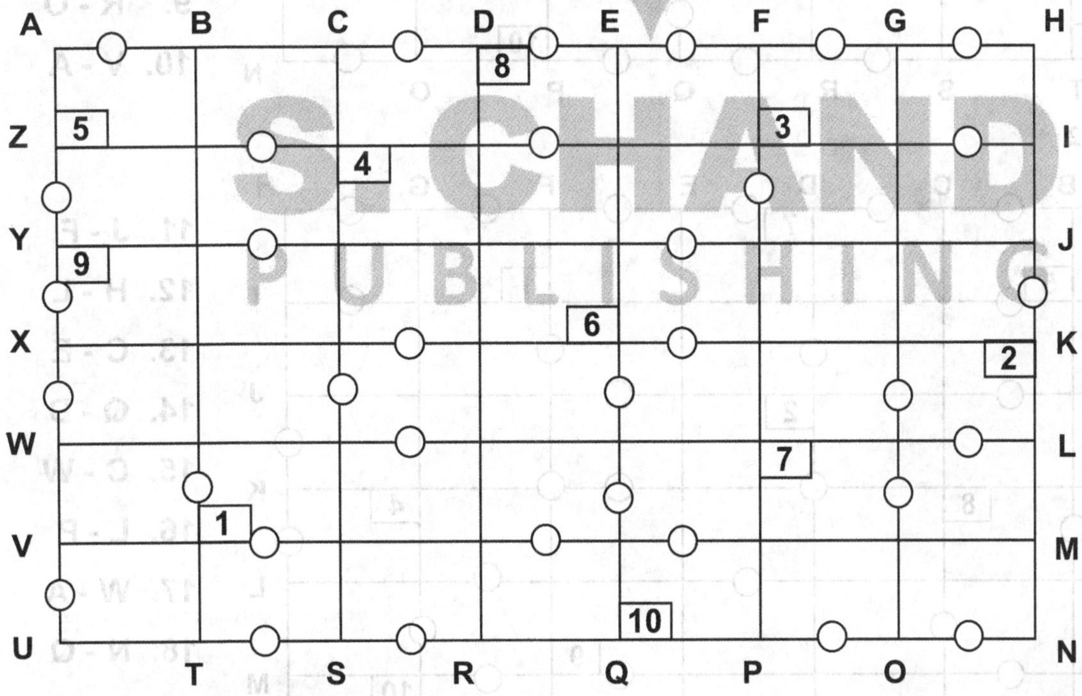

31. H - L
32. C - A
33. T - Y
34. C - X
35. E - R
36. O - J
37. R - D
38. P - J
39. N - Q
40. E - J

PRACTICE SET-5

Total Ques.- 40
Time - 5 or 8 Min.

निर्देश : (प्रश्न 1–40) इस अभ्यास में 40 प्रश्न दिए गए हैं जो चार उपखंडों 1, 2, 3 एवं 4 में 10–10 प्रश्नों (कुल 40 प्रश्न) के रूप में विभाजित है। प्रत्येक खण्ड के चित्रों को ध्यानपूर्वक देखकर दिए गए प्रत्येक प्रश्नों का उत्तर खोजकर अपने उत्तर-पत्रक में अंकित गोले को काला करें या माउस की सहायता से क्लिक करें और इसके लिए 5 या 8 मिनट का समय दिया जाता है।

Instructions: (Questions 1-40) : This exercise contains 40 questions, divided into four subsections: 1, 2, 3, and 4, each containing 10 questions (40 questions in total). Look carefully at the pictures in each section to find the answer to each question. Darken the circle on your answer sheet or click on it with the mouse. You are given 5 or 8 minutes for this.

उपखंड/Section-1

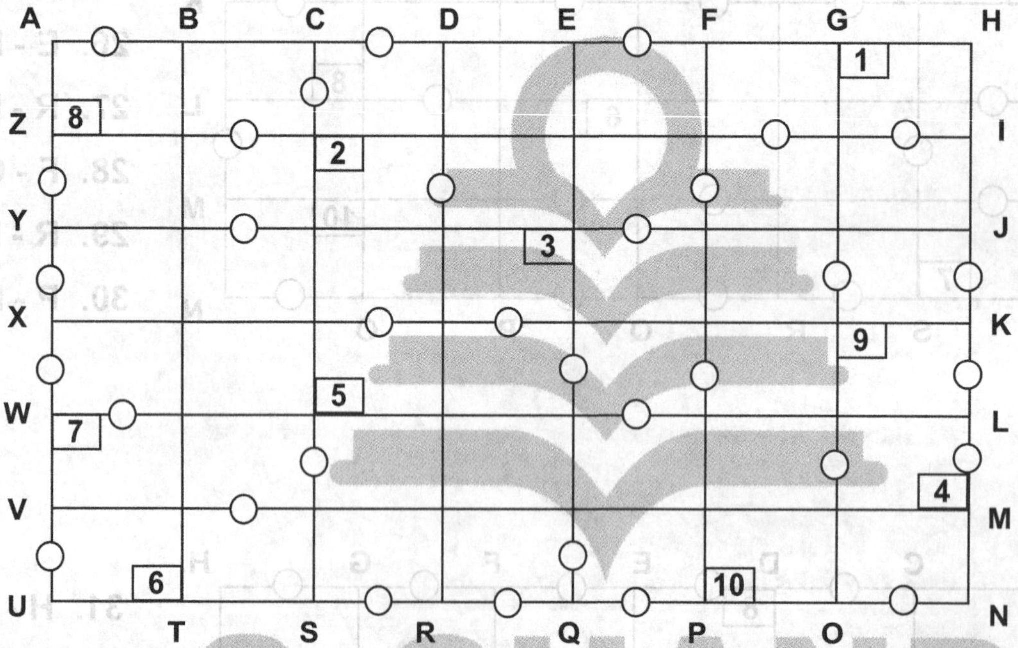

1. X - R
2. J - I
3. B - W
4. J - K
5. D - X
6. E - R
7. L - N
8. R - U
9. R - O
10. V - A

उपखंड/Section-2

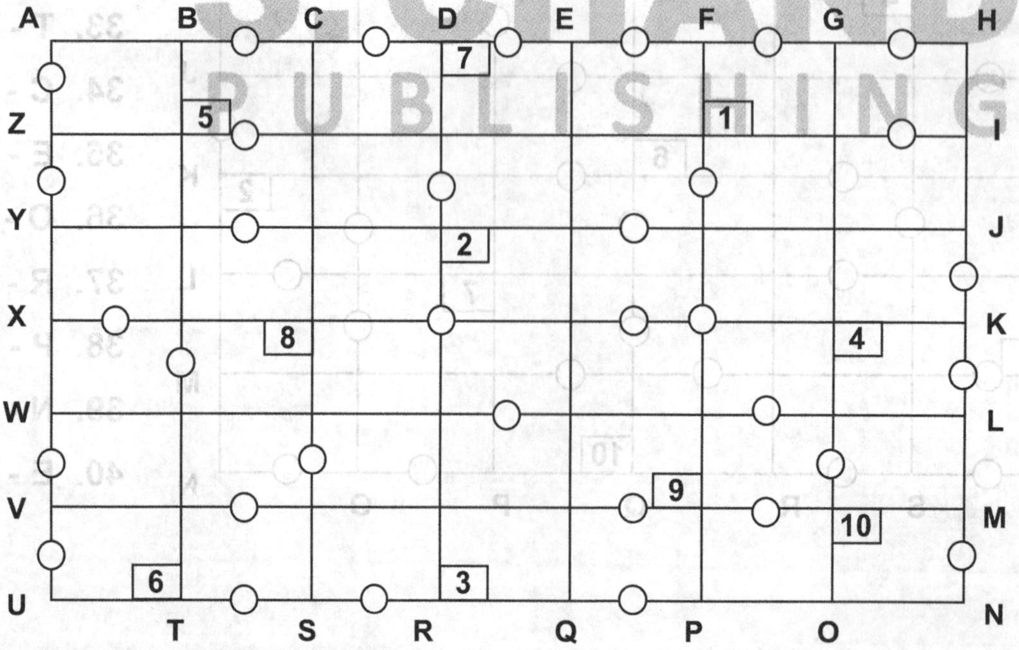

11. J - F
12. H - L
13. C - E
14. Q - D
15. C - W
16. L - P
17. W - A
18. N - Q
19. Y - U
20. Q - W

उपखंड/Section-3

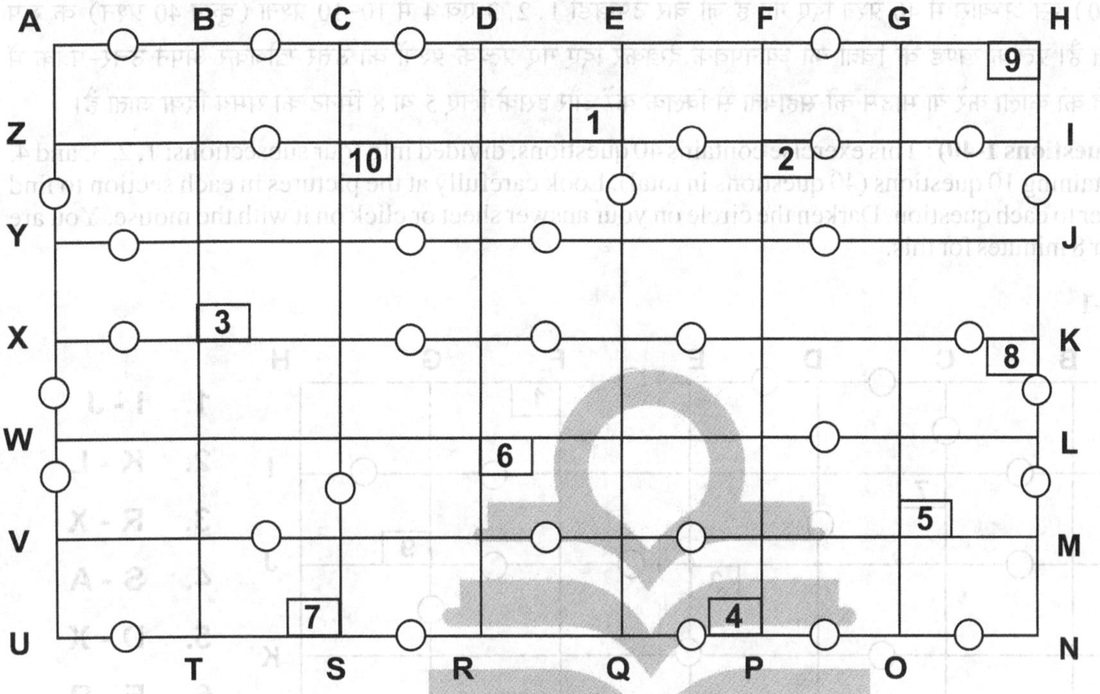

21. J - I
22. B - T
23. F - O
24. D - F
25. L - K
26. B - D
27. K - N
28. U - R
29. Q - P
30. D - R

उपखंड/Section-4

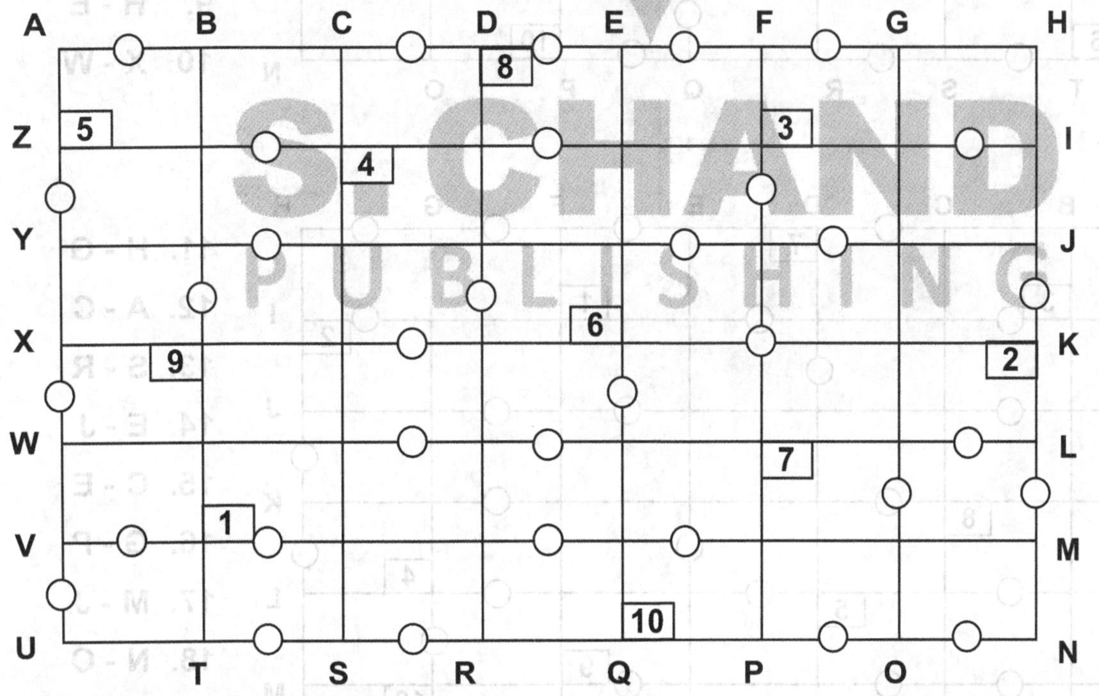

31. E - I
32. P - J
33. E - D
34. C - S
35. V - Y
36. H - L
37. N - R
38. U - S
39. X - A
40. E - R

PRACTICE SET-6

Total Ques.- 40
Time - 5 or 8 Min.

निर्देश : (प्रश्न 1-40) इस अभ्यास में 40 प्रश्न दिए गए हैं जो चार उपखंडों 1, 2, 3 एवं 4 में 10-10 प्रश्नों (कुल 40 प्रश्न) के रूप में विभाजित है। प्रत्येक खण्ड के चित्रों को ध्यानपूर्वक देखकर दिए गए प्रत्येक प्रश्नों का उत्तर खोजकर अपने उत्तर-पत्रक में अंकित गोले को काला करें या माउस की सहायता से क्लिक करें और इसके लिए 5 या 8 मिनट का समय दिया जाता है।

Instructions: (Questions 1-40) : This exercise contains 40 questions, divided into four subsections: 1, 2, 3, and 4, each containing 10 questions (40 questions in total). Look carefully at the pictures in each section to find the answer to each question. Darken the circle on your answer sheet or click on it with the mouse. You are given 5 or 8 minutes for this.

उपखंड/Section-1

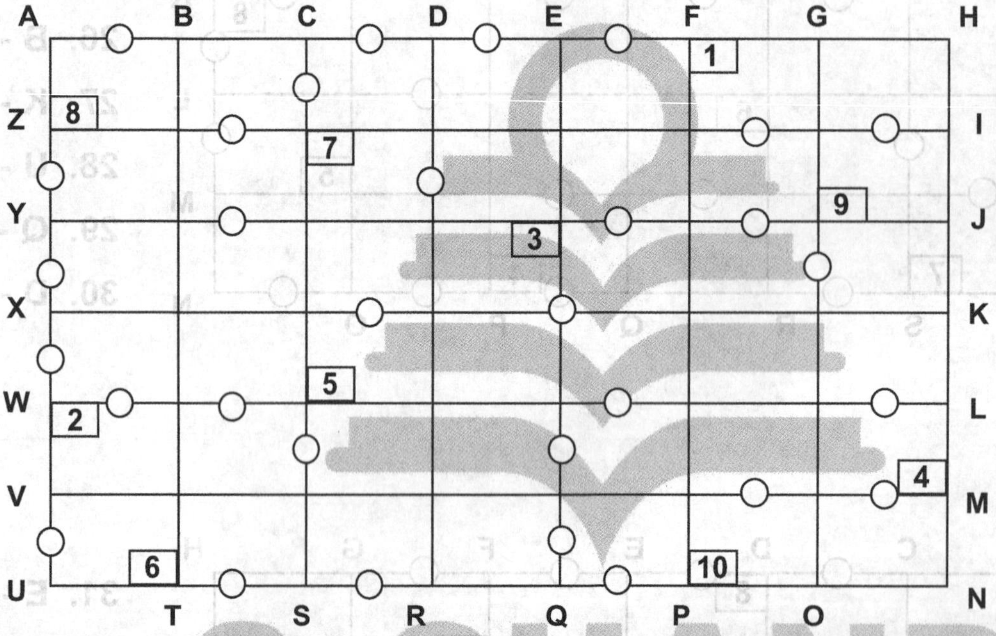

1. I - J
2. K - L
3. R - X
4. S - A
5. D - X
6. E - R
7. R - U
8. R - M
9. H - E
10. X - W

उपखंड/Section-2

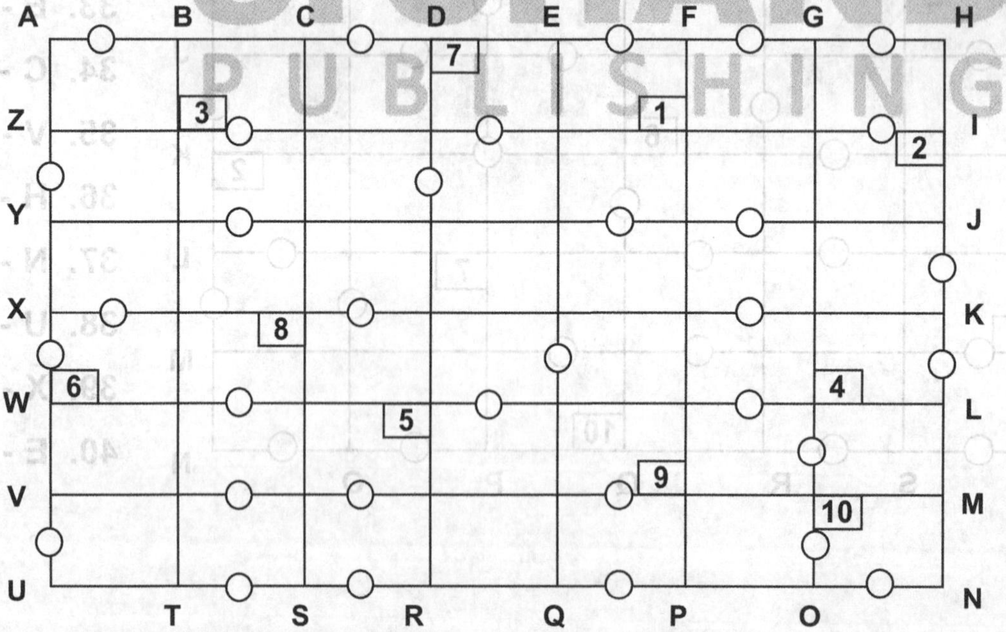

11. H - G
12. A - C
13. S - R
14. E - J
15. C - E
16. G - P
17. M - J
18. N - O
19. A - W
20. S - Y

उपखंड/Section-3

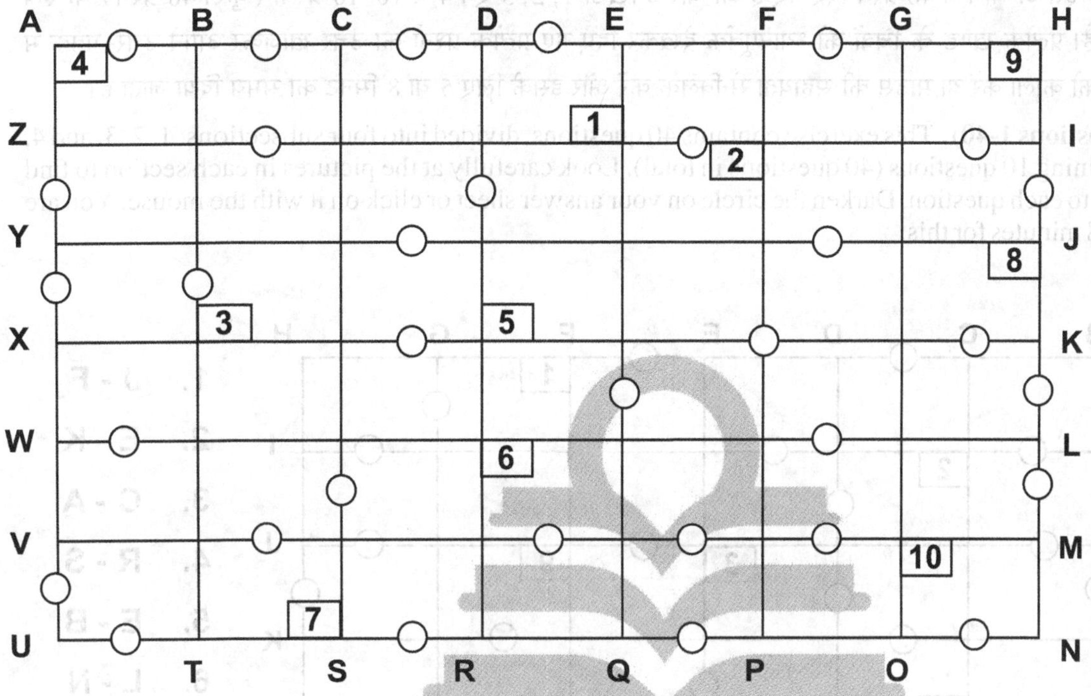

21. D - G
22. F - K
23. I - F
24. C - R
25. C - X
26. G - N
27. P - R
28. C - A
29. Q - S
30. I - F

उपखंड/Section-4

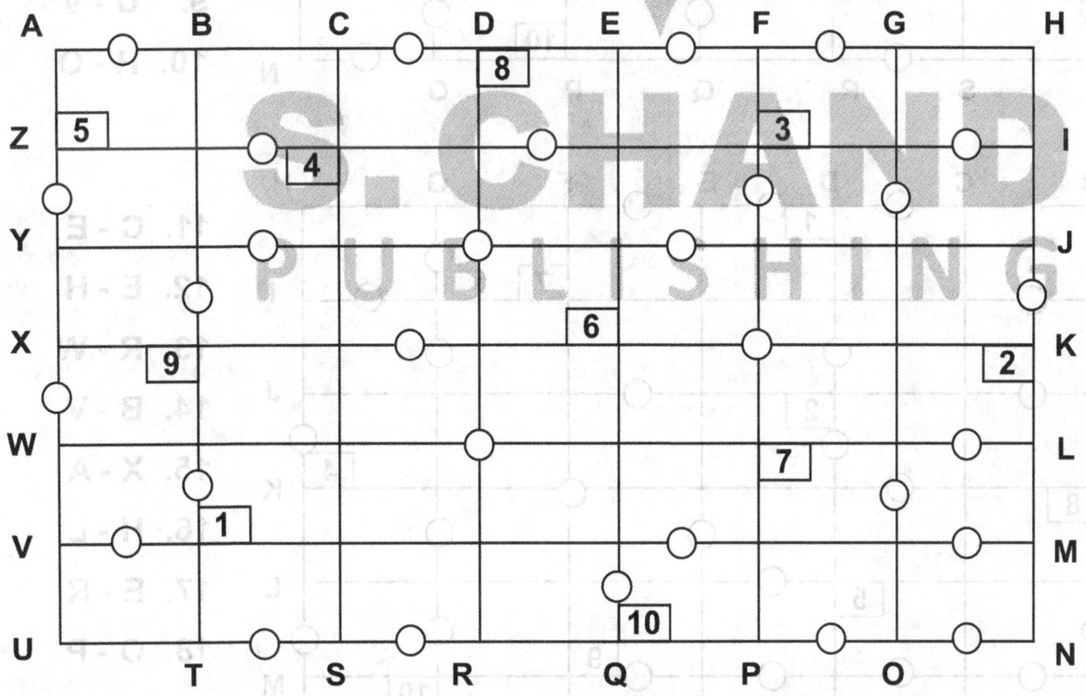

31. A - X
32. Y - U
33. N - H
34. E - I
35. S - C
36. U - R
37. R - O
38. E - B
39. P - J
40. E - R

PRACTICE SET-7

Total Ques.- 40
Time - 5 or 8 Min.

निर्देश : (प्रश्न 1–40) इस अभ्यास में 40 प्रश्न दिए गए हैं जो चार उपखंडों 1, 2, 3 एवं 4 में 10–10 प्रश्नों (कुल 40 प्रश्न) के रूप में विभाजित है। प्रत्येक खण्ड के चित्रों को ध्यानपूर्वक देखकर दिए गए प्रत्येक प्रश्नों का उत्तर खोजकर अपने उत्तर-पत्रक में अंकित गोले को काला करें या माउस की सहायता से क्लिक करें और इसके लिए 5 या 8 मिनट का समय दिया जाता है।

Instructions: (Questions 1-40) : This exercise contains 40 questions, divided into four subsections: 1, 2, 3, and 4, each containing 10 questions (40 questions in total). Look carefully at the pictures in each section to find the answer to each question. Darken the circle on your answer sheet or click on it with the mouse. You are given 5 or 8 minutes for this.

उपखंड/Section-1

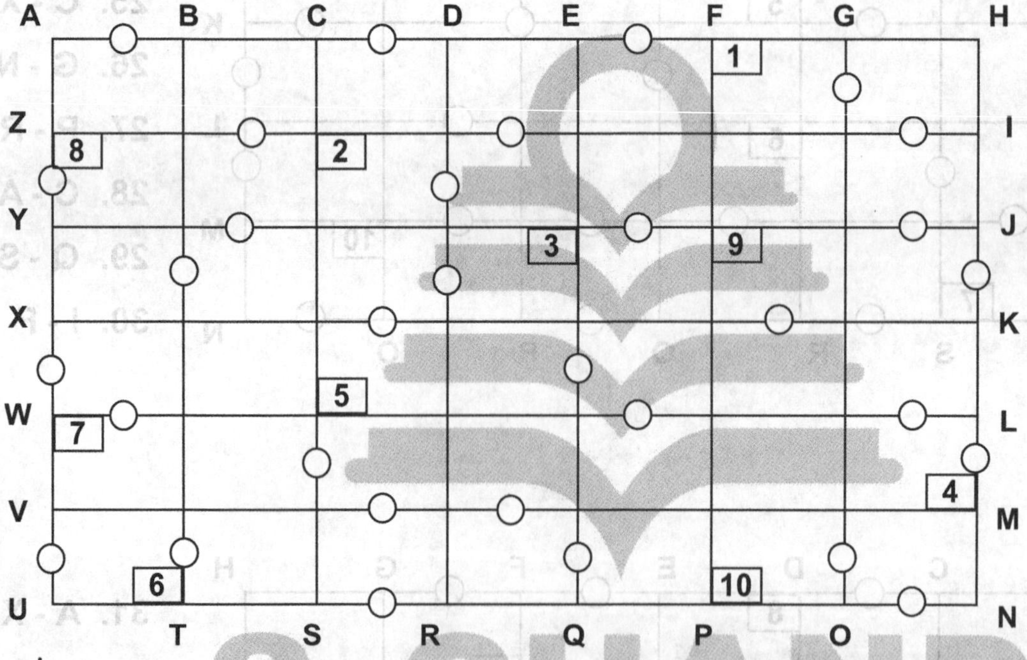

1. J - F
2. E - K
3. C - A
4. R - S
5. E - B
6. L - N
7. Y - W
8. E - R
9. U - V
10. R - O

उपखंड/Section-2

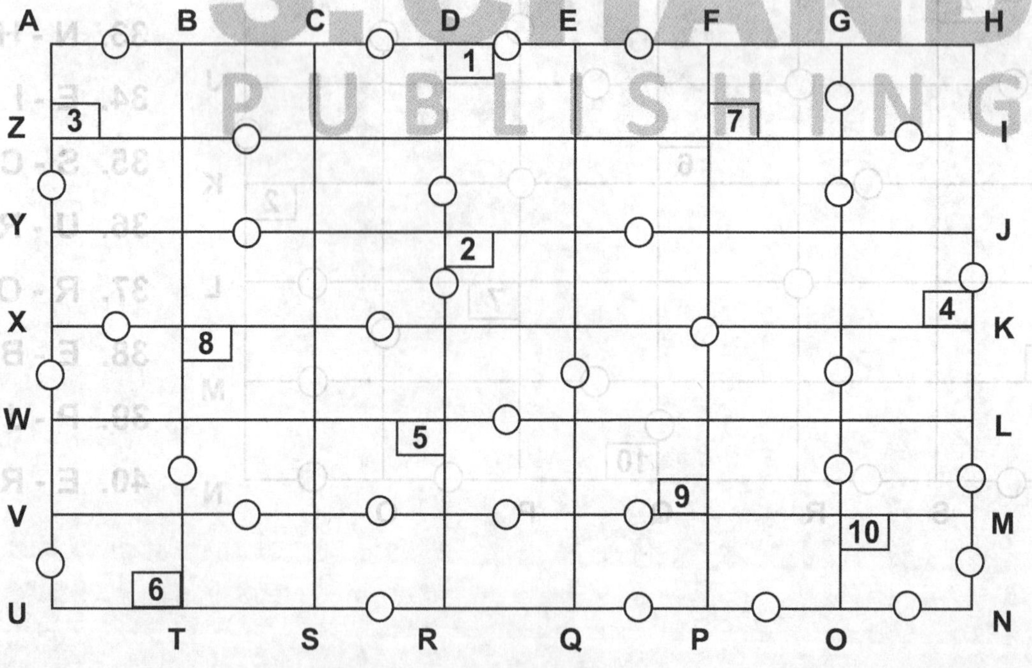

11. C - E
12. E - H
13. R - W
14. B - V
15. X - A
16. H - L
17. E - R
18. O - P
19. J - D
20. P - R

उपखंड/Section-3

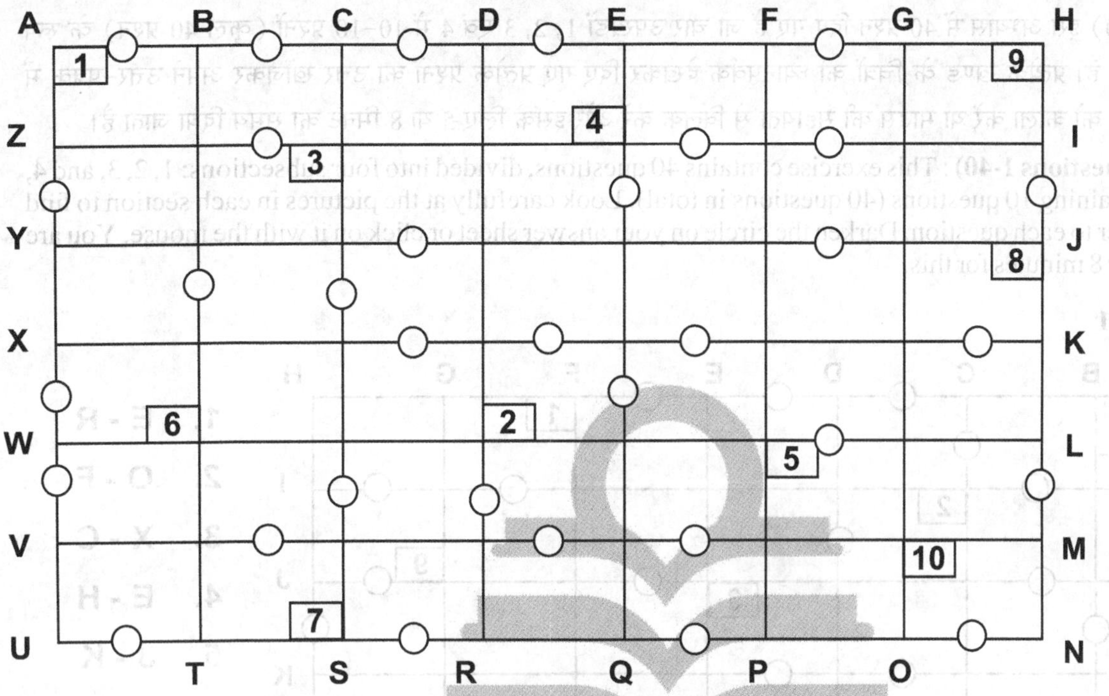

21. I - L
22. D - Q
23. F - C
24. F - J
25. D - Z
26. V - R
27. F - P
28. N - K
29. Y - U
30. X - A

उपखंड/Section-4

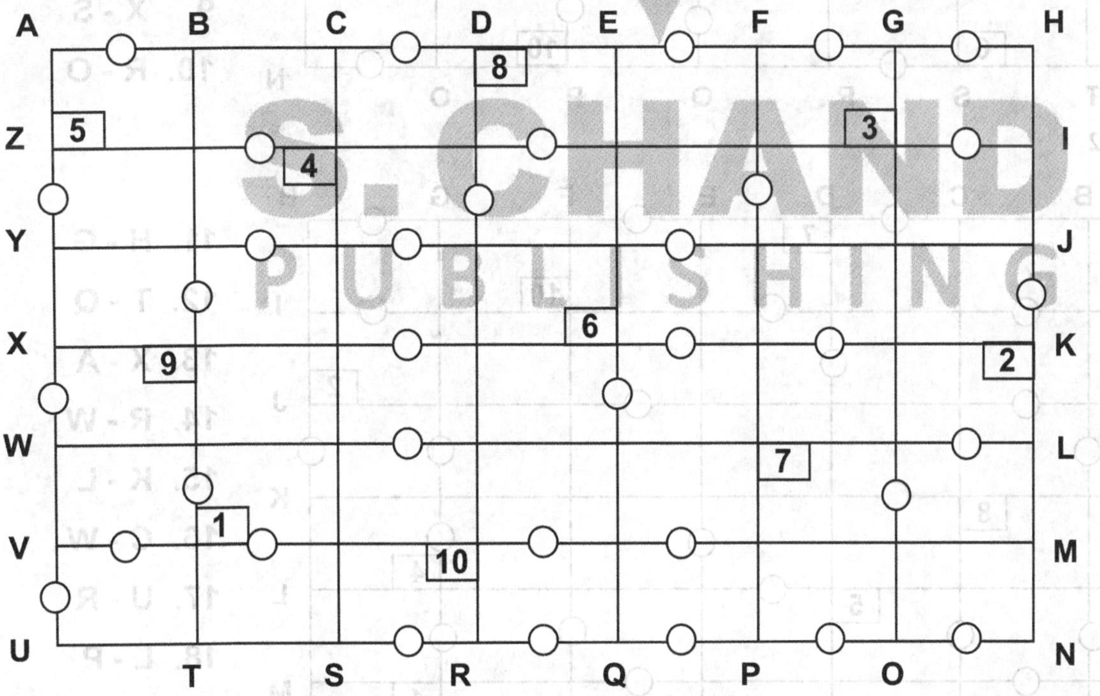

31. A - X
32. C - F
33. C - S
34. F - H
35. Y - V
36. E - Q
37. S - X
38. U - R
39. N - J
40. P - Q

PRACTICE SET-8

Total Ques.- 40
Time - 5 or 8 Min.

निर्देश : (प्रश्न 1-40) इस अभ्यास में 40 प्रश्न दिए गए हैं जो चार उपखंडों 1, 2, 3 एवं 4 में 10-10 प्रश्नों (कुल 40 प्रश्न) के रूप में विभाजित है। प्रत्येक खण्ड के चित्रों को ध्यानपूर्वक देखकर दिए गए प्रत्येक प्रश्नों का उत्तर खोजकर अपने उत्तर-पत्रक में अंकित गोले को काला करें या माउस की सहायता से क्लिक करें और इसके लिए 5 या 8 मिनट का समय दिया जाता है।

Instructions: (Questions 1-40) : This exercise contains 40 questions, divided into four subsections: 1, 2, 3, and 4, each containing 10 questions (40 questions in total). Look carefully at the pictures in each section to find the answer to each question. Darken the circle on your answer sheet or click on it with the mouse. You are given 5 or 8 minutes for this.

उपखंड/Section-1

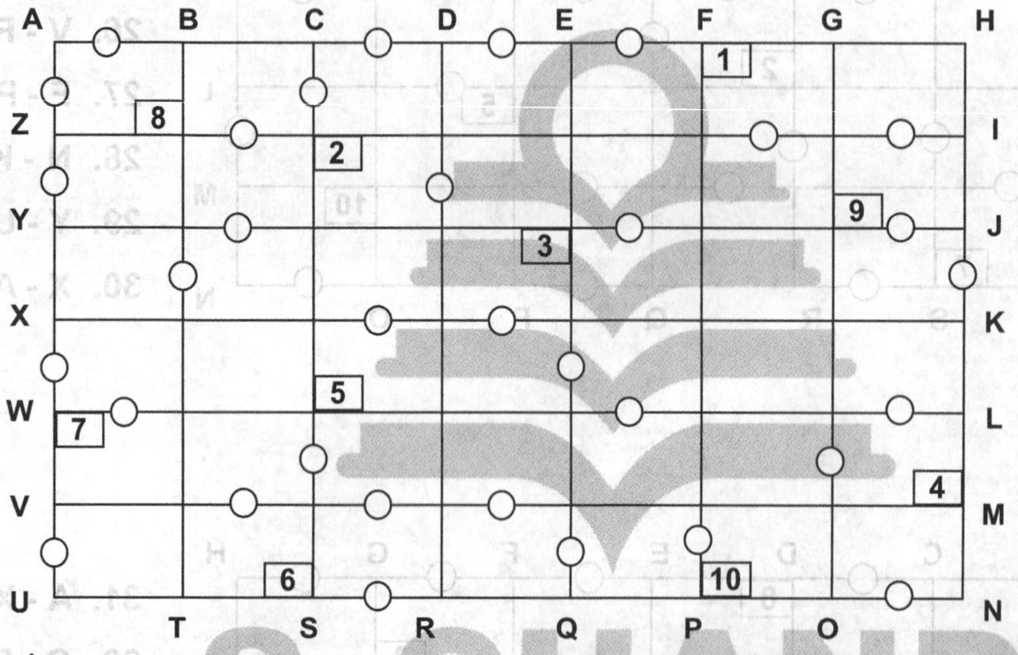

1. E - R
2. O - F
3. X - C
4. E - H
5. J - K
6. Y - W
7. R - X
8. K - O
9. X - S
10. R - O

उपखंड/Section-2

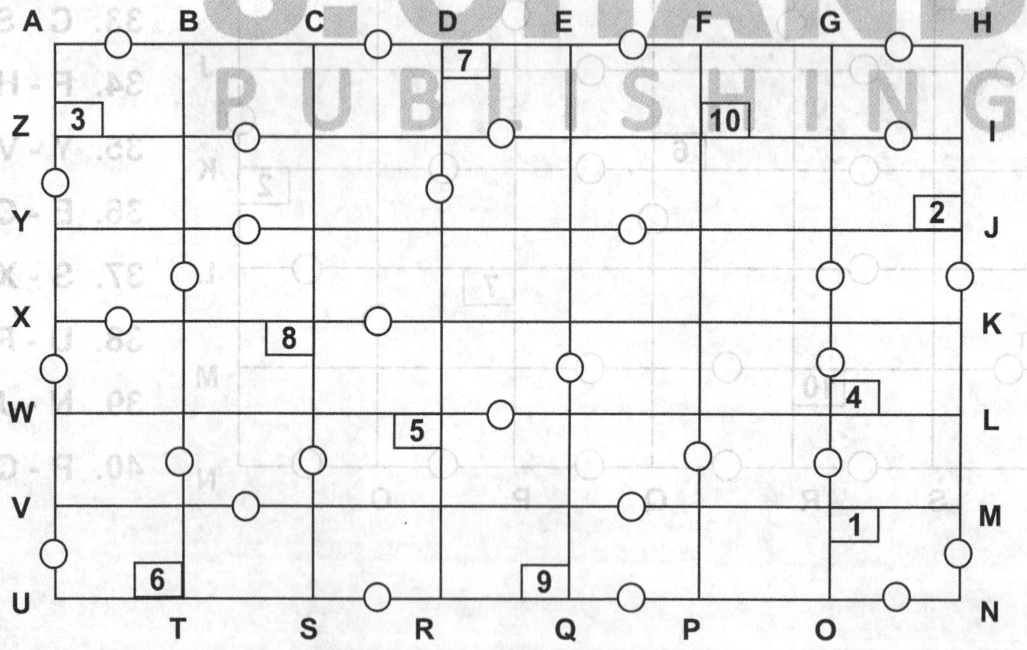

11. H - G
12. T - Q
13. X - A
14. R - W
15. K - L
16. C - W
17. U - R
18. L - P
19. B - E
20. K - F

उपखंड/Section-3

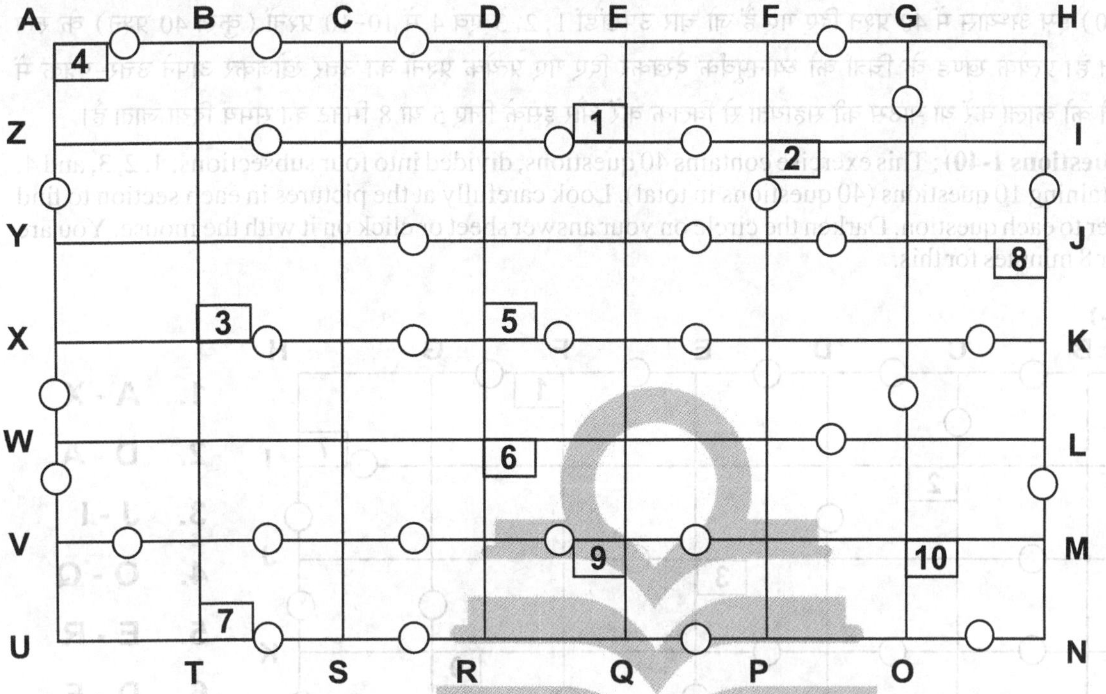

21. E - I
22. G - K
23. P - E
24. C - E
25. D - S
26. X - V
27. P - Q
28. R - S
29. N - K
30. B - W

उपखंड/Section-4

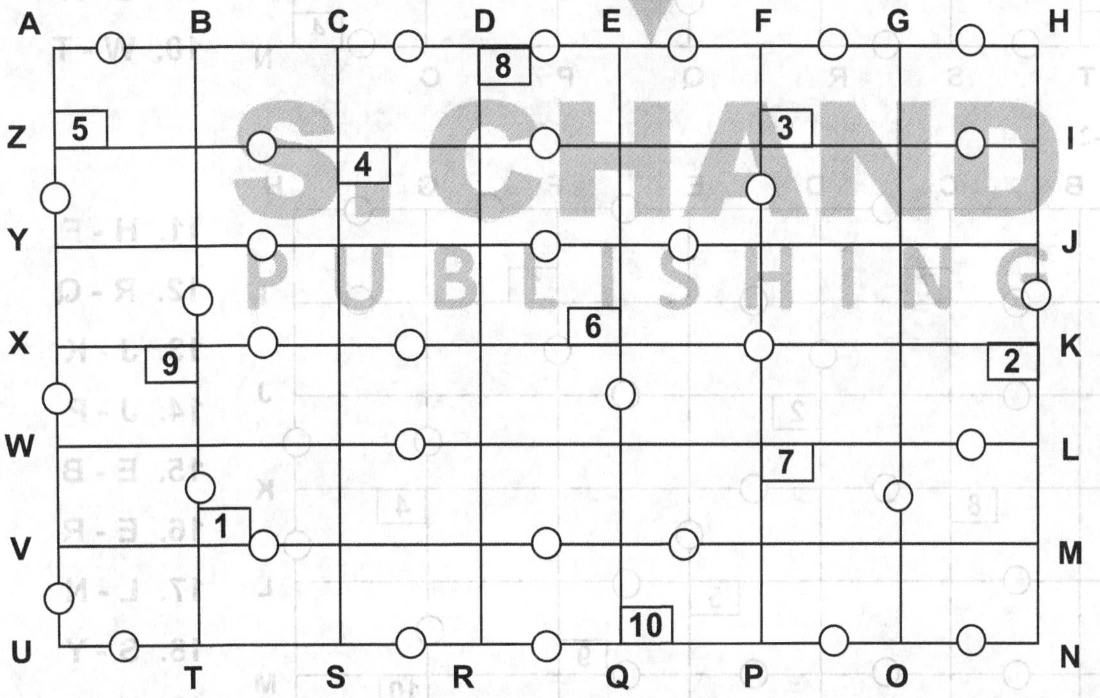

31. J - M
32. R - Q
33. E - R
34. J - F
35. R - D
36. R - X
37. P - J
38. C - S
39. N - Q
40. X - A

PRACTICE SET-9

Total Ques.- 40
Time - 5 or 8 Min.

निर्देश : (प्रश्न 1-40) इस अभ्यास में 40 प्रश्न दिए गए हैं जो चार उपखंडों 1, 2, 3 एवं 4 में 10-10 प्रश्नों (कुल 40 प्रश्न) के रूप में विभाजित है। प्रत्येक खण्ड के चित्रों को ध्यानपूर्वक देखकर दिए गए प्रत्येक प्रश्नों का उत्तर खोजकर अपने उत्तर-पत्रक में अंकित गोले को काला करें या माउस की सहायता से क्लिक करें और इसके लिए 5 या 8 मिनट का समय दिया जाता है।

Instructions: (Questions 1-40) : This exercise contains 40 questions, divided into four subsections: 1, 2, 3, and 4, each containing 10 questions (40 questions in total). Look carefully at the pictures in each section to find the answer to each question. Darken the circle on your answer sheet or click on it with the mouse. You are given 5 or 8 minutes for this.

उपखंड/Section-1

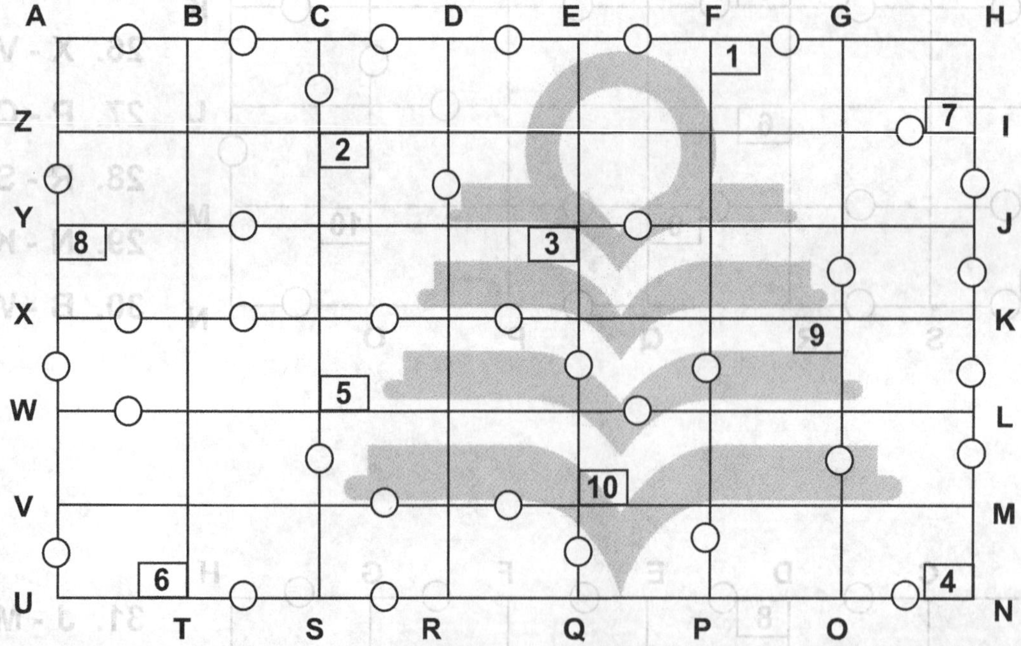

1. A - X
2. D - A
3. J - I
4. O - Q
5. E - R
6. D - F
7. K - O
8. R - S
9. L - N
10. W - T

उपखंड/Section-2

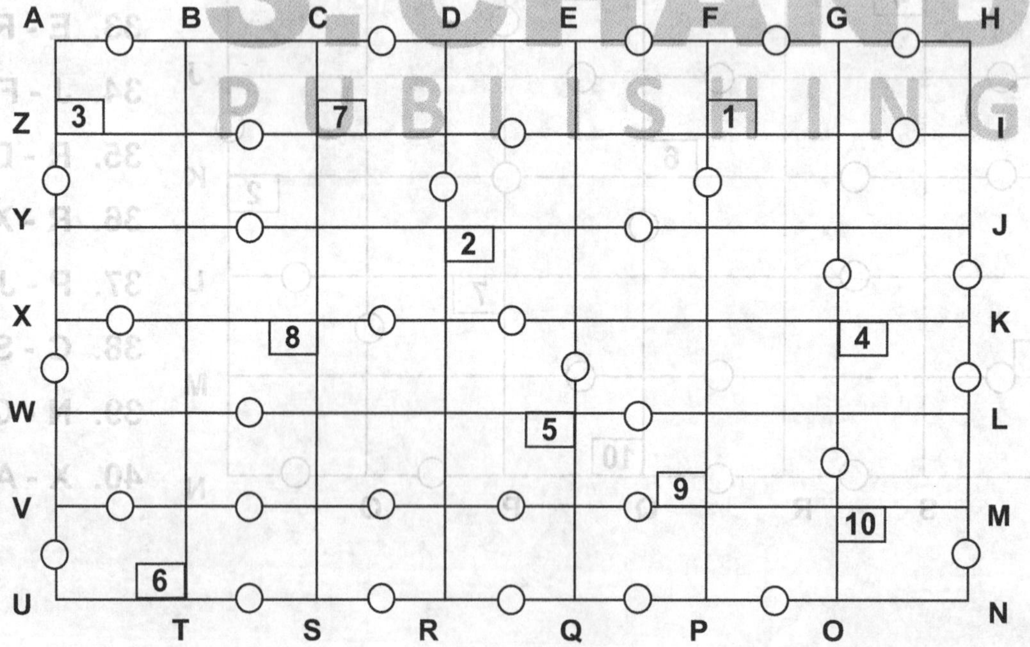

11. H - F
12. R - Q
13. J - K
14. J - P
15. E - B
16. E - R
17. L - N
18. S - Y
19. X - A
20. B - T

उपखंड/Section-3

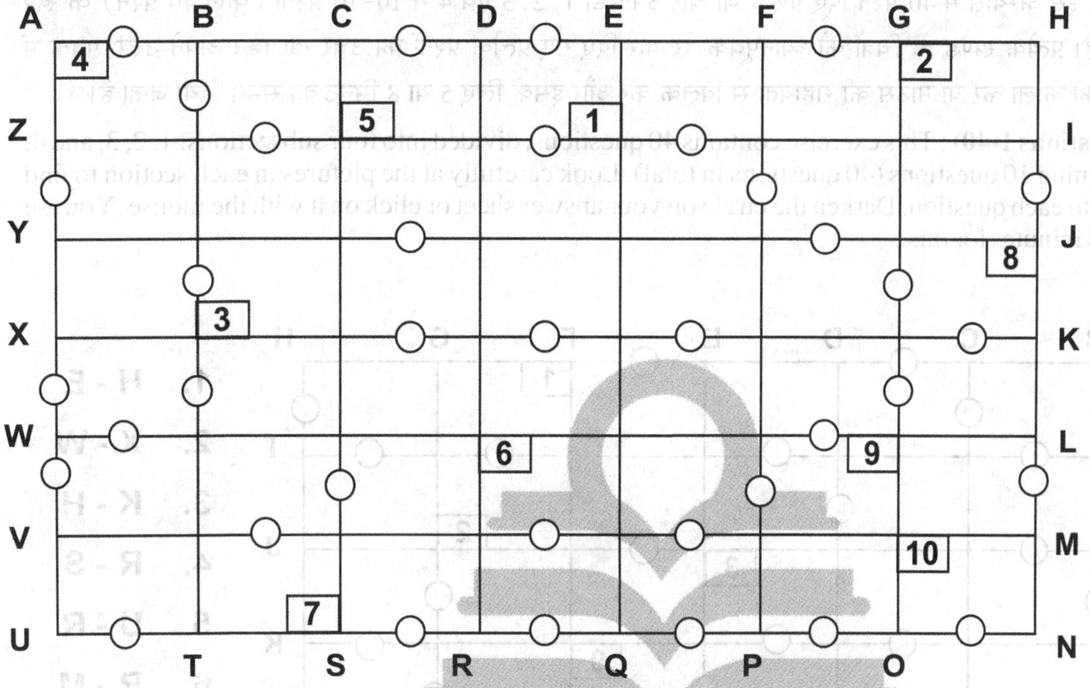

21. D - B
22. L - I
23. X - A
24. P - K
25. I - F
26. X - U
27. Q - E
28. D - Q
29. U - R
30. P - N

उपखंड/Section-4

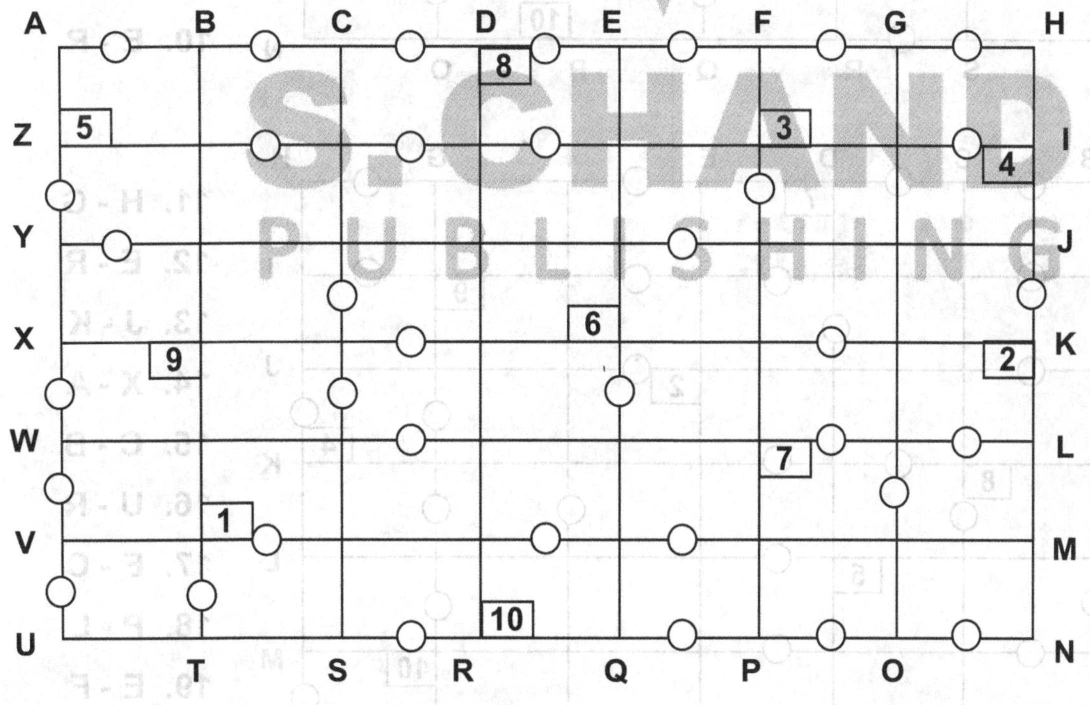

31. G - H
32. J - F
33. E - D
34. Y - W
35. G - P
36. A - C
37. N - J
38. V - S
39. P - Q
40. U - Q

PRACTICE SET-10

Total Ques.- 40
Time - 5 or 8 Min.

निर्देश : (प्रश्न 1-40) इस अभ्यास में 40 प्रश्न दिए गए हैं जो चार उपखंडों 1, 2, 3 एवं 4 में 10-10 प्रश्नों (कुल 40 प्रश्न) के रूप में विभाजित है। प्रत्येक खण्ड के चित्रों को ध्यानपूर्वक देखकर दिए गए प्रत्येक प्रश्नों का उत्तर खोजकर अपने उत्तर-पत्रक में अंकित गोले को काला करें या माउस की सहायता से क्लिक करें और इसके लिए 5 या 8 मिनट का समय दिया जाता है।

Instructions: (Questions 1-40) : This exercise contains 40 questions, divided into four subsections: 1, 2, 3, and 4, each containing 10 questions (40 questions in total). Look carefully at the pictures in each section to find the answer to each question. Darken the circle on your answer sheet or click on it with the mouse. You are given 5 or 8 minutes for this.

उपखंड/Section-1

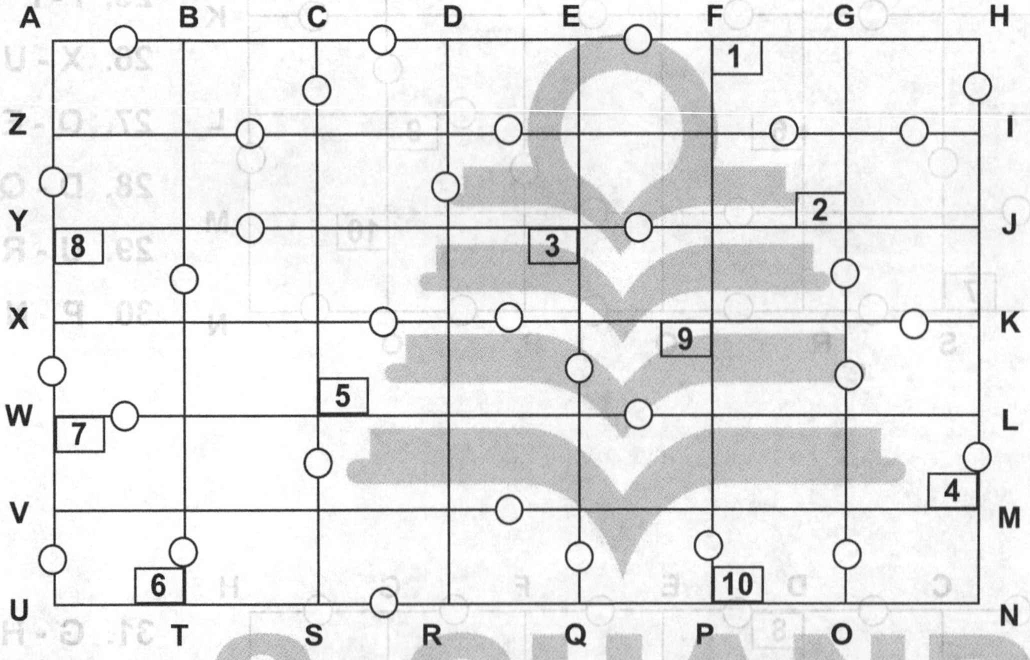

1. H - E
2. X - W
3. K - H
4. R - S
5. U - R
6. R - M
7. H - E
8. A - X
9. K - N
10. E - R

उपखंड/Section-2

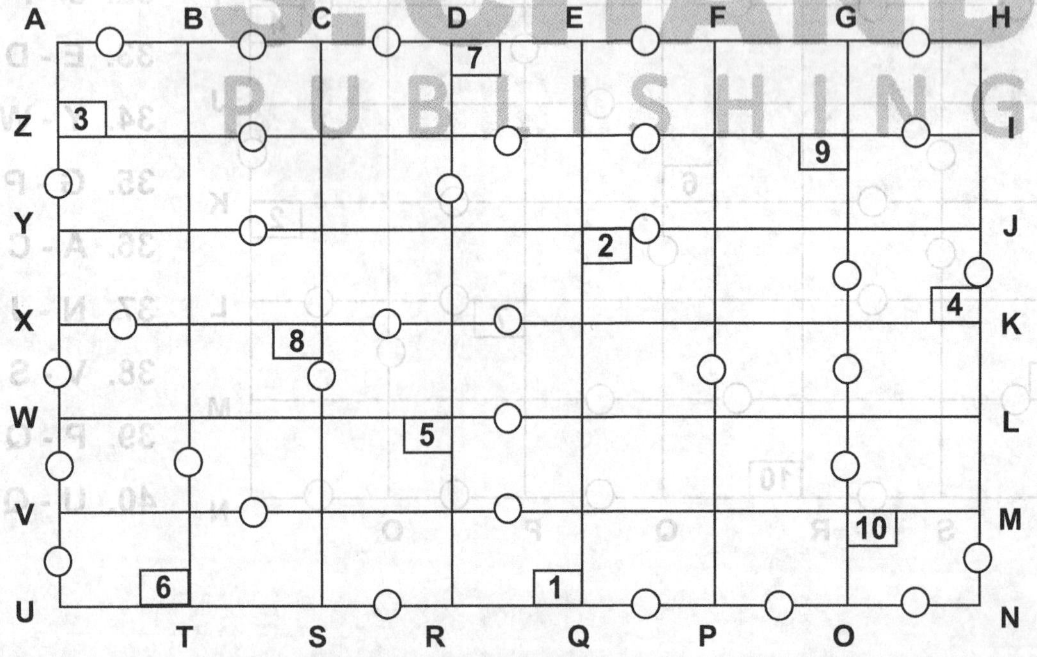

11. H - G
12. E - R
13. J - K
14. X - A
15. C - B
16. U - R
17. E - C
18. P - L
19. E - F
20. S - P

उपखंड/Section-3

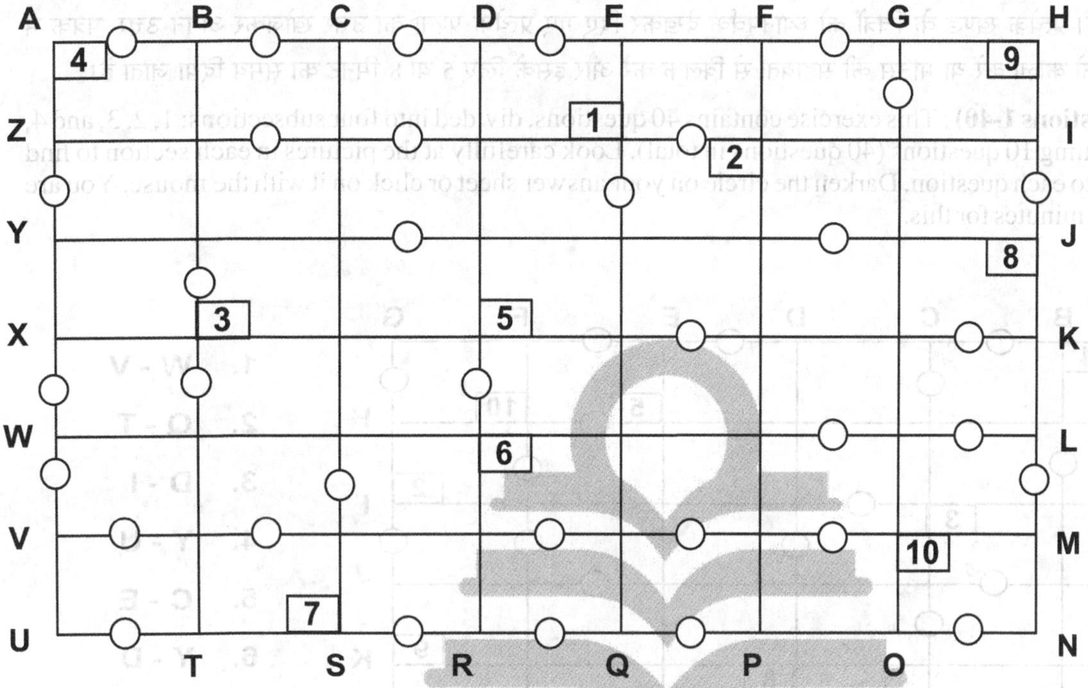

21. P - F
22. F - G
23. D - F
24. X - W
25. Q - R
26. X - A
27. L - I
28. D - C
29. R - T
30. N - Q

उपखंड/Section-4

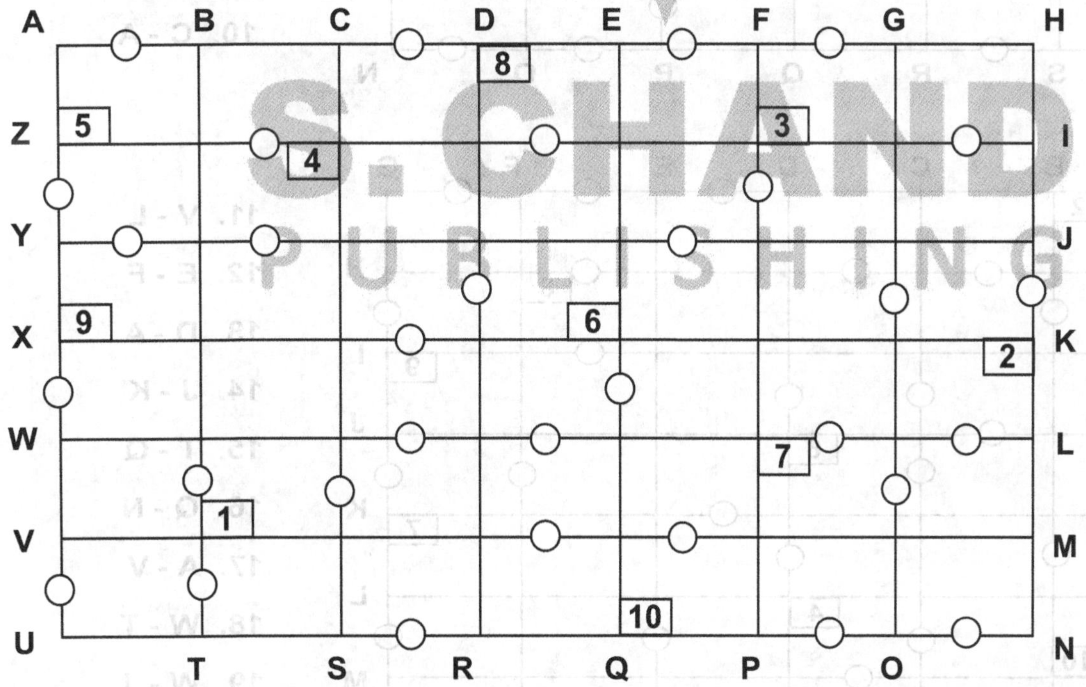

31. H - F
32. E - B
33. P - J
34. J - K
35. B - Y
36. E - R
37. W - A
38. S - P
39. V - Y
40. R - W

PRACTICE SET-11

Total Ques.- 40
Time - 5 or 8 Min.

निर्देश : (प्रश्न 1-40) इस अभ्यास में 40 प्रश्न दिए गए हैं जो चार उपखंडों 1, 2, 3 एवं 4 में 10-10 प्रश्नों (कुल 40 प्रश्न) के रूप में विभाजित है। प्रत्येक खण्ड के चित्रों को ध्यानपूर्वक देखकर दिए गए प्रत्येक प्रश्नों का उत्तर खोजकर अपने उत्तर-पत्रक में अंकित गोले को काला करें या माउस की सहायता से क्लिक करें और इसके लिए 5 या 8 मिनट का समय दिया जाता है।

Instructions: (Questions 1-40) : This exercise contains 40 questions, divided into four subsections: 1, 2, 3, and 4, each containing 10 questions (40 questions in total). Look carefully at the pictures in each section to find the answer to each question. Darken the circle on your answer sheet or click on it with the mouse. You are given 5 or 8 minutes for this.

उपखंड/Section-1

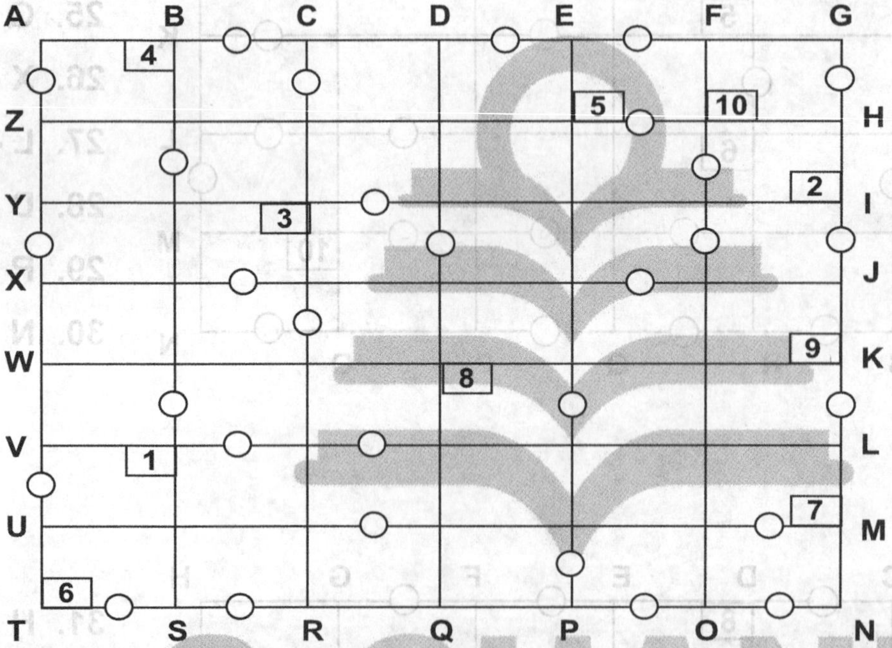

1. W - V
2. Q - T
3. D - I
4. Y - U
5. C - E
6. Y - D
7. P - N
8. D - Q
9. O - J
10. C - A

उपखंड/Section-2

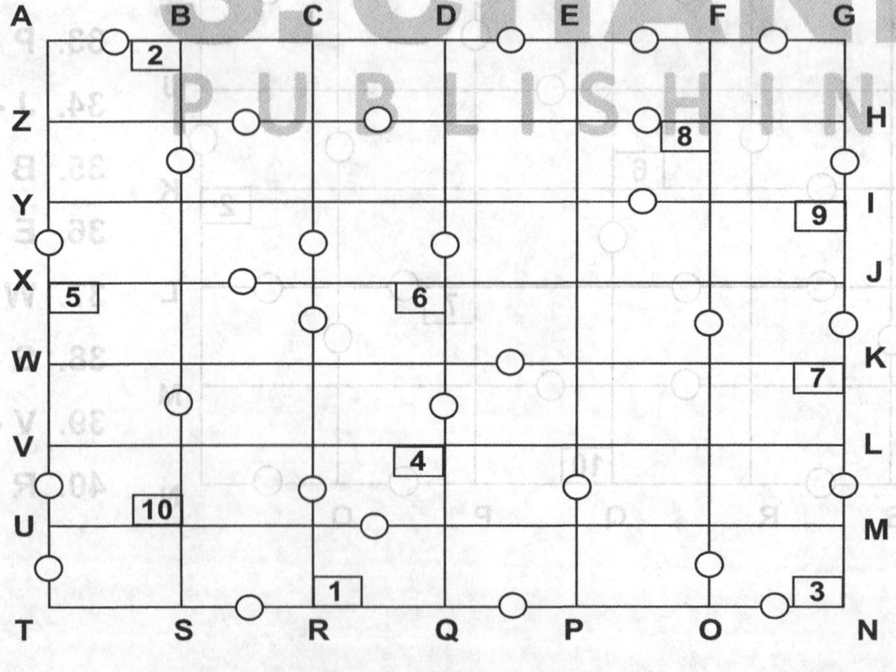

11. V - L
12. E - F
13. D - A
14. J - K
15. T - Q
16. Q - N
17. A - V
18. W - T
19. W - J
20. E - I

उपखंड/Section-3

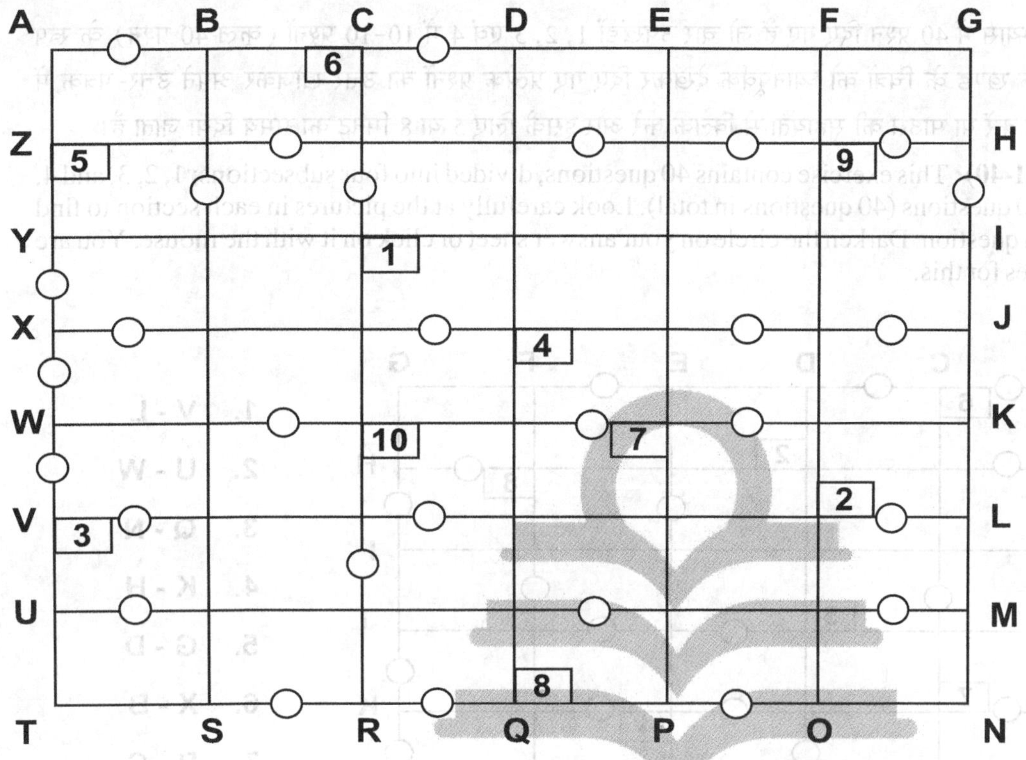

21. K - L
22. B - F
23. Y - I
24. D - E
25. O - R
26. K - G
27. E - P
28. H - J
29. W - V
30. W - A

उपखंड/Section-4

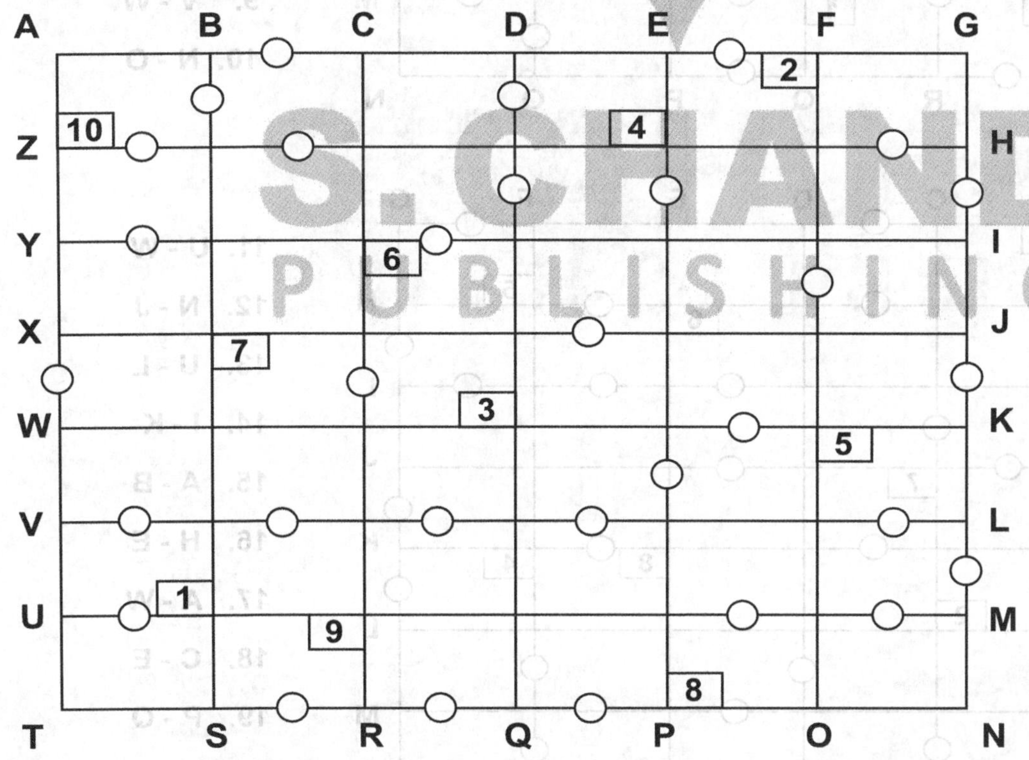

31. U - R
32. H - J
33. I - L
34. X - B
35. V - Y
36. I - E
37. X - I
38. M - P
39. W - J
40. M - L

PRACTICE SET-12

Total Ques.- 40
Time - 5 or 8 Min.

निर्देश : (प्रश्न 1-40) इस अभ्यास में 40 प्रश्न दिए गए हैं जो चार उपखंडों 1, 2, 3 एवं 4 में 10-10 प्रश्नों (कुल 40 प्रश्न) के रूप में विभाजित है। प्रत्येक खण्ड के चित्रों को ध्यानपूर्वक देखकर दिए गए प्रत्येक प्रश्नों का उत्तर खोजकर अपने उत्तर-पत्रक में अंकित गोले को काला करें या माउस की सहायता से क्लिक करें और इसके लिए 5 या 8 मिनट का समय दिया जाता है।

Instructions: (Questions 1-40) : This exercise contains 40 questions, divided into four subsections: 1, 2, 3, and 4, each containing 10 questions (40 questions in total). Look carefully at the pictures in each section to find the answer to each question. Darken the circle on your answer sheet or click on it with the mouse. You are given 5 or 8 minutes for this.

उपखंड/Section-1

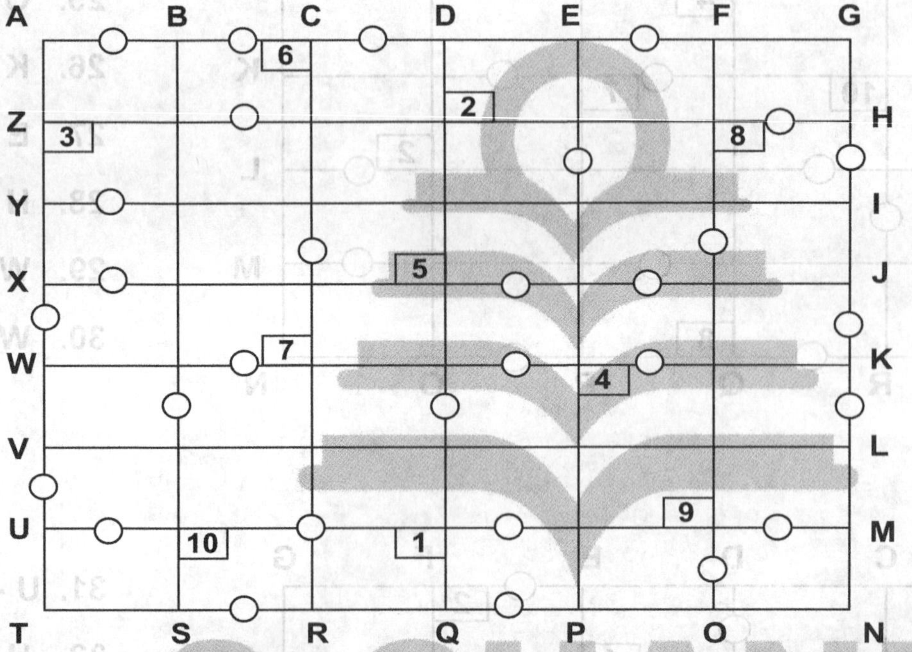

1. V - L
2. U - W
3. Q - N
4. K - H
5. G - D
6. X - B
7. B - C
8. F - J
9. V - W
10. N - O

उपखंड/Section-2

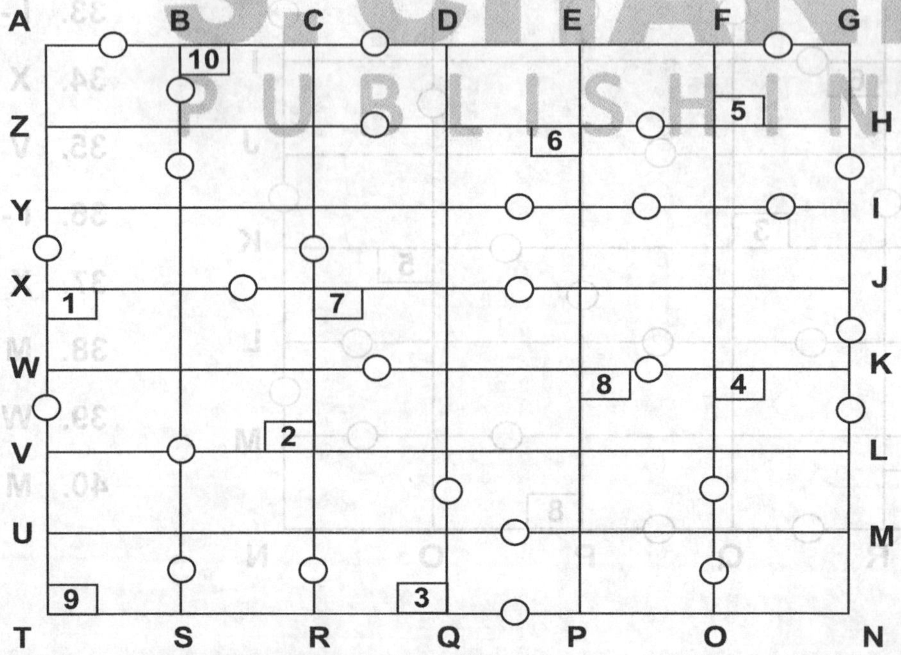

11. U - W
12. N - J
13. U - L
14. I - K
15. A - B
16. H - E
17. A - W
18. C - E
19. P - Q
20. C - P

उपखंड/Section-3

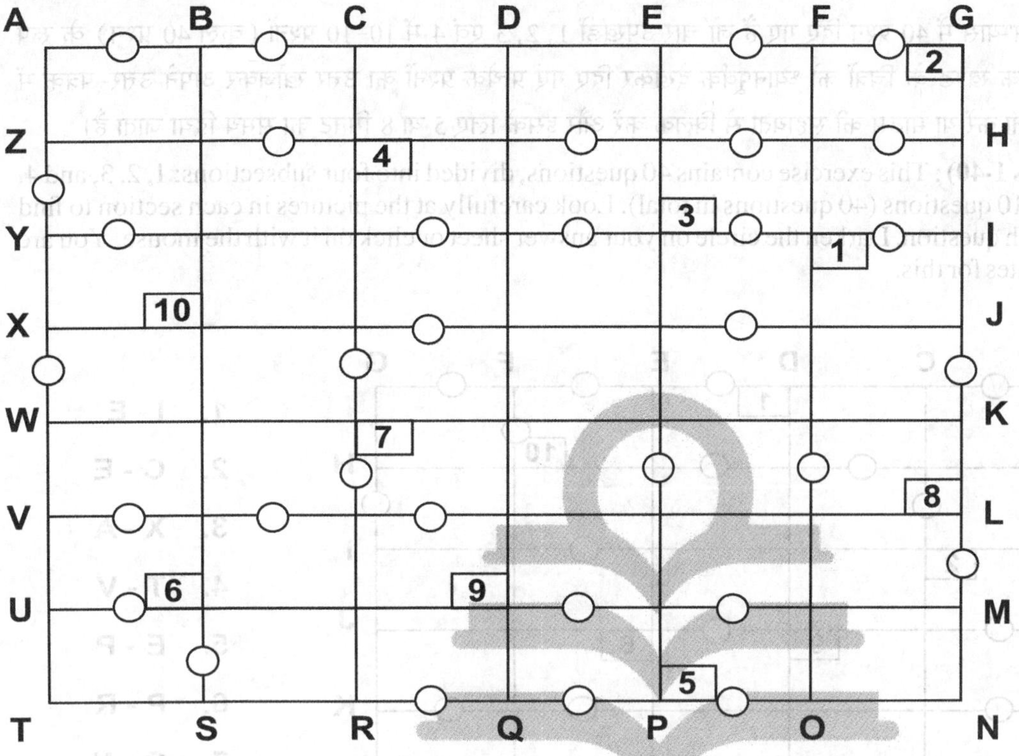

21. A - V
22. W - R
23. T - Q
24. E - K
25. W - K
26. J - F
27. D - Q
28. N - P
29. K - G
30. H - Q

उपखंड/Section-4

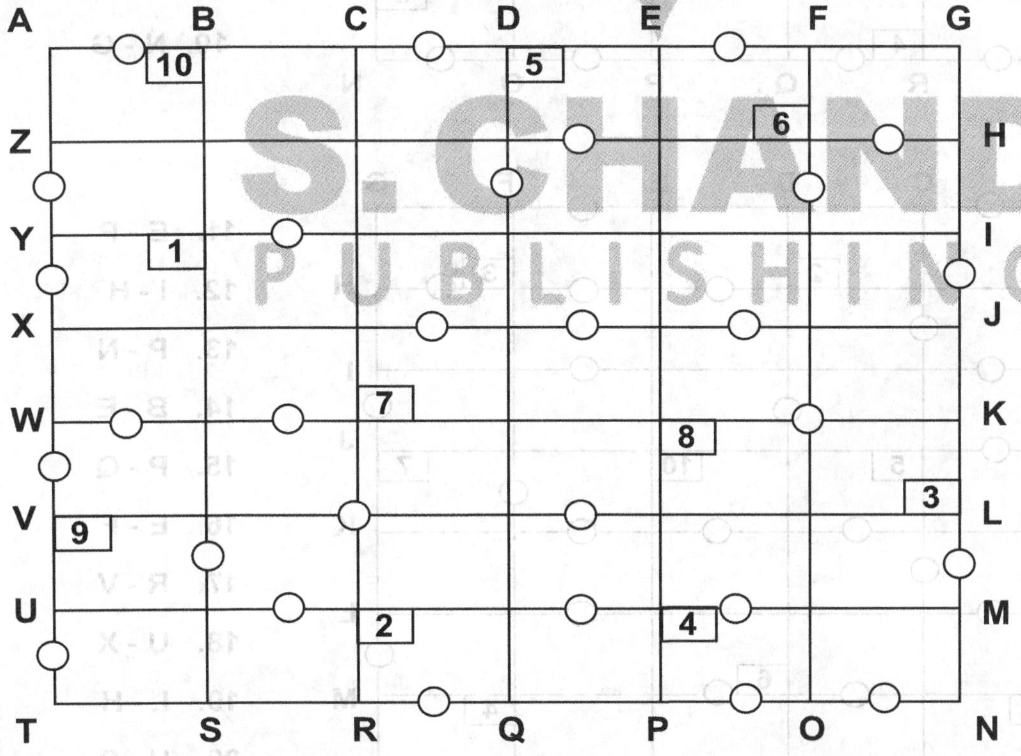

31. S - W
32. N - P
33. I - H
34. E - C
35. I - Y
36. C - Q
37. E - O
38. J - N
39. A - W
40. P - S

PRACTICE SET-13

Total Ques.- 40
Time - 5 or 8 Min.

निर्देश : (प्रश्न 1-40) इस अभ्यास में 40 प्रश्न दिए गए हैं जो चार उपखंडों 1, 2, 3 एवं 4 में 10-10 प्रश्नों (कुल 40 प्रश्न) के रूप में विभाजित है। प्रत्येक खण्ड के चित्रों को ध्यानपूर्वक देखकर दिए गए प्रत्येक प्रश्नों का उत्तर खोजकर अपने उत्तर-पत्रक में अंकित गोले को काला करें या माउस की सहायता से क्लिक करें और इसके लिए 5 या 8 मिनट का समय दिया जाता है।

Instructions: (Questions 1-40) : This exercise contains 40 questions, divided into four subsections: 1, 2, 3, and 4, each containing 10 questions (40 questions in total). Look carefully at the pictures in each section to find the answer to each question. Darken the circle on your answer sheet or click on it with the mouse. You are given 5 or 8 minutes for this.

उपखंड/Section-1

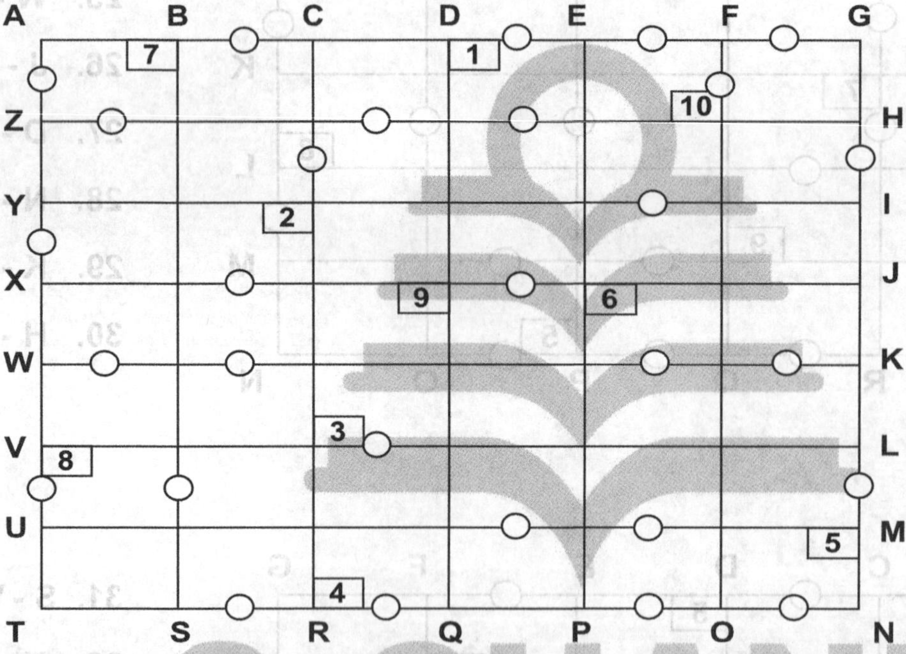

1. I - E
2. C - E
3. X - A
4. T - V
5. E - P
6. P - R
7. Q - N
8. Y - E
9. L - K
10. N - G

उपखंड/Section-2

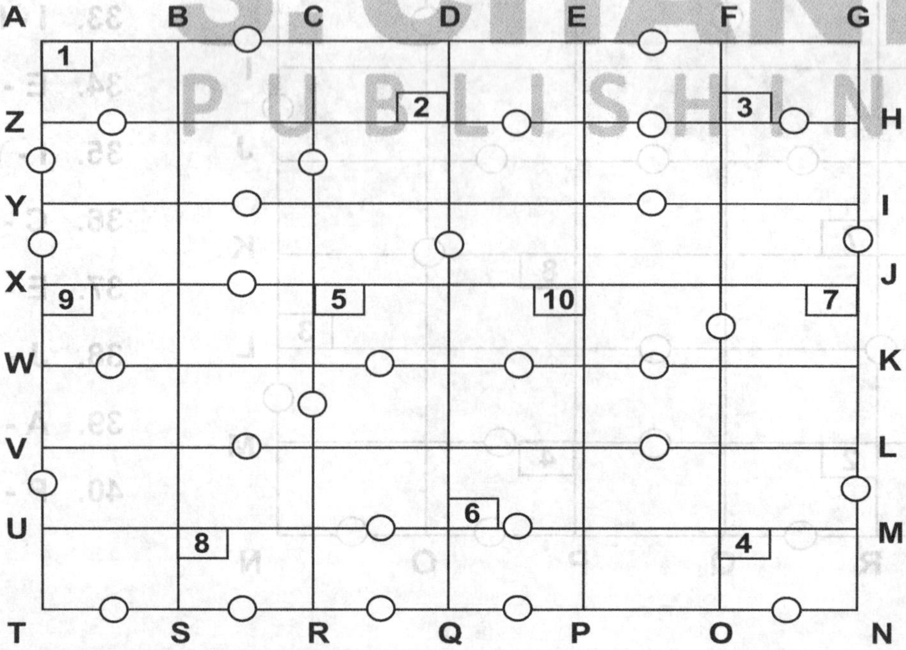

11. E - P
12. I - H
13. P - N
14. B - E
15. P - Q
16. E - F
17. R - V
18. U - X
19. L - H
20. U - P

उपखंड/Section-3

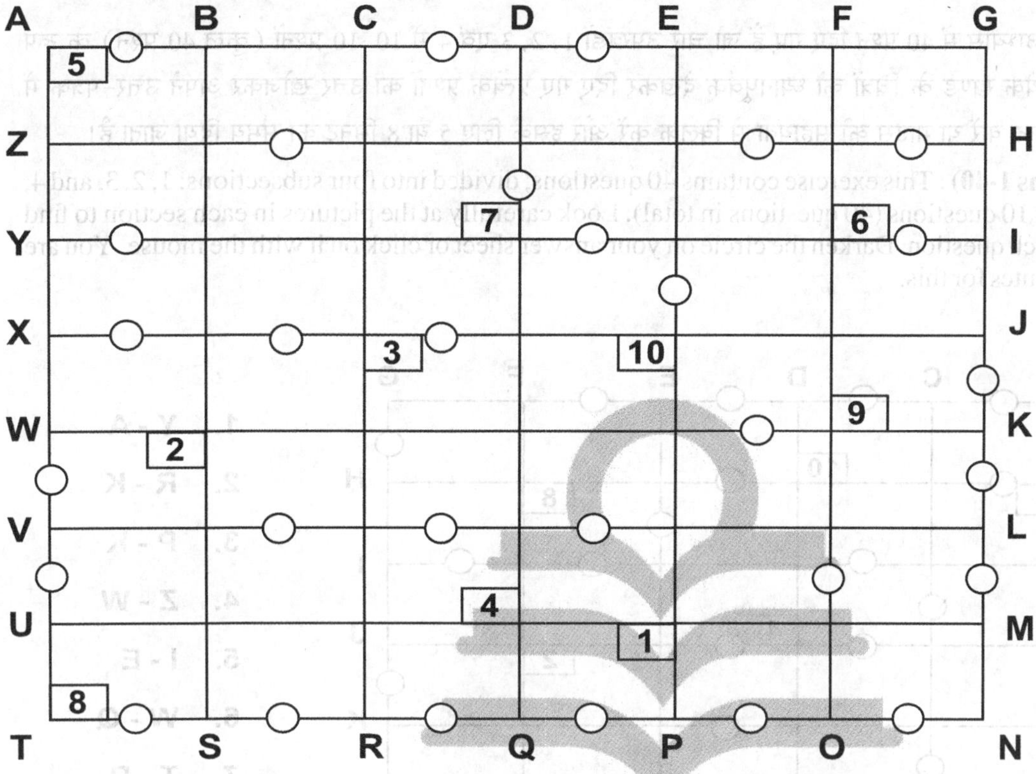

21. X - B
22. Y - U
23. N - K
24. N - P
25. C - R
26. E - H
27. W - L
28. N - Q
29. R - T
30. S - Q

उपखंड/Section-4

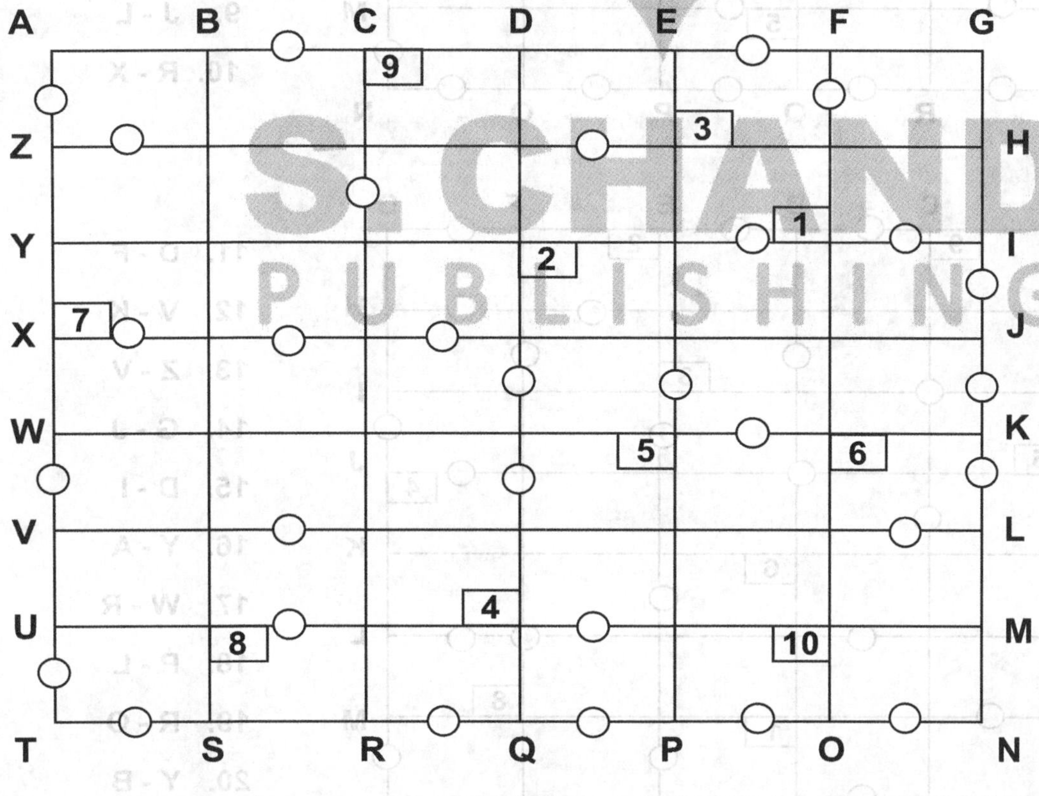

31. A - E
32. D - H
33. G - J
34. N - K
35. P - N
36. Y - J
37. A - W
38. R - P
39. R - W
40. P - Q

PRACTICE SET-14

Total Ques.- 40
Time - 5 or 8 Min.

निर्देश : (प्रश्न 1–40) इस अभ्यास में 40 प्रश्न दिए गए हैं जो चार उपखंडों 1, 2, 3 एवं 4 में 10–10 प्रश्नों (कुल 40 प्रश्न) के रूप में विभाजित है। प्रत्येक खण्ड के चित्रों को ध्यानपूर्वक देखकर दिए गए प्रत्येक प्रश्नों का उत्तर खोजकर अपने उत्तर-पत्रक में अंकित गोले को काला करें या माउस की सहायता से क्लिक करें और इसके लिए 5 या 8 मिनट का समय दिया जाता है।

Instructions: (Questions 1-40) : This exercise contains 40 questions, divided into four subsections: 1, 2, 3, and 4, each containing 10 questions (40 questions in total). Look carefully at the pictures in each section to find the answer to each question. Darken the circle on your answer sheet or click on it with the mouse. You are given 5 or 8 minutes for this.

उपखंड/Section-1

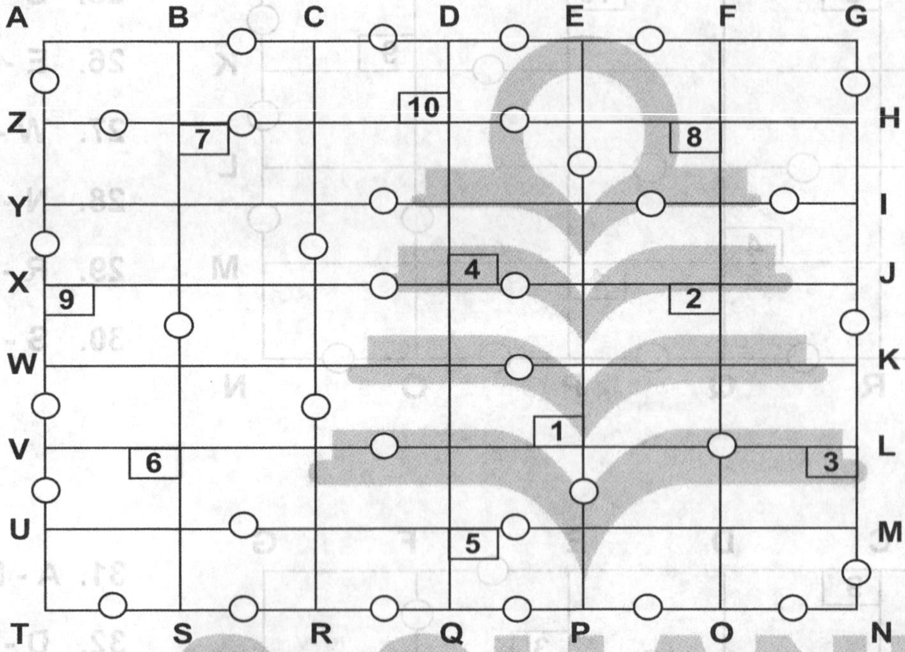

1. Y - A
2. R - K
3. P - K
4. Z - W
5. I - E
6. W - Q
7. T - R
8. Y - D
9. J - L
10. R - X

उपखंड/Section-2

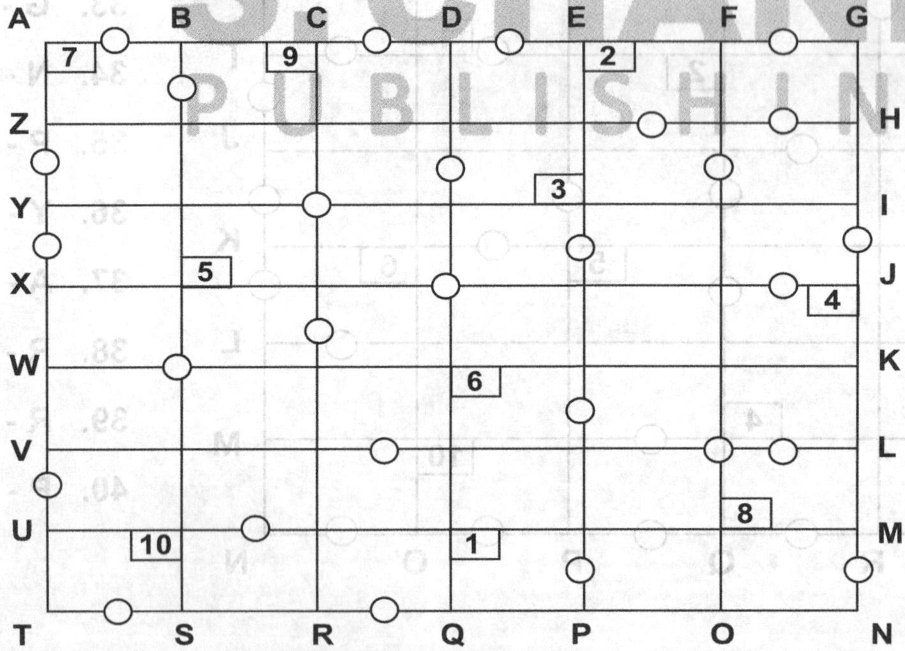

11. D - F
12. V - K
13. Z - V
14. G - J
15. D - I
16. Y - A
17. W - R
18. P - L
19. R - O
20. Y - B

उपखंड/Section-3

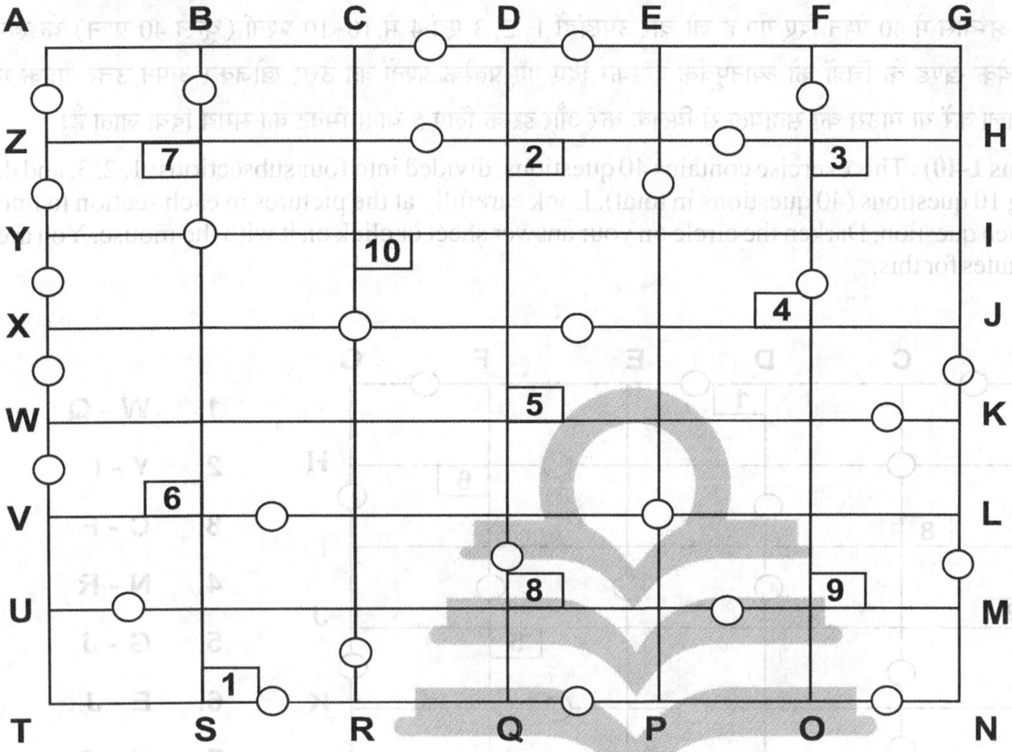

21. F - I
22. I - J
23. K - N
24. P - R
25. A - Z
26. C - I
27. W - L
28. X - U
29. K - P
30. T - Q

उपखंड/Section-4

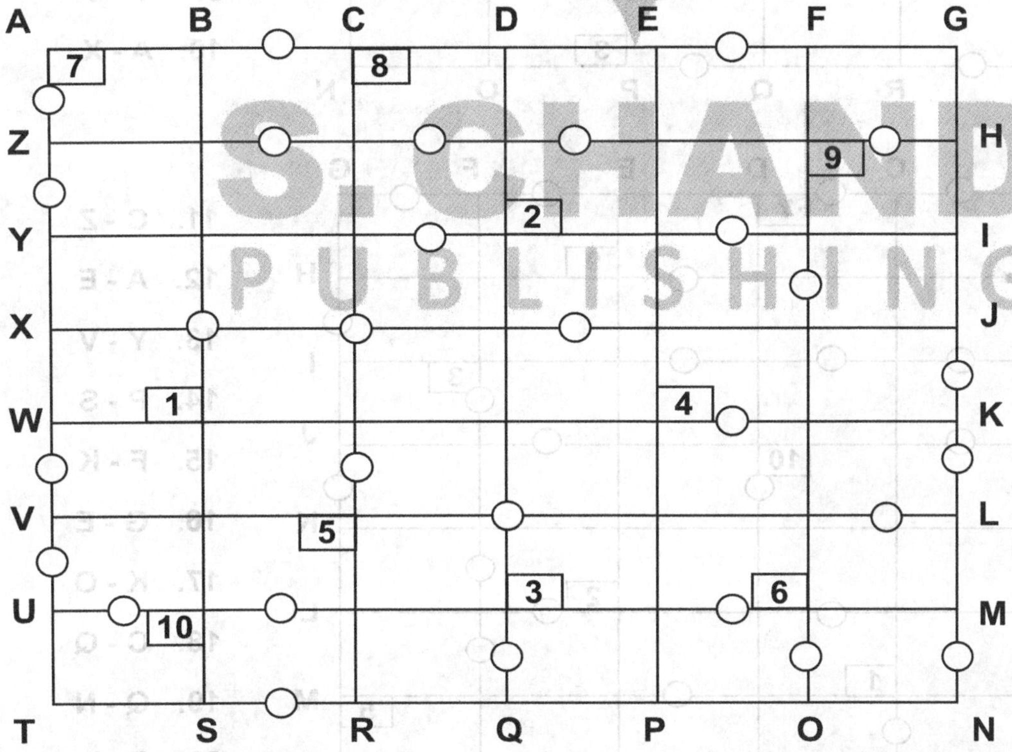

31. M - P
32. H - J
33. V - U
34. E - P
35. D - E
36. W - A
37. Y - D
38. V - Y
39. R - V
40. P - Q

PRACTICE SET-15

Total Ques.- 40
Time - 5 or 8 Min.

निर्देश : (प्रश्न 1-40) इस अभ्यास में 40 प्रश्न दिए गए हैं जो चार उपखंडों 1, 2, 3 एवं 4 में 10-10 प्रश्नों (कुल 40 प्रश्न) के रूप में विभाजित है। प्रत्येक खण्ड के चित्रों को ध्यानपूर्वक देखकर दिए गए प्रत्येक प्रश्नों का उत्तर खोजकर अपने उत्तर-पत्रक में अंकित गोले को काला करें या माउस की सहायता से क्लिक करें और इसके लिए 5 या 8 मिनट का समय दिया जाता है।

Instructions: (Questions 1-40) : This exercise contains 40 questions, divided into four subsections: 1, 2, 3, and 4, each containing 10 questions (40 questions in total). Look carefully at the pictures in each section to find the answer to each question. Darken the circle on your answer sheet or click on it with the mouse. You are given 5 or 8 minutes for this.

उपखंड/Section-1

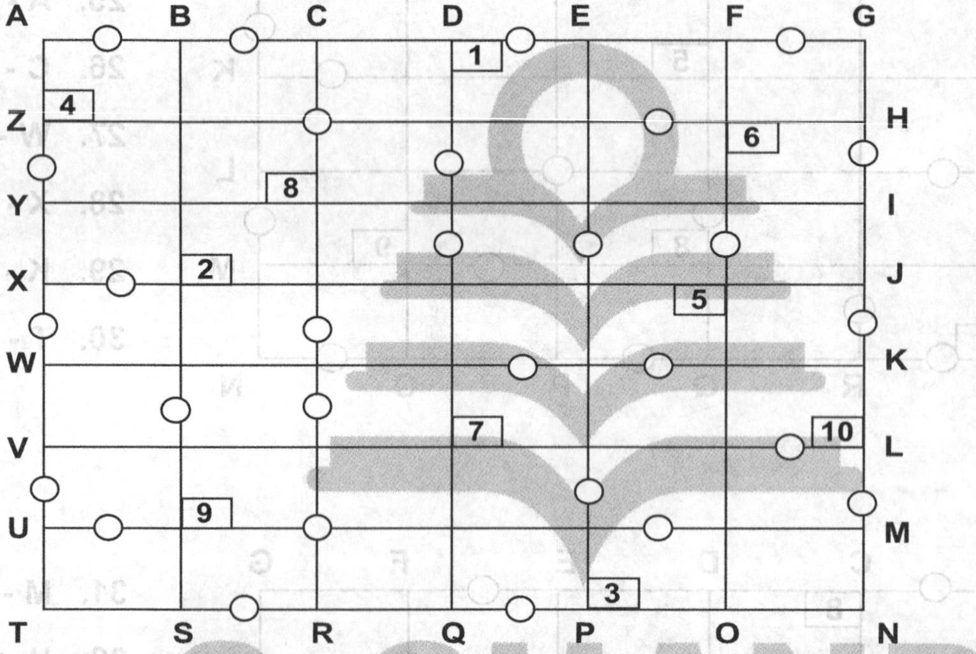

1. W - Q
2. Y - I
3. C - F
4. N - R
5. G - J
6. E - J
7. U - Q
8. W - U
9. Y - V
10. A - X

उपखंड/Section-2

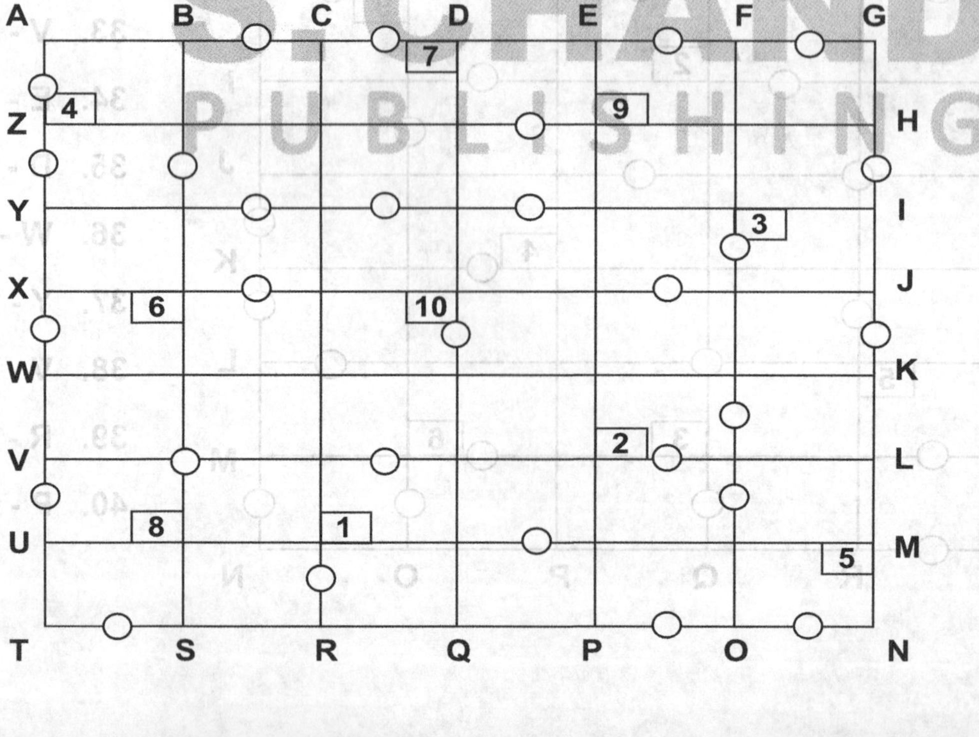

11. C - Z
12. A - E
13. Y - V
14. P - S
15. F - K
16. G - E
17. K - O
18. C - Q
19. Q - N
20. S - P

उपखंड/Section-3

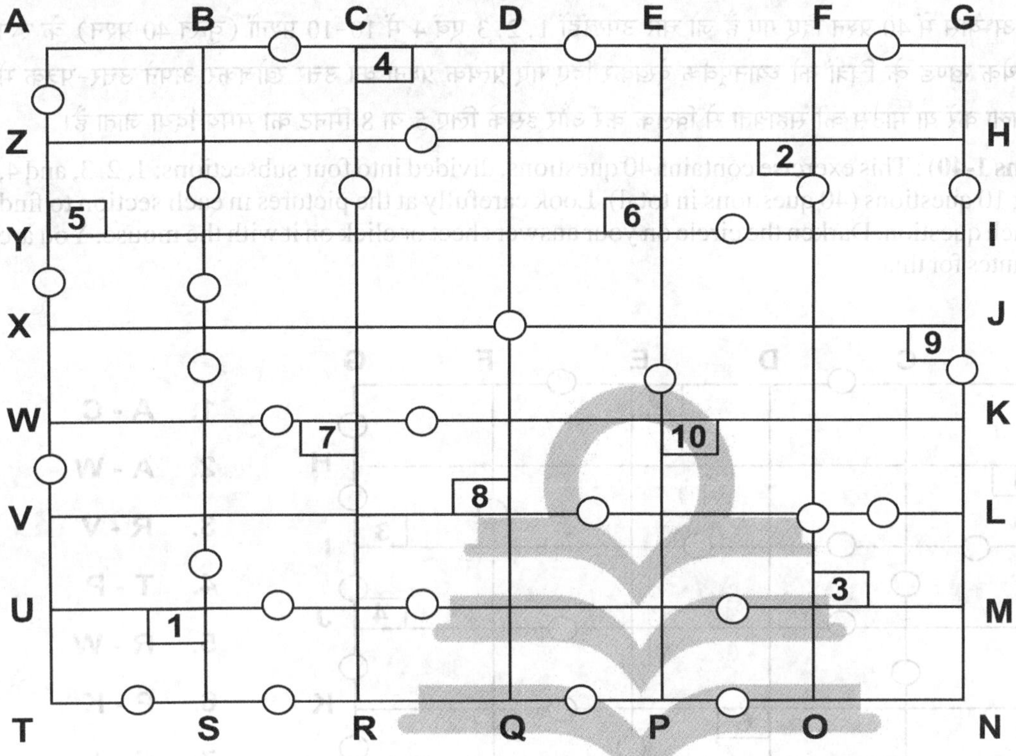

21. X - S
22. A - D
23. E - I
24. A - Y
25. X - W
26. V - Q
27. E - G
28. I - N
29. P - K
30. K - O

उपखंड/Section-4

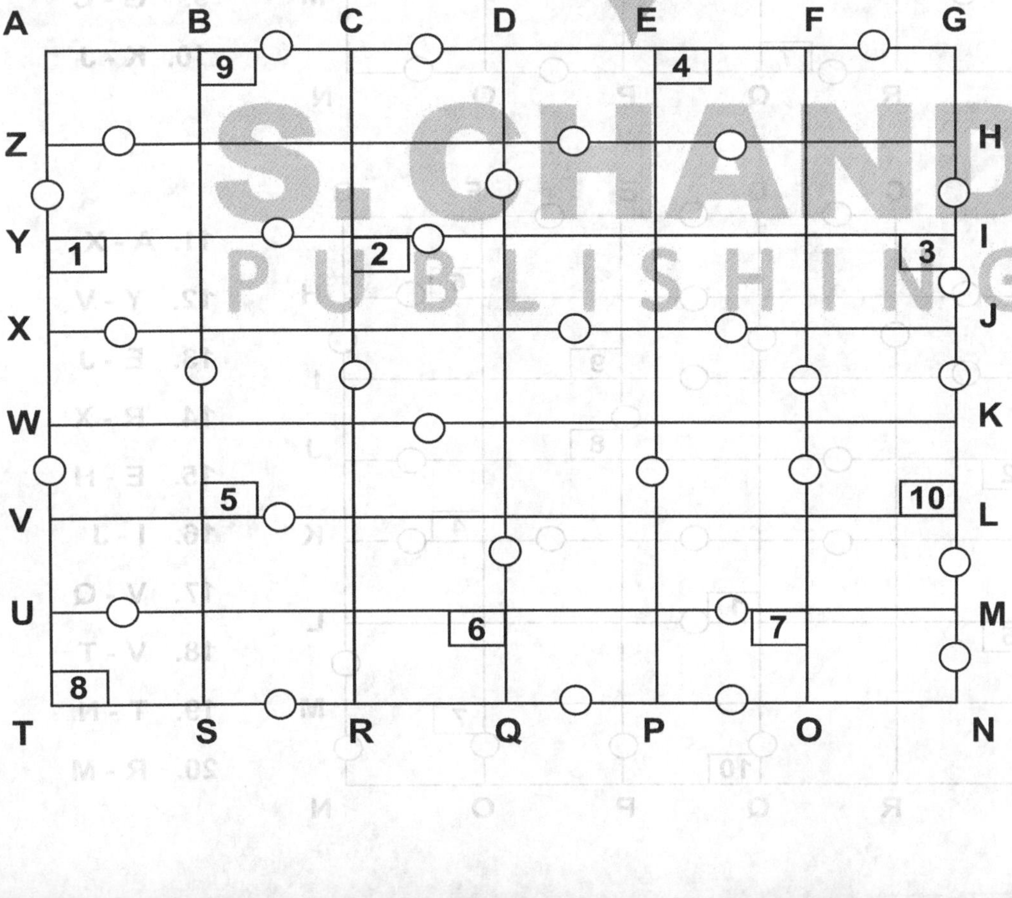

31. A - E
32. G - I
33. K - M
34. N - P
35. V - U
36. W - L
37. C - R
38. D - G
39. X - U
40. S - P

PRACTICE SET-16

Total Ques.- 40
Time - 5 or 8 Min.

निर्देश : (प्रश्न 1-40) इस अभ्यास में 40 प्रश्न दिए गए हैं जो चार उपखंडों 1, 2, 3 एवं 4 में 10-10 प्रश्नों (कुल 40 प्रश्न) के रूप में विभाजित है। प्रत्येक खण्ड के चित्रों को ध्यानपूर्वक देखकर दिए गए प्रत्येक प्रश्नों का उत्तर खोजकर अपने उत्तर-पत्रक में अंकित गोले को काला करें या माउस की सहायता से क्लिक करें और इसके लिए 5 या 8 मिनट का समय दिया जाता है।

Instructions: (Questions 1-40) : This exercise contains 40 questions, divided into four subsections: 1, 2, 3, and 4, each containing 10 questions (40 questions in total). Look carefully at the pictures in each section to find the answer to each question. Darken the circle on your answer sheet or click on it with the mouse. You are given 5 or 8 minutes for this.

उपखंड/Section-1

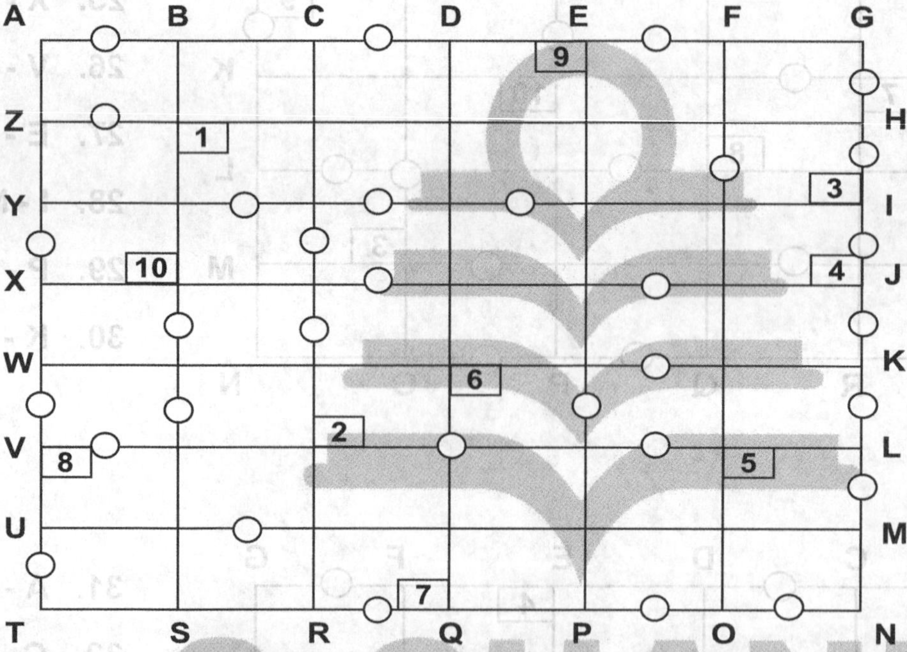

1. A - C
2. A - W
3. R - V
4. T - P
5. R - W
6. P - K
7. G - I
8. Y - H
9. G - C
10. K - J

उपखंड/Section-2

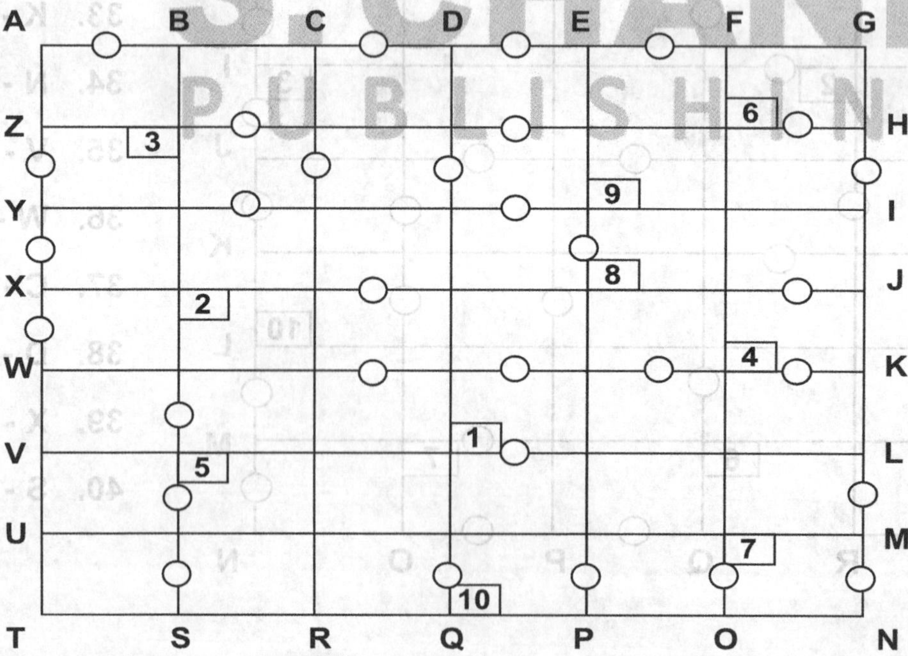

11. A - X
12. Y - V
13. E - J
14. R - X
15. E - H
16. I - J
17. V - Q
18. V - T
19. T - N
20. R - M

उपखंड/Section-3

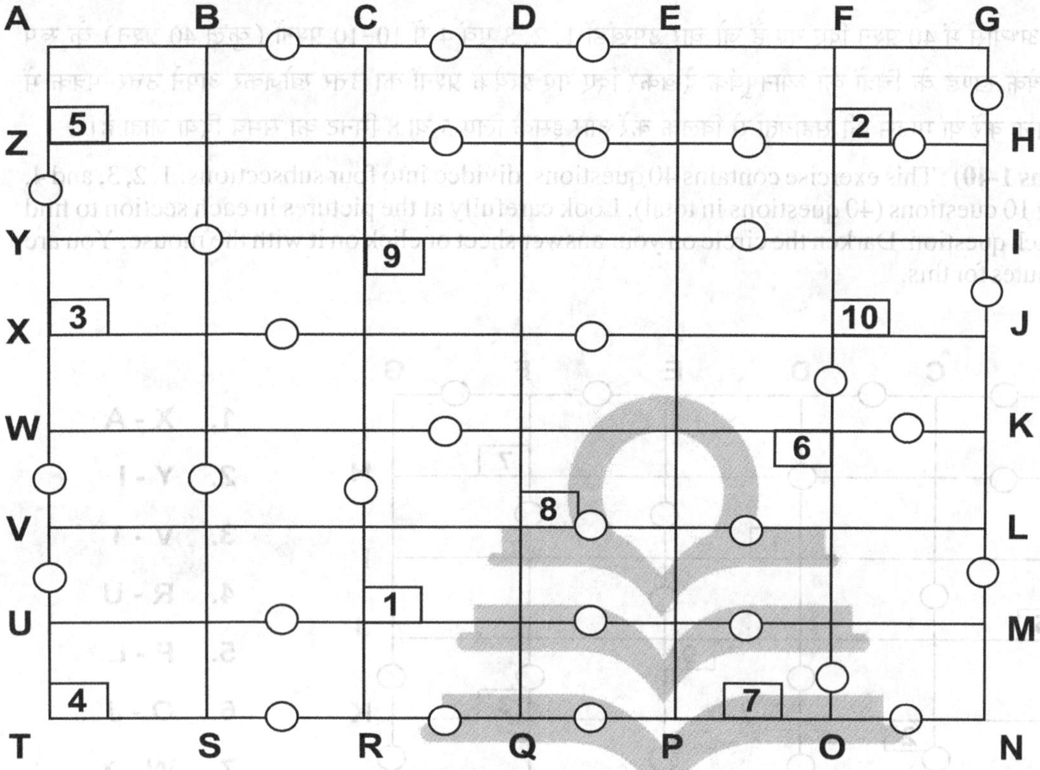

21. V - S
22. S - R
23. Q - P
24. E - O
25. L - P
26. H - G
27. D - Q
28. E - C
29. C - A
30. H - K

उपखंड/Section-4

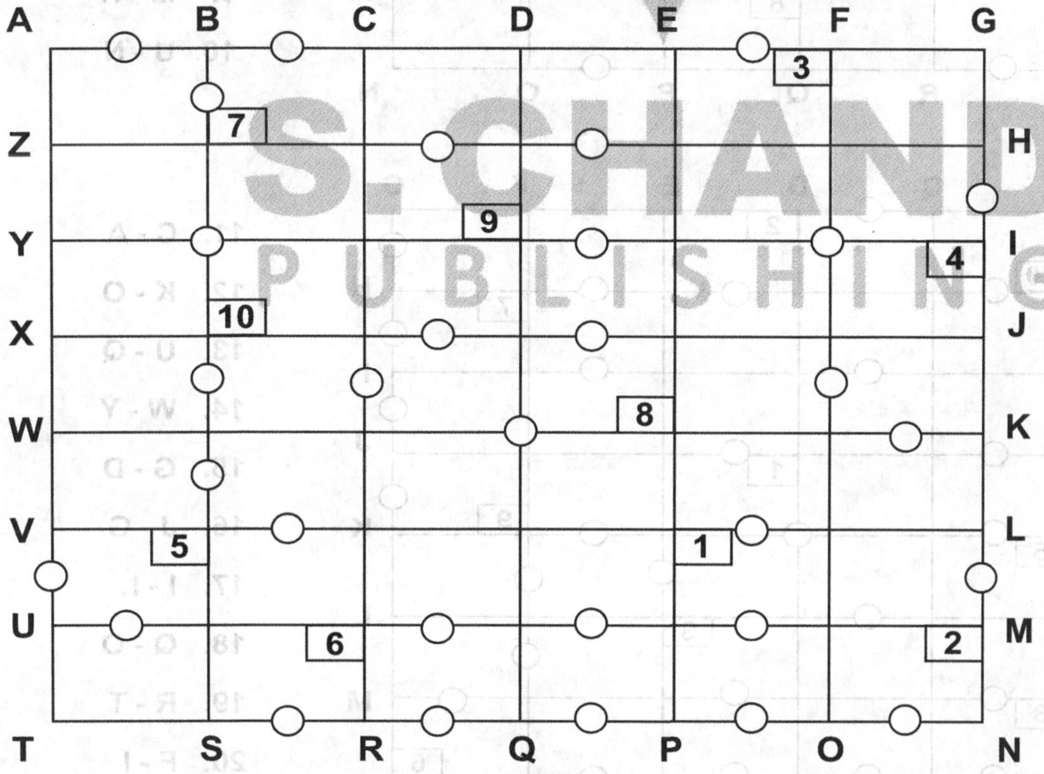

31. R - Q
32. H - I
33. J - N
34. L - J
35. P - O
36. L - I
37. D - C
38. W - R
39. X - U
40. A - D

PRACTICE SET-17

Total Ques.- 40
Time - 5 or 8 Min.

निर्देश : (प्रश्न 1–40) इस अभ्यास में 40 प्रश्न दिए गए हैं जो चार उपखंडों 1, 2, 3 एवं 4 में 10–10 प्रश्नों (कुल 40 प्रश्न) के रूप में विभाजित है। प्रत्येक खण्ड के चित्रों को ध्यानपूर्वक देखकर दिए गए प्रत्येक प्रश्नों का उत्तर खोजकर अपने उत्तर-पत्रक में अंकित गोले को काला करें या माउस की सहायता से क्लिक करें और इसके लिए 5 या 8 मिनट का समय दिया जाता है।

Instructions: (Questions 1-40) : This exercise contains 40 questions, divided into four subsections: 1, 2, 3, and 4, each containing 10 questions (40 questions in total). Look carefully at the pictures in each section to find the answer to each question. Darken the circle on your answer sheet or click on it with the mouse. You are given 5 or 8 minutes for this.

उपखंड/Section-1

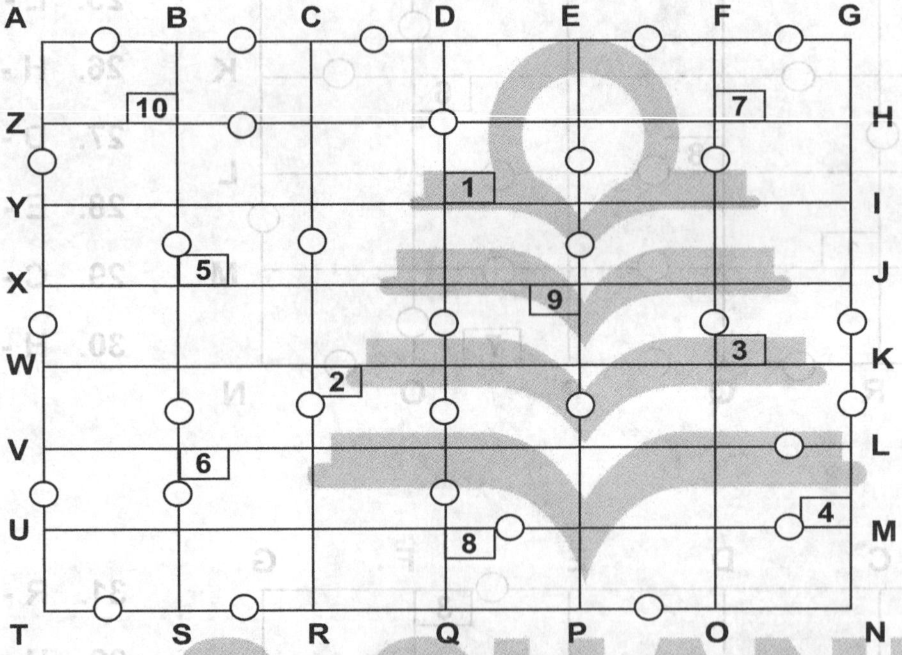

1. X - A
2. Y - I
3. V - T
4. R - U
5. P - L
6. O - J
7. W - X
8. J - E
9. M - K
10. U - N

उपखंड/Section-2

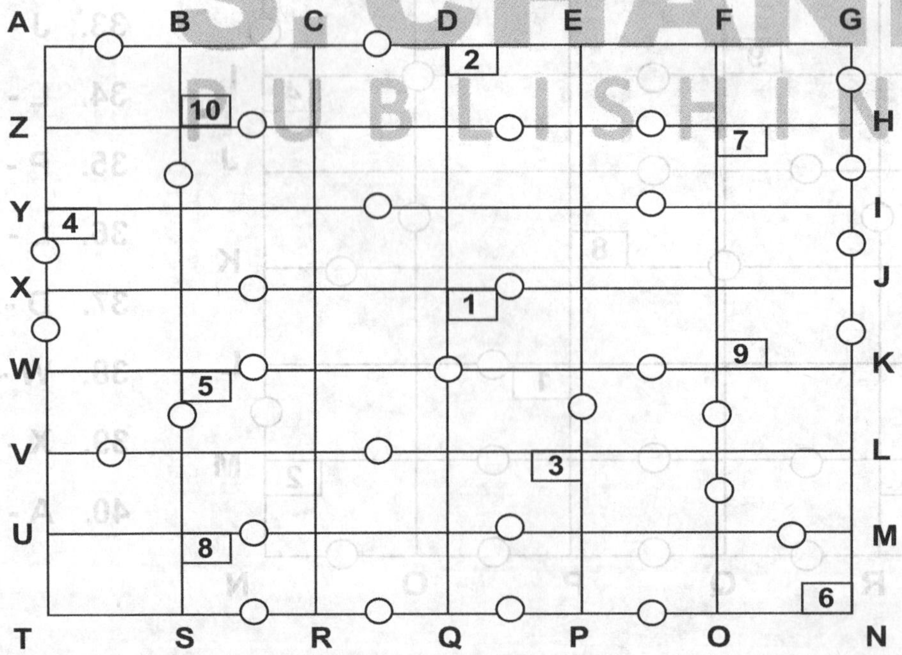

11. C - A
12. K - O
13. U - Q
14. W - Y
15. G - D
16. J - G
17. I - L
18. Q - O
19. R - T
20. F - I

उपखंड/Section-3

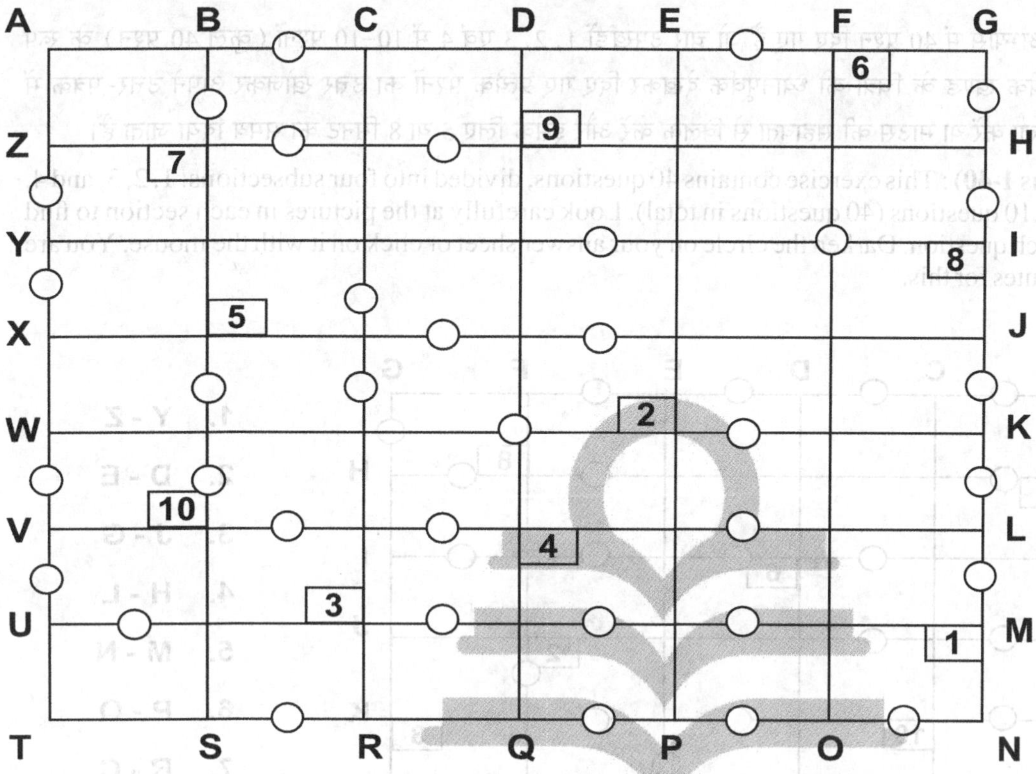

21. H - I
22. V - U
23. E - G
24. K - N
25. P - O
26. C - D
27. B - Y
28. Y - W
29. T - Q
30. P - Q

उपखंड/Section-4

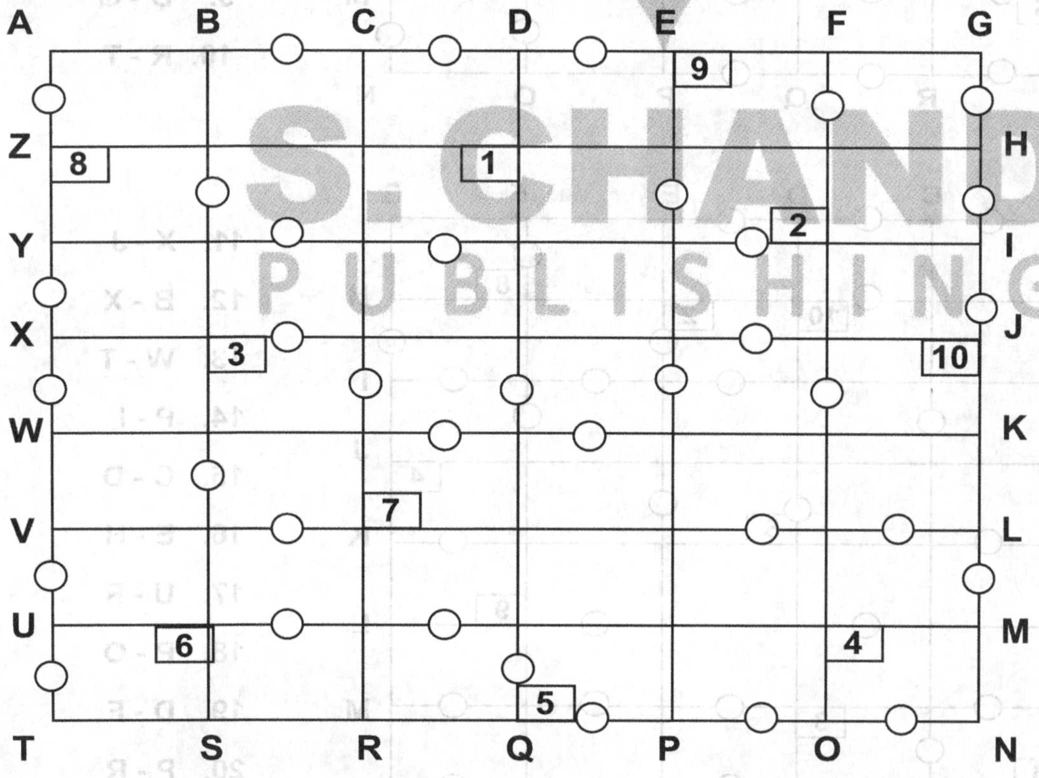

31. T - W
32. U - Q
33. R - P
34. L - N
35. D - G
36. X - A
37. D - C
38. L - I
39. P - R
40. I - H

PRACTICE SET-18

Total Ques.- 40
Time - 5 or 8 Min.

निर्देश : (प्रश्न 1–40) इस अभ्यास में 40 प्रश्न दिए गए हैं जो चार उपखंडों 1, 2, 3 एवं 4 में 10–10 प्रश्नों (कुल 40 प्रश्न) के रूप में विभाजित है। प्रत्येक खण्ड के चित्रों को ध्यानपूर्वक देखकर दिए गए प्रत्येक प्रश्नों का उत्तर खोजकर अपने उत्तर-पत्रक में अंकित गोले को काला करें या माउस की सहायता से क्लिक करें और इसके लिए 5 या 8 मिनट का समय दिया जाता है।

Instructions: (Questions 1-40) : This exercise contains 40 questions, divided into four subsections: 1, 2, 3, and 4, each containing 10 questions (40 questions in total). Look carefully at the pictures in each section to find the answer to each question. Darken the circle on your answer sheet or click on it with the mouse. You are given 5 or 8 minutes for this.

उपखंड/Section-1

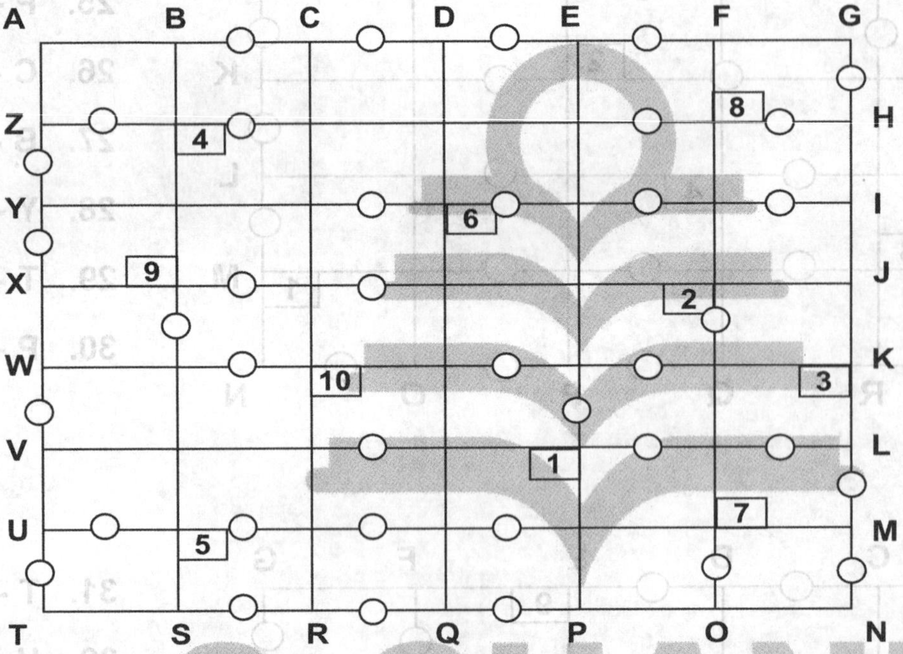

1. Y - Z
2. D - E
3. J - G
4. H - L
5. M - N
6. P - Q
7. R - C
8. J - E
9. D - Q
10. R - T

उपखंड/Section-2

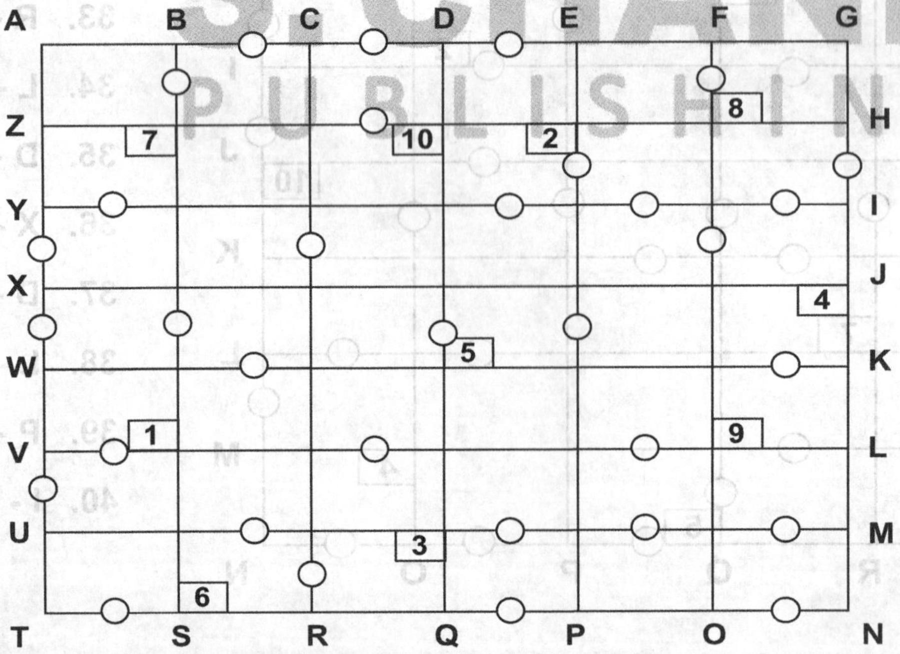

11. X - J
12. B - X
13. W - T
14. P - I
15. C - D
16. E - H
17. U - R
18. P - O
19. D - F
20. P - R

उपखंड/Section-3

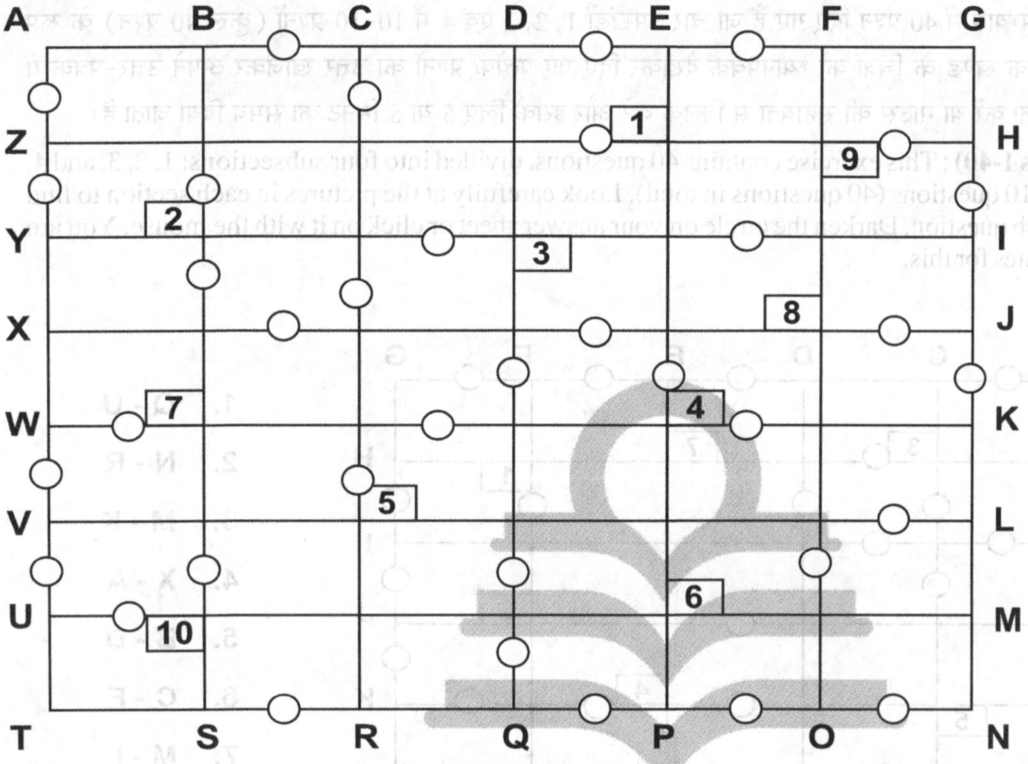

21. A - X
22. H - E
23. Y - V
24. D - Y
25. V - K
26. H - J
27. D - F
28. Q - U
29. R - O
30. O - R

उपखंड/Section-4

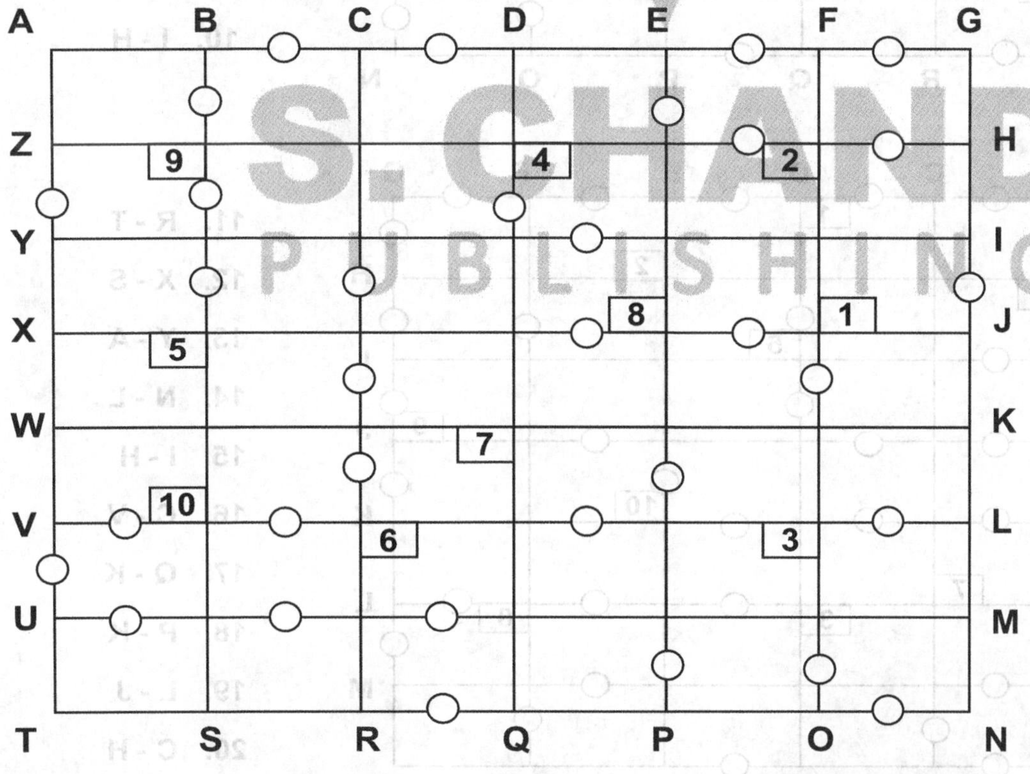

31. B - D
32. D - I
33. G - F
34. K - N
35. U - V
36. J - G
37. N - P
38. Q - S
39. W - K
40. Y - V

PRACTICE SET-19

Total Ques.- 40
Time - 5 or 8 Min.

निर्देश : (प्रश्न 1-40) इस अभ्यास में 40 प्रश्न दिए गए हैं जो चार उपखंडों 1, 2, 3 एवं 4 में 10-10 प्रश्नों (कुल 40 प्रश्न) के रूप में विभाजित है। प्रत्येक खण्ड के चित्रों को ध्यानपूर्वक देखकर दिए गए प्रत्येक प्रश्नों का उत्तर खोजकर अपने उत्तर-पत्रक में अंकित गोले को काला करें या माउस की सहायता से क्लिक करें और इसके लिए 5 या 8 मिनट का समय दिया जाता है।

Instructions: (Questions 1-40) : This exercise contains 40 questions, divided into four subsections: 1, 2, 3, and 4, each containing 10 questions (40 questions in total). Look carefully at the pictures in each section to find the answer to each question. Darken the circle on your answer sheet or click on it with the mouse. You are given 5 or 8 minutes for this.

उपखंड/Section-1

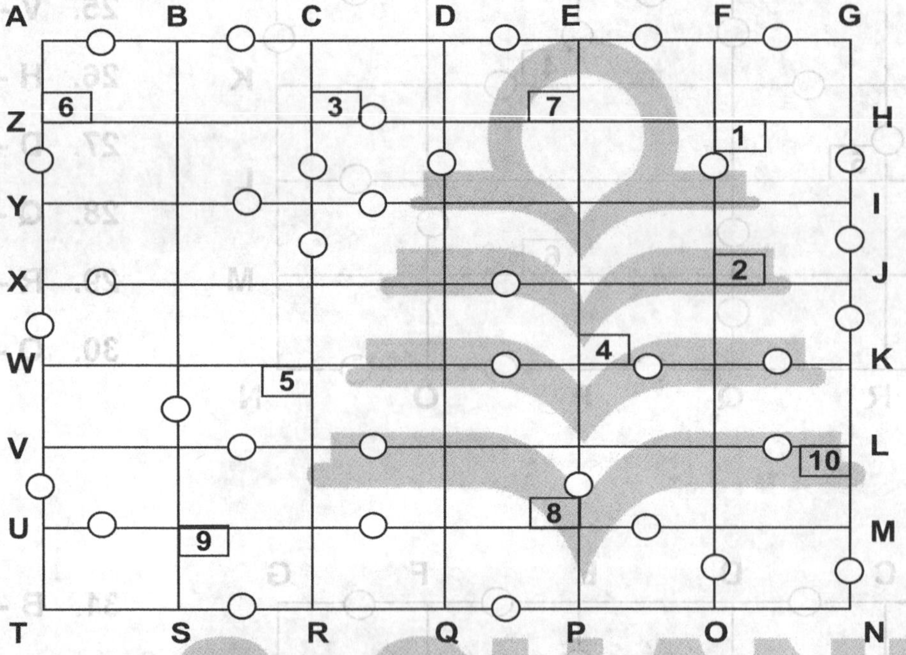

1. Q - U
2. N - R
3. M - K
4. X - A
5. B - D
6. C - F
7. M - I
8. W - Y
9. J - I
10. I - H

उपखंड/Section-2

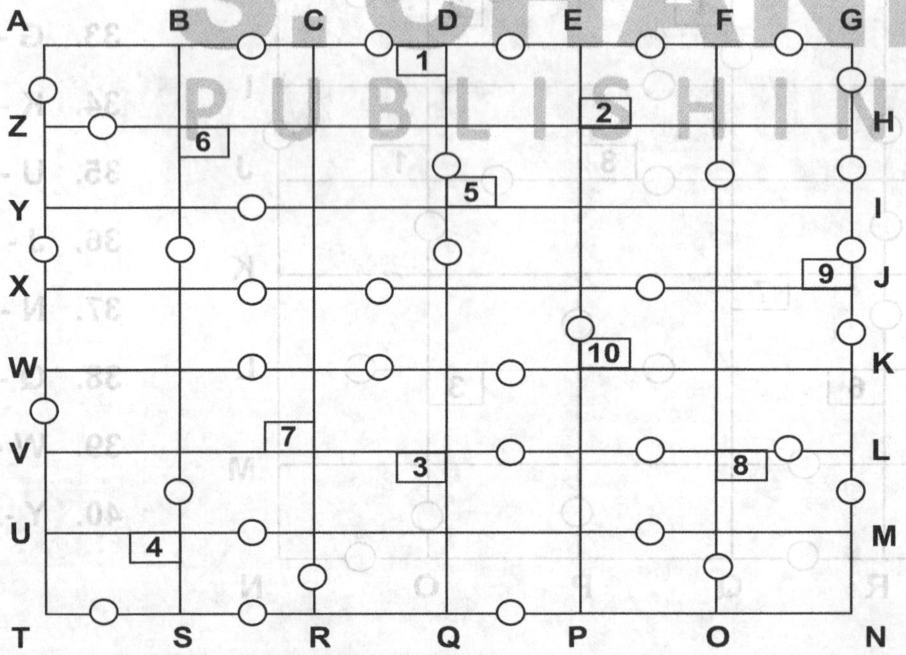

11. R - T
12. X - S
13. Y - A
14. N - L
15. I - H
16. C - V
17. Q - K
18. P - K
19. L - J
20. C - H

उपखंड/Section-3

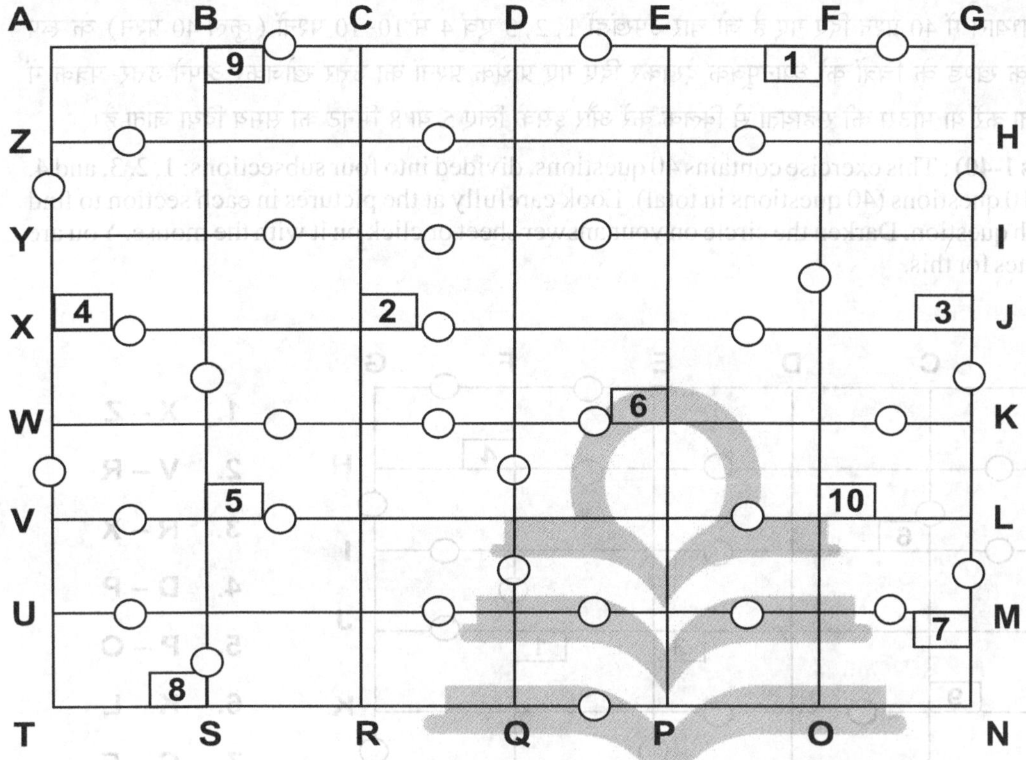

21. Z - D
22. E - I
23. C - R
24. V - R
25. W - R
26. E - P
27. O - K
28. P - M
29. G - J
30. C - X

उपखंड/Section-4

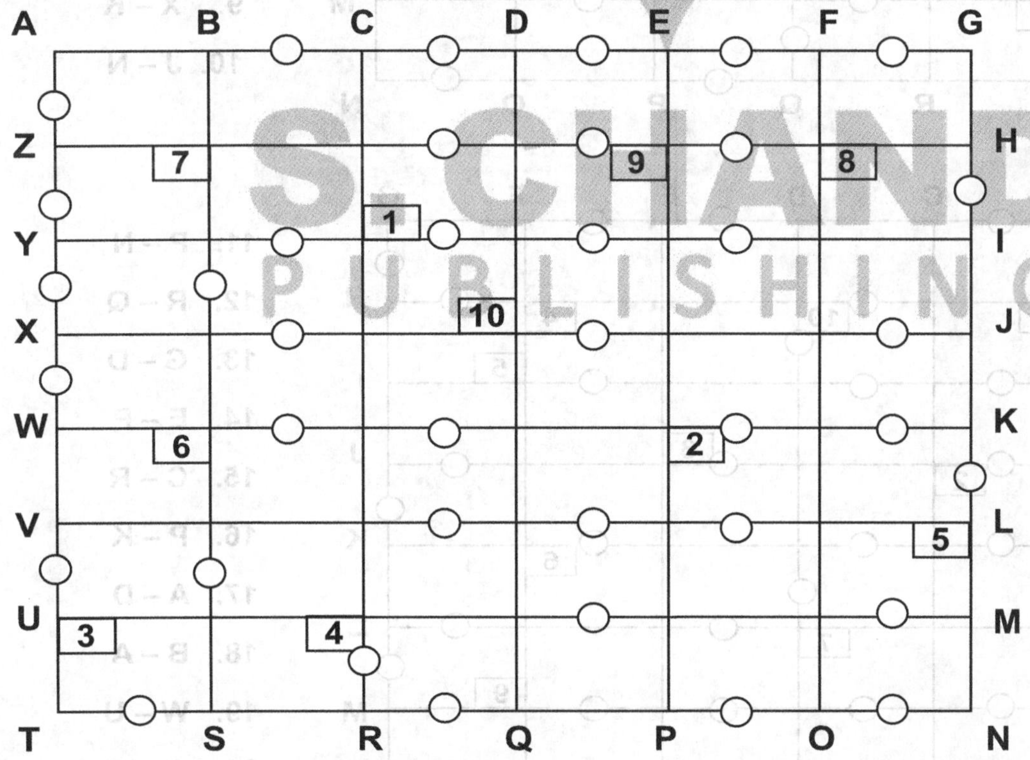

31. G - J
32. K - L
33. O - N
34. Q - E
35. P - Q
36. P - S
37. R - T
38. Q - W
39. V - Q
40. O - F

PRACTICE SET-20

Total Ques.- 40
Time - 5 or 8 Min.

निर्देश : (प्रश्न 1-40) इस अभ्यास में 40 प्रश्न दिए गए हैं जो चार उपखंडों 1, 2, 3 एवं 4 में 10-10 प्रश्नों (कुल 40 प्रश्न) के रूप में विभाजित है। प्रत्येक खण्ड के चित्रों को ध्यानपूर्वक देखकर दिए गए प्रत्येक प्रश्नों का उत्तर खोजकर अपने उत्तर-पत्रक में अंकित गोले को काला करें या माउस की सहायता से क्लिक करें और इसके लिए 5 या 8 मिनट का समय दिया जाता है।

Instructions: (Questions 1-40) : This exercise contains 40 questions, divided into four subsections: 1, 2, 3, and 4, each containing 10 questions (40 questions in total). Look carefully at the pictures in each section to find the answer to each question. Darken the circle on your answer sheet or click on it with the mouse. You are given 5 or 8 minutes for this.

उपखंड/Section-1

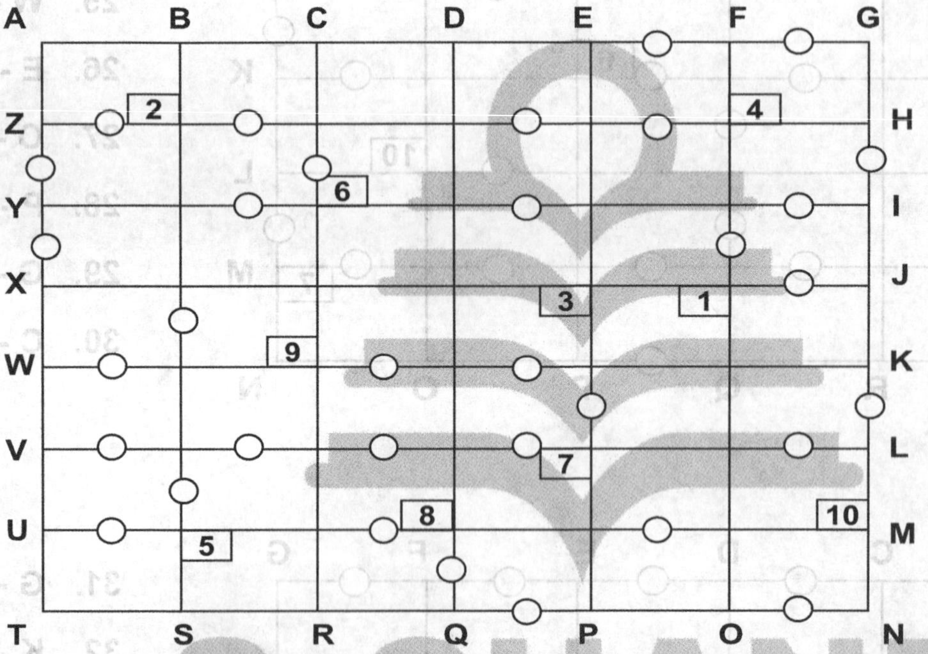

1. X – Z
2. V – R
3. R – X
4. D – P
5. P – O
6. K – L
7. G – E
8. E – D
9. X – K
10. J – N

उपखंड/Section-2

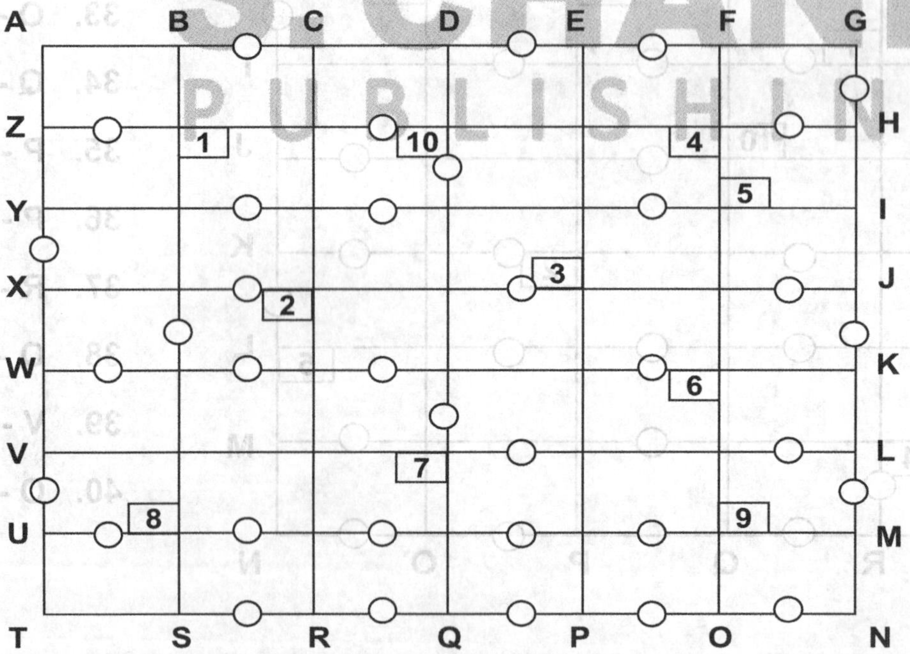

11. P – N
12. R – Q
13. G – D
14. E – P
15. C – R
16. P – K
17. A – D
18. B – A
19. W – U
20. J – K

उपखंड/Section-3

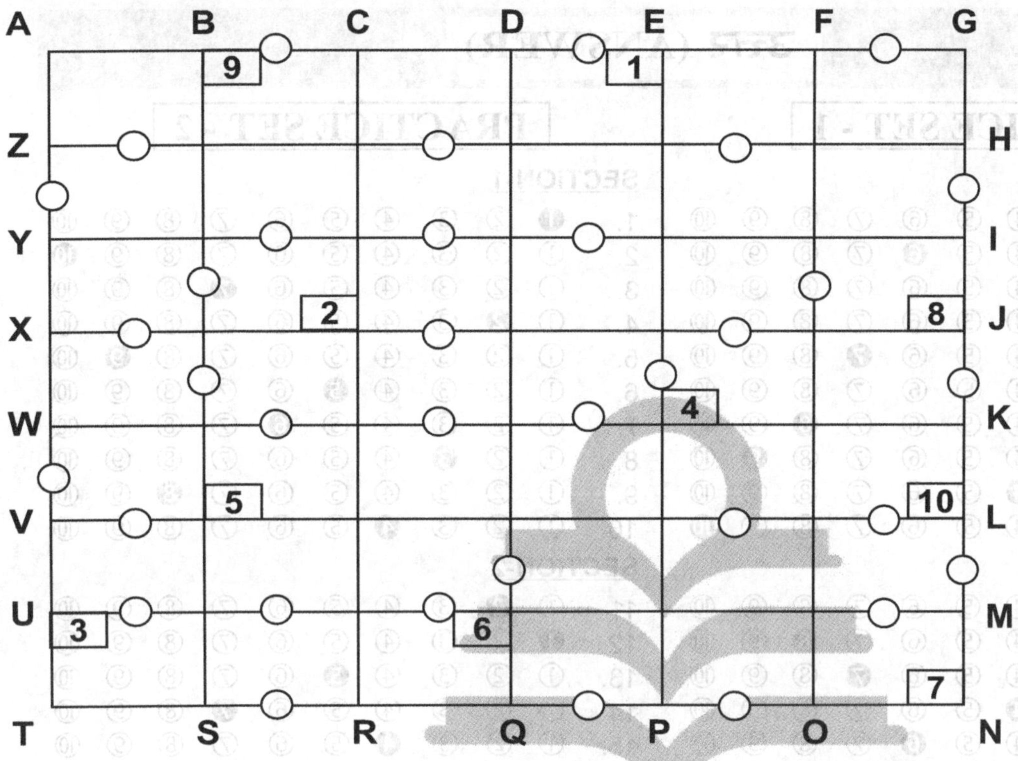

21. Z – X
22. X – S
23. P – M
24. D – G
25. H – K
26. O – L
27. C – R
28. R – P
29. P – O
30. V – S

उपखंड/Section-4

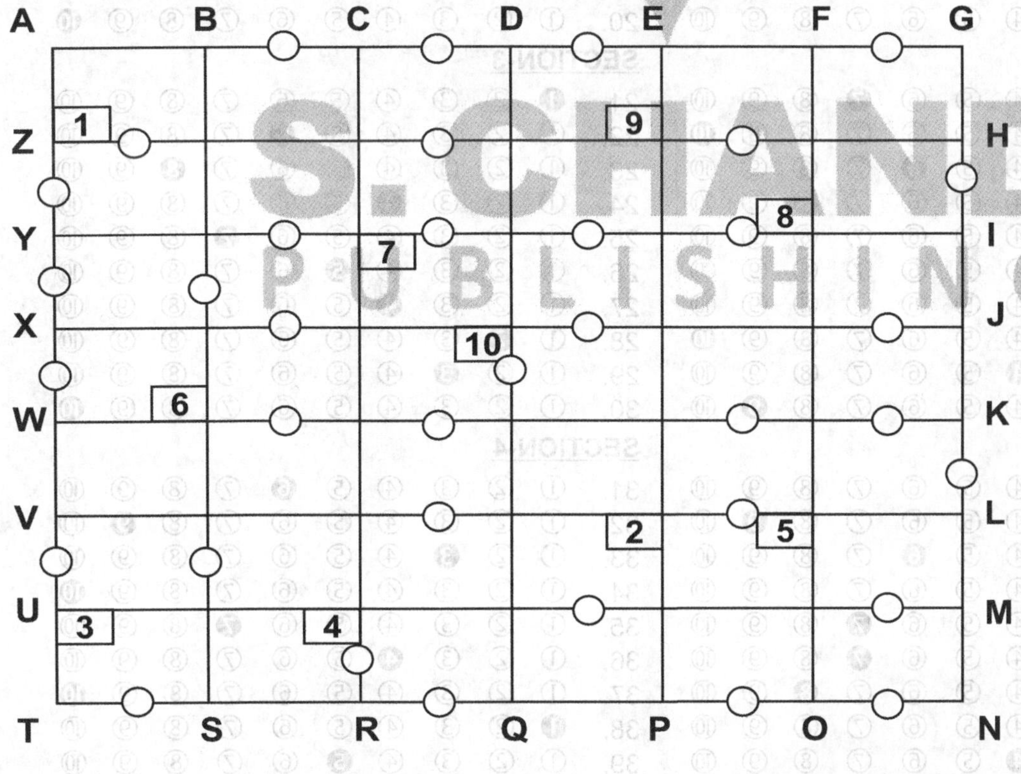

31. Y – Z
32. X – V
33. R – U
34. C – Q
35. S – P
36. Q – P
37. O – N
38. F – N
39. D – G
40. O – K

TEST FOR MEASURING SPATIAL SCANNING

उत्तर (ANSWER)

PRACTICE SET - 1

SECTION-1

1. ① ② ❸ ④ ⑤ ⑥ ⑦ ⑧ ⑨ ⑩
2. ① ② ③ ④ ⑤ ❻ ⑦ ⑧ ⑨ ⑩
3. ① ❷ ③ ④ ⑤ ⑥ ⑦ ⑧ ⑨ ⑩
4. ❶ ② ③ ④ ⑤ ⑥ ⑦ ⑧ ⑨ ⑩
5. ① ② ③ ④ ⑤ ⑥ ❼ ⑧ ⑨ ⑩
6. ① ② ❸ ④ ⑤ ⑥ ⑦ ⑧ ⑨ ⑩
7. ① ② ③ ④ ⑤ ⑥ ⑦ ❽ ⑨ ⑩
8. ① ② ③ ④ ⑤ ⑥ ⑦ ⑧ ❾ ⑩
9. ① ② ③ ❹ ⑤ ⑥ ⑦ ⑧ ⑨ ⑩
10. ① ② ③ ④ ⑤ ⑥ ⑦ ⑧ ⑨ ❿

SECTION-2

11. ① ❷ ③ ④ ⑤ ⑥ ⑦ ⑧ ⑨ ⑩
12. ① ② ③ ④ ⑤ ⑥ ⑦ ❽ ⑨ ⑩
13. ① ② ③ ④ ⑤ ⑥ ❼ ⑧ ⑨ ⑩
14. ① ② ③ ❹ ⑤ ⑥ ⑦ ⑧ ⑨ ⑩
15. ① ② ③ ④ ⑤ ❻ ⑦ ⑧ ⑨ ⑩
16. ❶ ② ③ ④ ⑤ ⑥ ⑦ ⑧ ⑨ ⑩
17. ① ② ③ ④ ⑤ ⑥ ⑦ ⑧ ⑨ ❿
18. ① ② ③ ④ ⑤ ⑥ ⑦ ⑧ ❾ ⑩
19. ① ② ❸ ④ ⑤ ⑥ ⑦ ⑧ ⑨ ⑩
20. ① ② ❸ ④ ⑤ ⑥ ⑦ ⑧ ⑨ ⑩

SECTION-3

21. ① ② ③ ④ ⑤ ⑥ ❼ ⑧ ⑨ ⑩
22. ① ② ③ ④ ⑤ ⑥ ⑦ ⑧ ⑨ ❿
23. ① ② ③ ④ ⑤ ❻ ⑦ ⑧ ⑨ ⑩
24. ① ② ③ ④ ⑤ ⑥ ⑦ ❽ ⑨ ⑩
25. ① ❷ ③ ④ ⑤ ⑥ ⑦ ⑧ ⑨ ⑩
26. ❶ ② ③ ④ ⑤ ⑥ ⑦ ⑧ ⑨ ⑩
27. ① ② ❸ ④ ⑤ ⑥ ⑦ ⑧ ⑨ ⑩
28. ① ② ③ ④ ⑤ ⑥ ⑦ ⑧ ⑨ ❿
29. ① ② ③ ❹ ⑤ ⑥ ⑦ ⑧ ⑨ ⑩
30. ① ② ③ ④ ⑤ ⑥ ⑦ ⑧ ❾ ⑩

SECTION-4

31. ① ❷ ③ ④ ⑤ ⑥ ⑦ ⑧ ⑨ ⑩
32. ① ② ③ ④ ⑤ ⑥ ⑦ ⑧ ❾ ⑩
33. ① ② ③ ④ ⑤ ❻ ⑦ ⑧ ⑨ ⑩
34. ❶ ② ③ ④ ⑤ ⑥ ⑦ ⑧ ⑨ ⑩
35. ① ② ③ ④ ⑤ ⑥ ❼ ⑧ ⑨ ⑩
36. ① ② ③ ④ ⑤ ⑥ ❼ ⑧ ⑨ ⑩
37. ① ② ③ ④ ⑤ ⑥ ⑦ ❽ ⑨ ⑩
38. ① ② ❸ ④ ⑤ ⑥ ⑦ ⑧ ⑨ ⑩
39. ① ② ③ ❹ ⑤ ⑥ ⑦ ⑧ ⑨ ⑩
40. ① ② ③ ④ ⑤ ⑥ ⑦ ⑧ ⑨ ❿

PRACTICE SET - 2

SECTION-1

1. ❶ ② ③ ④ ⑤ ⑥ ⑦ ⑧ ⑨ ⑩
2. ① ② ③ ④ ⑤ ⑥ ⑦ ⑧ ⑨ ❿
3. ① ② ③ ④ ⑤ ⑥ ❼ ⑧ ⑨ ⑩
4. ① ❷ ③ ④ ⑤ ⑥ ⑦ ⑧ ⑨ ⑩
5. ① ② ③ ④ ⑤ ⑥ ⑦ ⑧ ❾ ⑩
6. ① ② ③ ④ ❺ ⑥ ⑦ ⑧ ⑨ ⑩
7. ① ② ③ ④ ⑤ ❻ ⑦ ⑧ ⑨ ⑩
8. ① ② ❸ ④ ⑤ ⑥ ⑦ ⑧ ⑨ ⑩
9. ① ② ③ ④ ⑤ ⑥ ⑦ ❽ ⑨ ⑩
10. ① ② ③ ❹ ⑤ ⑥ ⑦ ⑧ ⑨ ⑩

SECTION-2

11. ① ❷ ③ ④ ⑤ ⑥ ⑦ ⑧ ⑨ ⑩
12. ❶ ② ③ ④ ⑤ ⑥ ⑦ ⑧ ⑨ ⑩
13. ① ② ③ ④ ❺ ⑥ ⑦ ⑧ ⑨ ⑩
14. ① ② ③ ④ ⑤ ⑥ ❼ ⑧ ⑨ ⑩
15. ① ② ③ ❹ ⑤ ⑥ ⑦ ⑧ ⑨ ⑩
16. ① ② ❸ ④ ⑤ ⑥ ⑦ ⑧ ⑨ ⑩
17. ① ② ③ ④ ⑤ ⑥ ⑦ ⑧ ❾ ⑩
18. ① ② ③ ④ ⑤ ⑥ ⑦ ❽ ⑨ ⑩
19. ① ② ③ ④ ⑤ ❻ ⑦ ⑧ ⑨ ⑩
20. ① ② ③ ④ ⑤ ⑥ ⑦ ⑧ ⑨ ❿

SECTION-3

21. ❶ ② ③ ④ ⑤ ⑥ ⑦ ⑧ ⑨ ⑩
22. ① ② ③ ④ ⑤ ❻ ⑦ ⑧ ⑨ ⑩
23. ① ② ③ ④ ⑤ ⑥ ⑦ ❽ ⑨ ⑩
24. ① ② ③ ❹ ⑤ ⑥ ⑦ ⑧ ⑨ ⑩
25. ① ② ③ ④ ⑤ ⑥ ❼ ⑧ ⑨ ⑩
26. ① ② ③ ④ ❺ ⑥ ⑦ ⑧ ⑨ ⑩
27. ① ② ③ ❹ ⑤ ⑥ ⑦ ⑧ ⑨ ⑩
28. ① ❷ ③ ④ ⑤ ⑥ ⑦ ⑧ ⑨ ⑩
29. ① ② ❸ ④ ⑤ ⑥ ⑦ ⑧ ⑨ ⑩
30. ① ② ③ ④ ⑤ ⑥ ⑦ ⑧ ⑨ ❿

SECTION-4

31. ① ② ③ ④ ⑤ ❻ ⑦ ⑧ ⑨ ⑩
32. ① ② ③ ④ ⑤ ⑥ ⑦ ⑧ ❾ ⑩
33. ① ② ❸ ④ ⑤ ⑥ ⑦ ⑧ ⑨ ⑩
34. ① ② ③ ④ ⑤ ⑥ ⑦ ⑧ ⑨ ❿
35. ① ② ③ ④ ⑤ ⑥ ❼ ⑧ ⑨ ⑩
36. ① ② ③ ❹ ⑤ ⑥ ⑦ ⑧ ⑨ ⑩
37. ① ② ③ ④ ⑤ ⑥ ⑦ ⑧ ⑨ ❿
38. ❶ ② ③ ④ ⑤ ⑥ ⑦ ⑧ ⑨ ⑩
39. ① ② ③ ④ ❺ ⑥ ⑦ ⑧ ⑨ ⑩
40. ① ❷ ③ ④ ⑤ ⑥ ⑦ ⑧ ⑨ ⑩

PRACTICE SET - 3

SECTION-1

1. ❶ ② ③ ④ ⑤ ⑥ ⑦ ⑧ ⑨ ⑩
2. ① ② ③ ❹ ⑤ ⑥ ⑦ ⑧ ⑨ ⑩
3. ① ② ③ ④ ⑤ ⑥ ⑦ ⑧ ❾ ⑩
4. ① ② ③ ④ ⑤ ⑥ ⑦ ⑧ ⑨ ❿
5. ① ② ③ ④ ⑤ ⑥ ❼ ⑧ ⑨ ⑩
6. ① ② ③ ④ ⑤ ⑥ ⑦ ❽ ⑨ ⑩
7. ❶ ② ③ ④ ⑤ ⑥ ⑦ ⑧ ⑨ ⑩
8. ① ② ③ ④ ❺ ⑥ ⑦ ⑧ ⑨ ⑩
9. ① ② ③ ④ ⑤ ❻ ⑦ ⑧ ⑨ ⑩
10. ① ② ❸ ④ ⑤ ⑥ ⑦ ⑧ ⑨ ⑩

SECTION-2

11. ① ② ③ ❹ ⑤ ⑥ ⑦ ⑧ ⑨ ⑩
12. ① ❷ ③ ④ ⑤ ⑥ ⑦ ⑧ ⑨ ⑩
13. ① ② ③ ④ ⑤ ⑥ ⑦ ⑧ ❾ ⑩
14. ① ② ③ ④ ⑤ ⑥ ❼ ⑧ ⑨ ⑩
15. ① ② ③ ④ ⑤ ⑥ ⑦ ❽ ⑨ ⑩
16. ① ② ③ ④ ⑤ ❻ ⑦ ⑧ ⑨ ⑩
17. ① ❷ ③ ④ ⑤ ⑥ ⑦ ⑧ ⑨ ⑩
18. ① ② ③ ④ ❺ ⑥ ⑦ ⑧ ⑨ ⑩
19. ① ② ❸ ④ ⑤ ⑥ ⑦ ⑧ ⑨ ⑩
20. ① ② ③ ④ ⑤ ⑥ ⑦ ⑧ ⑨ ❿

SECTION-3

21. ① ② ③ ④ ⑤ ⑥ ⑦ ⑧ ❾ ⑩
22. ① ❷ ③ ④ ⑤ ⑥ ⑦ ⑧ ⑨ ⑩
23. ① ② ③ ④ ⑤ ❻ ⑦ ⑧ ⑨ ⑩
24. ① ② ③ ④ ⑤ ⑥ ❼ ⑧ ⑨ ⑩
25. ① ② ③ ④ ⑤ ⑥ ⑦ ❽ ⑨ ⑩
26. ① ② ③ ❹ ⑤ ⑥ ⑦ ⑧ ⑨ ⑩
27. ❶ ② ③ ④ ⑤ ⑥ ⑦ ⑧ ⑨ ⑩
28. ① ② ③ ④ ❺ ⑥ ⑦ ⑧ ⑨ ⑩
29. ① ② ③ ④ ⑤ ⑥ ⑦ ⑧ ⑨ ❿
30. ① ② ❸ ④ ⑤ ⑥ ⑦ ⑧ ⑨ ⑩

SECTION-4

31. ① ② ③ ④ ⑤ ⑥ ⑦ ❽ ⑨ ⑩
32. ① ② ③ ❹ ⑤ ⑥ ⑦ ⑧ ⑨ ⑩
33. ① ② ③ ④ ❺ ⑥ ⑦ ⑧ ⑨ ⑩
34. ① ② ③ ④ ⑤ ⑥ ❼ ⑧ ⑨ ⑩
35. ① ② ③ ④ ⑤ ⑥ ⑦ ❽ ⑨ ⑩
36. ① ② ③ ④ ⑤ ❻ ⑦ ⑧ ⑨ ⑩
37. ① ❷ ③ ④ ⑤ ⑥ ⑦ ⑧ ⑨ ⑩
38. ① ② ❸ ④ ⑤ ⑥ ⑦ ⑧ ⑨ ⑩
39. ① ② ③ ④ ⑤ ⑥ ⑦ ⑧ ⑨ ❿
40. ❶ ② ③ ④ ⑤ ⑥ ⑦ ⑧ ⑨ ⑩

PRACTICE SET - 4

SECTION-1

1. ① ② ③ ④ ⑤ ⑥ ⑦ ⑧ ❾ ⑩
2. ❶ ② ③ ④ ⑤ ⑥ ⑦ ⑧ ⑨ ⑩
3. ① ② ③ ❹ ⑤ ⑥ ⑦ ⑧ ⑨ ⑩
4. ① ❷ ③ ④ ⑤ ⑥ ⑦ ⑧ ⑨ ⑩
5. ① ② ③ ④ ⑤ ⑥ ⑦ ❽ ⑨ ⑩
6. ① ② ❸ ④ ⑤ ⑥ ⑦ ⑧ ⑨ ⑩
7. ① ② ③ ④ ⑤ ⑥ ⑦ ⑧ ⑨ ❿
8. ① ② ③ ④ ⑤ ❻ ⑦ ⑧ ⑨ ⑩
9. ① ② ③ ④ ⑤ ❻ ⑦ ⑧ ⑨ ⑩
10. ① ② ③ ④ ⑤ ⑥ ❼ ⑧ ⑨ ⑩

SECTION-2

11. ① ② ③ ④ ⑤ ⑥ ❼ ⑧ ⑨ ⑩
12. ❶ ② ③ ④ ⑤ ⑥ ⑦ ⑧ ⑨ ⑩
13. ① ② ③ ④ ⑤ ⑥ ⑦ ❽ ⑨ ⑩
14. ① ② ③ ❹ ⑤ ⑥ ⑦ ⑧ ⑨ ⑩
15. ① ② ③ ④ ⑤ ⑥ ⑦ ⑧ ❾ ⑩
16. ① ② ③ ④ ❺ ⑥ ⑦ ⑧ ⑨ ⑩
17. ① ② ③ ④ ⑤ ⑥ ⑦ ⑧ ❾ ⑩
18. ① ② ❸ ④ ⑤ ⑥ ⑦ ⑧ ⑨ ⑩
19. ① ② ③ ④ ⑤ ⑥ ⑦ ⑧ ⑨ ❿
20. ① ❷ ③ ④ ⑤ ⑥ ⑦ ⑧ ⑨ ⑩

SECTION-3

21. ① ② ③ ④ ⑤ ⑥ ⑦ ❽ ⑨ ⑩
22. ❶ ② ③ ④ ⑤ ⑥ ⑦ ⑧ ⑨ ⑩
23. ① ② ❸ ④ ⑤ ⑥ ⑦ ⑧ ⑨ ⑩
24. ① ② ③ ④ ❺ ⑥ ⑦ ⑧ ⑨ ⑩
25. ① ❷ ③ ④ ⑤ ⑥ ⑦ ⑧ ⑨ ⑩
26. ① ② ③ ④ ⑤ ⑥ ⑦ ⑧ ❾ ⑩
27. ① ② ③ ④ ⑤ ⑥ ❼ ⑧ ⑨ ⑩
28. ① ② ③ ④ ⑤ ❻ ⑦ ⑧ ⑨ ⑩
29. ❶ ② ③ ④ ⑤ ⑥ ⑦ ⑧ ⑨ ⑩
30. ① ② ③ ④ ⑤ ⑥ ⑦ ⑧ ⑨ ❿

SECTION-4

31. ① ❷ ③ ④ ⑤ ⑥ ⑦ ⑧ ⑨ ⑩
32. ① ② ③ ④ ❺ ⑥ ⑦ ⑧ ⑨ ⑩
33. ① ② ③ ④ ⑤ ⑥ ⑦ ⑧ ❾ ⑩
34. ① ② ③ ❹ ⑤ ⑥ ⑦ ⑧ ⑨ ⑩
35. ① ② ③ ④ ⑤ ❻ ⑦ ⑧ ⑨ ⑩
36. ① ❷ ③ ④ ⑤ ⑥ ⑦ ⑧ ⑨ ⑩
37. ① ② ③ ④ ⑤ ⑥ ⑦ ❽ ⑨ ⑩
38. ① ② ③ ④ ⑤ ⑥ ❼ ⑧ ⑨ ⑩
39. ① ② ③ ④ ⑤ ⑥ ⑦ ⑧ ⑨ ❿
40. ① ② ❸ ④ ⑤ ⑥ ⑦ ⑧ ⑨ ⑩

PRACTICE SET - 5

SECTION-1

Q.	Answer
1.	5
2.	1
3.	7
4.	9
5.	2
6.	3
7.	4
8.	6
9.	10
10.	8

SECTION-2

Q.	Answer
11.	1
12.	4
13.	2
14.	7
15.	8
16.	10
17.	5
18.	9
19.	6
20.	3

SECTION-3

Q.	Answer
21.	9
22.	3
23.	2
24.	1
25.	5
26.	10
27.	5
28.	7
29.	4
30.	6

SECTION-4

Q.	Answer
31.	3
32.	7
33.	8
34.	4
35.	9
36.	2
37.	10
38.	1
39.	5
40.	6

PRACTICE SET - 6

SECTION-1

Q.	Answer
1.	9
2.	4
3.	5
4.	8
5.	7
6.	3
7.	6
8.	10
9.	1
10.	2

SECTION-2

Q.	Answer
11.	2
12.	3
13.	5
14.	1
15.	7
16.	9
17.	4
18.	10
19.	6
20.	8

SECTION-3

Q.	Answer
21.	1
22.	8
23.	9
24.	6
25.	3
26.	10
27.	6
28.	4
29.	7
30.	9

SECTION-4

Q.	Answer
31.	5
32.	9
33.	2
34.	3
35.	4
36.	1
37.	10
38.	8
39.	7
40.	6

PRACTICE SET - 7

SECTION-1

1. ❶ ② ③ ④ ⑤ ⑥ ⑦ ⑧ ⑨ ⑩
2. ① ② ③ ④ ⑤ ⑥ ⑦ ⑧ ❾ ⑩
3. ① ② ③ ④ ⑤ ⑥ ⑦ ❽ ⑨ ⑩
4. ① ② ③ ④ ❺ ⑥ ⑦ ⑧ ⑨ ⑩
5. ① ❷ ③ ④ ⑤ ⑥ ⑦ ⑧ ⑨ ⑩
6. ① ② ③ ❹ ⑤ ⑥ ⑦ ⑧ ⑨ ⑩
7. ① ② ③ ④ ⑤ ⑥ ❼ ⑧ ⑨ ⑩
8. ① ② ❸ ④ ⑤ ⑥ ⑦ ⑧ ⑨ ⑩
9. ① ② ③ ④ ⑤ ❻ ⑦ ⑧ ⑨ ⑩
10. ① ② ③ ④ ⑤ ⑥ ⑦ ⑧ ⑨ ❿

SECTION-2

11. ① ❷ ③ ④ ⑤ ⑥ ⑦ ⑧ ⑨ ⑩
12. ① ② ③ ④ ⑤ ⑥ ❼ ⑧ ⑨ ⑩
13. ① ② ③ ④ ❺ ⑥ ⑦ ⑧ ⑨ ⑩
14. ① ② ③ ④ ⑤ ⑥ ⑦ ❽ ⑨ ⑩
15. ① ② ❸ ④ ⑤ ⑥ ⑦ ⑧ ⑨ ⑩
16. ① ② ③ ❹ ⑤ ⑥ ⑦ ⑧ ⑨ ⑩
17. ① ② ③ ④ ❺ ⑥ ⑦ ⑧ ⑨ ⑩
18. ① ② ③ ④ ⑤ ⑥ ⑦ ⑧ ⑨ ❿
19. ❶ ② ③ ④ ⑤ ⑥ ⑦ ⑧ ⑨ ⑩
20. ① ② ③ ④ ⑤ ⑥ ⑦ ⑧ ❾ ⑩

SECTION-3

21. ① ② ③ ④ ⑤ ⑥ ⑦ ❽ ⑨ ⑩
22. ① ❷ ③ ④ ⑤ ⑥ ⑦ ⑧ ⑨ ⑩
23. ① ② ③ ❹ ⑤ ⑥ ⑦ ⑧ ⑨ ⑩
24. ① ② ③ ④ ⑤ ⑥ ⑦ ❽ ⑨ ⑩
25. ① ② ❸ ④ ⑤ ⑥ ⑦ ⑧ ⑨ ⑩
26. ① ② ③ ④ ⑤ ⑥ ❼ ⑧ ⑨ ⑩
27. ① ② ③ ④ ❺ ⑥ ⑦ ⑧ ⑨ ⑩
28. ① ② ③ ④ ⑤ ⑥ ⑦ ⑧ ⑨ ❿
29. ① ② ③ ④ ⑤ ❻ ⑦ ⑧ ⑨ ⑩
30. ❶ ② ③ ④ ⑤ ⑥ ⑦ ⑧ ⑨ ⑩

SECTION-4

31. ① ② ③ ④ ❺ ⑥ ⑦ ⑧ ⑨ ⑩
32. ① ② ③ ④ ⑤ ⑥ ⑦ ❽ ⑨ ⑩
33. ① ② ③ ❹ ⑤ ⑥ ⑦ ⑧ ⑨ ⑩
34. ① ② ❸ ④ ⑤ ⑥ ⑦ ⑧ ⑨ ⑩
35. ① ② ③ ④ ⑤ ⑥ ⑦ ⑧ ❾ ⑩
36. ① ② ③ ④ ⑤ ❻ ⑦ ⑧ ⑨ ⑩
37. ① ② ③ ④ ⑤ ⑥ ⑦ ⑧ ❾ ⑩
38. ① ② ③ ④ ⑤ ⑥ ⑦ ⑧ ⑨ ❿
39. ① ❷ ③ ④ ⑤ ⑥ ⑦ ⑧ ⑨ ⑩
40. ① ② ③ ④ ⑤ ⑥ ❼ ⑧ ⑨ ⑩

PRACTICE SET - 8

SECTION-1

1. ① ② ❸ ④ ⑤ ⑥ ⑦ ⑧ ⑨ ⑩
2. ❶ ② ③ ④ ⑤ ⑥ ⑦ ⑧ ⑨ ⑩
3. ① ② ③ ④ ⑤ ⑥ ⑦ ❽ ⑨ ⑩
4. ❶ ② ③ ④ ⑤ ⑥ ⑦ ⑧ ⑨ ⑩
5. ① ② ③ ④ ⑤ ⑥ ⑦ ⑧ ❾ ⑩
6. ① ② ③ ④ ⑤ ⑥ ❼ ⑧ ⑨ ⑩
7. ① ② ③ ④ ❺ ⑥ ⑦ ⑧ ⑨ ⑩
8. ① ② ③ ❹ ⑤ ⑥ ⑦ ⑧ ⑨ ⑩
9. ① ② ③ ④ ⑤ ❻ ⑦ ⑧ ⑨ ⑩
10. ① ② ③ ④ ⑤ ⑥ ⑦ ⑧ ⑨ ❿

SECTION-2

11. ① ❷ ③ ④ ⑤ ⑥ ⑦ ⑧ ⑨ ⑩
12. ① ② ③ ④ ⑤ ⑥ ⑦ ⑧ ❾ ⑩
13. ① ② ❸ ④ ⑤ ⑥ ⑦ ⑧ ⑨ ⑩
14. ① ② ③ ④ ❺ ⑥ ⑦ ⑧ ⑨ ⑩
15. ① ② ③ ❹ ⑤ ⑥ ⑦ ⑧ ⑨ ⑩
16. ① ② ③ ④ ⑤ ⑥ ⑦ ❽ ⑨ ⑩
17. ① ② ③ ④ ⑤ ❻ ⑦ ⑧ ⑨ ⑩
18. ❶ ② ③ ④ ⑤ ⑥ ⑦ ⑧ ⑨ ⑩
19. ① ② ③ ④ ⑤ ⑥ ❼ ⑧ ⑨ ⑩
20. ① ② ③ ④ ⑤ ⑥ ⑦ ⑧ ⑨ ❿

SECTION-3

21. ① ❷ ③ ④ ⑤ ⑥ ⑦ ⑧ ⑨ ⑩
22. ① ② ③ ④ ⑤ ⑥ ⑦ ❽ ⑨ ⑩
23. ❶ ② ③ ④ ⑤ ⑥ ⑦ ⑧ ⑨ ⑩
24. ❶ ② ③ ④ ⑤ ⑥ ⑦ ⑧ ⑨ ⑩
25. ① ② ③ ④ ❺ ⑥ ⑦ ⑧ ⑨ ⑩
26. ① ② ③ ④ ⑤ ⑥ ❼ ⑧ ⑨ ⑩
27. ① ② ③ ④ ⑤ ⑥ ⑦ ⑧ ❾ ⑩
28. ① ② ③ ④ ⑤ ❻ ⑦ ⑧ ⑨ ⑩
29. ① ② ③ ④ ⑤ ⑥ ⑦ ⑧ ⑨ ❿
30. ① ② ❸ ④ ⑤ ⑥ ⑦ ⑧ ⑨ ⑩

SECTION-4

31. ① ❷ ③ ④ ⑤ ⑥ ⑦ ⑧ ⑨ ⑩
32. ① ② ③ ④ ⑤ ⑥ ⑦ ⑧ ⑨ ❿
33. ① ② ③ ④ ⑤ ❻ ⑦ ⑧ ⑨ ⑩
34. ① ② ❸ ④ ⑤ ⑥ ⑦ ⑧ ⑨ ⑩
35. ① ② ③ ④ ⑤ ⑥ ⑦ ❽ ⑨ ⑩
36. ① ② ③ ④ ⑤ ⑥ ⑦ ⑧ ❾ ⑩
37. ① ② ③ ④ ⑤ ⑥ ❼ ⑧ ⑨ ⑩
38. ① ② ③ ❹ ⑤ ⑥ ⑦ ⑧ ⑨ ⑩
39. ① ② ③ ④ ⑤ ⑥ ⑦ ⑧ ⑨ ❿
40. ① ② ③ ④ ❺ ⑥ ⑦ ⑧ ⑨ ⑩

PRACTICE SET - 9

SECTION-1

1. ① ② ③ ④ ⑤ ⑥ ⑦ ❽ ⑨ ⑩
2. ① ❷ ③ ④ ⑤ ⑥ ⑦ ⑧ ⑨ ⑩
3. ① ② ③ ④ ⑤ ⑥ ❼ ⑧ ⑨ ⑩
4. ① ② ③ ④ ⑤ ⑥ ⑦ ⑧ ⑨ ❿
5. ① ② ❸ ④ ⑤ ⑥ ⑦ ⑧ ⑨ ⑩
6. ❶ ② ③ ④ ⑤ ⑥ ⑦ ⑧ ⑨ ⑩
7. ① ② ③ ④ ⑤ ⑥ ⑦ ⑧ ❾ ⑩
8. ① ② ③ ④ ❺ ⑥ ⑦ ⑧ ⑨ ⑩
9. ① ② ③ ❹ ⑤ ⑥ ⑦ ⑧ ⑨ ⑩
10. ① ② ③ ④ ⑤ ❻ ⑦ ⑧ ⑨ ⑩

SECTION-2

11. ❶ ② ③ ④ ⑤ ⑥ ⑦ ⑧ ⑨ ⑩
12. ① ② ③ ④ ❺ ⑥ ⑦ ⑧ ⑨ ⑩
13. ① ② ③ ❹ ⑤ ⑥ ⑦ ⑧ ⑨ ⑩
14. ① ② ③ ④ ⑤ ⑥ ⑦ ⑧ ❾ ⑩
15. ① ② ③ ④ ⑤ ⑥ ❼ ⑧ ⑨ ⑩
16. ① ❷ ③ ④ ⑤ ⑥ ⑦ ⑧ ⑨ ⑩
17. ① ② ③ ④ ⑤ ⑥ ⑦ ⑧ ⑨ ❿
18. ① ② ③ ④ ⑤ ⑥ ⑦ ❽ ⑨ ⑩
19. ① ② ❸ ④ ⑤ ⑥ ⑦ ⑧ ⑨ ⑩
20. ① ② ③ ④ ⑤ ❻ ⑦ ⑧ ⑨ ⑩

SECTION-3

21. ① ② ③ ④ ❺ ⑥ ⑦ ⑧ ⑨ ⑩
22. ① ② ③ ④ ⑤ ⑥ ⑦ ❽ ⑨ ⑩
23. ① ② ③ ❹ ⑤ ⑥ ⑦ ⑧ ⑨ ⑩
24. ① ② ③ ④ ⑤ ⑥ ⑦ ⑧ ❾ ⑩
25. ① ❷ ③ ④ ⑤ ⑥ ⑦ ⑧ ⑨ ⑩
26. ① ② ❸ ④ ⑤ ⑥ ⑦ ⑧ ⑨ ⑩
27. ❶ ② ③ ④ ⑤ ⑥ ⑦ ⑧ ⑨ ⑩
28. ① ② ③ ④ ⑤ ❻ ⑦ ⑧ ⑨ ⑩
29. ① ② ③ ④ ⑤ ⑥ ❼ ⑧ ⑨ ⑩
30. ① ② ③ ④ ⑤ ⑥ ⑦ ⑧ ⑨ ❿

SECTION-4

31. ① ② ③ ❹ ⑤ ⑥ ⑦ ⑧ ⑨ ⑩
32. ① ② ❸ ④ ⑤ ⑥ ⑦ ⑧ ⑨ ⑩
33. ① ② ③ ④ ⑤ ⑥ ⑦ ❽ ⑨ ⑩
34. ① ② ③ ④ ⑤ ⑥ ⑦ ⑧ ❾ ⑩
35. ① ② ③ ④ ⑤ ⑥ ❼ ⑧ ⑨ ⑩
36. ① ② ③ ④ ❺ ⑥ ⑦ ⑧ ⑨ ⑩
37. ① ❷ ③ ④ ⑤ ⑥ ⑦ ⑧ ⑨ ⑩
38. ❶ ② ③ ④ ⑤ ⑥ ⑦ ⑧ ⑨ ⑩
39. ① ② ③ ④ ⑤ ⑥ ❼ ⑧ ⑨ ⑩
40. ① ② ③ ④ ⑤ ⑥ ⑦ ⑧ ⑨ ❿

PRACTICE SET - 10

SECTION-1

1. ❶ ② ③ ④ ⑤ ⑥ ⑦ ⑧ ⑨ ⑩
2. ① ② ③ ④ ⑤ ⑥ ❼ ⑧ ⑨ ⑩
3. ① ❷ ③ ④ ⑤ ⑥ ⑦ ⑧ ⑨ ⑩
4. ① ② ③ ④ ❺ ⑥ ⑦ ⑧ ⑨ ⑩
5. ① ② ③ ④ ⑤ ❻ ⑦ ⑧ ⑨ ⑩
6. ① ② ③ ④ ⑤ ⑥ ⑦ ⑧ ⑨ ❿
7. ❶ ② ③ ④ ⑤ ⑥ ⑦ ⑧ ⑨ ⑩
8. ① ② ③ ④ ⑤ ⑥ ⑦ ❽ ⑨ ⑩
9. ① ② ③ ❹ ⑤ ⑥ ⑦ ⑧ ⑨ ⑩
10. ① ② ❸ ④ ⑤ ⑥ ⑦ ⑧ ⑨ ⑩

SECTION-2

11. ① ② ③ ④ ⑤ ⑥ ⑦ ⑧ ❾ ⑩
12. ① ② ③ ④ ❺ ⑥ ⑦ ⑧ ⑨ ⑩
13. ① ② ③ ❹ ⑤ ⑥ ⑦ ⑧ ⑨ ⑩
14. ① ② ❸ ④ ⑤ ⑥ ⑦ ⑧ ⑨ ⑩
15. ① ② ③ ④ ⑤ ⑥ ⑦ ❽ ⑨ ⑩
16. ① ② ③ ④ ⑤ ❻ ⑦ ⑧ ⑨ ⑩
17. ① ② ③ ④ ⑤ ⑥ ❼ ⑧ ⑨ ⑩
18. ① ② ③ ④ ⑤ ⑥ ⑦ ⑧ ⑨ ❿
19. ① ❷ ③ ④ ⑤ ⑥ ⑦ ⑧ ⑨ ⑩
20. ❶ ② ③ ④ ⑤ ⑥ ⑦ ⑧ ⑨ ⑩

SECTION-3

21. ① ❷ ③ ④ ⑤ ⑥ ⑦ ⑧ ⑨ ⑩
22. ① ② ③ ④ ⑤ ⑥ ⑦ ⑧ ❾ ⑩
23. ❶ ② ③ ④ ⑤ ⑥ ⑦ ⑧ ⑨ ⑩
24. ① ② ❸ ④ ⑤ ⑥ ⑦ ⑧ ⑨ ⑩
25. ① ② ③ ④ ⑤ ❻ ⑦ ⑧ ⑨ ⑩
26. ① ② ③ ❹ ⑤ ⑥ ⑦ ⑧ ⑨ ⑩
27. ① ② ③ ④ ⑤ ⑥ ⑦ ❽ ⑨ ⑩
28. ① ② ③ ④ ❺ ⑥ ⑦ ⑧ ⑨ ⑩
29. ① ② ③ ④ ⑤ ⑥ ❼ ⑧ ⑨ ⑩
30. ① ② ③ ④ ⑤ ⑥ ⑦ ⑧ ⑨ ❿

SECTION-4

31. ① ② ❸ ④ ⑤ ⑥ ⑦ ⑧ ⑨ ⑩
32. ① ② ③ ④ ⑤ ⑥ ⑦ ❽ ⑨ ⑩
33. ① ② ③ ④ ⑤ ⑥ ❼ ⑧ ⑨ ⑩
34. ① ❷ ③ ④ ⑤ ⑥ ⑦ ⑧ ⑨ ⑩
35. ① ② ③ ④ ⑤ ⑥ ⑦ ⑧ ❾ ⑩
36. ① ② ③ ④ ⑤ ❻ ⑦ ⑧ ⑨ ⑩
37. ① ② ③ ④ ❺ ⑥ ⑦ ⑧ ⑨ ⑩
38. ① ② ③ ④ ⑤ ⑥ ⑦ ⑧ ⑨ ❿
39. ① ② ③ ④ ⑤ ⑥ ⑦ ⑧ ❾ ⑩
40. ❶ ② ③ ④ ⑤ ⑥ ⑦ ⑧ ⑨ ⑩

PRACTICE SET - 11

SECTION-1

1. ❶ ② ③ ④ ⑤ ⑥ ⑦ ⑧ ⑨ ⑩
2. ① ② ③ ④ ⑤ ❻ ⑦ ⑧ ⑨ ⑩
3. ① ❷ ③ ④ ⑤ ⑥ ⑦ ⑧ ⑨ ⑩
4. ❶ ② ③ ④ ⑤ ⑥ ⑦ ⑧ ⑨ ⑩
5. ① ② ③ ④ ❺ ⑥ ⑦ ⑧ ⑨ ⑩
6. ① ② ❸ ④ ⑤ ⑥ ⑦ ⑧ ⑨ ⑩
7. ① ② ③ ④ ⑤ ⑥ ❼ ⑧ ⑨ ⑩
8. ① ② ③ ④ ⑤ ⑥ ⑦ ❽ ⑨ ⑩
9. ① ② ③ ④ ⑤ ⑥ ⑦ ⑧ ❾ ⑩
10. ① ② ③ ❹ ⑤ ⑥ ⑦ ⑧ ⑨ ⑩

SECTION-2

11. ① ② ③ ❹ ⑤ ⑥ ⑦ ⑧ ⑨ ⑩
12. ① ② ③ ④ ⑤ ⑥ ⑦ ❽ ⑨ ⑩
13. ① ❷ ③ ④ ⑤ ⑥ ⑦ ⑧ ⑨ ⑩
14. ① ② ③ ④ ⑤ ⑥ ❼ ⑧ ⑨ ⑩
15. ❶ ② ③ ④ ⑤ ⑥ ⑦ ⑧ ⑨ ⑩
16. ① ② ❸ ④ ⑤ ⑥ ⑦ ⑧ ⑨ ⑩
17. ① ② ③ ④ ❺ ⑥ ⑦ ⑧ ⑨ ⑩
18. ① ② ③ ④ ⑤ ⑥ ⑦ ⑧ ⑨ ❿
19. ① ② ③ ④ ⑤ ❻ ⑦ ⑧ ⑨ ⑩
20. ① ② ③ ④ ⑤ ⑥ ⑦ ⑧ ❾ ⑩

SECTION-3

21. ① ❷ ③ ④ ⑤ ⑥ ⑦ ⑧ ⑨ ⑩
22. ① ② ③ ④ ⑤ ❻ ⑦ ⑧ ⑨ ⑩
23. ❶ ② ③ ④ ⑤ ⑥ ⑦ ⑧ ⑨ ⑩
24. ① ② ③ ❹ ⑤ ⑥ ⑦ ⑧ ⑨ ⑩
25. ① ② ③ ④ ⑤ ⑥ ⑦ ❽ ⑨ ⑩
26. ① ② ③ ④ ⑤ ⑥ ⑦ ⑧ ❾ ⑩
27. ① ② ③ ④ ⑤ ⑥ ❼ ⑧ ⑨ ⑩
28. ① ② ③ ④ ⑤ ⑥ ⑦ ⑧ ❾ ⑩
29. ① ② ❸ ④ ⑤ ⑥ ⑦ ⑧ ⑨ ⑩
30. ① ② ③ ④ ❺ ⑥ ⑦ ⑧ ⑨ ⑩

SECTION-4

31. ① ② ③ ④ ⑤ ⑥ ⑦ ⑧ ❾ ⑩
32. ① ❷ ③ ④ ⑤ ⑥ ⑦ ⑧ ⑨ ⑩
33. ① ② ③ ④ ❺ ⑥ ⑦ ⑧ ⑨ ⑩
34. ① ② ③ ④ ⑤ ⑥ ⑦ ⑧ ⑨ ❿
35. ① ② ③ ④ ⑤ ⑥ ❼ ⑧ ⑨ ⑩
36. ① ② ③ ❹ ⑤ ⑥ ⑦ ⑧ ⑨ ⑩
37. ① ② ③ ④ ⑤ ⑥ ❼ ⑧ ⑨ ⑩
38. ① ② ③ ④ ⑤ ⑥ ⑦ ❽ ⑨ ⑩
39. ① ② ❸ ④ ⑤ ⑥ ⑦ ⑧ ⑨ ⑩
40. ① ② ③ ④ ❺ ⑥ ⑦ ⑧ ⑨ ⑩

PRACTICE SET - 12

SECTION-1

1. ① ② ③ ④ ⑤ ⑥ ⑦ ⑧ ❾ ⑩
2. ① ② ③ ④ ⑤ ⑥ ⑦ ⑧ ⑨ ❿
3. ❶ ② ③ ④ ⑤ ⑥ ⑦ ⑧ ⑨ ⑩
4. ① ② ③ ④ ⑤ ⑥ ⑦ ❽ ⑨ ⑩
5. ① ❷ ③ ④ ⑤ ⑥ ⑦ ⑧ ⑨ ⑩
6. ① ② ❸ ④ ⑤ ⑥ ⑦ ⑧ ⑨ ⑩
7. ① ② ③ ④ ⑤ ❻ ⑦ ⑧ ⑨ ⑩
8. ① ② ③ ④ ⑤ ⑥ ⑦ ❽ ⑨ ⑩
9. ① ② ③ ④ ⑤ ⑥ ❼ ⑧ ⑨ ⑩
10. ① ② ③ ④ ⑤ ⑥ ⑦ ⑧ ❾ ⑩

SECTION-2

11. ① ❷ ③ ④ ⑤ ⑥ ⑦ ⑧ ⑨ ⑩
12. ① ② ③ ❹ ⑤ ⑥ ⑦ ⑧ ⑨ ⑩
13. ① ② ③ ④ ⑤ ⑥ ⑦ ❽ ⑨ ⑩
14. ① ② ③ ❹ ⑤ ⑥ ⑦ ⑧ ⑨ ⑩
15. ① ② ③ ④ ⑤ ⑥ ⑦ ⑧ ⑨ ❿
16. ① ② ③ ④ ❺ ⑥ ⑦ ⑧ ⑨ ⑩
17. ❶ ② ③ ④ ⑤ ⑥ ⑦ ⑧ ⑨ ⑩
18. ① ② ③ ④ ⑤ ❻ ⑦ ⑧ ⑨ ⑩
19. ① ② ❸ ④ ⑤ ⑥ ⑦ ⑧ ⑨ ⑩
20. ① ② ③ ④ ⑤ ⑥ ⑦ ❽ ⑨ ⑩

SECTION-3

21. ① ② ③ ④ ⑤ ⑥ ⑦ ⑧ ⑨ ❿
22. ① ② ③ ④ ⑤ ❻ ⑦ ⑧ ⑨ ⑩
23. ① ② ③ ④ ⑤ ⑥ ⑦ ⑧ ❾ ⑩
24. ① ② ❸ ④ ⑤ ⑥ ⑦ ⑧ ⑨ ⑩
25. ① ② ③ ④ ⑤ ⑥ ❼ ⑧ ⑨ ⑩
26. ❶ ② ③ ④ ⑤ ⑥ ⑦ ⑧ ⑨ ⑩
27. ① ② ③ ④ ⑤ ⑥ ⑦ ⑧ ❾ ⑩
28. ① ② ③ ④ ❺ ⑥ ⑦ ⑧ ⑨ ⑩
29. ① ❷ ③ ④ ⑤ ⑥ ⑦ ⑧ ⑨ ⑩
30. ① ② ③ ④ ⑤ ⑥ ⑦ ⑧ ❾ ⑩

SECTION-4

31. ① ② ③ ④ ⑤ ⑥ ⑦ ⑧ ❾ ⑩
32. ① ② ③ ❹ ⑤ ⑥ ⑦ ⑧ ⑨ ⑩
33. ① ② ③ ④ ⑤ ❻ ⑦ ⑧ ⑨ ⑩
34. ① ② ③ ④ ❺ ⑥ ⑦ ⑧ ⑨ ⑩
35. ❶ ② ③ ④ ⑤ ⑥ ⑦ ⑧ ⑨ ⑩
36. ① ② ③ ④ ⑤ ⑥ ❼ ⑧ ⑨ ⑩
37. ① ② ③ ④ ⑤ ⑥ ⑦ ❽ ⑨ ⑩
38. ① ② ❸ ④ ⑤ ⑥ ⑦ ⑧ ⑨ ⑩
39. ❶ ② ③ ④ ⑤ ⑥ ⑦ ⑧ ⑨ ⑩
40. ① ❷ ③ ④ ⑤ ⑥ ⑦ ⑧ ⑨ ⑩

PRACTICE SET - 13

SECTION-1

1. ① ② ③ ④ ⑤ ⑥ ⑦ ⑧ ⑨ ❿
2. ❶ ② ③ ④ ⑤ ⑥ ⑦ ⑧ ⑨ ⑩
3. ① ② ③ ④ ⑤ ⑥ ❼ ⑧ ⑨ ⑩
4. ① ② ③ ④ ⑤ ⑥ ⑦ ❽ ⑨ ⑩
5. ① ② ③ ④ ⑤ ❻ ⑦ ⑧ ⑨ ⑩
6. ① ② ③ ❹ ⑤ ⑥ ⑦ ⑧ ⑨ ⑩
7. ① ② ③ ④ ❺ ⑥ ⑦ ⑧ ⑨ ⑩
8. ① ❷ ③ ④ ⑤ ⑥ ⑦ ⑧ ⑨ ⑩
9. ① ② ③ ④ ⑤ ❻ ⑦ ⑧ ⑨ ⑩
10. ① ② ③ ④ ❺ ⑥ ⑦ ⑧ ⑨ ⑩

SECTION-2

11. ① ② ③ ④ ⑤ ⑥ ⑦ ⑧ ⑨ ❿
12. ① ② ❸ ④ ⑤ ⑥ ⑦ ⑧ ⑨ ⑩
13. ① ② ③ ❹ ⑤ ⑥ ⑦ ⑧ ⑨ ⑩
14. ① ❷ ③ ④ ⑤ ⑥ ⑦ ⑧ ⑨ ⑩
15. ① ② ③ ④ ⑤ ❻ ⑦ ⑧ ⑨ ⑩
16. ① ② ❸ ④ ⑤ ⑥ ⑦ ⑧ ⑨ ⑩
17. ① ② ③ ④ ⑤ ⑥ ⑦ ❽ ⑨ ⑩
18. ① ② ③ ④ ⑤ ⑥ ⑦ ⑧ ❾ ⑩
19. ① ② ③ ④ ⑤ ⑥ ❼ ⑧ ⑨ ⑩
20. ① ② ③ ④ ⑤ ⑥ ⑦ ❽ ⑨ ⑩

SECTION-3

21. ① ❷ ③ ④ ⑤ ⑥ ⑦ ⑧ ⑨ ⑩
22. ① ❷ ③ ④ ⑤ ⑥ ⑦ ⑧ ⑨ ⑩
23. ① ② ③ ④ ⑤ ⑥ ⑦ ⑧ ❾ ⑩
24. ❶ ② ③ ④ ⑤ ⑥ ⑦ ⑧ ⑨ ⑩
25. ① ② ❸ ④ ⑤ ⑥ ⑦ ⑧ ⑨ ⑩
26. ① ② ③ ④ ⑤ ❻ ⑦ ⑧ ⑨ ⑩
27. ① ❷ ③ ④ ⑤ ⑥ ⑦ ⑧ ⑨ ⑩
28. ❶ ② ③ ④ ⑤ ⑥ ⑦ ⑧ ⑨ ⑩
29. ① ② ③ ④ ⑤ ⑥ ⑦ ❽ ⑨ ⑩
30. ① ② ③ ❹ ⑤ ⑥ ⑦ ⑧ ⑨ ⑩

SECTION-4

31. ① ② ③ ④ ⑤ ⑥ ⑦ ⑧ ❾ ⑩
32. ① ② ❸ ④ ⑤ ⑥ ⑦ ⑧ ⑨ ⑩
33. ❶ ② ③ ④ ⑤ ⑥ ⑦ ⑧ ⑨ ⑩
34. ① ② ③ ④ ⑤ ❻ ⑦ ⑧ ⑨ ⑩
35. ① ② ③ ④ ⑤ ⑥ ⑦ ⑧ ⑨ ❿
36. ① ❷ ③ ④ ⑤ ⑥ ⑦ ⑧ ⑨ ⑩
37. ① ② ③ ④ ⑤ ⑥ ❼ ⑧ ⑨ ⑩
38. ① ② ③ ❹ ⑤ ⑥ ⑦ ⑧ ⑨ ⑩
39. ① ② ③ ④ ⑤ ⑥ ⑦ ❽ ⑨ ⑩
40. ① ② ③ ❹ ⑤ ⑥ ⑦ ⑧ ⑨ ⑩

PRACTICE SET - 14

SECTION-1

1. ① ② ③ ④ ⑤ ⑥ ❼ ⑧ ⑨ ⑩
2. ❶ ② ③ ④ ⑤ ⑥ ⑦ ⑧ ⑨ ⑩
3. ① ② ❸ ④ ⑤ ⑥ ⑦ ⑧ ⑨ ⑩
4. ① ② ③ ④ ⑤ ⑥ ⑦ ⑧ ❾ ⑩
5. ① ② ③ ④ ⑤ ⑥ ⑦ ❽ ⑨ ⑩
6. ① ② ③ ④ ❺ ⑥ ⑦ ⑧ ⑨ ⑩
7. ① ② ③ ④ ⑤ ❻ ⑦ ⑧ ⑨ ⑩
8. ① ② ③ ④ ⑤ ⑥ ⑦ ⑧ ⑨ ❿
9. ① ❷ ③ ④ ⑤ ⑥ ⑦ ⑧ ⑨ ⑩
10. ① ② ③ ④ ⑤ ⑥ ⑦ ⑧ ❾ ⑩

SECTION-2

11. ① ❷ ③ ④ ⑤ ⑥ ⑦ ⑧ ⑨ ⑩
12. ① ② ③ ④ ⑤ ❻ ⑦ ⑧ ⑨ ⑩
13. ① ② ③ ④ ❺ ⑥ ⑦ ⑧ ⑨ ⑩
14. ① ② ③ ❹ ⑤ ⑥ ⑦ ⑧ ⑨ ⑩
15. ① ② ❸ ④ ⑤ ⑥ ⑦ ⑧ ⑨ ⑩
16. ① ② ③ ④ ⑤ ⑥ ❼ ⑧ ⑨ ⑩
17. ① ② ③ ④ ⑤ ⑥ ⑦ ⑧ ⑨ ❿
18. ① ② ③ ④ ⑤ ⑥ ⑦ ❽ ⑨ ⑩
19. ❶ ② ③ ④ ⑤ ⑥ ⑦ ⑧ ⑨ ⑩
20. ① ② ③ ④ ⑤ ⑥ ⑦ ⑧ ❾ ⑩

SECTION-3

21. ① ② ❸ ④ ⑤ ⑥ ⑦ ⑧ ⑨ ⑩
22. ① ② ③ ❹ ⑤ ⑥ ⑦ ⑧ ⑨ ⑩
23. ① ② ③ ④ ⑤ ⑥ ⑦ ⑧ ❾ ⑩
24. ① ② ③ ④ ⑤ ⑥ ⑦ ❽ ⑨ ⑩
25. ① ② ③ ④ ⑤ ⑥ ❼ ⑧ ⑨ ⑩
26. ① ② ③ ④ ⑤ ⑥ ⑦ ⑧ ⑨ ❿
27. ① ② ③ ④ ❺ ⑥ ⑦ ⑧ ⑨ ⑩
28. ① ② ③ ④ ⑤ ❻ ⑦ ⑧ ⑨ ⑩
29. ① ② ③ ④ ⑤ ⑥ ⑦ ⑧ ❾ ⑩
30. ❶ ② ③ ④ ⑤ ⑥ ⑦ ⑧ ⑨ ⑩

SECTION-4

31. ① ② ③ ④ ⑤ ❻ ⑦ ⑧ ⑨ ⑩
32. ① ② ③ ④ ⑤ ⑥ ⑦ ⑧ ❾ ⑩
33. ① ② ③ ④ ⑤ ⑥ ⑦ ⑧ ⑨ ❿
34. ① ② ③ ❹ ⑤ ⑥ ⑦ ⑧ ⑨ ⑩
35. ① ❷ ③ ④ ⑤ ⑥ ⑦ ⑧ ⑨ ⑩
36. ① ② ③ ④ ⑤ ⑥ ❼ ⑧ ⑨ ⑩
37. ① ② ③ ④ ⑤ ⑥ ⑦ ❽ ⑨ ⑩
38. ❶ ② ③ ④ ⑤ ⑥ ⑦ ⑧ ⑨ ⑩
39. ① ② ③ ④ ❺ ⑥ ⑦ ⑧ ⑨ ⑩
40. ① ② ❸ ④ ⑤ ⑥ ⑦ ⑧ ⑨ ⑩

PRACTICE SET - 15

SECTION-1

1. ① ② ③ ④ ⑤ ⑥ ❼ ⑧ ⑨ ⑩
2. ① ② ③ ④ ⑤ ⑥ ⑦ ❽ ⑨ ⑩
3. ❶ ② ③ ④ ⑤ ⑥ ⑦ ⑧ ⑨ ⑩
4. ① ② ❸ ④ ⑤ ⑥ ⑦ ⑧ ⑨ ⑩
5. ① ② ③ ④ ⑤ ❻ ⑦ ⑧ ⑨ ⑩
6. ① ② ③ ④ ⑤ ❻ ⑦ ⑧ ⑨ ⑩
7. ① ② ③ ④ ⑤ ⑥ ⑦ ⑧ ❾ ⑩
8. ① ② ③ ④ ⑤ ⑥ ⑦ ⑧ ❾ ⑩
9. ① ❷ ③ ④ ⑤ ⑥ ⑦ ⑧ ⑨ ⑩
10. ① ② ③ ❹ ⑤ ⑥ ⑦ ⑧ ⑨ ⑩

SECTION-2

11. ① ② ③ ❹ ⑤ ⑥ ⑦ ⑧ ⑨ ⑩
12. ① ② ③ ④ ⑤ ⑥ ❼ ⑧ ⑨ ⑩
13. ① ② ③ ④ ⑤ ❻ ⑦ ⑧ ⑨ ⑩
14. ❶ ② ③ ④ ⑤ ⑥ ⑦ ⑧ ⑨ ⑩
15. ① ② ❸ ④ ⑤ ⑥ ⑦ ⑧ ⑨ ⑩
16. ① ② ③ ④ ⑤ ⑥ ⑦ ⑧ ❾ ⑩
17. ① ② ③ ④ ❺ ⑥ ⑦ ⑧ ⑨ ⑩
18. ❶ ② ③ ④ ⑤ ⑥ ⑦ ⑧ ⑨ ⑩
19. ① ② ③ ④ ❺ ⑥ ⑦ ⑧ ⑨ ⑩
20. ❶ ② ③ ④ ⑤ ⑥ ⑦ ⑧ ⑨ ⑩

SECTION-3

21. ❶ ② ③ ④ ⑤ ⑥ ⑦ ⑧ ⑨ ⑩
22. ① ② ③ ❹ ⑤ ⑥ ⑦ ⑧ ⑨ ⑩
23. ① ② ③ ④ ⑤ ❻ ⑦ ⑧ ⑨ ⑩
24. ① ② ③ ④ ❺ ⑥ ⑦ ⑧ ⑨ ⑩
25. ① ② ③ ④ ⑤ ⑥ ❼ ⑧ ⑨ ⑩
26. ① ② ③ ④ ⑤ ⑥ ⑦ ❽ ⑨ ⑩
27. ① ❷ ③ ④ ⑤ ⑥ ⑦ ⑧ ⑨ ⑩
28. ① ② ③ ④ ⑤ ⑥ ⑦ ⑧ ❾ ⑩
29. ① ② ③ ④ ⑤ ⑥ ⑦ ⑧ ⑨ ❿
30. ① ② ❸ ④ ⑤ ⑥ ⑦ ⑧ ⑨ ⑩

SECTION-4

31. ① ② ③ ④ ⑤ ⑥ ⑦ ⑧ ❾ ⑩
32. ① ② ❸ ④ ⑤ ⑥ ⑦ ⑧ ⑨ ⑩
33. ① ② ③ ④ ⑤ ⑥ ⑦ ⑧ ⑨ ❿
34. ① ② ③ ④ ⑤ ⑥ ❼ ⑧ ⑨ ⑩
35. ① ② ③ ④ ⑤ ⑥ ⑦ ❽ ⑨ ⑩
36. ① ② ③ ④ ⑤ ⑥ ⑦ ⑧ ⑨ ❿
37. ① ❷ ③ ④ ⑤ ⑥ ⑦ ⑧ ⑨ ⑩
38. ① ② ③ ❹ ⑤ ⑥ ⑦ ⑧ ⑨ ⑩
39. ① ② ③ ④ ❺ ⑥ ⑦ ⑧ ⑨ ⑩
40. ① ② ③ ④ ⑤ ❻ ⑦ ⑧ ⑨ ⑩

PRACTICE SET - 16

SECTION-1

1. ❶ ② ③ ④ ⑤ ⑥ ⑦ ⑧ ⑨ ⑩
2. ① ② ③ ④ ⑤ ⑥ ⑦ ⑧ ⑨ ❿
3. ① ② ③ ④ ⑤ ⑥ ⑦ ❽ ⑨ ⑩
4. ① ② ③ ④ ⑤ ⑥ ❼ ⑧ ⑨ ⑩
5. ① ❷ ③ ④ ⑤ ⑥ ⑦ ⑧ ⑨ ⑩
6. ① ② ③ ④ ❺ ⑥ ⑦ ⑧ ⑨ ⑩
7. ① ② ❸ ④ ⑤ ⑥ ⑦ ⑧ ⑨ ⑩
8. ❶ ② ③ ④ ⑤ ⑥ ⑦ ⑧ ⑨ ⑩
9. ① ② ③ ④ ⑤ ⑥ ⑦ ⑧ ❾ ⑩
10. ① ② ③ ❹ ⑤ ⑥ ⑦ ⑧ ⑨ ⑩

SECTION-2

11. ① ② ❸ ④ ⑤ ⑥ ⑦ ⑧ ⑨ ⑩
12. ① ❷ ③ ④ ⑤ ⑥ ⑦ ⑧ ⑨ ⑩
13. ① ② ③ ④ ⑤ ⑥ ⑦ ⑧ ❾ ⑩
14. ① ❷ ③ ④ ⑤ ⑥ ⑦ ⑧ ⑨ ⑩
15. ① ② ③ ④ ⑤ ❻ ⑦ ⑧ ⑨ ⑩
16. ① ② ③ ❹ ⑤ ⑥ ⑦ ⑧ ⑨ ⑩
17. ① ② ③ ④ ❺ ⑥ ⑦ ⑧ ⑨ ⑩
18. ① ② ③ ④ ❺ ⑥ ⑦ ⑧ ⑨ ⑩
19. ① ② ③ ④ ⑤ ⑥ ⑦ ⑧ ⑨ ❿
20. ① ② ③ ④ ⑤ ⑥ ❼ ⑧ ⑨ ⑩

SECTION-3

21. ① ② ③ ❹ ⑤ ⑥ ⑦ ⑧ ⑨ ⑩
22. ❶ ② ③ ④ ⑤ ⑥ ⑦ ⑧ ⑨ ⑩
23. ① ② ③ ④ ⑤ ⑥ ⑦ ❽ ⑨ ⑩
24. ① ② ③ ④ ⑤ ⑥ ❼ ⑧ ⑨ ⑩
25. ① ② ③ ④ ⑤ ❻ ⑦ ⑧ ⑨ ⑩
26. ① ❷ ③ ④ ⑤ ⑥ ⑦ ⑧ ⑨ ⑩
27. ① ② ③ ④ ⑤ ⑥ ⑦ ❽ ⑨ ⑩
28. ① ② ③ ④ ⑤ ⑥ ⑦ ⑧ ❾ ⑩
29. ① ② ③ ④ ❺ ⑥ ⑦ ⑧ ⑨ ⑩
30. ① ② ③ ④ ⑤ ⑥ ⑦ ⑧ ⑨ ❿

SECTION-4

31. ① ② ③ ④ ⑤ ❻ ⑦ ⑧ ⑨ ⑩
32. ① ② ③ ❹ ⑤ ⑥ ⑦ ⑧ ⑨ ⑩
33. ① ❷ ③ ④ ⑤ ⑥ ⑦ ⑧ ⑨ ⑩
34. ① ② ③ ④ ⑤ ⑥ ⑦ ❽ ⑨ ⑩
35. ❶ ② ③ ④ ⑤ ⑥ ⑦ ⑧ ⑨ ⑩
36. ① ② ③ ❹ ⑤ ⑥ ⑦ ⑧ ⑨ ⑩
37. ① ② ③ ④ ⑤ ⑥ ⑦ ⑧ ❾ ⑩
38. ① ② ③ ④ ⑤ ❻ ⑦ ⑧ ⑨ ⑩
39. ① ② ③ ④ ❺ ⑥ ⑦ ⑧ ⑨ ⑩
40. ① ② ③ ④ ⑤ ⑥ ❼ ⑧ ⑨ ⑩

PRACTICE SET - 17

SECTION-1

Q.	Marked option
1.	10
2.	1
3.	6
4.	8
5.	4
6.	9
7.	5
8.	7
9.	3
10.	8

SECTION-2

Q.	Marked option
11.	10
12.	6
13.	8
14.	4
15.	2
16.	7
17.	9
18.	3
19.	8
20.	7

SECTION-3

Q.	Marked option
21.	8
22.	10
23.	6
24.	1
25.	2
26.	9
27.	7
28.	5
29.	3
30.	4

SECTION-4

Q.	Marked option
31.	6
32.	6
33.	7
34.	4
35.	9
36.	8
37.	1
38.	10
39.	7
40.	2

PRACTICE SET - 18

SECTION-1

Q.	Marked option
1.	4
2.	6
3.	8
4.	3
5.	7
6.	1
7.	10
8.	2
9.	6
10.	5

SECTION-2

Q.	Marked option
11.	4
12.	7
13.	1
14.	4
15.	10
16.	8
17.	6
18.	9
19.	2
20.	3

SECTION-3

Q.	Marked option
21.	2
22.	1
23.	7
24.	2
25.	5
26.	9
27.	3
28.	10
29.	6
30.	6

SECTION-4

Q.	Marked option
31.	9
32.	4
33.	2
34.	3
35.	10
36.	1
37.	3
38.	6
39.	7
40.	5

PRACTICE SET - 19

SECTION-1

1. ① ② ③ ④ ⑤ ⑥ ⑦ ⑧ ❾ ⑩
2. ① ② ③ ④ ⑤ ⑥ ⑦ ❽ ⑨ ⑩
3. ① ② ③ ④ ⑤ ⑥ ⑦ ⑧ ⑨ ❿
4. ① ② ③ ④ ⑤ ❻ ⑦ ⑧ ⑨ ⑩
5. ① ② ❸ ④ ⑤ ⑥ ⑦ ⑧ ⑨ ⑩
6. ① ② ③ ④ ⑤ ⑥ ❼ ⑧ ⑨ ⑩
7. ① ❷ ③ ④ ⑤ ⑥ ⑦ ⑧ ⑨ ⑩
8. ① ② ③ ④ ❺ ⑥ ⑦ ⑧ ⑨ ⑩
9. ① ❷ ③ ④ ⑤ ⑥ ⑦ ⑧ ⑨ ⑩
10. ❶ ② ③ ④ ⑤ ⑥ ⑦ ⑧ ⑨ ⑩

SECTION-2

11. ① ② ③ ④ ⑤ ⑥ ❼ ⑧ ⑨ ⑩
12. ① ② ③ ❹ ⑤ ⑥ ⑦ ⑧ ⑨ ⑩
13. ① ② ③ ④ ⑤ ❻ ⑦ ⑧ ⑨ ⑩
14. ① ② ③ ④ ⑤ ⑥ ⑦ ❽ ⑨ ⑩
15. ① ❷ ③ ④ ⑤ ⑥ ⑦ ⑧ ⑨ ⑩
16. ① ② ③ ④ ⑤ ⑥ ❼ ⑧ ⑨ ⑩
17. ① ② ③ ④ ⑤ ⑥ ⑦ ⑧ ⑨ ❿
18. ① ② ③ ④ ⑤ ⑥ ⑦ ⑧ ⑨ ❿
19. ① ② ③ ④ ⑤ ⑥ ⑦ ⑧ ❾ ⑩
20. ① ❷ ③ ④ ⑤ ⑥ ⑦ ⑧ ⑨ ⑩

SECTION-3

21. ① ② ③ ④ ⑤ ⑥ ⑦ ⑧ ❾ ⑩
22. ❶ ② ③ ④ ⑤ ⑥ ⑦ ⑧ ⑨ ⑩
23. ① ❷ ③ ④ ⑤ ⑥ ⑦ ⑧ ⑨ ⑩
24. ① ② ③ ④ ⑤ ⑥ ⑦ ❽ ⑨ ⑩
25. ① ② ③ ④ ❺ ⑥ ⑦ ⑧ ⑨ ⑩
26. ① ② ③ ④ ⑤ ❻ ⑦ ⑧ ⑨ ⑩
27. ① ② ③ ④ ⑤ ⑥ ⑦ ⑧ ⑨ ❿
28. ① ② ③ ④ ⑤ ⑥ ❼ ⑧ ⑨ ⑩
29. ① ② ❸ ④ ⑤ ⑥ ⑦ ⑧ ⑨ ⑩
30. ① ② ③ ❹ ⑤ ⑥ ⑦ ⑧ ⑨ ⑩

SECTION-4

31. ① ② ③ ④ ⑤ ⑥ ⑦ ❽ ⑨ ⑩
32. ① ② ③ ④ ❺ ⑥ ⑦ ⑧ ⑨ ⑩
33. ① ② ③ ④ ❺ ⑥ ⑦ ⑧ ⑨ ⑩
34. ① ② ③ ④ ⑤ ⑥ ⑦ ⑧ ❾ ⑩
35. ① ❷ ③ ④ ⑤ ⑥ ⑦ ⑧ ⑨ ⑩
36. ① ② ③ ❹ ⑤ ⑥ ⑦ ⑧ ⑨ ⑩
37. ① ② ❸ ④ ⑤ ⑥ ⑦ ⑧ ⑨ ⑩
38. ① ② ③ ④ ⑤ ❻ ⑦ ⑧ ⑨ ⑩
39. ① ② ③ ④ ⑤ ❻ ⑦ ⑧ ⑨ ⑩
40. ① ② ③ ④ ⑤ ⑥ ⑦ ❽ ⑨ ⑩

PRACTICE SET - 20

SECTION-1

1. ① ❷ ③ ④ ⑤ ⑥ ⑦ ⑧ ⑨ ⑩
2. ① ② ③ ④ ❺ ⑥ ⑦ ⑧ ⑨ ⑩
3. ① ② ③ ④ ⑤ ⑥ ⑦ ⑧ ❾ ⑩
4. ① ② ③ ④ ⑤ ⑥ ⑦ ❽ ⑨ ⑩
5. ① ② ③ ④ ⑤ ⑥ ❼ ⑧ ⑨ ⑩
6. ① ② ③ ④ ⑤ ⑥ ⑦ ⑧ ⑨ ❿
7. ① ② ③ ❹ ⑤ ⑥ ⑦ ⑧ ⑨ ⑩
8. ① ② ❸ ④ ⑤ ⑥ ⑦ ⑧ ⑨ ⑩
9. ① ② ❸ ④ ⑤ ⑥ ⑦ ⑧ ⑨ ⑩
10. ① ② ③ ④ ⑤ ⑥ ⑦ ⑧ ⑨ ❿

SECTION-2

11. ① ② ③ ④ ⑤ ⑥ ⑦ ⑧ ❾ ⑩
12. ① ② ③ ④ ⑤ ⑥ ❼ ⑧ ⑨ ⑩
13. ① ② ③ ❹ ⑤ ⑥ ⑦ ⑧ ⑨ ⑩
14. ① ② ❸ ④ ⑤ ⑥ ⑦ ⑧ ⑨ ⑩
15. ① ❷ ③ ④ ⑤ ⑥ ⑦ ⑧ ⑨ ⑩
16. ① ② ③ ④ ⑤ ❻ ⑦ ⑧ ⑨ ⑩
17. ❶ ② ③ ④ ⑤ ⑥ ⑦ ⑧ ⑨ ⑩
18. ❶ ② ③ ④ ⑤ ⑥ ⑦ ⑧ ⑨ ⑩
19. ① ② ③ ④ ⑤ ⑥ ⑦ ❽ ⑨ ⑩
20. ① ② ③ ④ ❺ ⑥ ⑦ ⑧ ⑨ ⑩

SECTION-3

21. ① ② ③ ④ ⑤ ⑥ ⑦ ⑧ ❾ ⑩
22. ① ② ③ ④ ❺ ⑥ ⑦ ⑧ ⑨ ⑩
23. ① ② ③ ④ ⑤ ⑥ ❼ ⑧ ⑨ ⑩
24. ❶ ② ③ ④ ⑤ ⑥ ⑦ ⑧ ⑨ ⑩
25. ① ② ③ ④ ⑤ ⑥ ⑦ ❽ ⑨ ⑩
26. ① ② ③ ④ ⑤ ⑥ ⑦ ⑧ ⑨ ❿
27. ① ❷ ③ ④ ⑤ ⑥ ⑦ ⑧ ⑨ ⑩
28. ① ② ③ ④ ⑤ ❻ ⑦ ⑧ ⑨ ⑩
29. ① ② ③ ❹ ⑤ ⑥ ⑦ ⑧ ⑨ ⑩
30. ① ② ❸ ④ ⑤ ⑥ ⑦ ⑧ ⑨ ⑩

SECTION-4

31. ❶ ② ③ ④ ⑤ ⑥ ⑦ ⑧ ⑨ ⑩
32. ① ② ③ ④ ⑤ ❻ ⑦ ⑧ ⑨ ⑩
33. ① ② ❸ ④ ⑤ ⑥ ⑦ ⑧ ⑨ ⑩
34. ① ② ③ ④ ⑤ ⑥ ❼ ⑧ ⑨ ⑩
35. ① ② ③ ❹ ⑤ ⑥ ⑦ ⑧ ⑨ ⑩
36. ① ❷ ③ ④ ⑤ ⑥ ⑦ ⑧ ⑨ ⑩
37. ① ② ③ ④ ❺ ⑥ ⑦ ⑧ ⑨ ⑩
38. ① ② ③ ④ ⑤ ⑥ ⑦ ❽ ⑨ ⑩
39. ① ② ③ ④ ⑤ ⑥ ⑦ ⑧ ❾ ⑩
40. ① ② ③ ④ ❺ ⑥ ⑦ ⑧ ⑨ ⑩

4 INFORMATION ORDERING TEST

(निर्देश समझ सकने की क्षमता परीक्षण)

परीक्षण निर्देश : रेलवे मनोवैज्ञानिक परीक्षण के अन्तर्गत **'निर्देश समझ सकने की क्षमता' (Information Ordering Test)** एक महत्वपूर्ण परीक्षण है। इस परीक्षण के द्वारा उम्मीदवारों की तार्किक क्षमता, सोचने की क्रमबद्धता, निर्देशों के अनुसार कार्य करने की योग्यता का मापन किया जाता है। इस परीक्षण में कुल 25 प्रश्न जिसके लिए 8 या 10 मिनट का समय दिया जाता है। इस प्रश्नों को हल करने के लिए **तालिका-1(Table-1)** और **तालिका-2 (Table-2)** की मदद की आवश्यकता होती है।

इस परीक्षण के अन्तर्गत प्रत्येक प्रश्न में जिसके बायीं ओर एक टेस्ट आकृति या प्रश्न आकृति दी होती है और दायीं ओर एक सीरीज में A से D तक चार प्रोसेस बॉक्स (Process Box) दिए होते हैं। प्रत्येक प्रोसेस बॉक्स भी तीन लेवल (Level) में विभाजित होते हैं। जिसे Level-1, Level-2 और Level-3 नाम दिया गया है। प्रोसेस बॉक्स के प्रत्येक लेवल में 'X' का चिह्न होगा या नहीं होगा। प्रोसेस बॉक्स में दिए गए लेवल में 'X' का चिह्न होगा तो उस लेवल में दिए गए तालिका-1 के अनुसार अंकों को जोड़ना अथवा घटाना होता है। जिस लेवल (Level) में 'X" का चिह्न नहीं होगा उस लेवल (Level) में कोई परिवर्तन नहीं करना होगा।

Test Instructions: As part of the Railway Psychological Assessment, the Information Ordering Test is an important Test. This test measures a candidate's logical ability, sequential thinking, and ability to follow instructions accurately. The test consists of 25 questions, with a time limit of 8 or 10 minutes. To solve these questions, you will need the assistance of Table-1 and Table-2.

Each question presents a test figure or problem figure on the left, and on the right, there is a series of four Process Boxes labelled A to D. Each Process Box is further divided into three levels: Level-1, Level-2 and Level-3.Each level may contain an 'X' mark or may be empty. If a level contains an 'X', you must add or subtract numbers according to Table-1 for that level. If a level does not contain an 'X', no change is required for that level.

Process Box (प्रोसेस बॉक्स)

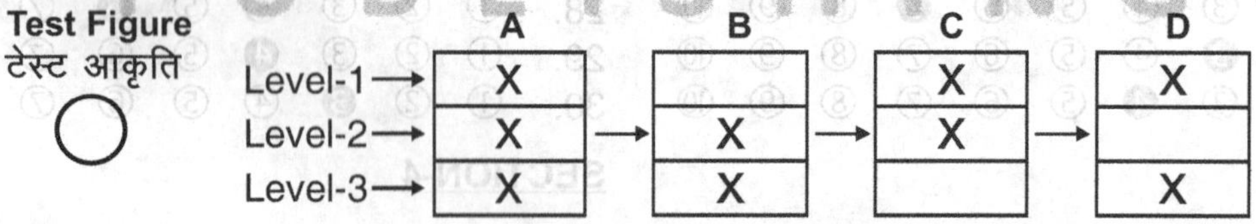

Process Box (प्रोसेस बॉक्स)

Table - 1/तालिका-1

	A		B		C		D	
Level-1 →	X	+1	X	+2	X	+2	X	–3
Level-2 →	X	–2 →	X	–3 →	X	–1 →	X	–2
Level-3 →	X	+3	X	–1	X	+3	X	+1

Table - 2/तालिका-2

Figures and their coreponding values

आकृति तथा सम्बन्धित मान तालिका

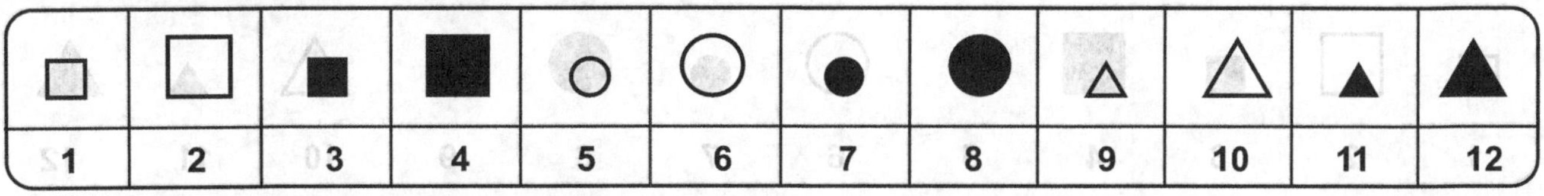

Steps to solve the test are :

परीक्षण को नीचे दिये क्रम के अनुसार हल करें :

परीक्षण को नीचे दिए विधि के अनुसार हल करें :-

1. सर्वप्रथम टेस्ट आकृति/प्रश्न आकृति का मूल्य (Value) आकृति तालिका (Table-2) से ज्ञात करें।
2. प्रश्न आकृति/टेस्ट आकृति के मूल्य 'X' के चिह्न वाले प्रत्येक प्रोसेस बॉक्स (Process Box) में A, B, C और D तक के Level के मूल्यों को तालिका (Table-1) के अनुसार जोड़े या घटाऐं।
3. प्रोसेस बॉक्स (Process Box) के अंतिम लेवल में प्राप्त संख्या के मूल्य (Value) से संबंधित आकृति, तालिका (Table-2) से मिलान करें।
4. इस प्रकार तालिका (Table-2) से प्राप्त आकृति दिए गए उत्तर विकल्प (Answer Option) क्रमशः 1, 2, 3, 4 और 5 में सही उत्तर ढूंढे।

Solve the test according to the following procedure:

1. First, find the value of the test figure/question figure from Table-2.
2. For each Process Box (A, B, C, and D), add or subtract the values of the levels marked with 'X' according to Table-1.
3. Match the final value obtained in the last level of the Process Box with the corresponding figure in Table-2.
4. Using Table-2, find the correct answer option (1, 2, 3, 4, or 5) for the given test figure.

उदाहरण/EXAMPLE-1 :

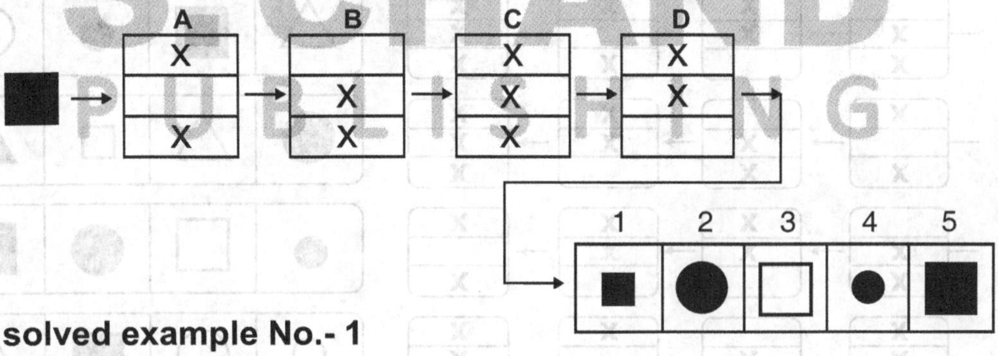

Step wise solved example No.- 1

क्रमवार हल किया हुआ उदाहरण 1

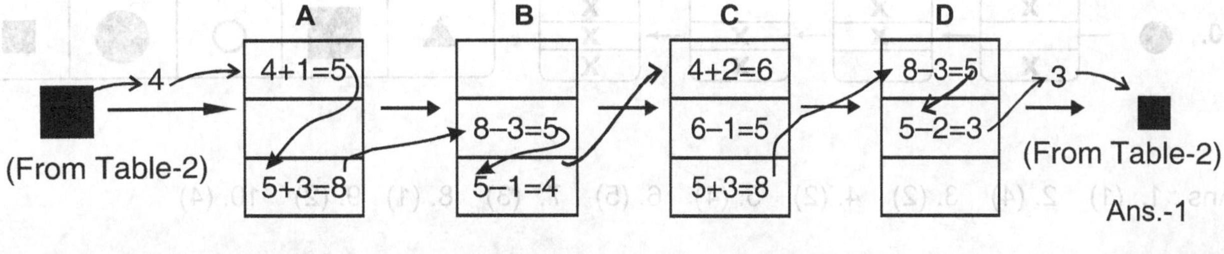

EXAMPLE

Table - 2

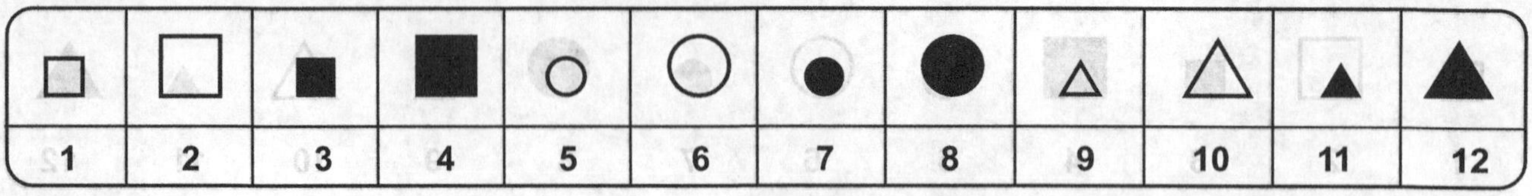

Table - 1

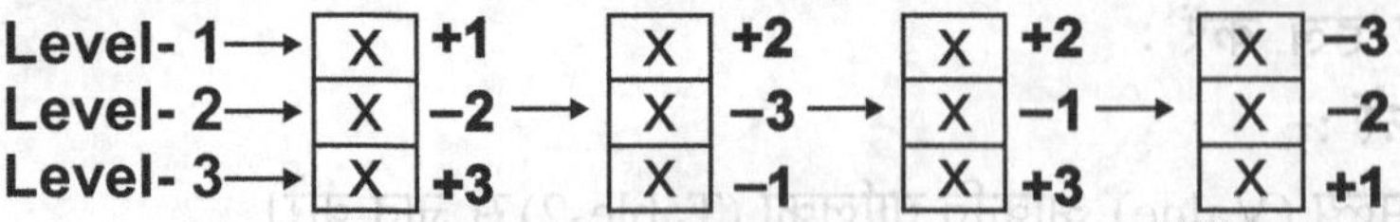

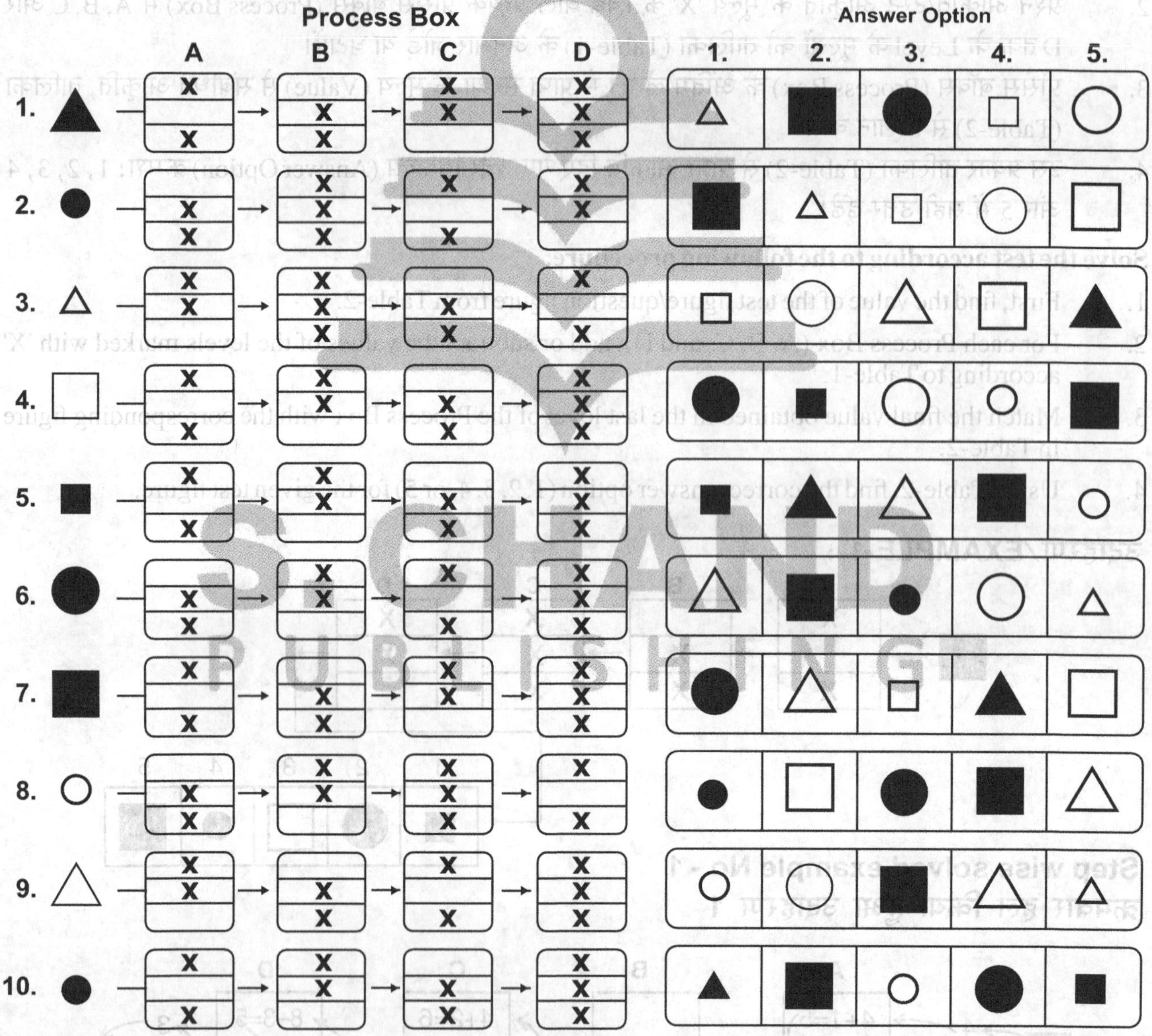

Ans.: 1. (1) 2. (4) 3. (2) 4. (2) 5. (4) 6. (5) 7. (3) 8. (1) 9. (2) 10. (4)

PRACTICE SET-1

Total Ques.- 25
Time - 8 or 10 Min.

Table - 2

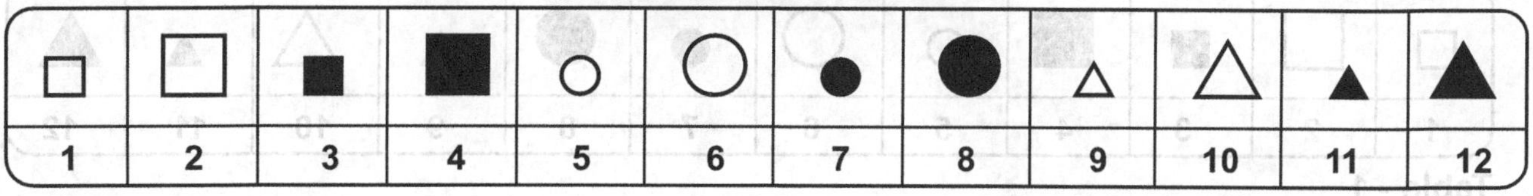

Table - 1

Level- 1→	X +1	X +2	X +2	X −3
Level- 2→	X −2 →	X −3 →	X −1 →	X −2
Level- 3→	X +3	X −1	X +3	X +1

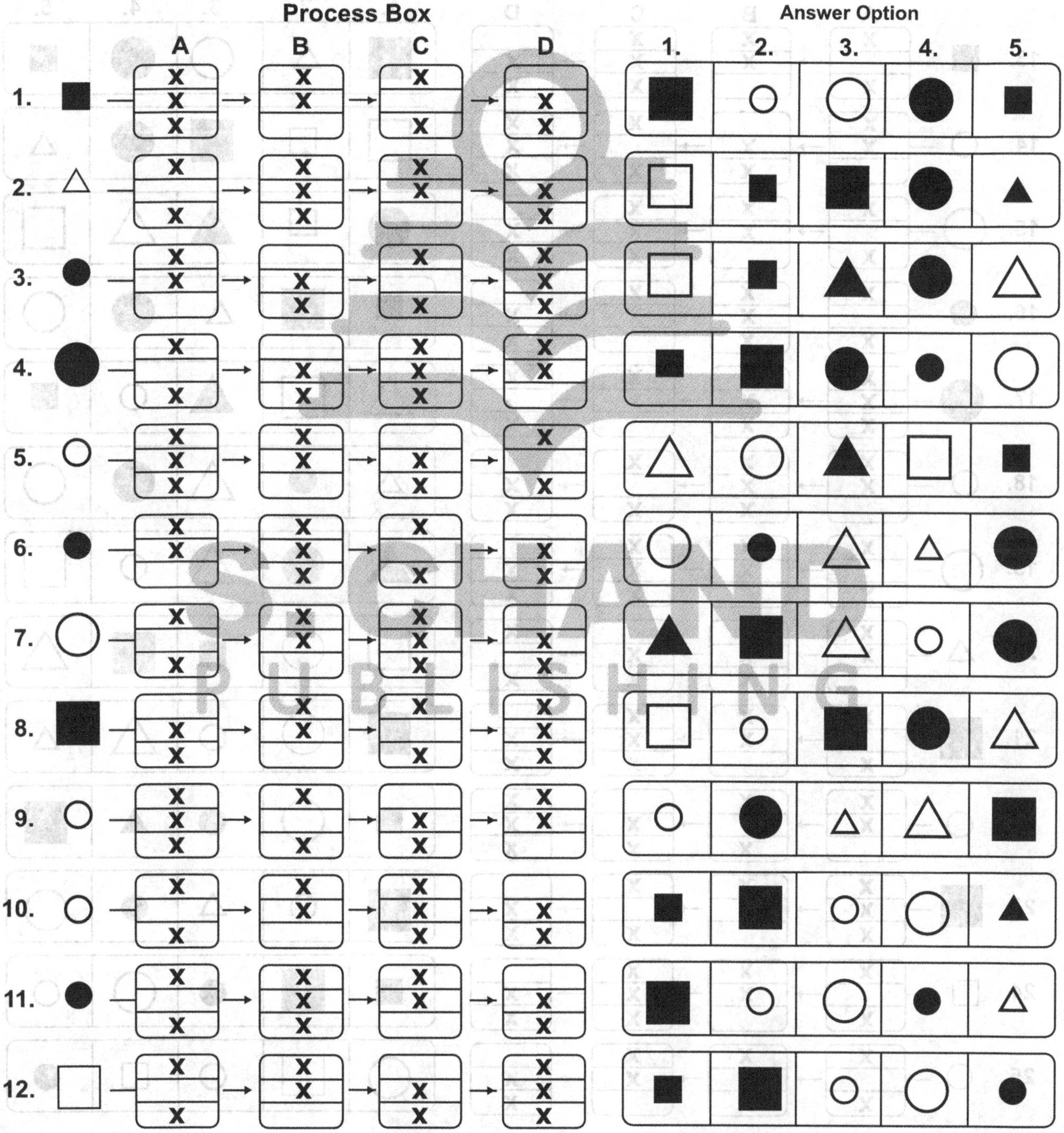

Table - 2

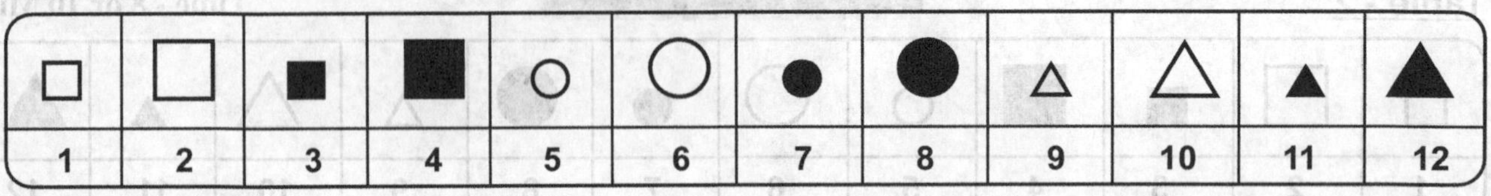

Table - 1

Level- 1 →	X +1	X +2	X +2	X −3
Level- 2 →	X −2 →	X −3 →	X −1 →	X −2
Level- 3 →	X +3	X −1	X +3	X +1

Process Box **Answer Option**

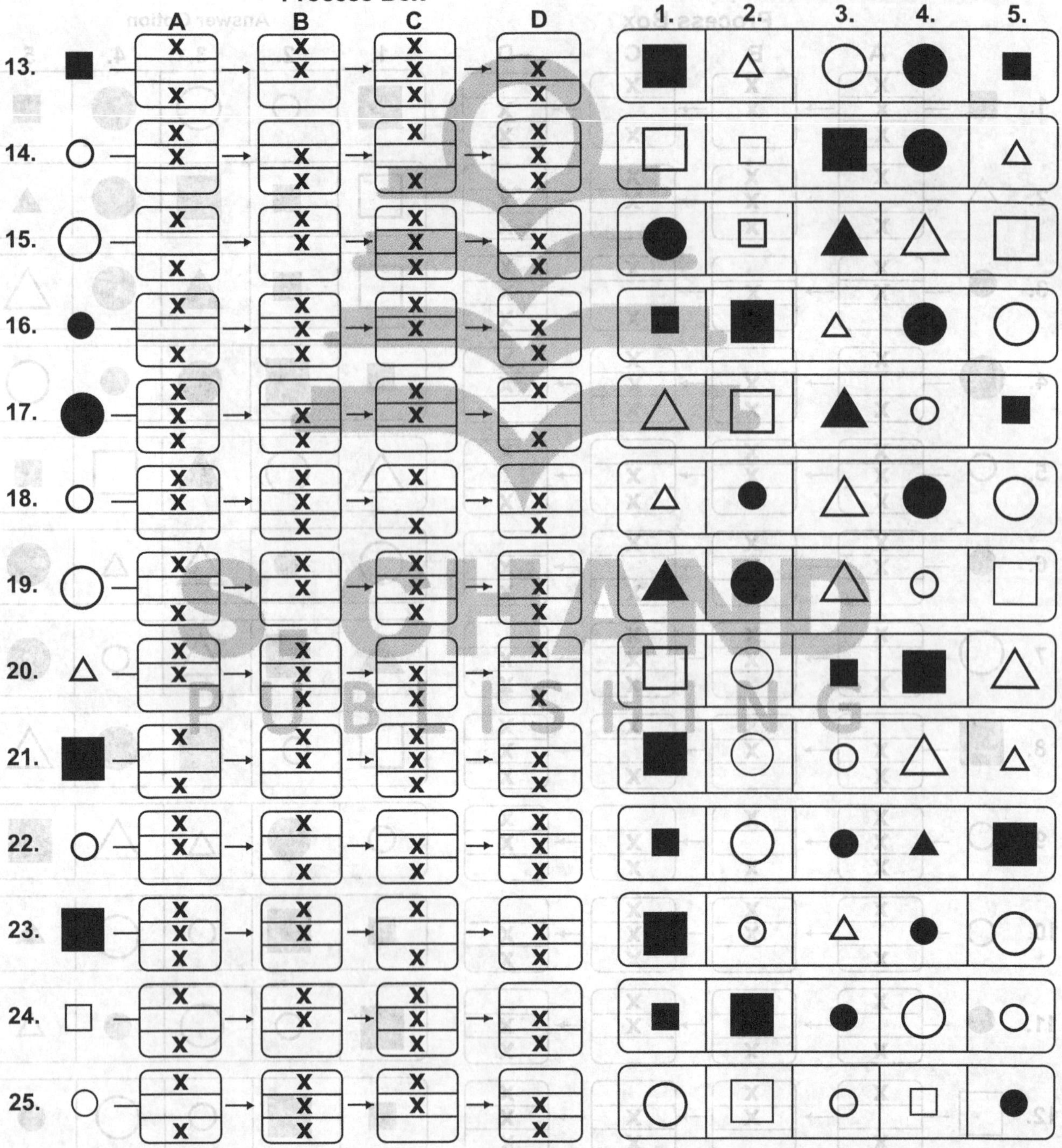

PRACTICE SET-2

Total Ques.- 25
Time - 8 or 10 Min.

Table - 2

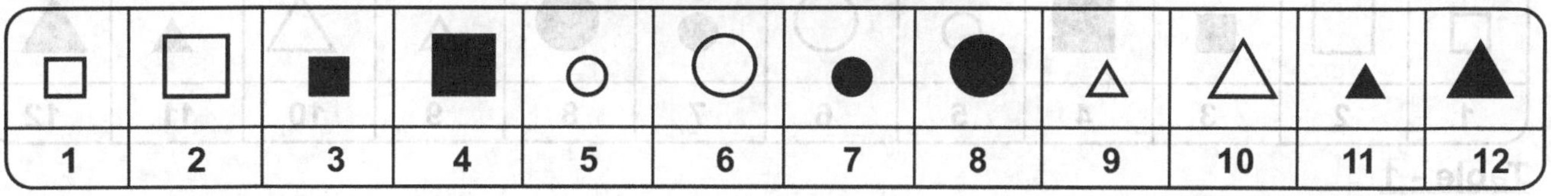

Table - 1

Level- 1 →	X +1	X +2	X +2	X −3
Level- 2 →	X −2 →	X −3 →	X −1 →	X −2
Level- 3 →	X +3	X −1	X +3	X +1

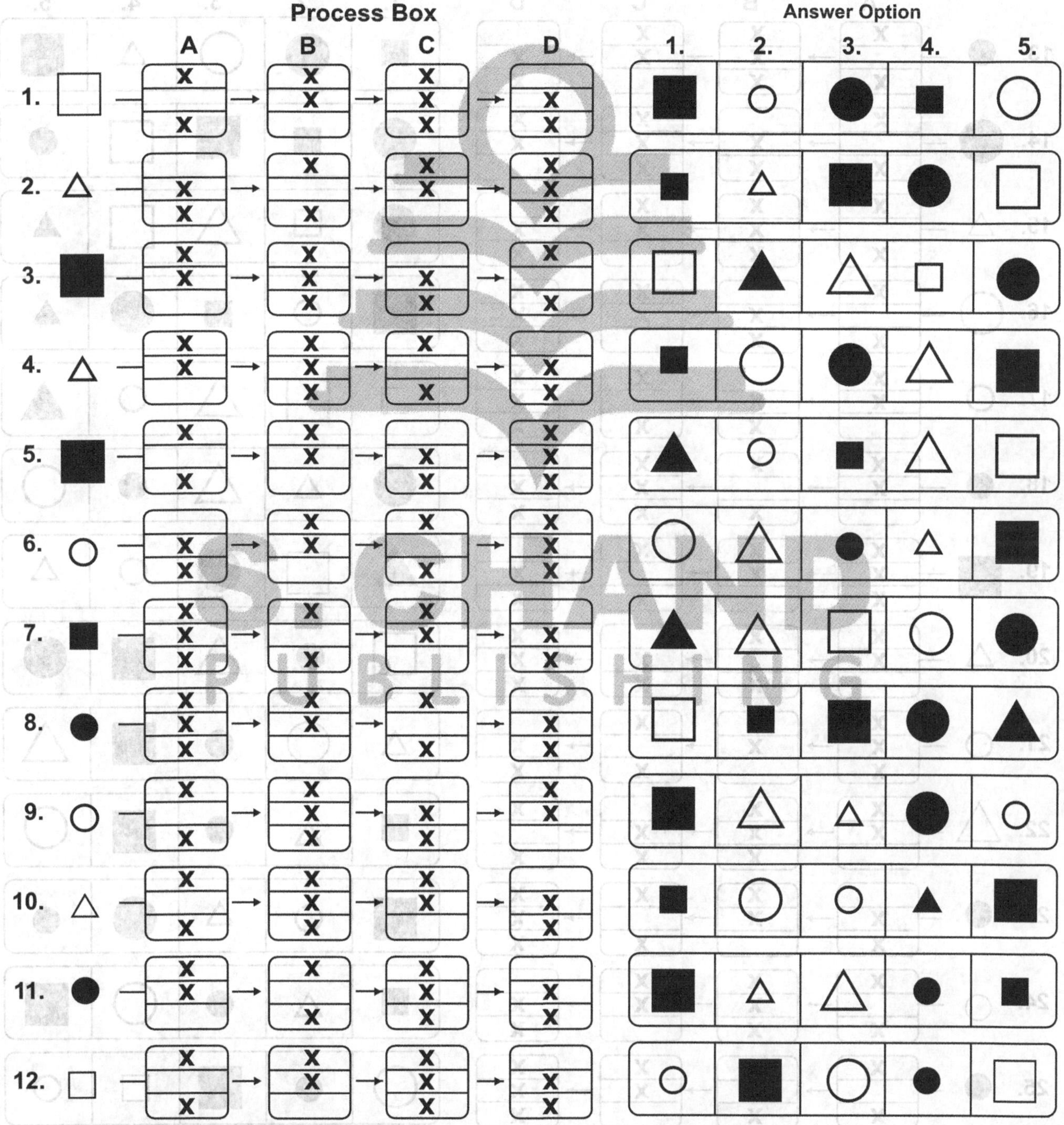

Table - 2

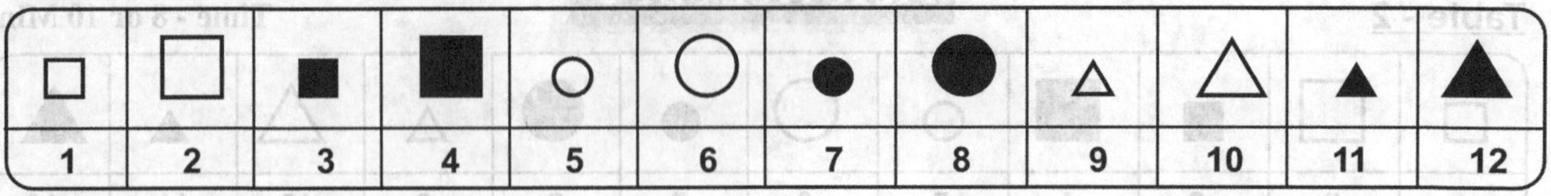

Table - 1

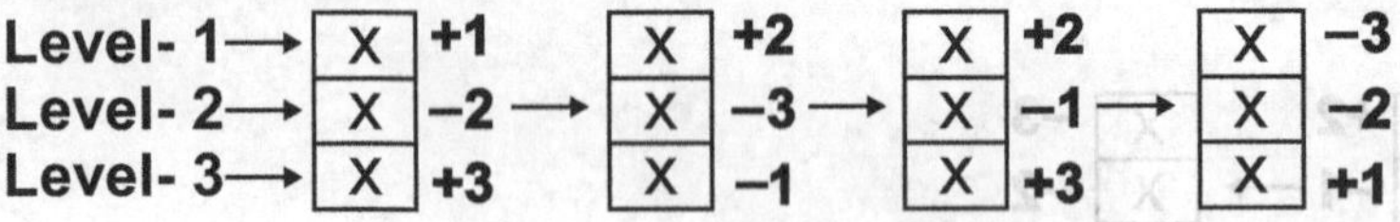

Process Box **Answer Option**

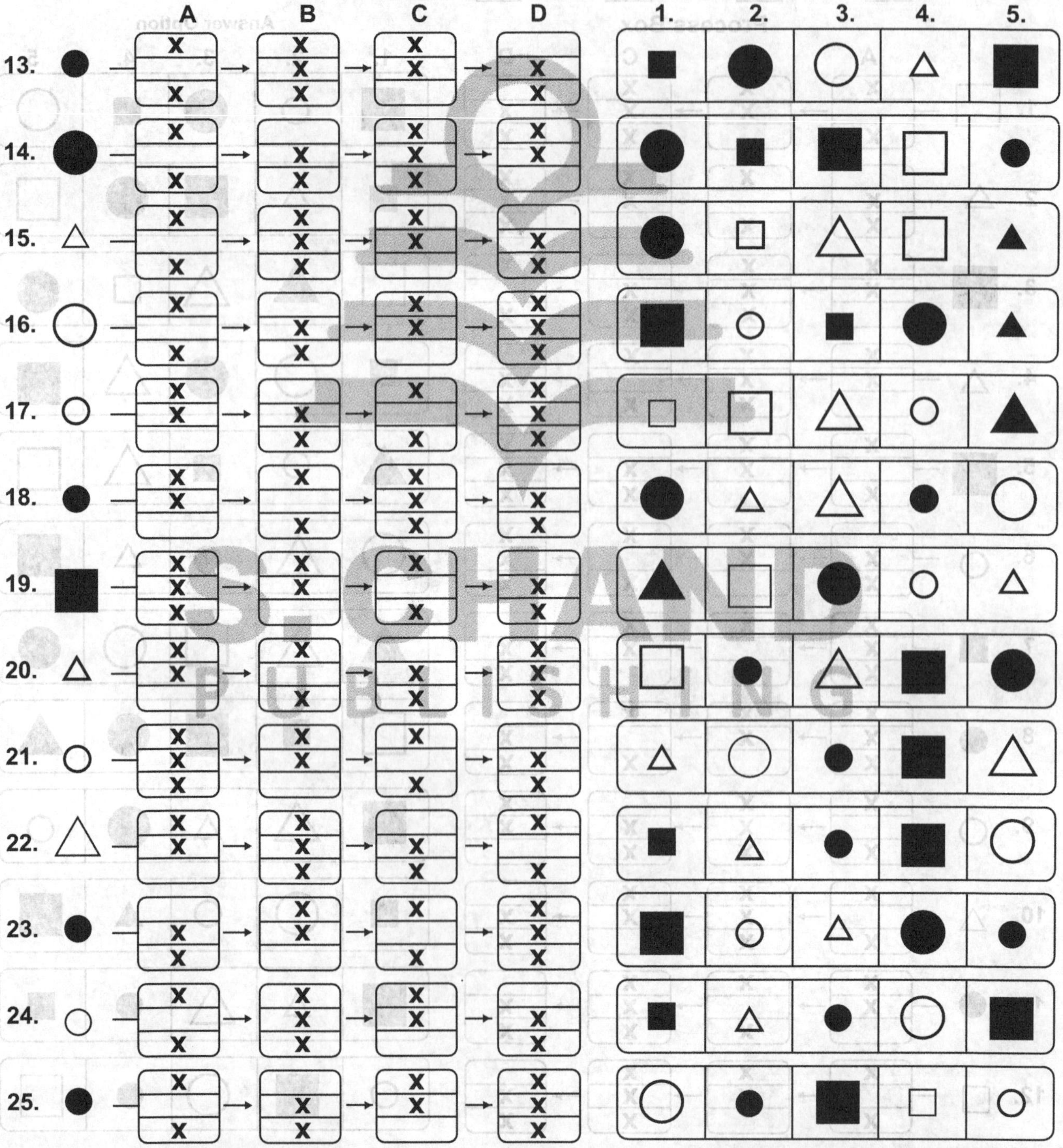

PRACTICE SET-3

Total Ques.- 25
Time - 8 or 10 Min.

Table - 2

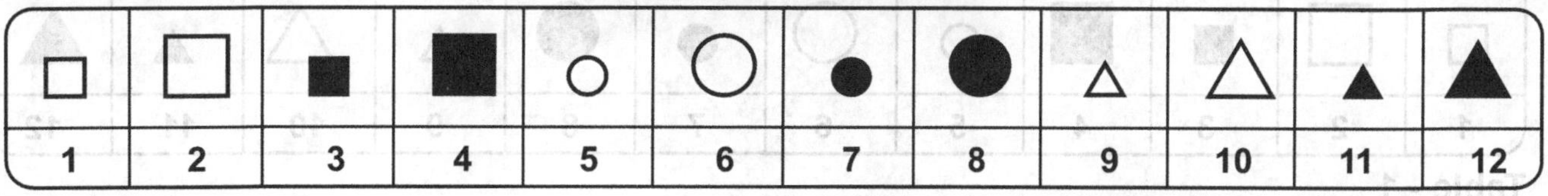

Table - 1

Level- 1 →	X +1	X +2	X +2	X −3
Level- 2 →	X −2 →	X −3 →	X −1 →	X −2
Level- 3 →	X +3	X −1	X +3	X +1

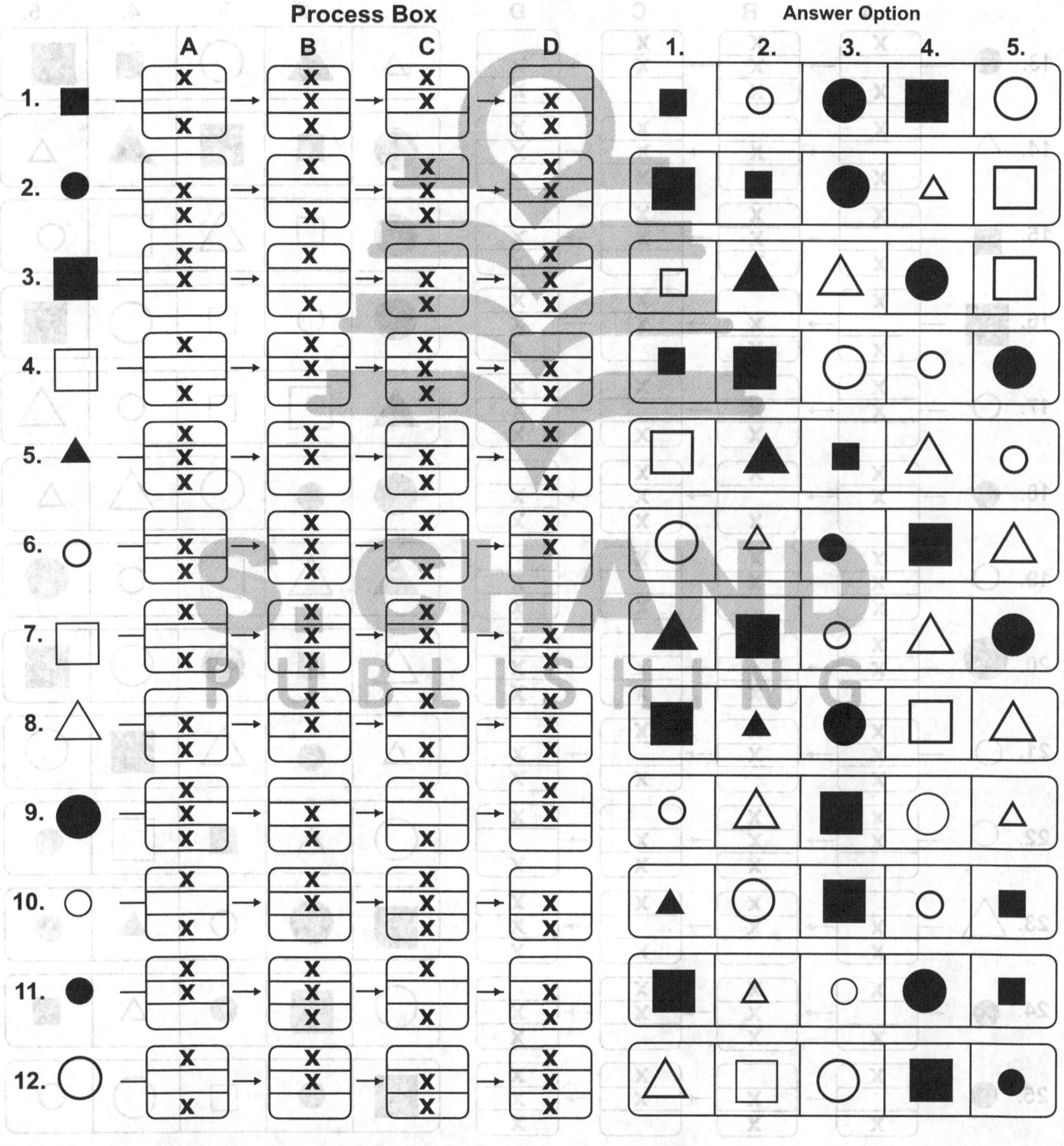

Table - 2

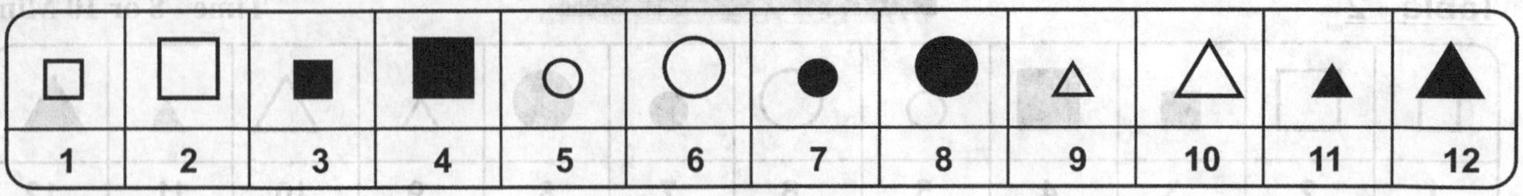

Table - 1

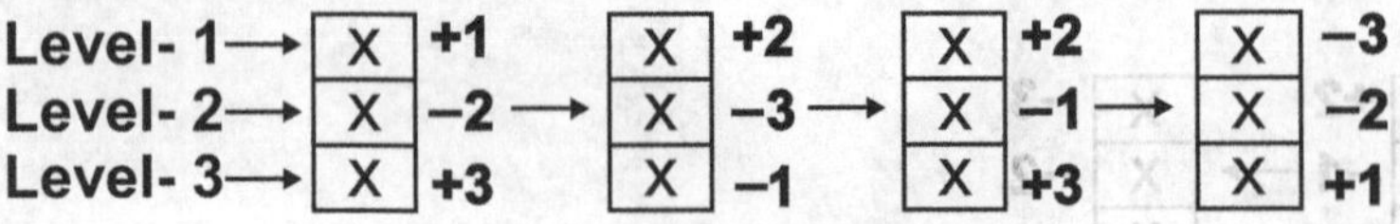

Process Box

Answer Option

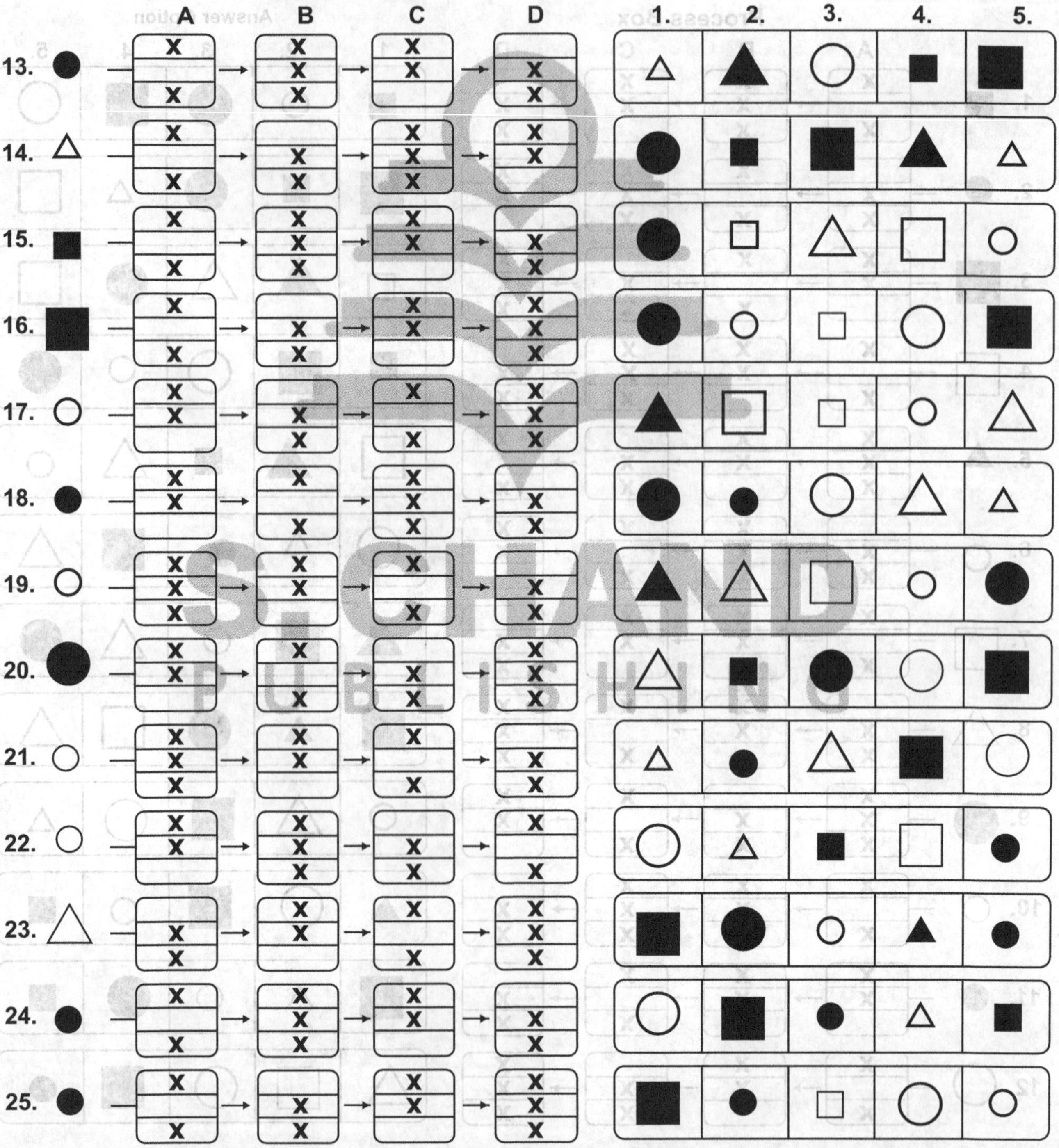

PRACTICE SET-4

Total Ques.- 25
Time - 8 or 10 Min.

Table - 2

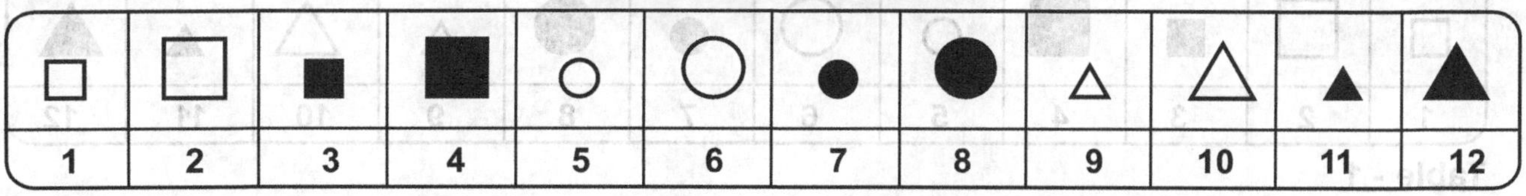

Table - 1

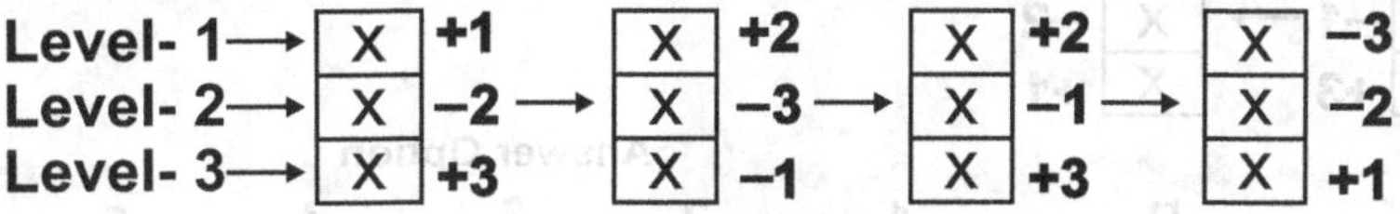

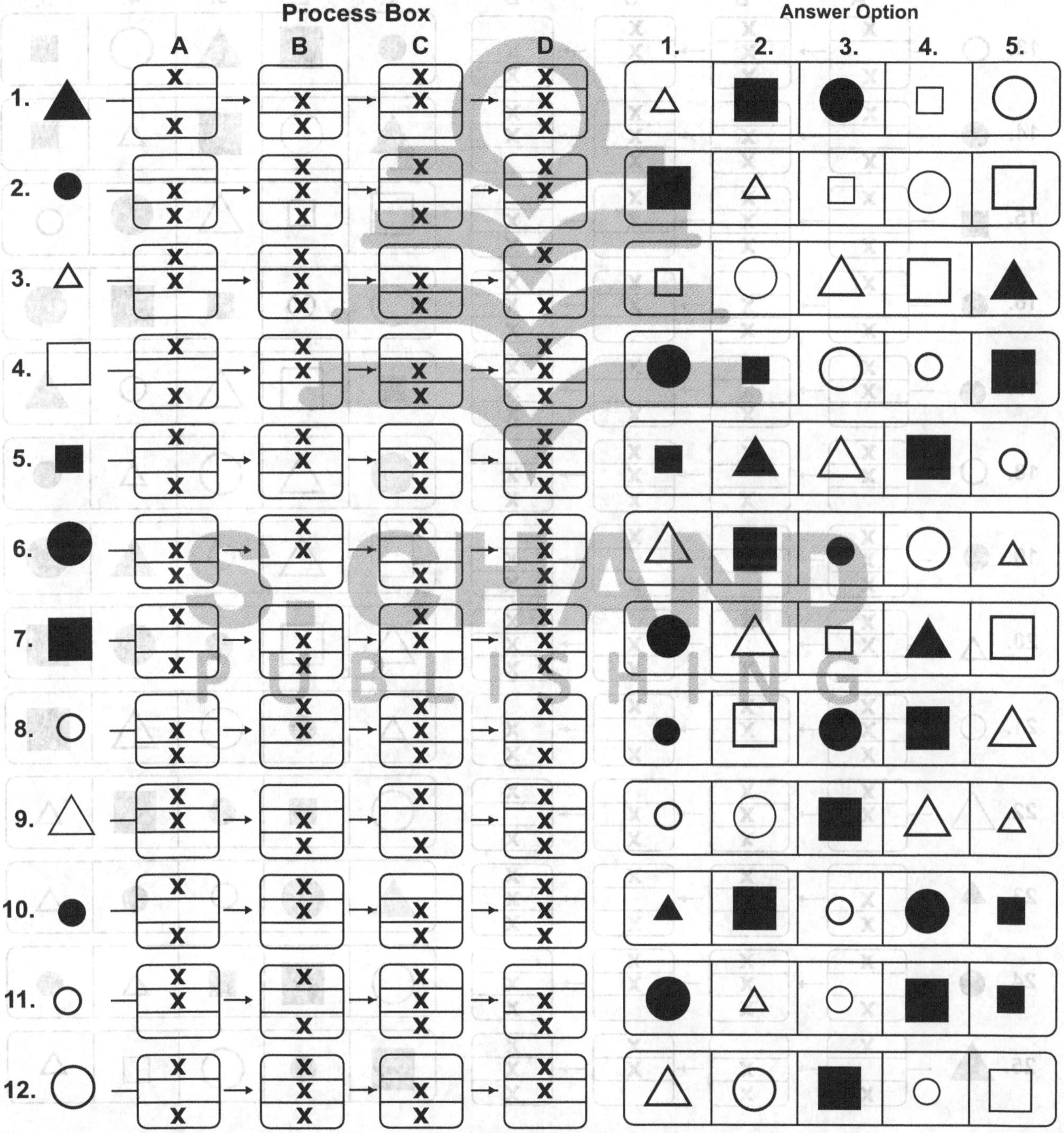

Table - 2

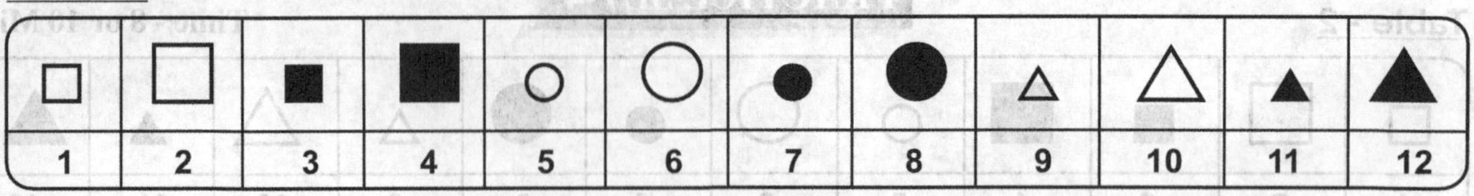

Table - 1

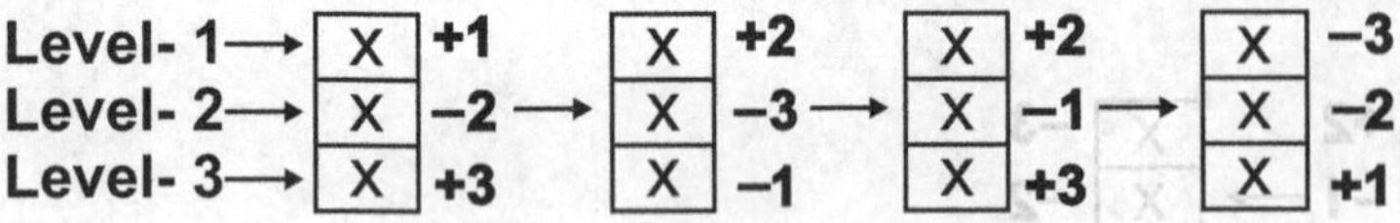

Process Box **Answer Option**

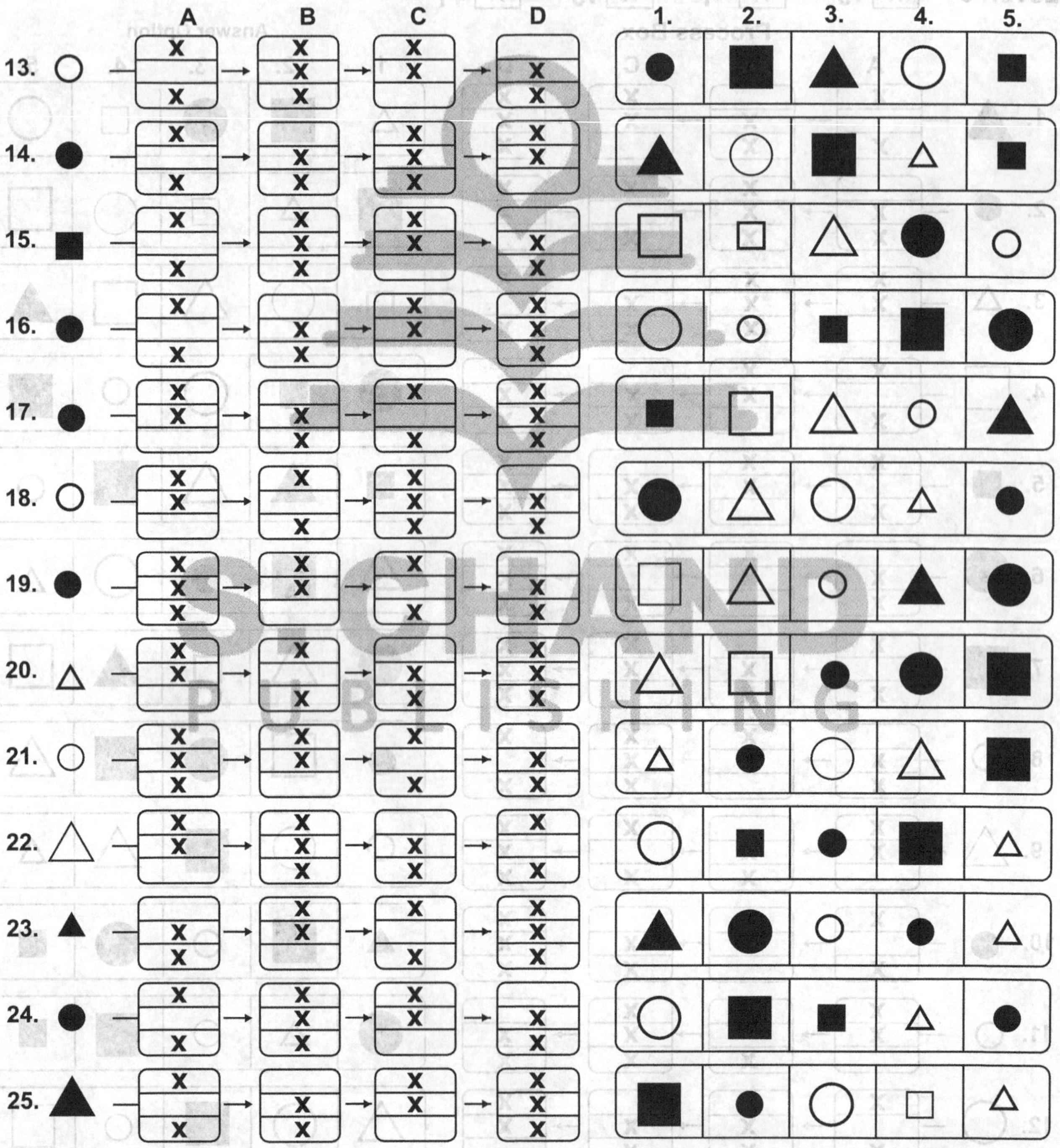

PRACTICE SET-5

Total Ques.- 25
Time - 8 or 10 Min.

Table - 2

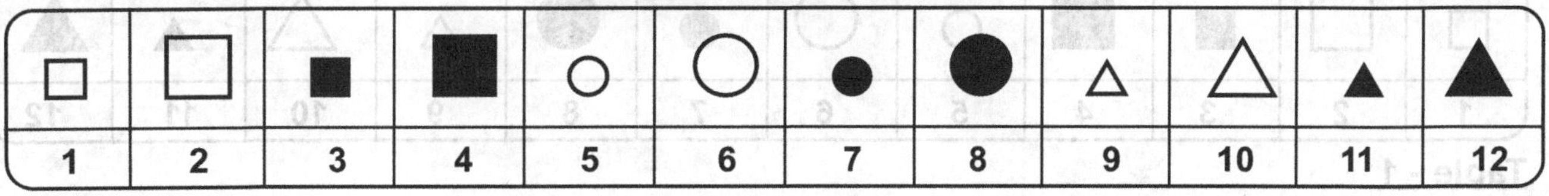

Table - 1

Level- 1→	X +1	X +2	X +2	X −3
Level- 2→	X −2 →	X −3 →	X −1 →	X −2
Level- 3→	X +3	X −1	X +3	X +1

Process Box | **Answer Option**

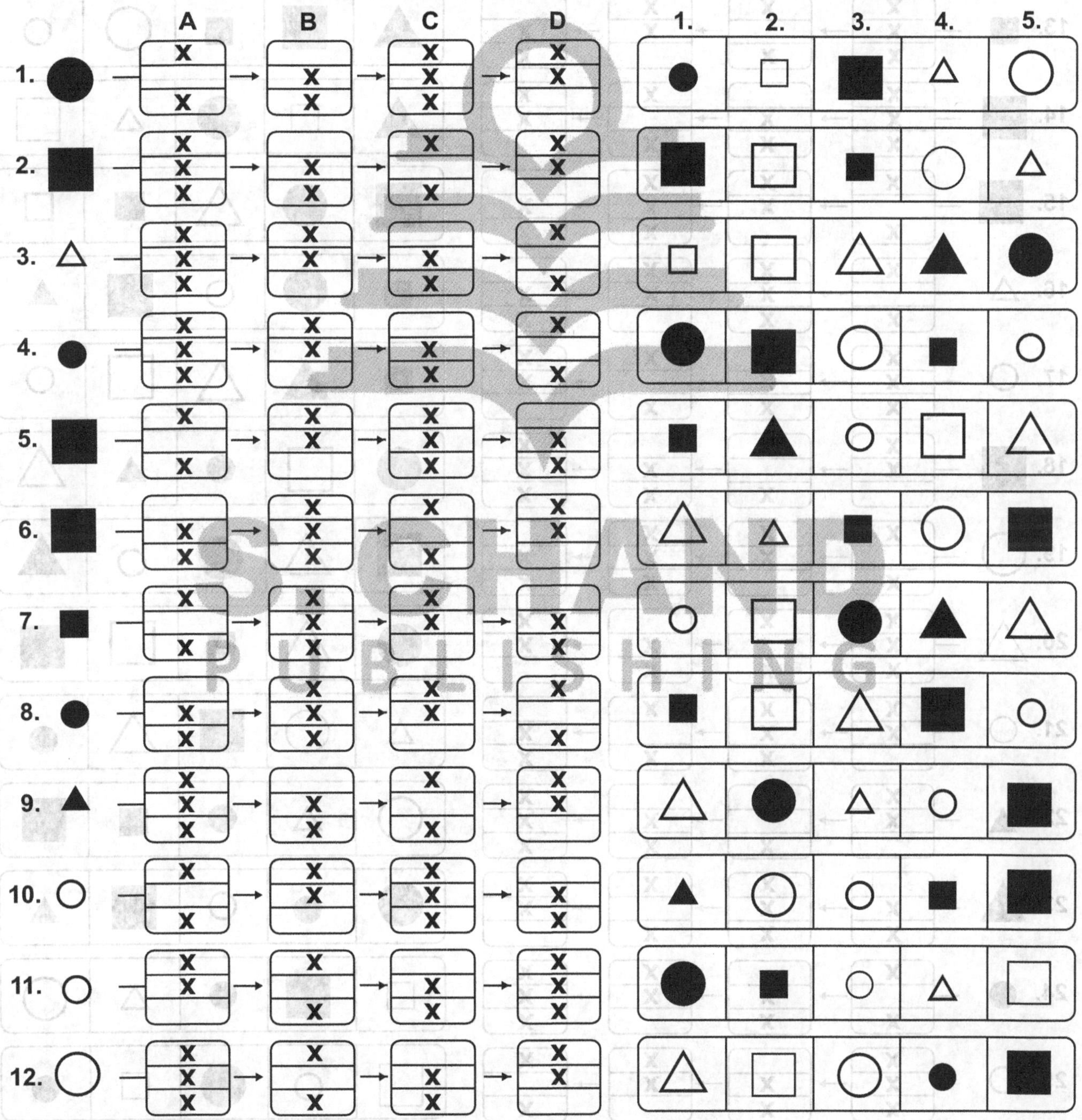

Table - 2

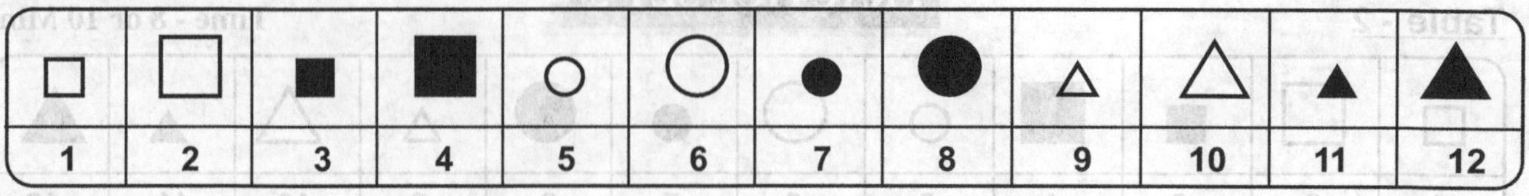

Table - 1

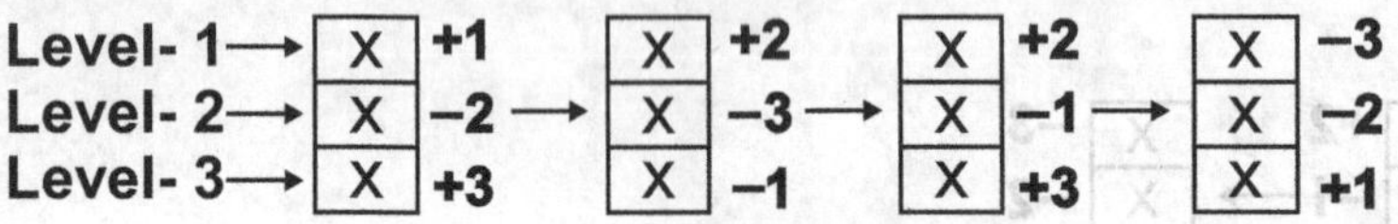

Process Box

Answer Option

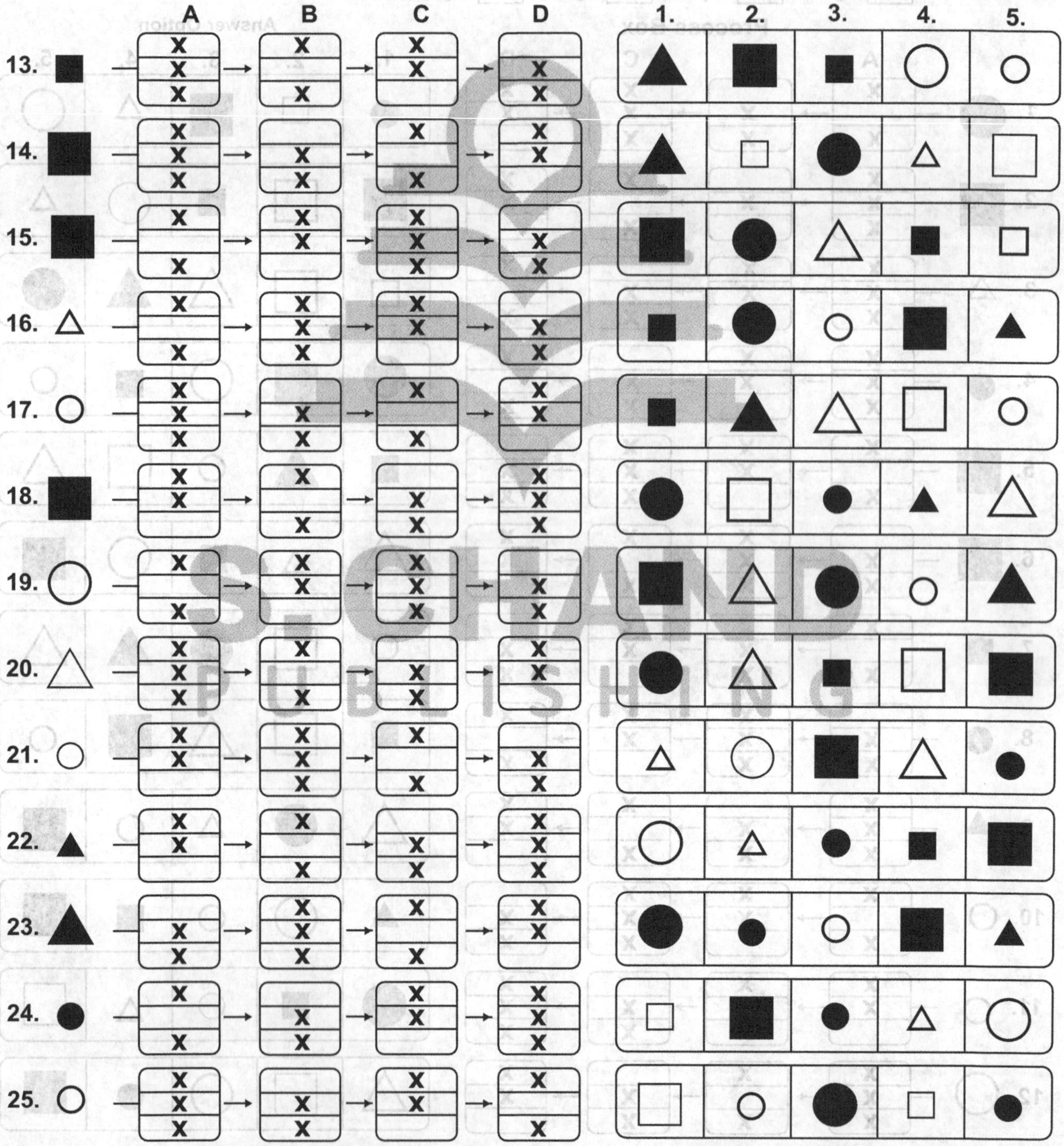

PRACTICE SET-6

Total Ques.- 25
Time - 8 or 10 Min.

Table - 2

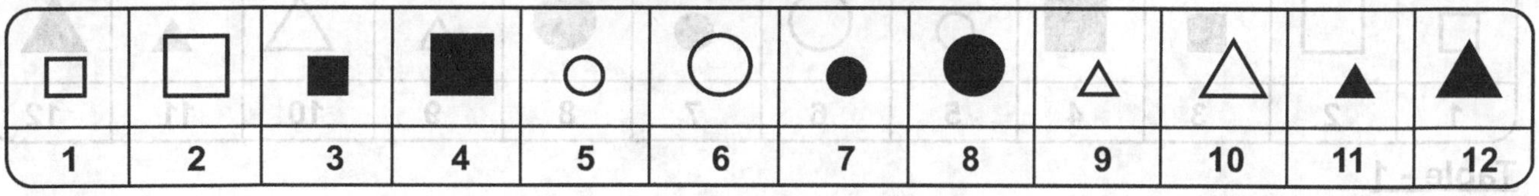

Table - 1

Level- 1 →	X	+1	X	+2	X	+2	X	−3
Level- 2 →	X	−2 →	X	−3 →	X	−1 →	X	−2
Level- 3 →	X	+3	X	−1	X	+3	X	+1

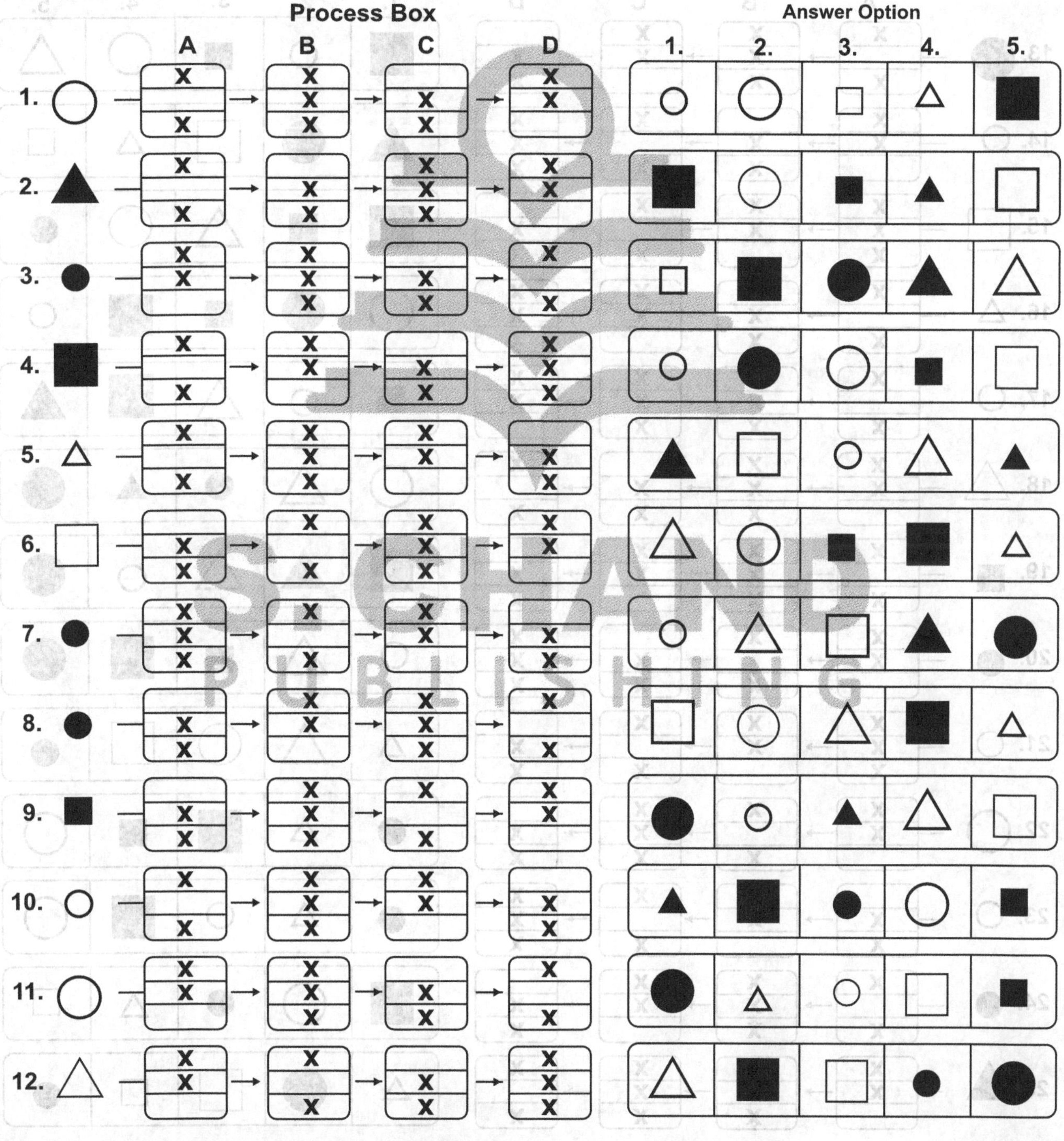

Table - 2

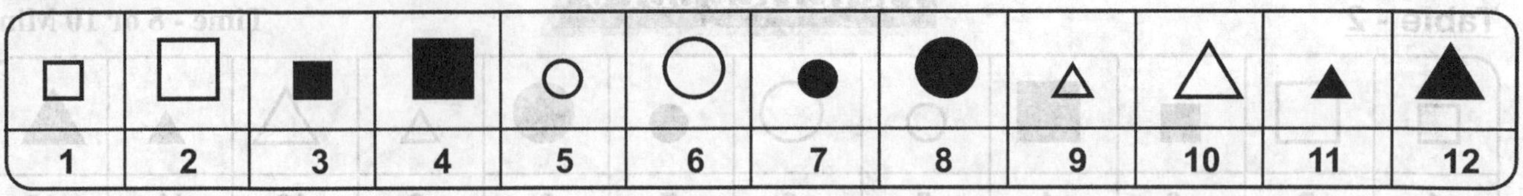

Table - 1

	Process Box			
Level- 1 →	X +1	X +2	X +2	X −3
Level- 2 →	X −2	X −3	X −1	X −2
Level- 3 →	X +3	X −1	X +3	X +1

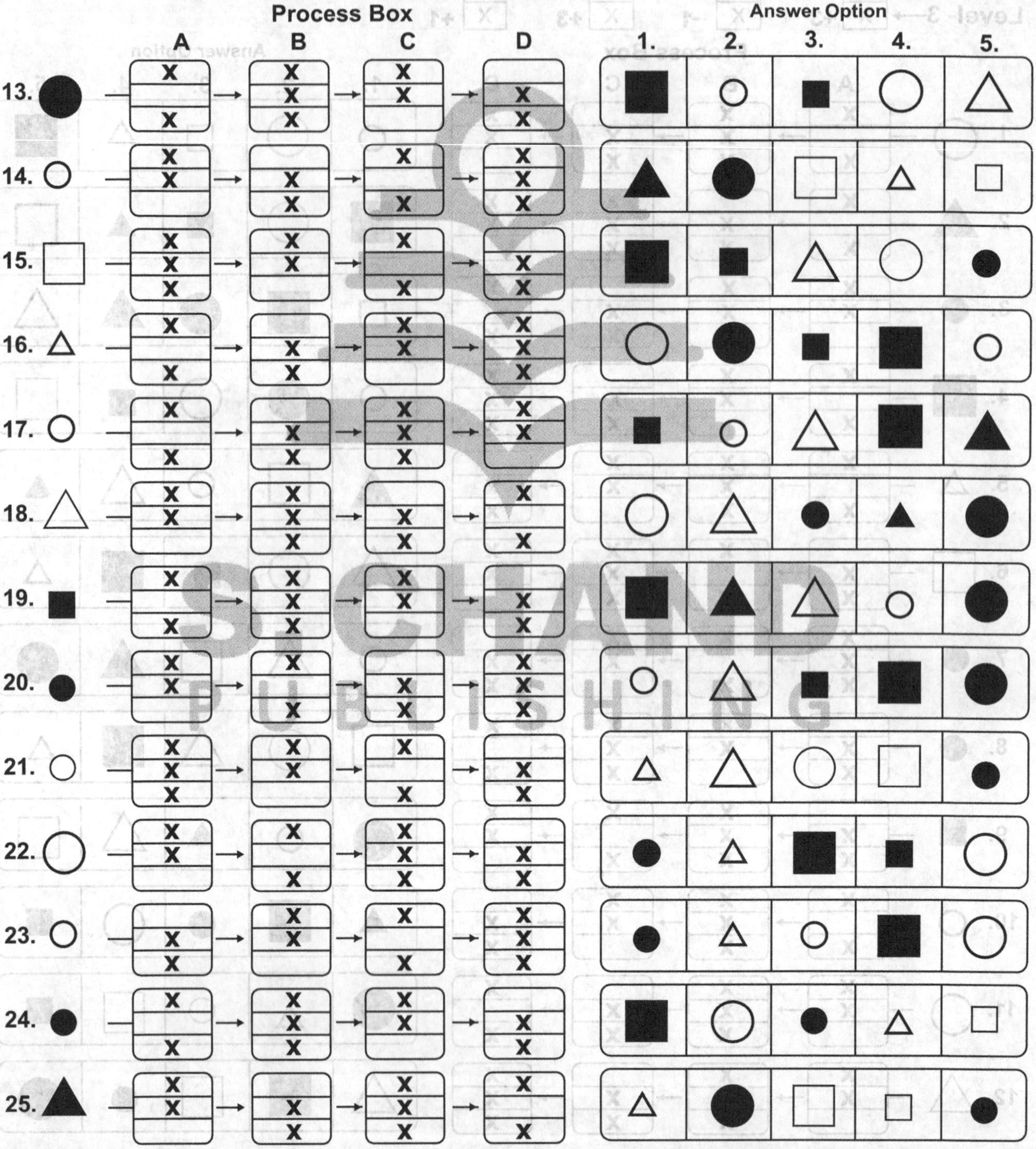

PRACTICE SET-7

Total Ques.- 25
Time - 8 or 10 Min.

Table - 2

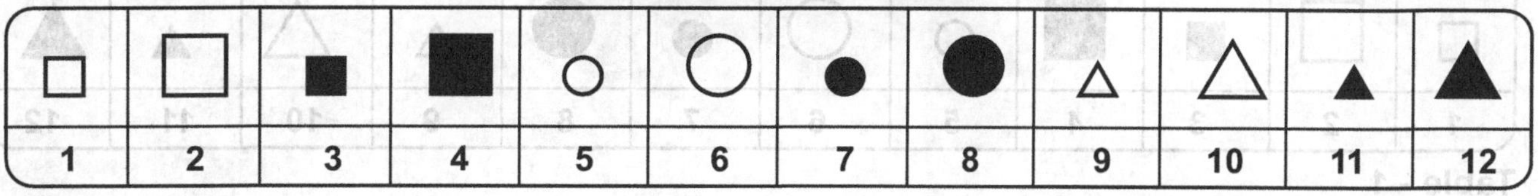

Table - 1

Level- 1 →	X +1	X +2	X +2	X −3
Level- 2 →	X −2 →	X −3 →	X −1 →	X −2
Level- 3 →	X +3	X −1	X +3	X +1

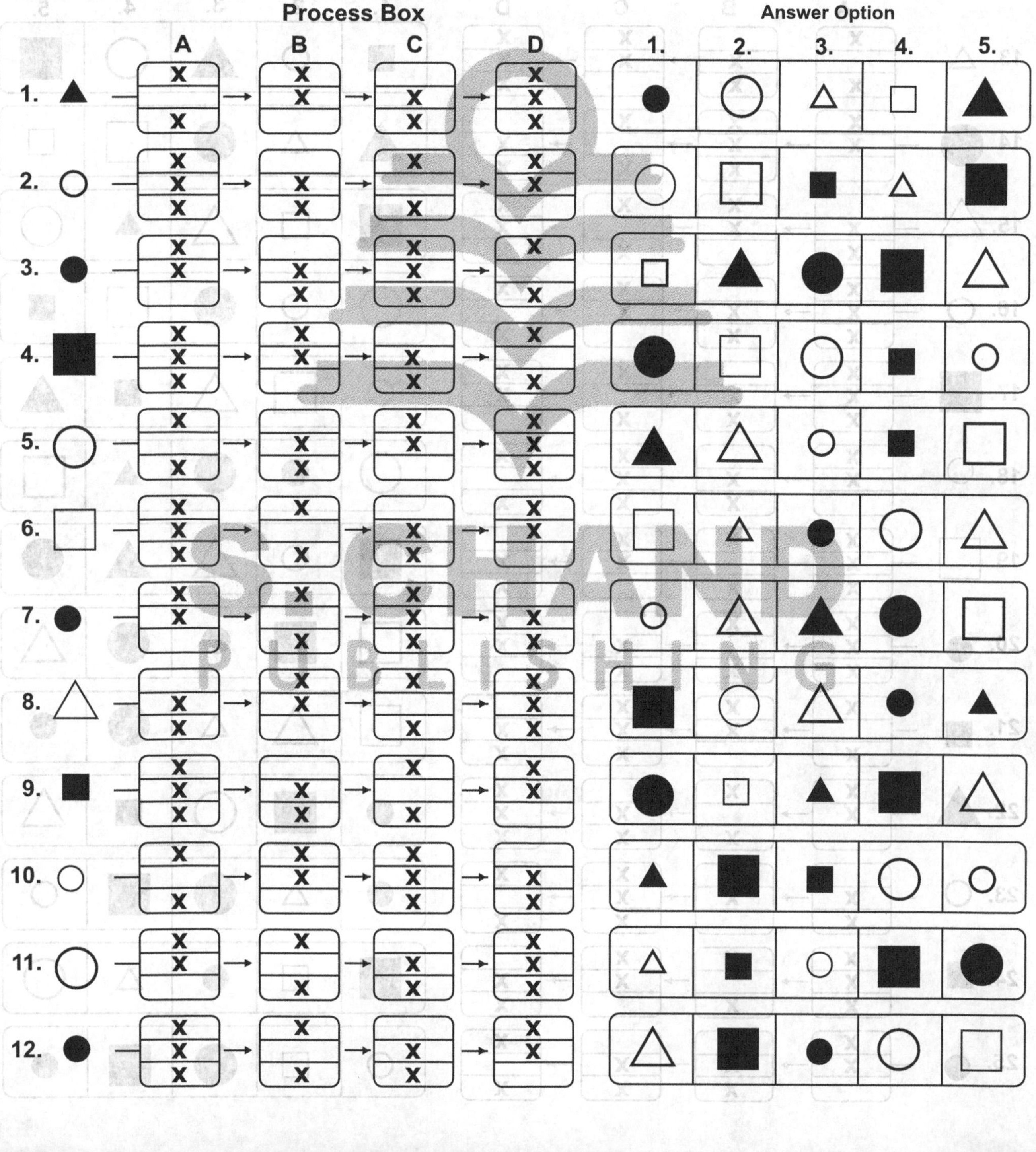

Table - 2

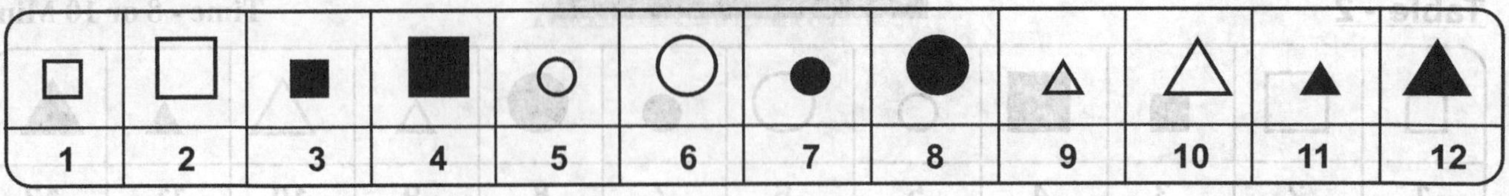

Table - 1

Level- 1 →	X +1	X +2	X +2	X −3
Level- 2 →	X −2 →	X −3 →	X −1 →	X −2
Level- 3 →	X +3	X −1	X +3	X +1

Process Box

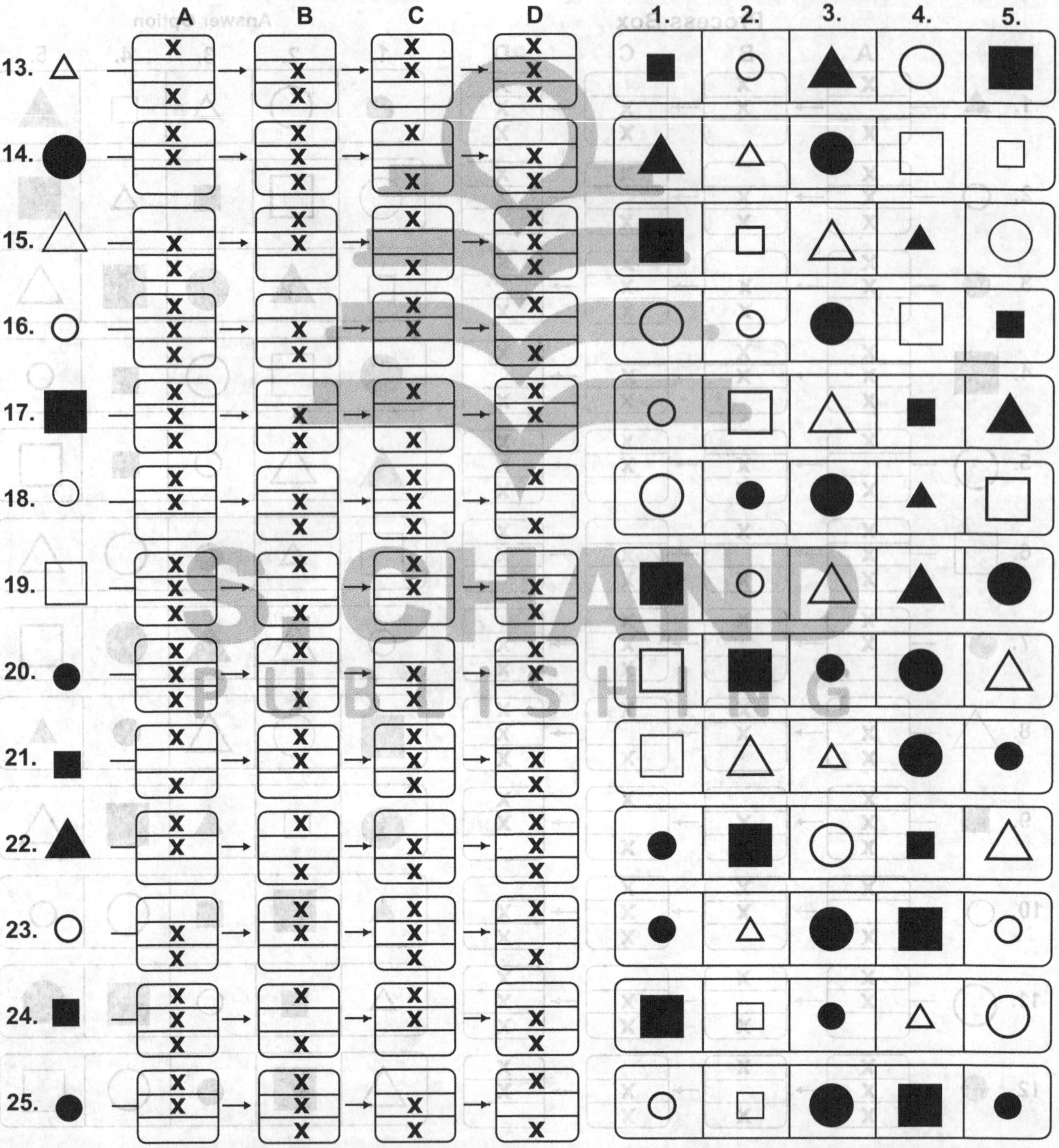

PRACTICE SET-8

Total Ques.- 25
Time - 8 or 10 Min.

Table - 2

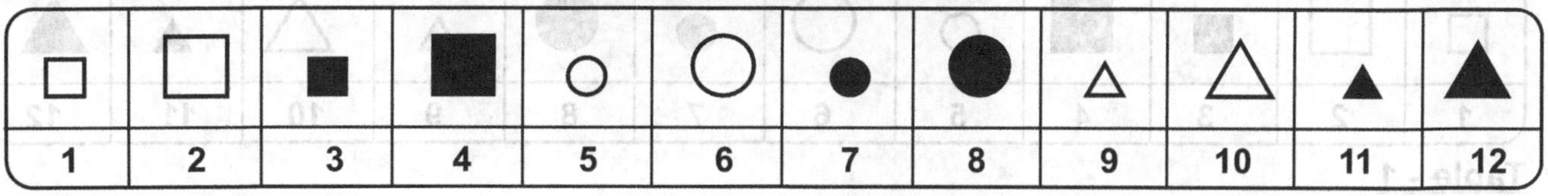

Table - 1

Level- 1 →	X +1	X +2	X +2	X −3
Level- 2 →	X −2 →	X −3 →	X −1 →	X −2
Level- 3 →	X +3	X −1	X +3	X +1

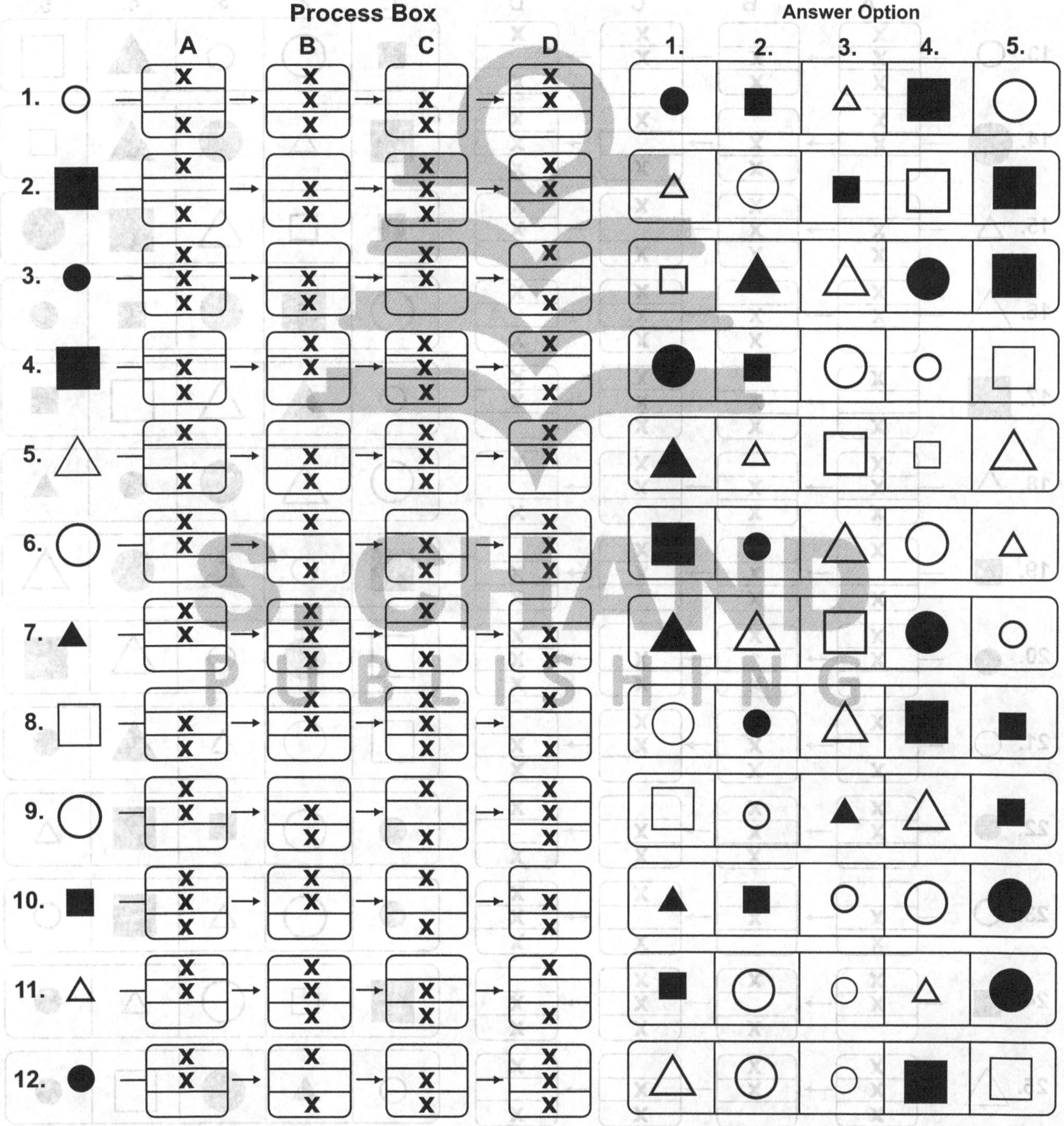

Table - 2

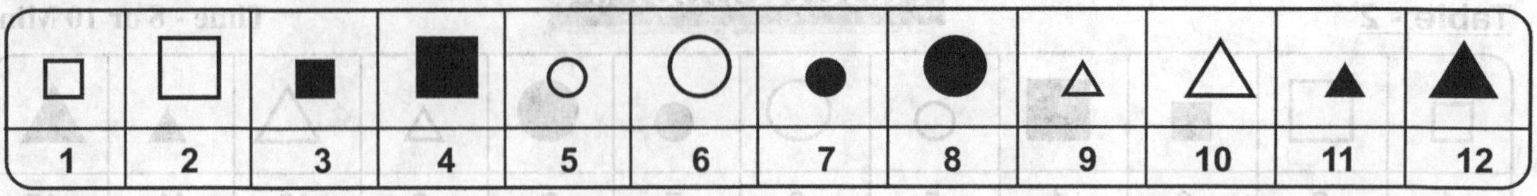

Table - 1

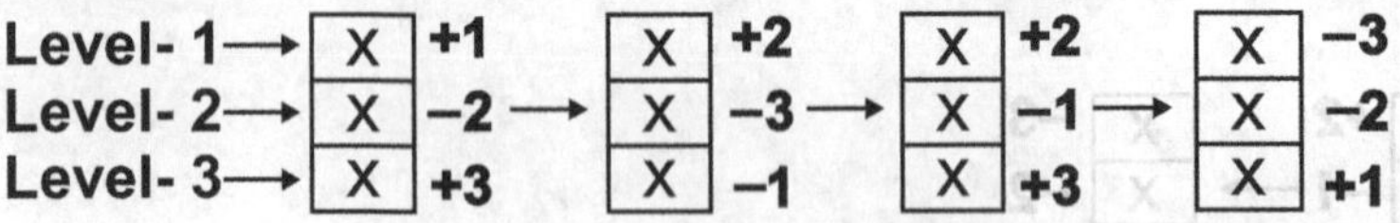

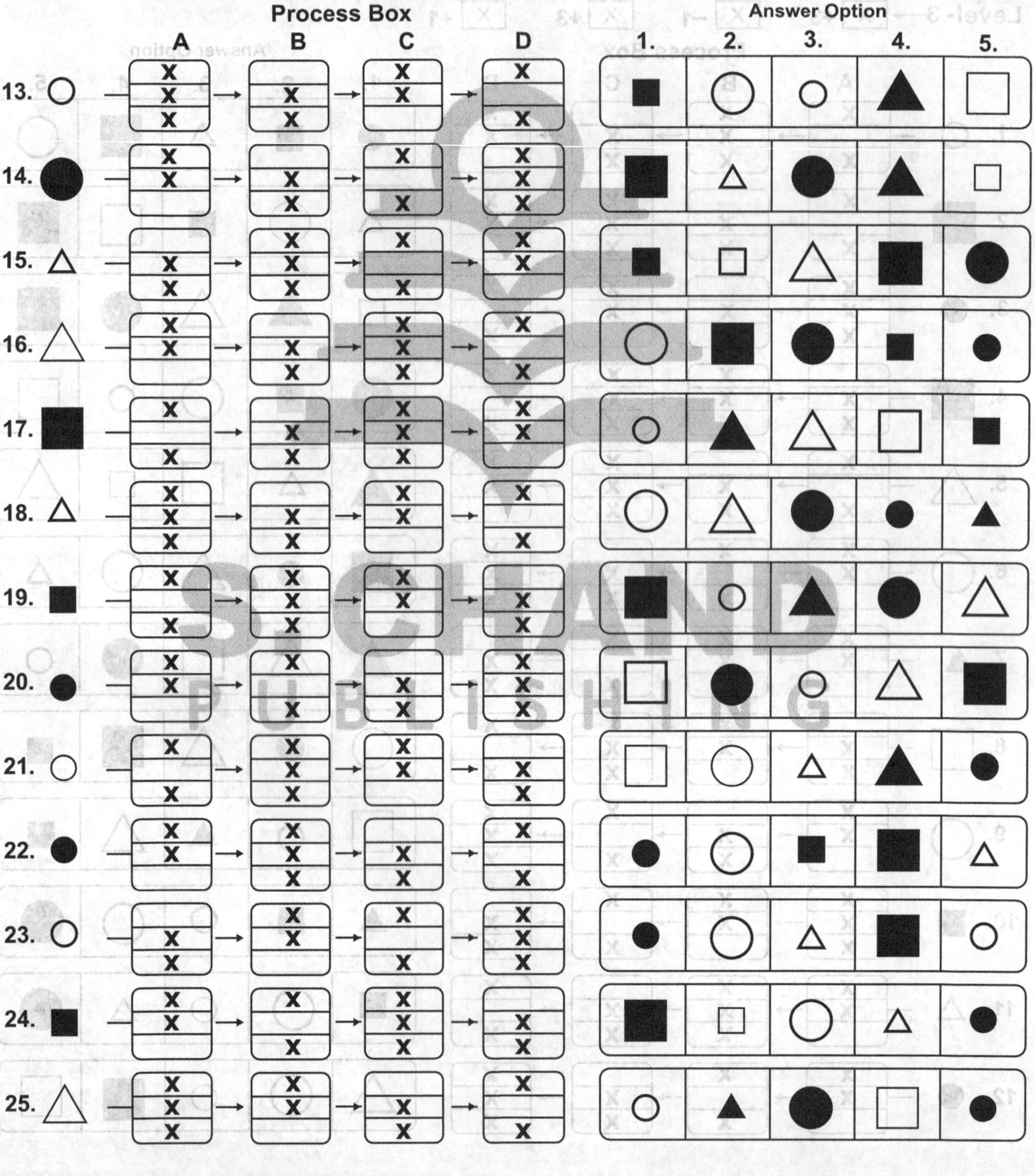

PRACTICE SET-9

Total Ques.- 25
Time - 8 or 10 Min.

Table - 2

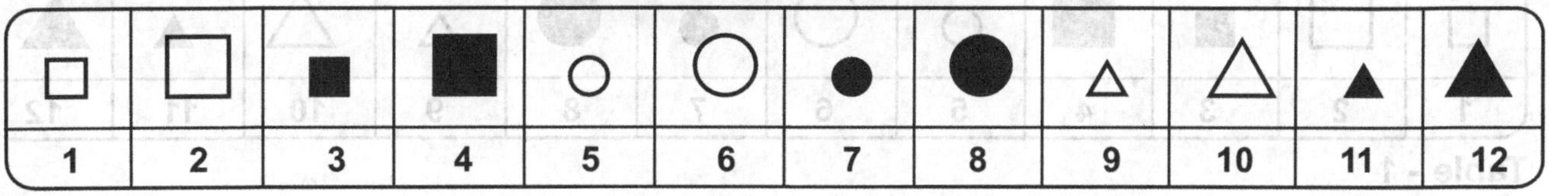

Table - 1

Level- 1	+1	+2	+2	–3
Level- 2	–2	–3	–1	–2
Level- 3	+3	–1	+3	+1

Process Box — **Answer Option**

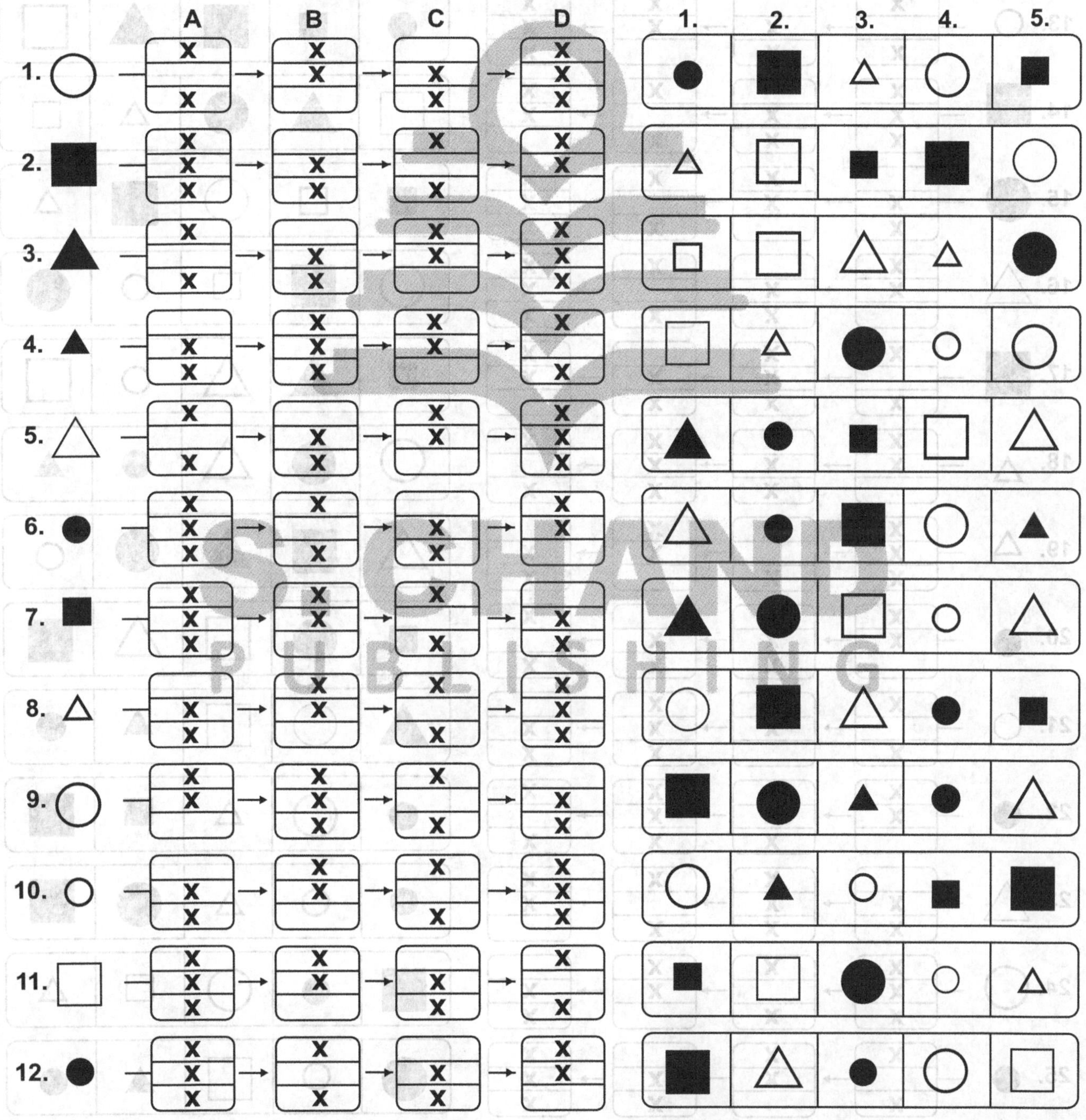

Table - 2

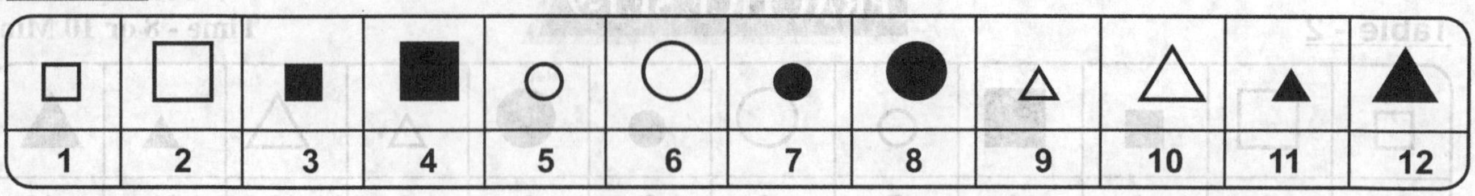

Table - 1

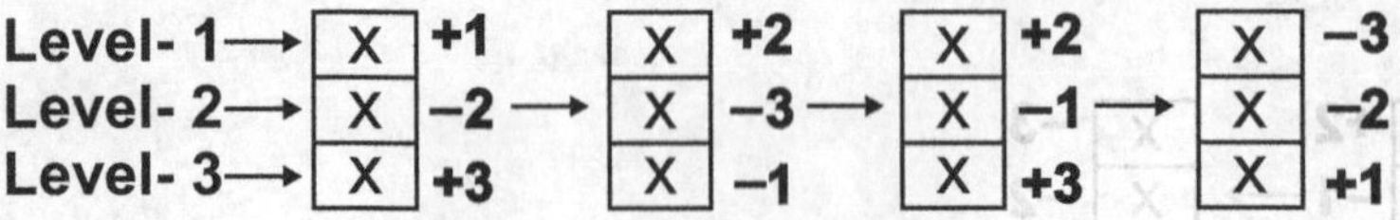

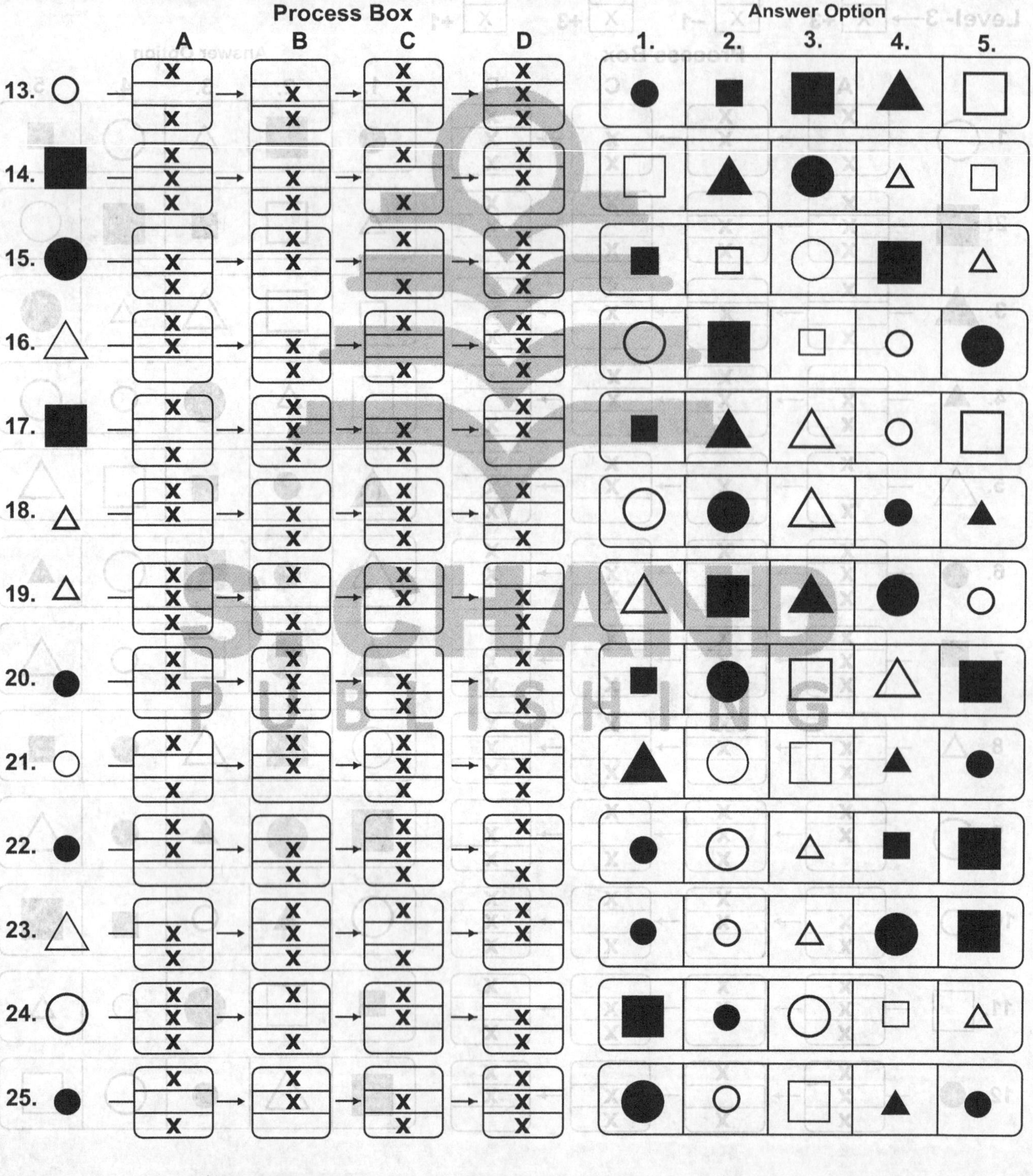

PRACTICE SET-10

Total Ques.- 25
Time - 8 or 10 Min.

Table - 2

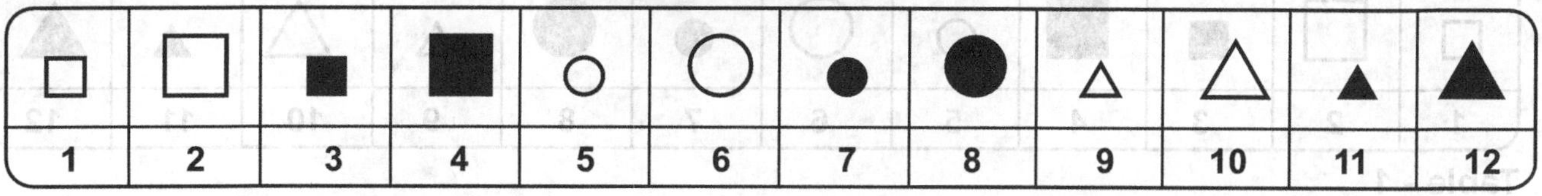

Table - 1

Level- 1 →	X +1	X +2	X +2	X −3
Level- 2 →	X −2 →	X −3 →	X −1 →	X −2
Level- 3 →	X +3	X −1	X +3	X +1

Process Box **Answer Option**

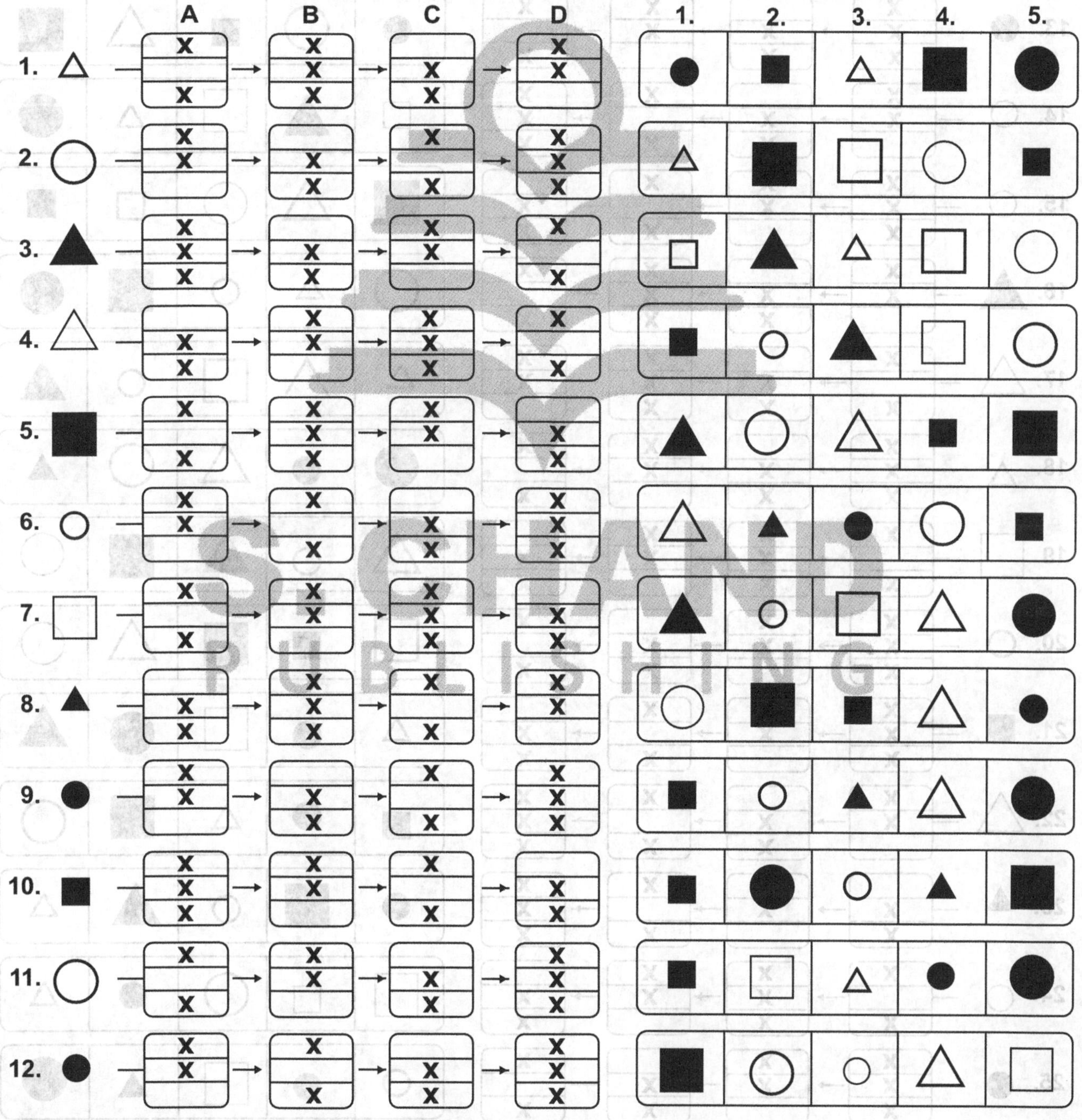

Table - 2

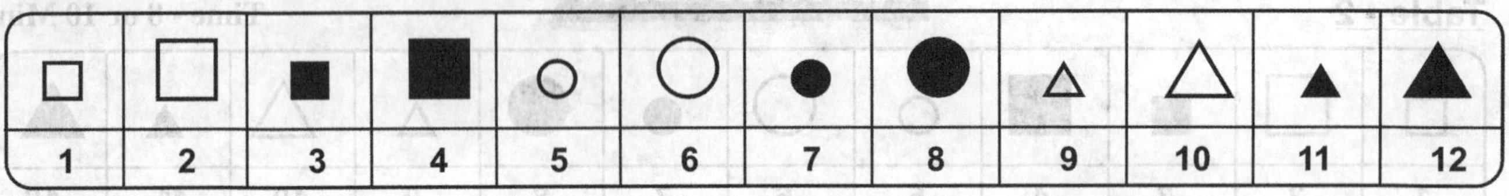

Table - 1

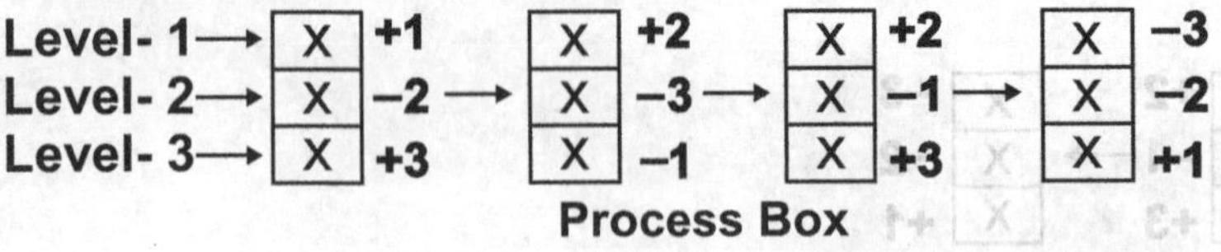

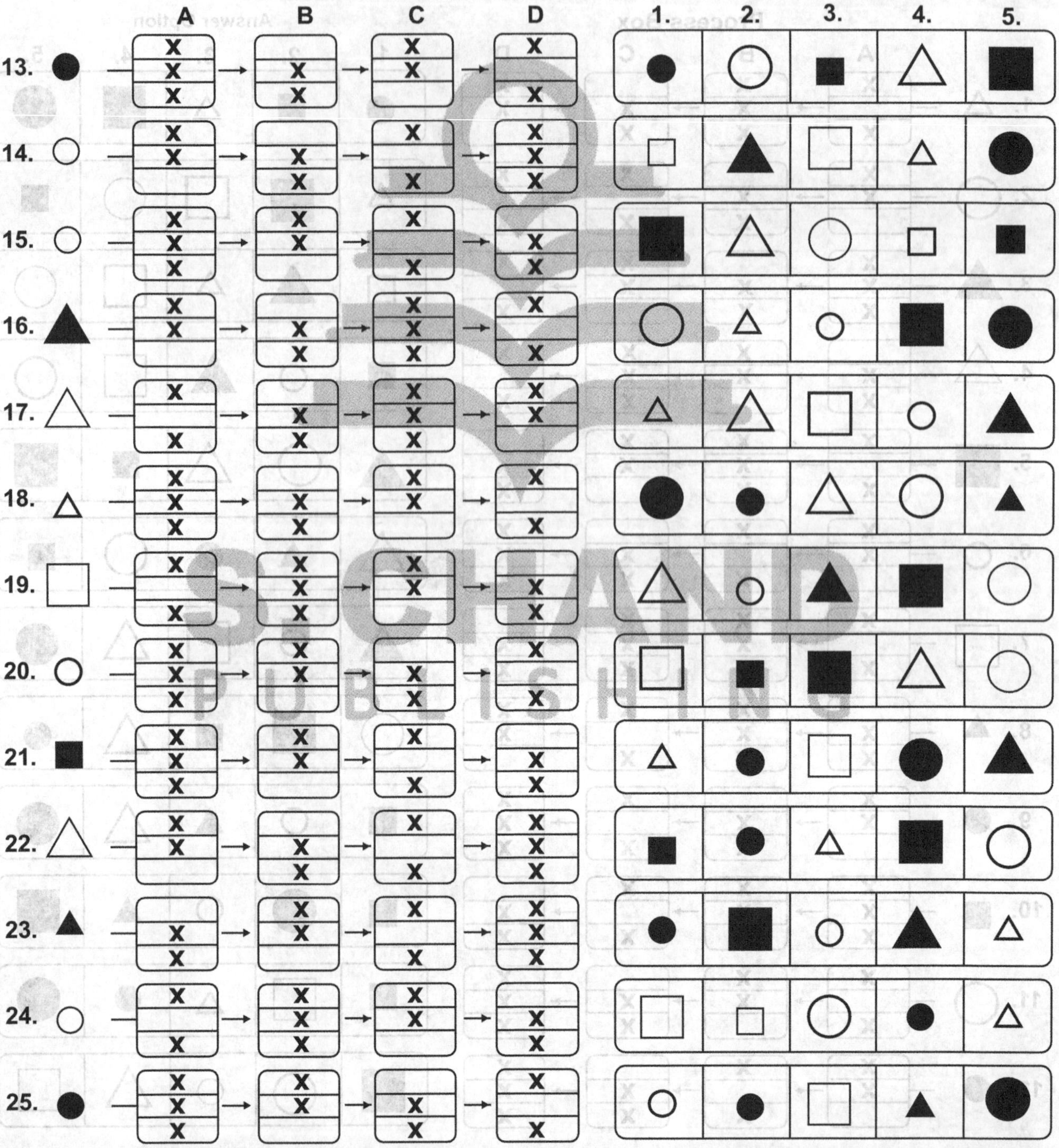

PRACTICE SET-11

Total Ques.- 25
Time - 8 or 10 Min.

Table - 2

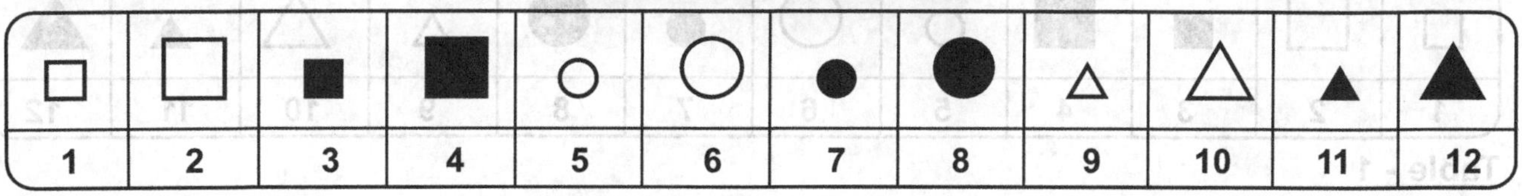

Table - 1

Level- 1	X +1	X +2	X +2	X –3
Level- 2	X –2	X –3	X –1	X –2
Level- 3	X +3	X –1	X +3	X +1

Process Box — Answer Option

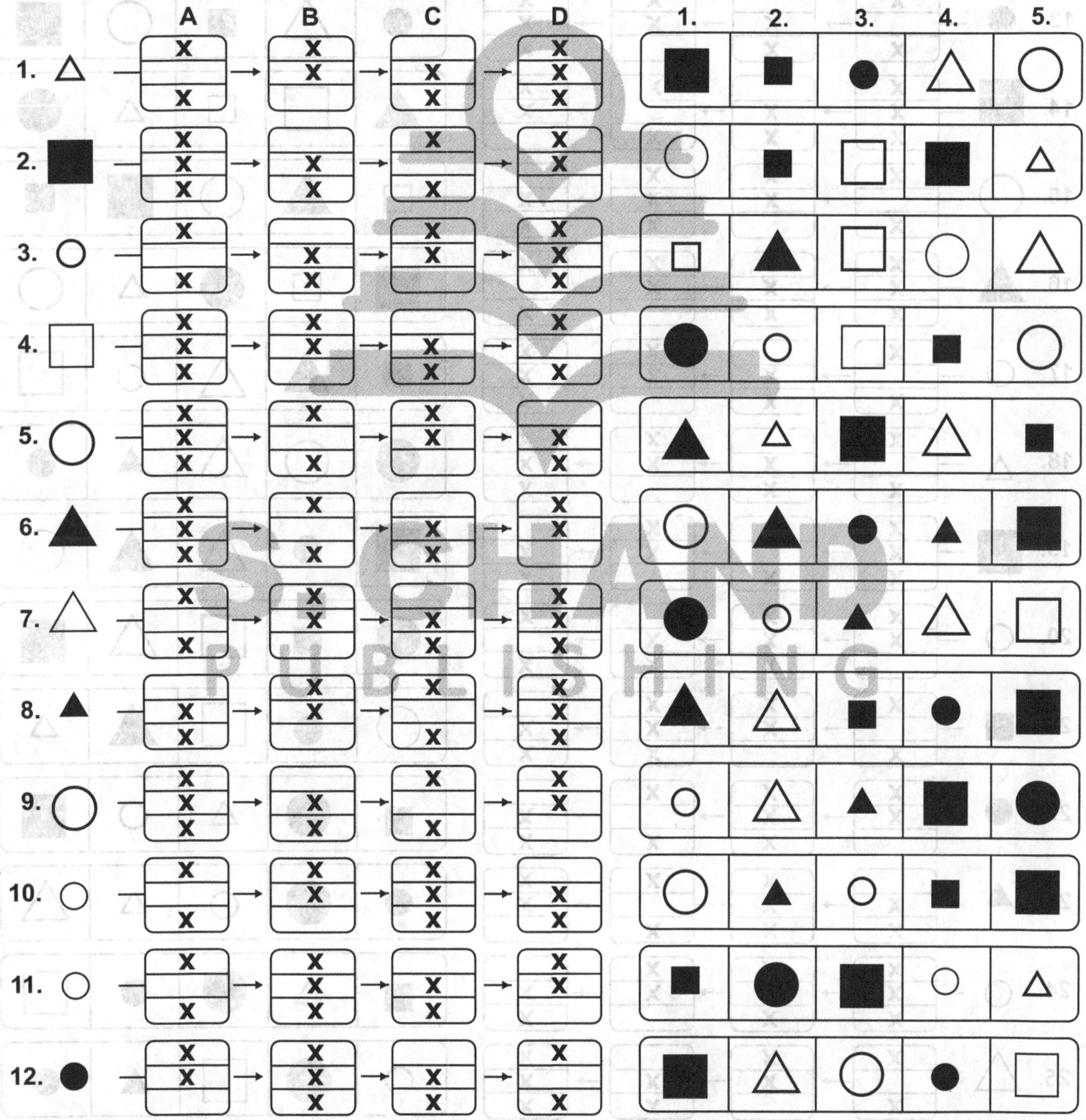

Table - 2

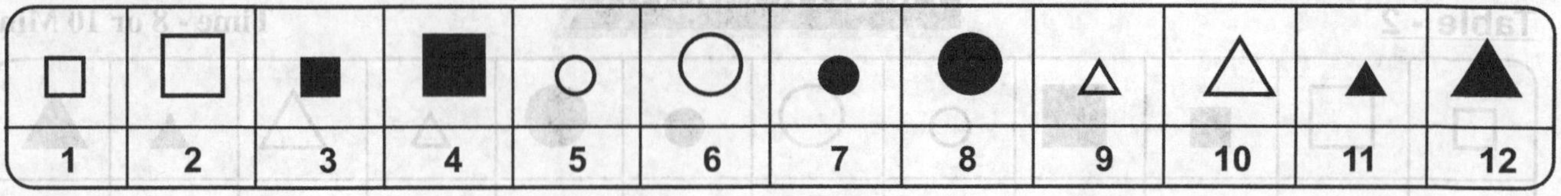

Table - 1

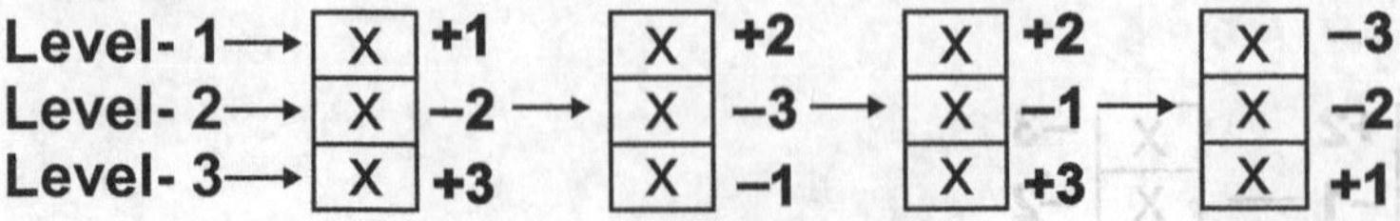

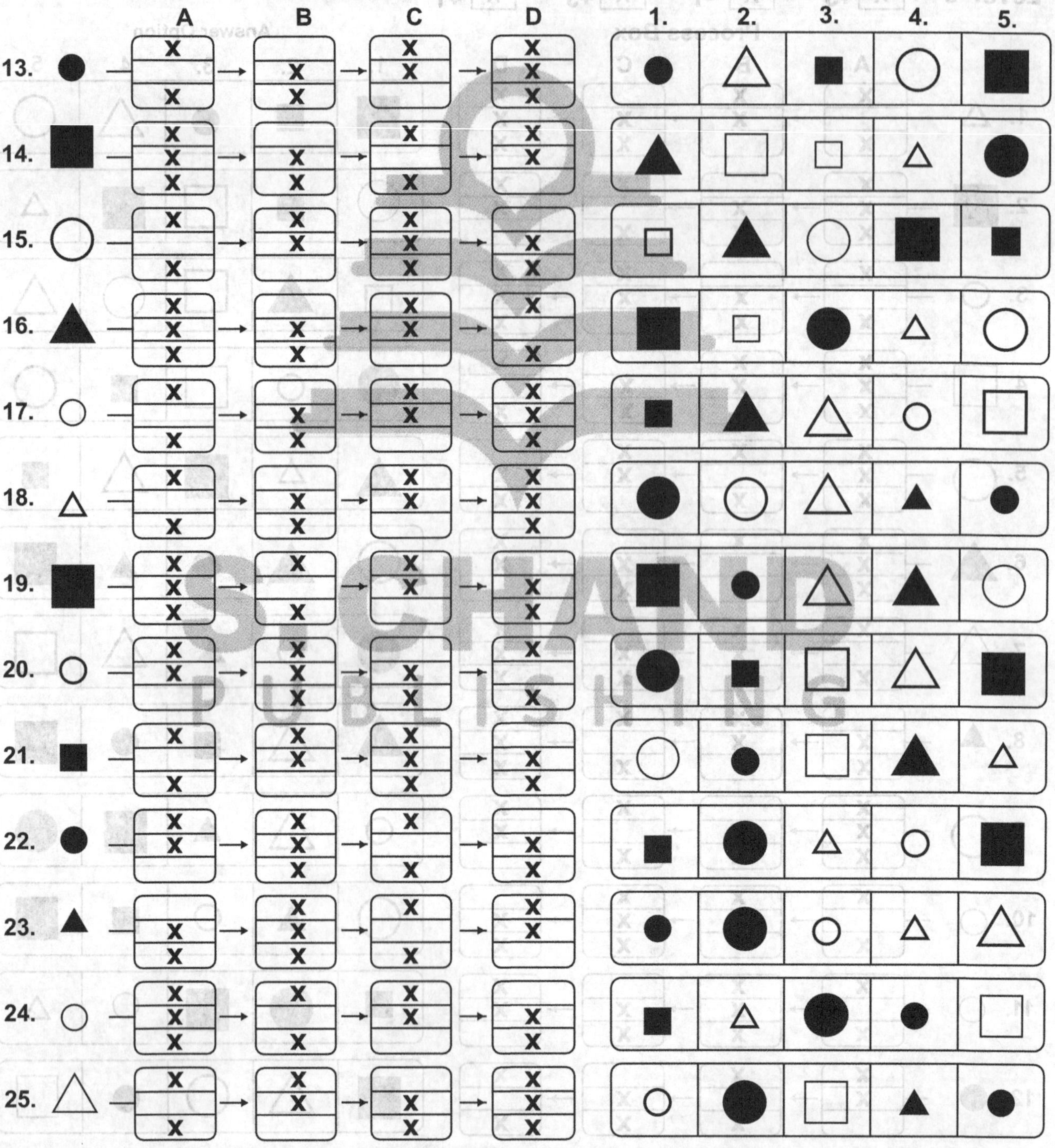

PRACTICE SET-12

Total Ques.- 25
Time - 8 or 10 Min.

Table - 2

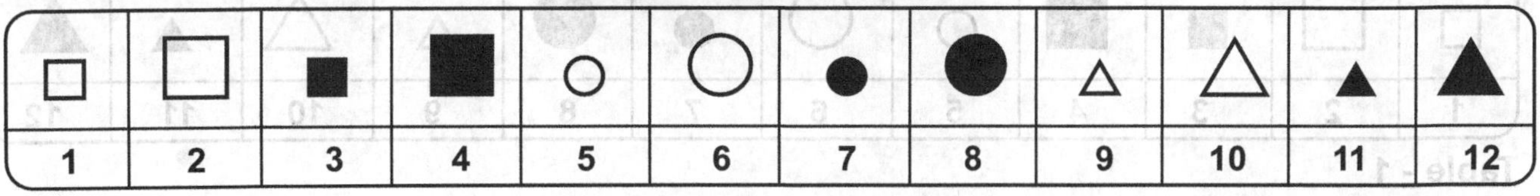

Table - 1

Level- 1 →	X +1	X +2	X +2	X –3
Level- 2 →	X –2 →	X –3 →	X –1 →	X –2
Level- 3 →	X +3	X –1	X +3	X +1

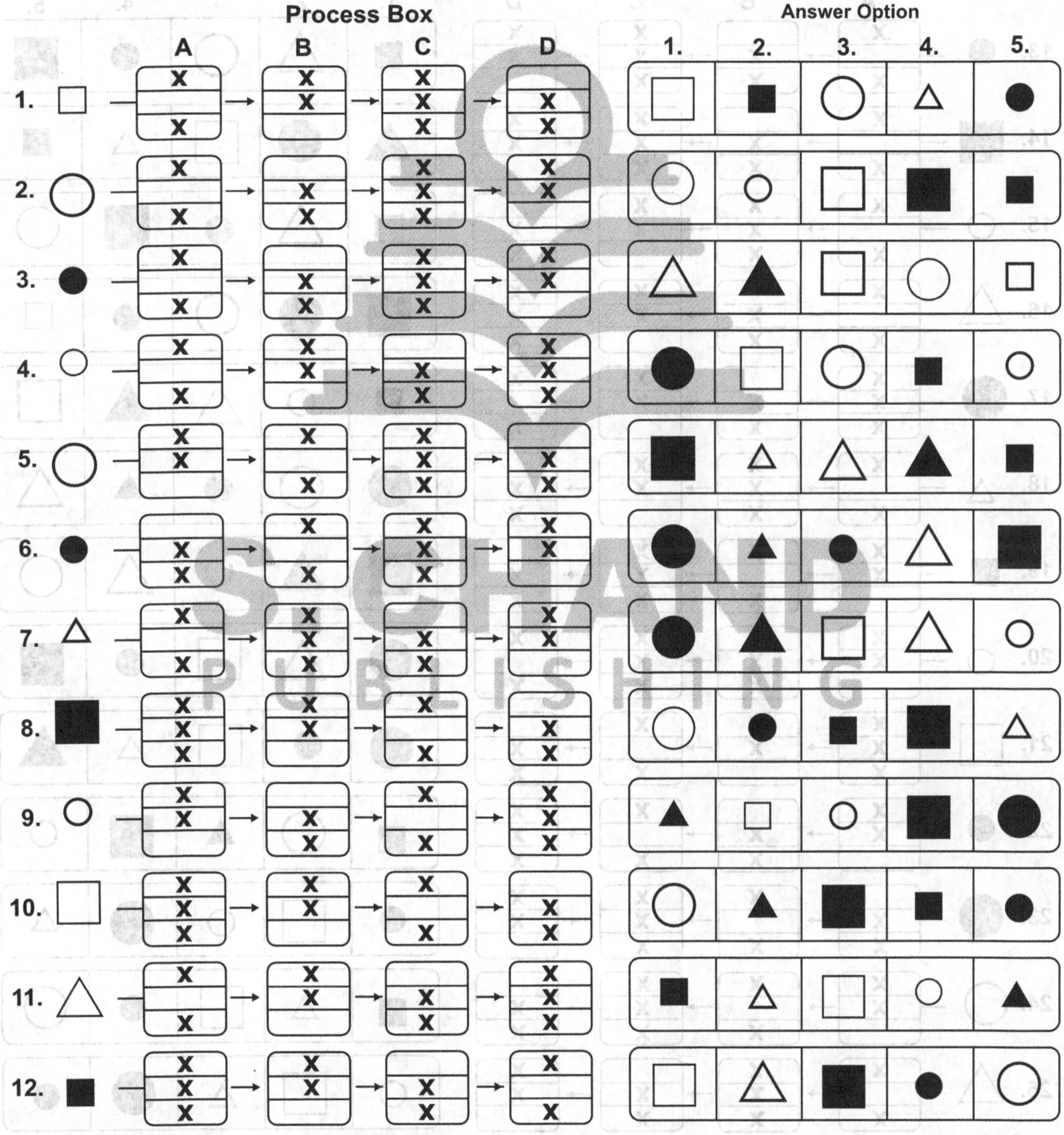

Table - 2

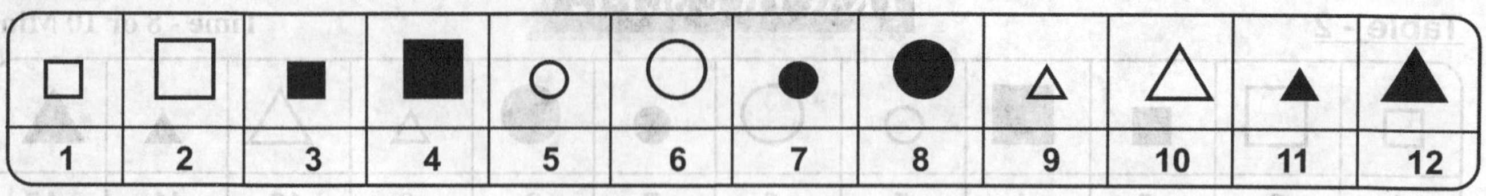

Table - 1

Level- 1 →	X +1	X +2	X +2	X –3
Level- 2 →	X –2 →	X –3 →	X –1 →	X –2
Level- 3 →	X +3	X –1	X +3	X +1

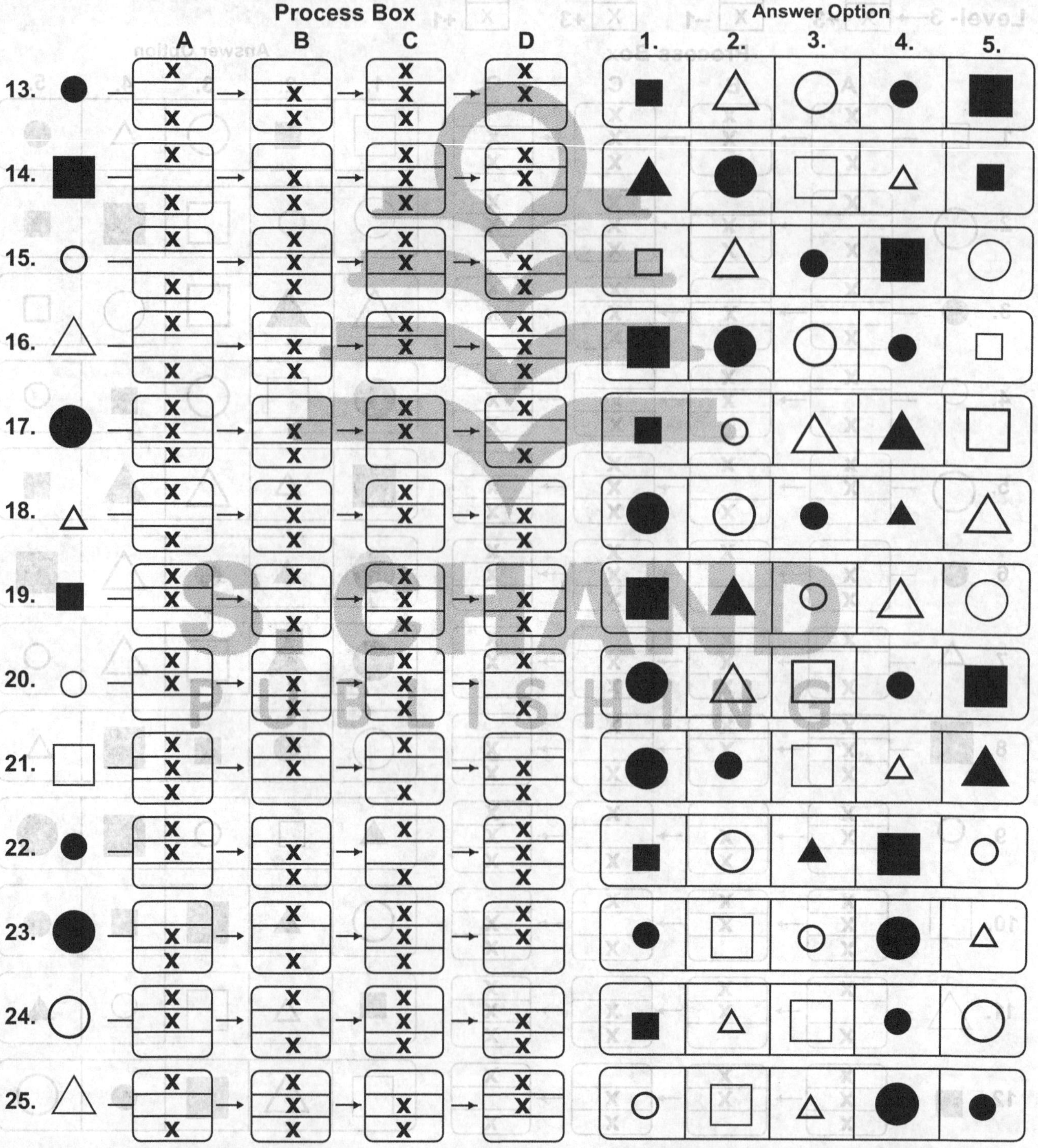

PRACTICE SET-13

Total Ques.- 25
Time - 8 or 10 Min.

Table - 2

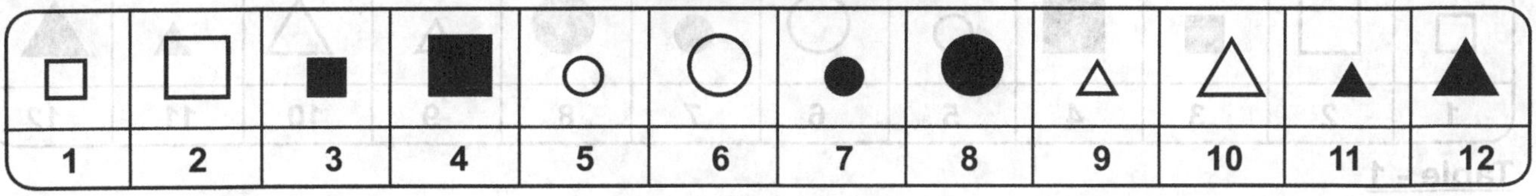

Table - 1

Level- 1→	X +1	X +2	X +2	X −3
Level- 2→	X −2 →	X −3 →	X −1 →	X −2
Level- 3→	X +3	X −1	X +3	X +1

Process Box **Answer Option**

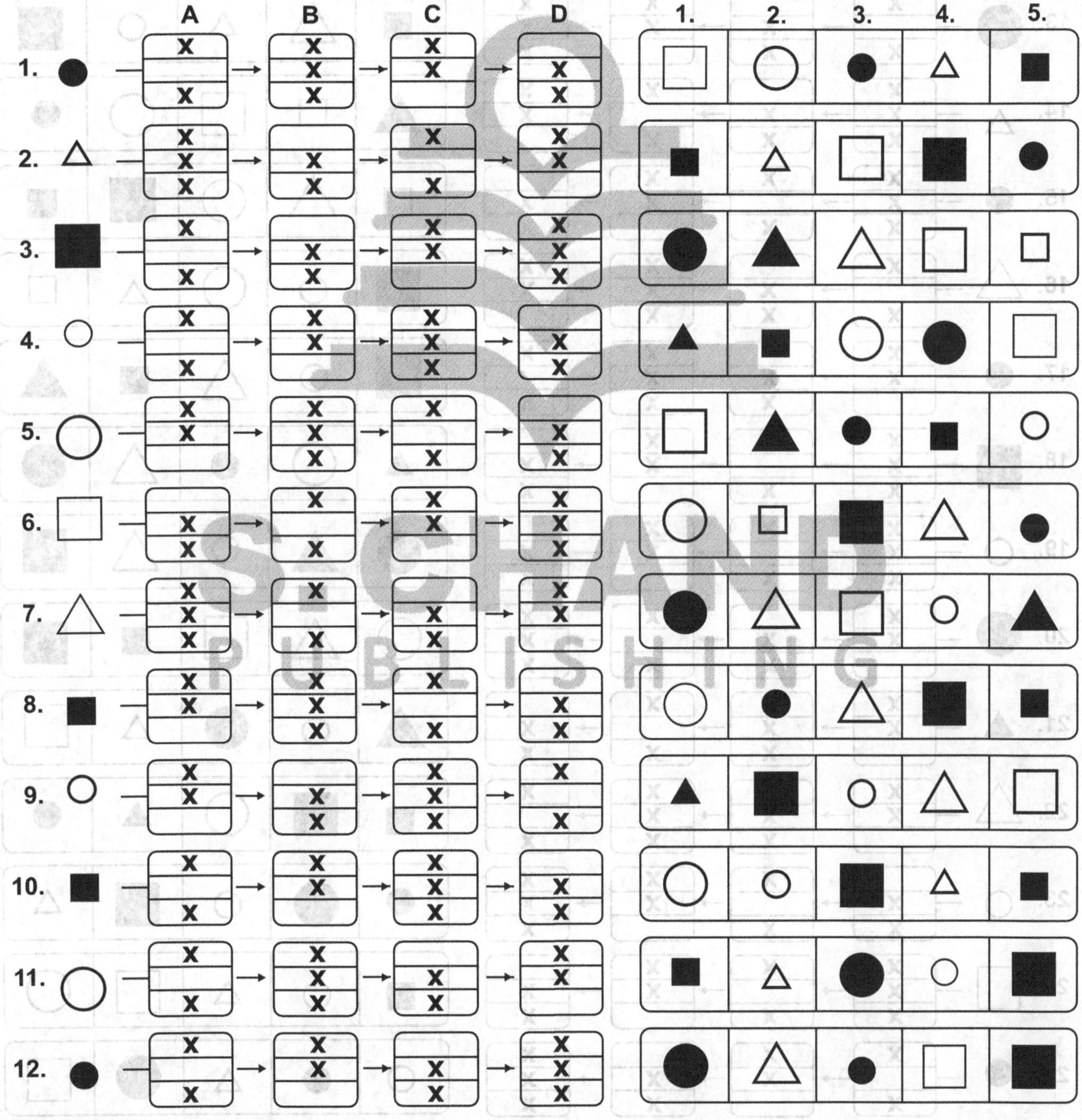

Table - 2

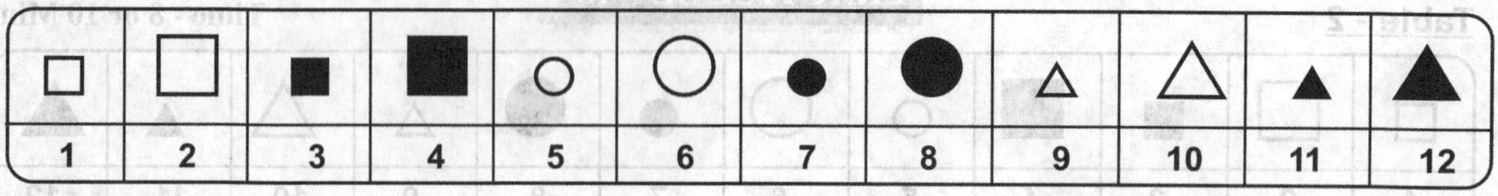

Table - 1

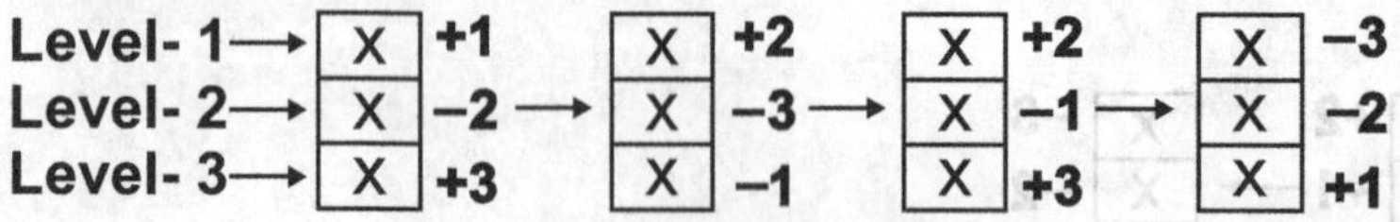

Process Box **Answer Option**

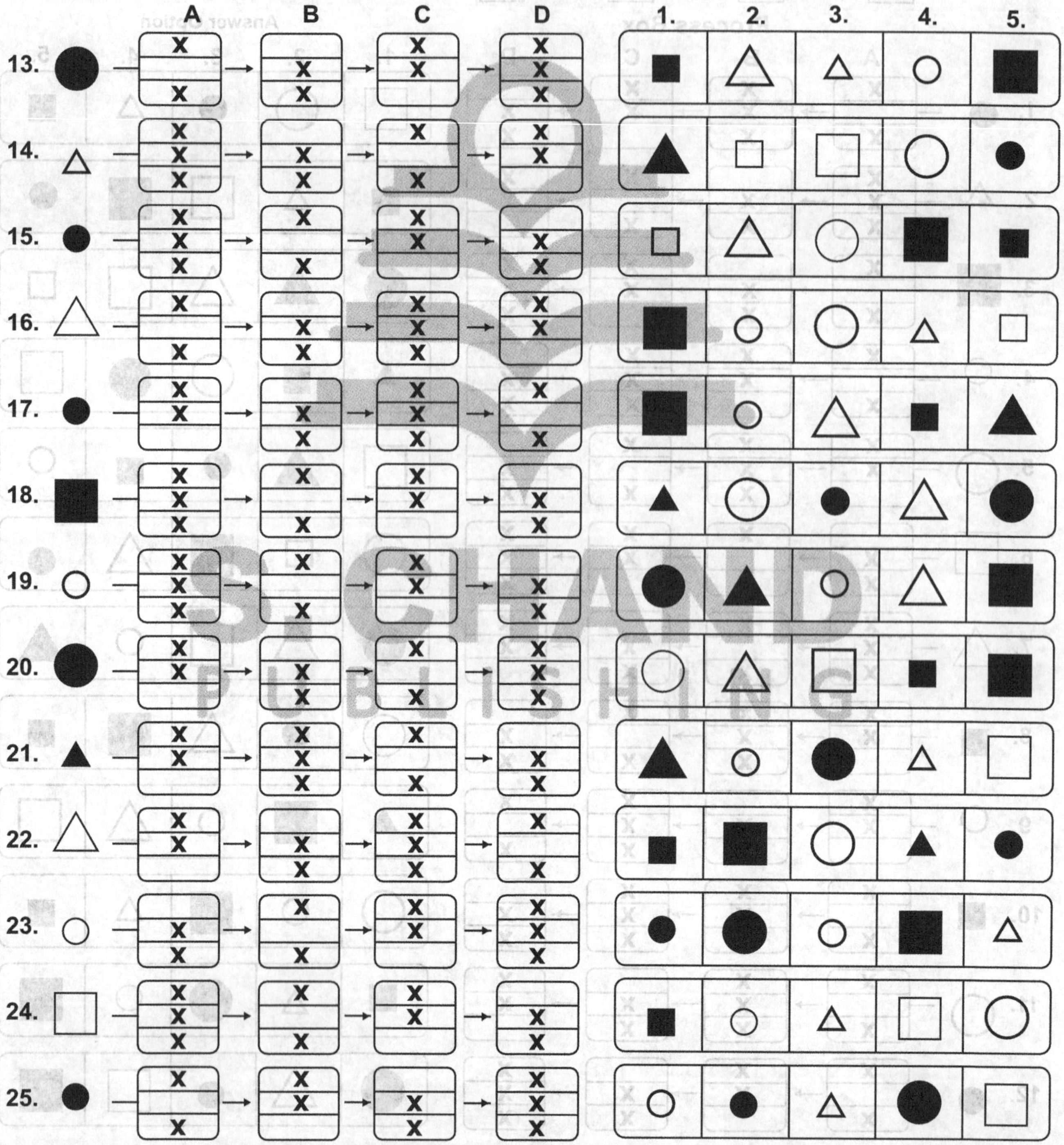

PRACTICE SET-14

Total Ques.- 25
Time - 8 or 10 Min.

Table - 2

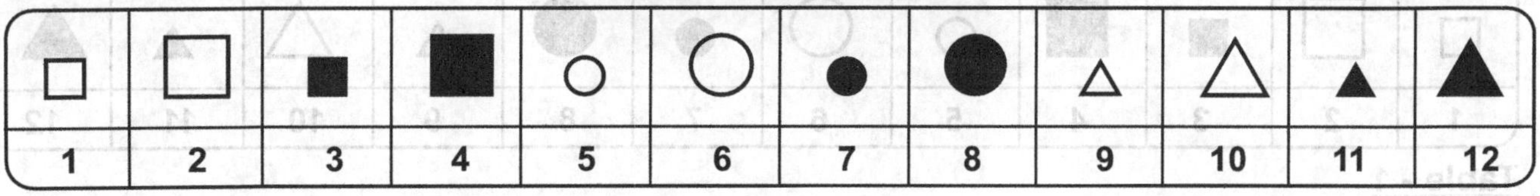

Table - 1

Level- 1 →	X +1	X +2	X +2	X −3
Level- 2 →	X −2 →	X −3 →	X −1 →	X −2
Level- 3 →	X +3	X −1	X +3	X +1

Process Box | **Answer Option**

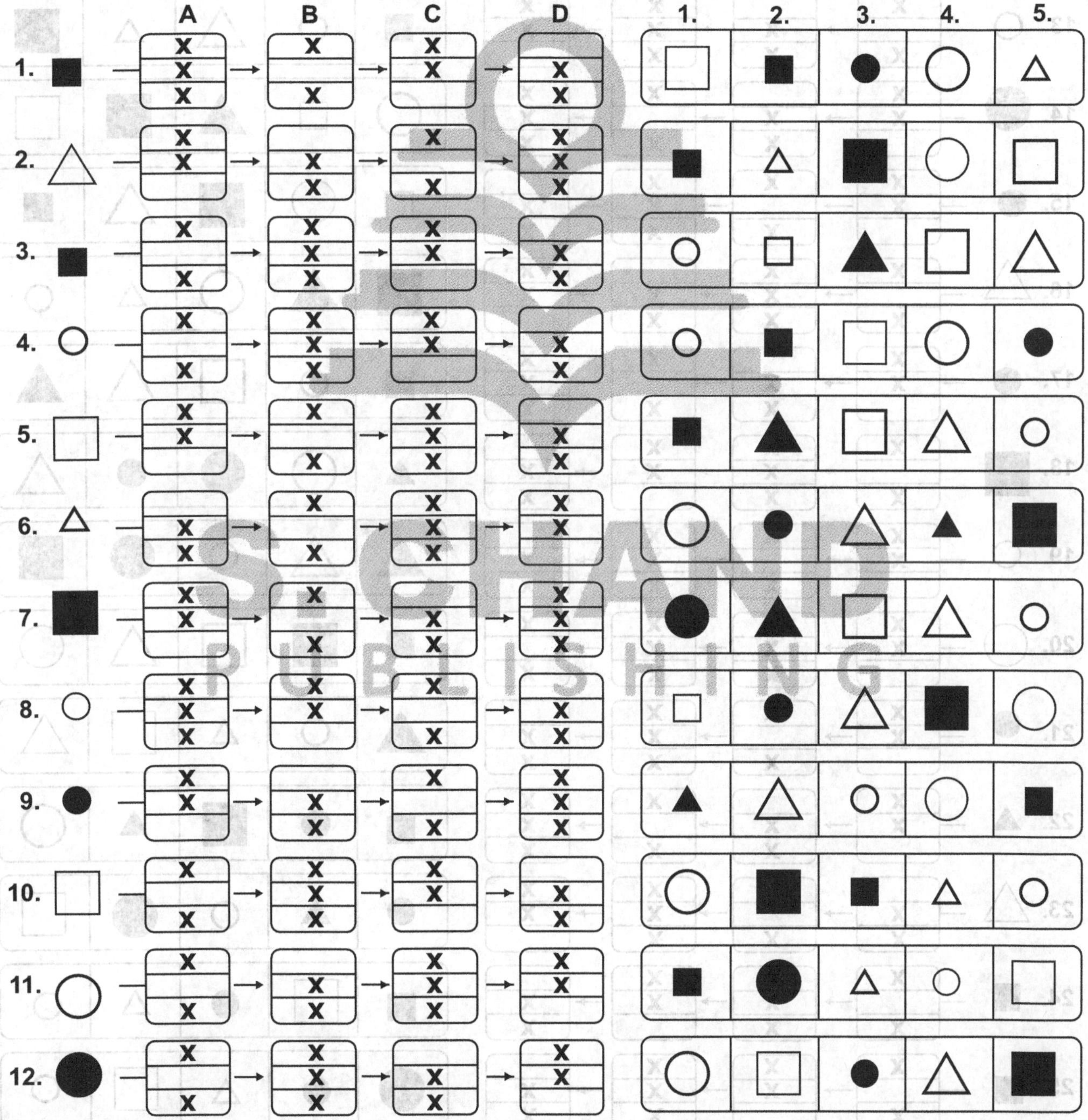

Table - 2

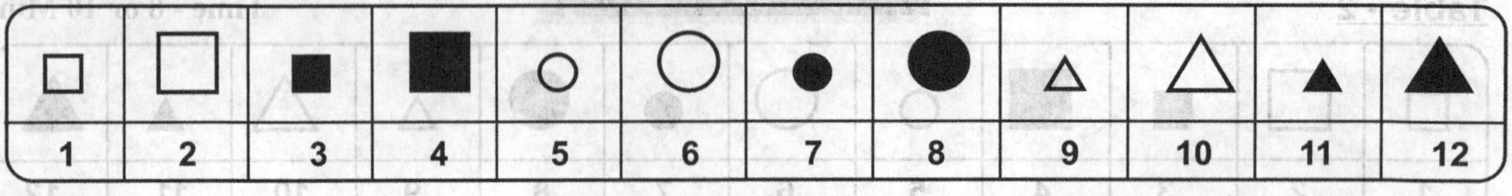

Table - 1

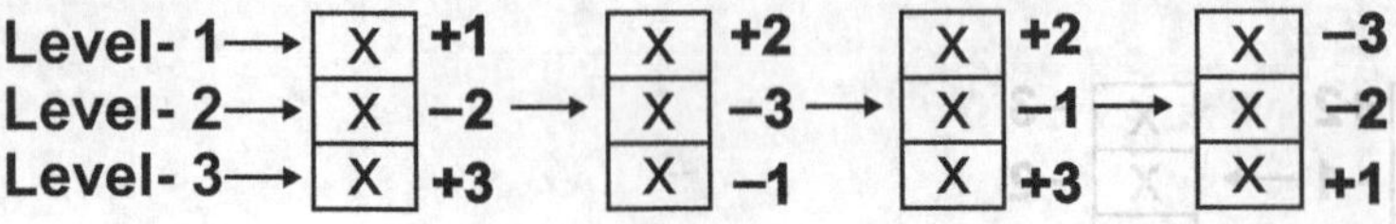

Process Box **Answer Option**

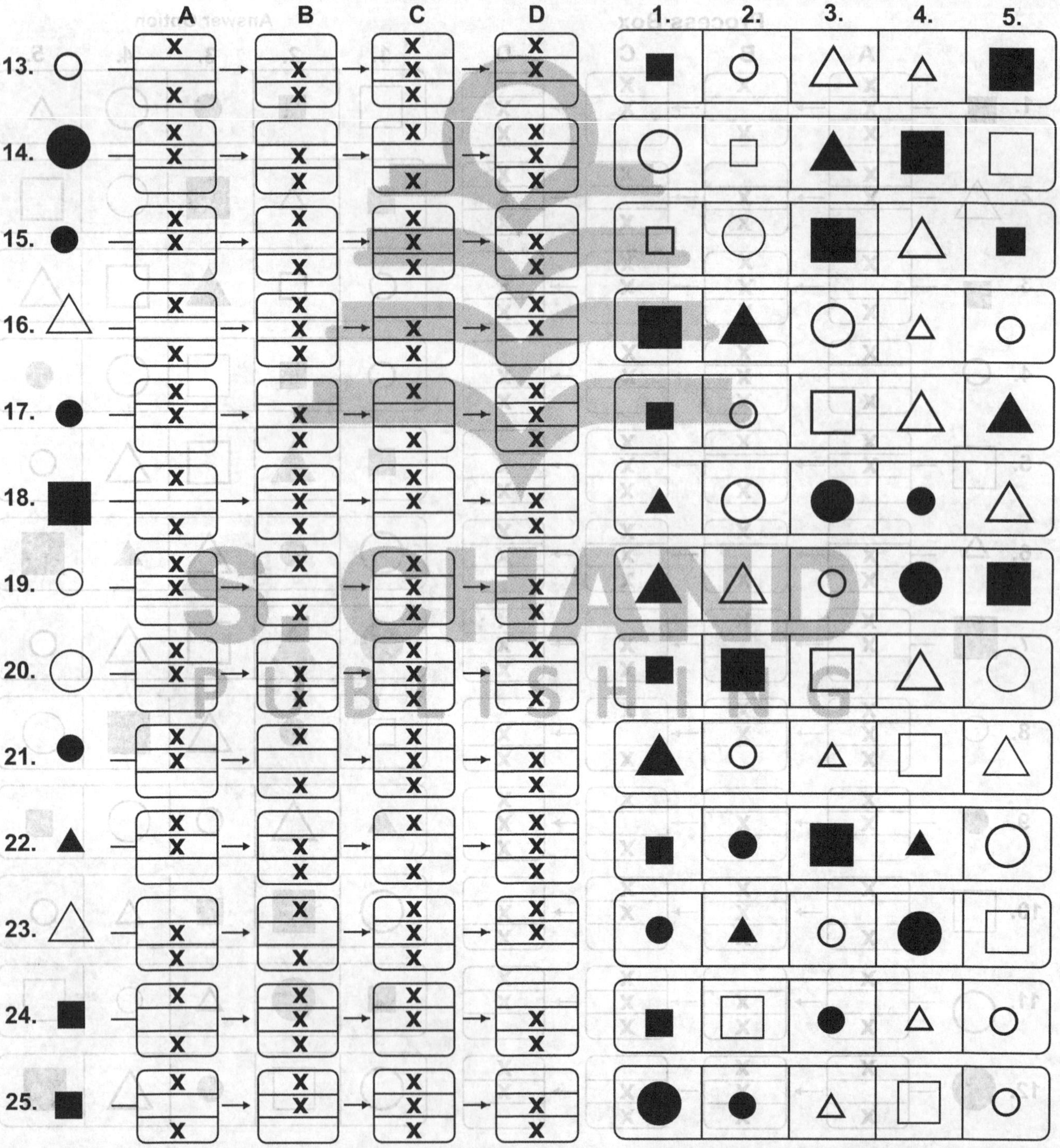

PRACTICE SET-15

Total Ques.- 25
Time - 8 or 10 Min.

Table - 2

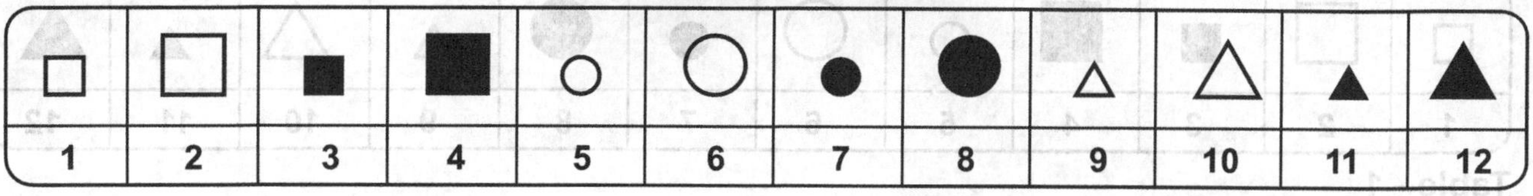

Table - 1

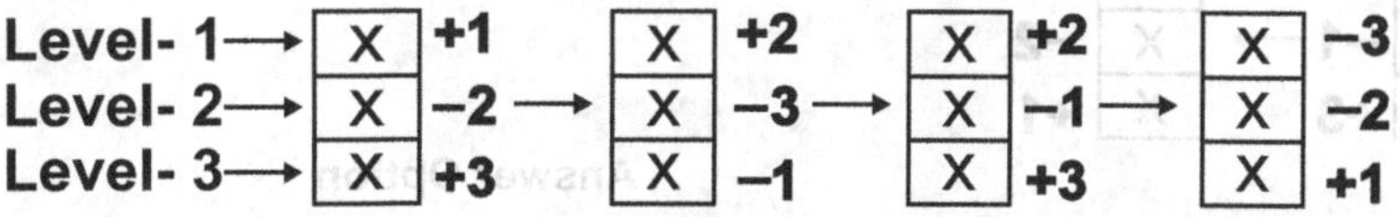

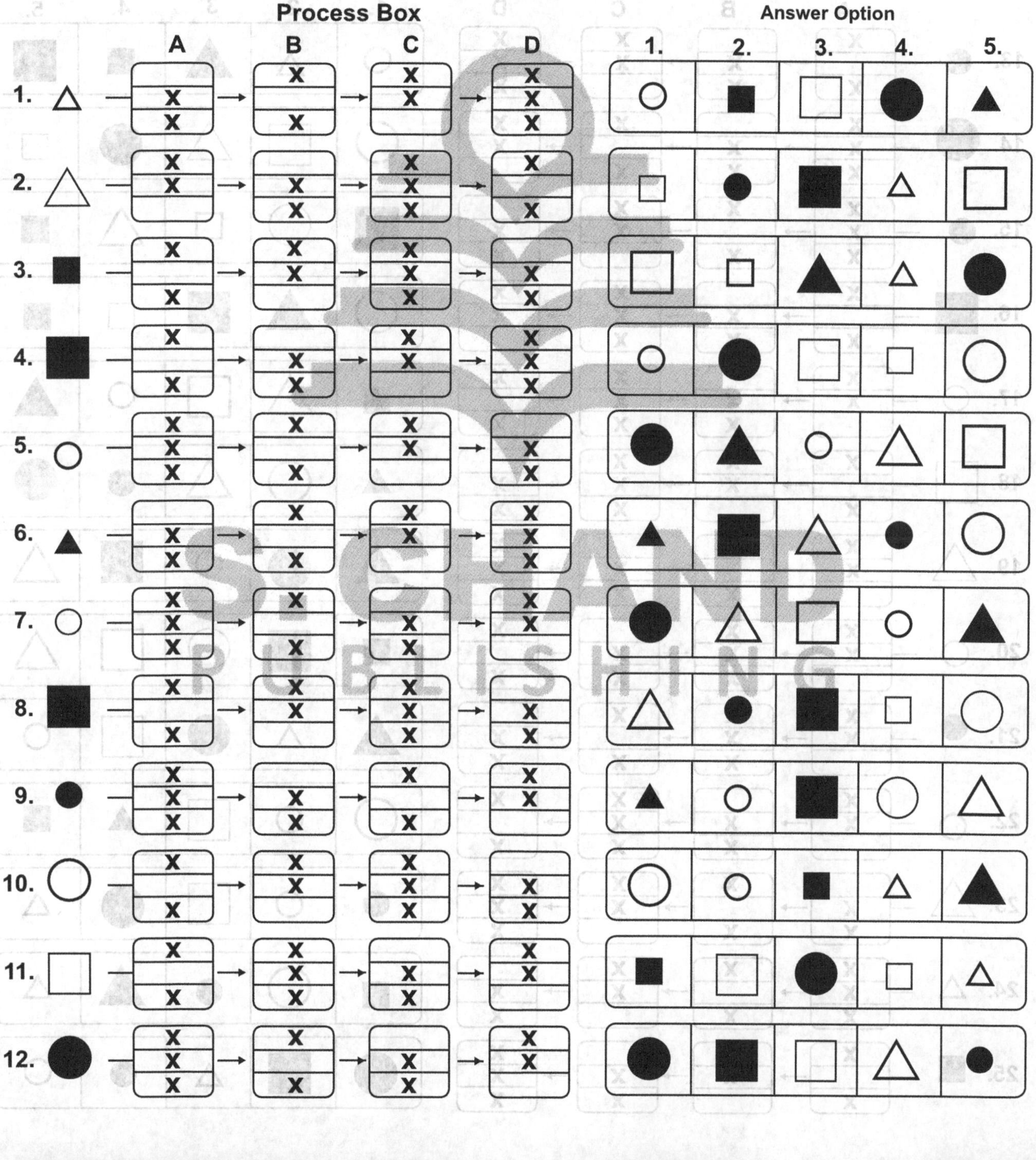

Table - 2

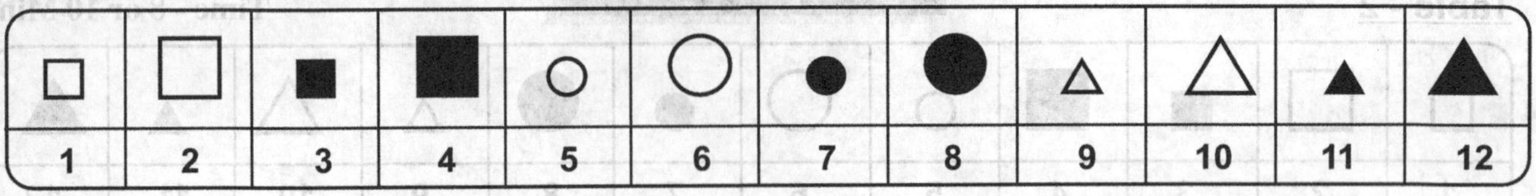

Table - 1

Level- 1 →	X +1	X +2	X +2	X –3
Level- 2 →	X –2 →	X –3 →	X –1 →	X –2
Level- 3 →	X +3	X –1	X +3	X +1

Process Box **Answer Option**

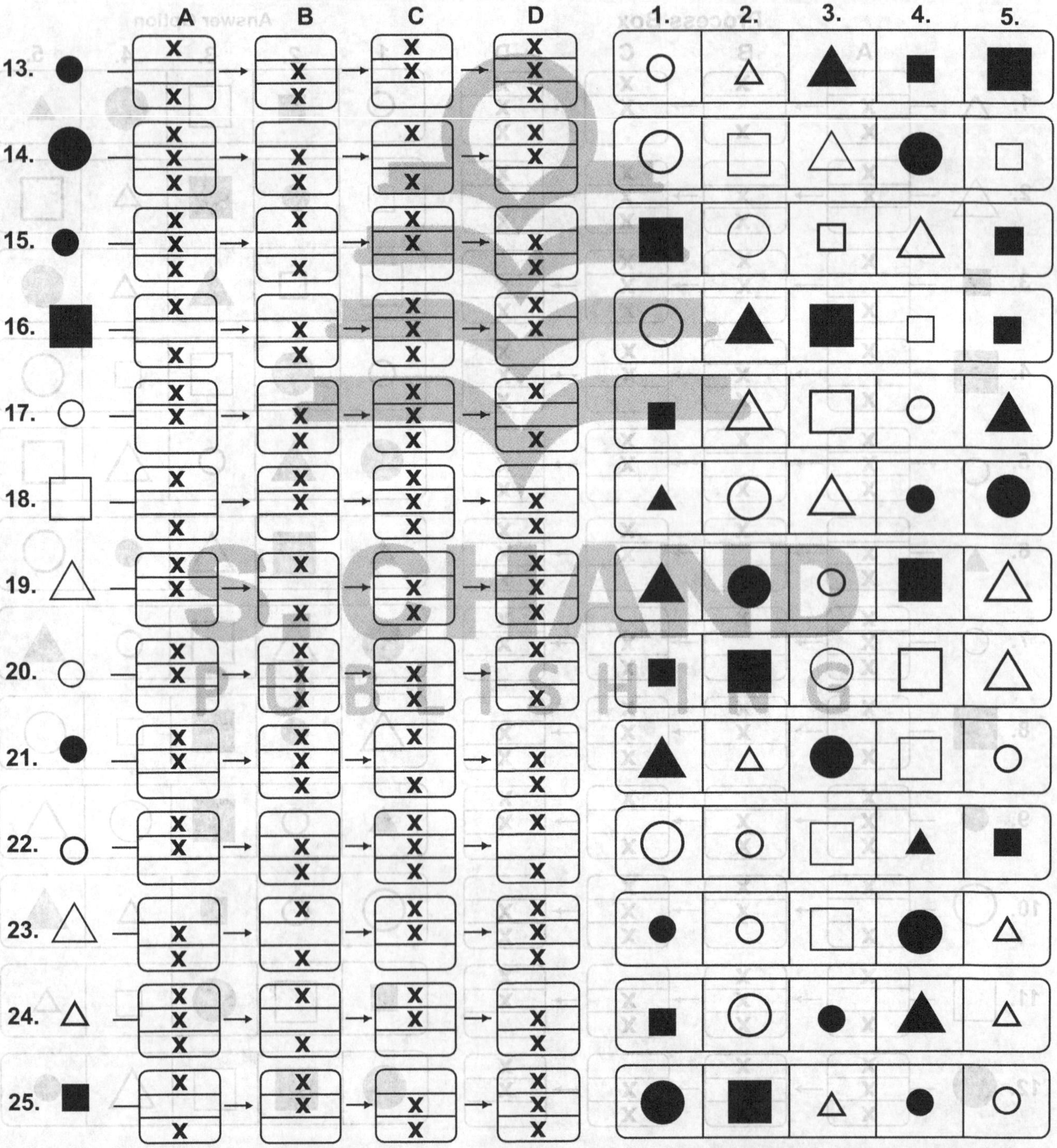

PRACTICE SET-16

Total Ques.- 25
Time - 8 or 10 Min.

Table - 2

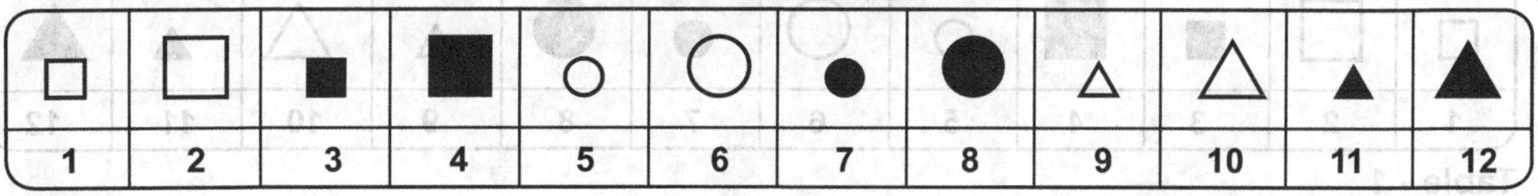

Table - 1

Level- 1→	X	+1	X	+2	X	+2	X	−3
Level- 2→	X	−2 →	X	−3 →	X	−1 →	X	−2
Level- 3→	X	+3	X	−1	X	+3	X	+1

Process Box **Answer Option**

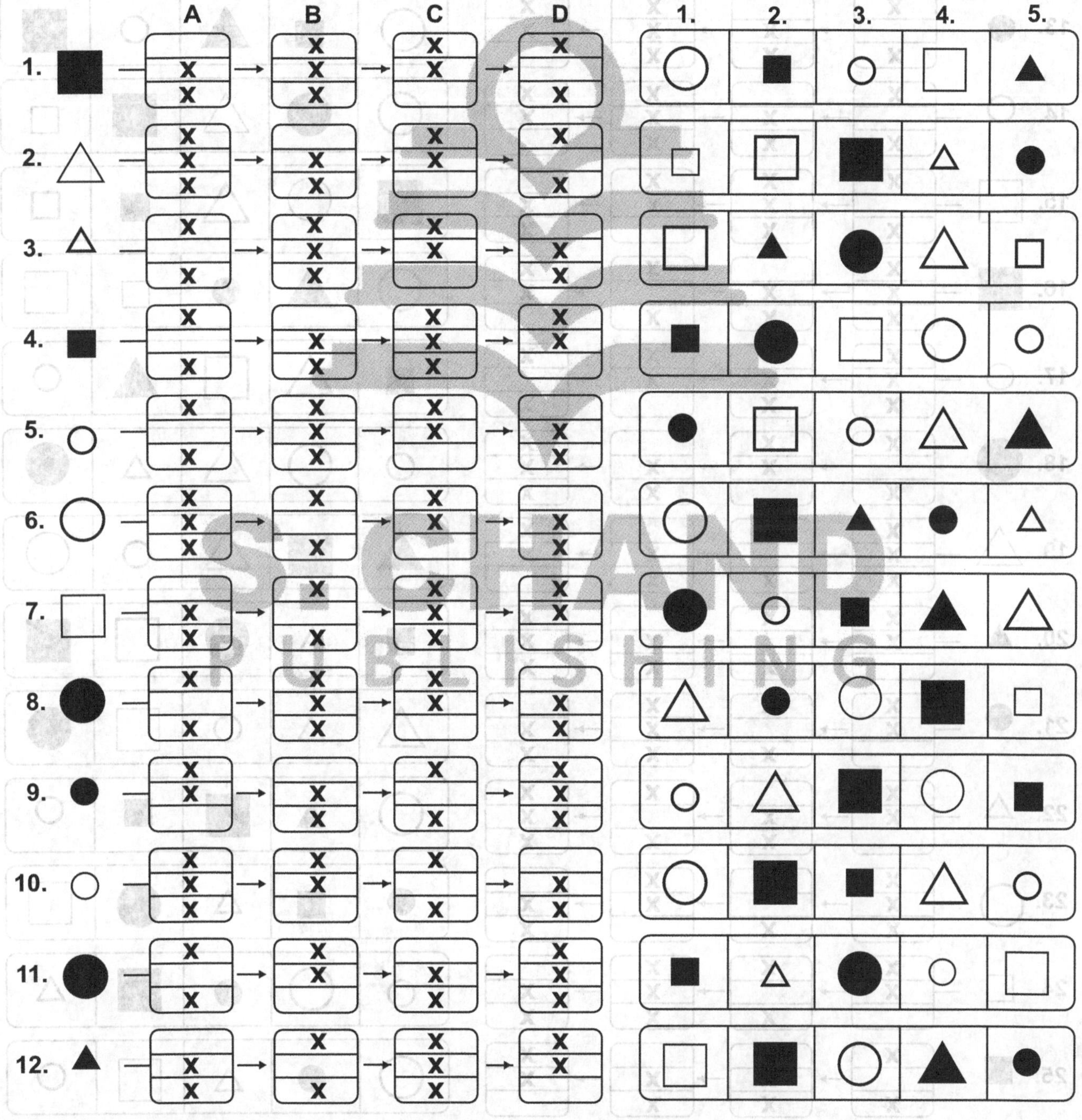

Table - 2

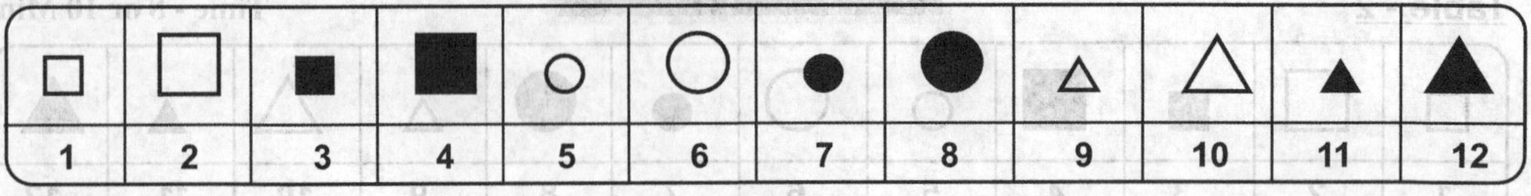

Table - 1

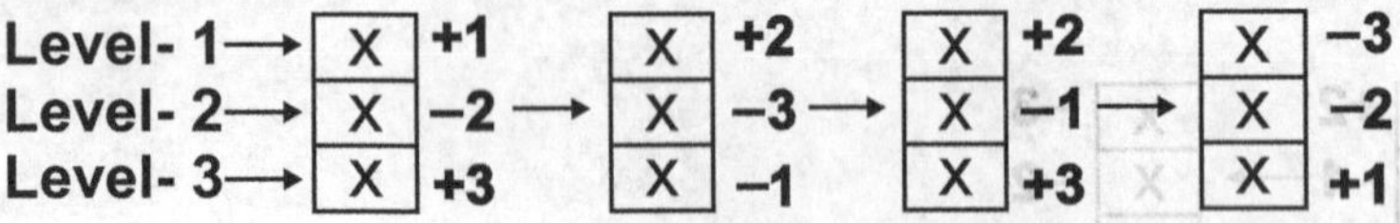

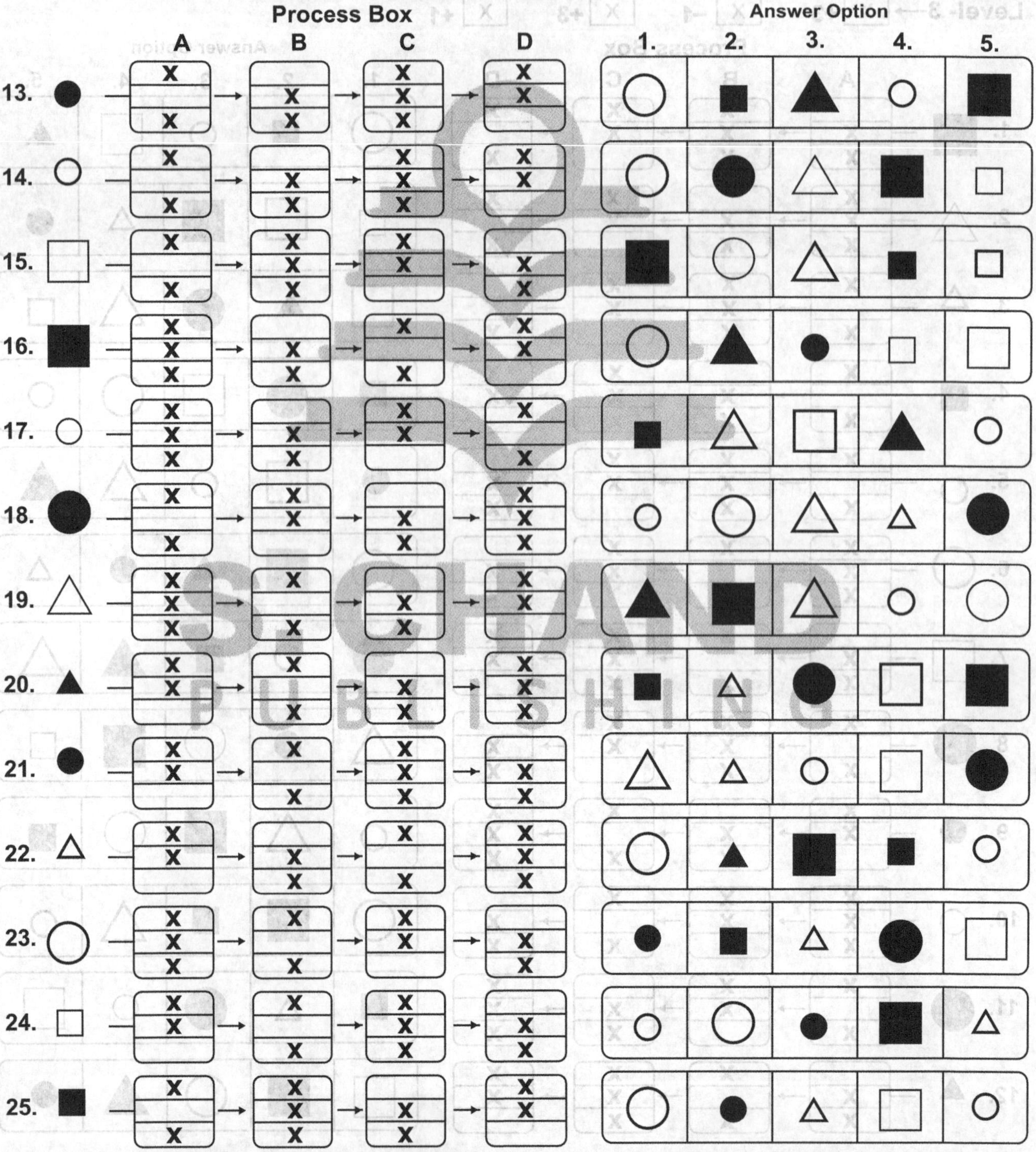

PRACTICE SET-17

Total Ques.- 25
Time - 8 or 10 Min.

Table - 2

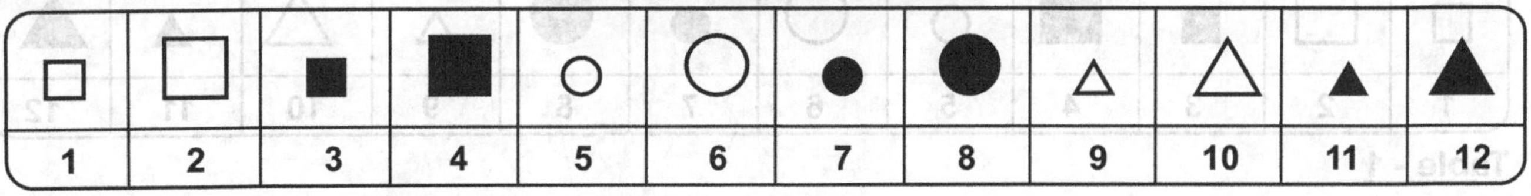

Table - 1

Level- 1 →	X +1	X +2	X +2	X −3
Level- 2 →	X −2 →	X −3 →	X −1 →	X −2
Level- 3 →	X +3	X −1	X +3	X +1

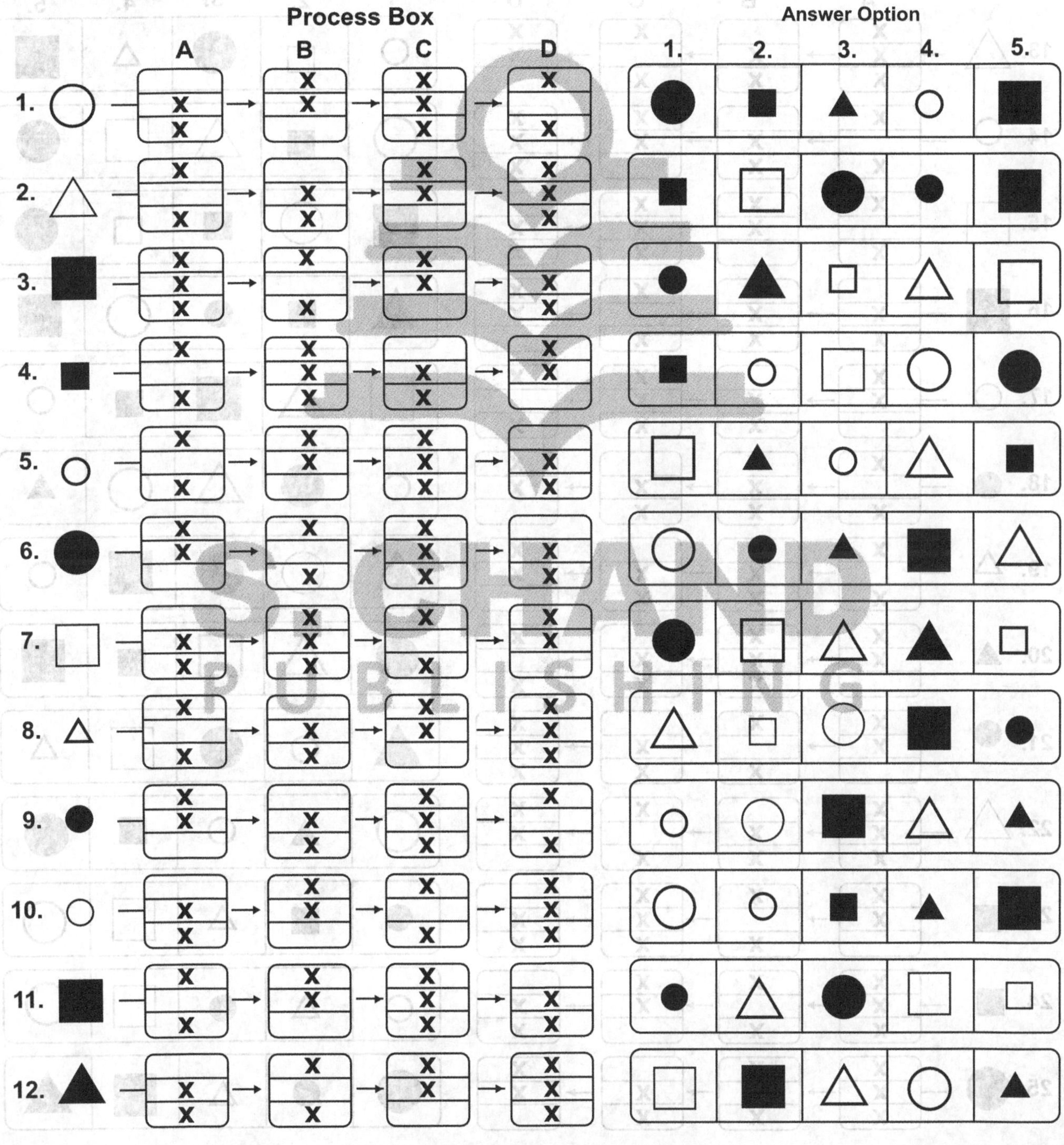

Table - 2

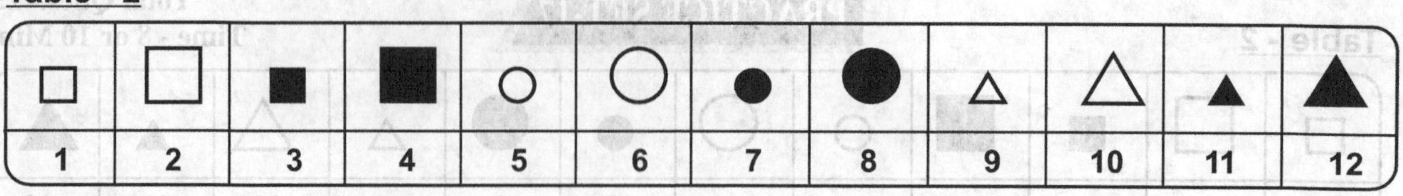

Table - 1

	A	B	C	D
Level- 1 →	X +1	X +2	X +2	X −3
Level- 2 →	X −2 →	X −3 →	X −1 →	X −2
Level- 3 →	X +3	X −1	X +3	X +1

Process Box

Answer Option

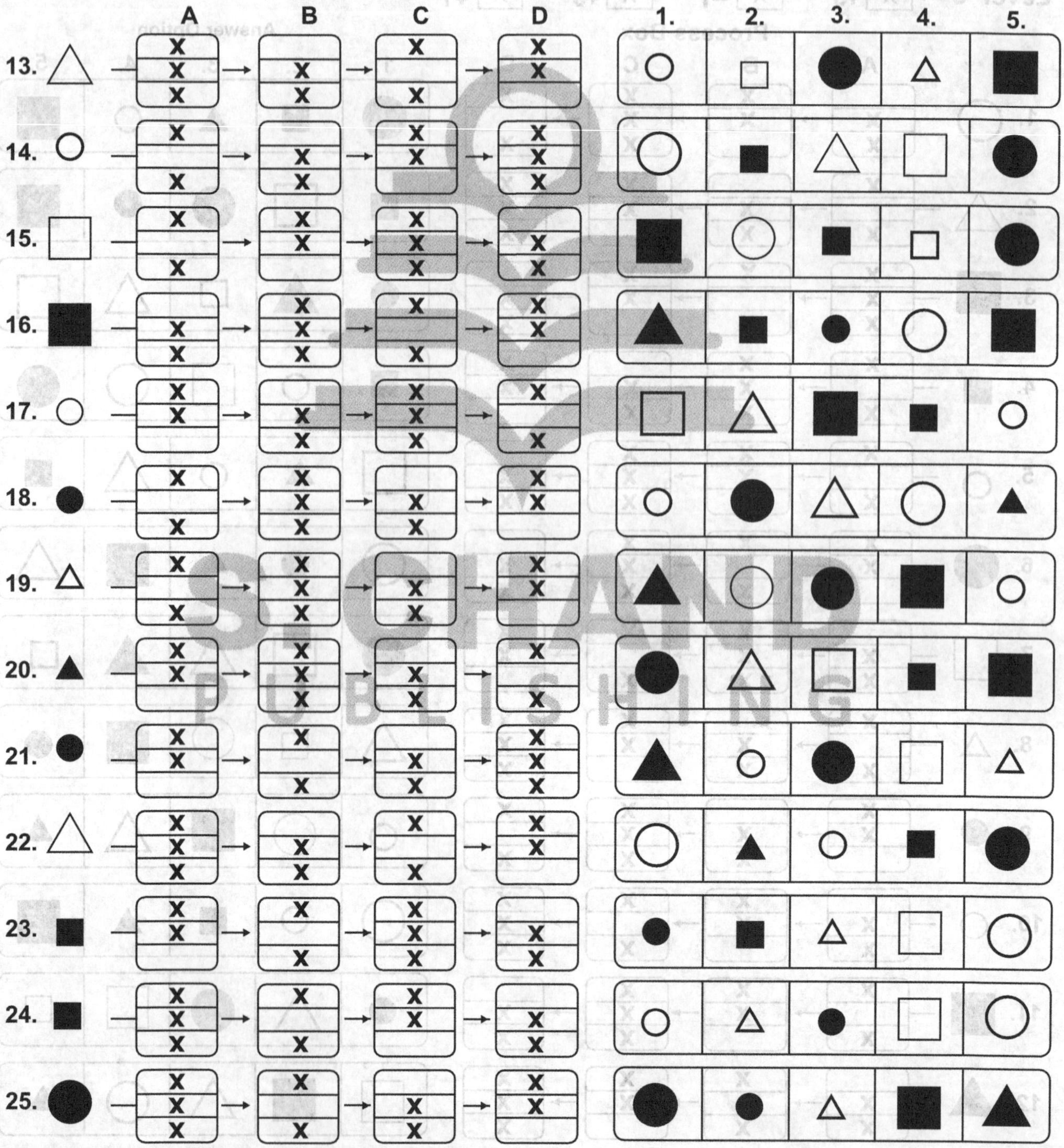

PRACTICE SET-18

Total Ques.- 25
Time - 8 or 10 Min.

Table - 2

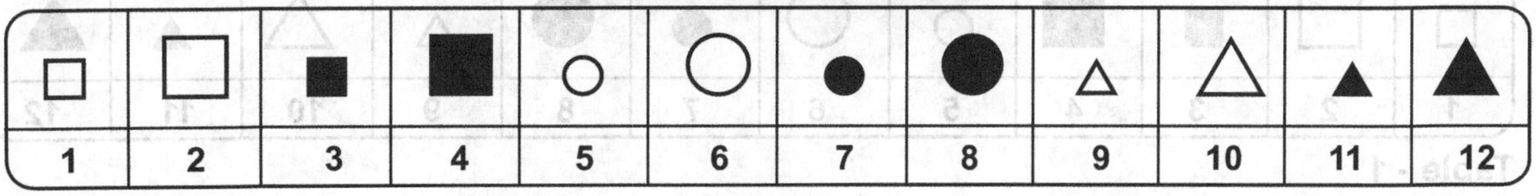

Table - 1

Level- 1→	X +1	X +2	X +2	X −3
Level- 2→	X −2 →	X −3 →	X −1 →	X −2
Level- 3→	X +3	X −1	X +3	X +1

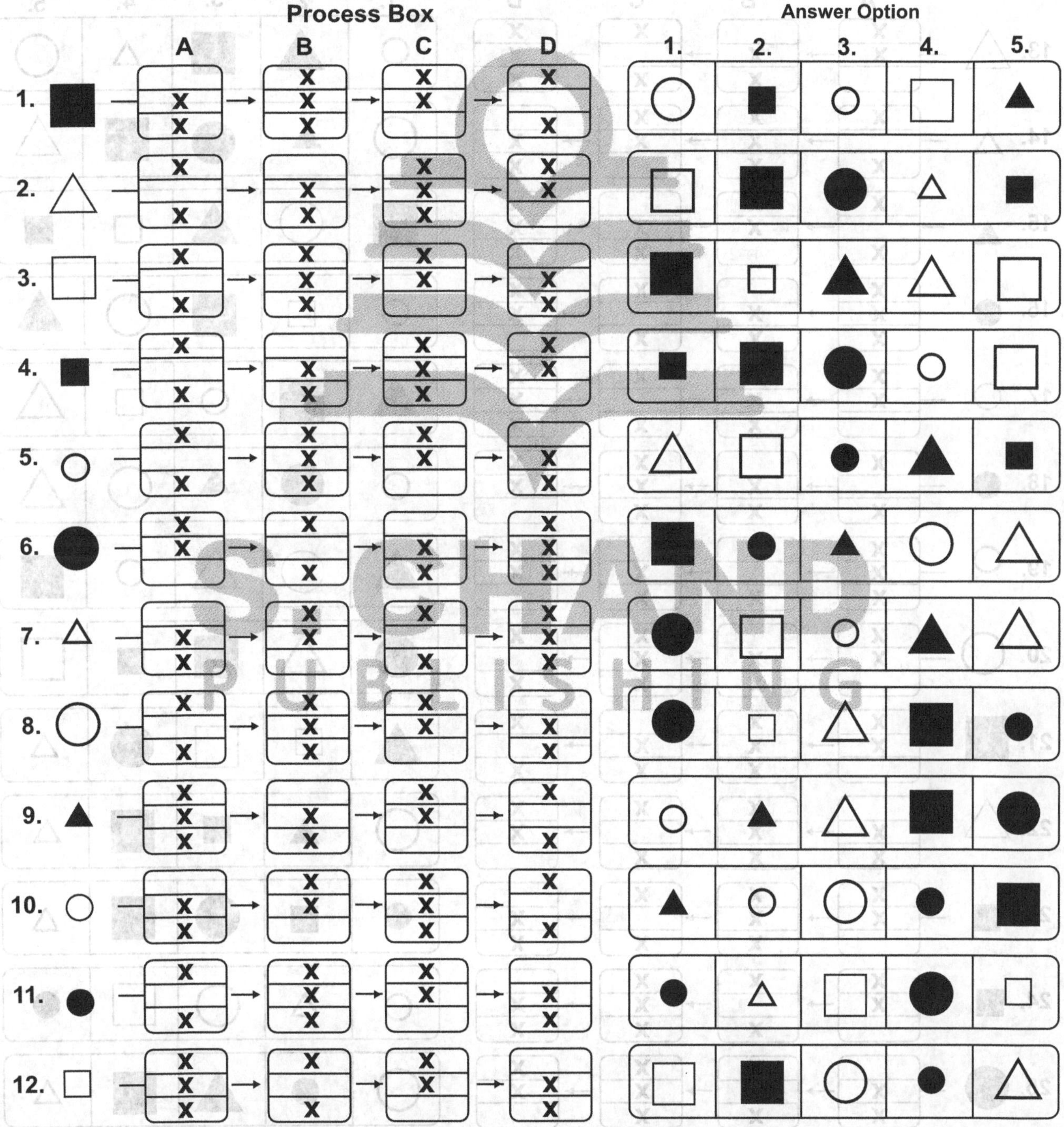

Table - 2

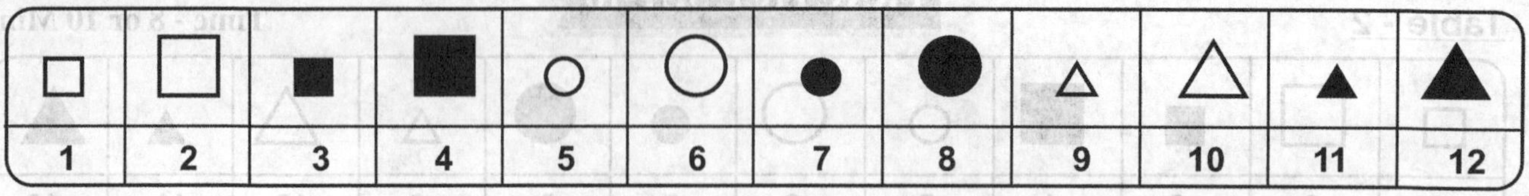

Table - 1

Level- 1 →	X +1	X +2	X +2	X −3
Level- 2 →	X −2 →	X −3 →	X −1 →	X −2
Level- 3 →	X +3	X −1	X +3	X +1

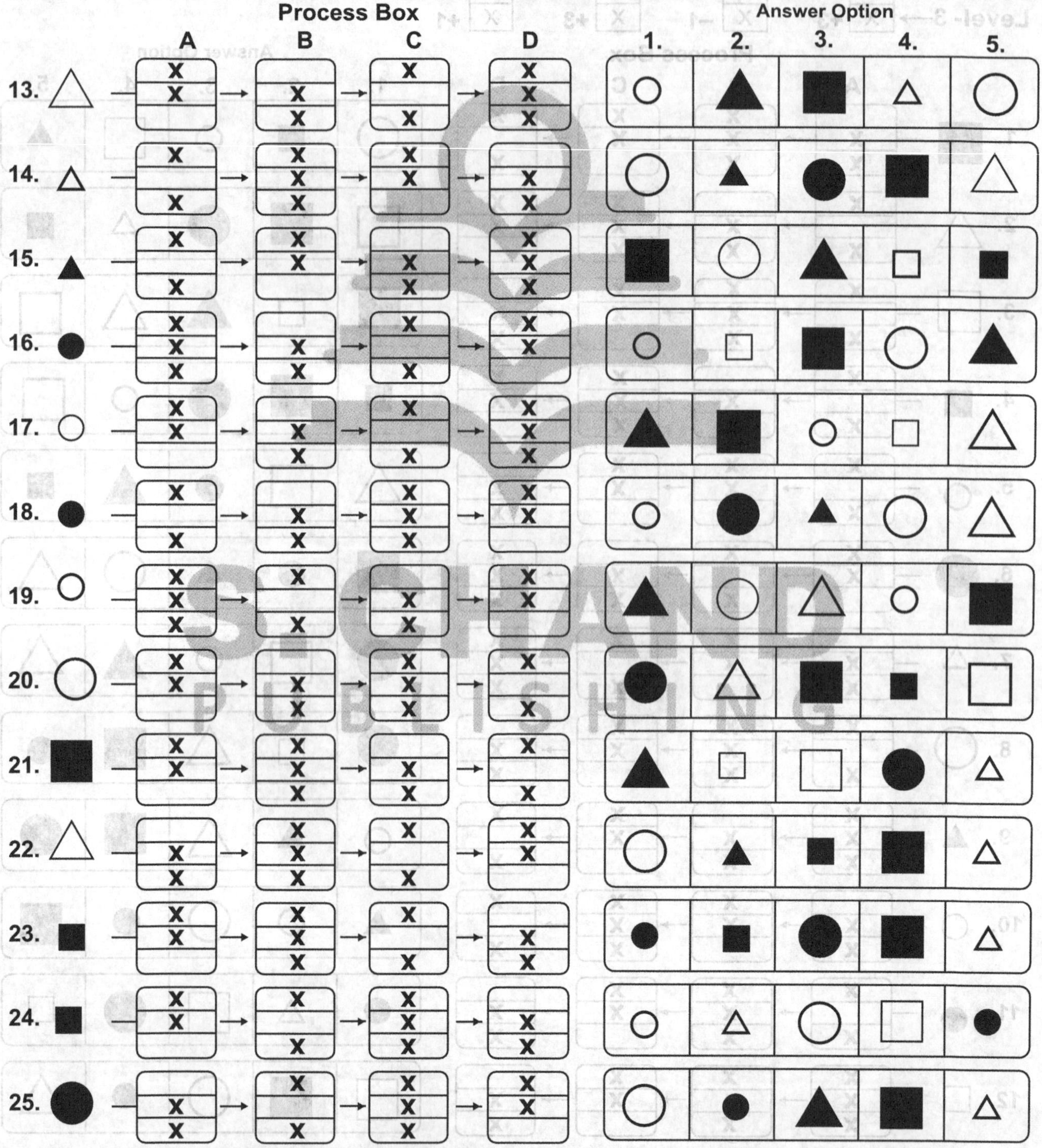

PRACTICE SET-19

Total Ques.- 25
Time - 8 or 10 Min.

Table - 2

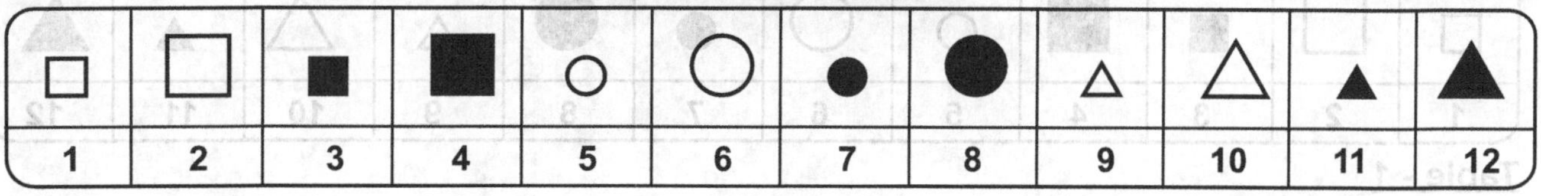

Table - 1

Level- 1 →	X +1	X +2	X +2	X –3
Level- 2 →	X –2 →	X –3 →	X –1 →	X –2
Level- 3 →	X +3	X –1	X +3	X +1

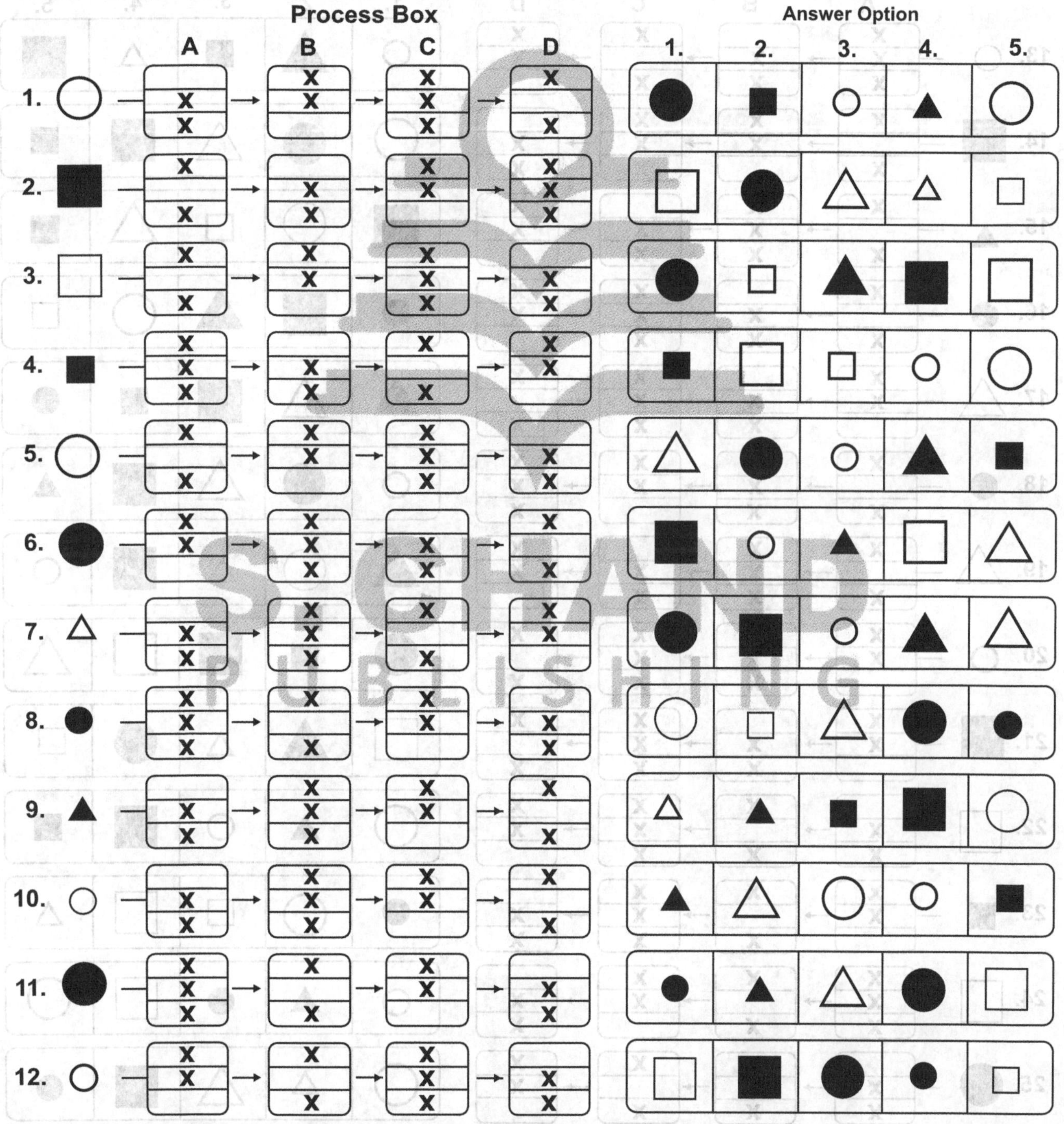

Table - 2

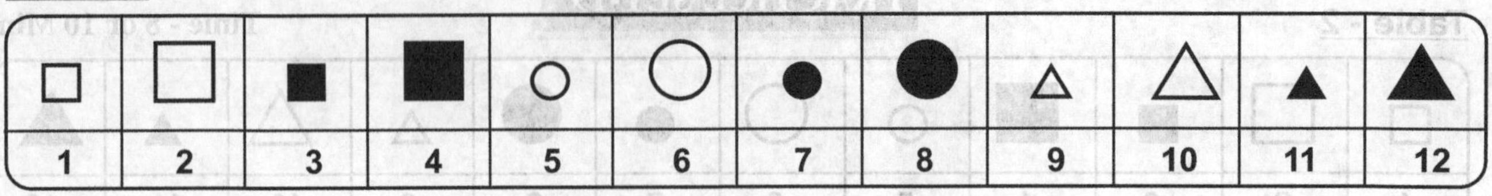

Table - 1

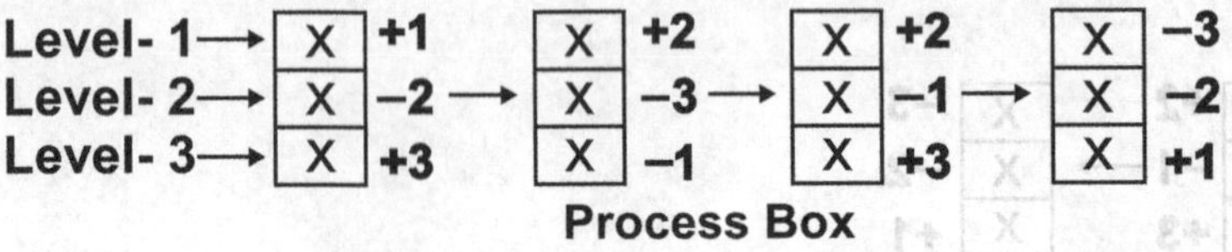

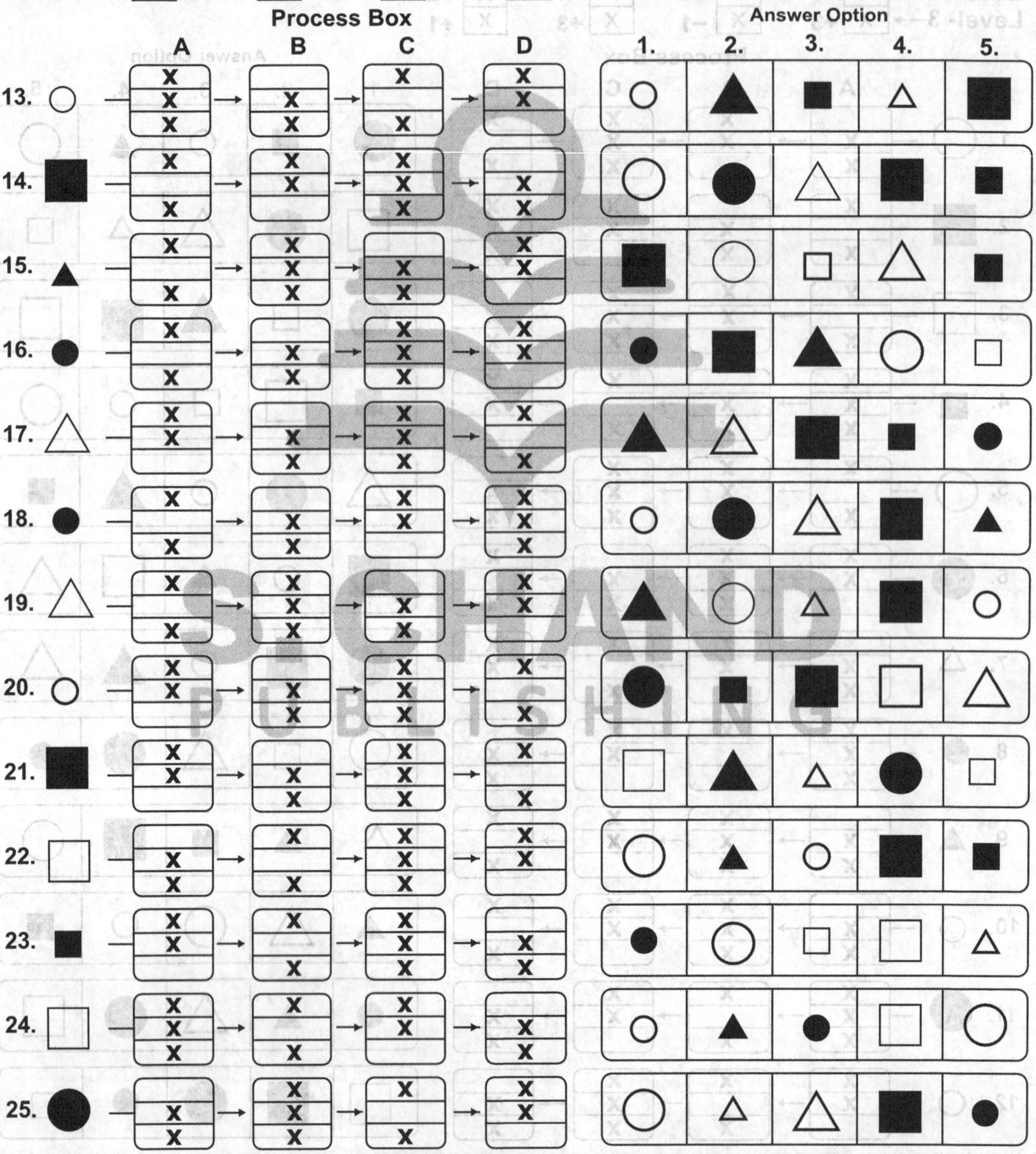

PRACTICE SET-20

Total Ques.- 25
Time - 8 or 10 Min.

Table - 2

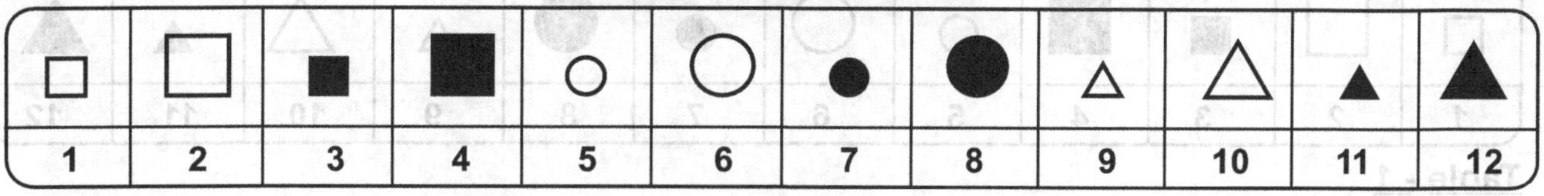

Table - 1

Level- 1 →	X +1	X +2	X +2	X −3
Level- 2 →	X −2 →	X −3 →	X −1 →	X −2
Level- 3 →	X +3	X −1	X +3	X +1

Process Box **Answer Option**

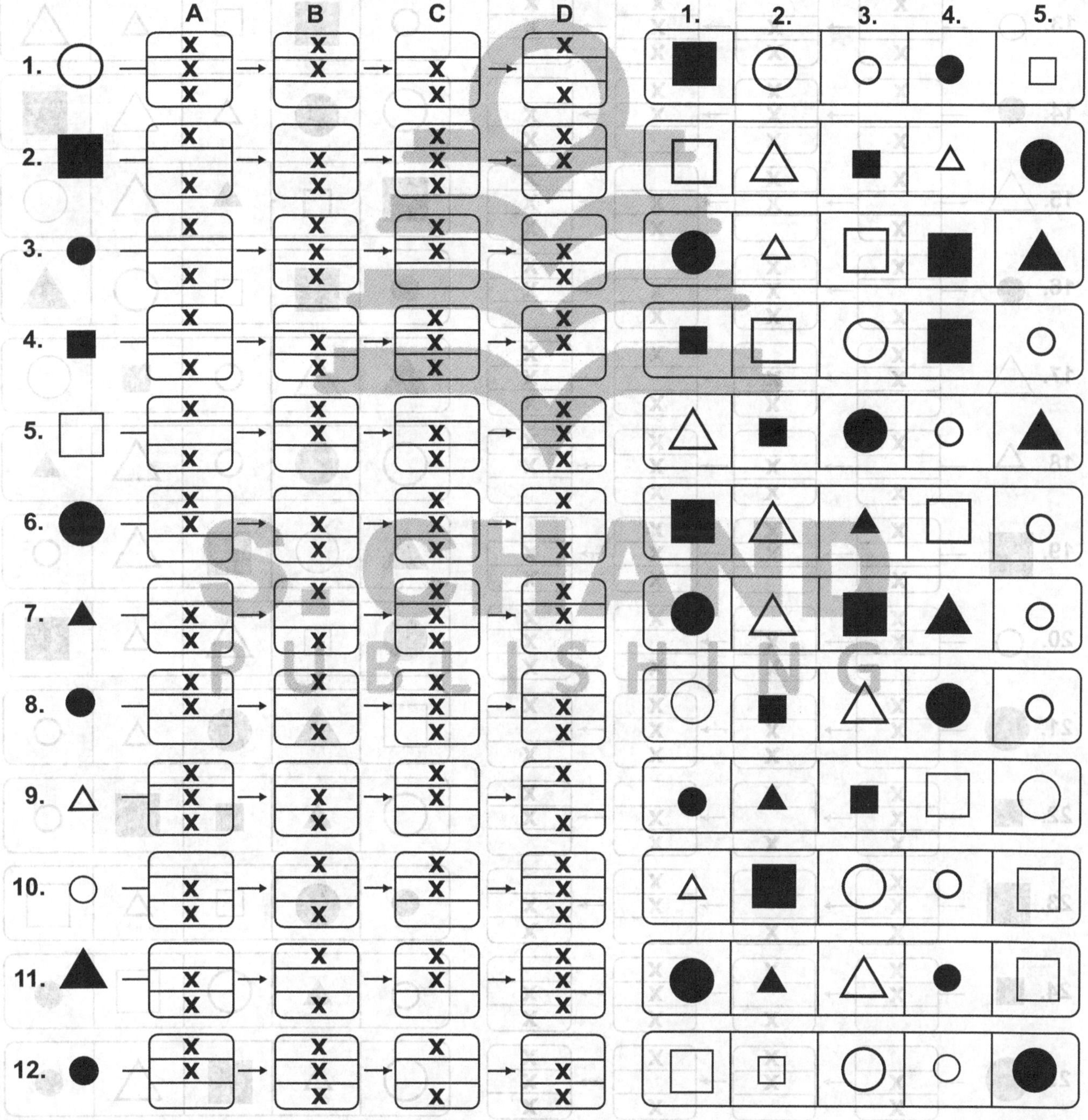

Table - 2

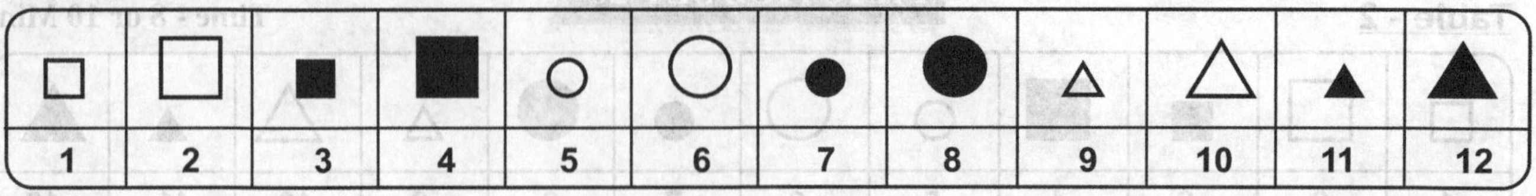

Table - 1

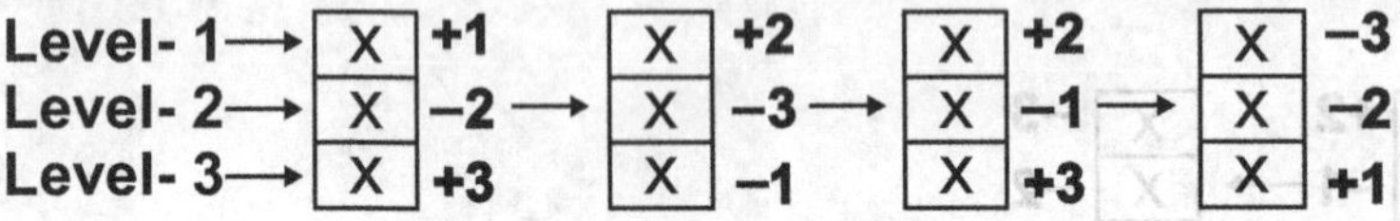

Process Box **Answer Option**

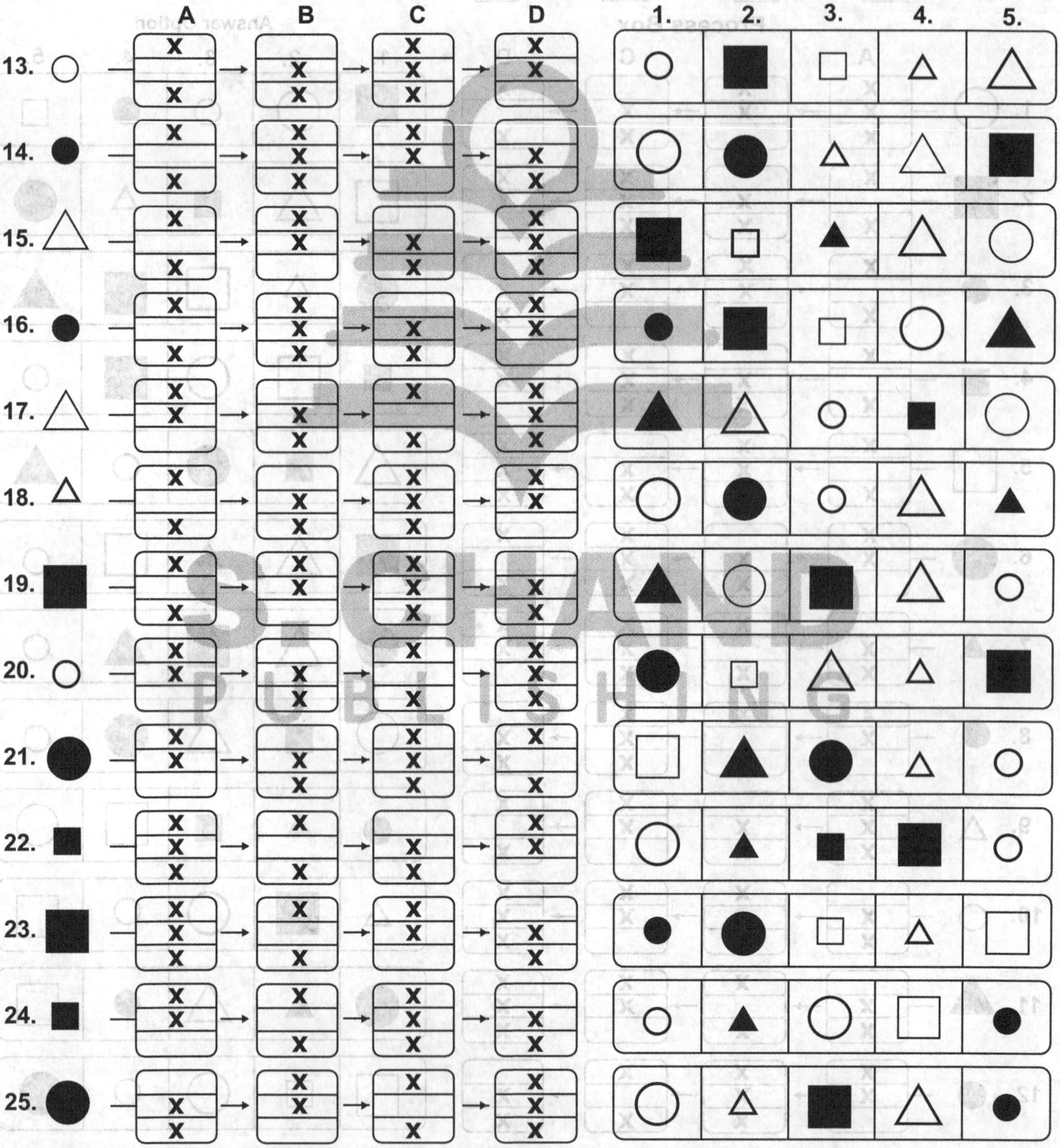

उत्तर (ANSWER)

PRACTICE SET - 1

1.	4	14.	2
2.	5	15.	3
3.	2	16.	3
4.	4	17.	4
5.	2	18.	5
6.	5	19.	1
7.	1	20.	2
8.	2	21.	4
9.	1	22.	1
10.	5	23.	3
11.	5	24.	3
12.	1	25.	5
13.	2		

PRACTICE SET - 2

1.	3	14.	5
2.	4	15.	5
3.	4	16.	3
4.	4	17.	1
5.	2	18.	3
6.	1	19.	5
7.	4	20.	2
8.	5	21.	5
9.	1	22.	3
10.	4	23.	4
11.	3	24.	3
12.	4	25.	3
13.	4		

PRACTICE SET - 3

1.	2	14.	1
2.	3	15.	5
3.	5	16.	3
4.	5	17.	3
5.	2	18.	4
6.	4	19.	2
7.	2	20.	4
8.	2	21.	3
9.	4	22.	4
10.	1	23.	4
11.	4	24.	4
12.	5	25.	1
13.	1		

PRACTICE SET - 4

1.	1	14.	2
2.	4	15.	5
3.	2	16.	4
4.	2	17.	1
5.	4	18.	1
6.	5	19.	4
7.	3	20.	3
8.	1	21.	4
9.	2	22.	3
10.	4	23.	1
11.	1	24.	4
12.	4	25.	5
13.	1		

PRACTICE SET - 5

1.	1	14.	5
2.	2	15.	3
3.	3	16.	5
4.	1	17.	1
5.	5	18.	2
6.	3	19.	5
7.	1	20.	2
8.	5	21.	2
9.	3	22.	2
10.	1	23.	5
11.	2	24.	2
12.	3	25.	1
13.	4		

PRACTICE SET - 6

1.	1	14.	5
2.	4	15.	5
3.	2	16.	1
4.	1	17.	4
5.	5	18.	3
6.	3	19.	4
7.	2	20.	1
8.	5	21.	2
9.	5	22.	2
10.	3	23.	5
11.	5	24.	4
12.	5	25.	1
13.	5		

उत्तर (ANSWER)

PRACTICE SET - 7

1.	5	14.	2
2.	3	15.	4
3.	4	16.	4
4.	5	17.	2
5.	4	18.	5
6.	1	19.	2
7.	2	20.	3
8.	5	21.	3
9.	2	22.	5
10.	1	23.	1
11.	4	24.	5
12.	3	25.	4
13.	4		

PRACTICE SET - 8

1.	4	14.	1
2.	3	15.	5
3.	5	16.	5
4.	3	17.	5
5.	2	18.	1
6.	1	19.	2
7.	1	20.	3
8.	4	21.	5
9.	1	22.	4
10.	5	23.	2
11.	2	24.	3
12.	3	25.	2
13.	5		

PRACTICE SET - 9

1.	1	14.	1
2.	2	15.	5
3.	4	16.	1
4.	2	17.	1
5.	2	18.	1
6.	2	19.	3
7.	2	20.	5
8.	3	21.	4
9.	4	22.	5
10.	1	23.	3
11.	1	24.	5
12.	3	25.	1
13.	5		

PRACTICE SET - 10

1.	5	14.	1
2.	3	15.	2
3.	3	16.	2
4.	3	17.	1
5.	2	18.	4
6.	5	19.	4
7.	5	20.	5
8.	4	21.	4
9.	1	22.	5
10.	2	23.	4
11.	4	24.	4
12.	3	25.	5
13.	5		

PRACTICE SET - 11

1.	4	14.	2
2.	3	15.	2
3.	3	16.	4
4.	4	17.	5
5.	2	18.	2
6.	2	19.	2
7.	3	20.	3
8.	1	21.	5
9.	4	22.	2
10.	2	23.	5
11.	3	24.	3
12.	1	25.	4
13.	5		

PRACTICE SET - 12

1.	5	14.	5
2.	2	15.	3
3.	4	16.	4
4.	3	17.	2
5.	2	18.	4
6.	1	19.	5
7.	1	20.	3
8.	5	21.	2
9.	2	22.	1
10.	5	23.	5
11.	5	24.	2
12.	3	25.	3
13.	3		

उत्तर (ANSWER)

PRACTICE SET - 13

1.	4	14.	5
2.	5	15.	2
3.	5	16.	4
4.	1	17.	1
5.	3	18.	3
6.	2	19.	1
7.	2	20.	5
8.	4	21.	1
9.	5	22.	5
10.	4	23.	4
11.	4	24.	2
12.	1	25.	4
13.	4		

PRACTICE SET - 14

1.	4	14.	4
2.	4	15.	4
3.	1	16.	4
4.	5	17.	1
5.	5	18.	2
6.	3	19.	4
7.	3	20.	1
8.	3	21.	5
9.	5	22.	2
10.	2	23.	2
11.	4	24.	5
12.	3	25.	3
13.	5		

PRACTICE SET - 15

1.	4	14.	1
2.	2	15.	4
3.	4	16.	5
4.	4	17.	3
5.	1	18.	5
6.	3	19.	2
7.	4	20.	4
8.	1	21.	3
9.	2	22.	3
10.	5	23.	5
11.	4	24.	4
12.	1	25.	2
13.	5		

PRACTICE SET - 16

1.	4	14.	4
2.	5	15.	1
3.	2	16.	5
4.	3	17.	3
5.	1	18.	4
6.	5	19.	3
7.	3	20.	2
8.	1	21.	1
9.	5	22.	5
10.	4	23.	3
11.	2	24.	4
12.	4	25.	4
13.	1		

PRACTICE SET - 17

1.	1	14.	4
2.	4	15.	5
3.	1	16.	2
4.	3	17.	1
5.	2	18.	4
6.	3	19.	3
7.	5	20.	1
8.	3	21.	2
9.	3	22.	5
10.	1	23.	5
11.	2	24.	5
12.	5	25.	1
13.	3		

PRACTICE SET - 18

1.	4	14.	2
2.	4	15.	3
3.	1	16.	1
4.	5	17.	4
5.	3	18.	4
6.	4	19.	4
7.	5	20.	4
8.	1	21.	2
9.	5	22.	5
10.	4	23.	4
11.	2	24.	3
12.	2	25.	5
13.	5		

उत्तर (ANSWER)

PRACTICE SET - 19

1.	1	14.	3
2.	5	15.	4
3.	1	16.	4
4.	3	17.	5
5.	4	18.	4
6.	2	19.	3
7.	1	20.	4
8.	3	21.	5
9.	1	22.	5
10.	5	23.	2
11.	2	24.	1
12.	3	25.	5
13.	3		

PRACTICE SET - 20

1.	4	14.	3
2.	3	15.	3
3.	2	16.	4
4.	2	17.	5
5.	2	18.	2
6.	5	19.	4
7.	4	20.	2
8.	3	21.	5
9.	5	22.	3
10.	2	23.	1
11.	2	24.	3
12.	5	25.	2
13.	2		

5 TEST FOR MEASURING YOUR PERSONALITY TEST

Personality Test (व्यक्तित्व परीक्षण)

रेलवे मनोवैज्ञानिक परीक्षण के अन्तर्गत व्यक्तित्व परीक्षण स्टेशन मास्टर पद के लिए बहुत महत्वपूर्ण परीक्षण है, जो उम्मीदवारों को त्वरित निर्णय लेने और उच्च दबाव वाली परिस्थितियों को प्रबंधित करने की क्षमता का मूल्यांकण करना होता है।

दिए गए इस व्यक्तित्व परीक्षण में कुल 35 प्रश्न होते हैं और इसे हल करने के लिए 15 मिनट का समय दिया जाता है। व्यक्तित्व परीक्षण के प्रत्येक प्रश्न में एक कथन (Statement) दिया होता है और इसके नीचे उत्तर के लिए तीन विकल्प दिए जाते हैं।

नोट : उम्मीदवारों को उत्तर अपनी अभिरूचि एवं दृष्टिकोण के आधार पर देना होता है। **दिए गए उत्तर के आधार पर अपने व्यक्तित्व के दो विभिन्न आयामों का मूल्यांकन किया जाएगा और इस परीक्षण के आधार पर दो अलग-अलग स्कोर निर्गत किए जाएंगे। इस परीक्षण में सफल होने वाले अभ्यर्थीयों को व्यक्तित्व के दोनों आयामों में उत्तीर्ण होना**

प्रश्नों का उत्तर देते समय नीचे लिखी इन बातों पर ध्यान रखें:-

1. आपको किसी प्रश्न पर ज्यादा सोचने-विचार करने की जरूरत नहीं है।
2. इस बात का ध्यान रहे कि कोई प्रश्न छूटने न पाये। जैसे भी हो सभी प्रश्नों का उत्तर आत्मकेन्द्रित होकर अपने समाजशीलता बुद्धिमता और निर्णय के आधार पर दें।
3. जो उत्तर आपके लिए सही है वही उत्तर सच्चाई और ईमानदारी से दें।
4. कठिन प्रश्नों पर समय ज्यादा नष्ट न करें।
5. निर्देशों को ध्यानपूर्वक पढ़ें।

The Personality Test is a crucial test for the Station Master position under Railway Psychological Testing. It assesses a candidate's ability to make quick decisions and manage high-pressure situations.This personality test consists of 35 questions with a 15-minute time limit. Each question in the personality test consists of a statement followed by three answer options.

Note : Candidates must answer based on their interest and perspective. **Based on the responses, two different dimensions of personality will be assessed and two separatescoreswill be generated. Candidates must pass in both personality dimensions to be considered successful in this test.**

While answering the questions, pay attention to the following points:

1. Do not overthink any question.
2. Be careful not to miss any questions. Answer all questions in a focused manner, based on your sociability, intelligence, and judgment.
3. Give the answer that is correct for you honestly and sincerely.
4. Do not waste too much time on difficult questions.
5. Read the instructions carefully.

नीचे दिए गए उदाहरणों के द्वारा इसे समझें :-

निर्देश :- प्रत्येक प्रश्न के लिए एक कथन (Statement) दी होती है और इसके नीचे उत्तर के तीन विकल्प दिए जाते हैं। उम्मीदवारों को आत्मकेन्द्रित होकर अपने समाजशीलता, बुद्धिमता और निर्णय के आधार पर सही उत्तर के लिए कोई एक विकल्प का चयन कर उत्तर-पत्रक में दिए गए गोले को काला या माउस की सहायता से

Example for understanding:

Instruction : For each question, a statement is given, followed by three answer options. Candidates should select the correct option based on their intelligence and judgment and fill the corresponding circle in the answer sheet or click using the mouse in a computer-based test.

1. ट्रेन परिचालन में सुरक्षा प्रोटोकॉल का पालन करना अति आवश्यक है।/It is very important to follow safety protocols in train operations.
   (A) मालूम नहीं/I don't know
   (B) हाँ/Yes
   (C) नहीं/No

2. अगर आपसे गलती होती है तो आप सरलता से स्वीकार करना चाहेंगे/If you make a mistake, you would like to admit it easily
   (A) हमेशा/Always (B) कभी नहीं/Never
   (C) कभी-कभी/Sometime

Ans.: (1) - B (2) - A

PRACTICE SET-1

Total Ques.- 35
Time - 15 Min.

निर्देश : (प्रश्न 1-35) प्रत्येक प्रश्न के लिए एक कथन (Statement) दी होती है और इसके नीचे उत्तर के तीन विकल्प दिए जाते हैं। उम्मीदवारों को अपने बुद्धिमता और निर्णय के आधार पर सही उत्तर के लिए कोई एक विकल्प का चयन कर उत्तर-पत्रक में दिए गए गोले को काला या माउस की सहायता से क्लिक (Click) करें।

Direction : (Questions 1–35) : For each question, a statement is given, followed by three answer options. Candidates should select the correct option based on their intelligence and judgment and fill the corresponding circle on the answer sheet or click using the mouse.

1. नकारात्मक विचारों को सकारात्मक में बदलने का प्रयास किया जाना चाहिए/Efforts should be made to change negative thoughts into positive ones.
(A) हाँ/Yes (B) नहीं/No
(C) कभी-कभी/Sometimes

2. नई कौशलों और ज्ञान को प्राप्त करने के लिए हरसंभव प्रयास किया जाना चाहिए/Every effort should be made to acquire new skills and knowledge-
(A) हाँ/Yes (B) नहीं/No
(C) कभी-कभी/Sometimes

3. छोटे और बड़े लक्ष्यों को निर्धारित कर उन्हें प्राप्त करने का प्रयास किया जाना चाहिए/Small and big goals should be set and efforts should be made to achieve them-
(A) हाँ/Yes (B) नहीं/No
(C) कभी-कभी/Sometimes

4. किसी भी कार्य को करने से पहले अच्छी तरह से तैयारी करना चाहिए/One should prepare well before doing any work-
(A) हाँ/Yes (B) नहीं/No
(C) कभी-कभी/Sometimes

5. दोस्तों और परिवार का समर्थन हमेशा लेना चाहिए/ Support of friends and family should always be taken
(A) हाँ/Yes (B) नहीं/No
(C) कभी-कभी/Sometimes

6. अपनी गलतियों को स्वीकारें ताकि सीखने का अवसर मिल सके/Accept your mistakes so that you get an opportunity to learn-
(A) हाँ/Yes (B) नहीं/No
(C) कभी-कभी/Sometimes

7. मन को शांत करने और तनाव को कम करने में एकाग्रता काफी मदद करता है/Concentration is very important in calming the mind and reducing stress It helps-
(A) हाँ/Yes (B) नहीं/No
(C) कभी-कभी/Sometimes

8. मानसिक योग्यता व्यक्ति की विचार के क्षमता को प्रभावित करती है, जिससे वे निर्णय लेने में सक्षम होते हैं/ Mental ability affects the thinking ability of a person, which enables them to take decisions-
(A) हाँ/Yes (B) नहीं/No
(C) कभी-कभी/Sometimes

9. शारीरिक और मानसिक स्वास्थ्य को बेहतर बनाने में योग मदद करता है/Yoga helps in improving physical and mental health-
(A) हाँ/Yes (B) नहीं/No
(C) कभी-कभी/Sometimes

10. कार्यो को व्यवस्थित करने और तनाव को कम करने में समय प्रबंधन काफी मदद करता है/Time manage-ment helps a lot in organizing tasks and reducing stress-
(A) हाँ/Yes (B) नहीं/No
(C) कभी-कभी/Sometimes

11. सकारात्मक सोच नकारात्मक विचारों को सकारात्मक में बदलने में काफी अहम भूमिका निभाती है/Positive thinking plays a very important role in changing negative thoughts into positive ones-
(A) हाँ/Yes (B) नहीं/No
(C) कभी-कभी/Sometimes

12. जाति की राजनीति से समाज के विकास में बाधा उत्पन्न होती है/Caste politics hinders the development of society-
(A) कभी नहीं/Never
(B) कभी-कभी/Sometimes
(C) हमेशा/Always

13. जनता के शिकायतों के समाधान हेतु सौहार्दपूर्ण कदम उठानी जानी चाहिए/Amicable steps should be taken to solve public grievances Should-
(A) हाँ/Yes (B) ऐसा नहीं/Not So
(C) कभी-कभी/Sometimes

14. परमाणु युद्ध पूरी दुनिया के विध्वंसकारी का कारण बनेगा/Nuclear war will cause destruction of the whole world-
(A) मालूम नहीं/don't know
(B) हो सकता है/It can happen
(C) ऐसा नहीं/It is not so

15. पारिवारिक तनाव कम करने के लिए आपस में विचार-विमर्श करना उचित समाधान है/Discussion among oneself is the right solution to reduce family tension-
(A) नहीं/No
(B) बिल्कुल सही/Absolutely right
(C) कभी-कभी/Sometimes

16. जंगलों में लगी आग, पर्यावरण के लिए खतरा का सूचक है/Forest fires are an indicator of danger to the environment-
(A) निश्चित/Certain
(B) अनिश्चित/Uncertain
(C) मालूम नहीं/Don't know

17. सरकार के द्वारा जाति जनगणना कराना उचित पहल है/Conducting caste census by the government is a right initiative-
(A) वोट की संख्या नहीं बढ़ेगी/Number of votes will not increase
(B) मालूम नहीं/Don't know
(C) सरकार की आर्थिक बोझ बढ़ेगा/Financial burden of the government will increase

18. मानसिक रूप से परेशान छात्र आत्महत्या करने को मजबूर हो जाते हैं/Mentally disturbed students are forced to commit suicide-
(A) बिल्कुल नहीं/Absolutely not
(B) हाँ/Yes
(C) मालूम नहीं/Don't know

19. लोकतंत्र में सत्ता स्थायी होना चाहिए/Power should be permanent in democracy-
(A) नहीं/No
(B) मालूम नहीं/Don't know
(C) कभी-कभी/Sometimes

20. विकसित भारत के निर्माण में भी हिन्दी भाषा की अहम भूमिका रहनी चाहिए/Hindi language also played an important role in the creation of developed India There should be-
(A) नहीं/No
(B) मालूम नहीं/Don't know
(C) हाँ/Yes

21. बुनियादी शिक्षा, विकसित भारत के लिए सशक्त होना जरूरी है/Basic education should be strong for a developed India-
(A) हाँ/Yes (B) नहीं/ No
(C) दोनों के बीच/Between the two

22. बुरे अनुभवों को अपने मस्तिष्क में रखना काम और सेहत दोनों को नुकसान पहुँचाता है/Keeping bad experiences in your mind harms both work and health-
(A) हमेशा/Always (B) ऐसा नहीं/Not so
(C) मालूम नहीं/Don't know

23. मेहनत से बड़ी से बड़ी सफलता हासिल की जा सकती है/The biggest success can be achieved by hard work-
(A) हमेशा/Always (B) नहीं/No
(C) कभी नहीं/Never

24. सरकार को लोक कल्याणकारी जीवन में फैसले सोच-समझकर योजनाओं का स्वरूप सशक्त कर लेना चाहिए/The government should strengthen the form of schemes by taking decisions in public welfare life-
(A) हाँ/Yes (B) नहीं/No
(C) कभी-कभी/Sometimes

25. रूकावट आने पर निराश होना एक सहज भाव है परन्तु स्वयं पर हावी होने नहीं देना चाहिए–/It is a natural feeling to get disappointed when there is an obstacle, but one should not let it dominate oneself-
(A) कभी नहीं/Never
(B) कभी-कभी/Sometimes
(C) हमेशा/Always

26. जानवरों के प्रति हमें प्रेम-भाव रखना चाहिए/We should have love towards animals-
(A) हमेशा/Always (B) नहीं/No
(C) कभी-कभी/Sometimes

27. अक्सर परीक्षा केन्द्रों पर कुप्रबंधन एजेंसियाँ का प्रभाव से विश्वसनीयता घटती जा रही है/Often the influence of mismanagement agencies at examination centres is reducing the credibility-
(A) कभी नहीं/Never (B) हाँ/Yes
(C) दोनों के बीच/

28. रेलवे परिवेश में हो रहे बदलाव और जटिल समस्याओं का निराकरण के बाद भी पूर्ण रूप से सुरक्षा का दायित्व निभाना कठिन समस्या है/Even after the changes taking place in the railway environment and solving complex problems, it is difficult to fulfill the responsibility of security completely-
(A) मालूम नहीं/ (B) ऐसा नहीं/
(C) बिल्कुल सही/Absolute Right

29. देश में प्रतिभा को बढ़ाने के लिए गुणवत्तापूर्ण शिक्षा और प्रशिक्षण प्रदान करना चाहिए/To increase talent in the country, quality education and training should be provided-
(A) कभी-कभी/Sometime
(B) देश में प्रतिभा की कमी/Lack of talent in the country
(C) हमेशा/Always

30. अक्सर राजनीतिक अस्थिरता और भ्रष्टाचार के कारण लोग स्वर्णिम भविष्य की तलाश में विदेशों का रूख अपनाते हैं/Often due to political instability and corruption, people turn to foreign countries in search of a golden future-
(A) नहीं/No
(B) कुछ लोग/Some People
(C) भ्रष्टाचार में कमी आई है/Corruption has decreased

31. भारत में बाढ़ भी एक विकराल समस्या बनती जा रही है/Floods are also becoming a huge problem in India-
(A) कभी नहीं/Never
(B) बिल्कुल सही/Absolutely Right
(C) हो सकता है/May be

32. बढ़ती महंगाई एक गंभीर आर्थिक समस्या है जो आम आदमी के जीवन पर पड़ती है/Rising inflation is a serious economic problem which affects the life of the common man-
(A) हाँ/Yes
(B) व्यक्ति की आय में वृद्धि हुई/Person's income increases
(C) महंगाई दर घटी है/Dearness rate r educed

33. आपदा के समय सरकारी, गैर सरकारी संगठन और स्थानीय समुदायों के साथ मिलकर काम करना चाहिए/At the times of disaster, government, non-governmental organiza-tions and local communities should work together.
(A) कभी नहीं/Never (B) दोनों/Both
(C) हाँ/Yes

34. अक्सर लोग फिल्मों को देखकर उसे अपनी जिंदगी में उतारने की कोशिश करते है/Often people watch films and try to implement them in their lives.
(A) हाँ/Yes (B) सभी लोग/All People
(C) नहीं/No

35. प्राकृतिक दृश्य मन को सकुन देता है–/Natural scenes give peace to the mind.
(A) हो सकता है/May be (B) हाँ/Yes
(C) कभी नहीं/Never

PRACTICE SET-2

Total Ques.- 35
Time - 15 Min.

निर्देश : (प्रश्न 1–35) प्रत्येक प्रश्न के लिए एक कथन (Statement) दी होती है और इसके नीचे उत्तर के तीन विकल्प दिए जाते हैं। उम्मीदवारों को अपने बुद्धिमता और निर्णय के आधार पर सही उत्तर के लिए कोई एक विकल्प का चयन कर उत्तर-पत्रक में दिए गए गोले को काला या माउस की सहायता से क्लिक (Click) करें।

Direction : (Questions 1–35) : For each question, a statement is given, followed by three answer options. Candidates should select the correct option based on their intelligence and judgment and fill the corresponding circle on the answer sheet or click using the mouse.

1. भारत देश नए युग में उर्जा के क्षेत्र में आत्मनिर्भर बनता जा रहा है/India is becoming self-sufficient in the field of energy in the new era-
(A) बिल्कुल सही/Absolutely Right
(B) ऐसा नहीं/Not So
(C) कभी-कभी/Sometimes

2. सौर उर्जा और पवन उर्जा सबसे सस्ते उर्जा श्रोत है/Solar energy and wind energy are the cheapest sources of energy-
(A) हाँ/Yes (B) नहीं/No
(C) कह नहीं सकते/Can't say

3. मानव अपने जीवन को कुछ समय के लिए साधना और ईश्वर के स्मरण में लगाना चाहिए/Humans should devote some time to meditation and remembrance of God-
(A) कभी-कभी/Sometimes
(B) हाँ/Yes (C) हमेशा/Always

4. किसी भी व्यक्ति का धर्म परिवर्तन कराना एक अपराध है/ Converting any person's is a crime-
(A) हाँ/Yes (B) नहीं/No
(C) मालूम नहीं/Don't know

5. वैसे काम जो कानून और मर्यादा के दायरे में किया जाय तो साम्प्रदायिक, सद्भाव व स्वास्थ्य को बल मिलता है/If such work is done within the limits of law and decorum, then communal harmony, cleanliness and health get strengthened-
(A) कभी-कभी/Sometimes
(B) हाँ/Yes (C) नहीं/No

6. सम्पूर्ण भारतवासियों को एकता और अनुशासन की आवश्यकता होती है–/All Indians need unity and discipline-
(A) हमेशा/Always (B) नहीं/No
(C) दोनों के बीच/Between the two

7. धर्म का काम किसी भावनाओं को ठेस नहीं पहुँचाना बल्कि उन्हें मान-सम्मान देना/The work of religion is not to hurt any feelings but to give them respect-
(A) कभी-कभी/Sometimes
(B) संभव नहीं/Not Possible
(C) बिल्कुल सही/ Absolute Right

8. धार्मिक पर्यटन आस्था के साथ-साथ अर्थव्यवस्था को भी मजबूत बनाती हैं/Religious tourism strengthens the economy along with faith-
(A) नहीं/No
(B) दोनों के बीच/Between the two
(C) हमेशा/Always

9. किसी भी समस्या के समाधान हेतु सकारात्मक पहल की आवश्यकता होती है/Positive initiative is required to solve any problem-
(A) हमेशा/Always
(B) कभी-कभी/Sometimes
(C) दोनों के बीच/Between the two

10. खान-पान अक्सर अपने सेहत को देखते हुए लेनी चाहिए/Food and drink should be taken keeping in mind one's health-
(A) कभी-कभी/Sometimes
(B) नहीं/No
(C) हमेशा/Always

11. नशे जैसी बुरी आदतें से छुटकारा पाने के लिए दृढ़ संकल्प और परिवार का प्यार होना आवश्यक है/To get rid of bad habits like addiction, it is necessary to have strong determination and love of family-
(A) दोनों के बीच/Between the two
(B) असत्य/False (C) सत्य/True

12. हमें हर दिन नए विकल्पों की तलाश करनी चाहिए/We have to look for new options every day Should be done-
(A) कभी-कभी/Sometimes
(B) नहीं/No (C) हमेशा/Always

13. शिक्षा मानव जीवन की ऐसी प्रक्रिया है जिससे उसे अच्छे व्यवहार और सही मार्गदर्शन में जाने के बाध्य करते देते है/Education is such a process in human life which forces him to follow good behaviour and right guidance-
(A) ऐसा नहीं/Not So (B) हाँ/Yes
(C) मालूम नहीं/Don't know

14. किसी भी देश के नागरिक को राष्ट्रहित की भावना से जुड़े हो तो उस देश का प्रगति यथासंभव अग्रसर होगा/If the citizens of any country are connected with the spirit of national interest, then the progress of that country will be as far as possible-
(A) कभी नहीं/Never (B) हमेशा/Always
(C) नहीं/No

15. व्यस्त जीवन के बीच मानसिक या भावनात्मक दबावों को दूर करने के लिए विराम की आवश्यकता होनी चाहिए/In the midst of a busy life, there should be a need for a break to remove mental or emotional pressures-
(A) कभी-कभी/Sometimes
(B) कभी नहीं/Never (C) हाँ/Yes

16. डिजिटल शिक्षा और कृत्रिम बुद्धिमता के इस दौर में गुरू का स्थान सर्वोपरि है/In this era of digital education and artificial intelligence, the place of the Guru is paramount-
(A) कभी-कभी/Sometimes
(B) ऐसा नहीं/Not So (C) हमेशा/Always

17. मन में शांति लाने के लिए अतीत को भूलने की आदत डालनी चाहिए/To bring peace in the mind, one should develop the habit of forgetting the past-
(A) कभी-कभी/Sometimes
(B) हमेशा/Always
(C) ऐसा नहीं/Not So

18. अतिक्रमण हटाने से शहर के विकास की संभावनाएँ बढ़ेगी/Removing encroachment will increase the possibilities of development of the city-
(A) कभी नहीं/Never (B) हाँ/Yes
(C) ऐसा नहीं/Not so

19. पर्यटन के प्रति बढ़ते रूझान सरकार की प्रभावशाली नीतियों और रोजगार के अवसर में अभूतपूर्व बढ़ोत्तरी की संभावनाएँ दिखती है/The increasing trend towards tourism, effective policies of the government and the possibilities of unprecedented increase in employment opportunities are visible Is-
(A) हाँ/Yes (B) ऐसा नहीं/Not so
(C) कभी-कभी/Sometimes

20. मीडिया लोकतंत्र की एक सशक्त स्तम्भ है जो प्रशासनिक कार्यो में पारदर्शिता, जन-जागरूकता बढ़ाने और सुधार की दिशा में अहम भूमिका निभाती है/Media is a strong pillar of democracy which plays an important role in increasing public awareness and improvement in administrative work-
(A) कभी-कभी/Sometimes
(B) नहीं/No
(C) मालूम नहीं/Don't know

21. सरकार को सरकारी कामकाज में पारदर्शिता लानी चाहिए/Government should bring transpa-rency in government work-
(A) कभी-नहीं/Never (B) हमेशा/Always
(C) मालूम नहीं/Don't know

22. पेयजल संकट के समाधान हेतु जल विभाग पर उचित कार्यवाई होनी चाहिए/Appropriate action should be taken against the water department to solve the drinking water crisis-
(A) अवश्य/Sure
(B) मालूम नहीं/Don't know
(C) दोनों के बीच/Between the two

23. लोकतांत्रिक देश में सरकार के जनादेश को सम्मान करना चाहिए/In a democratic country, the government should respect the mandate-
(A) कभी नहीं/Never
(B) कभी-कभी/Sometimes
(C) हमेशा/Always

24. विकसित भारत को लक्ष्य तक पहुँचने के शिक्षा का योगदान अति आवश्यक है/The contribution of education is very important for developed India to reach its goal-
(A) हाँ/Yes (B) नहीं/No
(C) मालूम नहीं/Don't know

25. मुफ्त रेबड़ी मामले में राजनीतिक दलों पर कार्यवाही होनी चाहिए/Free Rebdi case Action should be taken against political parties in-
(A) नहीं/No (B) हाँ/Yes
(C) मालूम नहीं/Don't know

26. नई पीढ़ी को धैर्य और साहस के साथ सौहार्दपूर्ण कदम उठाना चाहिए/The new generation should take cordial steps with patience and courage-
(A) कभी-कभी/Sometimes
(B) अवश्य/Of course (C) कभी-नहीं/Never

27. वर्तमान समय में निर्णय सोच-समझकर लेनी चहिए ताकि उसका परिणाम दूरगामी हो/In the present times, decisions should be taken after careful consideration so that their results are far-reaching.
(A) हाँ/Yes
(B) कभी-कभी/Sometimes
(C) मालूम नहीं/Don't know

28. वर्तमान समाज में शिकायतें और आलोचना की वृद्धि होने से प्रशंसा बनावटी लगती है/Due to increase in complaints and criticism in the present society, praise seems artificial.
(A) कभी नहीं/Never (B) हाँ/Yes
(C) मालूम नहीं/Don't know

29. अभिमानी व्यक्ति दूसरे की भावनाओं और जरूरतों को समझता है/A humble person understands the feelings and needs of others.
(A) हाँ/Yes (B) ऐसा नहीं/Not so
(C) कभी-नहीं/Never

30. शिकायतें और आलोचना नकारात्मक को बढ़ावा दे सकती है/Complaints and criticism can promote negative thoughts.
(A) कभी-कभी/Sometimes
(B) कभी नहीं/Never (C) हमेशा/Always

31. आधुनिक और तकनीकी शिक्षा के साथ-साथ रोजगार भी उपलब्ध कराना छात्रों का पलायन पर रोक लग सकता है/Providing employment along with modern and technical education can stop the migration of students.
(A) हाँ/Yes (B) कभी नहीं/Never
(C) नहीं/No

32. कठिन परिश्रम करने से भी सफलता मिल सकती है, चाहे व्यक्ति किसी उम्र का क्यों न हो/Hard work can also bring success, no matter what the age of the person is.
(A) बिल्कुल सही/Absolutely right
(B) कभी नहीं/Never No
(C) मालूम नहीं/Don't know

33. ईमानदारी, मेहनती व्यक्ति को अपने लक्ष्यों को प्राप्त करने और जीवन में सफलता प्राप्त करने में मदद करती है-/Honesty helps a hard working person to achieve his goal and achieve success in life.
(A) हमेशा/Always
(B) कभी-कभी/Sometime (C) नहीं/No

34. मेहनती और ईमानदार व्यक्ति को अपने काम और चरित्र पर विश्वास होता है, उन्हें किसी का डर नहीं होता है/A hard working and honest person has faith in his work and character, he has no fear of any one.
(A) नहीं/No (B) हाँ/Yes
(C) कभी नहीं/Never

35. रेलवे का उद्देश्य यात्रियों को सुरक्षित और बेहतर सेवाएँ प्रदान करना/The aim of railways is to provide safe and better services to passengers-
(A) नहीं/No (B) हाँ/Yes
(C) कुछ रेलकर्मी भरोसेमंद नहीं होते हैं/Some railway workers are not reliable

PRACTICE SET-3

Total Ques.- 35
Time - 15 Min.

निर्देश : (प्रश्न 1-35) प्रत्येक प्रश्न के लिए एक कथन (Statement) दी होती है और इसके नीचे उत्तर के तीन विकल्प दिए जाते हैं। उम्मीदवारों को अपने बुद्धिमता और निर्णय के आधार पर सही उत्तर के लिए कोई एक विकल्प का चयन कर उत्तर-पत्रक में दिए गए गोले को काला या माउस की सहायता से क्लिक (Click) करें।

Direction : (Questions 1–35) : For each question, a statement is given, followed by three answer options. Candidates should select the correct option based on their intelligence and judgment and fill the corresponding circle on the answer sheet or click using the mouse.

1. रेलवे देश की विविध भाषाओं और संस्कृतियों को जोड़ने का एक सशक्त साधन है–/Railways are a powerful means of connecting diverse languages and cultures of the country-
(A) हाँ/Yes (B) हो सकता है/May be
(C) रेलवे देश का सबसे बड़ा नेटवर्क है/Railways is the largest network in the country

2. रेलवे में राजभाषा नीति के तहत हिन्दी के उपयोग को बढ़ावा दिया जाना चाहिए–/The use of Hindi should be promoted in railways under the official language policy-
(A) नहीं/No
(B) मालूम नहीं/Don't know
(C) कुछ राज्य हिन्दी भाषा को नजरअंदाज करते हैं/Some states ignore Hindi language

3. देश के प्रत्येक रेलवे स्टेशन पर तिरंगे ध्वज होना चाहिए ताकि देशभक्ति और राष्ट्रीय एकता को बढ़ावा मिल सके–/There should be a tricolour flag at every railway station in the country so that patriotism and national unity can be promoted-
(A) हाँ/Yes (B) नहीं/No
(C) कुछ लोग देश के विरोधी हैं/Some people are opposed to the country

4. रेलवे यात्रियों को यथासंभव सब्सिडी प्रदान किया जाना चाहिए–/Railway passengers should be provided subsidy as far as possible-
(A) हमेशा/Always (B) नहीं/No
(C) केवल गरीबों के लिए/Only for the poor

5. अतिक्रमण और अवैध निर्माण भी जल जमाव का एक कारण है–/Encroachment and illegal construction is also a cause of waterlogging-
(A) कभी नहीं/Never (B) नहीं/No
(C) इसे हटाने से जल-जमाव की समस्या कम हो सकती है/Revolving it can reduce the problem of water logging

6. नागरिकों द्वारा कूड़ा और अन्य सामग्री को नालों और जल निकासी में नहीं प्रवाह करना चाहिए–/Citizens should not throw garbage and other material into drains and drainage-
(A) नहीं/No (B) हाँ/Yes
(C) कभी-नहीं/Never

7. प्रशासन को जल निकासी प्रणाली का सुधार करना चाहिए–/The administration should improve the drainage system-
(A) कभी नहीं/Never
(B) दोनों के बीच/Between the two
(C) हाँ/Yes

8. जल जमाव की समस्या का समाधान करने के लिए प्रशासन, नागरिकों और सामुदायिक भागीदारी की आवश्यकता होनी चाहिए–/To solve the problem of water logging, there should be a need for administration, citizens and community participation-
(A) कभी नहीं/Never (B) नहीं/No
(C) नागरिकों का योगदान भी आवश्यक है/The contribution of citizens is also necessary

9. नई तकनीको और शिक्षण विधियों का उपयोग करके शिक्षा की गुणवत्ता में सुधार करना चाहिए–/The quality of education should be improved by using new techniques and teaching methods-
(A) नहीं/No
(B) कभी-कभी/Sometimes
(C) गुणवत्ता में सुधार के लिए नई नीतियों की व्यवस्था होनी चाहिए/There should be a provision of new technologies to improve quality

10. रेलवे की गुणवत्ता बढ़ाने के लिए समय-समय पर जुड़े व्यक्ति को प्रशिक्षण और विकास कार्यक्रम आयोजित करने चाहिए–/To improve the quality of railways, the concerned workers should organize training and development programs from time to time-

(A) कभी नहीं/Never (B) हमेशा/Always
(C) नहीं/No

11. समाज की सांस्कृतिक धरोहर को समृद्ध किया जाना चाहिए–/The cultural heritage of the society should be enriched-
(A) कभी-कभी/Sometime (B) हाँ/Yes
(C) जरूरत नहीं/Not needed

12. समाज की सांस्कृतिक धरोहर को जीवंत रखा जाना चाहिए–/The cultural heritage of the society should be kept alive-
(A) नहीं/No (B) हमेशा/Always
(C) जरूरत नहीं/Not needed

13. बढ़ती आपराधिक घटनाएँ पुलिस प्रशासन के लिए–/The increasing criminal incidents are matter for the police administration-
(A) पुलिस प्रशासन के लिए सरदर्द बनती जा रही है/ Head pain is becoming for the Police Administrate
(B) आपराधिक घटना में कमी आई है/Criminal incident has decreased
(C) कुछ पुलिस भी शामिल हैं/Some Police are also involved

14. भागदौड़ भरी जिन्दगी और व्यस्त दिनचर्या तनाव का एक कारण बनता जा रहा है–/The hectic life and busy routine is becoming a cause of stress-
(A) कभी-कभी/Sometime (B) कभी नहीं/Never
(C) दोनों के बीच/Between the two

15. बढ़ते तापमान के दुष्प्रभाव के कारण बिमारियाँ फैलती जा रही है/Diseases are spreading due to the ill effects of increasing temperature-
(A) बिल्कुल सही/Absolutely right
(B) ऐसा नहीं/Not so
(C) मालूम नहीं/Don't know

16. छात्रों को सही और गलत के बीच अंतर करना सिखना चाहिए, ताकि समाज में जिम्मेदार नागरिक बनने में मदद मिल सके–/Students should learn to differentiate between right and wrong, so that they can become responsible citizens in the society.
(A) मालूम नहीं/Don't know
(B) नहीं/No (C) हाँ/Yes

17. हँसना या मजाक करना एक सकारात्मक ऊर्जा भी प्रदान करती है–/Laughing or joking gives also a positive energy.
(A) बिल्कुल नहीं/Not at all
(B) हाँ/Yes (C) कभी नहीं/Never

18. राजनेताओं को लागों को प्रेरित और एकजुट करने के लिए सकारात्मक भाषा का प्रयोग किया जाना चाहिए–/ Politicians should use positive language to motivate and unite people.
(A) कभी नहीं/Never (B) ऐसा नहीं/Not so
(C) एकजुट हो सके/So that they can unite

19. आपको निंदनीय शब्दों का प्रयोग करना चाहिए–/You should use derogatory words.
(A) कभी नहीं/Never (B) नहीं/No
(C) कभी-कभी/Sometimes

20. विफलता से सीखने के बाद नई रणनीति बनाना और उनके कारणों को समझना चाहिए–/After learning from failure, new strategies should be made and their reasons should be understood.
(A) निश्चित रूप से/Definitely
(B) ऐसा नहीं/Not so
(C) सीखने के समय/Learning Time

21. छात्रों को आत्महत्या करनी चाहिए–/Students should commit suicide-
(A) नहीं/No
(B) कभी-कभी/Sometimes
(C) कभी नहीं/Never

22. जाति जनगणना कराने से विभिन्न जातियों के बीच तनाव और विभाजन बढ़ने की सम्भावना बढ़ सकती है–/ Conducting caste census can increase the possibility of tension and division among different castes-
(A) बिल्कुल नहीं/Absolutely not
(B) ऐसा नहीं/Not so (C) हो सकता है/May be

23. सम्मान से आत्मविश्वास बढ़ता है और व्यक्ति अपने लक्ष्यों को प्राप्त करने के लिए अधिक प्रेरित होता है–/Respect increases self-confidence and a person is more motivated to achieve his goals-
(A) अवश्य/Of course
(B) कभी-कभी/Sometimes
(C) नहीं/No

24. सकारात्मक भावनाएँ हमारे जीवन में महत्वपूर्ण भूमिका निभाती है और लंबी आयु और स्वस्थ जीवन जीने में मदद करती है–/Positive emotions play an important role in our life and help in living a long and healthy life-
(A) जीवन में स्वस्थ रहना आवश्यक नहीं/It is not necessary to stay healthy in life
(B) बिल्कुल सही/Absolutely right
(C) ऐसा नहीं/Not so

25. देश की जीडीपी आर्थिक विकास का एक महत्वपूर्ण संकेतक है जो आर्थिक गतिविधियों को मापता है/The GDP of the country is an important indicator of economic development which measures economic activities-
(A) नहीं/No
(B) मालूम नहीं/Don't know
(C) हाँ/Yes

26. शिक्षक को बच्चों के भविष्य के आकार देने में महत्वपूर्ण भूमिका निभानी चाहिए/Teachers have to play an important role in shaping the future of children should-
(A) अवश्य/must
(B) कभी-कभी/sometimes
(C) ऐसा नहीं/not so

27. शिक्षक का कार्य विषय को रोचक और आकर्षक बनाना ताकि बच्चे उसमें रूचि ले सके/The teacher's job is to make the subject interesting and attractive so that children can take interest in it.
(A) बिल्कुल सही/Absolutely right
(B) ऐसा नहीं/Not so
(C) हो सकता है/Maybe

28. अच्छी बातें करना एक अच्छा गुण है, लेकिन अच्छाई को व्यक्ति के व्यवहार, क्रियाओं और इरादों से भी मापा जाना चाहिए/Talking well is a good quality, but goodness should also be measured by a person's behavior, actions and intentions.
(A) नहीं/No
(B) कभी-कभी/Sometimes
(C) हाँ/Yes

29. युवा पीढ़ी समाज की रचनात्मक और सांस्कृतिक धरोहर को बढ़ावा दिया जाना चाहिए/The creative and cultural heritage of the society should be promoted by the younger generation.
(A) हमेशा/Always (B) नहीं/No
(C) मालूम नहीं/Don't know

30. नई तकनीकों और शिक्षण विधियों का उपयोग करके शिक्षा की गुणवत्ता में सुधार करना चाहिए/The quality of education should be improved by using new techniques and teaching methods.
(A) कभी-कभी/Sometimes
(B) कभी नहीं/Never (C) हाँ/Yes

31. प्रशासन को जल निकासी प्रणाली का सुधार करना चाहिए / The administration should improve the drainage system.
(A) हमेशा/Always
(B) कभी-कभी/Sometimes
(C) हाँ/Yes

32. कोशिश जारी रखने से आत्मविश्वास बढ़ता है और व्यक्ति अपने लक्ष्यों को प्राप्त करने के लिए अधिक प्रेरित होता है/Continuing to try increases confidence and a person is more motivated to achieve his goals.
(A) ऐसा नहीं/Like this No
(B) बिल्कुल सही/Absolutely correct
(C) मालूम नहीं/I don't know

33. रेलवे में काम करने वाले लोगों को अक्सर टीम में करना पड़ता है, जिससे नेतृत्व और टीम वर्क के गुणों का विकास होता है/People working in railways often have to work in teams, which develops leadership and teamwork qualities
(A) हमेशा/Always (B) कभी नहीं/Never
(C) अक्सर टीम वर्क में काम नहीं होता है/Often teamwork doesn't work

34. दूसरों का सम्मान करना सीखना चाहिए/One should learn to respect others-
(A) कभी-कभी/Sometimes
(B) सम्मान करना अच्छे नागरिक का कर्त्तव्य नहीं है/ Respect is not the duty of a good citizen
(C) हमेशा/ Always

35. अपने शब्दों का चयन सावधानी से करना चाहिए/One should choose his words carefully-
(A) नहीं/No (B) कभी नहीं/Never
(C) हाँ/Yes

PRACTICE SET-4

Total Ques.- 35
Time - 15 Min.

निर्देश : (प्रश्न 1–35) प्रत्येक प्रश्न के लिए एक कथन (Statement) दी होती है और इसके नीचे उत्तर के तीन विकल्प दिए जाते हैं। उम्मीदवारों को अपने बुद्धिमता और निर्णय के आधार पर सही उत्तर के लिए कोई एक विकल्प का चयन कर उत्तर-पत्रक में दिए गए गोले को काला या माउस की सहायता से क्लिक (Click) करें।

Direction : (Questions 1–35) : For each question, a statement is given, followed by three answer options. Candidates should select the correct option based on their intelligence and judgment and fill the corresponding circle on the answer sheet or click using the mouse.

1. आत्मप्रेरणा और सकारात्मक सोच से सफलता प्राप्त करने में मदद मिलती है/Self-motivation and positive thinking help in achieving success-
   (A) कभी नहीं/Never
   (B) कभी-कभी/Sometimes
   (C) बिल्कुल नहीं/Not at all

2. दूसरों पर हँसने के बजाय समर्थन और सहानुभूति देना अधिक सकारात्मक हो सकता है/Instead of laughing at others, giving support and sympathy can be more positive-
   (A) हाँ/Yes (B) ऐसा नहीं/No
   (C) हँसने से तनाव मं कमी आती है/Laughing reduces stress

3. दूसरों की भावनाओं और परिस्थितियों को समझने की कोशिश करना चाहिए/One should try to understand the feelings and circumstances of others-
   (A) कभी नहीं/Never
   (B) कभी-कभी/Sometimes
   (C) हाँ/Yes

4. शिक्षा एक महत्वपूर्ण निवेश है जो व्यक्ति और समाज दोनों के लिए लाभदायक है/Education is an important investment which is beneficial for both the individual and the society-
   (A) कभी नहीं/Never
   (B) कभी-कभी/Sometimes
   (C) हमेशा/Always

5. बच्चों को सीखने के अवसर प्रदान करना और उन्हें नई चीजें सिखाने के लिए प्रोत्साहित करना चाहिए–/Children should be provided with opportunities to learn and encouraged to learn new things-
   (A) कभी-कभी/Sometimes
   (B) बच्चों के पास समय नहीं है/ Children do not have time
   (C) हमेशा/Always

6. अच्छी शिक्षा बौद्धिक क्षमता को विकसित करने में मदद करती है/Good education helps in developing intellectual capacity-
   (A) हाँ/Yes (B) नहीं/No
   (C) कभी नहीं/Never

7. लक्ष्य को हासिल करने के लिए हमें अपनी योजनाओं को कार्यान्वित करना चाहिए/To achieve the goal, we should implement our plans-
   (A) बिल्कुल सही/Absolutely right
   (B) योजना बनाना काफी कठिन है/ Planning is very difficult
   (C) नहीं/No

8. शिक्षकों को प्रशिक्षण प्रदान किया जाना चाहिए/ Teachers should be provided training-
   (A) कभी-कभी/Sometimes
   (B) हमेशा/Always
   (C) शिक्षकों में प्रशिक्षण की कमी है/ Lack of training in teachers

9. सभी छात्रों को समान अवसर मिले इसके लिए समान शिक्षा प्रदान करने का प्रयास किया जाना चाहिए–/Efforts should be made to provide equal education to all students so that they get equal opportunities.
   (A) समान शिक्षा जरूरी है/ Equal education is necessary
   (B) कभी-कभी/Sometimes
   (C) हमेशा/Always

10. अच्छी बातें करना एक अच्छा गुण है–/Speaking good things is a good quality.
    (A) कभी-कभी/Sometimes
    (B) कभी नहीं/Never (C) हमेशा/Always

11. निजीकरण से रेलवे के बुनियादी ढांचे में सुधार की संभावनाएँ बढ़ेगी/Privatisation will increase the possibilities of improvement in the infrastructure of railways.
(A) कभी-कभी/Sometimes
(B) हाँ/Yes
(C) रोजगार के अवसर में कमी आएगी/ Employment opportunities will decrease.

12. निजीकरण से रेलवे में रोजगार के अवसरों पर नकारात्मक प्रभाव पड़ सकता है/Privatisation can have a negative impact on employment opportunities in railways.
(A) ऐसा नहीं/Not so
(B) मालूम नहीं/Don't know
(C) हो सकता है/May be

13. रेलवे स्टेशनों का पुनर्विकास और आधुनिकीकरण होना चाहिए/Railway stations should be redeveloped and modernised.
(A) कभी-कभी/Sometimes
(B) ऐसा नहीं/Not so (C) हाँ/Yes

14. निजी कंपनियाँ रेल यात्रियों को बेहतर सुविधाएँ प्रदान कर सकती है-/Private companies can provide better facilities to railway passengers-
(A) नहीं/No (B) हो सकता है/Maybe
(C) कभी नहीं/Never

15. निजीकरण के बाद रेल यात्रा मंहगी होने की संभावना बढ़ेगी/After privatization, the possibility of rail travel becoming expensive will increase-
(A) नहीं/No (B) हमेशा/Always
(C) मालूम नहीं/Don't know

16. मित्रता हमें जीवन की चुनौतियों का सामना करने में मदद करती है/Friendship helps us to face the challenges of life-
(A) मालूम नहीं/Don't know
(B) हमेशा/Always (C) कभी नहीं/Never

17. मित्रता में विश्वास एक महत्वपूर्ण तत्व है जिससे विचारों और भावनाओं को साझा करने में सहज महसूस करते हैं/Trust is an important element in friendship due to which we feel comfortable in sharing thoughts and feelings-
(A) कभी-कभी/Sometimes
(B) मालूम नहीं/Don't know
(C) बिल्कुल सही/Absolutely right

18. आतंकवाद पर लगाम लगाने के लिए शिक्षा और जागरूकता भी एक महत्वपूर्ण कदम है/Education and awareness is also an important step to curb terrorism-
(A) नहीं/No (B) हाँ/Yes
(C) ऐसा नहीं/Not so

19. आतंकवाद अक्सर धार्मिक, राजनीतिक, सांस्कृतिक और आर्थिक मतभेदों के कारण भी उत्पन्न हो जाती है-/ Terrorism often arises due to religious, political, cultural and economic differences-
(A) नहीं/No (B) कभी नहीं/Never No
(C) हो सकता है/Maybe

20. आतंकवाद एक जटिल और खतरनाक समस्या है जो समाज को अस्थिर कर रही है/Terrorism is a complex and dangerous problem which is destabilizing the society.
(A) हाँ/Yes (B) नहीं/No
(C) मालूम नहीं/Don't know

21. भारतीय रेलवे दुनिया का सबसे बड़ा बाजार मुहैया करवाती है/Indian Railways has the largest market in the world.
(A) दुनिया में भारतीय रेल का बड़ा बाजार है/Indian Railways provides the world's largest market.
(B) ऐसा नहीं/Not so
(C) कभी-कभी/Sometimes

22. रेलों का नवनिर्माण का भारतीय जनता के जीवन, संस्कृति और अर्थव्यवस्था पर क्रांतिकारी प्रभाव पड़ा/The renovation of railways had a revolutionary impact on the lives, culture and economy of the Indian people.
(A) बिल्कुल सही/Absolutely right
(B) कभी नहीं/Never
(C) मालूम नहीं/Don't know

23. श्रम क्षेत्र में लैंगिक अंतर को कम करने से सकल घरेलू उत्पाद में महत्वपूर्ण वृद्धि हो सकती है/Reducing the gender gap in the labour sector can lead to a significant increase in GDP.
(A) नहीं/No (B) हाँ/Yes
(C) कह नहीं सकते/Can't say

24. परिवहन प्रणालियों में महिलाओं की पहुँच कार्यबल में उनकी भागीदारी बढ़ाती है–/Women's access to transport systems increases their participation in the workforce.
(A) हाँ/Yes (B) नहीं/No
(C) मालूम नहीं/Don't know

25. राष्ट्रीय अर्थव्यवस्था में परिवहन में अन्य साधनों की अपेक्षा रेल परिवहन सर्वोपरि हो गया है–/Rail transport has become paramount in the national economy as compared to other modes of transport. is
(A) हो सकता है/Maybe (B) नहीं/ No
(C) हाँ/Yes

26. रेल परिवहन प्रणाली का वर्तमान स्वरूप यात्रियों को आर्थिक केन्द्रों के बीच आवागमन की सुविधा प्रदान करना है–/The present form of rail transport system is to provide passengers the facility of movement between economic centres-
(A) हाँ/Yes
(B) बिल्कुल नहीं/Not at all (C) कभी नहीं/Never

27. बैंको द्वारा वित्तीय लेनदेन को सुगम बनाना चाहिए–/Financial transactions should be facilitated by banks-
(A) कभी नहीं/Never
(B) बैंक लोन देने में कठिनाईयाँ उत्पन्न करती है/ Banks create difficulties in giving loans
(C) हाँ/Yes

28. भारतीय बैंकिंग व्यवस्था को अर्थव्यवस्था की रीढ़ कहा जाता है–/Indian banking system is called the backbone of the economy-
(A) मालूम नहीं/Don't know
(B) नहीं/No
(C) हाँ/Yes

29. भारतीय रेलवे को अपने द्विपक्षीय और आर्थिक संबंधों को मजबूत करने के लिए अन्य देशों के साथ सहयोग करना चाहिए।/Indian Railways should cooperate with other countries to strengthen its bilateral and economic relations.
(A) कभी-कभी/Sometimes
(B) भारतीय रेलवे आर्थिक संसाधन में कमी है/Indian Railways is short of economic resources
(C) हमेशा/Always

30. भारतीय रेल देश के भीतर और बाहर व्यापार, पर्यटन और संस्कृति को बढ़ावा देती है–/Indian Railways promotes trade, tourism and culture within and outside the country-
(A) हमेशा/Always
(B) कभी-कभी/Sometimes
(C) मालूम नहीं/Don't know

31. विफलताओं से सीखना सफलता की कुंजी हो सकती है–/Learning from failures can be the key to success-
(A) नहीं/No (B) ऐसा नहीं/Not so
(C) हाँ/Yes

32. भारत सरकार ने रेलवे के बुनियादी ढांचे में सुधार और विकास के लिए व्यापक रूप से निवेश कर रही है–/The Government of India is investing extensively to improve and develop the infrastructure of railways-
(A) कभी नहीं/Never
(B) मालूम नहीं/Don't know
(C) हमेशा/Always

33. रेलवे में मनौवैज्ञानिक परीक्षण का उपयोग कर्मचारियों की एकाग्रता और कार्यक्षमता का मूल्यांकन करने में मदद करता है–/Use of psychological tests in railways helps in evaluating the concentration and efficiency of employees-
(A) कभी नहीं/Never
(B) कभी-कभी/Sometimes
(C) हमेशा/Always

34. मनौवैज्ञानिक परीक्षा के परिणामों के आधार पर, कर्मचारियों की सुरक्षा में सुधार हो सकता है, जिससे दुर्घटनाओं की संभावना कम हो सकती है–/Based on the results of psychological tests, the safety of employees can be improved, which can reduce the chances of accidents-
(A) बिल्कुल सही/Absolutely Correct
(B) नहीं/No
(C) दुर्घटना कभी भी हो सकता है/Accident can happen at any time

35. मनोविज्ञान में हम व्यवहार एवं अनुभव से संबंधित विविध समस्याओं का अध्ययन करते हैं–/In psychology, we study various problems related to behaviour and experience.
(A) नहीं/No
(B) हो सकता है/It can happe
(C) हाँ/Yes

PRACTICE SET-5

Total Ques.- 35
Time - 15 Min.

निर्देश : (प्रश्न 1-35) प्रत्येक प्रश्न के लिए एक कथन (Statement) दी होती है और इसके नीचे उत्तर के तीन विकल्प दिए जाते हैं। उम्मीदवारों को अपने बुद्धिमता और निर्णय के आधार पर सही उत्तर के लिए कोई एक विकल्प का चयन कर उत्तर-पत्रक में दिए गए गोले को काला या माउस की सहायता से क्लिक (Click) करें।

Direction : (Questions 1–35) : For each question, a statement is given, followed by three answer options. Candidates should select the correct option based on their intelligence and judgment and fill the corresponding circle on the answer sheet or click using the mouse.

1. व्यक्तित्व निर्माण एक सतत् प्रक्रिया है, जिसमें व्यक्ति अपने विचारों, भावनाओं और व्यवहारों को विकसित करता है–/Personality development is a continuous process in which a person develops his thoughts, feelings and behaviour-
(A) कभी-कभी/Sometimes
(B) कभी नहीं/Never (C) हमेशा/ Always

2. नकारात्मक सोच व्यक्तित्व को निखारता है–/Negative thinking enhances personality-
(A) हाँ/Yes (B) नहीं/No
(C) कभी-कभी/Sometimes

3. विनम्रता एक महान गुण है जो व्यक्तित्व को आकर्षक बनाए रखता है–/Humility is a great quality which keeps the personality attractive-
(A) सभी लोग विनम्र होते हैं/All people are humble
(B) बड़े लोग विनम्र नहीं होते हैं/Big people are not humble
(C) हमेशा/Always

4. धैर्य और शांत स्वभाव एक आलसी व्यक्तित्व का घोतक है–/Patience and calm nature are indicative of a lazy personality-
(A) हाँ/Yes (B) नहीं/No
(C) मालूम नहीं/Don't know

5. हमेशा सीखने और विकसित होने की इच्छा रखना एक ज्ञानी व्यक्ति को दर्शाता है।/Always having a desire to learn and develop shows a knowledgeable (literate) person.
(A) हाँ/Yes
(B) कभी-कभी/Sometimes
(C) नहीं/No

6. रेलवे ने भारत को जोड़ने और बदलने में महत्वपूर्ण भूमिका निभाई है, जिससे व्यापार, व्यवसाय और शहरीकरण में वृद्धि हुई है।/Railways have played a vital role in connecting and transforming India, leading to growth in trade, business and urbanisation.
(A) हाँ/Yes (B) कभी-नहीं/Never
(C) मालूम नहीं/Don't know

7. रेलवे ने औद्योगिक विकास को बढ़ावा दिया और परिवहन को आधुनिक बनाया है।/Railways have promoted industrial development and modernised transport.
(A) रेलवे का राजस्व बढ़ा है/Revenue of railways has increased
(B) ऐसा नहीं/Not so (C) कभी नहीं/Never

8. रेलवे की कठोर समय-सारणी और अनुशासन यात्रियों और कर्मचारियों दोनों में आत्म-अनुशासन और समयबद्धता की भावना को बढ़ावा देता है–/The strict timetable and discipline of railways promotes a sense of self-discipline and punctuality in both passengers and employees.
(A) हाँ/Yes
(B) कभी-कभी/Sometimes
(C) रेलवे की अनुशासन निम्न स्तर का है/Railway discipline is of low standard

9. रेलवे में काम करने वाले लोगों को अक्सर टीम वर्क में करना चाहिए।/People working in railways often have to work in teams.
(A) हाँ/Yes
(B) कभी नहीं/Never
(C) अक्सर टीम वर्क में काम नहीं होता है।/Discipline in railways is of poor standard

10. दूसरों का अपमान करना सीखना चाहिए।/One should learn to insult others.
(A) कभी-कभी/Sometimes
(B) सम्मान करना अच्छे नागरिकता का कर्त्तव्य है/ Respect is the duty of good citizenship
(C) हमेशा/Always

11. अपने विचारों का चयन सावधानी से करना चाहिए।/One should choose one's ideas carefully.
(A) नहीं/No (B) कभी नहीं/Never
(C) बिल्कुल सही/Absolutely right

12. आप सही दिशा, सही रणनीति और दिमागी ताकत लगाएँ, वो बिना ज्यादा मेहनत के भी बड़ा मुकाम पाया जा सकता है।/If you use the right direction, right strategy and brain power, you can achieve great heights even without much hard work.
(A) नहीं/No (B) हाँ/Yes
(C) मेहनत करना जरूरी नहीं है/Hard work is not necessary

13. सीमावर्ती क्षेत्रों में नागरिकों को आत्मसुरक्षा की प्रशिक्षण देनी चाहिए।/Citizens in border areas should be given self-defense training.
(A) सीमावर्ती क्षेत्रों के नागरिक भयभीत नहीं होते हैं/ Citizens in border areas are not scared
(B) कभी नहीं/Never
(C) संभव हो तो देनी चाहिए/If possible, it should be given

14. दूसरों के प्रति संवेदनशीलता और मदद करने की भावना रखना नैतिकता का आधार है।/Sensitivity towards others and a spirit of helping others is the basis of morality.
(A) बिल्कुल नहीं/Not at all
(B) बिल्कुल सही/Absolutely Right
(C) कभी-कभी/Sometimes

15. नैतिकता समाज को दिशा प्रदान करती है और अच्छे बुरे के बीच अंतर करने में मदद करने की कोशिश करती है।/ Morality (righteous) provides direction to society and tries to help differentiate between good and bad.
(A) हाँ/Yes (B) हो सकता है/Maybe
(C) मालूम नहीं/Don't know

16. शादी एक महत्वपूर्ण सामाजिक संस्था है जो हमारे समाज में एक महत्वपूर्ण भूमिका निभाती है। यह दो व्यक्तियों के बीच एक पवित्र बंधन है जो उनके जीवन को एक नई दिशा देता है।/Marriage is an important social institution which plays a vital role in our society. It is a sacred bond between two individuals which gives a new direction to their lives.
(A) कुछ लोग शादी से असंतुष्ट है/Some people are dissatisfied with marriage
(B) शादी के सामाजिक सम्मान नहीं मिलता है/ Marriage does not get social respect
(C) शादी के बाद नए जीवन की शुरूआत और पारिवारिक जीवन को मजबूती देता है/Marriage is the beginning of a new life and strengthens family life

17. प्रकृति के साथ संतुलन बनाने के लिए प्राकृतिक संसाधनों का संरक्षण करना, हरित जीवन शैली अपनाना और प्रकृति के साथ जुड़ना चाहिए/To create a balance with nature, we should conserve natural resources, adopt a green lifestyle and connect with nature.
(A) वर्तमान समय में प्रकृति के साथ छेड़छाड़ काफी किया जाता है/Pollution problem will increase
(B) हमेशा/Always
(C) प्रदूषण की समस्या बढ़ेगी/In present times, nature is tampered with a lot.

18. अपनी सामाजिक मर्यादा भंग नहीं करना चाहिए, इससे जीवन तनावग्रस्त हो जाता है।/We should not break our social limits, this makes life stressful.
(A) कभी-कभी/Sometimes
(B) हाँ/Yes
(C) मनुष्य को सामाजिक मर्यादा में रहना चाहिए/ Man should live within social limits.

19. दूसरों के साथ सकारात्मक व्यवहार और अच्छे संबंध बनाने की कोशिश करनी चाहिए।/We should try to have positive behavior and good relations with others.
(A) हमेशा/Always
(B) लोगों को स्वयं पर विश्वास नहीं होता है/People do not have confidence in themselves
(C) कभी नहीं/Never

20. हिंसात्मक फिल्में समाज पर एक महत्वपूर्ण प्रभाव डाल सकती है और वे समाज को गलत दिशा में भी ले जा सकता है।/Voilent Films can have a significant impact on society and they can also take society in the wrong direction.
(A) नहीं/No
(B) कभी-कभी/Sometimes
(C) हिंसात्मक फिल्में नहीं देखना चाहिए/One should not watch violet films

21. फिल्मों में सकारात्मक सामग्री को बढ़ावा देने से समाज पर सकारात्मक प्रभाव पड़ सकता है।/Promoting positive content in films can have a positive impact on society.
(A) नहीं/No
(B) ऐसा हो सकता है/This can happen
(C) मालूम नहीं/I don't know

22. अपना हित साधने के लिए झूठ और धोखा का सहारा लिया जाना चाहिए।/One should resort to lies and deception to fulfill one's own interests.
(A) नहीं/No
(B) कभी-कभी/Sometimes
(C) कभी नहीं/Never

23. विकास के नाम पर आदिवासियों को उनकी परम्पराओं से दूर किया जा रहा है।/In the name of development, tribals are being taken away from their traditions.
(A) कभी नहीं/Never
(B) हाँ/Yes
(C) आदिवासियों का संख्या कम होती जा रही है/ The number of tribals is decreasing

24. विवाद का मूल कारण वे लोग होते हैं जो अपने पक्ष को सही और दूसरे को गलत साबित करने की कोशिश करते हैं।/The root cause of disputes are those people who try to prove their side right and the other side wrong.
(A) हाँ/Yes
(B) ऐसा नहीं/This is not so
(C) कभी-कभी/Sometimes

25. शराब पीकर ट्रेन का लोको पायलट बेहतर तरीके से ट्रेन का परिचालन कर सकता है।/A loco pilot can operate a train better after drinking alcohol.
(A) कभी-कभी/Sometimes
(B) नहीं/No (C) कभी नहीं/Never

26. नशा शारीरिक और मानसिक क्षमता को बढ़ाता है–/ Intoxication increases physical and mental capacity-
(A) कभी-कभी/Sometimes
(B) ऐसा नहीं/Not so (C) हाँ/Yes

27. ट्रेन परिचालन में सुरक्षा प्रोटोकॉल का पालन करना अति आवश्यक है।/It is very important to follow safety protocols in train operations.
(A) मालूम नहीं/I don't know
(B) हाँ/Yes (C) नहीं/No

28. पति-पत्नी के रिश्ते की नींव विश्वास पर बनी होती है।/The foundation of the relationship between husband and wife is built on trust.
(A) ऐसा नहीं/Not so
(B) हो सकता है/May be (C) हाँ/Yes

29. नियम और कानून जनता के हित के लिए होने चाहिए, जिससे उनकी सुरक्षा, स्वतंत्रता और कल्याण सुनिश्चित हो सके।/Rules and laws should be for the benefit of the public, so that their safety, freedom and welfare can be ensured.
(A) बिल्कुल सही/Absolutely right
(B) जानकारी नहीं/I don't know
(C) जनता जागरूक हो चुकी है/The public has become aware

30. दूसरे की गलती पर प्रतिक्रिया देने के तरीके हमें सहानुभूति, सम्मान और सुधार के साथ प्रतिक्रिया देनी चाहिए।/Ways to react to others' mistakes We should react with sympathy, respect and correction.
(A) कभी-कभी/Sometimes
(B) नहीं/No (C) हमेशा/Always

31. किसी व्यक्ति के आत्मसम्मान को ठेस पहुँचाना चाहिए।/ One should not tolerate any self-esteem injury.
(A) नहीं/No
(B) कभी-कभी/Sometimes
(C) कभी नहीं/Never

32. आप अकेले ही कोई कार्य करना पसंद करते हैं।/You like to work alone.
(A) कभी-कभी/Sometimes
(B) मालूम नहीं/I don't know
(C) कभी नहीं/Never

33. टीम में कार्य करने से सदस्यों को बीच सहयोग और टीम वर्क की भावना बढ़ती है।/Working in a team increases the sense of cooperation and teamwork among the members.
(A) हमेशा/Always
(B) आपस में तालमेल में कमी दिखता है/There is lack of coordination among the members
(C) कभी नहीं/Never

34. ध्याण और योग तनाव को कम करने में मदद कर सकते हैं–/Meditation and yoga can help reduce stress.
(A) नहीं/No (B) कभी-कभी/Sometimes
(C) हमेशा/Always

35. आप तनाव को बेहतर तरीके से निपटाने के लिए सामाजिक परिस्थितियों में अच्छा व्यवहार कर सकते हैं।/You can behave well in social situations to deal with stress better.
(A) हाँ/Yes
(B) पारिवारिक तनाव काफी मुश्किल होती है/Family stress is very difficult
(C) तनाव के कारण स्वास्थ्य में गिरावट आती है/Stress causes deterioration in health

PRACTICE SET-6

Total Ques.- 35
Time - 15 Min.

निर्देश : (प्रश्न 1-35) प्रत्येक प्रश्न के लिए एक कथन (Statement) दी होती है और इसके नीचे उत्तर के तीन विकल्प दिए जाते हैं। उम्मीदवारों को अपने बुद्धिमता और निर्णय के आधार पर सही उत्तर के लिए कोई एक विकल्प का चयन कर उत्तर-पत्रक में दिए गए गोले को काला या माउस की सहायता से क्लिक (Click) करें।

Direction : (Questions 1–35) : For each question, a statement is given, followed by three answer options. Candidates should select the correct option based on their intelligence and judgment and fill the corresponding circle on the answer sheet or click using the mouse.

1. दूसरे के स्वभाव, शक्तियों और कमजोरियों को समझना महत्वपूर्ण है, क्योंकि इससे हम उनके साथ बेहतर तरीके से बातचीत कर सकते हैं और उनके साथ मजबूत संबंध बना सकते हैं।/It is important to understand the nature, strengths and weaknesses of others, as this helps us to interact with them better and build strong relationships with them.
   (A) नहीं/No (B) कभी नहीं/Never
   (C) हमेशा/Always
2. पड़ोसियों के साथ अच्छा संबंध बनाना चाहिए ताकि सुख-दुख में एक-दूसरे का सहयोग बना रहे।/Good relations should be maintained with neighbours so that they support each other in good and bad times.
   (A) हमेशा/Always
   (B) मालूम नहीं/Don't know
   (C) पड़ोसी एक दूसरे पर कटाक्ष करते हैं/Neighbours make sarcastic remarks at each other.
3. मानव व्यक्तित्व के विकास के लिए खुले विचारों और लचीलापन की आवश्यकता होती है, न कि रूढ़िवादिता की।/Human personality development requires open-mindedness and flexibility, not conservatism.
   (A) मालूम नहीं/Don't know
   (B) कह नहीं सकते/Can't say
   (C) हाँ/Yes
4. रूढ़िवादिता से व्यक्तित्व विकास में सहयोग की भावना उत्पन्न होती है।/Conservatism creates a feeling of cooperation in personality development.
   (A) हमेशा/Always
   (B) कभी नहीं/Never (C) नहीं/No
5. संस्कार और संस्कृति से हमें सामाजिक नियमों का पालन करने की शिक्षा मिलती है, जो हमारे समाज में रहने के लिए आवश्यक है-/Sanskar and culture teach us to follow social rules, which is necessary for living in our society.
   (A) पुरानी संस्कृति धीरे-धीरे समाप्त हो रही है/ Old culture is slowly vanishing
   (B) बच्चों को धार्मिक संस्कार नहीं दिया जाना चाहिए/ Babs should not be given religious sanskar
   (C) अच्छे संस्कार से नैतिक मूल्यों में बढ़ावा मिलेगी/ Good sanskar will promote moral values
6. सभी विषम परिस्थितियों में खुद को शांत रख सकते हैं।/We can keep ourselves calm in all adverse situations.
   (A) नहीं/No (B) हाँ/Yes
   (C) मालूम नहीं/Don't know
7. देश में नागरिक के रूप में हमें देश के प्रति निष्ठा रखनी चाहिए और देश के हितों को प्राथमिकता देनी चाहिए।/As citizens of the country, we should have loyalty towards the country and give priority to the interests of the country.
   (A) हमेशा/Always
   (B) कभी-कभी/Sometimes
   (C) कुछ लोग देश के प्रति निष्ठा नहीं रखते/Some people do not have loyalty towards the country
8. हमें नौकरी के साथ-साथ अपनी नागरिक जिम्मेदारियों का पालन करनी चाहिए।/We should fulfill our civic responsibilities along with our job.
   (A) वर्तमान समय में नौकरी नहीं मिल रही है/ Jobs are not available in the present time
   (B) नौकरी के लिए आरक्षण की जरूरत है/ Reservation is needed for jobs
   (C) हमेशा/Always
9. महापुरूषों के नाम पर ट्रेन का चलाया जाना उनके प्रति श्रद्धा और कृतज्ञता को प्रदर्शित करना और आनेवाली पीढ़ियों को उनके बारे में जानने का अवसर मिलता है।/Running trains in the name of great men shows respect and gratitude towards them and the coming generations get an opportunity to know about them.
   (A) लोग महापुरूषों के नाम भूल जाते हैं/People forget the names of great men
   (B) बिल्कुल सही/Absolutely correct

(C) ऐसा नहीं/Not so

10. इतिहास की महत्वपूर्ण घटनाओं और महापुरूषों के योगदान को याद रखा जाना चाहिए।/Important events of history and the contribution of great men should be remembered.
(A) बच्चों के इतिहास की जानकारी दी जानी चाहिए/ Children should be given information about history
(B) कभी-कभी/Sometimes
(C) पुरानी घटनाओं को याद रखना संभव नहीं/It is not possible to remember old events

11. फिल्मों में अनुचित सामग्री दिखाने से समाज में अनुचित व्यवहार को बढ़ावा मिल सकता है।/Showing inappropriate content in films can promote inappropriate behavior in society.
(A) बिल्कुल सत्य/Absolutely true
(B) असत्य/Untrue
(C) मालूम नहीं/Don't know

12. फिल्मों में हिंसा और अपराध को दिखाने से समाज में हिंसा और अपराध की दर बढ़ सकती है।/Showing violence and crime in films can increase the rate of violence and crime in society.
(A) कभी नहीं/Never
(B) ऐसा हो सकता है/It can happen
(C) अपराध की संख्या में कमी आयी है/The number of crimes will decrease

13. रेलवे के निजीकरण के बारे में निर्णय लेने से पहले गरीबों के लिए रेल यात्रा की सुविधा, रोजगार के अवसर और सेवाओं की गुणवत्ता पर विचार करना अति आवश्यक है।/ Before taking a decision about privatization of railways, it is very important to consider the convenience of rail travel for the poor, employment opportunities and quality of services.
(A) अमीरों को यात्रा करना काफी आसान होगा/ It will be very easy for the rich to travel
(B) रेलवे की आमदनी बढ़ जाएगी/The income of the railways will increase
(C) हाँ/Yes

14. सकारात्मक सोच लंबी आयु और स्वस्थ जीवन जीने में मदद करती है।/Positive thinking helps in living a long and healthy life.
(A) लंबी आयु जीने के लिए तनाव और अन्य नकारात्मक कारकों को दूर रखना चाहिए/To live a long life, stress and other negative factors should be kept away
(B) कभी-कभी/Sometimes
(C) वर्तमान समय में लोग लंबी आयु जीना नहीं चाहते है।/ In the present time, people do not want to live a long life.

15. निंदनीय शब्दों का प्रयोग सकारात्मक माहौल को बढ़ावा दे सकता है।/Use of condemnable words can promote a positive environment.
(A) हमेशा/Always
(B) कभी-कभी/Sometimes
(C) कभी नहीं/Never

16. काल्पनिक समस्याएँ वास्तविक समस्याओं से ध्यान भटका सकती है।/Imaginary problems can divert attention from real problems.
(A) हाँ/Yes
(B) मालूम नहीं/I don't know
(C) कह नहीं सकते/Can't say

17. कुछ पारम्परिक परिस्थितियों के कारण सही फैसले सही वक्त पर नहीं हो पाते हैं।/Due to some traditional circumstances, right decisions are not taken at the right time.
(A) नए विचारों पर सोचना चाहिए/New ideas should be thought of
(B) हाँ/Yes
(C) परिस्थितियाँ बदलती रहती है।/Circumstances keep changing.

18. बच्चों में सामाजिक भावना का विकास जन्म से ही होता है।/ Social feelings develop in a child from birth.
(A) कभी नहीं/Never
(B) हो सकता है/It may happen
(C) नहीं/No

19. वर्तमान शिक्षा प्रणाली में बच्चों को अधिक से अधिक ज्ञान प्रदान के लिए किताबों का बोझ बढ़ाया जा रहा है।/In the current education system, the burden of books is being increased to provide more and more knowledge to children.
(A) बच्चे में मोबाइल देखने की आदत कम जाएगी/The habit of watching mobile will decrease in the child.
(B) किताबें काफी मंहगी होती जा रही है/Books are becoming very expensive.
(C) हाँ/Yes

20. बच्चों के शारीरिक और मानसिक विकास को बेहतर बनाने के लिए आधुनिक शिक्षण के तरीके, खेलने का समय का प्रावधान, किताबों का चयन करके किया जा सकता है।/To improve the physical and mental development of children, modern teaching methods, provision of play time, selection of books can be done.
(A) बदलाव संभव नहीं है/Change is not possible
(B) बच्चों पर पढ़ाई का बोझ अधिक है/The burden of studies is more on children

(C) ऐसे तरीके अपनाने से बेहतर परिणाम हो सकते हैं।/ Adopting such methods can lead to better results.

21. नशा शारीरिक और मानसिक क्षमता को बेहतर बनाता है।/ Drug addiction improves physical and mental capacity.
(A) नशा कार्य करते वक्त करना चाहिए/Drug addiction should be done while working.
(B) नशा करने वाले का शरीर स्वस्थ रहता है/The body of a drug addict remains healthy.
(C) कभी नहीं/Never.

22. रेलवे यात्रा के दौरान विभिन्न पृष्ठभूमि के लोगों से मिलने और सामाजिक संपर्क बढ़ाने का अवसर प्रदान करती है।/Railway provides an opportunity to meet people of different backgrounds and increase social contact during travel.
(A) रेलवे यात्रा के दौरान यात्रियों से संपर्क नहीं बढ़ाना चाहिए/Contact with passengers should not be increased during railway travel.
(B) अच्छे लोगों की पहचान मुश्किल होती है/It is difficult to identify good people.
(C) हाँ/Yes.

23. दूसरों के साथ संवाद करते समय हमें अपनी भावना को नियंत्रित करना चाहिए।/We should control our feelings while communicating with others.
(A) कभी नहीं/Never.
(B) वार्तालाप करते समय ऐसी गलती हो जाती है/Such mistakes are made while conversing.
(C) हमेशा/Always.

24. जब कोई आपका अपमान करता है तो उस व्यक्ति के प्रति आपके विचार–/When someone insults you, your thoughts about that person-
(A) उसके प्रति दूषित हो जाता है/get polluted towards him.
(B) अच्छा लगता है/It feels good.
(C) नजरअंदाज कर लेते हैं/Ignore

25. सम्मान करने से हम दूसरे की भावनाओं और जरूरतों को समझने में मदद मिलती है।/Respect helps us to understand the feelings and needs of others.
(A) कभी-नहीं/Never
(B) कभी-कभी/Sometimes.
(C) हमेशा/Always

26. वृद्ध लोगों के प्रति सम्मानजनक व्यवहार और सकारात्मक सोच रखनी चाहिए।/We should have respectful behavior and positive thinking towards old people.
(A) कभी-कभी/Sometimes
(B) ऐसा नहीं/Not so (C) हमेशा/Always

27. ईमानदारी और सच्चाई हर परिस्थिति में सबसे अच्छी नीति है, इससे हम एक अच्छा इंसान बन सकते हैं।/Honesty and truth is the best policy in every situation, this can make us a good person.
(A) परिस्थिति बदलती रहती है/Situations keep changing
(B) बिल्कुल सही/Absolutely right
(C) वर्तमान समय में किसी व्यक्ति पर विश्वास नहीं करना चाहिए/One should not trust any person in the present time

28. व्यक्ति की याद्दाशत उम्र के साथ घटती और बढ़ती रहती है लेकिन स्वस्थ जीवन शैली और प्रर्याप्त नींद याद्दाशत को बेहतर बना सकती है।/A person's memory keeps on increasing and decreasing with age, but a healthy lifestyle and adequate sleep can improve memory.
(A) अवश्य/Of course (B) नहीं/No
(C) वृद्धावस्था में कोशिकाएँ धीरे-धीरे कमजोरी होने लगती है/In old age, cells gradually start weakening

29. बचपन और युवावस्था में याद्दाशत आमतौर पर सीखने और याद रखने की क्षमता अधिक होती है।/In childhood and youth, the ability to learn and remember is generally high.
(A) कभी-कभी/Sometimes
(B) हाँ/Yes
(C) मालूम नहीं/Don't know

30. रक्षा उत्पादन में निजी क्षेत्र की भागीदारी होनी चाहिए।/There should be participation of private sector in defense production.
(A) एक जटिल मुद्दा है/ It is a complex issue
(B) रोजगार का अवसर मिलेगा/Employment opportunities will be available
(C) मालूम नहीं/ Don't know

31. आज की दुनिया में प्रतिस्पर्धा के कारण सच्चाई को छोड़कर झूठ का सहारा लेकर लक्ष्यों को प्राप्त करते हैं।/In today's world, due to competition, people leave the truth and take the help of lies to achieve their goals.
(A) सभी लोग/Everyone
(B) कुछ लोग/Some people
(C) प्रतिस्पर्धा काफी कठिन है/Competition is very difficult

32. तकनीक और सोशल मीडिया ने हमारे जीवन को आसान बना दिया है।/Technology and social media have made our lives easier.
 (A) बिल्कुल सही/Absolutely right
 (B) चिंताजनक विषय है/It is a matter of concern
 (C) सोशल मीडिया काफी जागरूक हो गया/Social media has become very aware

33. अपने दैनिक जीवन में पर्यावरण संरक्षण के तरीकों को अपनाना चाहिए।/We should adopt methods of environmental protection in our daily lives.
 (A) हमेशा/Always
 (B) कभी-कभी/Sometimes
 (C) प्रदूषित हवा की मात्रा बढ़ी है/The amount of polluted air has increased

34. वायु की गुणवत्ता में सुधार कर पर्यावरण को हरा-भरा बनाया जाना चाहिए।/The environment should be made green by improving the quality of air.
 (A) फेक्ट्री में नियम-कानून सुधार होना चाहिए/There should be improvement in the rules and regulations in factories
 (B) ज्यादा पेड़-पौधे लगाकर पर्यावरण को हरे-भरे बना सकते हैं/We can make the environment green by planting more trees
 (C) मालूम नहीं/ Don't know

35. सम्मान करने से रिश्ते मजबूत और बेहतर तरीके से जुड़ जाते है।/Respect makes relationships stronger and better.
 (A) हमेशा/Always
 (B) ऐसा नहीं/It is not like this
 (C) रिश्ते टुटने पर जुड़ते नहीं है/Relationships do not mend when they break

PRACTICE SET-7

Total Ques.- 35
Time - 15 Min.

निर्देश : (प्रश्न 1–35) प्रत्येक प्रश्न के लिए एक कथन (Statement) दी होती है और इसके नीचे उत्तर के तीन विकल्प दिए जाते हैं। उम्मीदवारों को अपने बुद्धिमता और निर्णय के आधार पर सही उत्तर के लिए कोई एक विकल्प का चयन कर उत्तर-पत्रक में दिए गए गोले को काला या माउस की सहायता से क्लिक (Click) करें।

Direction : (Questions 1–35) : For each question, a statement is given, followed by three answer options. Candidates should select the correct option based on their intelligence and judgment and fill the corresponding circle on the answer sheet or click using the mouse.

1. वृक्षारोपण और वनस्पति संरक्षण से वायु की गुणवत्ता में सुधार कर सकते हैं/Air quality can be improved by tree plantation and vegetation conservation.
   (A) वायु की गुणवत्ता में सुधार असंभव है/Improving air quality is impossible.
   (B) बढ़ते औद्योगिकण से वायु प्रदूषित होती जा रही है/Air is getting polluted due to increasing industrialization.
   (C) अच्छी वायु प्राप्त करने के लिए वृक्षारोपण जरूरी है/Tree plantation is necessary to get good air.
2. दैनिक जीवन में पर्यावरण संरक्षण के तरीकों को अपनाना चाहिए/Environmental conservation methods should be adopted in daily life.
   (A) अवश्य/Of course (B) ऐसा नहीं/Not so
   (C) कभी-कभी/Sometimes
3. अपने कार्यों और निर्णयों में पारदर्शिता रखनी चाहिए/There should be transparency in one's actions and decisions.
   (A) कभी-कभी/Sometime
   (B) वर्तमान समय में ऐसा संभव नहीं है/This is not possible in the present time.
   (C) पारदर्शिता रखने से निर्णयों में विश्वास कर सकते है/By maintaining transparency, we can trust the decisions.
4. सरकारी अस्पतालों में निगरानी और जवाबदेही की व्यवस्था होनी चाहिए, ताकि मरीजों को समय पर ईलाज मिल सके/There should be a system of monitoring and accountability in government hospitals, so that patients can get timely treatment.
   (A) सरकारी अस्पतालों में डॉक्टरों और दवाओं की काफी किल्लत है/There is a huge shortage of doctors and medicines in government hospitals.
   (B) प्राईवेट नर्सिंग होम की संख्या में वृद्धि हो रही है/The number of private nursing homes is increasing.
   (C) ऐसा होना चाहिए/This should happen
5. सरकारी अस्पतालों में आधुनिक उपकरणों और सुविधाओं की सुनिश्चित करनी चाहिए/Modern equipment and facilities should be ensured in governmen hospitals-
   (A) कभी-कभी/Sometimes
   (B) हमेशा/Always
   (C) सरकार स्वास्थ्य सेवाओं पर खर्च करना नहीं चाहती/Government does not want to spend on health services
6. महिलाओं को उनके उत्कृष्ट कार्य के लिए पुरस्कार और सम्मान देनी चाहिए। ताकि अन्य महिलाओं को प्रोत्साहन मिल सके/Women should be given awards and honours for their excellent work. So that other women can get encouragement.
   (A) शहरी महिलाएँ तीव्र गति से सशक्त हो रही है/Urban women are getting empowered at a rapid pace
   (B) महिलाएँ पुरुषों की बराबरी नहीं कर सकती है/Women cannot be equal to men
   (C) महिलाओं को सम्मान मिलने से समाज में उनकी भूमिका मजबूत होती है/Women getting respect strengthens their role in the society.
7. महिलाओं को सशक्त बनाने के लिए शिक्षा और रोजगार के अवसर प्रदान करने चाहिए।/Education and employment opportunities should be provided to empower women.
   (A) पुरुषों में महिलाओं के प्रति आक्रोश बढ़ता है/Men's resentment towards women increases.
   (B) ऐसा नहीं/ Not so (C) हाँ/Yes
8. निजी उद्योग के विकास से आर्थिक विकास में वृद्धि हो सकता है, जो देश के नागरिकों के लिए लाभप्रद हो सकता है/The development of private industry can increase economic development, which can be beneficial for the citizens of the country.
   (A) ऐसा संभव नहीं/This is not possible
   (B) बेरोजगारी बढ़ेगी/Unemployment will increase
   (C) रोजगार के अवसर में वृद्धि होगी/Employment opportunities will increase

9. देश को आर्थिक और तकनीकी रूप से विकसित करने के लिए निजी उद्योग को बढ़ावा दिया जाना चाहिए/Private industry should be encouraged to develop the country economically and technologically.
(A) कभी नहीं/Never (B) हमेशा/Always
(C) निजी उद्योग की मनमानी बढ़ेगी/The arbitrariness of private industry will increase.

10. अधिकांश लोग सच्चाई के बजाय धन और संपत्ति को अधिक महत्व दे रहे हैं/Most people are giving more importance to money and property than truth.
(A) सभी लोग/ All people
(B) कुछ लोग लक्ष्यों को प्राप्त करने के लिए सच्चाई को छोड़कर झूठ का सहारा लेते हैं/Some people resort to lies instead of truth to achieve their goals.
(C) मालूम नहीं/Don't know.

11. जीवन में सच्चाई को महत्व देना चाहिए और इसे अपनाने का प्रयास किया जाना चाहिए/Truth should be given importance in life and efforts should be made to adopt it.
(A) हाँ/Yes
(B) कभी-कभी/Sometime
(C) सच्चाई को अपनाने से नाकारात्मक प्रभाव पड़ता है/ Adopting truth has negative effects.

12. बुनियादी ढांचे और नागरिकों की जिम्मेदारी भी जल-जमाव की समस्या का कारण हो सकती है/Infrastructure and responsibility of citizens can also be the cause of waterlogging problem.
(A) कभी नहीं/Never (B) हाँ/Yes
(C) प्रशासन इस समस्या को नजरअंदाज करती है/The administration ignores this problem.

13. शिक्षा विभाग को गुणवत्तापूर्ण शिक्षा प्रदान करने के लिए प्रयास किया जाना चाहिए। जिससे विद्यार्थी अपने लक्ष्यों को प्राप्त कर सके/The education department should make efforts to provide quality education so that students can achieve their goals.
(A) शिक्षा विभाग के पास पर्याप्त धन की कमी है/The education department lacks sufficient funds.
(B) प्रशिक्षित शिक्षक की कमी है/There is a shortage of trained teachers.
(C) गुणवत्ता में सुधार होने से विद्यार्थियों को बेहतर शिक्षा मिलेगी/Improvement in quality will provide better education to students.

14. विद्यार्थियों को उज्जवल भविष्य की इमारत बुलंद करने के लिए तत्पर रहना चाहिए/Students should be ready to build a bright future.
(A) हमेशा/Always
(B) कभी-कभी/Sometimes
(C) विद्यार्थियों के पास काफी चुनौतियाँ है/Students have many challenges.

15. आप एक स्टेशन मास्टर हैं और आपके स्टेशन के किसी प्लेटफार्म पर बम रखे होने की सूचना मिलती है तो आप क्या कदम उठायेंगे/If you are a station master and you get information about a bomb being placed on a platform of your station, what steps will you take?
(A) मैं तुरंत पुलिस (RPF) और सुरक्षा एजेंसियों को सूचित करूँगा/I will immediately inform the police (RPF) and security agencies.
(B) आने वाली ट्रेन को सुरक्षित करूँगा/I will secure the incoming train.
(C) उस शहर के थाना को सूचित करूँगा/I will inform the police station of that city.

16. स्टेशन मास्टर की भूमिका रेलवे के संचालन और प्रबंधन जैसे यात्रियों की सुविधा और सुरक्षा सुनिश्चित करने में महत्वपूर्ण योगदान होती है/The role of the station master plays an important role in the operation and management of railways, such as ensuring the convenience and safety of passengers.
(A) हाँ/Yes
(B) मालूम नहीं/I don't know
(C) स्टेशन मास्टर की व्यस्तता ज्यादा होती है/The station master is very busy.

17. एक पदाधिकारी या कर्मचारी का आचरण होना चाहिए/The conduct of an officer or employee should be-
(A) भ्रष्टाचार युक्त/Corrupt
(B) भ्रष्टाचार से मुक्त/Corruption-free
(C) दोनों के बीच/In between

18. यदि आपका चयन भारतीय रेलवे में स्टेशन मास्टर के पद पर हुआ है और प्रशिक्षण लेते समय कई प्रश्न समझ में नहीं आते हैं तो आप क्या कदम उठाऐंगे/If you have been selected for the post of Station Master in Indian Railways and you do not understand many questions during training, what steps will you take?
(A) स्टेशन मास्टर की प्रशिक्षण काफी कठिन होती है/The training of Station Master is quite difficult.
(B) प्रश्नों को विस्तार से समझाने के लिए आग्रह करेंगे/ You will request to explain the questions in detail.
(C) ऑनलाईन विडियो देखेंगे/You will watch online videos.

19. समस्या का समाधान करने से आत्मविश्वास और उत्साह बढ़ता है/Solving a problem increases confidence and enthusiasm-

(A) समस्या का समाधान मुश्किल है/Solution of problem is difficult.
(B) हमेशा/Always
(C) मालूम नहीं/I do not know.

20. आप अपने कार्यो का निष्पादन संलग्नता, बुद्धिमता व दक्षता के साथ करने का प्रयास करते हैं/You try to perform your tasks with involvement, intelligence and efficiency.
(A) कभी-कभी/Sometime
(B) कार्यो का निष्पादन से कार्यो में गुणवत्ता आती है/ Execution of tasks brings quality in work.
(C) नहीं/ No

21. यदि सफर के दौरान आपके पास बैठा व्यक्ति बेहोश हो जाता है, तो आप क्या कदम उठाऐंगे/If the person sitting next to you faints during the journey, what steps will you take?
(A) प्राथमिक चिकित्सा प्रदान करेंगे/Provide first aid
(B) सहायता के लिए रेलवे कर्मचारी को सूचना देंगे/ Inform the railway employee for help
(C) अगले रेलवे स्टेशन में रिपोर्ट करेंगे/Report at the next railway station

22. उत्तरदायित्व ग्रहण करने से कौशन और ज्ञान में सुधार करने का अवसर मिलता है/Taking responsibility provides an opportunity to improve skills and knowledge
(A) हमेशा/Always
(B) कभी-कभी/Sometime
(C) ऐसा नहीं/Not so

23. किसी भी कर्मचारी को पहली बार गलती करने पर नौकरी से निकाल देना चाहिए/Any employee should be fired from the job for the first time if he makes a mistake
(A) सुधरने का अवसर देना चाहिए/He should be given an opportunity to improve
(B) दूसरे कर्मचारी को गलती करने का मनोबल बढ़ेगा/ The morale of other employees to make mistakes will increase
(C) मालूम नहीं/Don't know

24. यदि आप स्टेशन मास्टर है और आपके परिसर में एक व्यक्ति नशे में बेहोश दिखता है तो आप क्या कदम उठाऐंगे/If you are a station master and you see a person unconscious due to intoxication in your premises, what steps will you take?
(A) उसे उठाकर रेल परिसर से बाहर फेंक देंगे/Pick him up and throw him out of the railway premises
(B) नजरअंदाज करेंगे/Ignore him
(C) पुलिस (RPF) को सूचना देंगे/Inform the police (RPF)

25. रेल कर्मचारी को रेलवे परिसर में यात्रियों का सुविधा, सुरक्षा मुहैया कराना चाहिए/Railway employee should provide convenience, security to passengers in railway premises
(A) कभी-कभी/Sometime
(B) नहीं/No
(C) हमेशा/Always

26. कार्य के दौरान कर्मचारियों को शिष्टाचार के साथ नही बाते करनी चाहिए/Employees should not talk politely during work
(A) कभी-नहीं/Never
(B) कभी-कभी/Sometimes
(C) हाँ/Yes

27. अच्छे विचार जीवन में सकारात्मक परिवर्तन ला सकते हैं/Good thoughts can bring positive changes in life.
(A) कभी-नहीं/Never (B) हाँ/Yes
(C) मालूम नहीं/Don't know

28. नए सुझावों का सम्मान करने से नए विचारों का आदान-प्रदान करने का अवसर मिलता है/Respecting new suggestions gives an opportunity to exchange new ideas.
(A) निश्चित रूप से/Definitely
(B) कह नहीं सकते/Can't say
(C) दोनों के बीच/Between the two

29. सत्य को छिपाना काफी आसान होता है/It is very easy to hide the truth
(A) हाँ/Yes
(B) कभी नहीं/Never
(C) दोनों के बीच/Between the two

30. झूठ बोलने से दूसरों का विश्वास खोना और रिश्ते को नुकसान पहुँचता है/Lying leads to losing the trust of others and damages the relationship.
(A) कभी-कभी/Sometime
(B) हाँ/Yes
(C) दोनों के बीच/Between the two

31. गलतियों को स्वीकार करना और उनसे सीखने के लिए तैयार रहना चाहिए/One should be ready to admit mistakes and learn from them.
(A) गलतियाँ किसी से भी हो सकती है/Anyone can make mistakes.
(B) कुछ लोग गलती स्वीकार नहीं करते/Some people do not admit mistakes.
(C) हाँ/Yes

32. गलतियों से सीखने से आत्मविश्वास और प्रदर्शन में सुधार कर सकते हैं/Learning from mistakes can improve confidence and performance.
   (A) कभी-कभी/Sometime
   (B) सीखने की इच्छा खत्म हो जाती है/The desire to learn ends.
   (C) अवश्य/must

33. दूसरों की नकारात्मक बातों को नजरअंदाज करना चाहिए/Negative comments of others should be ignored
   (A) हमेशा/Always
   (B) ऐसा नहीं/not like this
   (C) कभी नहीं/Never

34. सफलता से हमारी पहचान और प्रतिष्ठा भी बढ़ जाती/Success also increases our identity and prestige
   (A) कभी-कभी/ Sometime
   (B) अवश्य/must
   (C) दोनों के बीच/ in between

35. शुद्ध विचार और अच्छे इरादे वाले व्यक्ति को समाज में सम्मान मिलता है/A person with pure thoughts and good intentions gets respect in the society
   (A) ऐसे व्यक्ति सम्मान योग्य है/Such a person is worthy of respect.
   (B) कभी नहीं/Never
   (C) हो सकता है/may

PRACTICE SET-8

Total Ques.- 35
Time - 15 Min.

निर्देश : (प्रश्न 1–35) प्रत्येक प्रश्न के लिए एक कथन (Statement) दी होती है और इसके नीचे उत्तर के तीन विकल्प दिए जाते हैं। उम्मीदवारों को अपने बुद्धिमता और निर्णय के आधार पर सही उत्तर के लिए कोई एक विकल्प का चयन कर उत्तर-पत्रक में दिए गए गोले को काला या माउस की सहायता से क्लिक (Click) करें।

Direction : (Questions 1–35) : For each question, a statement is given, followed by three answer options. Candidates should select the correct option based on their intelligence and judgment and fill the corresponding circle on the answer sheet or click using the mouse.

1. समस्याओं का समाधान ढूँढने और सकारात्मक तरीके से आगे बढ़ने पर ध्यान देना चाहिए/We should focus on finding solutions to problems and moving forward in a positive way.
(A) समस्या का समाधान आसान नहीं/Solution to a problem is not easy
(B) सकारात्मक सोच से समस्या का समाधान हो सकता है/ Problems can be solved with positive thinking.
(C) मालूम नहीं/Don't know

2. विज्ञान की प्रगति को बढ़ावा देने और इससे प्राप्त लाभों को सभी तक पहुँचाने की कोशिश करनी चाहिए/We should try to promote the progress of science and make its benefits available to everyone
(A) विज्ञान शिक्षा को बढ़ावा नहीं देना चाहिए/Science education should not be promoted
(B) नए तकनीक आने से काम के प्रति रूझान में कमी आएगी/With the advent of new technology, the interest in work will decrease
(C) विज्ञान के लाभ से नए तकनीकों का उपयोग कर सकेंगे/With the benefits of science, we will be able to use new technologies

3. किसी भी क्षेत्र में सफलता के लिए निरंतर कार्य करना आवश्यक है, ताकि अपने लक्ष्यों को प्राप्त कर सके/To be successful in any field, it is necessary to work continuously so that we can achieve our goals.
(A) लक्ष्य प्राप्त करने के लिए कड़ी मेहनत की आवश्यकता है/Hard work is required to achieve the goal
(B) सफलता के लिए जश्न मनाना चाहिए/Success should be celebrated
(C) मालूम नहीं/Don't know

4. सफलता से आपकी पहचान और प्रतिष्ठा में वृद्धि होती है/ Success increases your identity and reputation
(A) हाँ/Yes
(B) कभी-कभी/Sometimes
(C) कुछ लोगों को पसंद नहीं है/Some people don't like it

5. ईमानदारी से संघर्ष करना जीवन में आगे बढ़ने के लिए आवश्यक है/Struggle with honesty is necessary to move forward in life
(A) ईमानदारी से कार्य करने पर जीवन सफल हो जाता है/ Life becomes successful if you work honestly
(B) मालूम नहीं/Don't know
(C) ईमानदारी से कार्य करने पर लक्ष्य की प्राप्ति नहीं होती/ Goal is not achieved if you work honestly.

6. उच्च तनाव, निजी जीवन की गुणवत्ता को कम कर सकता है/High stress can reduce the quality of personal life.
(A) ध्यान और मनन तनाव को कम नहीं करते हैं/ Meditation and contemplation do not reduce stress
(B) ऐसे तनाव से मनुष्य की आयु कम होने लगती है/ Such stress reduces the life span of a person
(C) मालूम नहीं/Don't know

7. साइबर अपराध एक बड़ा खतरा है जिसके लिए हमें जागरूक और सावधान रहना चाहिए/Cyber crime is a big threat for which we should be aware and careful.
(A) ऑनलाइन पेमेंट का उपयोग ज्यादा नहीं करें/Do not use online payment too much.
(B) मजबूत पासवर्ड का उपयोग करना चाहिए/ Strong passwords should be used(
(C) दोनों/Both

8. गुणवत्ता वाली शिक्षा सभी के लिए सुलभ और सस्ती होने से न केवल व्यक्तियों को लाभ होगा बल्कि समाज और देश के विकास में भी मदद मिलेगी/Quality education being accessible and affordable to all will not only benefit individuals but will also help in the development of society and the country.
(A) शिक्षा काफी महगी है/Education is very expensive.
(B) अच्छी शिक्षा ग्रामीण क्षेत्रों में नहीं पहुँचती है/Good education does not reach rural areas
(C) ऐसी शिक्षा से रोजगार के अवसर बढ़ेगा/Such education will increase employment opportunities

9. अपनी क्षमता और विश्वास करने से लक्ष्य की प्राप्ति होती है/By believing in your ability, the goal is achieved.
(A) हाँ/Yes (B) कभी-कभी/Sometime
(C) नहीं/No

10. भविष्य में कोई रेल दुर्घटना नहीं होनी चाहिए/There should not be any railway accident in future.
(A) कभी-कभी/Sometime
(B) हाँ/Yes
(C) रेल दुर्घटना कुछ क्षेत्रों में होती है/Railway accidents happen in some areas.

11. अचानक आपके कार्यालय में बिजली चली जाती है तो आप/If suddenly there is a power cut in your office, then you
(A) बिजली आने का इंतजार करते हैं/Wait for the power to come back.
(B) तुरंत टेक्नीशियन को सूचित करते हैं/Immediately inform the technician
(C) वास्तविक स्थिति का जायजा लेंगे/Take stock of the actual situation

12. कुछ लोग राजनीति को चुनौतिपूर्ण क्षेत्र मानते हैं/Some people consider politics a challenging field.
(A) हाँ/Yes
(B) सभी लोगों को राजनीति में जाने का अधिकार है/Everyone has the right to go into politics
(C) मालूम नहीं/Don't know.

13. बढ़ते तापमान के दुष्प्रभाव के कारण त्वचा कैंसर जैसी बिमारियाँ फैल रही है/Diseases like skin cancer are spreading due to the ill effects of rising temperatures.
(A) कैंसर रोगी की संख्या में वृद्धि नहीं हो रही है/The number of cancer patients is not increasing
(B) कुछ क्षेत्रों में /In some areas
(C) बढ़ते तापमान को रोकने की आवश्यकता है/There is a need to stop the rising temperature

14. बेहतर समाज निर्माण के लिए जनता और पुलिस के बीच आपसी समन्वय होना चाहिए/There should be mutual coordination between the public and the police for building a better society
(A) भरोसा की संभावना बढ़ेगी/The possibility of trust will increase
(B) दोनों एक-दूसरे को सहयोग नहीं करते हैं/Both do not cooperate with each other
(C) जनता जागरूक नहीं है/The public is not aware

15. जनता को पुलिस पर विश्वास बढ़ानी चाहिए ताकि पुलिस सहयोग के लिए प्रोत्साहित हो सके/The public should increase their trust in the police so that the police can be encouraged to cooperate
(A) नहीं/No (B) हाँ/Yes
(C) मालूम नहीं/Don't know

16. राजनीति में जाने से समाज के लिए योगदान और लोगों के जीवन में सुधार ला सकते हैं/By joining politics, one can contribute to the society and improve the lives of the people.
(A) कभी-कभी/Sometime
(B) हाँ/Yes
(C) चुनौतिपूर्ण काम है/It is a challenging job

17. स्वच्छता के लिए जागरूकता फैलानी चाहिए/Awareness should be spread for cleanliness
(A) हमेशा/Always (B) नहीं/No
(C) कभी-कभी/Sometime

18. नियमित व्यायाम करना और शारीरिक गतिविधियों में भाग लेना चाहिए/One should exercise regularly and participate in physical activities.
(A) नियमित व्यायाम संभव नहीं/Regular exercise is not possible
(B) कुछ लोग व्यायाम करते हैं/Some people exercise
(C) व्यायाम करने से मन संतुलित रहता है/Exercise keeps the mind balanced

19. यदि कोई कार्य पूर्ण नहीं होता है तो उसे उम्मीद छोड़ देनी चाहिए/If a task is not completed, one should give up hope.
(A) कभी-कभी/Sometime
(B) हाँ/Yes (C) नहीं/No

20. प्रगतिशील सोच के साथ बाधाएँ और असफलता भी सफलता का मूल-मंत्र बन जाता है/With progressive thinking, obstacles and failure also become the key to success.
(A) कभी-कभी/Sometime
(B) हाँ/Yes (C) ऐसा नहीं/Not so

21. नई चीजें सीखने और अपने कौशल को विकसित करने की इच्छा रखनी चाहिए/One should have the desire to learn new things and develop one's skills
(A) हमेशा/Always
(B) सीखने को पर्याप्त समय नहीं है/There is not enough time to learn
(C) कभी-कभी/Sometimes

22. तकनीकि शिक्षा और कौशल विकास से लोगों को बेहतर रोजगार के अवसर मिल सकते हैं/Technical education and skill development can provide better employment opportunities to people.
(A) कम पैसे देकर अधिक काम करवाते हैं/They get more work done by paying less money
(B) काम की गारंटी नहीं है/Work is not guaranteed
(C) इस अवसर से तंग जीवन में सुधार लाने में मदद मिल सकती है/This opportunity can help improve the cramped life

23. गरीबी को प्रभावी ढंग से निपटने के लिए आय को बढ़ाने की आवश्यकता है/Income needs to be increased to deal with poverty effectively
(A) आय बढ़ाने से गरीबी मिट जाएगी/Increasing income will eradicate poverty
(B) गरीब लोगों में शिक्षा की कमी है/Poor people lack education
(C) इससे निपटने के लिए आय का श्रोत विकसित करना पड़ेगा/To deal with this, a source of income will have to be developed

24. स्वच्छ भारत मिशन ने कचरे की समस्या को काफी हद तक सुलझाया है/Swachh Bharat Mission has solved the problem of garbage to a great extent
(A) स्वच्छता देश में काफी आवश्यक है/Cleanliness is very important in the country
(B) इस समस्या को दूर करने के लिए डिजिटल तकनीकों का उपयोग करना होगा/Digital technologies will have to be used to overcome this problem
(C) काफी कचरे की समस्या दूर हो चुकी है/Much of the problem of garbage has been solved

25. अपने कार्य को अधिक प्रभावी ढंग से पूरा करने के लिए एक रूपरेखा बनाने की आवश्यकता होती है/There is a need to create a framework to complete your work more effectively
(A) हाँ/Yes
(B) व्यर्थ समय लगता है/It takes time to waste
(C) कभी नहीं/Never

26. विकृत व्यक्तित्व वाले लोग आक्रामक व्यवहार प्रदर्शित करते हैं/People with personality disorder display aggressive behaviour
(A) नहीं/No
(B) कभी-कभी/Sometimes
(C) अक्सर/Often

27. आर्थिक असमानता समाज में तनाव और आक्रोश पैदा करती है/Economic inequality creates tension and resentment in the society
(A) हाँ/Yes (B) नहीं/No
(C) कभी-नहीं/Never

28. बुरे सामाजिक वातावरण में विकृत व्यक्तित्व का निर्माण होता है/A deformed personality is formed in a bad social environment
(A) कभी-नहीं/Never
(B) मालूम नहीं/Don't know (C) हाँ/Yes

29. कोई आपसे भीख मांगता है तो आप क्या करते हैं/What do you do if someone begs from you?
(A) देने से पहले सोचते हैं/You think before giving
(B) देना चाहिए/You should give
(C) नहीं देना चाहिए/You should not give

30. जो खेलने में होशियार होते हैं वे पढ़ने में कमजोर होते हैं/Those who are good in sports are weak in studies
(A) ऐसा हो सकता है/This can happen
(B) मालूम नहीं/Don't know
(C) पढ़ने का समय नहीं मिलता है/You don't get time to study

31. अगर आपसे गलती होती है तो आप सरलता से स्वीकार करना चाहेंगे/If you make a mistake, you would like to admit it easily
(A) हमेशा/Always (B) कभी नहीं/Never
(C) कभी-कभी/Sometime

32. व्यक्ति के व्यवहार से उनके व्यक्तित्व का पता चलता है/ A person's behavior reveals his personality
(A) सुन्दरता से व्यक्तित्व का मापन होता है/Personality is measured by beauty
(B) व्यक्ति का व्यवहार अच्छा होना चाहिए/A person's behavior should be good
(C) संवाद, आदतें और रूटीन से व्यक्तित्व का पता चलता है/Personality is revealed by communication habits and routine

33. कुछ यात्रियों को अधिक आरामदायक और सुविधाजनक यात्रा के लिए रेलवे को महंगी और शानदार गाड़ियों की संख्या बढ़ानी चाहिए/For more comfortable and convenient travel of some passengers, the railways should increase the number of expensive and luxurious trains.
(A) हाँ/Yes
(B) किराया काफी महंगी हो जाएगी/The fare will become very expensive
(C) संभव नहीं/Not possible

34. सकारात्मक दृष्टिकोण वाले व्यक्ति दूसरे की छोटी-मोटी बातें अपने दिल पे नहीं लेते है/People with a positive attitude do not take small things of others to heart
(A) मालूम नहीं/I don't know
(B) सकारात्मक दृष्टिकोण वाले व्यक्ति दिल के मजबूत होते हैं/People with a positive attitude are strong at heart
(C) अपने संबंधों में समस्याएँ पैदा कर सकता है/May create problems in our relations

35. भारत को विश्व के देशों से सैन्य-सामरिक क्षमताओं में प्रतिस्पर्द्धा करनी चाहिए/India should compete with the countries of the world in military strategic capabilities
(A) कभी नहीं/Never (B) हाँ/Yes
(C) जानकारी नहीं/Don't know

PRACTICE SET-9

Total Ques.- 35
Time - 15 Min.

निर्देश : (प्रश्न 1–35) प्रत्येक प्रश्न के लिए एक कथन (Statement) दी होती है और इसके नीचे उत्तर के तीन विकल्प दिए जाते हैं। उम्मीदवारों को अपने बुद्धिमता और निर्णय के आधार पर सही उत्तर के लिए कोई एक विकल्प का चयन कर उत्तर-पत्रक में दिए गए गोले को काला या माउस की सहायता से क्लिक (Click) करें।

Direction : (Questions 1–35) : For each question, a statement is given, followed by three answer options. Candidates should select the correct option based on their intelligence and judgment and fill the corresponding circle on the answer sheet or click using the mouse.

1. रेलवे को अपनी सुरक्षा प्रणालियों और प्रक्रियाओं में सुधार करने के लिए निरंतर प्रयास करनी चाहिए/Railways should make continuous efforts to improve their safety systems and procedures
   (A) रेलवे कर्मचारियों की लापरवाही होती है/Railway employees are negligent
   (B) इससे दुर्घटना होने की संभावना घटेगी/This will reduce the chances of accidents
   (C) मालूम नहीं/Don't know
2. रेलवे दुर्घटनाओं को रोकने के लिए रेलवे द्वारा कई कदम उठाए जाते हैं/Many steps are taken by the Railways to prevent railway accidents
   (A) कभी नहीं/Never (B) हाँ/Yes
   (C) रेलवे ट्रैक की सफाई जरूरी है/Cleaning of railway tracks is necessary
3. अच्छे सुझाव का सम्मान करना चाहिए/Good suggestions should be respected
   (A) कभी नहीं/Never
   (B) कभी-कभी/Sometimes
   (C) दोनों के बीच/Between the two
4. बच्चों को अच्छे संस्कार ही देना चाहिए/Children should be given good values
   (A) हाँ/Yes
   (B) कभी-कभी/Sometimes
   (C) हमेशा/Always
5. सत्य को छुपाना काफी आसान होता है/It is very easy to hide the truth
   (A) कभी नहीं/Never
   (B) कभी-कभी/Sometimes
   (C) हाँ/Yes
6. समाज के सबल वर्ग को सरकारी लाभ इसलिए नहीं मिलता है, क्योंकि वे समाज को सशक्त एवं प्रभावशाली वर्ग से हैं, इस कथन से आप/The strong section of the society does not get government benefits because they belong to the powerful and influential section of the society. With this statement you
   (A) सहमत हैं/agree
   (B) असहमत हैं/disagree
   (C) दोनों के बीच/Between the two
7. जो राजनीति के कार्यकर्त्ता हैं वे समाजसेवी भी है/Those who are workers in politics are also social workers
   (A) कभी नहीं/Never
   (B) हो सकता है/Can be
   (C) समाजसेवी राजनेता नहीं हो सकता है/A social worker cannot be a politician
8. गरीबों, कमजोरों तथा असहायों के प्रति करूणा व संवेदनशीलता का दृष्टिकोण रखना चाहिए/We should have an attitude of compassion and sensitivity towards the poor, the weak and the helpless
   (A) दोनों के बीच/Between two
   (B) कभी-कभी/Sometimes
   (C) हमेशा/Always
9. यदि कोई कार्य पूर्ण नहीं होता है तो हमें उम्मीद छोड़ देनी चाहिए/If a task is not completed, we should give up hope
   (A) कभी नहीं/Never (B) नहीं/No
   (C) हो सकता है/Maybe
10. आप अपने कार्यो का निष्पादन पूरी संलग्नता, बुद्धिमता व दक्षता के साथ करते हैं/You perform your tasks with full involvement, intelligence and efficiency
    (A) कभी-कभी/Sometimes
    (B) कभी नहीं/Never
    (C) हमेशा/Always
11. राष्ट्र की सुरक्षा, राष्ट्र की जनता पर निर्भर करती है/The security of the nation depends on the people of the nation
    (A) हमेशा/Always
    (B) राष्ट्र की सुरक्षा जरूरी है/Security of the nation is important
    (C) राष्ट्र की जनता जागरूक है/The people of the nation are aware

12. अपने देश के लिए समर्पण और प्रेम एक महत्वपूर्ण भावना है, जो हमें अपने देश के प्रति जिम्मेदार और संवेदनशील बनाती है/Dedication and love for our country is an important feeling, which makes us responsible and sensitive towards our country
(A) हाँ/Yes
(B) कभी-कभी/Sometimes
(C) लोगों में समर्पण की भावना नहीं दिखती है/People do not show the feeling of dedication

13. अपने देश के प्रति इतिहास, संस्कृति और मूल्यों के बारे में जागरूकता फैलानी चाहिए/Awareness should be spread about the history, culture and values of our country
(A) हाँ/Yes (B) कभी नहीं/Never
(C) देश के इतिहास काफी पुराना है/The history of the country is very old

14. प्रेम एक भावनात्मक जुड़ाव है जो हमें एक-दूसरे को साथ जोड़ता है/Love is an emotional bond that connects us with each other
(A) हमेशा/Always
(B) कभी-कभी/Sometimes
(C) कभी-नहीं/Never

15. बढ़ती डिजिटल अर्थव्यवस्था में आत्मनिर्भरता अपने लक्ष्यों और उद्देश्यों को प्राप्त करने के लिए स्वयं पर निर्भर होना है/ In the growing digital economy, self-reliance is to depend on oneself to achieve one's goals and objectives
(A) हाँ/Yes (B) ऐसा नहीं/Not so
(C) हो सकता है/May be

16. आत्मनिर्भरता अपने लक्ष्यों और उद्देश्यों को निर्धारित करने में मदद करता है/Self-reliance helps in setting one's goals and objectives
(A) हमेशा/Always
(B) कभी-कभी/Sometimes
(C) लक्ष्य और उद्देश्य निर्धारित नहीं हो पाते हैं/Goals and objectives are not determined

17. प्रेम मनुष्य का स्वभाव है, लेकिन इसे अभिव्यक्त करने की प्रक्रिया में वह विषय-वस्तु में उलझ जाता है/Love is a human being's nature, but in the process of expressing it, he gets entangled in the subject matter
(A) हाँ/Yes (B) नहीं/No
(C) मालूम नहीं/Don't know

18. अपनी गलतियों से सीखकर भी आगे बढ़ना चाहिए/One should move forward even after learning from one's mistakes
(A) कभी-कभी/Sometimes
(B) कभी नहीं/Never
(C) मालूम नहीं/Don't know

19. मंदिरों और मस्जिदों की संपत्ति का इस्तेमाल लोकहित में होना चाहिए/The property of temples and mosques should be used for public welfare
(A) कभी नहीं/Never (B) हाँ/Yes
(C) दोनों के बीच/Between two

20. मंदिरों और मस्जिदों से प्राप्त आमदनी लोकहित में इस्तेमाल करनी चाहिए/The income from temples and mosques should be used for public welfare
(A) कभी-नहीं/Never
(B) गरीबों के बीच वितरित करनी चाहिए/Distributed among the poor
(C) सरकार को हस्तक्षेप नहीं करनी चाहिए/The government should not interfere

21. अगर आपसे कोई गुस्से में बात करता है, तो उसे/If someone talks to you in anger, then
(A) नजरअंदाज करेंगे/Ignore him
(B) समझाने की कोशिश करेंगे/Try to explain
(C) प्रशासन को सूचना देंगे/Inform the administration

22. जब हम दूसरों की मदद करते हैं, तो हम अक्सर यह अपेक्षा रखते हैं कि वे बदले में हम मदद करेंगे/When we help others, we often expect that they will help us in return
(A) हाँ/Yes (B) नहीं/No
(C) निराश हो जाते हैं/Get disappointed

23. गलतियों से सीखने से हमारी निर्णय लेने की क्षमता में सुधार होता है/Learning from mistakes improves our decision-making ability.
(A) कभी नहीं/Never
(B) गलती स्वीकार नहीं करनी चाहिए/One should not admit mistakes
(C) हमेशा/Always

24. अपनी गलतियों से सीखना और आगे बढ़ना एक महत्वपूर्ण जीवन कौशल है/Learning from your mistakes and moving forward is an important life skill
(A) बिल्कुल सही/Absolutely correct
(B) गलतियाँ कभी भी किसी से हो सकती है/Mistakes can happen to anyone at any time
(C) कभी-कभी गलतियाँ हो जाती है/Sometimes mistakes happen

25. गरीब लोगों की मदद करने से उनकी स्थिति में सुधार के साथ-साथ सकारात्मक परिवर्तन आ सकता है/Helping poor people can bring about positive change along with improving their condition.

(A) कभी-नहीं/Never (B) अवश्य/Must
(C) गरीबी मिट नहीं सकती/Poverty cannot be eradicated

26. गरीब लोगों को रोजगार के अवसर प्रदान करने से उनकी मूलभूत आवश्यकताओं को पूरा करने में मदद मिल सकती है/Providing employment opportunities to poor people can help in fulfilling their basic needs.
(A) हमेशा/Always
(B) ऐसा नहीं/Not so
(C) गरीब लोगों के रोजगार की कमी नहीं है/There is no lack of employment for poor people

27. सरकार को कानून और संविधान के बारे में जागरूकता अभियान चलाये ताकि नागरिकों को जानकारी मिल सके/The government should run awareness campaigns about the law and the constitution so that citizens can get information
(A) कभी-कभी/Sometime
(B) कभी नहीं/Never
(C) कानून बदल नहीं सकता/The law cannot be changed

28. कानून और संविधान को सरल भाषा में लिखने से नागरिकों को समझने में आसानी होगी/Writing laws and constitution in simple language will make it easier for citizens to understand
(A) कठिन भाषा से नागरिक समझ नहीं पाते हैं/Citizens are not able to understand difficult language
(B) भारत का संविधान ज्यादा विस्तृत है/The Constitution of India is more detailed
(C) मालूम नहीं/Don't know

29. सरकार को प्लास्टिक बैग पर प्रतिबंध लगाना चाहिए/The government should ban plastic bags.
(A) कभी नहीं/Never
(B) बेरोजगारी बढ़ेगी/Unemployment will increase
(C) ऐसा होना चाहिए/This should happen

30. प्लास्टिक उपयोग कम करने से जल-प्रदूषण नियंत्रित किया जा सकता है/Water pollution can be controlled by reducing plastic use
(A) हाँ/Yes (B) कभी नहीं/Never
(C) मालूम नहीं/Don't know

31. दैनिक जीवन में कुछ वस्तुएँ के इस्तेमाल करने से पहले पर्यावरण पर प्रभाव के बारे में सोचना चाहिए/Before using some things in daily life, we should think about the impact on the environment
(A) कभी नहीं/Never
(B) कभी-कभी/Sometimes
(C) जानकारी नहीं/Don't know

32. भारतीय रेलवे को अपने देश के नागरिकों को समय-समय पर सुविधा और सुधार बढ़ानी चाहिए/Indian Railways should provide facilities and improvements to the citizens of the country from time to time
(A) रेलवे कर्मचारी सुधार नहीं चाहते/Railway employees do not want improvements
(B) कभी नहीं/Never
(C) बेहतर सुविधाओं की कमी है/There is a lack of better facilities

33. भारतीय रेलवे को आर्थिक स्थिति सुधारने के लिए व्यापार और वाणिज्य को विस्तार करनी चाहिए/Indian Railways should expand trade and commerce to improve the economic condition
(A) कभी नहीं/Never
(B) आर्थिक विकास में बढ़ोतरी होगी/Economic development will increase
(C) नहीं/No

34. गलत कार्यों के परहेज करने से आपकी सामाजिक प्रतिष्ठा बढ़ती है/Avoiding wrong deeds increases your social prestige
(A) कभी-कभी ऐसा करना चाहिए/Sometimes you should do this
(B) हमेशा/Always
(C) गलत कार्य करने के लिए लोग मजबूर हो जाते हैं/People are forced to do wrong things

35. आत्मनियंत्रण रखने से आप अपने विचारों और कार्यों को नियंत्रित कर सकते हैं/By having self-control, you can control your thoughts and actions
(A) नहीं/No
(B) कभी नहीं/Never
(C) हमेशा/Always

PRACTICE SET-10

Total Ques.- 35
Time - 15 Min.

निर्देश : (प्रश्न 1-35) प्रत्येक प्रश्न के लिए एक कथन (Statement) दी होती है और इसके नीचे उत्तर के तीन विकल्प दिए जाते हैं। उम्मीदवारों को अपने बुद्धिमता और निर्णय के आधार पर सही उत्तर के लिए कोई एक विकल्प का चयन कर उत्तर-पत्रक में दिए गए गोले को काला या माउस की सहायता से क्लिक (Click) करें।

Direction : (Questions 1–35) : For each question, a statement is given, followed by three answer options. Candidates should select the correct option based on their intelligence and judgment and fill the corresponding circle on the answer sheet or click using the mouse.

1. मैं ऐसे लोगों को पसंद करते हैं, जो दूसरे की भावनाओं को समझते और सहानुभूति रखते हैं/I like people who understand and sympathize with the feelings of others
   (A) कभी-कभी/Sometimes
   (B) हमेशा/Always (C) कभी नहीं/Never
2. सकारात्मक लोगों के साथ समय बिताने से आप गलत कार्यों से परहेज कर सकते हैं/By spending time with positive people, you can avoid wrong actions
   (A) नकारात्मक सोच वाले व्यक्ति दुष्ट स्वभाव के भी हो सकते हैं/People with negative thinking can also be of evil nature
   (B) दोनों/Both
   (C) गलत कार्यो से हमेशा दूर रहना चाहिए/One should always stay away from wrong actions
3. जो व्यक्ति अपने आप को श्रेष्ठ समझता है/The person who considers himself superior
   (A) घमंड या अहंकार का प्रदर्शन करता है/Displays pride or arrogance
   (B) दूसरे की भावनाओं को नहीं समझता/Does not understand the feelings of others
   (C) दोनों/Both
4. विनम्र व्यक्ति जो सामाजिक संबंधों में सुधार के साथ-साथ अच्छे संबंध बनाने की कोशिश करता है/A humble person who tries to improve social relations as well as build good relations
   (A) विनम्र की यही पहचान है/This is the identity of a humble person
   (B) दूसरों की भावनाओं और विचारों का सम्मान करना/ Respecting the feelings and thoughts of others
   (C) दोनों/Both
5. अक्सर ट्रेन छूट जाना एक आम समस्या है/Missing the train often is a common problem.
   (A) समय प्रबंधन की कमी के कारण/Due to lack of time management
   (B) यातायात में फंसना या रास्ता भटक जाना/Getting stuck in traffic or getting lost
   (C) दोनों/Both
6. आप अपने निर्णयों पर तुरंत कदम उठाने की कोशिश करते हैं/You try to act on your decisions immediately
   (A) कभी-कभी/Sometimes
   (B) कभी नहीं/Never
   (C) मालूम नहीं/Don't know
7. विकल्पों का मूल्यांकन करने से आप सर्वोत्तम निर्णय ले सकते हैं/By evaluating the options, you can make the best decision
   (A) नहीं/No
   (B) कह नहीं सकते/Can't say
   (C) कभी-कभी/Sometimes
8. नियमों का पालन करने से समाज में व्यवस्था और अनुशासन बनाए रखने में मदद करता है/Following the rules helps in maintaining order and discipline in the society
   (A) कभी नहीं/Never
   (B) हमेशा/Always
   (C) निष्पक्षता से नियम पालन नहीं होगा/Fairness will not follow the rules
9. रेलवे नियमों का सम्मान करना जिम्मेदार नागरिक का कर्त्तव्य है/Respecting railway rules is the duty of a responsible citizen
   (A) हाँ/Yes
   (B) कभी-कभी/Sometimes
   (C) दोनों/Both
10. नियमों का पालन करने से सुरक्षा में सुधार, दुर्घटनाओं और अपराधों को रोकने में काफी मदद मिलती है/Following rules helps a lot in improving safety, preventing accidents and crimes
    (A) हाँ/Yes
    (B) मालूम नहीं/Don't know
    (C) नियमों की जानकारी की कमी है/There is lack of knowledge of rules

11. आप जल्द घबरा जाते हैं/You get nervous easily
   (A) कभी नहीं/Never
   (B) हमेशा/Always
   (C) मालूम नहीं/Don't know

12. आप मुश्किल हालात में जल्द फैसले लेते हैं/You should take quick decisions in difficult situations
   (A) फैसले लेने से पहले सभी पहलुओं पर विचार किया जाना चाहिए/All aspects should be considered before taking a decision
   (B) सभी जानकारी और विकल्पों का मूल्यांकर किया जाना चाहिए/All information and options should be evaluated
   (C) दोनों/Both

13. जीवन में सफलता प्राप्त करने के लिए खुद पर भरोसा करना एक महत्वपूर्ण गुण है/Trusting yourself is an important quality to achieve success in life
   (A) इससे लक्ष्यों की प्राप्ति होती है/It helps in achieving goals
   (B) दोनों/Both
   (C) इससे आत्मविश्वास बढ़ता हुआ दिखता है/It seems to increase self-confidence

14. जब हम गलत काम को करते हुए देखते हैं तो गुस्सा हमें कारवाई करने का प्रेरित करता है/When we see someone doing something wrong, anger motivates us to take action
   (A) मालूम नहीं/I don't know
   (B) कभी-नहीं/Never
   (C) कभी-कभी/Sometimes

15. दिए गए कार्य को समय पर समाप्त कर दिया जाना चाहिए/The given work should be completed on time
   (A) कार्य को समय पर पूरा करना अनिवार्य है/It is mandatory to complete the work on time
   (B) कार्य का समय सीमा के अंदर समाप्त होना चाहिए/The work should be completed within the time limit
   (C) दोनों/Both

16. चुनौतिपूर्ण काम से नए अनुभव और विकास के अवसर मिलते हैं/Challenging work provides opportunities for new experiences and growth
   (A) हमेशा/Always (B) ऐसा नहीं/Not so
   (C) कभी-नहीं/Never

17. जिम्मेदारी वाली काम से मैं स्थिरता और अनुशासन सीखता हूँ/I learn stability and discipline from responsible work.
   (A) कभी नहीं/Never
   (B) कभी-कभी/Sometime
   (C) नहीं/No

18. हमेशा काम ईमानदारी और समर्पण के साथ करना चाहिए/Work should always be done with honesty and dedication
   (A) इससे सच्चाई और मेहनत दिखती है/This shows honesty and hard work
   (B) कभी-कभी/Sometime
   (C) लोग काम को नजरअंदाज करते हैं/People ignore work

19. विपरीत परिस्थितियों में निर्णय लेने में खुद को सक्षम मानते हैं/You consider yourself capable of taking decisions in adverse circumstances
   (A) इस परिस्थिति में भुलने की संभावना ज्यादा होती है/There is a high possibility of making mistakes in this situation
   (B) हाँ/Yes
   (C) घबराहट बढ़ जाती है/Anxiety increases

20. भ्रष्ट कर्मचारियों को नौकरी से निष्कासित कर देना चाहिए/Corrupt employees should be expelled from their jobs
   (A) हाँ/Yes
   (B) ऐसा नहीं निष्पक्ष जाँच कराना चाहिए/This should not be done, an impartial investigation should be conducted
   (C) भ्रष्टाचार में वृद्धि हुई है/Corruption has increased

21. सरकारी कार्यों में पारदर्शिता बढ़ाने के लिए ठोस कदम उठानी चाहिए/Concrete steps should be taken to increase transparency in government work
   (A) कभी-नहीं/Never
   (B) हमेशा/Always
   (C) जुर्माना बढ़ाना चाहिए/The penalty should be increased

22. आप ड्युटी को पहली प्राथमिकता देते हैं/You give first priority to duty.
   (A) अक्सर/Often
   (B) कभी-कभी/Sometime
   (C) कभी-नहीं/Never

23. ड्यूटी के समय निजी वार्तालाप करना चाहिए/One should have private conversations while on duty
   (A) कभी कभी/Sometime
   (B) कभी नहीं/Never
   (C) हमेशा/Always

24. कभी-कभी अपने विचारों और भावनाओं को व्यक्त करने से हमारे रिश्ते मजबूत होते जाते हैं/Sometimes expressing our thoughts and feelings strengthens our relationships

(A) नहीं/No
(B) रिश्ते मजबूत करने के लिए विचार और भावना खुली रखनी चाहिए/To strengthen relationships, we should keep our thoughts and feelings open
(C) कभी नहीं/Never

25. आप ज्यादा किसे महत्व देते हैं/What do you give more importance to?
(A) आराम से काम करना/Working comfortably
(B) समय पर काम पूरा करना/Completing work on time
(C) अच्छे रिश्ते बनाना/Building good relationships

26. अगर आपसे कोई काम करने में गलती होती है तो आप क्या करेंगे/If you make a mistake while doing any work, what will you do?
(A) छिपा लेंगे/Hide it
(B) गलती को बताकर सुधार करेंगे/Point out the mistake and correct it
(C) नजरअंदाज करेंगे/will ignore

27. मैं दबाव की स्थिति में भी शांत रहकर काम कर सकता हूँ/ I can work calmly even under pressure
(A) हमेशा/Always
(B) कभी नहीं/Never
(C) कानून बदल नहीं सकता/cannot change the law

28. दूसरों को आदेश देने से ज्यादा स्वयं काम करना पसंद है/ I like to work myself more than ordering others
(A) आदेश का पालन करना चाहिए/Must follow orders
(B) हाँ/Yes (C) कभी नहीं/Never

29. अगर कोई नियम-कानून तोड़ता है तो मैं उसे नजरअंदाज कर देता हूँ/If someone breaks the rules and laws, I ignore them
(A) हाँ/Yes (B) कभी नहीं/Never
(C) देखता रहता हूँ/Keep watching

30. आप नई परिस्थितियों में ढलने में अधिक आत्मविश्वास और सक्षम महसूस करते हैं/You feel more confident and capable of adapting to new situations
(A) नहीं/No (B) कभी नहीं/Never
(C) हाँ/Yes

31. अपना काम छोड़कर मुसीबत में घीरे एक व्यक्ति की मदद करनी हो तो आप क्या चुनेंगे/If you have to leave your work and help a person in trouble, what will you choose?
(A) उसे तुरंत मदद करने की कोशिश करेंगे/Try to help him immediately
(B) मदद के लिए दूसरे व्यक्ति को कहेंगे/Ask another person for help
(C) नजरअंदाज करेंगे/Ignore

32. निष्पक्ष न्याय देने से पहले सभी पहलूओं और परिणामों पर विचार करना आवश्यक है/It is necessary to consider all aspects and consequences before giving fair justice
(A) हमेशा/Always
(B) कभी कभी/Sometime
(C) दोनों में से कोई नहीं/Neither of the two

33. क्या स्टेशन मास्टर को ईमानदार और भरोसेमंद होने चाहिए/ Should a station master be honest and trustworthy?
(A) कभी कभी/Sometime
(B) कभी नहीं/Never
(C) अवश्य/Certainly

34. क्या आप अपने फायदे के लिए झूठ बोल सकते हैं/ Can you lie for your own benefit?
(A) कभी नहीं/Never
(B) कभी कभी/Sometime
(C) कुछ समय के लिए/For some time

35. आपके सहकर्मी से कोई गलती हो जाए तो आप क्या करेंगे/ What will you do if your colleague commits a mistake?
(A) उसे गलती का एहसास कराकर सुधारने की कोशिश करूँगा/I will try to correct him by making him realize his mistake
(B) उसे अकेला छोड़ दूँगा/I will leave him alone
(C) अधिकारी से शिकायत करूँगा/I will complain to the officer

PRACTICE SET-11

Total Ques.- 35
Time - 15 Min.

निर्देश : (प्रश्न 1-35) प्रत्येक प्रश्न के लिए एक कथन (Statement) दी होती है और इसके नीचे उत्तर के तीन विकल्प दिए जाते हैं। उम्मीदवारों को अपने बुद्धिमता और निर्णय के आधार पर सही उत्तर के लिए कोई एक विकल्प का चयन कर उत्तर-पत्रक में दिए गए गोले को काला या माउस की सहायता से क्लिक (Click) करें।

Direction : (Questions 1–35) : For each question, a statement is given, followed by three answer options. Candidates should select the correct option based on their intelligence and judgment and fill the corresponding circle on the answer sheet or click using the mouse.

1. अन्याय के खिलाफ प्रत्येक इंसान को आवाज उठानी चाहिए, ताकि समाज में सकारात्मक परिवर्तन भी ला सकते है/Every person should raise their voice against injustice, so that positive change can be brought about in society.
(A) नहीं/No
(B) कभी नहीं/Never (C) कभी कभी/Sometime

2. क्या गलत तरीके से पैसा कमाना बेहतर होता है?/Is it better to earn money through unfair means?
(A) कभी नहीं/Never (B) हाँ/Yes
(C) कभी कभी/Sometime

3. गलत तरीके से पैसे कमाने से न केवल चरित्र खराब होता है बल्कि समाज में नकारात्मक प्रभाव पड़ता है/Earning money through unfair means not only tarnishes character but also has a negative impact on society.
(A) वर्तमान समय में यही मांग है/This is what is demanded in the present times.
(B) नैतिक रूप से यह गलत है/It is morally wrong
(C) दोनों/Both

4. क्या ट्रेन प्लेटफार्म पर आने से पहले यात्री परेशान हो जाते हैं/Do passengers become anxious before the train arrives at the platform?
(A) नहीं/No
(B) कभी कभी/Sometime (C) दोनों/Both

5. अगर कोई कर्मचारी लगातार ड्यूटी में लापरवाही करते हुए दिखा तो आप की प्रतिक्रिया/If an employee is consistently neglecting their duties, how would you react?
(A) नजरअंदाज करेंगे/Ignore
(B) स्वयं काम करेंगे/Do the work yourself
(C) रिपोर्ट करेंगे/Report

6. आप समय की पाबंदी को महत्व देते हैं/You value punctuality
(A) कभी-कभी/Sometimes
(B) हमेशा/Always (C) नहीं/No

7. किसी को गलत काम करते हुए देखता हूँ तो मुझे गुस्सा आ जाता है/I get angry when I see someone doing something wrong
(A) कभी नहीं/Never
(B) नहीं/No (C) कभी-कभी/Sometime

8. ट्रेन विलंब होने से यात्री गुस्से में होते हैं, तो आपकी प्रतिक्रिया/If passengers are angry because a train is delayed, your reaction will be:
(A) अनदेखी करेंगे/Ignore it
(B) यात्रियों को शांत करने के लिए घोषणा करेंगे/Make an announcement to calm the passengers
(C) बहाना करेंगे/Make an excuse

9. खुद के लाभ से ज्यादा समाज के हित के बारे में सोचना चाहिए/You should prioritize the welfare of society over your own benefit
(A) कभी नहीं/Never (B) हमेशा/Always
(C) जानकारी नहीं/I don't know

10. अच्छे चरित्र वाले मनुष्य को समाज में सम्मान और इज्जत मिलता है/A person with good character gets respect and honor in the society
(A) कभी कभी/Sometime
(B) कभी नहीं/Never
(C) ऐसे व्यक्ति काफी गरीब होते हैं/Such people are very poor

11. क्या अच्छे संचार कौशल से आप अपने विचारों को प्रभावी ढंग से व्यक्त कर सकते हैं/Do good communication skills allow you to express your ideas effectively?
(A) नहीं/No (B) हमेशा/Always
(C) व्यक्त करना नहीं आता/I don't know how to express myself

12. चुनौतियों का सामना करने और असफलताओं से सीखने की क्षमता होनी चाहिए/One should have the ability to face challenges and learn from failures
(A) चुनौतियों का सामना मुश्किल है/Facing challenges is difficult

(B) असफल व्यक्ति काफी निराश होते हैं/People who fail are very disappointed
(C) हमेशा/Always

13. सरकारी कार्यों में पारदर्शिता बढ़ाने के लिए सख्त कदम उठाना चाहिए/Strict measures should be taken to increase transparency in government work
(A) कभी-नहीं/Never
(B) नहीं/No
(C) सरकारी कार्यों में भ्रष्टाचार की वृद्धि हुई है/Corruption in government work has increased

14. गरीबों को आर्थिक सहायता प्रदान करने से उन्हें अपनी बुनियादी जरूरतों को पूरा करने में मदद मिल सकती है/Providing financial assistance to the poor can help them meet their basic needs.
(A) गरीबों का उत्थान बहुत मुश्किल है/Uplifting the poor is very difficult
(B) गरीबी मिट नहीं सकती/Poverty cannot be eradicated
(C) मदद करने से कुछ सकारात्मक परिवर्तन आ सकता है/Helping can bring about some positive change

15. जो व्यक्ति ईमानदार, न्यायप्रिय और दयालु होते हैं, वे सकारात्मक प्रभावशाली वाले होते है/People who are honest, fair, and kind have positive influences
(A) कभी-नहीं/Never
(B) ऐसा नहीं/It's not like that
(C) हो सकता है/It's possible

16. अनुशासन और नियम के बिना जीवन में लक्ष्य पाना मुश्किल है/It's difficult to achieve goals in life without discipline and rules
(A) बिल्कुल सही/Absolutely right
(B) कभी-नहीं/Never
(C) कह नहीं सकते/Can't say

17. क्या जानबुझकर गलती होने पर भी अपने सहकर्मी को सहयोग करेंगे/Would you cooperate with your colleague even if he makes a mistake intentionally
(A) कभी-कभी/Sometime
(B) नहीं/No
(C) नजरअंदाज करेंगे/Ignore

18. क्या सभी दयालु व्यक्ति धनवान होते हैं/Are all kind people rich ?
(A) हाँ/Yes
(B) धनी व्यक्ति मदद नहीं करते हैं/Rich people don't help
(C) कुछ अमीर लोग दयालु भी होते है/Some rich people are kind too

19. अनुशासित व्यक्ति अपने कार्य को व्यवस्थित और समय प्रबंधन के साथ करता है/A disciplined person does their work systematically and with time management
(A) कभी-कभी/Sometime
(B) नहीं/No
(C) ऐसे व्यक्ति अपने जीवन में सफल हो सकते हैं/Such people can be successful in their lives

20. आजकल बिना किसी का नुकसान किए आपका लाभ नहीं हो सकता है/Nowadays, you can't benefit without harming someone
(A) हाँ/Yes (B) ऐसा नहीं/Not so
(C) मालूम नहीं/I don't know

21. भ्रम से जन्मी आशंका और अविश्वास आपसी रिश्ते को कमजोर बना देती है/Fear and distrust born of confusion weakens relationships
(A) नहीं/No
(B) हमेशा रिश्ते मजबूत होते हैं/Relationships always become stronger
(C) भ्रम फैलाने से रिश्ते भी टूटते हैं/Spreading confusion also breaks relationships

22. रिश्ते को मजबूत और मधुर बनाए रखने के लिए खुलकर ईमानदारी से और प्यार के साथ बातचीत करना बहुत जरूरी है/Open, honest, and loving communication is essential to maintaining a strong and harmonious relationship
(A) इससे आपसी कड़वाहट दूर हो जाती है/This eliminates bitterness
(B) ईमानदारी पर भरोसा करना चाहिए/Honesty should be trusted
(C) दोनों/Both

23. एक-दूसरे की भावनाओं को कद्र करना चाहिए ताकि मन में गलतफहमी की जगह विश्वास पैदा हो सके/We should respect each other's feelings so that trust can be created instead of misunderstanding
(A) नहीं/No
(B) कभी कभी/Sometime (C) हाँ/Yes

24. छोटे-छोटे मतभेद को आसानी से सुलझा देनी चाहिए/Minor differences should be resolved easily
(A) कभी नहीं/Never
(B) नहीं/No (C) हमेशा/Always

25. रिश्ते में अगर कोई बात खटक रही हो तो उसे दबाने के बजाय प्यार और इज्जत के साथ सामने रखना ही सबसे उत्तम रास्ता है/If something is bothering you in a relationship, the best way is to bring it up with love and respect rather than suppressing it.
(A) हाँ/Yes (B) कभी नहीं/Never
(C) कभी-कभी/Sometime

26. बिना सबुत के न विश्वास सही है, न शक, दोनों ही रिश्तों को कमजोर कर देते हैं/Without proof, neither trust nor suspicion is correct; both weaken relationships
(A) मालूम नहीं/ (B) हाँ/Yes
(C) कभी-कभी/Sometime

27. बेवजह शक रिश्तों में दरार डाल देता है/Unnecessary suspicion creates rifts in relationships
(A) हाँ/Yes (B) कभी नहीं/Never
(C) मालूम नहीं/I don't know

28. समय का सही उपयोग काम को आसान और तेज बना देता है/Proper use of time makes work easier and faster
(A) कभी नहीं/Never
(B) कभी-कभी/Sometime
(C) मालूम नहीं/I don't know

29. सफलता पाने के लिए मेहनत के साथ-साथ समय का सही उपयोग जरूरी है/To achieve success, along with hard work, proper use of time is essential
(A) हाँ/Yes (B) ऐसा नहीं/Not so
(C) कह नहीं सकती/Can't say

30. बिना संघर्ष कोई बड़ा सपना हकीकत नहीं बनता, क्योंकि कठिनाईयाँ ही इंसान को महान बनाती है/No big dream becomes reality without struggle, because difficulties are what make a person great
(A) नहीं/No
(B) कह नहीं सकते/Can't say
(C) बिल्कुल सही/Absolutely right

31. चुनौतियाँ हमें मजबुत और काबिल बनाती है/Challenges make us strong and capable
(A) हमेशा/Always (B) नहीं/No
(C) कभी नहीं/Never

32. कभी-कभी सफलता किस्मत से भी मिल जाती है, लेकिन उसे सभालने के लिए मेहनत जरूरी है/Sometimes success comes by luck, but hard work is necessary to maintain it
(A) सफलता के लिए मेहनत के साथ-साथ किस्मत भी जरूरी है/Along with hard work, luck is also necessary for success
(B) ऐसा नहीं/Not so
(C) केवल किस्मत से ही सफलता मिलती है/Success is achieved only by luck

33. अनुशासन और समय प्रबंधन की आदत डालनी चाहिए/Discipline and time management should be cultivated
(A) हमेशा/Always
(B) कभी कभी/Sometime
(C) कभी नहीं/Never

34. समय पर काम समाप्त होने से आत्मविश्वास बढ़ता है और तनाव कम होता है/Finishing work on time increases self-confidence andreduces stress
(A) यह प्रसन्नता को दर्शाता है/It reflects happiness
(B) कठिन काम में समय ज्यादा लगता है/Difficult tasks take more time
(C) ऐसा नहीं/Not so

35. नियमों का पालन करना बोझ नहीं, बल्कि जिम्मेदारी है जो इंसान को सच्चा और भरोसेमंद बनाता है/Following rules is not a burden, but a responsibility thatmakes a person truthful and trustworthy
(A) जिम्मेदारी नहीं लेनी चाहिए/One should not take responsibility
(B) नियमों का पालन करना काफी कठिन है/Following rules is very difficult
(C) बिल्कुल सही/Absolutely correct

PRACTICE SET-12

Total Ques.- 35
Time - 15 Min.

निर्देश : (प्रश्न 1-35) प्रत्येक प्रश्न के लिए एक कथन (Statement) दी होती है और इसके नीचे उत्तर के तीन विकल्प दिए जाते हैं। उम्मीदवारों को अपने बुद्धिमता और निर्णय के आधार पर सही उत्तर के लिए कोई एक विकल्प का चयन कर उत्तर-पत्रक में दिए गए गोले को काला या माउस की सहायता से क्लिक (Click) करें।

Direction : (Questions 1–35) : For each question, a statement is given, followed by three answer options. Candidates should select the correct option based on their intelligence and judgment and fill the corresponding circle on the answer sheet or click using the mouse.

1. समय के प्रति लापरवाह व्यक्ति पर भरोसा किया जाना चाहिए/A person who is careless about time should be trusted
(A) कभी कभी/Sometime
(B) कभी नहीं/Never (C) हमेशा/Always

2. अधिकारी और नियम के अनुरूप काम करना सिर्फ कर्त्तव्य नहीं, बल्कि सफलता और सम्मान की पहली सीढ़ी है/Working in accordance with the authorities and rules is not just a duty, but the first step to success and respect
(A) अधिकारी काम करनेवाले को ही परेशान करते हैं/ Officials harass those who work
(B) अधिकारी पर भरोसा नहीं है/I don't trust the authorities
(C) हाँ/Yes

3. घबराहट के बजाय धैर्य के साथ सही निर्णय लेना चाहिए/ Instead of panicking, one should make the right decisions with patience.
(A) नहीं/No
(B) दिमाग शांत नहीं रहता/The mind is not calm
(C) हमेशा/Always

4. स्थिरता और धैर्य के साथ काम करने से सफलता की मंज़िल तक पहुँच सकते हैं/Working with consistency and patience can lead to success
(A) कभी नहीं/Never
(B) स्थिरता और धैर्य दोनों सफलता की नींव है/ Consistency and patience are both the foundation of success
(C) लोगों के पास धैर्य की कमी है/People lack patience

5. रेल सुरक्षा की मजबूती अनुशासन और समय पालन पर ही टिकी है/The strength of railway safety depends on discipline and punctuality
(A) बिल्कुल सही/Absolutely correct
(B) ऐसा नहीं/Not so
(C) हो सकता है/It could be

6. रेल सुरक्षा की एक छोटी-सी लापरवाही भी बड़ी दुर्घटना का कारण बन सकती है/Even a small negligence in railway safety can cause a major accident
(A) कभी-कभी/Sometimes
(B) हमेशा/Always (C) कभी नहीं/Never

7. तनाव के समय खुद को स्थिर रखने की कोशिश करनी चाहिए ताकि निर्णय लेने और गलत प्रतिक्रिया से बचने में मदद मिलती है/One should try to remain composed during times of stress, as this helps in decision-making and avoids wrong reactions
(A) अक्सर लोग तनाव में गलत निर्णय ले लेते हैं/People often make wrong decisions under stress
(B) तनाव में घबराहट नहीं आती है/Stress does not cause panic
(C) जानकारी नहीं है/I don't know

8. क्या आप आदेशों का पालन करने में विश्वास रखते हैं/Do you believe in following orders
(A) नहीं/No (B) हाँ/Yes
(C) कभी-कभी/Sometime

9. संदेह ज्ञान व्यक्ति को भी परेशान कर देता है/Doubt can even trouble a knowledgeable person
(A) कभी नहीं/Never
(B) ज्ञानी व्यक्ति कभी परेशान नहीं होते हैं/Wise people are never troubled
(C) अवश्य/Sure

10. कभी-कभी ज्ञानी व्यक्ति भी बेचैनी, अस्थिरता और निर्णय न ले पाने की स्थिति में पहुँच जाता है/Sometimes, even a wise person finds himself in a state of restlessness, instability, and indecisiveness
(A) मालूम नहीं/I don't know
(B) हाँ/Yes (C) ऐसा नहीं/

11. जब जिम्मेदारी ज्यादा हो तो बड़े अधिकारी या अनुभवी व्यक्ति से प्रेरणा लेनी चाहिए/When the responsibility is high, one should seek inspiration from a senior or experienced person

(A) जिम्मेदारी नहीं लेनी चाहिए/One should not take responsibility
(B) कभी नहीं/Never
(C) हमेशा/Always

12. क्या आपको मुश्किल स्थिति में घबराहट होती है/Do you get nervous in difficult situations?
(A) हाँ/Yes (B) हमेशा/Always
(C) कभी-कभी/Sometime

13. टीम का नेतृत्व करना कठिन कार्य है, परन्तु क्या इसे आप पसंद करते हैं/Leading a team is a difficult task, but do you enjoy it?
(A) कभी नहीं/Never (B) हाँ/Yes
(C) कभी-कभी/Sometime

14. नेतृत्व आपको धैर्य, निर्णय, क्षमता और संवाद कौशल को और मजबूत करता है/Leadership strengthens your patience, judgment, competence, and communication skills.
(A) टीम में काम करने से अनुभव नहीं मिलता है/ Working in a team doesn't give you experience
(B) हाँ/Yes (C) नहीं/No

15. अच्छा नेता हमेशा जिम्मेदारी और न्यायप्रिय होने चाहिए/A good leader should always be responsible and fair
(A) हाँ/Yes
(B) मालूम नहीं/I don't know
(C) नेता कभी अच्छा नहीं होता है/A leader is never good

16. भारत डिजिटल अर्थव्यवस्था में अपनी स्थिति को मजबूत बनाने के लिए आत्मनिर्भर हो रहा है/India is becoming self-reliant to strengthen its position in the digital economy
(A) ऐसा नहीं/No (B) अवश्य/Of course
(C) कभी-नहीं/Never

17. अनुशासित व्यक्ति अक्सर अपने सिद्धांतों और मूल्यों पर चलते हैं जिससे समाज में अपमानित नहीं होना पड़ता है/ Disciplined people often adhere to their principles and values, which prevents them from being humiliated in society
(A) इससे सहमत हैं/I agree
(B) इससे असहमत हैं/I disagree
(C) मालूम नहीं/I don't know

18. नियमों का पालन करने से हमें सुरक्षा, स्थिरता और सफलता मिलती है/Following rules provides us with security, stability, and success
(A) हाँ/Yes (B) कभी नहीं/Never
(C) मालूम नहीं/Don't know

19. नियम तोड़ने के परिणामस्वरूप हमें न केवल व्यक्तिगत नुकसान हो सकता है, बल्कि संगठन पर नकारात्मक प्रभाव पड़ सकता है/Breaking rules can result in personal harm, but also negatively impact the organization
(A) नहीं/No
(B) कभी-कभी/Sometime
(C) हो सकता है/It may happen

20. रेलवे स्टेशन पर खासकर भीड़भाड़ वाले क्षेत्रों में सावधानी व धैर्यपूर्वक चलना चाहिए/One should walk carefully and patiently at a railway station, especially in crowded areas
(A) चोरी होने का डर होता है/There is a fear of theft
(B) अपने सामान पर ध्यान रखना चाहिए/One should take care of one's belongings
(C) दोनों/Both

21. कठिन परिश्रम से हमें अपने लक्ष्यों को प्राप्त करने में मदद मिलती है/Hard work helps us achieve our goals
(A) कभी-कभी/Sometime
(B) कभी नहीं/Never
(C) कठिन परिश्रम करना एक अच्छा विकल्प है/ Working hard is a good choice

22. संघर्षशील व्यक्ति जीवन में सफलता प्राप्त करने के लिए चुनौतियों का सामना और कड़ी मेहनत के लिए तैयार रहते हैं/Struggling people are ready to face challenges and work hard to achieve success in life
(A) ऐसे व्यक्ति अंदर से काफी मजबूत होते हैं/Such people are very strong from within
(B) कभी नहीं/Never
(C) सभी को सफलता नहीं मिलती है/Not everyone achieves success

23. भारतीय रेलवे के लिए समय का पालन करना हमेशा एक बड़ी चुनौती रही है/Punctuality has always been a big challenge for Indian Railways
(A) अवश्य/Of course (B) नहीं/No
(C) ट्रेनों का प्रबंधन एक समस्या है/Managing trains is a problem

24. जिसने संघर्ष किया है, वह जीवन की हर परिस्थिति में खुद को अच्छा और मजबूत रख सकता है/One who has struggled can keep himself strong and healthy in every situation of life
(A) संघर्षशील व्यक्ति हमेशा साहसी होता है/A struggling person is always courageous
(B) ऐसे व्यक्ति बुरे परिस्थितियों से नहीं डरते/Such people are not afraid of bad circumstances
(C) दोनों/Both

25. जिसने आँधियों में नाव चलाई है, वह छोटी लहरों से कभी नहीं डरता है/One who has sailed a boat in storms is never afraid of small waves
(A) आत्मविश्वासी होता है/Is self-confident
(B) हर स्थिति में शांत रहना सीखता है/Learns to remain calm in every situation
(C) दोनों/Both

26. संघर्ष इंसान को तोड़ता नहीं, बल्कि गढ़ता है/Struggle does not break a person, but rather shapes him
(A) कभी-कभी/Sometime
(B) ऐसा नहीं/Not so (C) हमेशा/Always

27. रेलवे में समय की लापरवाही सिर्फ देर नहीं है, यह सुरक्षा की बड़ी कीमत बन सकती है/In railways, punctuality isn't just about delay; it can be a huge safety risk
(A) हाँ/Yes (B) ऐसा नहीं/Not so
(C) कभी-कभी/Sometime

28. लापरवाही से लिया गया फैसला भी बड़े नुकसान में बदल सकता है/A careless decision can also result in significant losses
(A) कभी-कभी/Sometime
(B) कभी नहीं/Never (C) हमेशा/Always

29. जिम्मेदारी बढ़ना मतलब बोझ नहीं, बल्कि आपको और सतर्क होकर सही दिशा-निर्देश देना होता है/Increasing responsibility doesn't mean burden, but rather requires you to be morevigilant and provide proper guidance
(A) हाँ/Yes (B) नहीं/No
(C) मालूम नहीं/I don't know

30. रेल सुरक्षा केवल मशीनों पर निर्भर नहीं बल्कि कर्मचारियों के अच्छे तालमेल बनाए रखने से है/Railway safety doesn't depend solely on machines, but rather on maintaining good coordination among employees
(A) यात्रियों की सुरक्षा बढ़ानी चाहिए/Passenger safety should be increased
(B) शिक्षित कर्मचारी की कमी/Lack of educated staff
(C) हाँ/Yes

31. आप दूसरों से आदेश मानने के बजाय खुद निर्णय लेना पसंद करते हैं/You prefer to make your own decisions rather than accept orders from others
(A) कभी नहीं/Never
(B) निर्णय लेने में संकोच करते हैं/Hesitant to make decisions
(C) कभी-कभी/Sometime

32. आप अपने काम की जिम्मेदारी दूसरों पर डालते हैं/You shift the responsibility for your work onto others
(A) कभी नहीं/Never (B) हाँ/Yes
(C) कभी कभी/Sometime

33. स्टेशन मास्टर सिर्फ आदेश देने वाला नहीं, बल्कि सतर्क, धैर्यवाद और संतुलित दिमाग वाला होना चाहिए/The station master should not only be a person who gives orders, but also a person who is alert, patient, and level-headed
(A) ऐसा नहीं होने पर दुर्घटना की संभावना बढ़ेगी/ Failure to do so will increase the likelihood of accidents
(B) मालूम नहीं/I don't know
(C) इनकी ड्यूटी केवल आदेश देने वाला होता है/Their duty is to simply give orders

34. स्टेशन पर होनेवाली छोटी-सी घटना को गंभीरता से लेनी चाहिए/Even minor incidents at the station should be taken seriously
(A) हमेशा/Always (B) कभी नहीं/Never
(C) नहीं/No

35. अगर नियम कठोर और सख्त हो तो उसका अनुपालन करना हमारा कर्त्तव्य है/If the rules are strict and stringent, it is our duty to comply
(A) ऐसा नहीं/Not so
(B) हाँ/Yes
(C) नियम बदले जाते हैं/Rules change

PRACTICE SET-13

Total Ques.- 35
Time - 15 Min.

निर्देश : (प्रश्न 1–35) प्रत्येक प्रश्न के लिए एक कथन (Statement) दी होती है और इसके नीचे उत्तर के तीन विकल्प दिए जाते हैं। उम्मीदवारों को अपने बुद्धिमता और निर्णय के आधार पर सही उत्तर के लिए कोई एक विकल्प का चयन कर उत्तर-पत्रक में दिए गए गोले को काला या माउस की सहायता से क्लिक (Click) करें।

Direction : (Questions 1–35) : For each question, a statement is given, followed by three answer options. Candidates should select the correct option based on their intelligence and judgment and fill the corresponding circle on the answer sheet or click using the mouse.

1. शिक्षा वह कला है जो कठिन ज्ञान को सरल तरीके से सीखने में बदल देती है/Education is the art of transforming complex knowledge into simple learning
(A) हाँ/Yes
(B) ऐसा नहीं/Not so
(C) शिक्षा का विस्तार होनी चाहिए/Education should be expanded

2. जब सीखने की प्रक्रिया आसान हो तो आत्मविश्वास बढ़ती है/When the learning process is easy, self-confidence increases.
(A) हाँ/Yes (B) कभी नहीं/Never
(C) कभी-कभी/Sometime

3. शिक्षा हमें समस्या हल करने का तार्किक तरीके सिखाती है/Education teaches us logical ways to solve problems
(A) ऐसा नहीं/Not so
(B) निश्चित रूप से/Certainly
(C) हो सकता है/Maybe

4. समस्या आने पर उसे सुलझाने का प्रयास करना एक सकारात्मक एवं व्यवहारिक दृष्टिकोण है/Trying to solve a problem when it arises is a positive and practical approach
(A) कभी नहीं/Never
(B) कभी-कभी/Sometimes (C) हाँ/Yes

5. शिकायत करने की बजाय हल ढूँढने की दिशा में ऊर्जा लगानी चाहिए/Instead of complaining, energy should be focused on finding solutions
(A) अवश्य/Sure
(B) हो सकता है/Maybe (C) नहीं/No

6. हर समस्या हमें नया अनुभव और कौशल सिखाती है/Every problem teaches us new experiences and skills
(A) नहीं/No
(B) गंभीर समस्या कठिनाईयाँ पैदा करती है/Serious problems create difficulties
(C) हमेशा/Always

7. दोस्तों या परिवार के साथ हंसी साझा करने से रिश्तों में अपनापन भी बढ़ता है/Sharing laughter with friends or familyincreases closeness in relationships
(A) तनाव में भी कमी आती है/It also reduces stress
(B) रिश्ते खराब होते हैं/Relationships deteriorate
(C) कभी नहीं/Never

8. भरोसेमंद व्यक्ति से बात करने से मन का बोझ हल्का हो जाता है/Talking to a trusted person lightens the burden on the mind
(A) कभी कभी/Sometime
(B) कभी नहीं/Never
(C) ऐसा नहीं/Not so

9. दुखद घटनाऐं बार-बार याददाश्त करने से गहराई तक बस जाती है/Repeatedly remembering tragic events leaves a deep impact
(A) नहीं/No
(B) दु:खद घटनाऐं व्यायाम करने से कम होती है/ Memories of disappointment are like deep wounds
(C) निराशा की यादें गहरी चोट की तरह होती है/ Sad events are reduced by exercise

10. अनावश्यक बातों को भूल जाना एक अच्छा और सेहतमंद विचार है/It is a good and healthy idea to forget unnecessary things
(A) तनाव बढ़ता है/It increases stress
(B) कभी-कभी/Sometime
(C) हाँ/Yes

11. आलोचना करना एक नकारात्मक गतिविधि है लेकिन सही शब्दों और सही भावना के साथ यही आलोचना दवा का भी काम करती है/Criticism is a negative act, but with the right words and in the right spirit, it can also act as medicine
(A) हाँ/Yes (B) ऐसा नहीं/Not so
(C) मालूम नहीं/I don't know

12. लगातार दोष निकालना सामने वाले का आत्मविश्वास तोड़ देता है/Constantly finding fault breaks the other person's self-confidence
(A) तनाव में कमी आती है/It reduces stress
(B) कभी नहीं/Never
(C) इसे नाराजगी बढ़ती है/It increases resentment

13. रेलवे जैसी सेवाओं में मोबाईल उपयोग के लिए सख्त गाईडलाईन होती है, उनका अनुपालन अनिवार्य है/Services like the railways have strict guidelines for mobile phone use, and compliance with them is mandatory
(A) हमेशा/Always
(B) कभी-कभी/Sometime
(C) कभी नहीं/Never

14. काम और जिम्मेदारियों को सही समय पर करनी चाहिए/Work and responsibilities should be completed on time
(A) हाँ/Yes
(B) ऐसा नहीं/Not so
(C) लाभप्रद होनी चाहिए/It should be beneficial

15. स्टेशन मास्टर, लोको पायलट, गार्ड सभी को 'सेफ्टी फर्स्ट' की ट्रेनिंग दी जानी चाहिए/Station masters, loco pilots, and guards should all be trained in 'Safety First'
(A) हमेशा/Always
(B) कभी-कभी/Sometime
(C) व्यवस्था नहीं है/There is no provision

16. सुरक्षा नियमों की अनदेखी करने पर कानूनी कार्रवाई की जानी चाहिए/Legal action should be taken for ignoring safety rules
(A) कभी नहीं/Never
(B) समय देनी चाहिए/Time should be given
(C) हमेशा/Always

17. अपने विचार स्पष्ट रूप से रखने से आत्मसम्मान मजबूत होता है/Expressing your thoughts clearly strengthens self-esteem
(A) मुश्किल शब्दों से बचें/Avoid difficult words
(B) कभी नहीं/Never
(C) लंबी-लंबी बाते न करें/Don't talk at length

18. दया और सहानुभूति लोगों के बीच भरोसा और अपनापन बढ़ाती है/Kindness and empathy increase trust and closeness between people
(A) व्यक्ति को इज्जत और सम्मान मिलता है/A person receives respect and appreciation
(B) खुद में भी खुशी और संतोष बढ़ता है/Happiness and contentment increase within oneself
(C) दोनों/Both

19. समाज में गलत कार्यों को देखकर कुछ लोग गलत रास्ता भी चुन सकते हैं/Seeing wrongdoings in society may lead some peopleto choose the wrong path
(A) गलत कार्यों की संख्या बढ़ रही है/The number of wrongdoings is increasing
(B) कुछ लोग गुस्से में गलत कदम उठा सकते हैं/Some people may take wrong steps out of anger
(C) ऐसा नहीं/Not So

20. अपराध केवल कानून तोड़ता नहीं, बल्कि इंसानों को दिल और समाज की नींव को भी हिला देता है/Crime not only breaks the law, but also shakes the hearts of people and the foundations of society
(A) कभी नहीं/Never
(B) मालूम नहीं/I don't know
(C) हाँ/ Yes

21. नदियों का संरक्षण और पुनर्जीवन समाज, प्रकृति और आनेवाली पीढ़ियों के लिए बेहद महत्वपूर्ण है/Conservation and rejuvenation of rivers is extremely important for society, nature, and future generations
(A) हाँ/Yes
(B) हो सकता है/Maybe (C) नहीं/No

22. नदियों का अतिक्रमण और अंधाधुंध रेत खनन पर रोक लगानी चाहिए/River encroachment and indiscriminate sand miningshould be stopped
(A) हाँ/Yes
(B) रेत की कीमत में वृद्धि हुई है/The price of sand has increased
(C) बेरोजगारी में कमी आई है/Unemployment has decreased

23. लोगों को नदियों में कचरा नहीं डालने के लिए शिक्षित करना चाहिए/People should be educated not to dump garbage in rivers
(A) कभी-कभी/Sometime
(B) कभी नहीं/Never
(C) मालूम नहीं/Don't know

24. प्रशासन की सक्रियता अपराधियों के हौसले तोड़ती है और समाज में सुरक्षा का विश्वास जगाती है/The administration's proactiveness breaks the morale of criminals andinstills a sense of security in society
(A) कभी नहीं/Never (B) हाँ/Yes
(C) प्रशासन की सक्रियता की कमी है/There is a lack of proactiveness on the part of the administration

25. तेज कार्रवाई अपराधियों को डर और सजा का एहसास

कराती है/Swift action makes criminals feel fear and punishment
(A) नहीं/No
(B) इससे अपराधों में कमी आती है/It reduces crime
(C) मालूम नहीं/I don't know

26. क्या सक्रिय प्रशासन लोगों में सुरक्षा और भरोसा बनाए रखता है/Does active governance maintain security and trust among the people?
(A) कभी-नहीं/Never
(B) कभी-कभी/Sometimes
(C) नहीं/No

27. लगातार नाकारात्मक सोचने से दिमाग में/Constantly thinking negative thoughts
(A) उदासी बढ़ती है/increases sadness in the mind
(B) सही फैसला लेना मुश्किल होता है/makes it difficult to make the right decisions
(C) दोनों/Both

28. नकारात्मक सोच वाले व्यक्ति से नजदीकियाँ बनाए रखने चाहिए/One should maintain close relations with people who have negative thoughts
(A) हमेशा/Always
(B) कभी-कभी/Sometimes
(C) कभी नहीं/Never

29. योजनाबद्ध तरीके से काम करना अनावश्यक भटकाव/Working in a planned manner leads to unnecessary distractions
(A) कम होता है/less
(B) ज्यादा होता है/more
(C) दोनों/Both

30. बच्चों में उम्र बढ़ने के साथ-साथ उनमें तर्क विश्लेषण और निर्णय लेने की क्षमता धीरे-धीरे विकसित होती जाती है/As children grow older, their ability to reason, analyze, and make decisions gradually develops
(A) कभी-कभी/Sometime
(B) कभी नहीं/Never
(C) ऐसी परिपक्वता आती है/Such maturity comes

31. दूसरों की क्षमताओं की तुलना करने के बजाए/Instead of comparing one's abilities with others, one should
(A) उससे प्रेरणा लेनी चाहिए/draw inspiration from them
(B) ईर्ष्या करनी चाहिए/Should be jealous
(C) भगवान के भरोसे रहना चाहिए/Should rely on God

32. हर इंसान को सोचने-सीखने और करने की शैली अलग-अलग होती है/Every person has a different way of thinking, learning, and acting
(A) ऐसा नहीं/Not so
(B) हाँ/Yes
(C) मालूम नहीं/I don't know

33. बदलती परिस्थितियों में लचीलापन बच्चों को हर चुनौतियों का/Children should be taught to face all challenges
(A) सामना करना सिखाना चाहिए/Flexibility in changing circumstances
(B) केवल नौकरी के प्रति जागरूक करना चाहिए/ Should only be made aware of the job
(C) प्रोत्साहित नहीं करना चाहिए/Should not be encouraged

34. भविष्य की नौकरियों में केवल डिग्री नहीं बल्कि सीखते रहने की आदत डालनी चाहिए/For future jobs, the key should be to inculcate a habit of continuous learning, not just a degree
(A) हो सकता है/Maybe
(B) हमेशा/Always
(C) ऐसा नहीं/Not so

35. आज भी समाज में स्त्री और पुरूष के बीच भेदभाव एक आम समस्या है/Even today, discrimination between men and women is a common problem in society
(A) मालूम नहीं/Don't know
(B) हो सकता है/Maybe
(C) ऐसा नहीं/Not so

PRACTICE SET-14

Total Ques.- 35
Time - 15 Min.

निर्देश : (प्रश्न 1–35) प्रत्येक प्रश्न के लिए एक कथन (Statement) दी होती है और इसके नीचे उत्तर के तीन विकल्प दिए जाते हैं। उम्मीदवारों को अपने बुद्धिमता और निर्णय के आधार पर सही उत्तर के लिए कोई एक विकल्प का चयन कर उत्तर-पत्रक में दिए गए गोले को काला या माउस की सहायता से क्लिक (Click) करें।

Direction : (Questions 1–35) : For each question, a statement is given, followed by three answer options. Candidates should select the correct option based on their intelligence and judgment and fill the corresponding circle on the answer sheet or click using the mouse.

1. जीवन में सफल होने के लिए बुद्धिमानी और विद्यालय परीक्षा में अच्छा प्रदर्शन बेहद जरूरी है/Intelligence and good performance in school exams are essential for success in life.
   (A) हो सकता है/Maybe
   (B) ऐसा नहीं/Not so
   (C) बिल्कुल सही/Absolutely right.
2. गलत कामों के परहेज करने से आपका आत्म-सम्मान बढ़ता है/Avoiding wrongdoing increases your self-esteem.
   (A) कभी-कभी/Sometime
   (B) हमेशा/Always
   (C) मालूम नहीं/I don't know
3. जो लोग ईमानदार होते हैं वो अपने वादों को भी पूरा करते हैं/People who are honest also fulfill their promises
   (A) दोनों/Both
   (B) ईमानदार व्यक्ति उच्च विचार के होते हैं/Honest people have high ideals
   (C) ईमानदार व्यक्ति भ्रष्टाचार में लिप्त नहीं रहते हैं/Honest people don't engage in corruption
4. समय पर निकलने से आप ट्रेन छूटने से बच सकते हैं/Leaving on time can help you avoid missing a train
   (A) नहीं/No
   (B) कभी नहीं/Never (C) हाँ/Yes
5. किसी भी विशेष क्षेत्र में सफलता पाने के लिए प्रतिभा और क्षमता के साथ-साथ रुचि और उत्साह भी जरूरी है/To achieve success in any particular field, interest and enthusiasm are essential, along with talent and ability
   (A) मालूम नहीं/I don't know
   (B) कभी-कभी/Sometime
   (C) बिल्कुल सही/Absolutely right
6. भारतीय रेलवे को उदार बनाने के लिए नीतिगत सुधार करने चाहिए/Policy reforms should be made to liberalize the Indian Railways.
   (A) सुविधाएँ बढ़ेगी/Facilities will increase
   (B) दोनों/Both
   (C) विकास की संभावना बढ़ेगी/The potential for development will increase
7. पैसे की लालसा में लोग अक्सर अपनी नैतिकता और मूल्यों को भूल जाते हैं/In the pursuit of money, people often forget their morals and values
   (A) नैतिकता का पतन हो रहा है/Morality is declining
   (B) कभी-कभी/Sometimes
   (C) पैसे की कीमत में वृद्धि हुई है/The value of money has increased
8. दिव्यांगो के अधिकारों और जरूरतों के प्रति जागरूकता फैलाने में मदद करनी चाहिए/We should help spread awareness about the rights and needs of the disabled.
   (A) कभी कभी/Sometime
   (B) हमेशा/Always
   (C) समाज इन्हें नजरअंदाज करती है/Society ignores them
9. जीवन में कठिनाईयों का डटकर सामना करने से साहस और आत्मविश्वास बढ़ता है/Facing difficulties in life boldly increases courage and self-confidence.
   (A) हाँ/Yes
   (B) कभी कभी/Sometime
   (C) मालूम नहीं/Don't know
10. नियमित हस्तक्षेप से हम व्यवस्था को अधिक प्रभारी और जवाबदेह बना सकते हैं/Through regular intervention, we can make the system more responsible and accountable.
   (A) कह नहीं सकते/Can't say
   (B) कभी-कभी/Sometime
   (C) कभी नहीं/Never
11. अत्यधिक शक्तिशाली और निरंकुश शासन जनता के अधिकारों का हनन और उत्पीड़न कर सकता है/Overly powerful and autocratic governance can violate and oppress the rights of the people

(A) कभी नहीं/Never (B) हाँ/Yes
(C) जनता समस्या से घिरी हुई है/The public is surrounded by problems

12. शासन में जवाबदेही, पारदर्शिता और नागरिकों की भागीदारी होनी चाहिए/Accountability, transparency, and citizen participation in governanceshould be there.
(A) हाँ/Yes (B) कभी नहीं/Never
(C) मालूम नहीं/Don't know

13. सरकारी दफ्तरों में अनियमितता और भ्रष्टाचार की समस्या भी आम है/Irregularities and corruption are also common in government offices.
(A) सरकारी दफ्तर लेट से खुलते हैं/Government offices open late
(B) भ्रष्टाचार में कमी आई है/Corruption has decreased
(C) दोनों में से कोई नहीं/Neither of the two

14. वर्तमान समय में किसानों की स्थिति में कुछ सुधार हुआ है/The situation of farmers has improved somewhat these days.
(A) कभी नहीं/Never (B) हाँ/Yes
(C) टेक्नोलॉजी की कमी है/There is a lack of technology

15. अनियमित वर्षा, सूखा, अत्यधिक बारिश आदि की घटनाएँ बढ़ी है, जो फसल को काफी प्रभावित करती है/Incidents of irregular rainfall, drought, excessive rainfall, etc. have increased, significantly affecting crops.
(A) जलसंसाधन की कमी/Lack of water resources
(B) कभी नहीं/Never
(C) बिल्कुल सही/Absolutely correct

16. स्वस्थ समाज और मानवीय विकास के लिए हमें पर्यावरण का संरक्षण अवश्य करना चाहिए/For a healthy society and human development, we must protect the environment.
(A) हाँ/Yes
(B) कभी-कभी/Sometimes
(C) कभी नहीं/Never

17. कृत्रिम बुद्धिमता (AI) से मिली जानकारी कई बार गलत अधूरी या आपत्तिजनक हो सकती है/Information obtained from artificial intelligence (AI) can sometimes be inaccurate, incomplete, or objectionable.
(A) भ्रामक उत्तर हो सकता है/This could be a misleading answer
(B) सत् प्रतिशत सुरक्षित नहीं है/It's not 100% sure
(C) दोनों/Both

18. खुशमिजाज व्यक्तित्व वाले लोग समाज में साकारात्मक परिवर्तन लाते हैं/People with cheerful personalities bring about positive change in society.
(A) नहीं/No (B) कभी नहीं/Never
(C) हमेशा/Always

19. ध्यान और योग की पद्धति व्यक्तियों को तनाव प्रबंधन में मदद करती है/Meditation and yoga help individuals manage stress.
(A) नहीं/No
(B) तनाव में कुछ कमी आती है/It reduces stress somewhat
(C) मालूम नहीं/I don't know

20. बच्चों का स्वभाव और चरित्र प्रायः माता-पिता से मिलता-जुलता होता है/Children's temperament and character often resemble their parents.
(A) अवश्य/Of course
(B) मालूम नहीं/I don't know
(C) हो सकता है/It could be.

21. खाली समय में रचनात्मक कार्यों में मन लगाने से जीवन में संतुष्टि और आनन्द की अनुभूति मिलती है/Engaging in creative work in free time brings satisfaction and joy in life.
(A) कभी नहीं/Never (B) नहीं/No
(C) जीवन को आनन्दमद बनाने के लिए रचनात्मक कार्य जरूरी है/Creative work is essential to make life enjoyable

22. सरकारी कार्यों में पारदर्शिता बढ़ाने के लिए आवश्यक कदम उठाना चाहिए/Necessary steps should be taken to increase transparency in government work.
(A) कभी-कभी/Sometimes
(B) कभी नहीं/Never (C) हमेशा/Always

23. नई चीजें सीखने और अपने कौशल को विकसित करने की इच्छा रखनी चाहिए/One should have a desire to learn new things and develop one's skills.
(A) हमेशा/Always (B) नहीं/No
(C) नई-नई टेक्नोलॉजी विकसित हो रही है/New technologies are being developed

24. शिक्षा और कौशल विकास से लोगों को बेहतर रोजगार मिलने की संभावना हो सकती है/Education and skill development can provide people with the possibility of getting better jobs.
(A) कभी नहीं/Never
(B) बेरोजगार की संख्या में कमी आएगी/The number of unemployed will decrease
(C) मालूम नहीं/I don't know

25. अपने मूल्यों और विश्वासों के आधार पर हम बेहतर निर्णय

ले सकते हैं/We can make better decisions based on our values and beliefs.
(A) विश्वासों में कमी आयी है/Beliefs have decreased
(B) नहीं/No (C) हमेशा/Always

26. सरकार को प्लास्टिक के उपयोग को रोकने से पहले वैकल्पिक सामग्री जैसे कि कपड़े के बैग, पेपर बैग आदि को बढ़ावा दिया जाना चाहिए। अन्यथा/Before banning the use of plastic, the government should promote alternative materials such as cloth bags, paper bags, etc. Otherwise
(A) जल प्रदूषण में वृद्धि/Increase in water pollution
(B) स्वास्थ्य समस्याओं में वृद्धि/Increase in health problems
(C) दोनों/Both

27. भारतीय रेलवे को अपने देश के नागरिकों के प्रति बेहतर कदम उठाना चाहिए/Indian Railways should take better steps towards the citizens of our country
(A) आर्थिक विकास को बढ़ावा मिलेगा/This will promote economic development
(B) यात्री सेवा में सुधार को बढ़ावा मिलेगा/This will promote improvement in passenger service
(C) दोनों/Both

28. विकल्पों का मूल्यांकन करने से आप सर्वोत्तम निर्णय ले सकते हैं/Evaluating options helps you make the best decisions.
(A) मालूम नहीं/I don't know
(B) कभी-कभी/Sometimes
(C) नहीं/No

29. दुर्घटनाओं और अपराधों को रोकने के लिए नियमों का पालन करना अति आवश्यक है/It is essential to follow rules to prevent accidents and crimes.
(A) कभी-कभी/Sometime
(B) हाँ/Yes (C) ऐसा नहीं/Not so

30. कठोर निर्णय लेने से पहले सभी पहलूओं और परिणामों पर विचार करना अति आवश्यक है/It is essential to consider all aspects and consequences before making tough decisions.
(A) अवश्य/Of course
(B) कभी-कभी/Sometime
(C) कह नहीं सकते/Can't say

31. दूसरों का समर्थन और बड़ो का मार्गदर्शन लेना आवश्यक है/ It is essential to seek support from others and guidance from elders.
(A) कभी नहीं/Never
(B) कभी-कभी/Sometime
(C) मालूम नहीं/I don't know

32. समय का पालन करना भारतीय रेलवे के लिए एक बड़ी चुनौती रही है/Punctuality has been a major challenge for the Indian Railways.
(A) कभी-कभी/Sometime
(B) हमेशा/Always
(C) कभी नहीं/Never

33. आलस्य छोड़कर अनुशासन, मेहनत और सही योजना अपनाने से बड़ी सफलता मिलती है/Overcoming laziness and adopting discipline, hard work, and proper planning leads to great success.
(A) निश्चित रूप से/Definitely
(B) अनिश्चित रूप से/Uncertainly
(C) कभी नहीं/Never

34. अच्छे और सकारात्मक लोगों के साथ रहने से काम करने में ऊर्जा मिलती है/Being around good and positive people gives energy to work.
(A) नकारात्मक सोच में कमी आएगी/Negative thinking will reduce
(B) आत्मविश्वास बढ़ता है/Confidence increases
(C) दोनों/Both

35. ईमानदारी से काम करने पर लोगों में विश्वास और प्रतिष्ठा-/ Working honestly builds trust and reputation among people
(A) बढ़ती है/Increases
(B) घटती है/Decreases
(C) असंतोष मिलता है/Causes dissatisfaction

PRACTICE SET-15

Total Ques.- 35
Time - 15 Min.

निर्देश : (प्रश्न 1-35) प्रत्येक प्रश्न के लिए एक कथन (Statement) दी होती है और इसके नीचे उत्तर के तीन विकल्प दिए जाते हैं। उम्मीदवारों को अपने बुद्धिमता और निर्णय के आधार पर सही उत्तर के लिए कोई एक विकल्प का चयन कर उत्तर-पत्रक में दिए गए गोले को काला या माउस की सहायता से क्लिक (Click) करें।

Direction : (Questions 1–35) : For each question, a statement is given, followed by three answer options. Candidates should select the correct option based on their intelligence and judgment and fill the corresponding circle on the answer sheet or click using the mouse.

1. निजीकरण से गरीब और मध्यम वर्ग के लोगों पर नकारात्मक प्रभाव पड़ सकता है/Privatization can have a negative impact on the poor and middle class
   (A) किराए में वृद्धि हो सकती है/Fares may increase
   (B) रोजगार में/Employment
   (C) कभी-नहीं/Never
2. निजीकरण से रेलवे में नई तकनीकों और आधुनिक सुविधाओं का उपयोग हो सकता है/Privatization can lead to the use of new technologies and modern facilities in the railways
   (A) सत्य/True (B) असत्य/False
   (C) मालूम नहीं/I don't know
3. रेलवे के निर्देशों का पालन करने से यात्रियों और रेलवे कर्मचारियों की सुरक्षा बढ़ती है और दुर्घटनाओं के जाखिम को कम किया जा सकता है/Following railway instructions increases the safety of passengers and railway employees and reduces the risk of accidents
   (A) हमेशा/Always (B) नहीं/No
   (C) कभी नहीं/Never
4. योग एक प्राचीन पद्धति है जो शारीरिक, मानसिक और आत्मिक स्वास्थ्य को बेहतर बनाने में मदद करती है/Yoga is an ancient practice that helps improve physical, mental, and spiritual health
   (A) मालूम नहीं/Don't know
   (B) कभी कभी/Sometime (C) हाँ/Yes
5. योग के माध्यम से हम अपने शरीर और मन को संतुलित कर सकते हैं और तनाव, चिंता और कई समस्याओं से निजात पा सकते हैं/Through yoga, we can balance our body and mind and get relief from stress, anxiety, and many other problems.
   (A) बिल्कुल नहीं/Absolutely not
   (B) डॉक्टर इसकी सलाह नहीं देते हैं/Doctors do not recommend this
   (C) हो सकता है/It is possible
6. फलों का प्राकृतिक रंगों को देखकर उनकी पौष्टिकता का अनुमान लगाया जा सकता है/The nutritional value of fruits can be estimated by looking at their natural colors.
   (A) फलों के रंगों में विभिन्न पोषक तत्वों की उपस्थिति का संकेत मिलता है/The colors of fruits indicate the presence of different nutrients
   (B) ऐसा नहीं/It is not so
   (C) हो सकता है/It is possible
7. लोकतांत्रिक राज्य में, सभी नागरिकों को अपने अधिकारों और कर्त्तव्यों के प्रति जागरूक रहना चाहिए ताकि बिना भेदभाव के समान सामाजिक और आर्थिक न्याय मिले/ In a democratic state, all citizens should be aware of their rights and duties so that they can receive equal social and economic justice without discrimination.
   (A) इसे ही लोकतंत्र कहते है/This is called democracy
   (B) पूजा स्थल पर भेदभाव दिखता है/Discrimination is seen at places of worship
   (C) ग्रामीण क्षेत्रों में लोग आर्थिक रूप से सम्पन्न नहीं है/ People in rural areas are not economically well off
8. बच्चों को उनकी प्रतिभा को विकसित करने के लिए प्रोत्साहित करना चाहिए ताकि उनका आत्मविश्वास बढ़े और वे अपने लक्ष्यों को प्राप्त करने में सक्षम हो सके/Children should be encouraged to develop their talents so that their self-confidence increases and they are able to achieve their goals.
   (A) बच्चों के प्रतिभा का समर्थन करना चाहिए/ Children's talents should be supported
   (B) बच्चों की आयु बढ़ने से शौक और रूचियाँ बदलती रहती है/Children's hobbies and interests change as they grow older
   (C) दोनों/Both
9. अच्छे कपडों की चलन व्यक्ति की सामाजिक स्थिति, शैली और संस्कृति को भी दर्शा सकती है/The taste of good clothing can also reflect a person's social status,

style, and culture.
(A) कभी नहीं/Never (B) हो सकता है/Maybe
(C) मालूम नहीं/Don't know

10. शिक्षा को किसी जातिवाद से नहीं जोड़ना चाहिए, चाहे वह किसी भी धर्म, जाति या पृष्ठभूमि से हो, इससे/Education should not be linked to casteism, regardless of religion, caste, or background. This will
(A) सामाजिक समानता को बढ़ावा मिलेगा/Promote social equality
(B) सभी को समान अवसर मिलेगा/Provide equal opportunities to all
(C) दोनों/Both

11. शिक्षा को सभी वर्गों के लिए सुलभ और समान रूप से उपलब्ध होना चाहिए/Education should be accessible and equally available to all classes.
(A) उच्च एवं निम्न वर्गों के लोगों में ऐसी व्यवस्था नहीं है/ People in upper and lower classes do not have such a system
(B) शिक्षा महंगी है/Education is expensive
(C) दोनों/Both

12. देश में विकास की गति प्रदान करने के लिए महिलाओं और बालिकाओं को सामाजिक और आर्थिक रूप से सशक्त बनाने की जरूरत है/To accelerate development in the country, women and girls need to be socially and economically empowered.
(A) महिलाओं में आत्मनिर्भरता बढ़ेगी/Women's self-reliance will increase
(B) महिलाओं को सामाजिक प्रतिष्ठा बढ़ेगी/Women's social prestige will increase
(C) दोनों/Both

13. कौशल विकास योजनाएं के तहत महिलाओं को विभिन्न कौशलों संस्थान में प्रशिक्षण दिया जाना चाहिए। ताकि वे आत्मनिर्भर बन सके/Under skill development schemes, women should be trained in various skills at institutes so that they can become self-reliant.
(A) ऐसा नहीं/Not so
(B) कभी नहीं/Never (C) हाँ/Yes

14. राजनीति में कुछ लोग ऐसे आते हैं जो अपने सिद्धान्तों और मूल्यों के प्रति निष्ठावान रहते हैं/Some people enter politics who remain loyal to their principles and values.
(A) कभी कभी/Sometime
(B) हाँ/Yes (C) कभी नहीं/Never

15. सभी नेता समाज में सकारात्मक परिवर्तन लाने में महत्वपूर्ण भूमिका निभा सकते हैं/All leaders can play an important role in bringing positive change to society.
(A) हाँ/Yes (B) ऐसा नहीं/Not so
(C) कभी नहीं/Never

16. मनुष्यों को अपने दुर्गुणों का त्याग करने से आंतरिक शांति और संतुष्टि मिलती है/Humans find inner peace and satisfaction by abandoning their vices.
(A) बिल्कुल सही/Absolutely right
(B) ऐसा नहीं/Not so
(C) मालूम नहीं/I don't know

17. माता-पिता के व्यवहार, आदतें और मूल्य बच्चों पर गहरा प्रभाव डालते हैं और उनके गुण आत्मसात करते हैं/Parents' behavior, habits, and values have a profound impact on children, and they internalize their qualities.
(A) हो सकता है/Maybe
(B) कभी नहीं/Never (C) हाँ/Yes

18. झूठ और धोखे से अस्थायी सफलता मिल सकती है, लेकिन दीर्घकालिक रूप से यह नकारात्मक परिणामों का कारण बन सकता है/Lying and deceit may bring temporary success, but in the long run, they can lead to negative consequences.
(A) नहीं/No (B) हाँ/Yes
(C) मालूम नहीं/I don't know

19. झूठ और धोखे से दूसरों का विश्वास खोने का डर रहता है/ Lying and deceit can lead to losing others' trust.
(A) हमेशा/Always
(B) कभी नहीं/Never
(C) कभी कभी झूठ का सहारा लेना पड़ता है/Sometimes one has to resort to lying

20. अन्याय के खिलाफ आवाज उठाना और एकजुट होकर काम करना आवश्यक है/It is necessary to speak out against injustice and work together.
(A) इससे शिकार लोगों को न्याय मिल सकती है/ This can provide justice to victims
(B) लोगों में एकता और सहयोग की भावना बढ़ती है/ It increases the spirit of unity and cooperation among people
(C) दोनों/Both

21. औद्योगिक विकास से स्थानीय अर्थव्यवस्था को मजबूती मिलती है और रोजगार के अवसर बढ़ते हैं/Industrial development strengthens the local economyand increases employment opportunities.
(A) दोनों/Both
(B) जीवन में सकारात्मक परिवर्तन आता है/It brings positive changes in life
(C) बेरोजगारी में कमी आती है/It reduces unemployment

22. टीमवर्क में काम करने से सहयोग की भावना, नए विचार और समाधान मिलते है/Working in a team leads to a spirit of cooperation, new ideas, and solutions.

(A) निश्चित रूप से/Definitely so
(B) ऐसा नहीं/Not so
(C) गुणवत्ता में कमी आती है/It leads to a decline in quality

23. मरीजों की आपातकालीन सेवाओं में कुछ सरकारी योजनाएँ प्रदान करनी चाहिए/Some government schemes should be implemented to provide emergency services for patients.
(A) विषम परिस्थिति में बेहतर सुविधा मिल सके/To provide better facilities in difficult situations
(B) कम खर्च में ईलाज हो सके/To provide treatment at a lower cost
(C) दोनों/Both

24. देशभक्ति की भावना को जागृत करने के लिए छात्रों को आगे बढ़ाना/To foster a sense of patriotism, students should be encouraged to promote
(A) अच्छा विचार है/A good idea
(B) गलत विचार है/A bad idea
(C) मालूम नहीं/I don't know

25. छात्रों में देश के प्रति जिम्मेदारी और भविष्य में देश को नवनिर्माण में भूमिका निभानी चाहिए। ताकि/Students should be encouraged to play a role in the future reconstruction of the country.This will foster a sense of patriotism.
(A) देशभक्ति की भावना को बढ़ावा मिलेगा/To foster a sense of patriotism
(B) समाज में सकारात्मक परिवर्तन होगा/To bring about positive change in society
(C) दोनों/Both

26. छात्रों को देश के इतिहास, संस्कृति और मूल्यों के बारे में शिक्षित करना चाहिए/Students should be educated about the country's history, culture, and values.
(A) हमेशा/Always (B) नहीं/No
(C) कह नहीं सकते/Can't say

27. हमेशा कुछ नया करने से नए अवसरों की प्राप्ति होती है और सफलता के नए रास्ते खुलते हैं/Always doing something new opens up new opportunities and new paths to success.
(A) कभी नहीं/Never
(B) ऐसा नहीं/It's not like that
(C) ऐसा हो सकता है/It could be so

28. जिंदगी में चुनौतियों का सामना करने से आत्मविश्वास और साहस में वृद्धि होती है/Facing challenges in life increases self-confidence and courage.
(A) हमेशा/Always (B) नहीं/No
(C) कभी नहीं/Never

29. मुफ्त चिकित्सा शिविर का आयोजन करना गरीबों के लिए एक बहुत ही उपयोगी और सहायक कदम हो सकता है/Organizing free medical camps can be a very useful and helpful step for the poor
(A) स्वास्थ्य के प्रति जागरूकता बढ़ेगी/It will increase health awareness
(B) सरकार का बजट में बोझ बढ़ेगा/It will increase the government's budget burden
(C) कभी नहीं/Never

30. सरकार को बाढ़ प्रभावित क्षेत्रों में राहत कार्य करना और लोगों को आवश्यक सुविधाऐं प्रदान करना चाहिए/The government should carry out relief work in flood-affected areas and provide essential amenities to the people.
(A) कभी-कभी/Sometime
(B) कभी नहीं/Never (C) हमेशा/Always

31. बाढ़ की समस्या को भविष्य में रोकने के लिए योजनाएँ बनाना और उन्हें लागू करना चाहिए/Plans should be made and implemented to prevent future flood problems.
(A) बेरोजगारी में कमी आ रही है/Unemployment is decreasing
(B) बाढ़ की समस्या दिनोदिन बढ़ती जा रही है/The flood problem is increasing day by day
(C) कभी-कभी/Sometime

32. निजी क्षेत्र के प्रबंधन से रेलवे की कार्यक्षमता में सुधार हो सकता है/Private sector management can improve the efficiency of the railways.
(A) नहीं/No (B) हाँ/Yes
(C) कह नहीं सकते/Can't say

33. निजीकरण से रेलवे में आधुनिक तकनीक और सुविधाओं का समावेश हो सकता है/Privatization can bring modern technology and facilities to the railways.
(A) कभी नहीं/Never
(B) निश्चित रूप से/Definitely
(C) नुकसान भी हो सकता है/It can also be harmful

34. स्वस्थ खान-पान से कई बिमारियों का खतरा कम होता है/Healthy eating reduces the risk of many diseases.
(A) हाँ/Yes (B) नहीं/No
(C) बिमारियाँ नहीं आती है/Diseases don't occur

35. आप स्टेशन पर सुरक्षित और सुविधाजनक यात्रा करने के लिए स्टेशन के नियमों का पालन करना चाहिए/You should follow station rules for a safe and comfortable journey at the station.
(A) कभी-कभी/Sometime (B) हमेशा/Always
(C) खासकर भीड़भाड़ वाले इलाकों में/Especially in crowded areas

उत्तर (ANSWER)

PRACTICE SET - 1

1.	A	18.	B
2.	A	19.	A
3.	A	20.	C
4.	A	21.	A
5.	A	22.	A
6.	A	23.	A
7.	A	24.	A
8.	A	25.	C
9.	A	26.	A
10.	A	27.	B
11.	A	28.	C
12.	C	29.	C
13.	A	30.	B
14.	B	31.	B
15.	B	32.	A
16.	A	33.	C
17.	C	34.	A
		35.	B

PRACTICE SET - 2

1.	A	18.	B
2.	A	19.	A
3.	C	20.	A
4.	A	21.	B
5.	B	22.	A
6.	A	23.	C
7.	C	24.	A
8.	C	25.	B
9.	A	26.	B
10.	C	27.	A
11.	C	28.	B
12.	C	29.	C
13.	B	30.	C
14.	B	31.	A
15.	C	32.	A
16.	C	33.	A
17.	B	34.	B
		35.	B

PRACTICE SET - 3

1.	A	18.	C
2.	C	19.	A
3.	A	20.	A
4.	A	21.	C
5.	C	22.	C
6.	B	23.	A
7.	C	24.	B
8.	C	25.	C
9.	C	26.	A
10.	B	27.	A
11.	B	28.	C
12.	B	29.	A
13.	A	30.	C
14.	A	31.	A
15.	A	32.	B
16.	C	33.	A
17.	B	34.	C
		35.	C

PRACTICE SET - 4

1.	B	18.	B
2.	A	19.	C
3.	C	20.	A
4.	C	21.	A
5.	C	22.	A
6.	A	23.	B
7.	A	24.	A
8.	B	25.	C
9.	C	26.	A
10.	C	27.	C
11.	B	28.	C
12.	C	29.	C
13.	C	30.	A
14.	B	31.	C
15.	B	32.	C
16.	B	33.	C
17.	C	34.	A
		35.	C

PRACTICE SET - 5

1.	C	18.	B
2.	B	19.	A
3.	C	20.	B
4.	B	21.	B
5.	A	22.	C
6.	A	23.	B
7.	A	24.	A
8.	A	25.	C
9.	A	26.	C
10.	B	27.	B
11.	C	28.	C
12.	B	29.	A
13.	C	30.	C
14.	B	31.	C
15.	A	32.	A
16.	C	33.	A
17.	B	34.	C
		35.	A

PRACTICE SET - 6

1.	C	18.	B
2.	A	19.	C
3.	C	20.	C
4.	B	21.	C
5.	C	22.	C
6.	B	23.	C
7.	A	24.	A
8.	C	25.	C
9.	B	26.	C
10.	A	27.	B
11.	A	28.	A
12.	B	29.	B
13.	C	30.	A
14.	A	31.	B
15.	C	32.	A
16.	A	33.	A
17.	B	34.	B
		35.	A

उत्तर (ANSWER)

PRACTICE SET - 7

1.	C	18.	B
2.	A	19.	B
3.	C	20.	B
4.	C	21.	A
5.	B	22.	A
6.	C	23.	A
7.	C	24.	C
8.	C	25.	C
9.	B	26.	A
10.	B	27.	B
11.	A	28.	A
12.	B	29.	B
13.	C	30.	B
14.	A	31.	C
15.	A	32.	C
16.	A	33.	A
17.	B	34.	B
		35.	A

PRACTICE SET - 8

1.	B	18.	C
2.	C	19.	C
3.	A	20.	B
4.	A	21.	A
5.	A	22.	C
6.	B	23.	C
7.	C	24.	C
8.	C	25.	A
9.	A	26.	C
10.	B	27.	A
11.	C	28.	C
12.	A	29.	B
13.	C	30.	A
14.	A	31.	A
15.	B	32.	C
16.	B	33.	A
17.	A	34.	B
		35.	B

PRACTICE SET - 9

1.	B	18.	A
2.	B	19.	B
3.	B	20.	B
4.	C	21.	B
5.	A	22.	A
6.	A	23.	C
7.	B	24.	A
8.	C	25.	B
9.	A	26.	A
10.	C	27.	A
11.	A	28.	A
12.	A	29.	C
13.	A	30.	A
14.	A	31.	B
15.	A	32.	C
16.	A	33.	B
17.	A	34.	B
		35.	C

PRACTICE SET - 10

1.	B	18.	A
2.	B	19.	B
3.	C	20.	A
4.	C	21.	B
5.	C	22.	A
6.	A	23.	B
7.	C	24.	B
8.	B	25.	B
9.	A	26.	B
10.	A	27.	A
11.	A	28.	B
12.	C	29.	B
13.	B	30.	C
14.	C	31.	A
15.	C	32.	A
16.	A	33.	C
17.	B	34.	A
		35.	A

PRACTICE SET - 11

1.	C	18.	C
2.	A	19.	C
3.	B	20.	B
4.	B	21.	C
5.	C	22.	C
6.	B	23.	C
7.	C	24.	C
8.	B	25.	A
9.	B	26.	B
10.	A	27.	A
11.	B	28.	B
12.	C	29.	A
13.	C	30.	C
14.	C	31.	A
15.	C	32.	A
16.	A	33.	A
17.	B	34.	A
		35.	C

PRACTICE SET - 12

1.	B	18.	A
2.	C	19.	C
3.	C	20.	C
4.	B	21.	C
5.	A	22.	A
6.	B	23.	A
7.	A	24.	C
8.	B	25.	C
9.	C	26.	C
10.	B	27.	A
11.	C	28.	C
12.	C	29.	A
13.	B	30.	C
14.	B	31.	C
15.	A	32.	A
16.	B	33.	A
17.	A	34.	A
		35.	B

उत्तर (ANSWER)

PRACTICE SET - 13

1.	A	18.	C
2.	A	19.	A
3.	B	20.	C
4.	C	21.	A
5.	A	22.	A
6.	C	23.	A
7.	A	24.	B
8.	A	25.	B
9.	C	26.	B
10.	C	27.	C
11.	A	28.	C
12.	C	29.	A
13.	A	30.	C
14.	A	31.	A
15.	A	32.	B
16.	C	33.	A
17.	A	34.	B
		35.	B

PRACTICE SET - 14

1.	C	18.	C
2.	B	19.	B
3.	A	20.	A
4.	C	21.	C
5.	C	22.	C
6.	B	23.	A
7.	A	24.	B
8.	B	25.	C
9.	A	26.	C
10.	B	27.	C
11.	B	28.	B
12.	A	29.	B
13.	C	30.	A
14.	B	31.	B
15.	C	32.	B
16.	A	33.	A
17.	C	34.	C
		35.	A

PRACTICE SET - 15

1.	A	18.	B
2.	A	19.	A
3.	A	20.	C
4.	C	21.	A
5.	C	22.	A
6.	A	23.	C
7.	A	24.	A
8.	C	25.	C
9.	B	26.	A
10.	C	27.	C
11.	C	28.	A
12.	C	29.	A
13.	C	30.	C
14.	B	31.	B
15.	A	32.	B
16.	A	33.	B
17.	C	34.	A
		35.	B

MODEL SET - 1

Station Master (NTPC 2022) Psycho Exam.

(30-07-2022) का हल प्रश्न-पत्र (स्मृति पर आधारित) (Based on Memory)

TEST 1 TEST FOR MEASURING YOUR INTELLIGENCE

Total Ques.- 35
Time - 10 Min.

Classification Test (वर्गीकरण)

निर्देश : (प्रश्न 1–35) बुद्धिमापन परीक्षण के प्रत्येक प्रश्न में पाँच आकृतियाँ दिए जाते हैं जिसमें से चार आकृतियाँ में कुछ समानता और कोई एक आकृति अन्य चारों से भिन्न है वही भिन्न आकृति आपका उत्तर होगा जिसे दिए गए उत्तर-पत्रक में गोले को काला/माउस की सहायता से क्लिक करना होता है और इसके लिए 10 मिनट का समय दिया जाता है।

Instructions : (Questions 1–35) : Each question in the Intelligence Test consists of five figures, four of which have some similarity, and one that is different from the other four is your answer. You must click on the black circle on the answer sheet or using the mouse. You are given 10 minutes to complete the test.

A B C D E

1. 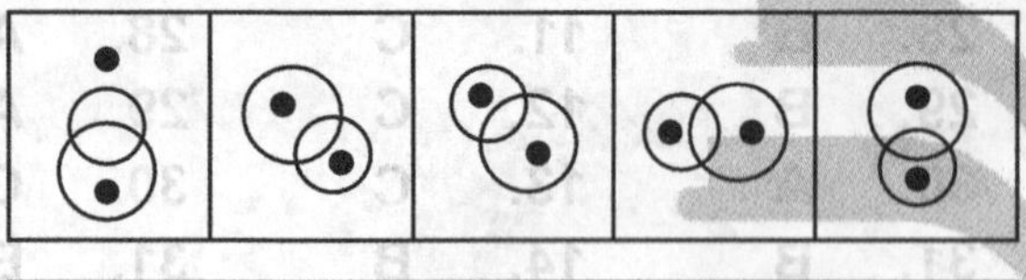

2. 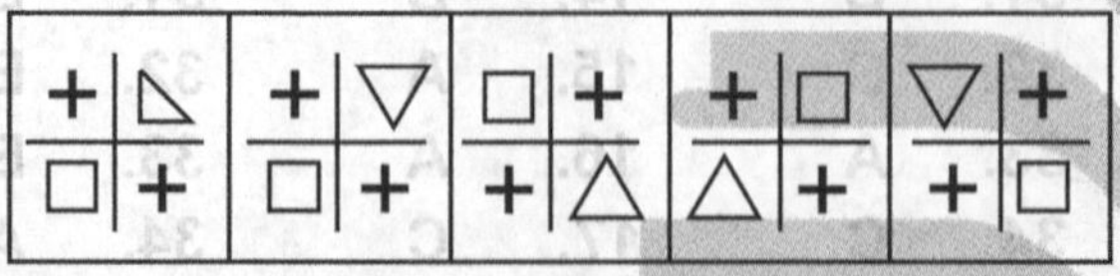

3. 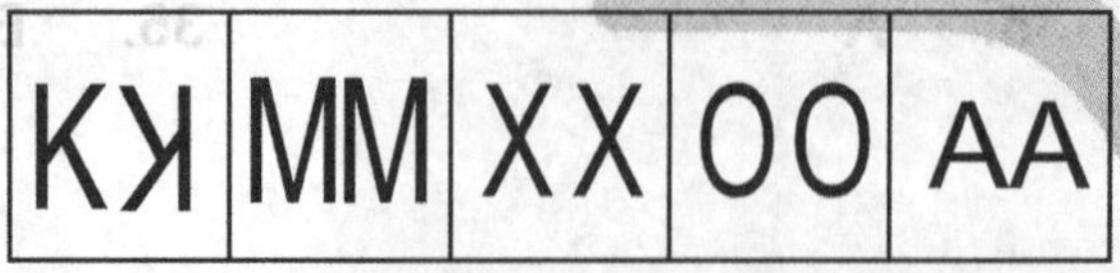

4. 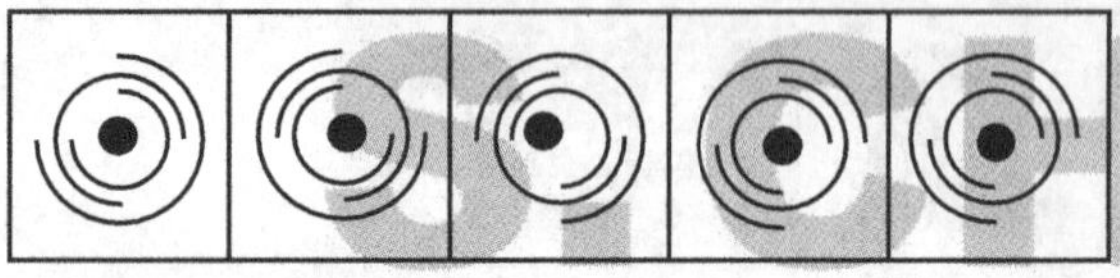

5. 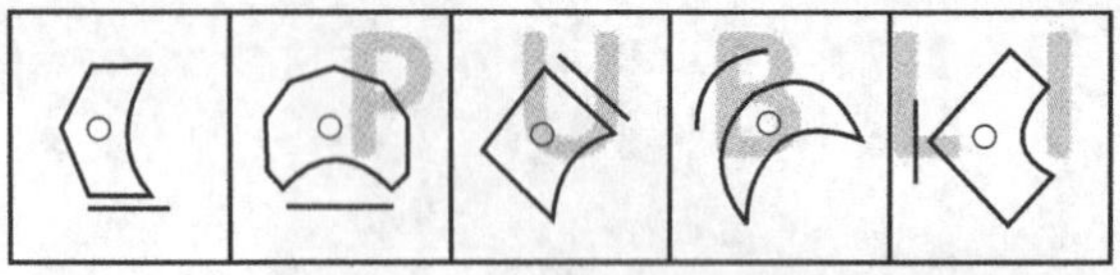

6. 

7. 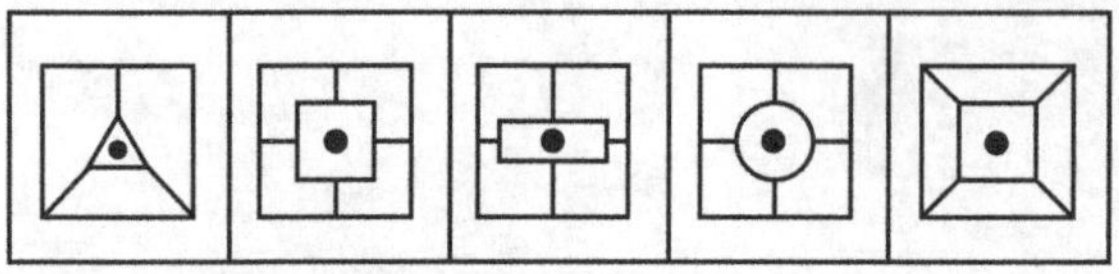

8. 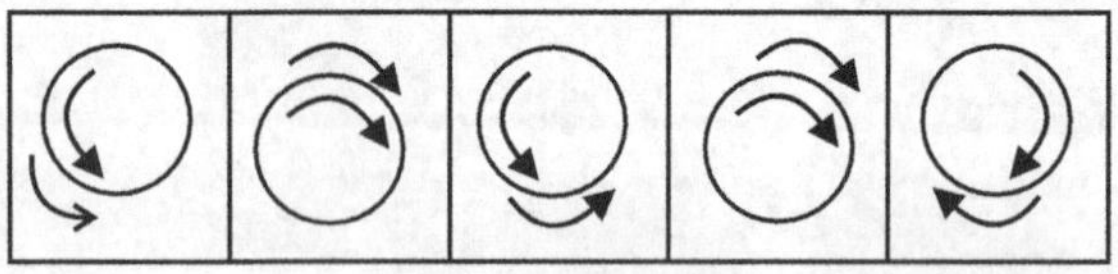

A B C D E

9. 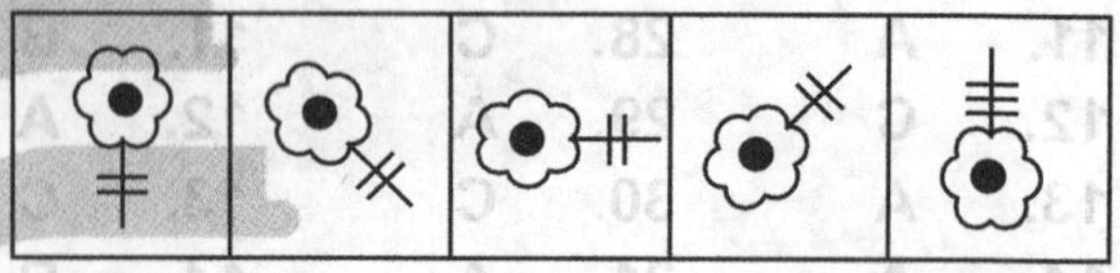

10. 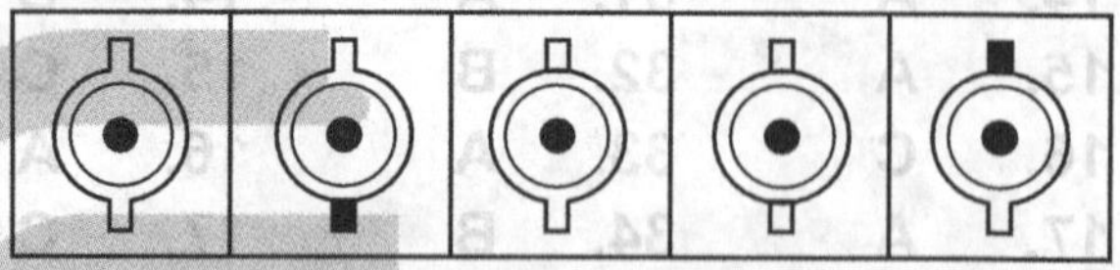

11. 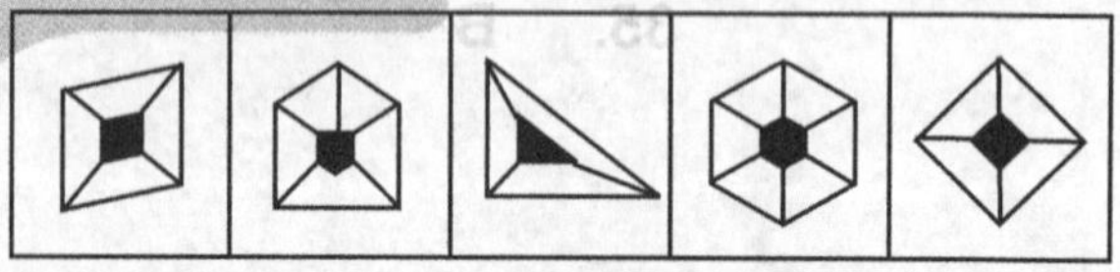

12. 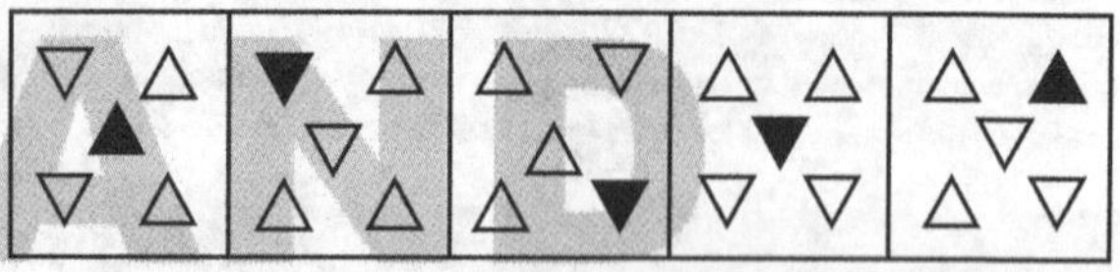

13. 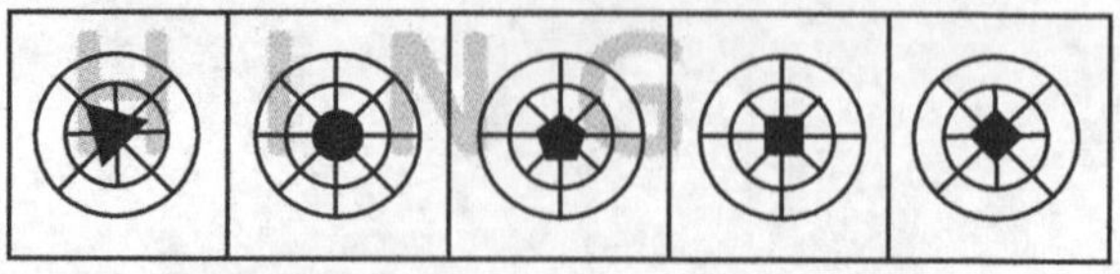

14. 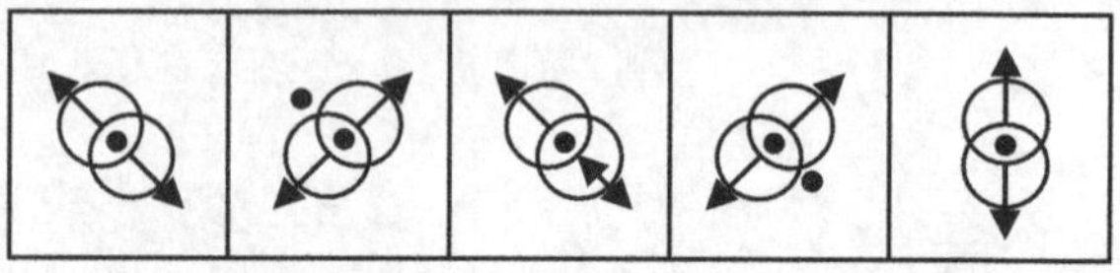

15. 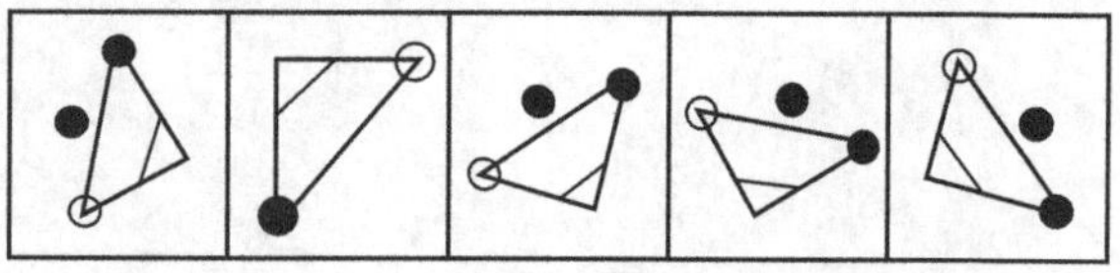

16. 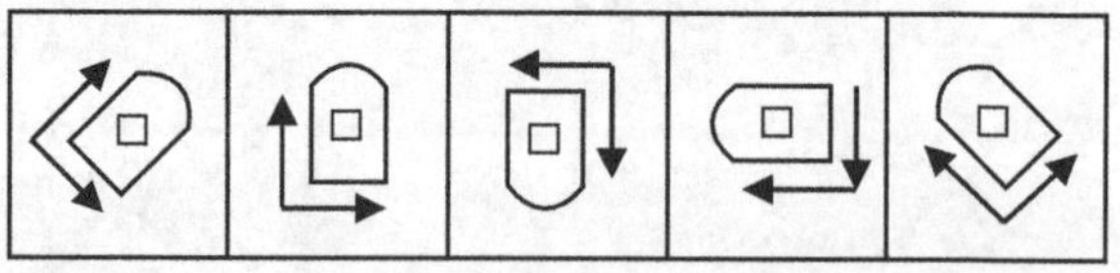

A B C D E

17.
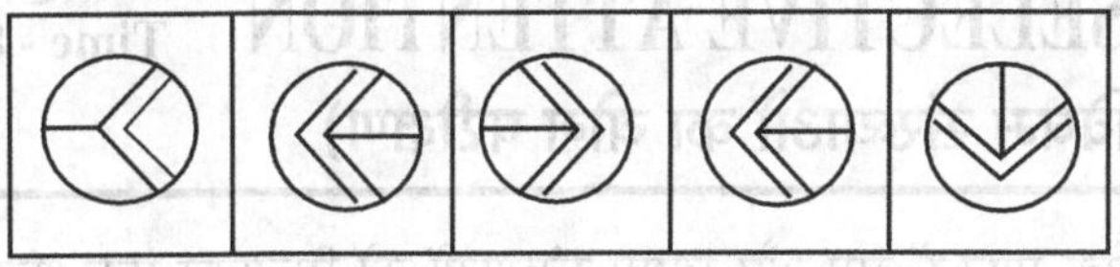

18.
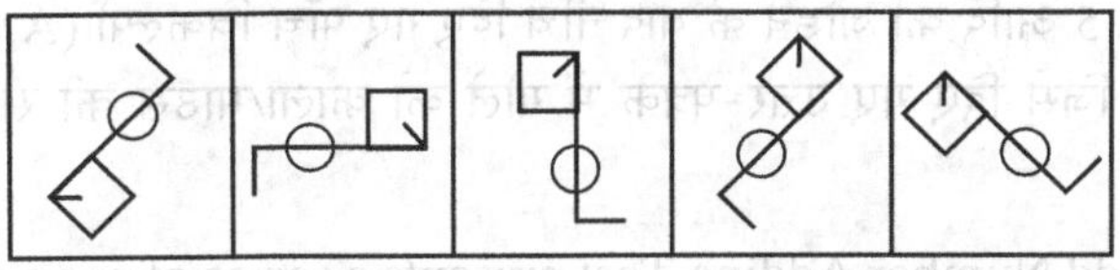

19.
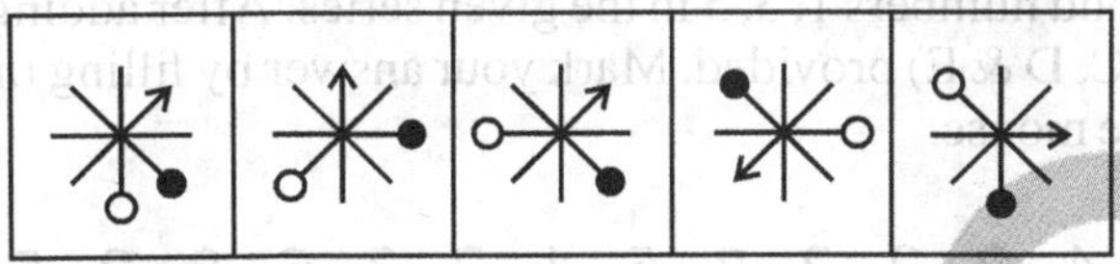

20.
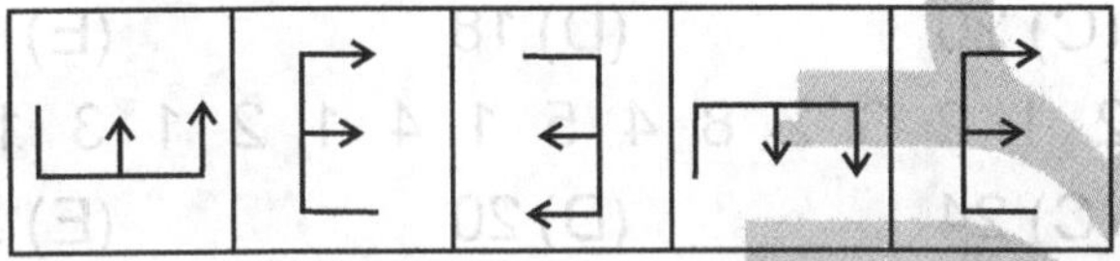

21.
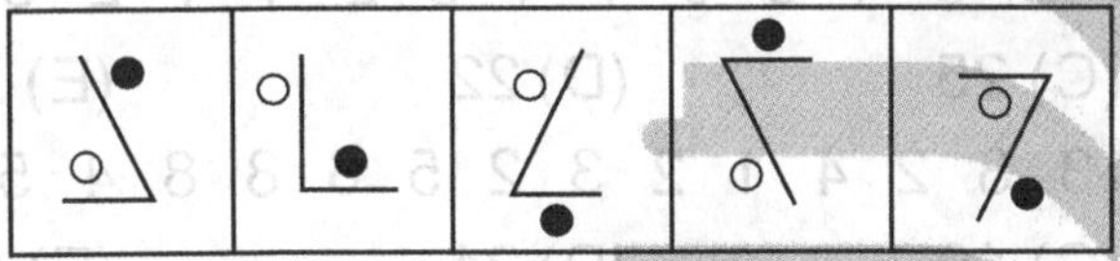

22.
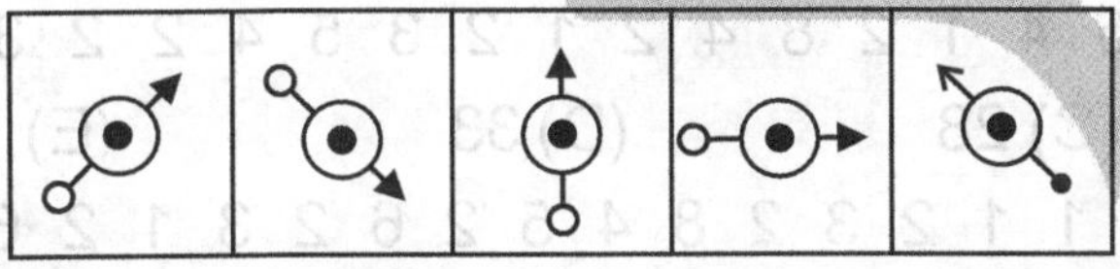

23.
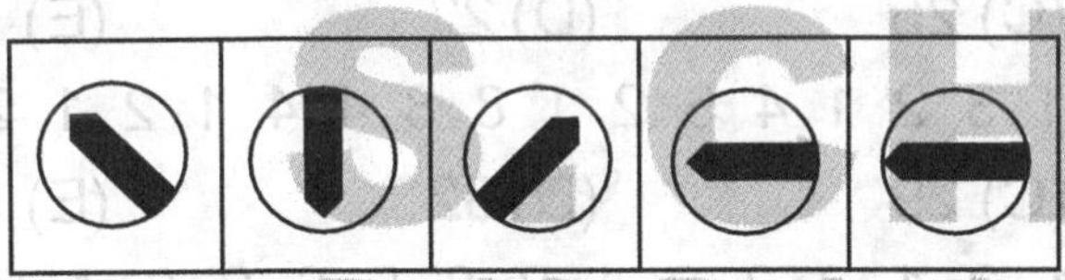

24.
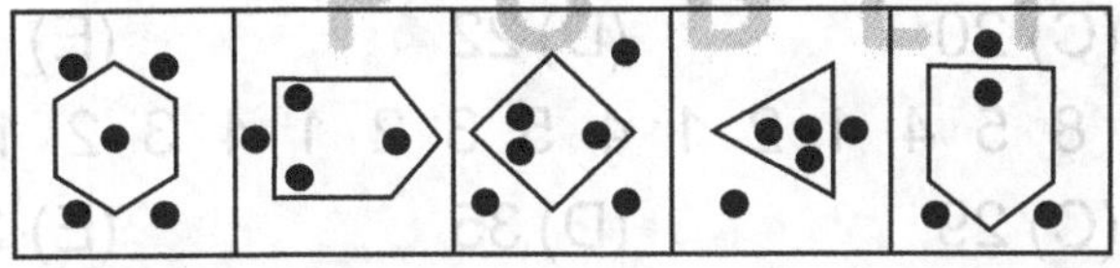

25.
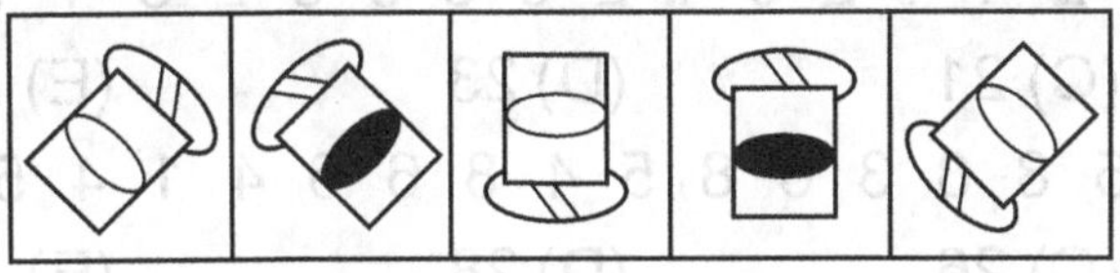

26.
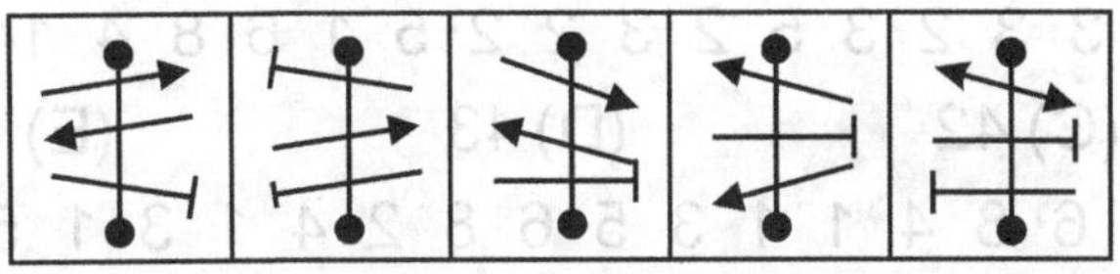

A B C D E

27.
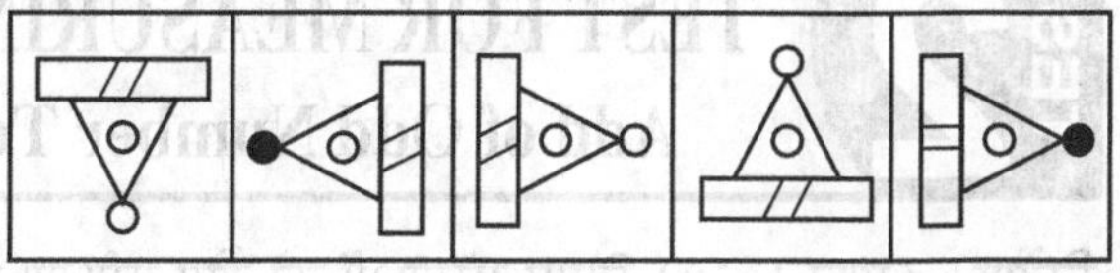

28.

A	B	C	D	E
T	E	M	B	D

29.

30.
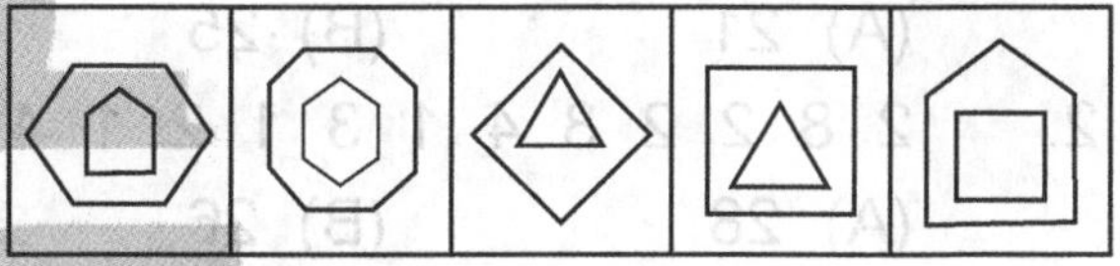

31.
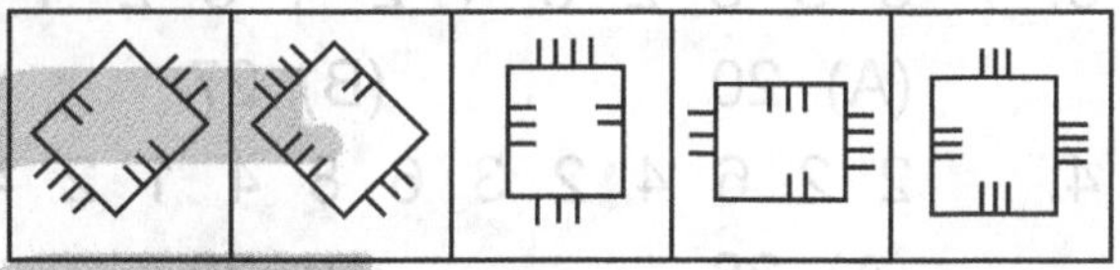

32.
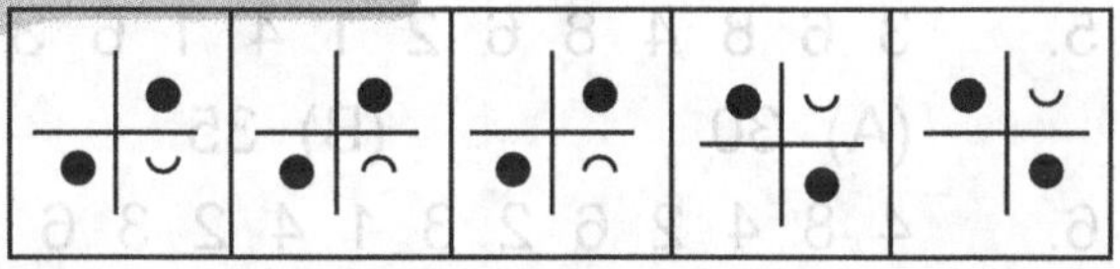

33.
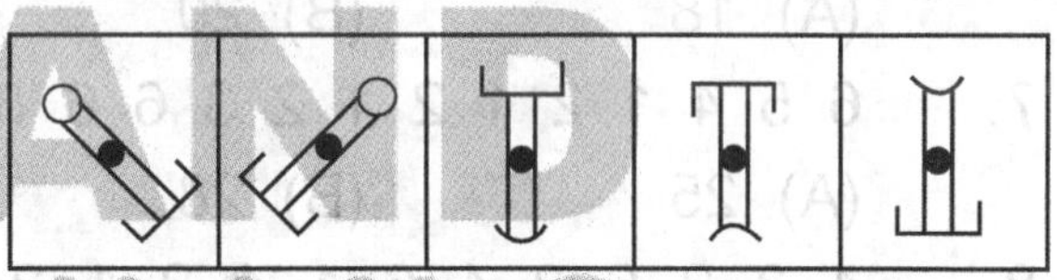

34.
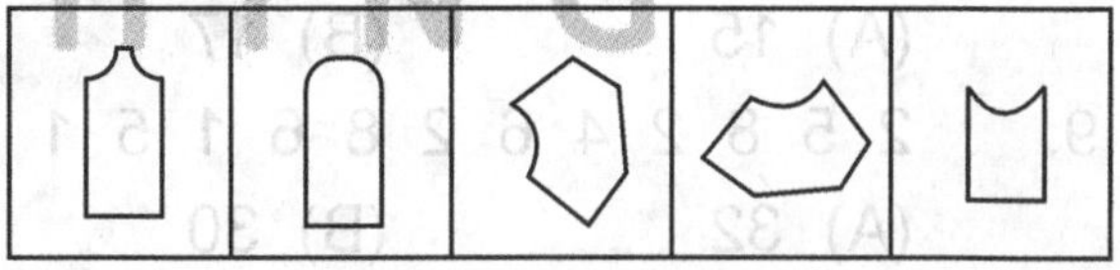

35.
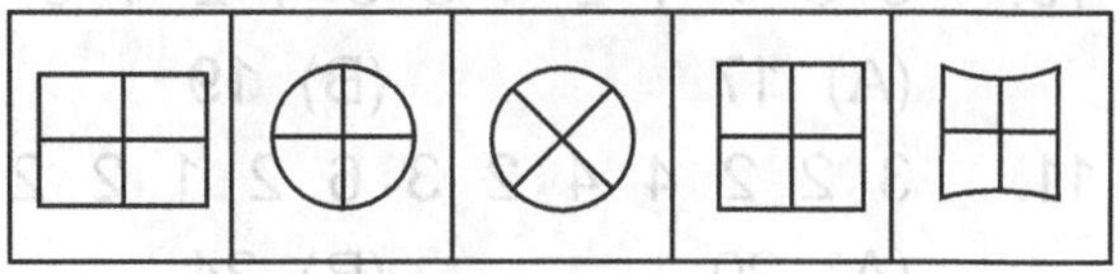

TEST 2 TEST FOR MEASURING SELECTIVE ATTENTION

Total Ques.- 30
Time - 8 Min.

Add of Odd Number Test (विषम संख्याओं का योग परीक्षण)

निर्देश : (प्रश्न 1-30) विषम संख्याओं को योग परीक्षण के प्रत्येक प्रश्न में सम और विषम संख्याओं को मिलाकर एक श्रृंखला दिया रहता है। इस श्रृंखला में प्रदत्त केवल विषम संख्या 1, 3, 5 आदि को जोड़ने के बाद नीचे दिए गए पाँच विकल्पों (A, B, C, D और E) में कोई एक सही विकल्प को ढूंढना होता है जिसे दिए गए उत्तर-पत्रक में गोले को काला/माउस की सहायता से क्लिक करना होता है।

Directions: (Questions 1–30) : Each question in the Odd Number Adding Test presents a series of even and odd numbers. You need to add the total number of odd numbers 1, 3, 5 in the given series. After adding, select the correct option from the five choices (A, B, C, D & E) provided. Mark your answer by filling the circle on the answer sheet or by clicking on it using the mouse.

1. 4 4 1 2 1 4 2 1 2 1 1 1 4 2 2 2 8 5 1 2 3 6 8 2 5 1 6
   (A) 21 (B) 25 (C) 20 (D) 18 (E) 23
2. 2 8 2 2 8 4 1 3 1 2 1 4 1 2 1 2 3 2 8 4 5 1 4 1 2 1 3 1 3 2
   (A) 28 (B) 26 (C) 24 (D) 20 (E) 27
3. 3 5 8 2 5 4 2 4 8 2 1 1 8 6 8 4 5 6 1 4 3 2 4 1 2 6 6 8
   (A) 20 (B) 27 (C) 25 (D) 22 (E) 28
4. 2 2 6 4 2 3 6 8 4 1 2 4 2 3 8 2 4 1 2 3 2 5 6 8 8 4 5 2 3
   (A) 28 (B) 22 (C) 19 (D) 24 (E) 26
5. 3 6 8 4 8 6 2 1 4 1 6 3 2 5 4 1 2 8 4 2 1 2 3 5 4 2 2 3 1 5
   (A) 30 (B) 35 (C) 28 (D) 33 (E) 32
6. 4 8 4 2 6 2 3 1 4 2 3 6 2 1 1 1 2 3 2 8 4 5 2 6 2 3 1 2 6 8 2
   (A) 18 (B) 20 (C) 25 (D) 22 (E) 23
7. 6 5 4 1 2 1 2 1 2 3 6 6 8 2 1 3 2 1 4 5 2 1 8 8 4 4 1 2 1 2 5 2
   (A) 25 (B) 28 (C) 29 (D) 32 (E) 30
8. 4 3 2 6 8 4 6 1 4 2 1 2 4 1 2 1 2 3 2 1 2 8 5 6 2 8 4 2 1 2
   (A) 15 (B) 17 (C) 20 (D) 22 (E) 18
9. 2 5 8 2 4 6 2 8 6 1 5 1 2 6 8 5 4 1 2 1 4 5 3 2 1 4 3 2 1 4 4
   (A) 32 (B) 30 (C) 29 (D) 35 (E) 33
10. 6 5 1 4 2 6 3 3 4 2 1 6 8 4 2 4 1 2 6 1 2 3 6 8 6 2 8 4 1 8 6
    (A) 17 (B) 19 (C) 21 (D) 23 (E) 20
11. 3 2 2 4 4 2 3 6 2 1 2 2 4 5 8 8 3 6 8 5 4 8 6 6 4 1 4 5 4 2
    (A) 20 (B) 24 (C) 26 (D) 28 (E) 31
12. 2 1 1 6 3 5 2 1 6 2 5 1 1 2 3 3 2 3 5 2 3 2 2 5 1 6 8 4 14 1 2
    (A) 40 (B) 45 (C) 42 (D) 43 (E) 47
13. 2 2 5 6 4 1 2 5 8 4 2 1 5 4 6 8 4 1 1 3 5 6 8 2 4 1 3 1 5 2 3
    (A) 38 (B) 36 (C) 43 (D) 46 (E) 40

14. 6 2 4 2 1 4 8 5 2 6 4 1 2 6 8 4 1 3 5 1 3 6 4 1 4 3 8
(A) 21 (B) 22 (C) 24 (D) 31 (E) 30

15. 6 2 3 5 6 8 2 5 3 8 2 5 3 5 2 2 1 5 6 2 2 2 4 5 8 1 5 2
(A) 46 (B) 42 (C) 47 (D) 43 (E) 48

16. 6 5 3 8 5 2 6 4 8 5 2 5 2 5 2 4 5 8 4 1 2 1 2 1 2 3 6 2 1
(A) 39 (B) 41 (C) 40 (D) 42 (E) 37

17. 8 4 2 3 2 5 3 4 1 2 3 2 5 4 1 5 2 6 4 8 5 6 4 1 3 2 6 2
(A) 34 (B) 35 (C) 36 (D) 33 (E) 32

18. 4 1 2 5 6 5 6 5 2 3 1 4 2 3 8 4 2 1 3 1 8 2 1 5 8 2 4 2 8 5
(A) 35 (B) 34 (C) 36 (D) 37 (E) 39

19. 5 2 3 1 3 1 2 5 2 3 5 8 6 4 4 8 2 2 4 5 2 5 2 8 4 1 2 1 8 2 8 2
(A) 37 (B) 40 (C) 39 (D) 38 (E) 36

20. 4 3 2 1 3 2 5 8 4 3 1 2 5 8 1 2 5 1 2 3 5 1 6 8 2 8 5 1 2 8
(A) 44 (B) 43 (C) 42 (D) 41 (E) 40

21. 2 2 3 2 5 2 1 4 2 1 5 4 2 1 2 3 2 1 4 4 2 4 4 5 6 5 2 1 4 1
(A) 32 (B) 35 (C) 36 (D) 37 (E) 38

22. 3 5 8 5 8 4 6 2 6 1 4 6 4 6 1 4 1 2 6 5 8 2 6 4 1 2 6 5 8 3 6
(A) 23 (B) 26 (C) 22 (D) 27 (E) 30

23. 6 6 8 3 4 1 2 5 8 4 1 2 2 5 1 3 6 5 2 1 4 2 1 3 6 2 4 1 4 2
(A) 26 (B) 27 (C) 28 (D) 29 (E) 30

24. 2 6 2 6 8 5 1 1 8 5 1 8 5 2 4 2 5 8 8 2 6 5 8 8 1 3 3 6 4 1
(A) 28 (B) 27 (C) 36 (D) 31 (E) 32

25. 6 2 8 4 1 2 2 1 4 1 2 4 3 8 4 1 6 4 2 4 2 1 3 2 2 6 6 1 2 4 1 2 2
(A) 15 (B) 19 (C) 17 (D) 13 (E) 11

26. 2 1 8 8 6 2 2 5 5 5 1 2 2 8 3 4 1 8 2 4 5 6 4 6 2 2 8 1 2 2
(A) 26 (B) 27 (C) 29 (D) 31 (E) 30

27. 1 5 3 2 4 6 2 1 2 6 8 8 4 5 8 4 6 8 4 1 3 3 3 2 2 3 3 2
(A) 32 (B) 33 (C) 34 (D) 30 (E) 31

28. 3 3 2 8 4 2 6 8 4 6 3 1 4 5 1 4 1 2 6 5 8 6 3 6 8 5 4 1 2 8 1
(A) 33 (B) 32 (C) 31 (D) 34 (E) 35

29. 4 1 4 3 2 4 4 2 4 4 2 6 1 5 8 4 1 4 2 6 4 6 3 2 3 6 5 2 1 6 3 1 1 1
(A) 23 (B) 26 (C) 27 (D) 29 (E) 24

30. 3 2 3 2 2 3 2 8 2 1 3 3 5 1 1 5 1 1 6 8 8 5 2 4 1 2 5 6 2 1
(A) 31 (B) 30 (C) 29 (D) 42 (E) 33

TEST 3 TEST FOR MEASURING SPATIAL SCANNING

Total Ques.- 40
Time- 8 Min.

Shortest Route Test (संक्षिप्त रास्ता परीक्षण)

निर्देश : (प्रश्न 1-40) इस अभ्यास में 40 प्रश्न दिए गए हैं जो चार उपखंडों 1, 2, 3 एवं 4 में 10-10 प्रश्नों (कुल 40 प्रश्न) के रूप में विभाजित है। प्रत्येक खण्ड के चित्रों को ध्यानपूर्वक देखकर दिए गए प्रत्येक प्रश्नों का उत्तर खोजकर अपने उत्तर-पत्रक में अंकित गोले को काला करें या माउस की सहायता से क्लिक करें और इसके लिए 5 या 8 मिनट का समय दिया जाता है।

Instructions: (Questions 1-40) : This exercise contains 40 questions, divided into four subsections: 1, 2, 3, and 4, each containing 10 questions (40 questions in total). Look carefully at the pictures in each section to find the answer to each question. Darken the circle on your answer sheet or click on it with the mouse. You are given 5 or 8 minutes for this.

उपखंड/Section-1

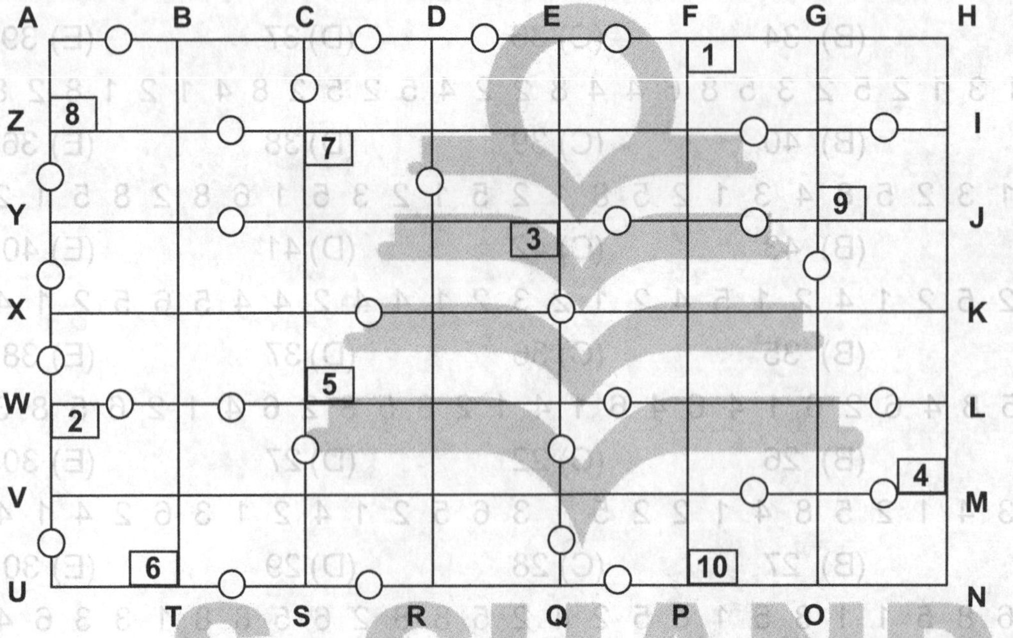

1. I - J
2. K - L
3. R - X
4. S - A
5. D - X
6. E - R
7. R - U
8. R - M
9. H - E
10. X - W

उपखंड/Section-2

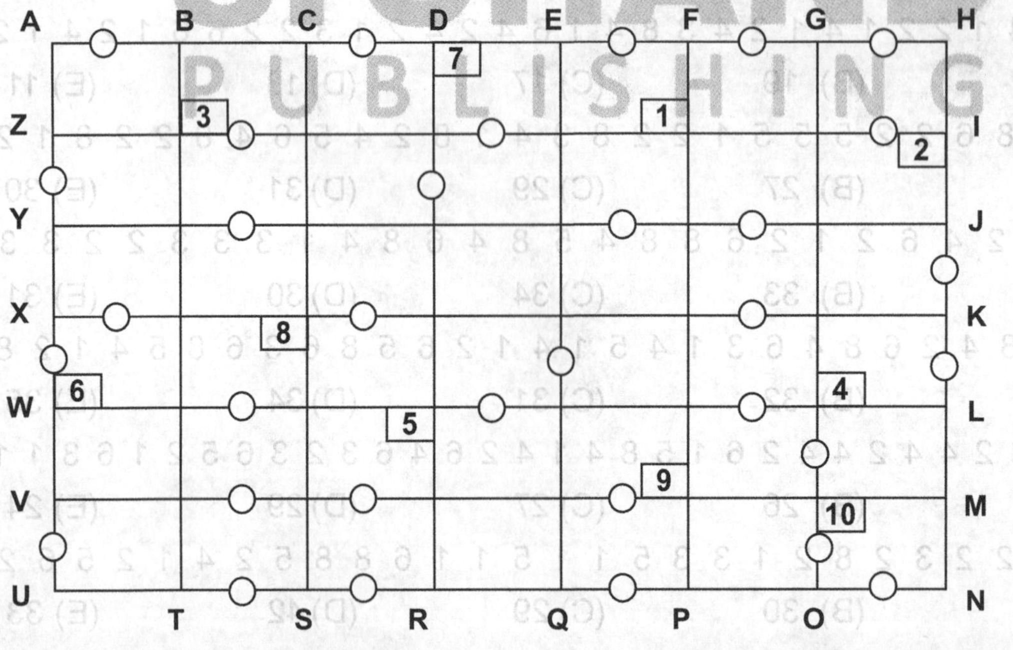

11. H - G
12. A - C
13. S - R
14. E - J
15. C - E
16. G - P
17. M - J
18. N - O
19. A - W
20. S - Y

उपखंड/Section-3

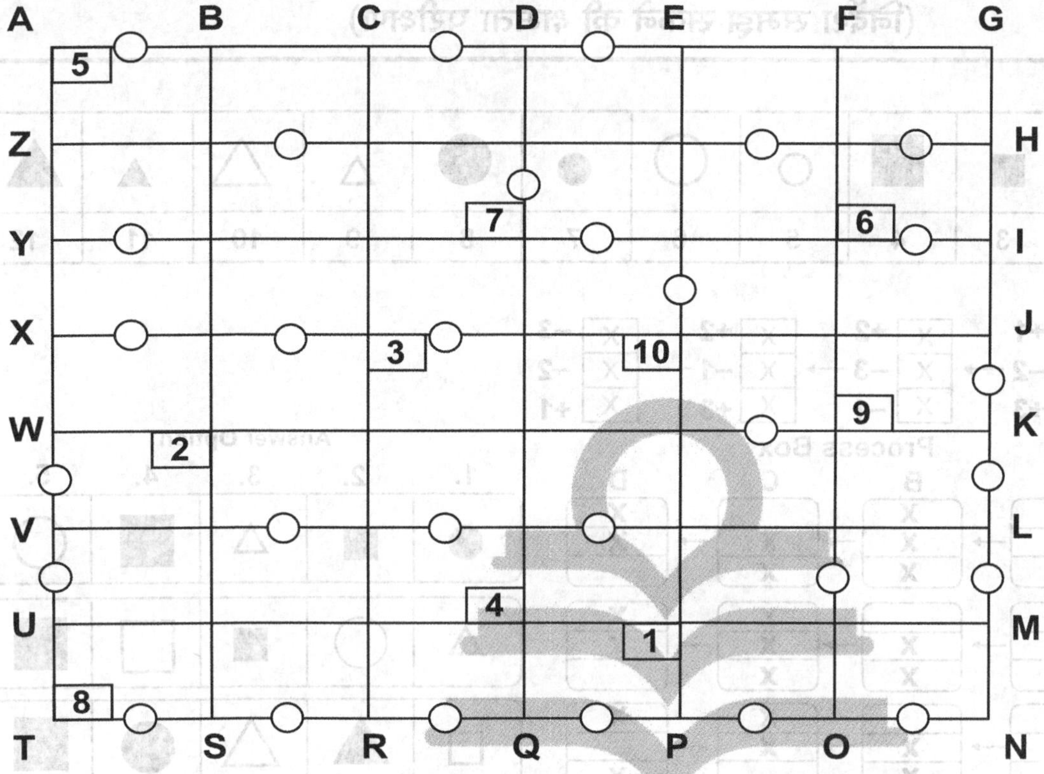

21. X - B
22. Y - U
23. N - K
24. N - P
25. C - R
26. E - H
27. W - L
28. N - Q
29. R - T
30. S - Q

उपखंड/Section-4

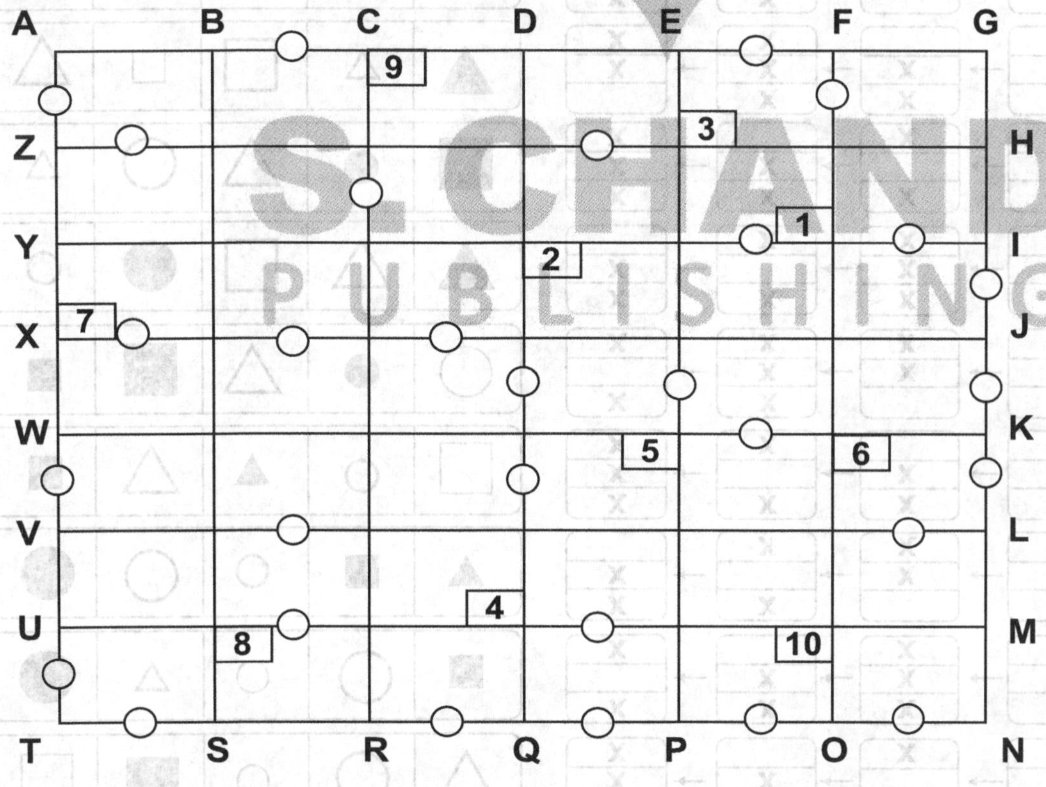

31. A - E
32. D - H
33. G - J
34. N - K
35. P - N
36. Y - J
37. A - W
38. R - P
39. R - W
40. P - Q

TEST 4

INFORMATION ORDERING TEST

(निर्देश समझ सकने की क्षमता परीक्षण)

Total Ques.- 25
Time - 8 Min.

Table - 2

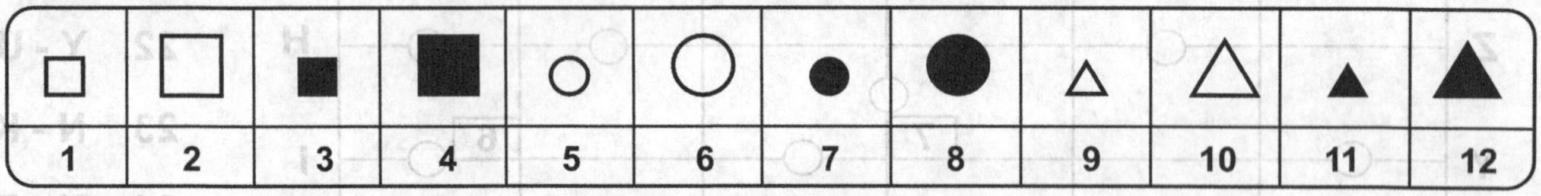

Table - 1

Level- 1 →	X +1	X +2	X +2	X −3
Level- 2 →	X −2	X −3	X −1	X −2
Level- 3 →	X +3	X −1	X +3	X +1

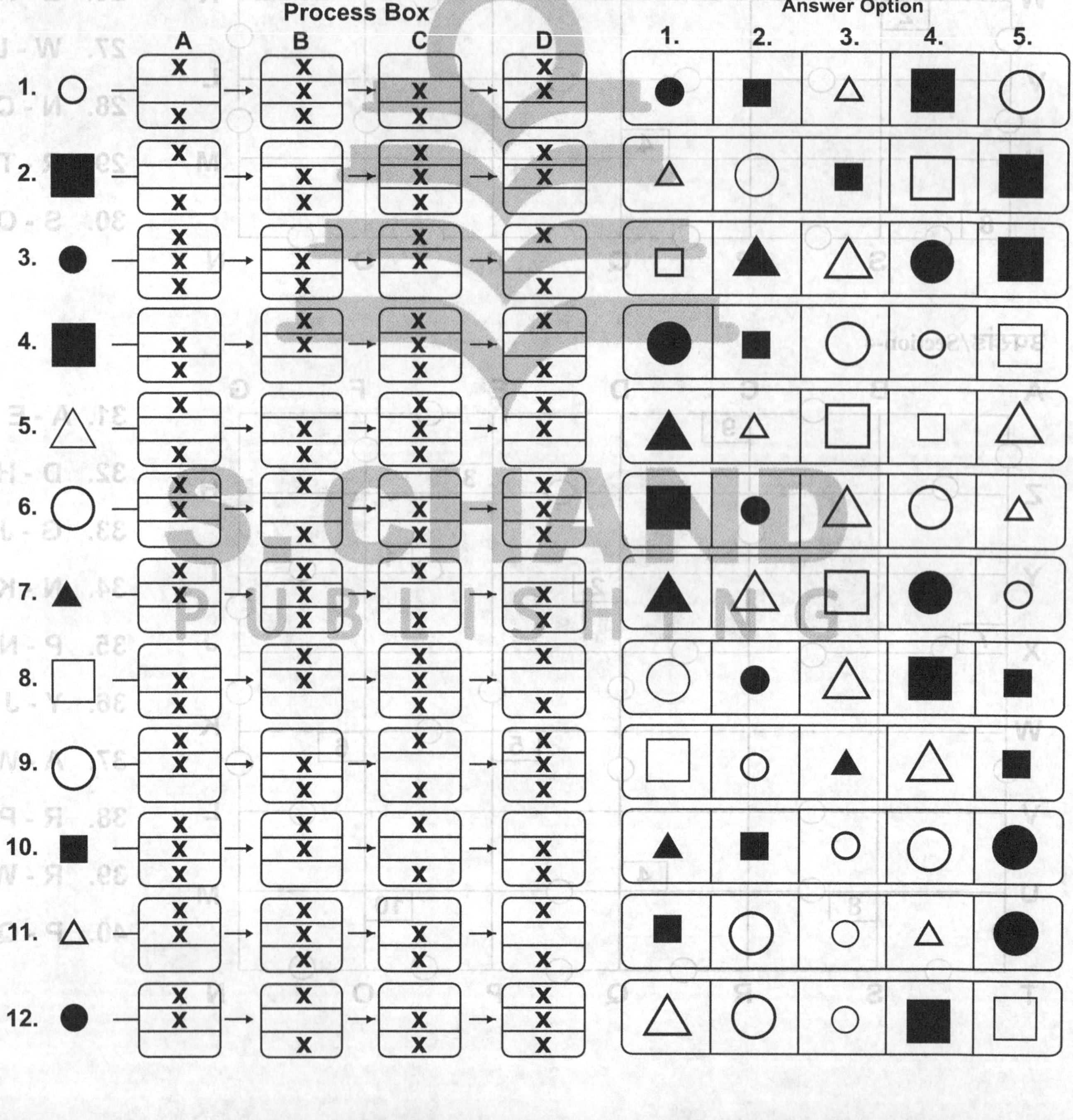

Table - 2

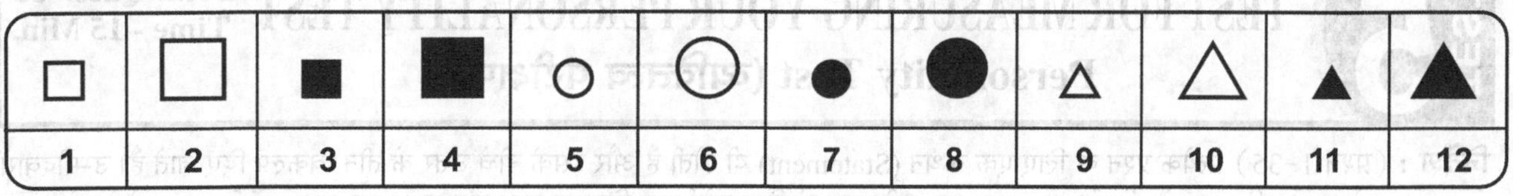

Table - 1

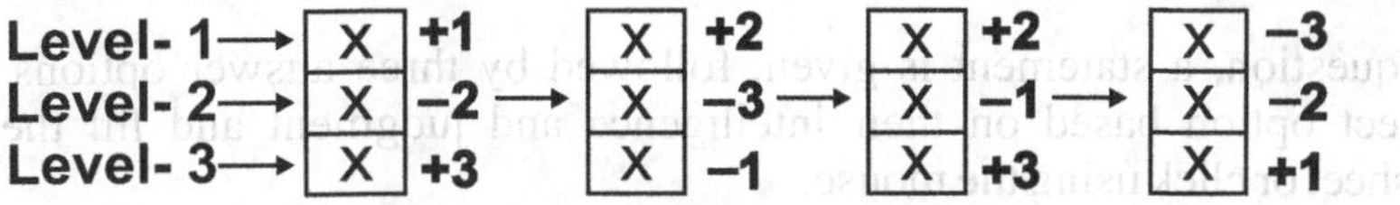

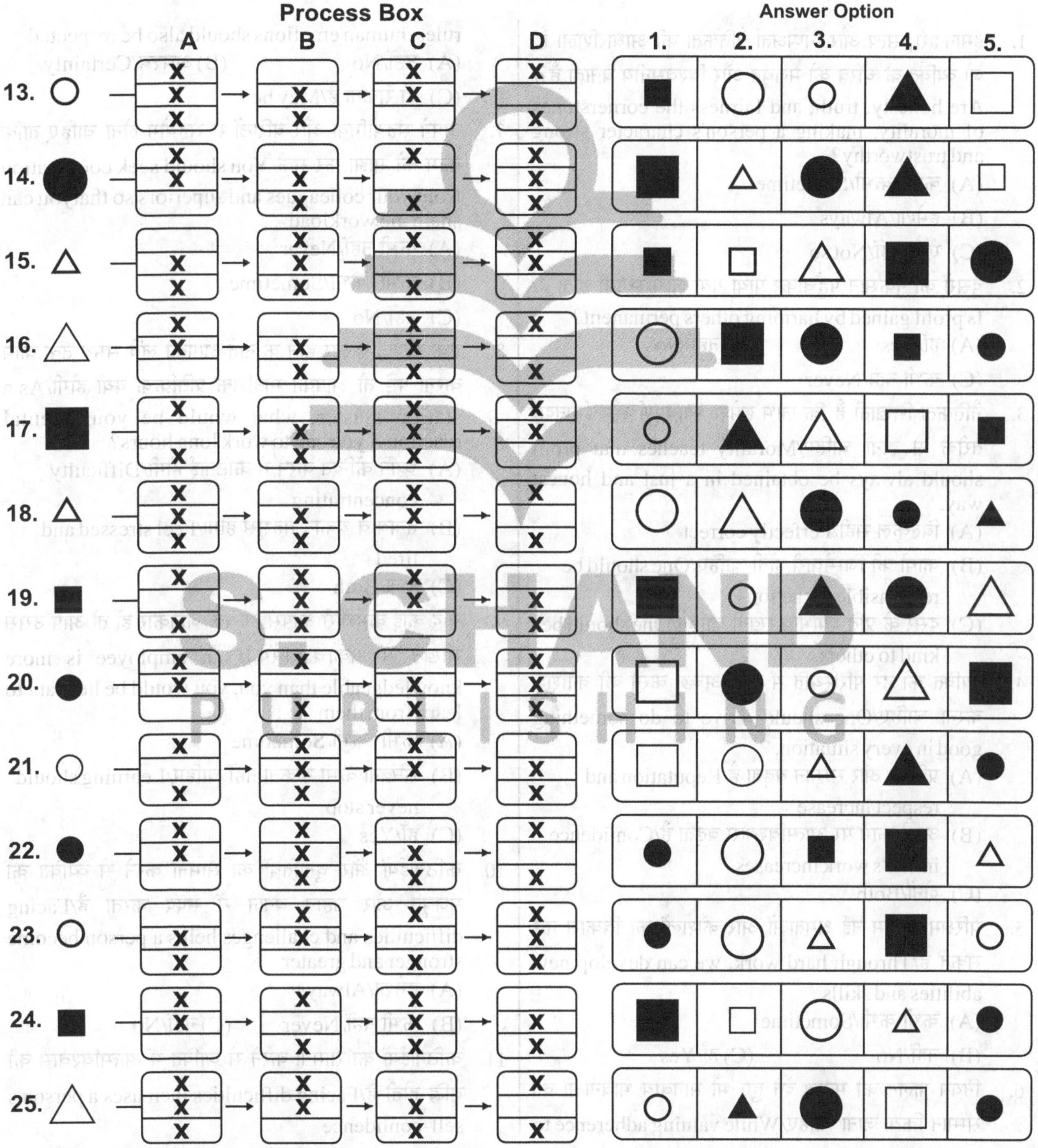

TEST 5 TEST FOR MEASURING YOUR PERSONALITY TEST

Total Ques.- 35
Time - 15 Min.

Personality Test (व्यक्तित्व परीक्षण)

निर्देश : (प्रश्न 1–35) प्रत्येक प्रश्न के लिए एक कथन (Statement) दी होती है और इसके नीचे उत्तर के तीन विकल्प दिए जाते हैं। उम्मीदवारों को अपने बुद्धिमता और निर्णय के आधार पर सही उत्तर के लिए कोई एक विकल्प का चयन कर उत्तर-पत्रक में दिए गए गोले को काला या माउस की सहायता से क्लिक (Click) करें।

Direction : (Questions 1–35) : For each question, a statement is given, followed by three answer options. Candidates should select the correct option based on their intelligence and judgment and fill the corresponding circle on the answer sheet or click using the mouse.

1. ईमानदारी, सत्य और निष्पक्षता नैतिकता की आधारशिला है, जो व्यक्ति के चरित्र को मजबूत और विश्वसनीय बनाती है?/ Are honesty, truth, and fairness the cornerstones of morality, making a person's character strong and trustworthy?
   (A) कभी-कभी/Sometime
   (B) हमेशा/Always
   (C) ऐसा नहीं/Not so
2. दूसरों को नुकसान पहुँचाकर पाया गया लाभ स्थायी होता है/ Is profit gained by harming others permanent?
   (A) हाँ/Yes (B) नहीं/No
   (C) कभी नहीं/Never
3. नैतिकता सिखाती है कि लाभ हमेशा न्यायपूर्ण और ईमानदार तरीके से होना चाहिए/Morality teaches that profit should always be obtained in a just and honest way.
   (A) बिल्कुल सही/Perfectly correct
   (B) कार्यो की जिम्मेवारी होनी चाहिए/One should be responsible for actions
   (C) दूसरे के प्रति दयाभाव रखनी चाहिए/One should be kind to others
4. व्यक्ति को हर परिस्थिति में कुछ अच्छा करने की कोशिश करना चाहिए/One should strive to do something good in every situation.
   (A) प्रतिष्ठा और सम्मान बढ़ता है/Reputation and respect increase
   (B) अपने काम पर आत्मविश्वास बढ़ता है/Confidence in one's work increases
   (C) दोनों/Both
5. परिश्रम से हम नई क्षमताओं और कौशलों का विकास कर सकते हैं/Through hard work, we can develop new abilities and skills
   (A) कभी कभी/Sometime
   (B) नहीं/No (C) हाँ/Yes
6. नियम पालन को महत्व देते हुए भी मानवीय भावनाओं का सम्मान किया जाना चाहिए/While valuing adherence to rules, human emotions should also be respected
   (A) नहीं/No (B) अवश्य/Certainly
   (C) हो सकता है/May be
7. अपने सहयोगियों और वरिष्ठों से सहयोग लेना चाहिए ताकि काम को साझा कर सके/You should seek cooperation from your colleagues and superiors so thatyou can share the workload
   (A) कभी नहीं/Never
   (B) कभी-कभी/Sometime
   (C) नहीं/No
8. एक स्टेशन मास्टर होने के नाते आपको लंबे समय तक काम करना पड़े तो आपकी मानसिक प्रतिक्रिया क्या होगी/As a station master, what would be your mental reaction if you had to work long hours?
   (A) ध्यान केन्द्रित करने में कठिनाई होगी/Difficulty concentrating
   (B) तनाव व थकान महसूस होगा/Feel stressed and tired
   (C) दोनों/Both
9. यदि कोई कर्मचारी आपसे अधिक जानकार हो तो आप उससे सीखने में संकोच करेंगे/If an employee is more knowledgeable than you, you would be hesitant to learn from them
   (A) कभी-कभी/Sometime
   (B) सीखना कभी रूकना नहीं चाहिए/Learning should never stop
   (C) हाँ/Yes
10. कठिनाईयों और चुनौतियों का सामना करने से व्यक्ति को मजबूत और महान बनाने में मदद करता है/Facing difficulties and challenges helps a person become stronger and greater
    (A) हमेशा/Always
    (B) कभी नहीं/Never (C) नहीं/No
11. कठिनाईयों का सामना करने से व्यक्ति में आत्मविश्वास की वृद्धि होती है/Facing difficulties increases a person's self-confidence

(A) हाँ/Yes (B) ऐसा नहीं/Not so
(C) मालूम नहीं/I don't know

12. यदि कोई अधिनस्थ आपकी बात नहीं मानता है तो आप क्या कदम उठाऐंगे/What steps will you take if a subordinate doesn't listen to you?
(A) शांत रहकर स्थिति को समझूंगा/I will remain calm and understand the situation
(B) स्पष्ट और प्रभावी ढंग से संवाद करूंगा/I will communicate clearly and effectively
(C) दोनों/Both

13. कर्मचारियों के साथ अच्छे संबंध बनाऐ रखना और उनके समस्या को समाधान करना चाहिए, इससे/Maintaining good relationships with employees and resolving their issues will help you
(A) तनाव में कमी आएगी/Reduce stress
(B) सकारात्मक दृष्टिकोण प्रदान होगा/Provide a positive attitude
(C) दोनों/Both

14. यदि किसी व्यक्ति का रवैया आपके प्रति नकारात्मक हो तो आप/If someone has a negative attitude towards you, will you:
(A) नजरअंदाज करेंगे/Ignore them
(B) उसे सुधारने का प्रयास करेंगे/Try to improve them
(C) दोनों/Both

15. यदि कर्मचारियों के बीच मतभेद हो जाए तो आप क्या कदम उठाऐंगे/What steps will you take if there is a disagreement between employees?
(A) दोनों पक्षों को समझाने की कोशिश करूँगा/I will try to make both parties understand
(B) उच्च अधिकारी को सूचित करूँगा/I will inform my superiors
(C) दोनों/Both

16. ड्यूटी के समय भीषण दुर्घटना होने पर आप क्या कदम उठाऐंगे/What steps would you take if a serious accident occurred while on duty?
(A) तुरंत अधिकारी को सूचना देंगे/I will immediately inform my superiors
(B) तुरंत आपातकालीन सेवाओं को सूचित करेंगे/I will immediately inform emergency services
(C) दोनों/Both

17. विनम्र एवं शांत स्वभाव वाला व्यक्ति दूसरे के साथ संवाद कर तनावपूर्ण माहौल को शांत कर सकता है/A person with a polite and calm demeanor can calm a tense situation by communicating with others
(A) कभी नहीं/Never
(B) ऐसे व्यक्ति क्रोधित कम होते हैं/Such people rarely get angry
(C) मालूम नहीं/I don't know

18. सम्मानजनक व्यवहार से व्यक्ति का अच्छे संस्कार और मानसिक अभिव्यक्ति दर्शाता है/Respectful behavior reflects a person's good values and mental expression
(A) ऐसे व्यक्ति आत्मविश्वासी होते हैं/Such people are self-confident
(B) ऐसे व्यक्ति कठोर स्वभाव वाले होते हैं/Such people are harsh
(C) मालूम नहीं/I don't know

19. आपकी गलती होने पर घबराहट के बजाय विश्लेषण कर सुधारने की सख्त जरूरत है/If you make a mistake, instead of panicking, you need to analyze and correct it
(A) ऐसी गलती नहीं इसके लिए सावधान रहूँगा/I will be careful not to make such a mistake
(B) कभी नहीं/Never (C) नहीं/No

20. नियमों का पालन करने से मतदाताओं का चुनाव प्रक्रिया में पारदर्शिता और निष्पक्षता बनी रहती है/Following the rules ensures transparency and fairness in the electoral process
(A) इससे विश्वास बढ़ता है/This increases voter trust
(B) वोट देने का सभी को अधिकार है/Everyone has the right to vote
(C) कभी-कभी/Sometime

21. दूसरों की भावनाओं को समझना और सहानुभूति दिखाना चाहिए/Understanding the feelings of others and showing empathyshould be done
(A) नहीं/No
(B) इससे व्यक्तिगत संबंध मजबूत होते हैं/This strengthens personal relationships
(C) अमीर लोग दयावान होते हैं/Rich people are compassionate

22. स्वस्थ खान-पान से कई बीमारियों का खतरा कम हो सकता है/Healthy eating can reduce the risk of many diseases
(A) अच्छे खाने-पीने के लिए लोगों के पास समय नहीं है/People don't have time for good food
(B) अच्छे खान-पान की कमी ही बिमारियाँ का कारण है/Lack of good food is the cause of diseases
(C) नहीं/No

23. निजीकरण से रेलवे में आधुनिक तकनीक और सुविधाओं का समावेश होगा/Privatization will bring modern technology and facilities to the railways
(A) बिल्कुल सही/Absolutely correct
(B) ऐसा नहीं/Not so
(C) कह नहीं सकते/Can't say

24. बाढ़ प्रभावित क्षेत्रों में राहत कार्य और आवश्यक सुविधाएँ

प्रदान करना चाहिए/Relief work and essential services should be provided in flood-affected areas.

(A) प्रभावित क्षेत्रों में रोजमर्रे की वस्तुएँ की आवश्यकता से वंचित हो जाते हैं/People in affected areas are deprived of daily necessities

(B) इन क्षेत्रों में आर्थिक स्थिति दयनीय हो जाती है/The economic situation in these areas becomes miserable

(C) दोनों/Both

25. गरीबों के स्वास्थ्य में सुधार के लिए समय-समय पर मुफ्त चिकित्सा शिविर का आयोजन किया जाना चाहिए/Free medical camps should be organized from time to time to improve the health of the poor

(A) गरीबों के लिए शिक्षा जरूरी है/Education is essential for the poor

(B) सरकार को आर्थिक मदद करनी चाहिए/The government should provide financial assistance

(C) हमेशा/Always

26. ध्यान और आराम करने से मानसिक शांति और तनाव में कमी आएगी/Meditation and relaxation will bring peace of mind and reduce stress

(A) हाँ/Yes (B) ऐसा नहीं/Not so

(C) लोगों के पास समय नहीं है/People don't have time

27. सच्चाई और ईमानदारी के साथ कार्य करना चाहिए/One should act with truth and honesty

(A) कभी-कभी/Sometime

(B) हमेशा/Always

(C) कभी नहीं/Never

28. बच्चों को नैतिकता, ईमानदारी और सहानुभूति जैसे मूल्यों की शिक्षा देनी चाहिए/Children should be taught values like morality, honesty, and empathy

(A) बच्चों में सकारात्मक सोच में वृद्धि हुई है/Positive thinking has increased in children

(B) इससे उनमें क्रोध, नकारात्मक विचार, ईर्ष्या जैसी भावनाएँ में कमी आएगी/This will reduce feelings like anger, negative thoughts, and jealousy

(C) दोनों/Both

29. समाज में सामाजिक न्याय की लड़ाई के लिए वंचित वर्गों को प्रोत्साहित करने चाहिए/Unprivileged sections of society should be encouraged to fight for social justice

(A) कभी-कभी/Sometime

(B) कभी नहीं/Never

(C) अवश्य/Certainly

30. घरेलु जिम्मेदारियाँ का दबाव बढ़ने से कामकाज की कार्यक्षमता पर नकारात्मक प्रभाव पड़ता है। जैसे कि/Increasing pressure from household responsibilities negatively impacts work efficiency. Such as:

(A) जिम्मेदारियाँ का बंटना/Dividing responsibilities

(B) समय प्रबंधन करना/Time management

(C) दोनों/Both

31. अपने देश के लिए देशभक्ति की भावना रखनी चाहिए/One should have a sense of patriotism for one's country

(A) हमेशा/Always

(B) ऐसा नहीं/Not so

(C) दोनों के बीच/Between two

32. रेलवे की इंजीनियरिंग विभाग की गड़बड़ी के कारण भी कई दुर्घटनाएँ हो जाती है/Many accidents also occur due to the negligence of the railway engineering department.

(A) कभी-कभी/Sometime

(B) ऐसा नहीं/Not so

(C) जानकारी नहीं/I don't know

33. विकृत व्यक्तित्व वाले लोग समाज में अपराध और हिंसा पैदा कर सकते हैं/People with personality disorders can cause crime and violence in society

(A) अक्सर/Often

(B) कभी नहीं/Never

(C) दोनों के बीच/Somewhere in between

34. स्वच्छता अभियान में सामुदायिक भागीदारी को बढ़ावा दिया जाना चाहिए/Community participation in cleanliness drives should be encouraged

(A) हाँ/Yes

(B) कभी नहीं/Never

(C) कभी कभी/Sometime

35. स्टेशन मास्टर की भूमिका यात्रियों, कर्मचारियों की सुरक्षा और रेलवे संचालन की प्रबंधन में महत्वपूर्ण योगदान शामिल है/The role of a station master involves significant contributions to the safety of passengers and staff, and the management of railway operations.

(A) अवश्य/Certainly

(B) नहीं/No

(C) दोनों के बीच/Somewhere in between

उत्तर (ANSWER)

SET - 1

1.	A	19.	A
2.	A	20.	A
3.	A	21.	B
4.	C	22.	E
5.	B	23.	E
6.	C	24.	C
7.	A	25.	D
8.	A	26.	E
9.	E	27.	E
10.	C	28.	B
11.	B	29.	C
12.	D	30.	B
13.	B	31.	E
14.	C	32.	A
15.	B	33.	C
16.	D	34.	A
17.	A	35.	E
18.	D		

SET - 2

1.	A	16.	C
2.	B	17.	B
3.	C	18.	E
4.	D	19.	D
5.	E	20.	B
6.	D	21.	A
7.	C	22.	E
8.	B	23.	E
9.	A	24.	C
10.	B	25.	D
11.	C	26.	B
12.	D	27.	E
13.	E	28.	B
14.	C	29.	D
15.	A	30.	D

SET - 3

SECTION-1

1. ① ② ③ ④ ⑤ ⑥ ⑦ ⑧ ❾ ⑩
2. ① ② ③ ❹ ⑤ ⑥ ⑦ ⑧ ⑨ ⑩
3. ① ② ③ ④ ❺ ⑥ ⑦ ⑧ ⑨ ⑩
4. ① ② ③ ④ ⑤ ⑥ ⑦ ❽ ⑨ ⑩
5. ① ② ③ ④ ⑤ ⑥ ❼ ⑧ ⑨ ⑩
6. ① ② ❸ ④ ⑤ ⑥ ⑦ ⑧ ⑨ ⑩
7. ① ② ③ ④ ⑤ ❻ ⑦ ⑧ ⑨ ⑩
8. ① ② ③ ④ ⑤ ⑥ ⑦ ⑧ ⑨ ❿
9. ❶ ② ③ ④ ⑤ ⑥ ⑦ ⑧ ⑨ ⑩
10. ① ❷ ③ ④ ⑤ ⑥ ⑦ ⑧ ⑨ ⑩

SECTION-2

11. ① ❷ ③ ④ ⑤ ⑥ ⑦ ⑧ ⑨ ⑩
12. ① ② ❸ ④ ⑤ ⑥ ⑦ ⑧ ⑨ ⑩
13. ① ② ③ ④ ❺ ⑥ ⑦ ⑧ ⑨ ⑩
14. ❶ ② ③ ④ ⑤ ⑥ ⑦ ⑧ ⑨ ⑩
15. ① ② ③ ④ ⑤ ⑥ ❼ ⑧ ⑨ ⑩
16. ① ② ③ ④ ⑤ ⑥ ⑦ ⑧ ❾ ⑩
17. ① ② ③ ❹ ⑤ ⑥ ⑦ ⑧ ⑨ ⑩
18. ① ② ③ ④ ⑤ ⑥ ⑦ ⑧ ⑨ ❿
19. ① ② ③ ④ ⑤ ❻ ⑦ ⑧ ⑨ ⑩
20. ① ② ③ ④ ⑤ ⑥ ⑦ ❽ ⑨ ⑩

SECTION-3

21. ① ❷ ③ ④ ⑤ ⑥ ⑦ ⑧ ⑨ ⑩
22. ① ❷ ③ ④ ⑤ ⑥ ⑦ ⑧ ⑨ ⑩
23. ① ② ③ ④ ⑤ ⑥ ⑦ ⑧ ❾ ⑩
24. ❶ ② ③ ④ ⑤ ⑥ ⑦ ⑧ ⑨ ⑩
25. ① ② ❸ ④ ⑤ ⑥ ⑦ ⑧ ⑨ ⑩
26. ① ② ③ ④ ⑤ ❻ ⑦ ⑧ ⑨ ⑩
27. ① ❷ ③ ④ ⑤ ⑥ ⑦ ⑧ ⑨ ⑩
28. ❶ ② ③ ④ ⑤ ⑥ ⑦ ⑧ ⑨ ⑩
29. ① ② ③ ④ ⑤ ⑥ ⑦ ❽ ⑨ ⑩
30. ① ② ③ ❹ ⑤ ⑥ ⑦ ⑧ ⑨ ⑩

SECTION-4

31. ① ② ③ ④ ⑤ ⑥ ⑦ ⑧ ❾ ⑩
32. ① ② ❸ ④ ⑤ ⑥ ⑦ ⑧ ⑨ ⑩
33. ❶ ② ③ ④ ⑤ ⑥ ⑦ ⑧ ⑨ ⑩
34. ① ② ③ ④ ⑤ ❻ ⑦ ⑧ ⑨ ⑩
35. ① ② ③ ④ ⑤ ⑥ ⑦ ⑧ ⑨ ❿
36. ① ❷ ③ ④ ⑤ ⑥ ⑦ ⑧ ⑨ ⑩
37. ① ② ③ ④ ⑤ ⑥ ❼ ⑧ ⑨ ⑩
38. ① ② ③ ❹ ⑤ ⑥ ⑦ ⑧ ⑨ ⑩
39. ① ② ③ ④ ⑤ ⑥ ⑦ ❽ ⑨ ⑩
40. ① ② ③ ❹ ⑤ ⑥ ⑦ ⑧ ⑨ ⑩

SET - 4

1.	4	14.	1
2.	3	15.	5
3.	5	16.	5
4.	3	17.	5
5.	2	18.	1
6.	1	19.	2
7.	1	20.	3
8.	4	21.	5
9.	1	22.	4
10.	5	23.	2
11.	2	24.	3
12.	3	25.	2
13.	5		

SET - 5

1.	B	18.	A
2.	C	19.	A
3.	A	20.	A
4.	C	21.	B
5.	C	22.	B
6.	B	23.	A
7.	B	24.	C
8.	C	25.	C
9.	B	26.	A
10.	A	27.	B
11.	A	28.	C
12.	C	29.	C
13.	C	30.	C
14.	C	31.	A
15.	C	32.	A
16.	C	33.	A
17.	B	34.	A
		35.	A

MODEL SET - 2

GDCE (09-06-2023) (Online Exam)

Station Master Psychological/Aptitude Test का हल प्रश्न-पत्र (Based on Memory)

TEST 1 — **TEST FOR MEASURING YOUR INTELLIGENCE** — **Total Ques.- 35** **Time - 10 Min.**

Classification Test (वर्गीकरण)

निर्देश : (प्रश्न 1-35) बुद्धिमापन परीक्षण के प्रत्येक प्रश्न में पाँच आकृतियाँ दिए जाते हैं जिसमें से चार आकृतियाँ में कुछ समानता और कोई एक आकृति अन्य चारों से भिन्न है वही भिन्न आकृति आपका उत्तर होगा जिसे दिए गए उत्तर-पत्रक में गोले को काला/माउस की सहायता से क्लिक करना होता है और इसके लिए 10 मिनट का समय दिया जाता है।

Instructions : (Questions 1–35) : Each question in the Intelligence Test consists of five figures, four of which have some similarity, and one that is different from the other four is your answer. You must click on the black circle on the answer sheet or using the mouse. You are given 10 minutes to complete the test.

A B C D E

1. 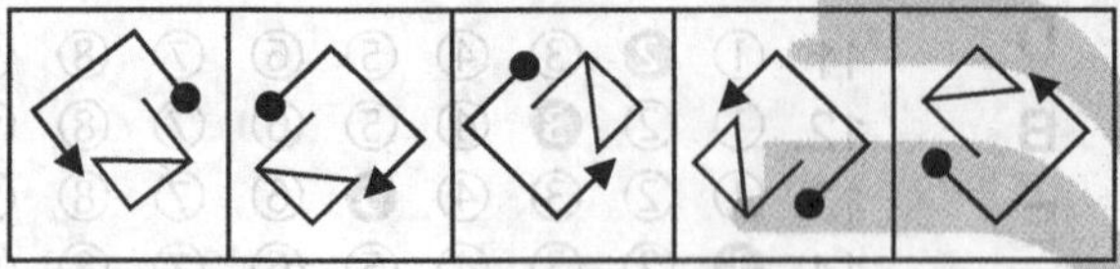

2. 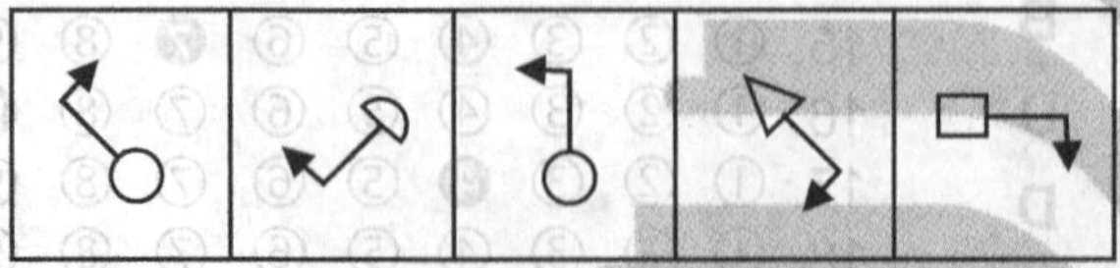

3. 

4. 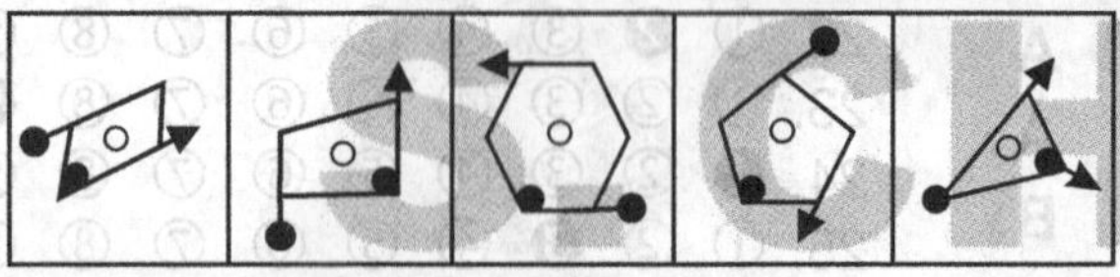

5. 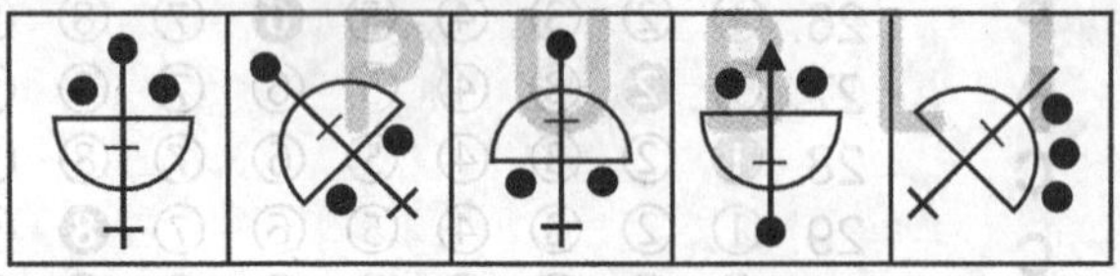

6. 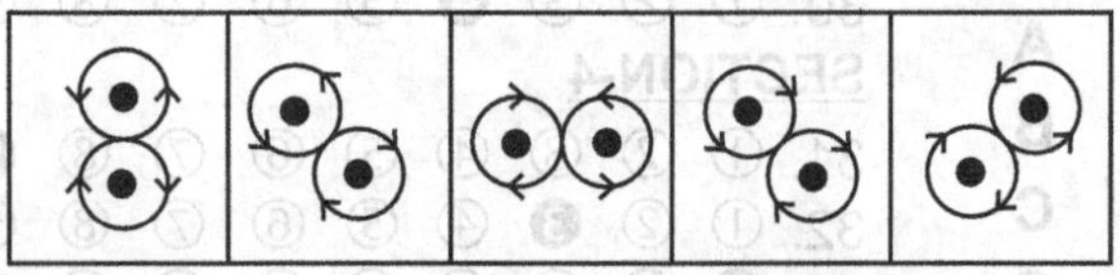

7. 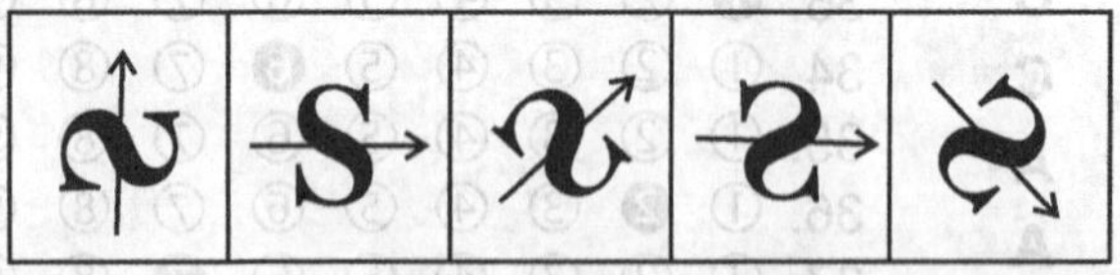

8. 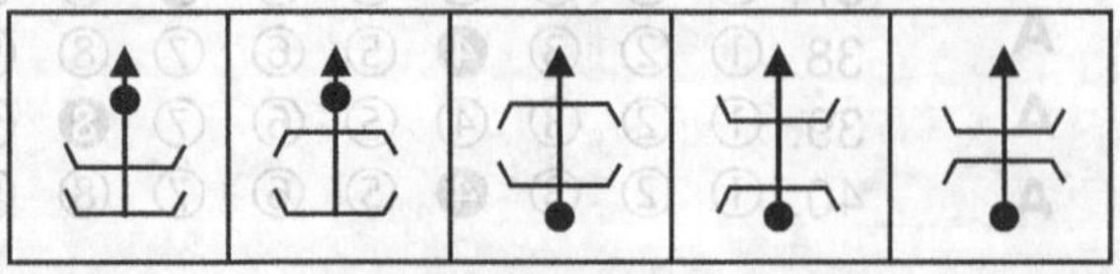

A B C D E

9. 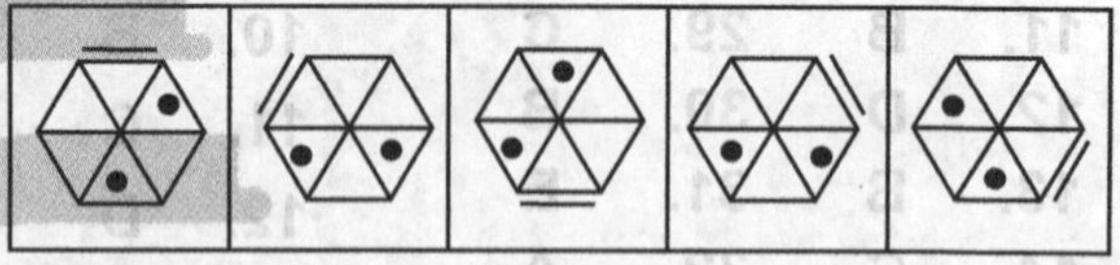

10. 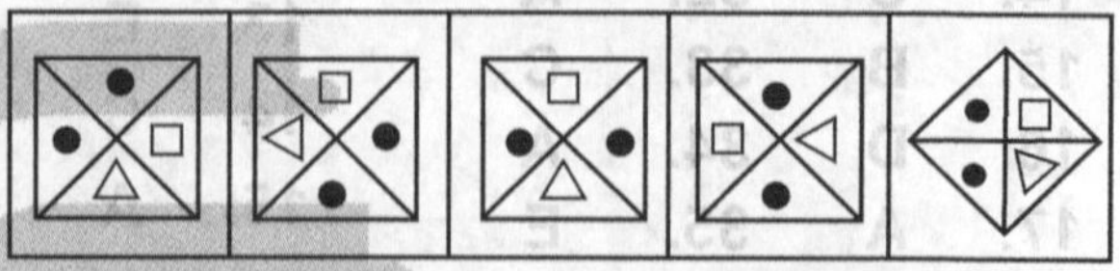

11. 

12. 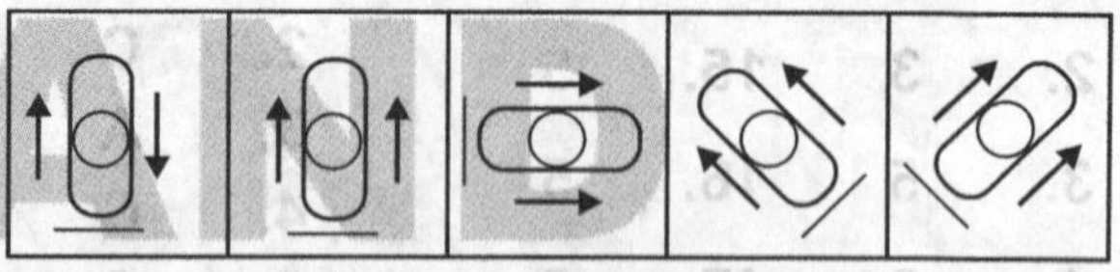

13. 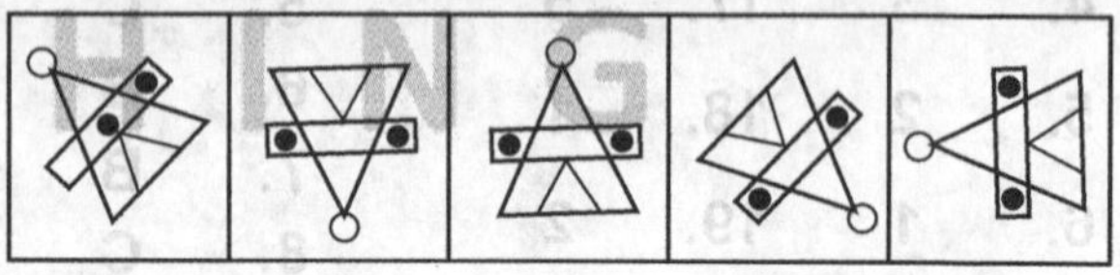

14. 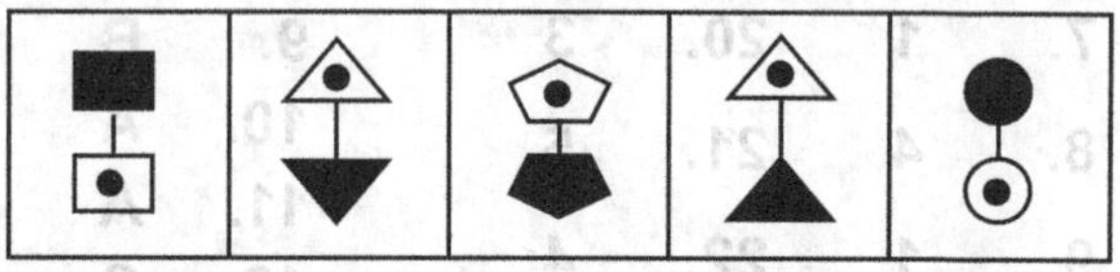

15. 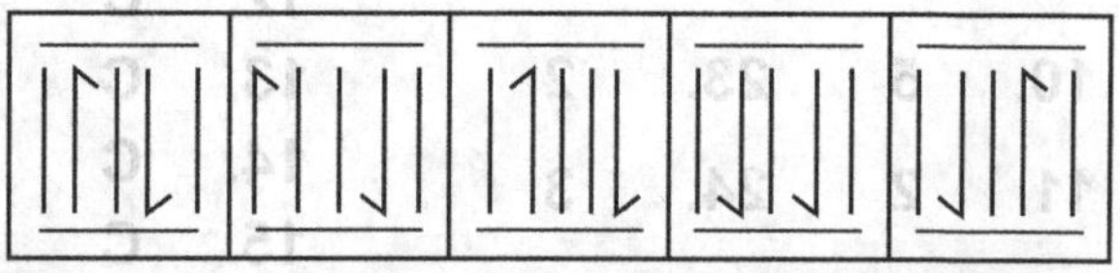

16. 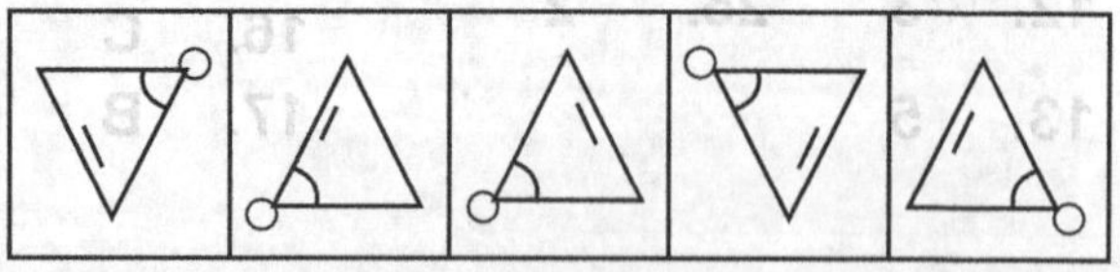

A B C D E

17.
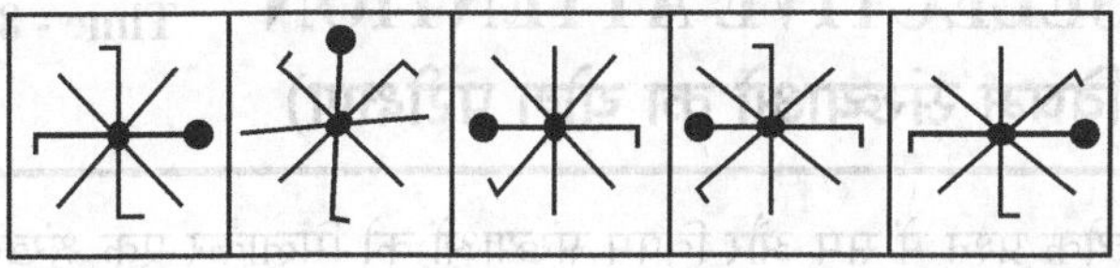

18.
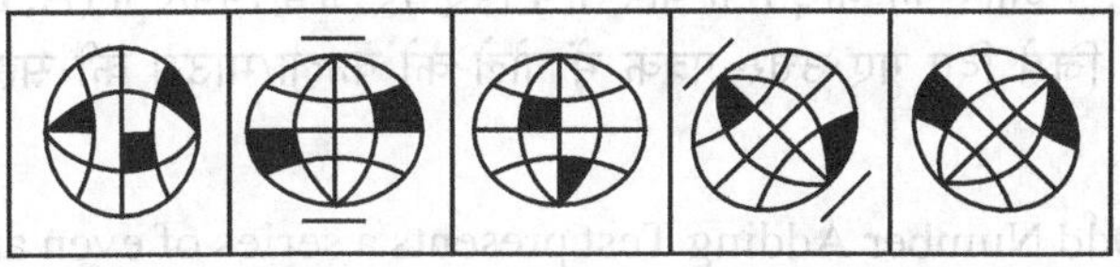

19.
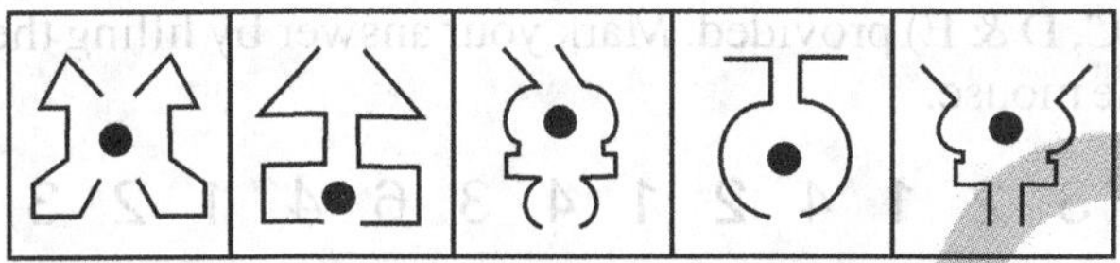

20.

21.
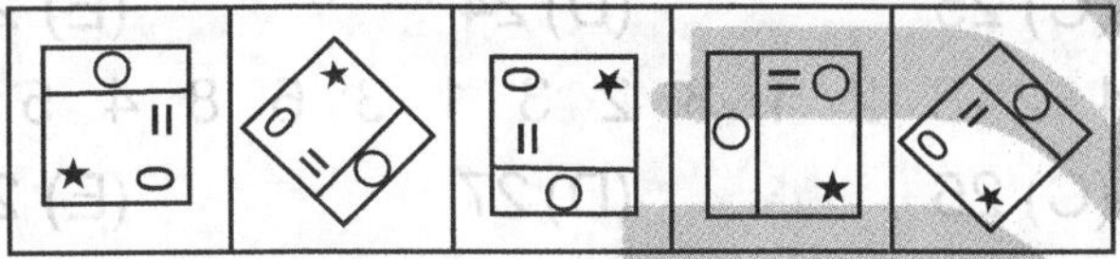

22.
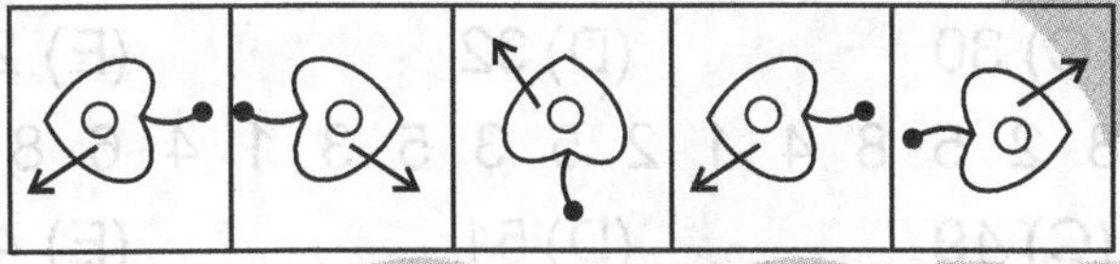

23.
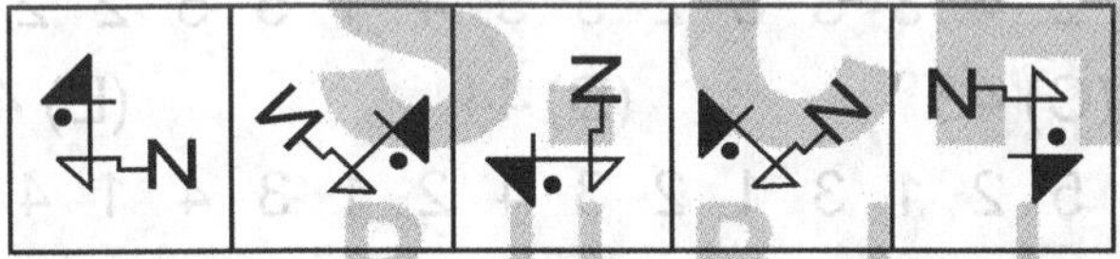

24.
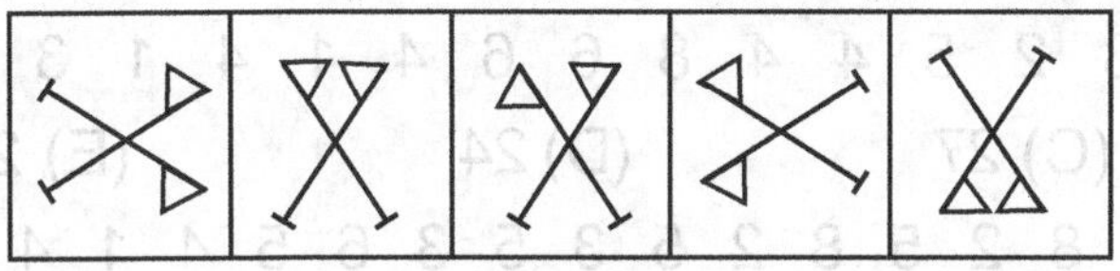

25.
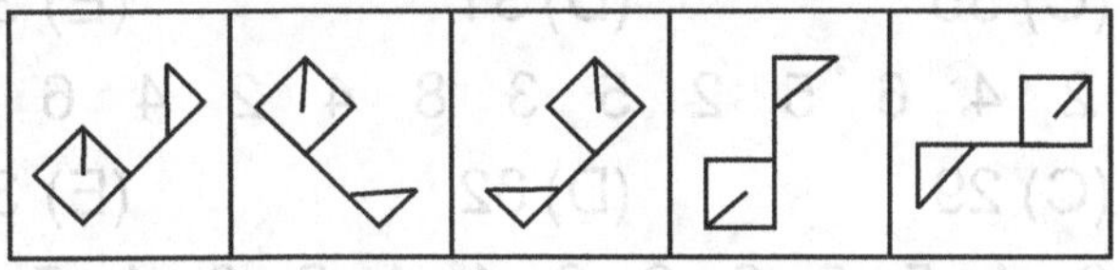

26.
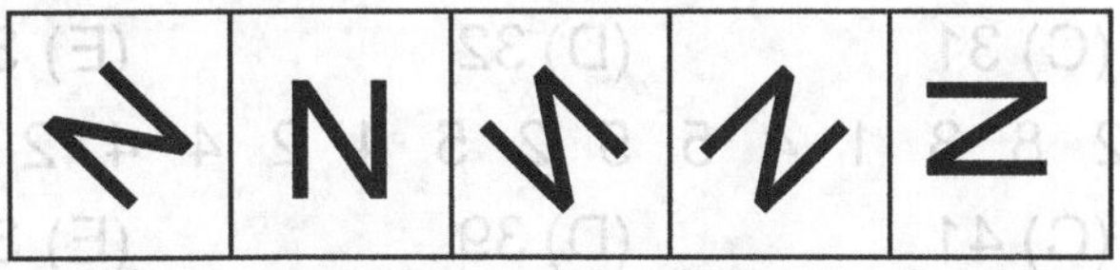

A B C D E

27.
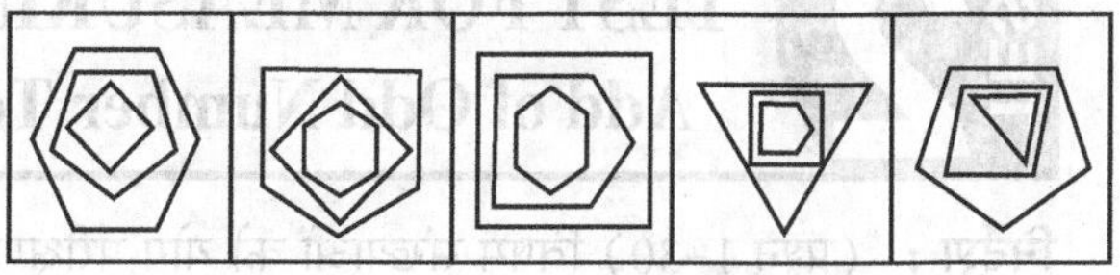

28.
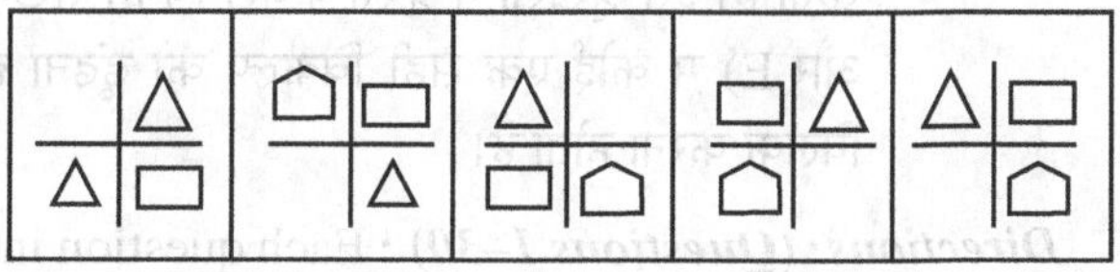

29.
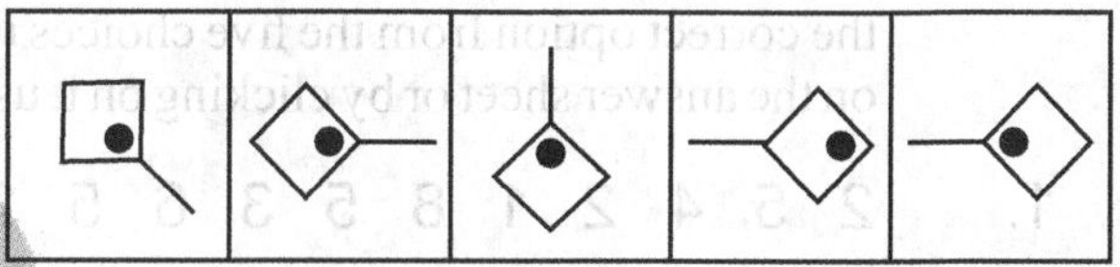

30.
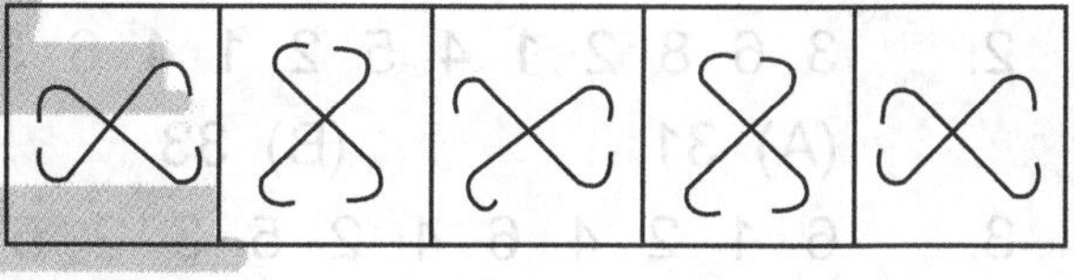

31.
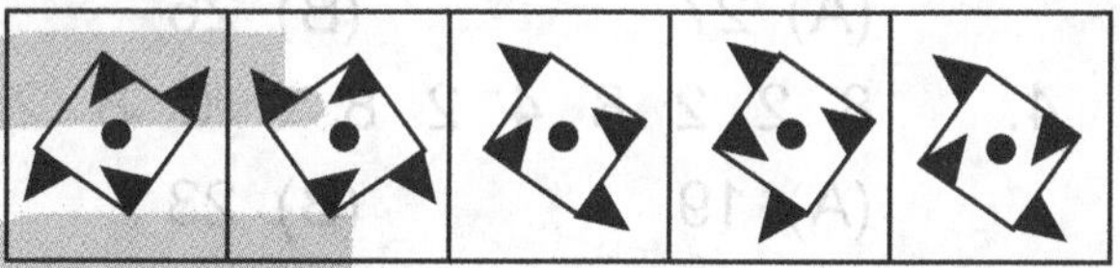

32.
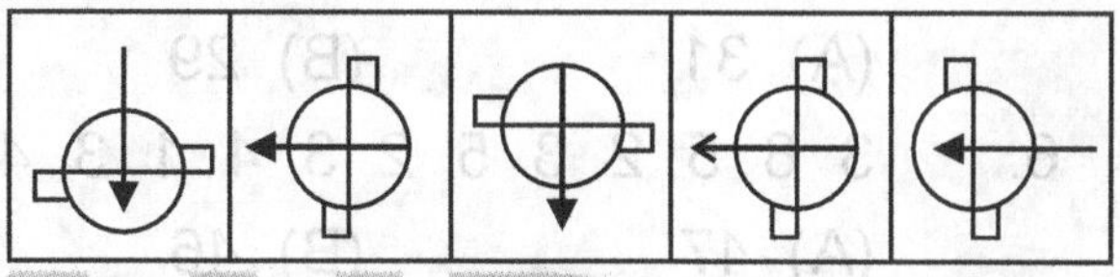

33.
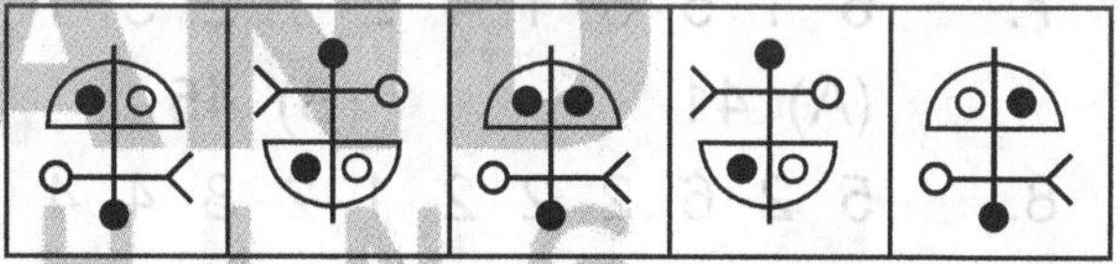

34.
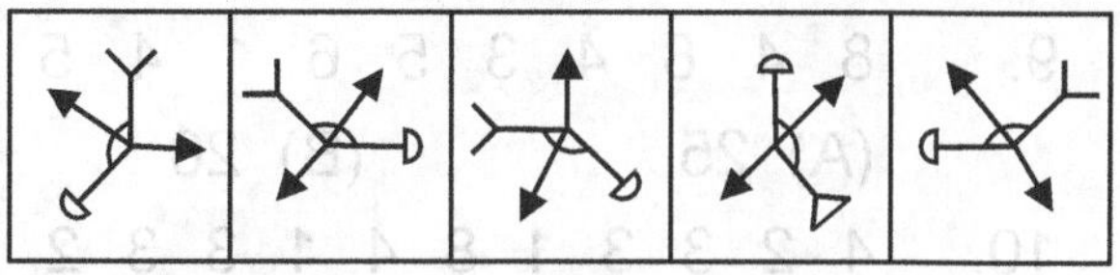

35.
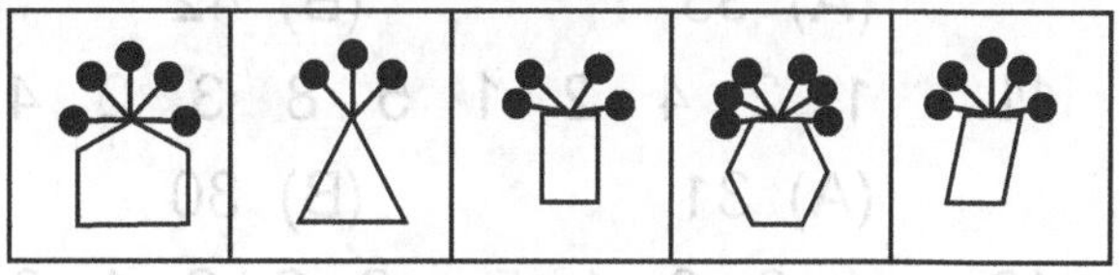

TEST 2 TEST FOR MEASURING SELECTIVE ATTENTION

Add of Odd Number Test (विषम संख्याओं का योग परीक्षण)

Total Ques.- 30
Time - 8 Min.

निर्देश : (प्रश्न 1-30) विषम संख्याओं को योग परीक्षण के प्रत्येक प्रश्न में सम और विषम संख्याओं को मिलाकर एक श्रृंखला दिया रहता है। इस श्रृंखला में प्रदत्त केवल विषम संख्या 1, 3, 5 आदि को जोड़ने के बाद नीचे दिए गए पाँच विकल्पों (A, B, C, D और E) में कोई एक सही विकल्प को ढूंढना होता है जिसे दिए गए उत्तर-पत्रक में गोले को काला/माउस की सहायता से क्लिक करना होता है।

Directions: (Questions 1–30) : Each question in the Odd Number Adding Test presents a series of even and odd numbers. You need to add the total number of odd numbers 1, 3, 5 in the given series. After adding, select the correct option from the five choices (A, B, C, D & E) provided. Mark your answer by filling the circle on the answer sheet or by clicking on it using the mouse.

1. 2 5 4 2 1 8 5 3 6 5 2 1 3 2 1 4 2 1 4 3 6 4 1 2 3 1 6
   (A) 34 (B) 33 (C) 31 (D) 30 (E) 32
2. 3 6 8 2 1 4 5 2 1 4 6 5 2 1 3 6 5 2 1 6 8 2 3 2 2 8 4 1 6 3
   (A) 31 (B) 33 (C) 35 (D) 34 (E) 32
3. 6 1 2 4 6 4 2 5 3 2 5 2 1 4 8 4 6 3 2 1 5 4 1 2 1 6 4 1
   (A) 27 (B) 26 (C) 25 (D) 24 (E) 23
4. 8 2 2 8 4 2 8 3 6 8 2 1 4 2 8 2 1 3 2 3 1 3 6 8 4 5 1 4
   (A) 19 (B) 23 (C) 25 (D) 27 (E) 21
5. 8 3 2 3 2 6 1 4 8 4 5 3 4 2 8 1 2 5 6 2 6 2 2 5 1 4 3 8 1
   (A) 31 (B) 29 (C) 30 (D) 32 (E) 28
6. 3 6 5 2 3 5 2 3 4 1 3 4 6 8 2 5 8 4 1 2 5 3 5 3 1 4 6 8 4 5
   (A) 47 (B) 46 (C) 49 (D) 51 (E) 48
7. 6 1 5 8 1 4 2 1 2 3 1 2 1 2 4 3 3 8 2 3 5 4 1 5 5 2 2 5 6
   (A) 41 (B) 45 (C) 43 (D) 44 (E) 40
8. 5 2 6 2 2 2 1 2 8 4 4 8 1 5 2 1 3 1 2 3 4 2 1 3 4 1 4 1 2
   (A) 25 (B) 26 (C) 24 (D) 23 (E) 27
9. 8 4 8 4 3 5 6 1 4 5 8 8 2 5 4 4 8 6 6 4 1 4 1 3 4 4
   (A) 25 (B) 26 (C) 27 (D) 24 (E) 23
10. 4 2 3 3 1 8 4 1 3 3 2 6 8 8 2 5 8 2 5 3 5 3 6 5 4 1 4 1 6
    (A) 33 (B) 42 (C) 35 (D) 31 (E) 37
11. 1 2 4 2 1 5 8 3 2 4 5 2 4 6 5 2 5 3 8 4 2 4 6 2 3
    (A) 31 (B) 30 (C) 29 (D) 32 (E) 33
12. 4 8 3 1 5 8 2 2 1 3 6 6 4 5 5 2 8 2 4 1 2 6 1 5 2 2
    (A) 29 (B) 30 (C) 31 (D) 32 (E) 33
13. 8 3 6 5 2 5 2 8 5 6 1 4 2 8 3 1 4 5 5 2 5 4 2 4 4 2 8 3
    (A) 43 (B) 42 (C) 41 (D) 39 (E) 37

14. 6 5 2 3 5 2 1 3 6 3 8 4 1 2 3 5 1 5 8 4 1 2 5 1 2 3 6 3 8

(A) 47 (B) 43 (C) 46 (D) 49 (E) 48

15. 5 8 4 5 2 1 4 8 5 4 1 2 3 6 8 2 4 1 2 3 2 4 1 2 5 6 2 8 4 1 2 2

(A) 30 (B) 33 (C) 31 (D) 32 (E) 29

16. 5 8 4 1 1 4 8 6 5 2 3 1 3 4 1 6 8 2 1 4 2 3 5 4 6 2 1 2 4 8 2

(A) 30 (B) 32 (C) 31 (D) 29 (E) 24

17. 8 5 4 1 2 2 3 6 5 2 6 8 4 2 3 2 1 1 1 1 2 2 3 3 3 6 8 3 6 6 2 6 5 2

(A) 36 (B) 37 (C) 35 (D) 38 (E) 39

18. 3 3 2 6 3 4 1 4 8 4 1 2 5 3 6 1 5 2 1 4 8 5 2 8 1 8 5 6 2 3 2

(A) 36 (B) 34 (C) 40 (D) 33 (E) 32

19. 6 5 2 1 5 8 4 1 2 1 3 8 6 2 3 2 4 1 3 6 5 2 1 8 4 2 6 2 4 1

(A) 29 (B) 28 (C) 27 (D) 30 (E) 31

20. 1 4 5 8 1 2 1 1 4 8 4 1 2 3 2 2 1 6 8 2 4 1 2 8 5 2 1 4 2 8

(A) 18 (B) 19 (C) 25 (D) 23 (E) 21

21. 4 6 2 6 8 5 2 1 3 2 1 2 5 1 1 2 8 2 4 1 2 6 8 5 3 3 2 1 8 1 1

(A) 41 (B) 33 (C) 35 (D) 32 (E) 37

22. 8 5 2 1 3 6 2 1 4 8 5 2 5 6 8 2 1 8 2 1 2 1 4 4 6 3 1 4 6

(A) 28 (B) 33 (C) 27 (D) 29 (E) 32

23. 6 5 8 2 4 1 3 2 1 3 5 1 4 8 1 2 3 2 1 8 4 4 1 3 6 8 5 2 1 5 8

(A) 38 (B) 39 (C) 37 (D) 36 (E) 40

24. 8 5 4 1 2 3 6 2 2 6 8 4 6 2 6 1 3 2 5 1 8 5 6 6 1 5 4 8 2 8 2 1

(A) 31 (B) 32 (C) 35 (D) 38 (E) 29

25. 2 5 1 4 2 1 3 4 2 1 8 1 4 2 3 5 2 1 6 3 2 5 8 4 1 2 6 1 8 4 6 1

(A) 30 (B) 32 (C) 33 (D) 35 (E) 37

26. 3 3 2 2 1 4 2 5 4 1 2 5 2 1 4 5 2 1 6 1 6 6 8 5 4 1 2 5 1 2 4

(A) 37 (B) 36 (C) 38 (D) 34 (E) 35

27. 3 2 5 8 5 2 2 2 4 1 6 2 3 2 3 3 3 2 6 5 2 2 1 8 4 1 2 5

(A) 39 (B) 33 (C) 35 (D) 38 (E) 40

28. 3 5 2 8 8 4 1 2 1 6 8 5 4 1 2 5 1 8 6 4 1 2 6 4 8 5 8 2 6

(A) 27 (B) 26 (C) 25 (D) 24 (E) 28

29. 2 3 2 1 4 1 4 8 5 2 1 3 4 1 2 6 8 6 2 1 3 2 1 4 3 6 3 8 2 1 1

(A) 25 (B) 27 (C) 29 (D) 28 (E) 30

30. 3 2 6 8 2 1 3 2 8 4 1 2 6 5 8 4 1 4 3 2 6 8 4 1 2 5 6 3 2 8 4 1

(A) 29 (B) 25 (C) 27 (D) 26 (E) 28

TEST 3 — TEST FOR MEASURING SPATIAL SCANNING

Total Ques.- 40
Time- 8 Min.

Shortest Route Test (संक्षिप्त रास्ता परीक्षण)

निर्देश : (प्रश्न 1-40) इस अभ्यास में 40 प्रश्न दिए गए हैं जो चार उपखंडों 1, 2, 3 एवं 4 में 10-10 प्रश्नों (कुल 40 प्रश्न) के रूप में विभाजित है। प्रत्येक खण्ड के चित्रों को ध्यानपूर्वक देखकर दिए गए प्रत्येक प्रश्नों का उत्तर खोजकर अपने उत्तर-पत्रक में अंकित गोले को काला करें या माउस की सहायता से क्लिक करें और इसके लिए 5 या 8 मिनट का समय दिया जाता है।

Instructions: (Questions 1-40) : This exercise contains 40 questions, divided into four subsections: 1, 2, 3, and 4, each containing 10 questions (40 questions in total). Look carefully at the pictures in each section to find the answer to each question. Darken the circle on your answer sheet or click on it with the mouse. You are given 5 or 8 minutes for this.

उपखंड/Section-1

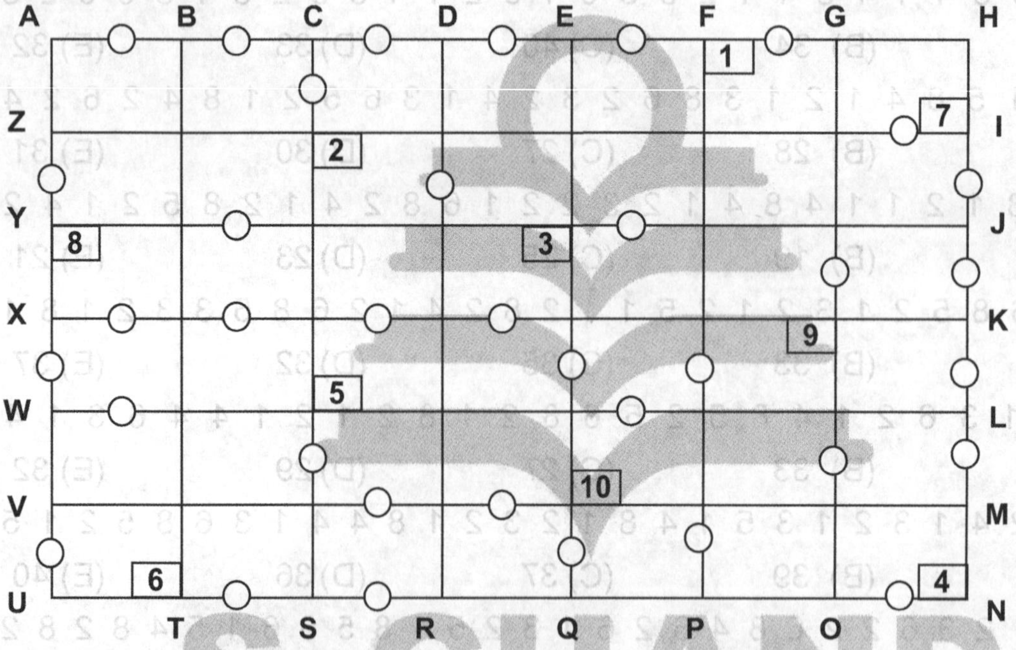

1. A - X
2. D - A
3. J - I
4. O - Q
5. E - R
6. D - F
7. K - O
8. R - S
9. L - N
10. W - T

उपखंड/Section-2

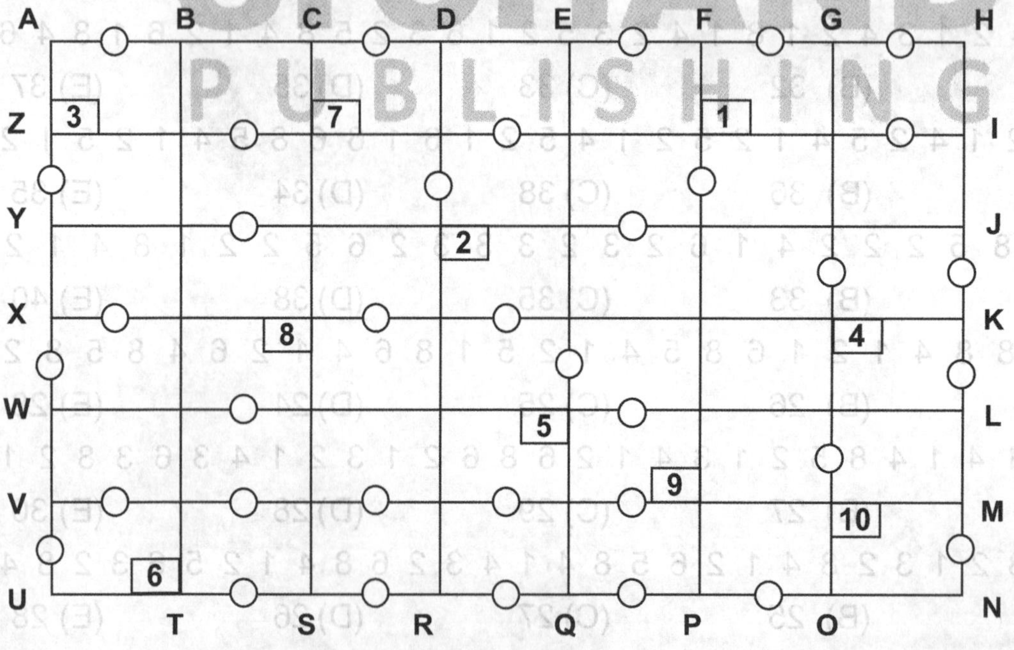

11. H - F
12. R - Q
13. J - K
14. J - P
15. E - B
16. E - R
17. L - N
18. S - Y
19. X - A
20. B - T

उपखंड/Section-3

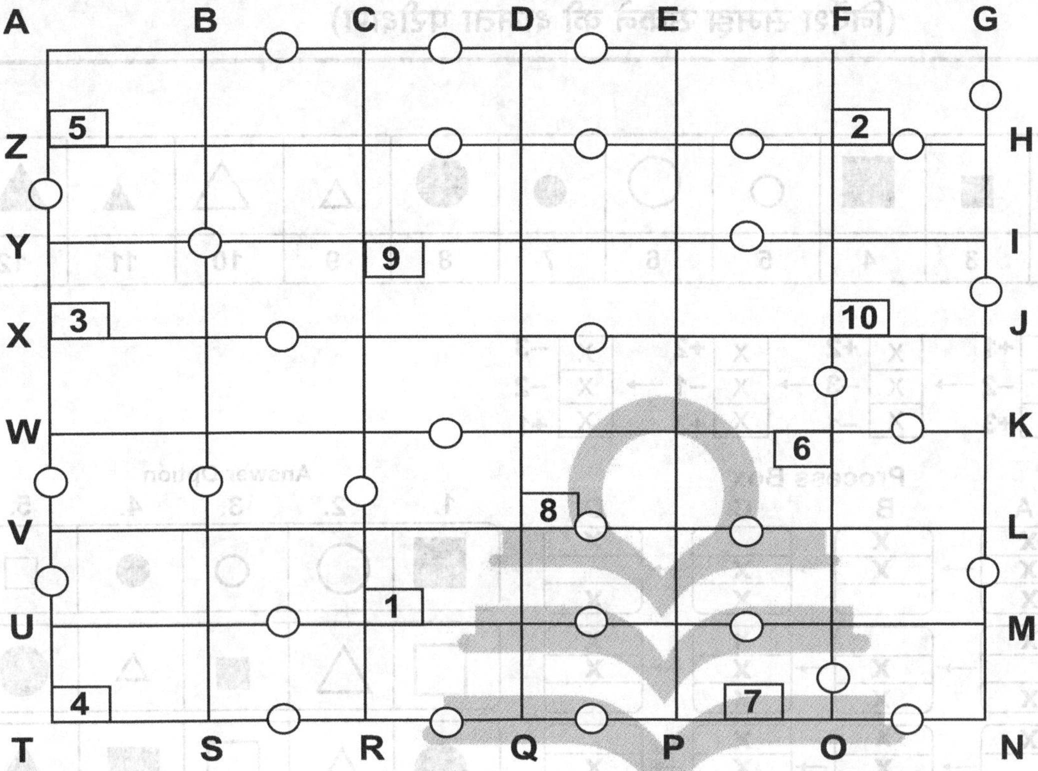

21. V - S
22. S - R
23. Q - P
24. E - O
25. L - P
26. H - G
27. D - Q
28. E - C
29. C - A
30. H - K

उपखंड/Section-4

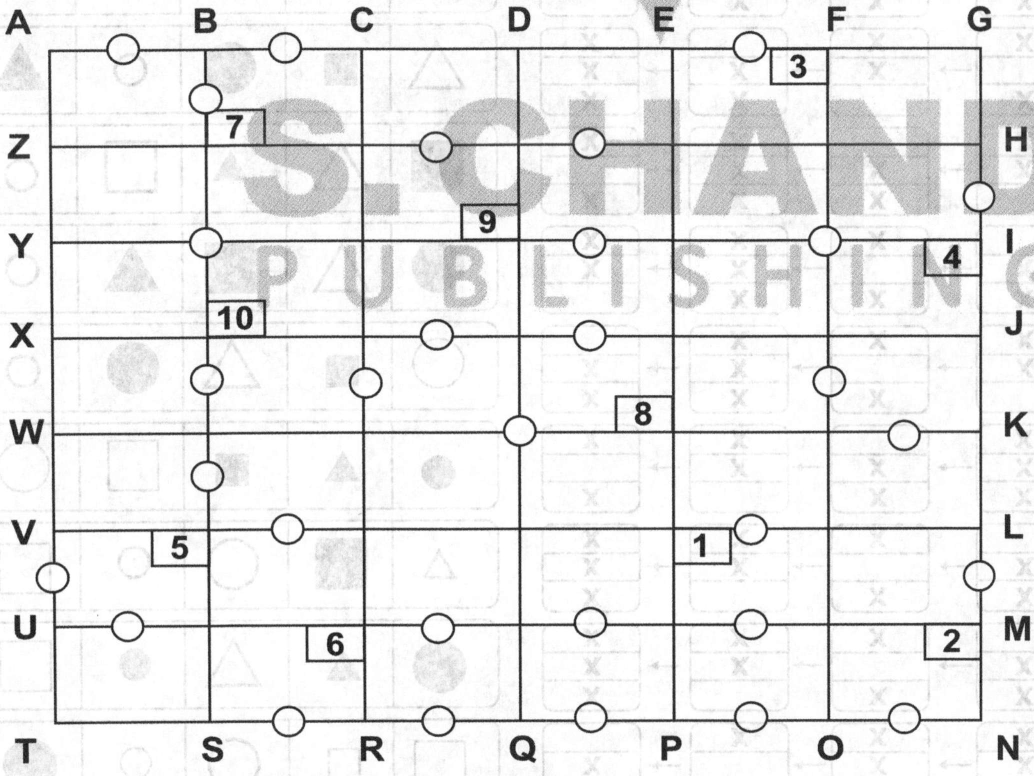

31. R - Q
32. H - I
33. J - N
34. L - J
35. P - O
36. L - I
37. D - C
38. W - R
39. X - U
40. A - D

TEST **4**

INFORMATION ORDERING TEST

(निर्देश समझ सकने की क्षमता परीक्षण)

Total Ques.- 25
Time - 8 Min.

Table - 2

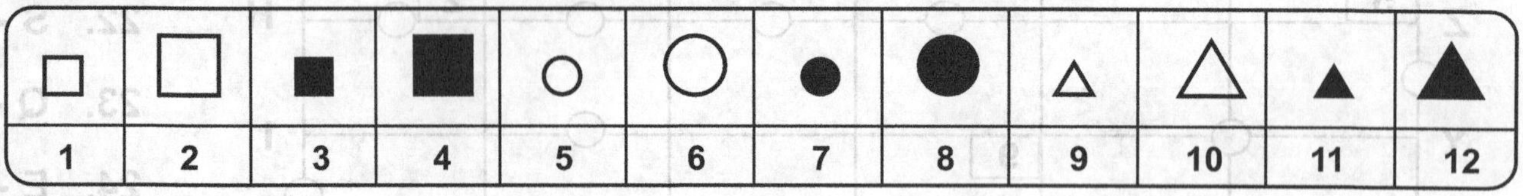

Table - 1

Level- 1 →	X +1	X +2	X +2	X −3
Level- 2 →	X −2 →	X −3 →	X −1 →	X −2
Level- 3 →	X +3	X −1	X +3	X +1

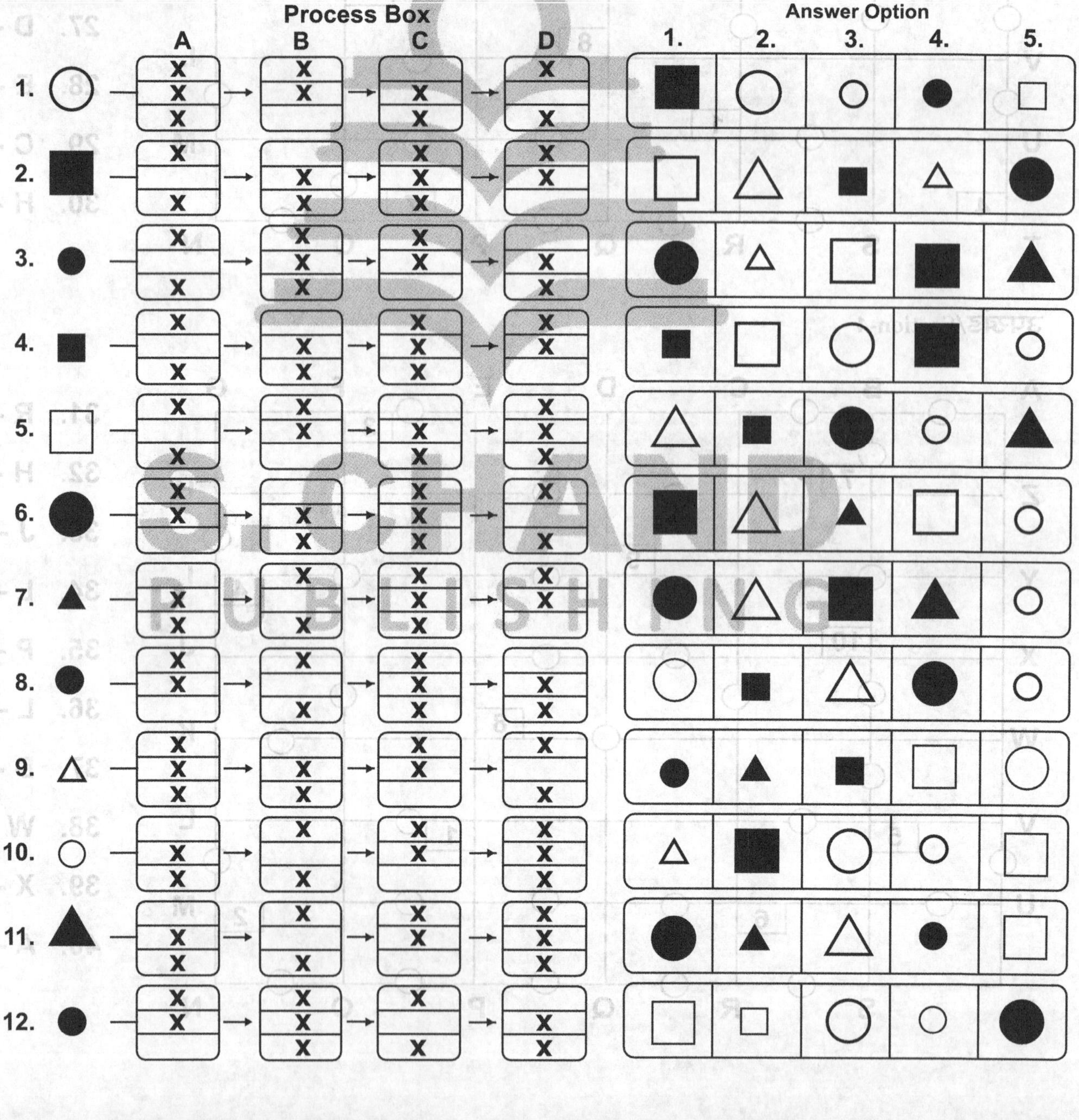

Table - 2

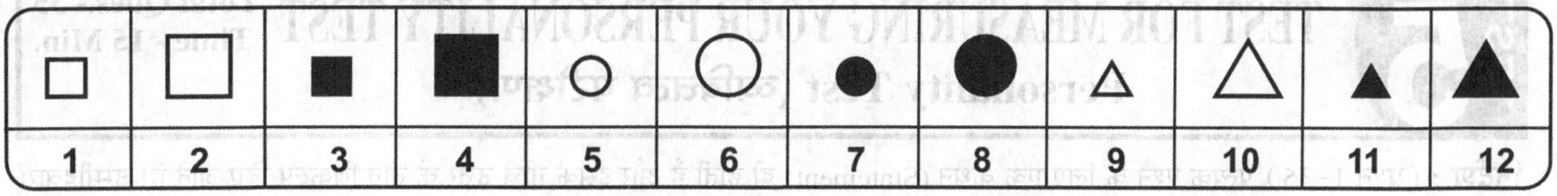

Table - 1

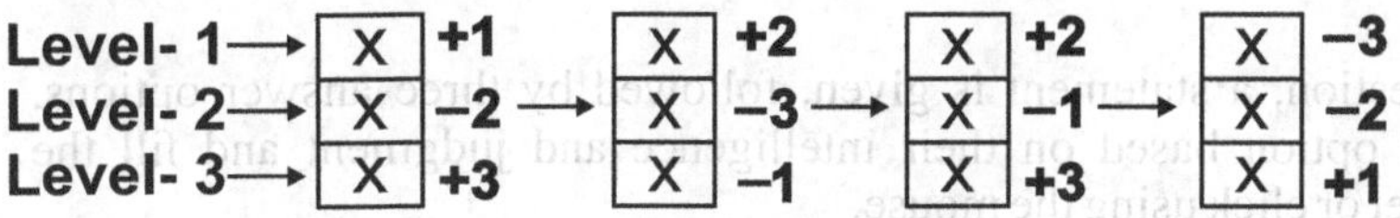

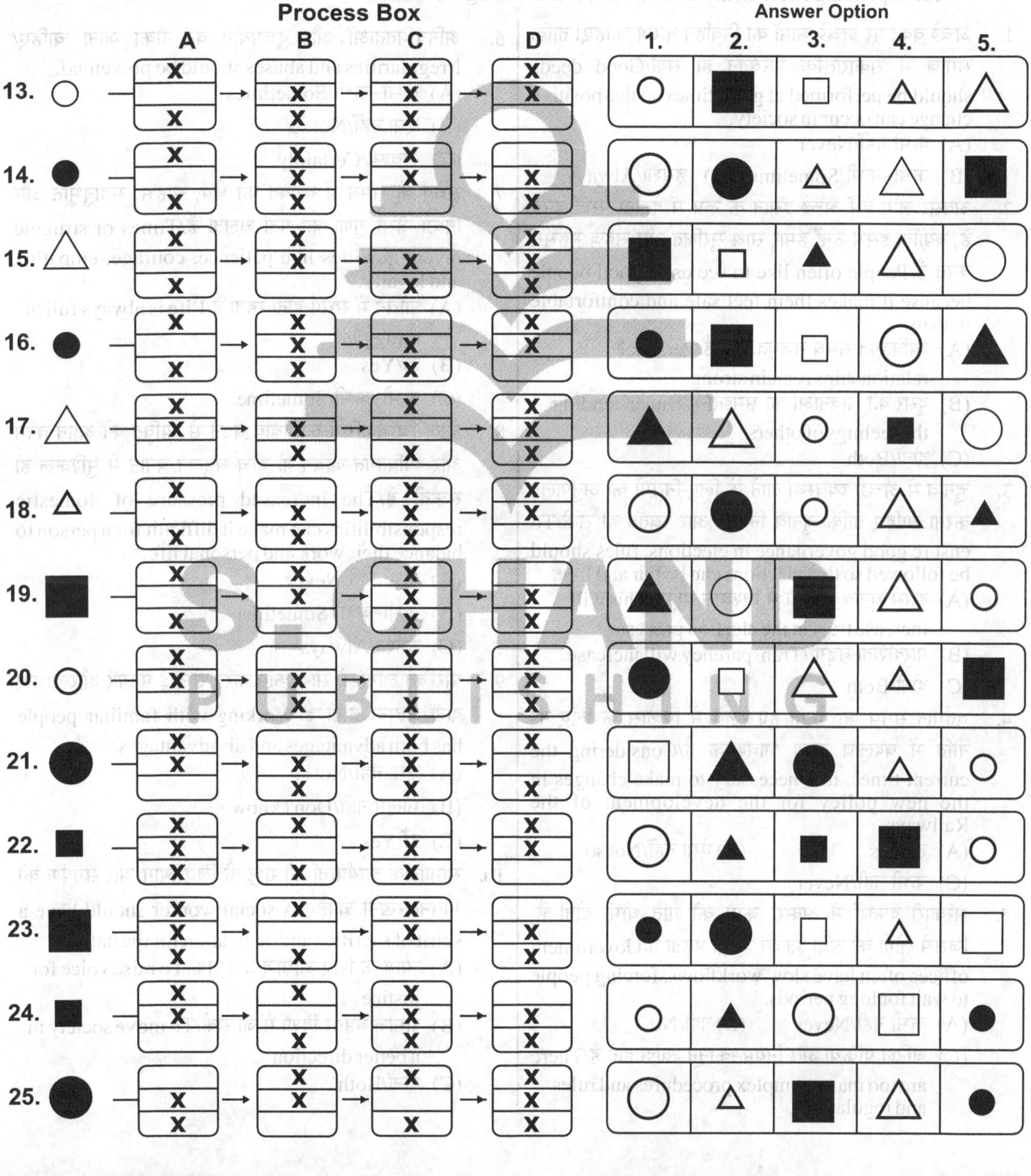

TEST 5 TEST FOR MEASURING YOUR PERSONALITY TEST

Total Ques.- 35
Time - 15 Min.

Personality Test (व्यक्तित्व परीक्षण)

निर्देश : (प्रश्न 1-35) प्रत्येक प्रश्न के लिए एक कथन (Statement) दी होती है और इसके नीचे उत्तर के तीन विकल्प दिए जाते हैं। उम्मीदवारों को अपने बुद्धिमता और निर्णय के आधार पर सही उत्तर के लिए कोई एक विकल्प का चयन कर उत्तर-पत्रक में दिए गए गोले को काला या माउस की सहायता से क्लिक (Click) करें।

Direction : (Questions 1–35) : For each question, a statement is given, followed by three answer options. Candidates should select the correct option based on their intelligence and judgment and fill the corresponding circle on the answer sheet or click using the mouse.

1. अच्छे वक्त पर अच्छे कामों का निर्वाहन करना चाहिए। ताकि समाज में सकारात्मक परिवर्तन हो सके/Good deeds should be performed at good times so thatpositive change can occur in society.
(A) कभी नहीं/Never
(B) कभी-कभी/Sometime (C) हमेशा/Always

2. अक्सर लोग हमें अच्छे इंसान के रूप में देखना पसंद करते हैं, क्योंकि इससे उन्हें हमारे साथ सुरक्षित और सहज महसूस करते हैं/People often like to see us as good people because it makes them feel safe and comfortable with us.
(A) व्यक्तिगत संबंध मजबूत रहते हैं/Personal relationships remain strong
(B) दूसरे की भावनाओं को समझते हैं/Understanding the feelings of others
(C) दोनों/Both

3. चुनाव में अच्छी व्यवस्था लाने के लिए नियमों का अनुपालन करना चाहिए ताकि चुनाव निष्पक्ष और स्वतंत्र हो सके/To ensure good governance in elections, rules should be followed so that elections can be fair and free.
(A) इससे चुनाव प्रक्रिया में विश्वास बढ़ेगा/This will increase trust in the election process
(B) पारदर्शिता बढ़ेगी/Transparency will increase
(C) दोनों/Both

4. वर्तमान समय को देखते हुए रेलवे में विकास के लिए नई नीति में बदलाव लाना आवश्यक है/Considering the current times, it is necessary to make changes in the new policy for the development of the Railways.
(A) हाँ/Yes (B) ऐसा नहीं/Not so
(C) कभी नहीं/Never

5. सरकारी दफ्तरों में अक्सर काम की गति धीमी होती है, जिससे लोगों को लंबा इंतजार करना पड़ता है/Government offices often have slow workflows, forcing people to wait for long periods.
(A) कभी नहीं/Never (B) नहीं/No
(C) जटिल प्रक्रिया और नियम-कानून ज्यादा होते है/There are too many complex procedures and rules and regulations

6. अनियमितताओं और दुरूपयोग को रोका जाना चाहिए/Irregularities and abuses should be prevented.
(A) कभी-कभी/Sometimes
(B) ऐसा नहीं/Not so
(C) अवश्य/Certainly

7. संघर्ष के समय में व्यक्ति की धैर्य, साहस, सहानुभूति और निष्ठा जैसी गुणों का पता चलता है/Times of struggle reveal qualities like patience, courage, empathy, and loyalty.
(A) जीवन में संघर्ष होता रहता है/Life is always full of struggle
(B) हाँ/Yes
(C) कभी-कभी/Sometime

8. घरेलू जिम्मेदारियाँ का दबाव बढ़ने से व्यक्ति को अपने काम और व्यक्तिगत जीवन के बीच संतुलन बनाने में मुश्किल हो सकती है/The increased pressure of domestic responsibilities can make it difficult for a person to balance their work and personal life.
(A) कभी नहीं/Never
(B) कभी-कभी/Sometime
(C) हमेशा/Always

9. परिचित लोगों के साथ काम करने से कई फायदे और बाधाऐं दोनों उत्पन्न होती है/Working with familiar people has both advantages and disadvantages.
(A) ऐसा नहीं/Not so
(B) मालूम नहीं/Don't know
(C) हाँ/Yes

10. सामाजिक कार्यकर्त्ता को राष्ट्र के लिए त्याग और समर्पण की भावना रखनी चाहिए/A social worker should have a spirit of sacrifice and dedication for the nation
(A) न्याय के लिए आवाज उठा सके/To raise voice for justice
(B) समाज बेहतर दिशा में जा सके/To move society in a better direction
(C) दोनों/Both

11. गरीबी से प्रभावी ढंग से निपटने के लिए आय बढ़ाने की सख्त आवश्यकता है/To effectively tackle poverty, there is a dire need to increase income.
(A) शिक्षा की सख्त आवश्यकता है/Education is a dire need
(B) आय की कमी ही गरीबी का मुख्य कारण है/Lack of income is the main cause of poverty
(C) ऐसा नहीं/Not so

12. किसी भी क्षेत्र में सफलता के लिए निरंतर प्रगति अति आवश्यक है/Continuous progress is essential for success in any field.
(A) हाँ/Yes (B) ऐसा नहीं/Not so
(C) कभी नहीं/Never

13. कौशल विकास योजनाऐं को तहत युवाओं को विभिन्न कौशल संस्थानों में प्रशिक्षण दिया जाना चाहिए। ताकि वे आत्मनिर्भर बन सके/Under skill development schemes, youth should be trained in various skill institutes so that they can become self-reliant.
(A) ऐसा नहीं/Not so
(B) कभी नहीं/Never (C) हाँ/Yes

14. क्या अच्छे कपड़े पहनने से व्यक्ति के व्यक्तित्व में बदलाव आ सकता है/Can wearing good clothes change a person's personality?
(A) कपड़े साफ होनी चाहिए/Clothes should be clean
(B) हो सकता है/Maybe
(C) मालूम नहीं/I don't know

15. अपनी ताकतों और उपलब्धियों पर ध्यान केन्द्रित करना चाहिए और सकारात्मक दृष्टिकोण अपनाना चाहिए ताकि सफलता प्राप्त करने में मदद हो सके/Focusing on your strengths and achievements and adopting a positive attitude can help you achieve success.
(A) लक्ष्यों को नहीं भूलना चाहिए/Goals should not be forgotten
(B) नकारात्मक विचारों से दूर रहना चाहिए/One should stay away from negative thoughts
(C) दोनों/Both

16. अपने लक्ष्य को प्राप्त करने के लिए जीवन में आगे बढ़ते रहना चाहिए/One should keep moving forward in life to achieve one's goals
(A) नहीं/No (B) कभी नहीं/Never
(C) हमेशा/Always

17. मजबूत नींव बच्चों को जीवन की चुनौतियों का सामना करने, सफलता प्राप्त करने और एक संतुष्ट सार्थक जीवन जीने में मदद करती है/A strong foundation helps children face life's challenges, achieve success, and live a satisfying and meaningful life.
(A) बिल्कुल सही/Absolutely right
(B) कभी नहीं/Never (C) नहीं/No

18. जब दो आदेशों में विरोधाभास होता है तब आप विवेक और तर्क के आधार पर स्वयं निर्णय ले सकते हैं/When two orders contradict, you can make your own decisions based on discretion and logic.
(A) कभी नहीं/Never (B) नहीं/No
(C) परिणामों का आकलन करना चाहिए/The consequences should be assessed

19. अगर आपके सीनियर से गलती होता है तो आप उसे सार्वजनिक रूप से नहीं बताना चाहिए/If your senior makes a mistake, you should not publicly report it.
(A) हमेशा/Always
(B) कभी नहीं/Never (C) हाँ/Yes

20. अपनी गलती से घबराने के बजाय उसे स्वीकार करके सुधारने का प्रयास करना चाहिए/Instead of being afraid of your mistakes, you should admit them and try to correct them.
(A) मालूम नहीं/I don't know
(B) कभी-कभी/Sometimes
(C) यही समझदारी की निशानी है/This is a sign of wisdom

21. सकारात्मक विचारों को अपनाकर अपने जीवन में अधिक सुखी और समृद्ध बना सकते हैं/By adopting positive thoughts, you can make your life happier and more prosperous.
(A) नकारात्मक विचारों को दूर रखना चाहिए/Negative thoughts should be kept away
(B) ऐसा नहीं/Not so
(C) कभी-कभी/Sometime

22. गलती करना गलत बात है, लेकिन उसे स्वीकार कर सुधारना ही असली बुद्धिमानी है/Making a mistake is wrong, but admitting and correcting them is true wisdom.
(A) गलतियाँ किसी से हो सकती है/Anyone can make mistakes
(B) ऐसे लोग भविष्य में बेहतर प्रदर्शन करते हैं/Such people perform better in the future
(C) गलतियाँ नहीं करनी चाहिए/Mistakes should not be made

23. गलती छिपाने से नहीं, उसे सुधारने से इंसान महान बनता है/A person becomes great not by hiding his mistakes but by correcting them.
(A) कभी नहीं/Never
(B) हो सकता है/Maybe
(C) बिल्कुल सही/Perfect

24. क्या आप अपनी भावनाओं को तनावपूर्ण परिस्थितियों में शांत रहकर निर्णय लेने की कोशिश करते हैं/Do you try to

control your emotions and make calm decisions in stressful situations?
(A) कभी नहीं/Never
(B) हमेशा/Always
(C) कभी-कभी/Sometime

25. अगर आपके सहकर्मी आपकी बात नहीं मानता है तो आपकी प्रतिक्रिया/If your coworker doesn't listen to you, your reaction will be:
(A) उसे निकाल देगें/Fire him/her
(B) तर्क और तथ्यों के साथ समझाऐंगे/Explain with logic and facts
(C) नजरअंदाज करेंगे/Ignore him/her

26. क्या आप दबाव में गलत निर्णय ले सकते हैं/Are you likely to make bad decisions under pressure?
(A) कभी नहीं/Never (B) नहीं/No
(C) कभी-कभी/Sometime

27. अगर किसी सहकर्मी की गलती से आपका काम में नुकसान होता है तो आप/If a colleague's mistake causes you harm at work, would you?
(A) शांत रहने की कोशिश करूँगा/I will try to remain calm
(B) आपस में मिलकर गलती सुधारने का प्रयास करूँगा/I will work together to correct the mistake
(C) दोनों/Both

28. क्या आप सकारात्मक आलोचना को बर्दाश्त करते हैं/ Do you tolerate constructive criticism?
(A) इसे सुधरने का मौका मिलेगा/I will give you a chance to improve
(B) कभी नहीं/Never
(C) कह नहीं सकते/I can't say no

29. अगर कोई आपकी गलती निकाल दे तो आप कैसा महसूस करेंगे/How would you feel if someone pointed out your mistake?
(A) गलती का एहसास करेंगे/I will realize my mistake
(B) बेहतर करने की कोशिश करेंगे/I will try to improve
(C) दोनों/Both

30. तनाव की स्थिति में आप खुद को कैसे संभालते हैं/How do you handle yourself in stressful situations?
(A) समस्या पर विचार करेंगे/I will think about the problem
(B) दिमाग को शांति की स्थिति में रखेंगे/I keep my mind calm
(C) दोनों/Both

31. अगर कोई आपको गुस्सा दिलाता है तो आपकी प्रतिक्रिया/If someone angers you, your reaction is:
(A) तुरंत जवाब देता हूँ/I respond immediately
(B) धैर्य के साथ उचित उत्तर देता हूँ/I respond patiently and appropriately
(C) पुलिस को सूचना देता हूँ/I inform the police

32. क्या आप अपने नीचे काम करने वाले से दूरी बनाकर रखना चाहिए/Should you maintain distance from your subordinates?
(A) हाँ/Yes
(B) कभी-कभी/Sometime
(C) मालूम नहीं/I don't know

33. आपातस्थिति में आप दूसरों के आदेश का इंतजार करने के बजाए स्वयं पहल करते हैं/In an emergency, you take initiative rather than waiting for orders from others.
(A) परिस्थिति के अनुसार निर्णय लेते हैं/I make decisions based on the situation
(B) स्थिति का मूल्यांकन करते हैं/I evaluate the situation
(C) दोनों/Both

34. जब अचानक कोई तकनीकि समस्या आ जाती है तो आप घबरा जाते हैं/When a technical problem suddenly arises, you get nervous.
(A) कभी नहीं/Never
(B) कभी कभी/Sometime
(C) हमेशा/Always

35. जल्दी-जल्दी निर्णय लेना या देर से सही निर्णय लेना बेहतर होता है/It is better to make a decision quickly than to make the right decision late.
(A) परिस्थिति का आकलन के आधार पर निर्णय लेना चाहिए/Decisions should be made based on an assessment of the situation
(B) मालूम नहीं/I don't know
(C) निर्णय लेने में अनुभव की आवश्यकता नहीं/No experience is required in making decisions

उत्तर (ANSWER)

SET - 1

1.	B	19.	C
2.	C	20.	E
3.	A	21.	D
4.	E	22.	B
5.	D	23.	B
6.	D	24.	C
7.	B	25.	A
8.	A	26.	C
9.	B	27.	B
10.	B	28.	A
11.	C	29.	D
12.	A	30.	C
13.	A	31.	D
14.	D	32.	D
15.	D	33.	C
16.	B	34.	D
17.	C	35.	E
18.	A		

SET - 2

1.	B	16.	A
2.	E	17.	B
3.	A	18.	C
4.	E	19.	D
5.	A	20.	E
6.	D	21.	D
7.	C	22.	C
8.	B	23.	B
9.	D	24.	A
10.	B	25.	B
11.	A	26.	C
12.	B	27.	D
13.	C	28.	E
14.	E	29.	D
15.	C	30.	C

SET - 3

SECTION-1

1. ① ② ③ ④ ⑤ ⑥ ⑦ ❽ ⑨ ⑩
2. ① ❷ ③ ④ ⑤ ⑥ ⑦ ⑧ ⑨ ⑩
3. ① ② ③ ④ ⑤ ⑥ ❼ ⑧ ⑨ ⑩
4. ① ② ③ ④ ⑤ ⑥ ⑦ ⑧ ⑨ ❿
5. ① ② ❸ ④ ⑤ ⑥ ⑦ ⑧ ⑨ ⑩
6. ❶ ② ③ ④ ⑤ ⑥ ⑦ ⑧ ⑨ ⑩
7. ① ② ③ ④ ⑤ ⑥ ⑦ ⑧ ❾ ⑩
8. ① ② ③ ④ ❺ ⑥ ⑦ ⑧ ⑨ ⑩
9. ① ② ③ ❹ ⑤ ⑥ ⑦ ⑧ ⑨ ⑩
10. ① ② ③ ④ ⑤ ❻ ⑦ ⑧ ⑨ ⑩

SECTION-2

11. ❶ ② ③ ④ ⑤ ⑥ ⑦ ⑧ ⑨ ⑩
12. ① ② ③ ④ ❺ ⑥ ⑦ ⑧ ⑨ ⑩
13. ① ② ③ ❹ ⑤ ⑥ ⑦ ⑧ ⑨ ⑩
14. ① ② ③ ④ ⑤ ⑥ ⑦ ⑧ ❾ ⑩
15. ① ② ③ ④ ⑤ ⑥ ❼ ⑧ ⑨ ⑩
16. ① ❷ ③ ④ ⑤ ⑥ ⑦ ⑧ ⑨ ⑩
17. ① ② ③ ④ ⑤ ⑥ ⑦ ⑧ ⑨ ❿
18. ① ② ③ ④ ⑤ ⑥ ⑦ ❽ ⑨ ⑩
19. ① ② ❸ ④ ⑤ ⑥ ⑦ ⑧ ⑨ ⑩
20. ① ② ③ ④ ⑤ ❻ ⑦ ⑧ ⑨ ⑩

SECTION-3

21. ① ② ③ ❹ ⑤ ⑥ ⑦ ⑧ ⑨ ⑩
22. ❶ ② ③ ④ ⑤ ⑥ ⑦ ⑧ ⑨ ⑩
23. ① ② ③ ④ ⑤ ⑥ ⑦ ❽ ⑨ ⑩
24. ① ② ③ ④ ⑤ ⑥ ❼ ⑧ ⑨ ⑩
25. ① ② ③ ④ ⑤ ❻ ⑦ ⑧ ⑨ ⑩
26. ① ❷ ③ ④ ⑤ ⑥ ⑦ ⑧ ⑨ ⑩
27. ① ② ③ ④ ⑤ ⑥ ⑦ ❽ ⑨ ⑩
28. ① ② ③ ④ ⑤ ⑥ ⑦ ⑧ ❾ ⑩
29. ① ② ③ ④ ❺ ⑥ ⑦ ⑧ ⑨ ⑩
30. ① ② ③ ④ ⑤ ⑥ ⑦ ⑧ ⑨ ❿

SECTION-4

31. ① ② ③ ④ ⑤ ❻ ⑦ ⑧ ⑨ ⑩
32. ① ② ③ ❹ ⑤ ⑥ ⑦ ⑧ ⑨ ⑩
33. ① ❷ ③ ④ ⑤ ⑥ ⑦ ⑧ ⑨ ⑩
34. ① ② ③ ④ ⑤ ⑥ ⑦ ❽ ⑨ ⑩
35. ❶ ② ③ ④ ⑤ ⑥ ⑦ ⑧ ⑨ ⑩
36. ① ② ③ ❹ ⑤ ⑥ ⑦ ⑧ ⑨ ⑩
37. ① ② ③ ④ ⑤ ⑥ ⑦ ⑧ ❾ ⑩
38. ① ② ③ ④ ⑤ ❻ ⑦ ⑧ ⑨ ⑩
39. ① ② ③ ④ ❺ ⑥ ⑦ ⑧ ⑨ ⑩
40. ① ② ③ ④ ⑤ ⑥ ❼ ⑧ ⑨ ⑩

SET - 4

1.	4	14.	3
2.	3	15.	3
3.	2	16.	4
4.	2	17.	5
5.	2	18.	2
6.	5	19.	4
7.	4	20.	2
8.	3	21.	5
9.	5	22.	3
10.	2	23.	1
11.	2	24.	3
12.	5	25.	2
13.	2		

SET - 5

1.	C	18.	C
2.	C	19.	A
3.	C	20.	C
4.	A	21.	A
5.	C	22.	B
6.	C	23.	C
7.	B	24.	B
8.	C	25.	B
9.	C	26.	A
10.	C	27.	C
11.	B	28.	A
12.	A	29.	C
13.	C	30.	C
14.	B	31.	B
15.	C	32.	B
16.	C	33.	C
17.	A	34.	A
		35.	A

MODEL SET - 3

Station Master (NTPC 2025) Psycho Exam.

(28-12-2025) का हल प्रश्न-पत्र (स्मृति पर आधारित) (Based on Memory)

TEST 1 TEST FOR MEASURING YOUR INTELLIGENCE

Total Ques.- 35
Time - 10 Min.

Classification Test (वर्गीकरण)

निर्देश : (प्रश्न 1–35) बुद्धिमापन परीक्षण के प्रत्येक प्रश्न में पाँच आकृतियाँ दिए जाते हैं जिसमें से चार आकृतियाँ में कुछ समानता और कोई एक आकृति अन्य चारों से भिन्न है वही भिन्न आकृति आपका उत्तर होगा जिसे दिए गए उत्तर-पत्रक में गोले को काला/माउस की सहायता से क्लिक करना होता है और इसके लिए 10 मिनट का समय दिया जाता है।

Instructions : (Questions 1–35) : Each question in the Intelligence Test consists of five figures, four of which have some similarity, and one that is different from the other four is your answer. You must click on the black circle on the answer sheet or using the mouse. You are given 10 minutes to complete the test.

A B C D E

1.
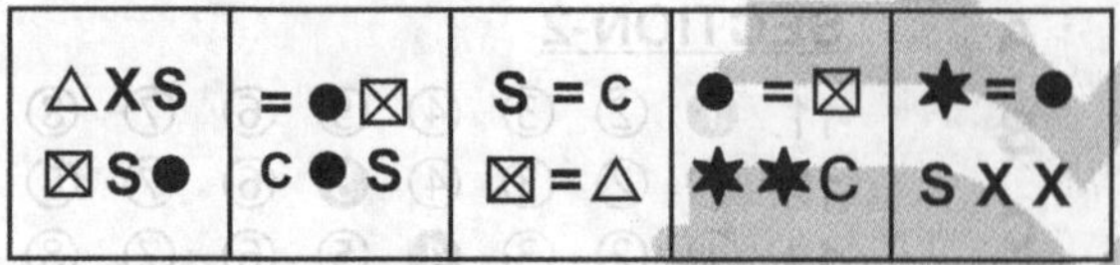

2.
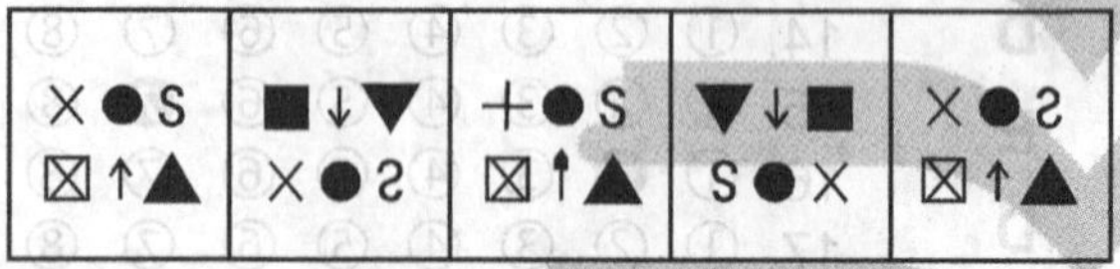

3.
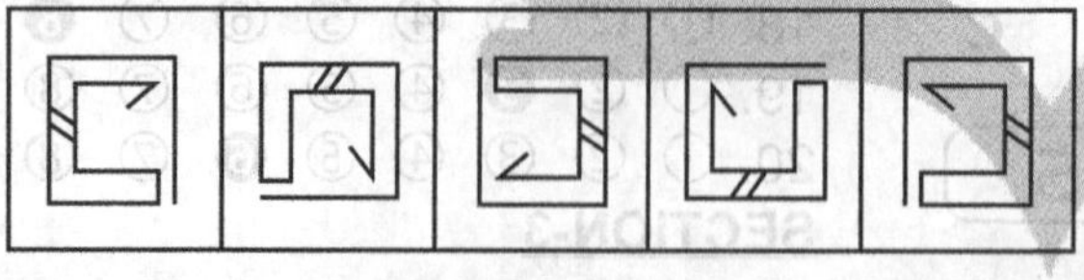

4.
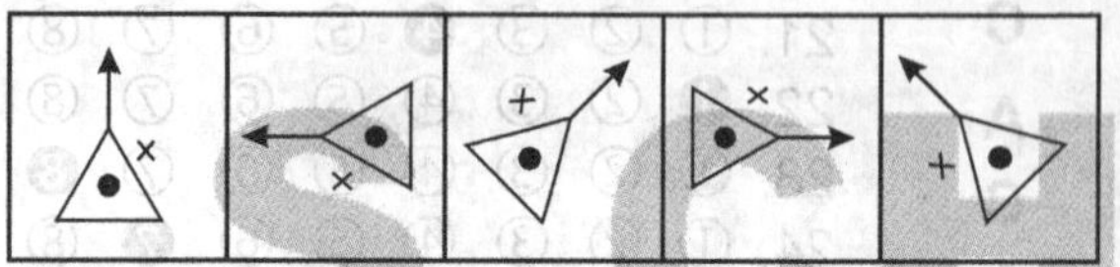

5.
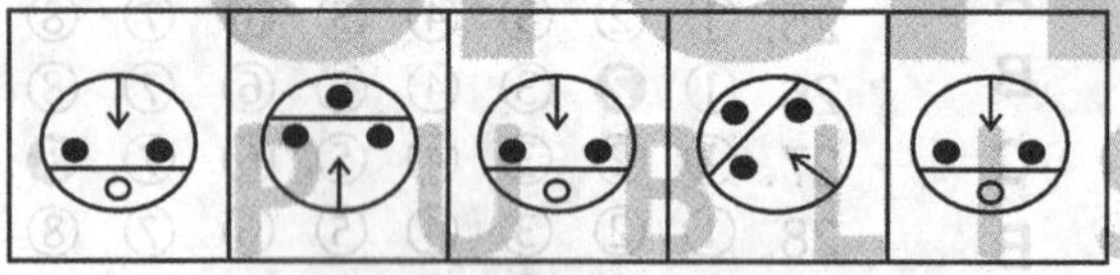

6.
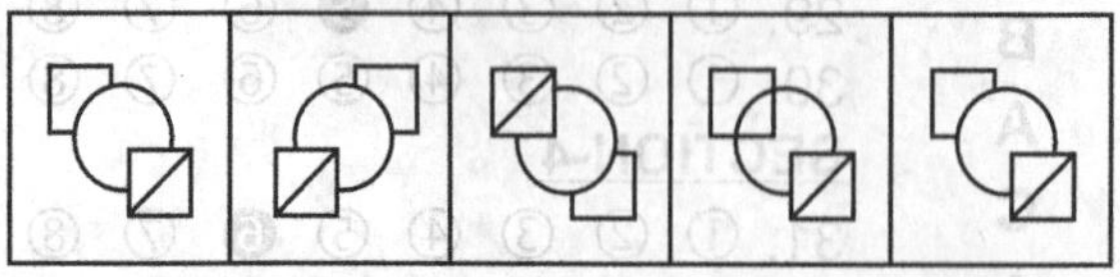

7.
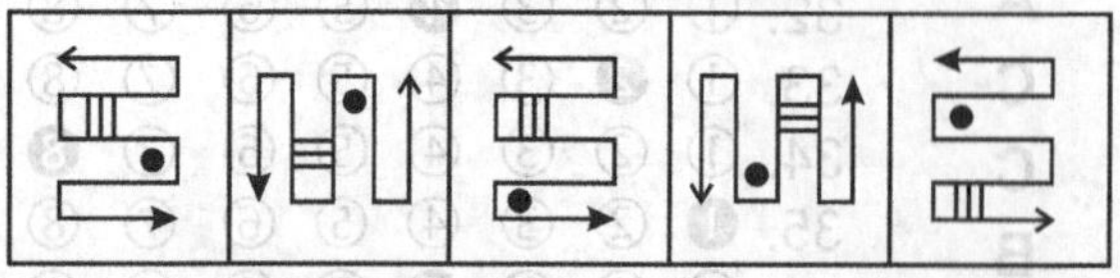

8.
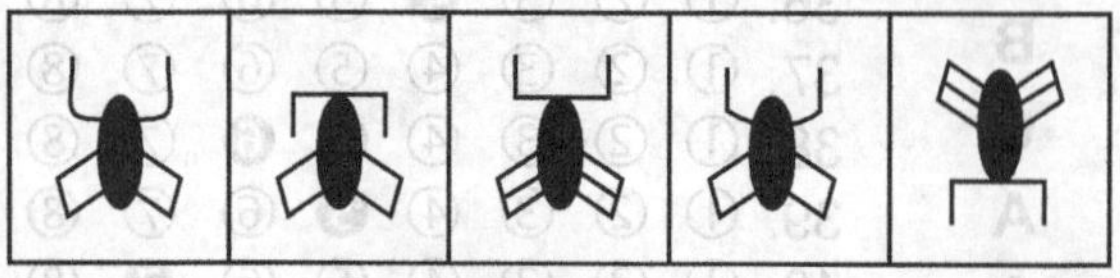

A B C D E

9.
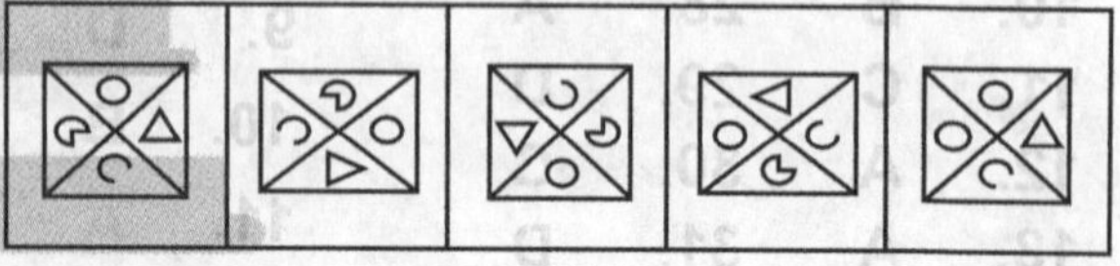

10.
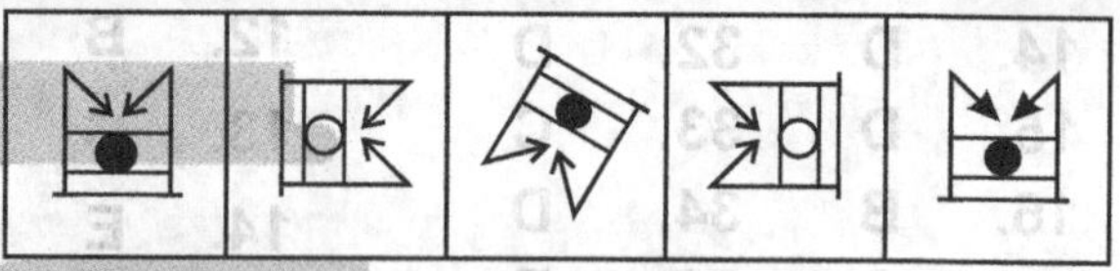

11.
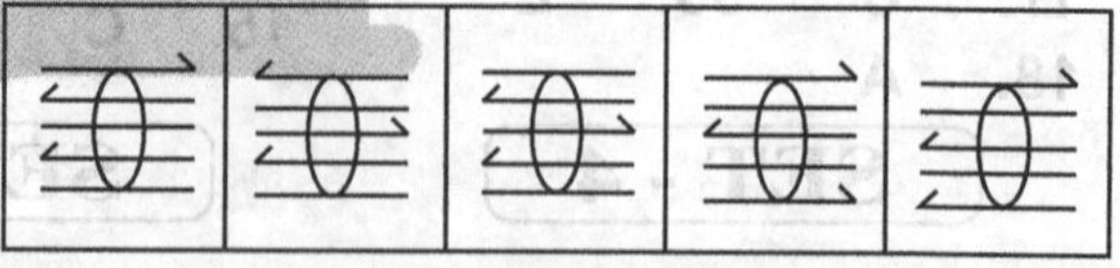

12.
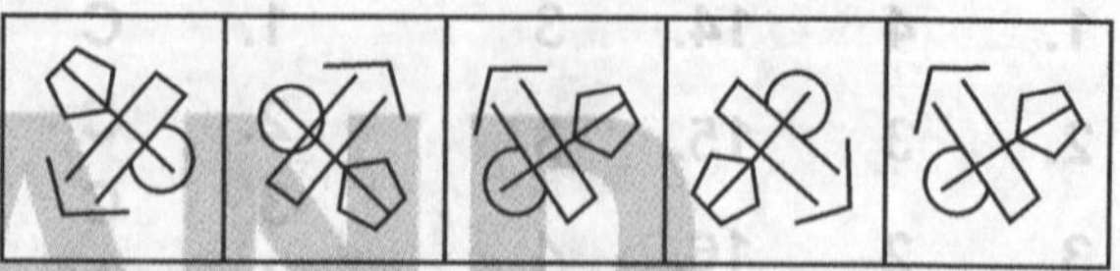

13.
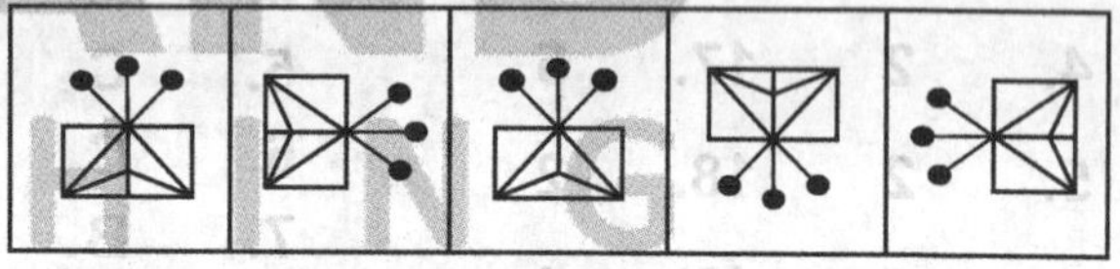

14.
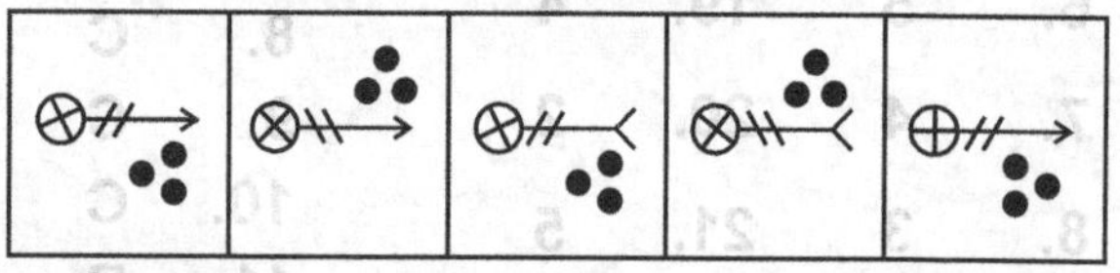

15.
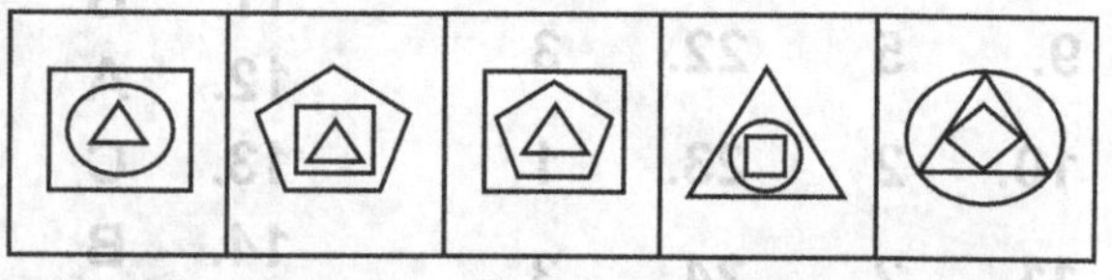

16.
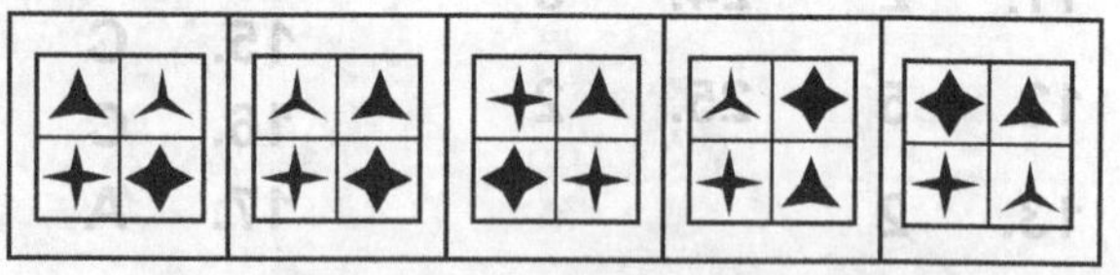

A B C D E

17. 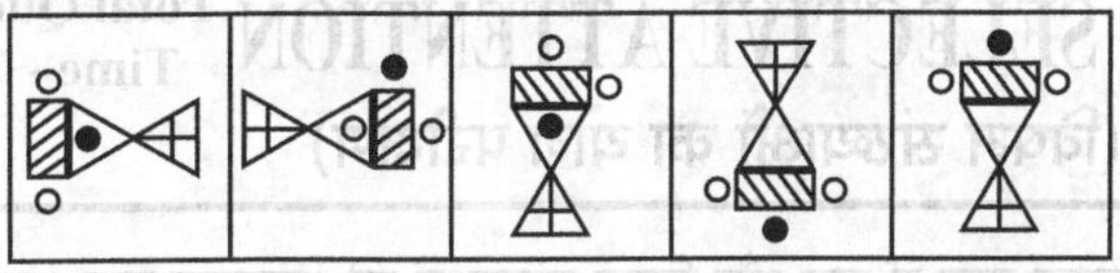

18. 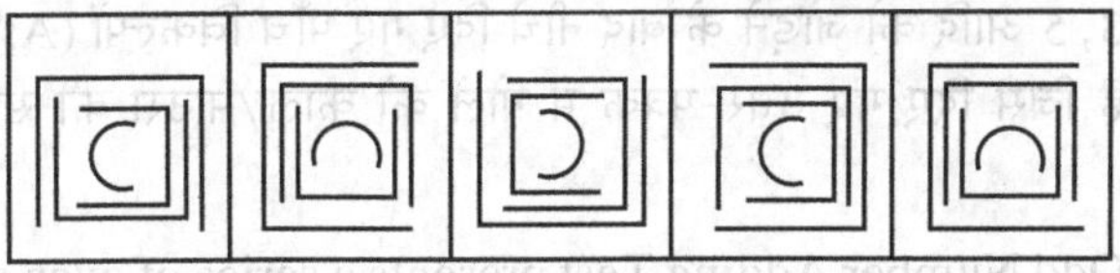

19. 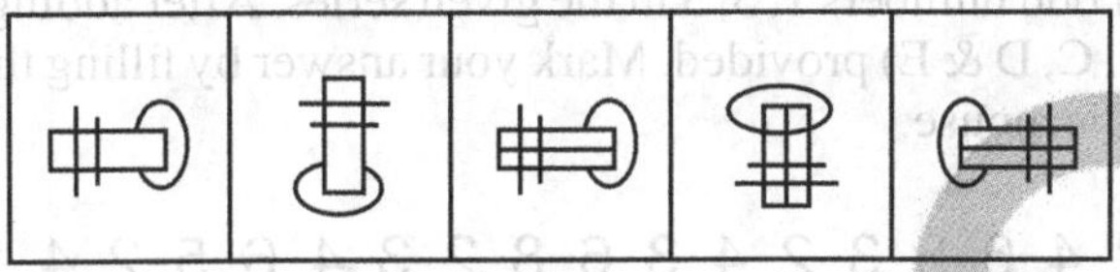

20. 

21. 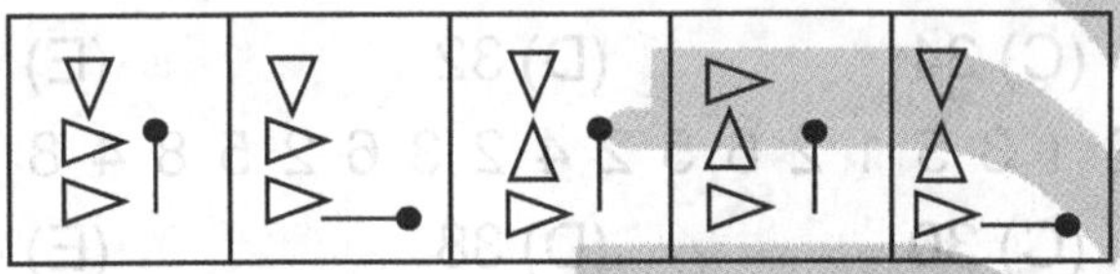

22. 

23. 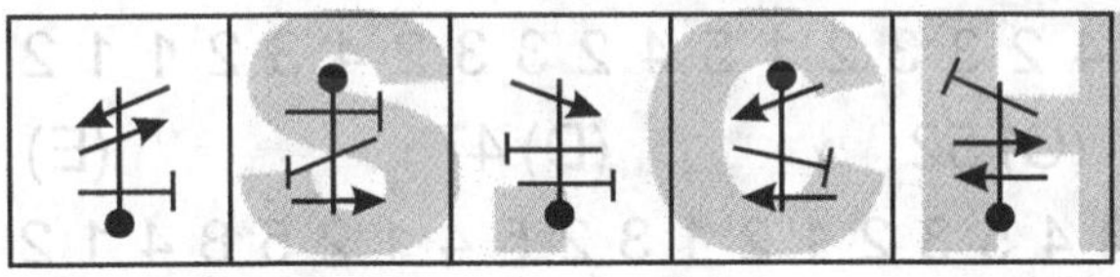

24. 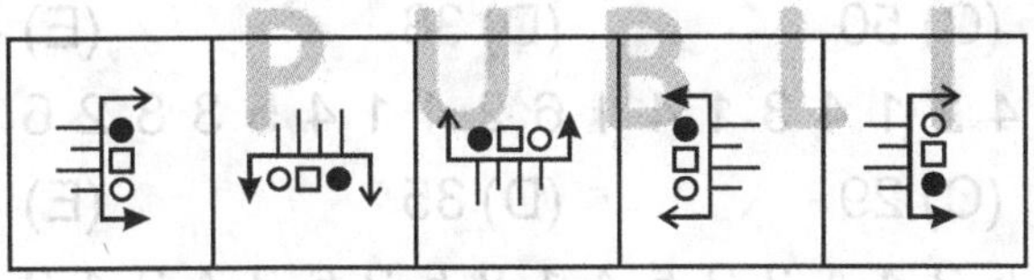

25. 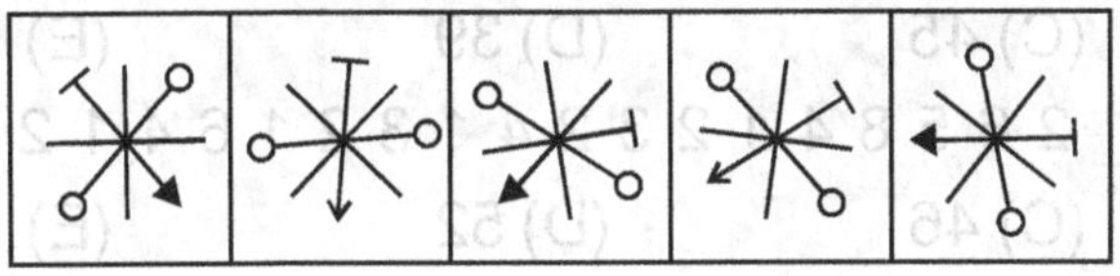

26. 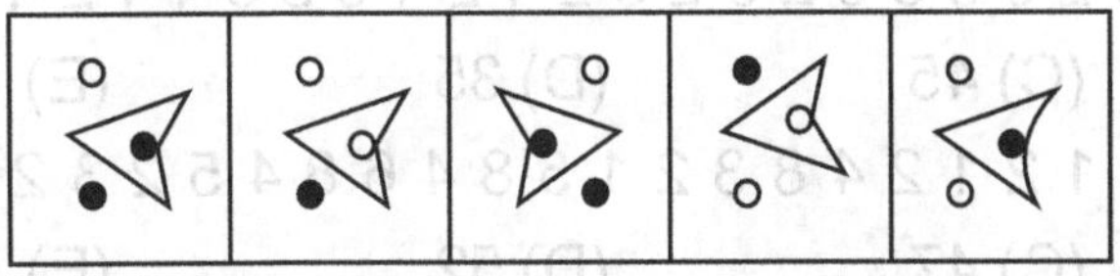

A B C D E

27. 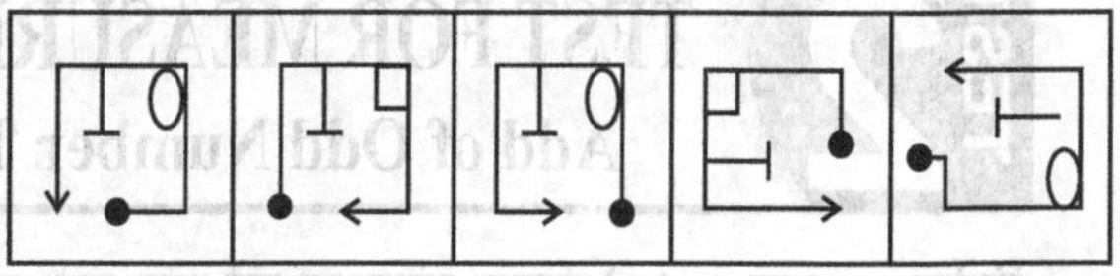

28. 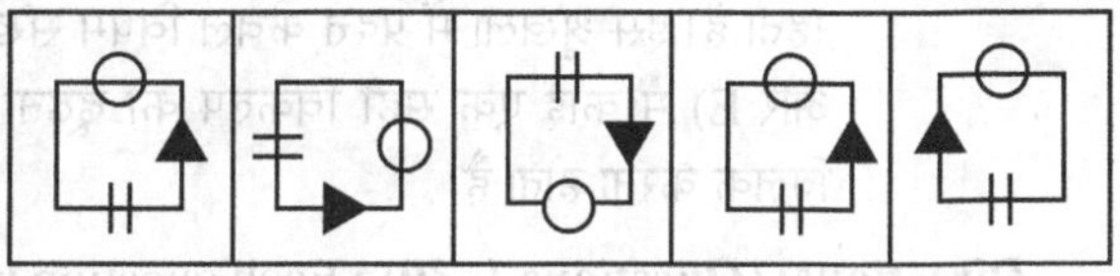

29. 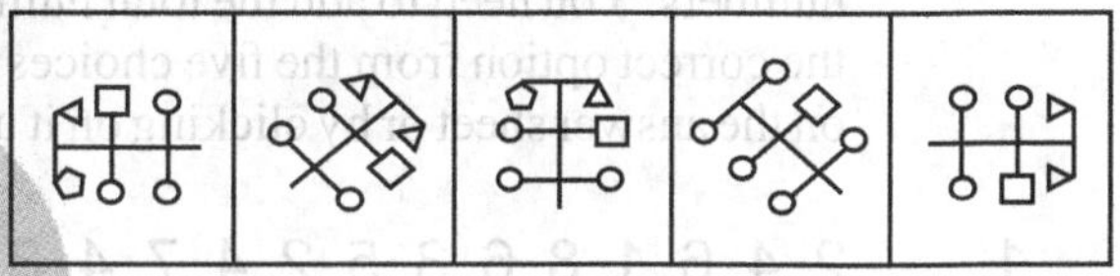

30. 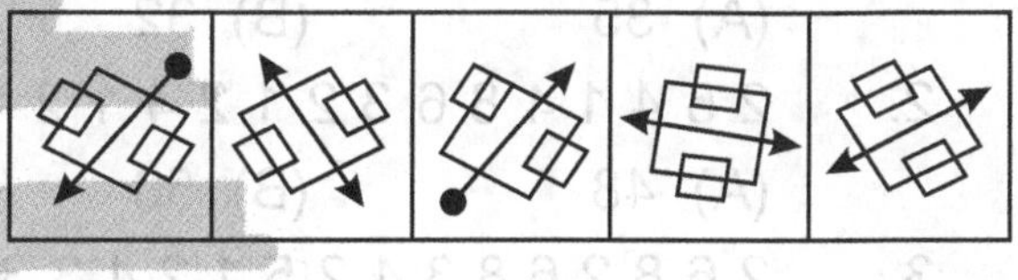

31. 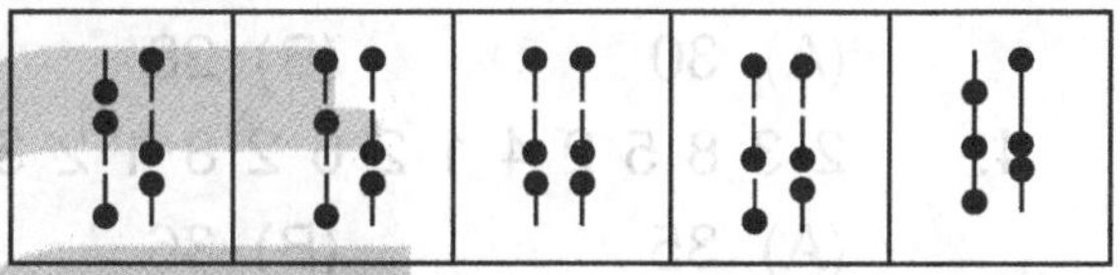

32. 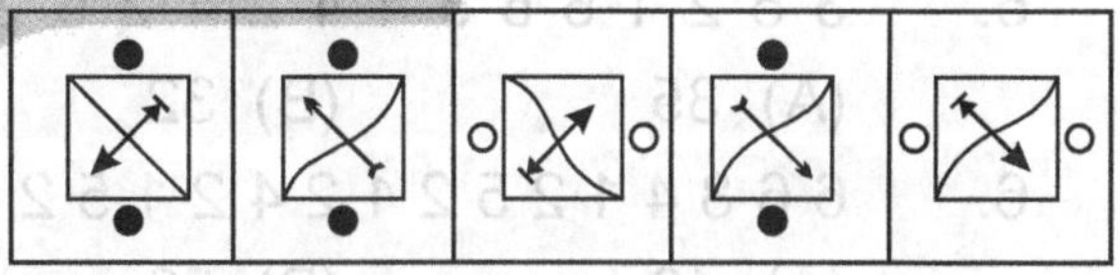

33. 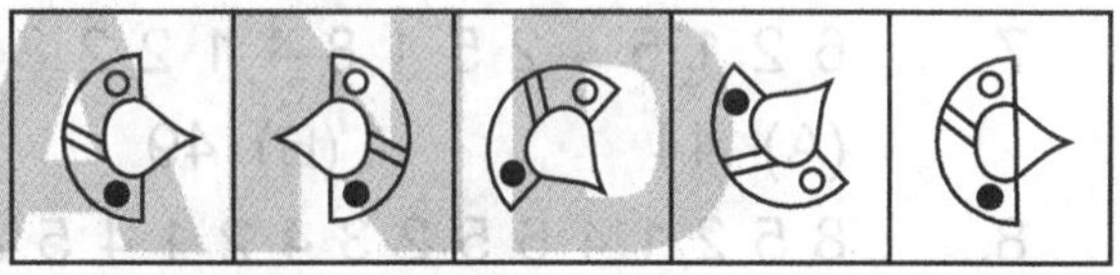

34. 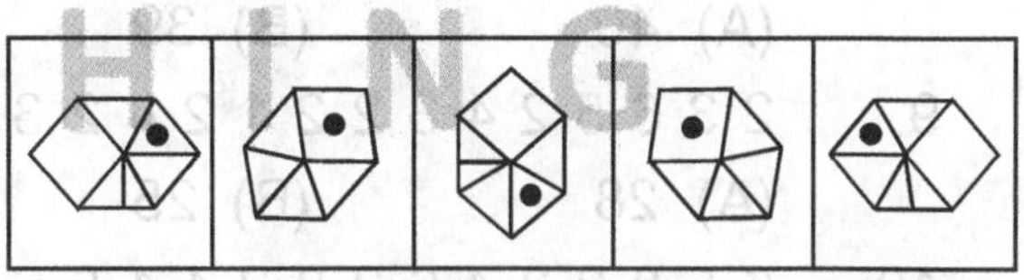

35. 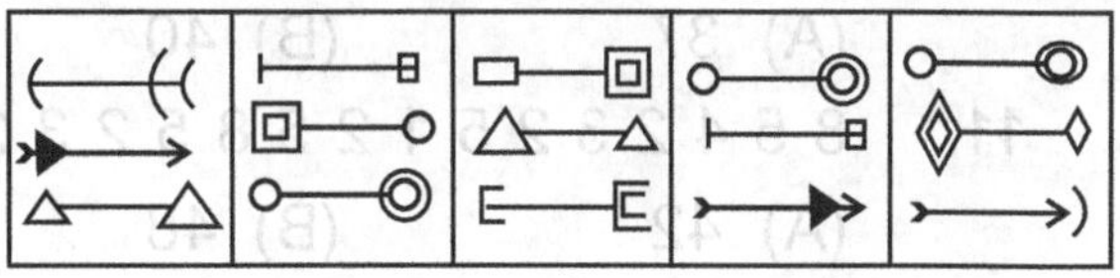

TEST 2 TEST FOR MEASURING SELECTIVE ATTENTION

Total Ques.- 30
Time - 7 Min.

Add of Odd Number Test (विषम संख्याओं का योग परीक्षण)

निर्देश : (प्रश्न 1-30) विषम संख्याओं को योग परीक्षण के प्रत्येक प्रश्न में सम और विषम संख्याओं को मिलाकर एक श्रृंखला दिया रहता है। इस श्रृंखला में प्रदत्त केवल विषम संख्या 1, 3, 5 आदि को जोड़ने के बाद नीचे दिए गए पाँच विकल्पों (A, B, C, D और E) में कोई एक सही विकल्प को ढूंढना होता है जिसे दिए गए उत्तर-पत्रक में गोले को काला/माउस की सहायता से क्लिक करना होता है।

Directions: (Questions 1–30) : Each question in the Odd Number Adding Test presents a series of even and odd numbers. You need to add the total number of odd numbers 1, 3, 5 in the given series. After adding, select the correct option from the five choices (A, B, C, D & E) provided. Mark your answer by filling the circle on the answer sheet or by clicking on it using the mouse.

1. 2 4 6 1 8 6 3 5 2 4 7 4 8 6 2 4 6 5 3 2 4 3 6 8 2 3 4 6 5 2 4 1 2 1
   (A) 35 (B) 32 (C) 34 (D) 37 (E) 36
2. 2 5 4 1 4 8 6 3 2 1 2 4 1 2 1 4 5 2 1 1 2 6 3 2 4 6 3 5 2 5 4 1 7 1 5 1 8 6
   (A) 48 (B) 50 (C) 47 (D) 45 (E) 52
3. 2 6 8 2 6 8 3 4 2 5 1 2 4 3 3 1 5 6 2 3 8 4 1 1 2 4 2 2 6 4 2 3 3 6 3 8 2 1 2
   (A) 30 (B) 28 (C) 34 (D) 32 (E) 36
4. 2 3 8 5 2 4 1 2 6 2 8 1 2 3 4 2 1 3 5 1 2 6 5 2 4 2 3 6 2 5 8 4 8 1 2 1
   (A) 35 (B) 36 (C) 30 (D) 38 (E) 40
5. 3 5 2 1 6 5 3 4 4 2 4 2 5 2 1 8 4 1 4 1 2 2 2 3 5 8 1 3 2 6 2 1 6 1 1 2
   (A) 35 (B) 32 (C) 42 (D) 46 (E) 40
6. 6 6 8 4 1 2 5 2 1 2 4 2 1 5 2 4 1 4 6 2 5 1 2 3 1 1 2 4 1 4 1 2 3 5 1 2 3 4 5 1
   (A) 42 (B) 50 (C) 45 (D) 55 (E) 41
7. 6 2 1 5 4 2 5 1 8 4 1 2 2 8 5 2 4 2 3 3 2 1 5 4 2 3 3 2 4 3 2 1 1 2 5 1 2
   (A) 44 (B) 49 (C) 52 (D) 47 (E) 56
8. 8 5 2 1 4 6 5 2 3 4 2 1 4 5 2 1 3 4 5 3 2 1 2 1 3 2 5 4 1 2 5 8 4 1 2 2 1 2
   (A) 40 (B) 39 (C) 50 (D) 38 (E) 42
9. 2 3 6 5 2 4 3 2 2 1 2 4 2 3 2 1 4 2 1 4 3 1 4 1 6 2 4 1 4 5 3 8 2 6 8 8 4
   (A) 28 (B) 25 (C) 29 (D) 35 (E) 31
10. 6 5 8 2 3 4 6 2 8 2 4 1 8 6 2 1 5 2 4 1 3 2 5 4 1 8 5 2 6 3 4 2 4 3 2 3 1
    (A) 37 (B) 40 (C) 45 (D) 39 (E) 38
11. 8 5 4 2 3 2 5 1 2 5 8 5 2 3 2 4 1 2 6 5 8 4 1 2 3 2 4 1 3 2 1 6 4 1 2 3 6 2
    (A) 42 (B) 48 (C) 46 (D) 52 (E) 52
12. 2 1 4 3 2 5 8 4 5 2 1 4 1 2 3 6 2 3 2 8 5 3 6 2 5 2 5 2 4 2 4 6 8 3 4 1 2 4 4 1 2
    (A) 40 (B) 41 (C) 45 (D) 35 (E) 36
13. 2 5 3 2 4 4 1 2 3 6 8 5 2 6 4 3 5 1 2 1 2 4 8 3 2 1 5 8 4 6 8 4 5 2 3 2 3 2 6
    (A) 50 (B) 49 (C) 47 (D) 52 (E) 56

14. 6 5 3 3 6 8 2 1 4 8 6 5 4 1 2 3 2 3 5 8 4 1 6 2 4 1 2 1 2 3 4 6 3 3 1 2 1 8

(A) 40 (B) 38 (C) 43 (D) 45 (E) 47

15. 5 8 4 8 2 4 1 3 2 5 2 1 3 4 6 3 8 4 1 5 2 3 2 4 1 4 2 5 6 2 8 4 1 2 3 5 1 2

(A) 42 (B) 36 (C) 41 (D) 46 (E) 48

16. 1 2 2 3 4 3 3 6 5 6 8 4 2 1 4 2 4 8 2 3 6 5 3 6 2 6 4 8 4 2 3 2 1 1 2 8 2

(A) 28 (B) 25 (C) 26 (D) 23 (E) 32

17. 1 2 5 3 6 2 6 2 1 5 2 8 3 4 5 4 1 2 3 6 6 2 1 4 8 4 2 1 2 4 8 5 2 8 2 6 5 2

(A) 32 (B) 39 (C) 41 (D) 43 (E) 45

18. 8 2 3 2 4 1 4 8 4 2 1 2 3 3 3 2 6 3 4 1 8 5 6 2 4 2 1 6 8 2 4 3 1 4 2 1 8

(A) 26 (B) 22 (C) 29 (D) 31 (E) 35

19. 4 5 2 4 1 8 4 2 3 2 4 1 2 6 4 2 6 5 8 6 2 4 3 2 3 4 1 3 6 1 4 5 8 4 1 2 1

(A) 28 (B) 30 (C) 35 (D) 38 (E) 33

20. 2 1 5 2 4 1 4 3 5 4 6 8 2 1 4 1 4 8 6 5 2 4 5 3 4 1 2 1 6 5 8 3 4 1 3 4 1 2

(A) 29 (B) 40 (C) 49 (D) 45 (E) 35

21. 4 1 4 3 8 1 4 1 5 2 3 5 6 8 2 5 2 1 4 3 6 1 3 3 2 1 6 4 2 8 2 4 1 2 6 4 8 1 2

(A) 30 (B) 35 (C) 36 (D) 38 (E) 42

22. 8 1 3 2 1 4 2 5 1 3 1 2 1 4 2 1 4 6 3 4 1 2 4 2 1 4 4 6 3 6 4 8 2 6 8 2 1 5 2

(A) 28 (B) 32 (C) 25 (D) 29 (E) 31

23. 6 2 1 8 5 2 1 6 4 6 5 8 4 4 1 2 4 2 1 5 4 3 2 5 8 4 1 4 2 3 6 8 5 4 2 8

(A) 34 (B) 32 (C) 30 (D) 28 (E) 36

24. 3 1 5 4 1 4 2 8 5 2 6 2 8 4 1 2 3 4 2 1 8 5 4 1 2 4 3 6 2 2 6 2 4 1 6 1

(A) 26 (B) 25 (C) 31 (D) 37 (E) 35

25. 4 2 4 5 6 2 6 1 4 3 2 1 4 2 4 1 4 2 1 8 5 2 4 3 6 1 8 4 6 8 4 3 5 1 4 3 1

(A) 32 (B) 34 (C) 40 (D) 45 (E) 36

26. 3 2 5 1 3 2 0 2 4 1 3 3 2 5 2 4 1 5 1 4 8 1 4 6 2 6 5 6 4 6 8 5 4 1 4 2 5 4

(A) 40 (B) 42 (C) 48 (D) 50 (E) 52

27. 3 3 2 4 1 2 1 2 4 3 6 5 2 1 8 8 4 3 8 5 8 5 2 4 2 5 4 1 3 3 1 3 2 4 2 5

(A) 51 (B) 48 (C) 46 (D) 42 (E) 40

28. 1 3 5 2 2 6 2 5 4 1 2 5 2 1 2 4 8 2 6 8 5 4 1 4 2 5 4 1 2 4 6 4 8 5 2 1 4

(A) 37 (B) 35 (C) 34 (D) 39 (E) 41

29. 2 3 4 1 8 2 4 1 3 5 8 4 1 2 6 3 2 1 2 4 8 2 6 2 1 3 5 2 2 1 4 3 6 8 2 1 1

(A) 28 (B) 27 (C) 35 (D) 39 (E) 33

30. 3 2 2 1 5 4 8 5 2 1 6 3 5 1 2 3 2 6 2 8 3 6 5 8 4 8 2 4 1 2 5 6 3 2 4 1

(A) 29 (B) 42 (C) 40 (D) 45 (E) 43

TEST 3 TEST FOR MEASURING SPATIAL SCANNING

Total Ques.- 40
Time - 6 Min.

Shortest Route Test (संक्षिप्त रास्ता परीक्षण)

निर्देश : (प्रश्न 1–40) इस अभ्यास में 40 प्रश्न दिए गए हैं जो चार उपखंडों 1, 2, 3 एवं 4 में 10–10 प्रश्नों (कुल 40 प्रश्न) के रूप में विभाजित है। प्रत्येक खण्ड के चित्रों को ध्यानपूर्वक देखकर दिए गए प्रत्येक प्रश्नों का उत्तर खोजकर अपने उत्तर-पत्रक में अंकित गोले को काला करें या माउस की सहायता से क्लिक करें और इसके लिए 6 मिनट का समय दिया जाता है।

Instructions: (Questions 1-40) : This exercise contains 40 questions, divided into four subsections: 1, 2, 3, and 4, each containing 10 questions (40 questions in total). Look carefully at the pictures in each section to find the answer to each question. Darken the circle on your answer sheet or click on it with the mouse. You are given 6 minutes for this.

उपखंड/Section-1

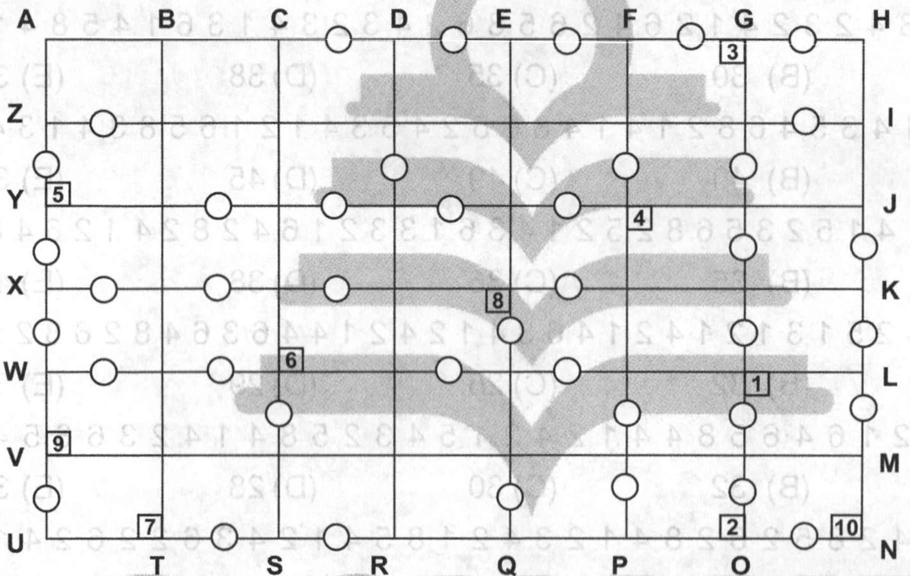

1. K - I
2. L - K
3. Z - G
4. M - O
5. P - T
6. E - R
7. B - W
8. F - Y
9. S - N
10. C - R

उपखंड/Section-2

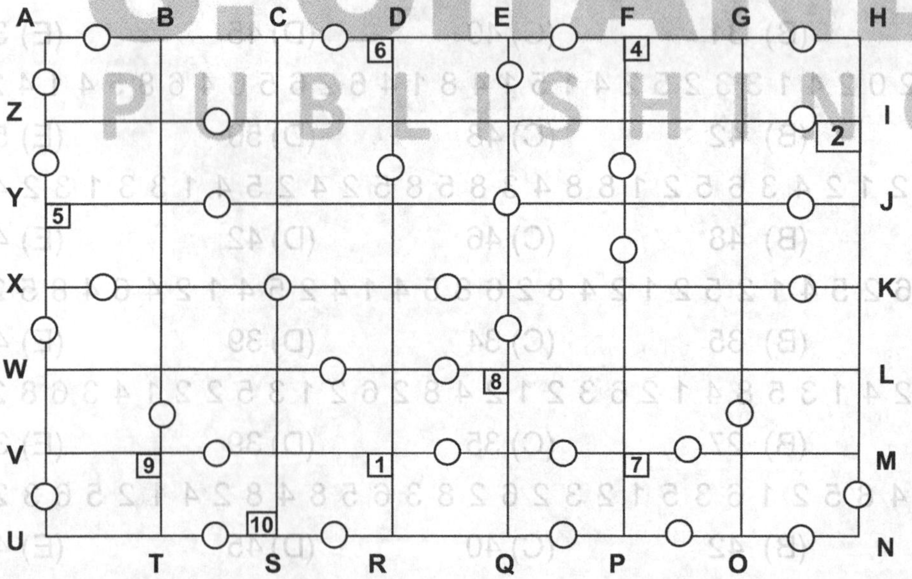

11. G - H
12. C - R
13. B - E
14. B - G
15. L - R
16. O - H
17. C - X
18. B - T
19. Z - S
20. O - P

उपखंड/Section-3

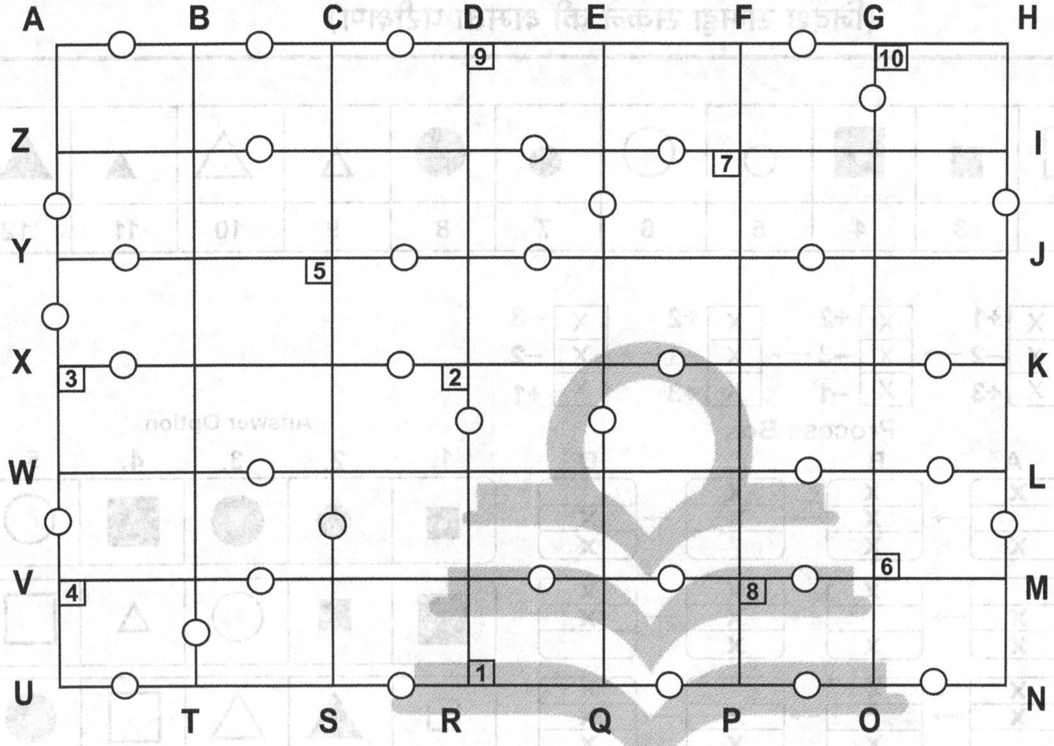

21. T - Q
22. Q - P
23. L - M
24. A - C
25. A - X
26. C - F
27. S - U
28. B - S
29. F - Q
30. L - G

उपखंड/Section-4

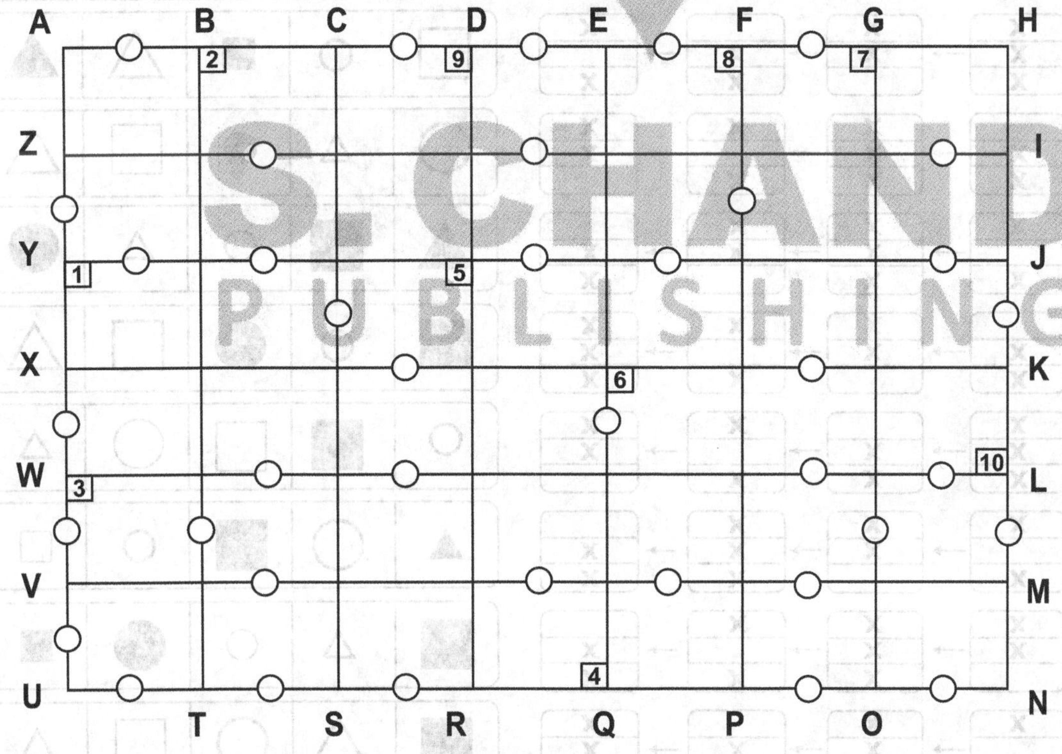

31. J - K
32. X - C
33. A - Y
34. S - W
35. K - F
36. H - E
37. C - R
38. E - P
39. S - P
40. P - L

TEST 4

INFORMATION ORDERING TEST

(निर्देश समझ सकने की क्षमता परीक्षण)

Total Ques.- 25
Time - 6 Min.

Table - 2

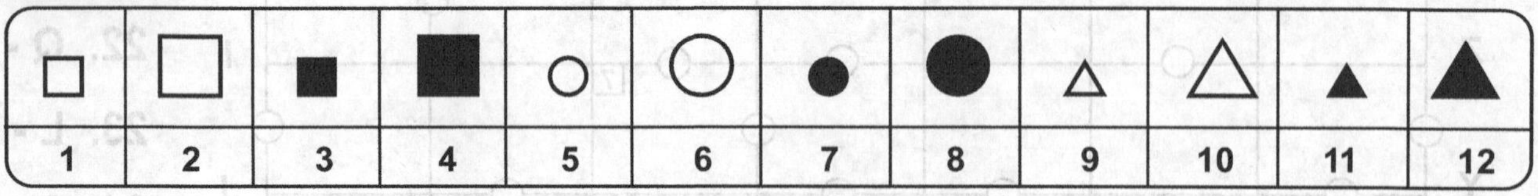

Table - 1

Level- 1 →	X +1	X +2	X +2	X −3
Level- 2 →	X −2 →	X −3 →	X −1 →	X −2
Level- 3 →	X +3	X −1	X +3	X +1

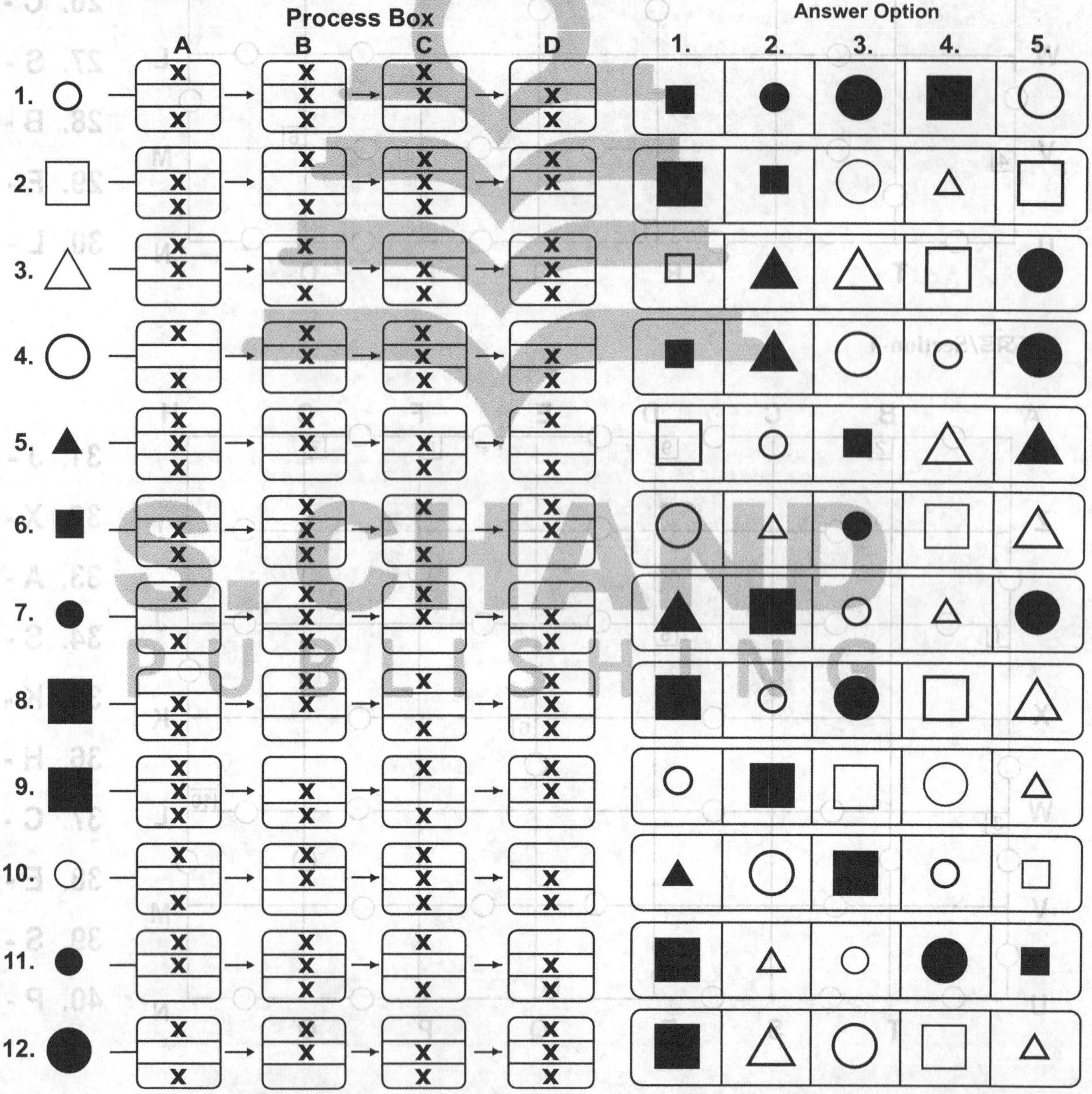

Table - 2

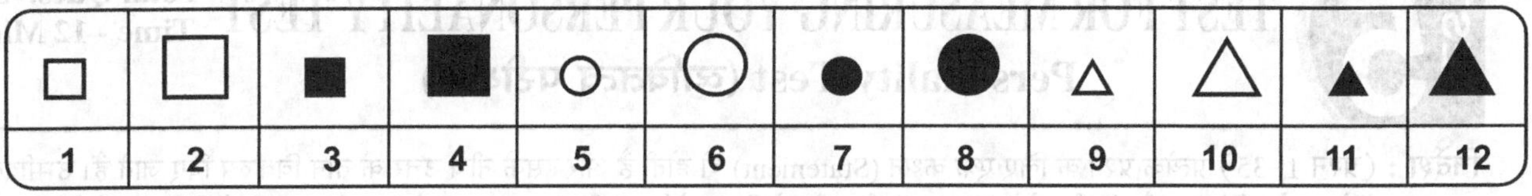

Table - 1

Level- 1 →	X +1 →	X +2 →	X +2 →	X –3
Level- 2 →	X –2 →	X –3 →	X –1 →	X –2
Level- 3 →	X +3	X –1	X +3	X +1

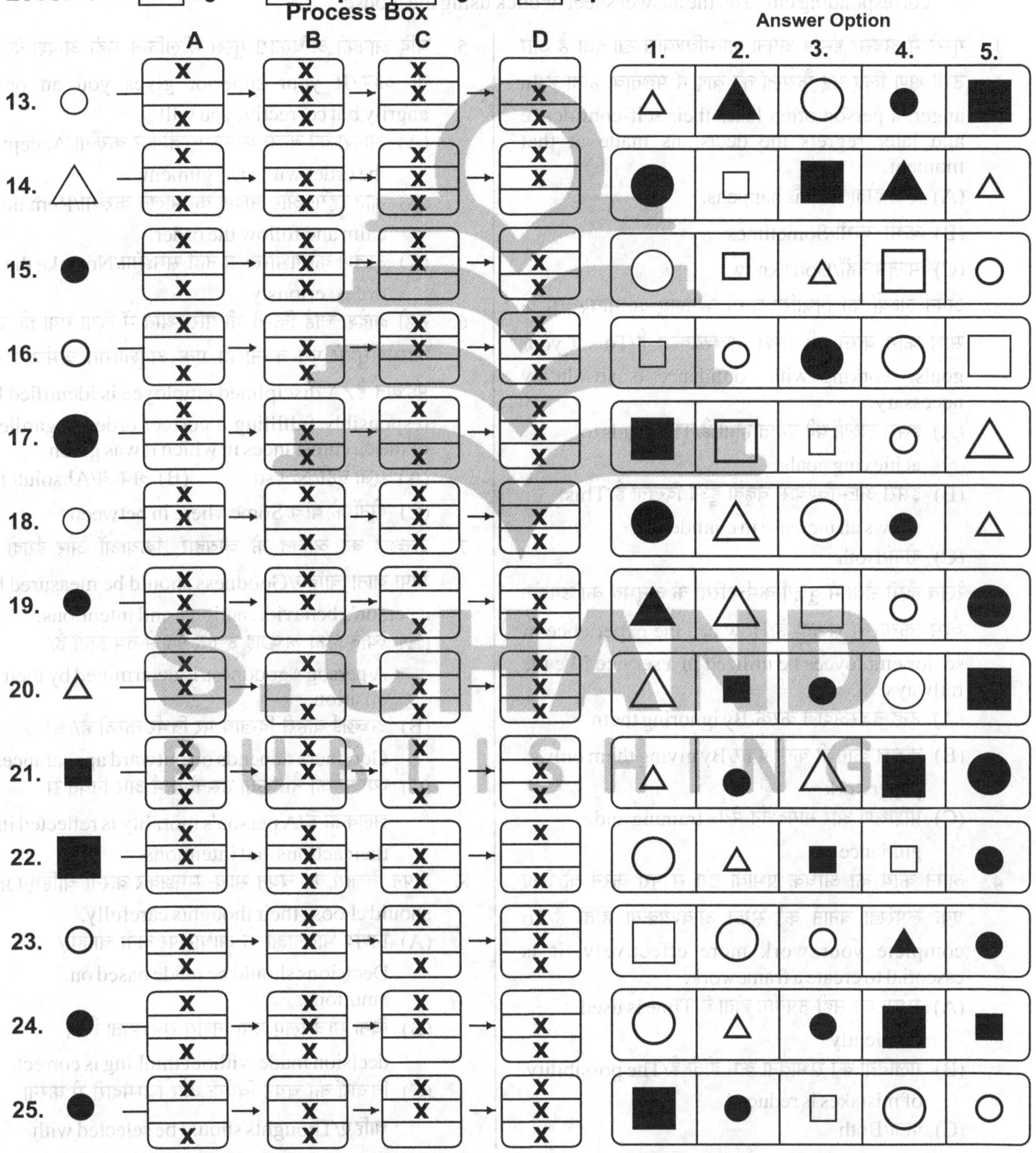

TEST 5 TEST FOR MEASURING YOUR PERSONALITY TEST

Total Ques.- 35
Time - 12 Min.

Personality Test (व्यक्तित्व परीक्षण)

निर्देश : (प्रश्न 1–35) प्रत्येक प्रश्न के लिए एक कथन (Statement) दी होती है और इसके नीचे उत्तर के तीन विकल्प दिए जाते हैं। उम्मीदवारों को अपने बुद्धिमता और निर्णय के आधार पर सही उत्तर के लिए कोई एक विकल्प का चयन कर उत्तर-पत्रक में दिए गए गोले को काला या माउस की सहायता से क्लिक (Click) करें।

Direction : (Questions 1–35) : For each question, a statement is given, followed by three answer options. Candidates should select the correct option based on their intelligence and judgment and fill the corresponding circle on the answer sheet or click using the mouse.

1. गुस्से में अक्सर इंसान अपना आत्मविश्वास खो देता है और उसी क्षण लिए गए फैसलों का बाद में पछतावा होता है/In anger, a person often loses their self-confidence and later regrets the decisions made at that moment.
(A) ऐसा होता है/This happens.
(B) कभी-कभी/Sometimes
(C) मालूम नहीं/Don't know

2. अपने लक्ष्यों को निर्धारित करने के लिए आत्मविश्वास के साथ काम करने की सख्त आवश्यकता है/To set your goals, working with confidence is absolutely necessary.
(A) इससे लक्ष्यों की प्राप्ति होती है/This leads to achieving goals.
(B) इससे आत्मविश्वास बढ़ता हुआ दिखता है/This shows an increase in confidence.
(C) दोनों/Both

3. रेलवे जैसी सेवा में बुजुर्ग कर्मचारियों के अनुभव का उपयोग कैसे किया जा सकता है/How can the experience of senior employees be utilized in a service like the railways?
(A) उन्हें नजरअंदाज करके/By ignoring them
(B) केवल कागजी काम देकर/By giving them only paperwork
(C) प्रशिक्षण और मार्गदर्शन में/In training and guidance

4. अपने कार्य को अधिक प्रभावी ढंग से पूरा करने के लिए एक रूपरेखा बनाने की सख्त आवश्यकता होती है/To complete your work more effectively, it is essential to create a framework.
(A) समय का सही उपयोग होता है/Time is used efficiently
(B) गलतियों की संभावना कम होती है/The possibility of mistakes is reduced
(C) दोनों/Both

5. यदि आपको अधिकारी गुस्से में लेकिन सही आदेश देता है तो आप/If your superior gives you an order angrily but correctly, you will
(A) आदेश को बहस के साथ स्वीकार करूँगा/Accept the order with an argument.
(B) शांत रहूँगा और आदेश का पालन करूँगा/Remain calm and follow the order.
(C) आदेश को गंभीरता से नहीं समझूँगा/Not take the order seriously.

6. सही आदेश चाहे किसी भी परिस्थिति में दिया गया हो, उसे जिम्मेदारी से पूरा करना ही एक अनुशासित कर्मचारी की पहचान है/A disciplined employee is identified by responsibly fulfilling a correct order, regardless of the circumstances in which it was given.
(A) ऐसा नहीं/Not so (B) अवश्य/Absolutely
(C) दोनों के बीच/Somewhere in between

7. अच्छाई को व्यक्ति के व्यवहार, क्रियाओं और ईरादों से मापा जाना चाहिए/Goodness should be measured by a person's behavior, actions, and intentions.
(A) व्यक्ति की अच्छाई उसके पद से तय होती है/A person's goodness is determined by their position.
(B) अच्छाई बाहरी दिखावे पर निर्भर करती है/Goodness depends on outward appearances.
(C) व्यक्ति की नैतिकता उसके कर्म और नियत से झलकती है/A person's morality is reflected in their actions and intentions.

8. अपने विचारों का चयन सोच-समझकर करना चाहिए/One should choose their thoughts carefully.
(A) निर्णय भावनाओं के आधार पर लेनी चाहिए/Decisions should be made based on emotions.
(B) बिना सोचे लिए गया निर्णय सही होता है/A decision made without thinking is correct.
(C) विचारों का चयन विवेक और जिम्मेदारी से करना चाहिए/Thoughts should be selected with discretion and responsibility.

9. क्या आपके दिमाग में ऐसे ख्याल आते हैं जो बहुत ही अजीबोगरीब हो, जिनको वास्तविक जीवन में करना सही नहीं हो/Do you have thoughts that are very strange, which would not be appropriate to act upon in real life?
(A) अक्सर/Often
(B) कभी-कभी/Sometimes
(C) कभी नहीं/Never

10. आप अपने विचारों को व्यवहारिक सकारात्मक और सामाजिक मर्यादाओं के अनुरूप रखना चाहिए ताकि किसी भी निर्णय लेने से पहले उसके परिणामों पर विचार करना चाहिए/You should keep your thoughts practical, positive, and in accordance with social norms, so that you consider the consequences before making any decision.
(A) ऐसा नहीं/Not so
(B) बिल्कुल सही/Absolutely correct
(C) कह नहीं सकते/Cannot say

11. यदि कोई व्यक्ति आपको गलत भाषा का इस्तेमाल करता है तो आप/If someone uses abusive language towards you, what will you do?
(A) आप भी गलत भाषा का इस्तेमाल करेंगे/You will also use abusive language.
(B) शांत, संयमित व सम्मानजनक तरीके से प्रतिक्रिया देंगे/You will react calmly, with restraint and respect.
(C) दोनों के बीच/Somewhere in between

12. दूसरों के प्रति संवेदनशीलता और सहायता की भावना नैतिकता का आधार है/Sensitivity and a spirit of helpfulness towards others are the foundation of morality.
(A) नैतिकता केवल नियमों से बनती है/Morality is only formed by rules.
(B) नैतिक व्यक्ति दूसरों की भावनाओं को समझकर सहायता करता है/A moral person understands the feelings of others and helps them.
(C) सहायता करना कष्टदायक प्रतीत होता है/Helping seems painful

13. आप किस तरह का उपन्यास पढ़ना पसंद करेंगे?/What kind of novel would you like to read?
(A) धर्म से संबंधित/Related to religion
(B) प्रेरणादायक और यथार्थपरम से संबंधित/Inspirational and realistic
(C) सामाजिक अलगाव से संबंधित/Related to social isolation

14. आपको ऐसे उपन्यास का सहारा लेना चाहिए जो जीवन-मूल्य, मानवीय संवेदनाओं, सामाजिक जिम्मेदारी और संघर्ष को दर्शाते हो/You should choose novels that depict life values, human emotions, social responsibility, and struggles.
(A) अनिश्चित/Uncertain
(B) निश्चित/Certain
(C) दोनों के बीच/Somewhere in between

15. आप किस तरह का काम करना पसंद करेंगे/What kind of work would you like to do?
(A) रासायनिक पदार्थों के प्रयोगशाला में रिसर्च/Research in a chemical laboratory
(B) होटल/इंश्योरेंस मैनेजर/Hotel/Insurance Manager
(C) योजनाबद्ध और टीम के साथ समन्वय बनाकर/Planned and coordinated with a team

16. यदि आपके पास ऐसी बंदुक है जिसमें गोली भरी हुई है, तो क्या आप उसे तुरंत खाली कर देंगे/If you have a loaded gun, would you immediately unload it?
(A) अनिश्चित रूप से/Uncertain
(B) निश्चित रूप से/Certainly
(C) दोनों के बीच/Somewhere in between

17. अधिकारी के प्रति सम्मान बनाए रखते हुए किसी भी कार्य को पूरी निष्ठा और ईमानदारी से करना चाहिए/Any work should be done with complete dedication and honesty while maintaining respect for the authority.
(A) अधिकारी को ज्यादा सम्मान नहीं दिया जाना चाहिए/The authority should not be given too much respect.
(B) अधिकारी का व्यवहार भरोसेमंद नहीं होते हैं/The behavior of the authority is not trustworthy.
(C) इससे कार्य की गुणवत्ता और आपसी विश्वसनीयता होता है/This improves the quality of work and mutual trust.

18. लोग आपको शक भरी नजरों से घुरते हैं तो क्या आपको उस समय घबराहट महसूस होती है/Do you feel nervous when people stare at you suspiciously?
(A) निश्चित रूप से/Definitely
(B) कभी-कभी/Sometimes
(C) कभी-नहीं/Never

19. जिम्मेदारी लेना और अपने काम को पूरी निष्ठा से पूरा करना ही सही मायने में प्रगति की कुजी है/Taking responsibility and completing your work with complete dedication is truly the key to progress.

(A) जिम्मेवार लोग कम होते हैं/Responsible people are few
(B) पूरी निष्ठा से किया गया कार्य हमेशा सफल होता है/Work done with complete dedication is always successful
(C) कुछ निष्ठावान व्यक्ति जिम्मेदारी लेने से घबराते हैं/Some dedicated individuals hesitate to take responsibility

20. स्टेशन मास्टर की जिम्मेदारी केवल समय का ध्यान रखना ही नहीं है, बल्कि दबाव की परिस्थिति में भी शांत रहकर अपने कर्त्तव्यों का निर्वाहन करना होता है/The station master's responsibility is not only to keep track of time, but also to remain calm under pressure and perform his duties
(A) दुर्घटना की संभावना में कमी आएगी/The possibility of accidents will decrease
(B) कुछ परिस्थितियाँ मजबूर कर देती है/Some circumstances are unavoidable
(C) पब्लिक का दबाव भी परेशानी का कारण है/Public pressure is also a cause of trouble.

21. यातायात के नियमों का कठोरता से पालन ही दुर्घटनाओं को कम करने और सुरक्षा को सुनिश्चित करने का प्रभावी उपाय है/Strict adherence to traffic rules is an effective way to reduce accidents and ensure safety.
(A) वाहनों की गहन जाँच होनी चाहिए/Vehicles should be thoroughly inspected.
(B) यातायात नियमों को प्रशासन सफल मानते हैं/The administration considers traffic rules successful
(C) दुर्घटनाओं को देखते हुए ऐसी कदम उठानी चाहिए/Such steps should be taken considering the accidents

22. सकारात्मक भावनाएँ हमारे जीवन में महत्वपूर्ण भूमिका निभाती है ये मन को शांत रखती है और आशावादी दृष्टिकोण विकसित करती है/Positive emotions play an important role in our lives; they keep the mind calm and develop an optimistic outlook.
(A) मानसिक शांति घटती है/Mental peace decreases
(B) अवश्य/Absolutely
(C) ऐसा नहीं/Not so

23. आप अपने परिवारों को समाज और देश के प्रति कर्त्तव्यों की भावना बतानी चाहिए/You should instill in your families a sense of duty towards society and the
(A) कोशिश करनी चाहिए/Should try
(B) हमेशा/Always
(C) कभी-कभी/Sometimes

24. RTI अधिनियम को मजबूत बनाया जाना चाहिए, ताकि लोगों को जानकारी प्राप्त करने में आसानी हो/The RTI Act should be strengthened so that people can easily obtain information.
(A) सरकारी कार्यों में बदलाव जरूरी है/Changes in government functioning are necessary.
(B) इससे पारदर्शिता आती है और भ्रष्टाचार समाप्त होगी/This brings transparency and reduces corruption
(C) RTI अधिानियम को और प्रभावी बनाना आवश्यक है/It is necessary to make the RTI Act more effective

25. आप अपने निवास स्थान पर ऐतिहासिक सामग्रियों को/You keep historical materials at your residence
(A) इसके पीछे समय लगाना अनुचित समझता हूँ/I consider it inappropriate to spend time on this
(B) यथोचित सजाकर रखता हूँ/I keep them properly arranged.
(C) बिखेरकर रखता हूँ/I keep them scattered.

26. आप निर्णय लेने में भावनाओं को महत्व देते हैं या नियमों को/Do you prioritize emotions or rules when making decisions?
(A) नियमों का प्राथमिक देना चाहिए/Rules should be given priority.
(B) कभी-कभी लोग भावनाओं में आकर गलत निर्णय लेते हैं/Sometimes people make wrong decisions based on emotions.
(C) उस समय अधिकारी से सलाह लेंगे/I would seek advice from a superior at that time.

27. नियम और मानवीय संवेदना में टकराव हो, तो आप/If there is a conflict between rules and human feelings, what would you do?
(A) केवल नियम देखेंगे/I would only consider the rules.
(B) केवल भावना देखेंगे/I would only consider the feelings.
(C) नियमों के अंदर मानवीय समाधान खोजेंगे/I would find a humane solution within the framework of the rules.

28. आपको लगता है कि आपसे गलती हो गई है, तो आप/If you realize you have made a mistake, what would you do?
(A) गलती छुपाने की कोशिश करेंगे/I would try to hide the mistake.
(B) दूसरों पर दोष डालेंगे/I would blame others.
(C) गलती स्वीकार कर सुधारात्मक कदम उठाएंगे/I would accept the mistake and take corrective action.

29. ड्यूटी के समय आपको व्यक्तिगत समस्या की जानकारी मिलती है, लेकिन स्टेशन पर भीड़ अधिक है तो आप/You receive information about a personal problem during duty hours, but the station is crowded, so you will:
(A) किसी और पर जिम्मेदारी डाल देंगे/Pass the responsibility to someone else.
(B) पहले ड्यूटी करके व्यवस्था संभालेंगे, फिर अधिकारी से उचित अनुमति लेंगे/First complete your duty and manage the situation, then seek proper permission from the officer.
(C) ड्यूटी के समय व्यक्तिगत समस्या पर विचार करेंगे/Consider the personal problem during duty hours

30. एक वरिष्ठ अधिकारी कहता है "मैं संभाल लूँगा, तुम नियमों की चिंता मत करो, तो आप/A senior officer says, "I will handle it, don't worry about the rules," so you will:
(A) आदेश मान लेंगे/Obey the order.
(B) विनम्रता से नियमों की जानकारी देकर लिखित आदेश मांगेंगे/Politely inform him about the rules and request a written order.
(C) अधिकारी से नियमों का बहस करेंगे/Argue with the officer about the rules.

31. भीड़ नियंत्रित करने के लिए पुलिस सख्ती दिखा रही है, यात्री डर रहे हैं, तो आप/The police are using force to control the crowd, and passengers are scared, so you will:
(A) स्थिति से दूर रहेंगे/Stay away from the situation.
(B) पुलिस को रोक देंगे/Stop the police.
(C) पुलिस से समन्वयकर मानवीय तरीके से व्यवस्था कराएंगे/Coordinate with the police and manage the situation in a humane manner.

32. आपको पता चलता है कि एक छोटी गलती से भविष्य में बड़ा खतरा हो सकता है तो, आप/You realize that a small mistake could lead to a major problem in the future, so you will:
(A) बाद में देखेंगे/Deal with it later.
(B) गलती छुपाने की कोशिश करेंगे/Try to hide the mistake.
(C) तुरंत रिपोर्ट कर सुधार करेंगे/Report it immediately and correct it.

33. यदि आप कोई काम करना शुरू करते हैं तो किस तरह से सोचते हैं/If you start a task, how do you think about it?
(A) जो आम जनता को कम पसंद लगे/Something that is less liked by the general public.
(B) जो परिवार के हित में हो/Something that is in the best interest of the family.
(C) जो दोस्तों को आनंद आए/Something that will bring joy to friends.

34. शिक्षित महिला अपने बच्चों की शिक्षा, स्वास्थ्य और भविष्य पर बेहतर ध्यान दे पाती है, इससे पूरा परिवार और अंततः समाज प्रगति करता है/An educated woman is better able to focus on her children's education, health, and future, which leads to the progress of the entire family and ultimately society.
(A) महिला शिक्षित होने से परिवार में विखराव बढ़ता जा रहा है/The education of women is leading to increased disintegration in families.
(B) महिलाओं में अभी भी जागरूकता की कमी है/There is still a lack of awareness among women.
(C) इससे महिलाओं में आत्मविश्वास, आत्मनिर्भर और निर्णय लेने की क्षमता बढ़ रही है/This is increasing self-confidence, self-reliance, and decision-making ability among women.

35. रेलवे के निजीकरण से गरीब वर्ग की रेल यात्रा प्रभावित होगी, इससे/The privatization of railways will affect rail travel for the poor, because:
(A) निजी कंपनियों का लक्ष्य बेहतर सामाजिक सेवा देना/Private companies aim to provide better social service.
(B) रेल किराया बढ़ने और रियायती टिकट योजनाएँ समाप्त हो सकती है/Rail fares may increase, and subsidized ticket schemes may be discontinued.
(C) निजिकरण से सभी वर्गों को लाभ मिलेगा/Privatization will benefit all sections of society.

उत्तर (ANSWER)

SET - 1

1.	A	19.	D
2.	C	20.	C
3.	E	21.	D
4.	A	22.	B
5.	D	23.	D
6.	D	24.	D
7.	E	25.	C
8.	B	26.	E
9.	E	27.	E
10.	E	28.	C
11.	D	29.	D
12.	B	30.	C
13.	C	31.	E
14.	E	32.	A
15.	E	33.	E
16.	C	34.	E
17.	B	35.	E
18.	D		

SET - 2

1.	D	16.	E
2.	B	17.	B
3.	E	18.	C
4.	D	19.	E
5.	E	20.	D
6.	C	21.	D
7.	D	22.	E
8.	C	23.	E
9.	E	24.	C
10.	B	25.	B
11.	C	26.	C
12.	C	27.	A
13.	C	28.	D
14.	C	29.	E
15.	D	30.	D

SET - 3

SECTION-1

1. ① ② ③ ❹ ⑤ ⑥ ⑦ ⑧ ⑨ ⑩
2. ❶ ② ③ ④ ⑤ ⑥ ⑦ ⑧ ⑨ ⑩
3. ① ② ❸ ④ ⑤ ⑥ ⑦ ⑧ ⑨ ⑩
4. ① ❷ ③ ④ ⑤ ⑥ ⑦ ⑧ ⑨ ⑩
5. ① ② ③ ④ ⑤ ⑥ ❼ ⑧ ⑨ ⑩
6. ① ② ③ ④ ⑤ ⑥ ⑦ ❽ ⑨ ⑩
7. ① ② ③ ④ ⑤ ⑥ ⑦ ⑧ ❾ ⑩
8. ① ② ③ ④ ❺ ⑥ ⑦ ⑧ ⑨ ⑩
9. ① ② ③ ④ ⑤ ⑥ ⑦ ⑧ ⑨ ❿
10. ① ② ③ ④ ⑤ ❻ ⑦ ⑧ ⑨ ⑩

SECTION-2

11. ① ❷ ③ ④ ⑤ ⑥ ⑦ ⑧ ⑨ ⑩
12. ❶ ② ③ ④ ⑤ ⑥ ⑦ ⑧ ⑨ ⑩
13. ① ② ③ ④ ⑤ ❻ ⑦ ⑧ ⑨ ⑩
14. ① ② ③ ❹ ⑤ ⑥ ⑦ ⑧ ⑨ ⑩
15. ① ② ③ ④ ⑤ ⑥ ⑦ ❽ ⑨ ⑩
16. ① ❷ ③ ④ ⑤ ⑥ ⑦ ⑧ ⑨ ⑩
17. ① ② ③ ④ ❺ ⑥ ⑦ ⑧ ⑨ ⑩
18. ① ② ③ ④ ⑤ ⑥ ⑦ ⑧ ❾ ⑩
19. ① ② ③ ④ ⑤ ⑥ ⑦ ⑧ ⑨ ❿
20. ① ② ③ ④ ⑤ ⑥ ❼ ⑧ ⑨ ⑩

SECTION-3

21. ❶ ② ③ ④ ⑤ ⑥ ⑦ ⑧ ⑨ ⑩
22. ① ② ③ ④ ⑤ ⑥ ⑦ ❽ ⑨ ⑩
23. ① ② ③ ④ ⑤ ❻ ⑦ ⑧ ⑨ ⑩
24. ① ② ③ ④ ❺ ⑥ ⑦ ⑧ ⑨ ⑩
25. ① ② ❸ ④ ⑤ ⑥ ⑦ ⑧ ⑨ ⑩
26. ① ② ③ ④ ⑤ ⑥ ⑦ ⑧ ❾ ⑩
27. ① ② ③ ❹ ⑤ ⑥ ⑦ ⑧ ⑨ ⑩
28. ① ② ③ ④ ❺ ⑥ ⑦ ⑧ ⑨ ⑩
29. ① ② ③ ④ ⑤ ⑥ ❼ ⑧ ⑨ ⑩
30. ① ② ③ ④ ⑤ ⑥ ⑦ ⑧ ⑨ ❿

SECTION-4

31. ① ② ③ ④ ⑤ ⑥ ❼ ⑧ ⑨ ⑩
32. ① ❷ ③ ④ ⑤ ⑥ ⑦ ⑧ ⑨ ⑩
33. ❶ ② ③ ④ ⑤ ⑥ ⑦ ⑧ ⑨ ⑩
34. ① ② ❸ ④ ⑤ ⑥ ⑦ ⑧ ⑨ ⑩
35. ① ② ③ ④ ⑤ ⑥ ⑦ ❽ ⑨ ⑩
36. ① ② ③ ④ ⑤ ⑥ ❼ ⑧ ⑨ ⑩
37. ① ② ③ ④ ❺ ⑥ ⑦ ⑧ ⑨ ⑩
38. ① ② ③ ④ ⑤ ❻ ⑦ ⑧ ⑨ ⑩
39. ① ② ③ ❹ ⑤ ⑥ ⑦ ⑧ ⑨ ⑩
40. ① ② ③ ④ ⑤ ⑥ ⑦ ⑧ ⑨ ❿

SET - 4

1.	2	14.	5
2.	2	15.	3
3.	5	16.	5
4.	2	17.	1
5.	5	18.	1
6.	4	19.	1
7.	4	20.	3
8.	2	21.	5
9.	3	22.	4
10.	1	23.	2
11.	4	24.	2
12.	5	25.	1
13.	4		

SET - 5

1.	A	18.	C
2.	C	19.	B
3.	C	20.	A
4.	C	21.	C
5.	B	22.	B
6.	B	23.	B
7.	C	24.	C
8.	C	25.	B
9.	C	26.	A
10.	B	27.	C
11.	B	28.	C
12.	B	29.	B
13.	B	30.	B
14.	B	31.	C
15.	C	32.	C
16.	B	33.	B
17.	C	34.	C
		35.	B